WALKER & WALKER'S
ENGLISH LEGAL SYSTEM

WALKER & WALKER'S

ENGLISH LEGAL SYSTEM

Tenth Edition

RICHARD WARD

Professor of Public Law and Head of Department of Law,
De Montfort University, Leicester

AMANDA AKHTAR

Senior Lecturer in Law, De Montfort University, Leicester

OXFORD

UNIVERSITY PRESS

OXFORD

UNIVERSITY PRESS

Great Clarendon Street, Oxford OX2 6DP

Oxford University Press is a department of the University of Oxford.
It furthers the University's objective of excellence in research, scholarship,
and education by publishing worldwide in

Oxford New York

Auckland Cape Town Dar es Salaam Hong Kong Karachi
Kuala Lumpur Madrid Melbourne Mexico City Nairobi
New Delhi Shanghai Taipei Toronto

With offices in

Argentina Austria Brazil Chile Czech Republic France Greece
Guatemala Hungary Italy Japan Poland Portugal Singapore
South Korea Switzerland Thailand Turkey Ukraine Vietnam

Oxford is a registered trade mark of Oxford University Press
in the UK and in certain other countries

Published in the United States
by Oxford University Press Inc., New York

Tenth edition 2008

British Library Cataloguing in Publication Data

Data available

Library of Congress Cataloging in Publication Data
Ward, Richard, LL.B.

Walker & Walker's English legal system / Richard Ward, Amanda
Akhtar. — 10th ed.
p. cm.
Includes bibliographical references and index.
ISBN 978–0–19–921487–7
1. Procedure (Law)—Great Britain.   2. Courts—Great Britain.
3. Law—Great Britain.   I. Wragg, Amanda.   II. Walker, Ronald Jack.
Walker & Walker's English legal system.   III. Title.   IV. Title:
English legal system.   V. Title: Walker and Walker's English legal system.
KD7100.W3 2008
347.42—dc22   2008021282

Typeset by Newgen Imaging Systems (P) Ltd., Chennai, India
Printed in Great Britain
on acid-free paper by
CPI Antony Rowe, Chippenham, Wiltshire

ISBN 978–0–19–921487–7

1 3 5 7 9 10 8 6 4 2

PREFACE

It is only two and half years since the Ninth edition. Despite that, the pace of change remains as frantic as ever.

The aim of the book remains unchanged; to provide an accessible and relatively concise expedition of the main principles, rules and issues. The aims may not have changed but much else has. Substantial rewriting in the area of the Human Rights Act 1998, the Tribunals, Courts and Enforcement Act 2007 and Legal Services has been needed. A multiplicity of detailed changes has occurred, necessitating judgments as to what is really valuable as opposed to more recent examples of the same. We have also tried to maximise the user-friendly nature of the book.

We are grateful for the comments of colleagues and reviewers alike which have helped us shape this new edition. Needless to say we alone are responsible for any errors or omissions.

We would like to thank the publishing team at OUP for their advice, support and efficiency.

On a more personal note Richard would like to thank Sarah for her support, encouragement and endless patience.

Amanda would like to thank her husband Jang and their beautiful daughter Laylah, to whom Amanda's contribution to this book is dedicated. Laylah was born shortly after the manuscript before this edition was completed, and so can genuinely claim to have written it with Amanda.

The manuscript was submitted in early January 2008, but it has been possible, with the indulgence of the publishers, to insert one or two later changes. In particular it has been possible to reflect, to some extent, some of the provisions of the Criminal Justice and Immigration Act 2008.

Richard Ward
Amanda Akhtar
May 2008

OUTLINE CONTENTS

DETAILED CONTENTS

PART I SOURCES OF ENGLISH LAW

PART III CIVIL PROCEDURE

PART IV   CRIMINAL PROCEEDINGS

TABLE OF CASES

TABLE OF STATUTES

TABLE OF STATUTORY INSTRUMENTS

TABLE OF EC LEGISLATION

PART I

SOURCES OF ENGLISH LAW

1

INTRODUCTORY ISSUES

INTRODUCTION

This introductory chapter is designed to give a general overview of the modern English legal system, and to put the current framework in its historical context. It will address the following:

- The historical development of the legal system and the evolution of the common law.
- The principal sources of law in the modern legal system.
- The importance of the distinction between civil and criminal law.
- The extent to which the boundary between civil and criminal law is becoming blurred in an age of anti-social behaviour orders (ASBOs), control orders and other developments.
- The administration of the legal system, and the respective roles of the Lord Chancellor, the Ministry of Justice, the Home Office and the Law Officers.

THE HISTORICAL CONTEXT

The current legal system of England and Wales[1] has evolved over many centuries and it has changed considerably during this time. Modern problems and needs have led to widespread changes in the court system, the organization of the legal profession, and the procedures followed by the courts. New courts have been created,[2] and a whole body of administrative justice has developed, meaning that many disputes between the state and the individual are now resolved in tribunals and inquiries rather than in the courts themselves.[3] Indeed, increasing emphasis is placed on seeking to avoid formal legal proceedings altogether, with the trend towards greater use of arbitration and mediation

---

[1] Scotland and Northern Ireland are separate jurisdictions with their own courts and laws. This book deals only with England and Wales.

[2] The Crown Court, for example, was created by the Courts Act 1971, and Part 3 of the Constitutional Reform Act 2005 provides for the creation of a new Supreme Court: see pp 20 and 253, *post*.

[3] See chapter 9.

procedures. Alongside this, old procedures have been developed and refined to meet modern needs.

Yet to concentrate exclusively upon modern developments would be to acquire an incomplete picture, for many institutions and procedures can only be understood in the light of an awareness of their historical background. Although the modern courts may be different from their predecessors, the court system is of ancient origins and many rules of procedure owe their existence to the nature of the institutions in which they first developed. For example, the fact that the modern criminal trial is still essentially oral in nature owes much to the old forms of trial for criminal offences, particularly trial by jury. Similarly, the current procedure of judicial review derives from powers exercised by the Crown since the twelfth century,[4] while modern principles of equity were developed in the old Court of Chancery. Moreover, the substantive rules of law are not immune from historical influence: the modern laws of contract and tort, for example, can best be understood in the light of their historical origins.

1 THE ROLE OF THE MONARCH

Historically, the sovereign was the fountain of justice in England, and the administration of justice was, and still is, one of the prerogative powers of the Crown.[5] In theory the Monarch continues to be the formal head of the legal system, and the Crown has a residual duty to ensure that justice is done[6] and that law and order is maintained.[7] The reality is that these functions are now exercised by or on behalf of ministers, and the role of the Monarch in the modern legal system is purely a nominal one. Historically, however, the Monarch's role was more direct, and the development of the common law arose through the unifying influence of those administering justice on his behalf. Specifically, it was the assumption of control over the administration of justice by the Monarch's representatives which led to local courts and jurisdictions being replaced with a centralized system.[8] The new courts that evolved as a result of this process were the King's courts, administering justice under the inherent power of the Crown. Even though the vast majority of courts now have a statutory basis, these historical origins remain important.

2 THE EVOLUTION OF COMMON LAW AND EQUITY

Common law and equity are two of the main historical sources of English law, the third being legislation. The term 'common law' reflects the fact that the law administered by the King's courts became the common law of England and Wales, gradually supplanting the mass of local custom that previously existed. The King's legal functions

---

[4] See chapter 7.   [5] This is discussed further in chapter 7.

[6] Consider, for example, the prerogative of mercy, discussed at p 214, *post*.

[7] For a modern example, see *R v Secretary of State for the Home Department, ex parte Northumbria Police Authority* [1989] QB 26, [1988] 1 All ER 556.

[8] See, generally: Baker, *An Introduction to English Legal History* (4th edn, 2002). Certain local courts survived formally until 1973, when they were abolished by the Courts Act 1971, s 43.

were originally performed by the King's Council and by the justices who travelled the country on his behalf. The jurisdiction of the King's Council gave rise to the emergence of the old common law courts of Exchequer, Common Pleas, and King's Bench, which continued to operate until they were abolished by the Judicature Acts 1873–75.[9]

As the common law grew more rigid, principally through the writ system, those who felt that they had suffered injustice as a result would petition the King to exercise his prerogative in their favour. These petitions were initially dealt with by the King in Council, but were later delegated to the King's chief minister, the Chancellor. Eventually the system became formalized, culminating in the development of rules of equity and the creation of the Court of Chancery. Equity then, evolved as a mechanism for remedying the deficiencies of the common law, and the Court of Chancery continued to be the principal forum for administering equity until its abolition in 1875.[10]

THE PRINCIPAL SOURCES OF LAW

1 LEGISLATION

The emergence of Parliament as the dominant force within the United Kingdom constitution[11] led to the growth of legislation as a major source of law, transcending both common law and equity in its importance. Its role today is unquestioned. Common law and equity are nowadays concerned essentially with the application and development of existing principles, and whilst this does involve the making of law,[12] courts generally take the view that the development of entirely new principles should be left to Parliament.[13] Legislation can also change or abolish existing common law principles, and amend or repeal earlier statutes.

The nature, creation, and interpretation of legislation are the subject of detailed consideration in chapter 2 of this book.

2 COMMON LAW

Despite the significance of legislation in modern times, common law is still one of the most important sources of legal rules, and its application through the doctrine of judicial precedent is the subject of detailed consideration in chapter 3.

---

[9] For the main courts prior to 1875, see pp 231–236, *post*.

[10] Principles of equity are now administered and applied by all courts.

[11] Through the development of the doctrine of the legislative supremacy of Parliament. Under this, no court can question the validity of an Act of Parliament: see *British Railways Board* v *Pickin* [1974] AC 765, [1974] 1 All ER 609.

[12] See further, p 78, *post*.

[13] See *Malone* v *Metropolitan Police Commissioner (No 2)* [1979] Ch 344, [1979] 2 All ER 620, and p 327, *post*.

The basic principle underpinning the early development of the common law was that a right only existed if there was a procedure for enforcing it *(ubi remedium ibi ius)*, and for this reason substantive law became inextricably bound up with procedure. The nature of the disputed right and the procedure through which it could be enforced determined which court dealt with the matter. Common law claims became highly technical, with the nature of the form of action often determining the content of the law and whether a particular claim could succeed. This rigid 'writ system' was effectively abolished by the Common Law Procedure Acts 1852 and 1854, and the law now strives to concentrate upon substance rather than form.

In criminal matters the common law developed the forms of trial which, in nature if not in detail, still exist today. Ancient procedures such as trial by battle may have disappeared,[14] but trial on indictment involving trial by jury[15] is of ancient origin, and was undertaken in the old courts of Assize.[16] In addition, the criminal law was also enforced summarily through trial by justices of the peace without a jury. Though procedures are much changed, these forms of trial are distinctly recognizable to modern eyes.

3   EQUITY

Equity developed primarily to correct deficiencies in the common law, and this inevitably meant that the two systems were frequently in conflict. Although the conflict was ultimately resolved in favour of equity,[17] the existence of two systems of law and two sets of courts, each with their own procedures, remedies, and routes of appeal, continued to cause problems of jurisdiction. The Judicature Acts 1873–75 were intended to bring about fundamental reform, and their immediate effect was to create a unified system of courts and procedure. The Acts did not merge the substantive rules and it is still correct to talk about 'principles of equity' or 'equitable remedies', but the unification of the courts did lead to considerable fusion between the two sets of rules. Courts can now apply both rules of common law and equity, irrespective of their origins, and it is often unclear to which of the two historical systems a rule owes its parentage. The effect of equity upon substantive law is therefore beyond doubt, particularly in relation to matters affecting property and trusts, the law of contract, and important remedies like the injunction.

4   THE EUROPEAN UNION

While the traditional sources of English law continue to be important, two European sources have become increasingly significant. One of these is the European Union. The Union was founded in 1992 upon the European Community,[18] a supra-national body

---

[14] Trial by battle was not formally abolished until the decision in *Ashford* v *Thornton* (1818) 1 B & Ald 405 reminded Parliament that it still theoretically existed.

[15] See pp 330 and 576, *post*.   [16] See p 233, *post*.   [17] *Earl of Oxford's case* (1615) 1 Rep Ch 1.

[18] Before the creation of the Union, this was known as the European Communities (plural), but the singular term 'Community' was adopted by the Maastricht Treaty in 1992.

with its own legal personality, institutions, and the capacity to make and enforce laws. The United Kingdom joined the European Community in 1972, and by virtue of the European Communities Act of the same year, Community laws were integrated into the English legal system. European Community law should therefore be regarded as a direct source of English law, and its importance is sufficient to warrant separate and more detailed treatment in chapter 4.

5 EUROPEAN CONVENTION ON HUMAN RIGHTS

The United Kingdom was one of the first signatories to the Convention for the Protection of Human Rights and Fundamental Freedoms in 1950.[19] This Convention, usually referred to as the European Convention on Human Rights (or ECHR), is a treaty of the Council of Europe, and unlike the law of the European Community it has never been incorporated directly into domestic law. While its principles have influenced the interpretation of statutes, the development of the common law, and decisions about the content of legislation, until recently its provisions could only be enforced by the European Court of Human Rights in Strasbourg. The position has now changed significantly as a result of the Human Rights Act 1998. This major piece of legislation obliges public authorities to act compatibly with Convention rights,[20] and in the event of a breach of those rights, it enables victims to seek a direct remedy in the domestic courts.[21] It also requires courts to interpret legislation in a manner compatible with Convention rights as far as it is possible to do so,[22] though it stops short of allowing the courts to disapply Acts of Parliament which cannot be interpreted in this way. Both the Human Rights Act and the Convention itself are the subject of more detailed discussion in chapters 5 and 6.

6 OTHER SOURCES

The following historical categories of law have now lost much of their original importance, and for this reason their content is not elaborated in detail in this book. They are not entirely without relevance, however, and their wider contribution to the development of the common law does merit some consideration.

(a) Custom

Though custom is no longer an important source of law in its own right, much of the early common law developed through the application by the courts of existing English customs. Thus customs such as monogamy, parental rights, the right to use the seashore for navigation and fishing,[23] and most of the early principles of criminal law, have either become part of the common law or have been incorporated in statute.

---

[19] The Convention came into effect in 1953.   [20] Section 6.
[21] Section 7.   [22] Section 3; see p 155, *post*.
[23] Though not for bathing or beachcombing; see *Alfred F Beckett Ltd* v *Lyons* [1967] Ch 449, [1967] 1 All ER 833. For a modern example of reliance on customary fishing rights, see *Anderson* v *Alnwick District Council* [1993] 3 All ER 613, [1993] 1 WLR 1156.

The word 'custom' may also be used in a more specific sense, to describe conventional trade or business usage. This is really a misuse of the word, however, since trade usage is usually relevant only to imply terms into contracts, and whether such terms can be implied in a particular case is a question of fact rather than law. Trade customs need not be ancient[24] provided that they can be proved to be certain. However, they must not be illegal or unreasonable and they may always be expressly excluded. Many trade customs were originally an elaborate method of granting discounts to purchasers; hence the 'baker's dozen' and the fact that 1,000 rabbits means 1,200 rabbits to rabbit-dealers.[25]

Another common use of the word 'custom' is to describe local custom; rules of law which apply only in a definite locality. This type of custom *is* a separate source of law, and it has two elementary and unvarying characteristics. First, it must be an exception to the common law, and second, it must be confined in its application to a particular locality or a class of persons within a locality, such as fishermen. Examples of the type of local customary right still existing include rights of way, rights to indulge in sports and pastimes on a village green,[26] and rights to dry fishing-nets on land within a parish.[27]

Local customary rights only exist in law when recognized by judicial decision and this means satisfying certain tests.[28] Firstly, the custom must have existed 'from time whereof the memory of man runneth not to the contrary' (time immemorial) and this has been fixed by statute at 1189.[29] In practice proof of existence in 1189 is rarely available, and the courts are usually satisfied by evidence that the custom has existed for a long time. It must have existed uninterrupted, however, and any interruption of the custom since 1189 defeats its existence. In addition, a custom can only exist by common consent. This means that it must not have been exercised by the use of force, nor secretly, nor under a revocable licence. Thus, where the right to fish depended upon the grant of a licence by the owners of an oyster fishery, it was held that there was no custom since enjoyment had never been as of right.[30] Other requirements are that the custom is certain, that it is consistent with other local customs, and that any duty imposed by the custom is obligatory. Finally, the most important test is that of reasonableness. A custom that is repugnant to the common law cannot be reasonable, and for this reason the House of Lords in one case rejected a custom which enabled a lord to undermine his tenant's land without compensating him for the resulting damage.[31]

(b) Canon law

Canon law, which is the law of the Western or Catholic Church, has influenced the growth of English law in two ways. First, it was the basis of many concepts formulated in the

---

[24] See *Noble* v *Kennoway* (1780) 2 Doug KB 510 at 513, per Lord Mansfield.

[25] *Smith* v *Wilson* (1832) 3 B & Ad 728.

[26] *New Windsor Corporation* v *Mellor* [1975] Ch 380, [1975] 3 All ER 44.

[27] *Mercer* v *Denne* [1905] 2 Ch 538.   [28] These tests owe their origins to the work of Blackstone.

[29] Statute of Westminster I 1275.

[30] *Mills* v *Colchester Corporation* (1867) LR 2 CP 476; see also *Alfred F Beckett Ltd* v *Lyons* [1967] Ch 449, [1967] 1 All ER 833.

[31] *Wolstanton Ltd and Duchy of Lancaster* v *Newcastle-under-Lyme Corporation* [1940] AC 860, [1940] 3 All ER 101.

law courts, and as such it is an original source of other, more modern sources. Examples include the nature of criminal law and its close association with moral fault, the use of imprisonment as a punishment for crime, and, of course, the nature of Christian marriage and family rights. Canon law also influenced the nature of equity, the strong moral content of which is attributable to the fact that the early Chancellors were clerics.

The second way in which canon law became a source of English law was by its application in the ecclesiastical courts. In this context it was a system of law wholly independent of the common law, and during the Middle Ages the ecclesiastical courts were completely outside the control of the King. Their jurisdiction remained separate from the common law except in the areas of probate and matrimonial jurisdiction, but since 1857 it has been confined to matters affecting members of the Church.[32]

(c) Roman law[33]

Roman law, the basis of most continental legal systems, is of surprisingly little importance as a source of English law. There was never a system of English courts applying solely Roman law and any influence that it did have was therefore indirect. The principal link between Roman law and common law is Bracton's treatise *De Legibus et Consuetudinibus Angliae*, written around 1250. Bracton was well versed in Roman law, and the civilian principles incorporated into his treatise owed much to the writings of the Roman jurist Justinian. Common law judges faced with a case of first impression have occasionally looked to Bracton for assistance, and in doing so have adopted Romanist principles. The leading example is the judgment of Holt CJ in *Coggs* v *Bernard*,[34] which classifies bailments according to Bracton's system.

(d) Textbooks

Unlike statutes and law reports, which are original literary sources of law, textbooks are merely a secondary source. Even the most highly regarded modern textbooks have little or no value as a source of law, since direct authority for a legal rule can almost always be found in a law report or Act of Parliament. However, in the infancy of law reporting textbooks were (and still are) the main source of authority for most common law rules. Indeed, during this period the line between a law report and a textbook opinion was often quite a narrow one, and Coke's *Institutes* (Inst) are generally accorded as much authority as his Reports. It will thus be apparent that there are two types of legal textbook. The first is the ancient textbook or 'book of authority', which is commonly used as an original source of common law. The second type is the modern textbook, which is not a source of law at all. The main functions of a modern textbook are to indicate where direct sources of law may be found and to provide an analysis of them. The dividing line between books of authority and modern textbooks is purely historical and depends on the availability of direct literary sources. Blackstone's *Commentaries on the Laws of England* is probably the watershed, in that although it is a book of authority, it was also the forerunner of the modern textbook.

---

[32] See p 287, *post*.   [33] See Lee, *Elements of Roman Law* (4th edn, 1986).
[34] (1703) 2 Ld Raym 909.

Books of authority. Of the many works produced as legal textbooks only about a dozen are accepted as books of authority, and it is no accident that almost all the authors of these works were judges. The academic lawyer in the modern sense did not appear until Blackstone in the eighteenth century, and Blackstone himself was also a judge.

Glanvill's treatise *De Legibus et Consuetudinibus Angliae* (concerning the laws and customs of England) was written in Latin in about 1187. It deals mainly with the subject of land law and is the first major commentary on the common law in existence. It is still cited as a book of authority,[35] though not as frequently as the larger and more comprehensive treatise of Bracton. The latter treatise, dating from around 1250, was also written in Latin and entitled *De Legibus et Consuetudinibus Angliae*. It draws many Roman law analogies and virtually all the principles of Roman law which have found their way into English law have done so via Bracton. Bracton was, however, primarily a chronicler of common law and his treatise stands as the major academic work on this subject prior to Coke's *Institutes*.

Littleton's *Of Tenures* was published in the late fifteenth century, and it was the first comprehensive study of English land law. It appears that the work was intended for use as a textbook and it was in fact used for this purpose for centuries after its composition. It is also notable as being the first major legal work to be printed rather than written. It was described by Coke as 'the most perfect and absolute work that ever was written in any human science'. Coke himself was probably the greatest of the early textbook writers, and his four *Institutes of the Laws of England* are, alongside his law reports, his great contribution to academic literature. The first Institute was published in 1628 and is a treatise on Littleton's *Of Tenures*. The second is a summary of the principal medieval statutes. The third is concerned with criminal law, and the fourth deals with the jurisdiction of the courts. The reason for the exalted position of the *Institutes* is Coke's mastery of the Year Books,[36] which has probably never been equalled. For this reason the Year Books are cited comparatively infrequently, while the Institutes have probably been cited to English courts more frequently than any other book of authority.

After Coke a large number of legal textbooks were produced. A few, such as those of Hawkins, Hale, and Foster are regarded as being particularly authoritative in the area of criminal law. In *Joyce v DPP*[37] for example, the House of Lords relied almost entirely on the work of Foster, Hale, Hawkins, East, and Coke, in deciding that a foreigner who enjoyed the protection of the Crown could be guilty of treason under the Treason Act 1351. More recently, in defining the common law offence of affray in the House of Lords, Lord Gardiner LC referred to Fitzherbert, Coke, Hale, Hawkins, and Blackstone.[38]

Blackstone's *Commentaries on the Laws of England*, published in 1765, deal with constitutional law, family law, the law of property, succession, contract, tort, criminal law, and civil and criminal procedure. It is, however, in the fields of tort and criminal law that Blackstone's authority is greatest. The *Commentaries* were probably the last work of

---

[35] *Warner v Sampson* [1959] 1 QB 297, [1959] 1 All ER 120.
[36] These are discussed further at p 103, *post*.   [37] [1946] AC 347, [1946] 1 All ER 186.
[38] *Button v DPP* [1966] AC 591, [1965] 3 All ER 587.

authority to be written, and in the event of an inconsistency with earlier works, the older authorities are almost bound to prevail. This is well illustrated by the case of *Button* v *DPP*,[39] in which Blackstone's assertion that a common law affray could occur only in a public place[40] was rejected by the House of Lords as inconsistent with earlier statements by Hale and Hawkins.

Modern textbooks. The growth of law reporting since Blackstone's era has made it unnecessary to look at more recent textbooks as a direct source of common law rules. Nineteenth-century works such as Stephen's *Commentaries on the Laws of England* are sometimes consulted, but only as guides rather than sources. There are nevertheless many standard textbooks which have considerable persuasive authority. Virtually every branch of the law has its standard work and a judge will think twice before dismissing a statement of law appearing in such a work. However, in the event of a textbook being inconsistent with a principle contained in a precedent or a statute, the latter will always prevail. For example, in *Button* v *DPP*[41] the House of Lords drew attention to errors in *Archbold's Pleadings, Evidence & Practice in Criminal Cases* and *Russell on Crimes and Misdemeanours*; both standard works on the criminal law. Similarly, in *Shenton* v *Tyler*[42] the Master of the Rolls referred to a dozen textbooks on evidence before deciding that they were all mistaken as to the scope of marital privilege. These are exceptional occurrences, however, and on the whole, the persuasive authority of a standard textbook is of considerable weight. There have been several cases in which a court has been willing to accept the view of a distinguished academic upon the law. Thus the Court of Appeal in *Re Ellenborough Park*[43] adopted the description of easements contained in Cheshire's *Modern Real Property*, while the House of Lords in *A-G* v *De Keyser's Royal Hotel Ltd*[44] expressly accepted Dicey's definition of the royal prerogative. To take this a step further, counsel for the respondents in *Rookes* v *Barnard*[45] suggested that the tort of intimidation had actually been created by Sir John Salmond in his work on the law of torts.

There used to be a rule of practice that a textbook could not be cited in court during the lifetime of its author, but this is no longer the case and several legal authors have had the satisfaction of seeing their opinions judicially endorsed during their lifetimes.[46] In *R* v *Shivpuri*, in which the House of Lords overruled one of its previous decisions in the face of considerable academic criticism, Lord Bridge (who had also been party to the earlier decision) ended his speech with the following tribute:[47]

> I cannot conclude this opinion without disclosing that I have had the advantage, since the conclusion of the argument in this appeal, of reading an article by Professor Glanville Williams entitled 'The Lords and Impossible Attempts, or *Quis Custodet Ipsos Custodies?*' [1986] CLJ 33. The language in which he criticises the decision in *Anderton* v *Ryan* is not conspicuous for its moderation, but it would be foolish, on

---

[39] Ibid.   [40] 4 Comm 145.   [41] [1966] AC 591, [1965] 3 All ER 587.
[42] [1939] Ch 620, [1939] 1 All ER 827.   [43] [1956] Ch 131, [1955] 3 All ER 667.
[44] [1920] AC 508.   [45] [1964] AC 1129, [1964] 1 All ER 367.
[46] See, e.g., *Read* v *J Lyons & Co Ltd* [1945] KB 216, [1945] 1 All ER 106 (affirmed [1947] AC 156, [1946] 2 All ER 471); *DPP* v *Humphrys* [1977] AC 1, [1976] 2 All ER 497.
[47] [1987] AC 1 at 23, [1986] 2 All ER 334 at 345.

that account, not to recognise the force of the criticism and churlish not to acknowledge the assistance I have derived from it.

In a recent Court of Appeal decision concerned with grazing rights,[48] counsel cited at least fourteen different textbooks spanning a period of more than three centuries. As there had not been a single reliably reported case in which the particular issue had formed part of the ratio, Robert Walker LJ clearly found these works helpful. After reviewing the various authorities, he stated:[49]

> In this case, [counsel for the plaintiffs] relies on textbook authority, not for an analysis of apparently conflicting decisions, but to make good a want of any clear decision. In those circumstances, and in such a technical area of the law of real property, textbooks may provide the court with valuable assistance.

He went on to conclude that:[50]

> [T]he preponderance of authority – both in reported cases and in classic textbooks – appears to me...to support the [plaintiff's case]. In my judgment the cumulative effect of this authority, even if it is not strictly binding, is so powerful that it should be followed.

THE DISTINCTION BETWEEN CIVIL AND CRIMINAL MATTERS

1 THE IMPORTANCE OF THE DISTINCTION

The law distinguishes between civil and criminal matters, and courts are sometimes classified into civil and criminal courts. This latter classification is useful for the purposes of exposition, but in reality it is not a valid one. Although certain courts do exercise a purely civil or criminal jurisdiction, most, including the House of Lords, Court of Appeal, High Court, Crown Court, and magistrates' courts, exercise jurisdiction in both civil and criminal matters.

This distinction between civil and criminal matters is important for several reasons. First, the terminology used is different. In civil proceedings a claimant (formerly called a plaintiff) sues a defendant or makes an application for a civil order, while in a criminal case a prosecutor prosecutes the accused.

Secondly, the burden and standard of proof differ. In a civil case the party asserting a particular matter bears the burden of proving it, usually to the civil standard of the

---

[48] *Bettison v Langton* [2000] Ch 54, [1999] 2 All ER 367 (affirmed [2001] UKHL 24, [2002] 1 AC 27, [2001] 3 All ER 417). See also *A v Secretary of State for the Home Department* [2004] UKHL 56, [2005] 2 WLR 87, in which Lord Walker relied heavily on academic literature in his discussion of the UK's anti-terror laws.

[49] [2000] Ch 54 at 64, [1999] 2 All ER 367 at 375.   [50] [2000] Ch 54 at 72, [1999] 2 All ER 367 at 382.

balance of probabilities.[51] In contrast, the burden of proof in a criminal case normally rests with the prosecution,[52] and the standard is that of proof beyond reasonable doubt.[53] However, this statement disguises the fact that even in a civil case the standard of proof may be high. In *R v Wolverhampton Coroner, ex parte McCurbin*,[54] an inquest (a civil inquiry into the cause of death by a coroners' court)[55] had to decide whether the death of an individual whilst being arrested amounted to an unlawful killing or death by misadventure. The Divisional Court upheld the coroner's view that the standard of proof needed to establish unlawful killing was the criminal standard, whilst that for establishing death by misadventure was the balance of probabilities. Findings of suicide in coroners' courts have also been held to require proof beyond reasonable doubt.[56] Similarly, in *Halford v Brookes*,[57] a civil case in which the defendant was effectively accused of murder, Rougier J observed:

> No-one, whether in a criminal or a civil court, should be declared guilty of murder, certainly not such a terrible crime as this, unless the tribunal was sure that the evidence does not admit of any other sensible conclusion.

More recently, in civil proceedings to obtain anti-social behaviour orders,[58] sex offender orders[59] and football banning orders,[60] it has been held that the standard of proof required for such purposes is indistinguishable from the criminal standard.

What is common to all of these situations is that they involve allegations of criminal or quasi-criminal conduct, even though the proceedings themselves are civil.[61] It is this allegation of wrongdoing which is said to necessitate a more exacting standard of proof. Whether there are in fact two standards, or simply different levels of proof which vary according to what has to be determined, is a moot point. In *R (on the application of N) v M*[62] the Court of Appeal had to determine the standard to be applied when ordering

---

[51] The standard is not an absolute one: see *Hornal v Neuberger Products Ltd* [1957] 1 QB 247, [1956] 3 All ER 970; *R v Secretary of State for the Home Department, ex parte Khawaja* [1984] AC 74, [1983] 1 All ER 765.

[52] See *Woolmington v DPP* [1935] AC 462. For exceptions, see *Bratty v Attorney-General for Northern Ireland* [1963] AC 386, [1961] 3 All ER 523 (the defence of insanity); Magistrates' Courts Act 1980, s 101; and other specific statutory exceptions.

[53] For the meaning of this phrase, see *Miller v Minister of Pensions* [1947] 2 All ER 372, per Lord Denning. In a case where the burden of proof is on an accused the standard is the civil standard of the balance of probabilities: *R v Carr-Briant* [1943] KB 607, [1943] 2 All ER 156.

[54] [1990] 1 WLR 719, [1990] 2 All ER 759.   [55] See p 276, *post*.

[56] *R v West London Coroner, ex parte Gray* [1988] QB 467, [1987] 2 All ER 129. Cf. *Dunbar (administrator of Dunbar, dec'd) v Plant* [1998] Ch 412, [1997] 4 All ER 289, where in civil proceedings it was held that the standard of proof for establishing that a party had aided and abetted a suicide was the civil standard.

[57] (1991) *The Times* 3 October.

[58] *R (on the application of McCann) v Manchester Crown Court and others* [2002] UKHL 39, [2003] 1 AC 787, [2002] 4 All ER 593.

[59] *B v Chief Constable of Avon and Somerset* [2001] 1 All ER 562, [2001] 1 WLR 340.

[60] *Gough v Chief Constable of Derbyshire* [2002] EWCA Civ 351, [2002] QB 1213, [2002] 2 All ER 985.

[61] Different considerations apply where allegations of serious criminal conduct are made in the context of a care proceedings application. The welfare of the child is the paramount consideration in such a case, and the standard of proof is therefore the balance of probabilities: *Re U (A Child) (Serious Injury: Standard of Proof)* [2004] EWCA Civ 567, [2005] Fam 134, [2004] 3 FLR 263.

[62] [2002] EWCA Civ 1789, [2003] 1 WLR 562, [2003] 1 FLR 667.

that a person detained under the Mental Health Act 1983 could be treated without his consent. A European Court of Human Rights case[63] was cited, in which it had been said that proof of necessity must be 'convincingly shown', but the Court of Appeal maintained that this did not amount to using the criminal standard:[64]

> [The defendant] submits that the test is, in effect, the same as the criminal standard of proof. We disagree. It seems to us that no useful purpose is served by importing the language of the criminal law. The phrase 'convincingly shown' is easily understood. The standard is a high one. But it does not need elaboration or further explanation.

This case should, however, be compared with the recent decision in *R (on the application of McCann)* v *Manchester Crown Court*, which concerned the making of anti-social behaviour orders.[65] The House of Lords considered it impractical to leave individual magistrates to determine precisely what was required by a 'heightened civil standard' of proof: in the interests of pragmatism Lord Steyn concluded that the standard in all such cases should be the criminal one.[66]

The categorization of a matter as civil or criminal is not only relevant to the burden of proof; it also determines which rules of evidence apply to the case. The rules of evidence followed in civil proceedings often differ from those applicable in criminal cases. This was well illustrated in *R* v *Governor of Brixton Prison, ex parte Levin*[67] where the House of Lords held that because extradition proceedings were to be treated as criminal proceedings, they were subject to rules in the Police and Criminal Evidence Act 1984. Similarly, the finding in *R (on the application of McCann)* v *Manchester Crown Court*[68] that proceedings to obtain an anti-social behaviour order were civil in nature, meant that the court could accept hearsay evidence as to the conduct alleged. This would not have been the case if the same allegations had been made at that time in criminal proceedings, though it should be noted that the Criminal Justice Act 2003 now provides for hearsay evidence to be more widely admissible in criminal cases.[69]

Finally, the fact that proceedings are criminal or are to be regarded as such, will affect the procedures to be followed and the standards that those procedures have to meet. Article 6 of the European Convention on Human Rights[70] specifies a number of minimum rights for the protection of those 'charged with a criminal offence'. It also requires such charges to be subject to a presumption of innocence. These rights have assumed added importance since the coming into force of the Human Rights Act 1998, as courts and public authorities are now obliged by domestic law to discharge their functions in a manner compatible with Convention rights.

---

[63] *Herczegfalvy* v *Austria* (1993) EHRR 437.

[64] [2002] EWCA Civ 1789 at [18], [2003] 1 WLR 562 at [18], per Dyson LJ.

[65] [2002] UKHL 39, [2003] 1 AC 787, [2002] 4 All ER 593.

[66] Ibid at [18].   [67] [1997] AC 741, [1997] 3 All ER 289.

[68] [2002] UKHL 39, [2003] 1 AC 787, [2002] 4 All ER 593.

[69] See Part 11 of the Act.   [70] See p 185, *post*.

2 DECISION AS TO WHETHER A MATTER IS CIVIL OR CRIMINAL

This decision is not always easy to make, and it cannot be made simply by asking whether the court that deals with the matter is a civil or a criminal court. An example of a case in which a court had to determine such a question is *ex parte Levin*.[71] The House of Lords had to decide whether extradition proceedings before a magistrates' court were civil or criminal in nature, since this was crucial to determining which rules of evidence applied. In an earlier case[72] a Divisional Court had apparently concluded that such proceedings were not criminal, and the court noted counsel's argument that they were *sui generis* (i.e. a type of their own). Lord Hoffmann, giving the decision of the House, disagreed with this view, pointing to a contrary body of authority[73] and a statutory requirement to conduct extradition proceedings 'as near as may be' as if they were committal proceedings before magistrates.[74]

The difficulty facing the court in *Levin* is far from unique, and it is increasingly possible to identify areas where the boundary between criminal and civil proceedings has become blurred. For example, the same acts or omissions may give rise to both civil and criminal proceedings. Thus, while a motorist who causes damage, injury or loss of life may well be prosecuted for a motoring offence, that same motorist will almost certainly be liable in damages if sued by the aggrieved party. The relatives of a person who has been unlawfully killed, but in respect of whose death no prosecution has been brought, may sue in tort; ostensibly for compensation, but in reality to provide a forum in which the culpability of the defendant can be established. Similarly, if a rape victim sues his[75] or her assailant, the assailant is liable irrespective of whether he has been successfully prosecuted. Another example is contempt of court, which can be both civil and criminal in nature.[76]

The growing tendency for formal links to be made between civil and criminal procedures is perhaps of greater significance. Increasingly, the lines between civil and criminal have become blurred, as the government has sought to address certain types of behaviour by a mix of civil and criminal proceedings. Several examples illustrate this point:

- The Protection from Harassment Act 1997, makes it a criminal offence to pursue a course of conduct amounting to harassment of a person, or which causes a person to fear that violence will be used against him. However, section 3 creates a civil remedy in tort for a person who is (or may be) the victim of harassment, and a restraining order can be made. Similarly, a criminal court may make a restraining order when sentencing a person for an offence, or, under the Domestic Violence,

---

[71] [1997] AC 741, [1997] 3 All ER 289.

[72] *R v Governor of Belmarsh Prison, ex parte Francis* [1995] 3 All ER 634, [1995] 1 WLR 1121.

[73] *Amand v Secretary of State for Home Affairs* [1943] AC 147, [1942] 2 All ER 381, where Viscount Simon LC said that a matter may be 'criminal' even though a person is not charged with a breach of the criminal law.

[74] Extradition Act 1989, s 9(2) and Schedule 1, para 6(1).

[75] The offence of rape extends to male victims: Sexual Offences Act 2003, s 1.

[76] See p 246, *post*.

Crime and Victims Act 2004, even after acquittal. In each of these situations, even though the order is civil, breach of it is a criminal offence.

- The Crime and Disorder Act 1998[77] and Sexual Offences Act 2003[78] permit magistrates' courts to make anti-social behaviour orders (ASBOs) and sexual offences prevention orders respectively. These are civil orders which can either be made in civil proceedings or, following conviction for a criminal offence, at the time of sentencing.[79] Non-compliance with such an order without lawful excuse amounts to a criminal offence triable before a magistrates' court.

- The Proceeds of Crime Act 2002 establishes an Assets Recovery Agency with the power to instigate civil proceedings to recover property obtained by criminal conduct. It even allows any income generated by such conduct to be taxed. The exercise of these powers clearly involves proof of criminal activity, but as the proceedings are civil the standard is that of the balance of probabilities.

- Civil proceedings to protect an 'associated person' can be brought under the Family Law Act 1996, and they can lead to a non-molestation order being made. This is a civil order, but under the Domestic Violence, Crime and Victims Act 2004 breach of such an order will in many circumstances amount to a criminal offence. The criminal law is thus used to provide a means of enforcing a civil order.

- The control order powers in the Prevention of Terrorism Act 2005 provide another interesting example. These powers may be used to impose unprecedented restrictions on individual liberties. Yet a court can confirm even the most serious orders if it is satisfied 'on the balance of probabilities' that the controlled person is or has been involved in terrorist-related activities.[80] Contravention of a control order 'without reasonable excuse' is a criminal offence punishable by imprisonment for up to five years.[81]

The impact of the Human Rights Act 1998

As already noted, one consequence of the Human Rights Act 1998 is that courts and public authorities must now comply with the European Convention on Human Rights. Article 6 of this Convention concerns the right to a fair trial, and it contains a number of safeguards which apply specifically to those charged with criminal offences. Thus while the boundary between civil and criminal law is now becoming increasingly blurred, the ability to make the distinction is perhaps more important than ever.

The European Court of Human Rights has previously confirmed that the term 'criminal' has an autonomous meaning for these purposes. This means that while a State's classification of a matter as civil or criminal is undoubtedly important, it cannot be conclusive: the content of what is alleged and the nature of any penalty must also be taken

---

[77] Sections 1 and 1C; see also the Anti-social Behaviour Act 2003.
[78] Section 104; this replaces the sex offender order provisions in the Crime and Disorder Act 1998, s 2.
[79] See e.g. *R v Boness*; *R v Bebbington* [2005] EWCA Crim 2395, [2006] 1 Cr App R (S) 120.
[80] Section 4(7) of the 2005 Act; for further discussion, see p 184, *post*.
[81] Ibid, s 9; it is also punishable by a fine.

into account.[82] It has previously been established that proceedings for non-payment of council tax are 'criminal' for the purposes of the Convention,[83] as are proceedings for binding over to keep the peace.[84] In contrast, the House of Lords used the Convention test to determine that ASBOs are not criminal in nature.[85] Crucial to this decision was the finding that there was no 'penalty' involved in the making of such an order: the House observed that there appeared to be no case in which the European Court of Human Rights had classified proceedings as 'criminal' in the absence of a penalty. It also noted that an ASBO cannot be entered as a conviction on a defendant's record.[86] The decision has been criticized for attaching insufficient weight to the fact that in common with most criminal sanctions, the purpose of an ASBO is to prevent behaviour detrimental to the public interest. Moreover, such orders arguably *do* have both a punitive and a deterrent element.[87] Nevertheless, the House of Lords has since applied a similar approach[88] to proceedings under section 4A of the Criminal Procedure (Insanity) Act 1964. A boy charged with indecent assault was declared incompetent to stand trial, and in the section 4A proceedings that followed, a second jury found that he had committed 'the act' in question. He was therefore required to register as a sex offender.[89] The House of Lords concluded that there was no incompatibility with Article 6 of the Convention, since the section 4A procedure did not involve the 'determination of a criminal charge' and therefore did not violate the presumption of innocence. Lord Bingham delivered the judgment for a unanimous House:[90]

> Whether one views the matter through domestic or European spectacles, the answer is the same: the purpose and function of the s 4A procedure is not to decide whether the accused person has committed a criminal offence. The procedure can result in a final acquittal, but it cannot result in a conviction and it cannot result in punishment. Even an adverse finding may lead, as here, to an absolute discharge . . . It is, indeed, difficult if not impossible to conceive of a criminal proceeding which cannot in any circumstances culminate in the imposition of any penalty, since it is the purpose of the criminal law to proscribe, and by punishing to deter, conduct regarded as sufficiently damaging to the interests of society to merit the imposition of penal sanctions.

[82] *Engel* v *The Netherlands (No 1)* (1979–1980) 1 EHRR 647 at [678]–[679].

[83] *Benham* v *United Kingdom* (1996) 22 EHRR 293.

[84] See *Steel* v *United Kingdom* (1999) 28 EHRR 603. Cf. *Williamson* v *Chief Constable of West Midlands* [2003] EWCA Civ 337, [2004] 1 WLR 14, in which the Court of Appeal held that breach of the peace is not 'an offence' for the purposes of the Police and Criminal Evidence Act 1984. The court pointed out that since the term 'criminal offence' has an autonomous meaning within Convention jurisprudence, it is not essential for breach of the peace to be categorized as an offence in domestic law. On this view, what matters is not the classification of an act but whether any Convention rights are violated as a consequence of that classification.

[85] *R (on the application of McCann)* v *Manchester Crown Court and others* [2002] UKHL 39, [2003] 1 AC 787, [2002] 4 All ER 593. For a discussion, see Bakalis, 'Asbos, "Preventative orders" and the European Court of Human Rights' [2007] EHRLR 427.

[86] See the Rehabilitation of Offenders Act 1974, s 1.

[87] See Bakalis, 'Anti-Social Behaviour Orders – Criminal Penalties or Civil Injunctions' [2003] 62(3) CLJ 583.

[88] *R* v *H (Fitness to Plead)* [2003] UKHL 1, [2003] 1 All ER 497, [2003] 1 WLR 411. See also p 631, *post.*

[89] Under the Sex Offenders Act 1997, s 1(1)(b); now repealed.

[90] [2003] UKHL 1 at [18]–[19], [2003] 1 All ER 497 at [18]–[19], [2003] 1 WLR 411.

The idea that the possibility of punishment is a distinguishing feature of a criminal act is consistent with conventional wisdom.[91] Nevertheless, being subjected to an ASBO or required to register as a sex offender must surely have adverse consequences, and it is safe to assume that such matters will continue to be hotly debated.

Finally, it was recently confirmed[92] that an application to confiscate the proceeds of criminal activity does not amount to a criminal charge and does not engage the protection of Article 6(2).[93] Thus, although confiscation proceedings are subject to a lesser standard of proof and impose a 'persuasive' burden on the person whose assets are disputed, they do not give rise to a breach of the Convention.[94]

THE ADMINISTRATION OF THE ENGLISH LEGAL SYSTEM

As outlined at the beginning of this chapter, the English legal system has developed in a piecemeal way over many centuries, with the result that no single institution has had overall responsibility for its administration. The creation of the Ministry of Justice in 2007 went some way towards addressing this, but other government departments and a growing number of executive agencies and other bodies continue to play a role. For example, the police,[95] Crown Prosecution Service,[96] Prison Service,[97] Youth Justice Board[98] and Parole Board[99] all perform important functions with regard to the criminal justice system. In addition, Her Majesty's Courts Service provides administrative support for the major courts,[100] while the Legal Services Commission plays a central role in the funding of legal actions.[101] The work of most of these smaller bodies is now overseen by the Ministry of Justice, the principal functions and responsibilities

---

[91] See, for example, Glanville Williams, 'The Definition of Crime' (1955) 8 CLP 107.

[92] *R v Benjafield* [2002] UKHL 2, [2003] 1 AC 1099, [2002] 1 All ER 815. The application in question was made under s 4(3) of the Drug Trafficking Act 1994.

[93] The Privy Council had previously reached the same conclusion in *HM Advocate* v *McIntosh (Sentencing)* [2001] UKPC D1, [2003] 1 AC 1078, [2001] 2 All ER 638.

[94] The House of Lords also found that even if Article 6(2) had been engaged there would have been no breach. This was because, when interpreted in the light of the Human Rights Act, the burden on the defendant was a 'persuasive' rather than a legal one.

[95] See chapter 13.   [96] See p 383, *post.*

[97] This became an executive agency of the Home Office in 1993 and is now the responsibility of the Ministry of Justice.

[98] Established under the Crime and Disorder Act 1998, s 41. Its principal functions are to monitor and set standards for the work of the youth justice system; see p 547, *post.*

[99] This is an executive non-departmental public body sponsored by the Ministry of Justice: see Criminal Justice Act 2003, s 239.

[100] Except for the House of Lords and the future Supreme Court. The agency was launched in March 2005 when the functions of Magistrates' Courts Committees were integrated into the existing Courts Service: see p 269, *post.*

[101] See chapter 12.

of which are discussed below. The roles of the Home Office and Law Officers are also briefly considered.

1 THE LORD CHANCELLOR AND THE MINISTRY OF JUSTICE

(a) The Lord Chancellor

For centuries, much of the responsibility for the administration of the legal system has rested with the Lord Chancellor. In modern times the holder of this office has exercised a wide range of functions, including those of Cabinet Minister, senior judge and 'speaker' of the House of Lords. Responsibility for overseeing the administration of the Supreme Court, Court of Protection, county courts and magistrates' courts[102] has also fallen within his remit, along with the task of appointing Court Rule Committees and allowing or disallowing their rules.[103] Other functions have included making or advising on judicial appointments, appointing and providing training for justices of the peace, overseeing the funding of legal services, appointing a Legal Services Ombudsman, and maintaining the National Archives[104] and Land Registry.

The Lord Chancellor's ministerial role acquired a new significance when his Department was asked to oversee the implementation of the Human Rights Act 1998. This was followed by the decision to transfer responsibility for constitutional affairs from the Home Office to the Lord Chancellor's Department.[105] These developments increasingly brought the Lord Chancellor into the political spotlight, and questions were raised about whether his role was compatible with the concept of an independent judiciary.[106] In *McGonnell* v *UK*[107] the European Court of Human Rights ruled that the right to a fair trial was breached when the Guernsey Royal Court Bailiff adjudicated in a planning case, having also been involved in making the applicable legislation. It was easy to see the parallels between the Bailiff's position and that of the Lord Chancellor.

On 13 June 2003 the Prime Minister announced plans to abolish the office of Lord Chancellor and transform his Department into a new Department for Constitutional Affairs. The proposal was part of a package of reforms designed to 'redraw the relationship between the Judiciary, the Government and Parliament'.[108] The idea was that the head of the new Department would inherit the Lord Chancellor's ministerial functions and hold the title of Secretary of State for Constitutional Affairs. The Lord Chancellor's judicial functions would be transferred to the Lord Chief Justice, and the mechanics of making judicial appointments would be handed to a new Judicial Appointments Commission. Plans to transfer the judicial functions of the House of Lords to a new Supreme Court were also part of the package.

---

[102] Courts Act 2003, s 1.   [103] For the most recent provisions, see Part 7 of the Courts Act 2003.

[104] Formerly the Public Record Office.

[105] Transfer of Functions (Miscellaneous) Order 2001, SI 2001/3500.

[106] The right to a fair trial under Article 6, ECHR includes the right to have one's rights and obligations determined by 'an independent and impartial tribunal'.

[107] (2000) 30 EHRR 289; see also *Starrs* v *Ruxton* 2000 JC 208, 2000 SLT 42.

[108] Department for Constitutional Affairs, *Constitutional Reform: Reforming the Office of the Lord Chancellor* (2003) CP 13/03.

Lord Falconer was immediately appointed as both Lord Chancellor and Secretary of State, with the intention being that he would hold both titles concurrently until the programme of reform was complete. He explained the rationale for the changes as follows:[109]

> It can no longer be appropriate for a senior judge to sit in Cabinet or for a Government Minister to be our country's senior judge. I have myself made it clear that I shall not sit judicially, but it is now time to bring such anachronistic and questionable arrangements to an end.

Some of the Lord Chancellor's ministerial responsibilities were transferred to the Secretary of State within weeks,[110] and provisions to redistribute his remaining functions were included in the Constitutional Reform Bill. The Bill attracted formidable opposition when it was introduced in the House of Lords. The proposed Judicial Appointments Commission was relatively uncontroversial and a majority of the Lords were also prepared to accept the plans for a Supreme Court: what they could not accept, however, was the idea of abolishing the historic office of Lord Chancellor.[111] By the time the Bill had its first reading in the House of Commons the government had been forced to make significant concessions. Instead of insisting that the office of Lord Chancellor should be abolished, it was now prepared to see the office continue in a modified form. This was a highly embarrassing climb-down but its practical significance should not be overstated. Although the title of Lord Chancellor has been retained, the effect of what is now the Constitutional Reform Act 2005 is that the holder of the officer no longer has a judicial role. During the Commons stages of the Bill, the Courts Minister explained the government's position:[112]

> Whether the post holder is called 'Secretary of State for Constitutional Affairs', 'Lord Chancellor', or has both titles, is not of great significance [...] what matters most is the substance of the post, the nature of the job, and whether it is reformed so that the post holder no longer has conflicting duties.

Having gained acceptance of the idea that a senior Minister should not also be a judge, the government took the view that it was no longer essential for the Lord Chancellor to have a legal qualification and sit in the House of Lords.[113] Section 2 of the Act thus provides that the person appointed as Lord Chancellor must be 'qualified by experience', and in deciding a person's suitability for the role his experience as a practitioner or academic is merely a factor to be 'taken into account'.[114] Experience gained as a Minister or MP in either House of Parliament may also be considered, along with any 'other expe-

---

[109] Ibid, foreword.   [110] Secretary of State for Constitutional Affairs Order 2003, SI 2003/1887.

[111] Most of the concerns related to the possible impact on judicial independence: see p 301, *post*.

[112] 430 HC Official Report (6th Series), coll 621–622, 31 January 2005, Christopher Leslie MP.

[113] This particular change was rejected by the Lords at the first time of asking, but it was eventually passed by a majority of just twelve.

[114] This provision is surely only enforceable at a political level – the idea of a court judicially reviewing the power to make Ministerial appointments is unthinkable: see p 218, *post*.

rience that the Prime Minister considers relevant'.[115] The person appointed has a duty to uphold the continued independence of the judiciary and to refrain from seeking to influence particular judicial decisions. He must also have regard to the need to *defend* judicial independence.[116]

Under the new arrangements[117] the Lord Chief Justice has assumed the title of 'President of the Courts of England and Wales', and the task of representing the judiciary's views to Parliament and the government now falls to him.[118] He is also responsible for overseeing the deployment of individual judges, allocating work within the courts,[119] issuing Practice Directions,[120] and ensuring that appropriate structures are in place for the training and support of judges.[121] The Lord Chancellor on the other hand, continues to be responsible for determining the geographical and jurisdictional boundaries of individual courts, and for ensuring an efficient and effective system to support them.

(b) The Ministry of Justice

In 2007, four years after the creation of the Department for Constitutional Affairs, it was transformed into a Ministry of Justice with a much wider remit.[122] This resulted from the government's decision to 're-focus' the work of the Home Office, following the Home Secretary's declaration that his Department was 'unfit for purpose'.[123] His view was that the Home Office had too many functions and had become too big and unwieldy, and the solution adopted effectively meant splitting it in half. The Home Office has retained responsibility for matters relating to terrorism, immigration and the prevention of crime and anti-social behaviour, but matters relating to criminal law, sentencing, prisons and probation are now the responsibility of the new Ministry of Justice. The Ministry is headed by the Lord Chancellor, who now holds the additional title of Secretary of State for Justice, and its remit includes:

- the administration of courts and tribunals through Her Majesty's Court Service and the Tribunals Service;
- sponsoring and overseeing the work of the Prison Service, the Probation Service, the Youth Justice Board and the Parole Board;
- taking the lead in matters relating to criminal, civil, family and administrative law;
- sentencing policy;

[115] In June 2007 Jack Straw replaced Lord Falconer and became the first Lord Chancellor in history to be appointed from the Commons benches. He did, however, have experience as both a barrister and former Home Secretary.

[116] Section 3.

[117] The details are set out in Schedule 4 of the Act, the blueprint for which was the 'Concordat' agreed between the Lord Chancellor and the Lord Chief Justice in January 2004: DCA, *The Lord Chancellor's Judiciary-Related Functions: Proposals.*

[118] Sections 5(1), 7(1) and 7(2)(a). The fate of the Lord Chancellor's judicial functions is discussed further in chapter 10.

[119] Section 7(2)(c).   [120] Schedule 2, Part 1.   [121] Section 7(2)(b).

[122] With effect from 9 May 2007.   [123] *Guardian,* 29 March 2007.

- Legal Aid and support for the Community Legal Service and Legal Services Commission;
- providing support for the judiciary and the Judicial Appointments Commission; and
- constitutional affairs and human rights.

2 THE HOME OFFICE

Before the creation of the Ministry of Justice, responsibility for criminal justice policies rested with the Home Office. This meant that in addition to his many other duties, the Home Secretary was responsible for matters such as sentencing policy, the prison service, and the maintenance of police standards. Under the new arrangements the Ministry of Justice is expected to take the lead in matters relating to criminal law and sentencing policy, and the prison service and probation service also fall within its remit. The Home Secretary, however, remains responsible for the government's overall strategy for dealing with crime, and his Department still has the power to propose new criminal offences and changes to sentencing powers. Responsibility for the police and related matters also rests with the Home Office, and in areas where both departments have an interest the Office for Criminal Justice Reform has an important role in helping to co-ordinate their efforts.[124] How effectively the new arrangements will work in practice remains to be seen, however, as there are clearly a number of areas in which the roles of the two Departments are difficult to separate. The Home Office, for example, is expected to take the lead on preventing and responding to youth crime, while the Ministry of Justice has primary responsibility for reducing youth re-offending.[125]

3 THE LAW OFFICERS

(a) The Attorney-General

The Law Officers' Department is headed by the Attorney-General and the Solicitor-General, both of whom are Ministers and legal advisers to the Crown.

In addition to his political duties, which include advising government departments and answering questions in Parliament, the Attorney-General is responsible for appointing the Director of Public Prosecutions and for overseeing the work of the Serious Fraud Office and Treasury Solicitors Office. He represents the Crown in major international litigation, certain civil proceedings, and trials for treason and other offences with a constitutional element. Mention may also be made of 'relator' proceedings in which the Attorney-General appears on behalf of a section of the public; proceedings to restrain a public nuisance being one such example. In addition, the consent of the

---

[124] *Home Office – Ministry of Justice Protocol*, 11 May 2007: available at http://www.homeoffice.gov.uk/ documents/new-ho-moj-protocol1. See also, p 544–545, *post*.

[125] Ibid.

Attorney-General is required for the prosecution of certain categories of offence,[126] and he is able to terminate prosecutions on indictment by the entry of a *nolle prosequi*.[127]

The future of the Attorney-General's role is currently under review due to concerns about the perceived tension between his different functions.[128] On the one hand he is a Cabinet Minister who holds office at the whim of the Prime Minister, yet in his capacity as legal adviser to the government and guardian of the public interest, he is required to act with independence and impartiality. This tension is illustrated by the controversy surrounding his advice about the legality of war in Iraq, and in a consultation paper published in July 2007 the government invited views on various options for reform. These include:[129]

- separating the role of chief legal adviser from that of Minister, with the former being exercised by a non-political official;

- modifying the Attorney-General's ministerial role so as to limit his political involvement. He could, for example, cease to attend Cabinet meetings unless his legal advice is required;

- allowing the Attorney-General's legal advice to the government to be published, by removing the client privilege attaching to that advice;

- requiring the Attorney-General to act as legal adviser to Parliament – or the public – instead of the government, or appointing another official to act in this capacity;

- clarifying the Attorney-General's role in relation to individual prosecutions, so that he is no longer able to give directions as to whether a particular prosecution should be brought;

- transferring responsibility for overseeing the prosecuting authorities to a different government department.

At the time of writing it is unclear which, if any, of these options the government will pursue. However, the current Attorney-General has already indicated that she 'will not make key prosecution decisions in individual criminal cases except where the law or national security requires it'.[130]

(b) The Solicitor-General

The Solicitor-General's role used to be to act as the Attorney-General's deputy, and to carry out those functions that had been delegated by the latter. This position has now changed, and the two Ministers are able to decide for themselves how to divide their various functions.[131]

---

[126] Including some offences under the Official Secrets Act 1989, the Public Order Act 1986, and the Anti-Terrorism, Crime and Security Act 2001.

[127] This is a prerogative power; see p 214, *post*.

[128] See, e.g.: House of Commons Constitutional Affairs Select Committee, *Constitutional Role of the Attorney-General: Fifth Report of Session 2006–07*, HC 306, July 2007.

[129] *The Governance of Britain: A Consultation on the Role of the Attorney-General*, Cm 7179, 2007.

[130] Ibid, at p 3. [131] Law Officers Act 1997, s 1.

(c) The Director of Public Prosecutions

The Director of Public Prosecutions is a barrister or solicitor of not less than ten years' standing, who is appointed by the Attorney-General[132] to head the Crown Prosecution Service (CPS). His duties under section 3 of the Prosecution of Offences Act 1985 include the following:

(a) taking over the conduct of all criminal proceedings instituted on behalf of a police force or immigration officer;

(b) instituting and conducting criminal proceedings where the importance or difficulty of the case makes it appropriate that the Director should institute the proceedings;

(c) taking over binding over proceedings brought by a police force;[133]

(d) giving advice to police forces on all matters relating to criminal offences; and

(e) appearing in certain appeals.

Thus the Director and the Crown Prosecution Service effectively control the prosecution process. They do not control the process of investigation – that is a matter for the police – but they may direct that certain enquiries be made. The work of the Law Officers and the CPS is considered in more detail in chapter 12.

FURTHER READING

BAKALIS, 'Anti-Social Behaviour Orders – Criminal Penalties or Civil Injunctions' [2003] 62(3) CLJ 583

BAKALIS, 'Asbos, "Preventative orders" and the European Court of Human Rights' [2007] EHRLR 427

BAKER, *An Introduction to English Legal History* (Butterworths: 4th edn, 2002)

Department for Constitutional Affairs, *Constitutional Reform: Reforming the Office of the Lord Chancellor* (2003) CP 13/03

Department for Constitutional Affairs, *The Lord Chancellor's Judiciary-Related Functions: Proposals* (2004) [also known as 'The Concordat']

GLANVILLE WILLIAMS, 'The Definition of Crime' (1955) 8 CLP 107

The Governance of Britain: A Consultation on the Role of the Attorney-General, Cm 7179, 2007

---

[132] Prosecution of Offences Act 1985, s 2.   [133] See p 429, *post*.

2

LEGISLATION

INTRODUCTION

This chapter focuses on legislation as one of the two main sources of law within the domestic legal system. Under the United Kingdom constitution Parliament is recognized as being legislatively supreme, and for centuries this has meant that the validity of an Act of Parliament cannot be challenged in any court. When interpreting an Act a court therefore has a duty to seek to give effect to Parliament's intentions, though there are different approaches to this task and the duty has been modified somewhat by developments in European law and human rights. Secondary legislation, by contrast, does not have the same 'supreme' status as Acts of Parliament, and it may therefore be subject to a greater level of judicial scrutiny. This chapter will look at the characteristics of both types of legislation, in addition to examining the principles governing their interpretation by the courts. In particular, it will address the following:

- The distinction between primary and secondary legislation, and the different purposes for which legislation may be made.
- The law-making process.
- The impact of EC law and the Human Rights Act 1998 on the legislative supremacy of Parliament.
- The geographical and temporal operation of statutes.
- Approaches to statutory interpretation and the impact of the Human Rights Act 1998.
- Specific presumptions and other aids which may influence statutory interpretation.

LEGISLATION AND LAW REFORM

The broad function of all legislation is to create, alter, or revoke law to give effect to the intention of the legislative body. The functions of Acts of Parliament, which are by far the most important form of legislation, may be classified as follows.

1 LAW REFORM

Although all statutes are concerned with law revision in the broadest sense, relatively few are concerned with altering or revising substantive rules of law. When statutes are passed to revise existing legal rules, it is usually because these rules have become stale and incapable of adaptation. A statute may also be passed to alter the law following an unpopular decision of a court, and there are many examples of Acts passed with the apparent intention of overruling a House of Lords decision.[1] However, the process of law reform is often more haphazard and piecemeal, and sometimes the impetus for change comes from ad hoc committees, departmental working groups, or Royal Commissions. The Police and Criminal Evidence Act 1984 is one such example, having been enacted following the report of the Royal Commission on Criminal Procedure.[2] More recently, major changes to the civil justice system were implemented following the report of a committee chaired by Lord Woolf.[3] Reviews of the criminal justice and tribunal systems by other committees have prompted similar reforms.[4]

An example of what can happen if law reform is not carefully considered is provided by attempts to reform the system of committal proceedings in criminal cases. Committals for trial were 'abolished' in 1994, to be replaced by a new system of transfers for trial. However, the government soon recognized the force of objections put by those who would have to operate the new system, and the transfer for trial provisions were repealed in 1996 without ever having been introduced. Further changes were included in a 1998 Act, and in 2003 Parliament once again changed the procedures for allocating criminal cases and sending them to the Crown Court.[5]

The Law Commission

A major addition to the machinery of law reform was made by the Law Commissions Act 1965, which established the Law Commissions.[6] Section 3(1) of the Act defines the duty of the Commissions thus:

> [I]t shall be the duty of each of the Commissions to take and keep under review all the law with which they are respectively concerned with a view to its systematic development and reform, including in particular the codification of such law, the elimination of anomalies, the repeal of obsolete and unnecessary enactments, the reduction of the number of separate enactments and generally the simplification and modernisation of the law.

---

[1] Examples are: Parliamentary Papers Act 1840; Limitation Act 1963; War Damage Act 1965; Criminal Evidence Act 1979.

[2] Cmnd 8092, 1981.

[3] Lord Woolf, *Final Report on Access to Justice* (1996): see Part 3 of this book for a detailed discussion.

[4] Lord Justice Auld, *Review of the Criminal Courts* (2001), discussed further in Part 4 of this book; Leggatt, *Tribunals for Users: One System, One Service* (2001), discussed in chapter 9.

[5] See p 580, *post*.

[6] Prior to 1965, the machinery for generating law reform consisted mainly of the Law Revision Committee and the Law Reform Committee, which considered, on their own initiative or at the invitation of the Lord Chancellor, branches of the law requiring change.

The creation of the Law Commissions was an important step forward in law reform. The Law Commission for England and Wales[7] has five full-time Commissioners and a full-time administrative staff, and it has produced a steady flow of reports, recommendations, and draft Bills, many of which have been implemented by Acts of Parliament.[8] By the time of its 37th Annual Report in 2003, the Law Commission had published 170 law reform reports.[9] Of these, around 120 had been implemented in full or in part, and of the thirty which were still outstanding, seventeen had been accepted by the government in principle.[10]

The mission of the Law Commission is to make the law simpler, fairer, and cheaper to use. Reform projects may be included in a programme of work submitted by the Commission to the Lord Chancellor, or they may be referred to the Commission by government departments. The process begins with a period of research and analysis of the relevant area of law, and the opinions of academics and professionals will often be canvassed. This is generally followed by the publication of a consultation paper, which will describe the existing problems with the law, and suggest possible solutions and reform options. Following a consultation period a final report is published, and this may include a draft Bill.

2 CONSOLIDATION OF ENACTMENTS

Where a branch of the law has evolved piecemeal, the existing law may effectively be re-enacted in a consolidating statute for the purpose of clarification. There are three sorts of consolidating Acts: (1) 'pure' consolidation (simple re-enactment); (2) consolidation under the Consolidation of Enactments (Procedure) Act 1949, which allows 'corrections and minor improvements';[11] and (3) consolidation with amendments recommended by the Law Commission. Many of the major consolidating Acts in recent years have fallen into the third category.[12]

Consolidation Acts are not subject to parliamentary debate, but there are special procedures designed to ensure that they do not depart from the provisions which are to be consolidated. The type of consolidation effected appears from the long title of the Act in question.[13] Substantive changes in the law will often be made before the process of

[7] There is a separate Commission for Scotland.

[8] See, for example, Landlord and Tenant Act 1988, Law of Property (Miscellaneous Provisions) Act 1989, Children Act 1989; Civil Evidence Act 1995; Contracts (Rights of Third Parties) Act 1999.

[9] Law Commission, *Annual Report 2002/03* (Law Com No 280), Appendix B, p 59.

[10] Ibid, Appendix C, p 61.

[11] These are defined by s 2 as amendments which have the effect of resolving ambiguities, removing doubts, bringing obsolete provisions into conformity with modern practice or removing unnecessary provisions or anomalies which are not of substantial importance, and amendments designed to facilitate improvement in the form or manner in which the law is stated. This category also covers any transitional provisions which may be necessary in consequence of such amendments.

[12] Examples are Water Industry Act 1991, Water Resources Act 1991, Social Security Contributions and Benefits Act 1992, Taxation of Chargeable Gains Act 1992.

[13] See, e.g., Employment Protection (Consolidation) Act 1978 (pure consolidation) (see, now, Employment Rights Act 1996); Road Traffic Act 1988 (Law Commission amendments); Juries Act 1974 (1949 Act 'corrections and improvements').

consolidation is undertaken. Thus, for example, section 106 of the Crime and Disorder Act 1998 has the side heading 'pre-consolidation amendments'.

Some believe that the idea of consolidation should be taken to the point of producing a consolidated statute book, in which the whole of our statute law would be arranged under titles and kept up to date by textual amendments. However, it is clear that this is not a reform likely to be implemented in the foreseeable future. In May 1973 the government set up the Renton Committee to review the form in which public Bills are drafted, 'with a view to achieving greater simplicity and clarity in statute law'. The Committee reported in 1975[14] and concluded that it would not be practical to consolidate the whole statute book within a limited number of years, nor to do so on the principle of 'one Act, one subject'.

3 CODIFICATION

Codification differs from consolidation in that an Act may only be said to consolidate statute law, whereas it may codify both statute law *and* case law. The processes are similar in function, however, in that the object is to simplify and clarify the existing law rather than to effect substantial alterations to it. Notable examples of major codifying statutes include the Sale of Goods Act 1893 (which was later consolidated in the Sale of Goods Act 1979) and the Marine Insurance Act 1906. Since then there has been very little codification, although one notable exception is the Police and Criminal Evidence Act 1984 (PACE). This statute radically altered and codified the existing common law and statutory rules relating to police powers of search, entry to premises, the treatment and questioning of suspects, and the admissibility of confession evidence.

There is a pressing need for codification in many areas of the law, and this is largely due to the manner in which Parliament approaches the task of amending statutes. Rather than producing a comprehensive re-enactment which would enable the law on a topic to be set out in a single Act, piecemeal amendments have often been made, with one statute dealing with a large number of different topics and amending an equally large number of earlier statutes. Subsequently the amending provision may itself be repealed, so that in order to discover what the law is, it becomes necessary to pick one's way through a maze of separate statutory provisions. This situation, in the field of industrial relations legislation, led Sir John Donaldson MR to make the following observation:[15]

> My plea is that Parliament, when legislating in respect of circumstances which directly affect the 'man or woman in the street' or the 'man or woman on the shop floor', should give as high a priority to clarity and simplicity of expression as to refinements of policy. Where possible, statutes, or complete parts of statutes, should not be amended but re-enacted in an amended form so that those concerned can read the rules in a single document. When formulating policy, ministers, of whatever political persuasion, should at all times be asking themselves and asking parliamentary counsel; 'Is this concept too refined to be capable of expression in basic English?'

[14] *The Preparation of Legislation*, Cmnd 6053 (1975).
[15] *Merkur Island Shipping Corporation* v *Laughton* [1983] 2 AC 570 at 594–5, [1982] 1 All ER 334 at 351.

Having to ask such questions would no doubt be frustrating for ministers and the legislature generally, but in my judgment this is part of the price which has to be paid if the rule of law is to be maintained.

Lord Diplock expressly adopted these remarks when the case reached the House of Lords.[16]

4 COLLECTION AND DISBURSEMENT OF REVENUE

The annual Finance Act implementing the Budget proposals is concerned primarily with the collection of revenue by the Crown. Other Acts, notably the Income and Corporation Taxes Act 1988, fulfil the same function. Conversely, public expenditure is authorized by Parliament annually through Consolidated Fund Acts (which authorize payments out of the Consolidated Fund), and the Appropriation Act (which appropriates public expenditure to specific purposes).

5 IMPLEMENTATION OF TREATIES

The United Kingdom, by entering into treaties, undertakes to implement the laws that form the subject matter of those treaties. For example, the directives and decisions of the European Community usually require implementation by statute or statutory instrument,[17] and the UK may also be obliged to legislate in order to give effect to decisions on the European Convention on Human Rights.[18] Examples of domestic legislation intended to implement other treaties and conventions include the Taking of Hostages Act 1982, the Employment Act 1989, and the Companies Act 1989.

6 SOCIAL LEGISLATION

These Acts are varied in their scope and functions but may be classified together as social legislation. Such Acts are concerned with regulating the day-to-day running of the social system rather than with creating criminal offences or rights and duties between individuals, although there is an increasing tendency for Parliament to delegate the power to make regulations of this nature to subordinate bodies.[19]

FORMS OF LEGISLATION[20]

Early legislation in England took several different forms, such as charters, provisions, ordinances, and statutes. At the present day, however, United Kingdom legislation may take one of three forms: Acts of Parliament, delegated legislation, and autonomic legislation.

---

[16] [1983] 2 AC 570 at 662, [1983] 2 All ER 189 at 198–9.
[17] See p 126, *post.*   [18] See p 147, *post.*   [19] See p 35, *post.*
[20] This chapter is confined to United Kingdom legislation. For EC legislation, see chapter 4, *post.*

1   ACTS OF PARLIAMENT

Subject to compliance with the overriding legislation of the European Community, Parliament is recognized as sovereign and as possessing unlimited legislative power. This has not always been so,[21] but in modern times it had not been seriously contended that the courts have any power to override the intention of the legislature until *British Railways Board* v *Pickin*.[22] In this case, an attempt was made to impugn the validity of the British Railways Act 1968, on the ground that the British Railway Board had fraudulently concealed certain matters from Parliament and had misled Parliament into an enactment which deprived the plaintiff of his land. If it was surprising that such a point should be pleaded, it was perhaps more surprising that the Court of Appeal should have held that it raised a triable issue.[23] The House of Lords, however, allowed the Board's appeal and restored the judge's order that the pleading be struck out as frivolous, vexatious, and an abuse of process. Accordingly, it is now clear that no court is entitled to go behind that which Parliament has enacted, and this rule is equally applicable to both public and private Acts.

The decision in *R (on the application of Jackson)* v *A-G* suggests that there may be a limited exception to this rule, in that the House of Lords was prepared to consider the validity of an Act made using the modified procedure set out in the Parliament Acts.[24] In addition, where there is a potential conflict between a United Kingdom Act and legislation of the European Community, the courts have power to restrain enforcement of the former. This occurred in *R* v *Secretary of State for Transport, ex parte Factortame (No 2)*.[25] The applicants, who were companies controlled by Spanish nationals, sought to challenge the validity of the Merchant Shipping Act 1988 on the basis that it contravened the EC Treaty and deprived them of their Community law rights. Since determination of this issue by the European Court of Justice was likely to take some time, the applicants applied for an interim injunction to restrain the Secretary of State from enforcing the Act. The House of Lords initially decided that they had no power to make such an order,[26] but following a reference to the European Court of Justice[27] they granted the applicants the interim relief sought. The effect of this unprecedented decision was to 'disapply' Part II of the Merchant Shipping Act. The decision was taken a stage further in *Equal Opportunities Commission* v *Secretary of State for Employment*,[28] where the House of Lords held that it was entitled to judicially review legislation to ensure that it

---

[21] See, e.g., dicta of Coke CJ in *Bonham's* case (1609) 8 Co Rep 113 and of Holt CJ in *City of London* v *Wood* (1701) 12 Mod Rep 669.

[22] [1974] AC 765, [1974] 1 All ER 609.

[23] [1973] QB 219, [1972] 3 All ER 923. For another unsuccessful attempt to have a statute declared ultra vires, see *Manuel* v *A-G* [1983] Ch 77, [1982] 3 All ER 822.

[24] [2005] UKHL 56, [2006] 1 AC 262, [2005] 4 All ER 1253. See further, p 33, *post*.

[25] [1991] 1 AC 603, [1991] 1 All ER 70. For the subsequent litigation see *R* v *Secretary of State for Transport, ex parte Factortame (No 3)* [1992] QB 680, [1991] 3 All ER 769; *R* v Secretary of *State for Transport, ex parte Factortame (No 4)* Case 48/93 [1996] QB 404, [1996] All ER (EC) 301; *R* v *Secretary of State for Transport, ex parte Factortame (No 5)* [2000] 1 AC 524, [1999] 4 All ER 906.

[26] *R* v *Secretary of State for Transport, ex parte Factortame (No 1)* [1990] 2 AC 85, [1989] 2 All ER 692.

[27] Case C-213/89 [1990] ECR I-2433, [1990] 3 CMLR 1.

[28] [1995] 1 AC 1, [1994] 1 All ER 910.

complied with European law. On the facts, provisions in the Employment Protection (Consolidation) Act 1978 were held to be contrary to European law, and a declaration to this effect was issued.

The impact of EC law on the legislative supremacy of Parliament was considered further in the recent case of *Thoburn v Sunderland City Council*.[29] The appellants had been convicted for selling produce in imperial measurements, contrary to delegated legislation implementing a European directive on the use of metric weights. The appeal by way of case stated centred on the claim that the Weights and Measures Act 1985 (which permitted the use of imperial weights) had, by implication, partially repealed section 2 of the European Communities Act 1972 (which authorizes the implementation of Community obligations by delegated legislation). The Divisional Court rejected this argument, and in doing so, Laws LJ sought to distinguish between 'constitutional statutes' such as the European Communities Act, and 'ordinary' Acts of Parliament:[30]

> There are now classes or types of legislative provision which cannot be repealed by mere implication. These instances are given and can only be given, by our own courts, to which the scope and nature of Parliamentary sovereignty are ultimately confided.

He continued:[31]

> In my opinion, a constitutional statute is one which (a) conditions the legal relationship between citizen and State in some general overarching manner, or (b) enlarges or diminishes the scope of what we would now regard as fundamental constitutional rights.

Other statutes said by Laws LJ to be immune from implied repeal include the Magna Carta, the Human Rights Act 1998, and the Scotland Act 1998.

In an earlier decision, Lord Hoffmann had made similar observations about Parliament's ability to legislate contrary to fundamental human rights principles:[32]

> The principle of legality means that Parliament must squarely confront what it is doing and accept the political cost. Fundamental rights cannot be overridden by general or ambiguous words...In the absence of express language or necessary implication to the contrary, the courts therefore presume that even the most general words were intended to be subject to the basic rights of the individual.[33]

(a) Public and Private Acts

Most Acts of Parliament are what are known as 'Public General Acts',[34] and the impetus for the vast majority of these comes from the government. Some may be based on specific manifesto pledges but many originate within government departments. They

---

[29] [2002] EWHC 195 (Admin), [2003] QB 151, [2002] 4 All ER 156.

[30] Ibid at [60].   [31] Ibid at [62].

[32] *R v Secretary of State for the Home Department, ex parte Simms* [2000] 2 AC 115 at 131, [1999] 3 All ER 400 at 412; see also Lord Steyn, 'Democracy through Law' [2002] EHRLR 723.

[33] See also the discussion at p 54, *post*.

[34] By virtue of the Interpretation Act 1978, s 3, every Act passed since 1850 is presumed to be a Public Act in the absence of a contrary provision.

are drafted by the Office of Parliamentary Counsel to the Treasury, in liaison with relevant Ministers. Occasionally, however, a Public General Act may begin life as a Private Members Bill. As the name indicates, such Bills are introduced by individual MPs rather than by Ministers acting on behalf of the government, and they rarely become law unless the government can be persuaded to lend its time and support. Examples of Private Members Bills which have been enacted with government support include the Obscene Publications Act 1959 (introduced by Roy Jenkins), the Abortion Act 1967 (David Steel), and the Public Interest Disclosure Act 1998 (Richard Shepherd).

Alongside Public General Acts there are also Private Acts, which are usually proposed by either local authorities (Local Acts) or large public companies and corporations (Personal Acts). Such Acts tend to affect only the interests of those who originally proposed them.

Acts of Parliament are published in Queens' Printers' Copy form by Her Majesty's Stationery Office and they are also made available electronically on the Office of Public Sector Information (OPSI) web site.[35] The Stationery Office publishes these statutes in annual volumes and also publishes an annual Index to the Statutes in Force, for reference purposes.

(b) The legislative process

Before a Bill is drafted the government may outline its intentions in a consultation paper, inviting feedback from interested parties on the range of options that is being considered. This consultation period will usually be followed by a White Paper setting out the government's revised proposals in detail. It is also becoming more common for Bills to be published in draft, providing an early opportunity for scrutiny and revision by the parliamentary Select Committees.

Once the government is satisfied with a Bill it will be introduced in Parliament. Money Bills and Bills dealing with politically contentious matters are usually presented to the House of Commons first, but less controversial Bills may begin life in the House of Lords. The title of the Bill will be read out in what is known as the first reading, and a date will be set for the second reading and a full debate on the Bill's merits.[36] At the end of this debate, the Bill and any amendments that have been proposed will be put to the vote. It is unlikely that any government sponsored Bill will be defeated at this stage, although on 17 January 2004 the government's Higher Education Bill survived its second reading in the Commons by a margin of just five votes. Assuming that a Bill does get this far, it will be referred to a Committee[37] for more detailed consideration. On occasion the Committee may receive evidence from experts and organisations. The Committee will then report back to the House in the report stage, before the Bill

---

[35] www.opsi.gov.uk.

[36] Section 19 of the Human Rights Act 1998 requires the Minister sponsoring a Bill to make a written statement before the Second Reading as to whether, in his view, its provisions are compatible with the rights specified in Schedule 1 of the 1998 Act: see p 162.

[37] In the House of Commons the committees involved in this stage of the legislative process have been known since 2006 as Public Bill Committees. In the House of Lords Bills are usually dealt with by either a Grand Committee or a Committee of the Whole House.

proceeds to the third reading and a final vote. If a simple majority of the House votes in favour of enacting the Bill it will be sent to the other House and the process is repeated.[38] Only when it has received the approval of both Houses can a Bill be presented for the Royal Assent and become an Act of Parliament.[39]

The Parliament Acts procedure. The Parliament Acts of 1911 and 1949 modify the principle that a Bill cannot be enacted without the approval of both the Commons and the Lords. Under the provisions of these Acts, the House of Lords no longer has the power of veto and can only delay Bills which have Commons support for a period of up to one year,[40] or in the case of money Bills, for up to one month.[41] If, at the end of this period the House of Lords rejects a Bill for a second time, the Commons can then invoke the Parliament Acts procedure and present the Bill for the Royal Assent. There is, however, no power enabling the House of Lords to legislate without the consent of the Commons. The Parliament Acts procedure has only been invoked on seven occasions, most recently to enact the Hunting Act 2004.[42]

In the case of *R (on the application of Jackson) v A-G*,[43] which concerned a challenge to the validity of the Hunting Act, it was argued that statutes made using the Parliament Acts procedure are in fact a form of delegated legislation. When the Parliament Act 1911 removed the Lords' power to veto legislation, it replaced it with the power to delay Public Bills for up to two years. The 1911 Act was then itself used to pass the Parliament Act 1949, which reduced this delaying period to one year. The argument advanced in *Jackson* was that the 1911 Act was an enabling Act which delegated law-making powers to the House of Commons and the Monarch.[44] It followed that the 1949 Act was a subordinate instrument made pursuant to the 1911 Act, and to the extent that it sought to amend its own 'parent Act', it was ultra vires: a subordinate body could not give itself greater powers than those originally conferred by Parliament. The applicant therefore sought a declaration that both the 1949 Act and the Hunting Act 2004 (which was made under it) were invalid. However, the House of Lords refused to grant the declaration and ruled that the effect of the Parliament Acts was to create an alternative way of enacting primary legislation:[45]

> To describe an Act of Parliament made by this procedure as 'delegated' or 'subordinate' legislation . . . would be an absurd and confusing mischaracterization. It would be equally inappropriate to liken the House of Commons to a 'delegate' or 'agent' when applying the 1911 Act procedure. The appropriate approach, rather, is to recognize that in enacting section 2 the intention of Parliament was to create a

---

[38] If any further amendments are proposed at this stage, the Bill must go back to the first House so that it can have the opportunity to vote on them.

[39] The usual procedure for this is set out in the Royal Assent Act 1967.

[40] Parliament Act 1911, s 2(1), as amended.   [41] Ibid, s 1.

[42] The Welsh Church Act 1914, the Government of Ireland Act 1920, the Parliament Act 1949, the War Crimes Act 1991, the European Parliamentary Elections Act 1999, and the Sexual Offences (Amendment) Act 2000 were also passed in this way.

[43] [2005] UKHL 56, [2006] 1 AC 262, [2005] 4 All ER 1253.

[44] Delegated legislation is discussed at p 35, *post*.

[45] [2005] UKHL 56 at [64], [2006] 1 AC 262 at [64], per Lord Nicholls.

second, parallel route by which...any public Bill introduced in the Commons could become law as an Act of Parliament. It would be inconsistent with this intention to interpret section 2 as subject to an inherent, over-arching limitation comparable to that applicable to delegated legislation.

Section 2 of the 1911 Act specifies a limited number of exclusions to the use of this modified procedure, most notably in respect of Bills purporting to extend the maximum duration of a Parliament. Their Lordships agreed in *Jackson* that a Bill passed in contravention of section 2 would not be an Act of Parliament, and that the courts would have the jurisdiction to declare such an 'Act' invalid. However, the question of whether there might be any *implied* exclusions to section 2, in addition to those expressly mentioned, was left unresolved.[46]

In most cases of disagreement between the two Houses a compromise can be reached without the need for the Parliament Acts to be invoked. Usually this involves the House of Lords voting in favour of a Bill in return for the House of Commons accepting certain amendments. Indeed, in one of the most extraordinary episodes in British political history Parliament sat through the night to debate what became the Prevention of Terrorism Act 2005. The Bill 'ping-ponged' between the two Houses four times before a compromise was finally reached. The deadlock was only broken when the government reluctantly agreed to give Parliament the opportunity to amend the Act at a later date.

(c) Citation

The mode of citation of statutes has undergone change. Early statutes were cited by the name of the place where Parliament met.[47] Subsequently statutes were cited by reference to their regnal year and chapter. Thus, for example, the Criminal Justice Act 1948 would be cited as 11 & 12 Geo 6, c 58 indicating that the Act was the fifty-eighth passed in the Parliamentary session extending over the eleventh and twelfth years of the reign of George VI. This exceedingly cumbersome method of citation was not abolished until 1962.[48] Although Acts still have chapter numbers (a legacy of the fiction that only one Act was passed in a parliamentary session), reference is now to the calendar year rather than to the regnal year. Acts are usually cited by reference to their short title, and this is permissible by section 2 of the Short Titles Act 1896.

(d) Enforcement of statutory duties

The creation of new rights and causes of action is virtually the prerogative of Parliament, and where a statute imposes a duty the question often arises whether a breach of that duty is actionable in tort. The issue in such cases is whether the legislature intended to confer a cause of action on the claimant, not whether the claimant belongs to a class which the provision was intended to protect. It might be thought that where a statute creates rules but provides no criminal penalty for their breach, Parliament must have

---

[46] Their Lordships were divided on this point. For further discussion see McHarg, 'What Is Delegated Legislation?' [2006] PL 539. As to the question of whether there might be any limits to parliamentary supremacy itself, see the discussion at p 131, *post*.

[47] e.g. Statute of Gloucester 1278; Provisions of Oxford 1258.

[48] Acts of Parliament Numbering and Citation Act 1962 (10 & 11 Eliz 2, c 34).

intended to create a right of civil action to a person who suffers as a result of a breach, 'for, if it were not so, the statute would be but a pious aspiration'.[49] This is not, however, invariably the case. Thus in *R v Deputy Governor of Parkhurst Prison, ex parte Hague*[50] the House of Lords held that the Prison Rules 1964 (made under the Prison Act 1952) conferred no right to sue for damages upon a prisoner who had been restrained in a manner not permitted by those Rules. The prisoner's remedies were to complain to the governor or board of visitors. He might also challenge any administrative decision of the Secretary of State or the governor by judicial review proceedings.

A similar approach was taken in *O'Rourke v Camden LBC*, where the House of Lords held that provisions in Part 3 of the Housing (Homeless Persons) Act 1977 did not confer private rights. The public duties imposed by the Act could be enforced through judicial review proceedings, but the Act did not suggest a legislative intention to create an additional remedy in private law:[51]

> Public money is spent on housing the homeless not merely for the private benefit of people who find themselves homeless but on grounds of general public interest: because, for example, proper housing means that people will be less likely to suffer illness, turn to crime or require the attention of other social services . . . It is not simply a private matter between the claimant and the housing authority. Accordingly, the fact that Parliament has provided for the expenditure of public money on benefits in kind such as housing the homeless does not necessarily mean that it intended cash payments to be made by way of damages to persons who, in breach of the housing authority's statutory duty, have unfortunately not received the benefits which they should have done . . .

Ultimately the matter depends on the construction of each individual statute, but if the duty is of a general administrative or regulatory nature, a right in tort is unlikely to be implied.[52]

2 DELEGATED LEGISLATION

'Delegated legislation' is the term used to describe the vast body of rules, orders, regulations, and byelaws, created by subordinate bodies under powers delegated through Acts of Parliament. Parliament has neither the time nor the expertise to enact all the legislation needed in a modern, complex society, and the use of delegated legislation enables legal rules to be made and altered quickly without taking up valuable parliamentary time.[53]

---

[49] *Cutler v Wandsworth Stadium Ltd* [1949] AC 398 at 407, [1949] 1 All ER 544 at 548, per Lord Simonds.

[50] [1992] 1 AC 58, [1991] 3 All ER 733.

[51] [1998] AC 188 at 193, [1997] 3 All ER 23 at 26, per Lord Hoffmann. A power to make delegated legislation will not necessarily include a power to create new enforceable rights: *Olutu v Home Office* [1997] 1 All ER 385, [1987] 1 WLR 328.

[52] *Capital and Counties plc v Hampshire County Council and others* [1997] QB 1004, [1997] 2 All ER 865 (duty to ensure a water supply under Fire Services Act 1947 did not confer enforceable right).

[53] In 2002 for example, a total of 2,959 Statutory Instruments applicable to the UK were made, compared with just 44 Public Acts of Parliament. Exceptionally, as many as 3,806 Statutory Instruments were made in 2001, but 597 of these related directly to the outbreak of Foot and Mouth disease in that year.

Orders in Council are the highest form of delegated legislation.[54] They are nominally made by the Privy Council, though in most cases the Privy Council merely sanctions Orders that have in practice been made by the government. Orders in Council made pursuant to statutory powers are published in statutory instruments,[55] as are the various regulations, orders, directions, and rules made by Ministers of the Crown and other subordinate bodies.[56] Statutory instruments are published by Her Majesty's Stationery Office and are cited by calendar year and number: for example, SI 2003/1660. They also have a short title. Failure to publish does not affect the validity of a statutory instrument, but it may provide a defence to any prosecution brought in respect of it.[57]

Local authority byelaws are another form of delegated legislation.[58] Alongside numerous powers to make byelaws on specific matters, local authorities also have a general power under the Local Government Act 1972 to make byelaws 'for good rule and government and suppression of nuisances'.[59]

As noted previously,[60] it has been suggested that legislation enacted using the Parliament Acts procedure is also a form of delegated legislation, but this view was rejected by the House of Lords in *R (on the application of Jackson) v A-G*.[61]

(a) The use of Henry VIII clauses and other wide-ranging powers

Delegated legislation is not a new phenomenon, and where it is concerned solely with implementing the detail of a general policy contained in an Act of Parliament it is useful and unexceptionable.[62] However, it is increasingly common for delegated powers to be defined in extremely wide terms,[63] with the effect of conferring extensive legislative power upon government departments. One example of this is section 2(2) of the European Communities Act 1972, which confers a wide power on Ministers or Her Majesty in Council to make delegated legislation giving effect to Community

---

[54] Note that Orders in Council can also amount to primary legislation pursuant to the royal prerogative: *Council of Civil Service Unions v Minister for the Civil Service* [1985] AC 374, [1984] 3 All ER 935.

[55] See the Statutory Instruments Act 1946. Statutes conferring subordinate legislative powers frequently provide that the statutory instrument made thereunder shall be laid before Parliament. In this event a copy of the instrument must be so laid before it comes into operation: s 4. Some statutory instruments cannot take effect until expressly approved by resolution, while others take effect immediately subject to cancellation by negative resolution within forty 'sitting' days.

[56] Not all statutory instruments are made by Ministers. The Courts Act 2003, for example, empowers the Criminal Procedure Rule Committee to make rules of practice and procedure for the criminal courts (s 69), and gives equivalent powers to a new Family Procedure Rule Committee (s 75). See also the Civil Procedure Act 1997, s 1, for the powers of the Civil Procedure Rule Committee.

[57] Statutory Instruments Act 1946, s 3; *R v Sheer Metalcraft* [1954] 1 QB 586, [1954] 1 All ER 542.

[58] Certain other bodies are also empowered to make byelaws. For example, s 210(1) and Schedule 25 of the Water Resources Act 1991 empower the Environment Agency to make byelaws for purposes connected with the carrying out of its functions.

[59] Section 235(1). Such byelaws only take effect when they are confirmed by the Secretary of State.

[60] See p 33, *ante*.

[61] [2005] UKHL 56, [2006] 1 AC 262, [2005] 4 All ER 1253.

[62] For example, many Acts of Parliament are brought into operation by Order in Council. An Act may be brought into force in this way, even though the power to make the Order derives from the Act itself; Interpretation Act 1978, s 13.

[63] Such powers tend to be very widely defined in time of war. See, for example, the extraordinarily wide powers conferred by the Supplies and Services (Transitional Powers) Act 1945 (now repealed).

obligations.[64] The potential scope of this power is vast. In 2003, for example, the government introduced a series of Regulations designed to give effect to two EC Directives on discrimination.[65] Entirely new grounds for challenging discrimination in employment were created,[66] and existing Acts of Parliament dealing with 'race', gender, and disability discrimination were substantially amended.[67] These reforms have had a significant impact on the entire field of anti-discrimination law; yet by relying on the enabling power in section 2(2) of the European Communities Act 1972, the government was able to bring about these changes without asking Parliament to enact further primary legislation.

There are numerous other examples of so-called 'Henry VIII clauses' which allow delegated legislation to amend Acts of Parliament. For instance, the Legislative and Regulatory Reform Act 2006 empowers Ministers to amend or repeal legislation in order to remove or reduce burdens resulting from it.[68] Another example can be found in the Human Rights Act 1998. Where a court has declared that a legislative provision is incompatible with a Convention right,[69] section 10 empowers a Minister to make such amendments to the legislation as he considers necessary to remove the incompatibility. In *R (on the application of H) v North and East London Regional Mental Health Tribunal* the Court of Appeal declared provisions of the Mental Health Act 1983 to be incompatible with the right to liberty under Article 5, ECHR.[70] The offending provisions were amended by the Mental Health Act 1983 (Remedial) Order 2001,[71] and because the Secretary of State considered that there were 'compelling reasons' for acting quickly he was able to make this Order without waiting for further parliamentary approval.[72]

---

[64] See p 125, *post*. The scope of s 2(2) is limited by Schedule 2, which excludes the power to make any provision imposing or increasing taxation, any retrospective provision or any criminal offence punishable with imprisonment for more than two years, or, on summary conviction with imprisonment for more than three months. Even with these limitations the power is far-reaching, and in 2003 138 statutory instruments affecting England and Wales were made pursuant to s 2(2) of this Act.

[65] EC Employment Directive (2000/78/EC); EC Race Directive (2000/43/EC).

[66] Employment Equality (Religion or Belief) Regulations 2003, SI 2003/1660; Employment Equality (Sexual Orientation) Regulations 2003, SI 2003/1661.

[67] Race Relations Act 1976 (Amendment) Regulations 2003, SI 2003/1626; Sex Discrimination Act 1975 (Amendment) Regulations 2003, SI 2003/1657; Disability Discrimination Act 1995 (Amendment) Regulations 2003, SI 2003/1673.

[68] Section 1. This replaces and extends the power previously contained in the Regulatory Reform Act 2001, though the power is still subject to certain limitations.

[69] A 'Convention right' means any of the rights contained in Articles 2 to 12 and 14 of the ECHR, Articles 1 to 3 of the First Protocol and Article 1 of the Thirteenth Protocol (Human Rights Act, s 1). Not all courts have the power to make such a declaration: see p 158, *post*.

[70] [2001] EWCA Civ 415, [2002] QB 1, [2002] 3 WLR 512. The provisions concerned the test to be applied when determining a restricted patient's entitlement to release from a secure hospital. The provision was held to be incompatible with Article 5 as the patient bore the burden of proving that his continued detention under the Act was no longer warranted.

[71] SI 2001/3712. See also the Naval Discipline Act 1957 (Remedial Order) 2004, SI 2004/66 and the Marriage Act 1949 (Remedial) Order 2007, SI 2007/438, discussed at pp 283 and 162, *post*.

[72] Human Rights Act 1998, s 10(2); Schedule 2, para 2(b).

(b) Scrutiny of delegated legislation

The vital feature that distinguishes Parliament from any other person or body with legis-lative powers is that only Parliament is sovereign. This means that delegated legislation is valid only if it is within the legislative powers conferred by Parliament (intra vires). Thus, while the courts have no power to declare Acts of Parliament invalid, delegated legislation *can* be declared invalid if it is ultra vires (outside the power). The scope of the courts' jurisdiction in such cases was considered in *R v Secretary of State for the Home Department, ex parte Javed*.[73] The case centred on an Order designating Pakistan as a country where there was 'no serious risk of persecution'.[74] The applicants were Pakistani asylum seekers who had been subjected to a fast-track procedure on the basis of this Order. The Court of Appeal confirmed that delegated legislation could be judicially reviewed on the grounds identified in the GCHQ case,[75] namely illegality, procedural impropriety, and *Wednesbury* unreasonableness.[76] The courts can also strike down subordinate legislation which is incompatible with the rights protected by the Human Rights Act,[77] unless the terms of the enabling Act make the incompatibility inevitable.[78] However, unless and until declared ultra vires by a final judgment in the courts, a statu-tory instrument must be treated as part of the law and enforced accordingly.[79]

Although any challenge to delegated legislation is usually made in an application for judicial review, it is also possible to raise the question of validity as a defence to a civil action[80] or a prosecution[81] in what is known as a 'collateral challenge'. However, the fact that part of delegated legislation is ultra vires does not necessarily invalidate the whole of that legislation. The valid part may be severable, meaning that the invalid part may be severed whilst the valid part remains intact and enforceable.[82]

Despite the possibility of judicial review, it must be remembered that the role of the court is limited to ensuring that the delegated legislation is authorized by the enabling Act. Where that Act has been drafted so as to confer very wide powers, the scope for judicial scrutiny of their exercise is necessarily limited. Such powers are always subject

---

[73] [2001] EWCA Civ 789, [2002] QB 129.

[74] Asylum (Designated Countries of Destination and Designated Safe Third Countries) Order 1996, SI 1996/2671. The Order was purportedly made under powers conferred by the Asylum and Immigration Appeals Act 1993.

[75] *Council of Civil Service Unions* v *Minister for the Civil Services* [1985] AC 374, [1984] 3 All ER 935. See further, p 216, *post*.

[76] *Associated Provincial Picture Houses Ltd* v *Wednesbury Corpn.* [1948] 1 KB 223, [1947] 2 All ER 680. The Court of Appeal in *Javed* held that the 1996 Order was void for unreasonableness. Delegated legislation may also be declared ultra vires where it breaches a fundamental right, such as the right of access to a court – see *R (on the application of Anufrijeva)* v *Secretary of State for the Home Department* [2003] UKHL 36, [2004] 1 AC 604, [2003] 3 All ER 827.

[77] A Minister or other body exercising a power to make delegated legislation is subject to s 6(1) of the Act, which makes it unlawful for a public authority to act incompatibly with Convention rights.

[78] s 6(2).

[79] Cf. *Hoffman-La Roche & Co AG* v *Secretary of State for Trade and Industry* [1975] AC 295 at 329, [1974] 2 All ER 1128; *Percy* v *Hall* [1997] QB 924, [1996] 4 All ER 523.

[80] *R* v *Reading Crown Court, ex parte Hutchinson* [1988] QB 384, [1988] 1 All ER 333.

[81] *Boddington* v *British Transport Police* [1999] 2 AC 143, [1998] 2 All ER 203. The House of Lords confirmed in *Boddington* that a collateral challenge could be based on either substantive or procedural ultra vires.

[82] *DPP* v *Hutchinson* [1990] 2 AC 783, [1990] 2 All ER 836.

to control by Parliament, and the Joint Committee on Statutory Instruments is able to consider the technical aspects of individual instruments and draw them to the attention of Parliament. In addition, most, though not all statutory instruments must be laid before Parliament for a period of forty days before they can take effect, and some require an affirmative resolution of both Houses.[83] The sheer volume of delegated legislation that is now being made and the inability of the Joint Committee to review its merits does raise doubts about the effectiveness of parliamentary scrutiny. However, the ultimate form of parliamentary control is that without the authority of an Act of Parliament there would be no power to make delegated legislation.

3 AUTONOMIC LEGISLATION

This differs from delegated legislation in that an autonomous body has an independent power to legislate for its own members, and in some cases, for members of the general public. Though this power is usually conferred by Parliament, this is not always so. However, in all cases the power is sanctioned by Parliament. Examples of autonomous legislative bodies are public undertakings such as transport authorities, and bodies created by Royal charter, such as universities, whose byelaws may affect the public at large. The Church of England, the General Medical Council, The Law Society, trade unions, and even limited companies are autonomous in the sense that they have power to control their own internal structures and to legislate for their members.

In almost all cases autonomic legislation is confined in its extent by an Act of Parliament and is therefore subject to the doctrine of ultra vires. An important exception, however, is the prerogative jurisdiction of the Privy Council. This jurisdiction is principally concerned with legislating by Order in Council for Crown Colonies. The power is subject to the ordinary rules of English law, though not to the doctrine of ultra vires.[84] It will thus be apparent that an Order in Council may be passed either under powers conferred by individual Acts or under a general prerogative power independent of statute. Both are subject to the power of the law to determine the existence and extent of the power to make the Order.[85]

4 CODES OF PRACTICE

Before leaving the topic of forms of legislation, it is necessary to refer to Codes of Practice, which are of increasing significance in certain legislative contexts. A number of Acts of Parliament specifically require or authorize the preparation of accompanying Codes of Practice, usually for the purpose of providing further guidance, instructions, or rules governing matters of practice and procedure. Whether such Codes are classifiable as 'legislation' is a moot point. In one sense they have the characteristic of

---

[83] For example, certain orders made under the Legislative and Regulatory Reform Act 2006 will be subject to an affirmative resolution procedure, while others may be subject to a *super-affirmative* resolution procedure involving a 60 day waiting period: see ss 12–18. Cf. Human Rights Act 1998, Schedule 2, para 2(b).

[84] *The Zamora* [1916] 2 AC 77.   [85] See p 215, *post*.

delegated legislation in that the power to issue them is conferred by statute,[86] and presumably a Code of Practice could be declared ultra vires. Certain codes must be laid before Parliament before they can come into operation, and some are even subject to an affirmative resolution procedure.[87] On the other hand, the very nature of Codes of Practice means that they do not have the force of law. As discussed below, however, this does not mean that they are without legal effect.

(a) Examples of particular Codes

In the context of the enforcement of the criminal law several Codes are of particular importance. Section 66 of the Police and Criminal Evidence Act 1984 (PACE) authorizes the Home Secretary to make Codes of Practice dealing with the different stages of police investigations. Codes dealing with the exercise of stop and search powers (Code A), the execution of search powers (Code B), the treatment and questioning of suspects (Code C), the identification of suspects (Code D), and the tape-recording of police interviews (Code E) have been in operation for some time. More recently, Codes dealing with the visual recording of interviews (Code F),[88] statutory powers of arrest (Code G), and the detention, treatment and questioning of terror suspects (Code H) have also been introduced.[89] The PACE Codes are important to both the practitioner and the police, and if there is a 'significant and substantial' breach of the Codes,[90] evidence obtained as a result of that breach may be excluded from consideration by the courts. The status of one of the PACE Codes was discussed by Lord Woolf CJ:[91]

> The Code has statutory backing under the Police and Criminal Evidence Act 1984. However, it remains a code and it does not have the status of subordinate legislation.

Another example is the Code of Practice on the preservation and disclosure of evidence, made under section 23 of the Criminal Procedure and Investigations Act 1996. This Code is intended to ensure that important material is made available to the prosecutor and disclosed to the defence if it may assist them.[92] In the context of the civil law, perhaps the most important example of a Code of Practice is that issued by the

---

[86] Not all Codes of Practice are issued pursuant to statutory powers. Numerous voluntary codes exist in both the private and public sectors, but these do not raise the same legal issues as those backed by a statutory framework.

[87] Codes of Practice made under s 66 of the Police and Criminal Evidence Act 1984 (PACE) can only be brought into force by a statutory instrument which has been approved by both Houses of Parliament (s 67(7)). However, revisions to existing Codes are not subject to affirmative resolution (s 67(7A)).

[88] Made pursuant to s 60A of the Act.

[89] New Codes A–E have effect from 1 February 2008.

[90] *R* v *Walsh* (1990) 91 Cr App R 161, [1989] Crim LR 822; *R* v *Aspinall* [1999] 2 Cr App R 115, (1999) 96(7) LSG 35. See further, p 440 et seq, *post*.

[91] *R* v *Sanghera (Rashpal)* [2001] 1 Cr App R 20 at 6, [2000] All ER (D) 1415. The Court of Appeal upheld the trial judge's decision not to exclude evidence obtained in breach of Code B because there was no doubt as to its reliability.

[92] See p 607, *post*. For discussion of the Code of Practice, see Card and Ward, *Criminal Procedure and Investigations Act 1996* (1996), ch 3, and p 607, *post*.

Advisory Conciliation and Arbitration Service (ACAS) under the Trade Union and Labour Relations (Consolidation) Act 1992. ACAS may issue Codes of Practice containing 'such practical guidance as the Service thinks fit for the purpose of promoting the improvement of industrial relations or for purposes connected with trade union learning representatives'.[93]

(b) The status of Codes of Practice

As already indicated, although Codes of Practice cannot be directly enforced through the courts they are not without legal effect. For example, Codes issued under the Trade Union and Labour Relations (Consolidation) Act 1992 are specifically admissible in any proceedings before a court, employment tribunal, or the Central Arbitration Committee.[94] Similarly, by section 67(11) of the Police and Criminal Evidence Act any Code under the Act is admissible in evidence, and if appearing to be relevant to any question arising in the proceedings, 'it shall be taken into account in determining that question'.

Codes of Practice approved or issued by the Health and Safety Commission have even greater force, since a failure to comply with such a Code amounts to prima facie proof of a breach of the Act's provisions for the purposes of any criminal proceedings.[95] Reference may also be made to the Highway Code, first issued pursuant to the Road Traffic Act 1930. Failure to comply with its provisions is not an offence in itself, but it may be relied upon by any party in civil or criminal proceedings.[96]

THE OPERATION OF STATUTES

In defining the scope of a statute it is necessary to advert both to its geographical area of operation and to the time during which it is operative.

1 GEOGRAPHICAL OPERATION

There is a presumption that an Act of Parliament is operative throughout the United Kingdom but not elsewhere unless a contrary intention appears in the Act itself.[97] The contrary intention may either limit or extend the geographical operation of the Act, and statutes frequently contain a section restricting their operation to exclude Scotland

---

[93] Section 199, as amended by the Employment Act 2002, s 43(1).

[94] Section 207(2), (3).

[95] Health and Safety at Work etc. Act 1974, ss 16 and 17(2).

[96] Road Traffic Act 1988, s 38(7).

[97] Since it lies within the prerogative power of the Crown to extend its sovereignty and jurisdiction across both land and sea, the words 'United Kingdom' incorporate such area of land or sea as may be formally declared by the Crown to be subject to its sovereignty and jurisdiction: see *Post Office v Estuary Radio Ltd* [1968] 2 QB 740, at 748, [1967] 3 All ER 663 at 680, per Diplock LJ.

or Northern Ireland. A similar reduction in geographical operation occurs with Acts which are expressed to apply only to a limited locality. Such Acts are described as 'Local Acts'.

Conversely an Act may expressly or by necessary implication extend outside the United Kingdom, though there is a presumption against this.[98] For example, section 57 of the Offences Against the Person Act 1861 provides that the crime of bigamy is committed 'whether the second marriage shall have taken place in England or Ireland, or elsewhere.' Another example is section 72 of the Sexual Offences Act 2003, which extends the jurisdiction of United Kingdom courts to allow trial in the UK of British citizens who commit sex offences abroad. However, an Act with extraterritorial operation will usually (but not always) apply only to British subjects or persons owing allegiance to the Crown.[99]

2 TEMPORAL OPERATION

(a) When a statute begins to be operative

Until 1793[100] a statute came into force on the first day of the parliamentary session in which it was passed. Consequently virtually all legislation was retrospective. The present law is that a statute comes into force on the day on which it receives the Royal Assent, unless some other date is specified in the Act itself. Increasingly, however, an Act may provide that it is to come into force on a 'day to be appointed' by statutory instrument, and different sections within an Act may be brought into force at different times. For example, most of the provisions of the Human Rights Act 1998 were brought into force in England and Wales approximately two years after the Act was passed, the commencement date having been effected by statutory instrument.[101] Certain provisions, however, came into effect as soon as the Act received the Royal Assent.[102]

There are portions of Acts in existence which have never been brought into force, and sometimes the decision not to implement is taken quite soon after the Act is passed. Thus, for example, sections 8 to 27 of the Crime (Sentences) Act 1997 introduced a new scheme for the early release of prisoners. Within months, and after a change of government, it was announced that the new scheme would not be implemented.[103]

---

[98] The presumption is particularly strong in criminal cases: see *Air-India* v *Wiggins* [1980] 2 All ER 593, [1980] 1 WLR 815.

[99] *Joyce* v *DPP* [1946] AC 347, [1946] 1 All ER 186. Cf. the Internationally Protected Persons Act 1978, under which attacks upon the person or property of protected persons (such as heads of state and their families) are offences justiciable in the United Kingdom, even though committed outside the United Kingdom by a person 'whether a citizen of the United Kingdom and Colonies or not' (s 1). See also the Suppression of Terrorism Act 1978, s 4 and the War Crimes Act 1991.

[100] Acts of Parliament (Commencement) Act 1793.

[101] For England and Wales – see s 22(3); Human Rights Act 1998 (Commencement No 2) Order, 2000 (SI 2000/1851).

[102] Sections 18 (appointment of judges to the European Court of Human Rights), 20 (the power to make supplementary orders) and 21(5) (abolition of the death penalty for certain military offences).

[103] See 299 HC Official Report (6th series) coll 342–350, 30 July 1997.

Sometimes the failure to bring a statutory provision into force may give rise to problems, as was vividly demonstrated in *R* v *Secretary of State for the Home Department, ex parte Fire Brigades' Union*.[104] The Criminal Justice Act 1988 provided for a statutory compensation scheme for victims of violent crime, this being intended to replace the ex gratia Criminal Injuries Compensation Scheme established under the royal prerogative.[105] The statutory provisions were not brought into force and in 1994 the Home Secretary purported to introduce a new scheme pursuant to the royal prerogative. The House of Lords held, by a majority, that the Home Secretary had acted unlawfully. Although he was not obliged to bring the statutory scheme into effect at any given time, he was under a duty to keep the matter under review. It was an abuse of prerogative power to exercise it in a manner inconsistent with bringing the statute into force. Lord Browne-Wilkinson observed that if the Home Secretary wanted to introduce a scheme inconsistent with that in the 1988 Act, he should have first asked Parliament to repeal the statutory provisions.

(b) Retrospective operation

As a general rule a statute only affects factual situations that arise during the period of its operation. There is a presumption against the statute being retroactive, although the courts have been keen to point out that it is in each case a question of ascertaining the intentions of Parliament.[106] The presumption is particularly strong where a statute creates criminal penalties or would operate to deprive a person of a vested right in property.[107] In the case of the former, the presumption can only have been strengthened by section 3 of the Human Rights Act 1998, under which the courts must try to interpret legislation in a manner compatible with the prohibition on retrospective criminal offences in Article 7, ECHR.[108] Parliament is sovereign, however, and statutes are occasionally expressed to be retrospective even where this operates to deprive a person of a vested right in property. A modern illustration was the War Damage Act 1965, which operated to remove rights to compensation from the Crown, and which was expressed to apply to proceedings commenced before the Act came into force.[109] A more recent example is provided by the provisions in Part 10 of the Criminal Justice Act 2003. These provisions bought about changes to the double jeopardy rule and are expressed to apply 'whether the acquittal was before or after the passing of this Act'.[110]

[104] [1995] 2 AC 513, [1995] 2 All ER 244; see p 216, *post*.

[105] Sections 108 to 117 and Schedules 6 and 7.

[106] *L'Office Cherifien des Phosphates* v *Yamashita-Shinnihon Steamship Co Ltd* [1994] 1 AC 486, [1994] 1 All ER 20; *Wilson* v *First County Trust (No 2)* [2003] UKHL 40, [2004] 1 AC 816, [2003] 4 All ER 97.

[107] *Yew Bon Tew* v *Kenderaan Bas Mara* [1983] 1 AC 553, [1982] 3 All ER 833. In *R* v *Fisher* [1969] 1 All ER 100, [1969] 1 WLR 8 the rule against retrospective operation operated *against* the accused, as he was convicted of an offence which had been abolished at some point between the commission of the offence and the date of his trial.

[108] See p 189, *post*. The Human Rights Act itself is presumed not to be retrospective, except to the extent that it can be relied upon in proceedings instigated by public authorities which concern events occurring before the Act came into force. See s 22(4); *R* v *Lambert* [2001] UKHL 37, [2002] 2 AC 545, [2001] 3 All ER 577.

[109] Section 1(2). The action affected was *Burmah Oil Co Ltd* v *Lord Advocate* [1965] AC 75, [1964] 2 All ER 348.

[110] Section 75(6).

An Act of indemnity, the purpose of which is to validate or legalize that which was initially invalid or illegal, must by its nature be retroactive.[111] Similarly, a statute which alters rules of evidence or procedure is always retroactive in the absence of a contrary intention, since the rules of evidence and procedure that a court is bound to observe are those in existence at the time of the hearing.[112] On the other hand, sentencing provisions usually apply only in respect of offences committed after the provisions were introduced.

Even if the statutory provision does not take effect retrospectively, it may nevertheless be held to entitle a court to have regard to what has occurred prior to its passage. Thus in *L'Office Cherifien des Phosphates* v *Yamashita-Shinnihon Steamship Co Ltd*,[113] the House of Lords held that an 'inordinate and inexcusable delay', which had occurred *before* section 13A of the Arbitration Act 1950 came into force, entitled an arbitrator to dismiss a claim.

(c) When a statute ceases to be operative

No statute becomes obsolete by the passing of time. Nevertheless there are many ancient statutes more honoured in the breach than in the observance. At one time the approach of the legislature was to do nothing until the need for repeal manifested itself. Thus, the plaintiff in a nineteenth-century case was no doubt disturbed to discover that his opponent had a right to claim trial by battle,[114] while resort to the Bill of Rights 1688 is by no means uncommon.[115] The present position is that the Law Commissions are expressly required to review 'obsolete and unnecessary enactments' with a view to repeal.[116] In consequence there are now regular Statute Law (Repeals) Acts, each of which repeals hundreds of obsolete enactments following recommendations of the Law Commissions.

Certain statutes are expressed to be operative only for a limited period, usually because they are experimental or transitional. However, temporary statutes may acquire a new lease of life by the passing of an Expiring Laws Continuance Act, which is effected solely for the purpose of renewing statutes which would otherwise expire. Thus Part I of the Commonwealth Immigrants Act 1962, an experimental measure expressed to last for only one year, was renewed annually until 1971 when the Immigration Act 1971 was passed to supersede it.

Unless it is expressed to be operative for a limited period, a statute ceases to have effect only when this is provided for by another statute, since only Parliament is competent to repeal (or authorize the repeal of) its own enactments.[117] Repeal of one statute does not

---

[111] Examples of Acts of indemnity are: Indemnity Act 1920; Indian Divorces (Validity) Act 1921.

[112] See *Blyth* v *Blyth* [1966] AC 643, [1966] 1 All ER 524; *R* v *Cruttenden* [1991] 2 QB 66, [1991] 3 All ER 242 (evidence); cf. *Yew Bon Tew* v *Kenderaan Bas Mara* [1983] 1 AC 553, [1982] 3 All ER 833 (limitation statute in Malaysia held not to revive statute-barred cause of action).

[113] [1994] 1 AC 486, [1994] 1 All ER 20.   [114] *Ashford* v *Thornton* (1818) 1 & Ald 405.

[115] See, e.g., *Rost* v *Edwards* [1990] 2 QB 460, [1990] 2 All ER 641; *R* v *Parliamentary Commissioner for Standards ex parte Al-Fayed* [1998] 1 WLR 669, [1998] 1 All ER 93.

[116] Law Commissions Act 1965, s 3(1).

[117] An enactment may be impliedly repealed by EC legislation: *Amministrazione delle Finanze dello Stato* v *Simmenthal SpA* [1978] ECR 629, [1978] 3 CMLR 263; see p 124 *post*. In addition, Parliament may confer power on a Minister to amend or repeal statutory provisions: see p 36, *ante*.

have the effect of reviving any earlier legislative provision, statutory or otherwise, unless the contrary intention is expressed by Parliament.[118]

Repeal may be express or implied. In modern times almost all repeal is express and it is common for a schedule of repeals to be incorporated into the body of an Act. Implied repeal is possible, however, and occurs where two statutory provisions are inconsistent with one another. In this situation the later provision impliedly repeals the earlier to the extent of the inconsistency.[119] The courts generally lean against implied repeal and will attempt to reconcile seemingly conflicting provisions wherever possible. Moreover, the recent decision of the Divisional Court in *Thoburn* v *Sunderland City Council and others* suggests that there is a certain class of legislation, labelled 'constitutional statutes', which can only be repealed expressly.[120] The European Communities Act 1972, the Human Rights Act 1998, and the Scotland Act 1998 are said to be examples of such legislation.[121]

THE INTERPRETATION AND CONSTRUCTION OF STATUTES[122]

1 THE NEED FOR INTERPRETATION AND CONSTRUCTION

Where the words of a statute are clear and unambiguous, persons affected by its provisions will be able to regulate their conduct according to its terms and the need for judicial interpretation will not arise. However, if the meaning or extent of a statute is uncertain or ambiguous the statute will fall to be interpreted. There is a technical distinction between interpretation and construction. 'Interpretation' is simply the process whereby a meaning is assigned to the words in a statute. 'Construction', on the other hand, is the process whereby uncertainties or ambiguities are resolved. It follows that every statute that comes before a court is interpreted, whereas only uncertain or ambiguous provisions require construction.

(a) The words of the statute

The need for interpretation or construction may arise for a variety of reasons. One may be careless drafting, or the form and content of the Act having been the subject of hasty or ill thought-out amendments during the parliamentary process. However, many issues of construction arise simply because of the very uncertainty of words themselves.

---

[118] Interpretation Act 1978, ss 15, 16(1).

[119] See, for example, *Smith* v *Benabo* [1937] 1 KB 518, [1937] 1 All ER 523; *Ellen Street Estates Ltd* v *Minister of Health* [1934] 1 KB 590; *Dryden* v *Dryden* [1973] Fam 217, [1973] 3 All ER 526.

[120] [2002] EWHC 195 (Admin) at [60], [2003] QB 151 at [60], [2002] 4 All ER 156, per Laws LJ.

[121] Ibid. See further, p 30, *ante*.

[122] See e.g., Cross, Bell and Engle, *Statutory Interpretation* (Butterworths: 3rd edn, 1995); Bennion and Goodall, *Bennion on Statutory Interpretation* (LexisNexis Butterworths: 5th edn, 2007).

In the drink-driving case of *DPP* v *Johnson*,[123] for example, the Divisional Court had to consider the meaning of the word 'consume' in section 5 of the Road Traffic Act 1988. As Schiemann LJ put it:

> It is not unusual to speak of a house being consumed by fire and it would not be strange to speak of a bottle of medical alcohol having been consumed by rubbing its contents into skin prior to administering an injection…One can also talk of consuming snuff by sniffing.

The meaning of a word depends on the context in which it is used. It was the context of section 5, together with the marginal note, that persuaded the court to reject the submission that 'consume' in section 5 meant 'consume by mouth'. It therefore held that a drink–drive offence could be committed even if the alcohol had, in part, been ingested by injection.

(b) Ambiguity

Ambiguity arises when words used in a statute are found to be capable of bearing two or more literal meanings. Language is an imprecise tool and even parliamentary draftsmen, in using words intended to convey one meaning, occasionally contrive to give rise to an alternative meaning which neither they nor the legislature envisaged. Thus the Restriction of Offensive Weapons Act 1959 made it an offence to 'offer for sale' certain offensive weapons, including 'flick knives'. A shopkeeper who displayed weapons of this type in his window was held not to be guilty of an offence under the Act, because the exhibition of goods in a shop window does not constitute an offer.[124]

Where a statute concerns an intrinsically complex area of law, such as landlord and tenant or income tax, it seems to be virtually impossible to choose language which is entirely free from ambiguity. Nevertheless the judiciary has on occasion been less than sympathetic to the draftsman's plight. Thus in *R* v *Royle*[125] section 16 of the Theft Act 1968 was described as being so obscure as to have 'created a judicial nightmare', while in *Central Asbestos Co Ltd* v *Dodd*, Lord Reid said that the Limitation Act 1963 had 'a strong claim to the distinction of being the worst drafted Act on the statute book'.[126]

(c) Uncertainty

Uncertainty is far more common than ambiguity. Uncertainty occurs where the words of a statute are intended to apply to various factual situations and the courts are called upon to decide whether the set of facts before them was envisaged by the Act. For

---

[123] [1995] 4 All ER 53, [1995] 1 WLR 728.

[124] *Fisher* v *Bell* [1961] 1 QB 394, [1960] 3 All ER 731. In reaching this decision, the Divisional Court relied heavily upon established common law principles of contract law: see also *Partridge* v *Crittenden* [1968] 2 All ER 421, [1968] 1 WLR 1204.

[125] [1971] 3 All ER 1359 at 1363, [1971] 1 WLR 1764 at 1767, per Edmund Davies LJ. The offending part of the section (s 16(2)(a)) was eventually repealed and replaced by the Theft Act 1978.

[126] [1973] AC 518 at 529, [1972] 2 All ER 1135 at 113; the Limitation Act 1975 (replacing that part of the 1963 Act) seemed to aim at similar distinction. The Acts concerned are now consolidated in the Limitation Act 1980.

example, the words 'an accident arising out of and in the course of his employment' in the Workmen's Compensation Acts were the source of innumerable cases, not because they were in any way ambiguous but because their scope was adaptable to endless permutations of facts and was therefore uncertain.[127]

The use of general and ostensibly straightforward words, such as 'road',[128] 'premises',[129] and 'board'[130] has created problems of construction that the legislature could not have envisaged. More recently, the courts have had to resolve such conundrums as whether the cremation of humans is 'the subjection of goods or materials to any process',[131] whether an orange squeezed by hand is a 'manufactured beverage',[132] whether a partner in a long-term homosexual relationship is a member of the other partner's 'family',[133] and whether a male to female transsexual is a 'female'.[134] Lord Denning once expressed the difficulty as follows:[135]

> It must be remembered that it is not within human powers to foresee the manifold sets of facts which may arise, and, even if it were, it is not possible to provide for them in terms free from all ambiguity.

2 JUDICIAL APPROACHES TO INTERPRETATION

The basic task of the judge is to ascertain the intention of Parliament. Nevertheless there are alternative approaches to this task. These approaches, which differ radically, are commonly known as the 'literal' approach and the 'purposive' approach. It is never possible to know in advance which approach any particular court will favour, and it may be that a court will adopt the approach which best enables it to reach the conclusion considered just in all the circumstances. In *Re M (A Minor) (Care Order: Threshold Conditions)*[136] Lord Templeman spoke of: 'ascertaining and giving effect to the intention of Parliament by construing a statute in accordance with the spirit rather than the letter of the Act.'

Both of these approaches to interpretation are discussed below, though they must now be considered in the light of the obligation arising from section 3 of the Human Rights Act 1998.[137]

---

[127] The words are still used in social security legislation (currently the Social Security Contributions and Benefits Act 1992, s 94) where they continue to cause trouble; see *Chief Adjudication Officer v Rhodes* [1999] ICR 178, [1999] IRLR 103.

[128] *Cutter v Eagle Star Insurance Co Ltd* [1998] 4 All ER 417, [1998] 1 WLR 1647.

[129] *Whitley v Stumbles* [1930] AC 544; *Maunsell v Olins* [1975] AC 373, [1975] 1 All ER 16.

[130] *Otter v Norman* [1989] AC 129, [1988] 2 All ER 897.

[131] *Bourne (Inspector of Taxes) v Norwich Crematorium Ltd* [1967] 2 All ER 576, [1967] 1 WLR 691.

[132] *Customs and Excise Commissioners v Savoy Hotel Ltd* [1966] 2 All ER 299, [1966] 1 WLR 948. For a delightfully sardonic exposition of the difficulty of ascertaining the 'right' meaning of words, see the judgment of Diplock LJ in *Slim v Daily Telegraph Ltd* [1968] 2 QB 157 at 171–2, [1968] 1 All ER 497 at 504.

[133] *Fitzpatrick v Sterling Housing Association Ltd* [2001] 1 AC 27, [1999] 4 All ER 705.

[134] *Bellinger v Bellinger* [2003] UKHL 21, [2003] 2 AC 467, [2003] 2 All ER 593.

[135] *Asher v Seaford Court Estates Ltd* [1949] 2 KB 481 at 499, [1949] 2 All ER 155 at 164.

[136] [1994] 2 AC 424, [1994] 3 All ER 298.

[137] The impact of the Human Rights Act on statutory interpretation is discussed at p 155, *post*. As to the interpretation of European Community legislation, see chapter 4, *post*.

(a) The literal approach

The basic approach to statutory interpretation, as already stated, is to ascertain the intention of the legislature. The literal approach to this task is that this intention must be found in the ordinary and natural meaning of the language used in the statute. In other words, the focus is on the 'objective' meaning of the words, not on the subjective intention that might lie behind their use. While this approach may be defended as respecting the proper boundaries between the judicial and legislative functions,[138] it does have certain obvious shortcomings. Firstly, it relies on an assumption that the 'ordinary and natural meaning' of a word or phrase can always be ascertained. Yet as discussed previously, this is not always the case and the courts have often had considerable difficulty in interpreting seemingly straightforward words.[139] Secondly, if the words used in a provision are capable of *alternative* ordinary and natural meanings, the court still needs to find a mechanism for choosing between these alternatives.

Despite these shortcomings, the literal approach will, in most cases, produce a reasonable interpretation of the statute. Difficulty arises, however, where a literal interpretation produces either an improbable result or a manifest absurdity. Where the result is merely less plausible than that which Parliament might be assumed to have intended, a strict application of the literal approach means that this interpretation ought nevertheless to be given. Thus in *Inland Revenue Commissioners* v *Hinchy*[140] the House of Lords was called upon to construe section 25(3) of the Income Tax Act 1952, which provided that any person delivering an incorrect tax return should forfeit 'treble the tax which he ought to be charged under this Act'. Although Parliament presumably intended a penalty of treble the *unpaid* tax,[141] the House of Lords took a literal approach to the subsection, and held that the respondent was liable to pay treble the *whole* amount of tax payable by him for the year. *Fisher* v *Bell*, cited earlier,[142] is a further example of the application of the literal rule producing a result which appeared contrary to the intention of the legislature.

The golden rule. The strict application of the literal approach may be modified by the use of 'the golden rule'. This means that where the literal approach would produce a manifestly absurd outcome, judges may depart from the ordinary meaning of the word(s), in favour of an interpretation which avoids the absurdity. Lord Blackburn explained this approach as follows:[143]

> [W]e are to take the whole statute and construe it all together, giving the words their ordinary signification, unless when so applied they produce an inconsistency

---

[138] See, e.g., the judgment of Viscount Dilhorne in *Kammins Ballrooms Co Ltd* v *Zenith Investments (Torquay) Ltd* [1971] AC 850, [1970] 2 All ER 871.

[139] See p 47, *ante*.   [140] [1960] AC 748, [1960] 1 All ER 505.

[141] The law was in fact changed shortly after this decision by the Finance Act 1960, s 44.

[142] [1961] 1 QB 394, [1960] 3 All ER 731; see p 47, *ante*. The Law Commission report, *The Interpretation of Statutes*, 1969 (Law Com No 21) recommended a statutory provision to the effect that a construction which would promote the general legislative purpose underlying the provision in question 'is to be preferred to a construction which would not'.

[143] *River Wear Commissioners* v *Adamson* (1877) 2 App Cas 743 at 764–5.

or absurdity or inconvenience so great as to convince the Court that the intention could not have been to use them in their ordinary signification, and to justify the court in putting them in some other signification, which, though less proper, is one which the Court thinks the words will bear.

The use of the golden rule is well illustrated by the unanimous decision of the House of Lords in *McMonagle* v *Westminster City Council*.[144] The appellant was charged with using premises as a 'sex encounter establishment' without a licence. The statutory definition of these words was 'premises at which performances which are not unlawful are given, which wholly or mainly comprise the sexual stimulation of persons admitted to the premises'. The appellant's defence was that the prosecution had failed to prove that the performances were not unlawful, and that if they were, according to the plain words of the statute a licence was not required. The House of Lords rejected this interpretation as manifestly absurd. Lord Bridge explained his reasoning:[145]

> I am satisfied that the main object of paragraph 3A(c) of Schedule 3 is to require any premises, not falling within the proviso, where live nude entertainment is provided to be licensed and that in order to avoid the substantial frustration of that object it is both necessary and legitimate that the words 'which are not unlawful' should be treated as surplusage and as having been introduced by incompetent draftsmanship for no other purpose than to emphasise that a licence confers no immunity from the ordinary criminal law.

Another example is provided by *Adler* v *George*.[146] In this case, a conviction for causing an obstruction *'in the vicinity of'* a prohibited place was upheld by the Divisional Court even though the incident had occurred *inside* the place in question. Similarly, in *R* v *Allen*[147] the court applied the golden rule to the statutory definition of bigamy in order to avoid a manifestly absurd outcome. Section 57 of the Offences Against the Person Act 1861 stated that, 'whosoever being married shall marry another person...shall be guilty of bigamy'. A literal interpretation of these words would have rendered it impossible to commit the offence, since any attempt to 'marry' whilst already being married to someone else would be ineffective. The court therefore interpreted the phrase 'shall marry' to mean 'shall go through a marriage ceremony'.[148]

The difficulty, of course, lies in drawing the line between a literal interpretation which appears to produce a 'manifest absurdity', and one which merely appears to be improbable. For those who advocate a literal approach to statutory interpretation, the adoption of a different meaning in the former case may be accepted as a legitimate extension of this approach. To depart from the ordinary meaning of words in the latter case, however, might be seen as unacceptable judicial activism. Lord Bridge is amongst

---

[144] [1990] 2 AC 716, [1990] 1 All ER 993.

[145] [1990] 2 AC 716 at 727, [1990] 1 All ER 993 at 998.

[146] [1964] 2 QB 7, [1964] 1 All ER 628.

[147] (1872) LR 1 CCR 367.

[148] This reasoning should be compared with that applied in *Whiston* v *Whiston* [1995] Fam 198, [1998] 1 All ER 423, to prevent a bigamist from claiming financial relief under the Matrimonial Causes Act 1973. (Cf. *Rampal* v *Rampal (No 2)* [2001] EWCA Civ 989, [2002] Fam 85, [2001] 3 WLR 795.)

those to have warned against the judiciary substituting its own judgment for that of the legislature:[149]

> It is one thing to abstain from giving to the language of a statute the full effect of its ordinary grammatical meaning in order to avoid some positively harmful or manifestly unjust consequence. This I would describe as a legitimate process of construction to avoid a positive absurdity. But it is quite another thing to read into a statute a meaning which the language used will not bear in order to remedy a supposed defect or shortcoming which, if not made good, will make the statutory machinery less effective than the court believes it ought to be in order to achieve its proper purpose.

A case which arguably stretches the limits of the golden rule is *DPP* v *McKeown*.[150] The House of Lords had to consider the meaning of section 69 of the Police and Criminal Evidence Act 1984, which allowed computer-generated documents to be admitted as evidence if the court was satisfied that any fault in the computer had not affected the production of the document or the accuracy of its contents. Because the computer's clock had been set inaccurately, the time stated on a document produced by the computer was wrong. On a literal interpretation, it was thus inadmissible: the contents were inaccurate. However, the House of Lords avoided this conclusion because it considered that Parliament could not have intended it – the inaccurate time shown on the document did not affect its reliability as proof of what was being disputed.

Finally, it should be noted that there is a residual category of cases in which a literal interpretation of a statute is rejected in order to avoid an outcome which would clearly be contrary to public policy. Thus in *Re Sigsworth*[151] the golden rule was applied to prevent a murderer from inheriting the estate of his victim, although he was, as her son, the 'sole issue' on a literal interpretation of the Administration of Estates Act 1925. In a later case, the Court of Appeal took a similar approach in rejecting the judicial review application of a double killer. The applicant had a psychotic illness which was known to involve extreme hatred of his adoptive parents. His application for a copy of his birth certificate was turned down by the Registrar General out of concern that he might use the information to find and harm his natural mother. Despite the fact that the ordinary words in the Adoption Act 1976 did not give the Registrar General any discretion to refuse the applicant's request, the Court of Appeal upheld his decision on the basis that Parliament could not have intended to facilitate the commission of a crime.[152]

(b) The purposive approach

The 'mischief rule', or rule in *Heydon*'s case,[153] is a form of purposive interpretation with a relatively long history. It means that where a statute was passed to remedy a

---

[149]   *R* v *Central Criminal Court, ex parte Francis & Francis* [1989] AC 346 at 375, [1988] 3 All ER 775 at 783.
[150]   [1997] 1 All ER 737, [1997] 1 WLR 295. The provision in question has now been repealed.
[151]   [1935] Ch 89.
[152]   *R* v *Registrar General, ex parte Smith* [1991] 2 QB 393, [1991] 2 All ER 88.
[153]   (1584) 3 Co Rep 7a.

mischief the court will, if possible, adopt the interpretation of the statute which will have the effect of correcting that mischief. In *Heydon*'s case itself, the rule was defined thus:

> four things are to be discussed and considered; (1) what was the common law before the making of the Act; (2) what was the mischief and defect for which the common law did not provide; (3) what remedy the Parliament hath resolved and appointed to cure the disease of the commonwealth; and (4) the true reason of the remedy.

In order to ascertain the mischief which the statute was passed to correct, the judge may legitimately have regard to the preamble of the statute, the long title, headings, and extrinsic sources which may indicate the state of the law before the passing of the Act.[154]

The rule has often been used to resolve ambiguities in cases where the literal rule would produce an unsatisfactory outcome. For example, a 'single woman' for the purposes of affiliation proceedings was held to be a woman with no husband to support her, not necessarily an unmarried woman – the relevant Acts were passed to remedy the mischief of women having illegitimate children without the means of supporting them.[155] Similarly, medically induced abortions brought about by nurses acting under the instruction of doctors constituted lawful 'termination by a registered medical practitioner'. This was because the statute in question was intended to correct the mischief of legal uncertainty and to ensure that abortions were carried out safely.[156]

Unlike in Heydon's day, most modern legislation is not specifically concerned with rectifying mischief but with the fulfilment of some more general policy objective:

> Even for the lawyer, the expression [the mischief rule] is unsatisfactory. It tends to suggest that legislation is only designed to deal with an evil, and not to further a positive social approach.[157]

The 'mischief rule' has therefore given way to the slightly broader notion of 'purposive' interpretation. This emphasizes the need to construe the wording of a statute in its wider context, so as to give effect to its underlying purpose. One criticism that could be made of the wide application of this purposive approach is that it is inherently subjective. The judge who decides that a literal interpretation is contrary to the intention of the legislature is, *ipso facto*, ascertaining its intention from some source other than the statute, and this might be regarded as going beyond the judicial function. Moreover, the judge may expose himself to the criticism that he is giving effect to his own views of what the policy of Parliament *ought* to be.[158] The contrary view, however, is that a consideration

---

[154] For further discussion of the use of both internal and external aids, see pp 64–74, *post*.

[155] *Kruhlak* v *Kruhlak* [1958] 2 QB 32, [1958] 1 All ER 154.

[156] *Royal College of Nursing* v *Department of Health and Social Security* [1981] AC 800, [1981] 1 All ER 545.

[157] Law Commission, *The Interpretation of Statutes* (Law Com No 21), 1969.

[158] See *Duport Steels Ltd* v *Sirs* [1980] 1 All ER 529, [1980] 1 WLR 142; *Shah* v *Barnet London Borough Council* [1983] 2 AC 309, [1983] 1 All ER 226.

of the context in which Parliament has used particular words can only enhance a judge's ability to ascertain their intended meaning:[159]

> The starting point is that language in all legal texts conveys meaning according to the circumstances in which it was used. It follows that the context must always be identified and considered before the process of construction or during it. It is therefore wrong to say that the court may only resort to evidence of the contextual scene when an ambiguity has arisen.

In *Shah* v *Barnet London Borough Council*,[160] the House of Lords offered *some* guidance as to when a purposive interpretation of a provision could be adopted in preference to its literal meaning. It concluded that this would only be legitimate where a clear expression of the legislative intention could be found in either the Act or permissible extrinsic sources.

Supplying omissions. The legitimacy of going beyond a literal interpretation of a statute is often called into question when a court is faced with a factual situation for which the statute does not provide. Such a situation is termed a *casus omissus*, and it can only be remedied by attributing to Parliament an intention that it never had. This amounts to a legislative act on the part of the judiciary, and it is a function which the more conservative judges are slow to adopt. Denning LJ, in the Court of Appeal, expressed his personal view of the judicial function as follows:[161]

> We sit here to find out the intention of Parliament and of Ministers and carry it out, and we do this better by filling in the gaps and making sense of the enactment than by opening it up to destructive analysis.

On appeal Lord Simonds condemned this approach, describing it as a 'naked usurpation of the legislative function under the thin disguise of interpretation'.[162] 'If a gap is disclosed,' Lord Simonds explained, 'the remedy lies in an amending Act.' However, in *Inco Europe Ltd* v *First Choice Distribution* the House of Lords was unanimous in confirming that the courts do have the power to correct obvious drafting errors:[163]

> Before interpreting a statute in this way the court must be abundantly sure of three matters: (1) the intended purpose of the statute or provision in question; (2) that by inadvertence the draftsman and Parliament failed to give effect to that purpose in the provision in question; and (3) the substance of the provision Parliament would have made, although not necessarily the precise words Parliament would have used, had the error in the Bill been noticed.

[159] *Westminster City Council* v *National Asylum Support Service* [2002] UKHL 38 at [5], [2002] 4 All ER 654 at [5], [2002] 1 WLR 2956, per Lord Steyn.
[160] [1983] 2 AC 309, [1983] 1 All ER 226.
[161] *Magor and St Mellons Rural District Council* v *Newport Corporation* [1950] 2 All ER 1226 at 1236.
[162] [1952] AC 189 at 191, [1951] 2 All ER 839 at 841.
[163] [2000] 2 All ER 109 at 115, [2000] 1 WLR 586 at 592, per Lord Nicholls. See also *Kammins Ballrooms Co Ltd* v *Zenith Investments (Torquay) Ltd* [1971] AC 850, [1970] 2 All ER 871.

(c) The trend towards purposive interpretation

While the literal and purposive approaches to statutory interpretation may be alternative models, it would be wrong to treat them as mutually exclusive. Firstly, a literal reading of a provision will not always be able to resolve an ambiguity, and secondly, even under a purposive approach the court's primary obligation is to interpret the words of the Act. As Lord Hoffman explained in one case:[164]

> There is ultimately only one principle of construction, namely to ascertain what Parliament meant by using the language of the statute.

Moreover, since these are merely approaches rather than strict rules, judges can, and do, adopt whichever method of interpretation they consider appropriate, and it is common to find elements of both approaches influencing the same decision. Thus, as Laws LJ observed, 'the difference in purposive and literal construction is in truth one of degree only,'[165] and the cases do not always fall neatly into distinct categories.

For some judges, the choice of approach is a matter of principle, and it is inextricably linked with ideas about the role of the courts within the framework of the constitution and the separation of powers.[166]

> [I]t cannot be too strongly emphasised that the British Constitution, though largely unwritten, is firmly based on the separation of powers. Parliament makes the laws, the judiciary interprets them. When Parliament legislates to remedy what the majority of its members at the time perceive to be a defect or lacuna in the existing law...the role of the judiciary is confined to ascertaining from the words that Parliament has approved as expressing its intention what that intention was, and giving effect to it. Where the meaning of statutory words is plain and unambiguous it is not for judges to invent fancied ambiguities as an excuse for failing to give effect to its plain meaning...Under our constitution it is Parliament's opinion on these matters that is paramount.

Increasingly, however, many judges take the view that the approach to interpretation must be determined on an individual basis, taking into account all the circumstances of a case. It is clear that the willingness to look beyond a strict literal approach is growing, and the decision to permit limited use of *Hansard* as an extrinsic aid is evidence of this. It is equally beyond doubt that the particular approach adopted by the court will turn not only on the inclinations of the individual judge, but also upon the context in which the matter is being decided. As will be seen later, the courts are always anxious to adopt a purposive approach to statutes in order to give effect to international obligations, and in the context of EC law they are under a legal obligation to do so. In addition, the Human Rights Act 1998 obliges the courts to take a more creative approach to statutory interpretation in all cases which could impact on the protection of ECHR rights.

---

[164] *MacNiven* v *Westmoreland Investments* [2001] UKHL 6, [2003] 1 AC 311, [2001] 1 All ER 865.
[165] *Oliver Ashworth (Holdings) Ltd* v *Ballard (Kent) Ltd* [2000] Ch 12 at 34, [1999] 2 All ER 791 at 805.
[166] *Duport Steels* v *Sirs* [1980] 1 All ER 529 at 541, [1980] 1 WLR 142 at 157, per Lord Diplock.

(d) Statutory interpretation under the Human Rights Act 1998[167]

The Human Rights Act 1998 adds a new dimension to the task of statutory interpretation.[168] The long title describes it as 'an Act to give further effect to rights and freedoms guaranteed under the European Convention on Human Rights', and one of the principal mechanisms by which it seeks to do this is contained in section 3(1). This provides that:

> So far as it is possible to do so, primary legislation and subordinate legislation must be read and given effect in a way which is compatible with the Convention rights.[169]

Section 3 applies to *all* legislation, whether enacted before or after the Human Rights Act,[170] and it significantly enhances the courts' powers of interpretation. However, it stops short of enabling them to disapply Acts of Parliament[171] and it does not affect the validity, continuing operation, or enforcement of any incompatible primary legislation. Nor does it affect the validity of incompatible subordinate legislation where primary legislation prevents removal of the incompatibility.[172] If a Convention compliant interpretation of an Act is not possible, a court[173] may issue a declaration of incompatibility but it must still give effect to the legislation as Parliament intended.[174] Thus, as Lord Steyn explained:[175]

> It is crystal clear that the carefully and subtly drafted Human Rights Act 1998 preserves the principle of Parliamentary sovereignty. In a case of incompatibility which cannot be avoided by interpretation under section 3(1), the courts may not disapply the legislation. The court may merely issue a declaration of incompatibility which then gives rise to a power to take remedial action.

---

[167] Much has been written about statutory interpretation under the Human Rights Act 1998. See for example, Clayton, 'The Limits of what's "Possible": Statutory Construction Under the Human Rights Act' [2002] EHRLR 559; Kavanagh, 'The Role of Parliamentary Intention in Adjudication under the Human Rights Act 1998' (2006) 26(1) OJLS 179; Lord Lester, 'The Art of the Possible – Interpreting Statutes Under the Human Rights Act' [1998] EHRLR 665; Marshall, 'The Lynchpin of Parliamentary Intention: Lost, Stolen or Strained?' [2003] PL 236; Van Zyl Smit, 'The New Purposive Interpretation of Statutes: HRA Section 3 after *Ghaidan* v *Godin-Mendoza*' (2007) 70(2) MLR 294.

[168] The overall significance of this major piece of legislation is discussed in chapter 5.

[169] Section 1(1) provides that 'Convention rights' are those ECHR rights contained in Articles 2 to 12 and 14, Articles 1 to 3 of the First Protocol and Article 1 Thirteenth Protocol. The text of these Articles is set out in Schedule 1 to the Act.

[170] Section 3(2).

[171] Cf. The European Communities Act 1972, s 2(4); discussed further in chapter 4, *post.*

[172] Section 3(2).

[173] For these purposes, the term 'court' means the House of Lords, the Judicial Committee of the Privy Council, the Court Martial Appeal Court, the Court of Appeal, the High Court, the Court of Protection, and the Scottish High Court of Justiciary (except when sitting as a trial court or Court of Session): s 4(5).

[174] Section 4. The effect of such a declaration is simply to bring the incompatibility to the attention of Parliament, and, where appropriate, to allow Ministers to take remedial action under s 10. Incompatible *subordinate* legislation may be declared invalid unless primary legislation prevents removal of the incompatibility. In the latter case a declaration of incompatibility may be issued.

[175] *R* v *DPP, ex parte Kebilene* [2000] 2 AC 326 at 333, [1999] 4 All ER 801 at 831.

Section 3 is more than just a 'tool' which judges may consider in the event of an ambiguity, and its effect is not simply to add yet another approach to existing canons of interpretation. Instead, it imposes an *obligation* on judges to seek a Convention compatible interpretation, regardless of whether the provision in question is ambiguous. Once it is established that Convention rights are engaged, courts are permitted to go far beyond previously accepted limits in seeking 'possible' meanings of words:[176]

> [Section 3] will require a very different approach to interpretation from that to which the English courts are accustomed. Traditionally, the search has been for the true meaning: now it will be for a possible meaning that would prevent the making of a declaration of incompatibility.

On the other hand, section 3 need not be considered at all unless an 'ordinary' reading of the disputed legislation would give rise to a Convention breach:[177]

> [U]nless the legislation would otherwise be in breach of the Convention section 3 can be ignored; so courts should always first ascertain whether, absent section 3, there would be any breach of the Convention...

Several cases decided since the Act came into force have considered the permissible boundaries of interpretation under section 3. In *Poplar Housing and Regeneration Community Association* v *Donoghue*, the Court of Appeal sought to distinguish between the tasks of legislation and interpretation:[178]

> [I]f it is necessary in order to obtain compliance to radically alter the effect of the legislation this will be an indication that more than interpretation is involved.

It is clear that 'reading down' legislation to narrow the effect of a provision, and reading additional words *in*, are both legitimate techniques in Human Rights Act cases. Thus, in *R* v *Lambert*[179] the House of Lords read down a provision of the Misuse of Drugs Act 1971, so as to impose an evidential rather than a legal burden on the accused and thereby avoid a breach of the presumption of innocence. Similarly, in *Ghaidan* v *Godin-Mendoza*[180] the phrase 'as his or her wife or husband' was construed to mean '*as if they were* his or her wife or husband', in order to avoid a conclusion that the Rent Act 1977 discriminated against same-sex partners.

The leading case on section 3 is *R* v *A (No 2)*.[181] The defendant was prosecuted for rape and sought to rely on the defence of consent. He wanted to adduce evidence of the

---

[176] Lord Cooke, 582 HL Official Report (5th series) col 1272, 3 November 1997. (Even before the Human Rights Act, there is evidence that some judges were prepared to take a more teleological approach to the interpretation of human rights provisions. See, e.g., the Privy Council's experience of interpreting written constitutions and Bills of Rights from other jurisdictions: *Huntley* v *Attorney-General for Jamaica* [1995] 2 AC 1, [1995] 1 All ER 308; *Attorney-General of Hong-Kong* v *Lee Kwong-kut* [1993] AC 951, [1993] 3 All ER 939.)

[177] *Poplar Housing and Regeneration Community Association Ltd* v *Donoghue* [2001] EWCA Civ 595 at [75], [2002] QB 48 at [75], [2001] 4 All ER 604, per Lord Woolf CJ. This approach was endorsed by Lord Hope in *R* v *A (No 2)* [2001] UKHL 25 at [58], [2002] 1 AC 45 at [58], [2001] 3 All ER 1.

[178] [2001] EWCA Civ 595 at [76], [2002] QB 48 at [76], [2001] 4 All ER 604, per Lord Woolf CJ.

[179] [2001] UKHL 37, [2002] 2 AC 545, [2001] 3 All ER 577.

[180] [2004] UKHL 30, [2004] 2 AC 557, [2004] 3 All ER 411.

[181] [2001] UKHL 25, [2002] 1 AC 45, [2001] 3 All ER 1.

complainant's sexual history in support of this defence, but the use of such evidence appeared to be precluded by section 41 of the Youth Justice and Criminal Evidence Act 1999. Defence counsel contended that a refusal to admit the evidence would breach the right of the accused to a fair trial under Article 6 of the Convention: the issue for the court was whether it was 'possible' to interpret section 41 in a manner compatible with that right. The House of Lords held that it was, interpreting it as being subject to an implied discretion to permit evidence of sexual history in order to ensure a fair trial. Lord Steyn explained the effect of section 3 as follows:[182]

> [T]he interpretive obligation under s 3 of the 1998 Act is a strong one. It applies even if there is no ambiguity in the language in the sense of the language being capable of two different meanings...Under ordinary methods of interpretation a court may depart from the language of the statute to avoid absurd consequences: s 3 goes much further. Undoubtedly, a court must always look for a contextual and purposive interpretation: s 3 is more radical in its effect. It is a general principle of the interpretation of legal instruments that the text is the primary source of interpretation: other sources are subordinate to it...Section 3 qualifies this general principle because it requires a court to find an interpretation compatible with Convention rights if it is possible to do so...In accordance with the will of Parliament as reflected in s 3 it will sometimes be necessary to adopt an interpretation, which linguistically may appear strained. The techniques to be used will not only involve the reading down of express language in a statute but also the implication of provisions.

Thus far, *R v A (No 2)* probably constitutes the 'high water mark' of judicial creativity under the Human Rights Act, and in subsequent decisions the courts have not always been willing to go quite this far. In *Re S (Children) (Care Order: Implementation of Care Plan)*[183] the Court of Appeal read words into the Children Act 1989 to give the courts increased discretionary powers concerning children taken into care. On appeal to the House of Lords, however, this use of section 3 was rejected, and their Lordships cautioned against reading words into an Act to the point of making it unintelligible or unworkable:[184]

> [Section] 3(2)(b) presupposes that not all provisions in primary legislation can be rendered convention compliant by the application of section 3(1)...For present purposes, it is sufficient to say that a meaning which departs substantially from a fundamental feature of an Act of Parliament is likely to have crossed the boundary between interpretation and amendment.

In *Ghaidan* v *Godin-Mendoza*[185] the House of Lords enthusiastically returned to the creative approach adopted in *R v A (No 2)*, and to date relatively few cases have resulted

---

[182] Ibid at [40].   [183] [2001] EWCA Civ 757, [2002] 2 FLR 582, [2002] HRLR 50.

[184] [2002] UKHL 10 at [38]–[43], [2002] 2 AC 291 at [38]–[43], [2002] 2 All ER 192, per Lord Nicholls. See also *International Transport Roth GmbH* v *Secretary of State for the Home Department* [2002] EWCA Civ 158, [2003] QB 728, [2002] HRLR 31. In this case the Court of Appeal was unable to find a compatible interpretation of provisions in the Immigration and Asylum Act 1999 without crossing the boundaries of legitimate interpretation. A declaration of incompatibility was issued.

[185] [2004] UKHL 30, [2004] 2 AC 557, [2004] 3 All ER 411.

in a declaration of incompatibility.[186] In *R (on the application of H) v North and East London Regional Mental Health Tribunal*, the Court of Appeal declared sections 72(1) and 73(1) of the Mental Health Act 1983 to be incompatible with the right to liberty under Article 5.[187] The offending provisions were subsequently amended by the Mental Health Act 1983 (Remedial) Order 2001.[188] In another case, the Court of Appeal issued a declaration of incompatibility in relation to provisions of the Immigration and Asylum Act 1999. The provisions imposed a fixed penalty of £2,000 per entrant on hauliers responsible for bringing illegal entrants into the UK.[189] The legislative response to this decision was to amend the offending provisions by Act of Parliament.[190] In *Bellinger v Bellinger*[191] a provision stating that a marriage shall be void if 'the parties are not respectively male and female'[192] was held to be incompatible with the rights of the transsexual applicant under Articles 8 and 12. Parliament's response was to enact the Gender Recognition Act 2004. Declarations of incompatibility have also been made in relation to provisions denying the possibility of review by the Parole Board to prisoners subject to deportation orders,[193] and provisions allowing the detention without trial of foreign nationals suspected of involvement in terrorism.[194]

3 RULES OF INTERPRETATION AND LANGUAGE

(a) The statute must be read as a whole

The meaning suggested by a word when used in isolation might be different from that suggested when used in conjunction with other words. A statute must therefore be read as a whole, and every section must be interpreted in the light of other sections. The decision of the House of Lords in *Beswick v Beswick* provides an interesting illustration of this.[195] The case concerned the interpretation of section 56(1) of the Law of

---

[186] Of these, a number have been overturned on appeal. See, e.g., *R (on the Application of Alconbury) v Secretary of State for the Environment, Transport and the Regions* [2001] UKHL 23, [2003] 2 AC 295, [2001] 2 All ER 929, reversing [2002] HRLR 2; *Matthews v Ministry of Defence* [2002] EWCA Civ 773, [2002] 3 All ER 513, [2002] 1 WLR 2621, reversing [2002] EWHC 13.

[187] [2001] EWCA Civ 415, [2002] QB 1, [2002] 3 WLR 512. Section 73 of the Mental Health Act 1983 concerns the test to be applied when determining a restricted patient's entitlement to release from a secure hospital. The provision was held to be incompatible with Article 5 as the burden of proof rested on the patient to show that his continued detention under the Act was no longer warranted.

[188] SI 2001/3712.

[189] *International Transport Roth GmbH v Secretary of State for the Home Department* [2002] EWCA Civ 158, [2003] QB 728, [2002] HRLR 31.

[190] Nationality, Asylum and Immigration Act 2002.

[191] [2003] UKHL 21, [2003] 2 AC 467, [2003] 2 All ER 593. Their Lordships noted that the government had already indicated its acceptance of the decision in *Goodwin v UK* (2002) 35 EHRR 18, in which the European Court of Human Rights had concluded that UK law was in breach of the Convention.

[192] Matrimonial Causes Act 1973, s 11.

[193] *R (on the application of Clift and others) v Secretary of State for the Home Department* [2006] UKHL 54, [2007] 1 AC 484, [2007] 2 All ER 1.

[194] *A v Secretary of State for the Home Department* [2004] UKHL 56, [2005] 2 WLR 87: see p 161, *post*.

[195] [1968] AC 58, [1967] 2 All ER 1197. Note that the law on privity of contract has now been substantially altered by the Contract (Rights of Third Parties) Act 1999.

Property Act 1925, which states that 'a person may take an interest in land or other property...although he may not be named as a party to the conveyance or other instrument'. The interpretation section of the same Act states that 'in this Act unless the context otherwise requires "property" includes "any thing in action"'.[196] It was argued that the combined effect of these provisions was to enable a stranger to a contract to enforce it, but the House of Lords rejected this argument. Their Lordships pointed out that section 56 is one of twenty-five sections in the Act grouped under the heading 'conveyances and other instruments', and in the context of the Act as a whole it was held that the word 'property' must be interpreted to mean 'real property'.

The general principle that a statute must be read as a whole has given rise to three specific presumptions concerning the use of language, each of which is known by a Latin title.

Noscitur a sociis. This translates as 'a thing is known by its associates', and in practical terms it means that where a provision contains a list of items, the meaning of each individual word in the list is coloured by the meaning of the others. In *Foster* v *Diphwys Casson Slate Co*[197] the court had to consider whether a statute prohibited the taking of explosives into a mine when carried in a cloth bag. The relevant statute stated that explosives could only be taken into a mine when carried in a 'case or canister'. Although in one sense a cloth bag might be thought of as a 'case', when interpreted in the context of the surrounding words it was held that the word only referred to containers of the same strength and solidity as a 'canister'.

Ejusdem generis. This rule means that general words which follow two or more particular words in an Act must be confined to a meaning of the same kind as the particular words. When the intention is to cover a wide range of similar circumstances, it is common drafting practice to use two or three particular examples, followed by a general expression such as 'or other place'. The effect of this is to extend the operation of the enactment to all circumstances within the same genus.

The operation of the rule can best be illustrated by two examples. Section 1 of the Betting Act 1853 prohibited the keeping of a 'house, office, room *or other place*' for the purposes of betting. In *Powell* v *Kempton Park Racecourse Co*[198] the issue was whether Tattersalls' ring at a racecourse was an 'other place' within the meaning of the Act. The House of Lords held that it was not, since the words 'house, office, room' created a genus of indoor places within which an outdoor place did not fall. *Brownsea Haven Properties Ltd* v *Poole Corporation*[199] concerned a power to make traffic orders 'in all times of public processions, rejoicings, or illuminations, *and in any case when the streets are thronged*

[196] Section 205(1).   [197] (1887) LR 18 QBD 428.
[198] [1899] AC 143; cf. *Culley* v *Harrison* [1956] 2 QB 71, [1956] 2 All ER 254.
[199] [1958] Ch 574, [1958] 1 All ER 205; see also *DPP* v *Jordan* [1977] AC 699, [1976] 3 All ER 775. Section 4(1) of the Obscene Publications Act 1959 provides a public good defence in the case of articles considered to be 'in the interests of science, literature, art or learning, or of other objects of general concern'. The House of Lords held that when construed ejusdem generis with the preceding words, the phrase 'other objects of general concern', did not include the psychotherapeutic value of pornography to sexual deviants.

or liable to be obstructed'. It was held that this did not confer power to create a one-way traffic system for the six months of the summer holiday season.

It should be noted that there must be at least two specific words to create a genus. Thus where an Act referred to 'theatres and other places of amusement', it was held that a funfair was within the Act even though not ejusdem generis with the word 'theatres'.[200] Similarly, the ejusdem generis rule does not apply where the particular words in a statute are sufficiently different that they do not create a genus at all.[201]

Expressio unius est exclusio alterius. This translates as 'to express one thing is to exclude another'. It means simply that where a provision includes an item or list which is *not* followed by general words such as 'or other place', it is presumed that Parliament did not intend any unspecified items to be included. Thus, in *R* v *Cuthbertson*[202] a power to order forfeiture of property following a conviction for 'an offence under *this* Act' did not authorize forfeiture for *conspiracy* to commit an offence: the offence of conspiracy was not created by that Act.[203]

(b) Interpretation Act 1978

This Act, which consolidated and amended the Interpretation Act 1889, prescribes definitions of certain words and phrases which are commonly encountered in Acts of Parliament. Thus, for example:

> unless the contrary intention appears: (a) words importing the masculine gender include the feminine; (b) words importing the feminine gender include the masculine; (c) words in the singular include the plural and words in the plural include the singular.[204]
>   ' "month" means calendar month'.[205]

However, these and other definitions are only presumptive and they yield to a contrary intention in the Act being interpreted. Thus, although the Interpretation Act defines the word 'person' to include a body corporate, a corporation carrying out legal work was not held to be not guilty of acting as an unqualified 'person': the statute concerned could only apply to persons who could qualify as solicitors.[206]

4 PRESUMPTIONS OF SUBSTANCE

It is possible to express almost any rule of statutory interpretation in the form of a presumption. The rules against retrospective and extraterritorial operation are often

---

[200] *Allen* v *Emmerson* [1944] KB 362, [1944] 1 All ER 344.
[201] For an illustration of this, see *Re C (A Minor) (Interim Care Order: Residential Assessment)* [1997] AC 489, [1996] 4 All ER 871.
[202] [1981] AC 470, [1980] 2 All ER 401.
[203] The statute in question was the Misuse of Drugs Act 1971.
[204] Section 6. For an illustration of this rule, see *Floor* v *Davis* [1980] AC 695, [1979] 2 All ER 677.
[205] Section 5 and Schedule 1.
[206] *Law Society* v *United Service Bureau Ltd* [1934] 1 KB 343. This lacuna was filled by the Solicitors Act 1957 (now Solicitors Act 1974, s 20).

expressed as presumptions, and the 'rules' concerning the interpretation of language can also be thought of as presumptions since their operation can be displaced by an express provision to the contrary. Nevertheless, although it is probably a mere matter of terminology, the following are always described as presumptions rather than rules.[207] Recent decisions indicate that these presumptions may simply be facets of the wider principle of legality:[208]

> Parliament does not legislate in a vacuum. Parliament legislates for a European liberal democracy founded on the principles and traditions of the common law. And the courts may approach legislation on this initial assumption. But this assumption only has prima facie force. It can be displaced by a clear and specific provision to the contrary.

(a) Penal provisions are construed narrowly

Where a statute imposes criminal liability or tax obligations (which are treated as penal) and the statute is ambiguous or uncertain, it should be construed in favour of the individual.[209] Thus it has been held that the offence of 'knowingly possessing an explosive' requires knowledge on the part of the accused that the substance possessed is explosive, not merely that he possesses the substance.[210] One aspect of this general rule is the presumption against the imposition of liability without fault.

However, this rule of interpretation is not strong enough to displace the literal rule. Consequently, where a statute unambiguously creates a criminal offence or a tax the court is bound to give effect to it. The provision will be regarded as unambiguous if the court considers the intention of Parliament to be clear, notwithstanding that the words are capable of bearing more than one meaning.[211]

(b) Presumption against the imposition of criminal liability without fault

At common law mens rea(intent) is an element in all crimes,[212] and although the legislature can, and does, create strict liability offences, the intention so to do must be clear

---

[207] For a useful discussion of several presumptions, see *Wilson* v *First County Trust (No 2)* [2003] UKHL 40 at [186]–[201], [2004] 1 AC 816 at [186]–[201], [2003] 4 All ER 97, per Lord Rodger.

[208] *R* v *Secretary of State for the Home Department, ex parte Pierson* [1998] AC 539 at 587, [1997] 3 All ER 577 at 603, per Lord Steyn. In *Wilson* v *First County Trust (No 2)* [2003] UKHL 40 at [153], [2004] 1 AC 816 at [153], [2003] 4 All ER 97, Lord Scott described the presumption against giving retrospective effect to legislation as 'part of a broader presumption that Parliament does not intend a statute to have an unfair or unjust effect.'

[209] *Kingston-upon-Hull Dock Co* v *Browne* (1831) 2 B & Ad 43; *D'Avigdor-Goldsmid* v *Inland Revenue Commissioners* [1953] AC 347, [1953] 1 All ER 403.

[210] *R* v *Hallam* [1957] 1 QB 569, [1957] 1 All ER 665.

[211] See, for examples, *Attorney-General's Reference (No 1 of 1988)* [1989] AC 971, [1989] 2 All ER 1; *Inland Revenue Commissioners* v *Hinchy* [1960] AC 748, [1960] 1 All ER 505. See also, p 46, *ante*.

[212] See *R* v *Tolson* (1889) LR 23 QBD 168; *Younghusband* v *Luftig* [1949] 2 KB 354, [1949] 2 All ER 72.

and unambiguous. In *Sweet* v *Parsley*[213] the House of Lords quashed a conviction for managing premises used for the smoking of cannabis, on the basis that the accused rented out the premises and did not know that her tenants were using drugs. Lord Reid explained the judicial approach as follows:[214]

> [O]ur first duty is to consider the words of the Act; if they show a clear intention to create an absolute offence, that is an end of the matter. But such cases are very rare. Sometimes the words of the section which creates a particular offence make it clear that mens rea is required in one form or another. Such cases are quite frequent. But in a very large number of cases there is no clear indication either way. In such cases there has for centuries been a presumption that Parliament did not intend to make criminals of persons who were in no way blameworthy in what they did. That means that, whenever a section is silent as to mens rea, there is a presumption that, in order to give effect to the will of Parliament, we must read in words appropriate to require mens rea.

The more serious the alleged offence, the more difficult it will be to rebut the presumption of the need for mens rea. Thus, in *B* v *DPP*[215] the House of Lords allowed the appeal of a fifteen year old boy who had pleaded guilty to inciting a child under the age of fourteen to commit an act of gross indecency: the boy had honestly believed that the girl was over fourteen.[216] In contrast, where a statute is silent on the question of mens rea, a court *may* be prepared to treat an offence as one of strict liability if this would help to further some general social objective and if the offence is not 'truly criminal' in character.[217]

An analogous presumption is that Parliament does not intend to create new criminal offences. In *R* v *Horseferry Road Justices, ex parte Independent Broadcasting Authority*[218] the Queen's Bench Divisional Court held that, 'the inference that Parliament did not intend to create an offence in the absence of an express provision to that effect is, nowadays, almost irresistible.' This is of very limited application, however, since when Parliament does intend to create a new criminal offence this is usually made clear by the fact that penalties for the offence are specified.

---

[213] [1970] AC 132, [1969] 1 All ER 347.

[214] [1970] AC 132 at 148, [1969] 1 All ER 347 at 349.

[215] [2000] 2 AC 428, 1 All ER 833.

[216] See also, *R* v *K (Age of Consent: Reasonable Belief)* [2001] UKHL 41, [2002] 1 AC 462, [2001] 3 All ER 897, where the same reasoning was applied to a charge of indecent assault under the Sexual Offences Act 1956, s 14(1). The fourteen year old alleged victim had in fact consented to the act and the defendant had a genuine belief that she was over the age of sixteen. The House of Lords reversed the Court of Appeal's finding and held that the prosecution was required to prove mens rea in respect of the girl's age. Interestingly, the Court of Appeal seems to have based its reasoning on an application of *expressio unius est exclusio alterius*: the Act expressly required mens rea in relation to other offences but was silent with regard to indecent assault: [2001] 1 Cr App R 35, [2001] Crim LR 134.

[217] See, for example, *R* v *Bezzina* [1994] 3 All ER 964, [1994] WLR 1057 (owning or handling a dog which is dangerously out of control in a public place); and *Harrow LBC* v *Shah* [1999] 3 All ER 302, [2000] 1 WLR 83 (selling a National Lottery ticket to a child under 16).

[218] [1987] QB 54 at 72, [1986] 2 All ER 666 at 674, per Lloyd LJ.

(c) Presumption against alteration of the law

Parliament, like the judiciary, is presumed to know the law. Consequently if an Act does not *expressly* alter the law it will be presumed that Parliament did not intend it to have that effect. In the words of Devlin J:[219]

> a statute is not to be taken as effecting a fundamental alteration in the general law unless it uses words which point unmistakably to that conclusion.

It is important to remember, however, that Parliament can and does make fundamental alterations to the common law, and if such a change appears from a literal interpretation of the words used, the use of any presumption to the contrary is out of place.

The presumption against fundamental change also applies in relation to statute law. One aspect of this is the presumption that where a provision is re-enacted in a consolidating statute, a modest change in the wording does not necessarily introduce a fundamental change in meaning. Conversely the mere fact that a provision *is* re-enacted cannot be assumed to mean that Parliament is endorsing judicial interpretations of the earlier enactment. The court must interpret the enactment as it stands, though if the scales are equally balanced, the fact that Parliament has re-enacted a provision which has been the subject of judicial interpretation might tip the balance in favour of that interpretation.[220]

(d) Presumptions against deprivation of liberty and property

There is a well-established presumption that in the absence of express provision the courts will not construe a statute as depriving a person of any property right vested in him before the statute came into operation. For example, every person has a right to the use and enjoyment of his own land. The remedy for infringement of this right is an action in trespass or nuisance, depending on the character of the interference. Consequently where a statute authorizes the performance of an act which constitutes a nuisance to the claimant, the statute will not be construed as removing the claimant's right unless it is clearly intended to have that effect.[221] There is an even stronger presumption against the deprivation of a person's liberty. Thus, in a case concerning detention under the Mental Health Act 1983, it was said that:[222]

> Parliament is presumed not to enact legislation which interferes with the liberty of a subject without making it clear that this was its intention.

Both presumptions must now be considered in the context of the Human Rights Act 1998, which requires legislation to be interpreted as far as possible in a manner compatible with the rights to liberty and to peaceful enjoyment of possessions.[223] Even in the Human Rights Act era, however, liberty and proprietary rights may be taken

---

[219] *National Assistance Board* v *Wilkinson* [1952] 2 QB 648 at 661, [1952] 2 All ER 255 at 260.

[220] See p 73, *post.*

[221] *Metropolitan Asylum District Managers* v *Hill* (1881) 6 App Cas 193.

[222] *R* v *Hallstrom, ex parte W* [1986] QB 1090 at 1104, [1986] 2 All ER 306, per McCullough J.

[223] Section 3: see p 55, *ante.* The rights to liberty (Article 5, ECHR) and the peaceful enjoyment of possessions (Article 1, Protocol 1, ECHR) are protected Convention rights under s 1 of the 1998 Act.

away by express words. In *R (on the application of H) v North and East London Regional Mental Health Tribunal*[224] the Court of Appeal found it impossible to interpret provisions of the Mental Health Act 1983 in a manner compatible with the right to liberty. A declaration of incompatibility was issued, but this did not, of course, alter the validity of the legislation.[225]

(e) Presumption against ousting the jurisdiction of the courts

Individuals cannot, by contract, exclude the jurisdiction of the courts. Although Parliament may exclude an individual's recourse to the courts, any provision purporting so to do must be absolutely clear and unambiguous since the courts are extremely wary about permitting interference with their jurisdiction.[226] So reluctant are the courts to see their jurisdiction ousted, that even seemingly clear words may not suffice. Thus in *Anisminic v Foreign Compensation Commission*,[227] a provision stating that any 'determination' of the Commission 'shall not be called into question in any court of law' did not prevent a court declaring that the Commission had made a fundamental error of law that deprived it of power to act. Because it had no power, no *valid* 'determination' was being called into question. Such legal sophistry can only be prevented by the clearest of words. An example of such words is the amended wording introduced following the *Anisminic* decision – section 3 of the Foreign Compensation Act 1969 prevents judicial review even of a 'purported determination'.

On the basis of this presumption, a provision stating that the decision of an inferior court, tribunal, or administrative body shall be 'final' will be held not to exclude the prerogative jurisdiction of the High Court to review the decision:

> if a tribunal goes wrong in law and the error appears on the face of the record, the High Court will interfere...to quash the decision. It is not to be deterred by the enactment that the decision is 'final'. The decision may be final on the facts but it is not final on the law.[228]

In contrast, a statute permitting challenge within a limited period is likely to be effective in preventing any review after that period. In *R v Cornwall County Council, ex parte Huntington*[229] a Divisional Court held that the terms of the Wildlife and Countryside Act 1981, which excluded judicial challenge after a forty-two-day period, prevented the court from engaging in judicial review of an order made under the Act.

---

[224] [2001] EWCA Civ 415, [2002] QB 1, [2001] 3 WLR 512.

[225] The offending provisions were subsequently amended by the Mental Health Act 1983 (Remedial) Order 2001, SI 2001/3712. See further, p 57, *ante*.

[226] See, for example, *Ealing London Borough v Race Relations Board* [1972] AC 342 at 353, [1972] 1 All ER 105 at 108. In this case the House of Lords held that the machinery established under the Race Relations Act 1968 for referring disputes to county courts did not exclude the inherent supervisory jurisdiction of the High Court.

[227] [1969] 2 AC 147, [1969] 1 All ER 208. See also, p 218, *post*.

[228] *Tehrani v Rostron* [1972] 1 QB 182 at 187, [1971] 3 All ER 790 at 793, per Lord Denning MR: see also *R v Medical Appeal Tribunal, ex parte Gilmore* [1957] 1 QB 574, [1957] 1 All ER 796, where the earlier authorities are reviewed. See also p 333, *post*.

[229] [1992] 3 All ER 566. The decision was upheld on appeal: see [1994] 1 All ER 694.

(f) Presumption that a statute does not bind the Crown

One of the few relics of the prerogative of the Crown is the rule that the Crown is not bound by a statute unless expressly named in it. The rule extends to the Crown and to its servants and agents, though not to nationalized industries.[230] The Crown Proceedings Act 1947 placed the Crown, with certain exceptions, in the same position as a private person in the law of torts. Consequently, statutes which affect common law rights and duties are usually expressed to bind the Crown. Examples are the Limitation Act 1980 and the Occupiers' Liability Act 1957. In practice the general trend of modern legislation is towards the removal of the Crown's privileges and immunities.

(g) Presumption that Parliament does not intend to violate international law

There is a presumption that Parliament does not intend to legislate in a manner incompatible with international law. The courts generally take a purposive approach when interpreting statutes designed to give effect to treaty obligations, the presumption being that Parliament intends such legislation to achieve its objectives.[231] Similarly, where a provision is genuinely ambiguous the courts may take account of a treaty when choosing between two equally reasonable interpretations, regardless of whether the statute was enacted for the purpose of giving effect to that treaty.[232] Of course, as with other presumptions, this is subject to the overriding principle that Parliament is legislatively supreme: clear and unambiguous words in the main body of an Act will take precedence over any inconsistent treaty obligations.[233]

> International obligations cannot alter the clear meaning of statutes. They may, however, be permitted to make clear which of more than one reasonable meaning was intended by Parliament.

5   MATERIAL AIDS TO CONSTRUCTION

Alongside the various approaches and presumptions that are applied in the process of statutory interpretation, there are also several aids to construction which may be considered in the event of ambiguity. There are two classes of aids to construction; internal aids and external aids. The extent to which these are used varies from case to case, but those who advocate a strict literal approach would generally regard the use of *external* aids as illegitimate.

---

[230] *Tamlin* v *Hannaford* [1950] 1 KB 18, [1949] 2 All ER 327; for an account of the history of this presumption and a recent illustration of its operation, see *Lord Advocate* v *Dumbarton District Council* [1990] 2 AC 580, [1990] 1 All ER 1.

[231] *Salomon* v *Commissioners of Customs and Excise* [1967] 2 QB 116, [1966] 3 WLR 1223. The interpretation of legislation designed to give effect to obligations of EC law is discussed in chapter 4.

[232] *R* v *Chief Immigration Officer, ex parte Salamat Bibi* [1976] 3 All ER 843, [1976] 1 WLR 979. It was held that where such an ambiguity arose, the courts had a discretion to take into account the UK's obligations under the European Convention on Human Rights. Since the introduction of the Human Rights Act 1998, however, courts have had a *statutory obligation* to seek an ECHR compatible interpretation of all legislation, whether it is ambiguous or not. See further, p 54, *ante*.

[233] *J. H. Rayner Ltd* v *Department of Trade and Industry* [1989] Ch 72 at 231, [1988] 3 All ER 257 at 342, per Ralph Gibson LJ (affirmed [1990] 2 AC 418, [1989] 3 All ER 523, HL).

(a) Internal aids

An internal (or intrinsic) aid is an aid that is to be found within the Queen's Printer's copy of the statute itself. The principle that a statute must be read as a whole means that those parts of the statute which form part of the enactment should always be consulted as part of the general process of interpretation. Certain other parts of the statute such as punctuation, headings, and marginal notes may also be used in cases of ambiguity, even though they are not strictly part of the enactment.

'Notes' of the type found in section 118 of the Criminal Justice Act 2003 fall into a different category. The Act makes significant changes to the rules governing the admissibility of hearsay evidence in criminal cases, and section 118 expressly preserves certain categories of evidence which were already admissible at common law. Thus section 118(2) preserves 'any rule of law under which in criminal proceedings evidence of a person's reputation is admissible for the purpose of proving his good or bad character'. This is qualified by a 'note', which states that the rule is 'preserved only so far as it allows the court to treat such evidence as proving the matter concerned.' Despite the label, this note is an integral part of the provision, and as such, it is likely to be crucial to its interpretation.[234]

Long title. The long title of an Act begins with the words 'an Act' and goes on to describe the general effect of the legislation. Thus the Law of Property Act 1925 has the long title; 'An Act to consolidate the enactments relating to Conveyancing and the Law of Property in England and Wales'. The long title is usually succinct rather than explanatory and it is unlikely to do more than identify the subject matter of the Act. However, as it forms part of the enactment and may be debated or amended by Parliament, it is regarded as a legitimate aid to interpretation and construction.[235] It is though, a minor aid: there have been conspicuously few cases in which it has been consulted and it certainly cannot prevail over an express provision in the body of the Act. Thus an Act to 'amend the law with respect to wills of personal estate made by British subjects' (Wills Act 1861) was held to apply to the will of an alien.[236] The long title should not be confused with the preamble, although preambles are rare in modern statutes and judges occasionally use the terms interchangeably.[237]

Short title. This is the title by which Acts are commonly, and properly, cited. In theory the short title is a valid aid to both interpretation and construction, but there appears to be no reported case in which the short title has been used to determine a point of construction. The short title could certainly not be used to introduce ambiguity into the body of the Act: indeed, the short titles of certain Acts do not reflect their content

[234] See also, s 118(3).
[235] See *Fielding* v *Morley Corporation* [1899] 1 Ch 1 at 3, per Lindley MR. Before the nineteenth century the long title did not form part of the enactment and therefore could not be used in this way.
[236] *Re Groos* [1904] P 269; see also *R* v *Bates* [1952] 2 All ER 842, [1953] 1 WLR 77; *R* v *Galvin* [1987] QB 862, [1987] 2 All ER 851.
[237] e.g. Winn LJ in *Crook* v *Edmondson* [1966] 2 QB 81 at 89, [1966] 1 All ER 833 at 835.

accurately. The Criminal Procedure Act 1865, for example, applies to both civil and criminal proceedings.

Preamble. The preamble is that part of the statute which precedes the enacting words and sets out the reason for the statute being passed. In old cases great weight was attached to the preamble as an aid to construction,[238] and important Acts such as the Statute of Frauds 1677 and the Parliament Act 1911 have long and instructive preambles. Probably the best known preamble is that of the Charitable Uses Act 1601, which, until recently, was regarded as containing the criteria to be adopted when considering whether a particular object is a 'charitable' one.[239] Modern statutes, however, rarely contain a preamble, and where one is included it is generally too brief to be of assistance. Moreover, as Lord Steyn made clear in *R (on the application of Jackson)* v *A-G*, arguments based on a preamble 'cannot possibly prevail against the clear language of the substantive provisions.'[240]

Headings. A section or group of sections in an Act may be preceded by a heading. Such headings are not part of the enactment and for that reason logic would suggest their exclusion. In fact, however, headings are often consulted as an aid to construction where the enactment is uncertain or ambiguous.[241] The modern judicial tendency appears to be to treat a heading as if it were a preamble.[242] In *DPP* v *Schildkamp*[243] Lord Upjohn was in favour of according greater weight to headings than were the other Law Lords. He observed:[244]

> In my opinion, it is wrong to confine their role to the resolution of ambiguities in the body of the Act. When the court construing the Act is reading it through to understand it, it must read the cross-headings as well as the body of the Act and that will always be a useful pointer as to the intention of Parliament in enacting the immediately following sections.

Marginal notes. Marginal notes or 'clause titles' are not part of an Act and are inserted by the draftsman purely for ease of reference. Sometimes a marginal note bears no relation to the content of a section that has been altered during the passage of the Bill, and sometimes it may simply be misleading. For example, the marginal note to section 143 of the Criminal Justice and Public Order Act 1994 referred to 'male rape and buggery', yet the provision itself only related to the latter.[245]

---

[238] *Belasco* v *Hannant* (1862) 3 B & S 13; *Sussex Peerage Case* (1844) 11 Cl & Fin 85.

[239] See, e.g. *McGovern* v *A-G* [1982] Ch 321, [1981] 3 All ER 493; *R* v *Radio Authority, ex parte Bull* [1996] QB 169, [1995] 4 All ER 481.

[240] [2005] UKHL 56 at [89], [2006] 1 AC 262 at [89], [2005] 4 All ER 1253. The preamble in question was that contained in the Parliament Act 1911.

[241] For an instructive case see *Crook* v *Edmondson* [1966] 2 QB 81, [1966] 1 All ER 833, in which the words 'immoral purposes' were construed in the light of the group of sections of the Sexual Offences Act 1956 in which those words occurred.

[242] *Martins* v *Fowler* [1926] AC 746; *Qualter, Hall & Co Ltd* v *Board of Trade* [1962] Ch 273, [1961] 3 All ER 389.

[243] [1971] AC 1, [1969] 3 All ER 1640.

[244] [1971] AC at 28, [1969] 3 All ER at 1656. See also *R* v *Montila* [2004] UKHL 50, [2004] 1 WLR 3141, [2005] 1 All ER 113, discussed below.

[245] The provision was eventually repealed by the Sexual Offences Act 2003.

For this reason the old rule was that marginal notes were not regarded as a legitimate aid to construction, even in the event of ambiguity. In *Re Woking Urban District Council (Basingstoke Canal) Act 1911* Philimore LJ explained that this was because they were not inserted into legislation by Parliament but by 'irresponsible persons'.[246] Now, however, it is clear that marginal notes can be taken into account, as explained by Lord Hope in *R v Montila*:[247]

> The question then is whether headings and sidenotes, although unamendable, can be considered in construing a provision in an Act of Parliament. Account must, of course, be taken of the fact that these components were included in the Bill not for debate but for ease of reference. This indicates that less weight can be attached to them than to the parts of the Act that are open for consideration and debate in Parliament. But it is another matter to be required by a rule of law to disregard them altogether...Subject, of course, to the fact that they are unamendable, they ought to be open to consideration as part of the enactment when it reaches the statute book.

The defendants in this case were being prosecuted for converting the proceeds of drug trafficking and criminal conduct, contrary to section 49 of the Drug Trafficking Act 1994 and section 93C of the Criminal Justice Act 1988.[248] The issue was whether the prosecution needed to *prove* that the property in question had its origins in drug trafficking and criminal conduct, or whether it was sufficient to show that the defendants knew or suspected that it did. The fact that the sidenotes accompanying the provisions referred to 'concealing or transferring proceeds' was one of several factors leading to the conclusion that the prosecution had to prove the illegal origins of the property. Similarly, in *DPP v Johnson*[249] it was held that the note accompanying section 8 of the Road Traffic Act 1988 provided evidence that Parliament's intention was to reduce the number of people driving with alcohol in their bodies. The note referred to: 'driving or being in charge of a motor vehicle with alcohol consumption above the prescribed limit', and on this basis the court construed the word 'consuming' widely to embrace the ingestion of alcohol by any method. The appellant had had alcohol injected into his body as a part of a pain-killing drug, and he was therefore guilty of an offence.

Punctuation. Acts of Parliament were not punctuated before 1850, and as punctuation tends to be left to the draftsman and is not scrutinized by Parliament there is some old authority for the proposition that punctuation cannot be taken into account as an aid to construction. Modern courts take a more realistic attitude, however, and following the observations of Lord Reid in *DPP v Schildkamp*,[250] the House of Lords has held that punctuation can and should be taken into account.[251]

[246] [1914] 1 Ch 300 at 322. See also *Chandler* v *DPP* [1964] AC 763, [1962] 3 All ER 142.
[247] [2004] UKHL 50 at [34], [2004] 1 WLR 3141 at [34], [2005] 1 All ER 113. See also the dicta of Upjohn LJ in *Stephens* v *Cuckfield Rural District Council* [1960] 2 QB 373 at 383, [1960] 2 All ER 716 at 720.
[248] Both provisions have since been repealed by the Proceeds of Crime Act 2002.
[249] [1995] 4 All ER 53, [1995] 1 WLR 728.
[250] [1971] AC 1 at 28, [1969] 3 All ER 1640 at 1654.
[251] *Hanlon* v *The Law Society* [1981] AC 124, [1980] 2 All ER 199; see also *Bodden* v *Commissioner of Police of the Metropolis* [1990] 2 QB 397, [1989] 3 All ER 833.

Interpretation sections. Most modern statutes include at least one interpretation section indicating the meaning that Parliament intended to be given to particular words. The context in which a word is used is still important, however, and where there is an inconsistency between the meaning given in an interpretation section and that suggested by the context, the latter prevails. This is especially so when the interpretation section uses the word 'includes'. In this case it will be regarded as extending rather than restricting the normal meaning of the words in question. Thus, in *R v Fulling*[252] the court defined the term 'oppression' in section 76 of the Police and Criminal Evidence Act 1984 by reference to its ordinary, natural meaning, as stated in the *Oxford English Dictionary*. It did not even cite the content of section 76(8) of that statute, which provides that oppression 'includes' inhuman or degrading treatment, torture, violence, or the threat of violence.

Another example is *Shimizu (UK) Ltd v Westminster City Council*.[253] In that case the House of Lords had to consider the meaning of the term 'listed building' in the Planning (Listed Buildings and Conservation Areas) Act 1990. Section 336 of the Town and Country Planning Act 1990 defined a 'building' as including 'part of a building', unless the context otherwise requires. That definition was incorporated into the Listed Buildings Act by section 91 of the Act. Despite that, Lord Hope was able to conclude that the expression 'listed building' included *part* of a listed building for the purposes of section 1 of the Act, but did not do so in respect of virtually all other provisions of that Act.

Schedules. Acts of Parliament often contain one or more schedules. They are always placed at the end of the Act and are usually used for prescribing forms, furnishing illustrations, listing repeals effected by the Act, and setting out transitional provisions. They cannot be regarded as altering the ordinary meaning of words used in the Act, but it is probable that they can be considered in cases of ambiguity.

The Consumer Credit Act 1974 utilized a novel concept in parliamentary drafting – the use of examples. Section 188(1) provides that 'Schedule 2 shall have effect for illustrating the use of terminology employed in this Act'. The Schedule contains twenty-four examples, each expressed in the form of a set of facts and an analysis of the application of the new terminology to those facts. The examples are expressed not to be exhaustive and section 188(3) provides that in the case of conflict between Schedule 2 and any other provision of the Act, the latter shall prevail.

When an Act of Parliament is passed to implement an international treaty, the text of that treaty will normally be included in a schedule to the Act. This may give rise to difficulties in interpretation if the treaty is in a foreign language or is set out in more than one language. A purposive approach will usually be adopted in such cases,[254] and the court may consult extrinsic sources such as dictionaries, *travaux préparatoires*, and the

---

[252] [1987] QB 426, [1987] 2 All ER 65.   [253] [1997] 1 All ER 481, [1997] 1 WLR 716.

[254] In one case involving a statute designed to give effect to a treaty, the Court of Appeal adopted the text of the treaty even though its meaning differed from the text used in the main body of the Act: *Corocraft Ltd v Pan American Airways Inc* [1969] 1 QB 616, [1969] 1 All ER 82.

decisions of foreign courts. The words used in the treaty will be construed so as to conform to the generally accepted meaning of the provision. As Lord Browne-Wilkinson put it in *Re H and others (Minors) (Abduction: Acquiescence)*:[255]

> An international convention, expressed in different languages and intended to apply to a wide range of differing legal systems, cannot be construed differently in different jurisdictions.

In *Fothergill* v *Monarch Airlines Ltd*[256] the House of Lords had to consider a provision of the Warsaw Convention contained in Schedule 1 to the Carriage by Air Act 1961. Reversing the decision of the Court of Appeal, it held that the loss of articles from a suitcase constituted 'damage' to baggage. It reached this conclusion by taking a purposive approach, and by looking at extrinsic sources to ascertain that the word 'avarie' (used in the French text) has a slightly wider meaning than the term 'damage' (used in the English): it is also capable of meaning 'loss'.

(b) External aids

An external (or extrinsic) aid to construction is an aid which is not to be found in the Queen's Printer's copy of the Act. The use of such aids is restricted and has always been controversial: those who favour a literal approach would generally reject their use on the basis that the courts should be concerned with what Parliament *actually* said, not what it *intended* to say. Even for advocates of a more purposive approach, the use of external aids is only legitimate to the extent that they can shed light on the intentions of Parliament:[257]

> '[T]he intention of Parliament' is an objective concept, not subjective. The phrase is a shorthand reference to the intention which the court reasonably imputes to Parliament in respect of the language used. It is not the subjective intention of the Minister or other persons who promoted the legislation. Nor is it the subjective intention of the draftsman, or of individual members of . . . either House.

Reports of parliamentary debates.[258] Since the function of the courts is to ascertain the intention of the legislature, it might be thought that they would readily refer to statements made in Parliament as to the intention of the member or party introducing the Bill. In fact, until recently the reports of debates on the Bill during its passage through Parliament were rigidly excluded.[259] However, in 1993 the House of Lords in *Pepper* v *Hart*[260] reconsidered the position, and held (Lord Mackay LC dissenting) that in certain

---

[255] [1998] AC 72, [1997] 2 All ER 225.

[256] [1981] AC 251, [1980] 2 All ER 696. Section 1(2) of the 1961 Act expressly provides that in the event of inconsistency between the English and French texts, the latter is to prevail.

[257] *R* v *Secretary of State for the Environment, Transport and the Regions, ex parte Spath Holme Ltd* [2001] 2 AC 349 at 387, [2001]1 All ER 195 at 206, per Lord Nicholls.

[258] For discussion see Kavanagh, '*Pepper* v *Hart* and Matters of Constitutional Principle' (2005) 121 LQR 98; Klug, 'The Human Rights Act 1998, *Pepper* v *Hart* and all that' [1999] PL 246; Lord Steyn, '*Pepper* v *Hart*: A Re-examination' (2001) 21 OJLS 59.

[259] *Assam Railways and Trading Co Ltd* v *Inland Revenue Commissioners* [1935] AC 445.

[260] [1993] AC 593, [1993] 1 All ER 42.

circumstances a court should be entitled to refer to parliamentary materials. The objection that by so doing the courts would be calling proceedings in Parliament into question, contrary to the Bill of Rights 1688, was rejected. The pre-conditions for the exercise of the power were stated by Lord Browne-Wilkinson:

> the exclusionary rule should be relaxed so as to permit reference to parliamentary materials where: (a) legislation is ambiguous or obscure, or leads to an absurdity; (b) the material relied upon consists of one or more statements by a Minister or other promoter of the Bill together if necessary with such other parliamentary material as is necessary to understand such statements, and their effect; (c) the statements relied upon are clear.

Only statements made in respect of a Bill passing through Parliament can be considered under this rule. The rule does not permit the use of statements to indicate a Minister's understanding of the law at the time;[261] nor does it permit the use of statements that are not concerned with the point at issue in the litigation.[262] Lord Mackay's dissenting speech expressed concern that the costs of litigation would be immensely increased by the onerous task of searching through *Hansard*, and the frequency with which the courts have been asked to apply *Pepper* v *Hart* lends support to these concerns.[263] The House of Lords recently endorsed the *Pepper* v *Hart* rule, but it also expressed scepticism as to its value, cautioning that recourse to *Hansard* should be permitted only exceptionally.[264] On a related matter, it has held that a court *is* entitled to have regard to ministerial statements and explanatory notes when determining the compatibility of legislation with the Human Rights Act 1998. A court should not, however, use extrinsic aids in a manner which amounts to questioning proceedings in Parliament:[265]

> The courts are now required to evaluate the effect of primary legislation in terms of Convention rights and, where appropriate, make a formal declaration of incompatibility...Sometimes the court may need additional background information tending to show, for instance, the likely practical impact of the statutory measure and why the course adopted by the legislature is or is not appropriate...Beyond this use of Hansard as a source of background information, the content of parliamentary debates has no direct relevance...The proportionality of a statutory measure is not

[261] *Hillsdown Holdings plc* v *Pensions Ombudsman* [1997] 1 All ER 862.

[262] *Pepper (Inspector of Taxes)* v *Hart* [1993] AC 593, [1993] 1 All ER 42; *Melluish (Inspector of Taxes)* v *BMI (No 3) Ltd* [1996] AC 454, [1995] 4 All ER 453; *Three Rivers District Council* v *Bank of England (No 2)* [1996] 2 All ER 363.

[263] See, e.g., *R* v *Warwickshire County Council, ex parte Johnson* [1993] AC 583, [1993 1 All ER 299 (reference made to Minister's speech in debate on a proposed amendment to Consumer Protection Act 1987, s 20); *Stubbings* v *Webb* [1993] AC 498, [1993] 1 All ER 322 (reference made to the speech of the chairman of the Committee upon whose report s 11 of the Limitation Act 1980 was based); *Mirvahedy* v *Henley* [2001] EWCA Civ 1749, [2002] QB 769, [2002] 2 WLR 566 (reference to ministerial statements to ascertain the scope of s 2(2) of the Animals Act 1971.)

[264] *R* v *Secretary of State for the Environment, Transport and the Regions, ex parte Spath Holme Ltd* [2001] 2 AC 349, [2001] 1 All ER 195. By a majority of four to one, the House of Lords held that the *Pepper* v *Hart* conditions were not satisfied.

[265] *Wilson* v *First County Trust (No 2)* [2003] UKHL 40 at [61]–[67], [2004] 1 AC 816 at [61]–[67], [2003] 4 All ER, per Lord Nicholls. Their Lordships permitted the Speaker of the House of Commons and the Clerk of Parliaments to make submissions expressing their concern about any expansion in the use of *Hansard*.

to be judged by the quality of the reasons advanced in support of it in the course of parliamentary debate, or by the subjective state of mind of an individual Minister or other member.

The courts tend to take a more flexible approach to the use of *Hansard* and other external aids when interpreting legislation designed to implement international or European obligations.[266] It may also be noted that most continental countries take a very positive view of extrinsic materials or *travaux préparatoires*, and they encourage consultation of the parliamentary and political history of the statute.

Explanatory notes. 'Explanatory Notes' are now published to accompany all Bills presented to Parliament.[267] These notes set out the purposes and key provisions of the Bill in clear and simple terms, and they may be revised as and when the Bill is amended during the legislative process. However, they do not form part of the enactment and Parliament has left it to the courts to determine what use, if any, can be made of them when construing legislation. Their status was considered by Lord Steyn in *Westminster City Council v National Asylum Support Service*.[268] Despite having made some rather sceptical extra-judicial comments about the merits of using *Hansard*,[269] he was more enthusiastic about the use of Explanatory Notes:[270]

> Insofar as the Explanatory Notes cast light on the objective setting or contextual scene of the statute, and the mischief at which it is aimed, such materials are ... always admissible aids to construction. They may be admitted for what logical value they have ... After all, the connection of Explanatory Notes with the shape of the proposed legislation is closer than pre-parliamentary aids which in principle are already treated as admissible.

Subsequently, Lord Hope has observed that 'it has become common practice for their Lordships to ask to be shown the Explanatory Notes when issues are raised about the meaning of words used in an enactment'.[271] It is recognized, however, that the distinction between legitimate and illegitimate uses of Explanatory Notes is a fine one:[272]

> If exceptionally there is found in Explanatory Notes a clear assurance by the executive to Parliament about the meaning of a clause, or the circumstances in which a power will or will not be used, that assurance may in principle be admitted against the executive in proceedings in which the executive places a contrary contention

[266] *Three Rivers District Council* v *Bank of England (No 2)* [1996] 2 All ER 363; *Pickstone* v *Freemans plc* [1989] AC 66, [1988] 2 All ER 803; *Fothergill* v *Monarch Airlines Ltd* [1981] AC 251, [1980] 2 All ER 696.
[267] See Select Committee on Modernisation of HC, 2nd Report: Explanatory Material for Bills, 1997–1998, HC 389, at pp 1–2. Before 1998, the practice was for a Bill to be accompanied by an explanatory document prepared by the sponsoring department and indicating its broad provisions and likely financial impact.
[268] [2002] UKHL 38, [2002] 4 All ER 654, [2002] 1 WLR 2956.
[269] '*Pepper* v *Hart*: A Re-examination' (2001) 21 OJLS 59.
[270] [2002] UKHL 38 at [5], [2002] 4 All ER 654 at [5].
[271] *R* v *Montila* [2004] UKHL 50 at [35], [2004] 1 WLR 3141 at [35], [2005] 1 All ER 113.
[272] [2002] UKHL 38 at [6], [2002] 4 All ER 654 at [6]. See also *Wilson* v *First County Trust (No 2)* [2003] UKHL 40, [2004] 1 AC 816, [2003] 4 All ER 97; Munday, 'Explanatory Notes and Statutory Interpretation' (2006) 170(8) JP 124.

before the court…What is impermissible is to treat the wishes and desires of the government about the scope of the statutory language as reflecting the will of Parliament. The aims of the government…cannot be attributed to Parliament. The object is to see what is the intention expressed by the words enacted.

Ministerial statements of compatibility. Section 19 of the Human Rights Act 1998 provides that before the Second Reading of a Bill, the Minister in charge of it must either: (a) make a statement that in his view the provisions of the Bill are compatible with Convention rights;[273] or (b) make a statement that although the Bill is *not* compatible, the government nevertheless wishes to proceed. Section 19 statements do not normally include an explanation as to *why* the Minister thinks that an Act is compatible or not, and for this reason their probative value is limited. Nevertheless, when a court is considering whether it is possible to interpret an Act in a Convention compliant manner,[274] a section 19 statement may have some value as a general indication of Parliament's intention.

Section 19 came into effect on 24 November 1998, and it is perhaps unsurprising that virtually all of the statements made under it have been to the effect that legislation is compatible. The exception is the Communications Act 2003. The Minister responsible for introducing the Bill felt unable to make a statement of compatibility as it included provisions prohibiting political advertising in broadcasting. The advertising ban was at odds with a decision of the European Court of Human Rights,[275] though the Minister made it clear that she did not consider an incompatible interpretation inevitable:[276]

> [G]iven the existence of the Swiss precedent, I must ask the House to consider this Bill with a section 19(l)(b) of the Human Rights Act 1998 statement attached to it. That does not mean that we believe the Bill to be incompatible with the ECHR, and we would mount a robust defence if it were legally challenged.

When the provisions in question were challenged the Administrative Court refused to make a declaration of incompatibility, holding that the restriction on freedom of expression fell within the UK's margin of appreciation.[277] In reaching this decision the court did not appear to give any direct weight to the Minister's statement, but Ousley J attached 'great weight' to the fact that Parliament had 'expressed a considered view, having grappled with the human rights implications' of the provisions.[278]

Dictionaries. Words in statutes are presumed to bear their ordinary and natural meaning, and it is legitimate to consult a dictionary when interpreting words with no

---

[273] By section 1, 'Convention rights' are those ECHR rights contained in Articles 2 to 12 and 14, Articles 1 to 3 of the First Protocol and Article 1 of the Thirteenth Protocol.

[274] Under s 3 of the 1998 Act: see further, pp 55 and 155.

[275] *VgT Verein gegen Tierfabriken* v *Switzerland* (2002) 34 EHRR 4.

[276] Tessa Jowell, MP (Secretary of State for Culture, Media and Sport), 395 HC Official Report (6th series) col 789, 3 December 2002.

[277] *R (on the application of Animal Defenders International)* v *Secretary of State for Culture, Media and Sport* [2006] EWHC 3069 (Admin), [2007] HRLR 9. For a discussion of the concept of 'margin of appreciation', see p 151, *post*.

[278] Ibid, at [114].

particular legal meaning. Dictionaries bear only slight weight, however, and in context the dictionary meaning may not be the one which Parliament intended. In a Court of Appeal case concerning the interpretation of the word 'ethnic' in the Race Relations Act 1976, Lord Denning MR rejected a 1972 dictionary definition in favour of one from 1934.[279] The House of Lords in the same case rejected both definitions and came to its own conclusions about the meaning of the word.[280] Words and phrases with a particular legal meaning are described as 'terms of art', and they do not necessarily bear the meaning which laymen would attribute to them.[281] In interpreting the foreign text of a convention, a court is entitled to consult foreign dictionaries, textbooks, and articles, and even to receive expert evidence.[282]

Reports of committees. Reports of the Law Commissions, Law Reform Committees, and similar bodies are legitimate aids to discovering the state of the pre-existing law and the mischief which a statute was passed to remedy.[283] Once again, however, if the words of a statute are unambiguous, it is not legitimate to interpret them otherwise in order to accord with the recommendations of a Committee. Thus in *Letang* v *Cooper*[284] the Court of Appeal held that the words 'negligence, nuisance or breach of duty' in the Law Reform (Limitation of Actions) Act 1954 were wide enough to embrace the tort of trespass to the person. This was despite the fact that the Tucker Committee report,[285] which preceded the 1954 Act, expressed an intention to exclude this form of action from the shorter limitation period recommended in that report.

Other statutes. Where the words of one statute are ambiguous or uncertain, assistance as to their meaning may be gained from considering the way in which similar words have been used in statutes dealing with the same subject matter. Thus in *R* v *Wheatley*[286] the question before the Court of Appeal was whether a pipe bomb filled with a mixture of sodium chlorate and sugar was an 'explosive' substance within the meaning of section 4 of the Explosive Substances Act 1883. The defendant's expert evidence was to the effect that the materials would produce only a pyrotechnic effect, and not an explosive one. The judge directed the jury that this was no defence, having regard to the definition of 'explosive' in section 3(1) of the Explosives Act 1875, which included a substance used to produce a 'pyrotechnic effect'. It was held that this direction was correct, since the long title of the 1883 Act indicated that it was intended to amend the 1875 Act and both Acts dealt with the same subject matter. It followed that what was an explosive substance

---

[279] *Mandla* v *Dowell Lee* [1983] QB 1 at 12.   [280] [1983] 2 AC 548, [1983] 1 All ER 1062, HL.

[281] See *Barclays Bank Ltd* v *Cole* [1967] 2 QB 738, [1966] 3 All ER 948 on the meaning of the word 'fraud', and compare *Lloyds Bank Ltd* v *Marcan* [1973] 2 All ER 359, [1973] 1 WLR 339.

[282] *Fothergill* v *Monarch Airlines Ltd* [1981] AC 251, [1980] 2 All ER 696.

[283] See, e.g., *Rookes* v *Barnard* [1964] AC 1129, [1964] 1 All ER 367; *Black-Clawson International Ltd* v *Papierwerke Waldhof-Aschaffenburg AG* [1975] AC 591, [1975] 1 All ER 810.

[284] [1965] 1 QB 232, [1964] 2 All ER 929.

[285] Cmnd 7740. See also *Sagnata Investments* v *Norwich Corporation* [1971] 2 QB 614, [1971] 2 All ER 1441, in which the report of the Royal Commission on Betting, Lotteries and Gaming (Cmnd 8190, 1951) was used as an aid to the construction of the Betting, Gaming and Lotteries Act 1963.

[286] [1979] 1 All ER 954, [1979] 1 WLR 144.

for the purposes of the 1883 Act was to be determined by applying the definition used in its 1875 equivalent.

(c) Judicial precedents

Where a superior court has already interpreted words in an Act, an inferior court is bound to adopt that interpretation if faced with the same words in the same Act. Similarly, the Court of Appeal and Divisional Courts are bound to follow their own previous decisions on the interpretation of statutes to the same extent as they are bound to follow any of their other previous decisions. In addition, if an Act employs words or phrases that have been the subject of interpretation in an earlier statute dealing with the same subject matter, it may be inferred that they are intended to bear the same meaning. For example, the House of Lords, in assigning a meaning to the word 'wreck' in the Merchant Shipping Act 1925, adopted the interpretation of that word which had been given in a case decided on the Merchant Shipping Act 1894.[287]

This is, however, no more than a possible inference, and it must not be supposed that by re-enacting a provision which has been the subject of judicial interpretation Parliament is necessarily giving statutory force to that interpretation. If it is a wrong interpretation, then provided it is not binding on the court in accordance with the doctrine of precedent, the court is perfectly free to disregard it.[288] Moreover, where the earlier decision is upon similar words in a statute that does not deal with the same subject matter, or where the words are used in a different context, that decision is of little, if any, value.[289] Finally, where the earlier case was decided before the Human Rights Act 1998 came into effect, a court should not follow that decision if doing so would result in a finding that the legislation is in breach of Convention rights.[290]

6 INTERPRETATION OF EUROPEAN
COMMUNITY LEGISLATION

The techniques of interpretation which English courts have developed over the centuries have been described above. As already noted, approaches to interpretation have influenced approaches to legislative drafting, and vice versa. Community legislation

---

[287] *Barras v Aberdeen Steam Trawling and Fishing Co Ltd* [1933] AC 402. See also *R v Freeman* [1970] 2 All ER 413, [1970] 1 WLR 788: in this case the Court of Appeal held that since there was no relevant distinction between the definition of 'firearm' in s 57(1) of the Firearms Act 1968 and the definitions in earlier Firearms Acts, Parliament must be taken to have adopted the interpretation of the earlier Acts when enacting the 1968 statute.

[288] See *Dun v Dun* [1959] AC 272, [1959] 2 All ER 134; *R v Chard* [1984] AC 279, [1983] 3 All ER 637 (in which the House of Lords expressly disapproved dicta to the contrary in *Barras v Aberdeen Steam Trawling and Fishing Co Ltd* [1933] AC 402).

[289] *London Corporation v Cusack-Smith* [1955] AC 337, [1955] 1 All ER 302; *Brown v Bennett (No 1)* [2002] 2 All ER 273, [2002] 1 WLR 713.

[290] See *Ghaidan v Godin-Mendoza* [2002] EWCA Civ 1533, [2003] Ch 380, [2002] 4 All ER 1162, in which the Court of Appeal declined to follow the House of Lords' interpretation of a provision in the Rent Act 1977 (*Fitzpatrick v Sterling Housing Association Ltd* [2001] 1 AC 27, [1999] 4 All ER 705). For a discussion of the impact of the Human Rights Act on the doctrine of judicial precedent, see chapter 3, *post*.

is drafted in a different mould. It is expressed in terms of broad principle, leaving the courts to supply the detail by giving effect, in particular cases, to the general intention of the body that enacted the instrument in question. Thus regulations, directives, and decisions of the Council and Commission have to state the reasons on which they have been based. They must also refer to any proposals or opinions that were required to be obtained pursuant to the Treaties. These reasons are normally set out in the preamble to the instrument in question. Accordingly, English judges are required to take a purposive approach to the interpretation of Community legislation, referring points of law to the Court of Justice when necessary or required. The 'literal' approach plays little or no part in this process.[291]

FURTHER READING

BENNION and GOODALL, *Bennion on Statutory Interpretation* (LexisNexis Butterworths: 5th edn, 2007)

CLAYTON, 'The Limits of What's "Possible": Statutory Construction under the Human Rights Act' [2002] EHRLR 559

CROSS, BELL and ENGLE, *Statutory Interpretation* (Butterworths: 3rd edn, 1995)

KAVANAGH, '*Pepper* v *Hart* and Matters of Constitutional Principle' (2005) 121 LQR 98

KAVANAGH, 'The Role of Parliamentary Intention in Adjudication under the Human Rights Act 1998' (2006) 26(1) OJLS 179

KLUG, 'The Human Rights Act 1998, *Pepper* v *Hart* and all that' [1999] PL 246

LESTER, 'The Art of the Possible – Interpreting Statutes under the Human Rights Act' [1998] EHRLR 665

MARSHALL, 'The Lynchpin of Parliamentary Intention: Lost, Stolen or Strained?' [2003] PL 236

McHARG, 'What Is Delegated Legislation?' [2006] PL 539

MUNDAY, 'Explanatory Notes and Statutory Interpretation' (2006) 170(8) JP 124

STEYN, 'Democracy through Law' [2002] EHRLR 723

STEYN, '*Pepper* v *Hart*: A Re-examination' (2001) 21 OJLS 59

VAN ZYL SMIT, 'The New Purposive Interpretation of Statutes: HRA Section 3 after *Ghaidan* v *Godin-Mendoza*' (2007) 70(2) MLR 294

---

[291] The interpretation of Community law is discussed in more detail in chapter 4, *post*.

3

CASE LAW, PRECEDENTS, AND LAW REPORTS

INTRODUCTION

This chapter considers the operation of the doctrine of precedent within the English legal system. The notion that judges should look to earlier cases when making decisions is established throughout the legal world, but the idea that a court might be *bound* to follow an earlier precedent is a particular feature of common law systems. In England and Wales, the principles derived from earlier cases constitute one of the two main sources of law – the common law – and this means that the rules of precedent are themselves of great significance. It also means that a system of reliable and comprehensive law reporting is a necessity. This chapter will therefore examine both the rules of judicial precedent and the law reports upon which those rules depend. The specific areas addressed will include:

- The historical development of the doctrine of precedent and its place in the modern legal system.

- The impact of the Human Rights Act 1998 on the doctrine.

- The different elements of a judicial decision, and the distinction between the *ratio decidendi* and *obiter dicta*.

- Binding and persuasive precedents.

- What it means to 'reverse', 'overrule' or 'distinguish' an earlier case.

- The relationship between the doctrine of precedent and the hierarchy of the courts.

- The modern system of law reporting and the rules governing the citation of cases in court.

THE RELATIONSHIP BETWEEN LAW REPORTS AND THE DOCTRINE OF PRECEDENT

The operation of the doctrine of precedent is inextricably bound up with law reporting. Precedents are almost always contained in law reports, and the modern doctrine of binding precedent did not develop until an integrated system of law reporting evolved in the nineteenth century. Nevertheless, until recently, any decision could be cited in court provided that it was vouched for by a barrister, solicitor, or other qualified person[1] who was present when the judgment was delivered, and decisions did not need to be reported in order to be relied upon in court. However, in the face of concern about the over-citation of cases, particularly those which are unreported, the judiciary is now seeking to limit the use of unreported decisions. In *Roberts Petroleum Ltd* v *Bernard Kenny* Lord Diplock caused considerable consternation among some sections of the profession by stating that:[2]

> [T]he time has come when your Lordships should adopt the practice of declining to allow transcripts of unreported judgments of the Civil Division of the Court of Appeal to be cited on the hearing of appeals to this House unless leave is given to do so...such leave should only be granted on counsel's giving an assurance that the transcript contains a statement of some principle of law, relevant to an issue in the appeal to this House, that is binding on the Court of Appeal and of which the substance, as distinct from the mere choice, of phraseology, is not to be found in one of the generalised or specialised series of reports.

The Court of Appeal has since adopted much the same approach[3] and in 2000 it issued a Practice Direction restricting the range of cases that can be cited in the civil courts.[4] The effect of this is that: (a) applications attended by one party only; (b) applications for permission to appeal; (c) decisions that an application is arguable; and (d) decisions of the county court,[5] cannot be cited unless there is a clear indication that the decision in question purports to establish a new principle or extend the present law.[6] The Practice Direction also discourages reliance on cases from foreign jurisdictions other than those of the European Court of Human Rights and European Court of Justice. Lord Woolf CJ explained the reasons for these changes:[7]

> The current weight of available material causes problems both for advocates and for courts in properly limiting the nature and amount of material that is used in the preparation and argument of subsequent cases...Recent and continuing efforts to increase the efficiency, and thus reduce the cost, of litigation, whilst maintaining the interests of justice, will be threatened if courts are burdened with a weight of inappropriate and unnecessary authority.

It is important to distinguish a law report from a court record. A court record consists of the names of the parties, the pleadings, and the decision or order of the court. A law report contains most of these, along with the judgment of the court setting out the reasoning upon which the decision was based. It is this reasoning which is important for

---

[1] Courts and Legal Services Act 1990, s 115. See p 375, *post*.

[2] [1983] 2 AC 192 at 200–2, [1983] 1 All ER 564 at 566–8.

[3] *Practice Statement (Court of Appeal: Authorities)* [1996] 3 All ER 382, [1996] 1 WLR 854.

[4] *Practice Direction (Citation of Authorities)* [2001] 2 All ER 510, [2001] 1 WLR 1001.

[5] A county court decision may be cited if it deals with a point of law in respect of which no higher authority is available, or in order to illustrate the measure of damages in a personal injury case.

[6] Since the Practice Direction, if a decision falling into one of these categories does extend the law or establish a new principle it must include an express statement to this effect in the judgment.

[7] [2001] 2 All ER 510 at [1]–[2], [2001] 1 WLR 1001 at [1]–[2].

the purposes of the doctrine of precedent, and court records are therefore of little value in this context.

One might suppose that because the doctrine of precedent is the cornerstone of the English legal system, the courts would have created a methodical system of producing law reports. In fact, however, this has never been done and law reporting has been left entirely to private enterprise. There is still an element of chance in the matter of whether or not a case is reported, although the growth of electronic legal databases means that few cases decided by the superior courts[8] (other than the Crown Court) escape the scrutiny of researchers. In addition, certain key tribunal decisions and Crown Court rulings become known to practitioners and academics through specialist journals and encyclopaedias.

THE OPERATION OF THE DOCTRINE OF PRECEDENT

1 THE DOCTRINE OF BINDING PRECEDENT

The traditional view of the function of an English judge has been that it is not to make law but to decide cases in accordance with existing legal rules. The doctrine of binding precedent (or *stare decisis*), whereby the judge is not merely referred to earlier decisions for guidance but is also bound to apply rules of law decided by those cases, was founded on this 'declaratory' view of the judicial process. However, few would now deny that judges have a powerful law-making function.

> The theoretical position has been that judges do not make or change law: they discover and declare the law which is throughout the same. According to this theory, when an earlier decision is overruled the law is not changed: its true nature is disclosed, having existed in that form all along. This theoretical position is, as Lord Reid said in the article 'The Judge As Law Maker' (1972–1973) 12 J.S.P.T.L. (N.S.) 22, a fairy tale in which no-one any longer believes. In truth, judges make and change the law. The whole of the common law is judge-made and only by judicial change in the law is the common law kept relevant in a changing world.[9]

The operation of the doctrine depends upon the hierarchy of the courts. All courts stand in a definite relationship to one another. A court is bound by decisions of courts above itself in the hierarchy and, usually, by courts of equivalent standing. Given that the doctrine of precedent has binding force within this framework, the question naturally arises of how the law may develop if cases are always to be determined according to ageless principles. In practice there are several ways in which the doctrine retains its

---

[8] See chapter 8, *post*.

[9] *Kleinwort Benson* v *Lincoln City Council* [1999] 2 AC 349 at 358, [1998] 4 All ER 513 at 518, per Lord Browne-Wilkinson.

flexibility. These are dealt with in detail below, but two basic principles should be noted: first, that superior courts have power to overrule decisions of inferior courts and, in certain cases, to overrule their own earlier decisions; and second, that any rule of law may be changed by statute. Consequently every rule of law is subject to change, either by the judges themselves or by Parliament.

The advantages of the precedent system are said to be certainty, precision, and flexibility.[10] Legal certainty is achieved, at least in theory, because judges are bound to deal with like situations in a consistent way. Precision is achieved by the sheer volume of reported cases which provide specific solutions to innumerable factual problems. Finally, flexibility is achieved by the possibility of decisions being overruled or distinguished, thus allowing the law to adapt to new or previously unforeseen circumstances. The obvious disadvantages of the system are its inherent rigidity, which can occasionally cause hardship, and the vast and ever-increasing bulk of cases to which courts must refer in order to determine what the law is. Indeed, it is this latter concern which has led the courts to impose restrictions on the citing of certain types of case as precedents.[11]

Finally, it is self-evident that there cannot be an infinite regression. Every rule of law must have its origin, and if it was not created by statute then it must have been created by a court. Even in modern times cases arise for which there is no precedent, and the court's decision in such a case must inevitably be based on general principles. These cases are described as cases of first impression and they require the judge to make law rather than to simply apply it.[12] Although he will do this by reference to analogous principles, even legal principles must have their origin. The failure to properly account for this is an inherent weakness of the declaratory theory.[13]

2 THE IMPACT OF THE HUMAN RIGHTS ACT 1998
ON THE DOCTRINE OF PRECEDENT

Under the Human Rights Act 1998,[14] courts and tribunals are obliged to perform their functions in accordance with Convention rights,[15] and they must interpret legislation in a manner compatible with these rights so far as it is possible to do so.[16] Not only does this sanction the appellate courts to overrule incompatible precedents in the ordinary

[10] See the observations of Russell LJ in *Gallie v Lee* [1969] 2 Ch 17 at 41, [1969] 1 All ER 1062 at 1076, and of Lord Hailsham in *Cassell & Co Ltd v Broome* [1972] AC 1027 at 1054, [1972] 1 All ER 801 at 809 ('in legal matters, some degree of certainty is at least as valuable a part of justice as perfection').

[11] See p 77, *ante*.

[12] e.g. *Philips v Brooks Ltd* [1919] 2 KB 243; *Malone v Metropolitan Police Commissioner (No 2)* [1979] Ch 344, [1979] 2 All ER 620; *Midland Bank Trust Co Ltd v Green (No 3)* [1982] Ch 529, [1981] 3 All ER 744; *Parker v British Airways Board* [1982] QB 1004, [1982] 1 All ER 834.

[13] See Lord Simon's observations on the declaratory theory of common law in *Jones v Secretary of State for Social Services* [1972] AC 944 at 1026, [1972] 1 All ER 145 at 198, quoted at p 321, *post*.

[14] The overall significance of this major piece of legislation is discussed in chapter 5, *post*.

[15] Section 6. Convention rights are defined in s 1.

[16] Section 3(1). The effect of the Act on statutory interpretation is discussed further in chapter 2, *ante*.

way, it also permits a 'year zero' approach to *stare decisis*.[17] This is because a court's obligations under the Act must prevail over any duty to obey the normal rules of precedent. In other words, a pre-Human Rights Act decision of a higher court cannot stand in the way of a lower court coming to a different conclusion in order to give effect to Convention rights. For example, the Court of Appeal has already declined to follow a previous decision of the House of Lords, in order to avoid the conclusion that a provision of the Rent Act 1977 was in breach of Article 14 of the Convention.[18] Similarly, in order to comply with Article 6 the same court[19] made a 'modest adjustment' to the test for bias established by the House of Lords in *R v Gough*.[20] The modified approach adopted in this case was later approved by the House of Lords in *Porter v Magill*.[21]

This does not mean, however, that a court can decline to follow a precedent on the grounds that it conflicts with a decision of the European Court of Human Rights. Domestic courts and tribunals must take *account* of the Strasbourg Court's decisions when determining Convention cases,[22] but they are not required to treat those decisions as binding precedents.[23]

3   THE BINDING ELEMENT IN PRECEDENTS

(a) The *ratio decidendi*

Strictly speaking, it is a misstatement to say that a 'decision' is binding on anyone other than the parties to the case in question. Similarly, it is not technically correct to regard a 'decision' as having been overruled. It is not the decision which binds (or is overruled); it is the rule of law contained within the decision. This element of the decision is termed the *ratio decidendi*, and not every statement of law made by a judge in the case forms part of this *ratio*.

Every decision contains the following basic ingredients:

(1) findings of material facts, both direct and inferential;[24]

(2) statements of the principles of law applicable to the legal problems disclosed by the facts; and

(3) a judgment (or judgments) based on the combined effect of (1) and (2).

---

[17] See Mead, 'Swallowing the Camel, Straining at the Gnat: The Implications of *Mendoza v Ghaidan*' [2003] 5 EHRLR 501 at 509.

[18] *Ghaidan v Godin-Mendoza* [2002] EWCA Civ 1533, [2003] Ch 380, [2002] 4 All ER 1162 (affirmed: [2004] UKHL 30, [2004] 2 AC 557, [2004] 3 All ER 411). The House of Lords decision in question was *Fitzpatrick v Sterling Housing Association Ltd* [2001] 1 AC 27, [1999] 4 All ER 705.

[19] *Director General of Fair Trading v Proprietary Association of Great Britain* [2001] 1 WLR 700, [2001] HRLR 17; *sub nom Re Medicaments and Related Classes of Goods (No 2)*.

[20] [1993] AC 646, [1993] 2 All ER 724.

[21] [2001] UKHL 67, [2002] 2 AC 357, [2002] 1 All ER 465.

[22] Human Rights Act 1998, s 2.

[23] *Kay v Lambeth LBC*; *Leeds City Council v Price* [2006] UKHL 10, [2006] 2 AC 465, [2006] 4 All ER 128. See further, pp 147 and 152, *post*.

[24] An inferential finding of fact is the inference which the judge (or jury) draws from the direct or perceptible facts. For example, negligence may be inferred from the direct facts of the speed of a vehicle, the length of skid marks, and the state of the road. Negligence is thus an inferential finding of fact.

For the purposes of the parties themselves, (3) is the material element in the decision, for it is what ultimately determines their rights and liabilities in relation to the subject matter of the case. However, for the purpose of the doctrine of precedent, (2) is the vital element in the decision, and it is this which is termed the *ratio decidendi*. Thus the *ratio decidendi* may be defined as the statement of law applied to the legal problems raised by the facts, upon which the decision is based.

The two other elements in the decision are not precedents at all: the findings of fact are not binding on anyone, and the judgment is only binding on the parties to the case in question.[25] This means that even where the direct facts of a case appear to be identical to those before the court in an earlier decision, the judge or jury is not bound to draw the same inferences. *Qualcast (Wolverhampton) Ltd* v *Haynes*[26] is a good example of this point. In that case an employee sued his employers for negligence in failing to provide a safe system of work. At first instance the county court judge held himself bound to fol-low earlier cases in which employers who had acted in a similar manner had been held liable. The House of Lords held that this was not the correct approach, since the cases relied upon by the judge were based upon inferences of fact which were not binding. Otherwise, as Lord Somervell observed:[27]

> the precedent system will die from a surfeit of authorities.

Not every statement of law in a judgment is binding. Only those statements which are based upon the facts and upon which the decision is based are binding. Any other state-ment of law is, strictly speaking, superfluous and is described as an *obiter dictum* (some-thing said 'by the way'). It should not, however, be concluded from this that *obiter dicta* are of little or no weight or importance.

(b) *Obiter dicta*

There are two types of *obiter dicta*. Firstly, a statement of law is regarded as *obiter* if it is based upon facts which either were not found to be material or were not found to exist at all. For example, the famous statement of equitable estoppel contained in the judgment of Denning J in *Central London Property Trust Ltd* v *High Trees House Ltd*[28] is clearly *obiter* since it applied to a set of facts which were not found to be present in the case. Similarly, in *Rondel* v *Worsley*[29] the House of Lords expressed opinions to the effect that a barrister might be held liable in tort when acting outside the province of litigation, and that a solicitor acting as an advocate might enjoy immunity from action. Since the case concerned only the liability of a barrister when acting as an advocate, these opinions were necessarily *obiter*.

---

[25] See *R* v *Secretary of State for the Home Department, ex parte Ku* [1995] QB 364, [1995] 2 All ER 891.

[26] [1959] AC 743, [1959] 2 All ER 38.

[27] [1959] AC 743 at 758, [1959] 2 All ER 38 at 43. In the tort of negligence, only the existence of a duty of care is a question of law; whether or not the defendant has broken this duty is a question of fact.

[28] [1947] KB 130, [1956] 1 All ER 256n.

[29] [1969] 1 AC 191, [1967] 3 All ER 993. The House of Lords has since overruled its decision in this case in *Arthur J S Hall* v *Simons and others* [2002] 1 AC 615, [2000] 3 All ER 673; see p 398, *post*.

Secondly, even where a statement of law *is* based on the facts as found, it will be regarded as *obiter* if it does not form the basis of the decision. A statement of law made in support of a dissenting judgment is an obvious example. Similarly, where a court makes statements of law leading to one conclusion but then comes to a contrary conclusion for a different reason, those statements are necessarily *obiter* since they do not support the decision. An example is provided by the seminal case of *Hedley Byrne & Co Ltd* v *Heller & Partners*.[30] The central proposition of law in that case was that the maker of a statement owes a duty of care, in certain circumstances, to persons whom he may expect to rely upon that statement. Strictly speaking, however, this statement was *obiter*, as on the facts of the case it was found that the bank which had given the disputed advice was protected by a disclaimer of responsibility. That being so, the further statement as to what rule of law *would* have been applied but for the disclaimer cannot be regarded as essential to the decision. Nevertheless, *Hedley Byrne* illustrates that the strict rules for isolating the *ratio* of a case are sometimes of limited value, since the reasoning of the House of Lords undoubtedly represents the present state of the law:[31]

> When five members of the House of Lords have all said, after close examination of the authorities, that a certain type of tort exists, I think that a judge of first instance should proceed on the basis that it does exist without pausing to embark on an investigation whether what was said was necessary to the ultimate decision.

Hedley Byrne has since been expressly applied by the Court of Appeal and approved by the House of Lords.[32] It seems reasonable to conclude that where the House of Lords states a rule of law and expressly rejects earlier contrary decisions, that statement will be treated as binding even though not strictly essential to the decision.

(c) Ascertaining the *ratio decidendi*

Although the distinction between *obiter dicta* and the *ratio* of a case is clear enough in theory, drawing this distinction in practice is often fraught with difficulty. First of all, a case may be argued on more than one ground. If the court is willing to decide the case on one ground it will usually refrain from expressing an opinion on any other point of law, but sometimes a court may feel compelled to deal with every point of law raised. Isolating the *ratio decidendi* in such a case may be extremely difficult. The problem is often particularly acute in the case of appellate decisions, since different members of the court may arrive at the same conclusion for different reasons. The starting point in this situation is that a reason adopted by a majority of the court is presumed to be *ratio*, whereas a reason adopted only by a minority is usually regarded as non-essential to the decision and therefore not binding. The position becomes complicated where no one reason is favoured by a majority, yet every case must be assumed to have a *ratio decidendi*. The answer seems to be that it depends upon which of the alternative reasons subsequent courts are prepared to accept as *rationes*. One classic example is the decision

[30] [1964] AC 465, [1963] 2 All ER 575.
[31] *W B Anderson and Sons Ltd* v *Rhodes* [1967] 2 All ER 850 at 857, per Cairns J.
[32] *Arenson* v *Casson, Beckman, Rutley & Co* [1977] AC 405, [1975] 3 All ER 901.

of the House of Lords in *Sinclair* v *Brougham*.[33] It was held in this case, that once the creditors of a society had been paid in full by agreement, the assets remaining were to be divided between depositors and members of the society in accordance with the proportion of new payments to the society. The reasons for this conclusion were far from clear, with one member of the court concurring with a judgment based on reasons which were at odds with his own.[34] The multiplicity of opinion and reasoning was sufficient to provoke Lord Browne-Wilkinson to observe in a later case that it was:[35]

> a bewildering authority: no single *ratio* can be detected; all the reasoning is open to serious objection, it was only intended to deal with cases where there were no trade creditors in competition and the reasoning is incapable of application where there are such creditors.

In so far as the decision of the court in *Sinclair* v *Brougham* was discernible at all, it was overruled.

A further difficulty is that what may initially be considered to be *obiter dicta*, even by the court itself, may subsequently be viewed differently. Thus, in *Luc Thiet Thuan* v *R*[36] the court considered that what may have been an *obiter dictum* in *R* v *Ahluwalia*[37] 'certainly ripened' into *ratio decidendi* in *R* v *Dryden*.[38]

It is certainly possible for a case to have two or more *rationes decidendi*. The case of *Fairman* v *Perpetual Investment Building Society*[39] is an example. The House of Lords in that case gave two reasons for its decision, both of which were accepted as binding by the House in *Jacobs* v *London County Council*.[40] On the other hand, in *Read* v *J Lyons & Co Ltd*.[41] the House of Lords advanced two reasons for its decision that the defendants were not liable under the rule in *Rylands* v *Fletcher*:[42] (1) that the rule did not apply in the absence of an escape of the dangerous substance from the defendant's occupation or control; and (2) that the rule did not apply unless the plaintiff had an interest in land affected by the escape. The second reason, which is principally contained in the speech of Lord Macmillan, was, in a later case,[43] treated by the Court of Appeal as *obiter*, on the basis that it was not essential to the decision. The position is further complicated by the fact that the Court of Appeal's statement on this point was itself *obiter*, because the plaintiff's action failed for another reason. The question of whether the second reason in *Read* v *J Lyons & Co Ltd* is *ratio* or *obiter* was therefore left unresolved.[44]

---

[33] [1914] AC 398, [1914–1915] All ER Rep 622.   [34] Lord Dunedin.

[35] *Westdeutsche Handesbank Girozentrale* v *Islington LBC* [1996] AC 669 at 713, [1996] 2 All ER 961 at 996.

[36] [1997] AC 131, [1996] 2 All ER 1033. See also, *St John the Evangelist, Chopwel* [1995] Fam 254, [1996] 1 All ER 275. In this case, the judge said that statements made in *Re St Thomas, Pennywell* [1995] Fam 50, [1995] 4 All ER 167, 'were not strictly necessary to that decision but now I adopt them as part of the *ratio decidendi* of the present case.'

[37] [1992] 4 All ER 889, (1993) 96 Cr App R 133.

[38] [1995] 4 All ER 987.   [39] [1923] AC 74.

[40] [1950] AC 361, [1950] 1 All ER 737. The case is particularly notable in that one of the two reasons given in *Fairman*'s case was clearly not essential to the decision.

[41] [1947] AC 156, [1946] 2 All ER 471.   [42] (1868) LR 3 HL 330.

[43] *Perry* v *Kendricks Transport Ltd* [1956] 1 All ER 154, [1956] 1 WLR 85.

[44] The Court of Appeal in *Dunne* v *North-Western Gas Board* [1964] 2 QB 806, [1963] 3 All ER 916, expressly left the point open.

A variation of this problem can arise if a majority of the judges in a case favour a reason which does not actually support the court's decision. The reason cannot be a *ratio* because it does not support the decision, yet on the other hand it seems logically odd to conclude that the *ratio* can be found in the contrary reasoning of the minority. The occasions on which such a dilemma will arise are likely to be very rare, but the decision of the House of Lords in *Central Asbestos Co Ltd* v *Dodd*[45] was such an occasion. The question before the House turned on the construction of the ill-drafted provisions of section 7(3) of the Limitation Act 1963. Lords Reid and Morris took one view of the law, Lords Simon and Salmon a different view. The fifth member of the court, Lord Pearson, was in favour of deciding the appeal in the same way as Lords Reid and Morris, but his view on the point of law substantially supported that of Lords Simon and Salmon. It was not long before the Court of Appeal was called upon to decide the point of law which had arisen in *Dodd*'s case, and it concluded that since the case had no discernible *ratio* at all, it would go back to the law contained in the earlier cases.[46]

4 PRECEDENTS WHICH ARE NOT BINDING

(a) Persuasive authorities

Obiter dicta. Although *obiter dicta* lack binding authority, they may nevertheless have a strong persuasive influence. This is particularly so where the statement in question has come from a court of high authority and is a deliberate statement of law as opposed to a casual expression of opinion. Such a dictum will usually be followed in the absence of any binding authority to the contrary. In the case of *Adams* v *Naylor*[47] for example, the House of Lords disapproved the practice of government departments setting up a nominal defendant to avoid the Crown's immunity from actions in tort. Although this disapproval was *obiter*, the Court of Appeal in *Royster* v *Cavey*[48] adopted it and refused to sanction this long-standing practice. *Hedley Byrne & Co Ltd* v *Heller & Partners*[49] provides another example of *obiter dicta* which has subsequently had considerable influence, but perhaps the most striking example of all is the 'neighbour principle' propounded by Lord Atkin in *Donoghue (or M'Alister)* v *Stevenson*.[50] This statement of law has become the basis of the modern tort of negligence and has been cited and applied on occasions too numerous to mention, yet the statement was far wider than the case itself required and it was therefore strictly *obiter*.

Decisions of inferior courts. Decisions of courts lower in the hierarchy may have some persuasive authority for those courts above them. Court of Appeal decisions, for example, are generally regarded as having persuasive authority in the House of Lords.

[45] [1973] AC 518, [1972] 2 All ER 1135.
[46] *Harper* v *National Coal Board* [1974] QB 614, [1974] 2 All ER 441.
[47] [1946] AC 543, [1946] 2 All ER 241.
[48] [1947] KB 204, [1946] 2 All ER 642. This decision precipitated the passing of the Crown Proceedings Act 1947, which enabled the Crown to be sued in tort.
[49] [1964] AC 465, [1963] 2 All ER 575; see p 82, *ante*.   [50] [1932] AC 562.

Decisions of the Judicial Committee of the Privy Council. 'Decisions' of the Judicial Committee of the Privy Council are not strictly binding on any English court,[51] and in theory, even a first instance judge may legitimately decline to follow a Privy Council decision.[52] In practice, however, such decisions are of very great persuasive authority for the obvious reason that the Judicial Committee is composed of the same persons who usually sit in the House of Lords. There had not been any suggestion that Privy Council authorities were of equivalent weight to House of Lords cases until the decision in *Doughty* v *Turner Manufacturing.*[53] In this case, the Court of Appeal expressed the view that its own decision in *Re Polemis*[54] was no longer good law in the light of the subsequent Privy Council decision in *The Wagon Mound.*[55] Similarly, when the Court of Appeal in *Worcester Works Finance Ltd* v *Cooden Engineering Co Ltd.*[56] was faced with a conflict between one of its own decisions and a later decision of the Privy Council, it had no hesitation in preferring the latter.

Since Privy Council decisions are merely persuasive it cannot be assumed that they will always be followed, and in *R* v *Smith*[57] both the Court of Appeal and the House of Lords declined to follow a Privy Council decision concerning the defence of provocation to murder.[58] However, in the truly exceptional case of *R* v *James (Leslie)*[59] the Court of Appeal declined to follow the House of Lords decision in *Smith*, preferring instead to follow a later decision of the Privy Council.[60] Although this was a very unusual and radical step, it should not be taken to signal a more general departure from the established rules of precedent. The decision in *Smith* had been widely criticized, and the nine Law Lords who were party to the Privy Council's decision made it clear that they intended it to resolve a question of English law. The Privy Council normally follows House of Lords decisions when deciding cases where the applicable law is English,[61] but this was clearly a case where their Lordships felt that an exception should be made:[62]

> This appeal, being heard by an enlarged board of nine members, is concerned to resolve this conflict and clarify definitively the present state of English law, and hence Jersey law, on this important subject.

---

[51] Privy Council decisions on 'devolution questions' affecting Wales, Scotland and Northern Ireland *are* binding, even on the House of Lords. However, when the House of Lords is replaced by a new Supreme Court it is intended that the new court will assume jurisdiction in such matters: see p 253, *post.*

[52] Diplock J did so in *Port Line Ltd* v *Ben Line Steamers Ltd* [1958] 2 QB 146, [1958] 1 All ER 787; see also *Dulieu* v *White* [1901] 2 KB 669.

[53] [1964] 1 QB 518, [1964] 1 All ER 98.   [54] [1921] 3 KB 560.

[55] *Overseas Tankship (UK) Ltd* v *Morts Dock and Engineering Co Ltd* [1961] AC 388, [1961] 1 All ER 404.

[56] [1972] 1 QB 210, [1971] 3 All ER 708.

[57] *R* v *Smith* [1999] QB 1079, [1998] 4 All ER 387, CA; [2001] 1 AC 146, [2000] 4 All ER 289, HL.

[58] The decision in question was *Luc Thiet Thuan* v *R* [1997] AC 131, [1996] 2 All ER 1033.

[59] [2006] EWCA Crim 14, [2006] QB 588, [2006] 1 All ER 759. Cf. *Re Spectrum Plus Ltd. (In Liquidation)* [2004] EWCA Civ 670, [2004] Ch 337, [2004] 4 All ER 995 (affirmed: [2005] UKHL 41, [2005] 2 AC 680, [2005] 4 All ER 209).

[60] *Attorney General for Jersey* v *Holley* [2005] UKPC 23, [2005] 2 AC 580, [2005] 3 All ER 371.

[61] *Tai Hing Cotton Mill Ltd* v *Liu Chong Hing Bank Ltd* [1986] AC 80, [1985] 2 All ER 947.

[62] [2005] UKPC 23 at [1], [2005] 2 AC 580 at [1], per Lord Nicholls.

The Court of Appeal in *James* had no doubt what the outcome would be if the case ended up in the House of Lords, and this was, after all, a homicide case in which the liberty of the subject was at stake:[63]

> What are the exceptional features in this case which justify our preferring the decision in Holley's case to that in the Morgan Smith case? We identify the following. (i) All nine of the Lords of Appeal in Ordinary sitting in Holley's case agreed in the course of their judgments that the result reached by the majority clarified definitively English law on the issue in question. (ii) The majority in Holley's case constituted half the Appellate Committee of the House of Lords…(iii) In the circumstances, the result of any appeal on the issue to the House of Lords is a foregone conclusion.
>
> We doubt whether this court will often, if ever again, be presented with the circumstances that we have described above. It is those circumstances which we consider justify the course that we have decided to take, and our decision should not be taken as a licence to decline to follow a decision of the House of Lords in any other circumstances.

Decisions of the European Court of Human Rights. Section 2 of the Human Rights Act 1998 requires any court or tribunal determining a matter involving a Convention right, to take into account any judgment, decision, or advisory opinion of the European Court of Human Rights, along with certain decisions of the Commission and Committee of Ministers, in so far as they may be relevant. Decisions of the European Court of Human Rights and the other institutions are thus given the status of persuasive precedents, and it is left to individual courts and tribunals to decide whether they should be followed in any particular case. The suggestion that courts ought to be bound by the Strasbourg jurisprudence was rejected by the government during the passage of the Human Rights Bill through Parliament. The Lord Chancellor explained that to make the Strasbourg jurisprudence binding on domestic courts would be inconsistent with the spirit of the Convention itself:[64]

> We must remember that Clause 2 requires the courts to take account of all the judgments of the European Court of Human Rights, regardless of whether they have been given in a case involving the United Kingdom…the United Kingdom is not bound in international law to follow that Court's judgments in cases to which the United Kingdom had not been a party, and it would be strange to require courts in the United Kingdom to be bound by such cases.

The precise effect of section 2 was subsequently considered by Lord Slynn in the leading case of *R (on the Application of Alconbury) v Secretary of State for the Environment, Transport and the Regions*:[65]

> In the absence of some special circumstances it seems to me that the court should follow any clear and constant jurisprudence of the European Court of Human Rights.

---

[63] [2006] EWCA Crim 14 at [43]-[44], [2006] QB 588 at [43]-[44], per Lord Phillips of Worth Matravers CJ. For further discussion see Conaglen and Nolan, 'Precedent from the Privy Council' (2006) 122 *LQR* 349.

[64] Lord Irvine of Lairg, 583 HL Official Report (5th series) col 511, 18 November 1997.

[65] [2001] UKHL 23 at [26], [2003] 2 AC 295 at [26], [2001] 2 All ER 929. For an example of a case in which the Strasbourg jurisprudence was *not* followed, see *R v Spear and others; R v Saunby and others* [2002] UKHL 31, [2003] 1 AC 734, [2002] 3 All ER 1074.

If it does not do so there is at least a possibility that the case will go to that court which is likely in the ordinary case to follow its own constant jurisprudence.

As stated previously, however, taking account of Strasbourg case law does not mean disregarding binding decisions of the domestic courts. The House of Lords recently confirmed that in the event of a conflict between a domestic decision and a decision of the Court of Human Rights, the normal rules of precedent will still apply.[66] This means that a court cannot decline to follow the binding precedent of a court higher in the legal hierarchy, even where that precedent is inconsistent with a more recent decision of the Strasbourg court. There may, however, be cases where the facts are of such an 'extreme character' that a departure from an otherwise binding precedent is justified.[67] *D v East Berkshire Community Health NHS Trust* is an example of such a case.[68] Here the Court of Appeal declined to follow a pre-1998 House of Lords decision[69] on the basis that the policy considerations underlying that decision had been largely eroded by the introduction of the Human Rights Act. An additional factor was that the claimants whose case had been rejected as unarguable by the House of Lords had later succeeded in establishing a breach of the Convention before the Court of Human Rights.[70]

Decisions from other jurisdictions. A third class of persuasive authorities consists of the decisions of Scottish, Irish, Commonwealth, and foreign courts. There is an increasing tendency on the part of English lawyers and judges to draw analogies from other legal systems, and decisions from other jurisdictions – particularly Scotland, Ireland, the USA, Australia, Canada, and New Zealand – are frequently cited. In an effort to reduce the sheer volume of cases being used in this way, the Court of Appeal felt compelled to take steps discouraging reliance on foreign cases except where they genuinely have something to add to existing domestic law.[71] At the same time, however, the Lord Chief Justice acknowledged that 'cases decided in other jurisdictions can, if properly used, be a valuable source of law.'[72]

(b) Statements of law made *per incuriam*

The Court of Appeal in the leading case of *Young v Bristol Aeroplane Co Ltd*[73] established that it was entitled to depart from one of its previous decisions if satisfied that the decision in question was reached *per incuriam* (through lack of care). When a decision is described as having been made *per incuriam*, this usually, though not always, means that some relevant statutory provision or precedent which would have led the court to a

---

[66] *Kay v Lambeth LBC; Leeds City Council v Price* [2006] UKHL 10 at [40]–[44], [2006] 2 AC 465 [40]–[44], [2006] 4 All ER 128, per Lord Bingham.

[67] Ibid, at [45].

[68] [2003] EWCA Civ 1151, [2004] QB 558, [2003] 4 All ER 796 (affirmed [2005] UKHL 23, [2005] 2 AC 373, [2005] 2 All ER 443).

[69] *X (Minors) v Bedfordshire CC* [1995] 2 AC 633, [1995] 3 All ER 353.

[70] *Z v United Kingdom* (2002) 34 EHRR 3.

[71] *Practice Direction (Citation of Authorities)* [2001] 2 All ER 510 at [9.1], [2001] 1 WLR 1001 at [9.1], per Lord Woolf CJ.

[72] Ibid.

[73] [1944] KB 718, [1944] 2 All ER 293 (affirmed [1946] AC 163, [1946] 1 All ER 98); see p 96, *post*.

different conclusion, was not brought to the court's attention.[74] Although the principle in *Young's* case was expressed to apply only to the Court of Appeal, it has since been applied in other courts. Thus in *R v Northumberland Compensation Appeal Tribunal, ex parte Shaw*[75] a Divisional Court of the King's Bench Division declined to follow a Court of Appeal decision on the ground that the latter had been reached *per incuriam*, a relevant House of Lords decision not having been cited to the Court of Appeal. However, when the Court of Appeal refused to follow a House of Lords decision on exemplary damages[76] which it considered to have been made *per incuriam*, it was roundly condemned by the House of Lords for having done so.[77] Lord Hailsham LC, in the course of the leading speech for the majority, asserted that:[78]

> it is not open to the Court of Appeal to give gratuitous advice to judges of first instance to ignore decisions of the House of Lords in this way. The course taken would have put judges of first instance in an embarrassing position, as driving them to take sides in an unedifying dispute between the Court of Appeal and the House of Lords.

These words proved to be prophetic because in *Miliangos v George Frank (Textiles) Ltd*,[79] Bristow J found himself in the embarrassing position foreseen by Lord Hailsham. This was because the Court of Appeal in *Schorsch Meier GmbH v Hennin*[80] had held that the rule of law whereby money judgments could only be expressed in sterling had ceased to exist, notwithstanding clear House of Lords authority for the existence of the rule. Bristow J preferred to follow the House of Lords authority, but the Court of Appeal later stated that he was wrong to do so because *Schorsch Meier* was binding upon him. On appeal[81] the House of Lords decision in question[82] was overruled, although not on any of the grounds cited by the Court of Appeal.

The *per incuriam* principle is of limited application, and few decisions have subsequently been regarded as having been reached in this way.[83] The mere fact that a case was not fully or expertly argued,[84] or that it was argued on one side only (as *Schorsch Meier* was), does not entitle a court to disregard it as having been made *per incuriam*. Similarly, a case cannot be considered *per incuriam* solely because the court appeared to misunderstand the law or was not aware of the policy considerations behind a

[74] *Duke v Reliance Systems Ltd* [1988] QB 108, [1987] 2 All ER 858 (affirmed [1988] AC 618, [1988] 1 All ER 626).

[75] [1951] 1 KB 711, [1951] 1 All ER 268. See also *Hughes v Kingston upon Hull City Council* [1999] QB 1193, [1999] 2 All ER 49.

[76] *Rookes v Barnard* [1964] AC 1129, [1964] 1 All ER 367. This decision had already been subjected to devastating criticism in the courts of the Commonwealth and had been repudiated by the Privy Council; see *Australian Consolidated Press Ltd v Uren* [1969] 1 AC 590, [1967] 3 All ER 523.

[77] *Cassell & Co Ltd v Broome* [1972] AC 1027, [1972] 1 All ER 801.

[78] [1972] AC 1027 at 1054, [1972] 1 All ER 801 at 809.

[79] [1975] QB 487, [1975] 1 All ER 1076.   [80] [1975] QB 416, [1975] 1 All ER 152.

[81] [1976] AC 443, [1975] 3 All ER 801.

[82] *Re United Railways of the Havana and Ragla Warehouses Ltd* [1961] AC 1007, [1960] 2 All ER 332 (a decision to which Lord Denning himself had been a party).

[83] For two recent examples, see *Royal Bank of Scotland v Etridge (No 2)* [1998] 4 All ER 705 and *R (on the application of W) v Lambeth LBC* [2002] EWCA Civ 613, [2002] 2 All ER 901.

[84] *Joscelyne v Nissen* [1970] 2 QB 86, [1970] 1 All ER 1213; *Morelle Ltd v Wakeling* [1955] 2 QB 379, [1955] 1 All ER 708.

statute.[85] However, if it appears to a court that a previous interpretation of a statute was clearly wrong, then it would seem that the duty of the later court is to apply a correct interpretation.[86] Whether this is an example of the *per incuriam* doctrine or simply an illustration of a judge's general obligations concerning the interpretation of statutes is a moot point. In *IM Properties v Cape & Dalgleish*,[87] the Court of Appeal was referred to an earlier House of Lords decision[88] which it considered to be based on an incorrect interpretation of section 35A of the Supreme Court Act 1981. The Court of Appeal held that in these circumstances it had no option but to depart from the earlier decision, and it is clear that it regarded this as an application of the *per incuriam* doctrine:[89]

> [U]nder these circumstances we are not bound by this aspect of the *Westdeutsche* decision and...we are entitled to determine this appeal upon what we consider is the correct construction of s 35A.

(c) Precedents embodying former rules of international law

The decision in *Trendtex Trading Corporation Ltd v Central Bank of Nigeria*[90] indicates that there may be a further limited exception to the doctrine of binding precedent in respect of that part of English law which embodies current international law. In this case the Court of Appeal held that the defendant bank could not claim sovereign immunity from action because, inter alia, as a matter of international law the doctrine of state immunity was not applicable to ordinary commercial transactions. In reaching this decision the court declined to follow an earlier Court of Appeal decision which would otherwise have been considered binding, the majority holding that the rule of *stare decisis* could not stand in the way of giving effect to changes in international law. The point does not appear to have been judicially considered since this case, and the decision must therefore be taken as an accurate statement of the current law.

5 REVERSING, OVERRULING, AND DISTINGUISHING

(a) Reversing

Reversing occurs when one of the parties to a case appeals against the decision of a lower court and the appellate court then reaches a different conclusion. The effect of this is

---

[85] *Farrell v Alexander* [1976] QB 345, [1976] 1 All ER 129 (decision reversed [1977] AC 59, [1976] 2 All ER 721); but see *Industrial Properties (Barton Hill) Ltd v Associated Electrical Industries Ltd* [1977] QB 580, [1977] 2 All ER 293. In the latter case, the Court of Appeal declared one of its previous decisions *per incuriam* where the court had misunderstood an earlier case because of deficiencies in the law report to which it had been referred. See also *Dixon v BBC* [1979] QB 546, [1979] 2 All ER 112 in which one *ratio* of an earlier case was treated as *per incuriam* on the ground that the statutory provision under construction had been considered in isolation rather than in context. See also, *R (on the application of W) v Lambeth LBC* [2002] EWCA Civ 613, [2002] 2 All ER 901.

[86] Ibid.   [87] [1999] QB 297, [1998] 3 All ER 203.

[88] *Westdeutsche Handesbank Girozentrale v Islington LBC* [1996] AC 669 at 713, [1996] 2 All ER 961 at 996.

[89] [1999] QB 297 at 308–9, [1998] 3 All ER 203 at 212, per Hobhouse LJ.

[90] [1977] QB 529, [1977] 1 All ER 881. The question at issue in the case has now been resolved by the State Immunity Act 1978, s 3(1).

literally to 'reverse' the lower court's decision in the case and to alter the outcome for the parties concerned. The process of reversing a decision must be carefully distinguished from that of 'overruling', since the latter does not change the outcome in the case that is overruled.

(b) Overruling

Overruling occurs when a court in one case makes a decision affecting the rule of law upon which the decision in a *different* case was based. This means that semantically, it is not correct to describe a decision as having been 'overruled' since it is only the rule of law contained in the decision which is affected, and not the decision itself.

A decision may be overruled either by statute or by a higher court. If overruled by a court, the earlier decision is deemed to have been based on a misunderstanding of the law, and on a strict application of the declaratory theory, the earlier rule is deemed never to have existed. On this view the common law is never changed; it is merely restated correctly. However, such a rationalization ignores the reality that judges do make law, and often change the law because of changing circumstances or attitudes. An example of such a decision is that of *R* v *R*,[91] in which the House of Lords held that the long-established rule that a husband cannot be criminally liable for raping his wife no longer formed part of English law.

Whatever the theoretical basis, judicial overruling operates retrospectively, and this is one important respect in which it differs from most instances of overruling by statute.[92] Another difference between overruling by the courts and overruling by statute is that statutes do not expressly name the decisions that they overrule. Nevertheless it is not usually difficult to identify the cases which are overruled by a statute, particularly where the statute follows closely upon an unpopular decision of a superior court.[93]

The United States Supreme Court has the power to overrule decisions prospectively. This means that it may overrule an existing legal rule for the benefit of future decisions, yet still apply it to the particular case before it.[94] This power is said to be based on the common law, but until recently it had never been recognized in this country. In *Jones* v *Secretary of State for Social Services*,[95] Lord Simon suggested that the most satisfactory method of dealing with the case would have been to allow the appeal on the basis that it was covered by an existing precedent, but to then overrule that precedent prospectively. In the event, he simply concurred with the majority of the House of Lords and decided to allow the appeal, observing that any extension of judicial power to include prospective overruling should preferably be left to Parliament.[96] However, the House of Lords has

---

[91]   *R* v *R (Rape: Marital Exemption)* [1992] 1 AC 599, [1991] 4 All ER 481; see p 323, *post*.

[92]   The War Damage Act 1965 is a rare example of an Act which was expressly stated to be retrospective, and which was passed with the apparent intention of overruling a House of Lords decision (*Burmah Oil Co Ltd v Lord Advocate* [1965] AC 75, [1964] 2 All ER 348). The presumption against the retrospective operation of statutes is discussed further in chapter 2.

[93]   Ibid.   [94]   *Linkletter* v *Walker* 381 US 618 (1965).

[95]   [1972] AC 944, [1972] 1 All ER 145; see p 93, *post*.

[96]   [1972] AC 944 at 1026–7, [1972] 1 All ER 145 at 198; Lord Simon advanced similar suggestions in *Miliangos v George Frank (Textiles) Ltd* [1976] AC 443 at 490, [1975] 3 All ER 801 at 832.

revisited the question of whether there is a power to prospectively overrule in a hand-ful of recent cases,[97] and in *Re Spectrum Plus Ltd (In Liquidation)* their Lordships were unanimous in holding that such a power existed:[98]

> There could be cases where a decision on an issue of law, whether common law or statute law, was unavoidable but the decision would have such gravely unfair and disruptive consequences for past transactions or happenings that this House would be compelled to depart from the normal principles relating to the retrospective and prospective effect of court decisions... If, altogether exceptionally, the House as the country's supreme court were to follow this course I would not regard it as tres-passing outside the functions properly to be discharged by the judiciary... Rigidity in the operation of a legal system is a sign of weakness, not strength... 'Never say never' is a wise judicial precept...

On the facts of the case, however, their Lordships held that there were no grounds for postponing the effect of their ruling.

A precedent does not lose its authority with the passing of time. Indeed the strength of a precedent arguably increases with age, and courts tend to be reluctant to overrule long-standing authorities unless they are clearly wrong. Apart from the desirability of attaining certainty, the main reason for the reluctance of judges to overrule old decisions is the fact that this might have the effect of disturbing existing financial arrangements, depriving persons of vested proprietary rights, or even imposing criminal liability retro-spectively. In *Re Compton*,[99] for example, the Court of Appeal was unwilling to overrule a long line of old authorities concerning charitable trusts, even though it considered these cases to be anomalous. Similarly, although the rule in *Pinnel's case*[100] is plainly anomalous, even the House of Lords has refused to overrule it. Thus, in *Foakes* v *Beer*[101] Lord Fitzgerald expressed doubt about the merits of the rule but felt that because of its longevity the House would not be justified in overruling it.[102]

On the other hand, the courts generally have little hesitation in overruling decisions which they consider to be clearly wrong. Thus, in *Bourne* v *Keane*[103] the House of Lords overruled a series of long-standing decisions on the law of trusts, even though this had the effect of disturbing many existing trusts and settlements. In *Button* v *DPP*[104] it held

---

[97] Including *Kleinwort Benson Ltd* v *Lincoln City Council* [1999] 2 AC 349, [1998] 4 All ER 513; and *R* v *Governor of Brockhill Prison, ex parte Evans (No 2)* [2001] 2 AC 19 at 26, [2000] 4 All ER 15 at 19. In the latter case Lord Slynn stated that in his view, 'there may be situations in which it would be desirable, and in no way unjust, that the effect of judicial rulings should be prospective or limited to certain claimants'.

[98] [2005] UKHL 41 at [40]-[41], [2005] 2 AC 680 at [40]-[41], [2005] 4 All ER 209, per Lord Nicholls.

[99] [1945] Ch 123, [1945] 1 All ER 198.   [100] (1602) 5 Co Rep 117a.

[101] (1883–84) LR 9 App Cas 605.

[102] Ibid at 630. The rule has, of course, been undermined by the doctrine of equitable estoppel; see *D & C Builders Ltd* v *Rees* [1966] 2 QB 617, [1965] 3 All ER 837. See also *Re Selectmove* [1995] 1 WLR 474, [1995] 2 All ER 531.

[103] [1919] AC 815. On the other hand, in *Prudential Assurance Co Ltd* v *London Residuary Body* [1992] 2 AC 386, [1992] 3 All ER 504, the House of Lords felt unable to overrule ancient authorities requiring the maximum duration of a term of years to be determinable at the outset. This conclusion was reached on the ground that overruling the earlier authorities might upset long-established titles, yet the House itself acknowledged that it led to a 'bizarre outcome' in the instant case.

[104] [1966] AC 591, [1965] 3 All ER 587.

that the common law offence of affray could be committed in a private place, and thus overruled a line of authority to the effect that the offence could occur only in a public place. Similarly, in the leading case of *Miliangos* v *George Frank (Textiles) Ltd*[105] the House of Lords effectively overruled a decision which embodied one of the clearest and most firmly entrenched rules of English law, namely that judgment must be given in sterling.[106]

(c) Distinguishing

The process of 'distinguishing' is probably the major factor in enabling the doctrine of precedent to remain flexible and adaptable. Cases are distinguished on their facts. The *ratio decidendi* of a case is, by definition, based upon the material facts of that case, and courts are only bound to apply precedents which share the same material facts. Consequently, if a court is willing to regard as material any fact which is not common to both the case before it and the precedent cited, the two cases can be distinguished. The law reports are full of strained distinctions where the court was evidently anxious not to follow an apparently binding precedent. In theory it is possible to distinguish virtually any precedent, since factual situations will almost never precisely duplicate themselves. Nevertheless there are practical limits beyond which the court will be unlikely to go. Cases which are indistinguishable are described as being 'on all fours' with one another.

To illustrate how fine a distinction may be drawn between ostensibly parallel factual situations, reference may be made to two cases concerning the tort of conversion. In *England* v *Cowley*[107] the defendant refused to allow the claimant to remove goods from his, the defendant's, premises. This was held not to be conversion since there was no absolute denial of title. This case was distinguished by the Court of Appeal in *Oakley* v *Lyster*,[108] in which the defendant refused to allow the claimant to remove material from his (the defendant's) land, and in addition asserted his own title to the material. This was held to be an act of conversion, the assertion of title apparently making the denial of title absolute.

6 THE HIERARCHY OF THE COURTS

It has already been noted that the doctrine of binding precedent rests upon the underlying principle that the courts form a hierarchy, with each court standing in a definite position in relation to every other court. The structure of this hierarchy must now be considered for the purposes of the doctrine of precedent.

(a) European Court of Justice[109]

In matters concerning: (1) the interpretation of the Treaties; (2) the validity and interpretation of acts of the Community institutions; and (3) the interpretation of the statutes of bodies established by an act of the Council, the Court of Justice of the European Communities is the supreme tribunal. Accordingly, its decisions in these areas of

---

[105] [1976] AC 443, [1975] 3 All ER 801.
[106] *Re United Railways of the Havana and Regla Warehouses Ltd* [1961] AC 1007, [1960] 2 All ER 332.
[107] (1873) LR 8 Exch 126.   [108] [1931] 1 KB 148.
[109] See chapter 4, *post*.

jurisdiction will be binding on all English courts. Indeed section 3(1) of the European Communities Act 1972 expressly provides that:

> for the purpose of all legal proceedings any question as to the meaning or effect of any of the Treaties, or as to the validity, meaning or effect of any Community instrument, shall be treated as a question of law (and, if not referred to the European Court, be for determination as such in accordance with the principles laid down by and any relevant decision of the European Court or any court attached thereto).

The European Court of Justice does not observe a doctrine of binding precedent and does not regard itself as bound by its previous decisions. This does not, however, mean that its previous decisions have no influence upon it.

(b) House of Lords

The House of Lords stands at the summit of the English hierarchy of courts, and decisions of the House of Lords are binding upon all other courts trying civil or criminal cases.

Formerly, the House of Lords regarded itself as strictly bound by its own earlier decisions, which were thus immutable except by legislation.[110] However, in 1966 Lord Gardiner LC issued a Practice Statement to the effect that their Lordships would in future be willing to depart from their earlier decisions 'when it appears right to do so'.[111] They would, however, bear in mind the danger of disturbing financial arrangements and proprietary rights retrospectively, and the especial need for certainty as to the criminal law. The Lord Chancellor made it clear, moreover, that this statement was not intended to apply elsewhere than in the House of Lords.

The practical consequences of this change in the law were, at first, slight. In the five years following Lord Gardiner's statement the House of Lords did not overrule any of its previous decisions. This reticence is aptly demonstrated by *Jones* v *Secretary of State for Social Services*.[112] In this case, a seven-member House declined to overrule one of its previous decisions[113] even though a majority of their Lordships were of opinion that the earlier decision was wrong. Since there was no suggestion that the earlier authority could be distinguished it might appear that there was no alternative but to overrule it, and three members of the House were prepared to do this. Lord Simon, however, gave several reasons why he thought that it would be wrong to depart from the earlier case, even though he agreed that it had been wrongly decided. In particular, he emphasized that the power to depart from a previous decision 'is one to be most sparingly exercised', and he concluded that a variation of view on a matter of statutory construction would rarely provide a suitable occasion. The wait for a suitable occasion was not a long one, however, and in *British Railways Board* v *Herrington*[114] the House refused to follow a precedent which had stood for over forty years,[115] concerning the duty of care owed by an occupier of land to trespassers.

---

[110] This principle was established in *London Tramways Co* v *London County Council* [1898] AC 375.
[111] [1966] 3 All ER 77, [1966] 1 WLR 1234.   [112] [1972] AC 944, [1972] 1 All ER 145.
[113] *Minister of Social Security* v *Amalgamated Engineering Union* [1967] 1 AC 725, [1967] 1 All ER 210.
[114] [1972] AC 877, [1972] 1 All ER 749.
[115] *Robert Addie & Sons (Collieries) Ltd* v *Dumbreck* [1929] AC 358.

In *R* v *Secretary of State for the Home Department, ex parte Khawaja*[116] the House of Lords rejected a previous decision which had unduly restricted the power of the courts to review the detention and removal of suspected illegal immigrants.[117] Lord Scarman stated that the House must be satisfied of two things before it was entitled to take such a step:[118]

> [T]he House must be satisfied not only that adherence to the precedent would involve the risk of injustice and obstruct the proper development of the law, but also that a judicial departure by the House from the precedent is the safe and appropriate way of remedying the injustice and developing the law. The possibility that legislation may be the better course is one which, though not mentioned in the [Practice] Statement, the House will not overlook.

Both conditions were clearly satisfied on the facts of the case because the liberty of the subject was at stake and the decision raised fundamental issues about the ability of the courts to review executive decisions.

A more recent example is provided by the case of *Arthur JS Hall & Co* v *Simons*,[119] in which the House of Lords departed from the precedent set in *Rondel* v *Worsley*[120] and removed the immunity of advocates from liability in tort. While their Lordships did not doubt that *Rondel* v *Worsley* had been correctly decided at the time, it was felt that the original justifications for the immunity no longer applied and that it was therefore in the interests of public policy for the immunity to be removed.[121]

Notwithstanding the especial need for certainty as to the criminal law, the House in *R* v *Shivpuri*[122] departed from its own previous decision in *Anderton* v *Ryan*[123] on the law of criminal attempts. *Anderton* had been decided less than a year earlier but had meanwhile been the subject of devastating academic criticism. Lord Bridge (who had also been a party to the earlier decision) gave the following reasons:[124]

> Firstly, I am undeterred by the consideration that the decision in *Anderton* v *Ryan* was so recent. The 1966 Practice Statement is an effective abandonment of our pretention to infallibility. If a serious error embodied in a decision of this House had distorted the law, the sooner it is corrected the better. Secondly, I cannot see how, in the very nature of the case, anyone could have acted in reliance on the law as propounded in *Anderton* v *Ryan* in the belief that he was acting innocently and now find that, after all, he is to be held to have committed a criminal offence.

Despite these and other examples,[125] the House of Lords' power to depart from its previous decisions continues to be exercised sparingly. As Lord Reid observed in one case:[126]

> our change of practice in no longer regarding previous decisions of this House as absolutely binding does not mean that whenever we think a previous decision was

---

[116] [1984] AC 74, [1983] 1 All ER 765.
[117] *R* v *Secretary of State for the Home Department, ex parte Zamir* [1980] AC 930, [1980] 2 All ER 768.
[118] [1984] AC 74 at 106, [1983] 1 All ER 765 at 778.   [119] [2002] 1 AC 615, [2000] 3 All ER 673.
[120] [1969] 1 AC 191, [1967] 3 All ER 993.   [121] This is discussed further in chapter 12, *post*.
[122] [1987] AC 1, [1986] 2 All ER 334.   [123] [1985] AC 560, [1985] 2 All ER 355.
[124] [1987] AC 560 at 23, [1986] 2 All ER 355 at 345.
[125] See *The Johanna Oldendorff* [1974] AC 479, [1973] 3 All ER 148; *Vestey* v *Inland Revenue Commissioners* [1980] AC 1148, [1979] 3 All ER 976; *Murphy* v *Brentwood District Council* [1991] 1 AC 398, [1990] 2 All ER 908.
[126] *Knuller (Publishing, Printing and Promotions) Ltd* v *Director of Public Prosecutions* [1973] AC 435 at 455, [1972] 2 All ER 898 at 903; see also, *Fitzleet Estates Ltd* v *Cherry* [1977] 3 All ER 996, [1977] 1 WLR 1345.

wrong we should reverse it. In the general interest of certainty in the law we must be sure that there is some very good reason before we so act.

As the recent decision in *R* v *Kansal*[127] confirms, the House will not overrule its own decisions lightly, and a belief that an earlier case was wrongly decided will not necessarily be a sufficient justification. In *Kansal*, the House declined to overrule a decision which it had reached only four months earlier,[128] despite a majority of the House agreeing that the earlier case had been wrongly decided. The unwillingness of their Lordships to invoke the Practice Statement on this occasion was largely due to the fact that the cases concerned the status of the Human Rights Act 1998 during the transitional period before it came into force. The decisions were therefore unlikely to have any long-term significance.

Apart from the possibility of the House of Lords being prepared to depart from its own earlier decisions, there are now four other means by which a House of Lords decision may lose its authority. Firstly, and most obviously, it may be overruled by statute or as a result of a decision of the European Court of Justice. Secondly, the potential scope of a House of Lords decision may be lessened if it can be distinguished. The process of distinguishing applies in the House of Lords as in other courts. Indeed, before the 1966 Practice Statement it was applied with more force in the House of Lords than elsewhere because there was no other judicial means of avoiding a precedent which the House felt to be wrong. Thirdly, the House of Lords may reject one of its own previous decisions if it was made *per incuriam*. This is, however, of limited application, since it would be virtually inconceivable in modern times for a case to progress through the House of Lords with a crucial authority being overlooked. Moreover, it is doubtful whether this option is open to other courts. As noted earlier, the Court of Appeal in *Broome* v *Cassell & Co Ltd*[129] regarded a House of Lords decision as being given *per incuriam* on the basis that two House of Lords authorities were not cited to the House. Not only did the House of Lords disapprove the Court of Appeal's application of the *per incuriam* doctrine, Lord Diplock stated clearly that the Court of Appeal had no power to treat a House of Lords' decision in this way:[130]

> The Court of Appeal found themselves able to disregard the decision of this House in *Rookes* v *Barnard* by applying to it the label *per incuriam*. That label is relevant only to the right of an appellate court to decline to follow one of its own previous decisions, not to its right to disregard a decision of a higher appellate court or to the right of a judge of the High Court to disregard a decision of the Court of Appeal.

This dictum has been approved in subsequent cases[131] and it may therefore be assumed to be authoritative. Finally, the status of certain House of Lords decisions may be

---

[127] *R* v *Kansal (No 2)* [2001] UKHL 62, [2002] AC 69, [2002] 1 All ER 257.

[128] *R* v *Lambert* [2001] UKHL 37, [2002] 2 AC 545, [2001] 3 All ER 577. *Kansal* has since been applied in *R* v *Benjafield* [2002] UKHL 2, [2003] 1 AC 1099, [2002] 1 All ER 815.

[129] [1971] 2 QB 354, [1971] 2 All ER 187; see p 88, *ante*.

[130] *Cassell & Co Ltd* v *Broome* [1972] AC 1027 at 1131, [1972] 1 All ER 801 at 874.

[131] See *Baker* v *R* [1975] AC 774, [1975] 3 All ER 55; *Miliangos* v *George Frank (Textiles) Ltd* [1976] AC 443 at 479, [1975] 3 All ER 801 at 822–3, per Lord Simon. Cf. *Hughes* v *Kingston upon Hull City Council* [1999] QB 1193, [1999] 2 All ER 49, in which the Divisional Court of the Queen's Bench Division rejected a *per incuriam* decision of the Court of Appeal.

undermined by the application of the Human Rights Act 1998. As discussed earlier in this chapter, the Human Rights Act obliges courts to act consistently with the ECHR, and to interpret legislation in a Convention compatible way wherever it is possible to do so. Thus, a court may have no option but to depart from a precedent which would otherwise be binding upon it, in order to reach a decision which is consistent with its obligations under the Human Rights Act. This is so, even if the precedent concerned was established by the House of Lords.[132]

(c) Court of Appeal

Civil Division. Decisions of the Court of Appeal are binding on all inferior courts trying civil or criminal cases, including divisional courts.[133] The Court of Appeal itself is bound by decisions of the European Court, the House of Lords,[134] and by its own earlier decisions.[135] The last principle was established in *Young* v *Bristol Aeroplane Co Ltd*.[136] In delivering the judgment in this case, Lord Greene MR cited three exceptional circumstances in which an earlier decision of the Court of Appeal would not be regarded as binding:

(1) **Where there are two conflicting decisions, the court may choose which it will follow and the decision not followed will be deemed to have been overruled.** Thus, in *Fisher* v *Ruislip-Northwood Urban District Council*[137] the court had to choose between conflicting decisions on the liability of local authorities to motorists who collided with unlit air-raid shelters. Similarly, in *Tiverton Estates Ltd* v *Wearwell Ltd*[138] the Court of Appeal was able to avoid following its decision in *Law* v *Jones*[139] because it conflicted with earlier decisions of the court.

(2) **The court is bound to refuse to follow a decision of its own, which, though not expressly overruled, cannot stand with a later House of Lords decision.** It is notable that in *Young* this exception was said to apply to cases in which a Court of Appeal decision was inconsistent with a *later* House of Lords decision. There was no mention of what should happen in the event of a conflict with an earlier decision of that House. It may be that Lord Greene did not envisage that such a situation would ever arise, or, alternatively, he may have assumed that any such situation would be covered by the third of his exceptions. In the recent case of *Iqbal* v *Whipps Cross University Hospital NHS Trust*,[140] the Court of Appeal held

---

[132] See, e.g., the decision of the Court of Appeal in *Ghaidan* v *Godin-Mendoza* [2002] EWCA Civ 1533, [2003] Ch 380, [2002] 4 All ER 1162, discussed further at pp 56 and 80, *ante*.

[133] *Brownsea Haven Properties Ltd* v *Poole Corporation* [1958] Ch 574, [1958] 1 All ER 205.

[134] Subject to such decisions being compatible with EC law and with the Human Rights Act 1998; see p 99, *post*.

[135] The Court of Appeal is also bound by the decisions of courts which exercised equivalent jurisdiction prior to 1875: the Court of Exchequer Chamber and the Chancery Court of Appeal; see *Re Stevens, ex parte M'George* (1882) 20 Ch D 697.

[136] [1944] KB 718, [1944] 2 All ER 293 (affirmed [1946] AC 163, [1946] 1 All ER 98).

[137] [1945] KB 584, [1945] 2 All ER 458.   [138] [1975] Ch 146, [1974] 1 All ER 209.

[139] [1974] Ch 112, [1973] 2 All ER 437.

[140] [2007] EWCA Civ 1190.

that it was bound to follow its own decision in *Croke (A Minor)* v *Wiseman*,[141] even though that decision was inconsistent with *two* earlier decisions of the House of Lords.[142] The situation was not covered by the *per incuriam* exception as the court in *Croke* had been referred to the earlier decisions, but in the Court of Appeal's view any error in its reasoning could only be corrected by the House of Lords:[143]

If the first Court of Appeal has considered the decision of the House of Lords and either wrongly distinguished it or misinterpreted its effect the second Court of Appeal would be simply disagreeing with the reasoning of the first Court of Appeal; something which the doctrine of *stare decisis* forbids.

(3) **The court is not bound to follow a decision of its own if that decision was given *per incuriam*.** Thus, in *Royal Bank of Scotland* v *Etridge (No 2)*[144] the court refused to follow its own decision in *Royal Bank of Scotland* v *Etridge (No 1)*[145] because it had not, in the earlier case, been referred to two previous decisions by which it ought to have been bound.

If a decision is described as having been given *per incuriam* this usually means that the court has overlooked a relevant statutory provision or a binding precedent,[146] but there is a residual category of other cases in which the principle may be invoked. Thus, in *Williams* v *Fawcett*[147] the Court of Appeal rejected a number of earlier authorities on the grounds that there had been a 'manifest slip or error' affecting the liberty of the subject, and it was unlikely that the House of Lords would have the opportunity to correct this error. The court applied the same test in *Rickards* v *Rickards*[148] and refused to follow an earlier decision involving a wrongful rejection of jurisdiction by the court. In the circumstances of the case there was no possibility of an appeal to the House of Lords.

While he was Master of the Rolls, Lord Denning engaged in a tireless but ultimately unsuccessful campaign to give the Court of Appeal the freedom to depart from its previous decisions at will. In *Gallie* v *Lee*[149] he made the following assertion:

We are, of course, bound by the decisions of the House [of Lords], but I do not think we are bound by prior decisions of our own, or at any rate, not absolutely bound. We are not fettered as it was once thought. It was a self-imposed limitation; and we who imposed it can also remove it. The House of Lords have done it. So why should not we do likewise?

---

[141] [1982] 1 WLR 71, [1981] 3 All ER 852.

[142] *Pickett* v *British Rail Engineering Ltd* [1980] AC 136, [1979] 1 All ER 774; *Gammell* v *Wilson* [1982] AC 27, [1981] 1 All ER 578.

[143] [2007] EWCA Civ 1190 at [57], per Gage LJ. See also *Miliangos* v *George Frank (Textiles) Ltd* [1976] AC 443 at 479, [1975] 3 All ER 801 at 823, per Lord Simon. Cf. *Turton* v *Turton* [1988] Ch 542, [1987] 2 All ER 641.

[144] [1998] 4 All ER 705.   [145] [1997] 3 All ER 628.

[146] See p 87, *ante*.   [147] [1986] QB 604, [1985] 1 All ER 787.

[148] [1990] Fam 194, [1989] 3 All ER 193.

[149] [1969] 2 Ch 17 at 37, [1969] 1 All ER 1062 at 1072 (affirmed *sub nom Saunders* v *Anglia Building Society* [1971] AC 1004, [1970] 3 All ER 961).

This was, however, a minority opinion. Russell LJ saw the position of the House of Lords in quite a different light, saying of the Master of the Rolls:[150]

> I think that in one respect he has sought to wield a broom labelled 'for the use of the House of Lords only'. I do not support the suggestion that this court is free to override its own decisions...the availability of the House of Lords to correct error in the Court of Appeal makes it in my view unnecessary for this court to depart from its existing discipline.

In *Barrington v Lee*,[151] a case concerned with liability in respect of an estate agent's default over a deposit, Lord Denning again made the bold statement that the Court of Appeal was not bound by a previous decision on similar facts. Again, however, he found himself in the minority: while Edmund Davies and Stephenson LJJ felt able to distinguish the earlier case and to concur with Lord Denning on the result of the appeal, they both reaffirmed the principles set out in *Young v Bristol Aeroplane*. Faced with such opposition, Lord Denning was constrained to resile from the statements he had made in this case and *Gallie v Lee*, and in *Miliangos v George Frank (Textiles) Ltd*[152] he expressly applied the principles in *Young v Bristol Aeroplane Co Ltd*. Nevertheless in *Davis v Johnson*,[153] a controversial case dealing with the power of the courts to protect battered wives, Lord Denning led the full Court of Appeal in yet another attack on *Young*. This attack was repulsed when the case reached the House of Lords,[154] and the rule in *Young* was, in Lord Diplock's words, 'expressly, unequivocally and unanimously' reaffirmed.

The general rule that the Court of Appeal is bound to follow its previous decisions is now well-settled, and in the light of the unequivocal House of Lords decision in *Davis v Johnson* it is difficult to envisage the Court making any further attempt to free itself from this position. This does not, however, preclude the possibility of adding to the list of recognized exceptions, and the Court of Appeal's willingness to depart from a previous decision in order to give effect to changes in international law may be regarded as one such example.[155] The Court of Appeal has also held that it is not bound by its previous decisions on applications for permission to appeal,[156] though an earlier finding that it was not obliged to follow interlocutory decisions made by only two judges[157] has now been rejected.[158]

[150] [1969] 2 Ch 17 at 41, [1969] 1 All ER 1062 at 1082. The third member of the court, Salmon LJ, took a middle view and stated that any change in policy would require a pronouncement of the whole Court of Appeal. Nevertheless, in *Davis v Johnson* [1979] AC 264, [1978] 1 All ER 1132, Lord Salmon and other members of the House of Lords expressly reaffirmed *Young*'s case.
[151] [1972] 1 QB 326 at 338, [1971] 3 All ER 1231 at 1238; see also *Hanning v Maitland (No 2)* [1970] 1 QB 580 at 587, [1970] 1 All ER 812 at 815.
[152] [1975] QB 487, [1975] 1 All ER 1076.   [153] [1978] 2 WLR 182, [1978] 1 All ER 841.
[154] [1979] AC 264, [1978] 1 All ER 1132.
[155] *Trendtex Trading Corporation Ltd v Central Bank of Nigeria* [1977] QB 529, [1977] 1 All ER 881; see p 89, *ante*.
[156] *Clark v University of Lincolnshire and Humberside* [2000] 3 All ER 752, [2000] 1 WLR 1988. This is, of course, consistent with the current rule of practice that decisions on applications for permission to appeal cannot normally be cited as precedents in the civil courts; *Practice Direction (Citation of Authorities)* [2001] 2 All ER 510, [2001] 1 WLR 1001.
[157] *Boys v Chaplin* [1968] 2 QB 1, [1968] 1 All ER 283; *Welsh Development Agency v Redpath Dorman Long* [1994] 1 WLR 1409, [1994] 4 All ER 10.
[158] *Cave v Robinson Jarvis and Rolfe* [2001] EWCA Civ 245, [2002] 1 WLR 581.

Two further exceptions to the rule that the Court of Appeal is obliged to follow its previous decisions have arisen as a result of statutory intervention. Firstly, as already noted,[159] the Human Rights Act 1998 has important implications for the doctrine of precedent. Given that the Court of Appeal has already refused to follow an earlier House of Lords decision in order to give effect to Convention rights,[160] it seems certain that the Court will not hesitate to depart from its own previous decisions in similar circumstances. Secondly, when faced with a conflict between one of its own decisions (or a decision of the House of Lords) and a decision of the European Court of Justice, section 3 of the European Communities Act 1972 obliges the Court of Appeal to follow the latter.

It may be noted finally that a 'full court' of five or more judges of the Civil Division is sometimes convened to hear cases involving particularly important or difficult points of law. The full court has, however, no greater authority than the normal court and its decisions carry no more weight as precedents.[161]

Criminal Division. Decisions of the Criminal Division of the Court of Appeal are binding on all inferior courts, including the Divisional Court of the Queen's Bench Division. The Division regards itself as bound by decisions of its predecessor, the Court of Criminal Appeal, and also by decisions of the Civil Division of the Court of Appeal, subject to the exceptions contained in *Young* v *Bristol Aeroplane Co Ltd*. Thus in *DPP* v *Merriman*[162] the Criminal Division reluctantly allowed an appeal which was totally lacking in merit, because of the existence of a direct authority of the Court of Criminal Appeal in favour of the appellant. However, the court certified a point of law of general public importance and granted leave to appeal to the House of Lords. The appeal was subsequently allowed and the earlier authority was overruled.[163]

The Court of Criminal Appeal formulated the principle that it would not be bound by its own previous decisions where this would cause injustice to an appellant, the rationale being that the desire for justice transcends the desirability of certainty. In *R* v *Taylor*, Lord Goddard CJ explained the rule as follows:[164]

> This court...has to deal with questions involving the liberty of the subject, and if it finds, on reconsideration, that, in the opinion of a full court assembled for that purpose, the law has been either misapplied or misunderstood in a decision which it has previously given, and that, on the strength of that decision, an accused person has been sentenced and imprisoned, it is the bounden duty of the court to reconsider

[159] See p 79, *ante.*

[160] *Ghaidan* v *Godin-Mendoza* [2002] EWCA Civ 1533, [2003] Ch 380, [2002] 4 All ER 1162, discussed further at pp 55 and 80, *ante.*

[161] *Young* v *Bristol Aeroplane Co Ltd* [1944] KB 718, [1944] 2 All ER 293. Likewise the authority of a two-judge court is no less than that of a three-judge court: *Langley* v *North West Water Authority* [1991] 3 All ER 610, [1991] 1 WLR 697.

[162] [1971] 2 QB 310, [1971] 2 All ER 1424. [163] [1973] AC 584, [1972] 3 All ER 42.

[164] [1950] 2 KB 368, [1950] 2 All ER 170. See also *DPP* v *Merriman* [1973] AC 584 at 605, [1972] 3 All ER 42 at 58, per Lord Diplock; *R* v *Howe* [1986] QB 626, [1986] 1 All ER 833 (affirmed [1987] AC 417, [1987] 1 All ER 771). Cf. *R* v *Charles* [1976] 1 All ER 659, [1976] 1 WLR 248 (affirmed *sub nom Metropolitan Police Commissioner* v *Charles* [1977] AC 177, [1976] 3 All ER 112).

the earlier decision with a view to seeing whether that person had been properly convicted. The exceptions which apply in civil cases ought not to be the only ones applied in such a case as the present.

This rule was adopted by the Criminal Division of the Court of Appeal in *R* v *Gould*.[165] A recent example of the application of the rule is the case of *R* v *Simpson*,[166] in which the Criminal Division declined to follow its previous decision in *R* v *Palmer (John)* because it considered that the law in the earlier case had been misunderstood and misapplied.[167] The exceptional case of *R* v *James (Leslie)*, in which the Criminal Division followed a Privy Council decision instead of an earlier House of Lords ruling, can also be considered in this context.[168]

In the past, decisions of the Court of Criminal Appeal were somewhat less reliable as precedents than the decisions of other appellate courts. This is accounted for by the fact that the court rarely reserved judgment, only one judgment was usually given, and dissenting opinions were not recorded. Although section 59 of the Supreme Court Act 1981 expressly provides that separate judgments may be pronounced on a question of law, precedents of the Criminal Division of the Court of Appeal are still regarded with more circumspection than decisions of the Civil Division.

(d) High Court

Divisional courts. In civil matters, divisional courts are bound by decisions of the House of Lords and Court of Appeal. They are also bound by their own previous decisions to the same extent as the Court of Appeal, and this means that they are entitled to rely on the exceptions established in *Young* v *Bristol Aeroplane* and elsewhere.[169] Thus, when faced with a conflict between two of their previous decisions divisional courts can choose which one to follow, and they need not follow previous decisions which are incompatible with EC law, the Human Rights Act 1998, or any decision of the Court of Appeal, House of Lords, or ECJ. Divisional courts can also depart from their own previous decisions if they are regarded as having been made *per incuriam*, and occasionally, they have even rejected Court of Appeal decisions on this basis.[170] Divisional court

---

[165] [1968] 2 QB 65, [1968] 1 All ER 849. The necessity for a 'full court' of five or more judges seems to have been tacitly abolished, though *R* v *Newsome* [1970] 2 QB 711, [1970] 3 All ER 455 suggests that a court of five has a greater power to depart from earlier decisions. On occasions when the need to choose between conflicting decisions arises, a full court is sometimes convened; see, e.g., *R* v *Jackson* [1974] QB 802, [1974] 1 All ER 640. See also, Zellick, 'Precedent in the Court of Appeal, Criminal Division' [1974] Crim LR 222.

[166] [2003] EWCA Crim 1499, [2004] QB 118, [2003] 3 All ER 531. See also *R* v *Rowe* [2007] EWCA Crim 635, [2007] 3 WLR 177, [2007] 3 All ER 36.

[167] [2002] EWCA Crim 2202, [2003] 1 Cr App R (S) 12.

[168] [2006] EWCA Crim 14, [2006] QB 588, [2006] 1 All ER 759.

[169] See p 97, *ante*; *Huddersfield Police Authority* v *Watson* [1947] KB 842, [1947] 2 All ER 193.

[170] *R* v *Northumberland Compensation Tribunal, ex parte Shaw* [1952] 1 KB 338, [1952] 1 All ER 122; *Hughes* v *Kingston upon Hull City Council* [1999] QB 1193, [1999] 2 All ER 49. Cf. *Cassell & Co Ltd* v *Broome* [1972] AC 1027 at 1131, [1972] 1 All ER 801 at 874, in which Lord Diplock asserted that the *per incuriam* doctrine did not entitle either the Court of Appeal or the High Court to disregard any decision of a higher appellate court.

decisions in civil cases are binding on judges of the same division of the High Court sitting alone, and possibly on judges of other divisions.[171]

In criminal cases the position of the Divisional Court of the Queen's Bench Division is analogous to that of the Criminal Division of the Court of Appeal. Thus it is free to depart from its own decisions in the same circumstances as in that court.

Finally, when exercising its supervisory jurisdiction, a Divisional Court is in the same position as a High Court judge sitting alone, and it may depart from one of its own previous decisions if convinced that the decision is wrong. The above principles appear from the judgment of the Queen's Bench Divisional Court, delivered by Goff LJ in *R v Greater Manchester Coroner, ex parte Tal*.[172]

Judges at first instance. Decisions of High Court judges sitting alone at first instance are binding on inferior courts but not on other High Court judges. For this reason, principles of law contained only in first instance decisions should not be relied upon too heavily. Naturally, however, they are of persuasive authority and a High Court judge will hesitate before 'not following' the decision of one of his brethren, if only for reasons of comity. Nevertheless, where a first instance judge is clearly convinced that an earlier decision at first instance is wrong, he will be free to refuse to follow that decision.

There have been several direct clashes between judges deciding cases at first instance. A notable example concerned the question of whether a failure to wear a seat belt in a motor vehicle should be treated as contributory negligence in the event of an accident in which injury is sustained. This question divided the judges of the Queen's Bench Division in some fourteen reported cases between 1970 and 1975, before the Court of Appeal finally resolved the conflict in *Froom v Butcher*.[173]

It is sometimes said that Chancery Division judges are less willing than judges of other divisions to depart from decisions of their brethren. However, this is only true in the sense that there is often a greater risk in Chancery Division cases that departing from an earlier decision might disturb financial arrangements or deprive a person of a proprietary right.

High Court judges are bound by the decisions of divisional courts, the Court of Appeal, and the House of Lords. However, as with the appellate courts, the strict application of the *stare decisis* doctrine must be considered in the light of the High Court's statutory obligations to give effect to EC law and to decide cases in accordance with the Human Rights Act 1998.[174]

---

[171] *Re Seaford, Seaford v Seifert* [1967] P 325, [1967] 2 All ER 458 (reversed [1968] P 53, [1968] 1 All ER 482) in which a judge of the Probate, Divorce and Admiralty Division regarded himself as bound by a decision of the Divisional Court of the Queen's Bench Division. Cf. *Elderton v United Kingdom Totalisator Co Ltd* (1945) 61 TLR 529 (affirmed [1946] Ch 57, [1945] 2 All ER 624).

[172] [1985] QB 67, [1984] 3 All ER 240. A 'full' Divisional Court of five or more judges has no greater authority than a court of two or three: *Younghusband v Luftig* [1949] 2 KB 354, [1949] 2 All ER 72.

[173] [1976] QB 286, [1975] 3 All ER 520; all of the reported cases on the subject are reviewed in the judgment of Lord Denning MR in this case. The Court of Appeal concluded that failure to wear a seat belt *did* amount to contributory negligence. For another illustration of clashes between judges at first instance, see *Esso Petroleum Co Ltd v Harper's Garage (Stourport) Ltd* [1965] 3 WLR 469, [1965] 2 All ER 933 and *Petrofina Ltd v Martin* [1965] Ch 1073, [1965] 2 All ER 176.

[174] See pp 79 and 99, *ante*.

(e) County courts, magistrates' courts, the Crown Court

Magistrates' courts and county courts are bound by the decisions of all superior courts, including first instance decisions of the High Court. Judges deciding cases in the Crown Court are also bound by these decisions, despite the bold assertion of one circuit judge that he was not bound by decisions of the Divisional Court.[175] The decisions of one inferior court do not bind other inferior courts, chiefly because they are unlikely to address new legal principles and are rarely reported. Decisions made by Crown Court judges *are* occasionally reported, however, and they may have persuasive authority for other inferior courts, especially when the Crown Court is presided over by a High Court judge.

(f) Tribunals

Lower tribunals do not set binding precedents for themselves or for any other court, and they are bound by the decisions of the appellate tribunals and superior courts. The Employment Appeal Tribunal and other appellate tribunals are bound by decisions of the Court of Appeal and House of Lords, but they do not generally regard themselves as being bound by their own decisions.

7 SUMMARY

In conclusion, it would be optimistic to state categorically that the doctrine of binding precedent achieves certainty while retaining flexibility. Its operation depends, as with the interpretation of statutes, on each judge or court's conception of the judicial function. The rules for determining the *ratio decidendi* of a case and the hierarchy of the courts are sufficiently well defined to achieve legal certainty. On the other hand, the *per incuriam* doctrine, the process of distinguishing, the capacity of superior courts to overrule decisions, and the absolute power of Parliament to change the law, all serve to keep the doctrine flexible. In the last analysis the doctrine of precedent is usually seen to operate fairly, though how far this is attributable to the inherent qualities of the doctrine and how far to the good sense of English judges is a matter of debate.

LAW REPORTING

As stated at the beginning of this chapter, the doctrine of binding precedent became a part of English law only when the system of law reporting had become comprehensive. The doctrine of precedent, as such, is of far greater antiquity but it was only in the nineteenth century that precedents became binding rather than merely persuasive. If it were

---

[175] *R v Colyer* [1974] Crim LR 24. The judge's refusal to follow a decision of the Queen's Bench Divisional Court must surely have been incorrect, given that decisions of the divisional courts are even binding upon themselves.

possible to mark the turning point, the decision in *Mirehouse* v *Rennell*[176] in 1833 would appear to herald the evolution of the modern system.

The history of law reporting can be roughly divided into three periods: the period of the Year Books extending approximately from 1272 to 1535; the period of the private named reporters extending from 1535 to 1865; and the modern, semi-official system of reporting which began in 1865.

1 THE YEAR BOOKS

The Year Books are the first available law reports. They were first compiled during the reign of Edward I and their exact purpose is uncertain. They were certainly not intended for use by the judges as precedents, and were probably just notes compiled by students and junior advocates as guides to pleading and procedure. However, there are indications that they may have been used by some judges as a direct source of precedent. Thus in 1310 Stanton J referred to a case decided at least ten years earlier,[177] while Bereford CJ in 1312 cited a decision some twenty-five years old.[178] By the fifteenth century there are many examples of Year Book cases in which the judge is reported as having relied upon a number of old authorities, and there is ample evidence that judges were conscious of their decisions being recorded for use as precedents.[179] Compilation of printed Year Books ceased in about 1535.[180] With the introduction of printing in the fifteenth century, many Year Book manuscripts were printed in the so-called 'Black Letter' editions. The most widely used modern versions of the Year Books are the Rolls Series (RS) and the Selden Society Series (SS), both of which date from the early twentieth century. They contain the original text of the Year Book manuscripts, which are in 'law French', a peculiar combination of Norman French, English, and Latin, together with an English translation.

2 THE PRIVATE REPORTS

As soon as the compilation of the Year Books ceased, private sets of reports began to be produced and published under the name of the law reporter. These reports proliferated in the period of 1535 to 1865, and the citation of precedents became progressively more common as the reports became more comprehensive.

The standard of reporting varied greatly. At one end of the scale were those whose reports contain what are still regarded as classic expositions of the common law, with Coke being the most notable example. Coke's Reports (Co Rep) are so well known as to be citable merely as 'reports' (Rep), and they contain comprehensive expositions of virtually every aspect of the common law. Published between 1600 and 1658, Coke's Reports contain many of the great constitutional cases of the seventeenth century, such

---

[176] (1833) 1 Cl & Fin 527.
[177] *Kembeare* v *K* YB 4 Edw 2 (SS iv), 153. Note the method of citation by regnal year.
[178] *Anon* YB 6 Edw 2 (SS xiii), 43.
[179] For examples see Allen, *Law in the Making* (7th edn), pp 190 *et seq.*
[180] Although manuscript Year Books continued to be produced into the seventeenth century.

as *Prohibitions del Roy*,[181] *Proclamations*,[182] and *Magdalen College*.[183] Alongside Coke, other highly regarded law reporters include Dyer, Plowden, and Burrow. Burrow's Reports of cases in the Court of King's Bench are widely regarded as the first set of law reports produced in the modern pattern, since they contain headnotes and the argument of counsel is carefully separated from the judgment.

It must not be thought that every one of the private law reporters was a Plowden or a Coke. At the other end of the scale were reporters such as Barnardiston, Atkyns, and Espinasse, whose reports became virtually uncitable so low were they held in judicial esteem.[184] Indeed, Lord Mansfield would not permit certain series of reports to be cited to him, while Holt CJ famously complained that 'these scrambling reports will make us appear to posterity for a parcel of blockheads'.[185]

The private reports are cited by the name of the reporter (usually abbreviated) and a volume and page number. The date of the report is not part of the reference but is usually inserted in ordinary round brackets. Thus the reference to the case of *Pillans* v *Van Mierop* (1765) 3 Burr 1664 indicates that the case can be found in the third volume of Burrow's Reports at page 1664. In practice most law libraries have the reports of the private reporters in the reprinted edition known as 'the English Reports' (ER or Eng Rep).

3 THE PRESENT SYSTEM OF LAW REPORTING

(a) The Law Reports

In 1865 the system of private reporting gave way to current system. A Council was established to publish reports of superior court decisions as cheaply as possible, and it was, from its inception, under professional control. The Council was incorporated in 1870 as the Incorporated Council of Law Reporting for England and Wales.[186] It now produces the Law Reports, the Weekly Law Reports (WLR), the Industrial Cases Reports (ICR), and the Law Reports Statutes. The Law Reports are not an official publication, but judges are given the opportunity to revise reports of their own judgments and they are the series of reports to which counsel should refer when citing a case which is reported in them.[187] One advantage of these Reports over other series is that legal argument, as well as the judgments, is published. Where the court has adjourned to take time to consider its decision, judgment is said to be 'reserved'. This fact is indicated in the reports by the words *curia advisari vult, cur ad vult* or *cav*, and reserved judgments are generally accorded greater weight than *ex tempore* judgments.

Before 1875, cases published in the Law Reports were cited by reference to the court in which they were decided and a serial number dating from 1865, prefixed by the letters

---

[181] (1607) 12 Co Rep 63.   [182] (1610) 12 Co Rep 74.   [183] (1615) 11 Co Rep 66b.

[184] See Allen, *Law in the Making* (7th edn), pp 221 *et seq.*   [185] *Slater* v *May* (1704) 2 Ld Raym 1071.

[186] The Council is a charity: *Incorporated Council of Law Reporting for England and Wales v A-G* [1972] Ch 73, [1971] 3 All ER 1029.

[187] *Practice Note (CA: Reports: Citations)* [1991] 1 All ER 352; *Practice Direction (Citation of Authorities)* [2001] 2 All ER 510, [2001] 1 WLR 1001. The House of Lords has stated that counsel may refer to a report in Tax Cases, rather than the Law Reports: *Bray* v *Best* [1989] 1 All ER 969, [1989] 1 WLR 167.

LR. The date was not part of the reference and was therefore inserted in ordinary round brackets. Thus *Irving* v *Askew* (1870) LR 5 QB 208 was reported in the fifth volume of Reports of cases in the Court of Queen's Bench, at page 208. Between 1875 and 1890 citation was by an abbreviation of the appropriate division of the High Court (Ch D; QBD; PD; CPD; Ex D[188]) or App Cas for an appeal case. The prefix LR was dropped but the date was still not part of the reference and the serial number dated from 1875. An example of citation during this period is *Symons* v *Rees* (1876) 1 Ex D 416.

In 1891 the date was made part of the reference in place of a serial number and the letter D (for Division) was dropped. The fact that the date is part of the reference is signified by its inclusion in square brackets. There is a separate volume of Reports for each division of the High Court (QB; Ch; Fam),[189] and a separate volume for House of Lords and Privy Council cases (AC).[190] Court of Appeal decisions are reported in the volume for the division of the High Court from which the appeal came. County court appeals and appeals to the Criminal Division of the Court of Appeal are usually reported in the volume for the Queen's Bench Division. There is thus nothing in the reference to distinguish a Court of Appeal decision from a decision at first instance.

(b) The Weekly Law Reports

The Weekly Law Reports have been published since 1953 and they include a report of every decision which will ultimately appear in the Law Reports proper.[191] The cases are reported in full, but legal argument is omitted because of the restriction on space. In addition, many cases are published in the Weekly Law Reports which are not subsequently included in the Law Reports. These cases make up Volume 1, whereas cases destined to reach the Law Reports can be found in Volumes 2 and 3.

The year is part of the reference for cases published in the Weekly Law Reports, and it therefore appears in square brackets. There is, however, no attempt to classify cases by the court in which they were decided. All cases appear in 1 WLR, 2 WLR or 3 WLR irrespective of whether they are House of Lords or first instance decisions.

(c) Other series of reports

The All England Reports. Perhaps the most important of the commercially published reports are the All England Law Reports.[192] These are published on a weekly basis by

[188] The last two were abolished in 1880; see p 233, *post*.

[189] When the Family Division was named the Probate, Divorce and Admiralty Division, this volume of Reports was cited by the letter P.

[190] Before 1974 when a case reached the House of Lords, the Privy Council, or a Divisional Court on appeal, the appellant's name used to be cited first. Thus, for example, the case known in the Court of Appeal as *Lever Brothers Ltd* v *Bell* [1931] 1 KB 557 became *Bell* v *Lever Brothers Ltd* [1932] AC 161 in the House of Lords. This practice was altered in 1974, and petitions for leave to appeal and appeals to the House of Lords carry the same title that they had at first instance; [1974] 1 All ER 752, [1974] 1 WLR 305. In criminal cases this had the effect of terminating the practice whereby the Director of Public Prosecutions was substituted for *Rex* (or *Regina*).

[191] These replaced the 'Weekly Notes' (WN), which were published in the form of a current précis and were not strictly citeable as reports; see *Re Loveridge* [1902] 2 Ch 859 at 865, per Buckley J.

[192] The Law Journal Reports (LJ) and Law Times Reports (LT) have been incorporated in the All England Law Reports.

LexisNexis-Butterworths, and are eventually collated in annual volumes. Their virtue lies principally in the speed with which they follow decisions and the fact that they include many cases which do not find their way into the Law Reports. The All England Law Reports are cited by the year in square brackets, followed a volume number,[193] the abbreviation All ER and a page number.

'Official' reports. Several series of reports are published under government authority and they concentrate on reporting cases in certain specialized areas. These series include Reports of Tax Cases, Reports, of Patent, Design and Trade Mark Cases, and Immigration Appeal Reports.

Specialist reports published commercially. There are many series of specialist reports published commercially. For example, the Criminal Appeal Reports (CAR or Cr App R), first published shortly after the creation of the Court of Criminal Appeal, are still produced and include a number of criminal cases not reported elsewhere. Similarly Lloyd's List Law Reports (Lloyd's Rep) contain a number of commercial cases not reported elsewhere, while the Road Traffic Reports (RTR) contain, as the title would suggest, reports of road traffic cases. Other specialist series in general use are Local Government Reports (LGR), Building Law Reports (BLR), Simon's Tax Cases (STC), Property and Compensation Reports (PCR), Industrial Relations Law Reports (IRLR), Housing Law Reports (HLR), Fleet Street Patent Law Reports (FSR), and Human Rights Law Reports (HRLR).

European cases. European Community law decisions are to be found principally in the European Court Reports (ECR) published by the European Court of Justice, and the Common Market Law Reports (CMLR) which are an unofficial source. The main source of decisions of the European Court of Human Rights is the European Human Rights Reports series (EHRR).

Newspapers and periodicals. A number of legal periodicals such as the Solicitors Journal, Justice of the Peace, Estates Gazette, Criminal Law Review, New Law Journal, and Current Law include notes of cases to which reference may be made in the absence of a full report in a recognized series. In addition, *The Times,* the *Guardian*, and the *Independent* also publish reports of decided cases, and while these are inevitably brief, they may be cited in court in the absence of an alternative source.

(d) Electronic sources

Many of the different series of law reports are now available electronically, either on CD Rom or on the Internet, and the use of this technology allows lawyers to access an increasingly large volume of case law, often within a relatively short time of the decisions being made. Important examples of commercially produced online databases include LexisNexis, Westlaw, Lawtel and Casetrack. In addition, the decisions of several courts,

---

[193] There are usually three or four volumes published each year.

including the House of Lords[194] and Privy Council,[195] can be accessed through official web sites,[196] as can cases decided by the European Court of Justice[197] and the European Court of Human Rights.[198]

(e) Neutral citation of judgments

With effect from 11 January 2001, the Lord Chief Justice issued a Practice Direction[199] establishing a new system of neutral citation for cases decided by the Administrative Court and Court of Appeal. Under this system an official number is assigned to each new decision, and when used in conjunction with the year and the abbreviation for the court issuing the decision, this gives each case a unique reference. In addition, judgments of the courts concerned are now issued with numbered paragraphs instead of page numbers. Thus, to adopt the example used in the Practice Direction, paragraph 30 of the tenth case decided by the Civil Division of the Court of Appeal in 2001 would be cited as [2001] EWCA Civ 10 at [30]. The Practice Direction further provides that when used in court, the neutral citation of a judgment should be given before the citation from the law report series. Lord Woolf CJ explained the reasons for this new system as follows:[200]

> The main reason of these changes is to facilitate the publication of judgments on the World Wide Web and their subsequent use by the increasing numbers of those who have access to the Web. The changes should also assist those who use and wish to search judgments stored on electronic databases.

Although not covered by the Practice Direction, the House of Lords, the Privy Council, and even the Immigration Appeals Tribunal have adopted the same approach, and the system of neutral citation has now been extended to all divisions of the High Court.[201] The correct form of citation for these courts is illustrated in the examples below:

R v *Lambert* [2001] UKHL 37	(House of Lords)
A v *B* [2002] EWCA Civ 337	(Court of Appeal, Civil Division)
R v *Barker* [2002] EWCA Crim 1508	(Court of Appeal, Criminal Division)
Percy v *DPP* [2001] EWHC 1125 (Admin)	(Administrative Court)
Douglas v *Hello* [2003] EWHC 786 (QB)	(High Court, Queen's Bench Division)
Re B [2002] EWHC 429 (Fam)	(High Court, Family Division)[202]
B v *Auckland District Law Society* [2003] UKPC 38	(Privy Council)
S v *Secretary of State for the Home Dept.* [2003] UKIAT 3	(Immigration Appeals Tribunal)

---

[194] www.parliament.uk/judicial_work/judicial_work.cfm
[195] www.privy-council.org.uk   [196] See also: www.courtservice.gov.uk
[197] http://www.curia.europa.eu/en/index.htm   [198] www.echr.coe.int
[199] *Practice Direction (Sup Ct: Form of Judgments)* [2001] 1 All ER 193, [2001] 1 WLR 194.
[200] Ibid at [3].
[201] *Practice Direction (Sup Ct: Judgments: Neutral Citations)* [2002] 1 All ER 351, [2002] 1 WLR 346.
[202] Other categories of High Court decision use the following abbreviations in place of (Fam): Chancery Division (CH); Patent's Court (Pat); Commercial Court (Comm); Admiralty Court (Admlty); Technology and Construction Court (TCC).

(f) Weaknesses in the present system of reporting

The most obvious criticism that can be made of the present system of law reporting in England is that it remains informal and the selection of cases for reporting is entirely at the discretion of the law reporters. While there cannot be many important cases which escape the elaborate net of the law reporters, there are undoubtedly some: the Court of Appeal, for example, decides about 3,000 cases every year, of which only a small proportion are reported. This has been remedied to an extent by the proliferation of commercial series of law reports, and coupled with the availability of computerized databases this means that in one sense there is now hardly ever an 'unreported' case.

While this may have gone some way towards addressing the risk that important decisions may be overlooked, it has, paradoxically, led some to suggest that *too many* cases are now available to practitioners. The citation of unreported cases and cases which do not appear in the Law Reports has become increasingly common, and concern at the effect of this on the length and cost of litigation has led the courts to restrict the use of unreported decisions as precedents.[203]

It can also be argued that the system involves an unnecessary duplication of effort, since many cases are reported in full in at least four different series of reports, in addition to being noted in newspapers and numerous periodicals.

On the initiative of the then Lord Chancellor, a Committee was set up to report on the state of law reporting. Its report, published in 1940, was somewhat negative in character. It rejected the proposal to grant a monopoly to the Incorporated Council of Law Reporting, being content to state that the Law Reports should be cited in preference to any other series. The Committee also rejected a proposal that law reporters should be subject to a system of licensing. Most of the positive recommendations in the 1940 Report were contained in the minority report of Professor Goodhart, the main suggestion being that each court should produce an authenticated transcript which would be filed with the court records. Copies of these transcripts would be available for sale to law reporters and other interested persons, which would in effect make law reports 'official'. However, the majority of the Committee rejected this proposal as expensive and inconvenient, and the system of law reporting in England continues to operate on an unofficial and informal basis.

FURTHER READING

ALLEN, *Law in the Making* (Oxford University Press: 7th edn, 1966)

CONAGLEN and NOLAN, 'Precedent from the Privy Council' (2006) 122 LQR 349

CROSS and HARRIS, *Precedent in English Law* (Clarendon Press: 4th edn, 1991)

MEAD, 'Swallowing the Camel, Straining at the Gnat: The Implications of *Mendoza* v *Ghaidan*' [2003] 5 EHRLR 501 at 509

---

[203] *Roberts Petroleum Ltd* v *Bernard Kenny* [1983] 2 AC 192, [1983] 1 All ER 564; *Practice Direction (Citation of Authorities)* [2001] 2 All ER 510, [2001] 1 WLR 1001. See p 77, *ante*.

PRIME and SCANLAN, 'Stare Decisis and the Court of Appeal: Judicial Confusion and Judicial Reform' (2004) 23 CJQ 212

ZANDER, *The Law-Making Process* (Cambridge University Press: 6th edn, 2004)

ZELLICK, 'Precedent in the Court of Appeal, Criminal Division' [1974] Crim LR 222

4

EUROPEAN LAW[1]

INTRODUCTION

This chapter looks at the role of European law within the English legal system. Since the UK joined what is now the European Community in 1970, it has become an increasingly important source of domestic legal rules. In addition, the doctrine of the supremacy of European over national law has significant implications for the UK's established constitutional orthodoxy. Any work on the English legal system would therefore be incomplete without some discussion of the role of European law within it. The specific areas addressed by this chapter will include:

- The history and development of the European Community and European Union.
- The general scope of European law and the principles of subsidiarity and proportionality.
- The structure and functions of the main European institutions.
- The different types of European law and the concepts of direct and indirect effect.
- The relationship between European and domestic law.
- The role of the European Court of Justice and the Article 234 procedure.

A BRIEF HISTORY

On 1 January 1973 the UK became a Member State of the European Communities. There were originally three communities: the European Coal and Steel Community (ECSC), the European Atomic Energy Community (Euratom), and the European Economic Community (EEC). The EEC, which was by far the most ambitious and significant of the three projects, was officially renamed 'the European Community' (EC) by the Treaty on European Union in 1992. The ECSC expired on 23 July 2002, leaving Euratom and

---

[1] See generally, Steiner, Woods and Twigg-Flesner, *EU Law* (9th edn, 2006); Hartley, *The Foundations of European Community Law* (6th edn, 2007); Wyatt and Dashwood, *European Union Law* (5th edn, 2006); Craig and De Búrca, *EU Law: Text, Cases and Materials* (4th edn, 2007).

the EC as the two remaining elements of the European Communities. Further changes will take effect once the process of ratifying the Treaty of Lisbon is completed.[2] From this point onwards the European Community will be replaced and succeeded by the European Union, and the Treaty establishing the European Community – the Treaty of Rome – will be renamed 'the Treaty on the Functioning of the European Union'.

Created in 1957 by the Treaty of Rome,[3] the European Community (or the EEC as it then was) initially comprised six members,[4] but has since expanded to its current composition of twenty-seven Member States.[5] The Treaty reflected a post-war desire to achieve stability through European unity, and the aim set out in the Preamble was to create an 'ever closer union' amongst the peoples of Europe. This was to be achieved through common action in the economic field. The Community was to have its own institutions, along with laws that could regulate the powers and obligations of Member States in economic matters.

1 THE SINGLE EUROPEAN ACT AND THE TREATY ON EUROPEAN UNION

The Community has now developed far beyond the original aims set by the Treaty of Rome. In 1987 the Single European Act was adopted,[6] which amended the Treaty and established the objective of making 'concrete progress towards European unity'. The process of amendment and reform was continued by the Treaty on European Union (TEU), which is more commonly referred to as the Maastricht Treaty. The UK ratified this Treaty in 1993 after considerable political controversy,[7] and it was given effect in law by the European Communities (Amendment) Act 1993. Not only did the Maastrich Treaty formally re-name the EEC as the 'European Community', it also radically amended the Treaty of Rome in order to achieve its aims. These aims are stated in the Preamble to be a continuation of the process of 'ever closer union', economic and monetary union, the development of a single currency,[8] common citizenship, common foreign and defence policies, and the enhancement of the democratic functions of Community institutions.

The effects of the Maastricht Treaty were significant. Firstly, it extended the area of legal competence of the Community: it created a common citizenship, expanded existing rights of movement and voting, increased co-ordination of general economic policy,

---

[2] This is due to happen by 1 January 2009: see p 113, *post*.

[3] The provisions of this Treaty were reorganized and renumbered by the Treaty of Amsterdam (in force since 1 May 1999). This chapter will adopt the current numbers when referring to those provisions, unless otherwise indicated. The Treaty provisions are due to be renumbered again under the Treaty of Lisbon: see p 113, *post*.

[4] Belgium, France, Germany, Italy, Luxembourg, and the Netherlands.

[5] Denmark, Ireland and the UK became members in 1973; Greece in 1981; Portugal and Spain in 1986; Finland, Austria and Sweden in 1995; Cyprus, the Czech Republic, Estonia, Hungary, Latvia, Lithuania, Malta, Poland, the Slovak Republic, and Slovenia in 2004; and Bulgaria and Romania in 2007. The number of Member States could rise to thirty if negotiations with Croatia, Turkey, and Macedonia come to fruition.

[6] Despite the name, this is a Treaty and should not be confused with an Act of the UK Parliament.

[7] For an unsuccessful challenge to the incorporation of the Treaty, see *R v Secretary of State for Foreign Affairs, ex parte Lord Rees-Mogg* [1994] QB 552, [1994] 1 All ER 457.

[8] The UK and Denmark reserved their positions on aspects of economic and monetary union, as did Sweden when it joined in 1995. The other 12 states adopted the Euro in 1999, and their national currencies ceased to be legal tender three years later.

established a Central Bank, and increased the rights of workers. Secondly, the Treaty established a European Union (EU), founded on the existing Member States of the European Communities. The EC and its body of laws formed one of the three pillars of the European Union, the other two being concerned with (a) establishing a common foreign and security policy, and (b) achieving co-operation in justice and home affairs. These other two pillars did not form part of the EC framework, with the result that decisions made under them have thus far been made at a political level and have not been subject to the jurisdiction of the European Court of Justice. More recent reforms mean that this position is now changing.

2   THE TREATY OF AMSTERDAM[9]

The next significant step was the signing of the Treaty of Amsterdam in 1997. The Treaty came into force on 1 May 1999 and made substantive amendments to both the EC Treaty and the Treaty on European Union. It also made specific commitments to a number of important non-economic goals, including human rights, environmental protection, and equality. Another important objective was to simplify the existing treaties by removing obsolete provisions, and most of the provisions in the earlier treaties were renumbered as a result.[10] The position of the European Parliament was also strengthened.[11] Economic co-operation still lay at the heart of the 'closer Europe' objective, but this was now balanced against other important aims.

From a legal perspective, one of the most important changes brought about by the Treaty of Amsterdam was the re-drawing of the boundaries between the EC and the EU. The Justice and Home Affairs pillar of the EU was re-titled 'Police and Judicial Co-operation in Criminal Matters', and a large part of it was brought within the framework of the EC pillar, making it susceptible to the jurisdiction of the European Court of Justice. Article 6(2) is another EU provision which was expressly made justiciable by the Treaty of Amsterdam. This provides that:

> The Union shall respect fundamental rights as guaranteed by the European Convention on Human Rights and Fundamental Freedoms...as general principles of Community law.

However, the second EU pillar – the Common Foreign and Security Policy – still lies beyond the jurisdiction of the Court of Justice.

3   THE TREATY OF NICE AND THE CHARTER
OF FUNDAMENTAL RIGHTS

The Treaty of Nice was signed by the Member States on 26 February 2001 but it did not come into force until 1 February 2003.[12] Unlike its predecessors this Treaty was

---

[9] Given effect in the UK by the European Communities (Amendment) Act 1998.

[10] See n 3, *ante*.   [11] See p 118, *post*.

[12] The process of ratification was initially delayed when the Irish rejected the Treaty in a referendum in June 2001. The Irish government was eventually able to proceed with ratification following a second referendum in October 2002. The Treaty was given effect in the UK by the European Communities (Amendment) Act 2002.

primarily concerned with institutional reform, and it paved the way for the number of Member States to be increased from fifteen. In anticipation of the likelihood that achieving unanimity would become more difficult as the EU expanded, it also provided for more measures to be adopted by qualified majority.[13]

Another important document to be agreed when the European Council met in Nice was the Charter of Fundamental Rights of the European Union. The Charter sets out a number of economic and social rights of the kind that one might expect from an organization founded on an economic agenda. Thus it includes the right to education, the right to engage in work, the right not to be dismissed unjustifiably, and the right to collective bargaining. However, it also includes many of the civil and political rights found in most other international human rights agreements,[14] along with more novel ones such as the right to protection of family data. The civil and political rights correspond closely with those found in the ECHR,[15] and to avoid any inconsistency the Charter states that:[16]

> In so far as this Charter contains rights which correspond to rights guaranteed by the Convention for the Protection of Human Rights and Fundamental Freedoms, the meaning and scope of those rights shall be the same as those laid down by the said Convention. This provision shall not prevent Union law providing more extensive protection.

The Charter was signed in December 2000. At that time it was not expressed to be legally binding, but the Treaty of Lisbon has since provided for a new Article 6(1) to be added to the Treaty on European Union. This will give the rights, freedoms and principles set out in the Charter the same legal value as the Treaties, meaning that they will be binding on EU institutions as well as on the Member States when they are implementing EU law. The UK and Poland, however, have both negotiated exemptions.

4 THE TREATY OF LISBON: A CONSTITUTION IN ALL BUT NAME?

In 2004, almost three years after the idea was first accepted in principle, the Heads of State and Government formally signed the EU Constitutional Treaty. The intention was that this document should replace the four major treaties on which the Union is founded, and that the EU should be given a distinct legal personality. The idea was to formally merge the EU with the EC and abolish its pillar structure, in addition to incorporating the Charter of Fundamental Rights into the main body of European Law. The Constitution was also intended to make the EU more democratic, and to this end many of its provisions were concerned with institutional reform.

The Constitution was an ambitious and controversial project, and despite being ratified by several Member States, it was effectively derailed by rejection in national referenda in both France and the Netherlands. The UK's referendum plans were postponed

---

[13] See p 118, *post*.
[14] For example, it includes provisions on equality, freedom of expression, and privacy.
[15] See chapter 6.   [16] Article 52(3).

indefinitely, and the President of the European Commission acknowledged that the Constitution had probably been dealt a fatal blow:[17]

> It is difficult to see what a renegotiation would achieve. It is highly unlikely it would produce a radically different or better document. The Constitution is already the best possible compromise. It represents a delicate balance of competing views, which contains many improvements to the way in which the EU carries out its business. That is why there is no plan B.

A 'plan B' eventually did emerge in the shape of the Treaty of Lisbon, and although billed as an 'amending' treaty it will bring about many of the changes intended by the ill-fated Constitution. It will significantly amend both the Treaty on European Union and the Treaty of Rome (to be known in future as the Treaty on the Functioning of the European Union), and as stated previously, it will give legal effect to the Charter of Fundamental Rights. It provides for the EU to formally replace and succeed the EC, and it will give the EU a distinct legal personality. It also incorporates many of the institutional and democratic changes originally set out in the Constitution: it will, for example, reduce the size of the European Commission, redistribute the seats within the European Parliament, and give the Parliament an enhanced role. National Parliaments will also have a greater role, as they will have the opportunity to consider proposals for new EU legislation directly. The EU will be forced to reconsider any proposed laws which are deemed by at least a third of national Parliaments to infringe the principle of subsidiarity,[18] and if a majority of national Parliaments oppose a proposal it may be struck down altogether.

The Treaty was signed by representatives from each Member State in December 2007, but it will not take effect until all twenty-seven states have ratified it. This is scheduled to happen by 1 January 2009.

THE SCOPE OF EUROPEAN LAW

Far from being a separate system of law, European law is now a significant source of English law. In *Bulmer Ltd* v *J Bollinger SA*, Lord Denning MR stated:[19]

> The treaty does not touch any of the matters which concern solely the mainland of England and the people in it. These are still governed by English law. They are not affected by the treaty. But when we come to matters with a European element, the treaty is like an incoming tide. It flows into the estuaries and up the rivers. It cannot be held back. In future, in transactions which cross the frontiers we must no longer speak or think of English law as something on its own. We must speak or think of Community law, of Community rights and obligations, and we must give effect to them.

---

[17] Jose Manuel Barroso, speaking at the National Forum on Europe, Dublin, 30 June 2005.

[18] 'Subsidiarity' means that decisions must be taken at a level which is as close as possible to the citizens of the Union.

[19] [1974] Ch 401 at 418, [1974] 2 All ER at 1231; see p 142, *post*.

This statement significantly underestimated the involvement of Community law beyond matters that 'cross frontiers', and today does not at all reflect the true legal position. Transactions which concern 'solely the mainland of England and the people in it' may nevertheless be affected by Community provisions. Some aspects of EC law concern obligations of an economic character, which are imposed on Member States rather than on individuals. Others, however, create individually enforceable rights, even within litigation that appears on its face to have no European context. Article 141, for example, concerns equality of treatment between male and female employees, while Article 174 provides for the regulation of environmental matters. Even where the implementation of Community obligations is achieved by domestic legislation, it is clear that the influence of European law is significant.

The scope of the Community's legal competence is subject only to the limits imposed by the EC Treaty, and many of its provisions are drafted in very wide terms. For example, legitimate areas of Community activity under Articles 3 to 5 include the elimination of restrictions on the free movement of goods and services, a common commercial policy, the creation of an internal market, free movement of persons, common agricultural, fisheries and transport policies, competition policy, social and environmental policies, consumer protection, and measures in the spheres of energy, civil protection, and tourism. In addition, Article 94 empowers the Council to issue directives for the approximation of laws, regulations, or administrative provisions directly affecting the common market, and the European Community may enter into treaties and international agreements in order to fulfil its objectives.[20]

1 THE PRINCIPLE OF SUBSIDIARITY

Article 5 of the EC Treaty outlines the Community's relationship with its Member States by reference to the principle of subsidiarity:[21]

> In areas which do not fall within its exclusive competence, the Community shall take action, in accordance with the principle of subsidiarity, only if and in so far as the objectives of the proposed action cannot be sufficiently achieved by the Member States and can therefore, by reason of the scale or effects of the proposed action, be better achieved by the Community.

The wording of this provision is arguably inconsistent with the principle that EC law is supreme, since this principle suggests that the Community should have the final word on *any* matter within its competence, regardless of whether this competence is 'exclusive' or not. Moreover, there is no agreed method for determining whether the Community's competence in a particular matter *is* exclusive. In *UK* v *EU Council*[22] the UK challenged the Working Time Directive made under Article 118a (now 138) of the Treaty, arguing that it conflicted with the principle of subsidiarity. In the UK's view there was no evidence

---

[20] See Article 133; to be renumbered Article 207 by the Treaty of Lisbon.

[21] This will be replaced by a new Article 3b of the Treaty on European Union once the Treaty of Lisbon is implemented. However, the new provision will not significantly alter the meaning of the principle.

[22] Case C-84/94, [1996] All ER (EC) 877.

that the aims of the Directive could not instead be achieved by action at a domestic level. However, the Court of Justice rejected this argument on the basis that Health and Safety issues fell within the Council's competence and the Council had an obligation to adopt minimum standards.[23]

The Member States sought to clarify the subsidiarity principle in a Protocol to the Treaty of Amsterdam. This provides that:[24]

> Subsidiarity is a dynamic concept and should be applied in the light of the object-
> ives set out in the Treaty. It allows Community action within the limits of its powers
> to be expanded where circumstances so require, and conversely, to be restricted or
> discontinued where it is no longer required.

The Protocol also introduced a requirement for new legislative proposals to include state-ments detailing their compliance with the principles of subsidiarity and proportional-ity. The Treaty of Lisbon will build on these changes by enabling national Parliaments to call for a review of any draft legislation which is thought to contravene the principle of subsidiarity.[25]

THE INSTITUTIONS

The EC and the EU operate through four main institutions, though these institutions have only a limited role with regard to foreign and security policy and certain other aspects of EU business. These institutions are the Council, the Commission, the Court of Justice, and the European Parliament.

1 THE COUNCIL

The Council of the European Union, formerly known as the Council of Ministers,[26] is the EU's main legislative and decision-making body. Article 202 of the EC Treaty states that its task is to ensure that the Treaty's objectives are obtained, and that the general economic policies of the Member States are co-ordinated. It also empowers the Council to 'take decisions', which primarily means approving legislation proposed by the Commission.[27] The Council is also responsible for negotiating with non-EU states, approving the EU budget, and making decisions under the second and third pillars.[28]

---

[23] The Court also rejected an argument that the Directive should have been made under a different provi-sion which would have given the UK a power of veto.

[24] The Protocol on the Application of the Principles of Subsidiarity and Proportionality.

[25] See Article 6 of the new Protocol on the Application of the Principles of Subsidiarity and Proportionality.

[26] It was re-named in 1993: Council Decision 93/592. It should not be confused with the European Council, which consists of the Heads of State and foreign ministers of the EU countries, together with the President and the President of the Commission. Under the Treaty of Lisbon the European Council will become a full EU institution with a permanent President.

[27] Under Article 208 (to be renumbered Article 241 by the Treaty of Lisbon) the Council may also initiate legislation by asking the Commission to examine a particular issue and submit its proposals.

[28] See p 111, *ante*.

The Council is composed of the ministers from each Member State,[29] with the precise composition at any given time being determined by the matter under discussion. For example, a Council meeting to discuss environmental issues would be attended by the environment Minister from each state and it would be referred to as 'the Environment Council'. For the purposes of continuity, a permanent committee of officials (COREPAR)[30] conducts much of the Council's routine work for later ratification. In addition, the Treaty of Lisbon provides that in future the Council will be assisted by a High Representative of the Union for Foreign Affairs and Security Policy.[31] The Presidency of the Council is held by each State in turn for a period of six months. The main functions of the Presidency are to convene and chair meetings of the Council, and also to determine the agendas.

The Treaty requires decisions on certain matters to be unanimous, but in most areas the Council operates on the basis of qualified majority voting (QMV).[32] Each Member State is entitled to cast a certain number of votes, with the numbers being weighted to give the most votes to the most populous countries. The current QMV rules date from 2004, when the EU was expanded from fifteen states. The UK, France, Germany, and Italy now have twenty-nine votes each, followed by Spain and Poland with twenty-seven. The least populous state, Malta, has just three. A qualified majority requires at least 72 per cent of the available votes and the approval of a majority (or sometimes a two-thirds majority) of the Member States.[33] In addition, a Member State can ask for confirmation that the votes cast in favour represent at least 62 per cent of the EU's population. This means that if a handful of large countries act together, they will be able to veto measures which have the support of the remaining states.

The Treaty of Lisbon provides for QMV to become the default method of decision-making within the Council,[34] and this means that it will be extended to a whole new range of policy areas. From 2014 a new system of 'double majority voting' will be phased in. Under this system, a qualified majority will require at least 55 per cent of the members of the Council (i.e. fifteen out of the twenty-seven states) to vote in favour of a measure. Those voting in favour will also have to represent at least 65 per cent of the EU's population.

2 THE COMMISSION

The powers of the Commission are set out in Article 211 of the EC Treaty.[35] They principally concern the formulation of legislative proposals and the implementation and enforcement of measures adopted by the institutions. The Commission can investigate potential breaches of Community law and may refer them to the European

---

[29] Article 203; to be replaced by provisions in a new Article 9B of the TEU once the Treaty of Lisbon is implemented.

[30] Article 207; to be renumbered Article 240 by the Treaty of Lisbon.

[31] See the proposed new Article 9B(2) of the TEU.

[32] Article 205; to be renumbered Article 238 by the Treaty of Lisbon. The Council can make certain decisions by a simple majority on the basis of one vote per State, but this is generally limited to decisions about procedural matters.

[33] See Article 3 of the Protocol on EU Enlargement, attached to the Treaty of Nice.

[34] By inserting a new Article 9C into the TEU.

[35] To be repealed and superseded by a new Article 9D of the TEU once the Treaty of Lisbon is ratified.

Court of Justice,[36] although frequently it is able to resolve such issues through political negotiations. The Commission can even impose its own sanctions where it finds breaches of competition law, fining states and large companies which are found to have engaged in anti-competitive behaviour.[37] Finally, the Commission is also responsible for managing the EU budget, and acting together with the Council it is able to represent the EU at an international level.

The Commissioners hold office for a renewable term of five years,[38] with each one being responsible for a particular policy area. There is currently one Commissioner per country,[39] but the Treaty of Lisbon provides for this number to be reduced from 2014 onwards. In future only two-thirds of Member States will have a Commissioner at any given time, based on a system of equal rotation.[40]

3 THE PARLIAMENT

Although originally comprising members nominated by Member States, the European Parliament has been directly elected since 1979.[41] Elections are held every five years, with the total number of MEPs now standing at 785. The UK currently contributes seventy-eight MEPs, but this number will be reduced to seventy-two from 2009 onwards.[42] The Treaty of Lisbon provides for the total number of MEPs to be capped at 751 (including the President), and when this comes into effect each state will be represented by between six and ninety-six MEPs.[43] The Parliament holds plenary sessions in both Strasbourg and Brussels, although much of the preparatory work is done in committees. The General Secretariat and its departments are based in Luxembourg.

In the original Article 137 of the EC Treaty (now 189), the role of the Parliament was stated to be 'advisory and supervisory'. Its position has since been considerably strengthened and it now has much greater involvement in the legislative process. It also has important roles in approving the Community budget and scrutinizing the other institutions. There are different legislative procedures for different areas of EC law, and many of them now require the approval or involvement of the Parliament. The most significant of these is the co-decision procedure established under Article 251, which, although rather complicated, effectively gives the Parliament a power of veto in a wide range of matters. The range of measures made by this procedure will increase considerably once the Treaty of Lisbon is ratified; so much so that it will be known in future as 'the ordinary legislative procedure'.[44] Despite this welcome development, however, the Parliament will still lack the power to legislate independently.

---

[36] Article 226; to be renumbered Article 258 by the Treaty of Lisbon.

[37] See Articles 81–83; to be renumbered Articles 101–103 by the Treaty of Lisbon.

[38] Article 214; to be replaced by provisions in a new Article 9D of the TEU under the Treaty of Lisbon.

[39] Article 4 of the Protocol on EU Enlargement.

[40] As provided by the new Article 9D(5) of the TEU, to be inserted by the Treaty of Lisbon.

[41] In 1999 a system of proportional representation was introduced in the UK for the election of MEPs: European Parliamentary Elections Act 1999 (replaced by the European Parliamentary Elections Act 2002).

[42] Article 190, as amended following the accession of Bulgaria and Romania.

[43] See the proposed new Article 9A(2) of the TEU.

[44] Article 2(2)(c), Treaty of Lisbon.

In addition to its legislative role, the Parliament can ask questions of the Commission and Council, and it can even censure the Commission and remove it on a motion passed by a two-thirds majority.[45] Though the power of censure was once regarded as a largely theoretical sanction, a significant milestone was reached in 1999 when the *threat* of a vote of no confidence forced the entire Commission to resign. This action followed a damning report into accusations of maladministration and fraud in matters for which the Commission was responsible. Had the Commission not resigned of its own accord the Parliament would undoubtedly have forced it to do so by passing a motion of no confidence.[46]

4 THE COURT OF JUSTICE

The Court of Justice consists of one judge from each Member State, assisted by eight Advocates-General. It can sit either in chambers of three or five judges, in a Grand Chamber of thirteen judges, or exceptionally, in plenary session.[47] It has a crucial role in enforcing Community obligations and in ensuring the uniform interpretation of European law throughout the Community.[48] Cases reach the Court either through direct actions or through references from national courts on points of Community law. Member States are obliged to apply its principles within their own jurisdictions, and the UK gives effect to this obligation by virtue of the European Communities Act 1972.

A Court of First Instance was created in 1988 to ease the problems of workload and delay which had bedevilled the Court of Justice.[49] The Court of First Instance deals with disputes between the Community and its servants, along with actions for judicial review brought by natural or other legal persons. Since the Treaty of Nice came into force on 1 February 2003, it has also been able to deal with some references from national courts under the Article 234 procedure. The work of both the Court of First Instance and the Court of Justice is considered in more detail later in this chapter.[50]

THE SOURCES OF COMMUNITY LAW

1 LEGISLATION

The Treaties are the primary source of European law, and they create a wide framework of powers, duties, and individual rights. Their provisions are framed in broad terms,

---

[45] Article 201; to be renumbered Article 234 by the Treaty of Lisbon.

[46] See Craig, 'The Fall and Renewal of the Commission: Accountability, Contract and Administrative Organisation' (2000) 6 ELJ 98.

[47] Article 221; to be renumbered Article 251 by the Treaty of Lisbon. See also, the proposed new Article 9F of the TEU.

[48] *Van Gend en Loos v Nederlandse Administratie de Belastingen* Case 26/62 [1963] ECR 1, [1963] CMLR 105; *R v Secretary of State for Transport, ex parte Factortame* Case C-213/89 [1990] ECR I-2433, [1990] 3 CMLR 1.

[49] Article 225; to be renumbered Article 251 by the Treaty of Lisbon.

[50] See p 135, *post*.

requiring further legislative action and subsequent interpretation by the Court of Justice. By Article 249[51] the Community institutions are empowered to issue regulations, directives, decisions, recommendations, and opinions. These are the instruments through which the policies inherent in the Treaties are achieved. Regulations, directives, and decisions may be classed as 'secondary' or 'delegated' Community legislation, and their legality may be challenged in the Court of Justice. However, national courts have no power to declare Community measures invalid unless they have already been declared as such by the Court of Justice.[52] If the legality of a Community measure is raised as an issue in a domestic case, the national court may make a reference to the Court of Justice for a ruling on the matter. In some circumstances it will be under a duty to do so.[53]

The differences between the types of instrument set out in Article 249 are as follows:

> A regulation shall have general application. It shall be binding in its entirety and directly applicable in all Member States.
>
> A directive shall be binding, as to the result to be achieved, upon each Member State to which it is addressed, but shall leave to the national authorities the choice of form and methods.
>
> A decision shall be binding in its entirety upon those to whom it is addressed.[54] Recommendations and opinions shall have no binding force.

There is thus a distinction between regulations and decisions on the one hand, and directives, recommendations, and opinions on the other. Only the former are immediately binding, although the doctrine of direct effects may confer a similar status on directives in practice. Where a measure is not immediately binding the task of implementation is left to the Member States. It should also be noted that only regulations and decisions may be challenged directly by individuals under Article 230:[55]

> Any natural or legal person may...institute proceedings against a decision addressed to that person or against a decision which, although in the form of a regulation or decision addressed to another person, is of direct and individual concern to the former.

2 CASE LAW

The other important source of Community law is the case law of the Court of Justice. The doctrine establishing the supremacy of Community law owes its origins to the court's

---

[51] To be renumbered Article 263 by the Treaty of Lisbon.

[52] *Firma Foto-Frost v Hauptzollamt Lübeck-Ost* Case 314/85 [1987] ECR 4199, [1988] 3 CMLR 57.

[53] Article 234; see p 138, *post*.

[54] Once the Treaty of Lisbon takes effect, this part of the Article will be reworded as follows: 'a decision shall be binding in its entirety. A decision which specifies those to whom it is addressed shall be binding only on them'.

[55] Note that in applying this provision, the Court of Justice has regard to the substance rather than the form of the measure; see, e.g. *Confédération Nationale des Producteurs de Fruits et Légumes v Commission* Case 16/62 [1962] ECR 471; *Salamander AG v Parliament and Council* Cases T-172 and 175–77/98 [2000] 2 CMLR 1099. This part of the Article will be reworded by the Treaty of Lisbon as follows: 'any natural or legal person may...institute proceedings against an act addressed to that person or which is of direct and individual concern to them, and against a regulatory act which is of direct concern to them and does not entail implementing measures'.

creativity, as does the concept of direct effect. In addition, the Treaties are framed in broad terms and it is the duty of the court to interpret and apply Community law in ways that fulfil their underlying spirit and policy. Besides this interpretative role, the court has developed a number of general principles:

(a) Legal certainty and legitimate expectations. The principle of legal certainty applies in various ways: a measure may not be altered once it has been adopted and it will be presumed that provisions do not operate retrospectively. In *Officier van Justitie* v *Kolpinghuis Nijmegen BV*[56] the Dutch authorities sought to rely in criminal proceedings on a directive that had not been implemented. The Court of Justice held that criminal liability could not be imposed in this way. The legitimate expectations[57] of individuals who are affected by Community measures will also be protected, though not to the point of fettering the Community's freedom of action.[58]

(b) Natural justice. Community bodies are required to give reasons for their actions, and not to act arbitrarily.[59]

(c) Equality of treatment in comparable situations.[60] Until recently, European legislation did not set out any general principle of equality, although there were specific provisions on gender discrimination in employment and on the free movement of workers regardless of (EC) nationality.[61] A wider principle was established by the Court of Justice, however, to the effect that comparable situations should be treated in the same way and different situations should be treated differently.[62] This principle has now been reinforced by Article 13 of the EC Treaty, which was inserted by the Treaty of Amsterdam.[63] The Article does not in itself prohibit discrimination, but instead empowers the EC institutions to:

> take appropriate action to combat discrimination based on sex, racial or ethnic origin, religion or belief, disability, age or sexual orientation.

The Article has already generated two major directives.[64]

---

[56] Case 80/86 [1987] ECR 3969, [1989] 2 CMLR 18.

[57] The phrase is borrowed from English law. See Usher: 'The Influence of National Concepts on Decisions of the European Court' [1976] 1 EL Rev 359. For an example, see *EC Commission* v *EC Council* Case 81/72 [1973] ECR 575.

[58] *ATB* v *Ministero per le Politiche Agricole* Case C-402/98 [2000] ECR I-5501. For a domestic example, see *R* v *Ministry of Agriculture and Fisheries, ex parte Hamble Fisheries* [1995] 2 All ER 714, [1995] 1 CMLR 533.

[59] *Transocean Marine Paint Association* v *EC Commission* Case 17/74 [1974] ECR 1063.

[60] See generally: Bell, *Anti-Discrimination Law and the European Union* (2002).

[61] Articles 2 and 12 EC Treaty; Equal Treatment Directive 76/207; Regulation 1612/68.

[62] *Sabbatini* v *European Parliament* Case 20/71 [1972] ECR 345; *Graff* v *Hauptzollamt Köln-Rheinau* Case C-351/92 [1994] ECR-I-3361.

[63] To be renumbered Article 19 by the Treaty of Lisbon.

[64] EC Employment Directive 2000/78; EC Race Directive 2000/43. Statutory instruments to implement these measures in UK law have now been introduced: SI 2003/1626 (race), SI 2003/1657 (sex), SI 2003/1660 (religion or belief), SI 2003/1661 (sexual orientation), and SI 2003/1673 (disability); SI 2006/1031 (age).

(d) Proportionality. Obligations may not be imposed on an individual except to the extent necessary to achieve the purpose of the measure.[65] This concept applies not only in respect of Community measures, but also in determining the legality of the actions of Member States. Thus Hoffman J in *Stoke-on-Trent City Council* v *B & Q plc* had to determine whether the restrictions on Sunday trading in the Shops Act 1950 were proportionate to those permitted by Article 30.[66] The question was ultimately decided in the affirmative by the House of Lords. The concept of proportionality may apply equally to the remedy that the court is being asked to grant. In *Taittinger* v *Allbev*,[67] the court granted an injunction restraining the use of the expression 'Elderflower Champagne' on the basis that it infringed a Community directive. The Court of Appeal rejected a submission that the remedy was disproportionate to the infringement.

(e) Fundamental rights.[68] The original Treaties of the European Communities did not include specific human rights provisions, but the protection of fundamental rights was nevertheless considered important. A Joint Declaration in 1977[69] stressed the role of the European Convention on Human Rights (ECHR), and in *Nold* v *Commission* the Court of Justice stated that:[70]

> [T]he Court is bound to draw inspiration from constitutional traditions common to the Member States, and it cannot therefore uphold measures which are incompatible with fundamental rights recognised and protected by the Constitutions of those States. Similarly, international treaties for the protection of human rights on which the Member States have collaborated or of which they are signatories, can supply guidelines which should be followed within the framework of Community law.

In respect of national legislation which falls outside the scope of Community law, the Court does not have any general power to examine its compatibility with the ECHR.[71] However, the Court is increasingly prepared to take a generous approach to the question of whether Community law is engaged. Thus in the *Familiapress*[72] case the Court ruled that since a ban on the distribution of a magazine obstructed the free movement of goods, any justification for the ban would need to be compatible with the right to freedom of expression under Article 10 of the ECHR.

---

[65] *Internationale Handelsgessellschaft GmbH* v *Einfuhr- und Vorratsstelle für Getreide* Case 11/70 [1970] ECR 1125, [1972] CMLR 255; *Johnston* v *Chief Constable of the RUC* Case 222/84 [1987] QB 129, [1986] 3 All ER 135.

[66] [1991] Ch 48, [1991] 4 All ER 221. Article 30 will be renumbered Article 36 under the Treaty of Lisbon.

[67] [1994] 4 All ER 75, [1993] 2 CMLR 741.

[68] See Alston, Heenan and Bustelo, *The EU and Human Rights* (1999).

[69] Joint Declaration by the European Parliament, Council and Commission ([1977] OJ C103/1). See also *Prais* v *Council* Case C-130/75 [1976] ECR 1589.

[70] Case 4/73 [1974] ECR 491 at para 13; see Drzemczewski 'The Domestic Application of the European Human Rights Convention as European Community Law' (1981) 30 ICLQ 118.

[71] *Demirel* v *Stadt Schwabisch Gmund* Case 12/86 [1987] ECR 3719, [1989] 1 CMLR 421; *Kremzow* v *Austria* Case C-299/95 [1997] ECR I-2629.

[72] *Vereingte Familiapress Zeitungsverlags- und Vertriebs GmbH* v *Heinrich Bauer Verlag* Case C-368/95 [1997] ECR-I-3689, [1997] 3 CMLR 1329.

Following the lead of the Court of Justice, the Member States included a provision in the Treaty on European Union stating that the ECHR 'shall be respected by Member States'.[73] Though the provision was initially not justiciable, it was expressly brought within the Court's jurisdiction by the Treaty of Amsterdam. The wording was also strengthened, and Article 7 made it possible for the voting rights of Member States to be suspended in the event of a 'serious and persistent' breach of human rights principles. The suggestion that the EU might itself become a signatory to the ECHR was mooted,[74] but in 1994 the Court of Justice advised that any move in this direction would require amendments to the Treaty.[75] Such amendments have now been included in the Treaty of Lisbon. Once this treaty is ratified Article 6(2) of the TEU will provide for the Union to accede to the ECHR, while Article 6(3) will give Convention rights the status of 'general principles of the Union's law'. In a corresponding move, the Council of Europe has agreed an amendment to the ECHR paving the way for the EU's accession.[76]

Quite apart from the developments outlined above, each EU Member State is already a Convention signatory in its own right, and a number of states have been challenged under the Convention in relation to aspects of EC law and procedure.[77] A German company fined by the EU Commission for a breach of competition laws recently challenged *all* of the EU Member States before the Court of Human Rights. The essence of the claim was that by refusing to suspend the fine pending the outcome of a hearing, the Commission had violated the presumption of innocence and the right to a fair trial under Article 6 of the ECHR.[78] The Court of Human Rights declared the claim inadmissible because by this stage the Court of First Instance had quashed the fines: the company was not a 'victim' of anything.[79] The rather more difficult question of whether the states *could* be collectively liable in this way was neatly side-stepped, but it is notable that the Strasbourg court did not rule out this possibility. From the other side, the European Court of Justice recently directed its attentions to the compatibility of its own institutions with Article 6, concluding that the involvement of the Advocate-General in cases before the court did not give rise to any breach of this provision.[80]

Finally, in December 2000 the Member States signed the Charter of Fundamental Rights of the European Union. Though the Charter was not initially expressed to be

---

[73] Article 6.

[74] See Harmsen, 'National Responsibility for EC Acts under the ECHR: Recasting the Accession Debate' (2001) 7 EPL 625.

[75] *Re Accession of the Community to the European Human Rights Convention (Opinion 2/94)* [1996] 2 CMLR 265.

[76] An amendment to Article 59, ECHR, will be made by the new Protocol 14: see p 198, *post*.

[77] *Matthews* v *UK* (1999) 28 EHRR 361; *JS* v *Netherlands* (1995) 20 EHRR CD 41; *Pafitis* v *Greece* (1999) 27 EHRR 566; see Canor, 'Primus Inter Pares: Who is the Ultimate Guardian of Fundamental Rights in Europe?' (2000) 25(1) EL Rev 3.

[78] *Senator Lines* v *15 EU Member States* (2004) 39 EHRR SE3; see also *Senator Lines GmbH* v *Commission* Case C-364/99 [1999] ECR I-8733, [2000] 5 CMLR 600.

[79] Whether there had been a breach initially was irrelevant, because until the company's case had been considered by the CFI its legal remedies had not been exhausted: see p 209, *post*.

[80] *Emesa Sugar* v *Aruba* Case C-17/98 [2000] ECR I-665. The role of Advocates-General is discussed at p 136, *post*.

legally binding,[81] the Treaty of Lisbon provides for a new Article 6(1) to be added to the Treaty on European Union, and once in force this will give the rights, freedoms and principles set out in the Charter the same legal value as the Treaties. It should be noted, however, that the UK and Poland have both negotiated exemptions.

THE RELATIONSHIP BETWEEN COMMUNITY AND NATIONAL LAW

1   THE GENERAL APPROACH OF THE COURT OF JUSTICE

In a series of important decisions the Court of Justice has developed the doctrine of supremacy of Community over national law. In *Van Gend en Loos* v *Nederlandse Administratie der Berlastingen*[82] it stated that Member States had 'limited their sovereign rights, albeit within limited fields'. Then, in *Costa* v *ENEL*[83] it held that:

> The transfer by the states from their domestic legal system to the Community legal system of the rights and obligations arising under the Treaty carries with it a permanent limitation of their sovereign rights, against which a subsequent unilateral act incompatible with the concept of the Community cannot prevail.

The supremacy of Community law means that national courts must enforce Community rights even if this involves overriding national legislation.[84] Thus, in the event of a conflict directly applicable Community law prevails. In addition, Member States have a duty to take any action necessary to implement Community law. Article 10 of the EC Treaty states:[85]

> Member States shall take all appropriate measures, whether general or particular, to ensure fulfilment of the obligations arising out of this Treaty or resulting from actions taken by the institutions of the Community. They shall facilitate the achievement of the Community's tasks. They shall abstain from any measure which could jeopardise the attainment of the objectives of this Treaty.

In *R* v *Secretary of State for Transport, ex parte Factortame*[86] the Court of Justice held that national courts must ensure the legal protection of rights derived from directly applicable Community law: i.e. those arising from the Treaty, Regulations, or rulings of

---

[81]   See p 113, *ante*; Arnull, 'From Charter to Constitution and Beyond: Fundamental Rights in the New European Union' [2003] PL 774.

[82]   Case 26/62 [1963] ECR 1, [1963] CMLR 105.   [83]   Case 6/64 [1964] ECR 585, [1964] CMLR 425.

[84]   *Amministrazione delle Finanze dello Stato* v *Simmenthal* Case 106/77 [1978] ECR 629, [1978] 3 CMLR 263.

[85]   This Article will be repealed by the Treaty of Lisbon once it is ratified. It will be replaced by an almost identically worded provision in a new Article 3a of the TEU, with the word 'Union' being substituted for 'Community' where it appears.

[86]   Case C-213/89 [1990] ECR I-2433, [1990] 3 CMLR 1. For the *Factortame* litigation generally, see pp 132–3, *post*.

the Court of Justice. Where rules of national law prevent this, they must be set aside. In cases where the Community and national authorities share jurisdiction, national courts must avoid reaching conclusions at variance with the Community institutions. They must also avoid the adoption of national procedural rules which render the exercise of Community rights virtually impossible or extremely difficult.[87]

2 DIRECT APPLICABILITY AND DIRECT EFFECT

(a) Identifying the concepts

Direct applicability. The Treaties, regulations, and some decisions of European law are said to be directly applicable. This means that they are automatically incorporated into domestic legal systems and come into force without the need for any further action on the part of Member States. Achieving direct applicability in the UK initially required an Act of Parliament: the UK is a dualist state and treaties do not become part of domestic law without specific legislation to implement them. Thus the European Communities Act 1972 was enacted, section 2(1) of which states that:

> All such rights, powers, liabilities, obligations and restrictions from time to time created or arising by or under the Treaties, and all such remedies and procedures from time to time provided for by or under the Treaties, as in accordance with the Treaties are without further enactment to be given legal effect or used in the United Kingdom shall be recognised and available in law, and shall be enforced, allowed and followed accordingly; and the expression 'enforceable Community right'[88] and similar expressions shall be read as referring to one to which this subsection applies.

The wording of this provision is cumbersome and does not fully convey its immense significance, but since it came into force all directly applicable European laws have automatically formed part of UK law without any further legislation to incorporate them being needed.

Not all European laws are directly applicable: directives and most decisions usually require an act of implementation by the Member State before they can take effect. In the UK, the power to implement such provisions by statutory instrument is contained in section 2(2) of the 1972 Act. The scope of this section is limited by Schedule 2, which excludes the power to do any of the following:

(a) make any provision imposing or increasing taxation; or

(b) make any provision taking effect from a date earlier than that of the making of the instrument containing the provision; or

---

[87] *SCS Peterbroeck van Compeenhout and Cie v Belgium* Case 312/93 [1996] All ER (EC) 242. In deciding this, the basic principles of the domestic judicial system must be considered: *Van Schijndel v Stichling Pensioenfonds* [1996] All ER (EC) 259; *Van der Weerd v Minister van Landbouw, Natuur en Voedselkwaliteit* Case C-222/05 [2007] 3 CMLR 7.

[88] The European Union (Amendment) Bill, introduced in December 2007, proposes to replace 'enforceable Community right' with 'enforceable EU right' in the event of the Treaty of Lisbon being ratified.

(c) confer any powers to legislate by means of orders, rules, regulations or other subordinate instrument, other than rules of procedure for any court or tribunal; or

(d) create any new criminal offence punishable with imprisonment for more than two years or punishable on summary conviction with a fine or imprisonment for more than three months.[89]

Even with these limitations the power is far-reaching: in 2003 alone, 138 statutory instruments affecting England and Wales were made pursuant to section 2(2).

Direct effect. In the context of European law, a provision is said to have 'direct effect' if it creates rights that an individual can rely upon in court. The courts have sometimes used the terms 'directly applicable' and 'direct effect' interchangeably,[90] but they are not, strictly speaking, synonymous.[91] Many directly applicable provisions can be described as having 'direct effect' because they are capable of creating rights enforceable by individuals. It does not necessarily follow, however, that *all* directly applicable provisions will have such an effect. In order for a provision to have direct effect, certain criteria must be satisfied. These were set out in the important case of *Van Gend en Loos*:[92]

(a) it must not relate to inter-state relations alone;

(b) it must be clear and precise;

(c) no further action by the state for implementation must be necessary; and

(d) it must not be conditional at the time of enforcement.

Whether a particular provision fulfils these criteria is a question of interpretation, to be determined as a question of European law.

(b) The Treaties

Treaty provisions are directly applicable and therefore require no further implementation. However, in order for a Treaty provision to have direct effect and give rise to individual rights, the *Van Gend en Loos* criteria must be satisfied.

A number of Articles of the Treaty of Rome have been held by the Court of Justice to be directly effective, and they must therefore be taken to create rights and obligations within English law. These include Article 25,[93] which prohibits the introduction of new customs duties; Article 90, which prevents Member States from imposing

---

[89] Obligations in these areas can only be implemented by Act of Parliament or through some other enabling provision.

[90] See, e.g., *Johnston* v *Chief Constable of the RUC* Case 222/84 [1987] QB 129, [1986] 3 All ER 135; *Van Duyn* v *Home Office* Case 41/74 [1975] Ch 358, [1975] 3 All ER 190.

[91] See Winter, 'Direct Applicability and Direct Effects' (1972) 9 CML Rev 425; Hilson and Downes, 'Making Sense of Rights: Community Rights in EC Law' (1999) 24 EL Rev 121.

[92] *Van Gend en Loos* v *Nederlandse Administratie der Belastingen* Case 26/62 [1963] ECR 1, [1963] CMLR 105; see further, Lenaerts and Corthaut, 'Of Birds and Hedges: The Role of Primacy in Invoking Norms of EU Law' (2006) 31(3) EL Rev 287.

[93] To be renumbered Article 30 by the Treaty of Lisbon.

discriminatory taxes on the products of other Member States;[94] Article 141, which states that men and women should receive equal pay for equal work;[95] and Article 39, which is concerned with the free movement of workers.[96]

These cases should be compared with the decision in *Zaera v Institutio Nacionale de la Seguriad Social*.[97] In this case the Court ruled that the commitment in Article 2 to 'raising the standard of living' was simply an aim of the Community and was insufficiently precise to confer enforceable rights.

(c) Regulations

Article 249 of the EC Treaty provides that regulations are to be directly applicable and binding in their entirety.[98] They automatically form part of UK law by virtue of section 2(1) of the European Communities Act 1972, and by their very nature they are likely to have the characteristics needed for direct effect.[99] There are, however, exceptions. In a recent case challenging the labelling of supermarket produce as 'Parma ham', the House of Lords held that the applicable regulation was intended to establish rights over brand marks that could be relied upon in Member States and was therefore directly effective.[100] However, the ECJ ruled that 'notwithstanding the principle of the direct effect of regulations... a Community measure is capable of creating individual rights only if it is sufficiently clear, precise and unconditional'.[101] As the regulation in question sought to impose conditions derived from another instrument which had not been properly publicized, those conditions could *not* be directly enforced by the applicants.

(d) Directives

Unlike regulations, directives do not necessarily have immediate binding force. They are addressed to Member States but it is left to individual national authorities to implement them, and in the UK this is normally done by an Order in Council or statutory instrument under section 2(2) of the European Communities Act 1972. This means that although directives are binding on Member States as to the result to be achieved, they are not directly applicable, and for this reason it was initially assumed that they could not have direct effect. However, in *Grad v Finanzampt Traunstein*[102] the Court of Justice ruled that a directive *could* create rights which would be enforceable by individuals. This was confirmed in *Van Duyn v Home Office*:[103]

> [W]here the Community authorities have, by directive, imposed on Member States the obligation to pursue a particular course of conduct, the useful effect of such an

---

[94] To be renumbered Article 110; *Alfons Lütticke GmbH v Hauptzollamt Saarlouis* Case 57/65 [1966] ECR 205.

[95] To be renumbered Article 157; *Defrenne v Sabena* Case 43/75 [1976] ECR 455, [1976] 2 CMLR 98.

[96] To be renumbered Article 45; *Van Duyn v Home Office* Case 41/74 [1975] Ch 358, [1975] 3 All ER 190.

[97] Case 126/86 [1987] ECR 3697.   [98] To be renumbered Article 288 by the Treaty of Lisbon.

[99] *Commission v Italy* Case 39/72 [1973] ECR 101; *Antonio Muñoz v Frumar Ltd* Case C-253/00 [2003] Ch 328, [2003] All ER (EC) 56.

[100] *Consorzio del Prosciutto di Parma v Asda Stores Ltd* [2001] UKHL 7, [2001] CMLR 43.

[101] Case 108/01 [2003] ECR I-5121, at para. 85.   [102] Case 9/70 [1970] ECR 825, [1971] CMLR 1.

[103] Case 41/74 [1975] Ch 358 at 376–7, [1975] 3 All ER 190 at 205.

act would be weakened if individuals were prevented from relying on it before their national courts and if the latter were prevented from taking it into consideration as an element of Community law.

There are, however, various limitations to the doctrine. Firstly, the conditions for direct effect must be fulfilled, and this means that the directive must be precise and unconditional as set out in *Van Gend en Loos*.[104] In addition, a directive cannot have direct effect until the deadline for implementation has expired. In *Publico Ministero* v *Ratti*[105] the Court of Justice held that whilst one directive could have direct effect and prevent the Italian authorities from relying on domestic laws relating to solvents, another could *not* have this effect because the date for implementation had not yet passed.

Even where these conditions are satisfied, directives only have 'vertical' direct effect: in other words, they can only be enforced against the state.[106] They do not have 'horizontal' direct effect and therefore cannot be enforced against private individuals. This was confirmed in *Marshall* v *Southampton and South West Hampshire Area Health Authority*, where it was stated that:[107]

> [T]he binding nature of a directive, which constitutes the basis for the possibility of relying on the directive before a national court, exists only in relation to 'each Member State to which it is addressed.' It follows that a directive may not of itself impose obligations on an individual...

Marshall itself concerned a challenge to an employer's policy of operating different retirement ages for men and women. Female employees were normally required to retire at the age of sixty, whereas their male colleagues were able to continue working until they reached sixty-five. This policy potentially violated the Equal Treatment Directive,[108] and since Miss Marshall's employer happened to be a state body, it was held that she was entitled to rely upon the directive as having direct effect. Yet if Miss Marshall had been employed by a private company she would have had no remedy.

The meaning of 'the state' for these purposes was considered in *Foster* v *British Gas*,[109] which, like *Marshall*, was a case concerning discriminatory retirement ages. On a reference under Article 234 of the EC Treaty, the Court of Justice ruled that the Equal Treatment Directive could be relied upon against a body if it provided a public service under the control of the state and exercised special powers for that purpose. In applying this guidance to the facts, the House of Lords held[110] that British Gas (at a time when it was a public corporation) was provided by statute with the duty of performing a public service. It had a monopoly power and it was also under the control of the state,

---

[104] Case 26/62 [1963] ECR 1, [1963] CMLR 105: see p 126, *ante*. See also, *Becker* v *Finanzamt Münster-Innenstadt* Case 8/81 [1982] ECR 53, [1982] 1 CMLR 499.

[105] Case 148/78 [1979] ECR 1629, [1980] 1 CMLR 96.

[106] Note that the doctrine does not operate the other way round and a state cannot enforce an unimplemented directive against an individual; see *Officier van Justitie* v *Kolpinghuis* Case 80/86 [1987] ECR 3969, [1989] 2 CMLR 18.

[107] Case 152/84 [1986] QB 401 at 422, [1986] 2 All ER 584, at 600. For the subsequent litigation, see *Marshall* v *Southampton and South West Hampshire Area Health Authority (No 2)* [1994] 1 AC 530, [1994] 1 All ER 736.

[108] Directive 76/207.   [109] Case C-188/89 [1991] 1 QB 405, [1990] 3 All ER 897.

[110] [1991] 2 AC 306, [1991] 2 All ER 705.

since the state could dictate its policies and reclaim revenue. The directive was therefore directly effective.

Though not definitive, *Foster* is the leading case in this area and is the starting point for any consideration of whether a body is 'an emanation of the state'. On the basis of the *Foster* test, the governing body of a voluntary-aided school in receipt of state funding has been held to be an emanation of the state,[111] as has a privatized water company.[112] On the other hand, in *Doughty v Rolls-Royce*[113] it was held that Rolls Royce was *not* a state body, even though the Crown owned 100 per cent of the company's shares at the time. More recently, the approach of the Court of Justice in *Kampelmann*[114] seems to suggest that the criteria set out in *Foster* are alternative rather than cumulative, and that a body may be regarded as an emanation of the state as long as *some* of these criteria can be satisfied.

This distinction between vertical and horizontal direct effect causes difficulties, not only in determining when a body is under the control of the state, but also in applying the rules evenly. For example, it has already been noted that rights in employment law may depend upon whether the employer is within the public or private sector, and the fact that cases can hinge on such matters has led to considerable criticism.[115] However, in the light of case law establishing that directives can also have '*indirect* effect', this distinction between vertical and horizontal effect has lost some of its significance.

Indirect effect. In *von Colson v Land Nordrhein-Westfalen*[116] the Court of Justice stated:

> [I]n applying the national law and in particular the provisions of a national law specifically introduced in order to implement [a directive], national courts are required to interpret their national laws in the light of the wording and the purpose of the directive in order to achieve the result referred to in the third paragraph of Article 189.

This approach was strengthened by the decision in *Marleasing SA v La Comercial Internacional de Alimentación SA*:[117]

> [I]n applying national law, whether the provisions concerned pre-date or post-date the directive, the national court asked to interpret national law is bound to do so in every way possible in the light of the text and the aims of the directive to achieve the results envisaged by it and thus comply with Article 189(3) of the Treaty.

The Court of Justice has since endorsed this strong interpretive obligation in a number of other cases,[118] and as far as possible, national courts must now interpret all legislation in a manner consistent with the provisions of directives. In adopting this approach the

---

[111] *National Union of Teachers v Governing Body of St Mary's Church of England (Aided) Junior School* [1997] 3 CMLR 630, [1997] IRLR 242.

[112] *Griffin v South-West Water Services Ltd.* [1995] IRLR 15.

[113] [1992] 1 CMLR 1045, [1992] ICR 538.

[114] *Kampelmann v Landschaftsverband Westfalen-Lippe* Cases C 253–258/96 [1997] ECR I-6907 at para 46.

[115] See, e.g. Lenz A-G *in Faccini Dori v Recrab Srl* Case C-91/92 [1994] ECR I-3325, [1995] All ER (EC) 1; Arnull, 'The Direct Effect of Directives: Grasping the Nettle' (1986) 35 ICLQ 939.

[116] Case 14/83 [1984] ECR 1891, [1986] 2 CMLR 430. The Article 189 in question is now Article 249 of the EC Treaty. It will be renumbered again (to 288) once the Treaty of Lisbon takes effect.

[117] Case C-106/89 [1990] ECR I-4135, [1992] 1 CMLR 305; ibid.

[118] See *Centrosteel v Adipol* Case C-456/98 [2000] ECR I-6007.

Court of Justice has undoubtedly reduced the significance of the direct effect doctrine,[119] but it should be remembered that the obligation described in *Marleasing* is merely one of interpretation. Its application depends upon whether a compatible interpretation of national law is 'possible', and the Court of Justice has generally left it to the domestic courts to answer this question.[120]

Damages. In some circumstances the failure of a Member State to implement a directive may give rise to an action for damages. In *Francovich* v *Italian Republic*[121] the Court of Justice ruled that an individual could claim for financial loss resulting from the non-implementation of a directive if three conditions were satisfied:

(1) The directive must have been intended to confer individual rights.

(2) It must be possible to identify the content of those rights on the basis of the provisions of the directive.

(3) There must be a causal link between the breach of the state's obligation and the damage suffered.

English law was slow to accept the right to seek damages in such cases,[122] but the decision in *R* v *Secretary of State for Transport, ex parte Factortame*[123] made it clear that domestic courts have a duty to confer effective protection for Community rights. The position was put beyond doubt by the decisions in *Brasserie du Pêcheur SA* v *Germany* and *R* v *Secretary of State for Transport ex parte Factortame (No 4)*.[124] In the first of these two companion cases, it was alleged that a German law relating to the purity of beer contravened European law, whilst in the second, the breach of Community law had already been established.[125] The Court of Justice confirmed the approach in *Francovich* and ruled that even where the infringement of Community law had resulted from the legislation of a national Parliament, liability for damages could still arise. The general principle to emerge from these cases is that if a state is responsible for a breach of Community obligations – even if those obligations derive from a measure which does not have direct effect – the state may be liable in damages for any losses that result. In determining whether a breach of Community law is sufficient to warrant compensation, the decisive test is whether the state manifestly and gravely disregarded the limits of its discretion. Factors to be considered by the court include: (a) the clarity and precision of the rule breached; (b) the measure of discretion left to the authorities; (c) whether the

---

[119] See Craig, 'Directives: Direct Effect, Indirect Effect and the Construction of National Legislation' (1997) 22 EL Rev 519; Drake, 'Twenty Years after Von Colson: The Impact of "Indirect Effect" on the Protection of the Individual's Community Rights' (2005) 30 EL Rev 329.

[120] *Faccini Dori* v *Recrab Srl* Case C-91/92 [1994] ECR I-3325, [1995] All ER (EC) 1; *Alcatel Austria* v *Bundesministerium für Wissenschaft und Verkehr* Case C-81/98 [1999] ECR I-7671. For the approach of the English courts, see p 136, *post*.

[121] Case C-6, 9/90 [1991] ECR I-5357, [1993] 2 CMLR 66. Note that in *Emmott* v *Minister for Social Welfare* Case C-208/90 [1993] ICR 8 the Court of Justice ruled that where a State fails to implement a directive properly the individual may sue the state in reliance on that directive (if directly effective) until proper implementation occurs.

[122] *Bourgoin SA* v *Ministry of Agriculture Fisheries & Food* [1986] QB 716, [1985] 3 All ER 585.

[123] Case C-213/89 [1990] ECR I-2433, [1990] 3 CMLR 1.

[124] Cases C-46/93 and 48/93 [1996] QB 404, [1996] All ER (EC) 301.   [125] See p 132, *post*.

infringement and the damage caused was intentional; (d) whether any error of law was excusable; and (e) whether the position taken by a Community institution may have contributed to the omission. In reliance on the guidelines established in these cases, the House of Lords in *Factortame (No 5)* accepted the duty to provide a remedy for breaches of Community obligations and entered judgment for the claimant.[126]

In *R v HM Treasury, ex parte British Telecommunications plc*[127] the Court of Justice stated that in order for a Member State to be liable in damages:

> [T]he rule of law infringed must be intended to confer rights on individuals; the breach must be sufficiently serious; and there must be a direct causal link between the breach of the obligation resting on the state and the damage sustained by the injured parties.

On the facts of the case, which concerned the incorrect implementation of a directive, it was held that the breach was not sufficiently serious to give rise to damages: the UK had acted in good faith and the wording of the directive was imprecise. By contrast, in *R v Ministry of Agriculture, Fisheries and Food, ex parte Hedley Lomas*[128] the breach was blatant. The UK had refused to grant a licence for the export of sheep for slaughter in Spain, without any legal justification for doing so. The fact that the UK believed the Spanish abattoir to be operating in breach of Community law was irrelevant. More recently, it was held that a breach of a directly effective Treaty Article concerning anti-competitive agreements could give rise to an action for compensation to cover damage caused by a non-state party.[129] The full implications of this decision are still, as yet, uncertain.[130]

(e) Decisions

Decisions may be made by the Council and Commission as a formal method of enunciating policies or initiating actions. They are binding upon those to whom they are addressed, and like directives, they are capable of having direct effect.

THE IMPACT UPON ENGLISH COURTS

1 THE QUESTION OF SUPREMACY

The insistence of Community law that it shall prevail over conflicting national law presents distinct challenges to the UK's constitutional orthodoxy. It was this potential

---

[126] [2000] 1 AC 524, [1999] 4 All ER 906.

[127] Case C-392/93 [1996] QB 615 at 655, [1996] All ER (EC) 411 at para 39.

[128] Case C-5/94 [1996] ECR I-2553, [1996] All ER (EC) 493.

[129] *Courage v Crehan* Case C-453/99 [2002] QB 507, [2001] All ER (EC) 886; see also *Manfredi v Lloyd Adriatico Assicurazioni SpA* Case C-295/04 [2006] ECR I-6619, [2006] 5 CMLR 17. Both cases concerned Article 81 of the EC Treaty.

[130] For a discussion, see Drake, 'Scope of *Courage* and the Principle of "Individual Liability" for Damages: Further Development of the Principle of Effective Judicial Protection by the Court of Justice' (2006) 31 EL Rev 841.

conflict that led to the unsuccessful attempt in *Blackburn* v *AG*[131] to challenge the UK's accession to the Treaty of Rome and the passage of the 1972 Act. The Court of Appeal ruled that the treaty-making power of the Crown was beyond challenge, though it also confirmed that Parliament retained the theoretical power to legislate in any way that it saw fit: if it chose to do so it could repeal the 1972 Act.

Implementation of the Treaty in English law was achieved by the passage of section 2(1) of the Act. In addition, section 2(4) states that:

> [A]ny enactment passed or to be passed, other than one contained in this part of this Act, shall be construed and have effect subject to the foregoing provisions of this section.

Directly applicable Community obligations therefore take precedence over conflicting national law. By these means Parliament has ensured that most conflicts between English law and European law are resolved in favour of the latter. The constitutional challenge can be avoided by relying on the will of Parliament itself. In *Macarthys Ltd* v *Smith*[132] the majority of the court held that the individual rights arising under what was then Article 119 (now 141)[133] should prevail over the clear and unambiguous words of the Equal Pay Act 1970. By contrast Lord Denning used the Article as an aid to construction, concluding that the terms of the 1970 Act were capable of bearing a meaning that would allow compliance with Community obligations. Alternatively he considered that if Parliament had intended to derogate from its obligations under the Treaty, it would (and could) do so by express words: in the absence of such words, an intention to comply with Treaty obligations would be presumed.

The authority conferred by the 1972 Act has enabled courts both to quash executive actions and to declare delegated legislation invalid. More fundamentally, the courts have now accepted that it may even require them to declare the provisions of a subsequent Act of Parliament to be inoperative. This occurred in *Factortame* v *Secretary of State for Transport (No 2)*.[134] The applicants, who were companies controlled by Spanish nationals, sought to challenge the validity of the Merchant Shipping Act 1988 on the basis that it contravened the EC Treaty and deprived them of their Community law rights. The Divisional Court had made a reference to the Court of Justice under Article 234 (then 177), but since determination of the issues was likely to take some time, the applicants applied for an interim injunction to restrain the Secretary of State from enforcing the Act. The House of Lords initially held that it had no power to make such an order,[135] but following a further reference to the Court of Justice[136] it granted an interim injunction to suspend the operation of the 1988 Act. Lord Bridge stated:[137]

> Whatever limitation of its sovereignty Parliament accepted when it enacted the European Communities Act 1972 was entirely voluntary. Under the terms of the 1972 Act it has always been clear that it was the duty of a United Kingdom court,

---

[131] [1971] 2 All ER 1380, [1971] 1 WLR 1037.   [132] [1979] 3 All ER 325, [1979] 1 WLR 1189.
[133] To be renumbered Article 157 by the Treaty of Lisbon.
[134] [1991] 1 AC 603, [1991] 1 All ER 70.   [135] [1990] 2 AC 85, [1989] 2 All ER 692.
[136] Case C-213/89 [1990] ECR I-2433, [1990] 3 CMLR 1.
[137] [1991] 1 AC 603 at 659, [1991] 1 All ER 70 at 107.

when delivering final judgment, to override any rule of national law found to be in conflict with any directly enforceable rule of Community law...[T]here is nothing in any way novel in according supremacy to rules of Community law in those areas to which they apply, and to insist that, in the protection of rights under Community law, national courts must not be inhibited by rules of national law from granting interim relief in appropriate cases is no more than a logical recognition of that supremacy.

Whether such an injunction will be granted depends upon the merits of the particular case, and it is certainly not automatic. A significant factor will be the likelihood of the Court of Justice giving a ruling which favours one party or the other. If a trial judge considers that this likelihood is evenly balanced, he is entitled to decide that the applicant's interest in having the Act of Parliament struck down is outweighed by the public interest in enforcing it.[138]

The impact of EC law on the legislative supremacy of Parliament was revisited in the recent case of *Thoburn v Sunderland City Council and others*.[139] The appellants had been prosecuted for selling produce in imperial measurements, contrary to delegated legislation implementing a directive on the use of metric weights. The appeal by way of case stated centred on the claim that the Weights and Measures Act 1985 (which permitted the use of imperial weights) had, by implication, partially repealed section 2 of the European Communities Act 1972. The Divisional Court rejected this argument, and in doing so, Laws LJ stated expressly what many had assumed for some time:[140]

There are now classes or types of legislative provision which cannot be repealed by mere implication. These instances are given and can only be given, by our own courts, to which the scope and nature of Parliamentary sovereignty are ultimately confided.

In the view of Laws LJ, the European Communities Act forms part of this special class of legislative provisions, which he collectively termed 'constitutional statutes', and it is therefore immune from implied repeal.[141] Although not a decision of the House of Lords, *Thoburn* is the strongest indication yet that as far as the national courts are concerned, the supreme status of European law is still dependent on the authority of the 1972 Act. However, unless and until Parliament chooses to expressly repeal that Act, it seems that any conflict between domestic and European law will be resolved in favour of the latter.

The supremacy of Community law has thus been achieved, and in appropriate cases the courts will be prepared to disapply Acts of Parliament in order to give it proper effect. In an action for judicial review, a court may also consider a declaration to the effect that the UK is in breach of its Community obligations.[142]

---

[138] Ibid; see also *R v Secretary of State for the National Heritage, ex parte Continental Television BV* [1993] 3 CMLR 387.

[139] [2002] EWHC 195 (Admin), [2003] QB 151, [2002] 4 All ER 156.

[140] Ibid. at [60].   [141] See p 31, *ante*.

[142] *Equal Opportunities Commission v Secretary of State for Employment* [1995] 1 AC 1, [1994] 1 All ER 910. On the facts, provisions in the Employment Protection (Consolidation) Act 1978 were declared to be contrary to the Equal Pay Directive (57/117) and Article 141 (then 119) of the Treaty.

2 INTERPRETATION

In most of the cases to come before the domestic courts, judges have been able to avoid confronting the issue of supremacy. The approach of Lord Denning in *Macarthys Ltd* v *Smith* was to use European law as an aid to construction, and it is this interpretative approach that has generally found favour with English judges. In *Garland* v *British Rail Engineering*, Lord Diplock stated:[143]

> [I]n the instant case the words of section 6(4) of the Sex Discrimination Act 1975 that fall to be construed, 'provision in relation to retirement', without any undue straining of the ordinary meaning of the language used, are capable of bearing either the narrow meaning accepted by the Employment Appeal Tribunal or the wider meaning preferred by the Court of Appeal but acknowledged by that court to be largely a matter of first impression. Had the attention of the court been drawn to Article 119 of the EEC Treaty and the judgment of the European Court of Justice in *Defrenne* v *Sabena* I have no doubt that, consistently with statements made by Lord Denning MR in previous cases, they would have construed section 6(4) so as not to make it inconsistent with Article 119.

The same approach was adopted in *Pickstone* v *Freeman's plc*,[144] where the House of Lords considered that an amendment to the Equal Pay Act 1970, which was intended to give effect to the ruling of the Court of Justice in *Marshall*,[145] was capable of being so construed. Although on a literal reading the amendment did not achieve its objective, the House of Lords felt able to read words into the legislation to give effect to the clear intention of Parliament. In *Litster* v *Forth Dry Dock and Engineering Co Ltd*[146] regulations were made to give effect to a directive. The claimant could not rely on the directive itself because the defendant company was not an organ of the state and there was thus no direct effect. Nevertheless, in a clear application of the *von Colson* principle, the House of Lords accepted that it had a duty to interpret the regulation in a manner consistent with the directive.

In both *Pickstone* and *Litster*, the courts were concerned with the interpretation of laws which had been made or amended to give effect to European law. This was not the case in *Duke* v *GEC Reliance*, however,[147] and the House of Lords refused to distort the meaning of a statute to give effect to a Community provision which was not directly effective. The House held that in such circumstances it was required by English law to give the words of the statute their ordinary and natural meaning, and that the *von Colson* ruling[148] was not applicable because the court had no discretion as to the approach to interpretation. The reasoning in this case is unconvincing, and in *Marleasing*[149] the Court of Justice confirmed that the duty to interpret national law in the light of European law is not confined to measures passed with the intention of implementing European provisions.

---

[143] [1983] 2 AC 751 at 771. What was Article 119 is now Article 141 of the EC Treaty. It will be renumbered again (to 157) once the Treaty of Lisbon takes effect.

[144] [1989] AC 66, [1988] 2 All ER 803.

[145] Case 152/84 [1986] QB 401, [1986] 2 All ER 584. See p 128, *ante*.

[146] [1990] 1 AC 546, [1989] 1 All ER 1134.   [147] [1988] AC 618, [1988] 1 All ER 626.

[148] Case 14/83 [1984] ECR 1891, [1986] 2 CMLR 430; see p 129, *ante*.

[149] Case C-106/89 [1990] ECR I-4135, [1992] 1 CMLR 305; see p 129, *ante*. For criticism of the *Duke* decision, see Foster, 'The Effect of the European Communities Act 1972, s 2(4)' (1988) 51 MLR 775.

The House of Lords returned to this issue in *Webb v EMO Air Cargo (UK) Ltd*. The claimant in this case had been hired to cover for another employee who was on maternity leave, but she was dismissed when she too became pregnant. Her situation did not appear to fall within the scope of the Sex Discrimination Act 1975, but she argued that it *was* covered by the Equal Treatment Directive and that the 1975 Act should be interpreted in the light of the latter instrument. The House of Lords accepted the principle expressed in *Marleasing*, but emphasized that the obligation to interpret statutes in a manner compatible with European law applied only to the extent that a compatible interpretation was 'possible'.[150]

> It is for a United Kingdom court to construe domestic legislation in any field covered by a Community directive so as to accord with the interpretation of the directive as laid down by the European Court, *if that can be done without distorting the meaning of the domestic legislation*. [emphasis added]

The House of Lords initially took the view that a compatible interpretation was *not* possible in this case. However, following a reference to the Court of Justice,[151] it accepted that the provision could be interpreted so as to comply with the directive without distorting the meaning of the Act.[152]

THE EUROPEAN COURT OF JUSTICE

1 COMPOSITION AND PROCEDURE

The Court of Justice comprises one judge for each Member State, assisted by eight Advocates-General.[153] Both the judges and the Advocates-General are appointed for a renewable period of six years, and appointments are staggered so that a proportion of the court is replaced or re-appointed every three years. Article 223 of the EC Treaty[154] provides that members of the Court shall:

> be chosen from persons whose independence is beyond doubt and who possess the qualifications required for appointment to the highest judicial offices in their respective countries or who are jurisconsults of recognised competence.

Article 223 further stipulates that the judges must nominate one of their number as President of the Court. The President holds office for a renewable term of three years, and is responsible for directing the judicial business of the Court and for overseeing its

---

[150] [1992] 4 All ER 929 at 939, [1993] 1 CMLR 259 at 270, per Lord Keith of Kinkel.
[151] Case C-32/93 [1994] QB 718, [1994] 4 All ER 115.
[152] *Webb v EMO Air Cargo (UK) Ltd (No 2)* [1995] 1 WLR 1454, [1996] 4 All ER 577.
[153] Articles 221 and 222 of the EC Treaty; to be renumbered Articles 251 and 252 by the Treaty of Lisbon. The nationality of the judges is not specified at present but it is assumed that each state will be represented. The proposed new Article 9F of the TEU will make this explicit, by providing that 'the Court of Justice shall consist of one judge from each Member State'.
[154] To be renumbered Article 253 by the Treaty of Lisbon.

administration. The Court also appoints its own registrar and lays down rules governing his service.

The Court may sit either in chambers of three or five judges, in a Grand Chamber of thirteen judges, or exceptionally, in plenary session.[155] Its organization and procedures are set out in the Statute of the Court (annexed to the EC Treaty) and in the Rules of Procedure adopted by the court itself.

(a) Advocates-General

The role of Advocate-General has no direct parallel within the English legal system. Comparisons with counsel acting as *amicus curiae* are inexact, because despite the name, an Advocate-General does not act on anyone's behalf. Instead his role is to present independent, reasoned conclusions on cases submitted to the Court, in order to assist the Court in performing its duties.[156] The opinion of the Advocate-General is not binding but it is clearly of persuasive value. It will be reported with the judgment of the Court and may therefore be important in assisting in the development of legal doctrine.

(b) The Court of First Instance

The Court of First Instance was created in 1988 in an attempt to ease the workload of the Court of Justice.[157] It deals mainly with disputes between the Community and its servants and with actions for judicial review brought under Article 230 of the EC Treaty.[158] Since the Treaty of Nice came into force in February 2003, it has also been able to deal with some references from national courts under the Article 234[159] procedure. The jurisdiction of the Court of First Instance will be further expanded under the Treaty of Lisbon, and it will in future be known as 'the General Court'.[160]

The Court has one judge for each Member State but there are no separate Advocates-General. In most other respects, the structure of the Court is very similar to that of the Court of Justice: judges are appointed for six years, they nominate a President who holds office for three years, and they normally sit in chambers of three or five. There is a right of appeal to the Court of Justice on a point of law.

2 JURISDICTION

The main jurisdiction of the Court of Justice is as follows:

(a) Judicial review of Community institutions. Under Article 230 of the EC Treaty[161] the Court can review the legality of an act of the Council or the Commission. Under Article 232[162] failures to act can also be challenged.

---

[155] Article 221.

[156] Article 222. The compatibility of the Advocate-General's role with the right to a fair trial was recently considered in *Emesa Sugar* v *Aruba* Case C-17/98 [2000] ECR I-665; see p 125, *ante*.

[157] Article 225; see Brown, 'The First Five Years of the Court of First Instance and Appeals to the Court of Justice' (1995) 32(3) CML Rev 743.

[158] To be renumbered Article 263 by the Treaty of Lisbon.

[159] To be renumbered Article 267 by the Treaty of Lisbon.   [160] Article 2(2)(n), Treaty of Lisbon.

[161] To be renumbered Article 263 by the Treaty of Lisbon.

[162] To be renumbered Article 265 by the Treaty of Lisbon.

Member States, the Council and the Commission have the status of privileged applicants, and may bring an action under these provisions on the grounds of lack of competence, infringement of an essential procedural requirement, infringement of Community law, or misuse of power.[163] An individual or 'non-privileged applicant' can only challenge (a) decisions addressed to him, and (b) decisions or regulations which are of direct and individual concern. The requirement for standing has been restrictively interpreted, and matters cannot be of direct concern to an individual if there is a discretion as to their implementation.[164] Where no real discretion exists, or where implementation is automatic, then the 'direct concern' test is satisfied.[165]

The established approach is typified by the decision in *Plaumann & Co v EEC Commission*.[166] Even though the applicants in this case imported clementines, they did not have standing to challenge a decision on the import duties on clementines, since any person could potentially be a clementine importer. Despite the restrictive effect of this ruling, it has been followed in numerous subsequent cases.[167] In the recent case of *Jégo-Quéré at Cie SA v Commission* the Court of First Instance adopted a more relaxed approach, citing the importance of providing an effective remedy for those affected by Community law.[168] However, the Court of Justice overturned this decision[169] and confirmed the *Plaumann* approach as correct.

Once the Treaty of Lisbon takes effect, words will be added to Article 230 to allow natural or legal persons to challenge any 'regulatory act which is of direct concern to them and does not entail implementing measures'. The absence of any reference to *individual* concern should make it easier to challenge certain EU acts.

(b) Direct actions against Member States. A Member State may be challenged directly in the Court of Justice for a failure to fulfil its Community obligations. Actions against Member States may be brought either by the Commission[170] or by other Member States.[171] Proceedings by the latter are extremely rare,[172] although the *threat* of a challenge from a Member State can sometimes lead the Commission to take action under Article 226. In 1999 for example, France refused to allow the importation of UK beef even though the Community had lifted a worldwide ban imposed in response to a health scare. The UK notified the Commission of its intention to bring an action against France, and the Commission responded by successfully challenging the ban itself under Article 226.[173]

---

[163] See, e.g. the challenge to the Working Time Directive in *UK v EU Council* Case C-84/94, [1996] All ER (EC) 877.

[164] *Alcan v EC Commission* Case 69/69 [1970] ECR 385.

[165] *International Fruit Co v NV Commission* Case 41–44/70 [1971] ECR 411.

[166] Case 25/62 [1963] ECR 95, [1964] CMLR 29.

[167] See, e.g. *Piraiki-Patraiki v Commission* Case 11/82, [1985] ECR 207. The approach to standing in such cases can be compared with that of the domestic courts on applications for judicial review; see p 220, *post*.

[168] Case T-177/01 [2002] All ER (EC) 932 at [51], [2002] 2 CMLR 44.

[169] Case C-263/02 [2005] QB 237, [2004] All ER (EC); see also *Unión de Pequeños Agricultores v Council* Case C-50/00 [2002] All ER (EC) 893, [2002] 3 CMLR 1.

[170] Article 226; to be renumbered Article 258 by the Treaty of Lisbon.

[171] Article 227; to be renumbered Article 229 by the Treaty of Lisbon.

[172] See *France v UK* Case 141/78 [1979] ECR 2923; *Belgium v Spain* Case C-388/95 [2000] ECR I-3121.

[173] *Commission v France; sub nom Re Ban on British Beef* Case C-1/00 [2001] ECR I-9989, [2002] 1 CMLR 22.

(c) Cases concerning the liability in damages of the Community and its servants. Under Articles 235 and 288,[174] the Court of Justice has jurisdiction over disputes concerning damage caused by the Community institutions and their servants in the performance of their duties. The Court of First Instance can also hear disputes between the Community and its servants.[175]

(d) Appeals from the Court of First Instance

(e) References from national courts requesting a preliminary ruling. This is a major source of work for the Court, and has important consequences for the courts of Member States. The jurisdiction is governed by Article 234 (formerly 177) of the EC Treaty and is considered in more detail below.

3 REFERENCES FOR A PRELIMINARY RULING UNDER ARTICLE 234[176]

Article 234 (formerly 177) of the EC Treaty creates a power, and in some circumstances imposes a duty, to refer questions concerning the interpretation of European law to the Court of Justice. This plays a key role in ensuring that the treaties and other instruments are applied consistently. Article 234 states:

(1) The Court of Justice shall have jurisdiction to give preliminary rulings concerning:

    (a) the interpretation of this Treaty;

    (b) the validity and interpretation of acts of the institutions of the Community *and of the European Central Bank;*[177]

    (c) *the interpretation of the statutes of bodies established by an act of the Council, where those statutes so provide.*

(2) Where such a question is raised before any court or tribunal of a Member State, that court or tribunal may, if it considers that a decision on the question is necessary to enable it to give judgment, request the Court of Justice to give a ruling thereon.

(3) Where any such question is raised in a case pending before a court or tribunal of a Member State, against whose decisions there is no judicial remedy under national law, that court or tribunal shall bring the matter before the Court of Justice.

---

[174] To be renumbered Articles 268 and 272 by the Treaty of Lisbon.

[175] Article 236; to be renumbered Article 270 by the Treaty of Lisbon.

[176] To be renumbered Article 267 by the Treaty of Lisbon. For a discussion of the provision, see Craig and De Búrca, *EU Law: Text, Cases and Materials* (4th edn, 2007), ch 11; Arnull, 'The Use and Abuse of Article 177, EEC' (1989) 52(5) MLR 622.

[177] The Treaty of Lisbon provides for the words in italics to be deleted, and for the following words to be added to the end of the Article: 'if such a question is raised in a case pending before a court or tribunal of a Member State with regard to a person in custody, the Court of Justice of the European Union shall act with the minimum of delay.'

(a) The power to refer

This power to refer matters under Article 234 is conferred upon courts and tribunals. It is for the Court of Justice to decide whether a body constitutes a 'court or tribunal', and the term has been held to include state bodies exercising judicial or quasi-judicial functions.[178]

(b) When is a reference mandatory?

If the interpretation of European law is raised as an issue in a case, the domestic court or tribunal involved in that case must decide whether to refer the matter to the Court of Justice. If the domestic court is one 'against whose decisions there is no judicial remedy', a reference to the Court of Justice will be mandatory. Thus if a matter falling within the scope of Article 234 is raised in a case before the House of Lords, that matter *must* be referred to the Court of Justice since there is no possibility of a further appeal. A reference is not only mandatory for courts whose decisions can *never* be challenged:[179] what matters is whether an appeal is possible in the particular case in question. On this basis, it could be suggested that the Court of Appeal would often be obliged to make a reference, since an appeal from a decision of this court is only possible with leave and leave may not be granted. However, if leave is not granted by the Court of Appeal it may still be requested from the House of Lords, and this means that the Court of Appeal usually has a discretion as to whether to seek a ruling:[180]

> Except... where the Court of Appeal is the court of last resort, the Court of Appeal is not *obliged* to make a reference to the ECJ... If the Court of Appeal does not make a reference to the ECJ, and gives its final judgment on the appeal, then the House of Lords becomes the court of last resort.

It should also be noted that the concept of a judicial remedy under Article 234 is wide enough to encompass judicial review. Since inferior courts and tribunals are under the supervisory jurisdiction of the High Court it would appear that such bodies will never be caught by the mandatory reference requirement, even if no right of appeal exists.[181]

(c) When is a decision on a point of European law 'necessary'?

Unless a decision on a point of European law is 'necessary' for the determination of a case, there is neither a duty nor a discretion to make a reference to the Court of Justice: necessity is a pre-condition to the use of the preliminary ruling procedure. In *HP Bulmer*

---

[178] *Broekmeulen* v *Huisarts Registratie Commissie* Case 246/80 [1981] ECR 2311; *De Coster* v *Collège des Bourgmestre et Échevins de Watermael-Boitsfort* Case C-17/00 [2001] ECR I-9445.

[179] Cf. Lord Denning in *HP Bulmer Ltd* v *J Bollinger SA* [1974] Ch 401, [1974] 2 All ER 1226, who suggested that only the House of Lords could be under an obligation to make a reference.

[180] *Chiron Corporation* v *Murex Diagnostics* [1995] All ER (EC) 88 at 93, per Balcombe LJ. See also *Lyckeskog* Case C-99/00 [2002] ECR I-4839, [2003] 1 WLR 9. The position is arguably different in the case of a Divisional Court which refuses to certify a point of law on appeal from a decision of a magistrates' court, since this extinguishes any possibility of taking the case further; see *SA Magnavision MN* v *General Optical Council (No 2)* [1987] 2 CMLR 262.

[181] See *Re a Holiday in Italy* [1975] 1 CMLR 184.

Ltd v *J Bollinger SA*, Lord Denning stressed that a decision on a matter is not 'necessary' if substantially the same point has already been decided by the Court of Justice or if the point is 'reasonably free from doubt'.[182] In the *CILFIT Case*[183] the Court of Justice stated that there is no need to refer a question if the answer to it 'can in no way affect the outcome of the case.' Other English courts have interpreted the phrase as meaning 'reasonably necessary' or 'substantially determinative' of the litigation.[184]

The doctrine of acte clair. Lord Denning's suggestion that a matter need not be referred if it is already reasonably free from doubt, mirrors the European law doctrine of *acte clair*. In *CILFIT* the Court of Justice stated:[185]

> [T]he correct application of Community law may be so obvious as to leave no scope for any reasonable doubt as to the manner in which the question raised is to be resolved. Before it comes to the conclusion that such is the case, the national court or tribunal must be convinced that the matter was equally obvious to the courts of the other Member States and to the Court of Justice.

The Court also stated that in determining whether a point is *acte clair*, regard should be had to the fact that Community law is drafted in different languages and may not always translate easily. In addition, it emphasized that Community concepts may bear different meanings from similar concepts in domestic law, and that such points need to be considered in the context of Community law as a whole. In *R* v *Pharmaceutical Society of Great Britain, ex parte the Association of Pharmaceutical Importers*[186] Kerr LJ observed that an English court should 'hesitate long' before concluding that a point of European law was so obvious as to leave no room for reasonable doubt. Note also that since a national court has no power to declare actions of the Community invalid, a reference under Article 234 may sometimes be necessary even where the point of law is clear.[187]

The existence of a 'precedent'. Though the Court of Justice does not operate a rigid doctrine of precedent, it does tend to follow its previous decisions in the interests of legal certainty. A national court may therefore consider it unnecessary to refer a point which has been answered by the Court of Justice in a previous case,[188] though much will depend on the national court's view of whether the earlier decision was correct. In *Da Costa*,[189] the Court of Justice suggested that an obligation to make a reference will

---

[182] [1974] Ch 401, [1974] 2 All ER 1226. He also suggested that the point of law must be conclusive of the case, but this goes too far and is inconsistent with the approach of the Court of Justice.

[183] *CILFIT Srl* v *Ministro della Sanita* Case 283/81 [1982] ECR 3415, [1983] 1 CMLR 472.

[184] *Customs and Excise Commissioners* v *Aps Samex* [1983] 1 All ER 1042.

[185] Case 283/81 [1982] ECR 3415 at para 16, [1983] 1 CMLR 472.

[186] [1987] 3 CMLR 951. See also the judgment of Bingham J in *Customs and Excise Commissioners* v *ApS Samex* [1983] 1 All ER 1042.

[187] *Firma Foto-Frost* v *Hauptzollamt Lubeck-Ost* Case 314/85 [1987] ECR 4199, [1988] 3 CMLR 57.

[188] *R* v *Secretary of State for the Home Department, ex parte A* [2002] EWCA Civ 1008, [2002] 3 CMLR 14; *Parfums Christian Dior* v *Evora BV* Case C-337/95, ECR I-6013, [1998] 1 CMLR 737.

[189] *Da Costa* v *Nederlandse Belastringadministratie* Cases 28–30/62 [1963] ECR 31, [1962] CMLR 224.

not arise where a 'precedent' exists, though there will still be a discretion to ask for a preliminary ruling.

(d) The discretion to refer

The discretion to refer is ultimately that of the national court or tribunal, and its decision will not be reviewable by the Court of Justice unless the reference is spurious or an abuse of process.[190] The Court of Justice will not, however, deliver advisory opinions or opinions on hypothetical questions.[191]

It will be for the national court to formulate the question to be answered, and it should also define the factual and legislative context. In one case,[192] the Court of Justice held that it could not rule on the questions posed by the national court as it had not been provided with sufficient information. In *Bulmer v Bollinger*[193] Lord Denning set out some guidelines for the exercise of the discretion by English courts, though these guidelines are not binding and the decision to make a reference must rest with the court or tribunal concerned:

(i)   the time needed to obtain a ruling;

(ii) the importance of not overloading the European Court with references;

(iii) the difficulty and importance of the point;

(iv) the expense involved; and

(v)   the wishes of the parties.

He also stated that the facts should be established first; an 'injunction of obvious merit'.[194] The importance of deciding the facts first is that they provide the legal context for the point at issue, and indeed may determine whether or not a reference is in fact necessary. However, as the Court of Justice stated in *Irish Creamery Milk Suppliers Association v Ireland*,[195] the national court has responsibility for giving judgment in the case and it is therefore in the best position to judge when a reference is required. There is nothing to prevent a reference being made at an interlocutory stage, and important issues were raised and resolved in this way in the *Factortame* litigation.[196] In each case, however, it is a matter for the discretion of the trial court. In *Henn and Darby v DPP*[197] Lord Diplock indicated that a reference in a criminal case should be dealt with if necessary *after* the trial, at the appellate stage. By contrast, in *R v Goldstein* it was said that in a criminal case the best time to deal with such a matter would be on a motion to

---

[190] *ICI Chemical Industries v Colmer (HM Inspector of Taxes)* Case C-264/96 [1998] ECR I-4695; *Foglia v Novello (No 2)* Case 244/80 [1981] ECR 3045.

[191] *Zabala Erasu v Instituto National de Empleo* Cases C-422–424/93 [1995] All ER (EC) 758.

[192] *Telemarsicabruzzo SpA v Circostel and others* Cases C-320–322/90 [1993] ECR I-393.

[193] [1974] Ch 401, [1974] 2 All ER 1226.

[194] *Customs and Excise Commissioners v ApS Samex* [1983] 1 All ER 1042 at 1055, per Bingham J.

[195] Case 36/80 [1981] ECR 735, [1981] 2 CMLR 455.

[196] *R v Secretary of State for Transport, ex parte Factortame* Case C-213/89 [1990] ECR I-2433, [1990] 3 CMLR 1.

[197] [1981] AC 850, [1980] 2 All ER 166.

quash the indictment.[198] It would seem that the real issue in all cases is whether the interests of justice provide a compelling reason for going ahead with the trial, pending determination of the reference.

Notwithstanding Lord Denning's guidelines, the workload of the Court of Justice appears not to be a relevant factor when deciding whether to make a reference. By contrast, expense *is* an important consideration. In *R v Pharmaceutical Society of Great Britain, ex parte Association of Pharmaceutical Importers*[199] Kerr LJ expected the case to reach the House of Lords, at which point a reference would become mandatory. He considered that an immediate reference would therefore save considerable time and costs. As Hodgson J observed in the *Factortame* case, if a reference is going to be made, 'the sooner it is done the better'.[200]

The wishes of the parties will be a relevant but not decisive factor, for it is the court's judgment as to the need for a reference that is important. However, where only one party wishes a reference to be made there is no inevitability: it will usually be the case that a reference will assist one party only. A reference may be appropriate even against the wishes of both parties. The court may also take into account the fact that the matter is one upon which the European Commission has strong views. Once a decision to make a reference is taken, however, the domestic court is not at liberty to disregard the outcome, and it must apply the ruling of the Court of Justice to the facts before it.[201]

FURTHER READING

ALSTON, HEENAN and BUSTELO, *The EU and Human Rights* (Oxford University Press: 1999)

ARNULL, 'The Direct Effect of Directives: Grasping the Nettle' (1986) 35 ICLQ 939

ARNULL, 'The Use and Abuse of Article 177, EEC' (1989) 52(5) MLR 622

ARNULL, 'From Charter to Constitution and Beyond: Fundamental Rights in the New European Union' [2003] PL 774

CRAIG, 'Directives: Direct Effect, Indirect Effect and the Construction of National Legislation' (1997) 22 EL Rev 519

CRAIG and DE BÚRCA, *EU Law: Text, Cases and Materials* (Oxford University Press: 4th edn, 2007)

DRAKE, 'Twenty Years after Von Colson: The Impact of "Indirect Effect" on the Protection of the Individual's Community Rights' (2005) 30 EL Rev 329

DRAKE, 'Scope of *Courage* and the Principle of "Individual Liability" for Damages: Further Development of the Principle of Effective Judicial Protection by the Court of Justice' (2006) 31 EL Rev 841

DRZEMCZEWSKI, 'The Domestic Application of the European Human Rights Convention

---

[198] [1983] 1 All ER 434, [1983] 1 WLR 151.   [199] [1987] 3 CMLR 951.

[200] *R v Secretary of State for Transport, ex parte Factortame (No 1)* [1989] 2 CMLR 353 at 380.

[201] See *Arsenal v Reed* [2003] EWCA Civ 696, [2003] 3 All ER 865, which raises some interesting questions about the extent to which courts should follow any views expressed by the Court of Justice about the application of the law to the facts.

as European Community Law' (1981) 30 ICLQ 118

FOSTER, 'The Effect of the European Communities Act 1972, s 2(4)' (1988) 51 MLR 775

HARMSEN, 'National Responsibility for EC Acts under the ECHR: Recasting the Accession Debate' (2001) 7 EPL 625

HARTLEY, *The Foundations of European Community Law* (Oxford University Press: 6th edn, 2007)

HILSON and DOWNES, 'Making Sense of Rights: Community Rights in EC Law' (1999) 24 EL Rev 121

LENAERTS and CORTHAUT, 'Of Birds and Hedges: The Role of Primacy in Invoking Norms of EU Law' (2006) 31(3) EL Rev 287

STEINER, WOODS and TWIGG-FLESNER, *EU Law* (Oxford University Press: 9th edn, 2006)

WINTER, 'Direct Applicability and Direct Effects' (1972) 9 CML Rev 425

WYATT and DASHWOOD, *European Union Law* (Sweet and Maxwell: 5th edn, 2006)

5

THE HUMAN RIGHTS ACT 1998 AND THE EUROPEAN CONVENTION ON HUMAN RIGHTS

INTRODUCTION

This chapter focuses on the Human Rights Act 1998 and its impact on the English legal system. It was not until October 2000, exactly half a century after the UK became a signatory to the European Convention on Human Rights, that its provisions were explicitly given effect in domestic law by the Human Rights Act. Yet in the short time that the Act has been in force it has left an indelible impression on the legal landscape, and a recent government review described its impact as 'irreversible'. The specific issues addressed in this chapter will include:

- The history of the ECHR and its impact on the English legal system before 1998.
- The arguments in favour of incorporation, and the aims and objectives of the 1998 Act.
- The Act's key provisions and their impact on the role of the courts and other public authorities.
- The impact of the Act on disputes between private individuals: the issue of horizontal effect.
- The future of the Act and the current campaign for a 'British Bill of Rights'.

THE CONTEXT

1 THE CONVENTION AND ITS HISTORY[1]

The UK is a signatory to the Convention for the Protection of Human Rights and Fundamental Freedoms, usually referred to as the European Convention on Human Rights or ECHR. It is an instrument of the Council of Europe, which, like the European Community,[2] is an intergovernmental body formed in the aftermath of the Second World War. Since it was established in 1949 the membership of the Council of Europe has steadily increased from ten to forty-six states,[3] and it includes all of the current Member States of the EC. There are now plans for the EC itself to accede to the Convention,[4] but it is important to remember that the Council of Europe and the EC are separate bodies with their own separate treaties and institutions. Whereas the EC was initially established as a vehicle for greater economic co-operation, human rights were at the centre of the Council of Europe's agenda from the outset. The ECHR was the Council's first major project and is undoubtedly its single most important achievement. The UK played a significant role in the drafting process and was one of the first countries to sign the Convention in November 1950. It entered into force in the UK on 3 September 1953.

The emphasis of the Convention is on protecting basic 'human rights', along with what might be termed civil and political rights,[5] and its text is closely modelled on the UN's Universal Declaration on Human Rights, 1948. The key rights are the right to life (Article 2), freedom from torture (Article 3), freedom from slavery (Article 4), the right to liberty and security of the person (Article 5), the right to a fair trial (Article 6), the right not to be subject to retrospective criminal liability or penalties (Article 7), respect for private and family life (Article 8), freedom of thought, conscience, and religion (Article 9), freedom of expression (Article 10), freedom of assembly and association (Article 11), and the right to marry and found a family (Article 12). These rights are considered in more detail in chapter 6.

---

[1] For a comprehensive account, see Simpson, *Human Rights and the End of Empire: Britain and the Genesis of the European Convention* (2001).

[2] See chapter 4.

[3] Albania, Andorra, Armenia, Austria, Azerbaijan, Belgium, Bosnia and Herzegovina, Bulgaria, Croatia, Cyprus, the Czech Republic, Denmark, Estonia, Finland, France, Georgia, Germany, Greece, Hungary, Iceland, Ireland, Italy, Latvia, Liechtenstein, Lithuania, Luxembourg, Malta, Moldova, Monaco, the Netherlands, Norway, Poland, Portugal, Romania, Russia, San Marino, Serbia and Montenegro, Slovenia, the Slovak Republic, Spain, Sweden, Switzerland, Turkey, the former Yugoslav Republic of Macedonia, the Ukraine, and the UK.

[4] See p 123, *ante*. When brought into effect, Protocol 14 will amend Article 59 of the Convention so as to make this possible: Protocol 14 is discussed further later in this chapter.

[5] The European Social Charter (1961) addresses economic, social and cultural rights, but is not backed up by the same mechanisms for enforcement; see Gomien, Harris and Zwaak, *Law and Practice of the European Convention on Human Rights and the European Social Charter* (1996).

One other provision should be noted: Article 13 guarantees the availability of a remedy at national level to enforce the substance of Convention rights in whatever form they are secured in domestic law.

> [T]he remedy required by Article 13 must be 'effective' in practice as well as in law. In particular its exercise must not be unjustifiably hindered by the acts or omissions of the…respondent State.[6]

The list of Convention rights has been enhanced over the years by a number of additional protocols. Though acceptance of the Convention is now a prerequisite for Council of Europe membership, most of the protocols are optional,[7] and this has enabled the Convention to address issues which probably would not have been brought within its framework at all if unanimity had been required. To date, fourteen protocols have been added to the Convention. Some of these have been concerned solely with institutional reform, but others have added new substantive rights. Protocol 1 includes the right to peaceful enjoyment of possessions, to education, and to free elections, while Protocol 6 is concerned with the abolition of the death penalty in peace time. Both of these Protocols have been signed and ratified by the UK, as has Protocol 13, which strengthens Protocol 6 by banning the use of the death penalty in *any* circumstances. However, the UK has thus far not accepted Protocol 4 (which prohibits the imprisonment of debtors, the expulsion of nationals, and the collective expulsion of aliens), Protocol 7 (which, inter alia, guarantees equality between spouses and the right not to be tried more than once for the same offence), or Protocol 12 (which prohibits discrimination on a range of grounds).

What distinguishes the ECHR from most other international human rights treaties is not the catalogue of rights that it protects, but its machinery for enforcement. It established both a Commission and a Court of Human Rights, which together were given the task of ensuring that the Convention was observed. The Commission was abolished in 1998, but the Court, based in Strasbourg, has gone from strength to strength. It received around 50,000 individual complaints in 2006 alone.[8]

2   THE STATUS OF THE ECHR BEFORE THE HUMAN RIGHTS ACT 1998

Unlike the European Communities, the Council of Europe did not set out to establish a superior legal order, and the ECHR does not oblige Member States to directly incorporate its provisions into their national legal systems. The UK's constitutional arrangements mean that international treaties are not binding in domestic law unless accompanied by an Act of Parliament,[9] and it was not until the implementation of the

---

[6] *Keenan* v *UK* (2001) 33 EHRR 38 at para 122.

[7] Acceptance of Protocol 6 is now mandatory.

[8] European Court of Human Rights, *Survey of Activities, 2006.* The majority of applications are declared inadmissible or otherwise resolved: 1,560 judgments were delivered in 2006, twenty-three of which concerned the UK. See p 208, *post.*

[9] *R* v *Chief Immigration Officer, Heathrow Airport, ex parte Bibi (Salamat)* [1976] 3 All ER 843, [1976] 1 WLR 979.

Human Rights Act 1998 that it was possible for Convention rights to form the basis of a domestic legal challenge. Even before this Act, however, decisions of the Court of Human Rights provided the impetus for several pieces of legislation and Convention rights were occasionally taken into account by the national courts. In addition, the Convention was able to have a subtle and indirect influence through the decisions of the European Court of Justice.

(a) The impact of findings of the European Court of Human Rights

Since the UK accepted the jurisdiction of the European Court of Human Rights and the right of individuals to petition that court,[10] it has been found to be in breach of Convention rights on numerous occasions. States are obliged to give effect to any decision of the Court in cases to which they are parties, and several Acts of Parliament have been enacted in response to adverse findings in Strasbourg. For example, the Contempt of Court Act 1981 followed the decision in *Sunday Times* v *UK*[11] that the common law approach to contempt was incompatible with freedom of expression. Similarly, the finding in *Malone* v *UK*[12] that there was insufficient legal regulation of telephone tapping led to the enactment of the Interception of Communications Act 1985. Decisions in Strasbourg have also triggered changes in the procedures for dealing with life prisoners[13] and the abandonment of the policy preventing homosexuals from serving in the military.[14] Occasionally, the mere *likelihood* of an adverse finding has been enough to bring about legislative reform. Thus in anticipation that aspects of the courts-martial system would be found to breach the fair trial provisions in Article 6, the government introduced the Armed Forces Act 1996. This Act made a number of changes to the courts-martial system, though it did not, of course, prevent the Strasbourg court from finding a breach of Article 6 in the case in question.[15]

(b) An indirect influence on the domestic courts[16]

There is a presumption that Parliament does not intend to legislate in a manner incompatible with international law,[17] and where a statutory provision is genuinely ambiguous it is legitimate to take account of an international treaty when choosing between two equally reasonable interpretations. Thus even before the passage of the Human Rights Act, the ECHR could be taken into account as an aid to statutory interpretation. The position was discussed in *R* v *Chief Immigration Officer of Heathrow Airport, ex parte Bibi (Salamat)*. Immigration officials had refused to give the applicant leave to enter the

---

[10] On 14 January 1966.   [11] (1979–1980) 2 EHRR 245; see p 199, *post*.

[12] (1985) 7 EHRR 14. The 1985 Act was replaced by the Regulation of Investigatory Powers Act 2000 following further criticism in *Halford* v *UK* (1997) 24 EHRR 523.

[13] See p 183, *post*.

[14] *Smith and Grady* v *UK* (2000) 29 EHRR 493; *Lustig-Prean and Beckett* v *UK* (2000) 29 EHRR 548.

[15] *Findlay* v *UK* (1997) 24 EHRR 221; see p 285, *post*.

[16] See Beloff and Mountfield, 'Unconventional Behaviour? Judicial uses of the European Convention in England and Wales' [1996] EHRLR 467.

[17] See p 64, *ante*.

UK to join a man that she said was her husband, and this was alleged to constitute an interference with the right to respect for family life under Article 8 of the Convention. In the course of his judgment, Lord Denning stated that:[18]

> The position as I understand it is that if there is any ambiguity in our statutes, or uncertainty in our law, then these courts can look to the Convention as an aid to clear up the ambiguity and uncertainty...but I would dispute altogether that the Convention is part of our law. Treaties and declarations do not become part of our law until they are made law by Parliament.

The issue was also considered by the House of Lords in *R v Secretary of State for Home Affairs, ex parte Brind*.[19] The Home Secretary had made a directive prohibiting the broadcasting of statements by representatives of proscribed organizations, and the applicant argued that this contravened the right to freedom of expression under Article 10. In dismissing the applications, the House recognized that the Convention *could* be used for the resolution of a legislative ambiguity. However, it held that it did not require an administrative body such as the Home Office to exercise its discretion within the terms of the Convention. To conclude otherwise would amount to incorporation of the Convention by the judiciary, and this would be a usurpation of the legislative function.

The courts were more willing to use the Convention when interpreting statutes enacted to give effect to decisions of the Court of Human Rights,[20] or when considering the scope of the common law. In most cases, however, its effect (if any) was limited to reinforcing a conclusion which would have been reached in any event. For example, in *R v Secretary of State for the Home Department, ex parte Leech (No 2)*,[21] rule 33(3) of the Prison Rules was found to be ultra vires the Prison Act 1952 because it created an unrestricted right for a governor to read prisoners' correspondence. It thus interfered with the right to seek legal advice and to have unimpeded access to the courts. The court based its conclusion on the idea that access to the courts is a 'constitutional right', but it also noted that its approach was consistent with Article 8 of the Convention.

More often, the Convention had no decisive effect on domestic cases at all, and on a number of occasions the courts made it clear that they felt unable to use it to develop the common law. Thus in *Malone v Metropolitan Police Commissioner (No 2)*[22] Sir Robert Megarry considered the legality of the police interception of telephone calls. Even though not bound by any authority, and despite considering that the practice could breach Article 8 of the Convention,[23] he declined to develop the law in a way that

---

[18] [1976] 3 All ER 843 at 847, [1976] 1 WLR 979 at 984.

[19] [1991] 1 AC 696, [1991] 1 All ER 720.

[20] *R v Secretary of State for the Home Department, ex parte Norney* (1995) 7 Admin LR 861.

[21] [1994] QB 198, [1993] 4 All ER 539. Cf. the Human Rights Act case of *R (on the application of Daly) v Secretary of State for the Home Department* [2001] UKHL 26, [2001] 2 AC 532, [2001] 3 All ER 433; discussed at pp 167 and 225, *post*.

[22] [1979] Ch 344, [1979] 2 All ER 620.

[23] In that it was not prescribed by law. The Strasbourg court later agreed with this assessment: *Malone v UK* (1985) 7 EHRR 14. Parliament responded by enacting the Interception of Communications Act 1985.

would ensure compliance, suggesting that any reform in this area would be best left to Parliament.[24]

(c) An influence through the EC/EU

Though the EU itself has not acceded to the Convention,[25] its individual Member States are all signatories and the European Court of Justice has frequently asserted that Convention rights form part of its legal order. The rights guaranteed by the Convention are given express recognition in Article 6 of the Treaty on European Union, and the recent Treaty of Lisbon will give Convention rights the status of 'general principles of the Union's law'.[26] In addition, where national legislation falls within the scope of European law, the Court of Justice will examine its compatibility with the ECHR.[27] In the *Familiapress*[28] case, for example, the Court ruled that any justification for a ban on the distribution of a magazine would need to be compatible with the right to freedom of expression under Article 10, ECHR. This led some to conclude that a measure of indirect incorporation was being achieved through the influence of EC law:[29]

> There is no case in which the European Court [of Justice] has upheld the validity of actions which conflicted with the European Convention on Human Rights. It seems therefore, that in those areas affected by the EEC Treaties, the ECHR is already indirectly incorporated into English domestic law. The principles of the Convention form an integral part of EEC law and English domestic law is subject to EEC law.

3 BRINGING RIGHTS HOME

Despite the influence of the Convention on aspects of domestic law, its impact prior to 1998 was inevitably limited by the fact that it was merely an international treaty and could not be directly enforced in the national courts. This meant that a 'victim' of a Convention breach had to either depend on the processes of interpretation described above, or take the case through the long, slow procedures of the Court of Human Rights. Moreover, the fact that the government might choose to bring the law into line with rulings of the court did not provide an automatic remedy for those who were aggrieved. Calls to incorporate the ECHR into national law had been made for decades,[30] but it was

---

[24] [1979] Ch 344 at 380, [1979] 2 All ER 620 at 649.

[25] It seems increasingly likely that the EU will accede to the Convention in the near future: see p 123 and p 145, n 4 *ante*.

[26] By inserting a new Article 6(3) into the Treaty on European Union: see p 114, *ante*.

[27] *Johnston* v *Chief Constable of the RUC* Case C-222/84 [1987] QB 129, [1986] 3 All ER 135, *Prais* v *Council* Case C-130/75 [1976] ECR 1589; *Rutili* v *Minister of the Interior* Case C-36/75, [1975] ECR 1219.

[28] *Vereingte Familiapress Zeitungsverlags und Vertriebs GmbH* v *Heinrich Bauer Verlag* Case C-368/95 [1997] ECR-I-3689, [1997] 3 CMLR 1329.

[29] Browne-Wilkinson, 'The Infiltration of a Bill of Rights' [1992] PL 397 at p 401. See also Grief, 'The Domestic Impact of the European Convention on Human Rights as Mediated through Community Law' [1991] PL 555; Beyleveld, 'The Concept of a Human Right and Incorporation of the ECHR' [1995] PL 577.

[30] A detailed discussion of the campaign is beyond the scope of this work, but see Zander, *A Bill of Rights* (4th edn, 1996); Bingham, 'The European Convention on Human Rights: Time to Incorporate' [1993] LQR 390; Lester, 'The Mouse that Roared: The Human Rights Bill 1995' [1995] PL 198; Klug and Wadham, 'The

not until 1998 that the UK finally enacted legislation to give it domestic effect. The argument that the UK had an exemplary human rights record and that incorporation was therefore unnecessary did not stand up to scrutiny: by the time of the Human Rights Bill the UK had lost more cases in Strasbourg than any other state except Italy.[31] The government's White Paper explained the rationale for incorporation as follows:[32]

> The rights, originally developed with major help from the United Kingdom Government, are no longer seen as British rights. And enforcing them takes too long and costs too much. It takes on average five years to get an action into the European Court of Human Rights once all domestic remedies have been exhausted; and it costs an average of £30,000. Bringing these rights home will mean that the British people will be able to argue for their rights in the British courts – without this inordinate delay and cost. It will also mean that the rights will be brought much more fully into the jurisprudence of the courts throughout the United Kingdom, and their interpretation will thus be far more subtly and powerfully woven into our law. And there will be another distinct benefit. British judges will be able to make a distinct contribution to the development of the jurisprudence of human rights in Europe.

The remainder of this chapter will explore the content and structure of the Human Rights Act itself, while the interpretation of specific Convention rights will be considered in chapter 6.

THE HUMAN RIGHTS ACT 1998

The Human Rights Act 1998, which came fully into force on 2 October 2000,[33] is described in its long title as 'an Act to give further effect to rights and freedoms guaranteed under the European Convention on Human Rights'. The UK's constitutional framework means that the Act is not 'entrenched' in the same manner as the human rights documents adopted by many other states, but it is presumed that any attempt to repeal or amend its provisions would require the clearest possible words.[34]

The scheme of the Act is complex: it obliges public authorities to perform their functions in a manner compatible with Convention rights, and it gives the Convention and its jurisprudence a significant influence over the interpretation of domestic law. However, it stops short of allowing the courts to 'disapply' or invalidate incompatible

"Democratic" Entrenchment of a Bill of Rights: Liberty's Proposals' [1993] PL 579; Gardner, *Aspects of Incorporation of the European Convention on Human Rights* (1993).

[31] Lord Irvine (Lord Chancellor), 582 HL Official Report (5th series) col 1227, 3 Nov 1997.

[32] *Rights Brought Home: The Human Rights Bill*, Cm 3782, at para 1.14. See also: Straw and Boateng, 'Bringing Rights Home: Labour's Plans to Incorporate the European Convention on Human Rights into UK Law' [1997] 1 EHRLR 71.

[33] For England and Wales – s 22(3); SI 2000/1851. Sections 18, 20 and 21(5) came into force on the date of Royal Assent.

[34] *Thoburn v Sunderland City Council and others* [2002] EWHC 195 (Admin), [2003] QB 151, [2002] 4 All ER 156. The Act was described in this case as a 'constitutional statute'.

Acts of Parliament, and in this crucial respect it does not give the Convention primacy over domestic law.[35]

1 THE STATUS OF CONVENTION RIGHTS[36]
AND JURISPRUDENCE

(a) Section 1: The rights protected

Section 1 provides that the 'Convention rights' given effect shall be those contained in Articles 2 to 12 and 14 of the Convention, in Articles 1 to 3 of the First Protocol, and in Article 1 of the Thirteenth Protocol. These rights are reproduced in Schedule 1 of the Act. The 'missing' right, Article 13, is the right to a remedy for an infringement of the Convention. The government took the view that the very existence of the Human Rights Act was sufficient to give effect to Article 13, and that to expressly incorporate it would involve unnecessary duplication.[37]

(b) Section 2: The Strasbourg case law[38]

Section 2 requires any court or tribunal determining a matter involving a Convention right, to take into account any judgment, decision, or advisory opinion of the European Court of Human Rights, along with certain decisions of the Commission and Committee of Ministers, *in so far as they may be relevant*. It is clear from this wording that Strasbourg decisions do not bind the national courts, and they thus have the status of persuasive precedents. The fact that Parliament chose not to *oblige* the courts to follow the Strasbourg case law is entirely consistent with the Convention itself, as states are afforded a generous margin of appreciation in the application of its provisions. Moreover, domestic courts will frequently be required to decide human rights cases where the only relevant case law concerns other jurisdictions, and it would be illogical to prevent them from reaching their own conclusions in such cases.

The domestic courts have made it clear that in the absence of exceptional circumstances they are unlikely to depart from any 'clear and constant jurisprudence of the European Court of Human Rights'.[39] This means that so far, most judges have adhered fairly closely to the Strasbourg case law. For example, despite considering that mandatory and discretionary life sentences raised similar issues, the Court of Appeal in *R (on the application of Anderson)* v *Secretary of State for the Home Department*[40] followed the Strasbourg line and ruled that mandatory sentences were not subject to the same requirements as those which were discretionary. Their Lordships were clearly influenced

---

[35] Cf. the status given to EC law by the European Communities Act 1972: see chapter 4 for a discussion.

[36] The content of these rights is considered in greater depth in chapter 6.

[37] Jack Straw MP (Home Secretary), 312 HC Official Report (6th series) col 975, 20 May 1998.

[38] See also p 86, *ante*.

[39] *R (on the Application of Alconbury)* v *Secretary of State for the Environment, Transport and the Regions*: [2001] UKHL 23 at [26], [2003] 2 AC 295 at [26], [2001] 2 All ER 929, per Lord Slynn.

[40] [2001] EWCA Civ 1698, [2002] 2 WLR 1143.

by the knowledge that another case on this point was already pending before the Court of Human Rights:[41]

> In the end there are two factors which have persuaded me to regard the Strasbourg case law as for the present determinative. First, that whatever advantage we might enjoy through our domestic knowledge and experience of the mandatory life sentence regime could perhaps be thought balanced (or even conceivably outweighed) by the Court of Human Rights' deeper appreciation of the true ambit and reach of Articles 5(4) and 6(1) of the Convention...
>
> The second factor which weighs with me is that of comity. True, this court is not bound by Court of Human Rights judgments, any more than that court is bound by them. Where, however, as here, the Court of Human Rights itself is proposing to re-examine a particular line of cases, it would seem somewhat presumptuous for us, in effect, to pre-empt its decision. For my part, I shall be surprised if the present regime for implementing mandatory life sentences survives the Court of Human Rights' re-examination of the issue in Stafford. The final decision, however, I am persuaded should be theirs.

As predicted, when the Strasbourg court did have the opportunity to revisit the issue in *Stafford* v *UK*,[42] it departed from its previous jurisprudence and agreed that the regime for implementing mandatory life sentences infringed the Convention. Consequently, when the House of Lords heard the appeal in *Anderson*[43] it felt able to declare that the Home Secretary's power to determine the tariff for mandatory life prisoners was incompatible with the Convention. What is notable is that in reaching its conclusions in *Stafford*, the Court of Human Rights drew heavily on the opinions expressed by the domestic courts in both *Stafford*[44] and *Anderson*. Thus, although the Court of Appeal thought it appropriate to leave the final decision to Strasbourg, it was able to influence that decision through its own jurisprudence.

On occasions, the national courts have felt less constrained by the Strasbourg case law. For example, in dismissing a claim that the courts-martial system was incompatible with Article 6, Lord Steyn politely suggested that a recent Strasbourg case[45] on the point had been wrongly decided:[46]

> It goes without saying that any judgment of the European Court commands great respect, and section 2(1) of the Human Rights Act 1998 requires the House to take any such judgment into account, as it routinely does. There were, however, a large number of points in issue in *Morris*, and it seems clear that on this particular aspect the European Court did not receive all the help which was needed to form a conclusion.

Similar comments were made by Lords Bingham and Rodger. At the next opportunity[47] a unanimous Grand Chamber of the Strasbourg court took account of these judgments

---

[41] Ibid at [65]–[66], per Simon Brown LJ.   [42] (2002) 35 EHRR 32.
[43] [2002] UKHL 46, [2003] 1 AC 837, [2002] 4 All ER 1089.
[44] *R* v *Secretary of State for the Home Department, ex parte Stafford* [1999] 2 AC 38, [1998] 4 All ER 7, HL.
[45] *Morris* v *UK* (2002) 34 EHRR 52.
[46] *R* v *Spear and others; R* v *Saunby and others* [2002] UKHL 31 at [12], [2003] 1 AC 734 at [12], [2002] 3 All ER 1074.
[47] *Cooper* v *UK* (2004) 39 EHRR 8.

and again departed from its previous case law, declaring that there was, after all, no incompatibility with the Convention.

As this case demonstrates, the obligation to *consider*, rather than to *follow* Strasbourg decisions, means that there is at least the potential for the national courts to develop a human rights jurisprudence of their own. Moreover, the flexibility inherent in section 2 means that 'domestic courts are perfectly entitled to accord *greater* rights than those guaranteed by the Convention'.[48] Cases such as *R* v *Spear* remain the exception rather than the rule, however, and more recent decisions have emphasized the importance of following the Strasbourg line wherever possible. In *Kay* v *Lambeth LBC* Lord Bingham explained the rationale for this as follows:[49]

> [I]t is ordinarily the clear duty of our domestic courts . . . to give practical recognition to the principles laid down by the Strasbourg court as governing the Convention rights specified in section 1(1) of the 1998 Act. That court is the highest judicial authority on the interpretation of those rights, and the effectiveness of the Convention as an international instrument depends on the loyal acceptance by member states of the principles it lays down.

His Lordship had previously expressed the view that 'the duty of national courts is to keep pace with the Strasbourg jurisprudence as it evolves over time: no more, but certainly no less'.[50] Lord Brown has since suggested that 'no less, but certainly no more' might have been a better choice of words.[51]

(c) Sections 12 and 13: The special status of freedom of religion and freedom of expression

Section 12 applies when a court is considering whether to grant relief which could affect the right to freedom of expression. Section 12(2) provides that relief should not be granted against a party who is neither present nor represented unless the court is satisfied that all reasonable attempts to notify him have been made, or that there are compelling reasons for not notifying him. Section 12(3) adds that the publication of disputed material should not be restrained before trial unless the applicant is 'likely to establish that publication should not be allowed.' Finally, section 12(4) requires the court to have particular regard to the importance of freedom of expression. It states that when considering granting relief in relation to material which is 'journalistic, literary

---

[48] *Begum (Runa)* v *Tower Hamlets* [2003] UKHL 5 at [69], [2003] 2 AC 430 at [69], [2003] 1 All ER 731, per Lord Hoffmann. See also: Masterman, 'Taking the Strasbourg Jurisprudence into Account: Developing a "Municipal Law of Human Rights" Under the Human Rights Act' (2005) ICLQ 54(4) 907; Lewis, 'The European Ceiling on Human Rights' [2007] PL 720.

[49] [2006] UKHL 10 at [28], [2006] 2 AC 465 [28], [2006] 4 All ER 128.

[50] *R (on the application of Ullah)* v *Special Adjudicator* [2004] UKHL 26 at [20], [2004] 2 AC 323 at [20], [2004] 3 All ER 785. See also Lord Bingham in *R (on application of Gentle) The Prime Minister* (2008) UKHL 20.

[51] *R (on the application of Al-Skeini)* v *Secretary of State for Defence* [2007] UKHL 26 at [106], [2007] 3 WLR 33 at [106], [2007] 3 All ER 685. See also *R (on the application of Quark Fishing Ltd)* v *Secretary of State for Foreign and Commonwealth Affairs (No 2)* [2005] UKHL 57, [2006] 1 AC 529, [2006] 3 All ER 111, where Lord Bingham stated at [25] that: 'a party unable to mount a successful claim in Strasbourg can never mount a successful claim under . . . the 1998 Act'.

or artistic', it must take into account (a) the extent to which the material is (or is about to become) available to the public; (b) whether publication would be in the public interest; and (c) any relevant privacy code.

Section 12 was included in the Act in response to strong lobbying from sections of the media who were concerned that incorporation might be the catalyst for new rights of privacy. In fact, however, the provision has not been interpreted to give freedom of expression priority over other rights. In *Douglas* v *Hello! Ltd (No 1)*, for example, Sedley LJ stated that:[52]

> That Convention right, when one turns to it, is qualified in favour of the reputation and rights of others and the protection of information received in confidence. In other words, you cannot have particular regard to Article 10 without having equally particular regard at the very least to Article 8.

The irony here is that not only was it assumed that section 12 made Article 10 directly applicable between private parties, it was also assumed that it indirectly did the same for the right to respect for private life in Article 8. This led one commentator to observe that section 12 was proving to be 'largely irrelevant' in practice.[53]

In a recent breach of confidence case the Court of Appeal confirmed that section 12 does not require freedom of expression to take priority over other Convention rights: it simply means that any attempt to restrict free speech must be clearly justified:[54]

> It is one thing to say ... that the media's right to freedom of expression, particularly in the field of political discussion 'is of a higher order' than 'the right of an individual to his good reputation'; it is, however, another thing to rank it higher than competing rights.

This point was not challenged when the case went to the House of Lords, but it was held that section 12 nevertheless required a new approach to the granting of pre-trial injunctions.[55] Lord Nicholls concluded that in the light of section 12 it would not necessarily be sufficient for the party seeking an injunction to establish 'a real prospect of succeeding'[56] at trial. Instead, he stated that the courts should be 'exceedingly slow to make interim restraint orders where the applicant has not satisfied the court that he will *probably* ("more likely than not") succeed at the trial'.[57]

The other Convention right given a special status under the Human Rights Act is freedom of religion. Section 13(1) provides that if the determination of an issue under

---

[52] [2001] QB 967 at 1003, [2001] 2 All ER 289 at 322.

[53] Amos, 'Can We Speak Freely Now? Freedom of Expression under the Human Rights Act' [2002] 6 EHRLR 750 at 755.

[54] *Cream Holdings* v *Banerjee* [2003] EWCA Civ 103 at [54], [2003] Ch 650 at [54], [2003] 2 All ER 318, per Simon Brown LJ. See also *Venables and Thompson* v *News Group Newspapers* [2001] Fam 430, [2001] 1 All ER 908, where the Article 10 right had to give way to the Article 2 rights of individuals whose lives could be endangered if details of their whereabouts were published.

[55] [2004] UKHL 44, [2004] 4 All ER 617, [2004] 3 WLR 918.

[56] This is the test established in *American Cyanamid Co* v *Ethicon Ltd* [1975] AC 396, [1975] 1 All ER 504.

[57] [2004] UKHL 44 at [22], [2004] 4 All ER 617 at [22] (emphasis added). Their Lordships overturned the Court of Appeal's decision on the facts and discharged the injunction that had been granted. For a novel application of this decision, see *Browne* v *Associated Newspapers Ltd* [2007] EWCA Civ 295, [2007] 3 WLR 289.

the Act could affect the exercise by a religious organization or its members of the right to freedom of thought, conscience, and religion, a court must have particular regard to the importance of that right.[58] This provision was included in response to lobbying from church leaders, who were concerned that they may find themselves compelled to conduct gay marriages or to employ those whose lifestyles or beliefs were incompatible with their doctrines.[59] In fact, the churches probably overestimated the extent to which they would be affected by the Act. The guarantees under Article 9 are already sufficient to ensure that a minister of religion could not be compelled to perform a marriage ceremony against his conscience, and most of the functions of a church would not be caught by section 6 in any event.[60] Moreover, the interpretation given to section 12 makes it unlikely that section 13 will allow freedom of religion to trump other Convention rights. Having 'particular regard' to the right will therefore mean paying equal regard to the grounds upon which religious freedom can be restricted in Article 9(2).

2 THE IMPACT ON LEGISLATION

(a) Section 3: The interpretative obligation

One of the principal mechanisms by which the Act seeks to give effect to Convention rights is set out in section 3(1). This provides that:

> So far as it is possible to do so, primary legislation and subordinate legislation must be read and given effect in a way which is compatible with the Convention rights.

This interpretive obligation applies to *all* legislation, whether enacted before or after the Human Rights Act,[61] and it permits the courts to go far beyond previously accepted limits in seeking 'possible' meanings of words. Once it is established that a provision engages a Convention right, the court must then consider whether it appears on its face to be compatible with that right. Most Convention rights are not absolute and the interference with the right may be a legitimate one: if this is the case the court need do nothing except give effect to the provision in the ordinary way. If, however, the provision appears to be inconsistent with the Convention, section 3 obliges the court to seek a different interpretation.

It is important to note that section 3 does not authorize the courts to disapply Acts of Parliament,[62] and it does not affect the validity, continuing operation, or enforcement

---

[58] For a discussion, see Cumper, 'The Protection of Religious Rights under s 13 of the Human Rights Act' [2000] PL 254.

[59] A House of Lords amendment which would have allowed Article 9 to prevail over other Convention rights was removed in the Commons: what is now s 13 was inserted in its place.

[60] See *Aston-Cantlow and Wilcote with Billesley Parochial Church Council* v *Wallbank* [2003] UKHL 37 at [63], [2004] 1 AC 546 at [63], [2003] 3 All ER 1213. Lord Hope confirmed that a church council was not a 'core' public authority for the purposes of the Human Rights Act: see p 165, *post*.

[61] Section 3(2). The impact of the Act on statutory interpretation is discussed further at p 54, *ante*.

[62] Cf. The European Communities Act 1972, s 2(4); discussed further in chapter 4, *ante*.

of any incompatible primary legislation.[63] Nevertheless, it is clear that the interpretive obligation under section 3 is a strong one. In the leading case of *R v A (No 2)*, Lord Steyn explained that:[64]

> It applies even if there is no ambiguity in the language...In accordance with the will of Parliament as reflected in s 3 it will sometimes be necessary to adopt an interpretation, which linguistically may appear strained. The techniques to be used will not only involve the reading down of express language in a statute but also the implication of provisions.

The implications of this approach are potentially dramatic. In *R v A* itself, the disputed provision[65] had been specifically enacted to prevent defendants in sex offence cases from adducing evidence of a complainant's sexual history in cases such as this. Yet in reliance on section 3, the House of Lords interpreted the provision as being subject to an implied discretion to *allow* such evidence in the interests of a defendant's right to a fair trial. Section 3 does have its limits, however, and in other cases the courts have cautioned against reading words into an Act to the point of making it unworkable:[66]

> [I]f it is necessary in order to obtain compliance to radically alter the effect of the legislation this will be an indication that more than interpretation is involved.

In *Re S (Children) (Care Order: Implementation of Care Plan)*[67] the Court of Appeal read words into the Children Act 1989 to create new discretionary powers for the courts to supervise local authority care orders. On appeal, however, the House of Lords rejected this use of section 3 on the basis that it would have undermined a fundamental feature of the 1989 Act: namely, that 'the courts are not empowered to intervene in the way local authorities discharge their parental responsibilities under final care orders.'[68] Their Lordships also noted that the Court of Appeal had failed to identify any specific provision of the Children Act that was capable of being interpreted in the manner suggested.[69] Similarly, in *Bellinger v Bellinger*[70] the House of Lords held that section 11 of the Matrimonial Causes Act 1973 could not be interpreted so as to allow a male to female transsexual to marry a man. Such an interpretation would have represented a major change in the law and would have had far-reaching ramifications which were best left to Parliament to determine.[71]

---

[63] Nor does it affect the validity of incompatible subordinate legislation where primary legislation prevents removal of the incompatibility: s 3(2).

[64] [2001] UKHL 25 at [40], [2002] 1 AC 45 at [40], [2001] 3 All ER 1.

[65] Youth Justice and Criminal Evidence Act 1999, s 41.

[66] *Poplar Housing and Regeneration Community Association Ltd v Donoghue* [2001] EWCA Civ 595 at [76], [2002] QB 48 at [76], [2001] 4 All ER 604, per Lord Woolf CJ.

[67] [2001] EWCA Civ 757, [2002] 2 FLR 582, [2001] HRLR 50: *sub nom Re W and B (Children) (Care Plan)*.

[68] [2002] UKHL 10 at [42], [2002] 2 AC 291 at [42], [2002] 2 All ER 192, per Lord Nicholls.

[69] Ibid, at [43].   [70] [2003] UKHL 21, [2003] 2 AC 467, [2003] 2 All ER 593.

[71] At the time the House of Lords was aware that legislation to remedy the defect was imminent: the government had already accepted that UK law was in breach of the Convention following the decision in *Goodwin v UK* (2002) 35 EHRR 18.

Re S and *Bellinger* v *Bellinger* were initially seen as evidence of a shift away from the 'high water mark' of *R* v *A* towards a more restrictive approach,[72] but the subsequent decision in *Ghaidan* v *Godin-Mendoza*[73] confirmed that this was not the case. By a majority of 4:1, the House of Lords construed provisions in the Rent Act 1977 so as to confer the tenancy rights of spouses on same-sex partners, thus avoiding the conclusion that the Act was incompatible with the non-discrimination requirements in Article 14. Lord Nicholls confirmed that section 3 required a radical approach:[74]

> Section 3 enables language to be interpreted restrictively or expansively . . . It is also apt to require a court to read in words which change the meaning of the enacted legislation, so as to make it Convention-compliant. In other words, the intention of Parliament in enacting section 3 was that, to an extent bounded only by what is 'possible', a court can modify the meaning, and hence the effect, of primary and secondary legislation.

Lord Nicholls acknowledged that there would inevitably be cases in which a Convention-compliant interpretation was not possible, and both *Re S* and *Bellinger* v *Bellinger* were said to be examples:[75]

> Parliament . . . cannot have intended that in the discharge of this extended interpretative function the courts should adopt a meaning inconsistent with a fundamental feature of legislation. That would be to cross the constitutional boundary section 3 seeks to demarcate and preserve.

Nevertheless, the majority of the House felt that the Rent Act could be given a Convention-compliant interpretation without crossing this constitutional boundary, and all five Law Lords endorsed the decision in the earlier case of *R* v *A (No 2)*.

By contrast, in *R (on the application of Wilkinson)* v *Inland Revenue Commissioners* the House of Lords held that a provision of the Income and Corporation Taxes Act 1988 could not be interpreted as applying to 'widowers' as well as 'widows'.[76] Section 262 of the Act stated that 'where a married man whose wife is living with him dies, his widow shall be entitled . . . to an income tax reduction'. The applicant argued that as a widower he should be entitled to the same reduction, but despite endorsing the decision in *Ghaidan* v *Godin-Mendoza* the House of Lords held that it was not possible to interpret the provision in this way:[77]

> [T]here is no way in which any reasonable reader could understand the word 'widow' to refer to the more general concept of a surviving spouse. The contrary indications in the . . . Act are too strong.

It should be noted that extending widow's bereavement allowance to widowers would not, in their Lordship's view, have been sufficient to achieve compliance with

---

[72] Nicol, 'Statutory Interpretation and Human Rights after *Anderson*' [2004] PL 274. Cf. Kavanagh, 'Statutory Interpretation and Human Rights after *Anderson*: A More Contextual Approach' [2004] PL 537.

[73] [2004] UKHL 30, [2004] 2 AC 557, [2004] 3 All ER 411: see Van Zyl Smit, 'The New Purposive Interpretation of Statutes: HRA Section 3 after *Ghaidan* v *Godin-Mendoza*' (2007) 70(2) *MLR* 294.

[74] *Ghaidan* v *Godin-Mendoza* [2004] UKHL 30, at [32].   [75] Ibid, at [33].

[76] [2005] UKHL 30, [2005] 1 WLR 1718, [2006] 1 All ER 529.   [77] Ibid at [19], per Lord Hoffmann.

the Convention,[78] and their approach to section 3 must be considered in this context. Nevertheless, the decision serves as a reminder that although the interpretative obligation decreed by section 3 is of an 'unusual and far-reaching character',[79] there will always be cases in which a compatible interpretation of legislation is not 'possible'.

More recently, in an approach reminiscent of that taken in *R* v *A (No 2)*, a majority of the House of Lords held that provisions in the Prevention of Terrorism Act 2005 could be read down so as to ensure compatibility with the right to a fair trial.[80] AF was subject to a control order made on the basis of undisclosed material, and he challenged the order on the grounds that he did not know the nature of the case against him. Their Lordships agreed that the right of a person to be informed of the case against him could be limited in the interests of national security, and that any potential injustice might be mitigated by the use of special advocates or other procedural devices. However, the majority accepted that such devices might not always be sufficient to comply with Article 6, and on this basis they held that the provisions could, if necessary, be read down so as so take effect only where this would be consistent with fairness.

(b) Sections 4, 5 and 10 – Declarations of incompatibility and remedial orders

If a court[81] concludes that a compatible interpretation of a provision is not possible, it may issue a declaration of incompatibility under section 4 of the Act. The effect of a declaration is to bring the matter to the attention of the government so that a change in the law can be considered. It does not affect the validity, continuing operation, or enforcement of the statute, and the court must give effect to the incompatible provision as Parliament intended.[82] Nevertheless, where a court is contemplating such a step, the Crown is entitled to be given notice and the relevant Minister or his nominee is entitled to be joined as a party to the proceedings.[83]

Where a declaration of incompatibility has been made, or where the Strasbourg court has made an equivalent finding, section 10 empowers a Minister to make such amendments to the legislation as he considers necessary to remove the incompatibility. It is important to note that this is a power, not an obligation, and it only arises where the Minister considers that there are 'compelling reasons' for proceeding under this

[78] The allowance had been abolished altogether before the case even came to court.
[79] *Ghaidan* v *Godin-Mendoza* [2004] UKHL 30 at [30], [2004] 2 AC 557 at [30], [2004] 3 All ER 411, per Lord Nicholls.
[80] *Secretary of State for the Home Department* v *MB* [2007] UKHL 46, [2007] 3 WLR 681. See also *R* v *Holding (Terence Anthony)* [2005] EWCA Crim 315, [2006] 1 WLR 1040: provisions on election expenses in the Representation of the People Act 1983 read down so as to comply with Article 10.
[81] For these purposes, the term 'court' covers the House of Lords, the Judicial Committee of the Privy Council, the Courts-Martial Appeal Court, the Court of Appeal, the High Court, the Court of Protection and the Scottish High Court of Justiciary (except when sitting as a trial court or Court of Session): s 4(5). Even the lower courts are bound by s 3 and may occasionally need to decide that a compatible interpretation of legislation is impossible. However, as they have no power to make formal declarations of incompatibility, such decisions cannot trigger the power to make a remedial order under s 10.
[82] Incompatible *subordinate* legislation may be declared invalid unless primary legislation prevents removal of the incompatibility: s 3(2). In the latter case a declaration of incompatibility may be issued.
[83] Section 5.

section. The requirement for compelling reasons was inserted during the committee stage in the House of Lords, the idea being to limit this potentially far-reaching power.[84] Ironically, however, it has been argued that the amendment may be to the detriment of human rights:[85]

> The consequence of this unfortunate amendment could be that a breach of human rights may go uncorrected for want of parliamentary time or because it relates to an unpopular group or a controversial cause. But it is precisely this domination of majority over minority interests which human rights law is designed to prevent. The amendment therefore had the unfortunate effect of weakening the structure of the Act.

So far, relatively few declarations have been made, and some have been overturned on appeal.[86] What this tells us about the level of human rights protection has been the subject of considerable debate, and much has been written about the extent to which deference plays a part in the courts' decisions.[87] A detailed examination of these issues is beyond the scope of this work, but it is worth remembering that a declaration of incompatibility does not oblige Parliament or the government to take remedial action. If there is a reluctance to use section 4 because of a concern that elected bodies should have the final word on policy matters, it is therefore unwarranted. On the other hand, the desire to avoid declarations is not always due to excessive deference. From a human rights perspective, a declaration of incompatibility may be the least desirable outcome: it will not affect the validity of the legislation and there is no guarantee of remedial action. Even if remedial action is taken it will not assist those involved in the original case. A compatible interpretation under section 3 is potentially far more powerful because it means *giving effect* to the provision in a Convention-compliant way.

In the recent case of *Secretary of State for the Home Department* v *MB*, Baroness Hale had no doubt that the House of Lords had a duty to avoid making a declaration of incompatibility if at all possible. Having concluded that provisions governing the imposition of control orders could be interpreted in a Convention-compliant manner, she explained why this was desirable:[88]

> [W]hen Parliament passed the [Prevention of Terrorism Act 2005], it must have thought that the provisions with which we are concerned were compatible with the Convention rights. In interpreting the Act compatibly we are doing our best to make it work. This gives the greatest possible incentive to all parties to the case, and to the judge, to conduct the proceedings in such a way as to afford a sufficient and substantial measure of procedural justice. This includes the Secretary of State, who

---

[84] Remedial orders are normally subject to affirmative resolution but this may be avoided if the Minister certifies that a more urgent response is necessary. In the latter case, the remedial order will expire after 120 days unless it has been approved by an affirmative resolution of both Houses: Schedule 2.

[85] Wadham and Mountfield, *Blackstone's Guide to the Human Rights Act 1998* (2nd edn, 1999) at p 49.

[86] See, e.g., *R (on the Application of Alconbury)* v *Secretary of State for the Environment, Transport and the Regions* [2001] UKHL 23, [2003] 2 AC 295, [2001] 2 All ER 929, reversing [2001] HRLR 2; *Wilson* v *First County Trust (No 2)*; *sub nom Wilson* v *Secretary of State for Trade and Industry* [2003] UKHL 40, [2004] 1 AC 816, [2003] 4 All ER 97, reversing [2001] EWCA Civ 633, [2002] QB 74, [2001] 3 All ER 229.

[87] See p 166, *post.*   [88] [2007] UKHL 46 at [73], [2007] 3 WLR 681 at [73].

will, of course, be anxious that the control order be upheld. A declaration of incompatibility, on the other hand, would allow all of them to conduct the proceedings in a way which they knew to be incompatible.

Though critics argue that the courts have sometimes exceeded the permissible bounds of 'interpretation',[89] ministerial comments made during the debates on the Human Rights Bill support the idea that declarations of incompatibility should be made only in exceptional cases:[90]

[W]e want the courts to strive to find an interpretation of legislation that is consistent with Convention rights, so far as the plain words of the legislation allow, and only in the last resort to conclude that the legislation is simply incompatible with them.

On the other hand, the very existence of section 4 means that Parliament must have envisaged that a compatible interpretation would not always be 'possible'. The danger in placing so much emphasis on section 3 is that the courts may interpret Convention rights quite narrowly, in order to make a finding of compatibility easier. More generally, there is concern that some judges may be too ready to accept that an interference with a right is justifiable, thus avoiding the need to fully engage with either section.

Responding to declarations of incompatibility. In respect of the few declarations that have not been successfully challenged, the government has yet to refuse to take remedial action.[91] Thus, provisions of the Immigration and Asylum Act 1999 which were found to be incompatible with the Convention[92] were amended by the Nationality, Immigration and Asylum Act 2002, while laws which breached the Convention rights of transsexuals[93] were amended by the Gender Recognition Act 2004. In some cases, the offending legislation had already been repealed or amended by the time that the matter came to court. Widow's bereavement allowance, for example, was abolished several years before the Court of Appeal declared the relevant provisions to be incompatible with

---

[89] See e.g. Nicol (2004) *supra*, n 72; Ekins, 'A Critique of Radical Approaches to Rights Consistent Statutory Interpretation' [2003] EHRLR 641.

[90] Jack Straw MP (Home Secretary), 313 HC Official Report (6th series) coll 421–2, 3 June 1998. In *Ghaidan v Godin-Mendoza* [2004] UKHL 30 at [39], [2004] 2 AC 557 at [39], [2004] 3 All ER 411 Lord Steyn observed that in the first three and a half years of the Human Rights Act there had been at least as many declarations of incompatibility as there had been uses of section 3. On the basis of these statistics he suggested that the law may have taken 'a wrong turning'.

[91] At the time of writing, of the seventeen surviving declarations of incompatibility made before June 2007: twelve have been addressed by primary legislation, one has been addressed by a remedial order, two are the subject of legislation currently before Parliament, and the two remaining are still under consideration. Despite this, the Court of Human Rights does not consider a declaration of incompatibility to be an effective remedy for the purposes of Article 13. This may change, however, if evidence of a 'long standing and established practice' of giving effect to them emerges: *Burden v UK* (2007) 44 EHRR 51, at para 39.

[92] *International Transport Roth GmbH v Secretary of State for the Home Department* [2002] EWCA Civ 158, [2003] QB 728, [2002] HRLR 31. The provisions imposed a fixed penalty on hauliers responsible for bringing illegal entrants into the UK and were found to be incompatible with Article 6 and with Article 1 of the First Protocol.

[93] The inability of transsexuals to marry in accordance with their new gender was found to be incompatible with Articles 8 and 12 in *Goodwin v UK* (2002) 35 EHRR 18 and *Bellinger v Bellinger* [2003] UKHL 21, [2003] 2 AC 467, [2003] 2 All ER 593.

Article 14.[94] Similarly, provisions denying the possibility of parole to prisoners subject to deportation orders had already been repealed when they were declared incompatible with Articles 5 and 14,[95] though they continue to apply to offences committed before 4 April 2005.[96] Other declarations of incompatibility have taken rather longer to address. In 2004, for example, the High Court made a declaration in respect of section 185(4) of the Housing Act 1996. The provision requires local authorities to disregard persons subject to immigration control – including dependent children – when determining priority need for accommodation, and this was deemed to be incompatible with Articles 8 and 14.[97] Following an unsuccessful appeal[98] the government accepted the need for remedial action, but as of January 2008 the necessary legislative changes were still working their way through Parliament.[99]

A *v* Secretary of State for the Home Department. The government was presented with perhaps its most difficult Human Rights Act challenge to date by the decision of the House of Lords in *A v Secretary of State for the Home Department*.[100] The case was brought by a number of foreign nationals who had been detained without trial for almost three years under powers in the Anti-Terrorism, Crime and Security Act 2001.[101] The purpose of these powers was to enable the government to deal with those foreign nationals who were suspected of involvement in terrorism, but who could not be put on trial and who could not be deported for humanitarian reasons. The government had sought to pre-empt any legal challenge to these powers by derogating from the Article 5 right to liberty and security of the person.[102] However, by a majority of 8:1 their Lordships held that by singling out non-nationals for detention, the Act was interfering with the right to liberty in a discriminatory manner and was therefore in breach of both Article 5 *and* Article 14. The Court of Appeal had taken the view that the difference in treatment was justifiable because foreign nationals, unlike British nationals, had no right to remain in the UK.[103] In the House of Lords' view, however, the logic of this argument was flawed. Once it was accepted that the threat of terrorism was not confined to non-nationals, the different legal status of such persons could not provide an objective basis for the difference

---

[94] *R (on the application of Wilkinson)* v *Inland Revenue Commissioners* [2003] EWCA Civ 814, [2003] 1 WLR 2683, [2003] 3 All ER 719. Section 262 of the Income and Corporation Taxes Act 1988 was repealed with effect from 2000.

[95] *R (on the application of Clift and others)* v *Secretary of State for the Home Department* [2006] UKHL 54, [2007] 1 AC 484, [2007] 2 All ER 1. The provisions in question were sections 46(1) and 50(2) of the Criminal Justice Act 1991.

[96] Criminal Justice Act 2003 (Commencement No 8 and Transitional and Saving Provisions) Order 2005, SI 2005/950.

[97] *R (on the application of Morris)* v *Westminster City Council (No 3)* [2004] EWHC 2191 (Admin), [2005] 1 WLR 865, [2005] 1 All ER 351.

[98] [2005] EWCA Civ 1184, [2006] 1 WLR 505, [2005] HRLR 43.

[99] See clauses 161 and 162 of the Criminal Justice and Immigration Bill, which completed its Commons stages and had its first reading in the House of Lords on 9 January 2008.

[100] [2004] UKHL 56, [2005] 2 AC 68, [2005] 3 All ER 169.   [101] Section 23.

[102] The concept of derogation is discussed at p 177, *post*. The derogation in question was registered by the Secretariat General on 18 December 2001; SI 2001/4032.

[103] [2002] EWCA Civ 1502, [2004] QB 335, [2003] 1 All ER 816.

in treatment. A declaration of incompatibility was therefore granted, and the Order dealing with the derogation from Article 5 was quashed. The government did not release the detainees immediately but it did agree to seek alternative ways of dealing with them. Within three months the internment powers in the 2001 Act had been replaced with a system of 'control orders'. These control orders may involve restricting the movement or communications of suspected terrorists, but crucially they can be used in respect of both nationals and non-nationals.[104] The Home Office also agreed to seek assurances about human rights from other states, so that more suspected foreign terrorists could be deported.[105]

Remedial orders. To date there have been only three occasions on which ministers have considered it appropriate to make a remedial order under section 10, and only one of these resulted from a decision of a domestic court. The decision in question was a Court of Appeal case in which provisions of the Mental Health Act 1983 were found to be incompatible with the right to liberty under Article 5.[106] The Secretary of State was satisfied in this case that there were compelling reasons for acting quickly, and the offending provisions were amended by the Mental Health Act 1983 (Remedial) Order 2001.[107] The other two remedial orders made so far have followed decisions of the European Court of Human Rights.[108]

(c) Section 19: Ministerial statements of compatibility[109]

The courts may be aided in their efforts under section 3 by ministerial statements made under section 19 of the Act. This provides that before the Second Reading of a Bill, the Minister in charge of it must either: (a) make a statement that in his view its provisions are compatible with Convention rights; or (b) make a statement that although it is *not* compatible, the government nevertheless wishes to proceed. The purpose of section 19 is presumably to aid the legislative process and to enable incompatible Bills to be subjected to heightened scrutiny. However, governments will inevitably be reluctant to declare that they are advocating Bills which infringe human rights. Indeed, virtually all of the statements made under section 19 have been to the effect that legislation is compatible,[110] and as the section does not require a Minister to explain *how* he arrived at his conclusion, the probative value of these statements is greatly limited. For this reason, they risk

---

[104] Prevention of Terrorism Act 2005.

[105] Charles Clarke MP (Home Secretary), 430 HC Official Report (6th series) col 307, 26 January 2005.

[106] *R (on the application of H) v North and East London Regional Mental Health Review Tribunal* [2001] EWCA Civ 415, [2002] QB 1, [2001] 3 WLR 512. The provisions had effectively required a restricted patient seeking release from a secure hospital to prove that his continued detention was no longer warranted.

[107] SI 2001/3712.

[108] The Naval Discipline Act 1957 (Remedial) Order 2004, SI 2004/66, was introduced following the decision in *Grieves v UK* (2004) 39 EHRR 2: see p 283, n 382, *post*. The Marriage Act 1949 (Remedial) Order 2007, SI 2007/438, followed the decision in *B and L v United Kingdom* (2006) 42 EHRR 11.

[109] See also, p 72, *ante*.

[110] The knowledge that provisions of the Anti-Terrorism, Crime and Security Bill would almost certainly be *in*compatible led to a derogation from Article 5: see the discussion of *A v Secretary of State for the Home Department* [2004] UKHL 56, [2005] 2 AC 68, [2005] 3 All ER 169, above.

being seen as little more than labels of approval, giving no real indication as to the true human rights implications of the Bills concerned. Much will depend in practice on the willingness of MPs to engage with human rights issues, and to subject ministerial statements to proper scrutiny. The Joint Committee on Human Rights has an important role to play here:[111]

> The Joint Committee...is able to monitor the operation of section 19 of the HRA speedily and effectively, and reports to each House of Parliament its views as to the compatibility or lack of compatibility of legislative proposals.

The knowledge that a statement of compatibility must be made might also serve to concentrate the Minister's mind during the preparatory stages of a Bill. In addition, section 19 statements may be considered by the courts,[112] and it has been said that they will 'inevitably be a strong spur to the courts to find the means of construing statutes compatibly with the Convention'.[113] They are not, of course, binding, and a ministerial statement of compatibility does not prevent a court from making a declaration of *in*compatibility in the future. Indeed, the courts have so far made section 4 declarations in respect of two statutes enacted since the Human Rights Act came into force,[114] both of which were judged to be compatible with human rights by the ministers who introduced them. Nevertheless, the ministerial statement may give tacit encouragement to the judiciary to maximize the interpretive obligation under section 3. After all, if a Minister considers a Bill to be compatible, and Parliament enacts it on that basis, it might be suggested that Parliament must intend a compatible interpretation to be found. Baroness Hale may have been alluding to this when suggesting in *MB* that Parliament must have thought the Prevention of Terrorism Act 2005 to be compatible with Convention rights, though she did not refer specifically to section 19.[115]

Ironically, in the only case so far in which a minister has felt unable to make a statement of compatibility, a court has subsequently found the statute concerned to be Convention-compliant. The Communications Act 2003 prohibits political advertising in broadcasting, and this is at odds with the decision of the Court of Human Rights in *VgT* v *Switzerland*.[116] On this basis the Minister introducing the Bill felt unable to make a statement of compatibility, though she made it clear that she did not consider

---

[111] Lester, 'Parliamentary Scrutiny Under the Human Rights Act 1998' [2002] 4 EHRLR 432, at 437.

[112] *Wilson* v *First County Trust (No 2)*; *sub nom Wilson* v *Secretary of State for Trade and Industry* [2003] UKHL 40 at [61]-[67], [2004] 1 AC 816 at [61]-[67], [2003] 4 All ER 97, per Lord Nicholls.

[113] Lord Irvine of Lairg, 'The Development of Human Rights in Britain under an Incorporated Convention on Human Rights' [1998] PL 221.

[114] Section 23 of the Anti-Terrorism, Crime and Security Act 2001 (*A* v *Secretary of State for the Home Department* [2004] UKHL 56, [2005] 2 AC 68, [2005] 3 All ER 169) and section 19(3) of the Asylum and Immigration (Treatment of Claimants etc.) Act 2004 (*R (on the application of Baiai)* v *Secretary of State for the Home Department* [2007] EWCA Civ 478, [2007] 3 WLR 573, [2007] 4 All ER 199. A third declaration made in respect of the Prevention of Terrorism Act 2005 (*Secretary of State for the Home Department* v *MB* [2006] EWHC 1000 (Admin), [2006] HRLR 29) was overturned on appeal: [2006] EWCA Civ 1140, [2007] QB 415, [2006] HRLR 37; affirmed [2007] UKHL 46, [2007] 3 WLR 681.

[115] *Secretary of State for the Home Department* v *MB* [2007] UKHL 46 at [73], [2007] 3 WLR 681 at [73].

[116] *VgT Verein gegen Tierfabriken* v *Switzerland* (2002) 34 EHRR 4.

an incompatible interpretation to be inevitable.[117] In a subsequent challenge to the provisions the Administrative Court refused to make a declaration of incompatibility, holding that the restriction on freedom of expression fell within the UK's margin of appreciation.[118] In reaching this decision Ousley J attached 'great weight' to the fact that Parliament had 'expressed a considered view, having grappled with the human rights implications' of the provisions.[119]

3 DIRECT ENFORCEMENT OF CONVENTION RIGHTS

(a) Section 6: The duty of public authorities to act compatibly with the ECHR

Section 6(1) of the Act makes it unlawful for a public authority to act in a way which is incompatible with a Convention right. However, the authority will have a defence under section 6(2) if it can be shown that:

(a) as the result of one or more provisions of primary legislation, the authority could not have acted differently; or

(b) in the case of one or more provisions of, or made under, primary legislation which cannot be read or given effect in a way which is compatible with the Convention rights, the authority was acting so as to give effect to or enforce those provisions.

Section 6(3) makes it clear that neither House of Parliament constitutes a public authority for these purposes, and persons exercising functions in connection with proceedings in Parliament are also excluded. However, courts and tribunals are expressly included within the definition, and thus have an obligation to perform their functions in a manner compatible with Convention rights.

Identifying public authorities. The Act takes a functional approach to the meaning of 'public authority', and this means that even seemingly 'private' bodies may be subject to the Act if certain of their functions are public in nature.[120] A person or body may fall into one of three categories for these purposes: (1) 'standard' public authorities, which must act compatibly with the Convention at all times; (2) 'hybrid' or 'quasi-public' bodies, which are only caught by the Act when performing their public functions; and (3) private bodies, which are not subject to the duty under section 6(1) at all. The first category includes bodies such as government departments, the police, and local authorities, which are all self-evidently public in nature and present relatively few difficulties. The precise scope of the second category is rather more complex, and predictably the courts have drawn upon principles which were already established in the field of judicial

---

[117] Tessa Jowell, MP (Secretary of State for Culture, Media and Sport), 395 HC Official Report (6th series) col 789, 3 December 2002: see further, p 72, *ante.*

[118] *R (on the application of Animal Defenders International)* v *Secretary of State for Culture, Media and Sport* [2006] EWHC 3069 (Admin), [2007] HRLR 9. For a discussion of the concept of 'margin of appreciation', see p 176, *post.*

[119] Ibid, at [114].   [120] Section 6(3)(b).

review.[121] In one of its early Human Rights Act decisions, the Court of Appeal held that a registered social landlord was subject to section 6 in respect of its relationship with its tenants. The fact that the landlord performed functions which a public authority would otherwise have to carry out was relevant but not conclusive:[122]

> What can make an act, which would otherwise be private, public, is a feature or a combination of features which impose a public character or stamp on the act. Statutory authority for what is done can at least help to mark the act as being public; so can the extent of control over the function exercised by another body which is a public authority. The more closely the acts that could be of a private nature are enmeshed in the activities of a public body, the more likely they are to be public.

It was considered relevant that the housing association had been specifically created to take over a large proportion of residential council property.[123] It was also in receipt of state funding, had various statutory duties and was supervised by a statutory body. However, in the subsequent *Aston-Cantlow* decision, the House of Lords held that a parochial church council was not performing public functions when exercising a statutory power to compel a landowner to repair a church chancel:[124]

> It may be said that, as the church is a historic building which is open to the public, it is in the public interest that these repairs should be carried out. It is also true that the liability to repair the chancel rests on persons who need not be members of the church...But none of these factors leads to the conclusion that the PCC's act in seeking to enforce the lay rector's liability on behalf of the parishioners is a public rather than a private act. The nature of the act is to be found in the nature of the obligation which the PCC is seeking to enforce. It is seeking to enforce a civil debt. The function which it is performing has nothing to do with the responsibilities which are owed to the public by the State.

The decision in L *v* Birmingham.[125] The *Aston-Cantlow* case was the House of Lords' first opportunity to comment on the meaning of 'public authority', and although the decision was welcomed by some[126] it was also criticized for failing to make any express

---

[121] See, e.g., *R v Panel on Takeovers and Mergers, ex parte Datafin* [1987] QB 815, [1987] 1 All ER 564.

[122] *Poplar Housing and Regeneration Community Association Ltd v Donoghue* [2001] EWCA Civ 595 at [65], [2002] QB 48 at [65], [2001] 4 All ER 604.

[123] See also *R (on the application of Beer (t/a Hammer Trout Farm)) v Hampshire Farmers Markets Ltd* [2003] EWCA Civ 1056, [2004] 1 WLR 233: a company created by a local authority to manage a farmers' market was deemed to be exercising public functions when licensing stall-holders.

[124] *Aston-Cantlow and Wilcote with Billesley Parochial Church Council v Wallbank* [2003] UKHL 37 at [64], [2004] 1 AC 546 at [64], [2003] 3 All ER 1213, per Lord Hope. Other bodies deemed not to be public authorities include Network Rail (*Cameron v Network Rail Infrastructure Ltd (formerly Railtrack plc.)* [2006] EWHC 1133 (QB), [2007] 1 WLR 163, [2007] 3 All ER 241), and Lloyd's (*R (on the application of West) v Lloyd's of London* [2004] EWCA Civ 506, [2004] 3 All ER 251).

[125] [2007] UKHL 27, [2007] 3 WLR 112, [2007] 3 All ER 957.

[126] Meisel, 'The *Aston-Cantlow* Case: Blots on English Jurisprudence and the Public/Private Law Divide' [2004] PL 2.

reference to *Poplar*.[127] As a result, there is still some confusion as to where the line between hybrid and purely private bodies might be drawn, and the recent House of Lords decision in *L* v *Birmingham* has done little to clarify matters.

The issue in *L* was whether a private care home was subject to duties under section 6 when providing care and accommodation under a contract with a local authority. By a majority of 3:2 the House of Lords held that it was not.[128] All of the opinions emphasized the importance of a functional approach, and some expressly criticized the importance attached to institutional relationships in *Poplar*.[129] The conclusion of the majority was that the provision of care and accommodation in such cases is not an 'inherently governmental function',[130] and on this basis, the owners of the care home were held not to be exercising functions of a public nature.

Despite its status as a precedent of the House of Lords and its endorsement of *Aston-Cantlow*, the decision in *L* v *Birmingham* is unlikely to end the debate about section 6. Of the two dissenting judges, Baroness Hale had 'no doubt' that Parliament had intended care homes to be subject to the Human Rights Act,[131] while Lord Bingham agreed that the position on this matter was 'clear'.[132] By contrast, two of the majority opinions gave weight to the contractual and commercial motives of the care providers,[133] apparently adding another factor to the equation. Meanwhile, the Joint Committee on Human Rights is so concerned about the impact of this and other cases, that its chairman has introduced a Private Member's Bill aimed at reversing the trend and clarifying the scope of section 6.[134]

(b) Judicial deference and proportionality

In determining whether public authorities have acted in breach of Convention rights, the courts are required to assess the legitimacy of any interference with those rights and to measure the extent of the interference against the yardstick of proportionality. This concept is discussed further at p 225, but in essence it means that a balance must be struck between the general interests of the community and the rights of the individual,[135] and that any restriction on a right must be limited to the extent necessary

---

[127] See e.g.: Quane, 'The Strasbourg Jurisprudence and the Meaning of a "Public Authority" under the Human Rights Act' [2006] PL 106; *R (on the application of Beer (t/a Hammer Trout Farm))* v *Hampshire Farmers Markets Ltd* [2003] EWCA Civ 1056, [2004] 1 WLR 233.

[128] In doing so their Lordships endorsed a similar decision made by the Court of Appeal in respect of a charitable foundation: *R (on the application of Heather)* v *Leonard Cheshire Foundation* [2002] EWCA Civ 366, [2002] 2 All ER 936.

[129] Baroness Hale, for example, stated at [61] that the Court of Appeal had 'relied too heavily upon the historical links between the local authority and the registered social landlord'. It has since been suggested that registered social landlords are unlikely to be treated as having public functions in future: Landau, 'Functional Public Authorities after *YL*' [2007] PL 630, at 633.

[130] [2007] UKHL 27 at [115], [2007] 3 WLR 112 at [115], [2007] 3 All ER 957, per Lord Mance.

[131] Ibid, at [73].   [132] Ibid, at [2].

[133] Ibid, at [31] per Lord Scott, and at [116] per Lord Mance.

[134] The Human Rights Act 1998 (Meaning of Public Function) Bill, introduced by Andrew Dismore MP, had its first reading in the House of Commons on 18 December 2007. See also: *The Meaning of Public Authority under the Human Rights Act*, Ninth Report of the Session 2006–07, HL Paper 77 / HC 410, 24 March 2007.

[135] *Soering* v *UK* (1989) 11 EHRR 439.

to achieve a legitimate aim. The House of Lords confirmed at an early stage that the actions of public authorities in Human Rights Act cases must be measured against this principle of proportionality:[136]

> First, the doctrine of proportionality may require the reviewing court to assess the balance which the decision maker has struck, not merely whether it is within the range of rational or reasonable decisions. Secondly, the proportionality test may go further than the traditional grounds of review inasmuch as it may require attention to be directed to the relative weight accorded to interests and considerations. Thirdly...the intensity of the review...is guaranteed by the twin requirements that the limitation of the right was necessary in a democratic society, in the sense of meeting a pressing social need, and the question whether the interference was really proportionate to the legitimate aim being pursued.

These principles require a different level of scrutiny to that traditionally applied in judicial review cases, and the debate about how much judicial deference should be paid to the executive in human rights cases is ongoing.[137] In a recent House of Lords' decision Lord Walker endorsed an earlier attempt by Laws LJ to establish some general principles:[138]

(1) greater deference is to be paid to an Act of Parliament than to a decision of the executive or subordinate measure;

(2) there is more scope for deference where the Convention itself requires a balance to be struck, much less so where the right is stated in terms which are unqualified;

(3) greater deference will be due to the democratic powers where the subject-matter in hand is peculiarly within their constitutional responsibility, and less when it lies more particularly within the constitutional responsibility of the courts;

(4) greater or less deference will be due according to whether the subject matter lies more readily within the actual or potential expertise of the democratic powers or the courts.

The courts have certainly taken a more 'interventionist' stance under the 'due process' rights in Articles 5 and 6, which might be regarding as falling within their particular

---

[136] *R (on the application of Daly)* v *Secretary of State for the Home Department* [2001] UKHL 26 at [27], [2001] 2 AC 532 at [27], [2001] 3 All ER 433, per Lord Steyn. A blanket policy authorizing searches of a prisoner's cell and requiring his correspondence with his lawyer to be examined in his absence was *not* a proportionate response to the legitimate objective of maintaining prison discipline. (Judicial review is discussed further in chapter 7.)

[137] See Allan, 'Human Rights and Judicial Review: A Critique of Due Deference' (2006) 65(3) CLJ 671; Clayton, 'Judicial Deference and "Democratic Dialogue": the Legitimacy of Judicial Intervention under the Human Rights Act 1998' [2004] PL 33; Edwards, 'Judicial Deference under the Human Rights Act' (2002) 65 MLR 859; Jowell, 'Judicial Deference: Servility, Civility or Institutional Incapacity?' [2003] PL 592; Morris, 'Separating Human Rights Adjudication from Judicial Review' [2007] EHRLR 679; and Steyn, 'Deference: A Tangled Story' [2005] PL 346. See also, p 328, *post*.

[138] *R (on the application of ProLife Alliance)* v *BBC* [2003] UKHL 23 at [136], [2004] 1 AC 185 at [136], [2003] 2 All ER 977 (applying the judgment of Laws LJ in *International Transport Roth GmbH* v *Secretary of State for the Home Department* [2002] EWCA Civ 158, [2003] QB 728, [2002] HRLR 31). See also, the observations of Lord Hope in *R* v *DPP, ex parte Kebilene* [2000] 2 AC 326 at 381, [1999] 4 All ER 801 at 844.

sphere of expertise. Thus, in *A v Secretary of State for the Home Department*,[139] which concerned the right to liberty under Article 5, Lord Bingham stated that the courts were not 'precluded by any doctrine of deference from scrutinising the issues raised', even though those issues included decisions about national security. On the other hand, the courts have tended to concede a wider margin of discretion under Articles such as 8 and 10, which require individual rights to be balanced against the public interest and which leave more scope for restrictions on policy grounds. In the light of these principles, Lord Hoffmann has taken exception to the word 'deference' being used at all:[140]

> I do not think that its overtones of servility, or perhaps gracious concession, are appropriate to describe what is happening...The principle that the independence of the courts is necessary for a proper decision of disputed legal rights or claims of violation of human rights is a legal principle. It is reflected in Article 6 of the Convention. On the other hand, the principle that majority approval is necessary for a proper decision on policy or allocation of resources is also a legal principle. Likewise, when a court decides that a decision is within the proper competence of the legislature or executive, it is not showing deference. It is deciding the law.

(c) Horizontal effect

In keeping with the scheme of the Convention, the Act does not oblige private bodies and individuals to act compatibly with Convention rights, and it does not expressly require the courts to give effect to the Convention in developing the common law. However, given that the courts are clearly under a general duty to perform their functions in accordance with the Convention, there was much academic speculation from the outset about whether the Human Rights Act would have 'indirect horizontal effect'.[141] In other words, would the courts be obliged to give effect to the Convention in developing the common law, and would this mean that Convention rights could be directly enforced against private individuals?

It soon became apparent that Convention rights and principles would have an influence on judicial reasoning in common law cases. For example:[142]

> If there is an intrusion in a situation in which a person can reasonably expect his privacy to be respected then that intrusion will be capable of giving rise to liability in an action for breach of confidence unless the intrusion can be justified.

---

[139] [2004] UKHL 56 at [29] and [42], [2005] 2 AC 68 at [29] and [42], [2005] 3 All ER 169; see further p 161.

[140] *R (on the application of ProLife Alliance) v BBC* [2003] UKHL 23 at [75]–[76], [2004] 1 AC 185 at [75]–[76], [2003] 2 All ER 977. See also the comments of a unanimous House of Lords in *Huang v Secretary of State for the Home Department* [2007] UKHL 11 at [16], [2007] 2 AC 167 at [16], [2007] 4 All ER 15.

[141] Buxton, 'The Human Rights Act and Private Law' (2000) 116 LQR 48; Hunt, 'The "Horizontal Effect" of the Human Rights Act' [1998] PL 424; Phillipson, 'The Human Rights Act: "Horizontal Effect" and the Common Law: A Bang or a Whimper?' (1999) 62(2) MLR 825; Wade, 'Horizons of Horizontality' (2000) 116 LQR 217.

[142] *A v B; H v Associated Newspapers* [2002] EWCA Civ 337 at [11], [2003] QB 195 at [11], [2002] 2 All ER 545, per Lord Woolf CJ. See also *Douglas v Hello! Ltd (No 1)* [2001] QB 967, [2001] 2 All ER 289; *Venables and Thompson v News Group Newspapers* [2001] Fam 430, [2001] 1 All ER 908.

Thus far, however, the courts have stopped short of recognizing any new common law torts, preferring instead to take the Convention into account when applying established torts such as breach of confidence and nuisance. Thus in *Wainwright* v *Home Office* the House of Lords held that a new tort of privacy could only be recognized by Parliament, but that the courts could develop existing torts and remedies in order to satisfy Article 8.[143]

(d) Section 7: Challenging public authorities under the Act

Where a person claims that a public authority has acted (or is proposing to act) in breach of Convention rights, proceedings may be brought against that authority under section 7(1)(a) of the Act. However, such proceedings can only be brought by a person who is able to show that he is (or would be) 'a victim of the unlawful act'. This is consistent with the criteria for bringing a Strasbourg application under Article 34 of the Convention, but it is rather stricter than the 'sufficient interest' test applied in conventional judicial review cases.[144] Public interest groups with a particular interest and expertise in an area may have standing to bring a judicial review action on conventional grounds, but they will not be considered 'victims' under the Human Rights Act unless they are actually affected by a Convention breach. The government considered that the Strasbourg approach would help to prevent the courts from becoming clogged up with test cases, and it rejected the suggestion that the 'victim' test could lead to injustice:[145]

> If there is an unlawful action or if unlawful action is threatened, then there will be victims or potential victims who will complain and who will in practice be supported by interest groups. If there are no victims, the issue is probably academic and the courts should not be troubled.

In addition to being able to bring a direct action under section 7(1)(a), section 7(1)(b) allows a victim (or potential victim) of a Convention breach to raise the issue in proceedings which have been commenced on some other basis. Thus, a Convention issue may be raised by a party to a civil action involving a public authority, by a defendant in a criminal case, or by an applicant in a judicial review action based on other grounds. However, a 'judicial act' of a court or tribunal may only be challenged in judicial review proceedings or during the course of an appeal.[146] In addition, section 7(3) states that:

> If the proceedings are brought on an application for judicial review, the applicant is to be taken to have a sufficient interest in relation to the unlawful act only if he is, or would be, a victim of that act.

---

[143] [2003] UKHL 53, [2004] 2 AC 406, [2003] 4 All ER 969. Cf. *Peck* v *UK* (2003) 36 EHRR 41, which revealed significant deficiencies in the ability of domestic law to safeguard the right to respect for private life: see p 187, *post*.

[144] See, e.g., *R* v *Inspectorate of Pollution, ex parte Greenpeace (No 2)* [1994] 4 All ER 329; *R* v *Secretary of State for Foreign and Commonwealth Affairs, ex parte World Development Movement* [1995] 1 WLR 386, [1995] 1 All ER 611. See also Marriott and Nicol, 'The Human Rights Act, Representative Standing and the Victim Culture' [1998] EHRLR 730.

[145] Lord Irvine (Lord Chancellor), 583 HL Official Report (5th series) col 832, 24 Nov 1997.

[146] Section 9(1).

This provision is designed to prevent public interest groups from circumventing the victim requirement by raising Convention issues in judicial review proceedings brought on other grounds. Nevertheless, a court conducting a judicial review of statutory powers will be obliged to seek a Convention-friendly interpretation of those powers, even if the applicant is not a 'victim'.[147] It would also appear that if a court accepts a judicial review application from a public interest group, it will be obliged to act compatibly with the Convention when conducting that review, in order to fulfil its own obligations under section 6.

The time limit for bringing an action under section 7 creates a further anomaly. Actions for judicial review must normally be brought within three months,[148] whereas section 7(5) specifies a one-year time limit for actions brought under section 7(1)(a).[149] In this respect, an applicant whose complaint is based solely on a breach of Convention rights appears to be in a better position than an applicant seeking review on both Convention and non-Convention grounds. In addition, it has been persuasively argued that claims under section 7(1)(a) need not necessarily be brought by way of judicial review at all, and that they could instead take the form of an action for breach of statutory duty.[150] The comments of the Under-Secretary of State for the Home Department during the committee stage of the Bill seem to support this view:[151]

> Clause 7(1)(a) creates a cause of action, and the Bill would be open to criticism if it did not clearly state what limitation period was to apply to proceedings under that paragraph. As I have said, we believe that the right balance is provided by a 12-month period, with the power to extend it for the benefit of the complainant. Suggestions for a two or three-year period fail to take account of the existing three-month period for judicial review, to which *many* claims under clause 7(1)(a) will be *similar*. [emphasis added]

Finally, section 7(6) confirms that Convention issues may be raised in proceedings brought by or at the instigation of a public authority, or in any appeal against the decision of a court or tribunal. Most of the Act's provisions did not come into force until 2 October 2000, and a section 7 claim may only be brought against a public authority in respect of acts occurring on or after this date. However, section 22(4) states that where proceedings are instigated or brought by a public authority, a breach of the Convention may be challenged under section 7(1)(b) whenever the act in question took place. In other words, a demonstrator arrested for a public order offence in September 2000 would

[147] See, e.g., *R (on the application of Rusbridger)* v *Attorney-General* [2003] UKHL 38, [2004] 1 AC 357, [2003] 3 All ER 784. The House of Lords confirmed that the editor of the *Guardian* did not need to be a 'victim' in order to seek a declaration that s 3 of the Treason Felony Act 1848 was incompatible with the Convention. However, the action failed because the provision had not actually been applied and the issue was purely hypothetical: see p 198, *post*.

[148] See p 228, *post*.

[149] The courts have a discretion to allow a longer period if it is considered equitable.

[150] See, e.g. Fenwick, *Civil Liberties and Human Rights* (3rd edn, 2002) at p 168; Clayton and Tomlinson, *Human Rights Law* (2000) at p 1498.

[151] Mike O'Brien MP, 314 HC Official Report (6th series) coll 1095 and 1099, 24 June 1998. Mr O'Brien took the view that the standard three-month time limit would normally be appropriate *if* judicial review proceedings were used.

have been entitled to raise issues based on Articles 10 or 11 in the course of his defence. In *R v Lambert*,[152] however, the House of Lords gave a restrictive interpretation to this provision and held that where a person had actually been tried and convicted before the commencement of the Act, pre-commencement breaches of the Convention could not be raised in a subsequent appeal. Within months a differently constituted House suggested that *Lambert* had been wrongly decided, but it was nevertheless unwilling to overrule the decision.[153]

(e) Section 8: Remedies

Where a court or tribunal has found that a public authority has acted unlawfully under section 6(1), it may grant 'such relief or remedy, or make such order within its powers as it considers just and appropriate'.[154] An award of damages can only be made by a court which already has the power to award damages in civil proceedings,[155] and only where the court is satisfied that an award is necessary to afford 'just satisfaction'.[156] In exercising the power to award damages a court must take into account the principles applied by the European Court of Human Rights under Article 41 of the Convention.[157] Having done this in a recent decision on Article 6, the House of Lords indicated that the finding of a breach of Convention rights would often be an adequate remedy in itself:[158]

> [T]he Court [of Human Rights] has ordinarily been willing to depart from its practice of finding a violation of Art.6 to be, in itself, just satisfaction under Art.41 only where the Court finds a causal connection between the violation found and the loss for which an applicant claims to be compensated... and [it] has on the whole been slow to award such compensation.

In its 2006 *Review of the Implementation of the Human Rights Act*, the Department for Constitutional Affairs noted that section 8 had been interpreted 'so strictly' that 'it is now very difficult to obtain damages under the HRA'.[159] Indeed, in the five-and-a-half-year period covered by the *Review* there were only three reported cases in which damages under section 8 were awarded.[160]

---

[152] [2001] UKHL 37, [2002] 2 AC 545, [2001] 3 All ER 577.

[153] *R v Kansal (No 2)* [2001] UKHL 62, [2002] AC 69, [2002] 1 All ER 257; *R v Lyons; Parnes; Saunders* [2002] 2 Cr App R 210.

[154] Section 8(1). For a discussion of when an award of damages might be 'just and appropriate', see *Anufrijeva v Southwark LBC* [2003] EWCA Civ 1406, [2004] QB 1124, [2004] 1 All ER 833. See also Hartshorne, 'The Human Rights Act 1998 and Damages for Non-Pecuniary Loss' [2004] EHRLR 660; Clayton, 'Damage Limitation: The Courts and the Human Rights Act Damages' [2005] PL 429.

[155] Section 8(2).   [156] Section 8(3).   [157] Section 8(4).

[158] *R (on the application of Greenfield) v Secretary of State for the Home Department* [2005] UKHL 14 at [11], [2005] 1 WLR 673 at [11], [2005] 2 All ER 240, per Lord Bingham (with whom the other Law Lords agreed).

[159] DCA (July 2006), at p 18.

[160] Ibid: *R (Bernard) v Enfield London Borough Council* [2002] EWHC 2282 (Admin), [2003] HRLR 4 (£8,000 awarded to a disabled claimant required to live in unsuitable accommodation for 20 months); *R (on the application of KB) v Mental Health Review Tribunal* [2003] EWHC 193 (Admin), [2004] QB 936, [2003] 2 All ER 209 (damages ranging from £750 to £4,000 awarded following delays to tribunal hearings); and *Van Colle v Chief Constable of Hertfordshire* [2006] EWHC 360 (QB), [2006] 3 All ER 963 (damages of £50,000 awarded to parents of a witness murdered following inadequate police protection – reduced on appeal to £25,000: [2007] EWCA Civ 325, [2007] 1 WLR 1821, [2007] 3 All ER 122).

Section 9(3) of the Act states that courts and tribunals cannot be liable in damages for judicial acts done in good faith unless there has been a breach of Article 5(5). Where there has been such a breach the award must be made against the Crown and the 'appropriate person'[161] must be joined to the proceedings.

THE FUTURE: A BRITISH BILL OF RIGHTS?

In its *Review of the Implementation of the Human Rights Act*, the Department for Constitutional Affairs concluded that the effect of the Act 'has been far from marginal, and has involved the courts in a much more active and intense scrutiny of the Executive' than had been required prior to October 2000.[162] As Klug explains, the Act has been 'rather too successful at challenging the executive for the government's comfort',[163] and decisions on human rights have been at the centre of much of the recent tension between the courts and the government. The Act has been widely misunderstood and misinterpreted by both public servants and the public in general,[164] and even politicians have occasionally succumbed to some of the urban myths surrounding its impact. David Cameron, for example, in a speech to the Police Federation, made reference to 'a series of disgraceful incidents', including 'prisons given access to pornography' and 'burglars given Kentucky Fried Chicken'.[165] In fact, a challenge to a decision to deny a prisoner access to pornography was thrown out at the application stage, while the decision to supply a burglar with fast food was part of a routine negotiating strategy designed to coax him down from the roof where he had taken refuge. It was, in any event, taken by the police rather than the courts.[166]

Against this background it is perhaps not surprising that some have called for the Act to be amended or repealed, and in 2006 the leader of the opposition announced that his party would, if elected to government, seek to replace it with a 'British' bill of rights more 'in tune with British traditions about liberty'.[167] Ministers have also hinted at the possibility of making changes to the Act – almost invariably when judicial decisions have gone against them[168] – but outright repeal has never been suggested as official

---

[161] The 'appropriate person' is defined by s 9(5) to mean 'the Minister responsible for the court concerned, or a person or government department nominated by him'.

[162] At p 35.

[163] 'A Bill of Rights: Do We Need One or Do We Already Have One?' [2007] PL 701 at 714. See also the discussion at p 331, *post*.

[164] DCA, *Review of the Implementation of the Human Rights Act* (July 2006) at chapter 4. An example cited at p 31 of the *Review* is the widespread but false assumption that the Act makes it unlawful to film school nativity plays.

[165] Cited in JUSTICE, *A British Bill of Rights: Informing the Debate* (2007) at p 14.

[166] DCA (2006) *supra*, n 164, at pp 30–31.   [167] Reported in *The Observer*, 4 November 2007.

[168] While still Prime Minister, for example, Tony Blair suggested that there was a case for reviewing the Act (reported in *The Guardian*, 15 May 2006). His comments followed a High Court ruling preventing nine Afghan hijackers from being deported: *R (on the application of S) v Secretary of State for the Home Department*

government policy. The DCA's *Review* re-stated the government's commitment to the ECHR and the Human Rights Act, and listed several reasons why repeal of the Act has been 'comprehensively and publicly ruled out':[169]

> [Any attempt at repeal] is likely at best to be fruitless and at worst to introduce a damaging conflict with a judiciary unwilling to see the common law divorced from the protection of fundamental rights. It would also, probably, increase further the scrutiny received by the UK at Strasbourg.

However, the *Review* also suggested that 'in a number of key areas, and particularly when public safety is in issue, key decision takers may be getting the balance wrong by placing undue emphasis upon the entitlements of individuals'.[170] The government has now joined the bill of rights bandwagon, but instead of calling for the Human Rights Act to be scrapped it is proposing that it should be supplemented by a 'British Bill of Rights and Responsibilities':[171]

> [Such a Bill] could provide explicit recognition that human rights come with responsibilities and must be exercised in a way that respects the human rights of others. It would build on the basic principles of the Human Rights Act, but make explicit the way in which a democratic society's rights have to be balanced by obligations. The Government itself recognised, in its review last year of the implementation of the Human Rights Act, the importance which must attach to public safety and ensuring that Government Agencies accord appropriate priority to protection of the public when balancing rights. A Bill of Rights and Duties might provide a means of giving greater clarity and legislative force to this commitment. However, a framework of civic responsibilities – were it to be given legislative force – would need to avoid encroaching upon personal freedoms and civil liberties which have been hard won over centuries of our history.

Not all of those who support the idea of a bill of rights are motivated by a desire to qualify the scope of existing protection. JUSTICE, for example, has added its voice to the campaign for such an instrument, suggesting that the government should consider: whether any rights not covered by the 1998 Act 'are now ripe for inclusion'; whether a different model of entrenchment could be adopted; and whether the existing mechanisms for enforcement are satisfactory.[172]

At the time of writing it is not clear what form the government's proposed Bill might take: indeed, it is by no means certain that the proposal will be taken forward at all. Yet whatever the outcome of the current debate, it seems increasingly likely that the impact of the 1998 Act will prove to be irreversible.

[2006] EWHC 1111 (Admin), *The Times*, 14 June 2006. The decision was subsequently affirmed by the Court of Appeal: EWCA Civ 1157, *The Times*, 9 October 2006.

[169] DCA (2006) *supra*, n 164, at p 38.   [170] Ibid, at p 39.

[171] *The Governance of Britain*, Cm 7170, 2007, at para 210; for discussion see Le Sueur, 'Gordon Brown's New Constitutional Settlement' [2008] PL 21.

[172] JUSTICE, *A British Bill of Rights: Informing the Debate* (2007) at p 16.

FURTHER READING

ALLAN, 'Human Rights and Judicial Review: A Critique of Due Deference' (2006) 65(3) CLJ 671

BELOFF and MOUNTFIELD, 'Unconventional Behaviour? Judicial Uses of the European Convention in England and Wales' [1996] EHRLR 467

BINGHAM, 'The European Convention on Human Rights: Time to Incorporate' [1993] LQR 390

BUXTON, 'The Human Rights Act and Private Law' (2000) 116 LQR 48

CLAYTON, 'Judicial Deference and "Democratic Dialogue": The Legitimacy of Judicial Intervention under the Human Rights Act 1998' [2004] PL 33

CLAYTON, 'Damage Limitation: The Courts and the Human Rights Act Damages' [2005] PL 429

CUMPER, 'The Protection of Religious Rights under s 13 of the Human Rights Act' [2000] PL 254

Department for Constitutional Affairs, *Review of the Implementation of the Human Rights Act* (2006)

EDWARDS, 'Judicial Deference under the Human Rights Act' (2002) 65 MLR 859

EKINS, 'A Critique of Radical Approaches to Rights Consistent Statutory Interpretation' [2003] EHRLR 641

HARTSHORNE, 'The Human Rights Act 1998 and Damages for Non-Pecuniary Loss' [2004] EHRLR 660

HUNT, 'The "Horizontal Effect" of the Human Rights Act' [1998] PL 424

IRVINE, 'The Development of Human Rights in Britain under an Incorporated Convention on Human Rights' [1998] PL 221

JOWELL, 'Judicial Deference: Servility, Civility or Institutional Incapacity?' [2003] PL 592

KAVANAGH, 'Statutory Interpretation and Human Rights after *Anderson*: A More Contextual Approach' [2004] PL 537

LANDAU, 'Functional Public Authorities after *YL*' [2007] PL 630

LESTER, 'Parliamentary Scrutiny under the Human Rights Act 1998' [2002] 4 EHRLR 432

LEWIS, 'The European Ceiling on Human Rights' [2007] PL 72

MARRIOTT and NICOL, 'The Human Rights Act, Representative Standing and the Victim Culture' [1998] EHRLR 730

MASTERMAN, 'Taking the Strasbourg Jurisprudence into Account: Developing a "Municipal Law of Human Rights" under the Human Rights Act' (2005) ICLQ 54(4) 907

MEISEL, 'The *Aston-Cantlow* Case: Blots on English Jurisprudence and the Public/Private Law Divide' [2004] PL 2

MORRIS, 'Separating Human Rights Adjudication from Judicial Review' [2007] EHRLR 679

QUANE, 'The Strasbourg Jurisprudence and the Meaning of a "Public Authority" under the Human Rights Act' [2006] PL 106

NICOL, 'Statutory Interpretation and Human Rights after *Anderson*' [2004] PL 274

PHILLIPSON, 'The Human Rights Act: "Horizontal Effect" and the Common Law: A Bang or a Whimper?' (1999) 62(2) MLR 825

STEYN, 'Deference: A Tangled Story' [2005] PL 346

STRAW and BOATENG, 'Bringing Rights Home: Labour's Plans to Incorporate the European Convention on Human Rights into UK Law' [1997] 1 EHRLR 71

VAN ZYL SMIT, 'The New Purposive Interpretation of Statutes: HRA Section 3 after *Ghaidan* v *Godin-Mendoza*' (2007) 70(2) MLR 294

WADE, 'Horizons of Horizontality' (2000) 116 LQR 217

WADHAM et al, *Blackstone's Guide to the Human Rights Act 1998* (Oxford University Press: 4th edn, 2007)

6

CONVENTION RIGHTS[1]

INTRODUCTION

This chapter focuses on the rights protected by the European Convention on Human Rights and given effect in domestic law by the Human Rights Act 1998. The specific areas covered will include:

- The general characteristics of the rights protected.
- The concepts of proportionality and the margin of appreciation.
- Derogation.
- The scope of specific rights and their impact at both Strasbourg and domestic level.
- The European Court of Human Rights and its role in enforcing the Convention.

THE NATURE OF THE RIGHTS PROTECTED

The Convention only imposes obligations on states and it is not possible to bring an action against a private individual at Strasbourg level. However, where an individual interferes with a Convention right the state may be liable if it has failed to take appropriate steps to protect that right or if it has failed to provide an adequate remedy. In *Earl Spencer* v *UK*,[2] for example, the European Court of Human Rights was prepared to consider a claim based on alleged breaches of privacy by several newspapers, because the applicant had made an arguable case that UK law did not protect individual rights of privacy.

---

[1] See Harris, O'Boyle and Warbrick, *Law of the European Convention on Human Rights* (1995); Janis, Kay and Bradley, *European Human Rights Law: Text and Materials* (3rd edn, 2008); Van Dijk et al, *The Theory and Practice of the European Convention on Human Rights* (4th edn, 2006); Mowbray, *Cases and Materials on the European Convention on Human Rights* (2nd edn, 2007); Ovey and White (eds), *Jacobs and White: European Convention on Human Rights* (4th edn, 2006).

[2] (1998) 25 EHRR CD 105. The claim was ultimately unsuccessful because the applicants failed to demonstrate the inadequacy of domestic law. See also, *Halford* v *UK* (1997) 24 EHRR 523.

Most Convention rights are not absolute. Although the rights to freedom from torture and slavery are unqualified and non-derogable,[3] the other rights are subject to certain limitations. The doctrines of proportionality and the margin of appreciation are both important in determining the permissible extent of these limitations.[4]

1 PROPORTIONALITY[5]

Inherent in the Convention is the principle that a fair balance must be struck between the general interests of the community and the individual's fundamental rights.[6] Where limitations on specific rights are permitted, they are usually expressed to be subject to a requirement of necessity, and this is given effect in the court's jurisprudence by the application of the principle of proportionality. For example, Article 10(2) states that any limitation on the right to freedom of expression must go no further than is 'necessary in a democratic society'. In other words, the restriction must conform to a 'pressing social need' and the interference must be proportionate to the legitimate aim pursued.[7]

This principle applies equally to the other qualified rights in the Convention. Thus in *Dudgeon* v *UK*,[8] laws criminalizing homosexual acts between consenting adult males infringed the Article 8 right to respect for private life because they failed the test of proportionality. This was so, notwithstanding the fact that the state was pursuing the 'legitimate aim' of protecting vulnerable young members of society. The House of Lords has confirmed that the actions of public authorities in Human Rights Act cases must be measured against the principle of proportionality, and this involves a different level of scrutiny to that traditionally applied in judicial review cases.[9]

2 THE MARGIN OF APPRECIATION

The 'margin of appreciation' describes the degree of deference shown to States in areas where there is room for discretion in the interpretation of Convention provisions. It arises most often in the context of the 'personal freedom' provisions in Articles 8 to 11,[10] since these are subject to a range of possible exceptions and there is room for disagreement about their scope. The principle was clearly articulated in the *Handyside* case:[11]

> By reason of their direct and continuous contact with the vital forces of their countries, State authorities are in principle in a better position than the international

---

[3] See below.   [4] For the application of these principles in EC law, see p 122, *ante*.

[5] See Fordham and de la Mere, 'Identifying the Principles of Proportionality', in Jowell and Cooper (eds), *Understanding Human Rights Principles* (2001) at 27; Blake, 'Importing Proportionality: Clarification or Confusion?' [2002] EHRLR 19.

[6] *Soering* v *UK* (1989) 11 EHRR 439.

[7] See *Sunday Times* v *UK* (1979–1980) 2 EHRR 245; *Handyside* v *UK* (1979) 1 EHRR 737.

[8] (1982) 4 EHRR 149.

[9] *R (on the application of Daly)* v *Secretary of State for the Home Department* [2001] UKHL 26, [2001] 2 AC 532, [2001] 3 All ER 433: see the quotation from this decision at p 167, *ante*.

[10] See Yourow, *The Margin of Appreciation Doctrine in the Dynamics of European Human Rights Jurisprudence* (1996).

[11] *Handyside* v *UK* (1979) 1 EHRR 737 at para 48.

judge to give an opinion on the exact content of these requirements as well as on the 'necessity' of a 'restriction' or 'penalty' intended to meet them.

The existence or non-existence of common ground between the states is an important factor in determining the extent of any national margin,[12] but opinion is divided as to whether the doctrine is really an appropriate response to European diversity and national sovereignty. In a partly dissenting judgment in *Z v Finland*, De Meyer J stated that:[13]

> [W]here human rights are concerned, there is no room for a margin of appreciation which would enable the states to decide what is acceptable and what is not. On that subject the boundary not to be overstepped must be as clear and precise as possible. It is for the Court, not each state individually to decide that issue.

Domestic courts are not required to apply Convention rights to a diverse group of states, and the margin of appreciation doctrine therefore has no application in Human Rights Act cases.[14] However, the role of the courts in reviewing the actions of public authorities is essentially supervisory, and although the standard of scrutiny under the Human Rights Act is a heightened one, decision-makers are still afforded a measure of discretion. This is particularly relevant in cases which hinge on whether a restriction on a right is 'necessary',[15] though any restriction is, of course, subject to a requirement of proportionality.

3 DEROGATION

Most Convention rights are subject to the possibility of derogation in times of war or other public emergency.[16] The UK entered a derogation in respect of Article 5 following the decision[17] that provisions of the Prevention of Terrorism (Temporary Provisions) Act 1984 were in breach of the Convention. At the time the UK deemed the situation in Northern Ireland to constitute an 'emergency threatening the life of the nation', and the European Court of Human Rights was not prepared to disagree with this assessment.[18] The provisions were eventually replaced by more stringent measures in the Terrorism Act 2000 and the derogation was withdrawn in February 2001. However, in December of the same year, the UK once again derogated from Article 5 in respect

---

[12] *Rasmussen v Denmark* (1984) 7 EHRR 371.

[13] (1997) 25 EHRR 371 at 415. Jones suggests that the doctrine 'can only...devalue Convention rights and freedoms at the expense of the limitations': 'The Devaluation of Human Rights Under the European Convention' [1995] PL 430, at 449. Cf. Schokkenbroek, 'The Basis, Nature and Application of the Margin of Appreciation Doctrine in the Case-Law of the European Court of Human Rights' (1998) 19(1) HRLJ 30; Letsas, 'Two Concepts of the Margin of Appreciation' (2006) 26(4) OJLS 705.

[14] Singh et al, 'Is there a Role for the Margin of Appreciation in National Law after the Human Rights Act?' [1999] EHRLR 15.

[15] See e.g. *R (on the application of Samaroo) v Secretary of State for the Home Department* [2001] EWCA Civ 1139, [2001] UKHRR 1150.

[16] Derogation from Articles 3, 4(1) and 7 is not possible, and Article 2 is only derogable in respect of 'deaths resulting from lawful acts of war'.

[17] *Brogan v UK* (1989) 11 EHRR 117.

[18] *Brannigan and McBride v UK* (1994) 17 EHRR 539.

of the newly enacted power[19] to detain suspected foreign terrorists without trial. The public emergency this time was said to stem from the heightened threat of terrorism in the wake of September 11th and the presence of suspected international terrorists in the UK.[20] When this derogation was challenged, a majority of the House of Lords accepted the government's assertion that the UK was facing a public emergency, but in doing so they demonstrated far less deference than that generally exhibited by the Court of Human Rights:[21]

> The courts' power to rule on the validity of the derogation is another of the safeguards [contained in the Human Rights Act 1998]...It would be meaningless if we could only rubber-stamp what the Home Secretary and Parliament have done. But any sensible court, like any sensible person, recognises the limits of its expertise. Assessing the strength of a general threat to the life of the nation is, or should be, within the expertise of the Government and its advisers...Protecting the life of the nation is one of the first tasks of a Government in a world of nation states. That does not mean that the courts could never intervene. Unwarranted declarations of emergency are a familiar tool of tyranny. If a Government were to declare a public emergency where patently there was no such thing, it would be the duty of the court to say so. But we are here considering the immediate aftermath of the unforgettable events of 11 September 2001...

It was held that the government had failed to demonstrate the need to single out foreign nationals for detention in circumstances where British nationals posed an equally serious threat. The derogation was thus incompatible with the Convention, and the government's Derogation Order[22] was quashed.

SPECIFIC RIGHTS

1 ARTICLE 2: THE RIGHT TO LIFE

This states that 'everyone's right to life shall be protected by law' and that 'no-one shall be deprived of his life intentionally save in the execution of a sentence of a court following his conviction of a crime for which this penalty is provided by law'. This form of words originally allowed states to retain the use of capital punishment, but the possibility of imposing the death penalty in peace time has effectively been removed by

---

[19] Anti-Terrorism, Crime and Security Act 2001, s 23. The power was limited to circumstances in which the suspect could not be deported because of the risk that he or she would face persecution or torture.

[20] Declaration registered by the Secretariat General on 18 December 2001.

[21] *A v Secretary of State for the Home Department* [2004] UKHL 56 at [226], [2005] 2 WLR 87 at [226], per Baroness Hale. Lord Hoffmann dissented on this point, stating at [96] that 'terrorist violence, serious as it is, does not threaten our institutions of government or our existence as a civil community'. Judicial deference under the 1998 Act is discussed at p 161, *ante*.

[22] Human Rights Act (Amendment No 2) Order 2001, SI 2001/4032. Further derogations are contemplated by the Prevention of Terrorism Act 2005, though none have been made to date. See further, p 184, *post*.

Protocol 6. Acceptance of this Protocol is now mandatory,[23] and as of 1 January 2008, only Russia had still to ratify it. Forty states, including the UK, had also ratified the more extensive provisions in Protocol 13, which bans the use of the death penalty in *any* circumstances.

The remaining limitations on the right to life permit the use of force where this is necessary to defend a person from unlawful violence, to effect a lawful arrest, to prevent the escape of a lawfully detained person, or to quell a riot or insurrection. In *McCann* v *UK*[24] the SAS shot and killed three members of the Provisional IRA who were suspected of planning a terrorist attack in Gibraltar. Although the court accepted that force had been used in pursuit of a legitimate aim, it found a violation of the Convention because it was not persuaded that the use of lethal force had been absolutely necessary.[25] Where a state is mounting a legitimate security operation, a breach of Article 2 will be established if the state does not take all reasonable precautions to avoid or minimize loss of life.[26] However, no violation was found in *Stewart* v *UK*[27] when a teenager was killed by plastic baton rounds fired into a crowd during a riot.

Article 2 also imposes a procedural obligation to investigate deaths caused by state action or while the deceased was in the state's care. In *Jordan* v *UK*[28] the Court of Human Rights ruled that the holding of an inquest does not discharge this obligation, because an inquest is not a forum for determining the identity or culpability of those responsible for causing death. This decision triggered the government's Review of Coroner Services,[29] along with several domestic cases. In *R (on the application of Amin)* v *Secretary of State for the Home Department*[30] an inquest was held to be an inadequate forum to investigate the death of a prisoner at the hands of his racist cellmate. An inquest into the death of a prisoner suffering from heroin withdrawal was also unsatisfactory, because the jury was not invited to consider a verdict of systemic neglect.[31] Similarly, a breach of Article 2 was established in *Finucane* v *UK*, because allegations of RUC collusion in the murder of a solicitor were not properly investigated.[32]

In *Osman* v *UK*[33] the Court of Human Rights confirmed that Article 2 may impose a positive duty on states to protect life. The case challenged the failure of the police to

[23] Parliamentary Assembly, Resolution 1044 (1994).

[24] (1996) 21 EHRR 97. See also *Kelly* v *UK* (1993) 74 D & R 139 (use of fatal force against a joyrider at an army checkpoint).

[25] Cf. *Brady* v *UK* (2001) App 55151/00: the police shooting of an unarmed robbery suspect did not give rise to an admissible Article 2 claim because the officer had genuinely and reasonably believed that the suspect was reaching for a gun.

[26] *Ergi* v *Turkey* (2001) 32 EHRR 18.   [27] (1985) 7 EHRR CD 453.

[28] (2003) 37 EHRR 2 (an unarmed member of the Provisional IRA shot by RUC officers): see N Aoláin, 'Truth Telling, Accountability and the Right to Life in Northern Ireland' [2002] EHRLR 572.

[29] See p 279, *post*.

[30] [2003] UKHL 51, [2004] 1 AC 653, [2003] 4 ALL ER 1264. See also *R on the application of Khan)* v *Secretary of State for Health* [2003] EWCA Civ 1129, [2004] 1 WLR 971, [2003] 4 All ER 1239 (Article 2 breached by a failure to provide funds enabling Mr Khan to be legally represented at his daughter's inquest). These decisions prompted an amendment to the exceptional funding provisions in the Access to Justice Act 1999.

[31] *R (on the application of Davies)* v *HM Deputy Coroner for Birmingham* [2003] EWCA Civ 1739, [2004] HRLR 13: a finding of accidental death had been reached.

[32] (2003) 37 EHRR 29.   [33] (2000) 29 EHRR 245.

arrest a teacher who was known to have formed an obsessive attachment to a former pupil. The teacher later shot and killed the boy's father, and although the Court found no breach of Article 2 on the facts, it indicated that the UK *would* have been liable if the applicants had been able to establish that:[34]

> [T]he authorities knew or ought to have known at the time of the existence of a real and immediate risk to the life of an identified individual or individuals...and that they failed to take measures within the scope of their powers which, judged reasonably, might have been expected to avoid that risk.

The *Osman* decision was instrumental in persuading the High Court to award damages to the parents of a witness murdered following inadequate police protection.[35] It also influenced the decision to grant injunctions to the killers of James Bulger upon their release from prison, as the court was satisfied that they would face a real threat of revenge attacks if details of their whereabouts and new identities were published.[36] On similar grounds the House of Lords has emphasized that the right to life must underpin any determination of asylum applications.[37] In general, however, a failure to *protect* life will only breach Article 2 if the authorities knew or should have known of an imminent and specific threat. In *Younger* v *UK*[38] a failure to prevent a suicide in police custody did not violate the right to life because the police had no prior knowledge that the deceased was a suicide risk. In contrast, a failure to protect a mentally ill prisoner from being kicked to death by his cellmate did give rise to a breach of Article 2.[39]

Finally, the Court of Human Rights[40] has confirmed the decision in *R (on the application of Pretty)* v *DPP*[41] that Article 2 does not guarantee the right to *end* life. The applicant had motor neurone disease and wanted to end her life so as to avoid further suffering and loss of dignity. However, she was physically unable to commit suicide alone and the DPP refused to undertake not to prosecute her husband if he assisted. Both the House of Lords and the Strasbourg court stressed that Article 2 is concerned with the *protection* of life and does not confer any right to die. It does not, however, prevent a state from permitting the carrying out of lawful abortions;[42] nor does it prevent surgery to separate conjoined twins which will inevitably result in the death of one of them, but which is necessary to preserve the life of the other.[43]

---

[34] Ibid at para 116.

[35] *Van Colle* v *Chief Constable of Hertfordshire* [2006] EWHC 360 (QB), [2006] 3 All ER 963. The £50,000 awarded was reduced to £25,000 on appeal: [2007] EWCA Civ 325, [2007] 1 WLR 1821, [2007] 3 All ER 122.

[36] *Venables and Thompson* v *News Group Newspapers* [2001] Fam 430, [2001] 1 All ER 908.

[37] *R (on the application of Sivakumar)* v *Home Secretary* [2003] UKHL 14, [2003] 2 All ER 1097, [2003] 1 WLR 840.

[38] (2003) 36 EHRR CD 252.   [39] *Edwards* v *UK* (2002) 35 EHRR 19.

[40] *Pretty* v *UK* (2002) 35 EHRR 1. Claims under Articles 3, 8, 9, and 14 were also rejected. Mrs Pretty died from her illness twelve days after this decision. For an extended analysis see Morris, 'Assisted Suicide under the European Convention on Human Rights: A Critique' [2003] EHRLR 65.

[41] [2001] UKHL 61, [2002] 1 AC 800, [2002] 1 All ER 1.

[42] *Open Door Counselling* v *Ireland* (1993) 15 EHRR 244.

[43] *Re A (Children) (Conjoined Twins: Surgical Separation)* [2001] Fam 147, [2000] 4 All ER 961.

2 ARTICLE 3: THE PROHIBITION OF TORTURE AND INHUMAN OR DEGRADING TREATMENT

Article 3 is concerned with different levels of ill treatment. 'Degrading treatment' is treatment which grossly humiliates a person beyond the level of humiliation inherent in any punishment, or which drives him to act against his own will or conscience. 'Inhuman treatment' involves causing physical or mental suffering, while 'torture' is an aggravated form of deliberate inhuman treatment causing 'very serious and cruel suffering'.[44] Article 3 has been used on several occasions to provide a standard against which the treatment of suspects and prisoners can be judged. In *Ireland* v *UK* the use of certain interrogation techniques on suspected terrorists was found to constitute degrading treatment.[45] Article 3 was also breached in *Keenan* v *UK*,[46] when the authorities failed to provide adequate medical care to a mentally ill prisoner who eventually committed suicide. In another important decision, the House of Lords has held that a court must refuse to admit any evidence which it is satisfied was obtained under torture.[47]

The positive obligations imposed by Article 3 have been addressed in several immigration and asylum cases. Thus, in *Chahal* v *UK* it was held that to deport a Sikh separatist leader to India, in the face of a real risk that he would be ill-treated, would amount to a violation of Article 3.[48] In *R (on the application of Q)* v *Secretary of State for the Home Department* it was held that certain procedural safeguards must be met before late asylum seekers could lawfully be deprived of state support,[49] and in *R (on the application of Limbuela)* v *Secretary of State for the Home Department* it was held that the withdrawal of support would breach Article 3 if it resulted in an asylum seeker being left destitute.[50] Article 3 was also the basis of a successful challenge to the designation of Pakistan as a safe third country.[51]

The Article has also been used in more novel ways. In has been held, for example, that it may be breached by extraditing a man to a country where he could face the death penalty,[52] or by deporting an AIDS sufferer to a country with inadequate medical facili-

---

[44] *Ireland* v *UK* (1979) 2 EHRR 25.

[45] Ibid. Detainees were forced to wear hoods, to stand against a wall in an uncomfortable position, to go without food, drink and sleep for long periods, and to endure loud and continuous noise. In some cases the treatment of prisoners has been sufficiently cruel and severe to constitute torture: see *Aydin* v *Turkey* (1998) 25 EHRR 251 (the rape of a detainee by an official); *Aksoy* v *Turkey* (1997) 23 EHRR 553 (being stripped naked, hung by the arms, beaten and subjected to electric shocks).

[46] (2001) 33 EHRR 38 (an Article 2 claim failed). Cf. *R* v *Drew* [2003] UKHL 25, [2003] 4 All ER 557, [2003] 1 WLR 1213.

[47] *A* v *Secretary of State for the Home Department (No 2)* [2005] UKHL 71, [2006] 2 AC 221, [2006] 1 All ER 575.

[48] (1996) 23 EHRR 413. See also *Hilal* v *UK* (2001) 33 EHRR 2; *McPherson* v *Secretary of State for the Home Department* [2001] EWCA Civ 1955, [2002] INLR 139.

[49] [2003] EWCA Civ 364, [2004] QB 36, [2003] 2 All ER 905. Support was denied under the Nationality, Immigration and Asylum Act 2002 on the grounds that the applicants did not claim asylum as soon as reasonably practicable after arrival.

[50] [2005] UKHL 66, [2006] 1 AC 396, [2007] 1 All ER 951.

[51] *R* v *Secretary of State for the Home Department, ex parte Javed* [2001] EWCA Civ 789, [2002] QB 129.

[52] *Soering* v *UK* (1989) 11 EHRR 439.

ties.[53] The Article has even been considered in the context of a failure to protect an applicant from domestic violence,[54] and in relation to the use of corporal punishment in schools[55] and homes.[56]

3 ARTICLE 4: THE PROHIBITION OF SLAVERY AND FORCED LABOUR

Very few cases have arisen under Article 4 and until recently none had been successful. However, in *Siliadin* v *France* a Togolese national established a breach of the Article after enduring four years of domestic slavery.[57] She was just fifteen when she arrived in France, and having had her passport confiscated by her employer she was sent to work for a family who made her work fifteen-hour days with little rest and no pay. France was held to be in breach of Article 4 because of a failure to adequately safeguard her rights. In an earlier case a lawyer had unsuccessfully challenged an obligation to do pro bono work: his claim failed because he knew when he became a barrister that this would be expected.[58]

There is arguably scope for using Article 4 more widely in the context of human trafficking.[59] though as in *Siliadin* Article 4 would only be engaged where a state had failed to protect individuals from a specific, known risk of exploitation. A more novel use of Article 4 came in a recent case on compulsory jury service. Although it was not suggested that this amounted to a breach of Article 4 itself, the fact that the burden of jury service was inequitably distributed between the sexes meant that there had been a breach of Article 14 when read alongside the prohibition on forced labour.[60]

4 ARTICLE 5: THE RIGHT TO LIBERTY AND SECURITY OF THE PERSON

Article 5 provides that no-one shall be deprived of his liberty save in accordance with a procedure prescribed by law for one of the purposes specified in Article 5(1). These purposes include: (a) detention after conviction; (b) arrest or detention for failing to comply with a court order or legal obligation; and (c) arrest or detention for the purpose of bringing a person before a competent legal authority on reasonable suspicion of having committed an offence. With regard to the latter, the requirement for 'reasonable

---

[53] *D* v *UK* (1997) 24 EHRR 423.

[54] *Z* v *UK* (2002) 34 EHRR 3 (failure to remove children from a home in which they were known to be neglected and abused).

[55] *Tyrer* v *UK* (1979–1980) 2 EHRR 1; *Costello-Roberts* v *UK* (1995) 19 EHRR 112.

[56] *A* v *UK* (1999) 27 EHRR 611; *R* v *H (Reasonable Chastisement)* [2001] EWCA Crim 1024, [2001] 2 FLR 431, [2002] 1 Cr App R 7; Rogers, 'A Criminal Lawyer's Response to Chastisement in the European Court of Human Rights' [2002] Crim LR 98.

[57] (2006) 43 EHRR 16; see Mantouvalou, 'Servitude and Forced Labour in the 21st Century: The Human Rights of Domestic Workers (2006) 35(4) ILJ 395.

[58] *Van der Mussele* v *Belgium* (1984) 6 EHRR 163.

[59] See Drew, 'Human Trafficking: A Modern Form of Slavery?' [2002] EHRLR 481.

[60] *Adami* v *Malta* (2007) 44 EHRR 3.

suspicion' is an essential safeguard against arbitrary detention. An 'honest belief' that an offence has been committed will not suffice,[61] and this raises doubts about the legitimacy of those police powers that do not depend upon a reasonable suspicion.[62] The power to arrest for breach of the peace has also been challenged, but the Strasbourg court has found it to be compatible with Article 5 even though breach of the peace is not 'an offence'.[63] In another case, the House of Lords recently held that stop and search powers will not normally engage Article 5 at all, on the basis that the brief period of detention involved does not amount to a deprivation of liberty.[64]

Article 5 lists a number of procedural safeguards for the benefit of those lawfully detained: an arrested person must be informed promptly of the reasons for his detention in a language which he understands, and he must be brought promptly before a judge. A detainee is also entitled to trial within a reasonable time, or to release pending trial, and he must have the right to challenge his detention. These requirements have had a significant impact on the procedures for making decisions about life prisoners. In *Thynne, Wilson and Gunnell v UK*[65] the Court of Human Rights ruled that those serving discretionary life sentences were entitled to periodic reviews to determine whether their continued detention could be justified. A similar conclusion was reached in respect of juveniles detained at Her Majesty's Pleasure.[66] The Home Secretary's involvement in setting the 'tariff' in such cases was also contrary to Article 5(4), because it meant that the period of detention was not controlled by a court.[67] New arrangements have since been put in place for determining and reviewing such sentences.[68]

Mandatory life sentences were thought to raise different issues because the Strasbourg court had previously found that they were not indeterminate and did not need to be periodically reviewed.[69] However, in *Stafford v UK*[70] the Court concluded that there was no material difference between discretionary and mandatory life prisoners. In both cases the setting of the tariff was a sentencing exercise, and Articles 5 and 6 required that it should be performed by a court. Mr Stafford had in fact been released on life licence, but the Home Secretary had revoked the licence following his conviction for fraud. This also violated Article 5, because the original life sentence could not

---

[61] *Fox, Campbell and Hartley v UK* (1991) 13 EHRR 157; cf. *Murray v UK* (1995) 19 EHRR 193 (mere suspicion sufficient in circumstances where officers could demonstrate an objective basis).

[62] Mead, 'The Likely Effect of the Human Rights Act on Everyday Policing Decisions in England and Wales' (2000) 5(1) J Civ Lib 5; Fenwick, *Civil Liberties and Human Rights* (3rd edn, 2002) at pp 775–7.

[63] *Steel v UK* (1999) 28 EHRR 603: see *Williamson v Chief Constable of West Midlands* [2003] EWCA Civ 337, [2004] 1 WLR 14. Detention for longer than necessary to prevent an imminent breach of the peace or to bring a person before magistrates will be unlawful: *R (on the application of Laporte) v Chief Constable of Gloucester* [2004] EWHC 253 (Admin), [2004] 2 All ER 874 (affirmed on appeal, though without reliance on Article 5: [2006] UKHL 55, [2007] 2 AC 105, [2007] 2 All ER 529).

[64] *R (on the application of Gillan) v Commissioner of Police for the Metropolis* [2006] UKHL 12, [2006] 2 AC 307, [2006] 4 All ER 1041.

[65] (1991) 13 EHRR 666.   [66] *Hussain and Singh v UK* (1996) 22 EHRR 1.

[67] *T and V v UK* (2000) 30 EHRR 121. The 'tariff' (now known as 'the minimum term') is the portion of a prison sentence that must be served before a person can be considered for parole.

[68] Crime (Sentences) Act 1997, s 28; Powers of Criminal Courts (Sentencing) Act 2000, ss 82A.

[69] *Wynne v UK* (1995) 19 EHRR 333.   [70] (2002) 35 EHRR 32.

authorize a further period of detention for an unrelated, non-violent offence.[71] Shortly after this decision, the House of Lords concluded that it was impossible to interpret the mandatory life sentence powers in a manner compatible with Article 6 without doing 'judicial vandalism' to the legislation.[72] It therefore issued a declaration of incompatibility. Provisions to bring the arrangements for mandatory life prisoners into line with these judgments were included in Part 12 of the Criminal Justice Act 2003.[73]

Article 5 issues have also been raised in relation to the detention of suspected terrorists. In *Brogan* v *UK*[74] laws allowing suspected terrorists to be detained for up to seven days without being brought before a judicial authority were found to breach Article 5. Instead of amending the offending legislation the government derogated from Article 5,[75] and the derogation remained in force until February 2001. The withdrawal of the derogation followed the decision to replace the existing anti-terror laws with the Terrorism Act 2000. Following amendments made in 2006, this Act now permits detention without charge for up to 28 days, but judicial authority must be obtained for detentions in excess of 48 hours.[76]

The UK entered a further derogation from Article 5 following the enactment of the Anti-Terrorism, Crime and Security Act 2001.[77] This Act provided that where a foreign national was suspected of terrorism but could not be deported on humanitarian grounds, the Secretary of State could certify that he was believed to present a threat to national security. The suspect could then be detained indefinitely, without trial. The government sought to pre-empt any legal challenge by derogating from Article 5 immediately, but in *A* v *Secretary of State for the Home Department*[78] the House of Lords nevertheless made a declaration of incompatibility. It held that by singling out non-nationals for detention the Act was interfering with the right to liberty in a discriminatory manner, and that it was therefore in breach of Articles 5 *and* 14. The government's response was the Prevention of Terrorism Act 2005, which replaces the internment powers with a system of control orders. This Act avoids the element of discrimination inherent in the earlier legislation, by providing that the new powers may be exercised against *any* person suspected on reasonable grounds of involvement in terrorism-related activity. Nevertheless, the range of controls permitted can have serious consequences for individual liberties, and the Act contemplates the possibility that some control orders may require a further derogation. The only control orders made thus far have been 'non-derogating', and several attempts

---

[71] See also *Waite* v *UK* (2003) 36 EHRR 54 (revocation of licence following conviction for further offences); *R (on the application of Giles)* v *Parole Board* [2003] UKHL 42, [2004] 1 AC 1, [2003] 4 All ER 429 (no breach of Article 5(4) in respect of judicial powers to impose an extended determinate sentence on public safety grounds).

[72] *R (on the application of Anderson)* v *Secretary of State for the Home Department* [2002] UKHL 46 at [30], [2003] 1 AC 837 at [30], [2002] 4 All ER 1089, per Lord Bingham; Crime (Sentences) Act 1997, s 29. See Amos, '*R* v *Secretary of State for the Home Department, ex parte Anderson*: Ending the Home Secretary's Sentencing Role' (2004) 67(1) MLR 108; p 154, *ante*.

[73] See p 673, *post*.

[74] (1989) 11 EHRR 117; Prevention of Terrorism (Temporary Provisions) Act 1984, s 14.

[75] The derogation was unsuccessfully challenged in *Brannigan and McBride* v *UK* (1994) 17 EHRR 539.

[76] Terrorism Act 2000, s 41 and schedule 8; as amended by the Terrorism Act 2006.

[77] Declaration registered by the Secretariat General on 18 December 2001; SI 2001/4032.

[78] *A* v *Secretary of State for the Home Department* [2004] UKHL 56, [2005] 2 AC 68, [2005] 3 All ER 169; see p 308, *ante*.

to challenge them through the courts have been unsuccessful.[79] However, the House of Lords recently upheld a decision to quash six control orders, having likened their effect to being in indefinite solitary confinement.[80] The applicants had been subject to eighteen-hour curfews and were forced to reside in one-bedroom flats in unfamiliar areas. They were electronically tagged, their use of communications equipment was restricted to a single, land-line telephone, and they could not meet with anyone without Home Office clearance. By contrast, Article 5 was not infringed by an order involving a twelve-hour curfew, where the applicant was able to continue living in his family home and had fewer restrictions on his movements.[81]

Article 5(1)(e) expressly permits the lawful detention of persons of unsound mind, but the state must demonstrate an objective and reliable basis for the detention, and it must be subject to periodic review.[82] In a 2001 case[83] the Court of Appeal declared provisions of the Mental Health Act 1983 to be incompatible with Article 5, because the patient bore the burden of proving that his continued detention was no longer necessary. The Act was subsequently amended by remedial order.[84] Following the decisions in *Stafford* and *Anderson*, a further declaration of incompatibility was made in *R (on the application of D) v Secretary of State for the Home Department*,[85] because the Act failed to provide an adequate right of review to restricted patients serving prison sentences.

Article 5(1)(f) permits the detention of persons pending deportation or extradition, and for the purpose of preventing unauthorized entry into the country. In *R (on the application of Saadi) v Secretary of State for the Home Department* the policy of detaining asylum seekers at 'reception centres' was challenged, on the basis that it affects those whose applications have yet to be determined, and in respect of whom no decision to deport has been taken.[86] However, the House of Lords held that as asylum applicants were only detained where there was a reasonable belief that they might abscond, the policy was a lawful and proportionate means of controlling entry.

5 ARTICLE 6: THE RIGHT TO A FAIR TRIAL[87]

Article 6(1) concerns the right to a fair trial, the main elements of which are: (a) a fair and public hearing; (b) an independent and impartial tribunal; (c) a trial within a reasonable period of time; (d) a public judgment; and (e) a reasoned decision. It applies to all proceedings which involve a criminal charge or the determination of civil rights

---

[79] See, e.g. *Secretary of State for the Home Department v MB* [2007] UKHL 46, [2007] 3 WLR 681, discussed at p 159, *ante*.

[80] *Secretary of State for the Home Department v JJ* [2007] UKHL 45, [2007] 3 WLR 642.

[81] *Secretary of State for the Home Department v E* [2007] UKHL 47, [2007] 3 WLR 720.

[82] *Johnson v UK* (1997) 27 EHRR 296.

[83] *R (on the application of H) v North and East London Regional Mental Health Review Tribunal* [2001] EWCA Civ 415, [2002] QB 1, [2001] 3 WLR 512.

[84] Mental Health Act 1983 (Remedial) Order 2001, SI 2001/3712.

[85] [2002] EWHC 2805 (Admin), [2003] 1 WLR 1315. The Act has since been amended.

[86] [2002] UKHL 41, [2002] 4 All ER 785, [2002] 1 WLR 3131.

[87] See Ashworth and Strange, 'Criminal Law and Human Rights' [2004] EHRLR 121; Juss, 'Constitutionalising Rights without a Constitution: The British Experience under Article 6 of the Human Rights Act' (2006) 27(1) Stat LR 29.

and obligations. A broad view is taken of what constitutes 'civil rights and obligations', and it is not confined to matters regarded as 'civil' for other purposes. Administrative decisions affecting 'personal, economic and individual' rights are also covered,[88] and this means that decisions relating to social security,[89] planning,[90] care proceedings,[91] and welfare payments[92] have all been held to engage Article 6(1). Conventional wisdom suggests that the extent of any discretion in conferring a benefit is crucial to the question of whether a 'right' exists,[93] but the Convention jurisprudence is not entirely consistent.[94] The English courts have indicated a willingness to go further than Strasbourg in extending due process obligations to a range of 'public law' matters. However, they have also expressed concern that administrative decisions should not be subjected to an unreasonable level of review. In one case[95] a decision that a homeless person had unreasonably been refused accommodation was *assumed* to engage Article 6(1), but the point was left open for future consideration.

The term 'criminal' also has an autonomous meaning for Article 6 purposes, and the content of what is alleged and the nature of any penalty must be taken into account.[96] Proceedings for non-payment of council tax[97] and for binding over to keep the peace[98] are both considered to be 'criminal'. However, proceedings relating to anti-social behaviour orders,[99] control orders,[100] the revocation of a prisoner's release on licence,[101] the forfeiture of goods seized by customs and excise,[102] and the confiscation of the proceeds of criminal activity,[103] are not. Additional safeguards for the benefit of those charged with a criminal offence are set out in Article 6(2) and 6(3). These include the presumption of innocence, the right to be promptly informed of the nature of any charges, the right to adequate time and legal assistance in preparing a defence, and the right to call and examine witnesses.

[88] *Feldbrugge* v *Netherlands* (1986) 8 EHRR 425 at para. 37.   [89] Ibid.

[90] *R (on the Application of Alconbury)* v *Secretary of State for the Environment, Transport and the Regions* [2001] UKHL 23, [2003] 2 AC 295, [2001] 2 All ER 929.

[91] *McMichael* v *UK* (1995) 20 EHRR 205.

[92] *Mennitto* v *Italy* (2002) 34 EHRR 48.

[93] Cf. *O'Rourke* v *Camden LBC* [1998] AC 188, [1997] 3 All ER 23, where the existence of a discretion was a key factor in persuading the House of Lords that provisions of the Housing Act 1985 could not be subject to a private law action for damages.

[94] It is difficult to see, for example, why social security decisions are protected by Article 6(1), but not taxation decisions.

[95] *Begum (Runa)* v *Tower Hamlets* [2003] UKHL 5, [2003] 2 AC 430, [2003] 1 All ER 731. See Craig, 'The Human Rights Act, Article 6 and Procedural Rights' [2003] PL 753.

[96] *Engel* v *The Netherlands (No 1)* (1979–1980) 1 EHRR 647.

[97] *Benham* v *UK* (1996) 22 EHRR 293.

[98] *Steel* v *UK* (1999) 28 EHRR 603; *Hooper* v *UK* (2005) 41 EHRR 1. Cf. *Williamson* v *Chief Constable of West Midlands* [2003] EWCA Civ 337, [2004] 1 WLR 14. The civil/criminal distinction is discussed at p 12, *ante*.

[99] *R (on the application of McCann)* v *Manchester Crown Court and others* [2002] UKHL 39, [2003] 1 AC 787, [2002] 4 All ER 593.

[100] *Secretary of State for the Home Department* v *MB* [2007] UKHL 46, [2007] 3 WLR 681.

[101] *R (on the application of Smith)* v *Parole Board* [2005] UKHL 1, [2005] 1 WLR 350, [2005] 1 All ER 755.

[102] *R (on the application of Mudie)* v *Dover Magistrates Court* [2003] EWCA Civ 237, [2003] QB 1238, [2003] 2 All ER 631.

[103] *R* v *Benjafield* [2002] UKHL 2, [2003] 1 AC 1099, [2002] 1 All ER 815.

Article 6 provides an important yardstick against which to measure any aspect of the trial process, and it has generated far more case law than any other Convention right. The idea that there should be equality of arms between the parties to an action is an important theme. Amongst other things, it entails an obligation to ensure the disclosure of relevant evidence,[104] the ability to challenge that evidence,[105] and the ability to participate effectively in the proceedings. The latter requirement may be breached where a child is tried in an adult court[106] or where language difficulties prevent a party to an action from fully understanding the proceedings.[107] Article 6 may also be breached by the operation of certain evidential rules,[108] or by the admission of unfairly or covertly obtained evidence.[109] The right of unimpeded access to legal advice is also fundamental,[110] and the availability of legal aid is an important factor here. The requirement for legal aid to be available is more explicit where criminal charges are involved,[111] but the Court of Human Rights recently found a breach of Article 6(1) when legal aid was denied to the defendants in a complex libel action.[112] The 'McLibel Two' were sued for distributing leaflets containing allegations about the fast-food giant, McDonald's. Legal aid is generally unavailable in defamation cases, and although the defendants were helped by volunteer lawyers they represented themselves throughout the two-and-a-half-year trial. It was held that the complexity of the issues, the potential severity of the consequences,[113] and the applicants' capacity to defend themselves effectively against the resources of McDonald's, had all contributed to an unacceptable inequality of arms.

Several cases have examined the requirement for an 'independent and impartial tribunal', and decisions on this aspect of Article 6 have had a considerable influence on the English legal system. The principle that decisions should be free from bias is well established in English law, but when the Human Rights Act came into force the Court

---

[104] *Edwards* v *UK* (1992) 15 EHRR 417; *Rowe and Davis* v *UK* (2000) 30 EHRR 1.

[105] *R* v *A (No 2)* [2001] UKHL 25, [2002] 1 AC 45, [2001] 3 All ER 1.

[106] *T and V* v *UK* (2000) 30 EHRR 121.

[107] *Cuscani* v *UK* (2003) 36 EHRR 2. Cf. *Williams* v *Cowell (t/a The Stables)* [2000] 1 WLR 187, [2000] ICR 85 (EAT's refusal to conduct its proceedings in Welsh did not deprive the applicant of a fair trial because he had perfectly good English).

[108] *Trivedi* v *UK* (1997) App 31700/96 (exceptions to the hearsay rule); *Hoare* v *UK* (1997) App 31211/96 (the availability of expert evidence): both applications were found to be inadmissible on the facts.

[109] *R* v *Looseley*; *sub nom Attorney-General's Reference (No 3 of 2000)* [2001] UKHL 53, [2001] 4 All ER 897 (entrapment); *Teixeira de Castro* v *Portugal* (1999) 28 EHRR 101 (entrapment); *Khan* v *UK* (2001) 31 EHRR 45 (use of a covert listening device breached Article 8 but not Article 6); *Allan* v *UK* (2003) 36 EHRR 12 (placing an informant in a cell to obtain a confession infringed the privilege against self-incrimination); *R* v *Veneroso* [2002] Crim LR 306 (drugs found while officers were illegally on the defendant's premises were inadmissible on the basis of Article 8, though the judge indicated that the outcome might have been different if semtex had been found).

[110] *Brennan* v *UK* (2002) 34 EHRR 18 (Article 6 breached by police presence at a meeting between the defendant and his solicitor); *P, C and S* v *UK* (2002) 35 EHRR 31 (refusal to adjourn care proceedings to allow a mother to obtain legal advice).

[111] See Article 6(2)(c); *Benham* v *UK* (1996) 22 EHRR 293.

[112] *Steel and Morris* v *UK* (2005) 41 EHRR 22.

[113] The defendants had been ordered to pay damages of £76,000, although McDonald's had not sought to enforce the award.

of Appeal held that a 'modest adjustment' to the existing test was needed.[114] Article 6 was also instrumental in bringing about reforms to the procedures for dealing with life prisoners,[115] and the Armed Forces Act 1996 pre-empted a finding that the courts-martial system lacked sufficient guarantees of independence.[116] In addition, following the decision in *Lawal* v *Northern Spirit*,[117] barristers are no longer used as part-time EAT judges. However, it is the decision in *McGonnell* v *UK*[118] that may prove to be the most significant. The facts of the case were that the Guernsey Royal Court Bailiff had adjudicated in a planning case, having also been involved in making the applicable legislation. The Court concluded that this amounted to a breach of Article 6, and although the decision was not concerned with wider constitutional issues, it had clear implications for both the Appellate Committee of the House of Lords and the office of Lord Chancellor. It is partly because of this decision that the Constitutional Reform Act 2005 was introduced.[119]

The question of whether a trial has taken place within a 'reasonable time' can only be resolved by reference to both the circumstances of the case and the complexity of the issues. Nine-year delays in resolving legal disputes have been held to breach Article 6,[120] but in *R* v *James (David John)*, a five-year delay in dealing with a complicated fraud case was not considered unreasonable.[121] The principle that justice should be seen to be done is also highly valued, but it is subject to the proviso that publicity may be restricted where the interests of justice demand it. Private hearings may be necessary in order to protect the identity of vulnerable witnesses,[122] and fairness may also require the imposition of reporting restrictions pending the outcome of proceedings. In *R (on the application of the Telegraph Group plc)* v *Sherwood*[123] a decision to delay the reporting of one trial until a related trial had been concluded was held to be a justifiable and proportionate response to a substantial risk of prejudice.

The right to be presumed innocent of a criminal charge is expressly protected under Article 6(2), and in several Human Rights Act cases[124] the courts have modified the

---

[114] *Director General of Fair Trading* v *Proprietary Association of Great Britain; sub nom Re Medicaments and Related Classes of Goods (No 2)* [2001] 1 WLR 700, [2001] HRLR 17. The modification was subsequently approved by the House of Lords in *Porter* v *Magill* [2001] UKHL 67, [2002] 2 AC 357, [2002] 1 All ER 465.

[115] See p 183, *ante.*

[116] The Strasbourg court made such a ruling in *Findlay* v *UK* (1997) 24 EHRR 221: see p 285, *post.*

[117] [2003] UKHL 35, [2004] 1 All ER 187, [2003] ICR 856.

[118] (2000) 30 EHRR 289. See also *Starrs* v *Ruxton; sub nom Starrs* v *Procurator Fiscal* 2000 JC 208, 2000 SLT 42; p 344, *post.*

[119] The reforms brought about by this Act are considered in more detail in chapters 1, 8, and 10.

[120] *Darnall* v *UK* (1994) 18 EHRR 205; *Blake* v *UK* (2007) 44 EHRR 29.

[121] [2002] EWCA Crim 1119.

[122] See *X* v *UK* (1993) 15 EHRR CD 113 (witnesses testified from behind a screen where they could not even be seen by the defendant). See also *R* v *Lord Saville of Newdigate, ex parte A* [1999] 4 All ER 860, [2000] 1 WLR 1855; p 244, n 82, *post.*

[123] [2001] EWCA Crim 1075, [2001] 1 WLR 1983. Cf. *R* v *B* [2006] EWCA Crim 2692, [2007] HRLR 1, discussed at p 245.

[124] *R* v *Lambert* [2001] UKHL 37, [2002] 2 AC 545, [2001] 3 All ER 577 (provisions of the Misuse of Drugs Act 1971 read down so as to impose an evidential rather than a legal burden); *Attorney-General's Reference (No 4 of 2002)* [2004] UKHL 43, [2005] 1 AC 264, [2005] 1 All ER 237 (provisions of the Terrorism Act 2000 read down so as to impose an evidential rather than a legal burden); *International Transport Roth GmbH* v

interpretation of burden of proof provisions. Freedom from self-incrimination and the related idea of the right to silence are not specifically mentioned, but both principles have been held to be covered by the fair trial concept in Article 6(1). In *Saunders* v *UK* the Court of Human Rights considered the effect of provisions of the Companies Act 1985, under which Mr Saunders was compelled to answer questions put to him during a fraud investigation.[125] The use made of these answers at Mr Saunders' trial, and the fact that they had been obtained under compulsion, was held to infringe Article 6. The right to silence is not absolute, however, and allowing a court to draw adverse inferences from silence will not automatically involve a breach of the Convention. Thus, restrictions on the right to silence in *Murray* v *UK*[126] did not violate Article 6 because the weight of evidence meant that the drawing of inferences had not been unfair. Moreover, the case was tried by a single judge who was required to give a reasoned decision. The risk of unfairness is considered to be greater where a defendant is tried by jury: Article 6 may be breached if the judge does not ensure that appropriate weight is given to any explanation offered by the accused.[127]

6 ARTICLE 7: THE RIGHT NOT TO BE SUBJECT TO RETROSPECTIVE CRIMINAL LIABILITY OR PENALTIES

Article 7 prohibits the imposition of criminal liability for an act which was not an offence when it was carried out. Legislation imposing retrospective criminal liability is virtually unknown in modern times,[128] but issues may arise where offences are given a different interpretation to that which might have been expected. Article 7 may also be infringed if an offence is not sufficiently precise to enable an individual to regulate his conduct. In practice, however, it will be rare for this type of challenge to succeed. In *CR and SW* v *UK* for example, the applicants claimed that the removal of the marital rape exemption in *R* v *R*[129] amounted to the creation of a retrospective offence, contrary to Article 7. However, the Strasbourg court ruled that the applicants should have foreseen that their conduct would be considered criminal, and that there was therefore no breach of the Convention.[130] In *O'Carroll* v *UK*, the court pointed out that it was 'not possible

---

Secretary of State for the Home Department [2002] EWCA Civ 158, [2003] QB 728, [2002] HRLR 31 (a compatible interpretation of provisions in the Immigration and Asylum Act 1999 could not be found and a declaration of incompatibility was issued).

[125] (1997) 23 EHRR 313. The Companies Act was later amended by the Youth Justice and Criminal Evidence Act 1999. Cf. *Brown* v *Stott* [2003] 1 AC 681, [2001] 2 All ER 97 and *O'Halloran and Francis* v *UK* [2007] Crim LR 897 (requirement to answer potentially incriminating questions under the Road Traffic Act 1988 does not infringe the Convention).

[126] (1996) 22 EHRR 29.   [127] *Condron* v *UK* (2001) 31 EHRR 1; *Beckles* v *UK* (2003) 36 EHRR 13.

[128] See p 43, *ante*. The War Crimes Act 1991 is a notable exception but it is the type of legislation envisaged by Article 7(2). This allows the retrospective criminalization of acts which would have been recognized as criminal at the time under general principles of international law.

[129] *R* v *R (Rape: Marital Exemption)* [1992] 1 AC 599, [1991] 4 All ER 481: see p 323, *ante*.

[130] (1996) 21 EHRR 363. The Court of Appeal reached the same conclusion on similar facts in *R* v *C (Barry)* [2004] EWCA Crim 292, [2004] 1 WLR 2098, [2004] 3 All ER 1.

to attain absolute rigidity in the framing of laws', particularly where there was a need to keep pace with changing circumstances.[131] On this basis, a challenge concerning a conviction for an indecency offence was deemed to be manifestly ill-founded. The domestic courts have rejected similar arguments in relation to the offences of public nuisance[132] and gross negligence manslaughter.[133]

Article 7 also forbids the imposition of a heavier criminal penalty than that in force at the time of the offence. Most of the cases that arise in this context hinge on whether a particular requirement constitutes a penalty, and the purpose of the requirement is usually crucial to this determination. Compelling a person to register as a sex offender has been held not to constitute a penalty, even though non-compliance is a criminal offence, because the purpose of the requirement is not to punish.[134]

In *R (on the application of Uttley)* v *Secretary of State for the Home Department*, the defendant was sentenced to twelve years imprisonment more than a decade after committing a series of sex offences. He argued that his release on licence after eight years amounted to a breach of Article 7, on the grounds that if he had been given the same sentence at the time of his offences, he would have been released after the same number of years but *without* licence. His argument was rejected by the House of Lords on the basis that Article 7 was only concerned with the maximum 'applicable' sentence, and not with the sentence that a particular offender was likely to receive.[135]

7 ARTICLE 8: THE RIGHT TO RESPECT FOR A PERSON'S PRIVATE AND FAMILY LIFE, HIS HOME AND CORRESPONDENCE

Article 8 may be subject to limitations which are in accordance with law and which are necessary in a democratic society in the interests of national security, public safety or the economic well-being of the country, for the prevention of disorder or crime, for the protection of health or morals, or for the protection of the rights and freedoms of others. Although the Article covers four key areas – private life, family life, home, and correspondence – it is often unnecessary to distinguish clearly between them, and they can be 'read together as guaranteeing collectively more than the sum of their parts.'[136] For example, the right to respect for private life includes the right to develop personal relationships with others,[137] and relationships which do not establish a conventional 'family' may nevertheless fall within the scope of Article 8. Moreover, where national

---

[131] (2005) 41 EHRR SE1.

[132] *R* v *Rimmington (Anthony)* [2005] UKHL 63, [2006] 1 AC 459, [2006] 2 All ER 257 (the defendants' convictions were quashed, however, as the ingredients of the offence had not been made out).

[133] *R* v *Misra (Amit)* [2004] EWCA Crim 2375, [2005] 1 Cr App R 21.

[134] *Adamson* v *UK* (1999) App 42293/98.

[135] [2004] UKHL 38, [2004] 1 WLR 2278, [2004] 4 All ER 1. See also *Taylor* v *UK* (2003) 36 EHRR CD 104 (boy who committed a crime as a fourteen year old punished as a young offender because he was fifteen when sentenced: Article 7 not engaged).

[136] Ovey and White (eds), *Jacobs and White: European Convention on Human Rights* (3rd edn, 2002) at p 218.

[137] *Niemietz* v *Germany* (1993) 16 EHRR 97; *X and Y* v *Netherlands* (1986) 8 EHRR 235.

laws confer particular rights or benefits on family members, there may be a breach of Article 8 if the state's interpretation of what constitutes a family is too narrow. Thus, in *X, Y and X, Y and Z v UK*[138] the relationship between a woman, a female to male transsexual and a child that the woman had conceived through artificial insemination, was held to constitute a family. Similarly, in *Ghaidan v Godin-Mendoza*[139] the House of Lords upheld a ruling that the Rent Act 1977 should be interpreted to confer the rights of a 'spouse' on the surviving gay partner of a protected statutory tenant.

The ability to maintain family ties is of fundamental importance, and any denial of parental rights of access to a child will be subject to strict scrutiny.[140] Indeed, a failure to involve a parent in otherwise justified decisions about care and custody may amount to a breach of Article 8.[141] Article 8 may also be violated by immigration and deportation decisions which have a disproportionate impact on the ability to maintain family relationships.[142] However, states are not obliged to respect the choice of married couples as to their country of residence.[143]

Article 8 entails respect for personal identity and sexual preferences, and it has been used alongside Article 14 in several cases concerning discrimination against homosexuals and transsexuals. The decision in *Smith and Grady v UK*[144] forced the Ministry of Defence to abandon its ban on gays in the military, and judicial decisions in both the UK and Strasbourg provided the impetus for a new law conferring legal rights on transsexuals.[145] The Strasbourg court also found breaches of Articles 8 and 14 in a case concerning the UK's age of consent laws, though the offending laws were amended before the case was even decided.[146] Article 8 was successfully relied upon by a gay man prosecuted for gross indecency after videotaping consensual sex acts for his own private use.[147] However, the prosecution of a group of men who recorded themselves engaging in sado-masochism did not involve a similar breach.[148] The Court accepted that the interference in the latter case was in the interests of public health.

The effectiveness of Article 8 in protecting environmental and housing rights has been rather more measured.[149] In *Hatton v UK*,[150] for example, the Grand Chamber[151] overturned a finding that night flights from Heathrow Airport breached the Article 8 rights of local residents. In another case the House of Lords rejected a nuisance action

---

[138] (1997) 24 EHRR 143.   [139] [2004] UKHL 30, [2004] 2 AC 557, [2004] 3 All ER 411.

[140] *K and T v Finland* (2003) 36 EHRR 18.   [141] *TP and KM v UK* (2002) 34 EHRR 2.

[142] *Berrehab v Netherlands* (1989) 11 EHRR 322 (refusal of residence permit to a Moroccan national living in the Netherlands who maintained regular contact with his ex-wife and their child).

[143] *Abdulaziz, Cabales and Balkandali v UK* (1985) 7 EHRR 471.

[144] (2000) 29 EHRR 493; *Lustig-Prean and Beckett v UK* (2000) 29 EHRR 548.

[145] The Gender Recognition Act 2004, introduced following *Goodwin v UK* (2002) 35 EHRR 18 and *Bellinger v Bellinger* [2003] UKHL 21, [2003] 2 AC 467, [2003] 2 All ER 593.

[146] *B v UK* (2004) 39 EHRR 30. The age of consent for male homosexuals was eighteen; it was sixteen for heterosexuals. The age of consent was equalized at sixteen by the Sexual Offences (Amendment) Act 2000. The relevant law is now contained in s 9 of the Sexual Offences Act 2003. See also *Dudgeon v UK* (1982) 4 EHRR 149, discussed at p 176, *ante*.

[147] *ADT v UK* (2001) 31 EHRR 33.   [148] *Laskey v UK* (1997) 24 EHRR 39.

[149] See Sands, 'Human Rights, the Environment and the Lopez Ostra Case' [1996] 29 EHRLR 597; Cook, 'Environmental Rights as Human Rights' [2002] 2 EHRLR 196.

[150] (2003) 37 EHRR 28.   [151] See p 208, *post*.

brought by a householder whose property was flooded by water from the sewers.[152] In the latter case the defendant's activities were subject to scrutiny by an independent regulator, and the statutory regime was held to strike an appropriate balance between the rights of those such as the claimant and those who depended on the defendant for sewerage services. Nevertheless, it is clear that severe pollution affecting home and family life *is* capable of being addressed under Article 8,[153] and in certain circumstances the state may have a positive obligation to provide information about serious environmental hazards.[154]

Decisions concerning the occupation of land by gypsies will also raise Article 8 issues, and although the courts have generally found any interference with the right to a home to be legitimate,[155] the Court of Human Rights took a different stance in *Connors v UK*.[156] In this case a summary procedure used to evict a family from a local authority caravan site was found to be in breach of Article 8. In the view of the court, the serious consequences of eviction meant that 'particularly weighty reasons of public interest' were required by way of justification, and in this case the UK government had failed to provide any. The government had also failed to establish that there was any pressing social need to justify the summary nature of the rules, given that gypsies on privately owned sites enjoyed greater procedural safeguards. The House of Lords had previously taken a narrow approach to Article 8 in a case concerning a man whose ex-wife had unilaterally given notice on a house that they had shared. A majority of their Lordships held that the landlord had an unqualified statutory right to recover possession, and that it was unnecessary to establish a justification under Article 8(2).[157] The reasoning in *Connors* casts doubt on the correctness of this decision, but as the Strasbourg court declined to hear a complaint in the *Qazi* case[158] the issue has yet to be finally settled. In *Kay v Lambeth* the House of Lords unanimously rejected two further appeals involving possession actions, but their Lordships were divided on the more general question of whether *Qazi* and *Connors* were reconcilable.[159]

Article 8 has, of course, been applied in cases involving more 'conventional' privacy claims, and in an important line of domestic jurisprudence the national courts have considered whether the Human Rights Act requires them to develop a common law tort of privacy. It is clear that no such tort existed before the Act,[160] though it was possible to bring some privacy claims within the scope of existing torts such as breach of

---

[152] *Marcic v Thames Water Utilities* [2003] UKHL 66, [2004] 2 AC 42, [2003] 1 All ER 135.

[153] *Lopez Ostra v Spain* (1995) 20 EHRR 277; *Vetterlein v Hampshire CC* [2001] EWHC 560 (Admin), [2002] Env LR 8.

[154] *Guerra v Italy* (1998) 26 EHRR 357.

[155] *Buckley v UK* (1997) 23 EHRR 101; *Chapman v UK* (2001) 33 EHRR 18; *South Buckinghamshire DC v Porter (No 1)*; *sub nom Wrexham CBC v Berry* [2003] UKHL 26, [2003] 2 AC 558, [2003] 3 All ER 1.

[156] (2005) 40 EHRR 9.

[157] *Qazi v Harrow LBC* [2003] UKHL 43, [2004] 1 AC 983, [2003] 4 All ER 461.

[158] In a strong dissenting opinion in *Qazi*, Lord Steyn had suggested that any European challenge to the decision was likely to prove successful; ibid at [27].

[159] *Kay v Lambeth LBC*; *Leeds City Council v Price* [2006] UKHL 10, [2006] 2 AC 465, [2006] 4 All ER 128.

[160] *Kaye v Robertson* [1991] FSR 62.

confidence, nuisance and trespass. In the first post-Human Rights Act 'privacy' case to come before the national courts, Sedley LJ famously asserted that:[161]

> [W]e have reached a point where it can be said with confidence that the law recognises and will appropriately protect a right of personal privacy.

However, in subsequent decisions the courts have stopped short of recognising the existence of a new tort. In the first such case to reach the House of Lords it was held that the creation of new torts was a matter for Parliament, and that Article 8 could instead be given effect by developing established torts and remedies.[162] The Strasbourg court has rarely had to consider claims involving media intrusions, and it rejected Earl Spencer's claim that the government had failed to protect him from such interference because it was not convinced that he lacked a remedy in domestic law.[163] Recently, however, it found a breach of Article 8 when CCTV footage recorded shortly after the applicant's suicide attempt was broadcast on television.[164] The case highlighted significant weaknesses in the ability of domestic law to safeguard individual privacy, and further developments in this field now seem inevitable. The only question is whether Parliament will finally grasp the nettle before the judiciary's hand is forced:[165]

> The recent judgment in *Peck* v *United Kingdom*... shows that in circumstances where the law of confidence did not operate, our domestic law has already been held to be inadequate. That inadequacy will have to be made good and if Parliament does not step in then the courts will be obliged to. Further development by the courts may merely be awaiting the first post-Human Rights Act case where neither the law of confidence nor any other domestic law protects an individual who deserves protection.

Police and prison searches and the use of covert surveillance techniques will obviously give rise to privacy issues, but they will generally be justifiable on one of the grounds set out in Article 8(2). However, in order to avoid a breach of the Convention such actions must be in accordance with a lawful procedure and must satisfy the requirements of proportionality. Breaches of Article 8 have been established in several cases concerning the interception of prisoners' correspondence, on the basis that the authorities' objectives could have been achieved by less restrictive means.[166] Similarly, in *Wainwright* v *UK* Article 8 was held to have been breached by intimate searches of two

---

[161] *Douglas* v *Hello! Ltd (No 1)* [2001] QB 967 at 997, [2001] 2 All ER 289 at 316. For the final chapter in this long-running legal battle, see: *Douglas* v *Hello! Ltd (No 6)* [2005] EWCA Civ 595, [2006] QB 125, [2005] 4 All ER 128; [2007] UKHL 21, [2007] 2 WLR 920, [2007] 4 All ER 545.

[162] *Wainwright* v *Home Office* [2003] UKHL 53, [2004] 2 AC 406, [2003] 4 All ER 969. See also, *Venables and Thompson* v *News Group Newspapers* [2001] Fam 430, [2001] 1 All ER 908; *A* v *B*; *H* v *Associated Newspapers* [2002] EWCA Civ 337, [2003] QB 195, [2002] 2 All ER 545; *Campbell* v *MGN* [2004] UKHL 22, [2004] 2 AC 457, [2004] 2 All ER 995.

[163] *Earl Spencer* v *UK* (1998) 25 EHRR CD 105.

[164] *Peck* v *UK* (2003) 36 EHRR 41. See also *Wainwright* v *UK* (2007) 44 EHRR 40.

[165] *Douglas* v *Hello! Ltd (No 6)* [2003] EWHC 786 (Ch) at [229], [2003] 3 All ER 996 at [229], per Lindsay J. See Aplin, 'The Development of the Action for Breach of Confidence in a Post-HRA Era' [2007] IPQ 19; Mulheron, 'A Potential Framework for Privacy? A Reply to *Hello!*' (2006) 69(5) MLR 679; Singh and Strachan, 'Privacy Postponed' [2003] EHRLR Special Issue 12.

[166] *R (on the application of Daly)* v *Secretary of State for the Home Department* [2001] UKHL 26, [2001] 2 AC 532, [2001] 3 All ER 433; *Campbell* v *UK* (1993) 15 EHRR 137.

visitors to a prison. Although the searches had been conducted for the legitimate purpose of tackling a drug problem within the prison, the nature of the searches was wholly disproportionate and the prison officers had failed to comply with their own procedures.[167] In *Malone* v *UK*[168] the finding that police telephone tapping was not properly regulated led to the enactment of the Interception of Communications Act 1985, and further criticism in *Halford* v *UK* prompted a more comprehensive piece of legislation.[169] More recently, breaches of the Convention have been established in respect of an employer's monitoring of email and internet usage,[170] and the use of covertly obtained footage in a video identification parade.[171]

Article 8 rights have also been considered in the context of adoption decisions,[172] the condition of local authority housing,[173] the sale of electoral registers,[174] the destruction of embryos following the withdrawal of consent to IVF,[175] and the police retention of DNA samples and fingerprints.[176]

8 ARTICLE 9: THE RIGHT TO FREEDOM OF THOUGHT, CONSCIENCE, AND RELIGION

This right includes the freedom to change religion or belief, and the freedom to manifest one's religion or belief in worship, teaching, practice, and observance. The bare right to freedom of thought, conscience, and religion is absolute, but the right to *manifest* a religion or belief is qualified by Article 9(2). This permits the right to be restricted on the grounds of public safety, public order, the protection of health or morals, and the protection of the rights and freedoms of others. To comply with Article 9(2), any such restriction must be prescribed by law and must be 'necessary in a democratic society'.

The term 'religion or belief' has been interpreted widely to extend beyond purely theistic beliefs and beliefs with a metaphysical element:[177]

> [Article 9] is, in its religious dimension, one of the most vital elements that go to make up the identity of believers and of their conception of life, but it is also a precious asset for atheists, agnostics, sceptics and the unconcerned.

---

[167] (2007) 44 EHRR 40. The House of Lords had rejected the Article 8 complaint, in part because the Human Rights Act was not in force at the time of the incident: *Wainwright* v *Home Office* [2003] UKHL 53, [2004] 2 AC 406, [2003] 4 All ER 969.

[168] (1985) 7 EHRR 14.

[169] (1997) 24 EHRR 523; Regulation of Investigatory Powers Act 2000. See also *Khan* v *UK* (2001) 31 EHRR 45.

[170] *Copland* v *UK* (2007) 45 EHRR 37.   [171] *Perry* v *UK* (2004) 39 EHRR 3.

[172] *Re B (A Minor) (Adoption: Natural Parent)* [2001] UKHL 70, [2002] 1 All ER 641, [2002] 1 WLR 258; *Keegan* v *Ireland* (1994) 18 EHRR 342.

[173] *Lee* v *Leeds City Council* [2002] EWCA Civ 6, [2002] 1 WLR 1488.

[174] *R (on the application of Robertson)* v *Wakefield MDC* [2001] EWHC 915 (Admin), [2002] QB 1052, [2002] 2 WLR 889.

[175] *Evans* v *UK* [2007] 1 FLR 1990.

[176] *Attorney-General's Reference (No 3 of 1999)* [2001] 2 AC 91, [2001] 2 WLR 56; *R (on the application of S)* v *Chief Constable of South Yorkshire; R (on the application of Marper)* v *Chief Constable of South Yorkshire* [2004] UKHL 39, [2004] 1 WLR 2196, [2004] 4 All ER 139.

[177] *Kokkinakis* v *Greece* (1994) 17 EHRR 397 at para. 31.

Alongside major world faiths such as Islam[178] and Christianity,[179] pacifism,[180] Scientology,[181] atheism,[182] and Buddhism[183] have all been assumed to constitute protected beliefs. Thus far, however, most Article 9 cases have been unsuccessful: the Court or former Commission has generally found either that there has been no interference with a protected 'manifestation', or that any interference was justified.

'Manifestations' covered by Article 9 include worship,[184] proselytism,[185] observing dietary restrictions,[186] and religious education.[187] In *Arrowsmith* v *UK*,[188] however, the distribution of leaflets urging troops not to serve in Northern Ireland was held not to be a manifestation of pacifism because the leaflets were not actually an expression of the applicant's pacifist views.[189] In addition, although there is a positive obligation for states to ensure the peaceful enjoyment of religious freedom, there is no requirement to guarantee equality between religions or to prohibit religious discrimination.[190] It seems that religious discrimination will only violate Article 9 where there is an element of compulsion. Thus, where an individual has voluntarily put himself in a position where his religious freedom is restricted, the Strasbourg institutions have generally found either that there has been no interference with Convention rights, or that the interference is justified. In *X* v *UK*,[191] for example, the Commission agreed with the UK government that a law requiring Sikh motorcyclists to wear crash helmets was a 'necessary' restriction on religious freedom. However, the government subsequently changed its mind and turban-wearing Sikhs are now exempt from the law in question.[192] In another case[193] the Commission rejected the claim of a Muslim teacher who was dismissed for missing forty-five minutes of classes each week in order to attend the mosque. The Commission concluded that the teacher had accepted restrictions on his religious freedom when taking up his post.

Several recent decisions have dealt with restrictions on the freedom to observe a religious dress code. In *R (on the application of Begum)* v *Denbigh High School* a fourteen-year-old Muslim girl challenged a decision to exclude her from the defendant school for refusing to comply with its uniform policy. The policy allowed girls to wear a form of dress – the shalwar kameeze – which was acceptable to the vast majority of its Muslim students, but the applicant believed that she was obliged by her religion to wear a more loose-fitting garment, the jilbab. The Court of Appeal found that there had been a restriction on her freedom to manifest her religious beliefs, and that the school had failed to

---

[178] *Ahmad* v *UK* (1982) 4 EHRR 126.   [179] *Kokkinakis* v *Greece* (1994) 17 EHRR 397.
[180] *Arrowsmith* v *UK* (1978) 19 D&R 5.   [181] *X and Church of Scientology* v *Sweden* (1978) 16 D&R 68.
[182] *Angelini* v *Sweden* (1986) 51 D&R 41.   [183] *X* v *UK* (1974) 1 D&R 41.
[184] *Holy Monasteries* v *Greece* (1995) 20 EHRR 1.   [185] *Kokkinakis* v *Greece* (1994) 17 EHRR 397.
[186] *Cha'are Shalom Ve Tsedek* v *France* (2000) 9 BHRC 27.
[187] *Kjeldsen, Busk Madsen and Pedersen* v *Denmark* (1979–1980) 1 EHRR 711.
[188] (1978) 19 D&R 5.
[189] See also *R (on the application of Playfoot (a child))* v *Millais School Governing Body* [2007] EWHC 1698 (Admin), [2007] HRLR 34: Article 9 not engaged by ban on the wearing of a chastity ring as not a manifestation of Christian beliefs.
[190] Except in states which have ratified Protocol 12: the UK is not one of these states.
[191] (1978) 14 D&R 234.   [192] Road Traffic Act 1988, s 16(2).
[193] *Ahmad* v *UK* (1982) 4 EHRR 126; see also *Copsey* v *WWB Devon Clays* [2005] EWCA Civ 932, [2005] ICR 1789.

justify this restriction.[194] However, the decision was overturned by the House of Lords,[195] with the majority of the panel concluding that there had been no interference with the applicant's Article 9 rights: she and her family had chosen the defendant school with full knowledge of its uniform policy, and other schools in the area would have accepted her as a pupil and allowed her to wear the jilbab. In partly dissenting judgments Lord Nicholls and Baroness Hale held that the applicant's religious freedom *had* been restricted, but they agreed that her claim should be dismissed as they considered the restriction to be justifiable. In rejecting the idea that Ms Begum's Article 9 rights were even engaged in this case, the approach of the majority is arguably too narrow. The minority approach, however, would appear to be compatible with the Grand Chamber's decision in *Sahin* v *Turkey*.[196] In this case rules preventing university students from wearing headscarves were found to be compatible with Article 9, on the basis that they pursued the legitimate aim of protecting the rights and freedoms of others in a secular state.[197]

Despite the symbolic importance attached to freedom of religion by section 13 of the Human Rights Act,[198] *Begum* is one of only a handful of domestic cases to have addressed Article 9. Another example is *R (on application of Ullah)* v *Special Adjudicator*, in which it was held that a refusal to grant asylum to a person fleeing religious persecution could theoretically amount to a breach of this provision.[199] In another case[200] the House of Lords rejected an argument that the prohibition on corporal punishment in schools was in breach of the Article 9 rights of parents. Their Lordships were prepared to accept as religious the belief that physical chastisement was biblically mandated. They also agreed that a court should not seek to measure the validity of a belief by some objective standard:[201]

> It is not for the court to embark on an enquiry into the asserted belief and judge its 'validity' by some objective standard such as the source material upon which the claimant founds his belief or the orthodox teaching of the religion in question or the extent to which the claimant's belief conforms to . . . the views of others professing the same religion. Freedom of religion protects the subject belief of an individual.

It was held, however, that any interference with the Article 9 rights of parents could be justified by the need to protect the rights and freedom of children.

---

[194] [2005] EWCA Civ 199, [2005] 1 WLR 3372, [2005] 2 All ER 396.

[195] [2006] UKHL 15, [2007] 1 AC 100, [2006] 2 All ER 487.

[196] (2007) 44 EHRR 5: see Hill and Sandberg, 'Is Nothing Sacred? Clashing Symbols in a Secular World' [2007] PL 488; Lewis, 'What not to Wear: Religious Rights, the European Court, and the Margin of Appreciation' (2007) 56 ICLQ 395.

[197] See also: *R (on the application of X)* v *Headteachers and Governors of Y School* [2007] EWHC 298 (Admin), [2008] 1 All ER 249 (refusal to allow Muslim girl to wear niqab veil upheld on similar reasoning to that adopted by the minority in *Begum*);

[198] See p 156, *ante*.

[199] [2004] UKHL 26, [2004] 2 AC 323, [2004] 3 All ER 785. It was thought, however, that a refugee entitled to succeed under Article 9 would in any event be entitled to asylum on the ground of a well-founded fear of persecution.

[200] *R (on the application of Williamson)* v *Secretary of State for Education and Employment* [2005] UKHL 15, [2005] 2 AC 246, [2005] 2 All ER 1.

[201] Ibid, at [23], per Lord Nicholls.

9 ARTICLE 10: THE RIGHT TO FREEDOM OF EXPRESSION

Article 10 covers the right to hold opinions and to receive and impart information and ideas. The right may be restricted in the interests of national security, territorial integrity or public safety, for the prevention of disorder or crime, for the protection of health, morals or the rights and freedoms of others, in order to prevent the disclosure of confidential information, or in order to maintain the authority and impartiality of the judiciary.[202] Freedom of expression lies at the heart of the Convention system, and its importance is expressly recognized by section 12 of the Human Rights Act.[203] Protected forms of expression can include words, pictures, dress, and even conduct,[204] though some types of expression are more highly valued than others. Commercial speech, for example, does not attract the same level of protection as political speech.[205] In addition, Article 17 states that the Convention does not confer any right to engage in activities aimed at the destruction of protected rights and freedoms, and this provides a basis for denying protection to speech inciting racial or religious hatred.[206] In any event, laws aimed at restricting hate speech will generally fall within the exceptions permitted under Article 10(2), subject to the principle of proportionality.

The fact that certain ideas are controversial or may 'offend, shock or disturb',[207] is not a sufficient justification for preventing their expression. In a recent case, however, the BBC was held to have acted lawfully in refusing to broadcast an election video containing graphic images of aborted foetuses.[208] The House of Lords accepted that the video constituted a form of protected speech, but found the BBC's decision to be consistent with Article 10(2) and with its statutory duty not to offend against good taste and decency. Lord Walker explained that although material likely to cause 'a significant degree of revulsion' could potentially be justified by its purpose, the BBC had considerable experience in determining accepted standards of taste and decency and its decision was within the limits of its discretion.[209] The degree of deference shown to the BBC in this case has been criticized,[210] and in a strong dissenting judgment Lord Scott concluded that the restriction was not 'necessary':[211]

> A broadcasters' mind-set that rejects a party election television programme dealing with an issue of undeniable public importance such as abortion, on the ground that large numbers of the voting public would find the programme 'offensive' denigrates the voting public, treats them like children who need to be protected from

---

[202] Article 10(2)   [203] See p 153, *ante.*

[204] *Stevens v UK* (1986) D&R 245; *Steel v UK* (1999) 28 EHRR 603.

[205] *X and the Church of Scientology v Sweden* (1978) 16 D&R 68.

[206] *Norwood v UK* (2005) 40 EHRR SE11 (public display of an Islamophobic poster did not enjoy the protection of Article 10).

[207] *Handyside v UK* (1979) 1 EHRR 737 at 48; see also *Jersild v Denmark* (1995) 19 EHRR 1.

[208] *R (on the application of ProLife Alliance) v BBC* [2003] UKHL 23, [2004] 1 AC 185, [2003] 2 All ER 977.

[209] Ibid, at [122].

[210] MacDonald, 'R *(on the application of ProLife Alliance)* v *British Broadcasting Corporation*' [2003] 6 EHRLR 651; Barendt, 'Free Speech and Abortion' [2003] PL 580.

[211] [2003] UKHL 23 at [99], [2004] 1 AC 185 at [99], [2003] 2 All ER 977.

the unpleasant realities of life, seriously undervalues their political maturity and can only promote...voter-apathy.

In another case a man was convicted of a public order offence[212] after preaching in a city centre whilst displaying a sign with the words 'Stop Immorality. Stop Homosexuality. Stop Lesbianism.' The Administrative Court held that although the man had been motivated by sincerely held religious beliefs and had intended to preach rather than cause offence, his conviction was compatible with Article 10.[213]

Freedom of expression is limited in numerous ways by domestic law, but most of the restrictions seem to fall within the legitimate exceptions permitted under Article 10(2). Thus in *Handyside* v *UK*[214] a prosecution under the Obscene Publications Act 1959 was held to be a legitimate and proportionate means of protecting public morals: the court was prepared to grant a wide margin of appreciation in the absence of a uniform conception of morality. In another case,[215] the refusal to give a film certificate to an allegedly blasphemous video was found to be a legitimate way of protecting the rights and freedoms of others. Recently the House of Lords suggested that section 11 of the Terrorism Act 2000, which makes it an offence to profess membership of a proscribed organization, is consistent with Article 10 because it does not prohibit the holding of particular views and is a proportionate response to concerns about terrorism.[216] In another case the House was asked to issue a declaration as to whether a treason provision was compatible with the right to freedom of expression.[217] It declined to grant the relief sought because the applicants had already published a series of articles advocating the peaceful overthrow of the monarchy and no-one had attempted to prosecute them. Their freedom of expression had therefore not been inhibited, and the question before the court was purely hypothetical. Nevertheless, Lord Scott did not refrain from expressing his opinion on the matter:[218]

> It is plain as a pike staff to the respondents and everyone else that no-one who advocates the peaceful abolition of the monarchy...is at any risk of prosecution. Whatever may be the correct construction of s 3, taken by itself, it is clear beyond any peradventure first, that the section would now be 'read down' as required by s 3 of the Human Rights Act 1998...and second, that no Attorney-General or Director of Public Prosecutions would or could authorise a prosecution for such advocacy without becoming a laughing stock. To do so would plainly be an unlawful act under s 6(1) of the 1998 Act.

---

[212] The offence of causing harassment, alarm, or distress: Public Order Act 1986, s 5.

[213] *Hammond* v *DPP* [2004] EWHC 69 (Admin), (2004) 168 JP 601. (It was also compatible with Article 9.) See further: Turenne, 'The Compatibility of Criminal Liability with Freedom of Expression' [2007] Crim LR 866.

[214] (1979) 1 EHRR 737.

[215] *Wingrove* v *UK* (1997) 24 EHRR 1.

[216] *Attorney-General's Reference (No 4 of 2002)* [2004] UKHL 43, [2005] 1 AC 264, [2005] 1 All ER 237. However, the defence under s 11(2) had to be read down so as to impose an evidential rather than legal burden on the defendant.

[217] *R (on the application of Rusbridger)* v *Attorney-General* [2003] UKHL 38, [2004] 1 AC 357, [2003] 3 All ER 784; Treason Felony Act 1848, s 3.

[218] Ibid at [23].

The Strasbourg court has criticized the UK's blasphemy laws on the basis that they only apply to the Anglican faith and thus discriminate between religions, but it has also ruled that restrictions on blasphemous speech are not inherently incompatible with Article 10.[219] However, since the coming into force of the Human Rights Act it was extremely unlikely that the authorities would seek to prosecute the offence, and the High Court recently held that a magistrate had correctly refused to allow a private prosecution following the BBC's controversial screening of *Jerry Springer: The Opera*.[220] These issues are now of academic interest only, the offence of blasphemy being abolished by the Criminal Justice and Immigration Act 2008.[221]

Reporting restrictions pending the outcome of legal proceedings are permissible under the Convention, in the interests of protecting the rights and freedoms of others and maintaining the impartiality of the judiciary. However, any restrictions must be prescribed by law and proportionate to their objectives, and criticism that the common law contempt jurisdiction was too uncertain in scope[222] led to the enactment of the Contempt of Court Act 1981.[223] It has also been held that the law of defamation is compatible with freedom of expression, as long as the level of damages awarded in successful cases is not so high as to have a chilling effect on the essence of the right.[224]

Article 10 cases decided under the Human Rights Act include the related cases of *R v Shayler*[225] and *Attorney-General v Punch*.[226] In the first case a former MI5 officer was prosecuted under the Official Secrets Act 1989 for disclosing information obtained during the course of his employment. In a ruling on a preliminary matter, the House of Lords held that the restrictions on free speech fell within Article 10(2) because they were a legitimate and proportionate response to the interests of national security. Moreover, the House did not consider it necessary to read a public interest defence into the Act in order to render it compatible. In the second case a magazine published an article by David Shayler while proceedings against him were still ongoing. Injunctions had already been obtained to prevent Mr Shayler from publishing such information, and it was held that the publishers could be liable for contempt of court. The fact that they did not believe the material to be harmful to the national interest was no defence: the

---

[219] *Otto-Preminger Institut* v *Austria* (1995) 19 EHRR 34.

[220] *R (on the application of Green)* v *City of Westminster Magistrates Court* [2007] EWHC 2785 (Admin), (2007) 157 NLJ 1767.

[221] 2008 Act, s 79.

[222] *Sunday Times* v *UK* (1979–1980) 2 EHRR 245.

[223] A line of Human Rights Act cases is already developing concerning the circumstances in which reporting restrictions and injunctions should be imposed: see *Venables and Thompson* v *News Group Newspapers* [2001] Fam 430, [2001] 1 All ER 908. In *R (on the application of the Telegraph Group plc)* v *Sherwood* [2001] EWCA Crim 1075, [2001] 1 WLR 1983, the Court of Appeal suggested that the pre-Human Rights Act approach was already broadly compatible with the Convention.

[224] *Tolstoy Miloslavsky* v *UK* (1995) 20 EHRR 442. In *Steel and Morris* v *UK* (2005) 41 EHRR 22 it was held that Article 10 could also be infringed if the defendant in a defamation case had no access to legal aid and faced a significant inequality of arms: see p 187, *ante*.

[225] [2002] UKHL 11, [2003] 1 AC 247, [2002] 2 All ER 477.

[226] [2002] UKHL 50, [2003] 1 AC 1046, [2003] 1 All ER 289.

purpose of the injunction was to preserve the confidentiality of the information until its status had been determined, and the terms of the order were proportionate to this objective.

Article 10 was also considered in *R (on the application of Farrakhan)* v *Secretary of State for the Home Department*.[227] In this case the Home Office had refused to allow a controversial political figure to enter the UK on the basis that his radical views might inflame religious tensions and lead to disorder. The Court accepted that Article 10 was engaged, even though Mr Farrakhan remained outside the territorial jurisdiction of the Convention. However, it held that the decision to refuse entry had been legitimate. In other cases consideration has been given to the right of prisoners to speak to the media,[228] and freedom of expression has also played a significant role in the jurisprudence on Article 8.[229]

10   ARTICLE 11: THE RIGHT TO FREEDOM OF PEACEFUL ASSEMBLY AND FREEDOM OF ASSOCIATION WITH OTHERS

Article 11 expressly protects the right to 'form and join a trade union for the protection of one's interests', and states have a positive duty to create conditions in which the exercise of this right is possible.[230] Article 11 also protects the right *not* to join a union, though it may be that this right is only breached if the individual is opposed to union membership for reasons of conscience and principle.[231] Professional associations are not considered to be trade unions for these purposes, and requiring members of a profession to join a relevant association will not normally be contrary to Article 11.[232]

The rights set out in Article 11 may be subject to restrictions in the interests of national security or public safety, for the prevention of disorder or crime, for the protection of health or morals, or for the protection of the rights and freedoms of others.[233] Any such restrictions must be prescribed by law and necessary in a democratic society, and this means taking into account the rights of unions themselves. For example, a law preventing a union from expelling a member on the grounds of his involvement with the British National Party (BNP) was recently found to be incompatible with Article 11, because despite its legitimate aim, it had a disproportionate impact on the union's freedom to choose its own members.[234]

In addition to the specific protection given to union rights, Article 11 can also be used in the context of the right to peaceful protest. It has been held, for example, that

[227] [2002] EWCA Civ 606, [2002] QB 1391, [2002] 4 All ER 289.

[228] *Hirst* v *Secretary of State for the Home Department* [2002] EWHC 602 (Admin), [2002] 1 WLR 2929. See also the pre-HRA case of *R* v *Secretary of State for the Home Department, ex parte Simms* [2000] 2 AC 115, [1999] 3 All ER 400.

[229] See p 190, *ante*.   [230] *Swedish Engine Drivers Union* v *Sweden* (1979–1980) 1 EHRR 617.

[231] *Young* v *UK* (1982) 4 EHRR 38; cf. *Sibson* v *UK* (1994) 17 EHRR 193 (no breach in respect of a worker who simply wanted to change from one union to another and who had been offered redeployment).

[232] *Le Compte* v *Belgium* (1982) 4 EHRR 1.   [233] Article 11(2).

[234] *ASLEF* v *UK* (2007) 45 EHRR 44. See Ewing, 'The Implications of the *ASLEF* case' (2007) 36(4) ILJ 425.

a decision to arrest demonstrators for breach of the peace must be measured against the yardstick of proportionality,[235] and at Strasbourg level the power to bind over to keep the peace has been criticized as too vague to constitute a limitation 'prescribed by law'.[236] However, 'assemblies' will only be protected under Article 11 if they are of a type necessary to the proper functioning of a democracy, and gatherings for recreational or sporting purposes will not normally fall into this category. A recent challenge to the ban on hunting with dogs was rejected on this basis.[237]

11 ARTICLE 12: THE RIGHT TO MARRY AND FOUND A FAMILY

This Article provides that 'men and women of marriageable age have the right to marry and to found a family, according to the national laws governing the exercise of this right.' On its face the wording appears to restrict the right to marry to couples of the opposite sex, and it also gives states considerable scope to regulate the exercise of the right as they see fit. However, in *Goodwin* v *UK* it was held that the refusal to recognize the change in gender of a post-operative transsexual, and the negative impact of this decision on the right to marry, was a violation of Articles 8 and 12.[238] In the view of the Court, evidence of changing attitudes towards gender and marriage meant that there was less scope for affording a wide margin of appreciation, though states still have some discretion as to how the effects of a change in gender should be recognized.[239] Other relevant decisions include the ruling that laws prohibiting a man and his former daughter-in-law from marrying were incompatible with the Convention,[240] and the decision that laws designed to prevent certain classes of immigrant from entering into sham marriages had a disproportionate impact on Article 12 rights.[241]

There have been fewer cases concerning the 'right to found a family', though the courts have dealt with a handful of claims arising from restrictions on prisoners' access to facilities for artificial insemination. In *R (on the application of Mellor)* v *Secretary of State for the Home Department* a refusal to provide such facilities was deemed to be

[235] *R (on the application of Laporte)* v *Chief Constable of Gloucester* [2006] UKHL 55, [2007] 2 AC 105, [2007] 2 WLR 46. See also: Fenwick, 'The Right to Protest, the Human Rights Act and the Margin of Appreciation' (1999) 62 MLR 491.

[236] *Steel* v *United Kingdom* (1999) 28 EHRR 603.

[237] *R (on the application of Countryside Alliance)* v *Attorney-General* [2007] UKHL 52, [2007] 3 WLR 922.

[238] (2002) 35 EHRR 18; applied in *Bellinger* v *Bellinger* [2003] UKHL 21, [2003] 2 AC 467, [2003] 2 All ER 593. The Gender Recognition Act 2004 was introduced in response to these decisions.

[239] *R and F* v *UK* (2006) App 35748/05 (no breach in respect of a male-to-female transsexual who could not obtain a full Gender Recognition Certificate under the 2004 Act without first divorcing a woman to whom she wished to remain married.)

[240] *B and L* v *UK* (2006) 42 EHRR 11. The incompatibility identified was removed by the Marriage Act 1949 (Remedial) Order 2007, SI 2007/438.

[241] *R (on the application of Baiai)* v *Secretary of State for the Home Department* [2007] EWCA Civ 478, [2007] 3 WLR 573, [2007] 4 All ER 199. At first instance the High Court also issued a declaration of incompatibility in respect of Article 14, because the law did not apply to marriages conducted by the Church of England: the government responded by announcing that it would extend the scheme to Church of England marriages as well, so as to remove the element of discrimination.

lawful,[242] but in a more recent case the government's policy was found to be in breach of Article 8 because it failed to strike a fair balance between competing private and public interests.[243] On the other hand, Article 12 does not entitle a prisoner to receive conjugal visits.[244]

12 ARTICLE 14: THE RIGHT NOT TO BE DISCRIMINATED AGAINST WITH REGARD TO OTHER CONVENTION RIGHTS

The substantive rights set out in the Convention must, by virtue of Article 14, be respected and protected in a non-discriminatory way:

> The enjoyment of the rights and freedoms set forth in this Convention shall be secured without discrimination on any grounds such as sex, race, colour, language, religion, political or other opinion, national or social origin, association with a national minority, property, birth or other status.

The list of prohibited grounds of discrimination is broad and non-exhaustive, and the reference to 'other status' has enabled additional grounds such as sexual orientation[245] and illegitimacy[246] to be brought within its ambit. However, a class of persons will only enjoy a common 'status' if they share something akin to a personal characteristic: a mutual interest in hunting, for example, will not suffice.[247]

Article 14 does not create a free-standing right, and a breach of the non-discrimination principle can only be established in conjunction with another Convention right. However, although the link with another right must be more than merely tenuous,[248] it will be sufficient to demonstrate that an act or omission 'falls within its ambit'. This means that even where the Convention does not *require* a state to take positive steps to protect or enhance a particular freedom, if it *chooses* to do so in respect of *some* groups, Article 14 may demand that the benefit is extended to all. For example, *Abdulaziz, Cabales and Balkandali v UK*[249] concerned an immigration rule governing when spouses who were non-nationals would be granted indefinite leave to remain in the UK, and which treated men and women differently. There was no breach of Article 8 but the rule fell 'within the ambit' of the right to family life, and as it discriminated on gender grounds it was held that there had been a breach of Article 14.

---

[242] [2001] EWCA Civ 472, [2002] QB 13, [2001] 3 WLR 533.
[243] *Dickson v UK* [2007] 3 FCR 877. In the light of this, it was considered unnecessary to examine the claim under Article 12.
[244] *ELH v UK* (1998) 25 EHRR CD 158.
[245] *Smith and Grady v UK* (2000) 29 EHRR 493.
[246] *Marckx v Belgium* (1979–1980) 2 EHRR 330.
[247] *R (on the application of Countryside Alliance) v Attorney-General* [2007] UKHL 52, [2007] 3 WLR 922.
[248] *M v Secretary of State for Work and Pensions* [2006] UKHL 11, [2006] 2 AC 91, [2006] 4 All ER 929.
[249] (1985) 7 EHRR 471.

In *Wandsworth LBC* v *Michalak*, Brooke LJ stated that when considering a claim under Article 14, a court would normally be required to address four questions:[250]

> If the answer to any of the four questions is 'no', then the claim is likely to fail, and it is in general unnecessary to proceed to the next question. These questions are:
>
> (i)   Do the facts fall within the ambit of one or more of the substantive Convention provisions...
>
> (ii) If so, was there different treatment as respects that right between the complainant on the one hand and other persons put forward for comparison ('the chosen comparators') on the other?
>
> (iii) Were the chosen comparators in an analogous situation to the complainant's situation?
>
> (iv) If so, did the difference in treatment have an objective and reasonable justification...

However, in *Carson* v *Secretary of State for Work and Pensions* it was held that this approach may not be appropriate in every case.[251] Examples of laws and policies challenged successfully under Article 14 include the criminalization of homosexual acts in Northern Ireland,[252] the denial of rights to same-sex partners which would be afforded to other unmarried couples,[253] and the ban on gays in the military.[254]

13   PROTOCOL 1

Protocol 1 of the Convention is concerned with three distinct rights: the right to peaceful enjoyment of possessions, the right to education, and the right to participate in free and fair elections.

(a) Peaceful enjoyment of possessions

The right to peaceful enjoyment of possessions is set out in Article 1 of the First Protocol. It may be restricted 'in the public interest' and subject to the conditions provided for by domestic and international law. In addition, the right does not 'in any way impair the right of a State to enforce such laws as it deems necessary to control the use of property in accordance with the general interest or to secure the payment of taxes or other contributions or penalties.' The term 'possessions' has been interpreted quite widely,[255]

---

[250]   [2002] EWCA Civ 271 at [20], [2003] 1 WLR 617 at [20], [2002] 4 All ER 1136.

[251]   [2005] UKHL 37, [2006] 1 AC 173, [2005] 4 All ER 545. See also: McColgan, 'Cracking the Comparator Problem: Discrimination, "Equal" Treatment and the Role of Comparisons' [2006] EHRLR 650.

[252]   *Dudgeon* v *UK* (1982) 4 EHRR 149 (a breach of Articles 8 and 14 because of the disproportionate impact on private life).

[253]   See, e.g. *Ghaidan* v *Godin-Mendoza* [2004] UKHL 30, [2004] 2 AC 557, [2004] 3 All ER 411.

[254]   *Smith and Grady* v *UK* (2000) 29 EHRR 493.

[255]   For example, it is capable of including licences, patents, planning permission, leasehold interests, and even goodwill in a business: see *Van Marle and others* v *Netherlands* (1986) 8 EHRR 483; *Mellacher* v *Austria* (1990) 12 EHRR 391.

and includes entitlements to pensions, income support and other welfare benefits.[256]
On the other hand, the right is subject to a wide range of exceptions, and states are
afforded considerable discretion in deciding when a restriction is in the public interest.
For example, in *Wilson* v *First County Trust (No 2)* a provision of the Consumer Credit
Act 1974, which could render a credit agreement unenforceable if the amount of credit
was calculated incorrectly, was held to be a proportionate mechanism for achieving the
legitimate objective of consumer protection:[257]

> [Section] 127(3) may be drastic, even harsh, in its adverse consequences for a lender.
> He loses all his rights under the agreement, including his rights to any security which
> has been lodged. Conversely, the borrower acquires what can only be described as
> a windfall. He keeps his money and recovers his security. These consequences apply
> just as much where the lender was acting in good faith throughout and the error
> was due to a mistaken reading of the complex statutory requirements as in cases of
> deliberate non-compliance...
>
> [Nevertheless] it must be open to Parliament to decide that, severe though this
> sanction may be, it is an appropriate way of protecting consumers as a matter of
> social policy.

Claims under Article 1 of the Protocol are unlikely to succeed unless there is a clear lack
of proportionality or a defective procedure. As a consequence, such claims are often
made in conjunction with a claim under Article 6 or 14 of the Convention. For example,
differentials in welfare payments corresponding with differences in age or country of
residence were recently challenged under Article 1 of the Protocol and Article 14 of the
Convention. The differences were found to be justifiable, however, and the challenge
failed on both grounds.[258] The right to peaceful enjoyment of possessions was also considered in *Aston Cantlow* v *Wallbank*.[259] The defendant owned the freehold over a plot
of rectorial land, and the Parish Council sought to invoke section 2(1) of the Chancel
Repairs Act 1932, under which the owners of such land could be obliged to repair the
chancel of the parish church. The defendants claimed that this was a breach of both
Article 14 of the Convention and Article 1 of the First Protocol: they argued that requiring them to pay for the repairs was an arbitrary deprivation of property which discriminated against them as owners of the land. The defendants ultimately lost their
case because the House of Lords found that the Parish Council was not performing

---

[256] In *Carson* v *Secretary of State for Work and Pensions* [2005] UKHL 37, [2006] 1 AC 173, [2005] 4 All
ER 545 the House of Lords was prepared to assume that a range of benefits fell within Article 1 of the First
Protocol, though it had doubts about those which are not contributions-based. The Grand Chamber has since
held that *all* entitlements to welfare payments fall within the ambit of the First Protocol, regardless of any link
with personal contributions: *Stec* v *UK* (2005) 41 EHRR SE18.

[257] [2003] UKHL 40 at [72]–[77], [2004] 1 AC 816 at [72]–[77], [2003] 4 All ER 97, per Lord Nicholls. As the
credit company had never had a right to enforce the payments 'proprietary rights' were not even engaged in
this case. However, their Lordships did not need to decide this point because the agreement was made before
the Human Rights Act came into force.

[258] *Carson* v *Secretary of State for Work and Pensions* [2005] UKHL 37, [2006] 1 AC 173, [2005] 4 All ER 545.

[259] *Aston-Cantlow and Wilcote with Billesley Parochial Church Council* v *Wallbank* [2003] UKHL 37, [2004]
1 AC 546, [2003] 3 All ER 1213.

a public function.[260] However, it added that there would have been no interference with Convention rights in any event, because the defendant had acquired her property with full knowledge of the accompanying repair obligation. *International Transport Roth*[261] is an example of a challenged based on a procedural defect. The case centred on a penalty regime under which hauliers could be fined £2,000 for every clandestine immigrant brought into the country by their vehicles. The challenge was partly based on Article 6 because hauliers were required to prove that they had an effective scheme for preventing such incidents, and this amounted to a reversal of the burden of proof. However, there was also an issue under Article 1, Protocol 1, because officials were empowered to detain vehicles in order to ensure payment. The regime was found to be in breach of both provisions and a declaration of incompatibility was issued.

(b) The right to education

Article 2 of the First Protocol states that 'no person shall be denied the right to education', and it imposes an obligation on states to 'respect the right of persons to ensure such education and teaching in conformity with their own religious and philosophical convictions'. Upon signing the Protocol, the UK entered a reservation in respect of this Article, which provides that it is accepted 'only so far as it is compatible with the provision of efficient instruction and training and the avoidance of unreasonable public expenditure.' The wording of the first part of the Article is deliberately restrictive, referring to the negative right not to be denied education, rather than a positive right to receive it. This means that it is primarily concerned with ensuring that existing educational facilities are available on an equal basis: it does not, for example, include any positive right to have children educated in a particular language.[262] In *Campbell* v *UK*[263] the use of corporal punishment in a school was successfully challenged under this provision, on the basis that it contravened the applicant's right to have her child educated in accordance with her religious and philosophical beliefs. This can be contrasted with the decision in *R (on the application of Williamson)* v *Secretary of State for Education and Employment*.[264] In this case a ban on the use of physical chastisement in schools was held to be justifiable, notwithstanding the applicant's belief that corporal punishment was integral to a Christian upbringing.

(c) The holding of free elections

Article 3 of the First Protocol obliges states to hold 'free elections at reasonable intervals by secret ballot, under conditions which will ensure the free expression of the opinion of the people.' The Article does not expressly create any individual rights, but the right to participate in elections is implied. A breach of this implied right was established in *Hirst* v *UK*, which concerned the disenfranchisement of prisoners under section 3 of the

---

[260] See p 165, *ante*.

[261] *International Transport Roth GmbH* v *Secretary of State for the Home Department* [2002] EWCA Civ 158, [2003] QB 728, [2002] HRLR 31.

[262] *Belgian Linguistics Case (No 2)* (1979–1980) 1 EHRR 252.

[263] (1982) 4 EHRR 293.   [264] [2005] UKHL 15, [2005] 2 AC 246, [2005] 2 All ER 1.

Representation of the People Act 1983.[265] In a landmark ruling it was held that although section 3 pursued a legitimate aim, its blanket application to all prisoners could not be justified and the interference with the right to vote was disproportionate. The government accepted the decision but at the time of writing has yet to bring forward proposals to remedy this incompatibility.

THE EUROPEAN COURT OF HUMAN RIGHTS

With its highly legalistic character and its several decades of interpretive jurisprudence, the European Convention on Human Rights has engendered the most sophisticated jurisprudence of any of the international judicial instruments promulgated to protect human rights...in many respects, the theory and practice of the European Convention on Human Rights parallel the theory and practice of the United States Supreme Court more closely than any domestic system operating in Europe. The key to understanding the Convention lies in the case-law of the European Commission and Court, whose role it is to interpret the Convention...[266]

In its original form, the ECHR established both a Commission and a Court of Human Rights. The Commission's role was to examine applications under the Convention and to reject at an early stage those which were manifestly unfounded or otherwise inadmissible. Admissible claims were then subject to the Commission's attempts to negotiate a 'friendly settlement'. Only if a settlement could not be reached would the matter finally be referred to the Court, but not before the Commission had examined the case and prepared a written opinion as to the merits. In the 1990s the Committee of Ministers[267] decided to streamline the complaints procedure in order to cope with the growing number of applications that were being received each year. The reforms were set out in Protocol 11 and came into effect on 1 November 1998. After a brief transitional period to allow the resolution of cases that were already in the system, the Commission was abolished and a re-vamped, full-time Court now deals with all stages of a complaint.

Protocol 14

Further reforms are due to be implemented under Protocol 14,[268] which was opened for signature on 12 May 2004. However, the Protocol requires ratification by all forty-six member states before it can take effect, and the Russian Duma has thus far refused to accept its provisions.[269] Whereas Protocol 11 brought about wholesale changes to the

---

[265] (2006) 42 EHRR 41.

[266] Gomien, Harris and Zwaak, *Law and Practice of the European Convention on Human Rights and the European Social Charter* (1996) at p 19.

[267] The Council of Europe's political and executive body.

[268] For a discussion, see Greer, 'Protocol 14 and the Future of the European Court of Human Rights' [2005] PL 83.

[269] See Leach, 'Strasbourg's Oversight of Russia: An Increasingly Strained Relationship' [2007] PL 640.

Strasbourg system, the reforms set out in Protocol 14 will (if they are ever introduced) be rather more modest. The aim is to ease the pressure on the Court by allowing clearly inadmissible claims to be filtered out by a single judge at a preliminary stage.[270] The Protocol will also introduce an additional admissibility criterion for individual applications.[271] Several Convention Articles will be amended or renumbered as a result of these changes,[272] though none of the provisions dealing with substantive rights will be affected. (References in this chapter are to the old Article numbers: the new numbers are given in brackets where applicable.)

1 THE COMPOSITION AND PROCEDURE OF THE COURT

The number of judges of the Court is equal to the number of parties to the Convention, though judges are appointed to sit in an individual capacity and there are no requirements as to nationality.[273] Like their counterparts in the European Court of Justice,[274] judges are currently appointed for a renewable period of six years, but under the reforms introduced by Protocol 14 they will serve for a single nine-year term.[275] Judges are elected by the Parliamentary Assembly from a list of candidates supplied by each Member State,[276] and the Court is divided into four sections. Rule 25(2) of the Rules of Procedure provides that 'the composition of the Sections shall be geographically and gender balanced and shall reflect the different legal systems among the Contracting Parties.' The sections are headed by two Vice-Presidents and two Presidents of Section. The holders of these positions are elected by the judges from amongst their ranks, as is the Court's President.[277]

Applications to the Court may be made in any language used by the Member States, though once a case reaches the merits stage proceedings are normally conducted in English or French.[278] Each application is assigned to a section, and a rapporteur decides whether to refer the case directly to a Chamber of seven judges, or whether to allocate it to a three-member committee for a preliminary examination.[279] Committees perform a filtering role similar to that performed by the former Commission and may strike out inadmissible claims without a hearing.[280] Under the new system it will also be possible for claims that are clearly inadmissible or without merit to be struck out by a single judge.[281]

Applications not struck out at a preliminary stage are currently referred to a Chamber for a full determination. This will continue to be the case for most applications brought under the new system, but the committees will also have the power to decide both the

[270] See the new Article 27.   [271] Article 35, as amended; Protocol 14, Article 12.
[272] Article 24 will be deleted, the old Articles 25–27 will become Articles 24–26, and a new Article 27 will be inserted. Articles 22–29, 31–32, 35–36, 38–39, 46, and 59 will be amended.
[273] Articles 20 and 21, ECHR. The judge currently occupying Liechtenstein's seat in the court is Swiss.
[274] See p 135, *ante*.   [275] Article 23, as amended; Protocol 14, Article 2.
[276] Article 22, as amended.   [277] Rule 8, Rules of Procedure.
[278] Rule 34.   [279] Rule 49. Under rule 48, all inter-state applications must be referred to a Chamber.
[280] Article 28, as amended.
[281] New Article 27 (which has no equivalent in the old Convention structure). Where a single judge is used, he or she cannot be the judge elected in respect of the state with which the case is concerned.

admissibility *and* the merits of repetitive claims. Thus, 'if the underlying question in [a] case...is already the subject of well-established case law', it will be possible for a committee of three judges to deal with all aspects of it in a single judgment, instead of admissible claims automatically being referred to a Chamber.[282] Where a decision is made by a Chamber, its membership will include the section President or Vice-President and the judge elected in respect of the Member State concerned. During this stage it may be possible for the parties to negotiate a friendly settlement with the assistance of the Court's Registrar,[283] but if the case cannot be resolved the Chamber will deliver its judgment. Within three months of the judgment, any party may request that the case be referred to the Grand Chamber on the grounds that it raises a serious issue of interpretation or some other serious issue of general importance.[284] The Grand Chamber consists of seventeen judges, including the President, Vice-Presidents, and section Presidents, and is constituted for a period of three years.[285] Exceptionally, where a case raises sufficiently important issues, the Chamber may decline to deliver a judgment and may instead refer the case directly to the Grand Chamber for a ruling.[286]

By Article 41, if a violation of the Convention is established the Court can afford 'just satisfaction' to the injured party. This may involve an order for a state to pay compensation and costs. Final judgments of the Court are binding on the member states concerned, and the Committee of Ministers is responsible for overseeing their execution and for ensuring that any remedial action is taken. Failure to comply with a judgment might lead to a state being suspended from the Council of Europe, or, under Protocol 14, to the Committee of Ministers bringing proceedings in the Court for persistent infringement.[287]

2 THE ADMISSIBILITY OF COMPLAINTS

Complaints may be brought either by other Convention states or by individual victims of a Convention breach.[288] Inter-state applications are rare, but this is perhaps inevitable given the likely diplomatic consequences of bringing such an action. Most inter-state cases have been brought by countries directly connected to the 'victims' of the complaints,[289] but the *Greek Case* is a notable exception.[290] Several countries pursued this case when the 'regime of the colonels' seized power in Greece in a military coup. Specific complaints included the use of torture, the use of courts-martial to sentence

---

[282] Article 28; Protocol 14, Article 8.

[283] Article 38. (The relevant provisions are moved to Article 39 by Protocol 14, Article 14, and the changes introduced allow the Court to facilitate a friendly settlement at *any* stage in proceedings.)

[284] Article 43. See further: Mowbray, 'An Examination of the Work of the Grand Chamber of the European Court of Human Rights' [2007] PL 507.

[285] Article 27 (new Article 26), as amended; Protocol 14, Article 6.   [286] Article 30.

[287] Article 46; Protocol 14, Article 16. For a discussion of Russia's persistent infringement, see Leach (2007) *supra*, n 269.

[288] Recognition of the right of individual petition has been compulsory on Convention states since 1998: Article 34. The UK accepted this right on 14 January 1966.

[289] *Ireland* v *UK* (1979) 2 EHRR 25; see p 181, *ante*. See also *Cyprus* v *Turkey* (2002) 35 EHRR 30.

[290] (1969) 12 YB ECHR 196.

political prisoners, the prohibition of political activity, censorship of the press, and suspension of the rule of law. In total, violations of ten different Convention rights were established, forcing Greece to withdraw from the Council of Europe. It did not return until democracy was restored in 1974.

The vast majority of complaints lodged with the Court are from individual applicants. The basic admissibility criteria are set out in Article 35 of the Convention. This stipulates that the applicant must have already exhausted all effective remedies in his own country, and that he must have lodged his complaint within six months of a final decision by a national court or tribunal.[291] These criteria are applied fairly rigidly, though a journalist who was refused a job following a secret vetting process was able to make a later application because the alleged breach was not discovered until nine years later.[292] An additional admissibility criterion will be introduced by Protocol 14. This will empower the Court to declare an individual application inadmissible if the applicant 'has not suffered a significant disadvantage'. However, the case should still be examined on its merits if respect for human rights requires it.[293] The complainant must also be a victim or potential victim of a Convention breach,[294] and a 'victim' for these purposes is a person directly affected by a violation of a right, or someone who runs the risk of being directly affected in the future. In *Norris* v *Ireland*,[295] for example, a gay man who risked prosecution under a law criminalizing homosexual acts was considered to be a 'victim' for the purposes of Article 34.

FURTHER READING

AMOS, '*R* v *Secretary of State for the Home Department, ex parte Anderson*: Ending the Home Secretary's Sentencing Role' (2004) 67(1) MLR 108

APLIN, 'The Development of the Action for Breach of Confidence in a Post-HRA Era' [2007] IPQ 19.

ASHWORTH and STRANGE, 'Criminal Law and Human Rights' [2004] EHRLR 121

BARENDT, 'Free Speech and Abortion' [2003] PL 580

BLAKE, 'Importing Proportionality: Clarification or Confusion?' [2002] EHRLR 19

COOK, 'Environmental Rights as Human Rights' [2002] 2 EHRLR 196

CRAIG, 'The Human Rights Act, Article 6 and Procedural Rights' [2003] PL 753

DREW, 'Human Trafficking: A Modern Form of Slavery?' [2002] EHRLR 481

FENWICK, 'The Right to Protest, the Human Rights Act and the Margin of Appreciation' (1999) 62 MLR 491

FENWICK, *Civil Liberties and Human Rights* (Routledge Cavendish: 4th edn, 2007)

HARRIS, O'BOYLE and WARBRICK, *Law of the European Convention on Human Rights* (Butterworths: 1995)

---

[291] Article 35. There is no obligation to have recourse to remedies which are inadequate or ineffective: *Aksoy* v *Turkey* (1997) 23 EHRR 553.

[292] *Hilton* v *UK* (1988) 57 D&R 108.   [293] Article 35, as amended; Protocol 14, Article 12.

[294] Article 34.   [295] (1991) 13 EHRR 186.

HILL and SANDBERG, 'Is Nothing Sacred? Clashing Symbols in a Secular World' [2007] PL 488

JANIS, KAY and BRADLEY, *European Human Rights Law: Text and Materials* (Oxford University Press: 3rd edn, 2008)

JONES, 'The Devaluation of Human Rights under the European Convention' [1995] PL 430

JUSS, 'Constitutionalising Rights without a Constitution: The British Experience under Article 6 of the Human Rights Act' (2006) 27(1) Stat LR 29

LETSAS, 'Two Concepts of the Margin of Appreciation' (2006) 26(4) OJLS 705

LEWIS, 'What not to Wear: Religious Rights, the European Court, and the Margin of Appreciation' (2007) 56 ICLQ 395

MACDONALD, 'R (on the application of ProLife Alliance) v British Broadcasting Corporation' [2003] 6 EHRLR 651

MANTOUVALOU, 'Servitude and Forced Labour in the 21st Century: The Human Rights of Domestic Workers' (2006) 35(4) ILJ 395

McCOLGAN, 'Cracking the Comparator Problem: Discrimination, "Equal" Treatment and the Role of Comparisons' [2006] EHRLR 650

MEAD, 'The Likely Effect of the Human Rights Act on Everyday Policing Decisions in England and Wales' (2000) 5(1) J Civ Lib 5

MORRIS, 'Assisted Suicide under the European Convention on Human Rights: A Critique' [2003] EHRLR 65

MOWBRAY, *Cases and Materials on the European Convention on Human Rights* (Oxford University Press: 2nd edn, 2007)

MOWBRAY, 'An Examination of the Work of the Grand Chamber of the European Court of Human Rights' [2007] PL 507

MULHERON, 'A Potential Framework for Privacy? A Reply to *Hello!*' (2006) 69(5) MLR 679

NÍ AOLÁIN, 'Truth Telling, Accountability and the Right to Life in Northern Ireland' [2002] EHRLR 572

OVEY and WHITE (eds), *Jacobs and White: European Convention on Human Rights* (Oxford University Press: 4th edn, 2006)

ROGERS, 'A Criminal Lawyer's Response to Chastisement in the European Court of Human Rights' [2002] Crim LR 98

SCHOKKENBROEK, 'The Basis, Nature and Application of the Margin of Appreciation Doctrine in the Case-Law of the European Court of Human Rights' (1998) 19(1) HRLJ 30

SINGH et al, 'Is there a Role for the Margin of Appreciation in National Law after the Human Rights Act?' [1999] EHRLR 15

SINGH and STRACHAN, 'Privacy Postponed' [2003] EHRLR Special Issue 12

TURENNE, 'The Compatibility of Criminal Liability with Freedom of Expression' [2007] Crim LR 866

VAN DIJK et al, *The Theory and Practice of the European Convention on Human Rights* (Intersentia: 4th edn, 2006)

PART II

THE ADMINISTRATION OF JUSTICE

7

THE ROYAL PREROGATIVE AND JUDICIAL REVIEW

INTRODUCTION

This chapter examines the royal prerogative, which is the very foundation of our system of justice. Indeed, it is from this that the supervisory functions of the courts have developed. The chapter also explains the basic role of the courts in judicial review. Specific areas addressed include:

- The key role of the Crown in the administration of justice.

- The supervisory functions of the courts.

- The basic principles of judicial review and how they operate in the context of the administration of justice.

- The limits of judicial review: it does not extend to the work of the superior courts.

THE ROYAL PREROGATIVE

In name, the Crown is at the head of our modern system of justice. This stems from the historic position of the sovereign as the fountain of justice, exercising powers derived from the royal prerogative – the unique common law powers of the Crown. The administration of justice is thus, strictly speaking, a prerogative of the Crown, though this prerogative has been substantially whittled away. For example, in the case of *Prohibitions del Roy*[1] it was decided by Coke CJ that the King (James I) could not, in his own person, judge any case. In addition, the Crown no longer has a general power to create new courts by prerogative, and while it can, theoretically, create courts to administer only the common law,[2] there would be no money to finance them in the absence of statutory authority. The few immunities that the Crown had in civil proceedings have also been

---

[1] (1607) 12 Co Rep 63.
[2] *Re Lord Bishop of Natal* (1864) 3 Moo PCCNS 115. The Criminal Injuries Compensation Board was an example of a tribunal created by prerogative act: see p 300, *post*.

drastically curtailed (other than in respect of the Monarch as an individual). In short, the powers and privileges of the Crown are in modern times largely formal. Those that remain, though nominally vested in the Crown, are in reality those of its Ministers.[3]

1 DEFINITION AND EXAMPLES OF PREROGATIVE POWERS

Dicey defined the prerogative as follows:

> The prerogative is the name for the remaining portion of the Crown's original author-
> ity, and is therefore, as already pointed out, the name for the residue of discretion-
> ary power left at any moment in the hands of the Crown, whether such power be in
> fact exercised by the King himself or by his Ministers.[4]

Most of the remaining vestiges of prerogative control over the administration of justice are formal rather than substantive. The superior courts are termed the 'Queen's Courts' and the judges of those courts styled 'Her Majesty's Judges'. Criminal proceedings on indictment are pursued in the name of the Queen, and all criminal proceedings are conducted on behalf of the Crown. However, these so-called prerogatives are illusory in reality: there is no power in the Crown to intervene in civil proceedings, and any private individual may usually commence criminal proceedings.

The parts of the royal prerogative which have a substantive and continuing influ-ence on the legal system are therefore few. Among them may be included the power of the Attorney-General to stop a prosecution on indictment by entering a *nolle prosequi*, the power to pardon a convicted person, and the prerogative of mercy under which the Crown may, through the Home Secretary, suspend, commute, or remit any sentence.[5] By far the most significant example is the process of judicial review, which provides an important mechanism for judicial scrutiny and control over parts of the administration of justice. Although it is today governed by the rules and procedures set out in para-graph 54 of the Civil Procedure Rules,[6] it owes its origins to the historic supervisory role of the Crown.

2 THE SUPERVISORY ROLE OF THE COURTS AND THE HISTORICAL ORIGIN OF THE POWERS OF THE HIGH COURT

Historically, the superior common law courts controlled the conduct of inferior courts of record, in the name of the King and under the royal prerogative.[7] Indeed, the existence of the prerogative itself was a matter claimed to be within the province of the common law courts. In the *Case of Proclamations*[8] the court stated that 'the King hath no preroga-tive, but which the law of the land allows him'. The errors of these courts, whether errors

---

[3] In accordance with constitutional principle, they are exercisable by and on the advice of Ministers.

[4] *Introduction to the Study of the Law of the Constitution* (8th edn, 1915), p 421, cited with approval in *A-G v De Keyser's Royal Hotel Ltd* [1920] AC 508. See also: *Council of Civil Service Unions v Minister for the Civil Service (the GCHQ case)* [1985] AC 374, [1984] 3 All ER 935.

[5] See p 217, *post*.   [6] Supplemented by *Practice Direction (PD 54)*.

[7] See p 215, *post*.   [8] (1610) 12 Co Rep 74.

as to jurisdiction or errors of law within jurisdiction, were again controlled through the prerogative. This supervisory function was achieved through use of the prerogative writs, with the four main writs being as follows:[9]

- *prohibition*: inferior courts or administrative bodies could be prohibited from acting unlawfully or in excess of jurisdiction – now *prohibition orders*

- *mandamus*: an inferior court could be ordered to exercise jurisdiction where it was declining to do so, and an official could be ordered to perform a function which the law required of him – now *mandatory orders*

- *certiorari*: the record of an inferior court could be examined by the King's Bench and the proceedings quashed on the grounds of error of law, excess of jurisdiction, or abuse of process – now *quashing orders*

- *habeas corpus*: requiring a person holding another in custody to justify the confinement to the court.

The various forms of the writ of habeas corpus still exist and they are frequently used, often as a means of testing the validity of detention effected for the purpose of extradition. Procedural reforms have led to the old writs now becoming known, under the Civil Procedure Rules, as *prohibition orders, mandatory orders*, and *quashing orders*. Together with injunctions and declarations they form the armoury of the Administrative Court,[10] which performs the supervisory functions inherent in the term 'judicial review'.[11] An application for any of the orders named above, or for an injunction or declaration, must be made by way of application for judicial review. Damages *may* be awarded – perhaps where there is found to be a breach of contract or a tort committed by a public authority[12] – but this is quite rare, and damages are more appropriate remedies in private law actions.

JUDICIAL REVIEW

1 THE SCOPE OF JUDICIAL REVIEW

This has widened greatly in recent years. Despite occasional judicial confusions, it was always clear that judicial review lay against any inferior court or tribunal, and against any body exercising statutory functions affecting the rights of individuals. A striking recent example of this principle is provided by the case of *R v Lord Chancellor, ex parte Witham*.[13] The applicant in this case challenged the validity of regulations which

---

[9] A fifth, *Quo Warranto*, enabled a party to challenge the jurisdiction of a court or person in a public office purporting to exercise jurisdiction over him. It fell into disuse long before its abolition in 1938.

[10] Part of the Queen's Bench Division: see p 261, *post*.

[11] Under Part 54 CPR, and, formerly, under RSC Ord 53.

[12] See e.g.: *R v Northavon DC, ex parte Palmer* (1995) 27 HLR 576.

[13] [1998] QB 575, [1997] 2 All ER 779.

purported to repeal provisions contained in an earlier order. The earlier order had exempted litigants in receipt of certain state benefits from the obligation to pay court fees. The applicant was on income support and wished to bring proceedings for defamation, but without the exemption he would not have had the financial means to do so. The Divisional Court[14] upheld his challenge to the regulations, holding that access to the courts was a constitutional right at common law and could not be limited without the clear authority of an Act of Parliament. There was no such authority in this instance, and the regulations were therefore outside the power (ultra vires) of the Lord Chancellor and invalid. The scope of judicial review has also developed to allow challenges to actions affecting the legitimate expectations of individuals.[15]

2 JUDICIAL REVIEW OF THE ROYAL PREROGATIVE

Until comparatively recently, doubt remained about the reviewability of actions taken by or on behalf of the Crown under the royal prerogative. The traditional position was that though the court was entitled to rule as to the existence or extent of prerogative power, it was not entitled to review its exercise.[16] Thus an attempt in *Hanratty* v *Lord Butler*[17] to challenge the exercise of the prerogative power of mercy inevitably failed. After a period of judicial re-evaluation,[18] the matter was effectively put beyond doubt by the House of Lords in *Council of Civil Service Unions* v *Minister for the Civil Service*.[19] The litigation arose out of an instruction by the Minister, to the effect that the employment conditions of staff at Government Communications Headquarters (GCHQ) would be revised so as to prohibit membership of any trade union (other than an approved departmental staff association). This instruction was issued pursuant to power conferred upon the Minister by an Order in Council made under the royal prerogative.[20] The appellants applied for judicial review of the Minister's instruction. It was contended on behalf of the Minister that the instruction was not open to review by the courts because it came from a use of the prerogative. In the event, adjudication on this argument became unnecessary because the House of Lords held the instruction to have been justified on the ground of national security. This being so, any observations by their Lordships upon the contention raised were necessarily obiter. Nevertheless, the majority proceeded on the basis that the key question was not the source of the power, but whether it was of a nature suitable for judicial adjudication – i.e. whether it was justiciable.

[14] The court responsible for dealing with applications for judicial review prior to the creation of the Administrative Court.

[15] See Lord Diplock in the GCHQ case, *supra*, n 4. The legitimate expectation could concern the receipt of a benefit, or it could be an expectation of being dealt with according to a particular procedure.

[16] *Case of Saltpetre* (1606) 12 Co Rep 12; *Blackburn* v *A-G* [1971] 2 All ER 1380, [1971] 1 WLR 1037.

[17] (1971) 115 Sol Jo 386.

[18] See: *R* v *Criminal Injuries Compensation Board, ex parte Lain* [1967] 2 QB 864, [1967] 2 All ER 770 (though this case did not concern the direct exercise of prerogative powers); *Laker Airways Ltd* v *Department of Trade* [1977] 2 All ER 182, per Lord Denning.

[19] [1985] AC 374, [1984] 3 All ER 935.

[20] This is primary legislation, to be distinguished from the use of Orders in Council as delegated legislation: see p 36, *ante*.

Lord Roskill's speech identified certain prerogative powers as being of a type not suitable for judicial determination. These included the making of treaties, the defence of the realm, the prerogative of mercy, the grant of honours, the dissolution of Parliament, and the appointment of Ministers. However, the key issue is the nature of the matter to be determined by the court,[21] and Lord Roskill's list cannot be considered definitive. This is illustrated by the case of *R* v *Secretary of State for the Home Department, ex parte Bentley*, in which a Divisional Court held that the courts *did* have jurisdiction to review the exercise of the prerogative of mercy.[22] The Home Secretary, in considering whether or not to grant a posthumous free pardon to B, a person hanged in 1952 for murder, had failed to have regard to the fact that such a pardon might be used in a variety of circumstances and take different forms. It might constitute a full pardon, or, as might have been appropriate in this case, a conditional pardon substituting a lesser sentence for that in fact imposed. The Secretary of State thus had made an error of law by failing to have regard to all relevant considerations, and therefore his refusal was unlawful. In so deciding the court was applying the reasoning of the House of Lords in the GCHQ case. Even the exercise of the prerogative of mercy could be judicially reviewed if the grounds of challenge did not involve the court in deciding policy questions. Thus, whilst the policy to be adopted for the granting of pardons was not justiciable (suitable for review), the present decision was, because the Secretary of State had failed to recognize the extent of his powers.

The trend set by the GCHQ case has continued. Recent case law shows that it is now the nature of the function that matters, and which determines whether judicial review is available. In *R* v *Panel on Take-overs and Mergers, ex parte Datafin*[23] the court ruled that the absence of a statutory or prerogative power was not decisive: judicial review would lie in respect of any body performing a public law function.[24] In this case, the Take-Over Panel was acting 'governmentally' in engaging in regulatory functions which would otherwise be performed by a statutory body on behalf of the state.[25] However, the application of the *Datafin* principle is far from easy in practice. In *R* v *Disciplinary Committee of the Jockey Club, ex parte the Aga Khan*[26] the Court of Appeal decided that the Jockey Club was not a public body for the purposes of judicial review,

---

[21] *R (on the application of Abbasi)* v *Secretary of State for Foreign and Commonwealth Affairs* [2002] EWCA Civ 1598, *The Times*, 8 November 2002.

[22] [1994] QB 349, [1993] 4 All ER 442.   [23] [1987] QB 815, [1987] 1 All ER 564.

[24] Which is not simply a question of whether the body concerned is a public body: see *R* v *East Berkshire Area Health Authority, ex parte Walsh* [1985] QB 152, [1984] 3 All ER 425. For the relevant principles, see *McClaren* v *Home Office* [1990] ICR 824; *R* v *Lord Chancellor's Department, ex parte Nangle* [1992] 1 All ER 897. Significant overlaps exist with the cases dealing with the meaning of 'public authority' for the purposes of the Human Rights Act 1998, s 6. See p 164, *ante*, and *Poplar Housing and Regeneration Community Association Ltd* v *Donoghue* [2001] EWCA Civ 595, [2002] QB 48, [2001] 4 All ER 604; *Aston-Cantlow and Wilcote with Billesley Parochial Church Council* v *Wallbank* [2003] UKHL 37, [2004] 1 AC 546, [2003] 3 All ER 1213; *L* v *Birmingham City Council* [2007] UKHL 27, [2007] 3 WLR 112, [2007] 3 All ER 957.

[25] The effect of the *Datafin* decision appears weakened by subsequent cases; See *R* v *Chief Rabbi of the United Hebrew Congregations of Great Britain, ex parte Wachmann* [1992] 1 WLR 1036. In *R* v *Insurance Ombudsman Bureau, ex parte Aegon Life Assurance Ltd* [1994] COD 426, the court held that if the exercise of the power was consensual or contractual then it was not a public law matter, despite being woven into a system of governmental control.

[26] [1993] 2 All ER 853, [1993] 1 WLR 909. See also *R (on the application of Mullins)* v *Jockey Club Appeal Board* [2005] EWHC 2197 (Admin), *The Times*, 24 October 2005.

despite its important regulatory function in respect of horseracing. The key features in reaching this decision were the lack of integration into a scheme of public regulation, the fact that the Jockey Club was not a 'surrogate organ of government', the fact that its powers derived from consent, and the fact that effective private law remedies existed.

3   LIMITS TO JUDICIAL REVIEW

A statute may attempt to prevent judicial review by the use of a so-called 'ouster clause'. If the words of such a clause are clear then the courts will be bound by them. One example is section 29(3) of the Supreme Court Act 1981 (discussed below), which prevents judicial review of matters relating to trial on indictment. However, the courts generally seek, where possible, to construe ouster clauses restrictively. An example is *Anisminic* v *Foreign Compensation Commission*, which concerned a provision in the Foreign Compensation Act 1950.[27] The provision purported to prevent judicial review of any 'determination' of the Commission, but the House of Lords ruled that it could not prevent judicial review of a matter which the Commission had no power to deal with in the way it had. The Commission had, on the particular facts, made an error of law which deprived it of jurisdiction.[28] The courts are always reluctant to be deprived of their power to scrutinize the legality of a decision or action, but their ability to sidestep an ouster clause will depend on its extent and nature. A partial ouster clause is more likely to be upheld.[29] Such provisions must also be viewed in the light of the European Convention on Human Rights, as any interference with the liberty or rights of an individual, without some opportunity for review or appeal, may raise issues under Article 6.[30]

One key limitation on judicial review is the nature of the question to be decided by the court.[31] For example, many (though not all) of the prerogative powers involving the administration of justice may be beyond judicial review, because of their unsuitability for judicial determination. Simon Brown LJ observed in one case that, 'only the rarest cases will today be ruled strictly beyond the court's purview',[32] but it is clear that the role of the court is to examine matters of legality rather than matters which infringe upon the territory of the executive or Parliament. In other words, judicial review is not concerned with the merits of a decision.[33] A good illustration of this is *R* v *Secretary of State for the Home Department, ex parte Fire Brigades Union*,[34] where an attempt to replace the criminal injuries compensation scheme with an extra-statutory scheme under the royal prerogative was held to be unlawful. Provisions for the creation of the

---

[27] [1969] 2 AC 147, [1969] 1 All ER 208.

[28] For these purposes, the word 'jurisdiction' can be equated with 'power'.

[29] *R* v *Secretary of State for the Environment, ex parte Ostler* [1977] QB 122; *R* v *Cornwall County Council, ex parte Huntington* [1992] 3 All ER 566.

[30] See p 185, *ante*.

[31] See Lord Roskill in GCHQ case, *ante*. See also *R (on the application of the Campaign for Nuclear Disarmament)* v *Prime Minister* [2002] EWHC 2777 (Admin), [2002] All ER (D) 245; *Marchiori* v *Environment Agency* [2002] EWCA Civ 3, *Independent*, 31 January 2002.

[32] *R* v *Ministry of Defence, ex parte Smith* [1996] QB 517, [1996] 1 All ER 257.

[33] *R* v *Secretary of State for the Home Department, ex parte Brind* [1991] 1 AC 696, [1991] 1 All ER 720.

[34] [1995] 2 AC 513, [1995] 2 All ER 244.

statutory scheme were included in the Criminal Justice Act 1988 but were never actually implemented. It was held that even though the Minister had the right to decide whether, if at all, to bring the statutory scheme into force, he was not entitled to use prerogative powers to frustrate the will of Parliament. Had he wished to introduce an alternative scheme he should have sought to have the statutory provisions changed through the legislative process. In short, he was misusing his powers and acting unlawfully.

Whilst it is easy to draw this distinction in theory, the reality is rather different. When reviewing the exercise of a statutory discretion the court will seek to establish, or impute, the intention of Parliament. At first sight that might appear to be a simple question of construction and interpretation, but as already noted,[35] the principles governing statutory interpretation are sufficiently broad to give the court real choices. Thus in *Padfield v Minister of Agriculture, Fisheries and Food*[36] it was held that Parliament could not have intended a seemingly unlimited discretion under the Agricultural Marketing Act 1958 to be used in the way that it had. In addition, one effect of the Human Rights Act 1998 is that the courts are now required to have regard to questions of policy and proportionality.[37] The scope of judicial review has therefore widened, raising important questions about the proper role of the judiciary.[38]

Judicial review should be carefully contrasted with appeals: appeals are concerned with the merits of a decision or action, either on matters of fact or law, whereas judicial review is concerned with questions of legality. In the context of the administration of justice there is obviously an overlap. For example, the appropriate way of correcting an error of law made by a superior court is by an appeal on a point of law.[39] By contrast, errors of law made by inferior courts and tribunals may be corrected through judicial review if they are apparent on the face of the record.[40] Even then, however, if a matter of fact is in issue the better approach may be to bring an appeal by way of case stated on a point of law.[41]

4 JUDICIAL REVIEW OF MATTERS RELATING TO LAW ENFORCEMENT

The court's power to judicially review matters relating to policing and prosecution is limited, though it is clear that the power does exist. An example of this is judicial review of the prosecution process. In *R v Commissioner of Police for the Metropolis, ex parte Blackburn*[42] the applicant sought an order of mandamus[43] to compel the Commissioner to reverse a policy statement appearing to limit the enforcement of the gaming laws. The Court of Appeal held that mandamus might be appropriate if there was a complete

---

[35] See pp 47–57, *ante*.   [36] [1968] AC 997, [1968] 1 All ER 694.

[37] See p 166, *ante*. For proportionality as a ground of challenge, see p 225, *post*.

[38] See further, p 328, *post*.   [39] As to which, see chapters 18 and 24, *post*.

[40] *R v Crown Court at Knightsbridge, ex parte International Sporting Club (London) Ltd.* [1982] QB 304, [1981] 3 All ER 417; *R v Lord President of the Privy Council, ex parte Page* [1993] AC 682, [1993] 1 All ER 97.

[41] *R v Morpeth Ward JJ, ex parte Ward* (1992) 95 Cr App R 215. For appeals by way of case stated, see p 651, *post*.

[42] [1968] 2 QB 118, [1968] 1 All ER 763.   [43] See p 215, ante.

failure to perform a duty imposed by law, but it declined to make an order in the case in question because the policy had already been reversed. In a subsequent case involving the obscene publications laws,[44] the court stressed that the discretion was that of the Commissioner, and that the court could only intervene where there was effectively an abdication of function. By contrast, it will be much easier to justify judicial intervention where a decision affects the ability to exercise legally protected rights. *R v Coventry City Council, ex parte Phoenix Aviation* is an example of such a case.[45] Here, a failure of the police to stop demonstrators from obstructing the applicants' rights to export live animals was held to be reviewable. The application succeeded on the facts.

One area which has evolved in tune with modern approaches to judicial review concerns decisions to institute proceedings. The decisions of the Law Officers appear generally to be beyond challenge, and in *Gouriet v Union of Post Office Workers*[46] the power to enforce the criminal law through applications for injunctive relief was held to be for the Attorney-General alone. More recently, in *R v Solicitor-General, ex parte Taylor and Taylor*,[47] a Divisional Court held that the decision whether to bring proceedings for contempt of court was not justiciable. However, in the context of judicial review of the decision to prosecute, the courts are more willing to intervene. A distinction has, in the past, been drawn between decisions involving juveniles and those involving adults. In *R v Chief Constable of Kent, ex parte L*[48] the court stated that where a policy exists in respect of cautioning juveniles, a decision to commence or discontinue criminal proceedings will only be reviewable if it can be shown that it was made regardless of, or contrary to, that policy.[49] This approach was applied in *R v Commissioner of Police for the Metropolis, ex parte P*,[50] where it was held that the improper cautioning of a juvenile, in contravention of the Code for Crown Prosecutors, was judicially reviewable. The courts have also been prepared to consider reviewing decisions to prosecute adults. The challenge in *R v Inland Revenue Commissioners, ex parte Mead*[51] failed on the facts, because the prosecuting authority had considered the matter fairly and appropriately and had taken all relevant matters into account. More recently, the courts permitted a challenge to a decision not to prosecute police officers following the fatal shooting of an individual wrongly suspected of being a suicide bomber.[52] It had already been established that the Code for Crown Prosecutors was susceptible to judicial review,[53] but the court was satisfied that the DPP had acted within the Code and that his decision had not been unreasonable. The court concluded that there had been no breach of the right to life under Article 2 of the European Convention, and the challenge was therefore unsuccessful.

---

[44] *R v Commissioner of Police for the Metropolis, ex parte Blackburn (No 3)* [1973] QB 241, [1973] 1 All ER 324.

[45] [1995] 3 All ER 37.   [46] [1978] AC 435, [1977] 3 All ER 70.

[47] [1996] 1 FCR 206.   [48] [1993] 1 All ER 756.

[49] See *R v Havering Justices, ex parte Gould* (1993), unreported.

[50] (1996) 5 Admin LR 6, (1996) 160 JP 369.   [51] [1993] 1 All ER 772.

[52] *R (on the application of Da Silva) v Director of Public Prosecutions* [2006] EWHC 3204 (Admin), (2007) 157 NLJ 31.

[53] *R v Director of Public Prosecutions, ex parte Manning* [2001] QB 330, [2001] HRLR 3. For the Code, see p 568, *post*.

5 JUDICIAL REVIEW OF INFERIOR COURTS, TRIBUNALS AND OTHER BODIES

Moving to the actions of the courts themselves, judicial review is an effective mechanism for the control of the inferior courts, ensuring a means of challenge where failures to comply with jurisdictional requirements or principles of fair procedure have occurred. Judicial review also provides a remedy where no right of appeal against a decision exists.[54] A good example was seen in *R (on the application of DPP)* v *Camberwell Youth Court*.[55] This case concerned a series of decisions by youth courts to retain jurisdiction over the sentencing of young offenders instead of committing them to the Crown Court.[56] The DPP proposed to challenge some of these decisions by seeking voluntary bills of indictment,[57] in a procedure against which there can be no appeal.[58] However, on an application for judicial review the court deprecated this practice, holding that a more appropriate way for the DPP to proceed in such a case would be to seek judicial review of the youth court's decision.

Where a right of appeal does exist, permission to apply for judicial review may be declined unless the complaint raised is one of procedural impropriety, unfairness, or bias.[59] Similar principles apply in respect of the decisions of other 'judicial' bodies, such as public inquiries and tribunals. However, the regime introduced by the Tribunals, Courts and Enforcement Act 2007[60] will give powers of judicial review to the new Upper Tribunal.[61] This body will also have appellate powers from decisions of the First-Tier Tribunal, and in cases to which the new regime applies there will thus be a unified appeal and review structure. Judicial review is also available in respect of decisions of the Parole Board.[62]

6 JUDICIAL REVIEW OF SUPERIOR COURTS

Judicial review does not generally lie against superior courts, except in the case of the Crown Court when it is dealing with appeals from magistrates' courts. The reason for this exception is that when hearing such appeals the Crown Court is effectively exercising the jurisdiction of the lower court. Crown Court decisions are also subject to review in other cases, subject to the important limitation in section 29(3) of the Supreme Court Act 1981, which concerns judicial review 'in matters relating to trial on indictment'. The reason for this limitation is historical: the Crown Court took over the appellate

---

[54] Judicial review can only be prevented by the clearest of words: *Anisminic Ltd* v *Foreign Compensation Commission* [1969] 2 AC 147, [1969] 1 All ER 208.

[55] [2004] EWHC 1805, [2005] 1 WLR 810, [2004] 4 All ER 699.

[56] Under the Powers of Criminal Courts (Sentencing) Act 2000, s 91. See, further, p 700, *post*.

[57] See p 601, *post*.

[58] *R* v *Manchester Crown Court, ex parte Williams and Simpson* [1990] Crim LR 654, (1990) 154 JP 589.

[59] *R* v *Hereford Magistrates' Court, ex parte Rowlands* [1998] QB 110, [1997] 2 Cr App R 340; cf. *R* v *Peterborough Magistrates' Court, ex parte Dowler* [1997] QB 911, [1996] 2 Cr App R 561.

[60] See p 295, *post*.   [61] 2007 Act, s 15.

[62] *Smith* v *Parole Board* [2005] UKHL 1, [2005] 1 WLR 350, [2005] 1 All ER 755; *R (on the application of Girling)* v *Parole Board* [2005] EWHC 546 (Admin), [2006] 1 WLR 1917, [2006] 1 All ER 11.

jurisdiction of the old courts of Quarter Sessions, which were inferior courts and thus subject to judicial review. However, the application of section 29(3) has proved less than easy in practice. In *R v Crown Court at Sheffield, ex parte Brownlow* Lord Denning sought to interpret the subsection as preventing judicial review of any matter arising 'in the course of trial on indictment'.[63] This extremely narrow construction was not adopted by the majority of the court, which concluded that the provision prevented review where a decision arose out of, or was incidental to, the jurisdiction to try cases on indictment. On this view, a decision by the trial judge as to information concerning the jury panel was held to be caught by section 29(3) and thus was not judicially reviewable.

The approach taken by the majority in *Brownlow* has not been followed in subsequent cases. In *Smalley v Crown Court at Warwick*,[64] for example, the House of Lords considered a decision to forfeit a recognizance entered into by a witness to be judicially reviewable. Lord Bridge stressed the need to proceed on a case-by-case basis, and he suggested that the limitation in section 29(3) applied to 'any decision affecting the conduct of a trial on indictment'. However, he later stressed that this was merely a guideline and was not an attempt to re-write the words of the subsection.[65] Even so, the guideline is difficult to apply in practice. Decisions to allow counts on an indictment to effectively remain untried, applications to quash an indictment, decisions not to dismiss a charge under section 51 of the Crime and Disorder Act 1998,[66] and decisions to remand a witness in custody[67] are all examples of matters which have been held not to be reviewable.[68] Decisions relating to sentence also fall into this category,[69] even in cases where there is no alternative remedy for an obvious error.[70]

The problem has been extensively considered by the House of Lords in two further cases. The first was *R v Manchester Crown Court, ex parte DPP*,[71] where the court held that an order made upon an application to stay proceedings for abuse of process was an order affecting the conduct of the trial and was therefore covered by section 29(3). The second was *DPP v Crown Court at Manchester and Huckfield*,[72] where a decision to quash an indictment for lack of jurisdiction was held to be a matter 'relating to trial on indictment' and thus not judicially reviewable. A test suggested in this case is whether the decision concerns the issue between the Crown and the defendant as formulated by the indictment, including issues relating to costs. If it does, judicial review might

---

[63] [1980] QB 530, [1980] 2 All ER 444.   [64] [1985] AC 622, [1985] 1 All ER 769.

[65] *Sampson v Crown Court at Croydon* [1987] 1 All ER 609 at 611, [1987] 1 WLR 194 at 196, per Lord Bridge.

[66] *R (on the application of Snelgrove) v Woolwich Crown Court* [2004] EWHC 2172 (Admin), [2005] 1 Cr App R 18.

[67] Under the Criminal Procedure (Attendance of Witnesses) Act 1965, s 4(3): see *R (on the application of H) v Wood Green Crown Court* [2006] EWHC 2683 (Admin), [2007] 1 WLR 1670, [2007] 2 All ER 259.

[68] See *R v Central Criminal Court, ex parte Raymond* [1986] 2 All ER 379, [1986] 1 WLR 710; *R v Southwark Crown Court, ex parte Ward* [1996] Crim LR 123.

[69] *R (on the application of Lichniak) Secretary of State for the Home Department* [2001] EWHC 294 (Admin), [2002] QB 296, [2001] 4 All ER 934.

[70] *R (on the application of Crown Prosecution Service) v Guildford Crown Court* [2007] EWHC 1798 (Admin), [2007] 1 WLR 2886.

[71] [1994] AC 9; *sub nom DPP v Crown Court at Manchester and Ashton* [1993] 2 All ER 663.

[72] [1993] 4 All ER 928, [1993] 1 WLR 1524.

well lead to delay in the trial and the matter is probably caught by section 29(3). Their Lordships stressed that this test might not always be appropriate. In particular, they left open the question of whether judicial review would be available in respect of the procedures to be followed in serious fraud cases.[73] However, the test formulated by the court does have the effect of permitting judicial review where a court order affects a person other than the defendant,[74] or where the court is acting under a different jurisdiction.[75]

GROUNDS FOR JUDICIAL REVIEW

As already noted, judicial review is not a form of appeal.[76] The Administrative Court should not substitute its own decision for that of a court, tribunal, or other body simply because it appears to be 'wrong', and it is generally at pains to avoid doing so. However, section 141 of the Tribunals, Courts and Enforcement Act 2007 will make inroads into this principle in an important respect. Once in force, it will mean that where a decision is quashed on an application for judicial review, the Administrative Court will be able to either remit the matter to the original decision-making body, *or substitute its own decision for the decision in question.*[77] Although this new power will only apply in cases where the original decision was made by a court or tribunal, it is nevertheless controversial. It will, however, enable the courts to deal more efficiently with cases where it is clear that only one decision can lawfully be reached.

1 THE *WEDNESBURY* PRINCIPLES

The court will interfere with a decision where there was no power or jurisdiction to take it, or where there has been a failure to comply with the rules of natural justice and procedural fairness. Standards of procedural fairness vary from case to case, but they generally include the right of each party to state his case, a prohibition on a person being a judge in his own cause, the right to be informed of the reasons for a decision and, in some cases, the right to legal representation before a tribunal.[78] In respect of

---

[73] In *R v Central Criminal Court, ex parte Serious Fraud Office* [1993] 2 All ER 399, [1993] 1 WLR 949 such proceedings were held not to be caught by the restriction in s 29(3). See also: *R v Crown Court at Southwark* [1993] 1 WLR 764. For procedures relating to serious fraud cases see p 600, *post.*

[74] See *Smalley* v *Crown Court at Warwick* [1985] AC 622, [1985] 1 All ER 769 (forfeiture of recognizance of third party); *R v Crown Court at Maidstone, ex parte Gill* [1987] 1 All ER 129, [1986] 1 WLR 1405 (forfeiture of property of third party).

[75] See, e.g. *R v Crown Court at Inner London, ex parte Benjamin* (1986) 85 Cr App R 267 (binding over of acquitted person).

[76] For a good illustration of the difficulty of the distinction, see *Huang* v *Secretary of State for the Home Department* [2007] UKHL 11, [2007] 2 AC 167, [2007] 4 All ER 15.

[77] Amending s 31(5) of the Supreme Court Act 1981 (emphasis added).

[78] See *R v Board of Visitors of HM Prison, The Maze, ex parte Hone* [1988] AC 379, [1988] 1 All ER 321; *R v Secretary of State for the Home Department, ex parte Cheblak* [1991] 2 All ER 319, [1991] 1 WLR 890.

inferior courts and tribunals, the court can intervene by way of judicial review if there has been an error of law upon which the decision depends. In addition, in the case of an administrative person or body, the court can intervene when a discretion has been misused. This could have occurred because relevant matters have not been taken into account,[79] because the decision-maker has had regard to irrelevant matters, or because the discretion has been improperly fettered[80] or otherwise used contrary to the enabling power. These are often known as 'the *Wednesbury* principles'.[81] They are couched in legal terms, but they often bring the courts into a position where care has to be taken not to cross the boundary between legitimate executive judgment and proper judicial intervention. Finally, if a body makes a decision that no sensible authority could have reached, it may be held to be invalid on the grounds of '*Wednesbury* unreasonableness' – generally now referred to as 'irrationality'.[82]

These grounds of judicial review were described by Lord Diplock in the GCHQ case as: (1) 'illegality'; (2) 'irrationality' (i.e. *Wednesbury* unreasonableness); and (3) 'procedural impropriety'.[83] Whilst these terms are widely used and accepted, it is important to recognize that they amount to no more than convenient labels and do not create new grounds of challenge.[84] The meaning and scope of 'irrationality' has been the subject of some doubt, and it has been graphically described as applying to decisions which are so unreasonable as to 'jump off the page at you'.[85] It is a controversial ground that raises issues about the proper role of the judiciary, because in effect it requires the court to take a view as to the merits (or lack of merits) of the decision under review. Lord Lowry in *R v Secretary of State for the Home Department, ex parte Brind* summed up the issues well when he said:[86]

> [W]hat we are accustomed to call *Wednesbury* unreasonableness is a branch of the abuse, or misuse, of power: the court's duty is not to interfere with a discretion which Parliament has entrusted to a statutory body or an individual but to maintain a check on excesses in the exercise of discretion. That is why it is not enough if a judge feels able to say... 'I think that is unreasonable: that is not what I would have done.' It also explains the emphatic language which judges have used in order to drive home the message and the necessity... for the act to be 'so unreasonable that no reasonable [body] would have done it.' In that strong and necessary emphasis lies

---

[79] See, e.g. *R v Port Talbot BC, ex parte Jones* [1998] 2 All ER 207; *R v Barnet & Camden Rent Tribunal* [1972] 2 QB 342, [1972] 1 All ER 1185; *Roberts v Hopwood* [1925] AC 578.

[80] See, e.g.: *Wheeler v Leicester City Council* [1985] AC 1054, [1985] 2 All ER 1106; *R v Lewisham LBC, ex parte Shell UK Ltd* [1988] 1 All ER 938; *R v Coventry City Council, ex parte Phoenix Aviation* [1995] 3 All ER 37.

[81] *Associated Provincial Picture Houses Ltd v Wednesbury Corporation* [1948] 1 KB 223, [1947] 2 All ER 680. For examples see: *Padfield v Minister of Agriculture, Fisheries and Food* [1968] AC 997, [1968] 1 All ER 694; *Wheeler v Leicester City Council* [1985] AC 1054, [1985] 2 All ER 1106; *R v Sefton Metropolitan Borough Council, ex parte Help the Aged* [1997] 4 All ER 532.

[82] For discussion, see *R v Secretary of State for the Home Department, ex parte Brind* [1991] 1 AC 696, [1990] 1 All ER 469, CA; [1991] 1 AC 696, [1991] 1 All ER 720, HL.

[83] See p 223, *ante*.

[84] *R v Secretary of State for the Home Department, ex parte Brind* [1991] 1 AC 696 at 722, [1990] 1 All ER 469 at 480, per Lord Donaldson MR.

[85] *R v Lord Chancellor, ex parte Maxwell* [1996] 4 All ER 751.

[86] [1991] 1 AC 696 at 737, [1991] 1 All ER 720 at 765.

the danger. A less emotive but, subject to one qualification, reliable test is to ask: 'Could a decision-maker acting reasonably have reached that decision?' The qualification is that the supervising court must bear in mind that it is not sitting on appeal, but satisfying itself whether the decision-maker has acted within the bounds of his discretion...

These issues become even more acute in the context of decisions under the Human Rights Act 1998.

2 HUMAN RIGHTS ACT 1998

Lord Templeman in *Brind* and Simon Brown LJ in *R v Ministry of Defence, ex parte Smith*[87] both appeared to suggest that decisions would be more amenable to challenge on grounds of irrationality if they involved the fundamental rights of the individual. This was somewhat controversial and was not firmly settled by authority.[88] Lord Diplock had previously canvassed 'proportionality' as a possible fourth ground of challenge,[89] but this was rejected in *Brind*, with the House of Lords suggesting that 'proportionality' instead formed part of the process by which allegations of a breach of the *Wednesbury* principles might be judged.[90] In any event, proportionality is more likely to be relevant to the review of administrative actions or discretions than to the decisions of inferior courts.

There is now no doubt that the Human Rights Act 1998 widens the role and approach of the courts on judicial review, and that in human rights cases it does take the courts into questions of proportionality. *R (on the application of Daly) v Secretary of State for the Home Department* concerned the legality of a policy on the searching of prison cells, and the impact of that policy on prisoners' rights to private and confidential communication with their lawyers.[91] In allowing the challenge, the House of Lords confirmed that the doctrine of proportionality may require the court to consider the appropriateness of the balance struck by the decision-maker, and that it overlapped with the traditional grounds of review. The question was whether the measures designed to meet the legislative objective were proportionate to the needs of that objective, and whether they went no further than necessary.[92] This approach was confirmed as correct in *R (on the application of Pro-Life Alliance) v BBC*, where the balancing function under this wider role led to a limitation on a party political broadcast being upheld.[93] It was said that a court should review such decisions with a level of intensity appropriate to the circumstances of the case: the degree of latitude or deference to be given to the decision-maker will

---

[87] [1996] QB 517, [1996] 1 All ER 527. See, to similar effect: *R v Secretary of State for the Home Department, ex parte Bugdaycay* [1987] AC 514 at 531, per Lord Bridge.

[88] See e.g.: *R v Secretary of State for the Environment, ex parte National Association of Local Government Officers* (1993) 5 Admin LR 785, per Neill LJ; cf. *R v Secretary of State for Home Department, ex parte McQuillan* [1995] 4 All ER 400.

[89] *Council of Civil Service Unions v Minister for the Civil Service* [1985] AC 374, [1984] 3 All ER 935.

[90] [1991] 1 AC 696, [1991] 1 All ER 720.   [91] [2001] UKHL 26, [2001] 2 AC 532, [2001] 3 All ER 433.

[92] Citing with approval the formulation in *De Freitas v Permanent Secretary of Ministry of Agriculture, Fisheries, Lands and Housing* [1999] 1 AC 69, [1998] 3 WLR 675. See further, p 176, *ante*.

[93] [2003] UKHL 23, [2004] 1 AC 185, [2003] 2 All ER 977.

depend on the subject matter under review, and on whether it lies more readily within the actual or potential expertise of the court.[94]

PROCEDURE

1 EXCLUSIVITY

An application for one of the prerogative orders or for a declaration that a public law decision is unlawful must be made by way of application for judicial review. A pre-action Protocol[95] requires that (except in emergency cases) an applicant must send a letter before claim, seeking to establish whether litigation can be avoided and setting out details of the matter to be challenged. A defendant should normally respond within fourteen days, indicating which matters are contested and which conceded. It should also supply certain other information or copies of any relevant documents requested.

An application for judicial review is the normal (though not exclusive) means of challenge where questions of public law arise,[96] and historically, a failure to use the correct procedure could be fatal to the success of an application. Defects in the Order 53 RSC procedure which existed prior to 1977 often meant that proceeding by way of writ in the Queen's Bench Division was a more attractive option. Certain procedures such as discovery[97] and cross-examination of those who swore affidavits were not available on judicial review; nor was it open to a court dealing with such an application to make an award for damages or issue a declaration. These and other defects were remedied in 1977 when a revised Order 53 came into effect. As a result, in 1981 the House of Lords in *O'Reilly* v *Mackman* stated that the Order 53 procedure was to be the usual method of challenging public law decisions.[98] Lord Diplock stressed the advantages of the limited time for challenge under Order 53, and the safeguard created by the requirement for leave. To seek to avoid these safeguards by proceeding by writ would amount in most cases to an abuse of process, although Lord Diplock conceded that there would be exceptions to this general rule. Applications for judicial review are now governed by Part 54, CPR.

The distinction between public and private law matters has caused the courts considerable difficulty.[99] The position was somewhat clarified, if not entirely so, by the House of Lords in *Roy* v *Kensington and Chelsea and Westminster Family Practitioners*

---

[94] See the formulation and summary of Laws LJ in *International Transport Roth Gmbh* v *Secretary of State for the Home Department* [2002] EWCA Civ 158, [2003] QB 728, [2002] HRLR 31. See also, p 167, *ante*.

[95] As to which, see p 478, *post*. For the pre-action Protocol in judicial review, see www.hmcourts-service. gov.uk/cms/4319.htm

[96] Matters relating to the administration of justice are likely to be public law matters.

[97] See p 507, *post*, for the modern concept of disclosure.

[98] [1983] 2 AC 237, [1982] 3 All ER 1124; see also *Cocks* v *Thanet District Council* [1983] 2 AC 286, [1982] 3 All ER 1135.

[99] See the *cri de coeur* of Henry J in *Doyle* v *Northumbria Probation Committee* [1991] 4 All ER 294, [1991] 1 WLR 1340. For discussion of the issues, see: Lord Woolf, 'Public Law – Private Law: Why the Divide? A Personal View' [1986] PL 220.

Committee.[100] In that case a doctor commenced an action by writ in which he sought to obtain payments that he alleged were due to him, and which he claimed were being withheld by the defendant. The doctor's terms and conditions of employment were governed by regulations made pursuant to statute, and the defendant sought to have his action struck out on the basis that it raised public law matters which should be decided on an application for judicial review. The challenge initially succeeded but was eventually rejected by both the Court of Appeal and the House of Lords. The plaintiff was seeking to recover money allegedly owed to him, and this raised private law rights which could be enforced by private law action. In his speech, Lord Lowry identified two approaches. The 'narrow' approach was the one taken by the court in *O'Reilly v Mackman*: that the Order 53 procedure ought generally to be followed if there was a public law issue. The 'broad' approach was the one that he favoured: that the Order 53 procedure was only obligatory if no private law issue was involved. Ultimately, however, it was held that the case would fall within the exception to the general rule under either approach, and therefore the point was not conclusively decided.

2 A NEW APPROACH

The broad approach suggested in *Roy* is consistent with a series of cases where a claim for money was held to be a private law matter, even if the defence involved an assertion that the claim was being made pursuant to an ultra vires action.[101] The mere fact that one party to an action is a public body does not necessarily turn the issue into a public law matter.[102] The position was put on a much more sensible and pragmatic footing in 2000, with the decision of the Court of Appeal in *Clark v University of Lincolnshire and Humberside*.[103] A student sought to challenge a university's decision by bringing an action for breach of contract, but when this was held to be an inappropriate forum for contesting what were essentially matters of academic judgment, she was allowed to amend her pleadings. The court rejected the defendant's assertion that this amounted to an abuse of process, even though it might have been more appropriate for the claimant to have sought judicial review in the first place:[104]

> Where a student has...a claim in contract, the court will not strike out a claim which could more properly be made under [Part 54] solely on the basis of the procedure that has been adopted. It may, however, do so if it comes to the conclusion that in all the circumstances, including the delay in initiating the proceedings, there has been an abuse of the process of the court under the CPR.

Whatever the technical and analytical difficulties, the courts are looking to the practicalities. In *Trustees of the Dennis Rye Pensions Fund v Sheffield City Council* it was

---

[100] [1992] 1 AC 624, [1992] 1 All ER 705.
[101] See in particular: *Wandsworth London Borough Council v Winder* [1985] AC 461, [1984] 3 All ER 976; *Davy v Spelthorne Borough Council* [1984] AC 262, [1983] 3 All ER 278.
[102] *R v East Berkshire AHA, ex parte Walsh* [1985] QB 152, [1984] 3 All ER 425.
[103] [2000] 3 All ER 752, [2000] 1 WLR 1988.
[104] [2000] 3 All ER 752 at 761, [2000] 1 WLR 1988 at 1998, per Lord Woolf MR.

said that a court should look at the practical consequences and not merely at the technical distinctions between public and private law.[105] In the case before the court it was obvious that the issues, which related to a claim for payment for work done, could be dealt with more conveniently in a private law action than by an application for judicial review. More recently, in *R v Bedfordshire CC, ex parte Henlow Grange Health Farm Ltd* the court dismissed a judicial review application in respect of a planning decision which had been 'called in' (i.e. taken over) by the Secretary of State.[106] The applicant was effectively seeking an advisory declaration to influence the Secretary of State's decision, and that was an abuse of the Part 54 jurisdiction. The court also took into account the fact that the planning legislation provided a comprehensive scheme for dealing with the issues raised by the claimant. Given the trend towards encouraging settlement rather than litigation,[107] it is unsurprising that the courts should be reluctant to allow judicial review in respect of matters which could be resolved without the intervention of the courts.[108]

The authorities also show that it is open to a party to proceedings to raise the invalidity of a public law action as a defence to criminal proceedings. The extent to which this is permissible was, until recently, unclear. The right to use the invalidity of a by-law as a defence to criminal proceedings was accepted in the nineteenth century,[109] and confirmed in *R v Reading Crown Court, ex parte Hutchinson*.[110] More recently, in *Boddington v British Transport Police* the House of Lords held that a defendant in criminal proceedings is entitled to challenge the validity of subordinate legislation or an administrative decision made pursuant to it.[111] The only exception to this is where there is a clear Parliamentary intention to the contrary. The ability to challenge as part of one's defence (i.e. collateral challenge) does not depend on the grounds of challenge, nor on whether those grounds are of a substantive or procedural nature. To the extent that an earlier authority appeared to suggest the contrary, that authority was overruled.[112]

3 PROCEDURE

The procedure under Part 54 is supplemented by the requirements of a Practice Direction (PD 54). Together, they require that the applicant must apply promptly to the Administrative Court, and in any event within three months from the date when the grounds of the application first arise, unless the court considers that there is good reason for extending this period. The claimant requires permission (formerly known as leave) to apply, and this matter is normally dealt with without a hearing, though the

---

[105] [1997] 4 All ER 747. See also *R v Chief Constable of Warwickshire, ex parte Fitzpatrick* [1998] 1 All ER 65 (complainant should not challenge a search warrant by judicial review, which was unsuitable for a fact-finding exercise, but should instead rely on his private rights).
[106] [2001] EWHC Admin 179, [2001] JPL 1435 (Note).   [107] See p 466, *post*.
[108] *Frank Cowl and others v Plymouth CC* [2001] EWCA Civ 1935, [2002] 1 WLR 803.
[109] See, e.g. *Kruse v Johnson* [1898] 2 QB 91, [1895–1899] All ER Rep 105.
[110] [1988] QB 384, [1988] 1 All ER 333.
[111] [1999] 2 AC 143, [1998] 2 All ER 203. See also *R v Wicks* [1998] AC 92, [1997] 2 All ER 801.
[112] *Bugg v DPP* [1993] QB 473, [1993] 2 All ER 815.

judge can require a hearing if he wishes. If the application for permission is refused, the claimant may renew it by applying in criminal cases to the Administrative Court or, in any other case, to a single judge sitting in open court (or, if the court so directs, to the Administrative Court).

Applications for interlocutory orders, such as disclosure, interrogatories, and cross-examination of witnesses, may be made to a judge or master. However, it should be borne in mind that:

> [I]n the ordinary way judicial review is designed to deal with matters which can be resolved without resorting to these procedures.[113]

On the hearing of the application for judicial review the court will hear any party served with the motion or summons and any other person who appears to be a proper person to be heard. An applicant must have sufficient interest (formerly known as locus standi) in the matter sought to be reviewed. This is designed to prevent the court from being troubled by 'mere busybodies',[114] though standing is not confined to persons who have a legal or financial interest.[115] Whether standing exists ultimately turns on the nature of the statutory provision in question, and on the nature of the person or organization claiming a sufficient interest. In *R v HM Inspectorate of Pollution and Ministry of Agriculture Fisheries and Food, ex parte Greenpeace (No 2)*, the environmental organization Greenpeace was held to have standing to challenge a decision to vary an authorization to discharge radioactive waste. It was considered relevant that Greenpeace was a large organization with internationally recognized expertise in environmental matters.[116]

The court in a judicial review action has the power to make prohibitory, mandatory and quashing orders, and to grant injunctions and declarations. It can also award damages if an applicant could have recovered damages by bringing a civil action rather than an application for judicial review. In addition, the court has power to grant interim relief, such as interlocutory injunctions. Where the relief sought is a declaration, an injunction, or damages, the court may in certain circumstances order the proceedings to continue as if they had been commenced by writ. As already observed, the essential feature of judicial review is that it applies to public law rather than private law matters. Thus it is not appropriate where the applicant's complaint is of a purely private nature, such as, for example, where he has been wrongfully dismissed by his employer, even where that employer is a public authority. Conversely, if the applicant wishes to challenge a public law decision he must proceed by way of judicial review, and he cannot avoid the procedural requirements of Part 54 (notably the need for permission and the prescribed time-limit) by bringing an ordinary civil action.

---

[113] *R v Derbyshire County Council, ex parte Noble* [1990] 1 CR 808, [1990] IRLR 332, per Woolf LJ.

[114] See *R v Greater London Council, ex parte Blackburn* [1976] 3 All ER 184, [1976] 1 WLR 550; *R v Monopolies and Mergers Commission, ex parte Argyll Group* [1986] 2 All ER 257, [1986] 1 WLR 763.

[115] *Inland Revenue Commissioners v National Federation of Self Employed and Small Businesses* [1982] AC 617; *R v Secretary of State for the Environment, ex parte Rose Theatre Trust* [1990] 1 QB 5, [1990] 1 All ER 754.

[116] [1994] 4 All ER 329.

FURTHER READING

CRAIG, *Administrative Law* (Sweet & Maxwell: 5th edn, 2003)

FORDHAM, 'Judicial Review: The New Rules' [2001] PL 4

LESTER, 'Is Judicial Review Undemocratic?' [2007] PL 280

SMITH, LE SUEUR and JOWELL, DE SMITH, WOOLF and *Jowell's Judicial Review of*

Administrative Action (Sweet & Maxwell: 6th edn, 2007)

WADE and FORSYTH, *Administrative Law* (Oxford University Press: 9th edn, 2004)

WOOLF, 'Public Law – Private Law: Why the Divide? A Personal View' [1986] 2 PL 220

8

THE COURTS

INTRODUCTION

This chapter explores the role played by each of the major courts in the English legal system, and it will also seek to give an overview of the hierarchy within which they operate. In addition to affecting the general distribution of work within the system and determining the destination of appeals, this hierarchy also plays a crucial role in the doctrine of precedent. The chapter will begin with an outline of some of the courts which have been important historically, before going on to examine the work of their modern counterparts in some depth. In particular, it will address the following:

- The distinctions to be made between different types of court: civil or criminal, first instance or appellate, court or tribunal, etc.

- The administration of the courts: the roles played by the Ministry of Justice, Her Majesty's Courts Service and other bodies.

- The importance of open justice, and the implications of this principle for the conduct of proceedings in court. The law governing contempt of court will also be considered.

- The constitution and jurisdiction of each of the major courts and the distribution of work between them.

- The impact of recent reforms, including the redistribution of work within the civil justice system and plans for a new Supreme Court.

- The unique roles of coroners' courts and the Judicial Committee of the Privy Council.

- The work of courts-martial and ecclesiastical courts, as examples of courts with special jurisdiction.

HISTORICAL CONTEXT

Any examination of the modern legal system would be incomplete without an awareness of its historical background. As noted in chapter 1 the monarch had a pivotal role in the development of the early courts, and the exercise of regal power through the King's Council or Curia Regis is therefore a useful starting point for this analysis.

1 THE CURIA REGIS

In medieval times the King's Council exercised legislative, executive, and judicial functions, and it is therefore the predecessor of both Parliament and the courts. Over a period of time the courts began to assume an independent jurisdiction, and the three main common law courts – the Court of Exchequer, the Court of Common Pleas, and the Court of King's Bench – split off from the Council. Their judges exercised jurisdiction over civil disputes and major criminal cases in London and on assize, and the King's justices assumed jurisdiction over other criminal offences. The residual jurisdiction of the King persisted, however, and it was not until the seventeenth century that the Council finally discontinued its judicial function.

2 THE COURT OF EXCHEQUER

This was the first of the three main common law courts to split off from the Curia Regis. Originally its jurisdiction was confined to disputes between subjects and the Crown concerning revenue, but it later acquired jurisdiction over disputes between subjects, such as writs of debt and covenant.[1] It also appears to have exercised an equity jurisdiction in its early days. When the Court of Exchequer was finally abolished in 1875, its common law jurisdiction was transferred to the newly formed High Court. Its equity jurisdiction had already been transferred by statute to the Chancery in 1841.[2]

3 THE COURT OF COMMON PLEAS

While the King was determining civil disputes in Council, suitors were obliged to follow the court wherever it travelled. Because of the inconvenience this caused it became the practice for some judges to remain permanently in Westminster Hall to try Common Pleas.[3] These judges were senior advocates who were highly paid and had an exclusive right of audience in the court. The court had jurisdiction over disputes between subjects where the King's interest was not involved, and it therefore tried all real actions, the personal actions of debt, covenant, and *detinue*, and trespass actions where the title to land was involved. When the court was abolished in 1875, its jurisdiction was transferred to the High Court.

4 THE COURT OF KING'S BENCH

This was the last of the three central courts to break away from the Council, and through its close association with the King it acquired jurisdiction to issue the prerogative writs of

---

[1] These were the earliest personal actions recognized by the common law. Debt was an action for a fixed sum of money in return for consideration already given. Covenant lay for breach of any obligation entered into under seal. For more detailed discussion, see the 6th edition of this work, pp 22–29.

[2] 5 Vict, c 5.

[3] As opposed to Pleas of the Crown, which were based upon breaches of the King's peace and usually involved a fine or forfeiture.

mandamus, prohibition, and *certiorari*,[4] and thus to restrain abuses of power by inferior courts and public officials. It also had the power to issue the writ of *habeas corpus*, which was later of great constitutional importance in curbing the use of prerogative powers by the King. The court was presided over by the Chief Justice of England, and it had both original and appellate functions. The court's original jurisdiction was exercised principally in civil matters, covering most actions in tort and contract. Its appellate jurisdiction covered both civil and criminal cases, though the right of appeal was based on an error in procedure in the court below.[5]

5 THE COURTS OF EXCHEQUER CHAMBER

At different times there have been no less than four courts bearing the title 'Exchequer Chamber':

(1) The oldest was established in 1357 and its jurisdiction was solely as a court of error from the Exchequer.

(2) Even before 1357 there was a practice of judges reserving difficult points of law for consideration by a bench of judges. The meetings were relatively informal and initially the opinions delivered were purely persuasive, but by the fifteenth century its judgments were regarded as binding.[6] The court was known as the Court of Exchequer Chamber because that was where it usually sat, and many of the leading common law cases were decided in this court. It continued to determine civil cases until the seventeenth century, and decided criminal matters until the nineteenth century.

(3) A third Court of Exchequer Chamber was created by statute in 1585[7] as a court of error from the King's Bench. Thus, in addition to the House of Lords there were at this time three courts of error, and this complex hierarchy prevailed until the creation of the last Court of Exchequer Chamber in 1830.

(4) The court created in 1830[8] was the court of error from all three common law courts, and any appeal from this court lay to the House of Lords. It existed until 1875 when its jurisdiction was transferred to the Court of Appeal.

6 ASSIZES

Even in the Middle Ages it was impossible to hold all criminal trials in London, and Norman and Plantagenet monarchs adopted the system of sending out royal justices to hold 'assizes' (or sittings) of the royal courts. The jurisdiction of these courts was at first purely criminal but was later extended to civil matters. Assize judges held office under

---

[4] Now called mandatory orders, prohibiting orders, and quashing orders. This 'judicial review' jurisdiction is still exercised by the Queen's Bench Division of the High Court: see chapter 7.

[5] 31 Edw 3, St 1, c 12.

[6] In 1483 the Chief Justice of the Common Pleas followed a decision of the Exchequer Chamber even though he thought it wrong (Y1 Ric 3, Michs, no 2).

[7] 31 Eliz 1, c 1.   [8] 11 Geo 4 & 1 Will 4, c 70.

royal commission, and while most were judges of the common law courts they could also be serjeants-at-law or even prominent laymen. The system was organized on the basis of circuits, with each circuit consisting of a group of counties visited three or four times a year. The *Statute of Nisi Prius* 1285 extended the system to certain civil actions triable by jury, and the jurisdiction was further extended in the fourteenth and fifteenth centuries to cover all types of civil action.[9]

7   JUSTICES OF THE PEACE

Justices of the peace[10] originate from a royal proclamation of 1195, which created the knights of the peace to assist the sheriff in enforcing the law. Initially the office was administrative in nature, but it assumed a judicial function in the fourteenth century because of the declining criminal jurisdiction of the local courts and the inability of the assizes to deal with the growing number of offenders. By 1330, the holders of the office had become so powerful that they were given statutory power to punish the sheriff if he abused his powers of granting bail to prisoners.

Statutes of Labourers were passed from 1351 in an attempt to regulate wages, and the enforcement of these statutes was placed in the hands of 'justices of labourers'. In 1361 these justices were included in the same commissions as the keepers of the peace, and it is from this date that the office of 'justice of the peace' in its modern sense originates. The criminal jurisdiction of the new justices was at first exercised solely in the quarter sessions which they were compelled by statute[11] to hold, but in 1496[12] they were given jurisdiction to try offences out of sessions. This summary jurisdiction was exercised without a jury by what is now termed a 'magistrates' court'.[13] In 1590 justices in quarter sessions were given jurisdiction over all criminal offences, including capital felonies, and it was not until the Quarter Sessions Act 1842 that their jurisdiction was limited to exclude treason, murder, and felonies punishable with life imprisonment.

The administrative functions of justices of the peace declined as their criminal juris-diction grew, and most of these functions are now in the hands of local authorities. However, certain important functions remain; notably the power to issue warrants of arrest and summonses. The task of conducting preliminary investigations into indict-able offences was conferred on justices of the peace in 1554.[14]

8   THE STAR CHAMBER

The Star Chamber derived its jurisdiction from the King in the same way as the common law courts, but because it retained its links with the King in Council it administered the royal prerogative rather than the common law. It seems to have originated from sittings of the Council in a chamber in Westminster known as the Star Chamber, possibly on

---

[9] The assize system survived until 1 January 1972, when the Courts Act 1971 came into operation.

[10] The term dates from about 1327: Plucknett, *A Concise History of the Common Law* (5th edn, 1956), p 168.

[11] 36 Edw 3, st 1, c 12.   [12] 11 Hen 7, c 3.

[13] See p 268, *post*.   [14] 1 & 2 P & M, c 13 and 2 & 3 P & M, c 10.

account of its interior decor. It consisted of members of the Council, the Chancellor, Treasurer and Privy Seal and common law judges, and it had jurisdiction over a range of civil matters. It is, however, the Star Chamber's criminal jurisdiction which is of the greatest interest, since it recognized and tried many new offences, including riot, unlawful assembly, conspiracy, criminal libel, perjury, and forgery.

Procedure differed radically from that in the common law courts. Criminal proceedings were commenced by the Attorney-General and the defendant was examined in an inquisitorial procedure, sometimes under torture. Evidence was frequently given by affidavit, thus denying the accused any opportunity to cross-examine witnesses, and guilt or innocence was determined by members of the court rather than by a jury. Despite this, even Coke, that most noted champion of the common law, described the court as 'the most honourable Court (our Parliament excepted) that is in the Christian world.'[15] Eventually the court came to be seen as a symbol of prerogative power, and one of the first legislative acts of the Long Parliament was the abolition of the Star Chamber in 1641.

9 COURT OF CHANCERY

The development of principles of equity to supplement the common law has already been noted.[16] The Court of Chancery was the principal court of equity, and its most important jurisdiction was the recognition and enforcement of equitable principles. The office of Chancellor and the principles of equity are, historically, inexorably linked, and the nature and effectiveness of the court depended upon the characteristics of the particular Chancellor. The court was brought into disrepute in the seventeenth century by the sale of offices in the court,[17] and the scale of the corruption was so great that on the 'bursting' of the South Sea Bubble in 1725 (an eighteenth-century speculative venture) a deficiency of £100,000 in court funds was discovered.

A further defect in the court was its organization. It had an excess of court officials who attempted to extend their duties so as to increase their revenue, and this naturally made litigation extremely slow and expensive. The excess of court officers was equalled only by the paucity of judges. At first the Chancellor himself was the only judge, but by the sixteenth century he was accustomed to delegate his judicial functions to the Masters in Chancery. This did little to speed up the conduct of litigation, however, since the parties had a right to apply to the Chancellor for a rehearing. During Lord Eldon's time in office (1807–1827) there are records of judgments being reserved for months and even years, and in 1813 he approved the appointment of a Vice-Chancellor. The Court of Chancery was eventually abolished by the Judicature Acts 1873–1875, and most of its jurisdiction was transferred to the Chancery Division of the High Court.

In addition to its equitable jurisdiction, the court acquired jurisdiction over other miscellaneous matters. For example, the Crown had protective custody of all infants

---

[15] 4 Inst, p 65.   [16] See p 6, *ante.*
[17] The office of Master of the Rolls was apparently worth £6,000 in the eighteenth century. See *ex parte the Six Clerks* (1798) 3 Ves 589.

within the realm, and this jurisdiction, comprising such matters as the power to appoint guardians, was assigned to the Court of Chancery.[18] A similar concept existed in relation to persons of unsound mind, and this jurisdiction continues to be exercised by the Court of Protection.[19]

THE MODERN SYSTEM OF COURTS: AN OVERVIEW

The impact of the Judicature Acts 1873–1875 in sweeping away many of the old courts has already been noted, and the modern system is very different from that which preceded it. The superior courts in England and Wales continue to derive their jurisdiction from the Crown, but they are now heavily regulated by statute and some courts and tribunals owe their origins entirely to statutory intervention.

1 CLASSIFICATION OF THE COURTS

Courts can be classified in various ways. It is, for example, possible to classify them on the basis of the types of cases that they hear, or according to whether their jurisdiction is original or appellate. These divisions are not entirely satisfactory, however, since courts often do not fall neatly into one particular category and the divisions have little formal significance. Nevertheless, they do have some value for the purposes of exposition, and the principal divisions are therefore set out below.

(a) Civil and criminal courts

The most obvious division is between civil and criminal courts, but this classification is problematic because most English courts – including the House of Lords, Court of Appeal, High Court, Crown Court, and magistrates' courts – exercise jurisdiction in both civil and criminal matters.

(b) Courts of original jurisdiction and appellate courts

An alternative method of classification is to distinguish between appellate courts and courts of original jurisdiction. Again, however, it is not possible to place all courts into one category or the other. While courts such as the Court of Appeal exercise a purely appellate jurisdiction, and those such as magistrates' courts have no appellate role, many other courts have both original and appellate functions. Indeed, the Queens Bench Divisional Court is neither a court of first instance nor a court of appeal; it is primarily a court of review. In addition, although the Court of Justice of the European

---

[18] It is now exercised by the Family Division of the High Court: see p 263, *post*.
[19] See p 275, *post*.

Communities (the European Court of Justice) is not technically a court of appeal, its decisions are binding on all domestic courts.

(c) Courts and tribunals

Strictly speaking, the term 'tribunal' is an umbrella term capable of encompassing not only the bodies that generally use this name, but also those that are usually labelled 'courts'. It also has a narrower meaning, however, and when used in this sense it refers only to those tribunals which cannot be described as courts.

Whether a particular tribunal can properly be called a 'court' is sometimes a matter of dispute. The description becomes important in the context of contempt of court,[20] since as the name suggests, this offence can only be committed in relation to a 'court'. In *A-G v BBC*[21] the House of Lords held that a local valuation court[22] was not a 'court' for the purposes of the contempt jurisdiction, since its functions were essentially administrative and it was not established to exercise the judicial power of the state. By contrast, employment tribunals *have* been held to constitute 'courts' for these purposes.[23]

Whether a particular tribunal can be called 'a court' or not appears to be of no other practical significance: it is not central to the question of whether it is subject to the High Court's supervisory jurisdiction, and it does not determine whether it is under a duty to act judicially.

(d) Courts of record

Historically, the distinction between courts of record and other courts depended upon whether the court maintained records of its proceedings and preserved them in the Public Record Office. The central characteristic of a court of record now is that it has the power to punish for contempt. However, it should be noted that magistrates' courts, which are not courts of record, have a statutory power to punish contempts committed in the face of the court.[24] In addition, the High Court has a common law jurisdiction to punish contempts committed before courts which are not courts of record.[25]

(e) Superior and inferior courts

Traditionally, the most significant division has been between superior and inferior courts.[26] The jurisdiction of superior courts is limited neither by geography nor by the value of the cases that they can hear. The House of Lords, Court of Appeal, High Court,

---

[20] See p 246, *post*.   [21] [1981] AC 303, [1980] 3 All ER 161.

[22] These courts were replaced by valuation tribunals: Local Government Finance Act 1992.

[23] *Peach Grey & Co v Sommers* [1995] 2 All ER 513, [1995] ICR 549; applied in *Ewing v Security Services* [2003] EWCA Civ 581.

[24] Contempt of Court Act 1981, s 12: see p 249, *post*.   [25] *R v Davies* [1906] 1 KB 32.

[26] Whether a court is an inferior or a superior court can usually be ascertained by reference to its historical origins or, where applicable, to the terms of the statute creating it. If this does not settle the matter it is necessary to look at the nature and powers of the court to see whether they are analogous to those of a superior or an inferior court. See, e.g., *R v Cripps, ex parte Muldoon* [1984] QB 68, [1983] 3 All ER 72, in which the Queen's Bench Divisional Court held an election court (under the Representation of the People Act) to be an inferior court.

Crown Court, Privy Council, and Employment Appeal Tribunal are all superior courts. The most important of the inferior courts are the county courts and magistrates' courts. One of the distinctive features of inferior courts is that they are amenable to the supervisory jurisdiction of the High Court.[27] However, the Crown Court is also subject to this jurisdiction in the exercise of its appellate functions, even though it is a superior court.[28] The distinction is also important in relation to contempt of court, as the superior courts are able to inflict more stringent penalties than those available to the inferior courts.[29]

2 THE ORGANIZATION AND ADMINISTRATION OF THE COURTS

Leaving aside the work of tribunals,[30] the principal courts exercising jurisdiction in England and Wales are the Court of Appeal, the High Court, the Crown Court, the House of Lords, county courts, and magistrates' courts. The first three courts in this list collectively comprise the Supreme Court of England and Wales.[31] The constitution and jurisdiction of each of these courts is considered in detail later in this chapter, but their roles can be summarized as follows:

(1) First instance jurisdiction over civil matters is primarily shared between the county courts and the High Court. The Crown Court and magistrates' courts also have a limited civil jurisdiction.

(2) Jurisdiction over criminal cases at first instance is divided between magistrates' courts and the Crown Court.

(3) The Crown Court and High Court exercise certain appellate functions alongside their original jurisdiction.

(4) The Court of Appeal hears appeals from the decisions of courts lower down in the hierarchy, though not from the decisions of magistrates' courts.

(5) Except in matters of European law,[32] the House of Lords is the final court of appeal for England and Wales, Scotland, and Northern Ireland. However, in 2003 the government announced plans to transfer the judicial functions of the House of Lords to a new Supreme Court: the Constitutional Reform Act 2005 gives effect to these changes.[33]

As outlined in chapter 1, the English legal system has evolved in a piecemeal way over many centuries, and although the new Ministry of Justice has assumed responsibility

---

[27] See chapter 7.

[28] The Crown Court is only open to the supervisory jurisdiction of the Divisional Court where jurisdiction is expressly granted by the Supreme Court Act 1981, ss 28 and 29(1). Matters relating to 'trial on indictment' are not within that jurisdiction.

[29] See p 246, *post*.   [30] See chapter 9.

[31] They will be renamed 'the Senior Courts of England and Wales' when the Judicial Committee of the House of Lords is replaced by a new Supreme Court: see p 253, *post*.

[32] The jurisdiction and functions of the European Court of Justice and European Court of Human Rights are discussed in chapters 4 and 5 respectively. Note that the ECJ is not technically a court of appeal.

[33] See p 253, *post*.

for most of its components, its organizational structure remains complex.[34] The rules governing the procedure and jurisdiction of the courts are contained in a multitude of statutes, practice directions, court rules, and other statutory instruments, all of which seem to be subject to constant revision and amendment. The distribution of business between the courts has been revised many times, and the legal system has been the focus of numerous reports and recommendations. In 1996 for example, the Woolf Report on *Access to Justice* led to a major restructuring of the civil justice system less than a decade after fundamental changes had been brought about by the Courts and Legal Services Act 1990.[35] Lord Justice Auld's review of the criminal justice system produced similarly far-reaching recommendations,[36] and although the government rejected his proposal to replace the Crown Court and magistrates' courts with a unified criminal court, a number of his other recommendations were given effect by the Courts Act 2003.

In 1998 the Civil Justice Council was established, with a remit of keeping the civil justice system under review and considering new ways of making it accessible, fair and efficient.[37] A Family Justice Council and a Criminal Justice Council have since been created, and following the Auld Report[38] a Criminal Justice Board with responsibility for direction and strategy at a national level was also set up. The criminal justice agencies are now supported by the Office for Criminal Justice Reform (OCJR), which is a cross-departmental team reporting to the Ministry of Justice, the Home Office and the Office of the Attorney-General.

The absence of a truly national framework applicable to all courts has been criticized, and the focus of many of the recent reforms has been on achieving greater harmonization and efficiency. The Auld Report had much to say on this subject, describing the criminal justice system as 'structurally inefficient, ineffective and wasteful'.[39] Prior to the Woolf reforms the county courts and the High Court were subject to different procedural rules, despite the fact that their jurisdiction is largely concurrent. The Civil Procedure Act 1997 changed this by establishing a Civil Procedure Rule Committee with the authority to make Rules for the High Court, the county courts, and the Civil Division of the Court of Appeal.[40] The Courts Act 2003 has introduced a similar approach for the criminal justice system: instead of being subject to three different sets of rules, all criminal cases are now governed by new Criminal Procedure Rules regardless of which court they are heard in.[41] A Family Procedure Rule Committee has similar powers to make rules governing family proceedings.[42] All rule committees are subject to an overriding duty to ensure that the system is 'accessible, fair and efficient', and that any rules made are both 'simple and simply expressed'.[43]

---

[34] See p 18, *ante*.
[35] Most of Woolf's recommendations were adopted in the Access to Justice Act 1999 and the Civil Procedure Rules 1998, SI 1998/3132: see p 456, *post*.
[36] *Review of the Criminal Courts of England and Wales* (2001); see p 521, *post*.
[37] Civil Procedure Act 1997, s 6.   [38] See chapter 8 of the Report.
[39] At para 14.   [40] Civil Procedure Rules 1998, SI 1998/3132, or 'CPR'.
[41] 2003 Act, s 69; Criminal Procedure Rules 2005, SI 2005/384.
[42] 2003 Act, ss 75–77.   [43] Ibid, ss 69(4); 75(5); Civil Procedure Act 1997, s 1(3), as amended.

Under section 1(1) of the Courts Act 2003 the Lord Chancellor has a duty to ensure that there is an efficient and effective system to support the business of the Supreme Court, Court of Protection, county courts, and magistrates' courts. The Act also provides for England and Wales to be divided into separate local justice areas, with each area having its own Courts Board. Courts Boards are responsible for scrutinizing and reviewing the administration of the courts and for making recommendations to the Lord Chancellor.[44] The principal aim of the Courts Act is to provide a framework for a unified court structure, and to this end the Lord Chancellor has transferred administrative responsibility for all but one of the major courts to a single executive agency called 'Her Majesty's Court Service'.[45] This body administers all of the courts that were previously managed by the Courts Service – that is, the Crown Court, High Court, Court of Appeal, and county courts – and it has also assumed responsibility for managing the network of magistrates' courts.[46] This leaves the House of Lords (or its replacement) as the only major court not covered by the new agency. However, it is considered appropriate for the latter court to be administered separately because of its unique position as an appellate court for all parts of the United Kingdom. The new arrangements will allow for greater sharing of resources, making it easier, for example, to use the same facilities as a venue for magistrates' and county court business, as well as for sittings of the Crown Court. It also opens up the possibility of creating specialist centres where magistrates, county courts, and High Court judges can exercise their family jurisdiction under one roof.

Despite the wholesale changes of recent years, it seems inevitable that there will be further reforms in the near future. Indeed, while the House of Commons was still debating legislation that will lead to the creation of a new Supreme Court,[47] the Department for Constitutional Affairs was already looking at the possibility of combining the existing civil courts.[48]

3   THE PRINCIPLE OF OPEN JUSTICE[49]

'Open justice' is a key principle of the English legal system, and amongst other things it requires that the courts should sit in public. In the words of Lord Hewart CJ in *R v Sussex Justices, ex parte McCarthy*:[50]

> a long line of cases shows that it is not merely of some importance but is of fundamental importance that justice should not only be done, but should manifestly and undoubtedly be seen to be done.

---

[44] Sections 4 and 5.   [45] Formally launched on 1 April 2005.

[46] These were previously managed by forty-two separate Magistrates' Courts Committees: see p 260, *post*.

[47] Constitutional Reform Act 2005: see p 253, *post*.

[48] DCA, *A Single Civil Court? The Scope for Unifying the Civil Jurisdictions of the High Court, the County Courts and the Family Proceedings Courts* (2005) CP 06/05. Having considered the responses to this consultation document, the government announced that the creation of single Civil and Family Courts would be adopted as a 'long-term objective' – *A Single Civil Court? Responses to the Consultation* (2005) CP(R) 06/05, at p 42.

[49] For a detailed analysis, see Jaconelli, *Open Justice: A Critique of the Public Trial* (2002).

[50] [1924] 1 KB 256 at 259; see also *R v Denbigh Justices, ex parte Williams* [1974] QB 759, [1974] 2 All ER 1052; Supreme Court Act 1981, s 67.

The principle, and the circumstances which may justify departure from it, were set out by the House of Lords in *Scott v Scott*[51] and later explained by Lord Diplock in *A-G v Leveller Magazine Ltd*:[52]

> As a general rule the English system of administering justice does require that it be done in public: *Scott v Scott*. If the way the courts behave cannot be hidden from the public ear and eye this provides a safeguard against judicial arbitrariness or idiosyncrasy and maintains the public confidence in the administration of justice.

More recently the principle was endorsed by Butler-Sloss P, quoting from the work of Jeremy Bentham:[53]

> Publicity is the very soul of justice. It is the keenest spur to exertion and the surest of all guards against improbity. It keeps the judge himself while trying under trial.

From this it follows that if at all possible, proceedings should be held in open court and fair and accurate reports of those proceedings should be permissible. In *Storer v British Gas*[54] the Court of Appeal quashed the decision of an industrial tribunal because the hearing had taken place in an office which was kept locked and marked 'Private'. On the other hand, certain restrictions on the principle of open justice may be permitted where this is necessary to protect the administration of justice, or where Parliament has created a specific exception.

Article 6(1) of the European Convention on Human Rights is also relevant in this context, and has assumed added importance since the coming into force of the Human Rights Act 1998.[55]

> Article 6(1)
>
> In the determination of his civil rights and obligations or of any criminal charge against him, everyone is entitled to a fair and public hearing...Judgment shall be pronounced publicly but the press and public may be excluded from all or part of the trial in the interests of morals, public order or national security in a democratic society, where the interests of juveniles or the protection of the private life of the parties so require, or to the extent strictly necessary in the opinion of the court in special circumstances where publicity would prejudice the interests of justice.

(a) A hearing in open court

Statutory provisions. Parliament has granted a power to sit in camera in various types of proceedings. These include proceedings covered by the Children Act 1989,[56] applications relating to a caution for soliciting,[57] cases involving evidence of sexual capacity in

---

[51] [1913] AC 417.   [52] [1979] AC 440, [1979] 1 All ER 745.
[53] *Clibbery v Allan* [2002] EWCA Civ 45 at [16], [2002] Fam 261 at [16], [2002] 1 All ER 865.
[54] [2000] 2 All ER 440, [2000] 1 WLR 1237.
[55] See chapter 5. For an illustration of the correct approach to this issue under Article 6(1), see *B v UK* [2001] 2 FLR 261, (2002) 34 EHRR 19. It was found in this case that a county court hearing to determine the residence of a child did not breach the Convention, even though it was held in private.
[56] Section 97.   [57] Street Offences Act 1959, s 2.

suits for the annulment of marriage,[58] and proceedings under the Official Secrets Acts.[59] In addition, provisions designed to assist vulnerable witnesses in criminal proceedings are contained in the Youth Justice and Criminal Evidence Act 1999.[60] Part II of this Act enables courts to take 'special measures' to assist certain categories of witnesses (though not defendants) who might have difficulty giving evidence or who might be reluctant to do so. These categories include those under the age of seventeen, alleged victims of sex offences, those suffering from a mental or physical impairment likely to affect the quality of evidence given, and those whose evidence is likely to be impaired by fear or distress.[61] One of the special measures available to the courts is the power to allow a vulnerable witness to give evidence in camera,[62] subject to section 25(3) which states that one representative of the press must be allowed to stay. Other special measures include the possibility of screening the witness from the accused,[63] or allowing the witness to give evidence via a pre-recorded video or live video link.[64] Following research suggesting that a third of child witnesses would be unable to give evidence without the use of special measures,[65] the government is now exploring ways in which their use might be extended.[66] In response to the decision of the European Court of Human Rights in *SC* v *UK*[67] it is also looking at whether child defendants, who are largely excluded from the regime created by the 1999 Act, should have access to the same special measures as child witnesses.[68] Amendments to the Act have already been made to allow vulnerable child defendants to give evidence by live video link.[69]

Common law. In addition to these specific provisions, the courts also have a general jurisdiction to sit in camera where the presence of the public would render the administration of justice impracticable. This was confirmed in *R* v *Richards (Randall)*[70] when a judge decided to clear the court so that a witness to a murder could give evidence. The witness had refused to testify under any other circumstances, and in denying

---

[58] Matrimonial Causes Act 1973, s 48(2).   [59] Official Secrets Act 1920, s 8(4).

[60] Most of the relevant provisions have been in force since 24 July 2002; see Youth Justice and Criminal Evidence Act 1999 (Commencement No 7) Order 2002, SI 2002/1739.

[61] Sections 16 and 17.

[62] Section 25. This applies only to evidence given in relation to a sex offence, or where there are grounds for believing that the witness has been or may be intimidated. See also s 37 of the Children and Young Persons Act 1933. For an analysis of the 1999 Act, see Birch, 'A Better Deal for Vulnerable Witnesses?' [2000] Crim LR 223. The Home Office has produced its own guidelines on the new provisions: *Achieving Best Evidence in Criminal Proceedings: Guidance for Vulnerable and Intimidated Witnesses, including Children.*

[63] Section 23.

[64] Sections 24, 27, and 28. Note that the Criminal Justice Act 2003 makes provision for the use of both live and pre-recorded video evidence to be used in a wider range of circumstances. At the time of writing, however, these provisions had yet to be implemented.

[65] Hamlyn et al, *Are Special Measures Working? Evidence from Surveys of Vulnerable and Intimidated Witnesses* (London: Home Office Research Study No. 283; June 2004).

[66] Office for Criminal Justice Reform, *Improving the Criminal Trial Process for Young Witnesses: A Consultation Paper* (2007).

[67] (2005) 40 EHRR 10.   [68] Chapter 5.

[69] Section 33A, 1999 Act. The court must be satisfied that the ability of the accused to participate effectively in the proceedings is compromised by his level of intellectual ability or social functioning.

[70] [1999] Crim LR 764.

an application for leave to appeal, the Court of Appeal observed that courts have an inherent jurisdiction to do what is necessary for the proper administration of justice. In another case, the Court of Appeal upheld a decision to allow an in camera hearing concerning allegations that a defendant had been tortured whilst in detention in a foreign jurisdiction.[71] The defendant was on trial for conspiracy to cause terrorist explosions, and along with representatives of the media he argued that the evidence should be heard in open court. The Court of Appeal held, however, that the evidence could be heard in camera for reasons of national security and the avoidance of harm to the administration of justice. It also confirmed that the judge had been right to hear the defendant's application for leave to appeal *against* this ruling in camera. The judge's reasons for granting the in camera hearing were cited with approval:[72]

> [G]eneral publication of the relevant parts of [the evidence] could give rise to a substantial risk to national security. Additionally it could obstruct the identification of, and cause the Crown to be deterred from prosecuting in this and other cases, those who it is in the public interest should be tried.

However, the courts are not permitted to restrict open justice in circumstances where the fair administration of justice is not threatened. There is certainly no jurisdiction to hear a case in private purely for the convenience of the parties. Thus in *R v Evesham Justices, ex parte McDonagh*[73] it was held that a court could not prohibit publication of the defendant's address to save him from being harassed by his ex-wife. This case may be compared with that of *R v Malvern Justices, ex parte Evans*,[74] in which magistrates sat in camera to hear a mitigation plea in respect of a driving offence. The mental health of the defendant was such that if the court had not sat in camera, the defendant would have been inhibited in making her plea. An appeal against the making of the order was dismissed, but the Divisional Court observed that it would rarely be appropriate to make such an order, and doubted whether it had in fact been appropriate in this particular case.

(b) Withholding particular information or evidence from the public

The second aspect of open justice is the principle that all evidence should be communicated publicly. However, just as there are limitations on the principle that proceedings should be conducted in public, there are also circumstances which may justify a court restricting publicity of evidence. To give a common example, a court will usually permit a victim of blackmail to be identified during proceedings by a title such as 'Mr X', and to communicate his name and address to the court by writing it down.[75] There are also statutory provisions for preserving the anonymity of young witnesses,[76]

---

[71] *R (on the application of A) v Crown Court at the Central Criminal Court* [2006] EWCA Crim 4, [2006] 1 WLR 1361, [2006] HRLR 10. The judge's order did not prevent the defendant himself from giving evidence in open court of his alleged treatment.

[72] Ibid, at [7].   [73] [1988] QB 553, (1988) 87 Cr App R 28.   [74] [1988] QB 540, [1988] 1 All ER 371.

[75] *R v Socialist Worker Printer and Publishers Ltd, ex parte A-G* [1975] QB 637, [1975] 1 All ER 142.

[76] Youth Justice and Criminal Evidence Act 1999, s 45; see also the Children and Young Persons Act 1933, s 39. For the relevant principles, see *R v Leicester Crown Court, ex parte S* [1992] 2 All ER 659, [1993] 1 WLR 111; *Re S (A Child) (Identification: Restrictions on Publication)* [2004] UKHL 47, [2005] 1 AC 593, [2004] 4 All ER 683.

complainants in sex offence cases,[77] and other vulnerable parties.[78] Exceptionally, the identity of witnesses may be protected even from other parties to the proceedings. The obvious situation in which this may occur is where an informant has a genuine fear of reprisals if he gives evidence in a criminal case. Withholding relevant information from a defendant is an extreme step, however, and it would usually be assumed to compromise his right to a fair trial.[79]

The parties to proceedings will not normally be granted anonymity. The position was discussed by the Court of Appeal in *R* v *Legal Aid Board, ex parte Kaim Todner*,[80] where a firm of solicitors sought anonymity in judicial review proceedings against the Legal Aid Board. In rejecting any special rule relating to the legal profession, Lord Woolf MR stressed that any exception to the general rule in *Scott* v *Scott* could only be justified if this was necessary in the interests of justice. This was a matter for the court and could not be determined by any agreement of the parties in the case. As had been noted in *ex parte P*,[81] 'when both sides agreed that information should be kept from the public, that was when the court had to be the most vigilant'. Public scrutiny was necessary in order to deter inappropriate behaviour by the courts, and to maintain confidence in the administration of justice. In addition, members of the public could not come forward with relevant evidence if they were unaware of its relevance to proceedings. In deciding whether to protect the anonymity of a party to an action, it was not unreasonable for a court to assume that a party who initiated proceedings had accepted the normal consequences of that action. On the other hand, a witness with no interest in the proceedings would have a stronger claim if he or she would be prejudiced by publicity, though even this would not attract automatic anonymity.[82]

This area of law was also considered in *A-G* v *Leveller Magazine*.[83] The House of Lords accepted that a court was entitled to sit in private or to withhold the name of a witness if this was in the interests of the administration of justice. On the facts, however, the judge had not made a clear order restricting publication, and the identity of the witness could be readily ascertained from evidence which was freely reportable. The defendant's

---

[77] Sexual Offences (Amendment) Act 1992, s 1 (as amended). Once an allegation of an offence has been made, it is an offence to publish information likely to lead members of the public to identify the complainant unless the judge has lifted these restrictions under s 3.

[78] Youth Justice and Criminal Evidence Act 1999, s 46.

[79] The relevant principles are discussed in *R* v *Liverpool City Magistrates' Court, ex parte DPP* (1997) 161 JP 43; *R (on the application of Al-Fawwaz)* v *Governor of Brixton Prison* [2001] UKHL 69, [2002] 1 AC 556, [2002] 1 All ER 545; *R* v *Davis (Iain)* [2006] EWCA Crim 1155, [2006] 1 WLR 3130, [2006] 4 All ER 648.

[80] [1999] QB 966, [1998] 3 All ER 541.   [81] (1998) *The Times*, 31 March.

[82] An exceptional case in which there were sound reasons for preserving the anonymity of witnesses is *R* v *Lord Saville of Newdigate, ex parte A* [1999] 4 All ER 860, [2000] 1 WLR 1855. The Court of Appeal agreed with the Divisional Court that it had been unreasonable to deny anonymity to 17 members of the armed forces who were due to give evidence to the Bloody Sunday Inquiry. Though not strictly concerned with a trial, this decision indicates the principles to be applied when considering a restriction on open justice. On the facts, it was found that revealing the identity of the witnesses was not vital to the fairness of the inquiry, and in any event, the clear risk that the lives of the witnesses could be threatened if their identities were made public outweighed any other considerations.

[83] [1979] AC 440, [1979] 1 All ER 745.

conviction for contempt of court was therefore quashed.[84] Any such order will now be made pursuant to section 11 of the Contempt of Court Act 1981 unless restrictions are permissible at common law.[85] It is possible to appeal against the making of such an order,[86] and an order should only be made where the administration of justice justifies the restriction. Personal embarrassment is not a sufficient reason.[87]

(c) The reporting of proceedings in court

A final principle of open justice is that reports of judicial proceedings should not be prevented or discouraged, as long as they are fair, contemporaneous, and accurate. The publication of such reports is expressly permitted by section 4 of the Contempt of Court Act 1981, but the law recognizes that there are circumstances where a departure from the general rule may be justified. Section 11 for example, confers a power to prevent the reporting of details which have not been disclosed in open court. In addition, section 4(2) of the Act empowers a court to *postpone* reporting where this is necessary in the interests of justice.[88] If, however, those interests can be satisfied in less restrictive ways, the section 4(2) power should not be used. This was the approach before the Human Rights Act came into effect,[89] and the decision in *R (on the application of the Telegraph Group plc) v Sherwood* suggests that it is still correct.[90] The Court of Appeal in this case identified three key principles. Firstly, a judge has no discretion to restrict publication unless there is a substantial risk of prejudice to particular legal proceedings. Secondly, where such a risk exists, an order should not be made unless the judge is satisfied that it is the least restrictive means of avoiding that risk. Finally, any risk of prejudice must be balanced against the public interest in the proceedings being reported. On the facts of the case a decision to delay the reporting of one trial until a second, related trial had been concluded, was held to be a justifiable and proportionate response to a substantial risk of prejudice.[91] The decision in *Sherwood* should be compared with that in *R v B*.[92] In this case the defendant had pleaded guilty to conspiracy to commit murder,

---

[84] For a discussion of contempt of court, see below at p 246.

[85] See *R v Socialist Worker Printer and Publishers Ltd, ex parte A-G* [1975] QB 637, [1975] 1 All ER 142; *Re M (Wardship: Freedom of Publication)* [1990] 2 FLR 36.

[86] Criminal Justice Act 1988, s 159; *R v Crook* [1992] 2 All ER 687, (1991) 93 Cr App R 17.

[87] See, e.g. *R v Malvern Justices, ex parte Evans* [1988] QB 540, [1988] 1 All ER 371; *R v Dover JJ, ex parte Dover DC* (1992) 156 JP 433 (publicity embarrassing to a restaurant); *H v Ministry of Defence* [1991] 2 QB 103, [1991] 2 All ER 834 (publication of embarrassing medical evidence restrained).

[88] Note that the latter provision is concerned with avoiding prejudice to specific proceedings, and it does not provide a basis for restrictions to be imposed indefinitely: *R v Times Newspapers Ltd.* [2007] EWCA Crim 1925, *The Times*, 31 July 2007.

[89] In *Re Central Independent Television* [1991] 1 All ER 347, [1991] 1 WLR 4 an order prohibiting radio or television reporting whilst a jury was staying overnight at a hotel was held to be excessive. See also, *Ex parte Telegraph plc* [1993] 2 All ER 971, [1993] 1 WLR 980.

[90] [2001] EWCA Crim 1075, [2001] 1 WLR 1983. For a discussion of the effect of reporting restrictions on the Convention right to freedom of expression, see Cram, 'Reporting Restrictions in Criminal Proceedings and Article 10 of the ECHR' [1998] EHRLR 742.

[91] Cf. the earlier decision in *R v Beck, ex parte Daily Telegraph plc* [1993] 2 All ER 177, in which reporting restrictions were refused in similar circumstances. The court in the recent case felt able to distinguish *Beck* on the facts, however, and did not doubt that it was correctly decided.

[92] [2006] EWCA Crim 2692, [2007] HRLR 1.

and the judge had made an order postponing the reporting of the sentencing hearing until the trial of his alleged co-conspirators had taken place. Applying the three-stage approach outlined in *Sherwood*, the Court of Appeal held that the order should be quashed: although the right to a fair trial had primacy over all other considerations, the duties imposed on publishers by the Contempt of Court Act were deemed to be a sufficient safeguard of fairness, and the court had confidence in the integrity of juries and in their ability to focus on the evidence presented in court:[93]

> [T]he responsibility for avoiding the publication of material which may prejudice the outcome of a trial rests fairly and squarely on those responsible for the publication. In our view, broadcasting authorities and newspaper editors should be trusted to fulfil their responsibilities accurately to inform the public of court proceedings, and to exercise sensible judgment about the publication of comment which may interfere with the administration of justice.

The rules governing the reporting of legal proceedings are considered in more detail below, in the context of the law of contempt.

Given the high-technology age in which we now live, some would question whether allowing printed reports of legal proceedings is still sufficient to ensure that justice is done in public. The government is currently considering whether there is a case for allowing the television cameras to have access to the courts, but a recent consultation exercise found only limited support for the idea.[94] Although some respondents felt that television coverage might be useful in helping to increase understanding of the justice system, most were concerned about the possible implications of widespread reporting for the fair administration of justice.[95] On this basis it seems likely that if the government does decide to move in this direction it will proceed with extreme caution.

4 CONTEMPT OF COURT[96]

Judges have an inherent jurisdiction to punish conduct calculated to prejudice or interfere with the process of the law. Such conduct is termed a contempt of court and may be either criminal or civil in nature.

(a) Criminal contempt

Criminal contempt is an offence at common law and comprises conduct which interferes with the administration of justice or which creates a substantial risk that the course of justice will be prejudiced.[97] Thus, it is a criminal contempt to interfere with a juror

---

[93] Ibid, per Sir Igor Judge at [25].

[94] Department for Constitutional Affairs, *Broadcasting Courts* (2005) CP 28/04.

[95] DCA, *Broadcasting Courts: Responses to the Consultation* (2005) CP(R) 28/04, at p 42.

[96] See generally: Miller, *Contempt of Court* (Oxford University Press, 3rd edn, 2000); Eady and Smith, *Arlidge, Eady and Smith on Contempt* (Sweet & Maxwell: 3rd edn, 2005), Fenwick and Phillipson, *Media Freedom under the Human Rights Act* (Oxford University Press, 2006).

[97] *A-G v Times Newspapers Ltd* [1992] 1 AC 191, [1991] 2 All ER 398.

or witness,[98] or to prevent or unlawfully deter a party from pursuing a legal action.[99] A journalist who refuses to disclose his source of information when required to do so by a court may also be liable for contempt.[100] However, a court may only require disclosure if satisfied that this is necessary in the interests of justice, national security, or the prevention of crime or disorder.[101]

It is also a contempt to publish the name of a party or witness where publication is prohibited by statute or is contrary to a court order.[102] In *Attorney-General v Punch*[103] the publishers and editor of a magazine were convicted of contempt after publishing an article by the former MI5 officer, David Shayler. Mr Shayler was being prosecuted for disclosing intelligence obtained while working for the security services, and he was the subject of an injunction preventing him from making further disclosures while his case was still pending. The injunction did not apply to the defendants directly, but on appeal to the House of Lords it was held that their publication nevertheless amounted to a contempt of court:[104]

> The primary effect of such an injunction is to regulate the conduct of the person against whom it is made. But it also has an indirect effect upon the conduct of third parties. In general, it is a contempt of court for anyone, whether party to the proceedings or not, deliberately to interfere with the due administration of justice. One species of such interference . . . is the deliberate publication of information which the court has ordered someone else to keep confidential. Publication interferes with the administration of justice because it destroys the subject-matter of the proceedings. Once the information has been published, the court can no longer do justice between the parties by enforcing the obligation of confidentiality.

Their Lordships acknowledged that the injunction had implications for the right to freedom of expression, and that Article 10 of the ECHR was therefore engaged. Nevertheless, they emphasized that the Article 10 right could be lawfully restricted on a number of grounds, and held that the injunction in this case had been proportionate to the legitimate objective of protecting national security.[105] The defendants'

[98] *Re Attorney-General's Application* [1963] 1 QB 696, [1962] 3 All ER 326.
[99] *Raymond v Honey* [1981] QB 874, [1981] 2 All ER 1084 (prisoner unlawfully prevented from making an application to the High Court); *A-G v Hislop and Pressdram* [1991] 1 QB 514, [1991] 1 All ER 911 (defendant in a libel case published further articles to deter the claimant from pursing the action).
[100] In *DPP v Channel 4 Television Co Ltd* [1993] 2 All ER 517, fines totalling £75,000 were imposed on the defendant for failure to comply with an order to produce documents.
[101] Contempt of Court Act 1981, s 10; *X Ltd v Morgan-Grampian (Publishers) Ltd* [1991] 1 AC 1, [1990] 2 All ER 1; *Ashworth Hospital Authority v MGN Ltd* [2002] UKHL 29, [2002] 1 WLR 2033, [2002] 4 All ER 193, *Interbrew SA v Financial Times Ltd.* [2002] EWCA Civ 274, [2002] EMLR 24. Cf. *Goodwin v UK* (1996) 22 EHRR 123. See also, the discussion of Article 10, ECHR, at p 197, *ante*.
[102] *R v Socialist Worker Printers and Publishers Ltd, ex parte A-G* [1975] QB 637, [1975] 1 All ER 142; There must, however, be a clear direction and not merely a request: *A-G v Leveller Magazine Ltd* [1979] AC 440, [1979] 1 All ER 745.
[103] [2002] UKHL 50, [2003] 1 AC 1046, [2003] 1 All ER 289.
[104] Ibid at [66], per Lord Hoffmann.
[105] Other legitimate grounds for restricting freedom of expression include maintaining judicial independence and protecting the rights and freedoms of others. The right must also be balanced against the right to a fair trial under Article 6.

motive was not important and the fact that they did not believe the material to be harmful to national security was irrelevant: what mattered was that their conduct was intentional.

In addition to the common law rule, contempt of court may also be committed under certain statutory provisions. For example, it is a contempt to obtain, disclose or solicit any particulars of statements made, opinions expressed, arguments advanced, or votes cast by members of a jury in the course of their deliberations.[106] There is also a strict liability rule covering publications that are seriously prejudicial to a fair trial.

Strict liability contempt. The strict liability rule is set out in sections 1 and 2 of the Contempt of Court Act 1981, and it covers the publication of material which creates a substantial risk of impeding or prejudicing 'active'[107] legal proceedings. In assessing whether a risk of prejudice is substantial, it is relevant to take into account the lapse of time between the publication and the date of any trial, and the likelihood of the material being encountered by potential jurors.[108] A publication creating such a risk will amount to a contempt of court, regardless of whether there was any intention to interfere with the course of justice.[109] However, publications *intended* to prejudice the course of justice can still be dealt with at common law,[110] as can material published when proceedings are imminent but not active.[111]

There are three statutory defences to the strict liability rule: (a) innocent publication or distribution;[112] (b) fair and accurate reports of legal proceedings held in public, which are published contemporaneously and in good faith;[113] and (c) discussion of public affairs or other matters of general public interest, where the risk of prejudice to particular legal proceedings is incidental.[114] An illustration of the defence of incidental discussion is provided by the case of *Attorney-General* v *English*,[115] in which the House of Lords decided that an article discussing the merits of mercy killing did not amount to contempt, even though at the time of publication a doctor was on trial accused of the mercy killing of a disabled child.

Where a publication is sufficiently prejudicial to justify the quashing of a conviction or a stay of proceedings, a finding of contempt will usually be possible. However, the

---

[106] Contempt of Court Act 1981, s 8(1). Proposals to relax this rule to allow legitimate jury research are discussed at p 366, *post*.

[107] In criminal cases proceedings will be active from the time of an arrest, the issue of an arrest warrant, or the issue of a summons. In civil proceedings the relevant date will usually be the date of setting down for trial: ibid, Schedule 1. See also, *A-G* v *Hislop and Pressdram* [1991] 1 QB 514, [1991] 1 All ER 911.

[108] In *R* v *Taylor and Taylor* (1994) 98 Cr App R 361 it was held that the prejudicial impact of an article could be heightened by the use of photographs.

[109] The position was previously governed by common law, which made it an offence to publish material prejudging the issues to be determined in pending litigation: *A-G* v *Times Newspapers* [1974] AC 273, [1973] 3 All ER 54. The 1981 Act was passed following the ruling of the European Court of Human Rights in *Sunday Times* v *UK* (1979–1980) 2 EHRR 245, which found that the common law rule was too vague and imprecise and went further than was necessary in a democratic society.

[110] Contempt of Court Act 1981, s 6(c); *A-G* v *Punch* [2002] UKHL 50, [2003] 1 AC 1046, [2003] 1 All ER 289.

[111] *A-G* v *Times Newspapers* [1992] 1 AC 191, [1991] 2 All ER 398.   [112] 1981 Act, s 3(1).

[113] Ibid, s 4. Note that the court may order publication to be postponed under s 4(2): see p 245, *ante*.

[114] Ibid, s 5.   [115] [1983] 1 AC 116, [1982] 2 All ER 903.

case of *Attorney-General* v *MGN*[116] illustrates some of the difficulties that may arise. Criminal proceedings against the partner of a well-known actress were abandoned when highly prejudicial reports appeared in five tabloid newspapers. The court found that there was a risk of prejudice stemming from the cumulative effect of these reports, but that when considered separately, none of them were sufficiently prejudicial to satisfy the test for contempt. Conversely, a finding of contempt may be made in circumstances where a stay of proceedings is unnecessary, as in *Attorney-General* v *BBC and Hat Trick Productions*.[117] The case concerned satirical remarks about Robert Maxwell's sons, which were broadcast six months before the brothers stood trial on serious fraud charges. The judge in the fraud case refused to order a stay of proceedings, on the basis that the six-month gap and the likely length and complexity of the trial would concentrate the juror's minds on the evidence presented in court. Nevertheless, the broadcaster and producers of the programme were convicted of strict liability contempt.

Contempt in the face of the court. If judicial proceedings are actually disrupted, or a contempt is committed in the vicinity of the courtroom, this will constitute contempt in the face of the court. This offence may be committed by, for example, distributing leaflets and shouting during proceedings,[118] using a tape-recorder in court without leave,[119] taking a photograph or making an unauthorized sketch in court,[120] or refusing to give evidence when summoned as a witness.[121] In one case a man was sentenced to six months imprisonment after attacking his wife and her solicitor during a child custody hearing.[122] In addition, disobeying a witness summons is punishable as a contempt in the same way as if it had been committed in the face of the court.[123]

(b) Civil contempt

Civil contempt will occur where a party fails to comply with a court order. For example, a civil contempt may be committed by a failure to comply with an injunction, or by the failure of a solicitor to comply with an undertaking.[124] Mere failure to pay a judgment debt is not contempt, although wilful refusal to do so is.[125] In addition, if an alternative method of securing compliance with a court order is available, the Court of Appeal

---

[116] [1997] 1 All ER 456.

[117] [1997] EMLR 76. See also *A-G* v *Birmingham Post and Mail Ltd* [1998] 4 All ER 49, [1999] 1 WLR 361, where it was suggested that strict liability contempt requires a lesser degree of prejudice than would be needed to stay proceedings or quash a conviction.

[118] *Morris* v *Crown Office* [1970] 2 QB 114, [1970] 1 All ER 1079.

[119] Contempt of Court Act 1981, s 9.

[120] Criminal Justice Act 1925, s 41(1), as amended; *R* v *D (Contempt of Court: Illegal Photography)* [2004] EWCA Crim 1271, (2004) *The Times*, 13 May – the defendant in this case was given an immediate twelve months custodial sentence for using his mobile phone to take photographs during proceedings.

[121] *A-G* v *Mulholland* [1963] 2 QB 477, [1963] 1 All ER 767.

[122] *Wilkinson* v *Lord Chancellor's Department* [2003] EWCA Civ 95, [2003] 2 All ER 184, [2003] 1 WLR 1254.

[123] Criminal Procedure (Attendance of Witnesses) Act 1965, s 3, as amended.

[124] *Re Kerly* [1901] 1 Ch 467; *Re A Solicitor* [1966] 3 All ER 52, [1966] 1 WLR 1604.

[125] Debtors Act 1869, as amended by the Administration of Justice Act 1970, s 11.

has stated that this method should be adopted rather than sending the contemnor to prison.[126]

The House of Lords made an important decision on civil contempt in *M v Home Office*.[127] M was seeking leave to apply for judicial review of the Home Secretary's decision to refuse his asylum application. At the end of the hearing the judge made it clear that he wished M to remain in the country until his application had been determined, and he understood the Home Secretary to have given an undertaking not to deport him. M was nevertheless flown out of the country, and the judge made an order obliging the Home Secretary to return him to the jurisdiction. When the Minister failed to comply, he was found to be in contempt of court.

(c) Jurisdiction to punish contempt

The jurisdiction to punish for contempt is inherent in superior courts of record. Such courts may commit for contempt and can punish contempt in the face of the court by an immediate fine and a prison term of up to two years.[128] Although a county court is an inferior court, it is treated as a superior court for these purposes.[129] Most other contempts relating to inferior courts are dealt with by the Queen's Bench Division,[130] although inferior courts of record can punish contempt in the face of the court by an immediate fine and a prison term not exceeding one month.[131] In addition, although not courts of record, magistrates' courts have equivalent powers to punish the wilful interruption of magistrates' proceedings and other forms of misbehaviour in court.[132] Until 1960 there was no right of appeal against punishment for criminal contempt, but this position was altered by section 13 of the Administration of Justice Act 1960. Appeal lies to the Court of Appeal, Divisional Court or House of Lords, as the case may be.

Contempt may be punished by a summary procedure far removed from the ordinary processes of the law: no precise charges are put, the accused may have no opportunity to consult a lawyer, and the judge making the decision may have been the person insulted. Article 6 of the ECHR establishes certain safeguards for a person charged with a criminal offence, including the presumption of innocence, the right to be informed of the nature of any charges, the right to adequate time and legal assistance in preparing a defence, and the right to be dealt with by an independent and impartial tribunal. Doubts have been raised about the compatibility of the summary procedure with these

---

[126] *Danchevsky v Danchevsky* [1975] Fam 17, [1974] 3 All ER 934; *Re G (Contempt: Committal)* [2003] EWCA Civ 489, [2003] 1 WLR 2051.

[127] *Re M* [1994] 1 AC 377; *sub nom M v Home Office* [1993] 3 All ER 537.

[128] Contempt of Court Act 1981, s 14(1).   [129] Ibid, s 14(4A).

[130] *R v Davies* [1906] 1 KB 32. Note that this jurisdiction is limited to 'courts' properly so-called, and it may therefore be important to ascertain whether a particular tribunal is a court: *A-G v BBC* [1981] AC 303, [1980] 3 All ER 161: see p 237, *ante*.

[131] 1981 Act, s 14(1), (2).

[132] Ibid, s 12. Magistrates can also punish the making of insults against justices, witnesses, solicitors, barristers, and officers of the court.

requirements, and the Court of Appeal has indicated that it should not be used in the absence of a clear contempt that cannot wait to be dealt with:[133]

> Nearly all contempt proceedings require to be adjourned to a separate hearing, in many cases to a different judge, with the rest of the case continuing if possible. An adjournment will usually be necessary if the first judge has already heard evidence from the party alleged to be in contempt which he would not be obliged to give, for risk of self-incrimination, if he were faced with an allegation of contempt.

THE EUROPEAN COURT OF JUSTICE AND EUROPEAN COURT OF HUMAN RIGHTS

These courts play an increasingly important role in the English legal system, and their functions and powers are considered in detail in chapters 4 and 5.

THE HOUSE OF LORDS

1　THE HOUSE OF LORDS: CONSTITUTION AND PROCEDURE

Parliament is the oldest common law court, and its judicial functions have been exercised by the House of Lords since the fifteenth century. In theory an appeal to the House of Lords is an appeal to the whole House, and until the nineteenth century this was literally true in that any member of the House could and did vote in judicial sessions. Even those peers who were lawyers were rarely the most senior and well-respected judges of their day, and puisne judges were frequently invited to advise their Lordships on the law.[134] The convention against lay peers participating in judicial sittings of the House was not firmly established until the Appellate Jurisdiction Act 1876, which provided for the creation of salaried life peers to hear appeals. The new life peers were called Lords of Appeal in Ordinary ('Law Lords'), and their number was subsequently fixed at between seven and twelve.[135]

---

[133] *Re G (Contempt: Committal)* [2003] EWCA Civ 489 at [21], [2003] 1 WLR 2051 at [21], per Butler Sloss P. See also, *Balogh v St Albans Crown Court* [1975] QB 73, [1974] 3 All ER 283.

[134] The last case in which this appears to have happened was *Allen v Flood* [1898] AC 1.

[135] Appellate Jurisdiction Act 1947; Administration of Justice Act 1968, s 1(1)(a); Maximum Number of Judges Order 1994, SI 1994/3217. By custom, one or two Law Lords have always been from Scotland and one from Northern Ireland: these members have usually sat in appeals from the Court of Session and the Court of Appeal of Northern Ireland.

Appeals must be heard by at least three peers, and in addition to the Lords of Appeal other peers 'who hold or have held high judicial office' also have the authority to sit.[136] In practice most appeals are heard by a committee of at least five Lords of Appeal (or occasionally seven),[137] and they are generally argued in a committee room at the Palace of Westminster and not in the Chamber of the House itself. Each Law Lord is entitled to deliver a separate opinion, with the decision of the majority prevailing. In the unusual case of *Kennedy* v *Spratt*[138] Lord Upjohn, who was one of the five Law Lords to have heard the appeal, died before the judgment was delivered. This resulted in the vote being equally split and the appeal was therefore dismissed.[139]

2 HOUSE OF LORDS: JURISDICTION

(a) Original jurisdiction

In modern times the House of Lords has had very little original jurisdiction. The right of a peer to be 'tried by his peers'[140] was abolished by the Criminal Justice Act 1948, and while the House theoretically retains the jurisdiction to conduct impeachment proceedings, this has not been exercised since the impeachments of Warren Hastings and Viscount Melville in 1795 and 1805 respectively. Both the House of Lords and the House of Commons have jurisdiction over breaches of privilege, including contempt of the House, and either House may imprison the offender. Beyond this, the original jurisdiction of the House of Lords is limited to hearing disputed peerage claims through the Committee of Privileges.[141]

(b) Appellate jurisdiction

Civil cases. The House of Lords hears appeals in civil cases from the Court of Appeal, but only with leave of either the Court of Appeal or the Appeals Committee of the House itself.[142] Most cases to reach the House of Lords have involved points of law of public importance, though this is not a pre-requisite in civil cases.[143]

---

[136] Appellate Jurisdiction Act 1876, s 5, as amended. Prior to implementation of the Constitutional Reform Act 2005, the Lord Chancellor was also entitled to sit.

[137] The appeal in *A* v *Secretary of State for the Home Department* [2004] UKHL 56, [2005] 2 WLR 87 was of such significance that it was heard by nine Law Lords: see p 184, *ante*.

[138] [1972] AC 83, [1971] 1 All ER 805.

[139] Ibid. As it happens, the opinion written by Lord Upjohn before his death indicated that he was in favour of dismissing the appeal. Had his opinion indicated that he was in favour of allowing the appeal, an anomalous situation would have arisen whereby his death would have deprived the appellant of success. It is uncertain how their Lordships would have responded to this situation.

[140] This is thought to originate from the Magna Carta.

[141] For examples, see the *Ampthill Peerage* case [1977] AC 547, [1976] 2 All ER 411, and the *Annandale and Hartfell Peerage Claim* [1986] AC 319, [1985] 3 All ER 577.

[142] Administration of Justice (Appeals) Act 1934. The House also hears appeals from the equivalent civil courts of Scotland (Court of Session) and Northern Ireland (Court of Appeal).

[143] In *Johnson* v *Moreton* [1980] AC 37 at 53, [1978] 3 All ER 37 at 44, Lord Hailsham suggested that nine out of ten House of Lords cases concerned the construction of Acts of Parliament.

The Administration of Justice Act 1969 introduced a 'leap-frog' procedure, allowing appeals to bypass the Court of Appeal and go directly from the trial court to the House of Lords. A leapfrog appeal is only possible if two conditions are satisfied:[144]

(1) The trial judge must grant a certificate (with the consent of all parties) that the case involves a point of law of general public importance. The point of law must either relate wholly or mainly to the construction of an enactment, or it must be one in respect of which the judge would be bound by a previous decision of the Court of Appeal or House of Lords; and

(2) The House of Lords must grant leave.

Criminal cases. The House of Lords' jurisdiction in criminal cases is of comparatively modern origin, and it was not until the Court of Criminal Appeal was created in 1907[145] that there was any general right to appeal to the Lords in a criminal case. The right of appeal from the Queen's Bench Divisional Court was created by the Administration of Justice Act 1960, and appeal also lies from the High Court, the Courts-Martial Appeal Court, and the Court of Appeal of Northern Ireland.[146] There is no right of appeal to the House of Lords from Scotland's highest criminal court, the High Court of Justiciary.

3 REFORM: A SUPREME COURT FOR THE UNITED KINGDOM

On 12 June 2003 the government unexpectedly announced that it planned to transfer the jurisdiction of the House of Lords' Appellate Committee to a new Supreme Court. This was to be part of a package of measures aimed at modernizing the constitution and ensuring a more formal separation of powers. Other parts of the package included reforming the office of Lord Chancellor,[147] the creation of a government department with administrative responsibility for most major courts,[148] and the creation of an independent Judicial Appointments Commission.[149] A consultation paper explained that the idea behind the proposed new court was to formally separate the judiciary from Parliament and the executive. 'Transparency of independence' was cited as the key issue:[150]

> The considerable growth of judicial review in recent years has inevitably brought the judges more into the political eye. It is essential that our systems do all that they can to minimise the danger that judges' decisions could be perceived to be politically

[144] Sections 12 and 13.

[145] Criminal Appeal Act 1907. The jurisdiction of this court was transferred to the Criminal Division of the Court of Appeal by the Criminal Appeal Act 1966.

[146] The conditions required for an appeal are discussed at p 730, *post*.

[147] Department for Constitutional Affairs, *Constitutional Reform: Reforming the Office of the Lord Chancellor* (2003) CP 13/03. The original proposal was for abolition; see p 19, *ante*.

[148] The Department for Constitutional Affairs (DCA); ibid.

[149] DCA, *Constitutional Reform: A New Way of Appointing Judges* (2003) CP 10/03; see p 338, *post*.

[150] DCA, *Constitutional Reform: A Supreme Court for the United Kingdom* (2003) CP 11/03, at para 1.2. The proposed reforms were considered sufficiently fundamental for at least one journal to devote an entire edition to the issue: (2004) 24 Legal Studies.

motivated. The Human Rights Act 1998, itself the product of a changing climate of opinion, has made people more sensitive to the issues and more aware of the anomaly of the position whereby the highest court of appeal is situated within one of the chambers of Parliament.

In its published response to the consultation paper,[151] the Judges' Council broadly accepted the proposals, whilst making it clear that not all of its members were convinced of the need for change. The main area of disagreement concerned the proposal to remove the senior judges from the legislature entirely:[152]

> While the House of Lords remains wholly, or mainly, an appointed (rather than elected) body there is a strong case for the Lord Chief Justice of England and Wales, the Lord President of the Court of Session, the Lord Chief Justice of Northern Ireland and the President of the Supreme Court being members. It would not be sensible to exclude from a House of Lords those best placed to contribute to debates on the justice system and the judiciary. All other members of the Supreme Court, should cease to exercise any rights they may have to speak or vote in the House while they serve as judges.

The final blueprint for the new Court was included in the Constitutional Reform Act 2005. The Act reflects most of the preferences expressed by the Judges' Council as to the Court's membership, size, composition, and jurisdiction.[153] Crucially, however, the recommendation that some senior judges should continue to sit in the House of Lords has not been adopted. Section 23 provides that 'there is to be a Supreme Court of the United Kingdom', and that it shall consist of twelve judges.[154] The Court will be properly constituted when an uneven number of not less than three judges is sitting, more than half of whom must be permanent members.[155] The current Lords of Appeal will become the first members of the new Court, and at this point they will cease to be entitled to sit in Parliament.[156] They will be called 'Justices of the Supreme Court',[157] and the Court's two most senior members will hold the offices of President and Deputy President.[158] The President will be able to supplement the Court's permanent membership by asking other senior judges to sit on a temporary basis. Former Law Lords and Supreme Court Justices will also be eligible to sit.[159]

The Supreme Court will not be able to strike down legislation as unconstitutional or contrary to the ECHR, and its jurisdiction will be broadly the same as that currently exercised by the House of Lords.[160] It will, however, inherit jurisdiction over devolution matters from the Privy Council.[161] As it will hear appeals from all parts of the UK it will remain legally separate from the existing courts of England and Wales.

---

[151] Judges' Council Response to the Consultation Papers on Constitutional Reform (available online at www.dca.gov.uk/judicial/pdfs/jcresp.pdf). The Law Lords' response is discussed at p 338, *post*.

[152] Ibid, at para 17.

[153] Some of the Council's recommendations were *not* adopted. For example, the Act does not include provisions making the Lord Chief Justice, Master of the Rolls, Lord President of the Court of Session, and Lord Chief Justice of Northern Ireland *ex officio* members of the new court; nor does it prevent leapfrog appeals from the High Court in criminal cases.

[154] This number may be varied by Order in Council, subject to an affirmative resolution procedure.

[155] Section 42.   [156] Sections 24 and 137.   [157] Section 23(6).

[158] Sections 23(5) and 24.   [159] Sections 38 and 39.   [160] Section 40.

[161] Section 40(4)(b); Schedule 9. The Privy Council's jurisdiction is discussed at p 280, *post*.

Although the Constitutional Reform Act was passed in 2005, the provisions establishing the Supreme Court will not be brought into force until it can be properly housed.[162] The venue selected for the new Court is Middlesex Guildhall on London's Parliament Square, and work on the building is due to be completed in time for it to open in October 2009.

THE COURT OF APPEAL

The English superior courts were completely reorganized by the Supreme Court of Judicature Acts 1873–1875. The Acts created the Supreme Court of Judicature[163] and transferred to it the jurisdiction of the existing superior courts: the appellate jurisdiction was transferred to the Court of Appeal and the original jurisdiction was transferred to the High Court. The Crown Court was added to the list by the Courts Act 1971. The Supreme Court now consists of three courts: the Court of Appeal, the High Court, and the Crown Court. The relevant law is consolidated in the Supreme Court Act 1981.

1 CONSTITUTION

The Court of Appeal is split into Civil and Criminal Divisions, and is composed of a number of *ex officio* judges along with the Lord and Lady Justices of Appeal.[164] The *ex officio* judges comprise the Lord Chief Justice, the Master of the Rolls, the Presidents of the Queen's Bench and Family Divisions of the High Court, the Chancellor of the High Court, former Lord Chancellors,[165] and the Lords of Appeal in Ordinary.[166] Of these, only the Master of the Rolls (in civil cases) and the Lord Chief Justice (in criminal cases) usually sit, and they are in fact the Presidents of the Civil and Criminal Divisions respectively. In addition to the regular judges of the Court, any High Court judge or circuit judge may be required to sit.[167] Former High Court and Court of Appeal judges may also be asked to sit, but they cannot be compelled to do so.

The Civil Division may be duly constituted with only one judge present, but most cases are heard by three judges sitting together.[168] As to the Criminal Division, at least

---

[162] Section 148(4).

[163] Renamed 'the Supreme Court of England and Wales' by the Supreme Court Act 1981. It will become 'the Senior Courts of England and Wales' when the new Supreme Court is established: see above.

[164] Supreme Court Act 1981, s 2. Section 2(3) was amended by the Courts Act 2003 to permit the use of the title 'Lady Justice of Appeal' where appropriate. The maximum number of ordinary Court of Appeal judges is thirty-seven: Maximum Number of Judges Order, SI 2002/2837.

[165] Only those who held this office before 12 June 2003: see further, pp 19 and 318.

[166] The Court has sometimes been composed of three Law Lords: see *Mallett* v *Restormel Borough Council* [1978] 2 All ER 1057. The Lords of Appeal will become 'Justices of the Supreme Court' when the new Court is established.

[167] Supreme Court Act 1981, s 9: note that circuit judges can only sit in the Criminal Division.

[168] Ibid, s 54(2), as amended. The Master of the Rolls may give directions about the minimum number of judges needed for (a) any description of proceedings, or (b) any particular proceedings; s 54(3)–(4A).

two judges must be present to hear appeals against sentence,[169] and three or more judges are required for any of the following:[170]

(a) an appeal against conviction;

(b) an appeal against a verdict of not guilty by reason of insanity;

(c) an appeal against a finding of unfitness to plead;

(d) an application for leave to appeal to the House of Lords;

(e) a refusal of leave to appeal against conviction (or against any of the verdicts and findings referred to above), unless the application has already been refused by a single judge; or

(f) a review of a sentencing decision which has been referred by the Attorney-General under Part IV of the Criminal Justice Act 1988.

In addition, a single judge of the Criminal Division has jurisdiction under the Criminal Appeal Act 1968 to hear certain types of application; notably for leave to appeal.[171] Either division may occasionally convene a 'full court' of five or more members to hear appeals involving novel or difficult points of law. However, such a court has no wider powers than the normal court.

2 JURISDICTION

The Court of Appeal has consisted of a Civil and a Criminal Division since 1 October 1966, which is when the Criminal Appeal Act 1966 came into operation.

(a) Civil Division

The Civil Division exercises:

(a) all jurisdiction conferred on it by the Supreme Court Act 1981 or any other Act; and

(b) all jurisdiction exercisable by it prior to the commencement of the 1981 Act.[172]

Its jurisdiction is entirely civil and entirely appellate. Until recently, appeals in civil cases from both the county court and the High Court were generally heard by the Court of Appeal, but in 1997 a review carried out by Sir Jeffrey Bowman concluded that the Civil Division's workload was unnecessarily high.[173] Two of the Review's most important recommendations were that:

(a) any appeal against the first instance decision of a civil court should normally require leave;[174] and

---

[169] Ibid, s 55(4).   [170] Ibid; there must be an odd number. For details, see p 729, *post*.

[171] Section 31, as amended.   [172] Supreme Court Act 1981, s 15(2).

[173] *Report to the Lord Chancellor by the Review of the Court of Appeal* (Lord Chancellor's Department, 1997); see also Jacob J, 'Bowman Review of the Court of Appeal' (1998) 61(3) MLR 390. Similar recommendations were made in Woolf's *Final Report on Access to Justice* (1996).

[174] The Review recommended that an appeal should still be as of right in cases where the liberty of the subject was at stake, and in certain cases involving children.

(b) more appeals should be dealt with at a lower level, the guiding principle being simply that the judge or court hearing an appeal should have a superior jurisdiction to the first instance decision maker.

The main aim of these proposals was to reduce the workload of the Civil Division and to improve the speed and overall efficiency of the appeals process.

Reform under the Access to Justice Act 1999. The Bowman recommendations were broadly implemented by the Access to Justice Act 1999 and the Civil Procedure Rules, Part 52.[175] Under section 56 of the Act the Lord Chancellor is empowered to make more detailed rules for the allocation of civil appeals by way of statutory instrument.[176] Appeals against many county court decisions are now dealt with by High Court judges, whilst the Court of Appeal continues to hear appeals against final decisions in multi-track[177] and specialist proceedings cases.[178] In addition, there is a discretion to allow any civil appeal which would normally be heard by a lower court to be dealt with instead by the Court of Appeal.[179]

Any second appeal against the decision of a county court or High Court judge will also lie to the Court of Appeal, but second appeals can only be granted exceptionally and the Court of Appeal must be satisfied that either:

(a) the appeal would raise an important point of principle or practice; or

(b) there is some other compelling reason for hearing it.[180]

Finally, the Civil Division has jurisdiction to hear appeals on points of law from the Employment Appeal Tribunal and various other tribunals.

The appeal itself normally takes the form of a limited review unless the court considers that it would be in the interests of justice to hold a rehearing, or exceptionally, to order a new trial.[181] The appeals system applicable to civil cases is discussed further in chapter 18 of this book.

(b) Criminal Division

The Criminal Division of the Court of Appeal was established by the Criminal Appeal Act 1966 as the successor to the Court of Criminal Appeal.[182] Its jurisdiction is entirely

---

[175] SI 1998/3132, as inserted by SI 2000/221; in force since 2 May 2000. For a discussion of the key changes, see *Tanfern Ltd* v *Cameron-MacDonald* [2000] 2 All ER 801, [2000] 1 WLR 1311.

[176] An Order pursuant to this provision has been made: see the Access to Justice Act 1999 (Destination of Appeals) Order 2000, SI 2000/1071.

[177] Ibid, Article 4. Multi-track cases are discussed at p 496, *post*.

[178] Ibid. Specialist proceedings are those involving the Patents Court or Technology and Construction Court, commercial proceedings, admiralty matters, and proceedings under the Companies Acts.

[179] 1999 Act, s 57. This discretion may be exercised by either the Master of the Rolls or a court involved in the case.

[180] Ibid, s 55(1); SI 2000/1071, Article 5.

[181] Civil Procedure Rules, Part 52. The difference between a review and a re-hearing is considered in *Assicurazoni Generali Spa* v *Arab Insurance Group* [2002] EWCA Civ 1642, [2003] 1 WLR 577.

[182] Established by the Criminal Appeal Act 1907, to supersede the Court for Crown Cases Reserved.

criminal and entirely appellate. Its principal function is to hear appeals against conviction and sentence from persons convicted in the Crown Court. It can also consider sentencing decisions referred by the Attorney-General on the grounds that they are unduly lenient.[183] In addition, where a trial on indictment has ended in a conviction, a finding of not guilty by reason of insanity, or a finding that a person did the act in question but is under a disability, the case can be referred by the Criminal Cases Review Commission for determination as an appeal.[184]

Where a trial on indictment has ended in acquittal, the Attorney-General has the power to refer points of law arising from the case to the Court of Appeal.[185] However, the purpose of such a reference is simply to clarify the law for future cases, and the Court of Appeal's opinion on the matter does not affect the outcome for the defendant. Indeed, before the Criminal Justice Act 2003, a jury's decision to acquit a defendant was final and could not be challenged by the prosecution. However, the 2003 Act gives prosecutors new powers to appeal against the outcome of a trial on indictment. They can ask the Court of Appeal to quash an acquittal and order a re-trial, where a person has been tried for a qualifying offence and certain conditions are met.[186] The first such application was made in the case of *R* v *D*.[187] While serving a prison sentence for an unrelated offence, the defendant had admitted to prison officers that he had committed a murder for which he had previously been tried and acquitted. An application to quash his acquittal was granted, and the defendant subsequently pleaded guilty to murder. Prosecutors can also appeal against a judge's decision to terminate a prosecution or to make an evidentiary ruling which significantly weakens their case.[188] A more detailed discussion of the criminal appeals system is set out in chapter 25 of this book.

THE HIGH COURT

1   CONSTITUTION

The High Court was established by the Supreme Court of Judicature Acts 1873–75 and to it was transferred the jurisdiction of several existing superior courts. These included the three superior common law courts of first instance, the Court of Chancery, and the Courts of Admiralty, Probate, and Divorce and Matrimonial Causes.[189] The constitution

---

[183]   Criminal Justice Act 1988, s 36; see p 716, *post*.
[184]   Criminal Appeal Act 1995, s 9: see p 716, *post*. This power was formerly exercisable by the Home Secretary: Criminal Appeal Act 1968, s 17.
[185]   Criminal Justice Act 1972, s 36; see p 720, *post*.
[186]   2003 Act, s 76(1): see p 721, *post*. 'Qualifying offences' are listed in Schedule 5, part 1. For a more detailed analysis see Ward and Davies, *Criminal Justice Act 2003: A Practitioners' Guide* (2004).
[187]   [2006] EWCA Crim 1354, [2007] 1 WLR 1657, [2007] 1 All ER 593. See further, p 722, *post*.
[188]   Sections 58 and 62.
[189]   The jurisdiction of the Chancery Courts of the Counties Palatine of Lancaster and Durham was *not* transferred, but these courts were merged with the High Court under s 41 of the Courts Act 1971.

and jurisdiction of the High Court are now governed by the Supreme Court Act 1981. The court sits primarily in London, but by virtue of section 71 of the Act sittings may be conducted at any place in England or Wales.[190] The centres at which sittings are actually held are determined in accordance with the Lord Chancellor's directions, and ad hoc directions may be given to enable the Court to sit at a particular location. Thus, in a case concerning a disputed right of way in Iken, a small village in Suffolk,[191] the Lord Chancellor authorized the Court to sit at Iken so that the evidence of an elderly witness could be taken.

2 JURISDICTION

The jurisdiction of the High Court is both civil and criminal. In civil actions its jurisdiction is virtually unlimited and it is broadly concurrent with that of the county courts. However, there is a minimum financial limit for the value of claims that can be commenced in the High Court, and subject to any statutory exceptions this is currently £50,000 for personal injury actions, and £15,000 for other cases.[192] For claims exceeding these limits proceedings can be commenced in either court, and there are provisions for transferring appropriate cases from one court to the other.[193] Following the Woolf reforms, the allocation of cases between the High Court and the county courts now depends not only on the sums involved, but also on whether they are designated as 'small claims', 'fast track', or 'multi track' cases.[194] These reforms are the subject of more detailed analysis in chapter 16, but for present purposes it is sufficient to note that the majority of the High Court's workload now consists of multi-track cases, and most civil actions continue to be determined at county court level.

In addition to its original jurisdiction in civil cases, the High Court also has both appellate and supervisory functions. The historic role of the courts in supervising the actions of inferior bodies and tribunals has already been noted,[195] and this role is now performed mainly by a Divisional Court of the Queen's Bench Division. All three divisions of the High Court also have an appellate role, and this has increased since the restructuring of the civil appeals system in 1999.[196]

3 THE DIVISIONS

The High Court initially consisted of five divisions, but these were reduced in 1880 to the three that currently exist:[197] the Chancery Division, the Queen's Bench Division, and

---

[190] Evidence may be taken outside the jurisdiction. In *Tito* v *Waddell* [1975] 3 All ER 997, [1975] 1 WLR 1303 the judge visited two Pacific islands in order to view land at the centre of a legal dispute.

[191] *St Edmundsbury and Ipswich Diocesan Board of Finance* v *Clark* [1973] Ch 323, [1973] 2 All ER 1155.

[192] High Court and County Courts Jurisdiction Order 1991, SI 1991/724; High Court and County Courts Jurisdiction (Amendment) Order 1999, SI 1999/1014.

[193] CPR, Part 30.   [194] See p 496, *post*.

[195] See p 214, *ante*.   [196] See p 529, *post*.

[197] See now, the Supreme Court Act 1981, s 5. Section 7 of the Act provides that the number of divisions may be increased or reduced on the recommendation of the senior judges specified in s 7(2).

the Family Division.[198] Each division handles a different type of subject matter, though it is important to note that the divisions are of equal competence and they are not separate courts. Indeed, the inherent jurisdiction of the High Court judge may be exercised by a judge of any division,[199] and the fact that a matter falls within a particular division's class of business does not necessarily mean that that the matter must be allocated accordingly.[200] Moreover, in certain cases the jurisdiction of the divisions overlaps, and this means that claimants sometimes have a choice about where to commence their actions. Many actions for professional negligence for example, can be commenced in either the Queen's Bench Division or the Chancery Division.[201] Nevertheless, the overall effect of the relevant statutes and rules of procedure is to confer a distinct jurisdiction upon each division,[202] and suggestions that the divisions should be merged have thus far been rejected.[203]

(a) Chancery Division

The business of the Chancery Division is carried out by the Chancellor of the High Court and seventeen puisne judges.[204] Before 1972, sittings of the Chancery Division were held only in the Royal Courts of Justice in London, and Chancery judges did not go on assize. The Supreme Court Act 1981 authorizes sittings of the High Court to be held anywhere in England and Wales,[205] but most Chancery business is still heard in London.[206]

Jurisdiction. Section 34 of the Supreme Court of Judicature Act 1873 gave the Chancery Division jurisdiction over matters which were previously heard in the Court of Chancery. The distribution of High Court business is now governed by section 61 and Schedule 1 of the Supreme Court Act 1981, and under these provisions the Chancery Division is assigned jurisdiction over all causes and matters concerning:

(a) the sale, exchange or partition of land, or the raising of charges on land;

(b) the redemption or foreclosure of mortgages;

(c) the execution of trusts;

---

[198] The Family Division was originally called the Probate, Divorce and Admiralty Division, but was renamed by the Administration of Justice Act 1970, s 1. Its Admiralty jurisdiction was reassigned to the Queen's Bench Division and contentious probate business was assigned to the Chancery Division.

[199] Supreme Court Act 1981, s 5(5): see *Re L* [1968] P 119, [1968] 1 All ER 20.   [200] Ibid.

[201] The contract disputes in *Petrofina (Great Britain) Ltd* v *Martin* [1965] Ch 1073, [1965] 2 All ER 176 and *Esso Petroleum Co Ltd* v *Harper's Garage (Stourport) Ltd* [1965] 3 WLR 469, [1965] 2 All ER 933 may also be considered in this context. The two cases concerned very similar issues, yet the former was tried in the Chancery Division and the latter in the Queen's Bench Division.

[202] For the distribution of business between the divisions, see Supreme Court Act 1981, s 61 and Schedule 1.

[203] See, e.g. Woolf, *Final Report on Access to Justice* (1996), at p 261.

[204] *Judicial Statistics 2005*, p 129. The Lord Chancellor has historically been head of the Division but modern Lord Chancellors have rarely sat at first instance. When Lord Falconer was appointed in 2003 he announced that he did not intend to sit at all, and Part 2 of the Constitutional Reform Act 2005 has formally stripped the Lord Chancellor of all judicial functions: see pp 20 and 301. The Act also replaces the title Vice-Chancellor with that of 'Chancellor of the High Court'; Schedule 4, para 115.

[205] Section 71(1).

[206] Cases are also heard in Birmingham, Bristol, Cardiff, Leeds, Liverpool, Manchester, Newcastle-upon-Tyne, and Preston.

(d) the administration of estates of deceased persons;

(e) bankruptcy;

(f) the dissolution of partnerships or the taking of partnership or other accounts;

(g) the rectification, setting aside or cancellation of deeds or other instruments in writing;

(h) probate business, other than non-contentious or common form business;

(i) patents, trade marks, registered designs or copyright;

(j) the appointment of a guardian of a minor's estate; and

(k) matters relating company law.

Various other statutes and rules of procedure give the Chancery Division jurisdiction over revenue matters, town and country planning, and landlord and tenant disputes.

The appellate jurisdiction of the Chancery Division has always been limited, and has primarily related to taxation, insolvency and land registration. As stated previously, however, reforms since 1999 mean that many more appeals from county court decisions can now be determined at High Court level. The implications of these changes are discussed further in chapter 18, but their overall effect is to extend the appellate jurisdiction of all three divisions of the High Court to cover a broader spectrum of cases.

Patents Court. The Patents Court is part of the Chancery Division and is one of a number of 'specialist courts' within the High Court. It was established by the Patents Act 1977 and hears patent actions at first instance and on appeal from the Comptroller-General of Patents, Designs and Trademarks.

(b) Queen's Bench Division

At the time of writing, the Queen's Bench Division has seventy-two puisne judges[207] and is headed by the President of the Queen's Bench Division.[208] It has both a civil and a criminal jurisdiction, and performs original, appellate, and supervisory functions.

Civil jurisdiction. The most important aspect of this Division's business is its first instance jurisdiction over civil matters, and most of its workload consists of actions in contract and tort. Its role in the civil appeals system has always been very limited, though High Court judges of all divisions were given a greater appellate jurisdiction when the system was restructured in 1999.[209] In addition, a Divisional Court of the Queen's Bench Division, consisting of two or more judges, has a limited civil jurisdiction to hear appeals by way of case stated from the Crown Court and magistrates' courts.[210]

---

[207] *Judicial Statistics 2005*, p 129.

[208] Supreme Court Act 1981, s 5. Prior to implementation of the Constitutional Reform Act 2005, the Lord Chief Justice was head of the Division.

[209] See p 530, *post*.

[210] Appeals from magistrates' courts in family cases lie to the Family Division.

Commercial Court. This court has jurisdiction over commercial matters, and like the Patents Court, it is a specialist court operating within a division of the High Court. It was officially designated as a court by the Administration of Justice Act 1970,[211] though a 'commercial list' of cases has been maintained since 1895. The Court has its own rules of procedure[212] and is served by nominated puisne judges with particular expertise in this area of law.

Admiralty Court. This is also a specialist court, and it has jurisdiction over matters assigned to the Queen's Bench Division by section 20 of the Supreme Court Act 1981. Its business includes actions to enforce claims for damages arising out of collisions between ships, claims to the possession or ownership of ships, claims for loss of or damage to goods carried in a ship, towage claims, and other specified proceedings. When trying admiralty actions the judge often sits with lay assessors.

Technology and Construction Court. Since 1998 this specialist court has been responsible for dealing with disputes involving construction, engineering, surveying, and similar matters, along with certain cases concerning information technology, the sale of goods, trespass, and nuisance.[213] However, a dispute will only warrant allocation to this court if it involves technically complex questions of fact.

As a final point, it should be noted that judges of the Queen's Bench Division also exercise many other functions. Not only do they handle most of the business of the Criminal Division of the Court of Appeal, they also sit in the Courts-Martial Appeal Court and determine disputed parliamentary elections when sitting as an election court.[214] In addition, the 'first-tier' jurisdiction of the Crown Court is exercised principally by judges from this Division.[215]

Criminal jurisdiction. The criminal jurisdiction of the High Court is exercised exclusively by the Queen's Bench Division and is entirely appellate. It comprises appeals by way of 'case stated'[216] from magistrates' courts, and also from the Crown Court when acting in its capacity as an appellate court. These appeals are heard by a Queen's Bench Divisional Court consisting of at least two but often three judges.

Supervisory jurisdiction. The supervisory jurisdiction of the Queen's Bench Division is also exercised by a Divisional Court. It includes the power to make mandatory orders, prohibition orders, and quashing orders,[217] which compel inferior courts and tribunals to exercise their powers properly and within the scope of their authority (intra vires).

---

[211] Section 3(1).   [212] See CPR, parts 49 and 58, and the accompanying *Practice Direction 58.*

[213] Supreme Court Act 1981, s 68 and Schedule 2, as amended by the Civil Procedure Act 1997. The matters dealt with by the court were formally known as 'Official Referee's Business'.

[214] Representation of the People Act 1983, s 120. This is not actually part of the Queen's Bench Division: indeed, it is an inferior court and is therefore subject to judicial review (*R v Cripps, ex parte Muldoon* [1984] QB 68, [1984] 3 All ER 72).

[215] See p 258, *post.*

[216] Magistrates' Courts Act 1980, s 111; Supreme Court Act 1981, ss 28 and 28A. For details of the procedure, see p 684, *post.*

[217] Formerly known as orders of mandamus, prohibition, and certiorari.

It also includes the power to issue the prerogative writ of habeas corpus. The Division's supervisory jurisdiction is exercised through the procedure known as 'judicial review', which is currently governed by Part 54 of the Civil Procedure Rules.[218] These cases used to be dealt with as part of the Crown Office list, but the group of increasingly specialized judges who determine judicial review matters is now known as 'the Administrative Court'.[219]

(c) Family Division

The Family Division[220] consists of the President and nineteen nominated puisne judges,[221] who are assisted in their work by a number of district judges. Its jurisdiction is set out in the Supreme Court Act 1981, and is both original and appellate. The following functions are assigned to it by Schedule 1 of the Act:

(a) all High Court matrimonial causes and matters (whether at first instance or on appeal);

(b) all causes and matters (whether at first instance or on appeal) relating to:

   (i) legitimacy;

   (ii) the exercise of the inherent jurisdiction of the High Court with respect to minors, the maintenance of minors and any proceedings under the Children Act 1989, except proceedings solely for the appointment of a guardian of a minor's estate;

   (iii) adoption;

   (iv) non-contentious or common-form probate business;

(c) applications for consent to the marriage of a minor;

(d) proceedings on appeal from an order or decision made under section 63(3) of the Magistrates' Courts Act 1980 to enforce an order of a magistrates' court made in matrimonial proceedings or with respect to the guardianship of a minor;

(e) certain proceedings under the Family Law Act 1986;

(f) proceedings under the Children Act 1989;

(g) certain proceedings under the Childcare Act 2006;

(h) certain proceedings under the Gender Recognition Act 2004;

(i) civil partnership causes and matters; and

(j) proceedings under various other statutory provisions.[222]

---

[218] This replaces RSC, Ord 53: for more detail, see chapter 7.

[219] *Practice Direction (Administrative Court: Establishment)* [2000] 4 All ER 1071, [2000] 1 WLR 1654.

[220] Prior to the Administration of Justice Act 1970, it was known as the Probate, Divorce and Admiralty Division. Sir Alan Herbert described the jurisdiction as 'wills, wives and wrecks': of these, 'wills' have gone to the Chancery Division, and 'wrecks' (other than the wrecks of marriages) to the Queen's Bench Division.

[221] Supreme Court Act 1981, s 5; *Judicial Statistics 2005*, p 129. The President of the Family Division also holds the title of Head of Family Justice: Constitutional Reform Act 2005, s 9.

[222] Family Law Acts 1986 and 1996; Child Abduction and Custody Act 1985; Human Fertilisation and Embryology Act 1990; Welfare Reform and Pensions Act 1999; Child Support Act 1991.

The effect of these provisions is to give the Division exclusive High Court jurisdiction over matrimonial disputes and children, thus avoiding the conflicts which used to arise between the Family and Chancery Divisions before 1970.[223]

For proceedings arising under the Children Act 1989, magistrates' courts, county courts, and the Family Division each have jurisdiction.[224] The distribution of work between the three courts is governed by an order made by the Lord Chancellor,[225] which also provides for the transfer of cases between the three courts. In addition, the Courts Act 2003 establishes a Family Procedure Rule Committee with the power to make Family Procedure Rules governing practice and procedure across all three courts.[226] The creation of a single Family Court has now been adopted as a long-term government objective.[227]

The appellate business of the Family Division consists largely of appeals from family courts concerning matrimonial causes and children.

COUNTY COURTS

1 CONSTITUTION

The county courts were established by the County Courts Act 1846 to meet the need for a system to deal with small claims. There are currently 218 county courts in England and Wales, each serving a particular district. Every county court district is assigned at least one circuit judge and one district judge, and deputy district judges may also be appointed.[228] In theory, even High Court and Court of Appeal judges may be asked to sit,[229] but it is rare for such senior judges to be used in this capacity.

2 JURISDICTION

The jurisdiction of the county courts is entirely civil, and in terms of subject matter it is broadly concurrent with the civil jurisdiction of the High Court. Thus the County Courts Act 1984 gives them jurisdiction over cases involving tort, contract, land, equity, family law, probate, and even admiralty, whilst other statutes confer jurisdiction in matters such as discrimination, divorce, landlord and tenant, and insolvency.[230] However, as county courts owe their origins entirely to statute they only have jurisdiction in matters specifically assigned to them by legislation. They do not, for example, have any inherent

---

[223] See, e.g. *Hall* v *Hall* [1963] P 378, [1963] 2 All ER 140.   [224] Children Act 1989, s 92.

[225] Children (Allocation of Proceedings) Order 1991, SI 1991/1677, as amended. See also, the Family Law Act 1996 (Part IV) (Allocation of Proceedings) Order 1997, SI 1997/1896.

[226] Sections 75–81.

[227] DCA, *A Single Civil Court? Responses to the Consultation* (2005) CP(R) 06/05, at p 42.

[228] County Courts Act 1984, ss 1, 5, 6, and 8.   [229] Ibid, s 5.

[230] See, e.g. Race Relations Act 1976, s 57; Sex Discrimination Act 1975, s 66; Matrimonial and Family Proceedings Act 1984, s 33; Rent Act 1977, s 141; Insolvency Act 1986, ss 117 and 373.

jurisdiction to conduct judicial review proceedings; nor can they grant the associated prerogative remedies.[231]

Not all county courts deal with the full range of cases eligible for determination at this level: almost a quarter do not have jurisdiction to hear divorce petitions, and over a third do not deal with insolvency matters. In addition, some county courts have been designated as specialist centres for dealing with particular types of action. For example, whilst all county courts have jurisdiction to hear proceedings under the Children Act 1989, a number have been designated as specialist 'family hearing centres' to which difficult cases may be transferred.[232] One county court in London even specializes in patent cases. There is also a Bulk Centre at Northampton County Court, which processes computer-generated debt recovery claims from major claimants such as public utilities and mail order companies. The same court also processes a large volume of claims for unpaid car parking charges.

There are two further limitations on the county courts' jurisdiction, the first of which is geographical. Unlike the High Court, which is a single court with the jurisdiction to sit anywhere in England and Wales, each county court is a separate entity serving a particular district. Although most claims can be commenced in any county court, a defended action to recover a sum of money will normally be transferred to the defendant's home district. Other claims may also be transferred at the court's discretion.[233]

The second limitation is a financial one. County courts were created primarily to handle minor civil actions such as the recovery of small debts, and until 1991 their jurisdiction in tort and contract was limited to claims involving £5,000 or less. Reforms under the Courts and Legal Services Act 1990 led to this upper ceiling being removed,[234] and the emphasis shifted to setting *minimum* financial limits for cases commenced in the High Court. Cases involving less than £25,000 generally had to be commenced at county court level. Further reforms since 1999 mean that the allocation of cases between the two courts now depends not only on the financial value of the claim, but also on whether it is designated as a 'small claims', 'fast track', or 'multi track' case.[235] The allocation and management of civil cases is discussed further in chapters 15 and 16, but in essence, 'small claims' (involving less than £5,000) continue to be dealt with by the county courts, and other actions involving less than £15,000 (or £50,000 for personal injuries) must also begin life at this level. Most claims for higher amounts can be commenced in either court, and the decision about where a case is ultimately determined depends not only on the sums involved, but also on the importance and complexity of the issues. County courts now have unlimited jurisdiction in tort, contract, and land cases, but financial limits are still in place for certain other types of action. For example, in equity matters and contentious probate cases, the upper limit is currently £30,000.[236]

---

[231] See chapter 7.
[232] Children (Allocation of Proceedings) Order 1991, SI 1991/1677, as amended. The designated centres are listed in Schedule 1 of the Order.
[233] CPR, rr 30.2 and 26.2.
[234] Section 1; High Court and County Courts Jurisdiction Order 1991, SI 1991/724.
[235] See p 496, *post*.
[236] This is the effect of the County Courts Jurisdiction Order 1981, SI 1981/1123.

Finally, it should be noted that although the jurisdiction of the county courts is largely original, circuit judges do have jurisdiction to hear appeals from the decisions of district judges.[237]

THE CROWN COURT

1 CREATION OF THE CROWN COURT

The Crown Court was created by the Courts Act 1971 and came into operation on 1 January 1972. Before this date trials on indictment took place at quarter sessions or assizes. Both quarter sessions and assizes had local jurisdiction and were generally confined to dealing with offences that had been committed locally.

The assize courts were grouped into circuits and did not sit continuously: judges were sent out on circuit by royal commission and sat at each assize town for the duration of the assize. Their jurisdiction was equivalent to that of the High Court and at least two Queen's Bench Division judges were usually named in the commissions. County court judges and Queen's Counsel were also included, and even the Master of the Rolls and Lord Justices of Appeal could theoretically be asked to sit. The assize courts generally dealt with the most serious criminal offences, though they also handled a certain amount of civil work. Less serious offences tried on indictment were dealt with at quarter sessions. These were held four times a year at almost 150 different courts, and like the assizes they dealt with both civil and criminal cases. Quarter sessions also had jurisdiction to hear appeals from the decisions of magistrates' courts, and to sentence persons committed for sentencing following summary conviction. The whole of this jurisdiction was subsequently transferred to the Crown Court.

Before leaving the pre-1972 system, three other courts should also be mentioned. The Central Criminal Court – popularly known as the 'Old Bailey' – was the assize court with jurisdiction over indictable offences committed in Greater London and on the high seas. In addition, the Criminal Justice Administration Act 1956 established Crown Courts in Liverpool and Manchester. These courts exercised a criminal jurisdiction equivalent to that of the assizes and quarter sessions in their respective areas.

This plethora of courts with workloads determined largely by historical factors led to the establishment of a Royal Commission chaired by Lord Beeching. The Commission's recommendations[238] formed the basis for the system introduced by the Courts Act 1971. The Act abolished all courts of assize and quarter sessions, including the Crown Courts of Liverpool and Manchester and the Central Criminal Court in London.[239] It replaced

---

[237] See p 496, *post.*

[238] See *Report of the Royal Commission on Assizes and Quarter Sessions*, Cmnd 4153, 1969.

[239] The latter has been retained in name, however, as s 8(3) of the Supreme Court Act 1981 provides for the Crown Court to be known as the Central Criminal Court when sitting in London. The same section preserves the right of the Lord Mayor and Aldermen of the City to sit as judges with any High Court judge, circuit judge,

them with a single court, to be known as the Crown Court, which is part of the Supreme Court of England and Wales[240] and a superior court of record.[241] Its constitution and jurisdiction are now governed by the Supreme Court Act 1981.

2 CONSTITUTION

As already indicated, the essential feature of the Crown Court is that it has a national jurisdiction. There are not various Crown Courts throughout the country: there is just one Crown Court, sittings of which may be held anywhere, at any time.[242] There are currently seventy-eight permanent Crown Court centres in England and Wales,[243] and for administrative purposes they are grouped into six circuits. Each centre falls into one of three categories:

(1) 'First tier' centres – these deal with the full range of Crown Court business and also provide a venue for High Court judges to handle some of their civil work;

(2) 'Second tier' centres – these deal with the full range of the Crown Court's criminal work; and

(3) 'Third-tier' centres – High Court judges do not usually visit third-tier centres, which means that the workload of these venues is generally confined to less serious criminal cases.

The Supreme Court Act 1981 provides that the Crown Court's jurisdiction may be exercised by High Court judges, circuit judges, recorders, and district judges from magistrates' courts.[244] Deputy circuit judges may also be appointed.[245] The most serious or difficult cases are usually reserved for High Court judges, who in practice are almost invariably drawn from the Queen's Bench Division.[246] In addition to the regular judges of the Court, any judge of the Court of Appeal and any former Court of Appeal or puisne judge may also be asked to sit, though they cannot be compelled to do so.[247] Crown Court judges normally sit alone, but when hearing appeals from magistrates' courts they must sit with between two and four justices of the peace.[248] A judge may also sit with justices of the peace when hearing a case on indictment, unless the case has been listed for a plea of not guilty.[249] Where justices do sit they must play a full part in all decisions, and in the event of disagreement the decision of the majority prevails.[250]

recorder or district judge (magistrates' courts). The reasons for this are unclear, but a seat in the Old Bailey is still traditionally left vacant for the Lord Mayor.

[240] See p 255, *ante*.

[241] Supreme Court Act 1981, ss 1, 45(1). When exercising its appellate jurisdiction the Crown Court is subject to the High Court's supervisory jurisdiction as if it were an inferior court: s 29(3) (see p 221, *ante*). It is not, however, subject to this jurisdiction in matters relating to trial on indictment.

[242] Ibid, s 78.

[243] There are also several satellite centres, bringing the current number of locations to 92: *Judicial Statistics 2005*, at p 80.

[244] Section 8.   [245] Courts Act 1971, s 24.   [246] As to the distribution of business, see p 603, *post*.

[247] Supreme Court Act 1981, s 9.   [248] Ibid, ss 8 and 74(1).

[249] Ibid, s 75; *Practice Direction (Crown Court: Business)* [2001] 4 All ER 635 at 638, [2001] 1 WLR 1996 at 2000.

[250] If the court is evenly split, the regular judge has the casting vote: s 73(3).

3 JURISDICTION AND PROCEDURE

The Crown Court has exclusive jurisdiction over all trials on indictment, including proceedings on indictment for offences within the jurisdiction of the Admiralty in England.[251] Before the Criminal Justice Act 2003 all trials on indictment were tried by a judge sitting with a jury, but it is now possible for cases where there is a real risk of jury tampering to be tried by a judge sitting alone. A similar power has been introduced in relation to complex fraud cases, though this has yet to be implemented.[252] The jurisdiction formerly exercised by the quarter sessions is also vested in the Crown Court.[253] This includes hearing appeals against summary conviction from the magistrates' courts,[254] sentencing those committed for sentence following summary conviction,[255] and exercising a limited civil jurisdiction in relation to licensing appeals.

The Lord Chief Justice is empowered by section 75 of the Supreme Court Act to give directions for the distribution of Crown Court business. The current directions[256] establish three different classes of offence. Class 1 offences are the most serious, and must be tried by a High Court judge or specially authorized circuit judge. Class 2 offences must also be tried by a High Court judge unless a particular case is released by or on the authority of a presiding judge,[257] while all other offences fall into Class 3 and may be listed for trial by a High Court judge, circuit judge, or recorder.

MAGISTRATES' COURTS

A magistrates' court is defined by section 148 of the Magistrates' Courts Act 1980, as 'any justice or justices of the peace[258] acting under any enactment or by virtue of his or their commission or under the common law'. Magistrates currently sit in over 1,500 courtrooms throughout England and Wales.[259]

1 CONSTITUTION AND ORGANIZATION

Before April 2005, each area of England and Wales had a separate commission of the peace,[260] and each commission area was divided into petty session areas. Magistrates'

---

[251] Supreme Court Act 1981, s 46.

[252] Criminal Justice Act 2003, ss 43–49: see pp 626 and 624, *post*. See also the discussion of the use of sample counts, at p 626, *post*.

[253] Courts Act 1971, s 8, Schedule 1; though note that certain administrative functions were transferred to local authorities.

[254] See p 687, *post*.   [255] See p 672, *post*.

[256] *Consolidated Criminal Practice Direction*, Pt III, as amended: effective in this respect since 6 June 2005. For further details of the classification of offences, see p 603, *post*.

[257] A presiding judge is a High Court judge with special responsibility for a particular circuit.

[258] For the historical role of justices of the peace, see p 234, *ante*.

[259] *Magistrates' Courts Business Returns, Annual Report 2002–2003*, p 4.

[260] In December 2003 there were forty-seven such areas in England and a further five in Wales: Justices of the Peace (Commission Areas) (Amendment) Order 2001, SI 2001/696, Schedule.

Court Committees (MCCs)[261] were responsible for the 'efficient and effective administration' of the courts in each commission area, and magistrates were appointed on a local basis to exercise a local jurisdiction. All of this has now changed as a result of the Courts Act 2003, which is the latest in a long line of reforms to affect the magistrates' courts. Executive responsibility for magistrates' courts was transferred from the Home Office to the Lord Chancellor's Department in 1992, and in 1993 the Magistrates' Court Service Inspectorate was established. This was followed by the Police and Magistrates' Courts Act 1994, which reduced the size of the MCCs and attempted to give them a more clearly defined management role. It also empowered the Lord Chancellor to reduce the number of commission areas in order to improve efficiency. Prior to the 1994 Act, it had been suggested that the local committees should be abolished and replaced with a national executive agency,[262] but this proposal was widely opposed by magistrates and the government did not pursue it.

The Justices of the Peace Act 1997 was primarily a consolidating Act, but the process of reform continued under the Access to Justice Act 1999. A unified Greater London Magistrates' Courts Authority replaced the twenty-two MCCs in London, and the Lord Chancellor was given greater powers to alter commission areas. In the Explanatory Notes accompanying the Act, the government set out the need to develop a 'coherent geographical structure' for the criminal justice system, by moving towards common boundaries for the various agencies involved.[263] This meant that not only should MCCs be able to reorganize the petty session areas within their commission boundaries, but also that there should be greater alignment between the commission boundaries, police force areas, and Crown Prosecution areas.

Reform under the Courts Act 2003

In his review of criminal justice,[264] Lord Justice Auld made the radical recommendation that the Crown Court and magistrates' courts should be replaced with a single Criminal Court. The government rejected this particular proposal but accepted that the criminal courts should be more closely aligned. This provided the impetus for the White Paper *Justice for All*, and for the subsequent Courts Act 2003. The Act repeals the Justices of the Peace Act 1997, though many of its provisions are re-enacted.

The Courts Act establishes a single commission of the peace for England and Wales,[265] and gives magistrates a national jurisdiction. It also provides for magistrates to be assigned to local justice areas,[266] which means in practice that they will continue to sit locally. The MCCs and the Greater London Magistrates' Courts Authority have been abolished,[267] and the Lord Chancellor is now under a general duty to ensure that there is an efficient and effective system to support the Supreme Court, Court of Protection,

[261] Consisting of justices of the peace and other members co-opted by the committee or appointed by the Lord Chancellor: Justices of the Peace Act 1997, s 28.
[262] See the Home Office study, *Magistrates' Courts: Report of a Scrutiny* (HMSO, 1989).
[263] At paras 248–250.   [264] *Review of the Criminal Courts of England and Wales* (2001).
[265] Section 7.   [266] Sections 8 and 10(2); Local Justice Areas Order 2005, SI 2005/554, as amended.
[267] 2003 Act, s 6.

county courts, and magistrates' courts.[268] Magistrates' courts, like most other major courts, are now administered by Her Majesty's Courts Service, which is an executive agency of the Ministry of Justice.[269] An element of local accountability has been retained through the creation of Local Courts Boards, which are established and appointed by the Lord Chancellor.[270] The membership of these Boards must include at least one judge, at least two local representatives, at least two other persons with 'appropriate knowledge or experience', and two or more justices of the peace.[271] They are concerned not only with magistrates' courts but also with the Crown Court and county courts in their areas,[272] and they are responsible for scrutinizing the management of the courts and making recommendations where appropriate.

2 JUSTICES OF THE PEACE

The vast majority of justices of the peace are lay magistrates, who are currently appointed by the Lord Chancellor on the advice of Local Advisory Committees.[273] They are unqualified and unpaid, but they are required to attend training courses[274] and may claim allowances for travel, subsistence, and loss of earnings.[275] They are expected to be available for at least twenty-six half-days each year, and normally sit in pairs or groups of three.[276] A single lay justice has a limited jurisdiction and cannot order a person to pay more than one pound or impose imprisonment for more than fourteen days.[277] However, a single justice can hear proceedings to determine the allocation of cases that are triable either way, and can also transfer cases to the Crown Court for trial on indictment.[278] Under amendments made by the Criminal Justice Act 2003,[279] a single justice may also accept a guilty plea in a case which is to be dealt with summarily.

Appointments to the lay magistracy are intended to reflect all sections of the community, but there is persistent criticism that the majority of justices tend to be white, middle class, Conservative, and old.[280] In fact, research carried out by Morgan and Russell in 2000[281] found that around 4 per cent of lay magistrates were black or Asian, with a further 1 per cent coming from other ethnic minority backgrounds. Although this indicated that at a national level the magistracy was 'approaching ethnic representativeness',[282] in cities

---

[268] Ibid, s 1.   [269] This was launched on 1 April 2005: see p 239, *ante*.

[270] 2003 Act, s 4; Schedule 1.   [271] Ibid, Schedule 1.   [272] Ibid, s 5.

[273] The Constitutional Reform Act 2005 makes provision for justices of the peace to be selected by the Judicial Appointments Commission, but at the time of writing a timetable for transferring responsibility has not been agreed.

[274] Courts Act 2003, s 19 (replacing the Justices of the Peace Act 1997, s 64).

[275] Ibid, s 15 (replacing s 10 of the 1997 Act).   [276] Magistrates' Courts Act 1980, s 121(1).

[277] Ibid, s 121(5).   [278] Ibid, ss 17–18 (as amended).

[279] Ibid, ss 18 and 20(7) (as amended).

[280] See Darbyshire, 'For the New Lord Chancellor: Some Causes for Concern about Magistrates' [1997] Crim LR 861, at 862–6.

[281] *The Judiciary in the Magistrates' Courts* (2000), chapter 2. This study was jointly commissioned by the Home Office and the Lord Chancellor's Department.

[282] Ibid, at p 14. Figures published by the Ministry of Justice indicate that almost 7 per cent of lay magistrates were from minority ethnic backgrounds as of 31 March 2006: *Statistics on Race and the Criminal Justice System – 2006* (2007), at p 110.

with large ethnic minority populations the bench was still disproportionately white. The same study found that around 94 per cent of lay justices were aged between forty and seventy, and that they were 'disproportionately middle class, and almost certainly financially well-off, compared to the population at large'.[283] For example, 69 per cent of lay magistrates in the survey described their current or former occupation as 'professional or managerial', while only 3 per cent described themselves as skilled manual workers. Given that lay magistrates are unpaid, it should come as no surprise that those who are retired or in well-paid employment are more likely to volunteer their services, and Morgan and Russell concluded that achieving greater diversity would inevitably be costly:[284]

> A more socially representative magistracy could almost certainly be recruited, but:
>
> - the members would be unlikely to be so willing or able to sit as often as many lay magistrates do today
> - we believe that more socially representative recruits would be more likely to claim loss of earnings and expenses.
>
> Which is to say that a more socially representative lay magistracy would be a more expensive one.

Upon reaching the age of seventy, lay magistrates join the supplemental list and can no longer serve as justices of the peace.[285]

In April 2005 there were 28,865 lay justices in England and Wales, but the magistracy is also served by 139 District Judges (Magistrates' Courts) and around 169 Deputy District Judges (Magistrates' Courts).[286] These judges used to be called stipendiary magistrates, but they were renamed by section 78 of the Access to Justice Act 1999. The same provision also merged the metropolitan and provincial benches.[287] Unlike lay magistrates, District Judges (Magistrates' Courts) are legally qualified and serve on a full-time, professional basis. They have all the powers of two lay justices and therefore sit alone.[288]

3 JUSTICES' CLERKS AND JUSTICES'
CHIEF EXECUTIVES

Justices' clerks are responsible for advising magistrates on matters of law. They are appointed by the Lord Chancellor and must have either: (a) a five-year magistrates' court qualification;[289] (b) five years' experience as an assistant to a justices' clerk and a

---

[283] Morgan and Russell, *supra* n 281, at p 16.   [284] Ibid, at p 108.

[285] Courts Act 2003, ss 12 and 13. A younger magistrate may have his name added to this list at his own request or on the grounds of incapacity.

[286] As of 1 April 2007: see www.judiciary.gov.uk/keyfacts.

[287] The functions and terms of appointment of District Judges (Magistrates' Courts) are set out in the Courts Act 2003, ss 22–26 (replacing sections 10A–10E of the 1997 Act).

[288] Ibid, s 26 (replacing section 10D of the 1997 Act).

[289] Within the meaning of the Courts and Legal Services Act 1990, s 71.

qualification as a solicitor or barrister; or (c) previous experience as a justices' clerk.[290] The functions of a justices' clerk include:[291]

> [G]iving advice to any or all of the justices of the peace to whom he is clerk about matters of law (including procedure and practice) on questions arising in connection with the discharge of their functions, including questions arising when the clerk is not personally attending on them.

Most justices' clerks cover more than one court and it is impossible for them to personally advise every courtroom for which they are responsible. As a result, many of their functions are delegated to justices' clerks' assistants or 'court clerks', not all of whom are professionally qualified. Concerns have been raised in the past[292] about the number of lay magistrates being advised by unqualified clerks, and more stringent professional requirements have now been introduced. Since January 1999, all newly appointed court clerks must be qualified solicitors or barristers, and those in post before this date have until 2010 to reach the same standard.[293]

The primary function of a clerk is to provide legal advice, and he has a duty to offer such advice whenever he considers it appropriate, regardless of whether it has been specifically requested.[294] However, care must be taken to ensure that he does not appear to interfere with the magisterial function. This means that a clerk should not play any part in helping magistrates to make findings of fact, and that any legal advice given should normally be stated in open court.[295] In addition to his advisory functions, a justices' clerk may also perform many of the pre-trial functions otherwise carried out by a single judge. These include setting the date and time of a trial, giving directions for the conduct of the trial, and making an order for public funding to assist defendants in criminal cases.[296]

In the past justices' clerks were responsible for the general administration of magistrates' courts, in addition to their role as legal advisers. Concerns about this mixing of administrative and legal functions were partly addressed by the Police and Magistrates' Courts Act 1994, which created the new position of justices' chief executive. Many of the clerks' administrative functions were transferred to the holders of this new office,[297] leaving the clerks free to concentrate on their advisory and judicial roles. Each MCC was required to appoint its own chief executive, and his role was to ensure the efficient and effective administration of magistrates' courts in the area. The chief executive was responsible for allocating work between clerks, but the Act expressly provided that clerks

---

[290] Courts Act 2003, s 27.

[291] Ibid, s 28(4). This largely re-enacts s 45 of the Justices of the Peace Act 1997.

[292] See, e.g. Darbyshire, 'For the New Lord Chancellor: Some Causes for Concern about Magistrates' [1997] Crim LR 861 at 872.

[293] Section 27(1) of the Courts Act 2003 makes it possible for a clerk without professional qualifications to remain in post for the time being. However, s 27(6) confers a power to remove this exception at a future date. See also: Assistants to Justices' Clerks Regulations 2006, SI 2006/3405, as amended.

[294] Courts Act 2003, s 28(5); replacing s 45 of the 1997 Act.

[295] *Practice Direction (QBD: Justices: Clerk to Court)* [2000] 4 All ER 895, [2000] 1 WLR 1886.

[296] Crime and Disorder Act 1998, s 49; Justices' Clerks Rules 2005, SI 2005/545, Schedule.

[297] Many of those that remained were transferred by the Access to Justice Act 1999: s 90; Schedule 13.

should not be subject to his direction when performing their legal functions.[298] The emphasis on separating administrative and legal functions has been continued by the Courts Act 2003, and like its predecessors the Act includes an express guarantee of the clerks' independence.[299] However, now that Her Majesty's Courts Service has taken over the management of magistrates' courts,[300] the office of justices' chief executive has been abolished.[301]

4 JURISDICTION

It is common to suppose that the jurisdiction of magistrates' courts is entirely criminal, but they also have a wide and varied civil jurisdiction. In both civil and criminal cases, however, this jurisdiction is limited to relatively minor matters when compared with the cases heard by the High Court, county courts, and Crown Court. Before examining the jurisdiction of the magistrates' courts more closely, it should be noted that when justices of the peace exercise such important functions as the granting of bail and the issuing of summonses and warrants, they are not strictly acting as 'magistrates' courts'.

(a) Criminal jurisdiction

The criminal jurisdiction of magistrates' courts principally concerns summary offences, which are offences triable without a jury. All summary offences are created by statute, and all are of a fairly minor character. Indeed, most summary convictions are for road traffic offences, and so numerous are the convictions for speeding and unauthorized parking, that offenders are able to plead guilty by post.[302] Almost two million persons each year are found guilty of summary offences in England and Wales.

Before the Criminal Justice Act 2003, the maximum penalty that could be imposed for a summary offence was six months' imprisonment and a fine limited in amount.[303] However, the 2003 Act makes provision for the Secretary of State to set a maximum penalty of up to fifty-one weeks' imprisonment for a range of summary offences,[304] and for the sentencing powers of magistrates to be increased accordingly.[305] The Act also provides for a new 'custody plus' sentence, which (when eventually introduced) will replace all short prison sentences (except for intermittent custody) with a short period of imprisonment followed by a period of supervision in the community.[306]

In addition to their jurisdiction over summary offences, magistrates' courts also have jurisdiction over offences 'triable either way',[307] though this is subject to a defendant's right to insist on trial by jury. Where a defendant is convicted of an either-way offence,

---

[298] Section 78. Proposals to transfer justices' clerks to a system of fixed-term contracts and performance related pay only added to concerns about judicial independence, and were dropped from the 1994 Bill at an early stage.

[299] Courts Act 2003, s 29. [300] See p 270, *ante*. [301] 2003 Act, s 6.

[302] See p 668, *post* [303] See p 700, *post*. [304] Section 281(2).

[305] Section 154. Neither provision had been brought into force at the time of writing.

[306] Section 181.

[307] See Magistrates' Courts Act 1980, s 17; Schedule 1. For details of the procedure for determining the mode of trial of such offences, see p 580, *post*.

a magistrates' court may impose penalties similar to those which may be imposed following conviction for a summary offence.

(b) Youth courts and youth justice

Youth courts are magistrates' courts exercising jurisdiction over offences committed by children and young persons.[308] Until 1991 they were known as juvenile courts.[309] A youth court consists of up to three justices selected from a specially trained youth panel, and must normally include at least one man and one woman.[310] The chair of the court remains constant, although other members serve by rotation. A youth court may also consist of a District Judge (Magistrates' Courts), sitting alone.[311]

Youth courts aim to treat juvenile suspects differently from adult defendants, and the procedures adopted are deliberately less formal. The only persons admitted to the court are the court officers, witnesses, bona fide members of the press, the parties and their representatives, and other persons authorized by the court to be present. In addition, the media is normally prohibited from publishing or broadcasting the identity of any child or young person involved in the proceedings,[312] though the court may lift these reporting restrictions if it is in the public interest to do so. The terms 'conviction' and 'sentence' are avoided, and the terms 'finding of guilt' and 'order made upon a finding of guilt' are used instead.

The Crime and Disorder Act 1998 established in statutory form that the basic aim of the youth justice system is to prevent offending. It also contains provisions relating to youth justice services, a new Youth Justice Board, and youth offending teams. Further important changes are now made by the Criminal Justice and Immigration Act 2008. All of these are considered further in chapter 19.

(c) Civil jurisdiction

This aspect of the magistrates' courts' jurisdiction is extremely varied. It includes the recovery of certain civil debts such as income tax, national insurance contributions, council tax, and electricity, gas, and water charges. It also includes the licensing of pubs, clubs, and gambling establishments. However, the most important aspect of the magistrates' courts' civil workload is their jurisdiction over family law matters. This is exercised principally under the Family Law Act 1996 and Children Act 1989, in what are known as 'family proceedings courts'.

(d) Family proceedings courts

These courts were created by section 80 of the Domestic Proceedings and Magistrates' Courts Act 1978, and were then known as domestic courts. They were renamed 'family

---

[308] For these purposes a 'child' is a person under fourteen years, and a 'young person' is someone aged fourteen to seventeen: Children and Young Persons Act 1933, s 107.

[309] Criminal Justice Act 1991, s 70.

[310] Children and Young Persons Act 1933, s 45 (as amended); Youth Courts (Constitution of Committees and Right to Preside) Rules 2007, SI 2007/1611, r 10. Exceptionally, a case may be heard by an all-male/all-female panel if, due to unforeseen circumstances, no members of the opposite gender are available and it would not be in the interests of justice to order an adjournment.

[311] 1933 Act, s 45 (as amended); Courts Act 2003, s 66; SI 2007/1611, r 10.

[312] 1933 Act, s 49 (as amended).

proceedings courts' by the Children Act 1989.[313] They normally consist of two or three justices drawn from a specially trained panel, and as far as practicable they should include a man and a woman.[314] Nominated District Judges (Magistrates' Courts) may sit alongside one or two lay justices, though it is possible for a judge to deal with family proceedings matters when sitting alone.[315] The only persons who may be present during proceedings are officers of the court, the parties, their legal representatives, witnesses, newspaper representatives, and any other persons permitted by the court.[316]

Family proceedings courts have jurisdiction to deal with maintenance applications and to make various orders in respect of children, domestic violence, and the occupation of the family home. They also have a public law jurisdiction to deal with care proceedings brought by local authorities under the Children Act 1989. In fact, their jurisdiction under the Children Act is largely concurrent with that of county courts and the Family Division of the High Court, except that public law actions can only be commenced in a family proceedings court.[317] In view of their overlapping jurisdictions, the Courts Act 2003 established a new Family Procedure Rule Committee with the power to make procedural rules governing all three courts.[318] The government is now moving towards the creation of Family Courts Centres, which will bring together the administrative arrangements for county courts and family proceedings courts in particular areas. Where possible, both types of court will be located in the same building.[319] Ultimately, the long-term objective is to create unified Family Courts.[320]

COURT OF PROTECTION

Until recently, applications concerning the property and affairs of persons of unsound mind were dealt with within the Chancery Division, by judges sitting as the Court of Protection. Following implementation of the Mental Capacity Act 2005 the Court of Protection has been given enhanced powers, and it is now a superior court of record in its own right.[321] The President of the Family Division has been appointed as President of the new court, and it is also served by a Vice-President, a Senior Judge, and nominated High Court, circuit and district judges.[322]

---

[313] Section 92.

[314] Magistrates' Courts Act 1980, ss 66 and 67 (as amended). See also, Family Proceedings Courts (Constitution of Committees and Right to Preside) Rules 2007, SI 2007/1610.

[315] Magistrates' Courts Act 1980, ss 66 and 67 (as amended).   [316] Ibid, s 69(2).

[317] Children (Allocation of Proceedings) Order 1991, SI 1991/1677, Article 3(1). Such cases may be transferred to the county court or to the Family Division if they are sufficiently complex or serious, or where there would otherwise be an unacceptable delay.

[318] Sections 75–81.

[319] DCA, *Response to the Constitutional Affairs Select Committee Report – Family Justice: The Operation of the Family Courts Revisited*, Cm 6971, 2006, at pp 5–6.

[320] DCA, *A Single Civil Court? Responses to the Consultation* (2005) CP(R) 06/05, at p 42.

[321] 2005 Act, s 45 – effective from 1 October 2007.   [322] Ibid, s 46.

CORONERS' COURTS

1 THE OFFICE OF CORONER

This ancient office dates from the twelfth century, when it principally concerned the custody of revenue accruing to the King from fines and forfeiture. In addition, the coroner occasionally exercised the jurisdiction of the sheriff and enquired into treasure trove and unexplained deaths. Some of these functions have since been removed, and the primary role of the modern coroner is to hold inquests into unexplained deaths. The appointment and jurisdiction of coroners is now governed by statute.[323] They may be barristers, solicitors, or registered medical practitioners of not less than five years' standing, and they may be removed from office for misbehaviour or inability to discharge their duties.[324]

2 JURISDICTION

The coroner's jurisdiction is principally concerned with inquests into the deaths of persons 'whose bodies are lying within his district'.[325] The jurisdiction arises where there is reasonable cause to suspect that a person has died a violent or unnatural death, or has died suddenly from an unknown cause. Deaths in prison or police custody, and deaths occurring as a result of injury caused by a police officer in the purported execution of his duty, also fall within the coroner's jurisdiction.[326] The holding of an inquest in such cases is mandatory. In *R* v *West Yorkshire Coroner, ex parte Smith*[327] the Court of Appeal held that the phrase 'lying within his jurisdiction' (which was the form of words used prior to the passing of the Coroners Act 1988) applied to a body brought into the district from abroad. This is still the position, and in October 2007 inquests into the deaths of Diana, Princess of Wales and Dodi Al Fayed, both of whom died in Paris, were opened at the Royal Courts of Justice, concluding some six months later.

To hold an inquest the coroner may, and in some cases must, summon a jury of between seven and eleven members.[328] Witnesses attend and give evidence and the coroner has the power to compel their attendance if necessary. The procedure is inquisitorial, however, and although interested persons may be represented and may ask questions, it is the coroner who conducts the proceedings and no speeches are made to the jury. The jury's verdict need not be unanimous provided that there are not more than two dissentients. Detailed matters of procedure are governed by the Coroners Rules 1984.[329]

---

[323] Coroners Act 1988 (a consolidation Act).   [324] Ibid, s 3.

[325] Ibid, s 8. Coroners also retain their historical jurisdiction to hold inquests in relation to treasure (s 30: see the Treasure Act 1996), but the recent Review of Coroners' Services recommended that this should be removed: see n 343, *post*.

[326] 1988 Act, s 8.   [327] [1983] QB 335, [1982] 3 All ER 1098.

[328] 1988 Act, s 8.   [329] SI 1984/552, as amended.

Prior to the passing of the Criminal Law Act 1977 the jury might return a verdict of murder, manslaughter, or infanticide by a named person, and the coroner could then commit that person for trial. This was abolished by section 56 of the 1977 Act and a coroner's inquisition cannot now charge a person with any offence. Moreover, although coroners have the power to compel the attendance of witnesses, a witness cannot be obliged to answer questions 'tending to incriminate himself'.[330] These limitations have given rise to a number of cases under the ECHR and the Human Rights Act 1998,[331] and were among the issues considered by the Review of Coroner Services (discussed below).

Where criminal proceedings are in hand, any inquest relating to the same issues should be adjourned.[332] The coroner has a discretion to resume the inquest on conclusion of the criminal proceedings, but if he does so, any findings as to the cause of death must not be inconsistent with the outcome of the criminal case.[333] A coroner must also adjourn an inquest if he is informed that the circumstances surrounding a death are to be the subject of a public inquiry, unless there is an 'exceptional reason' for not doing so.[334]

There is no appeal from an inquest, but the proceedings are subject to judicial review and may be challenged if, for example, there is evidence of bias.[335]

The inquests into the deaths of Diana, Princess of Wales and Dodi Al Fayed

Issues of bias were among those considered in the recent case of *R (on the application of Paul) v Deputy Coroner of the Queen's Household and Assistant District Coroner for Surrey*.[336] The case concerned the inquests into the deaths of Diana, Princess of Wales and Dodi Al Fayed. The inquest into the death of the Princess was due to be heard by the coroner of the Queen's household,[337] with the inquiry into Mr Al Fayed's death being transferred to the coroner for Surrey. The inquests were initially adjourned pending Lord Stevens' inquiry into allegations that there had been a conspiracy to murder,[338] but they were resumed when the inquiry concluded that there was no evidence of such a conspiracy. Given the high profile nature of the case and the heavy workload involved, Baroness Butler-Sloss was simultaneously appointed as Deputy Coroner of the Queen's Household and Assistant Deputy Coroner for Surrey, with the intention being that she should conduct both inquests. She decided to transfer the Al Fayed inquest to the jurisdiction of the coroner for the Queen's household so that the two inquests could be heard together. She also decided that she should sit without a jury. These rulings were challenged in the Administrative Court on the grounds that: (a) she did not have the

---

[330] SI 1984/552, r 22.   [331] See pp 183 and 616 for further discussion of the issues.
[332] 1988 Act, s 16; the decision ultimately rests with the DPP.   [333] Ibid, s 16.
[334] Ibid, s 17A, as inserted by the Access to Justice Act 1999.
[335] For an example, see *R v Inner West London Coroner, ex parte Dallaglio* [1994] 4 All ER 139.
[336] [2007] EWHC 408 (Admin), [2007] 3 WLR 503, [2007] 2 All ER 509.
[337] See s 29 of the Coroners Act 1988.
[338] Metropolitan Police, *The Operation Paget Inquiry Report into the Allegation of Conspiracy to Murder Diana, Princess of Wales and Emad El-Din Mohamed Abdel Moneim Fayed* (2006).

authority to transfer jurisdiction over the inquests; (b) it would be inappropriate for the coroner of the Queen's household to hold the inquests because an informed bystander would perceive a real risk of bias; (c) her support for the publication of Lord Stevens' report had further compromised her independence and impartiality; and (d) the possibility that the deaths were caused in circumstances prejudicial to public safety meant that she should have considered sitting with a jury.

Having considered these arguments, the court concluded that the coroner had acted within the scope of her powers when transferring the Al Fayed inquest from one jurisdiction to another.[339] It was also felt that her support for the publication of Lord Stevens' inquiry would not give rise to a real possibility of bias in the eyes of the fair-minded and informed observer.[340] However, the same could not be said for her decision to hear the case as coroner for the Queen's household: the appearance that the use of this title might give to members of the public had to be considered, and the decision to sit in this capacity was therefore quashed.[341] The decision to conduct the inquests without a jury was also quashed, since the deaths had occurred in circumstances which might be prejudicial to the safety of a section of the public and the summoning of a jury was mandatory in such circumstances.[342] Baroness Butler-Sloss subsequently stood down from the inquests due to her lack of experience in hearing jury cases, and both inquests were heard by Scott Baker LJ – sitting with a jury – following his appointment to the office of Assistant Deputy Coroner for Inner West London.

3 THE REVIEW OF CORONERS' SERVICES, 2003[343]

In July 2001 the government announced that it was setting up a Review of Coroners' Services, to be chaired by Tom Luce. The Review was completed in April 2003 and it highlighted a number of 'critical defects' in the system. The fact that coroners operate 'in isolation from the mainstreams of medicine and justice administration' was identified as a particular weakness,[344] as was the fact that most coroners are part-time.[345] The Review also criticized the absence of a national structure for leadership and administration,[346] along with the lack of 'a clear and reliable process for clarifying the relationship between the inquest and other formal processes for investigating death'.[347] The reforms recommended by the Review would essentially remodel the coroners' service along the lines of the other major courts:[348]

> The death investigation service – the coroner service – should become a service of predominantly full-time legally qualified professionals, appointed, trained and supported to modern judicial and public service standards.

[339] [2007] EWHC 408 (Admin), at [29], per Smith LJ. See also, s 14 of the 1988 Act.
[340] Ibid, at [65].   [341] Ibid, at [62].
[342] Ibid, at [39] and [46]. See also, s 8(3)(d) of the 1988 Act.
[343] *Death Certification and Investigation in England, Wales and Northern Ireland: The Report of a Fundamental Review*, Cm 5831, 2003.
[344] Ibid, at para 2.4.e.
[345] The Review found that only twenty-three of the 123 coroners in England and Wales were full-time.
[346] Para 2.4.j.   [347] Para 2.4.k.   [348] Para 3.2.

Specific recommendations included:

(1) Making the Lord Chancellor responsible for appointing and supporting the coroners' service, in the same way as for other courts;

(2) Requiring coroners to be full-time and to be legally (rather than legally *or medically*) qualified;

(3) Appointing a 'Statutory Medical Assessor' (a doctor) to assist each coroner;

(4) Establishing a standing Rules Committee to formulate procedural rules for the conduct of inquests;

(5) Creating a statutory Coronial Council to oversee the work of the service; and

(6) Restructuring the service in England and Wales to create a single jurisdiction headed by a Chief Coroner.[349] The jurisdiction would be split into around sixty districts, based on the existing police areas.

Another issue for the Review group was how to respond to the decision in *Jordan* v *UK*.[350] Article 2 of the ECHR implies a duty on the state to investigate deaths occurring as a result of state action or while the deceased was in state custody. In *Jordan*, the European Court of Human Rights found that the holding of an inquest does not discharge this duty, because it is not a forum for determining the identity and culpability of those responsible for causing death. This decision has since been applied in a number of domestic cases under the Human Rights Act 1998.[351] The matter is further complicated by Article 6. For example, although the ability to compel witnesses to attend an inquest is necessitated by Article 2, the right to a fair trial under Article 6 would seem to require that a witness is not obliged to give evidence which could incriminate him.

The Review recommended that the rule preventing a witness from being compelled to answer incriminating questions should be removed. It proposed instead that there should be a limited immunity, preventing incriminating testimony given by a witness from being used against him in criminal or disciplinary (but not civil) proceedings.[352] More generally, it concluded that the scope of an inquest should be limited only by the proviso that its findings 'do not determine civil or criminal liability',[353] and that the inquest should be the 'default process' for handling the vast majority of Article 2 cases.[354]

The government's initial response to the report was to accept that some reform was needed, but to ask for further research and consultation.[355] A Draft Coroners' Bill was

---

[349] A second jurisdiction would cover Northern Ireland.

[350] (2003) 37 EHRR 2; see also *Finucane* v *UK* (2003) 37 EHRR 29.

[351] See *R (on the application of Amin)* v *Secretary of State for the Home Department* [2003] UKHL 51, [2004] 1 AC 653, [2003] 4 All ER 1264 (inquest into the death of a prisoner who had been murdered by his cellmate did not satisfy Article 2). See also *R (on the application of Khan)* v *Secretary of State for Health* [2003] EWCA Civ 1129, [2003] 4 All ER 1239 (Article 2 breached because Mr Khan was unable to obtain legal aid enabling him to be legally represented at his daughter's inquest). These decisions prompted an amendment to the exceptional funding provisions in the Access to Justice Act 1999. Further examples are discussed at p 179, *ante*.

[352] Para 9.38.   [353] Para 21.33.   [354] Para 10.61.

[355] In November 2003 Tom Luce was asked to link his findings to an inquiry into the failure of various institutions to prevent a GP from murdering his patients. See *The Shipman Inquiry's Third Report: Death Certification and the Investigation of Deaths by Coroners*.

eventually published in June 2006,[356] but this Bill ignored many of the Luce recommendations and was widely criticized for not going far enough.[357] The government now intends to make significant revisions before bringing the Bill before Parliament.

JUDICIAL COMMITTEE OF THE PRIVY COUNCIL

1 CONSTITUTION

Prior to the Judicial Committee Act 1833, the jurisdiction of the Privy Council was exercised principally by laymen. The 1833 Act[358] created the Judicial Committee, which at the time of writing consists of the Lord President of the Council, the Lord Chancellor, ex-Lord Presidents, the Lords of Appeal in Ordinary, and certain other members who have held high judicial office. From time to time membership has also been extended to persons who have held high judicial office in Commonwealth countries, though such persons may not sit when the Committee is determining 'devolution issues' under the Scotland Act 1998, the Government of Wales Act 1998, and the Northern Ireland Act 1998.

The Lord Chancellor and the Lords of Appeal in Ordinary are the members of the Committee who usually sit. Decisions of the Privy Council therefore enjoy great authority, though they are not strictly binding on English courts.[359] The transfer of the House of Lords' judicial functions to a new Supreme Court will necessarily affect the Privy Council's composition: when this happens, it is intended that the Justices of the Supreme Court should take the positions currently occupied by the Lords of Appeal in Ordinary.[360]

Appeals are heard at the bar of the Privy Council before not less than three – and usually five – members of the Committee.[361] The procedure is similar to that currently followed by the House of Lords.

2 JURISDICTION

Although all English courts derive their jurisdiction directly or indirectly from the sovereign, the Judicial Committee of the Privy Council is slightly different, in that its

---

[356] *Coroner Reform: The Government's Draft Bill – Improving Death Investigation in England and Wales*, Cm 6849, 2006.

[357] Reform of the Coroners' System and Death Certification: Government Response to the Constitutional Affairs Select Committee's Report, Cm 6943, 2006; DCA, *Coroner Reform: The Government's Draft Bill: Responses to Consultation*, (R) 6849/07 (2007).

[358] As amended by the Judicial Committee Act 1844, the Appellate Jurisdiction Acts 1876–1947 and other Acts. Further amendments will be made by Schedule 16 of the Constitutional Reform Act 2005.

[359] See p 85, *ante*. The Privy Council's decisions on devolution issues are, of course, binding in respect of Wales, Scotland and Northern Ireland.

[360] This will be the effect of the Constitutional Reform Act 2005, s 138; Schedule 16.

[361] A greater number has been known: see, e.g. *Pratt v A-G for Jamaica* [1994] 2 AC 1, [1993] 4 All ER 769, where a committee of seven judges declared gross delays in carrying out death sentences in Jamaica to amount to inhuman and degrading treatment.

jurisdiction is that of the sovereign in Council. Consequently the Privy Council does not pass judgment: it merely tenders advice to the sovereign, which is then implemented by Order in Council. Only one opinion is usually read and until recently dissents were not even recorded.[362] However, it is now provided by Order in Council that dissenting opinions may be delivered in open court.[363]

The main aspects of the Privy Council's jurisdiction are as follows:[364]

(a) *Appeals from courts outside the United Kingdom*. Since the sovereign is the fountain of justice for all her Dominions, the Privy Council has jurisdiction to hear appeals from the Isle of Man, the Channel Islands, independent Commonwealth countries, and British Colonies and Protectorates. However, since the Statute of Westminster 1931, many Commonwealth States have legislated to exclude appeal to the Privy Council.[365] Leave to appeal in criminal matters is only given in exceptional cases, and mere misdirection will not suffice: there must be some clear departure from the 'requirements of justice', or something which 'deprives the accused of the substance of fair trial and the protection of the law.'[366]

(b) *Admiralty jurisdiction*. Prior to 1875, appeal lay from the High Court of Admiralty to the Privy Council. Since the Judicature Acts most appeals from the High Court now lie to the Court of Appeal, but the Privy Council has retained its jurisdiction to hear appeals from the High Court when sitting as a 'prize court'.[367] A prize court is a court convened to determine issues concerning the ownership of ships and cargo, and the validity of their capture by enemy warships.

(c) *Appeals from ecclesiastical courts*. The jurisdiction of the ecclesiastical courts was drastically curtailed in 1857,[368] and is now confined to matters affecting the clergy and church buildings. Appeals from the highest ecclesiastical courts lie to the Privy Council.[369] Although archbishops and bishops are not members of the Privy Council, an archbishop (or the Bishop of London) and four other bishops are summoned to sit in an advisory capacity whenever the Council is hearing ecclesiastical appeals.

(d) *Devolution questions*. The Privy Council currently has jurisdiction over devolution questions arising under the Scotland Act 1998, the Government of Wales

---

[362] Cf. the Criminal Division of the Court of Appeal, which also delivers only one judgment but for different reasons.

[363] Judicial Committee (General Appellate Jurisdiction) Rules Order 1982, SI 1982/1676, Schedule 2, para 16. For a particularly vigorous dissent, see *Abbot* v *R* [1977] AC 755, [1976] 3 All ER 140.

[364] Until recently the Privy Council had jurisdiction to hear appeals from tribunals governing healthcare professionals, but this jurisdiction has been transferred to the High Court, Queen's Bench Division.

[365] Territories which have ended or ceased to recognize the Privy Council's jurisdiction include: Aden, Australia, Botswana, Burma, Canada, Cyprus, Ghana, Guyana, Hong Kong, India, Kenya, Malaysia, Malta, New Zealand, Nigeria, Pakistan, Sierra Leone, Singapore, Sri Lanka, Tanzania, and Uganda.

[366] *Ibrahim* v *R* [1914] AC 599 at 614–615, per Lord Sumner: see also *Prasad* v *R* [1981] 1 All ER 319, [1981] 1 WLR 469.

[367] Supreme Court Act 1981, s 16(2). By s 20, the High Court's jurisdiction to sit as a prize court is exercised by the Admiralty Court (part of the Queen's Bench Division); see p 262, *ante*.

[368] Court of Probate Act 1857; Matrimonial Causes Act 1857.

[369] Ecclesiastical Jurisdiction Measure 1963, s 1(3)(d); s 8.

Act 1998, and the Northern Ireland Act 1998. Matters relating to the functions of the devolved legislative and executive bodies may be referred directly to the Judicial Committee of the Privy Council, or they may reach it through the appeals process.[370] This jurisdiction was conferred on the Privy Council to avoid the House of Lords having to determine disputes in which it had an interest as part of the UK Parliament. This will cease to be an issue when the House of Lords' judicial functions are transferred to an independent Supreme Court, and the new court will therefore take over jurisdiction in devolution cases.[371]

(e) *Special references*. In addition to its appellate jurisdiction, the Privy Council is sometimes required to advise on matters of law at the request of the sovereign.[372] In the past it has advised on such diverse matters as the powers of colonial judges,[373] legislation in Jersey,[374] and the eligibility of a person to sit and vote in the House of Commons.[375]

COURTS OF PARTICULAR JURISDICTION[376]

Certain courts do not fit within the general hierarchy because they are concerned with matters outside the scope of the ordinary civil and criminal law. The authority of these specialist courts is usually limited to certain members of society who have impliedly agreed to submit to their jurisdiction, though in some instances it extends to all members of the community.

1 COURTS-MARTIAL[377]

Courts-martial exercise jurisdiction over members of the armed forces, and over their dependants if an alleged offence is committed overseas.[378] They cannot generally exercise jurisdiction over civilians, except where Her Majesty's forces are in armed occupation of hostile territory and a state of martial law has been declared. In addition,

---

[370] For an example, see *Brown v Stott* [2003] 1 AC 681, [2001] 2 ALL ER 97.

[371] Constitutional Reform Act 2005, Schedule 9, part 2; see p 253, *ante*.

[372] Judicial Committee Act 1833, s 4.   [373] *Re Wells* (1840) 3 Moo PCC 216.

[374] *Re Jersey States* (1853) 9 Moo PCC 185.   [375] *Re Macmanaway* [1951] AC 161.

[376] Prior to 1977 there were many courts of local jurisdiction, but the judicial functions of most of them were abolished by the Courts Act 1971, the Local Government Act 1972 and the Administration of Justice Act 1977. The few that remain are listed in the Law Commission report, *Jurisdiction of Certain Ancient Courts* (Law Com No 72).

[377] See generally, Lyon, 'After Findlay – A Consideration of Some Aspects of the Military Justice System' [1998] Crim LR 109; Lyon, 'Two Swords and Two Standards' [2005] Crim LR 850.

[378] The recent case of *Martin v UK* (2007) 44 EHRR 31 concerned a seventeen-year-old civilian who was convicted of the murder of another civilian by a courts-martial in Germany. The courts-martial system was used because the defendant was the son of an army corporal, but the procedure was found to be contrary to the right to a fair trial under Article 6, ECHR. See further, p 286, *post*.

civilians who are employed by the forces and are on active service outside the United Kingdom may be tried in 'standing civilian courts'.[379]

At the time of writing, the disciplinary systems of the three main armed services operate within separate statutory frameworks,[380] although there are many similarities between them. However, once in force the Armed Forces Act 2006 will repeal these separate pieces of legislation and replace them with a single, harmonized framework covering all members of the armed forces.[381]

Air Force and military courts-martial are already similar in constitution and procedure.[382] The accused may be arrested by a superior officer for any offence against military law. If the offence is merely a 'summary' one he will be tried by superior officers, but in other cases he has a choice as to whether to be tried summarily or by court-martial. Serious offences are always tried at courts-martial, except that murder, manslaughter, treason, and rape committed within the United Kingdom must be tried in the ordinary criminal courts. In all other cases, the jurisdiction of civilian and military courts is concurrent. However, a person who has already been convicted or acquitted by a civilian court cannot subsequently be tried by court-martial, and vice versa.[383]

(a) First-instance decisions

Courts-martial are currently convened on an ad hoc basis, and each one consists of a Permanent President of Courts-Martial (PPCM), a Judge Advocate from the Judge Advocate General's department[384] and at least two other officers. The Judge Advocate's role is to advise on questions of law and to give rulings and directions on matters of practice and procedure. The President and the other officers are the sole arbiters of fact. The trial itself takes place in open court and is in many ways similar to a trial in the ordinary criminal courts. It is subject to similar rules of evidence and procedure, and the accused is sent for trial on a charge sheet which may be compared with an indictment. The prosecution case is conducted by an officer, either personally or through a civilian counsel, and the accused may appear in person or be represented by counsel, solicitor, or a defending officer. There is no jury, however, and at the conclusion of the

---

[379] Armed Forces Act 1996, s 6. See now s 51 of the Armed Forces Act 2006, which, when in force, will establish a Service Civilian Court with jurisdiction to try service offences committed outside the British Islands by civilians.

[380] The Army Act 1955, the Air Force Act 1955 and the Naval Discipline Act 1957, all of which are supplemented and amended by the Armed Forces Act 1996.

[381] The existing statutory framework is currently set to continue in force until 8 November 2008: Armed Forces, Army, Air Force and Naval Discipline Acts (Continuation) Order 2007, SI 2007/2123.

[382] They are described in detail in the European Court of Human Rights' judgment in *Cooper v UK* (2004) 39 EHRR 8. Naval courts-martial currently follow similar procedures, but there are slight differences in their composition. These differences proved to be crucial in the recent case of *Grieves v UK* (2004) 39 EHRR 2. In *Cooper* the court accepted that the army and Air Force courts-martial were 'independent and impartial' tribunals for the purposes of Article 6, ECHR. In *Grieves,* however, the court concluded that the naval system fell short of the required standard because it had no permanent President and Judge Advocates were appointed by a serving naval officer. The government subsequently introduced delegated legislation to address the issues raised: Naval Discipline Act 1957 (Remedial) Order 2004, SI 2004/66.

[383] Army Act 1955, ss 133, 134; Air Force Act 1955, ss 133, 134; Naval Discipline Act 1975, s 129. This position will continue under the Armed Forces Act 2006: see ss 64 and 66.

[384] The corresponding department in the Navy is the Judge Advocate of the Fleet's department.

evidence the Judge Advocate summarizes the legal and factual issues before leaving the court to arrive at its decision. A majority decision is acceptable.[385] All guilty verdicts and sentences are subject to confirmation by a Reviewing Authority.[386] This body has the power to reduce sentences, quash convictions, and order retrials, but it cannot increase a sentence or interfere with an acquittal. Any person convicted by court-martial has a right to appeal against both conviction and sentence to the Courts-Martial Appeal Court.

The Armed Forces Act 2006. The government's view is that the existing system already works well, and that changes made since 1996 have established a robust, fair and effective system of law which is ECHR-compliant.[387] The main purpose of the 2006 Act is thus to establish a more modern and coherent legal framework, which is better suited to an era in which the three services increasingly work together. Thus, a Director of Service Prosecutions will be appointed to replace the three current authorities,[388] and the offices of Judge Advocate General and Judge Advocate of the Fleet will be merged.[389] A Court Martial will be established as a unified standing court with the jurisdiction to sit anywhere in the world,[390] and a Service Civilian Court will replace the separate 'standing civilian courts' which currently exist.[391] The new Court Martial will continue to operate under the principle of 'open justice',[392] and its rules on evidence and procedure will be largely unchanged. These rules will, however, be harmonized and will apply to cases involving all three services.[393]

In many respects the system will continue to operate as before, but one notable change concerns the court's composition. In order for the new court to be properly constituted, a Judge Advocate will normally be required to sit with between three and five lay members.[394] The court's findings will be determined by majority vote and, in the event of a decision on the verdict being evenly split, the defendant must be acquitted. As at present, the Judge Advocate's role will be to determine legal points, and he will not have a vote on the verdict itself. However, in the event of an equality of votes on the sentence the Judge Advocate will have the casting vote.[395] There will no longer be a role for the Reviewing Authority, but those convicted of an offence by the Court Martial will still have a right of appeal to the Court Martial Appeal Court.[396]

(b) Courts-Martial Appeal Court[397]

The Courts-Martial Appeal Court was established by the Courts-Martial (Appeals) Act 1951,[398] and in terms of composition and procedure it closely resembles the Criminal

---

[385] See, e.g. Army Act 1955, s 96.

[386] Army Act 1955, s 113; Air Force Act 1955, s 113; Naval Discipline Act 1957, s 70.

[387] MoD, *An Overview of the Military Criminal Justice System and the Armed Forces Act 2006* (2006), at pp 3–4.

[388] Armed Forces Act 2006, s 364.   [389] Ibid, s 362; schedule 17.

[390] Ibid, s 154.   [391] Ibid, s 51.   [392] Ibid, s 158.   [393] Ibid, s 163.

[394] Ibid, s 155. Court Martial Rules may provide for the court to sit with up to seven lay members – or without any – in prescribed circumstances.

[395] Ibid, s 160.   [396] Ibid, schedule 8.

[397] To be renamed 'the Court Martial Appeal Court' when the Armed Forces Act 2006 comes into effect: 2006 Act, schedule 8.

[398] It is now governed by the Courts-Martial (Appeals) Act 1968. Before 1951 there was no right of appeal against conviction.

Division of the Court of Appeal. It comprises the *ex officio* and ordinary members of the Court of Appeal, nominated[399] judges of the Queen's Bench Division, certain Scottish and Irish judges, and other persons of legal experience who may be appointed to sit. Appeals are heard by at least three judges, though only one judgment is delivered. Any subsequent appeal lies to the House of Lords and can only be made with leave.[400]

(c) Issues of fairness

In *Findlay* v *UK* the court-martial procedure was found to be incompatible with the fair trial provisions in Article 6, ECHR, because there were insufficient safeguards to guarantee impartiality.[401] At the time, several aspects of the courts-martial procedure were under the control of a 'Convening Officer'. This Officer had the task of selecting the President and other members of the court, and this usually meant selecting officers who were inferior in rank and perhaps even under his direct command. The Convening Officer was also responsible for procuring the attendance of witnesses, deciding which charges should be brought against the accused, and sending an abstract of the evidence to the prosecution. All of this gave the impression of a tribunal lacking in impartiality.

The Armed Forces Act 1996 anticipated the decision in *Findlay* and introduced changes designed to safeguard the independence of the system. It abolished the Convening Officer role and distributed his former functions between the prosecuting authority and the Commanding Officer, in liaison with the court-martial administration officer and the Reviewing Authority. However, despite these reforms, the court-martial procedure has been the subject of further Article 6 challenges. In *R* v *McKendry*, the Judge Advocate advised that the office of Permanent President of Courts-Martial (PPCM) was incompatible with the idea of an independent tribunal. He noted that PPCMs were appointed for a limited number of years and did not have any formal security of tenure. He also voiced concern that PPCMs could, as military officers, be subject to periodic review by their superiors.[402] The use of PPCMs was subsequently suspended, but in *R* v *Spear* the Courts-Martial Appeal Court held that the involvement of PPCMs in a number of earlier hearings had *not* violated Article 6.[403] In each of the appeals before the court, the PPCM had been in his last posting before retirement and was therefore unlikely to have been influenced by the prospect of promotion or preferment. The court noted that PPCMs effectively operated outside the military chain of command, that (in the army at least) they were no longer subject to periodic reviews, and that despite the absence of any written guarantees of tenure, no PPCM had ever actually been removed from his position. On this basis, the Courts-Martial Appeal Court was satisfied that each appellant had been tried by an independent and impartial tribunal.

Spear was given leave to appeal to the House of Lords. Before the appeal could be heard, however, the European Court of Human Rights in *Morris* v *UK*[404] decided that despite the improvements made since *Findlay*, the courts-martial system still fell short

---

[399] By the Lord Chief Justice.   [400] See p 730, *post*; Courts-Martial (Appeals) Act 1968, s 39.

[401] (1997) 24 EHRR 221. Procedures at the time were governed by the Armed Forces Act 1981.

[402] *R* v *McKendry* (unreported) 6 March 2000, Aldershot Court-Martial Centre.

[403] *R* v *Spear and others* [2001] EWCA Crim 2, [2001] QB 804, [2001] 2 WLR.

[404] (2002) 34 EHRR 52.

of what was required by Article 6. The Court noted that the roles of the PPCM and the Judge Advocate were important safeguards of independence, but it considered that they were not sufficient to exclude the risk of outside pressure being brought to bear on the other members. In particular, it expressed concern that (a) these other members received no legal training; (b) there were no statutory or other bars to prevent them from being subjected to external influence; and (c) they remained subject to army discipline and reporting.

Morris was not followed when *R v Spear* reached the House of Lords,[405] their Lordships having taken the view that the Strasbourg court had not had sufficient information upon which to base its decision. It was noted that although the ordinary courts-martial members were still subject to army discipline and reporting, their 'judicial' decisions were not evaluated or discussed as part of the reporting process: indeed, officers were prohibited from discussing their deliberations with anyone who was not a member of the court. It was also noted that any attempt to influence a court-martial would probably constitute the offence of attempting to pervert the course of justice. Lord Bingham concluded that:[406]

> In my opinion the rules governing the role of junior officers as members of courts-martial are in practice such as effectively to protect the accused against the risk that they might be subject to 'external army influence', as I feel sure the European Court would have appreciated had the position been more fully explained.

Lord Rodger concurred, pointing out that:[407]

> Article 6 does not require that the members of the tribunal should not share the values of the military community to which they belong, any more than it requires that the judge or members of the jury in a civil court should be divorced from the values of the wider community.

In *Cooper v UK*[408] a unanimous Grand Chamber of the Strasbourg court took account of these judgments and departed from its previous case law, declaring itself satisfied that there was, after all, no incompatibility with the Convention. However, the courts in both *Cooper* and *Spear* suggested that the role of the Reviewing Authorities was anomalous, and while they found no unfairness in the proceedings on the facts, they expressed concern that PPCMs in the RAF were still subject to review by their superior officers.[409]

In the more recent case of *Martin v UK*, the Court of Human Rights criticized the use of a court-martial to try a young civilian accused of murder.[410] The applicant was seventeen when the offence was committed, and he was living with his family in Germany where his father was serving in the British Army. The applicant contended that his trial by court-martial was inherently unfair and oppressive, and the Strasbourg court

---

[405] *R v Spear and others; R v Saunby and others* [2002] UKHL 31, [2003] 1 AC 734, [2002] 3 All ER 1074. For the status of European Court of Human Rights decisions as precedents, see pp 86 and 153, *ante*.

[406] Ibid at [12].   [407] Ibid at [57].   [408] (2004) 39 EHRR 8.

[409] See also the decision in *Grieves v UK* (2004) 39 EHRR 2, discussed at p 283, n 382, *ante*.

[410] *Martin v UK* (2007) 44 EHRR 31.

agreed that the requirements of a fair trial had not been met. The trial had taken place in 1994 – before the system was reformed by the 1996 Act – and by the time the case reached Strasbourg many of the issues raised had therefore been addressed. However, the court also raised more general concerns about the use of military courts to try civilians, suggesting that this could only be justified in 'very exceptional circumstances'.[411] In response to this decision, the Ministry of Defence has stated that the Rules of the new Court Martial will require its lay members to be civilians in cases where civilians are on trial.[412] In its view this 'civilianisation' of the Court Martial will address any outstanding concerns about the independence of the new system, and will thus ensure that it is ECHR-compliant.[413]

2 ECCLESIASTICAL COURTS

These courts have a history as old as the common law itself. Although they have been subject to control by the sovereign since the reign of Henry VIII, and their jurisdiction over laymen has been abolished, there remains a hierarchy of courts within the Church of England. In addition, the General Synod of the Church of England has statutory powers[414] to pass Measures concerning any matter affecting the Church of England, and even concerning Acts of Parliament. These Measures have statutory force upon receiving the Royal Assent.

Each diocese has a consistory court with jurisdiction over matters such as parochial libraries, the restoration of churches, and acts relating to land within the diocese.[415] Until recently these courts also had jurisdiction over disciplinary matters, but a Measure passed in 2003 and given effect in January 2006 establishes separate Disciplinary Tribunals for each diocese. These Tribunals have jurisdiction over priests and deacons, and can determine allegations of neglect of duty, conduct unbecoming a clerk in Holy Orders, and other forms of misconduct.[416] The Vicar-General's Court for each province continues to have jurisdiction over allegations of misconduct involving bishops.[417] Appeals from the above courts lie to the Arches Court of Canterbury or the Chancery Court of York: both of these are presided over by officers who must either be barristers of

---

[411] Ibid, at [44].

[412] This position is set out in a letter from the MoD to the Joint Committee on Human Rights, dated 22 February 2007. The letter is available online at: http://www.parliament.uk/documents/upload/ECtHR%20 20%20MOD%20220207.pdf

[413] Ibid.

[414] Under the Church of England Assembly (Powers) Act 1919, as amended by the Synodial Government Measure 1969, s 2(1).

[415] Ecclesiastical Jurisdiction Measure 1963, ss 1 and 6.

[416] Clergy Discipline Measure 2003, ss 2, 6(1), 7 and 22. It is clear from this Measure that the Church of England is not immune from the mood of reform that has swept through the legal system in recent years. Its effect will be to transform the ecclesiastical courts into something more recognisable as a judicial system. Amongst other things, it provides for the appointment of a President of Tribunals, the creation of a Disciplinary Commission with an advisory role, and the formulation of a Code of Practice. It also ensures that members of ecclesiastical courts enjoy greater security of tenure and cannot be removed from office without due process.

[417] Ibid, ss 6(2), 7 and 23.

ten years' standing, or persons who have held high judicial office.[418] Any further appeal lies to the Privy Council.[419]

The Court of Ecclesiastical Causes Reserved has jurisdiction over all members of the clergy in matters of 'doctrine, ritual or ceremonial'. This court is composed of five judges appointed by Her Majesty, and must include two persons who have held high judicial office.[420] Any appeal lies to a Commission of Review, which is currently composed of three Lords of Appeal in Ordinary and two Lords Spiritual.[421]

The ecclesiastical courts can impose a range of penalties, including removal from office. Such a penalty may be imposed when a clergyman is sentenced to imprisonment, or has a decree of divorce or order of separation pronounced against him on one of certain specified grounds.[422]

FURTHER READING

AULD LJ, *Review of the Criminal Courts of England and Wales* (2001)

BIRCH, 'A Better Deal for Vulnerable Witnesses?' [2000] Crim LR 223

CRAM, 'Reporting Restrictions in Criminal Proceedings and Article 10 of the ECHR' [1998] EHRLR 742

DARBYSHIRE, 'For the New Lord Chancellor: Some Causes for Concern about Magistrates' [1997] Crim LR 861

Department for Constitutional Affairs, *Constitutional Reform: Reforming the Office of the Lord Chancellor* (2003) CP 13/03

Department for Constitutional Affairs, *A Single Civil Court? The Scope for Unifying the Civil Jurisdictions of the High Court, the County Courts and the Family Proceedings Courts* (2005) CP 06/05

Department for Constitutional Affairs, *A Single Civil Court? Responses to the Consultation* (2005) CP(R) 06/05

Department for Constitutional Affairs, *Broadcasting Courts* (2005) CP 28/04

Department for Constitutional Affairs, *Broadcasting Courts: Responses to the Consultation* (2005) CP(R) 28/04

EADY and SMITH, *Arlidge, Eady and Smith on Contempt* (Sweet & Maxwell: 3rd edn, 2005)

FENWICK and PHILLIPSON, *Media Freedom under the Human Rights Act* (Oxford University Press: 2006)

HAMLYN, PHELPS, TURTLE, and SATTAR, *Are Special Measures Working? Evidence from Surveys of Vulnerable and Intimidated Witnesses* (London: Home Office Research Study No. 283; June 2004)

Home Office, *Death Certification and Investigation in England, Wales and Northern Ireland: The Report of a Fundamental Review,* Cm 5831, 2003

JACOB J, 'Bowman Review of the Court of Appeal' (1998) 61(3) MLR 390

JACONELLI, *Open Justice: A Critique of the Public Trial* (Oxford University Press: 2002)

---

[418] Ecclesiastical Jurisdiction Measure 1963, ss 1, 3, and 7.   [419] Ibid, s 8.

[420] Ibid, ss 5 and 10. The others must be bishops.   [421] Ibid, s 7.

[422] Clergy Discipline Measure 2003, ss 30 and 31.

Lyon, 'After Findlay – A Consideration of Some Aspects of the Military Justice System' [1998] Crim LR 109

Lyon, 'Two Swords and Two Standards' [2005] Crim LR 850

Miller, *Contempt of Court* (Oxford University Press: 3rd edn, 2000)

Morgan and Russell, *The Judiciary in the Magistrates' Courts* (Home Office: 2000)

Office for Criminal Justice Reform, *Improving the Criminal Trial Process for Young Witnesses: A Consultation Paper* (2007)

Ward and Davies, *Criminal Justice Act 2003: A Practitioners' Guide* (Jordans: 2004)

Woolf, *Final Report on Access to Justice* (Lord Chancellor's Department: 1996)

9

TRIBUNALS AND INQUIRIES

INTRODUCTION

The focus in this chapter is on the work of tribunals and inquiries. With all the attention given to courts it is easy to overlook the role of tribunals in the legal system, yet as revealed in a recent report they have a workload in the region of a million cases each year. Currently there are dozens of different tribunals, and they differ radically in structure and approach. However, recent legislation makes provision for a radical overhaul of the system, with the aim of producing a unified and integrated framework. This chapter aims to give an overview of the existing system, and to examine the key features of the current programme of reform. Consideration will also be given to the work of different types of inquiry. The specific areas addressed will be:

- The characteristics of tribunals and the differences between tribunals and courts.
- The ways in which tribunals are administered and controlled, including the roles of the Tribunals Service and the Administrative Justice and Tribunals Council.
- The Leggatt Report and the trend towards a more harmonized and integrated system.
- The Tribunals, Courts and Enforcement Act 2007, and the creation of two new tribunals.
- The work of some of the existing tribunals, including the Asylum and Immigration Tribunal and employment tribunals.
- The extent to which tribunals are subject to control and supervision by the courts.
- The work of inquiries and the different forms that inquiries may take.

TRIBUNALS: OVERVIEW

In 2001 Sir Andrew Leggatt reported that there were over seventy administrative tribunals operating in England and Wales,[1] in addition to a number of domestic tribunals and other regulatory bodies. The overwhelming majority of these were created

---

[1] *Tribunals for Users: One System, One Service – Report of the Review of Tribunals* (2001), overview, para 2.

during the twentieth century to provide cheap and informal mechanisms for resolving particular types of dispute. Most, though not all, adjudicate on matters involving the citizen and the state. Over the past half a century the Welfare State has grown rapidly, and virtually every aspect of life – from the economy and industry, to housing and the environment – is increasingly subject to governmental intervention and regulation. The potential for disputes between the citizen and the state has increased phenomenally, and this has been matched by an increase in the jurisdiction and workload of the tribunals. As far back as 1979, tribunals were dealing with almost six times as many cases as the courts.[2] They now handle around a million cases each year:[3]

> That number of cases alone makes their work of great importance to our society, since more of us bring a case before a tribunal than go to any other part of the justice system. Their collective impact is immense.

1 THE CHARACTERISTICS OF TRIBUNALS

The distinction between tribunals and courts is not a technical one. Both courts and tribunals have been described as 'machinery for adjudication',[4] and both have a duty to act judicially. Although the offence of contempt of court[5] can only be committed in relation to a court, some tribunals have been held to be 'courts' for these purposes,[6] and the Employment Appeal Tribunal is actually a superior court of record. The choice of terminology therefore has no formal significance, and in a general sense, *any* type of court or judicial body can be called a 'tribunal'. In the context of the English legal system however, the term is usually reserved for bodies which have more specialized areas of jurisdiction than the ordinary courts, and which often comprise both lawyers and expert lay members.

When compared to courts, tribunals are said to be relatively informal, accessible, quick, and inexpensive, but in fact there is enormous variation in the extent to which different tribunals possess these characteristics. Much depends on the nature of the matter being determined. Thus, employment tribunals are rather more formal than the Social Security and Child Support Appeals Tribunal, and the Lands Tribunal exhibits a degree of formality similar to that of the ordinary courts. There are also differences in the types of decisions that individual tribunals are required to make. Some tribunals deal with appeals against the decisions of government departments and public officials,[7] and some even hear appeals against the decisions of other tribunals.[8] Others have original jurisdiction to determine matters such as the discharge of patients in compulsory

---

[2] Royal Commission on Legal Services, Cmnd 7648, 1979.
[3] *Tribunals for Users* (2001) at para 1.1.
[4] Royal Commission on Legal Services, para 40.   [5] See p 246, *ante.*
[6] *Peach Grey & Co* v *Sommers* [1995] 2 All ER 513, [1995] ICR 549 (employment tribunals); applied in *Ewing* v *Security Services* [2003] EWCA Civ 581. *Pickering* v *Liverpool Daily Post and Echo Newspapers plc* [1991] 2 AC 370 [1991] 1 All ER 622 (Mental Health Review Tribunals).
[7] The Social Security and Child Support Appeals Tribunal, and the Asylum and Immigration Tribunal are just two examples.
[8] See e.g., the Employment Appeal Tribunal, discussed at p 307, *post.*

detention,[9] or the legal recognition of the gender of transsexual persons.[10] In addition, a small number of tribunals – notably employment tribunals – have jurisdiction to hear disputes between private citizens.

Although the jurisdiction of most tribunals concerns 'administrative' disputes, it would be a mistake to assume that these disputes are any less important than those coming before the courts. Some tribunals adjudicate on matters affecting fundamental rights, such as asylum decisions, claims of unlawful discrimination, and applications to be discharged from compulsory detention. Others, such as the Lands Tribunal, sometimes deal with claims involving very large sums of money. However, with the exception of the EAT,[11] tribunals are generally regarded as inferior to the ordinary courts, and they are subject to the supervisory jurisdiction of the High Court. In some cases they are also subject to the appellate jurisdiction of the High Court or Court of Appeal.[12]

2 COMPOSITION

The composition of most tribunals differs from that of the average court, and usually includes both legally qualified persons and lay people with relevant expertise. For example, an employment tribunal typically comprises a legally qualified chairman and two 'wing members'. One wing member will be a layman with experience of representing employers' interests; the other will have experience of representing the rights of workers. Similarly, experts in the fields of medicine, disability and finance sit alongside lawyers in the Social Security and Child Support Appeals Tribunal.

The lay members who serve on tribunals have, until now, generally been drawn from panels of experts appointed by government Ministers. As tribunals frequently have to adjudicate upon decisions made by those same Ministers, concerns have been raised about the extent to which panel members are genuinely independent. The arrangements for appointing the lay members of employment tribunals were the subject of a Human Rights Act challenge in *Scanfuture Ltd v Secretary of State for Trade and Industry*.[13] Before 1999 lay members were appointed by the Secretary of State on a short-term basis and they had no real security of tenure. The renewal of their contracts was entirely at the Secretary of State's discretion, and their remuneration was determined by the same Minister. The Employment Appeal Tribunal ruled that 'a fair-minded and informed observer' would justifiably fear that members appointed like this were not independent and impartial. For a tribunal including such members to determine a case involving the Minister was therefore incompatible with the right to a fair trial under Article 6 of the ECHR.[14]

The government had anticipated such a challenge,[15] and the arrangements for appointing the lay members of employment and other tribunals had already been reformed

---

[9] The Mental Health Review Tribunal.   [10] The Gender Recognition Panel.
[11] Employment Appeal Tribunal: see p 307, *post*.   [12] This is discussed further at p 533, *post*.
[13] [2001] ICR 1096, [2001] IRLR 416.   [14] Article 6 is discussed further at p 185, *ante*.
[15] It was clear from the decision in *Starrs v Ruxton* 2000 JC 208, 2000 SLT 42 that the terms upon which many part-time judges and tribunal members held office would have to be reviewed: see; p 337, *post*.

by the time that *Scanfuture* was decided. Under the current arrangements, the wing members of employment tribunals are appointed by the Lord Chancellor in consultation with the Secretary of State for Business, Enterprise and Regulatory Reform.[16] They are appointed for a fixed term which is automatically renewable, and they can only be removed from their posts on specified grounds.[17] The EAT in *Scanfuture* concluded that there is now 'no need or reason, if ever there was, for any lay member to think that... it would help him acquire a renewal of his office by his leaning in favour of the Secretary of State in any hearing.'[18] Thus, in the opinion of the EAT the current arrangements for appointing lay tribunal members are compatible with Article 6.

A similar issue arose in *Singh v Secretary of State for the Home Department*[19] in the context of a part-time immigration adjudicator. The adjudicator had been appointed for an initial term of one year, and although it was 'normal' for such appointments to be renewed on expiry, his conditions of service made it clear that renewal could not be guaranteed. They also stated that the Lord Chancellor reserved the right to terminate his appointment 'without cause' at one month's notice. The Scottish Court of Session held that these arrangements did not provide security of tenure and were therefore incompatible with both Article 6 and the existing common law test for bias. Again, however, the court noted that a modified appointments system had already been put in place, and it appeared that the new system provided the necessary safeguards.[20]

Sir Andrew Leggatt's review of tribunals[21] also raised concerns about independence, and it recommended that tribunal members should be appointed in the same way as members of the judiciary. Provisions to give effect to this recommendation were included in the Constitutional Reform Act 2005 and the Tribunals, Courts and Enforcement Act 2007. In future, most tribunal members will be selected by the Judicial Appointments Commission,[22] and the Lord Chancellor's role in approving or recommending its selections will be largely a formality.

3 ORGANIZATION AND CONTROL

There is a danger that tribunals might be viewed as part of the process of government rather than as part of a legal system providing an independent means of review. Extensive powers of adjudication have been granted to tribunals which are not demonstrably independent of government departments, and for almost a century concerns have been growing[23] about executive encroachment into the legislative and judicial

---

[16] The equivalent of what used to be the Secretary of State for Trade and Industry.

[17] These grounds are: (a) misbehaviour; (b) incapacity; (c) failure as to training; (d) failure to satisfy the sitting requirements; and (e) sustained failure to observe reasonably expected standards.

[18] *Scanfuture* v *Secretary of State for Trade and Industry* [2001] ICR 1096 at [41], [2001] IRLR 416 at [41], per Lindsay J.

[19] 2004 SLT 1058, (2004) *The Times* 23 January, Inner House.

[20] The composition of the Employment Appeal Tribunal was the subject of a different type of Article 6 challenge in *Lawal v Northern Spirit* [2003] UKHL 35, [2004] 1 All ER 187, [2003] ICR 856: see p 293, *post*.

[21] *Tribunals for Users* (2001) at para 2.32.   [22] See p 337, *post*.

[23] See, e.g., Lord Hewart CJ's reference to 'administrative lawlessness' in *The New Despotism* (1929).

areas. Some of these concerns were addressed by the Donoughmore Committee in 1932.[24] This recommended that:

    (a) the supervisory jurisdiction of the High Court over tribunals should be maintained;

    (b) tribunals should be compelled by the High Court to observe natural justice;

    (c) the reports of statutory inquiries should be published; and

    (d) there should be the possibility of an appeal from tribunals on a question of law.

These recommendations were generally given effect,[25] but concerns about independence persisted. Then, in 1957, the Franks Committee carried out a major review of administrative tribunals and inquiries.[26]

(a) The Franks Committee

The Franks Committee Report described tribunals as follows:[27]

> [They] are not ordinary courts, but neither are they appendages of Government Departments...tribunals should properly be regarded as machinery provided by Parliament for adjudication rather than as part of the machinery of administration. The essential point is that in all these cases Parliament has deliberately provided for a decision outside and independent of the Department concerned...and the intention of Parliament to provide for the independence of tribunals is clear and unmistakable.

The Report highlighted the need for tribunals to have the three key characteristics of openness, impartiality, and fairness. These are in fact the key principles underpinning the judicial system in England and Wales, and a court in an application for judicial review would consider them to be the basic standards of procedural fairness.[28] The Report also noted that tribunals have certain advantages over courts: cheapness, accessibility, informality, expert knowledge of their own areas of operation, and an ability to deal with cases relatively quickly. The volume of work, however, is now very substantial, and this militates against the speedy disposal of applications. By 1999, employment tribunals alone were dealing with in excess of 83,000 cases each year.[29]

(b) The Leggatt Review of Tribunals: One System, One Service

In 2000, Sir Andrew Leggatt was asked to chair the first major review of tribunals since the Franks Report. His objective was to recommend a system that would be 'coherent, professional, cost-effective and user-friendly',[30] and which would also be compatible

---

[24] *Report of the Committee on Ministers' Powers*, Cm 4060, 1932.

[25] The courts' supervisory jurisdiction over tribunals is discussed at p 309, *post*.

[26] *Report of the Committee on Administrative Tribunals and Enquiries*, Cmnd 218, 1957.

[27] Ibid, at para 2.45.

[28] See, e.g., *Doody v Secretary of State for Home Affairs* [1994] 1 AC 531, [1993] 3 All ER 92; *R v Board of Visitors of HM Prison, The Maze, ex parte Hone* [1988] AC 379, [1988] 1 All ER 321. See further, p 309, *post*.

[29] *Tribunals for Users* (*supra*, n 1), chapter on Employment Tribunals at para 3.

[30] Ibid, overview, para 1.

with the requirements for independence under Article 6 of the ECHR.[31] He reviewed the work of more than seventy different tribunals and concluded that they could not really be described as a 'system' at all:[32]

> [T]he present collection of tribunals has grown up in an almost entirely haphazard way. Individual tribunals were set up, and usually administered by departments, as they developed new statutory schemes and procedures. The result is a collection of tribunals, mostly administered by departments, with wide variations of practice and approach, and almost no coherence. The current arrangements seem to us to have been developed to meet the needs and conveniences of the departments and other bodies which run tribunals, rather than the needs of the user.

Leggatt expressed concern that most tribunals were still administered by the departments whose policies they had a duty to consider:[33]

> The very fact that a department is responsible for the policy and the legislation, under which cases are brought in the tribunal it sponsors, leads users to suppose that the tribunal is part of the same enterprise as its sponsoring department.

He concluded that greater independence and efficiency could be achieved by establishing a common administrative service with responsibility for *all* tribunals. A more coherent system could be developed by grouping the existing tribunals into nine divisions, with each division relating to a particular subject area. Thus, there should be divisions dealing with education, finance, health and social services, immigration, land and valuation, social security and pensions, transport, regulatory matters, and employment.[34] Each division should have a corresponding appellate or 'second-tier' tribunal, and there should be a right to appeal against first-tier decisions but only on a point of law. Any further appeal should lie to the Court of Appeal.[35] Leggatt also recommended a number of reforms designed to make tribunals more 'understandable, unthreatening and useful to users'.[36] These included training chairmen to provide better assistance to those presenting their own cases, improving tribunal procedures, making relevant information more accessible, and ensuring that voluntary and other advice groups were properly funded.

(c) Transforming Public Services: the Tribunals, Courts and Enforcement Act 2007

The Leggatt Review made a total of 361 separate recommendations and received a fairly cautious welcome from the government. A consultation paper published in August 2001 said that the government had an open-mind but wanted to consult more widely.[37] The responses to the consultation revealed very strong support for reform, and in July 2004 the Department for Constitutional Affairs published a White Paper setting out its own

---

[31] See p 187, *ante*. [32] *Tribunals for Users*, para 1.3.
[33] Ibid, overview, para 11. [34] Ibid, para 9.
[35] Ibid, para 14. [36] Ibid, para 6.
[37] Lord Chancellor's Department, *Tribunals for Users: Consultation Paper about the Report of the Review of Tribunals by Sir Andrew Leggatt* (2001).

vision for the future. This vision was described as 'different from, but compatible with' that of Leggatt:[38]

> We accept Sir Andrew Leggatt's key recommendation that tribunals provided by central government should be brought together into a unified system within what is now the Department for Constitutional Affairs. We believe that this will be more effective and efficient, and will firmly embed the principle of independence. But we see this new body as much more than a federation of existing tribunals. This is a new organisation and a new type of organisation. It will have two central pillars: administrative justice appeals, and employment cases. Its task, together with a transformed Council on Tribunals, will not be just to process cases according to law. Its mission will be to help to prevent and resolve disputes, using any appropriate method and working with its partners in and out of government, and to help to improve administrative justice and justice in the workplace, so that the need for disputes is reduced.

Transforming the existing network of tribunals into a unified and coherent system is a major undertaking, and at the time of writing the detail of the new system has yet to be worked out. However, the government has already taken a major step towards realization of this vision with the passage of the Tribunals, Courts and Enforcement Act 2007. Part 1 of this Act provides a new statutory framework under which all tribunals will eventually operate.

Section 1 of the Act extends to the tribunal judiciary the same guarantee of judicial independence set out in section 3 of the Constitutional Reform Act 2005. The Lord Chancellor and other Ministers now have a statutory duty to uphold the continued independence of tribunal judges, the Senior President of Tribunals,[39] and certain other tribunal officers, and they are specifically prohibited from seeking to influence particular judicial decisions through any special access to the judiciary. The Lord Chancellor is also required to have regard to the need to *defend* judicial independence, and to ensure that the judiciary have the support necessary to enable them to exercise their functions.[40] Section 2 of the Act creates the new post of Senior President of Tribunals, and the holder of this office is given a range of functions modelled on those performed by the Lord Chief Justice in relation to courts.[41] As to the shape of the new tribunals system, the government rejected Leggatt's proposal for a nine-division structure as unnecessary.[42] Instead, the 2007 Act provides for the creation of two generic tribunals into which most of the existing tribunal jurisdictions will be transferred.[43] Those jurisdictions will, however, be grouped into different 'chambers' within each tribunal, so that similar work can be dealt with by judges and tribunal members with relevant skills and experience.[44] The framework of the new tribunals' structure is discussed in more detail later on in this chapter.

---

[38] Department for Constitutional Affairs, *Transforming Public Services: Complaints, Redress and Tribunals*, Cm 6243, 2004, at para 1.14.

[39] See p 298, *post*.   [40] 2005 Act, s 3(6).   [41] See p 298, *post*.

[42] *Transforming Public Services* (*supra*, n 38) at para 6.38.

[43] Section 3.   [44] Section 7.

TRIBUNALS AND INQUIRIES 297

The Tribunals Service. The first stage in the reform process was to begin bringing the tribunals together within a single administrative framework, separate from their sponsoring departments. The Tribunals Service, which is an executive agency of the Ministry of Justice, was launched in April 2006 and already administers more than twenty-five different tribunals. They include all of the tribunals previously administered by the Department for Constitutional Affairs, together with employment tribunals, the Employment Appeal Tribunal, the Mental Health Review Tribunal, and others. More tribunals are expected to join the list in the near future, and the new tribunals created by the Tribunals, Courts and Enforcement Act 2007 will also fall within the Service's remit.

Establishing the Tribunals Service did not require new legislation, but it is a significant development nonetheless. Although tribunals have thus far been transferred to the Service in their existing state, it is envisaged that more will be done to integrate and modernize the system over the coming years. Plans to create a network of multi-jurisdictional hearing centres and administrative support centres are already under way, and 'proportionate dispute resolution procedures' will also be introduced with a view to reducing the number of cases proceeding to a full hearing.[45]

The Administrative Justice and Tribunals Council. One of the key recommendations of the Franks Report was the creation of a permanent statutory body to supervise and review the working of tribunals within its remit. This recommendation was given effect by the creation of the Council on Tribunals.[46] Its role was advisory and consultative, and its primary function was to keep the workings of tribunals under review and to report on them from time to time. It also gave advice on the appointment and training of tribunal members and on the rules under which they operate. Its influence was limited, however, and one commentator[47] suggested that its reports did 'little more than recite facts and make the occasional grumble'.

Under the Tribunals, Courts and Enforcement Act 2007, the Council on Tribunals has been transformed into a new body with enhanced powers. The Administrative Justice and Tribunals Council[48] (AJTC) was launched in November 2007, and it is charged with keeping the entire administrative justice system under review.[49] The 'administrative justice system' is defined to mean 'the overall system by which decisions of an administrative or executive nature are made in relation to particular persons, including: (a) the procedures for making such decisions; (b) the law under which such decisions are made; and (c) the systems for resolving disputes and airing grievances in relation to such decisions'.[50] The Parliamentary Commissioner for Administration is an *ex officio* member of the new body, and he is joined by between ten and fifteen other members appointed

---

[45] *Tribunals Service Strategic and Business Plan for 2007–08 – Delivering the Future: One System One Service* (2007) at p 6.
[46] Tribunals and Inquiries Act 1958: this was superseded by the Tribunals and Inquiries Act 1992.
[47] Lomas, 'The Twenty-Fifth Annual Report of the Council on Tribunals – An Opportunity Sadly Missed' (1985) 48 MLR 694.
[48] Established under s 44 of the 2007 Act.   [49] 2007 Act, Schedule 7, para 13.   [50] Ibid.

by the Lord Chancellor and Scottish and Welsh Ministers.[51] It is intended that the Council will focus first and foremost on the needs of users, and one of its duties is to consider ways of making the administrative justice system more accessible, fair and efficient.[52] Its other functions include: advising the Lord Chancellor and others on proposals for change and other matters;[53] reviewing the work of tribunals and scrutinizing relevant legislation;[54] and reviewing and reporting on the constitution and working of statutory inquiries.[55] The Council must also be consulted with regard to the procedural rules for tribunals within its remit,[56] and it is required to produce annual reports.[57]

The Senior President of Tribunals. The creation of this post was originally recommended by Leggatt, and section 2 of the Tribunals, Courts and Enforcement Act 2007 gives effect to his recommendation. The holder of the office sits 'at the apex of the tribunals' judiciary, giving a focus and leadership to those tribunals covered by the 2007 Act'.[58] There are two possible ways in which he can be appointed. One option is for the appointment to be made on the recommendation of the Lord Chancellor, following consultation with the Lord Chief Justice and his Scotland and Northern Ireland counterparts.[59] In this case the person selected must be a judge of the Court of Appeal, a judge of the Inner House of the Scottish Court of Session or a Lord Justice of Appeal in Northern Ireland. Alternatively, if the Lord Chancellor and those consulted cannot agree on a suitable candidate, the Judicial Appointments Commission will be asked to make a recommendation instead.[60] If this route is followed, the person recommended must satisfy the judicial-appointment eligibility requirement on a seven-year basis,[61] and as with other judicial appointments the Lord Chancellor will have only one right of rejection.[62]

Once the new tribunal framework is in place the Senior President will exercise a range of functions. He will have duties relating to the training, guidance and welfare of tribunal judges and members,[63] and together with the Lord Chancellor he will be responsible for determining the structure of tribunal chambers and the allocation of work between them.[64] He will have the power to issue practice directions,[65] and either the Senior President or his nominee will chair a Tribunal Procedure Committee with the power to make Tribunal Procedure Rules.[66] He will also be responsible for representing the views of tribunal members to Parliament, the Lord Chancellor and other Ministers.[67]

---

[51] Ibid, Schedule 7, para 1.   [52] Ibid, Schedule 7, para 13.   [53] Ibid.
[54] Ibid, Schedule 7, para 14.   [55] Ibid, Schedule 7, para 15.
[56] Ibid, Schedule 7, para 24.   [57] Ibid, Schedule 7, para 21.
[58] Ministry of Justice, *Transforming Tribunals: Implementing Part 1 of the Tribunals, Courts and Enforcement Act 2007* (2007) CP 30/07, at para 138.
[59] The appointment is technically made by the Monarch: see s 2(1) of the 2007 Act.
[60] 2007 Act, Schedule 1, para 2(5).
[61] Or have an equivalent status within the judiciary of Scotland or Northern Ireland: 2007 Act, schedule 1, para 3. See also p 338, *post.*
[62] 2007 Act, Schedule 1, para 3. See further, p 338, *post.*
[63] 2007 Act, Schedule 2, para 8; Schedule 3, para 9.   [64] Ibid, s 7.
[65] Ibid, s 23.   [66] Ibid, s 22; Schedule 5.   [67] Ibid, Schedule 1, para 14.

In carrying out his functions he will be required to have regard to the following: (a) the need for tribunals to be accessible; (b) the need for tribunal proceedings to be fair and to be handled quickly and efficiently; (c) the need for tribunal members to have expertise in their areas of jurisdiction; and (d) the need to develop innovative methods of dispute resolution.[68]

SPECIFIC TRIBUNALS

As outlined above, the Tribunals, Courts and Enforcement Act 2007 provides for the creation of two new generic tribunals, to which it is envisaged that the jurisdiction of most of the existing tribunals will be transferred. At the time of writing much of the detail of the new system has still to be worked out, but the basic framework is set out in the 2007 Act. The key features of the new tribunals, and those of two of the tribunals which they will eventually replace – the Appeals Service and the Criminal Injuries Compensation Appeals Panel – are discussed in the pages that follow. The major tribunals which are intended to remain separate under the new system – the Asylum and Immigration Tribunal, the employment tribunals and the Employment Appeal Tribunal – are also discussed.

1 THE APPEALS SERVICE

In 1998 the social security appeals tribunals[69] were combined with the disability appeals tribunals, medical appeal tribunals, vaccine damage tribunals, and child support appeal tribunals to form a unified system with a single jurisdiction.[70] The resulting Appeals Service – also known since 2006 as the Social Security and Child Support Appeals Tribunal – handles over 250,000 cases each year.[71] Its workload consists mainly of appeals against decisions concerning entitlement to welfare benefits and other payments. It has a President,[72] 70 salaried and legally qualified panel members, and around 1,800 other fee-paid panel members.[73] Those members who are not legally qualified are appointed for their expertise in the fields of medicine, finance, and dealing with the needs of the disabled.[74] The President's role is primarily managerial and administrative. He has a statutory obligation to provide panel members with training, and he produces an annual report on the standard of the Secretary of State's decision-making in cases reaching appeal.[75]

---

[68] Ibid, s 2(3).

[69] These tribunals were themselves born out of a merger, in that they were created by combining supplementary benefits tribunals and National Insurance tribunals: Health and Social Services and Social Security Adjudications Act 1983. The origins of the system can be traced back to the Court of Referees, created by the National Insurance Act 1911.

[70] Social Security Act 1998, s 4.   [71] *The Appeals Service Annual Report 2005–2006*, at p 8.

[72] 1998 Act, s 5.   [73] *The Appeals Service Annual Report 2005–2006*, at p 7.

[74] Social Security and Child Support (Decisions and Appeals) Regulations 1999, SI 1999/991, Schedule 3.

[75] Schedule 1 of the 1998 Act.

Certain cases can only be determined by a lawyer sitting with one or two other panel members, but many can be heard by a lawyer sitting alone.[76] The conduct of hearings is deliberately informal, and panel members are expected to be pro-active in eliciting the facts and applying the relevant law. This is extremely important because most applicants are not represented at the hearing[77] and many do not even attend.[78] An appeal to a Social Security or Child Support Commissioner on a point of law is possible, but only with the leave of the tribunal or its chairman.[79] Any further appeal from the decision of a Commissioner normally lies to the Court of Appeal.[80] Until recently, responsibility for administering the Appeals Service rested with the Department for Work and Pensions, but since April 2006 it has been administered by the Tribunals Service.

In certain respects the Appeals Service was the model for the unified tribunals service proposed by Leggatt.[81] Replacing five separate jurisdictions with one has enabled the Appeals Service to adopt common procedures, and allowed greater flexibility in the deployment of resources: tribunal members appointed to the single jurisdiction can now be allocated to any type of case for which they have suitable expertise. Although Leggatt did not suggest that all tribunals should be unified in this way, this is, in effect, the approach now being adopted under the Tribunals, Courts and Enforcement Act 2007.

2 THE CRIMINAL INJURIES COMPENSATION APPEALS PANEL

In 1964 the government used prerogative powers[82] to create a scheme for compensating the victims of violent crime. Claims were administered by the Criminal Injuries Compensation Board and were assessed on the same basis as common law damages.

The scheme was placed on a statutory footing in 1995[83] and the Board was replaced by the Criminal Injuries Compensation Authority.[84] Awards are now calculated by reference to a tariff, which sets minimum and maximum amounts for each type of injury. A claimant who is dissatisfied with the decision of a claims officer can apply in writ-

[76] Ibid, s 7.
[77] Public funding is not available for representation in Appeals Service cases. The proportion of applicants who are legally represented is therefore very small.
[78] See Wikeley, Ogus, and Barendt, *The Law of Social Security* (5th edn, 2002). The success rate for unrepresented applicants is quite low.
[79] 1998 Act, s 14. If a person considering an application for leave to appeal is satisfied that the decision is wrong in law, he has the power to set it aside and refer it for re-determination to the same or a differently constituted tribunal: s 13(2).
[80] Ibid, s 15.
[81] *Tribunals for Users (supra*, n 1), chapter on the Appeals Service, at para 16.
[82] See *R v Criminal Injuries Compensation Board, ex parte Lain* [1967] 2 QB 864, [1967] 2 All ER 770; for a discussion of the royal prerogative, see chapter 7.
[83] Criminal Injuries Compensation Act 1995. Provisions to establish a statutory regime were included in the Criminal Justice Act 1988 but were never actually implemented: see *R v Secretary of State for the Home Department, ex parte Fire Brigades Union* [1995] 2 AC 513, [1995] 2 All ER 244. The scheme created under the 1995 Act was later revised and the current version dates from 2001.
[84] The Board was abolished on 1 April 2000.

ing to have it reviewed by someone in a more senior position. If the review is unsuccessful the claimant then has ninety days in which to appeal to the Criminal Injuries Compensation Appeals Panel.

The Panel has a chairman and around 75 other members, just under half of whom are legally qualified. Appeals are heard by either two or three members, one of whom must be a lawyer. At the hearing the appellant must prove his case on a balance of probabilities. He may choose to have a legal adviser or other representative present, and he may call, examine and cross-examine witnesses. The procedure is informal and adjudicators are not bound by strict rules of evidence. The Leggatt Report found that around 60 per cent of claimants were represented at appeal hearings, although it praised the supportive and constructive way in which unrepresented appellants were dealt with.[85] There is no right of appeal against the Panel's decisions but they are subject to the possibility of judicial review.[86]

Administrative responsibility for the Panel has rested with the Tribunals Service since its launch in April 2006.

3   THE NEW TRIBUNALS

The framework established by the Tribunals, Courts and Enforcement Act 2007 provides for the creation of two new tribunals: the First-tier Tribunal and the Upper Tribunal.[87] Section 30 empowers the Lord Chancellor to transfer the jurisdictions of tribunals listed in Schedule 6 to either of these new tribunals. Most of the tribunal jurisdictions currently administered by central government are covered by Schedule 6, including those of the Appeals Service and the Criminal Injuries Compensation Appeals Panel. However, certain jurisdictions will remain outside the new framework: the Asylum and Immigration Tribunal because of its unique single-tier structure, and the employment tribunals and Employment Appeal Tribunal because they hear 'party and party' disputes as opposed to appeals against administrative decisions. Tribunals which are currently administered by local government fall outside the scope of the 2007 Act altogether.

The First-tier Tribunal. The First-tier Tribunal will have a broad jurisdiction and will undoubtedly be very large: it is anticipated that it will eventually have an annual workload in the region of 300,000 cases, and that it will be served by around 90 judges and 3,600 other members.[88] However, section 7 of the 2007 Act provides for the new Tribunal to be divided into distinct Chambers, so that similar types of jurisdiction can be grouped together. The government appears to envisage something akin to the divisional structure of the High Court, with tribunal members having a common jurisdiction but being assigned to particular types of work according to their expertise.[89] The Chamber structure is designed to be flexible, and the Lord Chancellor and Senior President will have

---

[85]   *Tribunals for Users (supra,* n 1) at paras 4 and 9.   [86]   See p 309, *post.*
[87]   Section 3.   [88]   *Transforming Tribunals (supra,* n 58), at para 149.
[89]   *Transforming Public Services (supra,* n 38), at para 717.

302 PART II THE ADMINISTRATION OF JUSTICE

the power to make changes as and when required.[90] Initially, however, the government is proposing to establish five Chambers covering the following areas: (1) social entitlement; (2) general regulatory; (3) health, education and social care; (4) taxation; and (5) land, property and housing.[91]

Each Chamber of the First-tier Tribunal will have one or two Presidents, and each Chamber President must also be a judge of the Upper Tribunal.[92] The tribunal's legally qualified members will be titled 'Judge of the First-tier Tribunal', and it is anticipated that those who are appointed for their expertise in other areas will be known as 'members'.[93] Section 31(2) provides that when tribunals are transferred to the new jurisdiction, their existing members may be appointed as 'transferred-in' judges or members of one of the new tribunals. Others may be appointed by the Lord Chancellor on the basis of their qualifications or experience, following selection by the Judicial Appointments Commission.[94] The judges and members of the employment tribunals and Asylum and Immigration Tribunal may also be requested to sit, and the holders of other judicial posts may also be called upon.[95]

The Upper Tribunal. The primary role of the Upper Tribunal will be to hear appeals against the decisions of the First-tier Tribunal. The idea is thus to create a common appeals structure for the tribunals system, with any further appeal lying to the Court of Appeal.[96] However, the Upper Tribunal may also be given a first instance jurisdiction in relation to certain types of case. The test will be whether it is thought appropriate for an appeal against the first instance decision to lie directly to the Court of Appeal.[97]

The Upper Tribunal will be a superior court of record,[98] and its decisions will be binding on lower tribunals and authoritative on points of law. Like the First-tier, it will be organized into Chambers dealing with particular areas of work.[99] The government's current proposal is that there should be three Chambers, dealing with administrative appeals, finance and tax, and land.[100] Each Chamber will have its own President,[101] and judges and members will be appointed in much the same way as for the First-tier.[102] The intention is that most of the Upper Tribunal's members will initially be transferred-in from existing appellate tribunals or drawn from the High Court bench.[103] Although it will have both judges and other members its decisions will frequently be based on points of law, and this means that non-judicial members will not always be required to sit.[104]

---

[90] 2007 Act, s 7.   [91] *Transforming Tribunals* (*supra*, n 58), at para 149.

[92] 2007 Act, s 7; Schedule 4.

[93] Section 4. At the time of writing the government is still considering whether the title 'member' is sufficient to designate those who are not judges. 'Expert member' is one of the alternatives mooted in its consultation paper: *Transforming Tribunals* (*supra*, n 58), at para 241.

[94] 2007 Act, Schedule 2.   [95] Ibid.

[96] Ibid, ss 11–14. The role of the courts in reviewing the decisions of tribunals is discussed further at p 309, *post.*

[97] *Transforming Tribunals* (*supra*, n 58), at para 203.   [98] 2007 Act, s 3(5).

[99] Ibid, s 7.   [100] *Transforming Tribunals* (*supra*, n 58), at para. 179.

[101] 2007 Act, s 7(2).   [102] Ibid, Schedule 3.

[103] *Transforming Tribunals* (*supra*, n 58), at para 186.   [104] Ibid, at para 220.

Many of the existing tribunals currently have limited or no rights of appeal, and section 11 of the new Act will create a general right to appeal from the First-tier to the Upper Tribunal on a point of law. This will merely be a default position, however, and the right of appeal may be excluded by the Lord Chancellor using delegated legislation. There is also provision for the Upper Tribunal to exercise a judicial review jurisdiction, and it will be able to grant the prerogative remedies already available to the High Court.[105] However, this jurisdiction will only apply to categories of case specified in directions made by the Lord Chief Justice, and to individual cases transferred by the High Court or Court of Session.[106] A further limitation is that only judges of the High Court, Court of Session and Court of Appeal will be able to hear such 'judicial review' cases.[107]

4 THE ASYLUM AND IMMIGRATION TRIBUNAL

Launched in April 2005, this tribunal has jurisdiction to hear appeals against Home Office decisions in matters relating to immigration and asylum.[108] Its predecessor, the Immigration Appellate Authorities (IAA) comprised two separate bodies: the Immigration Adjudicators and the Immigration Appeal Tribunal (IAT). The Adjudicators handled appeals from decisions made by entry clearance officials, immigration officers, and the Home Secretary, whilst the IAT had jurisdiction to hear second-tier appeals from decisions of the Adjudicators. Before 2002, appeals to the IAT could be based on grounds of both fact and law. This made it almost inevitable that an unsuccessful appeal to the Adjudicators would be the subject of a further challenge in the IAT. In his Review of Tribunals, Leggatt concluded that these arrangements had a negative effect on the perceived authority of the Adjudicators and contributed to a 'culture of challenge'. He also suggested that the expert contribution of non-lawyers was made too late in the process: all Immigration Adjudicators were legally qualified and usually sat alone, but appeals to the IAT were heard by a legally qualified chairman sitting with one or two lay members. Leggatt recommended that lay members and lawyers should sit together at the Adjudicator stage to determine both the facts and the law: any further appeal to the IAT should only be possible on a point of law and should therefore be determined by a lawyer sitting alone.[109] His recommendations were given partial effect by the Nationality, Immigration and Asylum Act 2002, which restricted the jurisdiction of the IAT to appeals based on points of law.[110] The involvement of lay members remained unchanged, however, with the rather odd result that they were only able to contribute to the appeals process at a stage where purely legal issues were being determined. Just two years after these reforms were introduced the entire system was radically overhauled by the Asylum and Immigration (Treatment of Claimants etc.) Act 2004. The system of second-tier appeals was ended, and both the Adjudicators and

---

[105] 2007 Act, s 15. [106] Ibid, ss 18(6),19 and 20. [107] Ibid, s 18(8).

[108] The key provisions are contained in Part 5 of the Nationality, Immigration and Asylum Act 2002 (as amended by the Asylum and Immigration (Treatment of Claimants etc.) Act 2004).

[109] *Tribunals for Users* (*supra*, n 1), Part III, recommendations 298–301.

[110] 2002 Act, s 101 (now repealed).

the IAT were replaced with a single-tier Asylum and Immigration Tribunal.[111] Due to the unique nature of this tribunal, its jurisdiction will not be transferred to the system created by the Tribunals, Courts and Enforcement Act 2007.

As with the previous system, the IAT Tribunal has no jurisdiction in respect of decisions taken on national security grounds,[112] and it cannot review asylum claims certified by the Home Secretary as being manifestly unfounded or as having originated in a country which is presumed safe.[113] The government had originally intended that the Tribunal's decisions should not be subject to judicial review, but its proposed ouster clause was withdrawn from the Asylum Bill in the face of considerable opposition.[114] The compromise eventually reached means that the Tribunal's decisions may be judicially reviewed on the grounds of an error of law, but any challenge must be made within five days of the original decision and only written submissions will be examined.[115] Where a Tribunal decision has already been reconsidered, any further challenge on a point of law lies to the Court of Appeal and can only be made with leave.[116]

The Tribunal itself comprises both lawyers and persons with suitable non-legal experience, and the Lord Chancellor is required to appoint a President and at least one Deputy President. It is for the President to determine how many members should hear particular cases or classes of case, having regard to their complexity and other circumstances.[117]

5   EMPLOYMENT TRIBUNALS

Employment tribunals are by far the most important example of 'party and party' tribunals – tribunals with jurisdiction to hear disputes between individuals.[118] One of the issues addressed by Leggatt was whether such tribunals should be linked more closely with the courts, but on balance he concluded that this would not be in the interests of the user:[119]

> There are arguments for . . . keeping party and party [tribunals] separate from those dealing with administrative law. They are the parts of the tribunal system closest in essential function to the ordinary courts. The need for a fundamentally adversarial approach to cases has produced similarities in procedure. There is therefore an argument for party and party tribunals either to be merged with the ordinary

---

[111] Ibid, s 81; as substituted by the 2004 Act, s 26.

[112] On this point see the powers and jurisdiction of the Special Immigration Appeals Commission, as conferred by the Special Immigration Appeals Commission Act 1997, ss 1 and 2.

[113] 2002 Act, s 94 (as amended). The 2004 Act extends the powers of the Secretary of State in this regard, allowing him to certify that all or part of a country is presumed safe for particular classes of person.

[114] See the discussion of clause 11 at p 333, *post*.

[115] 2002 Act, s 103A (inserted by the 2004 Act). Those applying from abroad must do so within twenty-eight days.

[116] Ibid, s 103B.

[117] Detailed rules regarding the Tribunal are set out in a new Schedule 4 to the 2002 Act, and in the Asylum and Immigration Tribunal (Procedure) Rules 2005, SI 2005/230.

[118] The Lands Tribunal is another example of a tribunal with 'party and party' jurisdiction.

[119] *Tribunals for Users* (*supra*, n 1), paras 3.18–3.19.

courts, or to remain a separate body of tribunals but in a closer relationship with the courts…[P]arty and party tribunals are falling behind the modern courts in terms of speed, active case management, the effective conduct of hearings, and even informality. A closer relationship might promote modernisation and further the development of the new civil procedures…

Against these arguments should be set the distinctive benefits for the user in having cases decided by tribunals: the opportunities if procedures and hearings are simple and informal enough for users reasonably to expect to handle cases themselves, if properly supported; and better decisions if they are taken jointly by lawyers and experts…This has led us to conclude that the features which are common to citizen and state tribunals and party and party tribunals are much more important than those which divide them. Both should therefore form part of the Tribunals System.

The government accepted the recommendation that party and party tribunals should remain part of the system, but in recognition of their distinctive role, employment tribunals will remain as separate entities when the new tribunals framework is established.

First created in 1964, and until 1998 known as industrial tribunals,[120] employment tribunals now have jurisdiction to hear more than eighty different types of complaint. Their jurisdiction includes most claims in damages for breach of an employment contract,[121] along with claims relating to unfair dismissal,[122] unlawful discrimination,[123] and equal pay.[124] Until recently they were administered by an agency of the Department of Trade and Industry, but they have now been integrated with the Tribunals Service.[125]

In common with many other tribunals, employment tribunals comprise both lawyers and expert lay members. The lawyers are now known as 'employment judges',[126] and they must be barristers or solicitors of seven years standing.[127] The lay members are divided into two panels: one comprising those with experience of representing workers; the other consisting of persons experienced in representing employers' interests.[128] Until recently, members of the lay panels were appointed by the Secretary of State for Trade and Industry, prompting concerns that they were not sufficiently independent of the Minister whose policies they often have to consider.[129] These concerns have now been addressed, and under the current arrangements the wing members of employment tribunals are appointed by the Lord Chancellor in consultation with the Secretary

---

[120] They were renamed by the Employment Rights (Dispute Resolution) Act 1998, s 1.

[121] Employment Tribunals Extension of Jurisdiction Order 1994, SI 1994/1623. Employment tribunals do not have jurisdiction over claims relating to personal injuries and certain other matters, and cannot make awards exceeding £25,000.

[122] Employment Rights Act 1996, s 111.

[123] Sex Discrimination Act 1975, Race Relations Act 1976, Disability Discrimination Act 1995, Employment Equality (Religion or Belief) Regulations 2003, SI 2003/1660; Employment Equality (Sexual Orientation) Regulations 2003, SI 2003/1661; Employment Equality (Age) Regulations 2006, SI 2006/1031.

[124] Equal Pay Act 1970.   [125] See p 294, *ante*.

[126] Employment Tribunals Act 1996, s 3A – as inserted by the Tribunals, Courts and Enforcement Act 2007.

[127] Employment Tribunals (Constitution and Rules of Procedure) Regulations 2004, SI 2004/1861, reg 8.

[128] Ibid.   [129] See p 295, *ante*.

of State for Business, Enterprise and Regulatory Reform.[130] Their conditions of service have also been modified to ensure that they have greater security of tenure.[131] In future, all those who sit on employment tribunals will be selected by the Judicial Appointments Commission.

The system is headed by a President of Employment Tribunals,[132] whose functions include determining the number and location of tribunals, selecting employment judges and lay members for hearings, and sitting as a chairman himself.[133] Section 4 of the Employment Tribunals Act 1996[134] provides that cases should normally be heard by an employment judge sitting with two lay members. Regulations[135] further stipulate that one lay member should be drawn from each of the two panels, so that both sides of the industry are represented. Decisions are made by majority, and the chairman may therefore be outvoted if the lay members agree with each other as to the appropriate conclusion. Certain types of case can be determined by a chairman sitting alone,[136] including breach of contract cases and cases concerning the minimum wage. In addition, the parties may consent to *any* case being heard by a chairman sitting alone or with one lay member,[137] though the tribunal can override their wishes if a three-member panel is considered more suitable.[138]

Hearings are conducted in much the same way as in the ordinary civil courts, with rules of evidence generally, though not always, being adhered to.[139] An applicant may appear in person or be represented by counsel, a solicitor, a representative of a trade union or employers' association, or any other person whom he desires to represent him.[140] Many parties do appear in person, but there is concern that it is becoming increasingly difficult for unrepresented parties to contest cases successfully; particularly where aspects of European or anti-discrimination law are involved.[141] Public funding is not currently available for legal representation at employment tribunals, and an obvious way of assisting users would be to lift this restriction. Such a move would be extremely costly, however,[142] and Leggatt suggested that it would be better to concentrate

---

[130] The equivalent of what used to be the Secretary of State for Trade and Industry.

[131] See p 292, *ante; Scanfuture* v *Secretary of State for Trade and Industry* [2001] ICR 1096, [2001] IRLR 416.

[132] For England and Wales. A President of the Scottish Employment Tribunals is also appointed.

[133] Employment Tribunals (Constitution and Rules of Procedure) Regulations 2004, SI 2004/1861, regs 4–9.

[134] This was originally called the Industrial Tribunals Act but was renamed by the Employment Rights (Dispute Resolution) Act 1998.

[135] SI 2004/1861, reg 9.   [136] These are set out in s 4(3) of the 1996 Act.

[137] Ibid, s 4(1)(b); s 4(3).

[138] *Sogbetun* v *London Borough of Hackney* [1998] IRLR 676, [1998] ICR 1264.

[139] See the 2004 Regulations: SI 2004/1861. See also, MacMillan, 'Employment Tribunals: Philosophies and Practicalities' (1999) 28(1) ILJ 4.

[140] Employment Tribunals Act 1996, s 6. The right to be represented by a person of one's choosing is unqualified and cannot be restricted by the tribunal: *Bache* v *Essex County Council* [2000] 2 All ER 847.

[141] For a recent study of the experiences of tribunal users, see Adler and Gulland, *Tribunal Users' Experiences, Perceptions and Expectations: A Literature Review* (2003). Earlier research by Genn and Genn suggested that the benefits of representation for the tribunal user were significant: 'The Effectiveness of Representation at Tribunals' (1989, Lord Chancellor's Department).

[142] In 2006/07, employment tribunals received 132,577 applications: *Employment Tribunal and EAT Statistics (GB): 1 April 2006 – 31 March 2007.*

on improving the informality and accessibility of the system.[143] On the other hand, the nature of employment law is such that the Employment Tribunal Taskforce has doubted whether a less formal and complex system can really be achieved.[144]

Appeals against the decisions of employment tribunals lie to the Employment Appeal Tribunal (EAT) on a point of law. The proportion of cases which are the subject of an appeal to the EAT is very low – around 4 per cent[145] – and this is probably due in part to the number of parties who contest employment cases without the benefit of professional advice.

6 THE EMPLOYMENT APPEAL TRIBUNAL

The Employment Appeal Tribunal (EAT) was established in 1976[146] to hear appeals against the decisions of employment tribunals. It is a superior court of record and has all the characteristics of a court.[147] It comprises a number of judges nominated from the High Court and the Court of Appeal, at least one judge from Scotland's Court of Session, and such other lay members as may be appointed.[148] One of the judges is appointed President. The lay members are persons with special knowledge or experience of industrial relations, and they hold the highest judicial office available to a person without legal qualifications. The EAT is duly constituted when sitting with a judge and either two or four lay members.[149] As with employment tribunals, the lay members must be drawn in equal numbers from panels representing both sides of industry.

Senior barristers have sometimes been used as part-time EAT judges, but this practice was called into question when a barrister appeared as an advocate before lay members with whom he had sat in a judicial capacity. The claimant complained that this situation gave rise to a real possibility of bias, and the EAT agreed that his appeal should be heard by a differently constituted tribunal. The issue of principle was eventually referred to the House of Lords,[150] which held that for a judge to appear as an advocate under these circumstances would be contrary to both the common law and the ECHR right to a fair trial:[151]

> Would...an observer consider that it was reasonably possible that the wing member[s] may be subconsciously biased? The observer is likely to approach the matter on the basis that the lay members look to the judge for guidance on the law, and can be expected to develop a fairly close relationship of trust and confidence with the judge.[152]

---

[143] *Tribunals for Users* (*supra*, n 1), chapter on Employment Tribunals, at para 11.

[144] *Report of the Employment Tribunal Taskforce* (2002), at para 8.25. [145] Ibid, para 8.47.

[146] Employment Protection Act 1975, s 87. Its predecessor, the National Industrial Relations Court, was established under the Industrial Relations Act 1971 and abolished after only three years.

[147] It can only punish for contempt with the consent of one of its judicial members: Employment Tribunals Act 1996, s 36.

[148] Employment Tribunals Act 1996, s 22.

[149] Ibid, s 28. With the consent of the parties cases may be heard by a judge and either one or three other members.

[150] *Lawal* v *Northern Spirit* [2003] UKHL 35, [2004] 1 All ER 187, [2003] ICR 856.

[151] European Convention on Human Rights, Article 6: see p 185, *ante*.

[152] [2003] UKHL 35 at [21], [2004] 1 All ER 187 at [21], per Lord Steyn.

Their Lordships noted that the chairmen of employment tribunals were not permitted to appear as advocates before other tribunals in the same region, and they recommended that the EAT should adopt the same policy. Following this decision, it was announced that the practice of allowing barristers to sit as part-time EAT judges would be phased out.

The EAT's rules of procedure[153] aim at informality: no-one appears robed, there is no bench or witness box, and parties and their advisers sit at tables and address the court seated. In most other respects however, EAT hearings are very similar to those found in the ordinary courts. A party may appear in person or he may be represented by counsel, a solicitor, a representative of a trade union or employers' association, or any other person whom he desires to represent him.[154] Although employment tribunals are not covered by the Community Legal Service scheme, eligible persons can apply for public funding for representation at EAT hearings. Any decision of the EAT on a question of fact is final, and as a superior court of record, its decisions are not subject to the High Court's supervisory jurisdiction.[155] Any appeal on a point of law lies to the Court of Appeal.[156] As with employment tribunals, the EAT is administered by the new Tribunals Service.[157]

7 DOMESTIC TRIBUNALS

A number of private and professional associations have set up their own bodies for resolving disputes between their members and enforcing internal discipline. As these bodies are concerned with matters of private rather than public importance, they are often referred to as 'domestic tribunals'. Their jurisdiction is based primarily on contract: by becoming a member of the association or professional body concerned, a person contracts to accept the jurisdiction of its governing tribunal. Nevertheless, in several cases these tribunals exist on a statutory basis with a right of appeal to the courts. Examples of domestic tribunals constituted under statute are the Solicitors Disciplinary Tribunal[158] and the Investigation Committee of the General Medical Council.[159] Examples of tribunals created by private bodies themselves include the Disciplinary Tribunal of the Bar[160] and the Football Association's Disciplinary Committee. The decisions of a non-statutory tribunal cannot be the subject of an appeal to the ordinary courts, and they will not be amenable to judicial review unless the tribunal concerned is a public body performing public functions.[161] It may, however, be possible to mount a legal challenge using some other means: this is considered in more detail below.

---

[153] Employment Appeal Tribunal Rules 1993, SI 1993/2854; Employment Appeal Tribunal (Amendment) Rules 2001, SI 2001/1128; Employment Appeal Tribunal (Amendment) Rules 2004, SI 2004/2526; Employment Appeal Tribunal (Amendment) Rules 2005, SI 2005/1871; *Practice Direction (EAT: Appeal Procedure)* [2005] IRLR 94.

[154] Employment Tribunals Act 1996, s 29.   [155] See p 261, *ante.*   [156] 1996 Act, s 37.

[157] See p 295, *ante.*   [158] Solicitors Act 1974, s 46: see p 393, *post.*

[159] Medical Act 1983, s 1(3), as amended.   [160] See p 394, *post.*

[161] *Law v National Greyhound Racing Club* [1983] 3 All ER 300, [1983] 1 WLR 1302; *R v Disciplinary Committee of the Jockey Club, ex parte the Aga Khan* [1993] 2 All ER 853, [1993] 1 WLR 909. The relevant test was established in *R v Panel on Take-overs and Mergers, ex parte Datafin plc* [1987] QB 815, [1987] 1 All ER 564. In *R v General Council of the Bar, ex parte Percival* [1991] 1 QB 212, [1990] 3 All ER 137 a decision of the Bar Council's Professional Conduct Committee was held to be judicially reviewable. See p 217, *ante.*

CONTROL OF TRIBUNALS BY THE COURTS

1 APPEALS FROM TRIBUNALS

There is no right to appeal against the decision of a tribunal at common law, but in some cases a right to appeal on a point of law is provided by statute. The Tribunals and Inquiries Act 1992 establishes a statutory right to appeal to the High Court[162] against the decisions of a number of tribunals. In addition, the EAT is a rare example of a tribunal from which an appeal to the Court of Appeal is currently possible.[163]

When the new tribunals framework is eventually introduced, it is intended that there should be a more uniform appeals structure, with the Upper Tribunal[164] serving as an appellate body for the rest of the system. There will be a general right to appeal from the First-tier to the Upper Tribunal on a point of law, though this right may be excluded by the Lord Chancellor in relation to particular categories of case.[165] Any further appeal will lie to the Court of Appeal, and will require the permission of either this court or the Upper Tribunal.[166] The Lord Chancellor intends to introduce legislation limiting such appeals to cases which raise important points of principle or practice, or which are justified by other compelling reasons.[167] The government has described the creation of the Upper Tribunal as 'the most significant innovation' in its reform programme.[168]

The present arrangements are illogical and incoherent, reflecting the piecemeal historical development of the tribunal system. Appeals routes from first instance tribunals in England and Wales vary between specialized tribunals, the High Court (Administrative Court or Chancery Division), and the Court of Appeal. In some cases there is no statutory right of appeal, but judicial review provides an alternative remedy in the Administrative Court; or judicial review may be required to fill the gaps in a restricted statutory scheme. There are similar variations in the form and nature of the appeal, for example: whether on law only, or on law and fact; whether leave is required; and whether the procedure is primarily oral or written.

The creation of the Upper Tribunal provides the opportunity not only to rationalize the procedures, but also to establish a strong and dedicated appellate body at the head of the new system. Its authority will derive from its specialist skills and its status as a superior court of record, with judicial review powers, presided over by the Senior President.

2 SUPERVISORY CONTROL

Administrative and 'party and party' tribunals are public bodies performing public functions, and they are amenable to the High Court's supervisory jurisdiction in the same way as the inferior courts. This common law jurisdiction provides a basis

---

[162] Section 11. These appeals are heard by a Divisional Court of the Queen's Bench Division.
[163] Employment Tribunals Act 1996, s 37.   [164] See p 302, *ante.*
[165] Tribunals, Courts and Enforcement Act 2007, s 11.   [166] Ibid, s 13.
[167] Ibid, s 13(6); *Transforming Tribunals* (*supra*, n 58), at para 178.
[168] *Transforming Tribunals*, at paras 177–178.

for challenging decisions which have been made ultra vires or which are contrary to principles of natural justice. It is usually exercised by issuing one of the prerogative orders[169] in an application for judicial review,[170] though these remedies are not available in respect of bodies whose functions are essentially private in nature.

The Tribunals, Courts and Enforcement Act 2007 makes provision for the Upper Tribunal to exercise a limited judicial review jurisdiction.[171] However, this jurisdiction will only apply to categories of case specified in directions made by the Lord Chief Justice, and to individual cases transferred by the High Court or Court of Session.[172] A further limitation is that only judges of the High Court, Court of Session and Court of Appeal will be able to hear such 'judicial review' cases.[173]

3 CHALLENGING THE DECISIONS OF 'PRIVATE' DISCIPLINARY BODIES

Few domestic tribunals have public functions, and most derive their authority from a contractual relationship with those under their supervision. The decisions of these private bodies cannot be the subject of a prerogative order,[174] but the courts still have jurisdiction to determine whether they have been made fairly and in accordance with natural justice. The High Court has shown an increased willingness to intervene in the affairs of bodies which can deprive individuals of their livelihoods, and an aggrieved party may be able to challenge a decision by seeking a declaration or injunction.[175] Thus, in *Korda* v *International Tennis Federation*[176] the court granted a declaration as to the correct interpretation of the Federation's rules. The defendant's Disciplinary Committee had sanctioned the claimant for a breach of its anti-doping policy, but a dispute arose concerning the circumstances in which the defendant could refer the matter to the Court of Arbitration in Sport. On this occasion the issue was resolved in the defendant's favour: the Court of Appeal found that the rules allowed the Federation to appeal against the decision on the grounds that it was too lenient.

In the absence of an express contractual relationship, the courts may be prepared to find the existence of an *implied* contract between the parties and then to make a ruling as to its terms. In *Modahl* v *British Athletic Foundation Ltd (No 2)*[177] the claimant failed a dope test and was banned from competing in events recognized by her sport's governing body. She successfully challenged the ban by using the defendant's own appeals process, but then commenced a civil action for damages. On appeal from the

---

[169] Mandatory orders, prohibiting orders and quashing orders. Declarations and injunctions are other possible remedies.

[170] See chapter 7.   [171] 2007 Act, s 15.   [172] Ibid, ss 18(6),19 and 20.

[173] Ibid, s 18(8).

[174] In *R* v *Football Association Ltd, ex parte Football League Ltd* [1993] 2 All ER 833 it was held that the FA was not susceptible to judicial review because it was a private body deriving its authority from a contractual relationship. See p 217, *ante*.

[175] In *Nagle* v *Feilden* [1966] 2 QB 633, [1966] 1 All ER 689 the Court of Appeal held that a person had an arguable right not to be arbitrarily excluded from his chosen profession by a governing body. See also: *Bonsor* v *Musicians Union* [1956] AC 104, [1955] 3 All ER 518.

[176] (1999) *The Independent*, 21 April.   [177] [2001] EWCA Civ 1447, [2002] 1 WLR 1192.

Queen's Bench Division, the Court of Appeal held that the claimant had an implied contract with the defendant, which derived from her participation in the defendant's events and her submission to its disciplinary rules and procedures. The Court of Appeal found that the defendant had not failed in its contractual obligation to provide a fair disciplinary process, and the action was therefore unsuccessful. Nevertheless, this decision demonstrates that that there is at least a theoretical possibility of a civil remedy being awarded in such circumstances.

INQUIRIES

Inquiries are established for the purpose of investigating specific issues and their role is one of fact-finding rather than adjudication. They are not generally required to adhere to strict rules of evidence[178] and the courts are slow to interfere with their decisions in the absence of a clear breach of natural justice:[179]

> In determining what is relevant to [an] inquiry, regard must be had to its investigatory character. Where broad terms of reference are given to it, as in this case, the [inquiry] is not determining issues between parties but conducting a thorough investigation into the subject matter. It may have to follow leads. It is not bound by rules of evidence. There is no set order in which evidence must be adduced... If [the inquiry] bona fide seeks to establish a relevant connection between certain facts and the subject matter of the inquiry, it should not be regarded as outside its term of reference by doing so...
>
> [A] court... should be very slow to restrain [an inquiry] from pursuing a particular line of questioning and should not do so unless it is satisfied... [that it] is going off on a frolic of its own.

1 STATUTORY INQUIRIES

Some statutes require a Minister or public authority to hold an inquiry before a particular type of decision can be taken. These 'statutory inquiries' are covered by the Tribunals and Inquiries Act 1992 and may be the subject of procedural rules made pursuant to section 9 of that Act. Inquiries held at a Minister's discretion will also be subject to the Act if they are designated as statutory inquiries by the Lord Chancellor.[180] Statutory inquiries are an integral part of town and country planning, compulsory purchase, and highways development schemes.[181] They are conducted by inspectors and are usually triggered when objections are lodged against the decisions of public authorities.

The conduct of a statutory inquiry will be governed by the statute under which it is held, though the inspector will often be left with considerable discretion. Any rights of appeal

---

[178] See *Bushell* v *Secretary of State for the Environment* [1981] AC 75, [1980] 3 WLR 22.
[179] *Ross* v *Costigan* (1982) 41 ALR 319 at 334–5, per Ellicott J; cited with approval by Lord Walker in *Mount Murray Country Club Ltd* v *MacLeod* [2003] UKPC 53 at [28], *The Times*, 7 July.
[180] Section 16(1).   [181] See, e.g. the Town and Country Planning Act 1990.

will also be governed by the particular statutory scheme and will usually be restricted to points of law. An aggrieved party may, however, have recourse to judicial review.[182]

2 TRIBUNALS OF INQUIRY

Some inquiries are instigated by Ministers for the purposes of investigating specific events or issues of public concern. A recent consultation paper described the rationale for such inquiries as follows:[183]

> There has been a long standing practice in the UK of setting up formal and open inquiries, where necessary, to look into matters that have caused public concern. Ministers are not under any statutory duty to set up such inquiries, but have found them to be a useful method of dealing with matters that have warranted formal, independent investigation.

Inquiries of this nature can fall into one of three categories:

(a) Inquiries instigated by Ministers acting under specific statutory provisions

An example of a provision conferring the power to order such an inquiry is section 49 of the Police Act 1996. This has enabled Home Secretaries to instigate local inquiries into matters connected with the policing of an area.[184] Sir William MacPherson's inquiry into the racially motivated killing of Stephen Lawrence is a striking example of an inquiry ordered under this provision.[185] The police had investigated certain individuals in relation to the killing, but the Crown Prosecution Service had declined to prosecute because of a lack of evidence. A private prosecution brought by the victim's family was thrown out by the judge for the same reason. The scope of the inquiry was limited to an examination of alleged failings in the police investigation. Attempts to question those suspected of the killing in order to establish their guilt were successfully challenged in the Divisional Court, and it was made clear that the inquiry was not a proper forum for conducting a murder trial.[186]

The Inquiry into the Southall rail accident in 1997 is another example of an inquiry set up under subject-specific legislation. The statutory basis for this inquiry was section 14 of the Health and Safety at Work etc. Act 1974.

(b) Inquiries established under the Inquiries Act 2005[187]

The Inquiries Act 2005 provides a framework under which a Minister can establish an inquiry into events that have caused public concern. The procedures adopted by such

---

[182] See chapter 7.
[183] Department for Constitutional Affairs, *Effective Inquiries* (2004) CP 12/04 at p 7.
[184] Such inquiries will in future fall within the scope of the Inquiries Act 2005, which repeals section 49: for a discussion, see p 327, *post*.
[185] *Inquiry into the Death of Stephen Lawrence*, 1997–1998.
[186] *R v Chairman of Stephen Lawrence Inquiry, ex parte A* (1988) *The Times*, 25 July.
[187] For a discussion, see: Requa, 'Truth, Transition and the Inquiries Act 2005' [2007] EHRLR 404; Quane, 'Challenging the Report of an Independent Inquiry under the Human Rights Act' [2007] PL 529.

an inquiry are for the chairman to determine, but the Act confers specific powers to compel the production of documents, to summon witnesses, and to receive evidence on oath.[188] Inquiries that are subject to the Act must generally sit in public and the proceedings may be broadcast or recorded at the chairman's discretion.[189] However, the chairman also has a discretion to restrict publicity if he considers this to be conducive to the inquiry or in the wider public interest.[190]

The predecessor to the 2005 Act – the Tribunals of Inquiry (Evidence) Act 1921 – was rarely used,[191] and its procedures were usually reserved for inquires into allegations of misconduct on the part of public authorities. The second Bloody Sunday Inquiry is a notable example: at the time of writing, this inquiry had been ongoing for almost ten years and its eventual cost was expected to reach £155 million.[192] In 1966 the Royal Commission on Tribunals of Inquiry[193] made a number of recommendations regarding inquiries under the 1921 Act. In particular, it recommended that any person affected by allegations against him should have the right to be legally represented and to cross-examine witnesses, and that any testimony given by such a person should not be admissible as evidence in subsequent criminal or civil proceedings.[194] It also recommended that the facts should be presented to the inquiry panel by independent counsel. To date none of these recommendations have been adopted, and the extent to which cross-examination and legal representation are permitted is still a matter for individual inquiry chairmen.[195]

(c) Non-statutory inquiries

Some inquiries are established on a non-statutory basis, which means that they lack any formal powers of investigation and can only be effective to the extent that those involved are willing to co-operate. Inquiries that could have national security implications or cause political embarrassment are often conducted in this way. They are usually chaired by senior judges and may sit in private, though their findings are generally made public. A good example of a non-statutory inquiry was the inquiry into the export of arms to Iraq in breach of international embargoes.[196] It was established when several prosecutions collapsed amid allegations that ministers had turned a blind eye to the illegal trade and that the businessmen involved had spied for the security services. The inquiry was chaired by Sir Richard Scott and took four years to complete. Its five-volume

---

[188] Sections 17 and 21.   [189] Section 18.   [190] Section 19.

[191] See Winetrobe, 'Inquiries after Scott: The Return of the Tribunal of Inquiry' [1997] PL 18.

[192] Department for Constitutional Affairs, *Effective Inquiries* (2004) CP 12/04, Annex B. The inquiry was commenced in 1998: although it finished hearing evidence in 2005, its final report is not expected until 2008. For the first inquiry, see *Inquiry into Disorders in Northern Ireland ('Bloody Sunday')* Cmd 556, which reported in 1972.

[193] Cmnd 3121. The Commission was chaired by Lord Justice Salmon.

[194] Similar recommendations have been made with regard to testimony given in coroners' courts: see p 269 *ante*.

[195] For an argument that there is already a presumption in favour of allowing legal representation, see Willmott, 'A Presumption of Legal Representation at Judicial Inquiries' (2003) 12(2) Nott LJ 34. Note also that s 40 of the new Act allows chairmen to award payments of 'reasonable amounts' to witnesses, including awards in respect of legal representation.

[196] *Inquiry into the Export of Defence Equipment and Dual-Use Goods to Iraq*, 1996.

report criticized both ministers and officials, and generated a considerable amount of academic literature.[197]

The Hutton Inquiry into the circumstances surrounding the death of Dr David Kelly was also conducted on a non-statutory basis.[198] The government had published an intelligence dossier on Iraq shortly before the second Gulf War, and a journalist made a number of highly critical statements about the dossier in an item broadcast on BBC radio. Dr Kelly was a government scientist and he later admitted to officials in the Defence Department that he had been the journalist's 'anonymous' source. He then found himself at the centre of a very public row between the BBC and the government, and he apparently took his own life after his identity was revealed by the media. Lord Hutton's inquiry was highly critical of both the BBC and its journalist, but the government's handling of the incident was largely vindicated. This prompted concerns that the credibility of public inquiries was being undermined, with some suggesting that Lord Hutton had interpreted his terms of reference too narrowly and failed to address the real issues. In the aftermath of the Hutton Report, the government established a further inquiry into the intelligence upon which it based its controversial dossier and its subsequent decision to go to war with Iraq. The inquiry was conducted by Privy Councillors under the chairmanship of Lord Butler and it reported in July 2004.[199]

A common criticism of non-statutory inquiries is that although their main function is to investigate concerns about government action, they can only be instigated by ministers. Moreover, it is for the Minister instigating an inquiry to appoint its chair and determine its terms of reference. As a matter of law, however, there is nothing to prevent a member of the public from setting up his own inquiry and finding someone to chair it: the real issue is whether anyone outside the government would be able to fund one and to persuade the relevant people to participate.

FURTHER READING

ADLER and GULLAND, *Tribunal Users' Experiences, Perceptions and Expectations: A Literature Review* (Council on Tribunals: 2003)

BLOM-COOPER, 'Witnesses and the Scott Inquiry' [1994] PL 1

BLOM-COOPER and MUNRO, 'The Hutton Inquiry' [2004] PL 472

Department for Constitutional Affairs, *Transforming Public Services: Complaints, Redress and Tribunals* (Cm 6243, 2004)

Department for Constitutional Affairs, *Effective Inquiries* (2004) CP 12/04

GENN and GENN, *The Effectiveness of Representation at Tribunals* (Lord Chancellor's Department: 1989)

[197] See, for example, Blom-Cooper, 'Witnesses and the Scott Inquiry' [1994] PL 1; Howe, 'Procedure at the Scott Inquiry' [1996] PL 445; Leigh and Lustgarten, 'Five Volumes in Search of Accountability: The Scott Report' (1996) 59(5) MLR 695; Scott, 'Procedures at Inquiries: The Duty to be Fair' (1995) 111 LQR 596.
[198] It reported in January 2004: see Blom-Cooper and Munro, 'The Hutton Inquiry' [2004] PL 472; Lord Hutton, 'The Media Reaction to the Hutton Report' [2006] PL 807.
[199] *Review of Intelligence on Weapons of Mass Destruction* (HC Paper 898 (2004)).

Howe, 'Procedure at the Scott Inquiry' [1996] PL 445

Hutton, 'The Media Reaction to the Hutton Report' [2006] PL 807

Leggatt, *Tribunals for Users: One System, One Service – Report of the Review of Tribunals* (2001)

Leigh and Lustgarten, 'Five Volumes in Search of Accountability: the Scott Report' (1996) 59(5) MLR 695

Lomas, 'The Twenty-Fifth Annual Report of the Council on Tribunals – An Opportunity Sadly Missed' (1985) 48 MLR 694

Lord Chancellor's Department, *Tribunals for Users: Consultation Paper about the Report of the Review of Tribunals by Sir Andrew Leggatt* (2001)

MacMillan, 'Employment Tribunals: Philosophies and Practicalities' (1999) 28(1) ILJ 4

Ministry of Justice, *Transforming Tribunals: Implementing Part 1 of the Tribunals, Courts and Enforcement Act 2007* (2007) CP 30/07

Quane, 'Challenging the Report of an Independent Inquiry under the Human Rights Act' [2007] PL 529

Requa, 'Truth, Transition and the Inquiries Act 2005' [2007] EHRLR 404

Scott, 'Procedures at Inquiries: the Duty to be Fair' (1995) 111 LQR 596

Willmott, 'A Presumption of Legal Representation at Judicial Inquiries' (2003) 12(2) Nott LJ 34

Winetrobe, 'Inquiries after Scott: The Return of the Tribunal of Inquiry' [1997] PL 18

10

THE JUDICIARY[1]

INTRODUCTION

The focus in this chapter is on the judiciary and its functions. Judges clearly have a central role in the legal system, being responsible for everything from the determination of disputed points of law to decisions on remedies and punishments. Above all else they have a duty to ensure the fair administration of justice in their courts, and if they are to discharge this duty effectively they must not only be competent but also fair, impartial and independent. The underlying theme of this chapter will be to examine how these qualities are ensured, and the following areas will be considered:

- The judicial hierarchy and the different jurisdictions of each judicial rank.
- The role of the Lord Chief Justice and other senior judges, and changes to the law which have removed the judicial functions of the Lord Chancellor.
- The nature of the judicial function in relation to both statute and common law, and the extent to which some judges also have an administrative role.
- The constitutional position of judges and the way in which this is evolving.
- The judicial appointments system and the rules governing eligibility for judicial office.
- Diversity within the judiciary.
- The importance of judicial independence and security of tenure.

THE JUDICIAL HIERARCHY

The twelve Lords of Appeal in Ordinary – the 'Law Lords' – perform the judicial functions of both the House of Lords[2] and the Privy Council,[3] and are currently the most senior judges in the United Kingdom. The Constitutional Reform Act 2005

---

[1] See generally: Pannick, *Judges* (1987); Griffith, *The Politics of the Judiciary* (5th edn, 1997); Malleson, *The New Judiciary: The Effects of Expansion and Activism* (1999); Stevens, *The English Judges: Their Role in the Changing Constitution* (2002).

[2] See p 251, *ante*.   [3] See p 280, *ante*.

provides for the creation of a new Supreme Court,[4] which means that both the Appellate Committee of the House of Lords and the title 'Lord of Appeal' are due to be abolished. Under the Act the current Law Lords will automatically become Justices of the new court, but they will also lose their entitlement to sit and vote in Parliament.[5]

Next in order of seniority are the thirty-seven Lord (and Lady) Justices of Appeal.[6] Along with a number of *ex officio* members they are the permanent Court of Appeal judges, and they also sit in the Courts-Martial Appeal Court and Employment Appeal Tribunal. They can even be asked to hear High Court, Crown Court, and county court cases, though it is very rare in practice to find such a senior judge sitting below High Court level.[7]

Next in line are the 106 full-time High Court judges or 'puisne judges'. All puisne judges have jurisdiction to sit anywhere in the High Court, although in practice each judge is assigned to a particular division.[8] Puisne judges also hear the most serious types of Crown Court case,[9] and frequently sit alongside Lord and Lady Justices in the Court of Appeal – usually in the Criminal Division. Deputy High Court judges are also appointed, and they exercise the same jurisdiction as their full-time counterparts.

Circuit judges and their deputies carry out the majority of Crown Court work,[10] and in 2005 they accounted for 76 per cent of all sitting days in this court. However, they are also responsible for around a quarter of sitting days in the county courts, and a similar proportion of High Court work. They can even sit in the Criminal Division of the Court of Appeal if called upon, and actually did so in approximately 4 per cent of the Division's cases in 2005.[11] Circuit judges are assisted in both their criminal and civil work by deputy circuit judges and recorders, although these judges do not have jurisdiction to sit in the Court of Appeal.

District judges and deputy district judges are responsible for most county court business,[12] in addition to hearing a small number of cases in the High Court. Finally, there are the District Judges (Magistrates' Courts) and their deputies.[13] These judges were formerly known as stipendiary magistrates, and as the name indicates, they have jurisdiction to sit as justices of the peace in magistrates' courts.[14]

---

[4] See Part 3 of the Constitutional Reform Act 2005, and the discussion at p 253, *ante*.

[5] Ibid, ss 24 and 137.

[6] See p 256, *ante*. The title 'Lady Justice' has been officially recognized since January 2004: Supreme Court Act 1981, s 2(3), as amended by the Courts Act 2003, s 63(1). The Court of Appeal's first female judge was originally referred to by the masculine title.

[7] In 2005, Lord and Lady Justices of Appeal collectively sat 250 days in the High Court, accounting for 2 per cent of all High Court sitting days. They did not sit in the Crown Court at all during this period, and they accounted for less than 1 per cent of county court sitting days: *Judicial Statistics 2005*, at pp 133–5.

[8] See p 260, *ante*. The maximum possible number of such judges is currently 108.

[9] See p 267, *ante*.

[10] Ibid. Section 151(4) of the Supreme Court Act 1981 provides that unless the context requires otherwise, a reference to a judge of the Supreme Court shall not include a reference to a judge of the Crown Court.

[11] Supreme Court Act 1981, s 9; *Judicial Statistics 2005*, at pp 134–5.

[12] See p 264, *ante*.   [13] See p 269, *ante*.

[14] They were renamed by the Access to Justice Act 1999, s 78: see p 269, *ante*.

(a) Specific judicial offices

The Lord Chancellor. Historically, the highest judicial office in the United Kingdom was that of Lord Chancellor, and the holder of this office was the most senior member of the Appellate Committee of the House of Lords. He was also an *ex officio* member of the Court of Appeal, head of the High Court's Chancery Division, 'speaker' of the House of Lords, and a Cabinet Minister. He was therefore a member of the judicial, legislative, *and* executive branches of the state, giving him a unique position within the constitution. However, his executive role always meant that he did not have the security of tenure enjoyed by other judges, and to this day he can be replaced at the whim of the Prime Minister in the same way as any other member of government.[15]

In June 2003, the government announced plans to abolish the office of Lord Chancellor in order to achieve a more formal separation of powers.[16] The intention was to transfer the Lord Chancellor's ministerial functions to the new office of Secretary of State for Constitutional Affairs, leaving his judicial functions to be performed by the Lord Chief Justice. Lord Falconer was given the task of implementing the changes, and he was simultaneously appointed as both Lord Chancellor and Secretary of State. There was, however, widespread criticism that the government had not consulted senior judges before making the announcement, and many felt that it had underestimated the implications of its decision.[17] The Lord Chief Justice was among those to express his concerns:[18]

> [T]he announcement of 12 June . . . clearly indicated an extraordinary lack of appreciation of the significance of what was being proposed. This was followed . . . without consultation, by the transfer of the Court Service from the Lord Chancellor to the Secretary of State for Constitutional Affairs. This last action could well have been due to oversight but it demonstrates there is a lack of appreciation of the significance of the independence of the judiciary in the corridors of government.

Several weeks *after* announcing its intentions, the government did publish a consultation paper.[19] The Lord Chief Justice was ultimately persuaded of the need for reform, and on behalf of the judiciary he negotiated a lengthy Concordat with the Secretary of State.[20] This document was intended as a blueprint for the future relationship between the courts and the government, and the subsequent Constitutional Reform Bill broadly reflected its contents. The Lord Chief Justice later said that if the Concordat was accepted in its entirety it would be 'a highly satisfactory outcome',[21] but not everyone

---

[15] In June 2003 for example, Lord Falconer was appointed Lord Chancellor when it became clear that his predecessor, Lord Irvine, did not support the government's plans for constitutional reform.

[16] For other aspects of the reform package, see p 253, *ante.*

[17] See Stevens, 'Reform in Haste and Repent at Leisure: Iolanthe, the Lord High Executioner and *Brave New World*' (2004) 24 LS 1.

[18] Lord Woolf, 'The Rule of Law and a Change in the Constitution' (2004) 63(2) CLJ 317, at p 323.

[19] Department for Constitutional Affairs, *Constitutional Reform: Reforming the Office of the Lord Chancellor* (2003) CP 13/03.

[20] DCA, *The Lord Chancellor's Judiciary-Related Functions: Proposals* (2004). The document is widely referred to as 'the Concordat'.

[21] 'The Rule of Law and a Change in the Constitution' (2004) 63(2) CLJ 317 at p 325.

was convinced that change was necessary. Many in the House of Lords felt that abolishing the Lord Chancellor's office would *damage* judicial independence rather than enhance it, and these sentiments were echoed by the Judges' Council:[22]

> The office has played a critical role in binding together the three arms of the State: the legislature, the executive and the judiciary. The office is a key pillar of the constitution. If it had not been for the office of Lord Chancellor, it is doubtful whether this country would have managed without a formal written constitution. The Lord Chancellor's wide range of responsibilities, including those of a Cabinet Minister with major responsibilities for the administration of justice, has resulted in him being a cohesive force. As Head of the Judiciary he has been able to represent the judiciary at the highest level within government...[he] has been the constitutional link between The Queen and the judiciary.

In the end the Judges' Council did not oppose the proposals, but many in the House of Lords did. By the time the Bill reached the House of Commons it had already been significantly amended: instead of abolishing the office of Lord Chancellor, Part 2 of what is now the Constitutional Reform Act 2005 provided for it to continue in a modified form. As a consequence, the Lord Chancellor no longer has any judicial functions but he has retained his role as a Member of Parliament and Cabinet Minister. The latter role was effectively expanded with the creation of a Ministry of Justice in May 2007, and the holder of the office of Lord Chancellor now holds the additional title of Secretary of State for Justice.[23] The 2005 Act also paved the way for Lord Chancellors to be appointed from the House of Commons rather than the House of Lords, and in June 2007 Jack Straw became the first Lord Chancellor in history to be appointed from the Commons benches. He is still responsible for overseeing the administration of most major courts,[24] and for appointing Court Rule Committees,[25] allowing or disallowing Court Rules,[26] overseeing judicial appointments,[27] and overseeing the funding of legal services.[28] He is not, however, eligible to sit in any court.

The Lord Chief Justice and other senior posts. The Lord Chief Justice is President of the Courts of England and Wales,[29] President of the Criminal Division of the Court of Appeal, and, following the decision to end the judicial role of the Lord Chancellor, the country's most senior judge. His office entitles him to sit in any of the ordinary courts in the jurisdiction[30] and it carries with it a number of responsibilities. These include overseeing the arrangements for judicial education,[31] supervising the deployment of judges and allocating work within the courts,[32] issuing Practice Directions

---

[22] Judges' Council Response to the Consultation Papers on Constitutional Reform, at para 21. The Response is available online at www.dca.gov.uk/judicial/pdfs/jcresp.pdf

[23] The post of Secretary of State for Constitutional Affairs was discontinued. See further, p 253, *ante*.

[24] With the exception of the Appellate Committee of the House of Lords: Courts Act 2003, s 1.

[25] See p 239, *ante*.

[26] Constitutional Reform Act 2005, s 12; Schedule 1.   [27] See p 336, *post*.

[28] See p 389, *post*. Some of the Lord Chancellor's other functions are considered at p 19, *ante*.

[29] A post created by the Constitutional Reform Act 2005, s 7(1).

[30] Ibid, s 7(3); (4).   [31] Ibid, s 7(2)(b).   [32] Ibid, s 7(2)(c).

(with the concurrence of the Lord Chancellor),[33] and representing the judiciary's views to Parliament and the government.[34]

The other Heads of Division are the Master of the Rolls (who heads the Civil Division of the Court of Appeal), the Chancellor of the High Court,[35] the President of the Queen's Bench Division, and the President of the Family Division. Other senior posts include those of Head and Deputy Head of Civil Justice,[36] Head and Deputy Head of Criminal Justice, Head and Deputy Head of Family Justice, and President and Deputy President of the Supreme Court.[37]

THE JUDICIAL FUNCTION

Most of the judges' work is 'judicial', in the sense that they have to adjudicate upon disputes. This means that they must deduce the facts from the evidence presented in court, and apply the law to the facts so that they can give the 'right decision'. Appellate courts have repeatedly pointed out that the judicial function goes no further than this, and that a court has no duty to seek out some 'independent truth'. Thus:[38]

> If [a] decision has been in accordance with the available evidence and with the law, justice will have been fairly done.

Having found the facts, a judge must apply the existing legal rules to those facts. This function has two elements: (a) the interpretation and construction of statutes; and (b) the application of precedent.

1   STATUTES

Where a case concerns a rule of statute law, the judge's task is to ascertain the intention of the legislature. Different approaches to this task have already been identified,[39] but the traditional view is that judges must interpret statutes in accordance with the literal meaning of the words used.[40] However, strict adherence to this rule is not always possible: the law being considered may be uncertain or ambiguous, and the Act may not

---

[33]   Ibid, s 13; Schedule 2.   [34]   Ibid, ss 5(1); 7(2)(a).

[35]   Formerly known as 'the Vice-Chancellor'. His new title and the formalization of his *de facto* role as Head of the High Court's Chancery Division were brought about by the Constitutional Reform Act 2005: Schedule 4, para 115.

[36]   Created by the Courts Act 2003, s 62. The current Head of Civil Justice is the Master of the Rolls.

[37]   Constitutional Reform Act 2005, ss 8, 9, and 24. The post of Head of Criminal Justice is to be held by the Lord Chief Justice or a person appointed by him: at the time of writing it was held by the President of the Queen's Bench Division. The President of the Family Division is *ex officio* Head of Family Justice.

[38]   *Air Canada v Secretary of State for Trade (No 2)* [1983] 2 AC 394 at 438, [1983] 1 All ER 910 at 919, per Lord Wilberforce.

[39]   See p 48, *ante*.

[40]   See, for example, the words of Lord Diplock in *Duport Steels Ltd v Sirs* [1980] 1 All ER 529 at 541, [1980] 1 WLR 142, at 157: quoted at p 53, *ante*.

provide for the circumstances in question. Judges must create new law in such cases, and this obviously raises questions about the limits of the judicial function. Most would accept that the role of the courts is to decide questions of law, and not to impinge upon the right of the executive to make and apply policy.[41] Yet deciding where this line should be drawn is not easy, particularly in the context of the Human Rights Act and in judicial review cases. In judicial review[42] for example, the courts are often required to determine whether executive bodies have acted within their statutory authority, and this means that they must engage in an interpretative function. Yet where the exercise of discretionary powers is concerned, Parliament's intention may be elusive.[43] Moreover, under section 3 of the Human Rights Act this intention may have to give way to an interpretation that is compatible with Convention rights.[44] The nature of these rights means that the courts may also have to take a view as to the proportionality of any action or provision interfering with them, and this inevitably requires a measure of policy evaluation.[45]

2 COMMON LAW

Traditional views are also changing in relation to the development of common law principles. In *Jones* v *Secretary of State for Social Services* Lord Simon stated:[46]

> In this country it was long considered that judges were not makers of law but merely its discoverers and expounders. The theory was that every case was governed by a relevant rule of law, existing somewhere and discoverable somehow, provided sufficient learning and intellectual rigour were brought to bear.... [T]he theory, however unreal, had its value in limiting the sphere of law-making by the judiciary (inevitably at some disadvantage in assessing the potential repercussions of any decision, and increasingly so in a complex modern industrial society), and thus also in emphasising that central feature of our constitution, the sovereignty of Parliament. But the true, even if limited, nature of judicial law-making has been more widely acknowledged of recent years.

Judges do sometimes establish new legal principles, and a good example of this is the judgment of Denning J in *Central London Property Trust Ltd* v *High Trees House Ltd*,[47] which effectively created the doctrine of equitable estoppel. Similarly, the 'neighbour principle' propounded by Lord Atkin in *Donoghue (or M'Alister)* v *Stevenson*[48] is widely acknowledged as the basis of the modern law of negligence. Indeed, it is fair to say that some judges deem the creation of new law to be part of the judicial function, but others believe that any far-reaching change should be left to Parliament. The latter approach

---

[41] See *R* v *Secretary of State for Home Affairs, ex parte Brind* [1991] 1 AC 696, [1991] 1 All ER 720.

[42] See p 215, *ante*.

[43] In some cases this intention may be ascertained from the records of parliamentary debates: see *Pepper* v *Hart* [1993] AC 593, [1993] 1 All ER 42.

[44] See e.g. *R* v *A (No 2)* [2001] UKHL 25 at [40], [2002] 1 AC 45 at [40], [2001] 3 All ER 1: discussed at p 157, *ante*.

[45] See the discussion at p 225, *ante*.

[46] [1972] AC 944 at 1026, [1972] 1 All ER 145 at 198. See also p 90, *ante*.

[47] [1947] KB 130, [1956] 1 All ER 256n.   [48] [1932] AC 562.

is exemplified by the vigorous dissenting speech of Lord Simon in *Miliangos* v *George Frank (Textiles) Ltd*:[49]

> I am sure that an expert committee, including or taking evidence from departmental officials, would apprehend a great number of not immediately apparent repercussions of the decision which my noble and learned friends propose to take. Such a committee might conclude that the repercussions make the decision unacceptable. Or they might suggest some means of mitigating any adverse effect. Or they might advise that the repercussions were on balance acceptable. But at least the crucial decision would be taken in the light of all the consequences involved.
>
> By contrast . . . judicial advance should be gradual. I am not trained to see the distant scene; 'one step enough for me' should be the motto on the wall opposite the judge's desk. It is, I concede, a less spectacular method of progression than somersaults and cartwheels; but it is the one best suited to the capacity and resources of a judge.

Lord Simon was a lone dissenting voice in this case, and the House of Lords effected a radical reform of the law by holding that English courts have the power to give judgments expressed in foreign currency. However, on other occasions judges have exercised restraint on the basis that the resolution of a problem is best left to Parliament. In *Malone* v *Metropolitan Police Commissioner (No 2)* for example, Sir Robert Megarry considered that the practice of telephone tapping 'cried out' for legislation, but he declined to develop common law rules to fill the vacuum:[50]

> I am not unduly troubled by the absence of English authority: there has to be a first time for everything, and if the principles of English law, and not least analogies from the existing rules, together with the requirements of justice and common sense, pointed firmly to such a right existing, then I think the court should not be deterred from recognising the right. On the other hand, it is no function of the courts to legislate in a new field. The extension of the existing laws and principles is one thing, the creation of an altogether new right is another.

Twenty-five years later, the House of Lords held that although the Human Rights Act had given greater recognition to the right to respect for private life,[51] this did not entitle the courts to create a new tort:[52]

> For the reasons so cogently explained by Sir Robert Megarry in *Malone* v *Metropolitan Police Comissioner*, this is an area which requires a detailed approach which can be achieved only by legislation rather than the broad brush of common law principle.

The earliest criminal offences were, of course, judge-made, but since the nineteenth century it has been accepted that judges have no power to create new criminal offences.[53]

---

[49] [1976] AC 443 at 481–2, [1975] 3 All ER 801 at 824–5.

[50] [1979] Ch 344 at 372, [1979] 2 All ER 620 at 642.   [51] Article 8, ECHR.

[52] *Wainwright* v *Home Office* [2003] UKHL 53 at [33], [2004] 2 AC 406 at [33], [2003] 4 All ER 969, per Lord Hoffman.

[53] This was virtually the only point upon which all five members of the House of Lords were agreed in *Knuller (Publishing, Printing and Promotions) Ltd* v *DPP* [1973] AC 435, [1972] 2 All ER 898. Lord Diplock's speech contains a useful account of the historical background: see [1973] AC 435 at 474, [1972] 2 All ER 898 at 918.

Nevertheless, they have occasionally sought to enforce public morality by declaring that the common law recognizes certain conduct to be criminal. Thus in *R v Manley*[54] the defendant falsely alleged that she had been attacked and robbed, and this put the police to considerable trouble and expense. She was convicted of the offence of public mischief, and despite counsel's protestations that no such offence was known to the law, her conviction was upheld on appeal. The decision of the House of Lords in *Shaw v DPP*[55] is equally striking. An agreement to publish the 'Ladies Directory', which advertised the names, addresses, and photographs of prostitutes, was held to constitute the offence of conspiracy to corrupt public morals. The following observation from the speech of Viscount Simonds has been widely quoted:[56]

> In the sphere of criminal law I entertain no doubt that there remains in the courts of law a residual power to enforce the supreme and fundamental purpose of the law, to conserve not only the safety and order but also the moral welfare of the State.

In *Knuller v DPP*[57] a similar publication aimed at the homosexual market was held to give rise to the same offence, and a majority of the House of Lords suggested that an offence of outraging public decency also existed. In the light of these authorities, the principle that judges have no power to create new offences would appear to be illusory. However, in *DPP v Withers*[58] the House of Lords explained that conspiracy to effect a public mischief is not an offence in itself, and that conduct such as that in *R v Manley* (above) is criminal only because it amounts to some other established offence.

The approach to such matters is not always consistent, and judicial activism sometimes comes to the fore. Thus, in *R v R* the House of Lords concluded that the rule that a husband could not be criminally liable for raping his wife was no longer part of English law.[59] Other examples of judicial creativity include the recognition of psychological harm as a form of assault,[60] the development of the law of provocation in the context of domestic violence,[61] and the decision that medical treatment may be lawfully withdrawn from a patient in a permanent vegetative state.[62] By contrast, in *C v DPP*[63] the House of Lords declined to abolish the *doli incapax* rule. The rule created a rebuttable presumption that a child under the age of fourteen could not possess criminal intent, and at first instance Laws J had said:[64]

> [T]his presumption at the present time is a serious disservice to our law. It means that a child over ten who commits an act of obvious dishonesty, or even grave violence, is to be acquitted unless the prosecution specifically prove...that he understands the obliquity of what he is doing...

---

[54] [1933] 1 KB 529.   [55] [1962] AC 220, [1961] 2 All ER 446.
[56] [1962] AC 220 at 267–268, [1961] 2 All ER 446 at 452.
[57] [1973] AC 435, [1972] 2 All ER 898. See also *R v Gibson* [1990] 2 QB 619, [1991] 1 All ER 439.
[58] [1975] AC 842, [1974] 3 All ER 984.   [59] [1992] 1 AC 599, [1991] 4 All ER 481.
[60] *R v Chan-Fook* [1994] 2 All ER 552, [1994] 1 WLR 689; *R v Ireland* [1997] QB 114, [1997] 1 All ER 112; *R v Constanza* [1997] 2 Cr App R 492, [1997] Crim LR 576.
[61] *R v Thornton* [1992] 1 All ER 306, (1993) 96 Cr App R 112; *R v Ahluwalia* [1992] 4 All ER 889, (1993) 96 Cr App R 133.
[62] *Airedale NHS Trust v Bland* [1993] AC 789, [1993] 1 All ER 821.
[63] [1996] AC 1, [1995] 2 All ER 43.   [64] [1994] 3 All ER 190 at 196–7.

In the House of Lords, Lord Lowery set out five general principles:

> (1) If the solution is doubtful the judges should beware of imposing their own rem-edy; (2) caution should prevail if Parliament has rejected opportunities of clear-ing up a known difficulty or has legislated while leaving the difficulty untouched; (3) disputed matters of social policy are less suitable areas for judicial intervention than purely legal problems; (4) fundamental legal doctrines should not lightly be set aside; (5) judges should not make a change unless they can achieve finality and certainty.

The application of these principles led him to conclude that the presumption should not be abandoned. It has, however, now been abolished by statute.[65]

Where a case gives rise to a potential Human Rights Act issue, different consider-ations apply. As discussed previously, the Act does not oblige private bodies to act com-patibly with the Convention, and it does not expressly require the courts to give effect to the Convention at common law. It does, however, oblige them to perform their functions in a manner consistent with Convention rights,[66] and since this is a statutory obligation it must prevail over any duty to obey established common law principles. A court may even conclude that it has no option but to depart from a precedent that would otherwise be binding, as when the Court of Appeal made a modest adjustment to the House of Lords' test for bias.[67] The open-textured language of Convention rights also leaves con-siderable room for interpretation, and on occasions judges have had to determine mat-ters that involve as many moral choices as they do legal ones. In *R (on the application of Pretty) v DPP*[68] for example, the House of Lords found itself grappling with the difficult question of whether the right to life also gave a terminally ill woman the right to die. Similarly, in *Re A*[69] a court had to consider whether the same right could prevent surgery to separate conjoined twins, in circumstances where this would inevitably result in the death of one of them.

Convention rights have undoubtedly had an influence on judicial reasoning, but as indicated above, the courts have thus far stopped short of asserting the authority to create new common law torts. They have, however, sought to give effect to Convention rights – notably the right to respect for private life – by developing established torts such as breach of confidence.[70]

---

[65] Crime and Disorder Act 1998, s 34.

[66] Section 6. Convention rights are defined in s 1 of the Act: see p 151 and chapter 6, *ante*.

[67] *Director General of Fair Trading* v *Proprietary Association of Great Britain (No 2)* [2001] 1 WLR 700, *sub nom Re Medicaments and Related Classes of Goods (No 2)* [2001] HRLR 17. The approach was subsequently approved by the House of Lords in *Porter* v *Magill* [2001] UKHL 67, [2002] 2 AC 357, [2002] 1 All ER 465.

[68] [2001] UKHL 61, [2002] 1 AC 800, [2002] 1 All ER 1: see p 180, *ante*.

[69] *Re A (Children) (Conjoined Twins: Surgical Separation)* [2001] Fam 147, [2000] 4 All ER 961.

[70] See, e.g. *A* v *B*; *H* v *Associated Newspapers*, [2002] EWCA Civ 337, [2003] QB 195, [2002] 2 All ER 545; *Douglas* v *Hello! Ltd (No 1)* [2001] QB 967, [2001] 2 All ER 289; *Campbell* v *Mirror Group Newspapers* [2004] UKHL 22, [2004] 2 AC 457, [2004] 2 All ER 995. These and other cases are discussed at pp 168 and 193, *ante*. Cf. *Wainwright* v *Home Office* [2003] UKHL 53, [2004] 2 AC 406, [2003] 4 All ER 969. Note also that in *Peck* v *UK* (2003) 36 EHRR 41, the European Court of Human Rights highlighted significant deficiencies in the ability of domestic law to protect privacy.

Finally, it should be noted that judges occasionally go beyond the function of dispute resolution by issuing guidelines for future cases. Thus the rates of interest to be awarded on damages in personal injury actions,[71] and the principles to be applied in determining applications for interim injunctions,[72] have both been the subject of House of Lords guidelines. Similarly, the Criminal Division of the Court of Appeal has established a practice of issuing sentencing guidelines to assist Crown Court judges.[73]

3 ADMINISTRATIVE FUNCTIONS

In addition to resolving disputes, judges also exercise certain administrative functions. This is particularly true of justices of the peace, whose functions include licensing and the issuing of summonses and warrants. The judges who sit in the Court of Protection administer the affairs of persons of unsound mind,[74] and in their capacity as 'visitors' of the Inns of Court, High Court judges hear appeals from the Senate of the Inns of Court and the Bar.[75] Courts also deal with various types of non-contentious business, such as the administration of trusts, the winding-up of companies, adoption, and legitimacy. In addition, judges issue Practice Directions, act as presiding judges[76] and Heads of Division, and sit on the various Court Rule Committees which make Rules for court practice and procedure.[77]

THE CONSTITUTIONAL POSITION OF JUDGES

Although there is some debate about whether judges are 'servants' of the Crown, there is no doubt that they cannot be controlled in the exercise of their office by either Parliament or the executive, and judicial independence is a fundamental principle of English law. This independence is essential if the courts are to perform their constitutional role of reviewing executive action. The idea is closely linked to the doctrine of the separation of powers, which for many judges is a cornerstone of the constitution:[78]

> It is a feature of the peculiarly British conception of the separation of powers that Parliament, the executive and the courts have each their distinct and largely exclu-

---

[71] See p 517, *post*.   [72] See p 503, *post*.

[73] This practice seems to have originated in *R v Turner* (1975) 61 Cr App R 67 in relation to sentences for robbery and has since been followed in many other sentencing areas. See, e.g., *R v Clarke (Linda)* [1982] 3 All ER 232, [1982] 1 WLR 1090 (partially suspended sentences); and *R v Armagh* (1982) 76 Cr App R 190 (drugs offences). See now, pp 692–693, *post*.

[74] This court is discussed at p 275, *ante*.

[75] For this general jurisdiction, see *R v Visitors to the Inns of Court, ex parte Calder and Persaud* [1994] QB 1, [1993] 2 All ER 876.

[76] Courts and Legal Services Act 1990, s 72.   [77] See pp 463 and 554, *ante*.

[78] *R v Secretary of State for the Home Department, ex parte Fire Brigades' Union* [1995] 2 AC 513 at 567, [1995] 2 All ER 244 at 267, per Lord Mustill. See also, *Duport Steels v Sirs* [1980] 1 All ER 529 at 541, [1980] 1 WLR 142 at 157, per Lord Diplock.

sive domain. Parliament has a legally unchallengeable right to make whatever laws it thinks right. The executive carries on the administration of the country in accordance with the powers conferred on it by law. The courts interpret the laws, and see that they are obeyed.

It is clear, however, that the separation of powers within the UK is incomplete,[79] and the *balance* of powers between the legislature, executive, and judiciary is unequal. The legislative supremacy of Parliament was described by Wade as 'the ultimate political fact' upon which the system hangs,[80] and the traditional view is that this supremacy is unrestricted.[81] The UK does not have a written constitution with a superior status to ordinary laws, and as 'the weakest and least dangerous department of government'[82] the judiciary has no authority to strike down legislation as unconstitutional or invalid.[83] Yet within this framework there is room for genuine debate about the limits of judicial authority, and about the proper relationship between the courts and the other 'departments of government'.

1 THE CHANGING POLITICAL CLIMATE

Since the 1940s most governments have enjoyed large majorities in the House of Commons, and this has enabled them to control the legislative agenda. The post-war era was characterized by political consensus, but the two main parties became more polarized and ideological during the 1970s, and the political climate since then has been distinctly adversarial. Successive governments have used their large majorities to steer controversial laws through Parliament, prompting Lord Hailsham's famous warning that the UK was becoming an 'elective dictatorship'.[84] Disputes with a political dimension have frequently come before the courts, and the courts have responded by developing more sophisticated principles of review. Since the 1980s, some Law Lords have felt compelled to break the convention against speaking in legislative debates,[85] and the rules preventing judges from commenting on matters of public interest have been abandoned.[86] These developments, along with the involvement of judges in several high-profile inquiries,[87] have created the impression that the judiciary is being drawn into the political arena.

---

[79] Given that the UK does not have a written constitution and that it draws its Ministers from the legislature, several academics have questioned whether there is a separation of powers at all: see, e.g. Hood Phillips, 'A Constitutional Myth: Separation of Powers' (1977) 93 LQR 11.

[80] Wade, 'The Basis of Legal Sovereignty' [1955] CLJ 172 at p 188.

[81] This view of parliamentary supremacy is closely associated with the work of Dicey; see *Introduction to the Study of the Law of the Constitution* (10th edn, 1959).

[82] See Lord Steyn: 'The Weakest and Least Dangerous Department of Government' [1997] PL 84.

[83] But see the discussion at p 327–33, *post*.

[84] In 1976: see Lewis, *Lord Hailsham: A Life* (1997) at p 136. Lord Hailsham ceased to voice such concerns when he was made Lord Chancellor a few years later.

[85] See: Stevens, *The English Judges: Their Role in the Changing Constitution* (2002) at pp 93–4.

[86] The so-called 'Kilmuir rules' (named after a former Lord Chancellor) were abandoned in 1989.

[87] See p 313, *ante*.

(a) Judicial inquiries

Governments often appoint senior judges to head inquiries into matters of public interest. A government with a difficult or sensitive issue to address may rely on the 'borrowed authority'[88] of a judge to conduct an independent review, and to use his forensic ability to examine witnesses and sift evidence. Inevitably, however, the outcome of an inquiry rarely pleases everyone, and judges cannot be expected to produce non-political solutions to political problems. The Denning Report into the Profumo scandal,[89] the Scott Inquiry into the sale of arms to Iraq,[90] and the Hutton Inquiry into the death of Dr David Kelly,[91] are just three examples of inquiries that have generated intense controversy,[92] and which have arguably had a negative impact on the appearance of judicial impartiality.

(b) Judicial review and judicial activism

Judicial review[93] is the principal mechanism for holding the executive accountable to the law, and it is therefore central to the constitutional role of the courts. Over the last twenty years the courts have developed more sophisticated principles of review, and in *GCHQ*[94] and other cases they have extended the application of these principles to new situations. The courts' powers of review have been further enhanced by the Human Rights Act 1998, and judicial review has thus assumed considerable importance in recent years. This partly explains why the last two decades have witnessed an unprecedented level of conflict between the judiciary and the government. Ministers have increasingly found themselves on the receiving end of adverse judicial comment, and owing to the nature of their responsibilities – and perhaps the personalities involved – Home Secretaries have been particularly susceptible. For example, when Kenneth Baker authorized the deportation of an asylum seeker and ignored a judge's order to return him to the jurisdiction, he became the first Minister in British legal history to be held liable for contempt of court.[95] In the Court of Appeal, Nolan LJ reminded him that:[96]

> [T]he proper constitutional relationship of the executive with the courts is that the courts will respect all acts of the executive within its lawful province, and that the executive will respect all decisions of the courts as to what its lawful province is.

Another Home Secretary, Michael Howard, was defeated in the House of Lords when he purported to use prerogative powers to establish a Criminal Injuries Compensation

---

[88] See Griffith, *The Politics of the Judiciary* (4th edn, 1991), at pp 52–5; Drewery, 'Judicial Inquiries and Public Reassurance' [1996] PL 368.

[89] Cmnd 2152, 1963.

[90] *Inquiry into the Export of Defence Equipment and Dual-Use Goods to Iraq*, 1996.

[91] This reported in January 2004: see p 314, *ante*.

[92] The Inquiries Act 2005 is aimed at making their procedures more efficient and effective: see Department for Constitutional Affairs, *Effective Inquiries: A Consultation Paper* (2004) CP 12/04.

[93] See chapter 7.

[94] *Council of Civil Service Unions* v *Minister for the Civil Service* [1985] AC 374, [1984] 3 All ER 935. In this case it was held that the use of prerogative powers was potentially amenable to judicial review.

[95] *Re M; sub nom M* v *Home Office* [1994] 1 AC 377, [1993] 3 All ER 537, HL: see p 250, *ante*.

[96] [1992] QB 270 at 314–15, [1992] 4 All ER 97 at 146.

scheme instead of implementing the scheme provided for by statute.[97] His attempts to extend the minimum prison term served by the killers of James Bulger were also thwarted by the courts.[98] On each occasion the courts asserted the importance of the separation of powers, but critics accused them of interfering in matters of policy. This was not, however, an argument accepted by Lord Steyn. Writing extra-judicially, he stated that:[99]

> [T]he principle of the separation of powers is an essential constitutional safeguard of judicial independence, and the integrity of the administration of justice. It exists not to eliminate friction between the judiciary and the executive. It exists not to promote efficiency. It exists for one reason only: to prevent the rise of arbitrary executive power.

Lord Steyn was not the only judge to express his views outside the courtroom. Home Office policies on crime and sentencing were publicly criticized by the Lord Chief Justice,[100] and Laws LJ wrote various articles about the constitution and the role of the courts within it.[101] Some judges even added their voices to campaigns for a written constitution and the incorporation of the European Convention on Human Rights.[102]

The Human Rights Act era. The European Convention on Human Rights was eventually given domestic effect by the Human Rights Act 1998, which requires the courts to balance individual rights against competing public interest claims.[103] It also requires them to engage in creative statutory interpretation, and, wherever possible, to give effect to legislation in a manner that is compatible with Convention rights. Decisions under the Act therefore require a greater level of scrutiny than that previously adopted in judicial review cases, and this has created further opportunities for clashes with the government.

The question of how much judicial 'deference' is appropriate in human rights cases is still unresolved, but it is clear that less deference will be shown where the courts regard the subject matter of a case as falling within their own sphere of expertise.[104] Once again, this has led to conflict between the judiciary and the Home Office. A series of cases, both domestically and in Strasbourg, have effectively wrestled control of sentencing

---

[97] *R* v *Secretary of State for Home Affairs, ex parte Fire Brigades Union* [1995] 2 AC 513, [1995] 2 All ER 244. The statute in question was the Criminal Justice Act 1988. Several Law Lords had spoken out against the scheme in Parliament, which effectively meant that they could not sit when this case reached the House of Lords.

[98] *R* v *Secretary of State for the Home Department, ex parte Venables and Thompson* [1998] AC 407, [1997] 3 All ER 97.

[99] 'The Weakest and Least Dangerous Department of Government' [1997] PL 84, at p 87.

[100] See Stevens, *The English Judges: Their Role in the Changing Constitution* (2002), at pp 50–2.

[101] See, e.g. 'Law and Democracy' [1995] PL 80; 'The Constitution: Morals and Rights' [1996] *PL* 622.

[102] See, e.g. Bingham, 'The European Convention on Human Rights: Time to Incorporate' [1993] LQR 390; Scarman, *Why Britain Needs a Written Constitution* (1992). Many academics and politicians were opposed to such developments on the basis that they would require the courts to make political judgments: see Griffiths, 'The Political Constitution' (1979) 42 MLR 1; Lyell, 'Whither Strasbourg? Why Britain Should Think Long and Hard Before Incorporating the European Convention on Human Rights' [1997] EHRLR 132.

[103] For a discussion, see p 176, *ante*.

[104] *R (on the application of Prolife Alliance)* v *BBC* [2003] UKHL 23 at [136], [2004] 1 AC 185 at [136], [2003] 2 All ER 977, per Lord Walker; *International Transport Roth GmbH* v *Secretary of State for the Home Department* [2002] EWCA Civ 158, [2003] QB 728, [2002] HRLR 31, per Laws LJ. For further discussion, see p 167, *ante*.

decisions from the Home Secretary.[105] The courts have also modified the interpretation of various statutes, so as to protect the right to a fair trial and to the presumption of innocence.[106] However, it is in the field of asylum and immigration that some of the most significant clashes have occurred. The government's policies in this area have been challenged in several recent cases, and at least one Home Secretary has responded by publicly attacking the courts' decisions. Thus, when Collins J held that six asylum seekers had been unlawfully denied state support,[107] the then Home Secretary, David Blunkett, complained that:[108]

> Frankly, I am personally fed up with having to deal with a situation where Parliament debates issues and the judges then overturn them. I don't want any mixed messages going out so I am making it absolutely clear that we don't accept what Justice Collins has said.

The same judge had previously ruled that detaining asylum seekers at 'reception centres' was unlawful.[109] This decision was later overturned on appeal,[110] but not before the Secretary of State had complained that his policies were being thwarted by unaccountable judges.[111] Mr Blunkett was further infuriated when the Special Immigration Appeals Commission – again chaired by Collins J – declared that the detention without trial of suspected foreign terrorists was incompatible with the Human Rights Act.[112] In a landmark decision the Commission's ruling was endorsed by the House of Lords,[113] forcing the government into a major rethink of its anti-terror laws. The internment provisions were subsequently replaced with a new system of control orders,[114] and all of those detained were eventually released. It was not long, however, before the new system fell under the judicial spotlight, and in *Secretary of State for the Home Department* v *JJ* a majority of the House of Lords quashed six control orders on the grounds that they too were in breach of the Human Rights Act.[115]

---

[105] See p 183, *ante*. See also: Amos, 'R v Secretary of State for the Home Department, ex parte Anderson: Ending the Home Secretary's Sentencing Role' (2004) 67(1) MLR 108.

[106] See, e.g. *R* v *A (No 2)* [2001] UKHL 25, [2002] 1 AC 45, [2001] 3 All ER 1; *R* v *Lambert* [2001] UKHL 37, [2002] 2 AC 545, [2001] 3 All ER 577.

[107] *R (on the application of Q)* v *Secretary of State for the Home Department* [2003] EWHC 195 (Admin), *The Times*, 20 February. See also, *R (on the application of Limbuela)* v *Secretary of State for the Home Department* [2004] EWHC 219 (Admin), *The Times*, 9 February, QBD; [2005] UKHL 66, [2006] 1 AC 396, [2007] 1 All ER 951, HL.

[108] These comments were made in a radio interview and reported by *The Independent*, 20 February 2003: see also Bradley, 'Judicial Independence Under Attack' [2003] PL 397. Justice Collins' decision was upheld by the Court of Appeal on slightly modified grounds: [2003] EWCA Civ 364, [2004] QB 36, [2003] 2 All ER 905.

[109] *R (on the application of Saadi)* v *Secretary of State for the Home Department* [2001] EWHC 670 (Admin).

[110] [2002] UKHL 41, [2002] 4 All ER 785, [2002] 1 WLR 3131.

[111] Stevens, *The English Judges: Their Role in the Changing Constitution* (2002) at pp 130–1.

[112] *A* v *Secretary of State for the Home Department* [2002] HRLR 45. Collins J later ordered the release of one detainee, having described evidence presented by the Home Office as 'inaccurate' and 'clearly misleading': *Secretary of State* v *M*, unreported, 8 March 2004.

[113] [2004] UKHL 56, [2005] 2 AC 68, [2005] 3 All ER 169. The significance of this case was such that it was heard by nine of the twelve Law Lords. Coincidentally, Mr Blunkett resigned as Home Secretary the day before their Lordships delivered their opinions, and it was left to his successor to plan the government's response.

[114] Prevention of Terrorism Act 2005: the background to this legislation is discussed further at pp 161 and 184, *ante*.

[115] [2007] UKHL 45, [2007] 3 WLR 642. See further p 185, *ante*.

Other decisions of note include the ruling that an asylum seeker's benefits could not be withdrawn without notification,[116] and the declaration that penalties applied to hauliers who assisted illegal immigrants were incompatible with Convention rights.[117]

The issues raised by these and other cases have continued to divide lawyers and politicians. Many feel that the courts have been seeking to uphold the rule of law, and they view the government's reaction to certain decisions as an affront to judicial independence. Indeed, when Lord Irvine was Lord Chancellor, he issued a tacit reminder to his own Cabinet colleagues about the need to respect judicial authority:[118]

> In a democracy under the rule of law, it is not mature to cheer the judges when a win is secured and boo them when a loss is suffered...
>
> [The Human Rights Act] was drafted sensitively to the balance of forces within our substantially unwritten constitution. And that means the government can accept adverse court decisions, not as defeats, but as steps on the road to better governance...
>
> In giving greater responsibility to our judges, we are merely confirming that ours is a society governed by the rule of law... We ask our judges to decide many difficult cases. Some are between private citizens. Some are criminal appeals. Others are against ministers; and of these, some are lost and some are won. That is neither avoidable nor unconstitutional. It is simply proof that 'be you ever so high, the law is above you'.

Others, however, would argue that the courts have at times undermined the will of Parliament, and that concerns about judicial independence are misplaced:[119]

> Once appointed, judges of the English High Court and above can be removed only on an address by both Houses of Parliament, which means that they are virtually irremovable. So, against whom does the judiciary need protection? Against the government? Yet, there has never been a time when government decisions have been struck down with greater abandon than now, and even Acts of Parliament have been savaged by the courts...
>
> The real loser is democracy. In a parliamentary democracy like the UK, legislation is intended to give expression to the will of the people. If it fails to do so, the people can turn the government out at the next election. But for unelected judges to make up the law as they go along is contrary not only to the doctrine of the separation of powers, but is also a usurpation of the role of Parliament.

Even Prime Ministers have occasionally succumbed to the urge to criticize the courts, with Tony Blair describing a ruling preventing nine Afghan hijackers from being deported[120] as 'an abuse of common sense'.[121] By the time that this case was decided, the

---

[116]   *R (on the application of Anufrijeva) v Secretary of State for the Home Department* [2003] UKHL 36, [2004] 1 AC 604, [2003] 3 All ER 827.

[117]   *International Transport Roth GmbH v Secretary of State for the Home Department* [2002] EWCA Civ 158, [2003] QB 728, [2002] HRLR 31.

[118]   'The Impact of the Human Rights Act: Parliament, the Courts and the Executive' [2003] PL 307, at pp 323–4.

[119]   Arnheim, 'The Rule of Law or the Rule of Lawyers?' (2004) 154 NLJ 776.

[120]   *R (on the application of S) v Secretary of State for the Home Department* [2006] EWHC 1111 (Admin), *The Times*, June 14 2006. The decision was subsequently affirmed by the Court of Appeal: EWCA Civ 1157, *The Times*, October 9 2006.

[121]   Reported in *The Observer*, 14 May 2006.

same Prime Minister who had presided over the enactment of the Human Rights Act in 1998 appeared to be having second thoughts, and in a letter to his Home Secretary he suggested that the Act should be reviewed.[122] David Cameron MP, as leader of the opposition, has been even more vociferous. He has repeatedly called for the Human Rights Act to be replaced with a 'British' bill of rights more 'in tune with British traditions about liberty',[123] and when asked to comment on a ruling that a convicted killer could not be deported at the end of his sentence[124] he declared that:[125]

> The fact that the Human Rights Act means he cannot be deported flies in the face of common sense. It is a shining example of what is going wrong in our country. He is someone who has been found guilty of murder and should be deported back to his country.

Although the government has indicated that this decision will be vigorously contested, it would seem that the current Prime Minister does not share the views of either Mr Cameron or Mr Blair on the Human Rights Act itself. Instead he has called for a 'British Bill of Rights and Responsibilities' which would build upon rather than replace the 1998 Act,[126] and his Lord Chancellor has firmly rejected the idea that the government views this Act as a hindrance:[127]

> We will do our utmost to secure the safety of the British people, and we all have to be prepared to limit individual liberties to the extent that is necessary. We have human rights and an independent judiciary to establish and marshall the lawful boundaries of our response. We do not need to resile from the ECHR nor the [Human Rights Act].

Whichever view is taken, the relationship between the government and the judiciary has undoubtedly been tested over the last two decades, and the Human Rights Act has been at the centre of much of the recent tension. Yet it is not only in the courtroom that clashes have occurred: the enactment of a number of recent statutes has also proved contentious, and two of these are discussed below.

(c) The Constitutional Reform Act 2005

The original aims of the Constitutional Reform Bill have been considered in detail elsewhere in this book, but they can be broadly summarized as follows:

(a) to abolish the post of Lord Chancellor and transfer his judicial responsibilities to the Lord Chief Justice, leaving his ministerial functions to the Secretary of State for Constitutional Affairs;

---

[122] Reported in *The Guardian*, 15 May 2006.
[123] Reported in *The Observer*, 4 November 2007.
[124] *Appellant v Secretary of State for the Home Department*, Appeal Number IA/13107/2006, 17 August 2007, unreported (Asylum and Immigration Tribunal). In fact the disputed decision was based primarily on the application of EU law, with Article 8 of the ECHR being very much a secondary issue.
[125] Reported in the *Guardian*, 22 August 2007.   [126] *The Governance of Britain*, Cm 7170, 2007.
[127] These comments were made in a lecture delivered at Cambridge University on 25 October 2007. The text of the lecture is available at: http://www.justice.gov.uk/news/sp251007a.htm

(b) to replace the Appellate Committee of the House of Lords with an independent Supreme Court, so that the most senior judges cease to occupy seats in Parliament; and

(c) to establish an independent Judicial Appointments Commission.

On its face, the Bill was intended to achieve a more formal separation of powers, and a judiciary that is more transparently independent of government. One might therefore have expected it to be well received by most judges, but in fact, initial reactions ranged from the mildly sceptical to the deeply suspicious. The government's failure to consult judges before announcing its decision didn't help matters, and the Lord Chief Justice could barely conceal his anger that the reforms were thought to be 'capable of being achieved by a press release'.[128] The biggest cause for concern was the proposed abolition of the Lord Chancellor's office.[129] The Judges' Council expressed serious reservations about this proposal, pointing out that the new Secretary of State would be a political figure, who would not be constrained by 'judicial responsibilities and constitutional conventions'.[130] The Law Lords agreed that the Lord Chancellor's role had been a safeguard of judicial independence, and that 'the constitution would be gravely weakened if that safeguard were removed and not replaced.'[131] The judiciary's main concern was whether a Secretary of State, who might not necessarily be a lawyer, could properly defend judicial interests within government. Their unease was exacerbated by the fact that certain politicians appeared not to respect their authority, and they had previously opposed plans to transfer the Court Service to the Home Office for similar reasons:[132]

> It was disturbing that – at that time – it was not appreciated within government that it was inappropriate for the department that most frequently had to defend proceedings for judicial review in the courts and that had to lead responsibility for criminal justice policy to be in charge of what should be seen as an impartial Court Service.

Judges were more ambivalent about the plans for a Supreme Court, but six of the twelve Law Lords publicly opposed the proposals, and eight were in agreement that if the reforms *did* go ahead, at least some of the Court's members should continue to sit in the House of Lords.[133] Lord Hobhouse, for example, argued that the Lord Chief Justice and other senior figures should retain their parliamentary seats so that they could continue to speak on behalf of the judiciary.[134] By the time that the Bill was presented to Parliament, many of the judges' preferences had been accommodated, and the Concordat[135] negotiated by the Lord Chief Justice had helped to allay some of their concerns.

[128] Lord Woolf, 'The Rule of Law and a Change in the Constitution' (2004) 63(2) CLJ 317, at p 320.
[129] See p 20, *ante*.
[130] Response to the Consultation Papers on Constitutional Reform; available at www.dca.gov.uk/judicial/pdfs/jcresp.pdf
[131] The Law Lords' Response to the Government's Consultation Paper on Constitutional Reform: A Supreme Court for the United Kingdom, CP 11/03 July 2003, at para 5.
[132] Lord Woolf, 'The Rule of Law and a Change in the Constitution' (2004) 63(2) CLJ 317 at p 323.
[133] The Law Lords' Response (*ante*, n 131), at paras 2 and 21.
[134] Ibid, at para F.2.   [135] See p 319, *ante*.

The proposed abolition of the Lord Chancellor's office also faced opposition from within Parliament, and the government was 'persuaded' to accept that the office should continue in a modified form. The Constitutional Reform Act 2005 thus removes the Lord Chancellor's judicial functions[136] whilst reminding him of the need to defend judicial independence.[137] It also removes the requirement for him to be either a lawyer or a peer,[138] meaning that he is, in effect, a Secretary of State in all but name. Indeed, the office of Lord Chancellor was recently combined with the new role of Secretary of State for Justice,[139] and it is currently held by a Member of the House of Commons: Jack Straw, MP. The suggestion that certain judges should retain their parliamentary seats was also rejected by the government, and the Act leaves it to the Lord Chief Justice to ensure that their interests are represented by other means.[140]

(d) The 'mother of all ouster clauses'

While the debate about constitutional reform was still ongoing, a second government Bill was generating further controversy. The main purpose of what is now the Asylum and Immigration (Treatment of Claimants) Act 2004 was to create a new, single-tier tribunal to deal with appeals in immigration and asylum cases.[141] In what was described as the 'mother of all ouster clauses',[142] clause 11 of the Bill purported to exclude the tribunal's decisions from any possibility of judicial review. Previous attempts to oust the jurisdiction of the courts have been interpreted narrowly: it has generally been assumed that Parliament would not have intended to prevent the review of a decision made without its authority.[143] Clause 11, however, was clearly drafted with the intention of making it 'judge-proof'.[144] If enacted, it would have expressly precluded the courts from considering claims based on: (i) lack of jurisdiction; (ii) irregularity; (iii) error of law; (vi) breach of natural justice; or (v) any other matter. Senior judges publicly condemned the clause, and the Lord Chief Justice was particularly scathing:[145]

> The provision has to be read to appreciate the lengths to which the government has gone to try and exclude the possibility of intervention by the courts. Extensive consultation took place with myself and other members of the judiciary before the Bill was introduced...our advice was that a clause of the nature now included in the Bill was fundamentally in conflict with the rule of law and should not be contemplated by any government if it had respect for the rule of law.
>
> We advised that the clause was unlikely to be effective and identified why. The result was that clause 11 was extended to close the loopholes we had identified, instead of being abandoned as we had argued...we pointed out that the danger of the proposed ouster clause was that it could bring the judiciary, the executive and the legislature into conflict. Apparently this was of little concern...

---

[136] Most of these are transferred to the Lord Chief Justice by Schedules 2 and 4.

[137] Section 3(6); s 3(5) prohibits *all* Ministers from seeking to influence judicial decisions.

[138] Section 2: see p 20, *ante*.   [139] See p 19, *ante*.

[140] Sections 5(1) and 7(2)(a).   [141] See p 303, *ante*.

[142] See Jowell, 'Heading for a Constitutional Crisis' (2004) 154 NLJ 401.

[143] *Anisminic v Foreign Compensation Commission* [1969] 2 AC 147, [1969] 1 All ER 208: see p 63, *ante*.

[144] Jowell, *ante*, n 142.

[145] Lord Woolf, 'The Rule of Law and a Change in the Constitution' (2004) 63(2) CLJ 317, at pp 328–9.

> I am not over-dramatising the position if I indicate that, if this clause were to become law, it would be so inconsistent with the spirit of mutual respect between the different arms of government that it could be the catalyst for a campaign for a written constitution... The response of the government and the House of Lords to the chorus of criticism of clause 11 will produce the answer to the question of whether our freedoms can be left in their hands under an unwritten constitution.

In the end, the level of opposition to the clause forced the government to withdraw it,[146] and the compromise reached means that the Tribunal's decisions can be reviewed on the grounds of an error of law.[147] It remains to be seen, however, whether a constitutional crisis was avoided or merely postponed.

2   A NEW BALANCE OF POWERS?

Lord Woolf is one of a small but growing number of judges to assert a more powerful role for the courts. Before he was appointed as Lord Chief Justice, he said that if Parliament was to do the unthinkable and attempt to abolish judicial review, he would:[148]

> [C]onsider there were advantages in making it clear that ultimately there are even limits on the supremacy of Parliament which it is the courts' inalienable responsibility to identify and uphold.

Similar comments have been made by Laws LJ:[149]

> [T]hose who exercise democratic political power must have limits set to what they may do: limits which they are not allowed to overstep...the doctrine of Parliamentary sovereignty cannot be vouched by Parliamentary legislation; a higher order law confers it and must limit it.

Lord Justice Sedley has presented an alternative view, based on:[150]

> [A] bi-polar sovereignty of the Crown in Parliament and the Crown in the courts, to each of which the crown's ministers are answerable – politically to Parliament, legally to the courts.

Not only are these judges asserting their own role within the constitution, they are also re-examining what is required by the rule of law.[151] Lord Steyn's judgment in *Pierson*, for example, suggests that in addition to requiring some lawful authority for

---

[146]   Lord Falconer, 659 HL Official Report (5th series) col 51, 15 March 2004. For a discussion, see Le Sueur, 'Three Strikes and it's out? The UK Government's Strategy to Oust Judicial Review from Immigration and Asylum Decision-Making' [2004] PL 225.

[147]   Nationality, Immigration and Asylum Act 2002, s 103A: discussed at p 303, *ante*.

[148]   Woolf, 'Droit Public – English Style' [1995] PL 57 at p 69.

[149]   Laws, 'Law and Democracy' [1995] PL 80.

[150]   Sedley, 'Human Rights: A Twenty-First Century Agenda' [1995] PL 386.

[151]   In a work of this nature it is not possible to give a detailed account of the issues, but see: Allan, 'The Limits of Parliamentary Sovereignty' [1985] PL 614; Allan, 'The Conceptual Foundations of Judicial Review: Conceptual Conundrum or Interpretative Inquiry?' (2002) 61(1) CLJ 87; Craig, 'Public Law, Political Theory and Legal Theory' [2000] PL 211.

government action, the rule of law might also be capable of tempering Parliament's supremacy:[152]

> Unless there is the clearest provision to the contrary, Parliament must be presumed not to legislate contrary to the rule of law. And the rule of law enforces minimum standards of fairness.

By arguing that Parliament must be *presumed* to legislate in accordance with the rule of law, Lord Steyn avoids making a direct challenge to Parliament's authority. Lord Justice Laws adopted a similar approach in *Thoburn v Sunderland City Council*, when he asserted that there are 'constitutional statutes' which can only be repealed by express words.[153] Lord Woolf's approach is more direct, however, and he suggests that the rule of law may impose modest but substantive limits on Parliament's ability to legislate.[154] The ideas expressed by these judges may seem radical, but they are a reminder of Hart's idea that supremacy is 'a rule of recognition',[155] and that its existence depends on Parliament's authority being accepted as legitimate. In other words, if Parliament purports to legislate in an arbitrary or unjust manner, its authority to do so may be called into question.

These views are by no means universally – or even generally – accepted,[156] and outside the field of European law[157] no judge in modern times has attempted to disapply an Act of Parliament. Moreover, even if it could be agreed that there *should* be limits on legislative power, many would dispute whether an unelected and unaccountable judiciary should have the authority to police those limits. Nevertheless, there are signs that the UK is 'inching towards becoming a constitutional state',[158] and if this trend continues it is likely to lead to a more influential – and perhaps more equal – role for the judges. At the very least, it could be argued that the recent tensions between the government and the judiciary are a sign of a healthy democracy rather than impending constitutional crisis. David Feldman, for example, has argued that:[159]

> Tension between institutions is ... desirable. A functioning constitution requires that the various institutions of the state should provide checks and balances, and checks and balances depend on maintaining a state of tension between institutions and

---

[152] *R v Secretary of State for the Home Department, ex parte Pierson* [1998] AC 539 at 575, [1997] 3 All ER 577 at 607. The rule of law is explicitly recognized as a 'constitutional principle' by s 1 of the Constitutional Reform Act 2005: the Act does not, however, attempt to define it.

[153] [2002] EWHC 195 (Admin) at [60], [2003] QB 151 at [60], [2002] 4 All ER 156. For a discussion, see p 30, *ante*.

[154] See the above extracts. Woolf has described the legislative intent approach as 'a harmless fairytale': see 'Droit Public – English Style' [1995] PL 57.

[155] *The Concept of Law* (1961).

[156] See, e.g. Lord Irvine of Lairg, 'Judges and Decision Makers: the Theory and Practice of Wednesbury Review' [1996] PL 59.

[157] See pp 29 and 132, *ante*.

[158] Steyn, 'Democracy through Law' [2002] EHRLR 723 at p 734. Stevens agrees that 'it is becoming slowly more accurate to describe Britain as a constitutional democracy rather than a parliamentary democracy': *The English Judges: Their Role in the Changing Constitution* (2002) at p 148.

[159] Feldman, 'Human Rights, Terrorism and Risk: The Roles of Politicians and Judges' [2006] PL 364, at p 383.

their constitutional positions. Tension between institutions is not pathological; as long as it does not tear the state apart, it is a precondition for a healthy constitution under the rule of law.

Moreover, in enacting the Human Rights Act Parliament has arguably left the judges with little option but to make controversial – and even 'political' – decisions. Like Feldman, Nicol argues that this is not necessarily bad for democracy:[160]

> [T]he Law Lords have shown ideological unity during the early years of the HRA. It is therefore not entirely fanciful to recast the Law Lords as a political faction. Their particular focus on individual rights may help draw Parliament's attention to a perspective it might otherwise neglect.

However, while Nicol considers it both desirable and inevitable that judges will at times be 'robust' in their condemnation of legislation or government decisions, he sees nothing wrong in politicians being equally robust in their criticism of the courts:[161]

> [W]hen parliamentarians disagree with judicial conceptions of rights they should say so – and say why – forthrightly, and should reiterate the compelling reasons of principle why Parliament, not the courts, remains sovereign. Frank speech...requires abandoning the convention that politicians never express disagreement with court judgments. This inhibition hails from a bygone era when courts were not politically centre-stage, when they were not perceived as 'doing politics'. It certainly should not apply to HRA decisions.

JUDICIAL APPOINTMENTS AND SECURITY OF TENURE

1 APPOINTMENTS

(a) The old system

Until 2006 district judges and lay magistrates were appointed directly by the Lord Chancellor, while High Court judges, circuit judges, recorders, and district judges (magistrates' courts) were appointed by the Queen on his advice. In the case of the Law Lords, Court of Appeal judges and Heads of Division, the Prime Minister was ultimately responsible for 'advising' the Queen on appointments, but in practice the Prime Minister would normally be guided by the Lord Chancellor's recommendations. Thus, the power to determine all judicial appointments rested, in effect, in the hands of senior members of the government.

---

[160] Nicol, 'Law and Politics after the Human Rights Act' [2006] PL 722, at p 743.
[161] Ibid, at p 746.

The idea of judicial independence is of fundamental importance, and many feel strongly that the power to appoint judges should not be in the government's hands. English judges are said to rank highly on any international scale of objectivity[162] and few would seriously contend that they are subject to direct political interference, but they are also predominantly male, white, middle-class, and middle-aged. Although the last two decades have witnessed a period of 'unprecedented antagonism between judiciary and government',[163] some argue that the judiciary as an institution has an inherent tendency to support 'conventional, settled and established interests'.[164] In addition, the right to a fair trial before an 'independent and impartial tribunal'[165] requires judges to not only *be* independent but to be demonstrably so, and once this right was given statutory effect by the Human Rights Act concerns about the judicial appointments system gained momentum.

(b) The reform agenda

In 1999 Sir Leonard Peach carried out an independent scrutiny of the system, and on the basis of his recommendations the government established a Commission for Judicial Appointments.[166] However, the Commission's role was merely advisory and supervisory and it had no direct role in making appointments. In 2003 it carried out an audit of appointments to the High Court bench and concluded that fundamental changes were needed:[167]

> Our review of the 2003 High Court appointment competition has left us convinced that radical change is needed, to bring the system into line with best practice in other fields. We would be concerned to see any further High Court Judge selection processes take place on the basis of the present system, which we have found to be seriously lacking in transparency and accountability.

By the time that the audit was completed, the government had already published a consultation paper setting out is plans for a more powerful commission:[168]

> In a modern democratic society it is no longer acceptable for judicial appointments to be entirely in the hands of a Government Minister. For example the judiciary is often involved in adjudicating on the lawfulness of actions of the Executive. And so the appointments system must be, and must be seen to be, independent of Government. It must be transparent. It must be accountable. And it must inspire public confidence.

---

[162] Stevens, *The English Judges: Their Role in the Changing Constitution* (2002) at p 82.

[163] Lord Irvine of Lairg, 'The Impact of the Human Rights Act: Parliament, the Courts and the Executive' [2003] PL 307, at p 323. Although Lord Irvine wrote these words as Lord Chancellor and was referring to the period before the Labour government took office, the antagonism between the courts and the executive has actually increased subsequently. For a discussion, see p 328, *ante*.

[164] Griffith, *The Politics of the Judiciary* (5th edn, 1997), at p 20.

[165] Article 6, ECHR: see p 185, *ante*.

[166] *Appointment Processes of Judges and Queen's Counsel in England and Wales*. The Commission was established in 2001. For a discussion, see The Law Society, *Broadening the Bench* (2000), ch 5.

[167] Her Majesty's Commissioners for Judicial Appointments, *Report of the Commissioners' Review of the High Court 2003 Competition* (2004) at para E.10.2.

[168] DCA, *Constitutional Reform: A New Way of Appointing Judges* (2003) CP 10/03, foreword.

More than half of those who responded to the consultation felt that the Commission should be able to make actual appointments, and a further 13 per cent (including the Bar Council, Law Society and Judges' Council) said that it should at least be able to make appointments to the lower ranks.[169] The government had emphasized the need for accountability, and its preference was for a 'recommending commission' which would leave the final decision to the Minister. However, it was persuaded that the Minister's discretion should be kept to a minimum, and this is reflected in the provisions that were eventually included in the Constitutional Reform Act 2005.

It should be noted, however, that not everyone was convinced of the need to reduce political involvement in the appointments process. Writing in 2002, more than a year before the government's proposals were announced, Robert Stevens argued that:[170]

> Judges choosing judges is the antithesis of democracy. In all major common law countries – the US, Canada, Australia and South Africa – the executive chooses the judiciary, although sometimes with advice from a Judicial Appointments Commission. To hand over the appointment of judges to a commission might well ensure bland appointments. The courts do have important political powers and responsibilities…the choice of judges is too important to be left to a quango…At the very least, if there is to be a Constitutional or Supreme Court, its judges must be chosen by elected officials and subject to examination by a democratic body.

(c) The new system: the Judicial Appointments Commission

The Constitutional Reform Act 2005 provides that the Judicial Appointments Commission (JAC) should comprise six lay members, five judges, a solicitor, a barrister, a tribunal member, and one lay justice. One of the lay members must be appointed as Chairman.[171] Twelve of the Commissioners are appointed through a process of open competition, with the other three – those who are senior judges – being selected by the Judges' Council.[172] The current Chairman is Baroness Usha Prashar CBE, who was appointed to the role in October 2005.

Eligibility for judicial office. At one time only experienced barristers were eligible for most judicial appointments, and solicitors could only be appointed at the level of recorder or district judge. The Courts and Legal Services Act 1990 removed some of these barriers by linking the criteria for appointment to its provisions on rights of audience,[173] but a consultation exercise carried out in 2004 suggested that the rules were still perceived as being unduly restrictive.[174]

---

[169] DCA, *Constitutional Reform: A New Way of Appointing Judges – Summary of Responses to the Consultation*, January 2004. See also: Malleson, 'Creating a Judicial Appointments Commission: Which Model Works Best?' [2004] PL 102; The Law Society, *Broadening the Bench* (2000).

[170] Stevens, *The English Judges: Their Role in the Changing Constitution* (2002) at p 144.

[171] See Schedule 12, part 1. This composition is more varied than that originally envisaged by the government: its consultation paper had proposed (at paras 118–121) that there should be five lay members, five judges, and five lawyers.

[172] Ibid.   [173] See p 377, *post*.

[174] DCA, *Increasing Diversity in the Judiciary* – Summary of Responses to the Consultation, March 2005, at p 6. For the original consultation paper, see DCA, *Increasing Diversity in the Judiciary* (2004) CP 25/04.

The issue of statutory eligibility requirements, both in terms of who could apply [for judicial office] and time served, attracted diverse and strong responses. Some respondents felt that the current arrangements were about right. However, the majority believed that broadening eligibility would widen the pool of potential judges and thus enhance diversity. A number of respondents felt that the current emphasis on rights of audience was too restrictive and that eligibility should be based on wider legal skills and experience (particularly given that advocacy skills are not relevant to judicial office). In addition some thought that 'time served' was not an appropriate judgement of a person's suitability for appointment.

The government's response to these findings was to amend the minimum eligibility requirements for judicial appointments. The new arrangements are set out in Part 2 and Schedule 10 of the Tribunals, Courts and Enforcement Act 2007, and they centre on the concept of the 'judicial-appointment eligibility condition'. Each level of judicial office is now subject to such a condition, and in order to satisfy it a candidate must: (a) have held a relevant qualification for a specified minimum period, and (b) have been gaining experience in law at the same time.[175] What will constitute a 'relevant qualification'[176] is determined by the nature of the post, and this means that certain judicial offices will be open to legal executives and others.[177] For many posts, the minimum period for which a qualification must have been held has also been reduced. However, the additional requirement to have gained *experience* of the law means that a barrister or solicitor who hasn't actually worked as a lawyer since qualifying will not satisfy the statutory criteria. According to section 52(2) of the Act, a person will be deemed to have gained experience in law by being 'engaged in law-related activities'. Being in practice or employment as a lawyer is just one way of doing this: section 52(4) also refers to things such as teaching or researching law, acting as an arbitrator or mediator, and being engaged in any other activity which the decision-maker considers to be broadly similar to one of those specified.

Once in force, these arrangements will mean that in order to be eligible for appointment as a Lord of Appeal (or Justice of the Supreme Court) a candidate will need to satisfy the judicial-appointment eligibility condition for a minimum of fifteen years.[178] A person seeking appointment as a Lord or Lady Justice will need to satisfy this condition on a seven-year basis or have experience as a High Court judge, and a candidate for the High Court bench will be subject to a seven-year eligibility condition unless he has at least two years' experience as a circuit judge.[179] The posts of circuit judge and recorder will also be subject to a seven-year condition, though applicants for the former post will be deemed eligible if they have held one of certain specified posts[180] for a minimum

[175] 2007 Act, s 50.   [176] Ibid, s 51.

[177] Ibid. Section 51(2) provides that in order to be deemed 'relevant' for these purposes, a qualification must have been awarded either by the Institute of Legal Executives or a body authorized under the Courts and Legal Services Act 1990 to confer rights of audience or rights to conduct litigation. Potentially then, patent agents and trade mark attorneys could be eligible to apply for certain appointments: see further, pp 376 and 373, *post*.

[178] Appellate Jurisdiction Act 1876, s 6; Constitutional Reform Act 2005, s 25 – as amended by the 2007 Act, s 50; Schedule 10.

[179] Supreme Court Act 1981, s 10(3), as amended.

[180] These include coroner, district judge, and certain tribunal offices.

of three years.[181] The eligibility condition applicable to the posts of district judge and district judge (magistrates' courts) will be five years.[182]

Selection procedures.　Under the arrangements put in place by the Judicial Appointments Commission, most judicial positions are widely advertised in both the national press and professional publications, and 'outreach' events are sometimes held to encourage potential applicants to apply. Checks are made as to the eligibility and 'good character' of all applicants, and, in the case of junior appointments, candidates may also be asked to complete a qualifying test or attend a selection day. Shortlisted candidates are then interviewed by a selection panel of Commissioners.

For appointments to the High Court bench and lower judicial ranks, the 2005 Act requires the Commission to recommend a single candidate to the Minister.[183] The Lord Chancellor does have the power to reject the initial selection and to ask the Commission to reconsider or put forward an alternative, but if he does this he must then appoint either: (a) the next candidate selected, or (b) the Commission's original choice.[184] If at the first stage the Lord Chancellor merely asks the Commission to *reconsider* its selection, he will be entitled to reject the candidate put forward at the second stage (who may or may not be the same person), but he *must* then appoint the next selection. Though the rules are complicated, they mean in essence that the Commission will never be required to put forward more than two or three selections for each post, and that the Lord Chancellor will only ever have one right of rejection. The Act sets out similar arrangements for the appointment of the Lord Chief Justice, Heads of Division, Lord and Lady Justices of Appeal, and Senior President of Tribunals,[185] but the Commission is required to convene a special selection panel before making any recommendation. The precise membership of this panel is determined by the nature of the appointment, but it would normally include the Chairman, the Lord Chief Justice, a senior judge and a lay member.[186] At all levels the Commission is required to make its selections on the basis of merit and good character,[187] and to take into account any guidelines issued by the Lord Chancellor.[188]

In the future, when a vacancy arises in the new Supreme Court[189] the Lord Chancellor will be required to convene a panel comprising the President of the Supreme Court, the Deputy President, and a member of each of the appointments bodies for England and Wales, Scotland, and Northern Ireland.[190] That panel will in turn be required to consult senior judges and the relevant Minister for each of the UK jurisdictions.[191] The Lord Chancellor will again have only one right of rejection,[192] and the actual appointment of

---

[181] Courts Act 1971, ss 16(3) and 21(2), as amended.

[182] County Courts Act 1984, s 9; Courts Act 2003, ss 22 and 24 – as amended.

[183] Section 88.　　[184] Section 90.

[185] This office is discussed further at p 298, *ante*.

[186] Sections 67–84. Slightly different configurations are adopted when appointing the Lord Chief Justice and Senior President of Tribunals.

[187] Section 63.　　[188] Section 65.

[189] See p 253, *ante*.　　[190] Schedule 8, part 1.

[191] Section 27: for England and Wales the Lord Chancellor is the relevant Minister.

[192] Section 29.

these judges will be formally made by the Prime Minister.[193] The Lord Chancellor's role will be to notify him of the selection.

As outlined previously, section 3 of the 2005 Act means that all Ministers have a duty to uphold judicial independence and to refrain from attempting to improperly influence judicial decisions. It further provides that the Lord Chancellor must have regard to the need to *defend* judicial independence and to ensure that judges have the support necessary to enable them to perform their functions. The Act also provides for the appointment of a Judicial Appointments and Conduct Ombudsman, with the power to investigate complaints about appointments and disciplinary matters.[194]

The government is now considering whether its reforms have gone far enough, and it recently invited views as to whether the Lord Chancellor's formal role in the appointments process might be further reduced.[195]

(d) Diversity in the judiciary

At present, members of the judiciary continue to be drawn from a fairly narrow section of society. The first female Law Lord was appointed in January 2004, but there were only two Lady Justices in the Court of Appeal at this time, and less than 7 per cent of High Court judges were women. Women were slightly better represented in the lower ranks, accounting for 11 per cent of circuit judges and almost 40 per cent of district judges,[196] but the figures for ethnic minorities were less encouraging. Ethnic minorities comprised just 3 per cent of district judges and 1.5 per cent of circuit judges, and not a single black or Asian judge was appointed above the level of the circuit bench.[197]

For obvious reasons, the composition of the judiciary has always mirrored that of the Bar, and although the number of female and ethnic minority barristers is increasing, it will be some time before this is reflected in the senior judicial ranks. The Lord Chancellor's 2003 appointments guidelines revealed his personal frustration at the slow rate of progress:[198]

> Appointments must and will be made on merit irrespective of ethnic origin, gender, marital status, political affiliation, sexual orientation, religion or disability. These are not mere words. They are firm principles...I want every vacancy on the Bench to be filled by the best person available, but I can only appoint the judiciary from among those who are ready and willing to do the job. I would like all eligible practitioners to have the confidence to apply.

The implication here is that suitably qualified female and ethnic minority lawyers may be less inclined than their white, male counterparts to apply for judicial office. This perception is borne out by at least some empirical research. Writing in 1991 for example, Hughes suggested that opening up the system to greater competition made it *less* likely that female judges would be appointed, because a sizeable proportion of women lawyers

---

[193] Section 26.   [194] Section 62; Schedule 13.
[195] Ministry of Justice, *The Governance of Britain: Judicial Appointments*, CP 25/07, October 2007.
[196] DCA, *Statistics: Women in the Judiciary* (2004).
[197] DCA, *Statistics: Ethnic Minorities in the Judiciary* (2004).
[198] *Judicial Appointments in England and Wales* (2003), at p 1.

would not put themselves forward without direct encouragement.[199] Similarly, while the Judges' Council broadly supported the creation of the new Judicial Appointments Commission, it argued that there should still be a place for headhunting:[200]

> The very best candidates frequently do not actively seek appointment. In practice, many judges take an appointment only when encouraged to do so out of a sense of duty.

On the other hand, it would be naïve to rely on such headhunting to remedy centuries of inequality and under-representation. Writing extra-judicially, Lady Justice Hale (as she then was) observed that, 'women have been entering the [legal] profession in significant numbers for a long time...But [there are]...systemic obstacles to making sufficient progress to be regarded as a serious candidate.'[201] The long hours culture, the fact that women's lifestyles may make it more difficult to devote time to 'networking', and the fact that High Court judges are still regularly appointed from a handful of elite chambers, are all cited as examples of such obstacles. A number of academics have argued that the overwhelmingly white, male culture of the judiciary has a real impact on both the development of the law, and the treatment of those who appear before the courts.[202] For Hale, however, the issue is even more fundamental:[203]

> Judges...are set in authority over others and can sometimes wield enormous power over individuals and businesses. In a democratic society, in which we are all equal citizens, it is wrong in principle for that authority to be wielded by such a very unrepresentative section of the population.

When the government proposed the creation of the new Judicial Appointments Commission, it also expressed a wider interest in finding new and more inclusive ways of selecting judicial candidates:[204]

> [T]he current judiciary is overwhelmingly white, male, and from a narrow social and educational background. To an extent, this reflects the pool of qualified candidates from which judicial appointments are made: intake to the legal professions has, until recently, been dominated by precisely these social groups.
>
> Of course the fundamental principle in appointing judges is and must remain selection on merit. However, the Government is committed to opening up the system of appointments, to attract suitably qualified candidates both from a wider range of social backgrounds and from a wider range of legal practice.

---

[199] *The Circuit Bench: A Women's Place* (1991). Cf. Malleson and Banda, *Factors Affecting the Decision to Apply for Silk and Judicial Office* (2000) Lord Chancellor's Department Research Series 02/00; Holland and Spencer, *Without Prejudice? Sex Equality at the Bar and in the Judiciary* (1992).

[200] Judges' Council Response to the Consultation Papers on Constitutional Reform, at para 76: see www.dca.gov.uk/judicial/pdfs/jcresp.pdf.

[201] Hale, 'Equality and the Judiciary: Why We Should Want More Women Judges' [2001] PL 489 at 492. See also, The Law Society, *Broadening the Bench* (2000).

[202] See, e.g.: Kennedy, *Eve Was Framed: Women and British Justice* (1992); Temkin, *Rape and the Legal Process* (1987); Genn, *Paths to Justice* (1997) at p 229; Smart (ed), *Law, Crime and Sexuality: Essays in Feminism* (1995).

[203] [2001] PL 489 at 502.

[204] DCA, *Constitutional Reform: A New Way of Appointing Judges* (2003), CP 10/03, foreword.

As this statement suggests, the link between rights of audience and eligibility for judicial office has greatly restricted the pool of potential applicants, and this was one of the main issues raised by the consultation on *Increasing Diversity in the Judiciary*. On the basis of the responses to this consultation, the Department for Constitutional Affairs concluded that:[205]

> The current requirements need to be reviewed, both in terms of the qualification required, and the length of time which must be served before an application for judicial appointment can be made. Examples of the type of people [the Secretary of State] has in mind as potentially having the right sort of skills and experience are legal executives, academics with a legal background; patent and trademark attorneys; and possibly lay magistrates with an appropriate legal qualification.

However, the consultation also revealed widespread support for other measures, such as doing more to attract and support disabled candidates, and allowing more scope for the introduction of flexible sitting arrangements and career breaks.[206] The changes to eligibility criteria being introduced as a result of this consultation will undoubtedly aid efforts to recruit a more diverse judiciary,[207] but the rate of change will also be influenced by the government's willingness to address these wider issues, and by the willingness of suitable candidates to put themselves forward.

2 TENURE

(a) Removal and discipline

Before Stuart times judges could be removed at the will of the King, but this position was altered by the Act of Settlement 1700. The Act provided that as long as they conducted themselves properly, judges of the superior courts could only be removed on an address by both Houses of Parliament,[208] and this rule still applies to judges of the High Court, Court of Appeal, and House of Lords.[209] No English judge has ever been removed under this procedure, although an Irish judge was removed in 1830 when he was discovered to have misappropriated court funds. Judges of the lower ranks can be removed by the Lord Chancellor without parliamentary approval, but this can only be done on the grounds of incapacity or misbehaviour and with the agreement of the Lord Chief Justice.[210] Judges of all ranks thus enjoy considerable security of tenure.

---

[205] DCA, *Increasing Diversity in the Judiciary* – Summary of Responses to the Consultation, March 2005, at p 76.

[206] Ibid, at p 8.

[207] See the discussion of the Tribunals, Courts and Enforcement Act 2007, at p 295, *ante*.

[208] The Lord Chancellor was always an exception: see p 318, *ante*.

[209] Supreme Court Act 1981, s 11(3) (High Court and Court of Appeal – it is for the Lord Chancellor to formally recommend the exercise of this power to the monarch; s 11(3A); Appellate Jurisdiction Act 1876, s 6 (House of Lords). Special provisions allow the Lord Chancellor to remove a judge who is disabled by permanent infirmity and who does not have the capacity to resign: see the 1981 Act, s 11(8).

[210] Courts Act 1971, s 17(4) (circuit judges); County Courts Act 1984, s 11 (district judges); Courts Act 2003, s 22 (district judges (magistrates' courts)). Lay justices have not previously enjoyed the same security of tenure as their professional counterparts, but this position was rectified by s 11 of the Courts Act 2003.

Serious judicial misconduct is almost unheard of in modern times. In 1983 a circuit judge was removed from office after being convicted of various smuggling offences, but this is an extreme example. On the rare occasions when judges have been disciplined, this has usually taken the form of a reprimand for a lesser 'offence' such as incompetence, neglect, unacceptable delay, or unacceptable personal behaviour.[211] Some judges have responded to allegations of such behaviour by offering their resignation, and others have been asked to do so. Thus, a High Court judge resigned in 1998 after being castigated by the Court of Appeal for taking twenty months to deliver a judgment:[212]

> Conduct like this weakens public confidence in the whole judicial process. Left unchecked, it would be ultimately subversive of the rule of law. Delays on this scale cannot and will not be tolerated.

(b) *Starrs* v *Ruxton* and the problem of fixed-term appointments

Unlike other judges, recorders are appointed on a part-time basis and for a specific term of office. Before 2000 the standard length of appointment was three years, and at the end of this period the Lord Chancellor had a discretion as to whether a contract should be renewed. These arrangements were called into question by the decision of the Scottish High Court of Justiciary in *Starrs* v *Ruxton*.[213] The court ruled that the use of temporary judges infringed Article 6 of the ECHR, because a judge without security of tenure could not be considered 'independent'. The case was concerned with the use of temporary sheriffs in Scotland, but it had obvious implications for the appointment of recorders and the Lord Chancellor was quick to respond. The terms upon which part-time judges hold office were reviewed, and all are now appointed for a minimum period of five years. They can only be removed on the grounds of misbehaviour, incapacity, failure to comply with sitting requirements, failure to comply with training requirements, or sustained failure to observe reasonably expected standards. In the absence of one of these grounds, contracts will normally be renewed automatically at the end of each five-year term.[214] The Lord Chancellor also took the opportunity to abolish the separate office of 'assistant recorder', and those who already held this title were re-appointed as recorders.

(c) Retirement

The standard retirement age for judges is seventy,[215] although a judge who has completed twenty years of service can retire with full pension rights at the age of sixty-five.[216]

---

[211] The *Judicial Appointments Annual Report 2002–2003* records that two formal reprimands were issued during the relevant period, although the Lord Chancellor received a total of 370 complaints relating to the personal conduct of judges: para 12.2. The Lord Chief Justice now has greater powers in this area: Constitutional Reform Act 2005, s 108.

[212] *Goose* v *Wilson Sandford & Co* (1998), *The Times*, February 19, per Peter Gibson LJ. The judge, Mr Justice Harman, had regularly featured at the top of a legal journal's 'Worst Judge' poll: see 'Controlling the Judges' (1998) 148 NLJ 234.

[213] 2000 JC 208, 2000 SLT 42, *sub nom Starrs* v *Procurator Fiscal*. See also: *Scanfuture* v *Secretary of State for Trade and Industry* [2001] ICR 1096, [2001] IRLR 416.

[214] Courts Act 1971, s 21.

[215] Judicial Pensions and Retirement Act 1993, s 26(1); Schedule 5.

[216] Judicial Pensions Act 1981. The twenty-year rule means that even if a judge continues until the age of seventy, he will be ineligible to receive a full pension unless he was called to the bench by the age of fifty.

In addition, a judge of the circuit bench or lower ranks may be asked to stay on until he reaches seventy-five,[217] and any retired judge below this age may sit on an ad hoc basis.[218] Lay magistrates also 'retire' at seventy, which is when their names are added to the supplemental list and they cease to be able to perform judicial functions.[219] They are, however, unsalaried, and unlike their professional counterparts they do not receive a pension.

(d) Salaries

Judicial salaries are determined by the Lord Chancellor with the consent of the Minister for the Civil Service (the Prime Minister). They are paid from the Consolidated Fund[220] and are not subject to a vote in Parliament. They are deliberately set at a high level so as to provide a further safeguard of independence, the idea being that a well-paid judge will not be vulnerable to bribery and corruption. In fact, however, the high earning capacity of the most successful practitioners means that accepting a judicial appointment will often involve a reduction in income. As of November 2007, district judges in both the magistrates' and the civil courts received a salary of £98,900, while High Court judges received £165,900 and the Lord Chief Justice got £230,400.[221] By contrast, the most successful barristers can earn over £500,000 per annum, although the income of the *average* barrister is much less than this.[222]

3 TRAINING

It was once assumed that those appointed to the Bench already had sufficient training and experience to enable them to perform judicial functions. It is now accepted that this is not inevitably the case, and in 1979 the Judicial Studies Board was established to provide training for both new and experienced judges. The Board is run by judges themselves, and through training courses and refresher courses it seeks to create an awareness of best practice and to equip judges to deal with common problems.[223] It also runs courses covering developments in procedure, substantive law, evidence, and sentencing, and in 1998 it began a major training programme to educate judges about the Human Rights Act. Judges are also exposed to related disciplines such as penology, and all judges now receive equal treatment training.

4 JUDICIAL IMMUNITY

The doctrine of judicial immunity is an offshoot of the principle of independence. Historically, the degree of immunity recognized has varied with the status of the judge,

---

[217] Judicial Pensions and Retirement Act 1993, s 26(5).   [218] Ibid, s 26(7).

[219] Courts Act 2003, ss 12 and 13 (replacing the Justices of the Peace Act 1997, s 7).

[220] Supreme Court Act 1981, s 12; Administration of Justice Act 1973, s 9.

[221] Ministry of Justice, *Judicial Salaries and Fees 2007–2008*.

[222] *Chambers Guide to the Legal Profession 2001–2002*, at p 1247.

[223] For a more detailed discussion, see Partington, 'Training the Judiciary in England and Wales' (1994) 13 CJQ 319; Malleson, *The New Judiciary: The Effects of Expansion and Activism* (1999), ch 5.

and the old cases distinguish between judges of superior and inferior courts. Superior court judges were immune from liability even if acting maliciously, while judges of the inferior courts enjoyed immunity only while acting within their jurisdiction. Thus, a recorder who unlawfully imprisoned a jury for ignoring his direction to convict was held immune from suit,[224] while an unfortunate county court judge was held liable in damages for making an innocent mistake of law.[225]

In the modern case of *Sirros v Moore* the Court of Appeal rejected the idea that the degree of immunity should depend upon the status of the court. The claimant was a foreign national who unsuccessfully appealed to the Crown Court against a recommendation that he should be deported. The circuit judge who rejected his appeal was under the mistaken impression that the claimant was in custody, and at the end of the hearing he ordered a police officer to arrest and detain him. The detention was clearly unlawful, and the claimant brought an action for false imprisonment against both the judge and the police officer. However, the Court of Appeal held that the judge was immune from liability, despite the fact that he was a judge of an inferior court. The police officer was also held to be immune on the basis that he was following the judge's orders. Lord Denning MR even suggested that the principle of immunity should extend to justices of the peace:[226]

> Every judge of the courts of this land from the highest to the lowest should be protected to the same degree, and liable to the same degree. If the reason underlying this immunity is to ensure 'that they may be free in thought and independent in judgment', it applies to every judge, whatever his rank. Each should be protected from liability to damages when he is acting judicially. Each should be able to do his work in complete independence and free from fear. He should not have to turn the pages of his books with trembling fingers, asking himself; 'If I do this, shall I be liable in damages?' So long as he does his work in the honest belief that it is within his jurisdiction, then he is not liable to an action.

In the later case of *McC v Mullan*,[227] the House of Lords questioned the assertion that inferior and superior courts are now subject to the same rules. It also confirmed that justices of the peace could be sued if they acted outside their jurisdiction. Nevertheless, *Sirros v Moore* remains good law, and justices of the peace now have statutory immunity for acts done in good faith and in the purported execution of their duty.[228] In addition, a judge cannot be compelled to give evidence of matters relating to the performance of his judicial functions, although he is a competent witness to such matters and may testify if he is willing to do so.[229]

The immunity that attaches to judicial proceedings is not personal to the judge. No civil action lies in respect of words spoken in the course of proceedings by parties,[230] witnesses,[231] or advocates;[232] nor can an action be brought in respect of the verdict of

---

[224] *Hamond v Howell* (1677) 2 Mod Rep 218.   [225] *Houlden v Smith* (1850) 14 QB 841.
[226] [1975] QB 118 at 136, [1974] 3 All ER 776 at 785.   [227] [1985] AC 528, [1984] 3 All ER 908.
[228] Courts Act 2003, ss 31 and 32.   [229] *Warren v Warren* [1997] QB 488, [1996] 4 All ER 664.
[230] *Astley v Younge* (1759) 2 Burr 807.
[231] *Hargreaves v Bretherton* [1959] 1 QB 45, [1958] 3 All ER 122.
[232] *Munster v Lamb* (1883) 11 QBD 588.

ajury.[233] In addition, media reports of judicial proceedings are absolutely privileged in the law of defamation. They must, however, be fair, accurate and contemporaneous.[234]

FURTHER READING

ALLAN, 'The Limits of Parliamentary Sovereignty' [1985] PL 614

ARNHEIM, 'The Rule of Law or the Rule of Lawyers?' (2004) 154 NLJ 776

BRADLEY, 'Judicial Independence under Attack' [2003] PL 397

CRAIG, 'Public Law, Political Theory and Legal Theory' [2000] PL 211

Department for Constitutional Affairs, *Constitutional Reform: A New Way of Appointing Judges* (2003) CP 10/03

Department for Constitutional Affairs, *Constitutional Reform: Reforming the Office of the Lord Chancellor* (2003) CP 13/03

Department for Constitutional Affairs, *Constitutional Reform: A New Way of Appointing Judges – Summary of Responses to the Consultation* (January 2004)

Department for Constitutional Affairs, *The Lord Chancellor's Judiciary-Related Functions: Proposals* (2004) – 'The Concordat'

Department for Constitutional Affairs, *Increasing Diversity in the Judiciary* (2004) CP 25/04

Department for Constitutional Affairs, *Increasing Diversity in the Judiciary – Summary of Responses to the Consultation* (March 2005)

DREWERY, 'Judicial Inquiries and Public Reassurance' [1996] PL 368

FELDMAN, 'Human Rights, Terrorism and Risk: the Roles of Politicians and Judges' [2006] PL 364

GRIFFITH, *The Politics of the Judiciary* (Fontana: 5th edn, 1997)

HALE, 'Equality and the Judiciary: Why We Should Want More Women Judges' [2001] PL 489

HOLLAND and SPENCER, *Without Prejudice? Sex Equality at the Bar and in the Judiciary* (TMS Management Consultants, 1992)

HUGHES, *The Circuit Bench: A Women's Place* (1991)

IRVINE, 'Judges and Decision Makers: The Theory and Practice of Wednesbury Review' [1996] PL 59

IRVINE, 'The Impact of the Human Rights Act: Parliament, the Courts and the Executive' [2003] PL 307

JOWELL, 'Heading for a Constitutional Crisis' (2004) 154 NLJ 401

Judges' Council, *Response to the Consultation Papers on Constitutional Reform* (2003) – available at www.dca.gov.uk/judicial/pdfs/jcresp.pdf

Law Lords, *Response to the Government's Consultation Paper on Constitutional Reform: A Supreme Court for the United Kingdom* (2003) – available at http://www.parliament.uk/documents/upload/JudicialSCR071103.pdf

LAWS, 'Law and Democracy' [1995] PL 80

Law Society, *Broadening the Bench* (2000)

LE SUEUR, 'Three Strikes and it's out? The UK Government's Strategy to Oust Judicial Review from Immigration and Asylum Decision-Making' [2004] PL 225

---

[233] *Bushell's Case* (1670) Vaugh 135.   [234] Defamation Act 1996, s 14.

MALLESON, *The New Judiciary: The Effects of Expansion and Activism* (Aldershot: 1999)

MALLESON, 'Creating a Judicial Appointments Commission: Which Model Works Best?' [2004] PL 102

Ministry of Justice, *The Governance of Britain: Judicial Appointments*, CP 25/07 (2007)

NICOL, 'Law and Politics after the Human Rights Act' [2006] PL 722

PANNICK, *Judges* (Oxford University Press: 1987)

PARTINGTON, 'Training the Judiciary in England and Wales' (1994) 13 CJQ 319

SCARMAN, *Why Britain Needs a Written Constitution* (Charter 88: 1992)

SEDLEY, 'Human Rights: A Twenty-First Century Agenda' [1995] PL 386

STEVENS, *The English Judges: Their Role in the Changing Constitution* (Hart: 2002)

STEVENS, 'Reform in Haste and Repent at Leisure: Iolanthe, the Lord High Executioner and *Brave New World*' (2004) 24 LS 1

STEYN, 'The Weakest and Least Dangerous Department of Government' [1997] PL 84

STEYN, 'Democracy through Law' [2002] EHRLR 723

WADE, 'The Basis of Legal Sovereignty' [1955] CLJ 172

WOOLF, 'Droit Public – English Style' [1995] PL 57

WOOLF, 'The Rule of Law and a Change in the Constitution' (2004) 63(2) CLJ 317

11

JURIES

INTRODUCTION

The focus in this chapter will be on the role of the jury in the modern English legal system. In the twenty-first century the majority of criminal cases are tried by magistrates rather than juries, and with the exception of trials for defamation, the use of the jury in civil cases is now almost unheard of. Yet the idea of trial by jury has always been seen as a cornerstone of the English legal system, and it remains the standard mode of trial for dealing with the most serious types of criminal case.

The following aspects of the jury and its role will be addressed in this chapter:

- The origins of the jury system and the use of the jury trial in both criminal and civil cases.

- The way in which juries are selected and empanelled and the rules governing excusal and disqualification.

- The extent to which the composition of a jury might be challenged by one of the parties to an action, and the powers available to judges when dealing with such challenges.

- The rules governing jury secrecy and their implications for research into jury decisions.

- The extent to which the use of juries is compatible with the idea of 'a fair trial'.

HISTORICAL GROWTH OF THE JURY SYSTEM

The trial of criminals by jury evolved in the thirteenth century to replace trial by ordeal, and by the middle of the fourteenth century the separate roles of the petty jury and grand jury were established.

The grand jury was not a 'trial jury' in the modern sense. Its original function was to present persons for trial at the start of assizes or quarter sessions,[1] but when the system of preliminary investigation by magistrates developed its role was reduced to a mere formality. The grand jury was finally abolished by the Criminal Justice Act 1948.[2]

---

[1] See p 233, *ante*.   [2] Section 31(3). Grand juries are still used in some United States jurisdictions.

The twelve member petty jury was the equivalent of the modern trial jury, though in its early stages jurors were summoned for their local knowledge and acted as witnesses rather than judges of fact. The petty jury's function changed gradually as the practice of examining independent witnesses grew and by the fifteenth century it had assumed its modern role as arbiter of fact. A landmark decision in 1670[3] established that jurors should decide cases according to their consciences and that they could not be punished for returning a verdict contrary to the evidence or the judge's direction.

In civil cases there was only ever one type of jury: the trial jury of twelve members. This had its origins in the Assize of Clarendon, 1166, and by 1304 it was established that all trespass actions in common law courts had to be tried with a jury. As with criminal juries, jurors in civil trials originally acted as witnesses, but a similar transition from witnesses to judges of fact took place. The steady decline of the jury in civil cases began with the Common Law Procedure Act 1854, which allowed common law actions to be tried without a jury if both parties agreed. The use of juries in civil cases is now extremely limited.[4]

THE COMPOSITION OF THE MODERN JURY

1   QUALIFYING FOR JURY DUTY

Eligibility for jury service used to depend upon the existence of a property qualification, and juries were criticized for being 'predominantly male, middle-aged, middle-minded and middle-class'.[5] Following the recommendations of the Morris Committee[6] the property qualification was abolished and the present system of selecting jurors from the electoral register was introduced.[7] The law was consolidated in the Juries Act 1974 and was most recently amended by the Criminal Justice Act 2003. Section 1 of the 1974 Act now provides that[8] a person will be qualified to serve as a juror and liable to attend for jury service when summoned, if:

(a)   he is registered as a parliamentary or local government elector and is not less than eighteen nor more than seventy[9] years of age;

(b)   he has been ordinarily resident in the United Kingdom, the Channel Islands or the Isle of Man for any period of at least five years since attaining the age of thirteen;

(c)   he is not a mentally disordered person; and

(d)   he is not disqualified for jury service.

---

[3] *Bushell's case* (1670) Vaugh 135.   [4] See p 362, *post*.

[5] Devlin, *Trial by Jury* (1956), at p 20.

[6] *Report of the Departmental Committee on Jury Service*, 1965, Cmnd 2627.

[7] Criminal Justice Act 1972. For the effect of these reforms on the composition of juries, see Baldwin and McConville, *Jury Trials* (1979) at p 94.

[8] As amended by the 2003 Act: with effect from 5 April 2004.

[9] The upper age limit was raised from sixty-five by the Criminal Justice Act 1988, s 119.

Thus, assuming that the residential and age qualifications are met, anyone listed on the electoral register may be required to serve as a juror unless he is *ineligible* by reason of mental disorder[10] or *disqualified* under Schedule 1, Part 2.[11]

Excusal and deferral

The government considers jury service to be 'one of the most important civic duties that anyone can be asked to perform'.[12] Those eligible have a legal obligation to attend if summoned unless they can satisfy the 'appropriate officer'[13] that there is a good reason to excuse or defer them.[14] In a recent Home Office study of 50,000 people summoned for jury duty,[15] 38 per cent of those in the sample were excused and nearly 17 per cent were granted a deferral.[16] The most common grounds for excusal were child-care responsibilities, illness, and work commitments. Recent guidelines[17] state that excusals should only be granted to those who can show good reason for not serving at any time within the following twelve months. Religious objections[18] or being out of the country are cited as examples of good reasons for excusal, but deferral is considered more appropriate for those with holiday plans or work commitments.

Before 5 April 2004, Members of Parliament, medical professionals and members of the armed forces were entitled to be excused from jury service as of right, the rationale being that such persons would generally have more pressing duties to perform elsewhere. Those aged over sixty-five and those belonging to religious societies with beliefs incompatible with jury service[19] could also insist on being excused. In addition, ministers of religion, members of the legal profession, and certain other persons involved in the administration of justice were *ineligible* to serve as jurors by reason of their occupation. The Morris Committee had suggested these occupational exclusions because of concerns that a clergyman or someone with professional knowledge of the justice system might exercise undue influence in a jury room. There was also an argument that

---

[10] This is defined in Schedule 1, Part 1 of the 1974 Act (as amended).

[11] There are three basic categories of disqualification. (1) A person who has been given an extended sentence, or who has been sentenced to a term of imprisonment or detention of five years or more, or to imprisonment or detention for public protection, is effectively disqualified from jury service for life. (2) A person who has served a period of imprisonment, youth custody or detention or who has been the subject of one of the community or rehabilitation orders listed in paragraph 7 of the Schedule is disqualified for ten years after completion of the sentence. (3) A person who is on bail in criminal proceedings is also disqualified.

[12] Department for Constitutional Affairs, *Jury Summoning Guidance* (consultation paper; 2003), *foreword*.

[13] In practice, this task now falls to the Jury Central Summoning Bureau: see p 352, *post*.

[14] Juries Act 1974, ss 9 and 9A. Failure to attend is a criminal offence punishable by a fine (s 20), although 'offenders' are rarely pursued: see Darbyshire, Maughan and Stewart, *What can the English Legal System Learn from Jury Research Published up to 2001? – Findings for the Criminal Courts Review* (2001) at p 6.

[15] Airs and Shaw, *Jury Excusal and Deferral*, Home Office Research Findings No 102 (1999), at p 1.

[16] A further 13 per cent were ineligible, disqualified or excused as of right, and 15 per cent had their summonses returned as 'undelivered' or simply did not attend.

[17] Issued in April 2004 under the new section 9AA of the Juries Act 1974: Department for Constitutional Affairs, *Guidance for Summoning Officers when considering deferral and excusal applications*.

[18] In *R v Crown Court at Guildford, ex parte Siderfin* [1990] 2 QB 683, [1989] 3 All ER 73 it was held that excusal on religious grounds should only be granted where the religious belief would stand in the way of proper performance of the jury function.

[19] Ibid.

someone working in the legal system might find it difficult to follow a judge's directions if this meant putting aside his own legal 'knowledge'.

In his *Review of the Criminal Courts* Lord Justice Auld concluded that despite the reforms of previous decades, juries still lacked diversity and were not sufficiently representative of the communities from which they were drawn. With a view to widening participation, he recommended that 'no-one should be automatically ineligible or excusable from jury service simply because he or she is a member of a certain profession or holds a particular office or job'.[20] This recommendation was given effect by the Criminal Justice Act 2003. The government dismissed concerns that the presence of lawyers in the jury room might be problematic:[21]

> In England and Wales, a large number of people with extensive knowledge of the criminal justice system – legal academics, law students and civil servants working in criminal justice – currently do jury service. There is no evidence to suggest that the involvement of any of these groups in jury service has been a problem. More generally, the diluting effect of the process of random selection, and the group dynamic of the jury, serve to protect the integrity of the deliberative process.

Those who would previously have been ineligible or excused as of right because of their occupations are now subject to the same regime as everyone else: if they wish to be excused from jury service they must persuade the summoning officer that they have a good reason. Even judges may now be called upon to serve as jurors and the Lord Chief Justice recently wrote to all judges offering advice on what to do if summoned.[22] The only persons automatically entitled to be excused are those who have served (or attended to serve) on a jury within the previous two years.[23] The Department for Constitutional Affairs estimates that a person's chances of doing jury service during his lifetime are roughly one in six.[24]

2 SELECTING AND SUMMONING JURORS

Before 2000, jurors were selected locally by the summoning officers for each court centre, but a Central Summoning Bureau has now been established at Blackfriars Crown Court. The Bureau operates on a national basis and randomly selects names from the electoral register by computer, taking into account the number of prospective jurors needed for each area. It is then responsible for issuing summonses and for dealing with applications for excusal or deferral. Under the old system many local summoning officers developed their own methods for selecting names from the electoral lists, and the approach to dealing with excusals and deferrals differed from area to area. The move to a centralized system has gone some way towards improving the randomness and consistency of

---

[20] *Review of the Criminal Courts of England and Wales* (2001) at para 5.14.
[21] DCA, *Jury Summoning Guidance*, (consultation paper; 2003) at p 9.
[22] The text of the letter can be accessed through the Department for Constitutional Affairs website: www.dca.gov.uk.
[23] Juries Act 1974, s 8. Lord Justice Auld's *Review of the Criminal Courts* (2001) recommended that this time-scale should be extended (at para 5.224).
[24] *Jury Summoning Guidance* (consultation paper; 2003) at p 6.

the selection process, and it should also enable automatic checks to be made to ensure that those disqualified by their criminal convictions do not serve. It does not, however, address the more fundamental criticism that thousands of otherwise eligible people do not qualify for jury service at all because their names do not appear on the electoral register. A particular concern here is that members of certain ethnic groups may be under-represented on jury panels because they are less likely to register to vote than those from other backgrounds. For example, research carried out for the Home Office in 1999 suggested that across the population as a whole the rate of non-registration was around 8 per cent, but for black people this figure was as high as 24 per cent.[25] In reliance on this research, Lord Justice Auld's Review of the Criminal Courts recommended that in racially sensitive cases there should be a modified selection procedure to ensure that up to three ethnic minority jurors were chosen.[26] However, this recommendation was rejected by the government as being potentially divisive, and a more recent and more comprehensive study commissioned by the Ministry of Justice found no real evidence that ethnic minorities were under-represented on juries:[27]

> [T]he survey revealed that the summoning process reaches BME [black and minority ethnic] groups in remarkable consistency to BME representation in the local popula-tion for virtually all Crown Courts. This indicates that the process of computerised random selection from the electoral lists provided by local authorities is successfully summoning ethnically representative groups of potential jurors for Crown Courts in England and Wales.

3 CHALLENGING THE COMPOSITION OF THE JURY

Once the summonses have been issued, the court officer prepares a 'panel' of prospective jurors and the parties have the right to inspect a list of their names and addresses. The names of those on the list are then put on cards and placed in a box. At the beginning of a trial, cards are drawn from the box by a ballot in open court[28] and those named on them are sworn in as jurors.[29] It is at this point that the parties may exercise their limited rights to challenge those selected.[30] However, as the parties are given no information about the panel except for a list of names and addresses,[31] they will generally have very little to go on. Characteristics such as gender and race are not legitimate grounds for

---

[25] Airs and Shaw, *Jury Excusal and Deferral*, Home Office Research Findings No 102 (1999), at p 2.

[26] *Review of the Criminal Courts of England and Wales* (2001) at para. 5.60.

[27] Thomas and Balmer, *Diversity and Fairness in the Jury System*, Ministry of Justice Research Series 2/07 (2007), at p 77. For further discussion of the issues surrounding the ethnicity of jurors, see p 356, *post*.

[28] Juries Act 1974, s 11. A jury should only be used once except where a second trial commences within twenty-four hours of the jury being constituted: s 11(5)(a). However, individual jurors may be returned to the pool at the conclusion of a trial and may try other cases if their names are drawn in subsequent ballots. The usual period of jury service is two weeks.

[29] For the manner of taking an oath for these purposes, see the Oaths Act 1978, ss 1 and 5.

[30] For a discussion, see Buxton, 'Challenging and Discharging Jurors – Part 1' [1990] Crim LR 225.

[31] It is legitimate to withhold the names of jurors from a court if there is a real risk of the jury being 'nob-bled'. However, the parties still have the right to challenge for cause and are entitled to insist on inspecting the list of names on the panel: *R v Comerford* [1998] 1 All ER 823, [1998] 1 WLR 191. Note however, that under sections 44 and 46 of the Criminal Justice Act 2003, a jury trial may be dispensed with altogether if there is a

a challenge,[32] and the parties are not permitted to question jurors to ascertain whether any other grounds exist. In exceptional cases a judge may agree to the use of a questionnaire to determine whether jurors have been influenced by pre-trial publicity,[33] but exposure to pre-trial publicity in itself is not a sufficient basis for a challenge.

The effect of this is that unless a potential juror happens to be personally known to the defendant or one of the witnesses, it is unlikely in practice that the defence will have any basis for a challenge. The prosecution, however, may have a slight advantage over the defence because of the controversial practice known as 'jury vetting'.

(a) Jury vetting

This practice came to light in 1978 when it was discovered that the prosecution in an official secrets trial had 'vetted' the names on the jury panel in order to identify those who might be 'disloyal'. The Attorney-General responded to the criticism that followed by publishing his guidelines on the use of the practice. The current guidelines date from 1988[34] and permit two types of checks. The first involves checking the names of potential jurors against police records to ensure that disqualified persons are excluded from the panel.[35] The second type of vetting is more controversial and involves making 'authorized checks' against the records of Special Branch and the security services. Authorized checks can only be made in national security and terrorism cases, and they require the personal consent of the Attorney-General. The aim is to identify potential jurors with extreme political views, on the basis that such persons might find it impossible to assess a case fairly, and might exert improper pressure on other jurors or reveal evidence heard *in camera*. If the checks reveal information about a juror which is of concern to the Director of Public Prosecutions, the prosecutor in the case may then seek to exclude that person by asking him or her to 'stand-by' for the Crown.

The legitimacy of jury vetting was challenged in *R v Sheffield Crown Court, ex parte Brownlow*, in which Lord Denning MR expressed the view that:[36]

> To my mind it is unconstitutional for the police authorities to engage in jury vetting. So long as a person is eligible for jury service, and is not disqualified, I cannot think it right that, behind his back, the police should go through his record so as to enable him to be asked to 'stand by for the Crown' or to be challenged for the defence. If this sort of thing is to be allowed, what comes of a man's right of privacy?

These comments were merely obiter however, and although jury vetting is not specifically sanctioned by the Juries Act it has been held that the practice is not unlawful.[37]

'real and present' danger of jury tampering which cannot be avoided by other measures. The defendant in such a case may be tried by a judge sitting alone.

[32] *R v Ford* [1989] QB 868, [1989] 3 All ER 445.

[33] In *R v Andrews (Tracey)* [1999] Crim LR 156 the Court of Appeal confirmed that this was a possibility, but it upheld the decision of the trial judge to refuse a questionnaire in Miss Andrews' case.

[34] *Practice Note (Juries: Right to Stand by: Jury Checks)* [1988] 3 All ER 1086, (1989) 88 Cr App R 123.

[35] The creation of the Central Summoning Bureau makes it possible for such checks to be made before jurors are even summoned and it is a criminal offence for a person who knows that he is disqualified from jury service to sit.

[36] [1980] QB 530 at 542, [1980] 2 All ER 444 at 453.   [37] *R v Mason* [1981] QB 881, [1980] 3 All ER 777.

(b) Standing by for the Crown

The prosecution has always had the right to request that a juror 'stand by for the Crown'. This means, in effect, that he will be moved to the back of the queue of potential jurors and will not be called upon for the trial unless and until the entire panel is exhausted. In this way the prosecution is able to prevent the juror from serving, without showing cause, as long as there are enough members of the panel left to form a jury. The most obvious situation in which this form of challenge may be used is in connection with jury vetting. The Attorney-General's guidelines[38] make it clear that jurors should only be stood by in exceptional cases. They also state that where jury vetting has revealed information which strongly suggests that someone on the panel may be biased against the defendant, the prosecution has a duty to make defence counsel aware of the risk.

The right of stand by is controversial because it is not open to the defence. Defence counsel used to have the right to exclude up to three jurors without showing cause in what was known as a peremptory challenge. However, this was abolished by the Criminal Justice Act 1988[39] and the only form of challenge now open to the defence is the right to challenge for cause.

(c) Challenging for cause

Both parties have the right to challenge any or all of the jurors for cause,[40] and this means establishing a good reason why the juror(s) in question should not be involved in the particular case. If prima facie grounds for a challenge can be shown, the issue will be tried by the judge.[41] The fact that a juror is ineligible or disqualified from jury service would clearly be grounds for a challenge,[42] but a juror may also be challenged on the ground of bias.

Bias. Before the implementation of the Human Rights Act 1998, the leading case on the meaning of bias was *R v Gough*.[43] The appellant in the case had been indicted on a single count that he had conspired with his brother to commit robbery. His brother's name and address had been disclosed in open court during the trial, and a photograph of both men had been shown to the jury. One of the jurors was a next-door neighbour of the brother but she did not realize this until he started shouting in court after the appellant was convicted. Gough appealed on the ground that a reasonable and fair-minded person would have had a reasonable suspicion that a fair trial was not possible under these circumstances. The appeal was dismissed, however, and the House of Lords held that no such danger arose on the facts of the case.

When the Human Rights Act came into force the Court of Appeal[44] made a 'modest adjustment' to the *Gough* test in order to satisfy the requirement that cases should

---

[38] *Practice Note (Juries: Right to Stand by: Jury Checks)* [1988] 3 All ER 1086, (1989) 88 Cr App R 123.

[39] Section 118.   [40] Juries Act 1974, s 12(1)(a); Juries Act 1825, s 29.   [41] Ibid, s 12(2).

[42] Ibid, s 12(4). If a person serves on a jury and is subsequently discovered to have been disqualified or unfit to serve, this will not constitute grounds for reversing the jury's verdict unless an objection was raised at the time: s 18(1).

[43] [1993] AC 646, [1993] 2 All ER 724.

[44] *Director General of Fair Trading* v *Proprietary Association of Great Britain; sub nom Re Medicaments and Related Classes of Goods (No 2)* [2001] 1 WLR 700, [2001] HRLR 17.

be determined by an 'independent and impartial tribunal'.[45] The modified approach makes the objective nature of the test more explicit and asks whether a 'fair-minded and informed observer' would conclude that there was 'a real possibility of bias'.[46] In *R v Pintori (Andrei)*[47] a conviction was quashed on the grounds that one of the jurors was a civilian police worker who had previously worked with some of the officers called as witnesses at the trial. The Court of Appeal held that in these circumstances a fair-minded and informed observer would conclude that there was a real possibility of the jury being biased. The court had no doubt that the bias test was satisfied as far as the individual juror was concerned, and it followed that there was a real risk of the entire jury's verdict being 'tainted' by her influence.[48]

The issue of race. The principle of random selection lies at the heart of the jury system, and jurors are not generally selected on the basis of gender or ethnic origin. As already noted, the government recently rejected a recommendation that juries in racially sensitive cases should be subject to an ethnic minority quota,[49] and there is still no lawful mechanism for interfering with the composition of a jury in order to achieve a racial balance.[50]

> In England and Wales there is virtually no mechanism to ensure that juror bias may be removed. Certainly there remains challenge for cause but the defence are given no facts about jurors upon which to base a challenge. Thus, short of a juror having a swastika tattoo in full view of the court, challenge for cause is practically redundant.[51]

The European Court of Human Rights has held that this position is not inherently incompatible with the right to a fair trial. Indeed, in *Gregory v UK*[52] the Strasbourg court held that a black defendant had received a fair trial even though the judge had refused to excuse a member of the jury following complaints of racial bias from another juror. The judge had reminded the jury of the importance of deciding the case according to the evidence, and this was held to be sufficient to satisfy Article 6. The Court of Appeal recently took a similar approach[53] in the case of a black defendant convicted of

---

[45] Article 6, ECHR.

[46] The modified test has since been approved by the House of Lords in *Porter v Magill* [2001] UKHL 67, [2002] 2 AC 357, [2002] 1 All ER 465.

[47] [2007] EWCA Crim 1700, [2007] Crim LR 997.

[48] The rules governing jury secrecy meant that the court had no way of knowing what role this juror had played in the deliberations, and what influence (if any) she had had over her fellow jurors. For further discussion of the jury secrecy rules, see p 363, *post*.

[49] See p 353, *ante*.

[50] *R v Ford* [1989] QB 868, [1989] 3 All ER 445. In the unreported case of *R v El Faisal* (20 Jan 2003), a judge excluded Hindu and Jewish jurors from the trial of a Muslim cleric accused of soliciting the murder of Hindus and Jews. This was, however, a truly exceptional case: see Tausz and Ormerod [2003] Crim LR 633.

[51] Darbyshire Maughan and Stewart, *What can the English Legal System Learn from Jury Research Published up to 2001? – Findings for the Criminal Courts Review* (2001) at p 18. The authors supported Auld's recommendation that special selection procedures should be used in racially sensitive cases.

[52] (1998) 25 EHRR 577. This decision was distinguished in the later case of *Sander v UK* (2001) 31 EHRR 44: see p 365, *post*.

[53] *R v Smith* [2003] EWCA Crim 283, [2003] 1 WLR 2229.

GBH by an all-white jury. The offence had been committed during a violent incident involving the defendant and a group of white men, but the Court of Appeal confirmed that the judge had no discretion to discharge jurors for the purposes of altering the jury's composition. Although the defendant framed his appeal in terms of the right to a fair trial, the court held that fairness was ensured by the principle of random selection.

The present system rests on the assumption that a randomly selected jury with twelve white members is not necessarily incapable of fairly trying a black defendant. Indeed, research done for the Commission for Racial Equality suggests that black defendants are marginally more likely to be acquitted by a jury than white ones,[54] and another recent study found no evidence that the verdicts of racially mixed juries were influenced by the ethnicity of either the defendant or the victim.[55] The latter study was based on case simulations in which 'juries' were asked to watch recorded footage of a real criminal trial. The juries were made up of real jurors who had just completed their jury service at Blackfriars Crown Court, and the trial footage was carefully edited so that aspects of the trial, including the ethnicity of both the defendant and the victim, could be systematically varied. Although the authors found that the decisions of some jurors did seem to be influenced by ethnicity,[56] with some displaying 'same race leniency' towards defendants in certain types of case,[57] they also found that ethnicity had no discernible impact on the decisions of juries as a whole.[58] Individual biases were effectively nullified by the process of collective deliberation and by the possibility of majority verdicts. Crucially, however, all of the 'juries' used in this study were racially mixed, and it is by no means clear whether all-white juries would be as effective in nullifying individual biases. As the report's authors acknowledge, demographic factors mean that 'most juries in most Crown Courts in England and Wales are likely to be "all-white juries"',[59] and further research will therefore be needed before we can conclude that ethnicity has no impact on jury decision-making.

Although racism undoubtedly exists,[60] since other forms of prejudice also exist it is questionable whether 'race' should be singled out for special treatment. On this point, Auld argued that:[61]

> [W]hite juries are, or are perceived to be, less fair to black than to white people. It is [the] quality of visible difference and the prejudice that it may engender that singles out race for different treatment from other special interest groups.

[54] Bridges, Choongh and McConville, *Ethnic-Minority Defendants and the Right to Elect Jury Trial* (2000). It is at least possible that black defendants are more likely than whites to be taken to trial on comparatively weak evidence. See also: Enright, 'Multi-racial Juries' (1991) 41 *NLJ* 992.

[55] Thomas and Balmer, *Diversity and Fairness in the Jury System*, Ministry of Justice Research Series 2/07 (2007). For a discussion of other aspects of this research, see p 353, *ante*.

[56] Ibid., at p 164. They found for example, that jurors were marginally more likely to vote to acquit black and ethnic minority defendants than white ones, and in this respect their findings lend some support to the research commissioned by the CRE. See n 54, *supra*.

[57] Those which lacked an explicit 'racial' element: jurors showed no such leniency in cases where the defendant was accused of a racially aggravated offence: *ibid*, at p 166.

[58] Ibid., at pp 167–8.   [59] Ibid., at p 190.

[60] In 1995, the victims of nearly 400,000 crimes considered the offences to have been racially motivated: Auld, *Review of the Criminal Courts of England and Wales* (2001), at para 5.56.

[61] Ibid, at para 5.59.

Auld's proposal for a modified selection procedure was confined to 'racially sensitive' cases: he did not think that a special procedure should be used simply because a defendant happened to be black. Yet there is surely a 'visible difference' between a white jury and a black defendant in a robbery case, just as there would be if the black defendant was accused of racially motivated violence. Moreover, the absence of a visible difference between the defendant and the jury would not guarantee a bias-free decision in other sensitive cases. It would not, for example, assist a gay man tried before a homophobic jury if the fact of his homosexuality was relevant to the case and revealed during the evidence. Similarly, a religious leader prosecuted for inciting violence towards 'non-believers' would not be able to conceal the fact of his religious difference from members of the jury.[62] Of course, judges already have a discretion to discharge any juror who is incapable of properly performing his functions,[63] and an alternative to Auld's proposal might be to allow questionnaires to be used in appropriate cases for the purpose of uncovering possible bias.[64] Such an approach would, however, mark a significant inroad into the principle of random selection.

(d) Challenging the array

At common law it is possible for either party to challenge the entire jury on the ground that the person responsible for summoning the jurors is biased or has acted improperly.[65] This is known as a challenge to the array. Such challenges are now extremely rare, although there was an unsuccessful attempt to challenge an all-white jury on this basis in *R v Danvers*.[66]

(e) The judge's discretion to discharge

Where there are doubts about the capacity of a person to act effectively as a juror because of language difficulties[67] or a physical disability,[68] the 1974 Act empowers a judge to discharge that person from jury service. Judges also have a residual discretion to prevent a person from serving in any other circumstances where it is proper to do so.[69] A judge may, for example, discharge a person who is manifestly unsuited for jury service because of illiteracy, or who might otherwise be the subject of a challenge for cause. It is implicit in section 16 of the Juries Act that a juror may also be discharged once a trial is underway. This may be necessary, for example, if he is taken ill or if it becomes apparent during the course of the trial that he may be biased. A judge may also discharge a juror who experiences professional or personal difficulties during the trial, and a recent

---

[62] See n 50, *ante*.   [63] See above.   [64] See p 355, *ante*.

[65] This common law power is expressly preserved by s 12(6) of the Juries Act 1974.

[66] [1982] Crim LR 680.   [67] Section 10.

[68] Section 9B, as inserted by the Criminal Justice and Public Order Act 1994, s 41. In *Re Osman* [1995] 1 WLR 1327, [1996] 1 Cr App R 126, a profoundly deaf person was discharged on the basis that he could only have understood the case with the assistance of an interpreter: as a non-juror, the interpreter could not have been allowed into the jury room. The Lord Chancellor subsequently indicated that he could see no objection to deaf people serving as jurors: Auld, *Review of the Criminal Courts* (2001), at para 5.56.

[69] *Mansell v R* (1857) 8 E & B 54; see Buxton, 'Challenging and Discharging Jurors – Part 1' [1990] Crim LR 225.

practice direction asks judges to be sensitive to the inconvenience that jury service may cause. However, it suggests that where a juror in a longer trial encounters a temporary difficulty such as a child-care problem or an urgent public service commitment, the judge may be able to avoid discharging the juror by allowing a short adjournment instead.[70]

In some circumstances, a failure to discharge a juror may constitute grounds for a subsequent appeal against conviction,[71] and as long as the number of jurors does not fall below nine it is possible for the trial to continue.[72] Exceptionally, the judge may discharge the entire jury if it appears that jury tampering has taken place,[73] or that the jury may be unable to reach a fair verdict because of adverse media reporting.[74]

THE USE OF THE JURY TRIAL AT THE PRESENT DAY

Before the present century the jury system was widely pronounced to be one of the chief safeguards against the abuse of prerogative and judicial power. The right to trial by jury was thought to be essential and inviolable, and Blackstone saw the jury in criminal cases as a barrier between the liberties of the people and the prerogative of the Crown.[75] Lord Camden, reflecting the mood of the age, observed:

> Trial by jury is indeed the foundation of our free constitution; take that away, and the whole fabric will soon moulder into dust.[76]

By the middle of the nineteenth century the idea that the jury trial was sacrosanct was disappearing, and the jury began to decline as a factor in both civil and criminal cases. The rapid growth in the volume of civil cases and the even more rapid growth of summary jurisdiction in criminal cases contributed to this decline, but there was also an increasing awareness that juries were both fallible and unpredictable. Yet although the use of the jury trial has steadily diminished, the debate about its merits continues, and the jury trial is still regarded by many as the hallmark of the English criminal justice system.

---

[70] *Practice Direction (Jury Service: Excusal (Amendment))* [2005] 1 WLR 1361, [2005] 3 All ER 89 (amending *Practice Direction (Criminal Proceedings: Consolidation)* [2002] 1 WLR 2870, [2002] 3 All ER 904).

[71] *R v Spencer* [1987] AC 128, [1986] 2 All ER 928.   [72] 1974 Act, s 16(1).

[73] Criminal Justice Act 2003, s 46. The judge must then decide whether to continue the proceedings without a jury (see p 339), or whether to terminate the trial.

[74] In 2001 the judge in the trial of four footballers prosecuted for attacking an Asian student ruled that there was no evidence of a racial motive for the assault. The jury was later discharged when a national newspaper ran a story alleging that the attack *was* racially motivated. Three of the footballers were eventually tried before a second jury but two were cleared of all charges. One was convicted of affray.

[75] 3 Comm 379.

[76] See Jackson, *The Machinery of Justice in England* (1989, 8th edn), pp 391 *et seq*.

1 CRIMINAL CASES

In criminal cases the loss of faith in the jury system has been less marked than in civil cases. Trial by jury is still the standard mode of trial for indictable offences, and where a defendant aged eighteen or over[77] is prosecuted for an either way offence, he or she normally has the right to insist on trial by jury. Nevertheless, the percentage of criminal cases actually tried by jury is surprisingly low. The vast majority of offences committed are triable only summarily, and not all defendants who have the right to insist on trial by jury actually do so.[78] In 2001, some 1.84 million defendants were tried summarily, compared with only 78,000 in the Crown Court.[79] Many of those whose cases are disposed of in the Crown Court plead guilty, and the proportion of defendants whose fate is actually determined by a jury is only around 1 per cent. Thus, although the jury trial still has great symbolic importance in the context of serious offences, in the overall scheme of things it actually plays a fairly minor role.

The right to trial by jury for either way offences has been under review for a number of years. Critics have pointed out that jury trials cost considerably more than the summary alternative, and that most defendants who opt for trial by jury eventually plead guilty.[80] However, attempts to remove or diminish the right have always met with stiff opposition.[81] The Auld Report[82] recommended that the final decision about mode of trial should rest with the court and not the defendant, but the changes eventually introduced by the Criminal Justice Act 2003 did not go this far. Instead, a variety of procedural changes were made to encourage more defendants to elect summary trial, together with increased sentencing powers for magistrates' courts.

Fraud cases. The Roskill Report in 1986 recommended that serious fraud cases should not be tried by jury at all, but should instead be tried by a judge sitting with two lay assessors. This was also advocated by the Auld Review.[83] In addition to allowing trial without jury in cases where there is a real and present danger of jury tampering,[84] the 2003 Act also makes provision for judge-only trials to be used in complex fraud cases. In order for a jury to be dispensed with in a fraud trial, the judge (with the approval of the Lord Chief Justice or his deputy) would have to be satisfied that it was in the interests of justice to hear the case without a jury.[85] At the time of writing this change had yet to be implemented, but the collapse of the 'Jubilee Line Extension' case in March 2005 once

---

[77] There are special provisions for children and young persons; see p 584, *post.*

[78] The procedure for the allocation of offences is discussed further at p 580, *post.*

[79] *Criminal Statistics 2001,* at p 18.

[80] See, e.g., the *Report of the Royal Commission on Criminal Justice,* Cm 2263, 1993; *The Review of Delay in the Criminal Justice System ('the Narey Report')* (1997).

[81] The Criminal Justice (Mode of Trial) Bill 1999 and the Criminal Justice (Mode of Trial) Bill (No 2) 2000, would both have removed the defendant's right to insist on jury trial for an either way offence. Both Bills were defeated in the House of Lords.

[82] *Review of the Criminal Courts of England and Wales* (2001) at para 5.166.

[83] Ibid., at para 5.192.

[84] Section 44. A clause which would have allowed a defendant charged with an indictable offence to request trial by judge alone was dropped from the Bill, following considerable opposition.

[85] Section 43.

again drew attention to the issue. The trial of six defendants on allegations of fraud had lasted for 272 days and had been thwarted by excessive delays and problems with the jury. By the time the trial was abandoned, one juror had already been discharged after becoming pregnant and another had been discharged on the grounds of financial hardship. A third juror had requested a discharge on medical grounds, and the health of one of the defendants was also deteriorating. The trial was discontinued at the prosecution's request, and an inquiry ordered by the Attorney-General.[86] On exactly the same day the Lord Chief Justice issued a Protocol for the Control and Management of Heavy Fraud and other Complex Cases. It provides that serious fraud and other complex trials should not normally be permitted to last longer than three months, although it acknowledges that a small number of exceptional cases may take longer than this. A practice direction issued at the same time reminds judges that they may occasionally need to use their discretion to adjourn a trial or discharge members of a jury. Where the length of a trial is expected to be particularly long, it is said to be good practice for the judge to enquire at the outset whether members of the jury panel foresee any difficulties with this.[87]

Trial by jury of sample counts. In a further inroad into the use of jury trials for serious offences, reforms implemented in January 2007 mean that where a defendant is charged with multiple counts on an indictment, the prosecution can request that the trial of some of those counts should be conducted without a jury.[88] As long as certain criteria are satisfied,[89] the judge can then order that a number of sample counts should be tried by jury in the ordinary way, with any remaining counts being tried later by a judge sitting alone.

Majority verdicts. The standard size of a jury in a criminal case is twelve, but if this figure is reduced because a juror dies or is discharged, it will still be validly constituted as long as the number does not fall below nine.[90] Where a jury has eleven or twelve members, a majority verdict can be accepted if at least ten jurors agree; if a jury has ten members, a majority of nine is acceptable.[91] The verdict of a nine-member jury must be unanimous. The possibility of a majority verdict reduces the likelihood of a jury's decision being affected by bias or tampering, because a single juror will not normally be able to force a re-trial. Before a majority verdict can be accepted, however, the jury must have deliberated for a minimum of two hours and the foreman of the jury must state in open court how many jurors agreed with it.[92]

---

[86] See Wooler, *Review of the Investigation and Criminal Proceedings Relating to the Jubilee Line Case* (HM Crown Prosecution Service Inspectorate, June 2006). The Review included an examination of the experiences and perspectives of the jurors: for a further discussion of this aspect, see Lloyd-Bostock, 'The Jubilee Line Jurors: Does their Experience Strengthen the Argument for Judge-only Trial in Long and Complex Fraud Cases?' [2007] Crim LR 255. The author of this article concludes (at p 273) that 'the "problem" with the Jubilee Line case was not the jury's ability to cope, but the unnecessarily excessive length of the case with its consequences for the jurors' lives, together with some aspects of their treatment at court.'

[87] *Practice Direction (Jury Service: Excusal (Amendment))* [2005] 1 WLR 1361, [2005] 3 All ER 89 (amending *Practice Direction (Criminal Proceedings: Consolidation)* [2002] 1 WLR 2870, [2002] 3 All ER 904).

[88] Domestic Violence, Crime and Victims Act 2004, s 17.

[89] Ibid. For a discussion see p 626, *post.*   [90] Juries Act 1974, s 16(1).

[91] Ibid, s 17.   [92] Ibid, s 17.

2 CIVIL PROCEEDINGS

It is in civil cases that the decline of the jury has been most marked. Until 1854 most civil actions in the common law courts were tried by jury, but the Common Law Procedure Act 1854 allowed cases to be tried by judge alone if both parties consented. The real turning point was the Administration of Justice (Miscellaneous Provisions) Act 1933, which limited the right to claim trial by jury in a civil action to cases of libel, slander, malicious prosecution, false imprisonment, seduction, breach of promise of marriage, and fraud.[93] So far as the Queen's Bench Division is concerned, the right to a jury trial in these cases is now governed by section 69 of the Supreme Court Act 1981. A jury may only be refused in such a case if the court considers that the trial will involve a scientific or local investigation or a prolonged examination of documents.[94] For all other types of case the grant of a jury is at the discretion of the court. This discretion was once absolute,[95] but in the leading case of *Ward* v *James*[96] the Court of Appeal established that it had to be exercised judicially. It also stated that unless there were special circumstances, trials in personal injury cases should be by judge alone. The court noted the unpredictability of damages awards in jury cases, and suggested that juries tended to make disproportionate awards because they often assumed that the substantive defendant was a deep-pocketed insurance company.

Immediately before *Ward* v *James*, approximately 2 per cent of trials in the Queen's Bench Division took place before a jury. The figure is now minimal. In *H* v *Ministry of Defence*[97] the court was able to identify only one personal injury case since *Ward* v *James* in which trial by jury had been ordered, and if the Law Commission's recommendations are implemented, the use of the jury in personal injury cases will disappear entirely.[98] Consequently, in little more than a century, jury trial in civil cases has been virtually superseded by trial by judge alone, the one notable exception being trials for defamation. Jury trials in the county courts are even less common, though it is still possible for a county court to try a case before an eight-person jury,[99] and this occasionally happens in civil actions involving the police. Juries of between seven and eleven persons are also used in coroners' cases.[100]

Coroners' cases aside, the role of juries in civil actions remains controversial, and the extremely large awards of damages made by juries in some defamation cases have attracted considerable criticism. The European Court of Human Rights has suggested that such awards could unlawfully restrict freedom of expression, contrary to Article 10

---

[93] Actions for seduction and breach of promise of marriage were abolished by the Law Reform (Miscellaneous Provisions) Act 1970.

[94] *Beta Construction* v *Channel Four Television* [1990] 2 All ER 1012, [1990] 1 WLR 1042; *Viscount De L'Isle* v *Times Newspapers* [1987] 3 All ER 499, [1988] 1 WLR 49.

[95] *Hope* v *Great Western Rly Co* [1937] 2 KB 130, [1937] 1 All ER 625.

[96] [1966] 1 QB 273, [1965] 1 All ER 563.   [97] [1991] 2 QB 103, [1991] 2 All ER 834.

[98] *Damages for Personal Injury: Non Pecuniary Loss* (HC Working Paper (1995) no 140), p 125. For an argument that there should still be a role for jury trials in personal injury cases, see Morris, 'Jury Trials in Personal Injury Claims – is there a Place for them?' [2002] 3 *Journal of Personal Injury Law* 310.

[99] County Courts Act 1984, s 66(3). A majority verdict of seven to one is acceptable in such a case: Juries Act 1974, s 17(2).

[100] See Coroners Act 1988, s 8(2)(a), and p 276, *ante*.

of the ECHR.[101] In *John* v *Mirror Group Newspapers*, libel damages awarded to the singer Elton John were reduced from £625,000 to £125,000 on appeal, leading the Master of the Rolls to observe that:[102]

> It is in our view offensive to public opinion...that a defamation plaintiff should recover damages for injury to reputation greater, perhaps by a significant factor, than if the same plaintiff had been rendered a helpless cripple.

In *Grobbelaar* v *News Group Newspapers*,[103] the House of Lords famously awarded damages of just £1 to a goalkeeper who sued for defamation when match-fixing allegations were published in a national newspaper. Their Lordships clearly took the view that the claimant was the author of his own misfortunes, and they also ordered him to pay his own costs. However, they refused to interfere with the jury's finding of liability on the facts, reversing the Court of Appeal's decision in this respect.

3 JURY SECRECY

A key principle of the jury system is that what takes place in the jury room must not be disclosed, and the secrecy of jurors' deliberations is protected by both common law and statute. Section 8(1) of the Contempt of Court Act 1981 makes it an offence to obtain, disclose, or solicit any particulars of statements made, opinions expressed, arguments advanced, or votes cast by members of a jury in the course of their deliberations. There are only two exceptions to this rule: (a) disclosures for the purpose of enabling the jury to arrive at and deliver its verdict;[104] and (b) disclosures made where an offence is alleged to have been committed in relation to the jury.[105] In *R* v *Miah*[106] section 8 was held to apply to 'anything said by one juror to another about the case from the moment the jury is empanelled, at least provided what is said is not overheard by anyone else who is not a juror.' Breach of this rule amounts to contempt of court, even if the breach is indirect. In *Attorney-General* v *Associated Newspapers*[107] a conviction for publishing the views of the jurors in a long and abortive fraud case was upheld, even though the appellants had obtained the information from a researcher and not directly from the jurors.

Evidence of improper conduct by the jury. At common law, the rule is that 'the court will not investigate, or receive evidence about, anything said in the course of the jury's

---

[101] *Tolstoy Miloslavksy* v *UK* (1995) 20 EHRR 442.

[102] [1997] QB 586 at 614, [1996] 2 All ER 35 at 54, per Sir Thomas Bingham MR. See also the comments of Lord Donaldson MR in *Sutcliffe* v *Pressdram Ltd* [1991] 1 QB 153, [1990] 1 All ER 269. Such cases are discussed further at p 537, *post*.

[103] [2002] UKHL 40, [2002] 4 All ER 732, [2002] 1 WLR 3024. Cf *Gleaner Co. Ltd* v *Abrahams* [2003] UKPC 55, [2004] 1 AC 628, in which the Privy Council held that the Court of Appeal had not erred in refusing to be guided by awards in personal injury actions when determining the quantum of damages in a defamation case.

[104] Section 8(2)(a). It is lawful, for example, for notes to be passed between the judge and jury for this purpose.

[105] Section 8(2)(b).   [106] [1997] 2 Cr App R 12 at 18, per Kennedy LJ.

[107] [1994] 2 AC 238, [1994] 1 All ER 556.

deliberations while they are considering their verdict in their retiring room.'[108] Evidence of the jury's behaviour *outside* the jury room can be admitted, however, and in *R v Young (Stephen)*[109] the Court of Appeal quashed a murder conviction after hearing that the jury had attempted to contact the deceased using a oujia board in a hotel room. The rationale for maintaining the secrecy of jury deliberations was explained by Atkin LJ in an earlier case:[110]

> [O]n the one hand it is in order to secure the finality of decisions arrived at by the jury, and on the other to protect the jurymen themselves and prevent their being exposed to pressure to explain the reasons which actuated them in arriving at their verdict.

It is also assumed that jurors are more likely to express their views honestly and frankly if they feel confident that their deliberations will remain confidential. On the other hand, the law operates with such rigidity that there is a serious risk of miscarriages of justice going undiscovered and unchallenged.

The scope of both the common law and statutory prohibitions was considered by the House of Lords in *R v Mirza (Shabbir Ali)*.[111] The defendant was a Pakistani man charged with six counts of indecent assault. As English was not his first language he was assisted in court by an interpreter, but the jury sent two separate notes to the judge, indicating that they found the use of the interpreter suspicious. The judge directed the jury that they should draw no adverse inference from the use of the interpreter, but a letter written by a juror six days after the defendant's conviction indicated that they had ignored these instructions and were possibly influenced by racial prejudice. The Court of Appeal dismissed the defendant's appeal against conviction. The issue for the House of Lords was whether a court was prevented, either at common law or under the 1981 Act, from considering evidence of jury deliberations indicating a breach of Article 6. In a partial departure from the previous case law,[112] their Lordships held that section 8 of the 1981 Act was addressed to third parties and did not prevent a court from investigating allegations of injustice. A court had a responsibility to ensure that the defendant received a fair trial and it could not be in contempt of itself. However, a majority of their Lordships also upheld the common law rule against receiving evidence of jury deliberations. Exceptions to this rule could only be made where it was alleged that the jury had been affected by 'extraneous influences' or had declined to deliberate at all.[113]

---

[108] *R v Mirza (Shabbir Ali)* [2004] UKHL 2 at [95], [2004] 1 AC 1118 at [95], [2004] 1 All ER 925, per Lord Hope.

[109] [1995] QB 324, [1995] 2 WLR 430.   [110] *Ellis v Deheer* [1922] 2 KB 113 at 121.

[111] [2004] UKHL 2, [2004] 1 AC 1118, [2004] 1 All ER 925.

[112] In *R v Young (Stephen)* [1995] QB 324, [1995] 2 WLR 430 the Court of Appeal held that it was prevented by s 8 from hearing evidence concerning improper conduct in the jury room: see p 342, *ante*. See also *R v Qureshi* [2001] EWCA Crim 1807, [2002] 1 WLR 518, [2002] 1 Cr App R 33, in which a juror made allegations of racial bias three days after the verdict. Leave to appeal was refused on the basis that the jury's verdict had been accepted by the trial judge and s 8 of the 1981 Act prevented any investigation into its deliberations.

[113] The 2005 consultation on jury research asks whether clarification of this area of law is needed, though it makes it clear that the government's own preference is to leave such matters to the courts: *Jury Research and Impropriety* CP 04/05, discussed at p 366, *post*.

This approach was applied in *R v Karakaya (Adem),*[114] where it was discovered that one of the jurors in a rape trial had done some 'research' on the internet and taken downloaded documents into the jury room during deliberations. The matter only came to light when the documents were found by the jury bailiff after the trial had concluded. The Court of Appeal had no hesitation in holding that it was entitled to examine the documents, but it did not consider it necessary to question the jurors about the matter: the presence of the extraneous material itself was enough to cast doubt on the safety of the verdict. After some deliberation, the Court also held that it was entitled to look at a handwritten note on the back of one of the documents – apparently written by one of the jurors – in order to form a 'preliminary view' as to whether it might have a bearing on the appeal.[115] In the end it decided that the note did *not* have a bearing on the case because it was merely a summary of the downloaded material. However, it is not clear what the Court would have done if the note had revealed details of the jury's deliberations. Moreover, the recent decision in *R v Marshall (Jay David)*[116] suggests that the discovery of extraneous material in the jury room will not always be grounds for quashing a conviction. Although it was clear in this case that at least one juror had brought downloaded documents with him to the jury's deliberations, the documents in question concerned sentencing tariffs and it was difficult to see how their use could have damaged the verdicts against the two defendants. On this basis the convictions were not unsafe.

The Article 6 dimension. The majority in *Mirza* clearly felt that the existing approach to jury secrecy was not incompatible with the right to a fair trial, but in a strong dissenting judgment, Lord Steyn argued that:[117]

> [T]here is a positive duty on judges, when things have gone seriously wrong in the criminal justice system, to do everything possible to put it right. In the world of today, enlightened public opinion would accept nothing less. It would be contrary to the spirit of these developments to say that in one area, namely the deliberations of the jury, injustice can be tolerated as the price for protecting the jury system.

In *Gregory v UK,*[118] the European Court of Human Rights accepted the rules governing the secrecy of jury deliberations as a crucial and legitimate feature of English trial law. Thus, a judge who refused to investigate a juror's allegations that another member of the jury had made racist remarks, and who dealt with the matter by reminding the jury to decide the case according to the evidence, was held to have satisfied Article 6. By contrast, a breach of Article 6 was established on similar facts in *Sander v UK.*[119] The judge in this case had responded to the original allegation of racism by asking the jurors

---

[114] [2005] EWCA Crim 346, [2005] 2 Cr App R 5.   [115] Ibid, at [13], per Judge LJ.

[116] [2007] EWCA Crim 35, [2007] Crim LR 562.

[117] [2004] UKHL 2 at [4], [2004] 1 AC 1118 at [4], [2004] 1 All ER 925.

[118] (1998) 25 EHRR 577 at 594.

[119] (2001) 31 EHRR 44. See also, *Remli v France* (1996) 22 EHRR 253 (breach of Article 6 established when a court failed to investigate allegations of juror bias which came to light after the verdict); Zander, 'The Complaining Juror' (2000) 150 NLJ 723.

to search their consciences, and after receiving a note from the entire jury refuting the allegations, he had declined to do anything further. The distinction between these cases is a fine one, but it would appear that as long as a judge takes reasonable steps to address allegations made during the course of a trial, the court's duty under Article 6 will have been satisfied.

On a related matter, Darbyshire and others have questioned whether the failure of the jury system to provide a defendant with a reasoned verdict is itself a breach of Article 6:[120]

> It is hard to see, in an era when every tribunal and magistrates' court provides a reasoned decision, how the secrecy of jury trials can survive.

Darbyshire concludes that juries should be required to respond to a series of written questions formulated by counsel and the judge, arguing that this would ensure compliance with Article 6 and would also help to reduce the scope for 'perverse verdicts'. The recommendation was endorsed by Lord Justice Auld in his Review of the Criminal Courts.[121] In his dissenting opinion in *Mirza*, Lord Steyn suggested that a jury is a judicial tribunal in its own right, and that its obligation to comply with the requirements of Article 6 is independent of any obligation on the judge.[122] This was not, however, a view endorsed by the majority.

Jury research. Section 8 of the 1981 Act has been criticized for severely restricting the scope for conducting research into the jury system, and in 1993 the Royal Commission on Criminal Justice proposed an amendment which would make legitimate jury research possible. In 2005 the Department for Constitutional Affairs revealed that such an amendment was finally being considered. The proposal outlined in its consultation paper would have allowed the Secretary of State to authorize specific research projects. These authorized projects would have been subject to strict conditions and governed by a Code of Conduct, while *unauthorized* research into jury deliberations would have remained unlawful.[123] However, following the consultation process the government concluded that there was scope for doing more research within the existing legal framework, and that the case for amending the 1981 Act had not been made out:[124]

> The Government is not opposed to amending section 8 of the Contempt of Court Act 1981 but does not believe that this should be done until there are specific and detailed questions to be answered that cannot be investigated without altering statute.

---

[120] Darbyshire, Maughan and Stewart, *What can the English Legal System Learn from Jury Research Published up to 2001? – Findings for the Criminal Courts Review* (2001) at p 39. See also, Pritchard, 'A Reform for Jury Trial?' (1998) 148 NLJ 45.

[121] (2001) at para 11.41.

[122] [2004] UKHL 2 at [6], [2004] 1 AC 1118 at [6], [2004] 1 All ER 925.

[123] *Jury Research and Impropriety* (2005) CP 04/05.

[124] *Jury Research and Impropriety: Response to Consultation* (Department for Constitutional Affairs, 08/11/05), at p 16.

In particular, the government supported the idea of conducting more research using mock or shadow juries,[125] the recent study commissioned by the Ministry of Justice[126] being one such example.

THE MERITS OF JURY TRIAL

Jury trial has been the subject of significant criticism in recent years, with the most contentious issue being what some regard as an unacceptably high acquittal rate in criminal cases.[127] Statistically, jury trials do result in proportionately more acquittals than magistrates' cases,[128] but the proportion of defendants acquitted by juries on all counts is still quite low.[129] In addition, it is difficult to make direct comparisons because the statistics are calculated differently and are influenced by different factors. For example, much of the business of magistrates' courts consists of strict liability offences where the scope for contesting guilt is reduced and the stakes are lower. The proportion of defendants pleading guilty in summary cases is therefore much higher than for cases in the Crown Court. Similarly, the acquittal rate for either way cases in the Crown Court may be at least partly explained by the fact that those with a comparatively weak defence are less likely to elect trial by jury because of the risk of receiving a stiffer sentence if convicted.

The reality is that too little is known about how juries work, and as stated previously, research into how juries reach their verdicts is currently prohibited by the Contempt of Court Act 1981. In an attempt to work around this restriction some research has been carried out using 'shadow juries', where a panel of 'shadow' jurors is asked to follow a real case.[130] Some anecdotal and personal accounts of real jurors have also been published, and in 2001 a group of academics carried out a comprehensive review of jury research published in the UK and elsewhere.

The merits of the jury system are sometimes stated in terms of the deficiencies of alternative modes of trial. Although the summary process in the magistrates' courts is relatively quick and cheap, it is by no means beyond criticism, and it is often

---

[125] Ibid.

[126] Thomas and Balmer, *Diversity and Fairness in the Jury System*, Ministry of Justice Research Series 2/07 (2007), discussed at pp 353 and 357, *ante*.

[127] See, e.g. Darbyshire, 'For the New Lord Chancellor: Some Causes for Concern about Magistrates' [1997] Crim LR 861.

[128] In 2002 just over 30 per cent of contested cases in the magistrates' courts were dismissed. In the same year, 65 per cent of those pleading not guilty in the Crown Court were either acquitted by the jury or had the case discharged by the judge – *Criminal Statistics 2002*, at p 16.

[129] In 2001, 8.6 per cent of cases committed for trial in the Crown Court resulted in the defendant being acquitted by a jury on all counts. A further 17.3 per cent were acquitted by or on the direction of the judge and 14.8 per cent were convicted on some or all counts after pleading not guilty. The majority of defendants – 56.3 per cent – pleaded guilty: *Judicial Statistics 2001*, at pp 68–9.

[130] See McCabe and Purves, *The Shadow Jury at Work* (1974); Thomas and Balmer (2007) *supra*, n 126.

thought that jury trial favours an accused. Other advocates of jury trial rely upon its constitutional importance, and on the safeguards that it is said to provide for defendants.[131] In *Ward* v *James*, Lord Denning MR explained the role of the modern jury as follows:[132]

> Let it not be supposed that this court is in any way opposed to trial by jury. It has been the bulwark of our liberties too long for any of us to seek to alter it. Whenever a man is on trial for serious crime, or when in a civil case a man's honour or integrity is at stake, or when one or other party must be deliberately lying, then trial by jury has no equal.

It was put more graphically by Lord Devlin, who described jury trial as 'the lamp that shows that freedom lives'.[133] Not all commentators are convinced by this romanticism, pointing out that this 'bulwark of our liberties' did not prevent any of the famous miscarriages of justice exposed in the 1990s.[134] Critics have also pointed to the potentially random factors that may affect a jury's deliberations. The fact that juries are laymen who are not required to explain their decisions leaves greater scope for them to be influenced by factors which have nothing to do with the law or the evidence. Thus, they may occasionally reach perverse verdicts because they have acted on the basis of prejudice and stereotypes, or because they have failed to properly understand the legal and evidential issues. Juries may also return verdicts motivated by conscience, and there are many well-known examples of cases in which juries are thought to have acquitted defendants on moral rather than legal grounds. In 1985 for example, a jury found Clive Ponting not guilty of committing official secrets offences, despite clear evidence that he had in fact done what he was accused of. Similarly, in 2000, a multiple sclerosis sufferer was acquitted on charges of possessing cannabis after the jury was told that the defendant used the drug to relieve the symptoms of the disease. For some, the ability of a jury to deliver a moral verdict in such cases is one of the system's great strengths, but for others, these perverse acquittals are an affront to the rule of law.

Academic opinion on the jury system may be divided, but it seems that jurors themselves are strongly in favour of it. A recent Home Office survey, based on interviews with those summoned for jury service in six courts, found that:[135]

> [T]he majority of respondents had a more positive view of the jury trial system after completing their service than they did before. Furthermore, virtually all jurors interviewed considered jury trials to be an important part of the criminal justice system.

---

[131] On this argument, see: Cornish, *The Jury* (1970).

[132] [1966] 1 QB 273 at 295, [1965] 1 All ER 563 at 571.

[133] Devlin, *Trial by Jury* (1956).

[134] See Darbyshire, 'The Lamp that Shows that Freedom Lives: Is it Worth the Candle?' [1991] Crim LR 740. Ironically, the primacy of jury trial has also been used as a justification for judicial non-interference with verdicts in alleged miscarriage of justice cases: see p 714, *post*.

[135] Matthews, Hancock and Briggs: *Jurors' Perceptions, Understanding, Confidence and Satisfaction in the Jury System: A Study in Six Courts* (2004) Home Office Research Study 227, at p 1.

FURTHER READING

AIRS and SHAW, *Jury Excusal and Deferral*, Home Office Research Findings No 102 (1999)

AULD, RT HON LORD JUSTICE, *Review of the Criminal Courts of England and Wales* (2001), chapter 5

BALDWIN and McCONVILLE, *Jury Trials* (Clarendon Press: 1979)

BRIDGES, CHOONGH and McCONVILLE, *Ethnic-Minority Defendants and the Right to Elect Jury Trial* (Commission for Racial Equality: 2000)

BUXTON, 'Challenging and Discharging Jurors – Part 1' [1990] Crim LR 225

CORNISH, *The Jury* (Penguin: 1970)

DARBYSHIRE, MAUGHAN and STEWART, *What Can the English Legal System Learn from Jury Research Published up to 2001? – Findings for the Criminal Courts Review* (2001)

DEVLIN, *Trial by Jury* (London, Stevens & Sons: 1956)

ENRIGHT, 'Multi-racial Juries' (1991) 41 NLJ 992

LLOYD-BOSTOCK, 'The Jubilee Line Jurors: Does their Experience Strengthen the Argument for Judge-only Trial in Long and Complex Fraud Cases?' [2007] Crim LR 255

MORRIS, 'Jury Trials in Personal Injury Claims – Is There a Place for Them?' [2002] 3 JPIL 310

PRITCHARD, 'A Reform for Jury Trial?' (1998) 148 NLJ 45

ROBERTSHAW, 'A Human Rights Conflict: Freedom of Expression versus Non-Disclosure of Jury Deliberations' (2003) 22 CJQ 265

THOMAS and BALMER, *Diversity and Fairness in the Jury System*, Ministry of Justice Research Series 2/07 (2007)

THORNTON, 'Trial by Jury: 50 Years of Change' [2004] Crim LR 683

WOOLER, *Review of the Investigation and Criminal Proceedings Relating to the Jubilee Line Case* (HM Crown Prosecution Service Inspectorate, June 2006)

ZANDER, 'The Complaining Juror' (2000) 150 NLJ 723

12

LEGAL SERVICES

INTRODUCTION

This chapter will examine the provision of legal services. The availability of high quality legal lawyers, and the ability to afford access to their services, is fundamental to the effectiveness of any system of law. It is a fast-changing topic, as government has addressed issues of how legal services should be provided, financed and regulated. Specific areas covered will include:

- How the legal profession is organized.
- What solicitors and barristers do, how they are organized, trained and regulated.
- How complaints against lawyers are resolved.
- The development and evolution of the legal aid schemes.
- The new funding arrangements.

THE LEGAL PROFESSION: THE ORGANIZATIONAL FRAMEWORK

1 AN OVERVIEW

A distinctive feature of the English legal system is the division of the legal profession into two separate branches: solicitors and barristers. Such a division is unknown outside Britain and the Commonwealth, and elsewhere all practitioners are simply described as 'lawyers'. The division dates back to around 1340, which is when professional advocacy first evolved:[1] attorneys, who were the forerunners of solicitors, were responsible for carrying out the preparatory stages of an action, but only serjeants and barristers had rights of audience in the common law courts. This basic distinction still exists at a formal level, but the differences between the two professions are rapidly diminishing in practice. Thus, while barristers are still thought of primarily as advocates, most spend a lot of time engaged in 'paper-work' such as the drafting of pleadings, opinions, and divorce

---

[1] For details see Baker, *An Introduction to English Legal History* (4th edn, 2002).

petitions. Employed barristers can even conduct litigation.[2] Similarly, while solicitors are still responsible for the preparatory stages of litigation, they also deal with a range of non-litigious matters such as conveyancing and the drafting of wills, and all solicitors have rights in audience in at least some courts and tribunals.[3]

The structure, function, regulation and financing of the legal profession has been the subject of ongoing review and change, often of a radical nature. In 1976 a Royal Commission was set up to inquire into the provision of legal services. Its report, published in 1979, suggested that the legal profession was performing its functions well.[4] The Report was broadly supportive of the status quo and did not advocate fusing the two branches of the profession.[5] It did, however, prompt further debate and discussion. Over the next ten years the government published White Papers on civil justice,[6] legal services,[7] the legal profession,[8] conveyancing services,[9] and contingency fees.[10] Eventually, in 1990, the Courts and Legal Services Act was passed. The passage of the 1990 Act did not bring to an end the spate of review and reform: far from it. Changes to funding regimes, in complaints mechanisms and in the way legal services are provided have all been at the heart of an agenda designed to create efficiency and effectiveness of legal provision. Most recently, the passage of the Criminal Defence Act 2006 and the Legal Services Act 2007 heralds a further sustained period of change. Change has been ongoing through a mixture of legislative, administrative and financial measures. But at the core of the change are several key pieces of legislation.

2 COURTS AND LEGAL SERVICES ACT 1990

The 1990 Act is based on a distinct philosophy, as set out in section 17(1):

> The general objective of this Part is the development of legal services in England and Wales (and in particular the development of advocacy, litigation, conveyancing and probate services) by making provision of new or better ways of providing such services, and a wider choice of persons providing them, while maintaining the proper and efficient administration of justice.

In addition to preserving the existing rights of audience of solicitors and barristers,[11] section 17(3) of the Act[12] established the 'general principle' that rights of audience should be linked to the following criteria:

(i) possession of appropriate qualifications;

(ii) membership of a professional body with effective and enforceable rules of conduct;

---

[2] See p 376, *post.*   [3] See p 377, *post.*
[4] Report of the Royal Commission on Legal Services (Cmnd 7648, 1979) – 'The Benson Report'.
[5] Ibid, paras 17.45–17.46.   [6] Report of the Review Body on Civil Justice, Cm 394, 1988.
[7] Legal Services: A Framework for the Future, Cm 740, 1989.
[8] The Workload and Organisation of the Legal Profession, Cm 570, 1989.
[9] Conveyancing by Authorised Practitioners, Cm 572, 1989.
[10] *Contingency Fees*, Cm 571, 1989.   [11] Sections 31 to 33.
[12] Repealed by Legal Services Act 2007, Schedule 23.

(iii) the existence of satisfactory arrangements for ensuring that legal services are not withheld on objectionable grounds; and

(iv) the existence of appropriate rules of conduct.

The Act provided a framework for solicitors to break the monopoly that barristers had enjoyed over advocacy work in the higher courts,[13] and it opened up the possibility that rights of audience might be extended to members of other professions.[14] The rules governing the provision of litigation[15] and probate[16] services were also relaxed, and section 66 of the Act removed the legal obstacles preventing solicitors from forming partnerships with non-solicitors.[17] The Act thus laid the foundations for significant changes to the way in which legal services were provided. It also provided for the appointment of a Legal Services Ombudsman[18] with the power to review complaints handling by the professional regulatory bodies.[19] All of these are now fundamentally affected by the Legal Services Act 2007.

3   THE ACCESS TO JUSTICE ACT 1999

The Access to Justice Act 1999 made important changes to the funding of legal services: it established two separate schemes to replace what used to be known as 'legal aid', and it relaxed some of the rules governing the remuneration of lawyers through private funds.[20] Part III of the Act continued the theme of the Courts and Legal Services Act, by establishing the general principle that all lawyers with appropriate qualifications should be able to exercise full rights of audience in all proceedings. It also simplified the procedure for approving any further changes to rights of audience and rights to conduct litigation,[21] in addition to conferring additional powers on the Legal Services Ombudsman.[22]

4   LEGAL SERVICES ACT 2007

The 2007 Act makes fundamental changes.[23] It changes the whole regulatory regime of the legal profession by creating a Legal Services Board. The Board is given objectives that the regulatory procedures and mechanisms should seek to achieve, and it is the duty of the Board to promote those objectives. It creates a framework for the conduct of legal activity, and the potential to license bodies to engage in legal activity. It defines what

---

[13] See p 377, *post.*

[14] Section 27: for more detailed discussion of rights of audience, see p 377, *post.*

[15] Section 28: see p 376, *post.*

[16] Section 55, which was not implemented until 2004: see p 376, *post.* Due to a lack of demand, provisions which would have further relaxed the rules governing conveyancing services have not been implemented at all: see p 376, *post.*

[17] There had been no such legal obstacles relating to barristers, though both solicitors and barristers have been prevented from entering into multi-disciplinary partnerships by their own professional rules.

[18] See p 394, *post.*   [19] See p 394, *post.*

[20] Sections 27–28: see p 400, *post.* In the context of funding of criminal cases, the 1999 Act has been significantly amended by the Criminal Defence Services Act 2006.

[21] See pp 401–2, *post.*   [22] See p 394, *post.*   [23] See p 395, post.

amounts to a 'reserved legal activity', and in section 13 deals with the question of who is entitled to carry on such an activity. It creates a new Office for Legal Complaints and provides in detail a structure for dealing with them. It contains a variety of miscellaneous provisions relating to, or affecting, lawyers. At the date of going to press the operative provisions of the Act were not yet in force.

5 THE NEW REGIME FOR THE CONDUCT OF LEGAL ACTIVITY

The provisions of the Legal Services Act 2007 are based largely on the proposals contained in the White Paper *The Future of Legal Services: Putting Consumers First*, published in 2005.[24] That itself was based on the recommendations of the Clementi Report. This review of the regulation of legal services,[25] chaired by Sir David Clementi, had two main terms of reference: (a) 'to consider what regulatory framework would best promote competition, innovation and the public and consumer interest in an efficient, effective and independent legal sector'; and (b) 'to recommend a framework which will be independent in representing the public and consumer interest, comprehensive, accountable, consistent, flexible, transparent, and no more restrictive or burdensome than is clearly justified'. The final report of the review was published in December 2004.[26]

The Report made a number of significant recommendations which have a profound effect on the legal landscape. Clementi's concerns fell into three main categories:

- concerns about the complexity and ineffectiveness of the existing regulatory framework;
- concerns about the current approach of the professions to the handling of complaints;
- concerns about the restrictive nature of current business practices.

The details of these issues will be discussed later.[27] The 2007 provides for a new framework to get rid of what the White Paper described as the 'regulatory maze', but also one which would encourage the creation of 'a legal services market that will enable lawyers and other professionals to work together to provide legal services in new ways'.[28] Clementi had recommended a range of alternative business structures. His key recommendation here was that steps should be taken to enable lawyers from different professional backgrounds to work together to provide legal services to the public. This could be achieved by lifting the restrictions preventing solicitors from entering into partnerships with those from other disciplines, and by the Bar Council changing

---

[24] Cm 6679: available at www.dca.gov.uk.

[25] *Competition and Regulation in the Legal Services Market – A Report following the Consultation 'In the Public Interest?'* (2003).

[26] *Final Report of the Review of the Regulatory Framework for Legal Services in England and Wales* (2004).

[27] See p 388, *post*.

[28] Department for Constitutional Affairs, *Consumers: 21st Century Legal Services* (2006).

its own rules to permit barristers to enter into partnerships with others. Such changes would mean, for example, that solicitors and barristers would be able to join together to create 'Legal Disciplinary Practices', in which non-lawyers performing a managerial or administrative role might also be partners. Several well-known companies have already expressed an interest in setting up legal services when they are entitled to do so. Clementi recognized, however, that if lawyers and non-lawyers were to be able to enter into partnerships, special safeguards would be needed to ensure the maintenance of ethical standards.[29] The Clementi Report was 'warmly welcomed' by the government, and its recommendations were broadly accepted. Even before it was published, the Lord Chancellor had made it clear that he was keen to explore new way of delivering legal services:[30]

> I want us to adopt the Heineken approach and find legal services which reach parts of the community that no other services have reached . . .
>   I want to see a market where everyone, except those with limited means who get free access, can get access to legal services at affordable cost in a modern setting. Shopping centres are the most obvious example of this, where clusters of problems such as employment, housing, debt and family problems can be dealt with together. And this leads to the use of employed solicitors by other businesses . . . for the legal profession to thrive and survive we must continue to be competitive in the legal market of today and we must not be frightened of innovation and change.

The Legal Services Act 2007 provides the framework to do this. Section 12 defines 'reserved legal activities'. These are rights of audience, the conduct of litigation, reserved instrument activities, probate activities, notarial activities and the administration of oaths. A person must be entitled to carry on a reserved activity, for otherwise he commits a criminal offence if he does so without being entitled to do so.[31] A person is 'entitled' if he or she is authorized to perform that activity. A lawyer, whether a solicitor or barrister, will be authorized by the relevant regulator for solicitors or barristers.[32] However, others may be able to perform that activity if they are 'exempt persons' under schedule 3 to the Act.

The overall effect of this therefore, is that the functions of solicitors and barristers set out below will, when the 2007 Act is fully in force, be performed within the framework of the new Act.

6 LICENSED BODIES

It should be evident from what we have just described that the intention is to encourage a wider range of providers of legal services. Part 5 of the 2007 Act is the part of the legislation that creates the framework of powers needed to achieve that. It defines those who are to be regarded as licensing authorities. These are the Legal Services

[29] Ibid, at paras F11 and F25.
[30] The quote is taken from a speech to the Law Society's Annual Conference, 26 September 2003.
[31] 2007 Act, ss 13, 14.   [32] 2007 Act, s 18. For the professional regulators, see p 385, post.

Board or an approved regulator designated to perform a licensing function.[33] Complex provisions exist about the designation of licensing authorities, procedure and the grant, modification and regulation of licences.[34] The relevant licensing authority will consider applications, and the effect of the grant of a licence, with or without conditions, will be, within the terms of the licence, to permit a non-authorized person to perform a relevant reserved activity. Through these means it will be possible for organizations owned or managed by a non-authorized person to provide reserved legal activities. It will allow solicitors to enter into partnerships with others. It would be possible, for example, for solicitors and barristers to join together to created a 'Legal Disciplinary Practice' in which non-lawyers performing a managerial or administrative role might also be partners It will allow organizations like, perhaps, the Co-op, Tesco, or the AA, to provide legal services as part of their 'product range', and, as already noted, facilitate the growth of multi-disciplinary companies or partnerships.

THE WORK OF SOLICITORS AND BARRISTERS

1 SOLICITORS

There are in excess of 100,000 practising solicitors in England and Wales.[35] For most people seeking legal services or advice, a solicitor will be their first point of contact. In addition to conducting the preparatory stages of litigation, solicitors as a profession provide a wide range of other services. These include conveyancing work, the drafting of wills, the supervision of trusts and settlements, the administration of estates, the provision of advice on matters such as welfare law, immigration, and divorce, and the provision of advice and assistance to persons in custody. In addition, all solicitors enjoy at least some rights of audience before the courts,[36] and advocacy is an increasingly important part of the work of many solicitors. There is thus considerable variety in the types of work that different solicitors do, but a very clear and growing trend towards specialization. For example, while many high-street firms offer a general range of services, others – particularly sole practitioners – elect to specialize in certain areas such as conveyancing or personal injury work. The funding arrangements for publicly funded legal work increasingly require cost efficiencies that can only be achieved through dealing with a large volume of matters of a similar type. At the other end of the scale, many solicitors now work in very large firms which deal only with corporate and commercial law, whilst others provide legal services as employees of local governments or Law Centres.[37]

---

[33] 2007 Act, s 73.   [34] 2007 Act, ss 73–91.

[35] The Law Society *Annual Statistical Report 2005* identified 101,000 practising solicitors. More than half had been in practice for less than ten years. Some 41,807 were female.

[36] See p 377, *post*.

[37] For a survey of recent trends, see the Law Society's *Annual Statistical Report, 2003*.

(a) The right to conduct litigation

The right to conduct litigation is defined in the Courts and Legal Services Act 1990 as the right:[38]

(a) to issue proceedings before any court; and

(b) to perform any ancillary functions in relation to proceedings (such as entering appearances to actions).

Section 28 of the Act[39] established the principle that any person should be entitled to conduct litigation where the right to do so has been conferred by an appropriate body. At that time, the only body authorized to confer the right was the Law Society, and the Act thus had the effect of preserving the monopoly that solicitors had enjoyed in this area. In 1999 the Bar Council and the Institute of Legal Executives were added to the list of 'authorized bodies' capable of granting litigation rights to their members.[40] However, the Bar Council has so far declined to grant such rights to barristers in independent practice.[41] The Act also established a process by which other organizations could apply to the Lord Chancellor for recognition as authorized bodies.[42] At the time of writing, two organizations had made successful use of this system: the Chartered Institute of Patent Agents and the Institute of Trade Mark Attorneys.[43]

When the 2007 Act is fully in force, authorization to conduct litigation will be granted either by an approved regulator, or by a licensing authority granting a licence.

(b) Other monopolies: conveyancing and probate

The monopoly of solicitors over conveyancing work was formally ended by the Administration of Justice Act 1985. Part II of that Act introduced a system of licensed conveyancers and established the Council for Licensed Conveyancers to regulate and oversee the new profession. Provisions in the Courts and Legal Services Act 1990[44] were designed to further liberalize the market and to create a new supervisory body, the Authorised Conveyancing Practitioners Board. The implementation of these provisions was postponed indefinitely due to a lack of demand. The Legal Services Act 2007 now provides a framework in which further expansion and diversity can be achieved.

Solicitors have also had a virtual monopoly over the right to perform probate work. Section 55 of the 1990 Act provided that any organization which has been 'approved' by the Lord Chancellor may authorize suitably qualified persons to provide probate services for reward. Section55, repealed by the 2007 Act, came into force in December 2004. The framework is thus in place for Licensed Conveyancers, banks, building societies, and insurance companies to offer probate services.

---

[38] Section 119 (as amended).   [39] Now repealed by the Legal Services Act 2007, Schedule 23.
[40] Access to Justice Act 1999, s 40.
[41] Such rights *have* been granted to employed barristers: see p 382, *post*.
[42] Courts and Legal Services Act 1990, s 29; Schedule 4 (as amended).
[43] Chartered Institute of Patent Agents Order 1999, SI 1999/3137; Institute of Trade Mark Attorneys Order 2005/240.
[44] Sections 34–53.

(c) Rights of audience

Solicitors may be slowly losing their monopolies over litigation, conveyancing, and probate work, but they themselves are also making in-roads into an area that has historically been the preserve of barristers: that of advocacy in the higher courts. Prior to the Courts and Legal Services Act 1990, solicitors had only limited rights of audience: they could appear on behalf of clients in magistrates' courts, county courts, and most tribunals, but barristers had exclusive rights of audience in most Crown Court and High Court cases and in all cases coming before the Court of Appeal and House of Lords.[45] The 1990 Act established the general principle that rights of audience should be determined on the basis of: (a) qualifications; and (b) membership of a properly regulated profession.[46] The Act did not affect the rights of audience acquired by solicitors and barristers on joining their respective professions, but it did authorize the Law Society and the Bar Council to confer rights of audience on their members. The Law Society's criteria for granting higher court rights of audience to solicitors were approved in 1994.[47]

The Bar Council had argued that their monopoly over higher court advocacy was necessary for the maintenance of high standards and for the preservation of a strong and effective Bar.[48] They had also noted that solicitors had no equivalent of the 'cab-rank' rule,[49] meaning that they had greater freedom than barristers in choosing which cases to accept. The Law Society had responded by pointing out that solicitors were already doing advocacy work in the lower courts, and that the cab-rank rule was often ineffective in practice.[50] In the end the new system appeared to satisfy no one. As Humphries observed in 1998:[51]

> The levels of competence, experience and training required to achieve the qualification have been kept so high that today only 624 out of more than 70,000 solicitors have the right to appear in the higher courts.

The Access to Justice Act 1999 simplified matters by providing that all solicitors who have complied with the Law Society's training requirements should have a full right of audience before every court.[52] By 2004 it was reported that around 2,000 solicitors had obtained higher court advocacy rights.[53]

The principle set out in section 36 applies equally to barristers, and the restrictions on rights of audience which had once been imposed on employed barristers have now been

---

[45] These limitations were derived from the practices of the courts themselves. See, e.g. *Practice Direction (Supreme Court: Solicitors: Rights of Audience)* [1986] 2 All ER 226, [1986] 1 WLR 545; *Practice Direction (Crown Court: Solicitors: Rights of Audience)* [1988] 3 All ER 717, [1988] 1 WLR 1427.

[46] Section 17(3): see p 371, *ante*.

[47] These rules required the approval of the Lord Chancellor, the Master of the Rolls, the Lord Chief Justice, and the Vice-Chancellor before they could take effect.

[48] Bar Council, *The Quality of Justice – The Bar's Response* (1989) at pp 128–46.

[49] See p 381, *post*.

[50] See *Striking the Balance: The Final Response of the Council of the Law Society on the Green Papers* (1989).

[51] 'Preparing for the New Order in Court', *The Lawyer*, 21 July 1998 at p 14.

[52] Section 36, which substitutes section 31(2)(a) of the Courts and Legal Services Act 1990.

[53] *Final Report of the Review of the Regulatory Framework for Legal Services in England and Wales* (2004) at para 6.

lifted for most purposes.[54] Note also that the Institute of Legal Executives, the Chartered Institute of Patent Agents, and the Institute of Trade Mark Attorneys have been designated as 'authorized bodies' by the Lord Chancellor.[55] This means that they are able to confer limited rights of audience on their members,[56] as will any other authorized regulator designated under the 2007 Act, or granted rights under licence.

(d) The relationship between solicitor and client

A solicitor's authority derives from the retainer given to him by his client, the effect of which is to create a contractual relationship. The precise scope of this relationship will depend on the terms of the retainer, but a solicitor will generally acquire the authority to act as an agent on his client's behalf,[57] and he will be entitled to remuneration on completion of the work agreed. The relationship is not governed solely by the law of contract, however, and it is circumscribed by a variety of statutory rules.[58]

The solicitor–client relationship is also a fiduciary one, which means that a solicitor has an obligation derived from equity to act in good faith in all dealings with his client. But the contractual context should not be overlooked. In *Hilton Barker Booth and Eastwood (a firm)*[59] Lord Walker observed:

> A solicitor's duty to his client is primarily contractual and its scope depends on the express and implied terms of his retainer...The relationship...is one in which the client reposes trust and confidence in the solicitor...it is a fiduciary relationship...a solicitor's duty of single-minded loyalty to his client's interest, and his duty to respect his client's confidences, do have their roots in the fiduciary nature of the solicitor-client relationship. But they may also have to be moulded and informed by the terms of the contractual relationship.

A solicitor who enters into a transaction with his client must ensure: (a) that he has made a full and honest disclosure of all facts within his knowledge; (b) that the financial terms are fair to the client; and (c) that the transaction was not procured by undue influence. A failure to do any of these things may result in the transaction being set aside.[60] A presumption of undue influence will also arise if a client gives his solicitor an inter vivos gift: in *Wright* v *Carter* it was held that this presumption could only be rebutted by evidence that the gift had been made or affirmed after the fiduciary relationship had ended.[61] The presumption of undue influence does not apply to gifts made by will, but where a solicitor prepares a will under which he receives a large benefit a court will require affirmative proof that the testator knew and fully approved of its contents.[62]

---

[54] Access to Justice Act 1999, s 37: see p 382, *post*.

[55] Courts and Legal Services Act 1990, s 27(9); Schedule 4.

[56] Institute of Legal Executives Order 1998, SI 1998/1077; Chartered Institute of Patent Agents Order 1999, SI 1999/3137; Institute of Trade Mark Attorneys Order 2005/240.

[57] See p 396, *post*.   [58] See generally, the Solicitors Act 1974, and p 399, *post*.

[59] [2005] UKHL 8 [2005] 1 All ER 651, cited with approval in *Conway* v *Patiou* [2005] EWCA Civ 1302, [2006] 1 All ER 571.

[60] *Wright* v *Carter* [1903] 1 Ch 27 at 60, per Stirling LJ.

[61] Ibid: evidence that the client had received independent advice from another solicitor did not suffice.

[62] *Wintle* v *Nye* [1959] 1 All ER 552, [1959] 1 WLR 284.

Another feature of this fiduciary relationship is the confidential nature of solicitor–client communications. This gives rise to two types of privilege: privilege in the tort of defamation and privilege from disclosure in evidence. This latter privilege, is known as legal professional privilege. It is, however, in the future not to be confined to solicitors or barristers. Section 190 of the Legal Services Act 2007 effectively extends the privilege to all authorized bodies providing advocacy, litigation, conveyancing and probate services. Legal professional privilege is to be regarded as fundamental.[63] Communications between solicitor and client[64] are privileged provided they were made in confidence and for the purposes of obtaining or giving legal advice about the client's rights, liabilities, obligations, or remedies. In the important case of *Three Rivers District Council* v *Bank of England (Disclosure)*[65] Lord Scott endorsed the view expressed by Taylor LJ in an earlier case:[66]

> [L]egal advice is not confined to telling the client the law; it must include advice as to what should prudently and sensibly be done in the relevant legal context.

The *Three Rivers* case itself concerned advice given to the Bank of England about its submissions to a public inquiry. Despite being largely presentational, the advice was held to be covered by legal professional privilege: the fact that the Bank may have been the subject of criticism by the inquiry gave the advice a legal context. On the other hand, their Lordships made it clear that not all communications between lawyer and client would necessarily be protected in this way. It was observed, for example, that advice relating to investments, finance, and other business matters would often lack a legal context.[67] This decision also confirms that legal professional privilege is absolute, and that once established it can only be waived by the client or overridden by statute.[68] Note finally that privilege also attaches to communications made in connection with current or contemplated litigation, and that in this context it may extend to cover communications with third parties.

2 BARRISTERS

(a) Inns of Court and entry to the Bar

A person may only practise as a barrister in England if he has been 'called to the Bar' of one of the four Inns of Court: Lincoln's Inn, the Inner Temple, the Middle Temple, and Gray's Inn. These Inns are as old as the profession itself and appear to have originated as living quarters for apprentices-at-law. Their jurisdiction derives from the judiciary and is subject to judicial control.[69]

---

[63] See *R* v *Derby Magistrates' Court, ex parte B* [1996] AC 487, [1995] 4 All ER 526; *Three Rivers District Council* v *Bank of England (Disclosure)* [2004] UKHL 48, [2004] 3 WLR 1274.

[64] Phrased this way for ease of reference: it will in future apply to all who perform these functions.

[65] [2004] UKHL 48 at [38], [2004] 3 WLR 1274 at [38].

[66] *Balabel* v *Air India* [1988] Ch 317 at 330, [1988] 2 All ER 246 at 254.

[67] [2004] UKHL 48 at [38], [2004] 3 WLR 1274 at [38], per Lord Scott.   [68] Ibid at [25].

[69] *R* v *Gray's Inn* (1780) 1 Doug K353, per Lord Mansfield; *Lincoln* v *Daniels* [1962] 1 QB 237 at 250, [1961] 3 All ER 740 at 745, per Sellers J.

Entry to the Bar has been the responsibility of the General Council of the Bar. The Bar Standards Board has been established and acts as the regulatory arm of the Bar Council.[70] It sets and monitors the standards for training for the Bar, which are currently under review.

A person seeking to qualify as a barrister must join one of the four Inns before he can begin the vocational stage of his legal training.[71] He must also keep a number of terms,[72] which means attending some of the dinners, educational days, and residential weekends that are organized by each Inn. The benchers of an Inn, who are judges or senior members of the Bar, have historically had absolute control over the admission of students and the call of barristers. As noted above, these are now matters for the Bar Standards Board. In principle the benchers also have jurisdiction over disciplinary matters, though for most purposes this jurisdiction is in practice delegated to the disciplinary tribunals appointed by the Inns Council. Any appeal against a decision of the benchers lies to the 'Visitors' of the Inns of Court – a domestic tribunal comprising the judges of the High Court.

Such an entrant also has to have appropriate academic qualifications, either a law degree, or another non-qualifying degree and have passed the Graduate Diploma in Law. Having passed the Bar Vocational Course, a pupil barrister must then complete twelve months' pupillage. During the second six months of that pupillage the pupil can spend some of the time on his or her own work.

(b) Practice at the bar

There are about 11,500 self-employed barristers.[73] Most barristers work in independent practice in sets of chambers, which are associations of barristers sharing common facilities and administrative support. The work of each barrister is organized and arranged by the barrister's clerk, who also plays a key role in re-allocating cases when a barrister is unable to appear because of other commitments. The role of the barrister is primarily that of an advocate, and barristers are deemed to have been granted rights of audience before every court in relation to all proceedings.[74] They also deal with matters such as the giving of advice and the drafting of legal documents, though self-employed barristers are currently prevented by Bar Council rules from conducting litigation.[75] The practice of wearing robes continues despite some debate as to its utility,[76] and counsel

---

[70] For details of its work see www.barstandsboard.org.uk

[71] The various stages of a barrister's training are discussed further at p xxx, *post*. For general review of entry to the Bar, see *Entry to the Bar Working Party Final Report* (2007) – 'the Neuberger Report': available at www.barcouncil.org.uk

[72] The current requirement is that a student should complete twelve 'qualifying units': a dinner counts as one unit, an educational day counts as two, and a residential weekend counts as three.

[73] Neuberger Report (2007), *supra* n 71, at para 6, p 14.

[74] Courts and Legal Services Act 1990, s 31(1).

[75] Code of Conduct of the Bar of England and Wales (8th edn, 2004) para 401: see also p 382, *post*.

[76] A recent survey commissioned by the Lord Chancellor's Department found strong support for the reform of court dress from both court users and members of the public. There was no consensus as to what form any change might take, though only 34 per cent of advocates favoured the retention of wigs: ORC International, *Public Perceptions of Working Court Dress in England and Wales* (2002). See also: Lord Chancellor's Department,

cannot generally be 'heard' in court unless they are dressed appropriately. The wearing
of wigs has now been discontinued in civil cases. They do not wear robes when appearing
before courts which are themselves unrobed, magistrates' courts being one example.

Barristers are divided into junior counsel and Queen's Counsel (QCs). The latter are
known as 'silks' because they wear silk gowns as opposed to the stuff gowns worn by jun-
iors. Appointments to the office of Queen's Counsel are made by the Crown on the advice
of the Lord Chancellor, and are based on ability and experience. Silks are instructed in
the most difficult, complex, or important of cases and are able to command much higher
fees than their junior counterparts. At one time they were subject to rules preventing
them from doing drafting work or giving written opinions on evidence, and they were
not permitted to appear in court without a junior. Such formal restrictions no longer
exist, though a QC is not obliged to accept instructions to act without a junior if he feels
that it would not be in the interests of his client to do so. The established practice has been
for appointments to the office of Queen's Counsel to be made annually, but in 2003 the
process was suspended pending the outcome of a consultation exercise.[77] Changes were
made to the selection process as a result of this consultation,[78] and the annual round of
appointments resumed in 2005. Although the consultation revealed *some* support for the
idea that a two-tier system works against the public interest, the overall conclusion was
that the title of QC serves as a useful 'kitemark' or indication of quality.[79]

(c) The relationship between barrister and client

Whereas the relationship between solicitor and client is to some extent regulated by
statute, a barrister's obligations towards his client are largely governed by self-imposed
standards.[80] The common law rule which historically prevented self-employed barristers from entering into contracts for the provision of their services was abolished in
1990.[81] However, it was not until 2001 that the Bar Council relaxed its own rules and
allowed barristers to accept instructions from solicitors on contractual terms.[82] Further
changes in 2004 mean that barristers can now accept instructions directly from lay
clients, though they are prohibited from doing so in certain types of case.[83] Barristers
may advertise their services by any means permitted by law, though the Bar Council's
Code of Conduct[84] prohibits them from publicising their success rates or making direct
comparisons with their competitors.

Consultation on Court Working Dress in England and Wales (2003) CP 05/03. At the time of writing it remains
unclear whether the practice will survive.

[77] Department for Constitutional Affairs, *The Future of Queen's Counsel* (2003) CP 08/03.

[78] QCs are now selected by a panel comprising solicitors, barristers, laymen, and a judge, with the Lord
Chancellor having no direct input into the decision.

[79] See Lord Falconer (Lord Chancellor), 661 HL Official Report (5th series) col WS54, 26 May 2004.

[80] See Code of Conduct of the Bar of England and Wales (8th edn, 2004).

[81] Courts and Legal Services Act 1990, s 61(1).

[82] See Annexe G2 of the Code of Conduct: 'The Contractual Terms of Work on Which Barristers Offer their
Services to Solicitors'.

[83] See Annexe F2 of the Code of Conduct: 'The Public Access Rules'.

[84] At para 710.

A barrister has an obligation to preserve the confidences of his client, and he is deemed to have the authority to conduct proceedings on his client's behalf. The scope of this authority is subject to the ordinary principles of agency,[85] and it includes the authority to compromise proceedings and to make admissions on the client's behalf in civil proceedings. Note should also be taken of the 'cab-rank' principle. In theory this obliges barristers to accept any brief in an area in which they practice, provided that they are available and are offered a proper fee. A busy barrister can easily be committed elsewhere, however, and the extent to which the cab-rank principle operates in practice is questionable.[86] Indeed, in 1973 some twenty-four QCs declined to accept briefs on behalf of the IRA Old Bailey bombers.[87] This is undoubtedly an extreme example and it is impossible to know the reasons given by those who were unable to accept the brief. Nevertheless, it seems unlikely that barristers are regularly forced to undertake work which they would not otherwise have accepted,[88] and in any event the cab-rank rule does not apply to work undertaken on the basis of a contract or conditional fee agreement.[89] In addition, barristers are required by the Bar's Code of Conduct to refuse to accept instructions which might cause 'professional embarrassment' or create a conflict of interests.

(d) Employed barristers

Although most barristers are self-employed and working in independent practice, a sizeable minority supply legal services as salaried employees. There are about 3,500 fully qualified barristers who are employed in the private sector, the Crown Prosecution Service, the Government Legal Service or Local Government.[90] Some are employed by solicitors' firms, but barristers are also employed in other sectors such as government and commerce. Employed barristers may not supply legal services for reward except in the course of their employment, and in most cases this means that they may only supply legal services to their own employers. However, a barrister in the employment of a solicitor, authorized litigator, legal advice centre, or the Legal Services Commission may also provide legal services for his employer's clients.[91]

All employed barristers are permitted by the Bar's Code of Conduct to conduct litigation,[92] provided that they comply with the relevant rules and have completed the necessary training.[93] In addition to performing the other functions normally undertaken by barristers, an employed barrister may also interview witnesses, take statements, and handle his employers' funds. However, a barrister who has never practised

---

[85] See p 398, *post.*

[86] See the survey covered by Walson, 'Advocacy for the Unpopular' (1998) 162 JP 499.

[87] Robertson, *The Justice Game* (1998) at p 379.

[88] See the observations of Lord Steyn in *Arthur JS Hall & Co v Simons* [2002] 1 AC 615 at 678, [2000] 3 All ER 673 at 759.

[89] Barristers have also voted to abandon the rule in certain public-funded cases: see p 400, *post.*

[90] Neuberger Report (2007), *supra* n 71, at para 6, p 14.

[91] Code of Conduct of the Bar of England and Wales, Part V. Employed barristers are not prohibited from supplying legal services to the public free of charge.

[92] At para 504: cf. the position of self-employed barristers, at p 376, *ante.*

[93] Code of Conduct, Annexe I: Employed Barristers (Conduct of Litigation) Rules.

in chambers may only exercise full rights of audience if he practises (or has practised) from the office of an experienced advocate for a period of at least three years.[94]

3 THE DIRECTOR OF PUBLIC PROSECUTIONS AND
THE CROWN PROSECUTION SERVICE

Before 1985 there was no national system for the prosecution of offences, and arrangements varied considerably from one police area to the next. Some forces relied on local authority solicitors or solicitors in private practice, but many had their own prosecuting solicitors departments. The role of the Director of Public Prosecutions (DPP) was supervisory and advisory, and he assumed responsibility for the prosecution of serious offences such as murder. The Royal Commission on Criminal Procedure[95] concluded that an independent system of public prosecutions was essential, and it recommended that once a police force had decided to prosecute, the conduct of that prosecution should be entrusted to a separate authority.[96] The Commission recommended that this new authority should be locally based,[97] but the government opted to create a national prosecution service under the control of the DPP. The government's decision was given effect by the Prosecution of Offences Act 1985, which established the Crown Prosecution Service (CPS).

Section 2 of the Act provides that the DPP must be a barrister or solicitor of not less than ten years' standing, and that he must be appointed by the Attorney-General. His duties are set out in section 3(2) of that Act, and they include the following:

(a) to take over the conduct of all criminal proceedings instituted on behalf of a police force;

(b) to institute and conduct criminal proceedings where the importance or difficulty of the case makes it appropriate that he should do so;

(c) to take over binding over proceedings brought by a police force;

(d) to give advice to police forces on all matters relating to criminal offences; and

(e) to appear in certain appeals.

Any member of the Crown Prosecution Service who is a barrister or solicitor may be designated by the DPP as a Crown Prosecutor.[98] Crown Prosecutors have all the powers of the DPP to institute and conduct proceedings, though they are subject to the direction of the DPP in the exercise of these powers.[99] Crown Prosecutors have the same rights of audience as solicitors, and since 2000 they have been able to appear before the higher courts if qualified to do so.[100] In 2006, the CPS completed its first in-house prosecution of a murder. This trend is regarded as an important strengthening of the prosecution

---

[94] He must also have completed a pupillage: see p 386, *post*. A person who has not completed a pupillage may be employed as a barrister without rights of audience if he was called to the Bar before 2002.

[95] Cm 8092, 1981.   [96] Ibid, at para 7.3.

[97] Ibid, at para 7.22.   [98] 1985 Act, s 1(3).   [99] Ibid, s 1(6).

[100] Courts and Legal Services Act 1990, s 31A (as inserted by the Access to Justice Act 1999).

process, assisting in communication with both the police and with victims.[101] The DPP may also confer limited rights of audience on CPS employees who are not Crown Prosecutors, and has done so within prescribed parameters.[102]

The CPS itself is a national organization with offices in regional centres in 43 CPS Areas. It employs 2,879 prosecutors and 4,908 caseworkers.[103] Its role is to prosecute offences and it does not control the process of investigation. Since it was established, however, the context within which it operates has changed significantly: levels of serious crime have risen and a series of high profile cases have raised concerns about its effectiveness. The Glidewell Report,[104] which reported in May 1998, concluded that the structure of the CPS should be reorganized so as to achieve greater devolution of responsibility. It proposed that each Area should be headed by a Chief Crown Prosecutor and supported by an Area Business Manager, with the CPS National Headquarters having responsibility for resourcing and monitoring. The Report suggested that each CPS 'Area' should be regarded as equivalent to a large legal firm specializing in criminal prosecution, and that it should enjoy a large degree of autonomy in carrying out its professional functions. These aims were broadly accepted by the government, and the CPS was the subject of major structural changes in 1999. In particular, the boundaries of CPS Areas have been realigned to correspond with police areas,[105] and CPS staff are increasingly being located in or close to police stations. Not only that, there is an effective 44th area through CPS Direct, which is a 24-hour telephone service available to advise the police.

Coupled with this structural review, Glidewell also considered the operational performance of the CPS. Statistics showed that more than half of all acquittals in the Crown Court resulted from an order or direction of the judge, and this was viewed with some concern. The Report also noted the suspicion that charges were sometimes dropped or downgraded in circumstances where such action was inappropriate, although it found no firm evidence that this actually occurred.[106] Glidewell took the view that where a case had been reviewed by the CPS it ought to be strong enough to put to a jury, and it recommended that the preparation of case files in future should be the responsibility of the CPS rather than the police. The idea that the CPS should become involved in the decision making at an earlier stage was given effect by the Criminal Justice Act 2003. Schedule 2 of the Act amends the Police and Criminal Evidence Act 1984,[107] with the result that the CPS now has much greater involvement in deciding whether a charge should be laid, and what the nature of any charge should be.[108] The approach now is that CPS and police work in partnership to ensure that the right decisions are made at the right time.

---

[101] CPS Annual Report, 2006, p 15.

[102] Prosecution of Offences Act 1985, s 7A (as inserted by then Crime and Disorder Act 1998). See 2006 Annual Report, Annex D. See also Criminal Justice and Imagination Act 2008.

[103] CPS Annual Report, 2006.   [104] Review of the Crown Prosecution Service (Cm 3960, 1998).

[105] See p 416, *post*.   [106] The power to discontinue proceedings is discussed at p 570, *post*.

[107] By amending s 37 and inserting new ss 37A, 37B, 37C and 37D.

[108] These reforms are discussed in greater detail at p 560, *post*.

4 THE LAW OFFICERS

The 'law officers' are the Attorney-General and the Solicitor-General. They are legal advisers to the Crown and *ex officio* members of the Bar Council, though they may not engage in private practice during their time in office. They are assisted by practising barristers known as Treasury Counsel.

Apart from his political duties, which include advising government departments and answering questions in Parliament, the Attorney-General represents the Crown in certain civil proceedings and in trials for treason and other offences with a political or constitutional element. He also exercises the prerogative power of staying prosecutions on indictment by the entry of a *nolle prosequi*, and certain criminal proceedings can only be commenced with his authority.

The Solicitor-General's position is basically that of the Attorney-General's deputy, and he may exercise any power vested by statute in the Attorney-General (unless the statute in question provides otherwise).[109]

THE EDUCATION AND TRAINING OF LAWYERS

1 SOLICITORS

Section 2 of the Solicitors Act 1974 provided that the Law Society may, with the concurrence of the Lord Chancellor, the Lord Chief Justice, and the Master of the Rolls, make regulations governing the education and training of solicitors. No person could be admitted as a solicitor without a certificate stating that he has complied with these training regulations and that the Society is satisfied as to his character and suitability.[110] The functions formerly exercised by the Law Society are now exercised by the Solicitors Regulation Authority.[111] This body sets the standards for qualifying as a solicitor, monitors training providers and administers the roll of solicitors.[112]

The current training regulations stem from changes made in 1990 and they divide the training process into three distinct stages: the academic stage, the vocational stage, and continuing professional development. For many would-be solicitors the academic stage of training is satisfied by graduating with a qualifying law degree.[113] Graduates with a non-qualifying degree can meet the Law Society's requirements by completing a one-year[114] Common Professional Examination course (CPE) or by obtaining a Graduate Diploma in Law (GDL). The only way for non-graduates to complete the academic stage is to follow the ILEX route, which involves working in a legal office and

---

[109] Law Officers Act 1997, s 1.   [110] Solicitors Act 1974, ss 1, 3.

[111] See, generally: www.sra.org.uk   [112] See, further, p 387, *post.*

[113] One which covers 'The Foundations of Legal Knowledge': Public Law, EU Law, Criminal Law, the Law of Obligations, Property Law, and Equity and the Law of Trusts. See the Joint Statement on Qualifying Law Degrees issued by the Law Society and the Bar Council (effective 1 September 2001).

[114] Or a longer period for part-time or distance-learning students.

passing the exams needed to qualify as a Member or Fellow of the Institute of Legal Executives. A Legal Executive who wishes to qualify as a solicitor can then undertake further training and go on to sit the CPE. The ILEX route is described by the Law Society as 'lengthy, demanding and academically challenging',[115] and in practice the overwhelming majority of solicitors enter the profession as graduates. Having completed the academic stage of training, a student can then commence the vocational stage, which means passing a practical-orientated Legal Practice Course and entering into a training contract.[116] The third stage of a solicitor's training – continuing professional development – is undertaken once a solicitor is actually qualified, but it is nevertheless compulsory.

2 BARRISTERS

The Bar Council has the Bar Standards Board as its regulatory arm, which governs entry to the Bar. It deals with the requirements for entry to the profession. As far as the academic stage is concerned, the requirements are essentially the same as for a would-be solicitor: they can be satisfied by obtaining either a qualifying law degree[117] or a non-qualifying degree followed by a CPE certificate or Graduate Diploma in Law. There is no equivalent for barristers of the ILEX route. The vocational stage of training comprises the one-year[118] Bar Vocational Course (BVC), which a student cannot commence until he or she has joined one of the Inns of Court.[119] This is followed by a twelve-month pupillage in chambers, the first half of which is spent shadowing a pupil supervisor. Pupils may accept instructions during the last six months of a pupillage, though not without the permission of their supervisors. It is only after each of these requirements has been fulfilled that a person can be called to the Bar and practise as a barrister. Like solicitors, barristers must also undertake continuing professional development activities on a regular basis.[120]

THE REGULATION OF LEGAL SERVICES

1 THE LAW SOCIETY

Up until recently, the Law Society was the professional regulatory body governing the work of solicitors. It received its first Royal Charter in 1831 and was originally called 'The Society of Attorneys, Solicitors, Proctors and others not being Barristers, practising in the Courts of Law and Equity of the United Kingdom'. Its name was officially changed to 'the Law Society' by the Supplemental Charter of 1903. It has a President,

---

[115] See the Law Society publication, 'Ways to Qualify as a Solicitor'.
[116] ILEX Fellows are exempt from the requirement to enter a training contract.
[117] See n 113, *ante*.   [118] If full-time: two years if part-time.   [119] See p 380, *ante*.
[120] This is a fairly recent innovation: CPD was not a requirement of all barristers until January 2005.

a Vice-President and a Deputy Vice-President, and it is governed by a Council of between 100 and 105 members. At present the Council has 105 members, comprising sixty-one solicitors representing regional constituencies, thirty-nine other solicitors, and five lay members.

The Law Society's regulatory powers affected all solicitors, and derived from the Solicitors Act 1974.[121] Their regulatory functions are now performed by the Solicitors Regulation Authority. It maintains the roll of solicitors. It sets requirements for continuing professional development, and monitors solicitors to ensure that they comply with the relevant professional rules. It has the powers to close down solicitor's firms, and to refer complaints to the Solicitors Disciplinary Tribunal.

The Law Society also looks after the welfare of solicitors generally and attempts to maintain good relations with other bodies and with the public. To this end the Council examines the activities of unqualified persons doing the work of solicitors, and in appropriate cases it institutes proceedings. It also performs educative and public relations activities.

2 THE BAR COUNCIL

The General Council of the Bar (usually referred to as the Bar Council) was founded in 1894, though it was reconstituted by the Bar and the Senate of the Inns of Court in 1987. Its membership of 115 barristers includes representatives of the Inns and Specialist Bar Associations, along with ex officio members such as the Attorney-General, Solicitor-General, and the Director of Public Prosecutions.

The Bar Council is both a representative and a regulatory body, and it has a wide range of functions. Its regulatory powers do not derive from statute but it is deemed to be an 'authorized body' for the purposes conferring rights of audience and rights to conduct litigation.[122] Other functions include compiling and implementing the Bar's Code of Conduct, maintaining and enhancing professional standards, and representing the interests of the profession to the government and other bodies. It also determines the Bar's policies on education and training and is thus able to regulate entry to the profession.

3 REVIEW BY THE COURTS

Solicitors are officers of the Supreme Court,[123] and judges of this court have an inherent jurisdiction to suspend a solicitor for misconduct or to strike his name from the Roll of Solicitors. In their capacity as officers of the court, solicitors may be ordered to meet any

---

[121] The constitution and general purposes of the Law Society are still governed by its Royal Charter of 1845, which refers to its role in 'promoting professional improvement and facilitating the acquisition of legal knowledge'.

[122] Courts and Legal Services Act 1990, ss 27(9); 8(5).

[123] To be renamed 'the Senior Courts of England and Wales' when a new 'Supreme Court' is established to replace the Appellate Committee of the House of Lords: see p 253, *ante*.

costs incurred as a result of improper, unreasonable, or negligent conduct,[124] and they may also be liable for any losses which are the natural and probable consequence of such conduct.[125] Barristers are not officers of the Supreme Court and have historically not been subject to this jurisdiction,[126] but since 1990 the major civil and criminal courts have had a statutory jurisdiction to order *any* legal representative to pay the whole or part of any wasted costs.[127] The courts also have an inherent jurisdiction to prevent abuse of their procedures, and in exercising this jurisdiction they could refuse to hear an advocate or restrain his participation in a particular trial. In practice, however, a court will only take such a drastic step in the most exceptional of cases.[128]

In addition to the above, a solicitor may incur liability as an officer of the court by giving an undertaking to the court,[129] or by giving an undertaking to an individual when acting in his capacity as a solicitor.[130] Such an undertaking will be enforced by the court summarily, not as a contractual obligation but in order to secure the proper conduct of its officers. Finally, both solicitors and barristers may be liable for contempt of court for acts done in a professional capacity.[131]

4 THE CLEMENTI REPORT AND THE LEGAL SERVICES ACT 2007 – CHANGE TO THE REGULATORY FRAMEWORK

(a) The Report and White Paper

We have already noted[132] that the Clementi Report recommended sweeping changes to the regulatory provision in respect of the legal profession, including changes to widen the provision of legal services. The Report recommended the creation of a new Legal Services Board with responsibility for overseeing the regulation of all legal service providers.[133] In addition to exercising regulatory powers in respect of the Law Society and Bar Council, the new body would also oversee the Institute of Legal Executives,

---

[124] This jurisdiction is preserved by the Solicitors Act 1974, s 50(2). See, e.g. *Holden & Co* v *Crown Prosecution Service* [1990] 2 QB 261, [1990] 1 All ER 368 (inherent jurisdiction to order defence solicitor to pay prosecution costs following a serious dereliction of duty); *Langley* v *North West Water Authority* [1991] 3 All ER 610, [1991] 1 WLR 697 (solicitor personally liable for costs resulting from failure to comply with county court Practice Direction).

[125] *Marsh* v *Joseph* [1897] 1 Ch 213.

[126] In *Metcalf* v *Wetherill (Wasted Costs Order)* [2002] UKHL 27, [2003] 1 AC 120, [2002] 3 All ER 721 the House of Lords suggested, obiter, that the inherent jurisdiction could be applied to any legal representative. However, it also accepted that the jurisdiction had largely been superseded by statute.

[127] Supreme Court Act 1981, s 51 (civil courts) as amended by the Courts and Legal Services Act 1990; Prosecution of Offences Act 1985, s 19A (criminal courts) as inserted by the 1990 Act. The principles to be applied were considered by the Court of Appeal in *Re A Barrister (Wasted Costs Order (No 1 of 1991))* [1993] QB 293, [1992] 3 All ER 429 and are discussed at p 521, *post*.

[128] *Geveran Trading Co* v *Skjevesland* [2002] EWCA Civ 1567, [2003] 1 WLR 912, [2003] 1 All ER 1.

[129] *D* v *A & Co* [1899] D 2136.

[130] *Re A Solicitor, ex parte Hales* [1907] 2 KB 539; *Re A Solicitor* [1966] 3 All ER 52, [1966] 1 WLR 1604.

[131] *Linwood* v *Andrews and Moore* (1888) 58 LT 612; *Alliance and Leicester Building Society* v *Ghahremani* [1992] NLJR 313 (1992) *The Times* 19 March; *Daw* v *Eley* (1868) LR 7 Eq 49.

[132] See p 373, *ante*.   [133] Ibid, at paras B70–B71.

the Council for Licensed Conveyancers, the Chartered Institute of Patent Agents, the Institute of Trade Mark Attorney, and the Office of the Immigration Services Commissioner. The existing professional bodies would still have front-line responsibility for regulating their own members, but the Legal Services Board would be able to intervene if standards were not being maintained. The Board would also assume a number of powers currently exercised by the Lord Chancellor, including the power to authorize bodies to confer rights of audience and the right to conduct litigation.[134] In addition, Clementi recommended that all front-line regulatory bodies should be required to 'separate out' their own regulatory and representative functions.[135] On the issue of complaints, the Report proposed the creation of an Office for Legal Complaints, which would be a single, independent body responsible for handling all consumer complaints. Matters of professional conduct and discipline, however, would continue to be dealt with by the existing professional bodies.[136]

The Clementi Report was welcomed by the government, although it did not consider it went far enough.[137] The reaction of the professions to this news was mixed. The proposal for a new complaints body received a particularly frosty reception from the Bar Council, which pointed out that its existing complaints system already had a good track record and did not need to be fixed. It also voiced concerns about the possible effect on standards and legal ethics if lawyers were to be allowed to join 'Legal Disciplinary Practices', and it stated that it would continue to oppose the idea of barristers being able to form partnerships with other barristers.[138] For its part, the Law Society was rather more enthusiastic. It had already begun to move towards the separation of regulatory and representative functions envisaged by Clementi, and the prospect of solicitors being able to form alternative business structures was particularly welcomed.[139]

The White Paper, published in 2005,[140] fully endorsed the recommendations of Clementi, and forms the basis for the Legal Services Act 2007.

(b) Legal Services Board

The 2007 Act creates the Legal Services Board. Figure 1[141] shows the role of the Board in the new structure.

The Board is an independent body corporate, which is accountable to the Lord Chancellor, and, through him, to Parliament.[142] It is at the head of the new regulatory regime. Day-to-day regulation is to be provided by Front Line Regulators, which will be authorized for this purpose by the Board if it is satisfied they are appropriate bodies who can perform this function. These will include the existing professional bodies, such as the Law Society, Bar Council, Council for Licensed Conveyancers, and the Institute of Legal Executives.

---

[134] See p 372, *ante*.   [135] Including the Law Society and the Bar Council: ibid, at para B39.
[136] Ibid, paras C88–C89.   [137] See p 373, *ante*.
[138] 'Clementi Must Not Be Used to Compromise the Independence of Lawyers' – press release from the Chairman of the Bar Council, 15 December 2004.
[139] 'The Future of Legal Services' – press release from the President of the Law Society, 22 March 2005.
[140] See n p 373, *ante*.   [141] Taken, with modifications from the White Paper, *op cit*, p 12.
[142] For composition, see Schedule 1 of the 2007 Act.

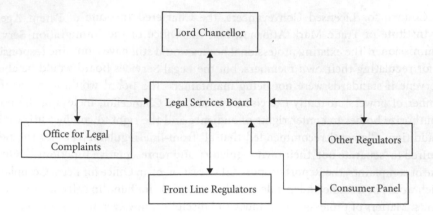

Fig. 1 Structure of the Legal Services Board

Section 1 of the Legal Services Act 2007 identifies seven regulatory objectives which the Board is under a duty to promote and comply.[143] These reflect the intention that the provision of legal services should be of high quality and best reflect the interests of consumers. They are:

- protecting and promoting the public interest;
- supporting the constitutional principle of the rule of law;
- improving access to justice;
- protecting and promoting the interests of consumers;
- promoting competition in the provision of legal services;
- encouraging an independent, strong, diverse and effective legal profession;
- increasing public understanding of the citizen's legal rights and duties.

A Consumer Panel is established.[144] The members of the Panel will have experience of consumer affairs. The Panel will report to the Board, and ensure that the views and concerns of consumers are heard.[145] The Board will also relate and interact with other regulatory Boards, such as the Office of Fair Trading.[146]

The powers of the Board enable it to effectively regulate the Front Line Regulators, although the 2007 Act gives to the Lord Chancellor the power to designate the Board itself as an approved regulator of one or more of the reserved legal activities in limited circumstances where a designation of a regulator has been cancelled or a new 'reserved legal activity' has been created.[147] The powers conferred by the 2007 Act are wide.[148] It may make rules, set performance targets, issue directions, publicly censure an approved regulator, impose financial penalties and intervene in respect of an approved regulators' function by the making of directions. Although it is intended that the Board and

---

[143] 2007 Act, ss 1, 3.   [144] Ibid, s 8.   [145] White Paper, *op cit*, para 5.3.
[146] 2007 Act, s 57.   [147] 2007 Act, s 82.   [148] Ibid, Part 4.

regulators will work together to improve areas of weakness,[149] it may recommend to the Lord Chancellor that a designation of an approved regulator be cancelled. It must issue a policy statement indicating how these powers are to be exercised.

COMPLAINTS AGAINST LAWYERS

Broadly speaking, complaints about lawyers fall into one of three main categories: (1) complaints involving allegations of professional misconduct; (2) complaints about inadequate professional service; and (3) complaints that a lawyer has acted with negligence. Both branches of the profession have their own internal mechanisms for dealing with complaints about misconduct and inadequate service, but a client who alleges that a lawyer has acted with negligence must generally look to the civil courts for a remedy.

These existing systems for the redress of complaints were considered inadequate by Clementi[150] and by the White Paper *The Future of Legal Services*.[151] The White Paper reviewed existing provision, and considered it fell short of what is required. Its recommendations are given effect by the Legal Service Act 2007. We first examine the existing regime, before explaining the new provisions.

1 SOLICITORS

(a) Complaint handling by the Law Society

In 1996 the Law Society replaced its existing Solicitor's Complaints Bureau with an Office for the Supervision of Solicitors (OSS). The OSS handled complaints about the quality of service provided by solicitors in addition to dealing with allegations of professional misconduct. It was also responsible for overseeing the Solicitors' Compensation Fund. Like its predecessor, the OSS was much criticized for its inefficiency and its perceived lack of independence: despite its semi-autonomous status and the inclusion of a number of lay members, it was directly funded by the Law Society and its membership included several solicitors who sat on the Law Society's Council. The OSS was widely criticized during its short history,[152] and in 2004 the Legal Services Ombudsman reported that the quality of its complaints handling was satisfactory in only 53.3 per cent of cases.[153] Three months before the Ombudsman's report was published, the OSS was replaced by two new bodies: the Consumer Complaints System and the Compliance Directorate. How

---

[149] White Paper, *op cit*, para 5.6.   [150] See p 373, *ante*.

[151] *Op cit*, at paras 3.3–3.4.

[152] See, e.g. Moorhead, Sherr and Rogers, 'Willing Blindness? OSS Complaints Handling Procedures (2000); DCA, Complaints and Regulation in the Legal Services Market: A Scoping Study' (2003).

[153] *In Whose Interest?* – Annual Report of the Legal Services Ombudsman for England and Wales, 2003/2004 at p 13. The role of the Legal Services Ombudsman is discussed further at p 394, *post*.

complaints are handled is monitored by the Office of the Legal Services Complaints Commissioner, established in 2004.

Complaints that a solicitor has provided an 'inadequate professional service' – e.g. by involving the client in unreasonable delays or failing to keep him informed – are handled by the Consumer Complaints Service (CCS). The CCS also offers a free service for checking that solicitors' bills are fair and reasonable, though this is only offered in respect of work that has not involved court proceedings. The emphasis of the CCS is on conciliation, but in appropriate cases it can reduce a solicitor's bill or order a solicitor to pay compensation of up to £5,000. Where some form of professional misconduct is alleged, such as a breach of lawyer-client confidentiality or the mishandling of client funds, the complaint is referred to the Society's Compliance Directorate. No compensation can be awarded in respect of such an allegation unless there is also an element of 'inadequate professional service'.[154] However, the Law Society can take disciplinary action against the solicitor concerned, place conditions on his practising certificate, or intervene in the solicitor's practice. Serious or persistent cases of professional misconduct may be referred to the Solicitors Disciplinary Tribunal.[155] The Law Society also has had an Independent Commissioner with responsibility for overseeing its handling of complaints. The Commissioner has no involvement in dealing with individual complaints but he produces an annual report on the Law Society's performance and has the power to make recommendations. His office is funded by the Law Society and has no statutory basis: his independence derives from the fact that he is appointed by the Master of the Rolls and is not a lawyer. The relationship between the Commissioner and the Law Society has not always been an easy one: in 2006 the Law Society was fined £250,000 for submitting an inadequate complaints-handling plan for 2007.

In dividing responsibility for complaints handling between the CSS and its Compliance Directorate, the Law Society was responding to the Independent Commissioner's recommendation that it should separate its regulatory function from its handling of 'consumer redress'.[156] However,[157] its efforts failed to impress the Legal Services Ombudsman:[158]

> Regardless of the precise motives or details of this latest reorganisation, there is no doubt that it represents a high profile change to the Law Society's complaints-handling operations. I was therefore extremely disappointed that the Law Society took such a radical step without any consultation or communication with either my Office ... or, as far as I am aware, with any other external stakeholders. This hardly represents the actions of a model regulator prepared to engage openly and transparently with its stakeholders.

---

[154] The Solicitors Act 1974 itself makes a distinction between 'conduct' and 'service' issues.

[155] See p 393, *post*.

[156] See Sir Stephen Lander, Independent Commissioner to the Law Society, *Redress or Rules? Whither the Consumer Redress Scheme?* (2003).

[157] See (2006) 156 NLJ 858, and Annual Report.

[158] See n 153, *supra*, at p 51.

The Ombudsman also pointed that 'the most obvious single contribution to improving client satisfaction ... would of course be to remove the causes that give rise to complaints in the first place'.[159]

Before the Law Society will consider a complaint about inadequate professional service, it will normally insist that a client has first made use of a solicitor's own 'in-house' complaints procedure. Rule 15 of the Solicitors Practice Rules requires all solicitors to have a complaints-handling procedure in place, and a breach of this rule may itself be a disciplinary matter. Both the Legal Services Ombudsman and the Independent Commissioner have indicated that the Law Society has not done enough to enforce this rule in the past, and the Society is now taking steps to address this.[160]

(b) The Solicitors Disciplinary Tribunal

Allegations of serious professional misconduct are dealt with by an independent Solicitors Disciplinary Tribunal. The Tribunal consists of 'solicitor members', who must be practising solicitors of not less than ten years' standing, and 'lay members', who are neither solicitors nor barristers.[161] It is independent of the Law Society and like other judicial tribunals it may receive evidence on oath and compel the attendance of witnesses. It is properly constituted when at least three members are present, the majority of whom must be solicitor members. There must also be at least one lay member present.[162]

Most of the Tribunal's caseload consists of referrals from the Law Society, though it can also hear applications from solicitors, judges, and members of the public. In addition to dealing with a variety of disciplinary matters it can hear any application to strike a solicitor's name from the Roll, or to reinstate a solicitor who has previously been struck off or suspended.[163] It can also hear applications concerning the conduct of solicitors' employees.[164] The Tribunal can dispose of an application involving a solicitor by making any such order as it thinks fit:[165] in particular, an adverse finding may result in a solicitor being struck off, suspended, reprimanded, fined, or prevented from carrying out work funded by the Legal Services Commission.[166] In the case of an application concerning a solicitor's employee the Tribunal may make an order preventing that person from being employed or remunerated by a solicitor without the Law Society's written permission.[167] Any appeal against a refusal to revoke such an order lies to the Master of the Rolls, and his decision is final.[168] The Master of the Rolls also hears appeals against decisions relating to the reinstatement of a solicitor who has been

---

[159] Ibid, at p 52.
[160] See *In Whose Interest?* – Annual Report of the Legal Services Ombudsman for England and Wales, 2003/2004 at p 53; Annual Report of the Independent Commissioner to the Law Society 2003, Annex III, recommendation 3. See also Moorhead, 'Self-Regulation and the Market for Legal Services' – paper published by the Cardiff Centre for Ethics, Law and Society (Cardiff University, 2004).
[161] Solicitors Act 1974, s 46.   [162] Ibid, s 46(6).   [163] Ibid, s 47(1).
[164] Ibid, s 43.   [165] Ibid, s 47(2).   [166] Ibid, ss 47(2); 47(2A).
[167] Ibid, s 43(2).   [168] Ibid, ss 49(1)(a); 49(6).

struck off or suspended.[169] Appeals in all other cases lie to the High Court, and from there (with leave) to the Court of Appeal.[170]

2 BARRISTERS

Although barristers have always been subject to the disciplinary jurisdiction of the Inns of Court, the Bar Council did not have a system for dealing with complaints from lay clients until the appointment of a Complaints Commissioner in 1997. The Commissioner is an independent non-lawyer and his function is to examine all complaints received by the Bar Council and to filter out those that are clearly without justification. Complaints which appear to have merit are referred by the Commissioner to the Council's Professional Conduct and Complaints Committee (PCCC). If the PCCC agrees that the complaint may be justified it will refer the matter to another body for a final determination. Complaints which only raise issues of inadequate professional service are referred to an Adjudication Panel comprising the Commissioner, a layman, and two barristers: if a complaint is upheld the barrister may be ordered to repay his fees or to pay compensation of up to £5,000. Where a complaint is based wholly or partly on an allegation of professional misconduct[171] the PCCC has three options: (1) to refer the matter to an informal hearing; (2) to refer it to a summary procedure panel; or (3) to refer it to a disciplinary tribunal comprising a judge, two barristers and two laymen. Disciplinary tribunals deal with the most serious cases and can disbar or suspend a barrister if appropriate. A barrister can appeal against the decision of a tribunal or summary procedure panel to the Visitors of the Inns of Court (the High Court Judges).

3 THE LEGAL SERVICES OMBUDSMAN

The Ombudsman is an independent non-lawyer appointed for a renewable term of three years.[172] Her role is to investigate allegations made by persons who are dissatisfied at the handling of their complaints by the professional bodies. The focus of any investigation will be on the handling of the complaint itself, and the Ombudsman's role is not to review the actions of the lawyer who was originally the subject of that complaint.[173] Depending on the outcome of her investigations, the Ombudsman has the power to require that a complaint is reconsidered and/or that compensation is paid by the professional body or the lawyer concerned. She may also make recommendations of a more general nature.[174] In 2003/2004 the Ombudsman's Office completed 1,731 investigations and ordered compensation payments totalling £199,840.[175]

---

[169] Ibid.
[170] Ibid, s 49(1)(b). See, e.g. *Langford v Law Society* [2002] EWHC 2802 (Admin); [2003] 153 NLJR 176.
[171] The Code of Conduct of the Bar of England and Wales states that any failure to comply with the Code shall amount to professional misconduct (8th edn, 2004; para 901). It would be unusual however, for very minor breaches to be dealt with as misconduct in practice.
[172] Courts and Legal Services Act 1990, s 21; Schedule 3.
[173] The Ombudsman's functions are set out in detail in s 22 of the 1990 Act.   [174] Ibid, ss 23–24.
[175] *In Whose Interest?* – Annual Report of the Legal Services Ombudsman, 2003/2004 at p 13.

4 LEGAL SERVICES ACT 2007

(a) Background and overview

We identified above the growing concern about the adequacy of existing complaints resolution mechanisms. The White Paper[176] observed that consumers did not have enough confidence in the current system, and were not convinced of its independence. It stressed the need for timeliness and consistency, and noted that professional bodies still largely set their own standards, but these did not always represent 'best practice'. It recommended the creation of a single complaints body, the Office for Legal Complaints (OLC). This is established by section 114 of the Legal Services Act 2007.

The OLC is under a duty to comply with the regulatory objectives already described.[177] It is to administer an Ombudsman scheme. It reports to the Legal Services Board which, in turn, reports to the Lord Chancellor. The statutory Ombudsman scheme will supersede regulatory regimes of any approved regulator, such as the Law Society or Bar Council, in respect of 'redress'.[178] However, authorized regulators will be expected to have complaints resolution procedures, or participate in procedures established by others, as a condition of its authorization,[179] and the Act makes clear, in section 158, that aurhorized persons can be required by their regulatory body, to have in place a complaints regime as required by section 158. Thus, existing requirements in respect of individual solicitors' firms can continue in place, subject to such modifications as may be required from time to time. The offices of the Legal Services Complaints Commissioner and the Legal Services Ombudsman are abolished. The Act also envisages the OLC establishing voluntary schemes to supplement the Ombudsman scheme.

(b) OLC and the Ombudsman

The OLC will appoint a Chief Ombudsman[180] to run the new redress and complaints system. The jurisdiction of the Ombudsman is defined by sections 125 to 128 of the 2007 Act. The Ombudsman may deal with any complaint if the complainant and respondent are within the scheme, and the complaint is not excluded from the scheme. A complaint is excluded if the complainant has not first used the respondent's complaints procedures. The individuals within the scheme[181] must be the recipients of services provided by an authorized person of a reserved legal activity. Another provider of a reserved legal activity, or a public body is not an eligible complainant. It is not entirely clear why a public authority, such as a local authority, police authority or CPS should not be entitled to rely on the Ombudsman scheme in respect of inadequate legal services.

The Ombudsman scheme rules may exclude specific type of complaints, but may not exclude any complaint on the ground that it relates to a matter which could have been the subject of disciplinary action by the respondent's authorizing complaint. Thus a

---

[176] Op cit, paras 3.4–3.5.   [177] See p 390, *ante*.   [178] 2007 Act, s 157.
[179] Ibid, s 112.   [180] Who may delegate to his staff: ibid, s 134.
[181] Section 128(3)(b) envisages that the Lord Chancellor may make persons (other than individuals) eligible by Order.

complaint against a solicitor cannot be excluded by virtue of the fact that disciplinary proceedings have been, or could be, taken.

The details of the Scheme are to be set out in rules, to regulate in detail the matters identified by section 133. These will relate to matters in respect of evidence and procedure, matters to be taken into account by the Ombudsman, costs and dismissal of complaints. Authorized regulators, and, through rules made by them, authorized persons, are under an obligation to provided specified information to the OLC, and there is a duty imposed on authorized persons to cooperate with investigations. The Ombudsman must report any failure to cooperate to the relevant regulatory authority, and may, as a last resort, report to the OLC. Detailed provisions provide for the disclosure of information or documents.[182] The Ombudsman must deal with a complaint in any way that is fair and reasonable in all the circumstances of the case.[183] This might be an apology, limitation of fees, compliance with a requirement made to give effect to a direction, or the payment of compensation. The maximum limit of compensation ordered to be paid is, initially, £30,000.[184]

(c) Voluntary scheme

The 2007 Act permits the creation of voluntary arrangements being reached by the Legal Services Board to provide assistance in the improving of legal services and promoting legal services. It envisages the establishment of voluntary complaint-resolution schemes, providing quick and informal resolution of such complaints.[185] These schemes, as and when approved, will be quicker and more informal than the formal procedures of the Ombudsman. The legislation provides the framework. A complaint can only be dealt with under a voluntary scheme if the complainant is a legible person, which will depend on the voluntary scheme established. He or she must agree. The respondent must be a participant in the scheme. The terms of the scheme will be determined by the OLC when approving the scheme.

CIVIL LIABILITY

1 SOLICITORS

(a) Liability to the client

A solicitor's authority derives from the retainer given to him by his client, the effect of which is to create a contractual relationship between the two parties. This relationship is subject to the ordinary law of contract and in particular to that part of contract law concerning agency.[186] Consequently the solicitor has a right to be indemnified by his client for acts done within the scope of his authority, and he is entitled to be put in funds

---

[182] 2007 Act, ss 147–153.   [183] Ibid, s 137.   [184] Ibid, s 138.
[185] Ibid, ss 137, 138.   [186] See the discussion of liability to third parties, above.

for disbursements. If he is engaged to conduct contentious business he may also require payment of a reasonable sum on account of costs.[187] Beyond this, however, the general rule is that a solicitor undertakes to complete the transaction for which he was retained, and he is not entitled to remuneration until the transaction is completed. In addition to his liability in contract, a solicitor who fails to act with due skill and care may also incur liability in tort. In *Midland Bank Trust Co Ltd* v *Hett, Stubbs and Kemp*[188] it was held that the relationship between solicitor and client was a 'special relationship' of the kind envisaged in *Hedley Byrne* v *Heller.*[189] A solicitor could thus be liable in tort for negligent advice given in the context of such a relationship. A solicitor may also be liable to his client if incompetent counsel is instructed,[190] or if counsel is not given adequate instructions upon which to act.[191]

(b) Liability to third parties

Where a solicitor contracts on behalf of a client with the knowledge of the other party, the transaction will be subject to the ordinary law of agency: contractual liability to the third party will be assumed by the client rather than the solicitor.[192] This principle applies equally to contracts made by the solicitor with the *ostensible* authority of his client: if the solicitor's actual authority to act is disputed, his liability will be to the client rather than the third party.[193] A solicitor will, however, be contractually liable to a third party if he fails to disclose that he is acting on someone else's behalf.[194] He will also incur liability to a third party if he purports to act with the authority of a client but no such authority exists.[195]

A solicitor may be liable in tort for any tortious act to which he has been a party, whether or not he was acting with the authority of a client. For example, a solicitor who fraudulently induces a third party to buy an estate with a defective title commits the tort of deceit. In some circumstances a solicitor may even be liable to a third party for economic loss caused by his negligence. This occurred in *White* v *Jones,*[196] where a solicitor's negligence in failing to draft a new will deprived the intended beneficiaries of an inheritance.

2 BARRISTERS

(a) Liability

As noted previously, barristers were historically prevented from entering into contractual relationships with clients, but this rule has now changed.[197] Since 2004 it has been

---

[187] Solicitors Act 1974, s 65(2).

[188] [1979] Ch 384, [1978] 3 All ER 571. See also *Ross* v *Caunters* [1980] Ch 297, [1979] 3 All ER 580.

[189] [1964] AC 465, [1963] 2 All ER 575.   [190] *Re A (A Minor)* [1988] Fam Law 339.

[191] *Dauntley* v *Hyde* (1841) 6 Jur 133.

[192] *Wakefield* v *Duckworth & Co* [1915] 1 KB 218 (solicitor not liable for failure to pay a photographer).

[193] A solicitor has ostensible authority to do any act which is within the scope of his retainer, and thus may bind his client to compromise of an action whether or not he has the client's actual authority so to do: *Waugh* v *HB Clifford and Sons Ltd* [1982] Ch 374, [1982] 1 All ER 1095.

[194] *Foster* v *Cranfield* (1911) 46 L Jo 314.   [195] *Yonge* v *Toynbee* [1910] 1 KB 215.

[196] [1993] 3 All ER 481, [1993] 3 WLR 730.   [197] See p 380, *ante.*

possible for barristers who comply with certain criteria to undertake 'public access' work, which means that they may accept instructions directly from lay clients. The relationship between barrister and client in such a case will normally be contractual, and the barrister may thus be liable in contract for any failure to perform.

Barristers were historically assumed to be immune from liability in negligence, and in *Rondel* v *Worsley*[198] the House of Lords accepted that this immunity could be justified. Various public policy arguments were cited: it was pointed out, for example, that barristers have an overriding duty to the court which could potentially conflict with a client's wishes, and the fact that barristers are not free to pick and choose their clients was also noted. A particular concern was that disgruntled clients might attempt to sue their barristers as a way of reopening cases that had already been lost. Some of their Lordships also thought that barristers might be inhibited in carrying out their duties if they had to operate under the threat of being sued. Although their Lordships differed in the emphasis that they placed on each of these grounds, they were agreed that barristers should continue to enjoy immunity in respect of their conduct at trial.

In the subsequent case of *Saif Ali* v *Sydney Mitchell & Co*[199] the House of Lords was once again called upon to consider the scope of barristers' immunity, but this time in relation to work done in chambers in the course of litigation. The effect of this decision was to limit the immunity to matters of pre-trial work which were intimately connected with the conduct of the case in court. Since the barrister's advice and pleadings in the instant case had prevented the claimant's dispute from coming to court at all, it was not within the sphere of a barrister's immunity. Finally, in *Arthur JS Hall & Co* v *Simons*[200] the House of Lords departed from *Rondel* v *Worsley*[201] and abolished the controversial immunity altogether. Though their Lordships accepted that some of the justifications for it had merit, they concluded that none of them were sufficient to outweigh the interests of the client in having a remedy for the negligence of his advocate. They pointed out that doctors have no such immunity despite being bound by an ethical code, and they also stressed that a barrister would never be deemed negligent for acting in accordance with his duty to court. Concerns that barristers acting in criminal cases might be particularly at risk from unmeritorious claims persuaded a minority of the House that the immunity should only be lifted in respect of civil litigation. The majority, however, shared Lord Hoffman's view that 'it would ordinarily be an abuse of process for a civil court to be asked to decide that a subsisting conviction was wrong',[202] and as Lord Millett pointed out:[203]

> [To retain the immunity for criminal cases] would mean that a party would have a remedy if the incompetence of his counsel deprived him of compensation for (say) breach of contract or unfair dismissal, but not if it led to his imprisonment for a crime he did not commit and the consequent and uncompensated loss of his job.

The majority thus concluded that the immunity should be removed across the board.

---

[198] [1969] 1 AC 191, [1967] 3 All ER 993.   [199] [1980] AC 198, [1978] 3 All ER 1033.
[200] [2002] 1 AC 615, [2000] 3 All ER 673.   [201] [1969] 1 AC 191, [1967] 3 All ER 993.
[202] [2002] 1 AC 615 at 706, [2000] 3 All ER 673 at 785.
[203] [2002] 1 AC 615 at 752, [2000] 3 All ER 673 at 829.

(b) Liability to third parties

In principle, barristers are in the same position as solicitors with regard to their potential liability to third parties. In one case for example, a barrister who gave negligent advice about the setting up of a trust was successfully sued in tort by its trustees.[204] In practice, however, the nature of the barrister's role means that third party liability is much less likely to be an issue. One specific point to note is that the standard terms on which a barrister would normally accept a brief from a solicitor do not give rise to any contractual liability. There is, however, nothing to stop barristers from accepting a retainer on contractual terms.[205]

THE FUNDING OF LEGAL SERVICES

1 THE REMUNERATION OF LAWYERS

The remuneration of solicitors is subject to a variety of statutory and other rules, the application of which depends upon whether the work done by the solicitor is contentious or non-contentious. 'Contentious business' is defined in section 87(1) of the Solicitors Act 1974 as:

> Business done, whether as solicitor or advocate, in or for the purpose of proceedings begun before a court or before an arbitrator appointed under the Arbitration Act [1996], not being business which falls within the definition of non-contentious or common form probate business in the Supreme Court Act 1981, s 128.

The essence of the test is whether proceedings have begun: if they have, then all business relating to those proceedings is contentious. Section 59 of the Solicitors Act authorizes solicitors to enter into agreements with their clients to regulate remuneration in contentious business. In the absence of such an agreement a solicitor may submit either a Bill containing detailed items or one charging a gross sum.[206] The client is entitled to apply to the High Court for a detailed assessment (formerly known as 'taxation') of his bill.[207] If the application is granted the bill will be assessed on an 'indemnity' basis,[208] which means that all costs which have been reasonably incurred and are reasonable in amount will be allowed.[209] Different rules apply where a bill is to be paid from Legal Services Commission funds.

Work done in respect of a dispute which is settled before proceedings are commenced is regarded as 'non-contentious business'. This term also covers a wide range of other matters, such as conveyancing and the drafting of wills and settlements. Save in certain

[204] *Estill v Cowling* [2000] Lloyd's Rep PN 378.
[205] Code of Conduct of the Bar of England and Wales, Annexe G2: The Contractual Terms of Work on which Barristers Offer their Services to Solicitors, 2001.
[206] Solicitors Act 1974, s 64.   [207] Ibid, s 70.   [208] See p 525, *post*.
[209] RSC , Ord 62, r 12(2).

exceptional cases under specific enactments,[210] remuneration for non-contentious business is regulated by an order made under section 56 of the 1974 Act. The basis of remuneration under the current order[211] is that the solicitor's costs must be fair and reasonable, having regard to all the circumstances of the case. Particular regard must be had to the complexity of the matter, the skill, specialized knowledge and responsibility involved, the number of documents, the time involved, the value of any property or amount of any sum involved, whether any land was registered, and the importance of the matter to the client.[212] As with contentious business the parties are at liberty to make their own agreement as to costs,[213] but any such agreement may still be subject to review by the courts.

Barristers are not covered by the same regulatory regime as solicitors, and they may be remunerated on any basis agreed by the parties as long as it is permitted by law. Again, the principles that apply are often different in respect of work funded by the Legal Services Commission. In addition, counsel's fees may come under scrutiny when costs fall to be considered at the end of a trial and a barrister will not be permitted to charge for work which he has not been instructed to do.[214]

(a) Conditional fee agreements

Conditional fee arrangements are now a fundamentally important way of funding legal services. They shift the burden of financing many types of litigation from the state to the individual person or company.[215] A conditional fee agreement is defined by section 58(2)(a) of the Courts and Legal Services Act 1990 as:

> [A]n agreement with a person providing advocacy or litigation services which provides for his fees and expenses, or any part of them, to be payable only in specified circumstances.

In other words, a lawyer who enters into a conditional fee agreement will only be paid for his services in certain circumstances. The vast majority of such agreements are entered into on what is described as a 'no win, no fee' basis, which means that the solicitor does not receive a fee from his client if he loses the case, but is paid a 'success fee' if he wins. A success fee is an amount which increases the standard fee by a given percentage.[216] Conditional fee agreements were once thought to be contrary to public policy, but the Courts and Legal Services Act 1990 legitimized their use in certain classes of case. These classes are designated by Order and were originally fairly limited, but current legislation permits the use of conditional fees in the vast majority of cases. The only remaining statutory exceptions are: (a) criminal cases; and (b) specified family proceedings cases.[217] For a conditional fee agreement to be enforceable it must be in writing and its effects must have been made clear to the client. In particular, the agreement must specify the

---

[210] Preserved by s 75 of the 1974 Act.

[211] Solicitors' (Non-Contentious Business) Remuneration Order 1994, SI 1994/2616.

[212] Ibid, Article 3.   [213] 1974 Act, s 57.

[214] *Loveday* v *Renton (No 2)* [1992] 3 All ER 184.

[215] See Lord Hoffmann in *Campbell* v *MGN (No 2)* [2005] UKHL 61, [2005] 4 All ER 393, at para 17.

[216] Courts and Legal Services Act 1990, ss 58(2)(b); 58(4)b.   [217] Ibid, s 58A.

circumstances in which the client may be liable to pay the legal representative's costs, and it must also state what percentage increase (if any) is attributable to a success fee.[218] The maximum percentage increase permitted by the regulations is currently 100 per cent of the normal fee.[219] The existence of a conditional fee agreement places most of the financial risks of litigation with the lawyer, and it is on this basis that an increase in the standard fee is said to be justified. In *Campbell v MGN (No 2)*[220] the House of Lords observed that success fees were to be regarded as the contribution that unsuccessful litigants make to enable lawyers to take on other cases which might not otherwise be successful but which would provide access to justice for people who could not otherwise afford to sue. It was a proportionate response by the state to secure a valid objective. For that reason, in this libel action a success fee was held not to contravene the right of freedom of expression conferred by Article 10 of the European Convention.[221] This was so even though the claimant was a wealthy celebrity who could well afford to fund her own action, and even though the amount of the success fee went beyond that which might be regarded as fair and reasonable when calculating costs in the normal way.[222]

Even with such an arrangement in place, however, there will still be some element of risk for the client: the unsuccessful litigant may not have to pay his own lawyer but he will generally be liable to pay the other side's costs. He may also be liable for court fees, the cost of obtaining expert reports, and so on. The current regulations require the lawyer to explain this risk to the client and to advise him as to how this risk might be offset. The result is that most litigants who enter into these arrangements are protected by some form of insurance policy covering any potential liability for costs. In principle, both the lawyer's success fee and the cost of after-the-event insurance are recoverable from the losing party to an action. Ultimately, however, this is a matter for the court's discretion.[223]

Note finally that conditional fee agreements must be carefully distinguished from other types of contingency agreement, such as those common in the United States which involve the lawyer receiving a percentage of any damages awarded. This type of arrangement has historically been unenforceable in England and Wales on public policy grounds.[224] The argument is that a contingency arrangement would give a lawyer an incentive to try to win at all costs and might therefore encourage unscrupulous conduct. In fact, the same argument could be made in respect of conditional fee agreements, and the Middleton Report recommended that the case for contingency fees should be reconsidered.[225]

---

[218] Ibid, s 58; Conditional Fee Agreement Regulations 2000, SI 2000/692. See also the decision in *Sharratt v London Central Bus Co Ltd (No 1)*; *Hollins v Russell* [2003] EWCA Civ 718, [2003] 1 WLR 2487, [2003] 4 All ER 590, in which the Court of Appeal held that a conditional fee arrangement will normally be enforceable as long as the general purpose of the statutory rules designed for the client's protection has been complied with.

[219] Conditional Fee Agreements Order 2000, SI 2000/823.

[220] [2005] UKHL 61, [2005] 4 All ER 793.   [221] As to which, see p 200, *ante*.

[222] For the reasonableness of success fees, see p 526, *post*.

[223] See p 518, *post* for more detail on the recovery of costs.

[224] *Aratra Potato Co Ltd v Taylor Jaynson Garrett (A Firm)* [1995] 4 All ER 695.

[225] Review of Civil Justice and Legal Aid: A Report to the Lord Chancellor (1997), at para 5.50.

(b) Litigation funding agreements

'Litigation funding agreements' are a variation on conditional fee agreements. They are made not with lawyers but with third-party funders such as insurance companies, the idea being that these funders agree to bear the financial risk of litigation, in return for which they can claim a success fee if their clients win. This type of arrangement is provided for in principle by section 28 of the Access to Justice Act 1999, which will insert a new section 58B into the Courts and Legal Services Act 1990. At the time of writing, however, this provision has yet to be implemented.

2 THE COST OF THE LAW

Access to legal advice is a fundamental right under the European Convention on Human Rights, and this right has now been given direct effect in English law.[226] Without access to advice an individual may remain unaware of his legal rights and obligations, and he may be unable to make effective use of the courts. Yet the cost of exercising this 'right' is high: the Woolf Report[227] found the average cost of litigation in medical negligence cases to be £38,252, while in personal injury cases it was £20,413. The majority of defendants in criminal cases are in receipt of public funding, but the cost of such cases may still be considerable. In 2003/2004, one barrister reportedly earned £800,000 in fees for work done for the Criminal Defence Service[228] and in recent years the Lord Chancellor has 'named and shamed' barristers considered to earn excessive amounts from doing publicly funded work.[229] However, the cost of justice is not solely a matter of lawyers' fees: court fees and other expenses may also be significant, and achieving access to justice in this climate is a real challenge for government.

One of the aims of the Woolf civil justice reforms[230] has been to reduce cost with a view to improving access to justice.[231] In addition, many lawyers have sought to address some of these difficulties by not charging for work done on behalf of financially strapped clients, *pro bono* work. In the past it was common for solicitors to tender initial advice free of charge, and the Bar's Free Representation and Pro Bono schemes have provided free legal services to many deserving clients. The Legal Services Act 2007 recognizes the importance of this type of work by permitting a court in certain circumstances to make a payment to a 'specified charity'.[232] The work done by bodies such as Law Centres and Citizens' Advice Bureaux is also important.

Conditional fee agreements, linked with legal expenses insurance, have become a major response to meeting the costs of legal services, making inroads into the position of legal aid as the major source of funding in a climate of spiralling costs. One government response to these pressures has been to try and recoup money by raising court fees. In 1996 it also sought to repeal certain rules which had exempted persons in receipt of state

---

[226] Article 6: given effect by the Human Rights Act 1998 and discussed at p 185, *ante*.
[227] Access to Justice: Interim Report, Annex III, pp 251–6.
[228] 227 Law Society Annual Conference, London (26 September 2003).
[229] See 'Fat Cats': The Facts Behind 'those Figures', *Counsel*, June 1998 at 12. See also p 526, *post*.
[230] See p 456, *post*.   [231] See pp 456–9 *post*.
[232] 2007 Act, s 194. See, further, p 408, *post*.

benefits from paying such fees.[233] However, in *R v Lord Chancellor, ex parte Witham*[234] its authority to take such action was successfully challenged. Witham was in receipt of income support and wished to bring proceedings for defamation, but since legal aid was unavailable and he was apparently no longer entitled to an exemption, he did not have the financial means to issue proceedings. Laws J upheld his claim that the change in the rules was ultra vires, stressing that access to the courts was a constitutional right at common law, and that it could not be abrogated without the clear and specific authority of an Act of Parliament. The Lord Chancellor had claimed that such authority was provided by section 130 of the Courts and Legal Services Act 1990, but Laws J disagreed and found the regulations in question to be invalid.

3 THE DEVELOPMENT OF LEGAL AID

Since the Second World War, legal aid has been the most important mechanism for ensuring affordable access to justice. Pressure on resources has inevitably increased as actions have become more complex and legal costs have risen, and these pressures have forced successive governments to keep the operation of the legal aid system under review. In 1991, the expenditure on legal aid was some £682 million. By 1997, this figure had increased to £1,477 million,[235] and by 2004 the total expenditure on publicly funded legal services was almost £2 billion.[236]

A civil legal aid scheme was introduced in the aftermath of the Second World War as part of the creation of a Welfare State.[237] It was not fully implemented, and its impact was limited, but the system expanded in subsequent decades as further legislation was enacted.[238] Criminal legal aid came later,[239] followed by the introduction of the duty solicitor scheme.[240] Eventually, the Legal Aid Act 1988 established a more comprehensive scheme covering both civil and criminal matters.[241] Section 3 of the Act created a Legal Aid Board to administer the new system and ensure the availability of advice, assistance, and representation.[242] The Board was responsible for managing the scheme in its application to civil matters, and also for maintaining a legal aid fund.[243] It could contract with law centres, Citizens Advice Bureaux, and other information agencies, in addition to entering into franchise arrangements with individual firms of solicitors.

The Act incorporated the 'Green Form' scheme, which was originally established under the Legal Advice and Assistance Act 1972. It was applicable to both civil and criminal matters and was designed to secure the availability of legal advice and information to those who would otherwise be unable to afford it. It covered oral or written

---

[233] Supreme Court Fees (Amendment) Order 1996, Article 3, SI 1996/3191.
[234] [1998] QB 575, [1997] 2 All ER 779.   [235] See Middleton Report, p 404, *post*.
[236] Legal Services Commission, *Annual Report 2003–04*, preface.
[237] Legal Aid and Advice Act 1949.
[238] See the Legal Advice and Assistance Act 1972 and the Legal Aid Acts of 1960, 1964, 1974, and 1979.
[239] Criminal Justice Act 1967.   [240] See p 410, *post*.
[241] See Legal Aid in England and Wales – A New Framework (Cmnd 118, 1987).
[242] 1988 Act, s 3(2). For the meaning 'advice', 'assistance', and 'representation' see s 2.
[243] Ibid, s 6.

advice given by a legal representative[244] in relation to any question of English law,[245] and a person who met the criteria for eligibility could obtain assistance equivalent to two hours' worth of work. 'Assistance by way of representation' was also available.[246] In principle, this could cover any steps taken on behalf a person in the institution or conduct of proceedings before a court, tribunal, or statutory inquiry, whether by representing him in those proceedings or otherwise. However, the precise application of the scheme was subject to more detailed rules,[247] and not all proceedings were actually covered. The scheme did not, for example, cover representation in defamation cases.[248]

The framework governing legal aid in criminal cases was set out in Part V of the Act, and as under the previous system the scheme was administered by the courts.[249] In principle, where legal aid was granted it could cover representation by a solicitor and counsel, in addition to the provision of advice. In magistrates' courts, however, the cost of representation by counsel would only be covered where a case concerned an unusually grave or difficult indictable offence. In both civil and criminal cases, an assisted person could be ordered by the court to pay such contribution as appeared reasonable, having regard to his commitments and resources. Such means-testing did not apply to the duty solicitor scheme, however,[250] which continued to fund the provision of free legal advice in police stations and magistrates' courts.

4 'ACCESS TO JUSTICE': THE NEW FUNDING REGIME

(a) The Middleton Committee

The Middleton Committee, which reported in 1997,[251] identified a number of weaknesses in the Legal Aid scheme. In particular, it raised serious concerns about the rapid growth in the cost of the scheme and its inability to target resources on priority areas. The Committee reported that expenditure on Legal Aid had risen from £682 million in 1991 to £1,477 million in 1997, an increase of some 115 per cent.[252] Some 90 per cent of that expenditure was said to have gone on lawyers' fees. In civil legal aid, expenditure since 1993 had increased by 43 per cent, yet the number of people assisted had gone down by 9 per cent. On the basis of such evidence, the Report concluded that significant reforms were needed. It proposed that the Legal Aid Board should use its purchasing power to contract for legal services in a pro-active way, setting requirements of quality, access, and value for money. Only contracted suppliers should be able to do legal aid work, and consideration should be given to the possibility of the Board employing its own lawyers to provide legal services. Users of the system should be required to contribute as much as they could afford to the costs of their case, and everyone should be required to pay something. The Middleton Report was followed by publication of the government's own

[244] *R v Legal Aid Board, ex parte Bruce* [1992] 1 All ER 133, [1991] 1 WLR 1231.
[245] 1988 Act, s 2(2).   [246] Ibid, ss 2(3); 8(2).
[247] Legal Advice and Assistance (Scope) Regulations 1989, SI 1989/550, reg 9.
[248] 1988 Act, Schedule 2, Part II, para 1.   [249] See p 403, *ante*.
[250] Legal Advice and Assistance (Scope) Regulations 1989, SI 1989/340.
[251] Review of Civil Justice and Legal Aid: A Report to the Lord Chancellor (1997).
[252] Ibid, at para 3.3.

plans for the reform of Legal Aid.[253] These plans were part of a package of measures which would result in significant changes to the entire civil justice system.[254] In the government's view it was important to reduce the cost of civil justice for all users, so as to ensure greater accessibility and better value for money for both the taxpayer and the individual litigant. The government's proposals drew heavily on the Middleton Report and were given effect by the Access to Justice Act 1999. These are dealt with below.

Some seven years later, in 2006, the Carter Report concluded that further fundamental change was necessary. We discuss his analysis later.[255]

(b) The Legal Services Commission

Section 1(1) of the Access to Justice Act 1999 established a new Legal Services Commission (LSC) to replace the Legal Aid Board. The Commission is required by the Act to 'establish, maintain and develop' two separate services: (a) the Community Legal Service;[256] and (b) the Criminal Defence Service.[257] It consists of between seven and twelve members,[258] who are appointed for their knowledge and experience in matters such as the provision of legal services, the work of the courts, consumer affairs, social conditions, and management.[259] The Commission has a wide range of powers and responsibilities and it may do anything which it considers necessary or appropriate for the discharge of its functions.[260] It is required to publish an annual plan setting out how it intends to fund its services for the forthcoming year, and at the end of that year it must also publish a report on its performance. Both documents must be submitted to the Lord Chancellor and laid before Parliament.[261]

The aim of the LSC is not only to improve the public's access to advice, but to ensure that the advice available is of good quality. It has therefore introduced a range of Quality Marks to recognize high standards in the delivery of different types of service. Three different standards of Quality Mark are available: (a) information; (b) general help; and (c) specialist help. Within these categories there are specific Quality Marks for things such as mediation and telephone advice, and there is also a Quality Mark for the Bar. The 'specialist help' standard is aimed at legal professionals and other specialized agencies, and without this Quality Mark it is not possible to obtain LSC funding. It will be apparent from this that the other Quality Mark standards enable the LSC to accredit a range of services which it does not actually fund.

Contracts. Under the old Legal Aid system the vast majority of funding was provided on a case-by-case basis. Any lawyer could undertake legal aid work and there were no restrictions on the amount that he could do. A new scheme had been introduced in 1994 whereby practitioners could apply for a Legal Aid franchise in one or more areas of law. Those operating under a franchise had to comply with strict quality and auditing requirements, in return for which they were able to undertake legal aid work on more

[253] *Modernising Justice* (White Paper), December 1998.
[254] See the discussion at p 455, *post*.   [255] See p 411, *post*.
[256] 1999 Act, ss 1(2)(a); 4(1). See p 406, *post*.
[257] Ibid, ss 1(2)(b); 12(1). See p 409, *post*.   [258] Ibid, s 1(3).
[259] Ibid, s 1(5).   [260] Ibid, s 3(1).   [261] Ibid, schedule 1, paras 14–15.

favourable terms and without seeking prior approval for each case. At this stage the scheme was voluntary, and those who were unwilling (or unable) to obtain a franchise could still do legal aid work on the same terms as before. Since the launch of the Legal Services Commission, however, things have changed significantly.

The position now is that publicly funded legal services can only be provided by those who hold LSC contracts. The terms of these contracts restrict the categories of law in which LSC-funded services can be offered, and they also limit the volume of cases that a provider can undertake. In this way, the LSC is able to exercise much greater control over expenditure than its predecessor: by regulating the types of contract awarded it can concentrate its funds on the areas in which they are most needed, and by auditing contracted suppliers it can ensure that proper standards are being maintained. In the government's view, this approach is the key to ensuring a high quality of service for the client and better value for money for the taxpayer.

(c) The Community Legal Service

The Community Legal Service (CLS) was established under section 1(2)(a) of the 1999 Act and is the responsibility of the Legal Services Commission. Its statutory purpose is to promote the availability of a range of services, and to secure access to those services so as to effectively meet individual needs.[262] The services specifically falling within its remit concern: (a) the provision of information about the law and the legal system; (b) the provision of help and advice about the application of the law to particular circumstances; (c) the provision of help in preventing, settling or otherwise resolving disputes about legal rights and duties; (d) the provision of help in enforcing decisions about the resolution of such disputes; and (e) the provision of help in relation to legal proceedings not relating to disputes.[263] The Commission must decide how to prioritize the allocation of its resources, but it must do so within the framework of directions laid down by the Lord Chancellor.[264] Priorities identified thus far include proceedings under the Children Act 1989 and other proceedings concerning child welfare, civil proceedings where the client is at real risk of loss of life or liberty, domestic violence proceedings, and proceedings which allege serious breaches of human rights on the part of public authorities. The Commission is required to maintain a separate fund to support the provision of such services in accordance with the terms of the Act,[265] and in this sense the Community Legal Service can be seen as a replacement for civil legal aid.

What work is covered by Community Legal Service contracts? The Funding Code issued under section 8 of the 1999 Act lists seven levels of service that may be provided by contracted suppliers:

    (1)   Legal help (this covers the provision of advice as to the application of the law and assistance in resolving disputes – in essence it replaces the old Green Form scheme);[266]

---

[262] Ibid, s 4(1).   [263] Ibid, s 4(2).
[264] Ibid, s 6(1); Community Legal Service Fund Funding Priorities (2000).   [265] Ibid, s 4(5).
[266] See p 403, *ante*, for a brief explanation of the Green Form scheme.

(2) Help at court (help and advocacy for a client in relation to a particular hearing but falling short of formal legal representation);

(3) Approved family help (legal help and some types of representation in family disputes);

(4) Legal representation (including litigation and advocacy services and related preparatory work);

(5) Support funding (assistance with representation in cases which are otherwise privately funded);

(6) Family mediation;

(7) Such other services as may be authorized by the Lord Chancellor.

Precisely which services are available is determined by the nature of the client's case and the terms of the provider's contract with the LSC. Work done under a Community Legal Service contract may be 'controlled' or 'licensed'. Controlled work is work for which the contract provides full authorization, and for which the supplier does not need to seek approval before accepting each new case. It encompasses all 'legal help' and 'help at court', in addition to covering 'legal representation' before certain tribunals.[267] All other work done under a general contract is known as 'licensed work', and it must be authorized on a case-by-case basis. In 2003/2004, 93 per cent of all solicitors holding General Civil Contracts had been allocated a quota of controlled work.[268] The LSC's total expenditure on controlled work was £383.3 million.[269] In the same year the LSC spent £514.1 million funding licensed work, the majority of which involved legal representation.[270] The Carter Report envisages the potential for longer-term contracts, driven by minimum standards and peer-review.[271] The effect of that may be, by April 2009, to cause some restructuring as 'suppliers of inadequate quality legal services are forced to improve or withdraw from the market'.

Work which falls outside the general contract altogether may be authorized separately under an 'individual case contract', and there are special arrangements for remunerating work done in 'high cost' cases. As with the Legal Aid scheme, however, there are certain types of work for which Community Legal Service funding is not available at all. These exclusions are listed in Schedule 2 of the 1999 Act, and they comprise: (a) most claims in negligence (except those relating to clinical negligence); (b) conveyancing; (c) boundary disputes; (d) the making of wills; (e) matters of trust law; (f) defamation or malicious falsehood; (g) matters of company or partnership law (h) other business matters; and (i) asylum decisions. Many areas of work *are* covered by CLS funding, including (a) family; (b) housing; (c) debt; (d) immigration; (e) employment; (f) contract and consumer law; (g) welfare law; (h) community care; (i) clinical negligence; (j) education; (k) mental health; (l) public law; and (m) actions against the police. However,

---

[267] Mental Health Review Tribunals and the Asylum and Immigration Tribunal: Funding Code, para A3.

[268] Legal Services Commission, *Annual Report 2003–04*, p 21.

[269] Ibid, p 79.   [270] Ibid, p 78.

[271] Carter, *Legal Aid: A Market-Based Approach to Reform* (2006) – 'the Carter Report' – at p 3. This report is available at: www.legalaidprocurementreview.gov.uk/docs/carter-review-p1.pdf

funding for advocacy is only available in relation to certain courts and certain types of proceedings,[272] with the result that representation before most tribunals is not covered by the scheme.

Eligibility for Community Legal Service assistance. An individual must satisfy both a merits test and a means test in order to obtain services from the CLS. The merits test derives from section 8 of the Access to Justice Act and from the Funding Code issued under it. Factors to be considered include: (a) the potential benefit to the client of providing the service in question and the likely cost to the CLS of funding it; (b) the availability and suitability of other sources of funding, such as conditional fee agreements; (c) the prospects of any legal action being successful; (d) the principle that mediation is often better than litigation in family cases; and (e) the public interest. 'High cost' cases and cases in areas such as clinical negligence and judicial review are subject to additional considerations.[273]

The rules governing financial eligibility are set out in regulations made under section 7 of the 1999 Act. The current regulations date from 2000,[274] though they have recently undergone considerable revision.[275] Different types of service used to be subject to different eligibility limits, but standard limits have now been introduced. Those with very low incomes and little capital will be entitled to full CLS assistance,[276] while those who are slightly better-off will be required to pay a contribution towards certain services.[277] The financial limits are reviewed each year and are increased by Statutory Instrument. More people qualify for assistance under the current regime than were covered by the Legal Aid system,[278] but the means test is still set at quite a low level – so much so that the Director of the Legal Aid Practitioner's Group has suggested that 'only loan sharks would loan money to someone who is poor enough to qualify for legal aid'.[279]

Not-for-profit organizations and Community Legal Service Partnerships. It should not be assumed that the CLS is only about the work done by solicitors' firms. Bodies like Shelter and the Citizens' Advice Bureaux can hold General Civil Contracts and receive LSC funding in much the same way as the private sector. In fact the LSC is increasingly looking to the not-for-profit sector as the number of solicitors doing publicly funded work declines, and in 2003/2004 it funded almost a million caseworker hours.[280] Another important feature of the new system is that it requires the LSC to work with

---

[272] Access to Justice Act 1999, Schedule 2.   [273] See generally, parts 6 to 13 of the Funding Code.

[274] Community Legal Service (Financial) Regulations 2000, SI 2000/516.

[275] Community Legal Service Financial (Amendment) Regulations 2005, SI 2005/589; Community Legal Service (Financial) (Amendment No 2) Regulations 2005, SI 2005/1097.

[276] Capital is not taken into account if the client is a pensioner or if the capital is the subject matter of the dispute. Those on Income Support and certain other benefits automatically qualify for full assistance.

[277] Services for which no contribution is required include: the provision of general information about the law and legal services; the provision of Legal Help or Help at Court; and Legal Representation in some cases involving children or asylum and immigration disputes – SI 2000/516, Article 3 (as amended).

[278] Controversial proposals to treat the equity in a person's home as 'capital' for these purposes were recently abandoned: see LSC, *A New Focus for Civil Legal Aid – Consultation Outcomes* (2005).

[279] Miller, 'Getting the Focus Right for Civil Legal Aid' (2004) NLJ 1673.

[280] Legal Services Commission, *Annual Report 2003–04*, p 78.

other bodies and organizations to find ways of improving access to justice.[281] To this end it has brought solicitors together with law centres, Citizens Advice Bureaux, and local authority advice agencies to establish over 200 Community Legal Service Partnerships. A key function of these Partnerships is to identify areas of 'unmet legal need' and to find ways of addressing them at a local level.[282] These developments are supported by the recommendations of the Carter Report[283] which stress that there should not be one single model for community legal advice centres, which should be encouraged to develop in a flexible way meeting the needs of local communities.

(c) The Criminal Defence Service

The other service managed by the LSC is the Criminal Defence Service (CDS). This was established under section 1(2)(b) of the Access to Justice Act 1999 and its role is to secure advice, assistance, and representation to persons involved in criminal investigations or proceedings.[284] All solicitors providing services for the CDS[285] must hold a General Criminal Contract and a Specialist Quality Mark. In this respect the CDS operates in a similar way to the Community Legal Service, although work done on behalf of the CDS is not subject to strict quotas.[286] In March 2004, 2,669 solicitors' firms were operating under General Criminal Contracts.[287] The Carter Report[288] envisaged significant change to criminal legal aid provision and financing. The new contract with LSC would permit efficient providers of criminal legal aid services to do greater amounts of work, achieving greater efficacy and expertise. This is being accompanied by a greater reliance on a system of fixed fees, and changes to graduated fees for advocacy in the Crown Court, to encourage better preparation of cases at the earlier parts of the trial process.

Three basic levels of service may be provided: (1) advice and assistance; (2) advocacy assistance; and (3) representation. All services funded by the CDS are subject to some form of merits test, though many of them are not means-tested. With regard to initial advice and assistance, the merits test will automatically be satisfied if a suspect or defendant has a statutory right to legal advice,[289] but the provision of any additional assistance must be justified on a case-by-case basis.

One of the most important functions of the CDS is to provide duty solicitor schemes in police stations and magistrates' courts. These schemes cover the provision of 'advice and assistance' to persons who are held in police custody or who are appearing before magistrates in certain types of proceedings.[290] Their services are provided free of charge on

---

[281] 1999 Act, s 4(6).

[282] The Director of JUSTICE has concluded that not-for-profit bodies have benefited considerably from the creation of the CLS: Smith, *Paper for Legal Services Authority Conference on the Future of Community Legal Services: Law for those in Disadvantage* (4 October 2002) at para 44.

[283] *Op cit*, p 8, Recommendations 3.5–3.8.

[284] 1999 Act, s 12(1). For these purposes the term 'criminal proceedings' includes proceedings relating to sentencing, appeals, extradition, binding over, and contempt of court: s 12(2).

[285] With the exception of those employed by the Public Defender Service: see p 410, *post*.

[286] Cf. the concept of 'controlled work' under CLS contracts, discussed at p 406, *ante*.

[287] Legal Services Commission, *Annual Report 2003–04*, p 6.

[288] Carter Report (2006) *supra* n 271, p 4.   [289] See p 411, *post*.

[290] Including bail applications and applications relating to anti-social behaviour and sex-offender orders.

a non-means-tested basis, and for the most part they are supplied by solicitors working in private practice. Recent changes to the General Criminal Contract mean that advice to those detained in connection with less serious offences will normally be provided by telephone only. Face-to-face assistance will be available if a police interview or identification procedure is to take place, or where the client is a young or vulnerable person, requires the assistance of an interpreter, or has complained of serious mistreatment. It may also be offered if the duty solicitor is already present at the police station. A pilot scheme for telephone advice, *CDSDirect*, was commenced in October 2005 in certain pilot areas.[291] It involves the provision of telephone advice for some offences, reducing the need for attendance at the police station by the duty solicitor. In 2006 the annual savings to the legal aid fund from the pilot scheme were estimated to be £3.9 million, with 99 per cent of calls attempted by CDSDirect within 30 minutes.[292] However, surveys into the pilot have shown some cause for concern in terms of practical operation, in particular with the response rates and times of the police in response to CDSDirect calls, with a significant number of calls from CDSDirect remaining unanswered, and also with aspects of the quality of service provided.[293]

Court duty solicitors may provide 'advocacy assistance' in connection with bail applications and binding-over proceedings, and *any* CDS-contracted solicitor may provide advocacy assistance in relation to ASBOs and certain other court orders, or in cases where a person risks imprisonment for non-payment of fines. Representation is subject to a merits test and will only be funded where a representation order has been made by a court or the LSC. It is not means-tested at the point of access but the Crown Court has the power to make a Recovery of Defence Costs Order at the conclusion of a case. In 2005 the government proposed changes which are now to be found in the Criminal Defence Service Act 2006. These reintroduce means testing in magistrates' courts and require convicted defendants to repay their defence costs if they can afford to do so.

The Public Defender Service. In addition to delivering services through contracted lawyers in private practice, the CDS is also able to provide legal services through lawyers in its own employment.[294] A Public Defender Service has been launched, which now has offices in Birmingham, Cheltenham, Chester, Darlington, Liverpool, Middlesbrough, Pontypridd, and Swansea. Public Defenders participate in local duty solicitor schemes, and provide other CDS services – including representation – directly to their own clients. Public Defenders are an established feature of the legal system in the US and other jurisdictions, but they are a radical new development for England and Wales. There are concerns about the extent to which Public Defenders can be genuinely independent, though the Code of Practice established under section 16 of the Act aims to address some of these concerns. More fundamentally, there are questions concerning the long-term role and remit of the Public Defender Service. In 2007 an evaluation of the pilot

---

[291] Certain parts of Liverpool and Lincolnshire.
[292] See www.legalservices.gov.uk/criminal/cds_direct.asp
[293] See (2006) 156 NLJ 205.
[294] 1999 Act, s 13(2)(f) (advice and assistance); s 14(2)(f) (representation).

scheme was undertaken.[295] It concluded that it was unlikely that the scheme could be seen as a large-scale provider of general criminal defence services, or as a means of competition which would provide a cost benchmark against which private criminal firms could be measured in the context of the Carter reforms.[296] The value was recognized of the Public Defender Service as a way of providing services in areas less well serviced by private practice, and by way of developing the quality of criminal defence work undertaken efficiently:

> We can envisage a wider role for the PDS as an essential guarantor of quality standards, minimum costs and client choice of representative in a more 'managed market' for such services.[297]

The Public Defender Service is thus an important innovation.

5 WHAT HAS THE NEW REGIME DELIVERED? 'ACCESS TO JUSTICE' OR JUSTICE DENIED? THE CARTER REPORT

The task faced by the LSC has been undoubtedly a difficult one. The cost of funding legal services has been rising for many years, placing an increasing strain on public finances. Expenditure on legal aid per head of population in England and Wales is greater than anywhere else in the world.[298] Legal aid expenditure rose from £1.5 billion in 1997 to over £2 billion in 2006, costing each taxpayer nearly £100 per year. Delivering access to justice in this climate is not easy, and defenders of the changes would argue that the LSC has made a number of improvements. Changes to the means-test have enabled more people to benefit from LSC services than were covered by the old Legal Aid system, and the idea of concentrating funds on early dispute resolution has much to commend it in principle. The increase in funding for not-for-profit organizations has been welcomed, as has the greater emphasis on quality and accountability. There have also been many completely new initiatives, such as the development of Community Legal Advice (formerly known as Community Legal Service Direct),[299] the introduction of Housing Possession Duty Court Schemes,[300] and the launch of the Public Defender Service.

Critics, however, argue that in spite of the LSC's efforts to target funds where they are most needed, access to justice has actually diminished since its launch. The contract system has limited the number of suppliers who are able to provide publicly funded services, and those who do hold contracts are subject to considerable regulatory and administrative burdens. The professional bodies continue to complain that public funded work is poorly remunerated, and all of these factors are having a negative effect

---

[295] Bridges, Cape, Fenn, Mitchell, Moorhead and Sherr, *Evaluation of the Public Defender Service in England and Wales* (2007): available at www.legalservices.gov.uk/docs/pds/Public_Defenders_Report

[296] As to which, see below.   [297] Bridges et al (2007), *supra* n 295, chapter 8.

[298] Carter Report (2006) *supra* n 271, at p 3.

[299] Formerly called 'Just Ask!', this web site provides the public with information about how to get advice, and it also includes a national directory of service providers: www.communitylegaladvice.org.uk/.

[300] Which make housing advisers available in courts; cf. the duty solicitor scheme: see p 409, *ante*.

on the number of providers willing to work in this sector. A survey by Citizens' Advice found that 68 per cent of their bureaux experienced difficulties in finding Community Legal Service lawyers to do immigration work, with 60 per cent facing similar problems in the field of housing law.[301] Some 39 per cent of bureaux said that they were operating in 'an advice desert',[302] and the overall conclusion of the report was that publicly funded legal services were declining in all parts of the country.[303]

In an effort to tackle rising costs and to make its budget go further, the LSC introduced a mandatory system of fixed fees covering all types of controlled[304] civil work except immigration. By rewarding service providers for 'outputs' rather than for the actual time spent on each case, the new system will be more cost efficient and will ensure that payments to suppliers reflect market conditions.[305] It remains to be seen whether the profession will see things this way: when graduated fixed fees were introduced for family and criminal work, barristers took the view that they were being denied 'proper remuneration' and they voted to abandon the cab-rank rule for cases which were subject to this system.

Statistics suggest that some lawyers engaged in public funded work are not impoverished. In 2003/2004, one barrister reportedly earned £800,000 in fees for work done for the Criminal Defence Service, while another barrister was paid £606,000 by the Community Legal Service over the same period. These figures add weight to a point made by the Lord Chancellor in a speech to the Law Society in 2003:[306]

> I know lawyers complain about remuneration rates but may I point out that over the last ten years the average cost per family case in civil representation has gone up by 91 per cent. Inflation in the same period was 30 per cent. I do *not* argue that this is all to the benefit of lawyers. But it does show that arguments about rates are not as straightforward as they first appear.

It is likely that lawyers and politicians will continue to disagree about the fees paid for public funded work, but there is a growing consensus about the need to correct the imbalance between the civil and criminal budgets. It was for that reason, and because of ongoing concerns about the affordability of provision of legal service, and whether they are being provided efficiently, that the Carter Review was established. It reported in 2006.[307] Carter identified the fact that more is spent per head on legal aid in England and Wales than anywhere else in the world, with legal aid expenditure increasing from £1.5 billion in 1997 to over £2 billion in 2006. He concluded that this increase in costs was not, of itself, down to wastefulness, but resulted from the way legal aid services were procured. He identified potential efficiencies which would save £100 million 'without compromising quality and access to services…' Mindful of an imbalance between civil and criminal legal aid, he considered that his recommendations would reduce spending on criminal legal aid by 20 per cent over four years.

---

[301] *Geography of Advice* (2004) at para 2.15.   [302] Ibid, at para 2.14.
[303] Ibid, at para 5.1.   [304] See p 406, *ante.*
[305] Legal Services Commission, *Tailored Fixed Fee Scheme Consultation Paper: Civil (Non-Immigration) Controlled Work* (2004). The system became mandatory on 1 April 2005.
[306] Law Society Annual Conference, London (26 September 2003).
[307] Carter Report (2006) *supra* n 271.

These aims were to be achieved by, in civil work, to a wholesale move to fixed fees, with graduations to reflect levels of difficulty and complexity. In the area of criminal legal aid, a movement to preferred contractors, based on fixed fees, again subject to increase to reflect complexity and effort, minimum thresholds for the number of cases handled, peer review of quality, and measuring efficiency against performance indicators. Carter envisaged fewer providers, with 'preferred suppliers' of defence representation.

Work is now ongoing in terms of implementation of the Carter reforms, and, in particular, the fee earning regime for criminal cases. At the heart of this, however, is the ever-increasing demands on state funding and how these may be controlled whilst maintaining client choice and effective representation. The Carter approach is to try and achieve this balance through an ever-more efficient system. It remains to be seen how effective as a strategy this will be.

FURTHER READING

BAKER, *An Introduction to English Legal History* (Butterworths: 4th edn, 2002)

Bar Council, *The Quality of Justice – The Bar's Response* (1989)

Bar Council, *Entry to the Bar Working Party Final Report* (2007) – 'the Neuberger Report'

BRIDGES, CAPE, FENN, MITCHELL, MOORHEAD and SHERR, *Evaluation of the Public Defender Service in England and Wales* (2007): available at www.legalservices.gov.uk/docs/pds/Public_Defenders_Report

CARTER, *Legal Aid: A Market-Based Approach to Reform* (2006) – 'the Carter Report'

CLEMENTI, *Final Report of the Review of the Regulatory Framework for Legal Services in England and Wales* (2004)

Department for Constitutional Affairs, *Consumers: 21st Century Legal Services* (2006)

KRAMER, *Bewigged and Bewildered: A Guide to Becoming a Barrister in England and Wales* (Hart: 2007)

LAVER, *Blackstone's Guide to Becoming a Solicitor* (Blackstone Press: 2000)

Lord Chancellor's Department, *The Workload and Organisation of the Legal Profession* (Cm 570, 1989)

Lord Chancellor's Department, *Contingency Fees* (Cm 571, 1989)

Lord Chancellor's Department, *Legal Services – A Framework for the Future* (Cm 740, 1989)

MILLER, 'Getting the Focus Right for Civil Legal Aid' (2004) NLJ 1673

ROBERTSON, *The Justice Game* (Chatto & Windus: 1998)

WALSON, 'Advocacy for the Unpopular' (1998) 162 JP 499

13

THE POLICE AND LAW ENFORCEMENT[1]

INTRODUCTION

This chapter explores the role of the police in the English legal system, in addition to giving a brief overview of the work of civilian officers and other law enforcement agencies. The jurisdiction of England and Wales is currently served by forty-three separate police forces, and the organizational structure of these forces, along with the mechanisms for ensuring their accountability will be the focus of the first part of this chapter. The latter part will give an overview of some of the most important police powers. The specific areas covered will include:

- The organizational structure of the police, including the roles of central government, local police authorities, chief constables, and individual officers.

- The trend towards greater centralization of certain aspects of policing, and the expansion of the role of civilian officers and non-police employees.

- Mechanisms for ensuring police accountability, including rules of evidence, the work of the Independent Police Complaints Commission, and the possibility of civil or criminal proceedings.

- Basic concepts such as breach of the peace, reasonable suspicion and reasonable force.

- Specific examples of some of the most important police powers, including powers relating to stop and search, arrest, and detention.

---

[1] The literature on the police is extensive. See e.g. the Report of the Royal Commission on Criminal Procedure, and the research studies listed in Annex D (Cmnd 8092, 1981); Lustgarten, *The Governance of the Police* (1986); Reiner, *The Politics of the Police* (3rd edn, 2000); English and Card, *Police Law* (10th edn, 2007); Newburn (ed), *Handbook of Policing* (2003); Newburn and Reiner, 'From PC Dixon to Dixon plc: Policing and Policing Powers since 1954' [2004] Crim LR 601.

THE LAW ENFORCEMENT FUNCTION

Law enforcement functions in England and Wales are performed primarily, but not exclusively, by the jurisdiction's forty-three local police forces. These forces are served by over 140,000 full-time police officers, each one of whom exercises the legal powers and privileges of a 'constable'.[2] These salaried officers are assisted by around 14,000 'special constables', who serve on a part-time, unpaid basis. Since 2002, a number of civilian officers have also been designated, though their 'powers and privileges' are less extensive.[3]

In addition to local police forces, several other organizations perform law enforcement functions. The Ministry of Defence Police, the British Transport Police and the Civil Nuclear Constabulary are examples of specialist police forces, and their officers hold the office of constable within their jurisdictions.[4] The Serious Organised Crime Agency, which was formed in 2006,[5] also operates at a national level. In addition, the Director of the Serious Fraud Office has wide ranging powers to assist in the investigation of complex or serious fraud cases,[6] and bodies such as the Inland Revenue and the Health and Safety Executive also have important investigative roles. It is, however, the police who perform the bulk of investigatory and law enforcement work.

1 THE ROLE OF THE INDIVIDUAL

All individuals have a duty to preserve the peace, though this is a duty of 'imperfect obligation' and there is generally no sanction for its breach. In *Albert* v *Lavin*[7] Lord Diplock stated:

> Every citizen in whose presence a breach of the peace is being, or reasonably appears to be about to be, committed has the right to take reasonable steps to make the person who is breaking or threatening to break the peace refrain from doing so; and those reasonable steps in appropriate cases will include detaining him against his will. At common law this is not only the right of every citizen, it is also his duty, although, except in the case of a citizen who is a constable, it is a duty of imperfect obligation.

Citizens also have powers of arrest in respect of indictable offences which are being (or have been) committed,[8] and it is these powers that are used by store detectives, doormen and private security officers.

---

[2] Police Act 1996, s 30.   [3] Police Reform Act 2002, s 38; Schedule 4. See p 420, *post*.

[4] Ministry of Defence Police Act 1987, s 2; Railways and Transport Safety Act 2003, s 31; Energy Act 2004, s 56.

[5] Serious Organised Crime and Police Act 2005, part 1: see p 418, *post*. Parts of the Immigration Service and Her Majesty's Customs and Excise have also been incorporated into the new Agency.

[6] Criminal Justice Act 1987, s 2; see *Smith* v *Director of Serious Fraud Office* [1992] 3 All ER 456.

[7] [1982] AC 546 at 565, [1981] 3 All ER 878 at 880.

[8] Police and Criminal Evidence Act 1984, s 24A: see p 436, post.

Beyond this, however, a citizen has no general duty to assist the police. The law proceeds on the basis that individuals have a 'right to silence',[9] and a person is generally under no obligation to answer police questions or to co-operate with any investigation.[10] There is, however, a duty not to mislead or hinder an investigation: intentional, positive acts which make it more difficult for an officer to do his job may constitute the offence of wilfully obstructing a constable in the execution of his duty.[11] In *Rice* v *Connolly* Lord Parker CJ stated that whilst it was not unlawful to refuse to answer police questions, deliberately giving a false story undoubtedly *could* constitute an offence.[12] More recently, the Administrative Court rejected appeals from two men convicted of wilful obstruction after they ran away from officers who wanted to question them about suspicious activity.[13] Although the court conceded that the appellants were under no legal duty to assist the police and would have been entitled to remain silent when questioned, it was held that running off before the officers could apprehend them amounted to an offence of wilful obstruction. The rationale seems to have been that if the suspects had simply refused to assist the police instead of running away the officers could have considered making an arrest, but this is a controversial decision nonetheless. More straightforward is the decision in *Ingleton* v *Dibble*.[14] In this case a motorist who was about to be breathalysed grabbed a whisky bottle from another man and took a swig from it. His intention was clearly to make it impossible to ascertain whether he had been intoxicated whilst driving, and it was held that his actions amounted to a wilful obstruction of an officer in the execution of his duty. In another case a motorist was convicted of the same offence after ignoring a constable's order to reverse the wrong way down a one-way street to allow an ambulance to pass.[15]

Note finally, that since 2006 police officers have had the power in certain circumstances to compel persons to answer questions or disclose relevant documents and information. The use of these powers is confined to the investigation of specific serious offences, and the consent of the Attorney-General or Director of Revenue and Customs Prosecutions is required.[16] Similar powers are available to the Serious Fraud Office.

2 THE ORGANIZATION OF THE POLICE

The structures and organization of the police were radically changed by the Police Act 1964, the Police and Criminal Evidence Act 1984 and the Police and Magistrates' Courts Act 1994. The relevant provisions were consolidated by the Police Act 1996, and further changes have since been made by the Police Act 1997, the Police Reform Act 2002 and the Police and Justice Act 2006. Policing is, for the most part, organized on a local basis, and each of the forty-three police areas[17] in England and Wales

---

[9] Though see p 448, post.   [10] *Rice* v *Connolly* [1966] 2 QB 414, [1966] 2 All ER 649.
[11] Police Act 1996, s 89(2): see p 426, post.   [12] [1966] 2 QB 414 at 420, [1966] 2 All ER 649 at 652.
[13] *Sekfali* v *DPP* [2006] EWHC 894 (Admin), (2006) 170 JP 393.
[14] [1972] 1 QB 480, [1972] 1 All ER 275.   [15] *Johnson* v *Phillips* [1976] 1 WLR 65, [1975] 3 All ER 682.
[16] See part 2 of the Serious Organised Crime and Police Act 2005. It is not normally possible to use statements made under such compulsion as evidence in any criminal proceedings against their maker: s 65.
[17] See schedule 1 of the Police Act 1996 for a list of police areas outside London.

has its own police authority.[18] Most police authorities outside London have seventeen members, comprising members of local authorities, justices of the peace and certain other nominated persons.[19] The Metropolitan Police Authority has twenty-three members, but is otherwise similarly constituted.[20] Slightly different arrangements exist for the City of London area, where the Common Council performs the functions of a police authority.[21]

There is no direct democratic element in the management of policing, though democratic input is achieved indirectly through the representatives of local authorities. In addition, section 96 of the Police Act 1996 states that:

> (1) Arrangements shall be made for each police area for obtaining –
>
>> (a) the views of people in that area about matters concerning the policing of the area, and
>>
>> (b) their co-operation with the police in preventing crime and anti-social behaviour in that area.

The primary duty of a police authority is 'to secure the maintenance of an efficient and effective police force for its area'.[22] To this end, the authority is required to appoint a Chief Constable[23] and to produce a plan setting out its objectives and its proposed arrangements for policing the area.[24] In addition, although the appointment of individual police officers is a matter for the Chief Constable,[25] it is for the police authority to decide how many officers are needed for its area. Despite this apparent local autonomy, there are numerous mechanisms for ensuring the accountability of local police forces to central government, and the last two decades have seen an increasing trend towards centralization.

(a) Police authorities and central government

A police authority cannot appoint, remove or suspend a Chief Constable without the approval of the Home Secretary,[26] and the Home Secretary can require a Chief Constable to retire in the interests of efficiency.[27] The Home Secretary can also direct that a police force be given assistance or reinforced in the interests of justice, safety or public order, and he can do this with or without the agreement of the police authority.[28] Indeed, the Home Secretary has a wide range of powers that can be used to 'promote the efficiency and effectiveness of the police',[29] and it is to him that police authorities must send their

---

[18] Police Act 1996, ss 3; 5B.   [19] Ibid, s 4; Schedule 2.

[20] Ibid, s 5C; Schedule 2A.   [21] Ibid, s 101.   [22] Ibid, s 6(1)(a).

[23] Ibid, s 11: any appointment requires the Home Secretary's approval. The Metropolitan Police Authority is subject to different arrangements: both the Authority and the Mayor of London have the power to recommend a person for appointment as the Metropolitan Police Commissioner, but the actual appointment is made by the Monarch on the advice of the Home Secretary: 1996 Act, s 9B.

[24] Ibid, s 8. (Section 8 will be repealed and policing plans will be governed by a new section 6ZB of the Act when the Police and Justice Act 2006 is brought into force.)

[25] Ibid, s 13(3).   [26] Ibid, s 11: see also, n 23, above.

[27] Ibid, s 42(1).   [28] Ibid, s 24.   [29] Ibid, s 36(1).

plans and reports.[30] The Inspectorate of Constabulary also reports to the Secretary of State,[31] and if the Secretary of State is satisfied that a police authority or its force is failing to discharge its functions effectively he can require the authority to take remedial measures.[32] The Secretary of State also determines the size of the central government grant made to each police authority,[33] and the threat to withhold funds can be used as a lever to secure changes in the way a force is run.

For his part the Secretary of State has the power to determine 'strategic priorities' for each police area,[34] and he can direct police authorities to establish performance targets.[35] He can also issue Codes of Practice[36] and make regulations for the use of equipment.[37] In addition to these statutory powers, the royal prerogative allows the Home Secretary to take all reasonably necessary steps to ensure the preservation of the Queen's peace. In *R v Secretary of State for the Home Department, ex parte Northumbria Police Authority*[38] the Court of Appeal considered the scope of section 41 of the Police Act 1964. At the time, this was the provision authorizing the Home Secretary to provide and maintain services for promoting the efficiency of the police. The Court held that this provision entitled the Home Secretary to supply riot control equipment from central stores, without the approval of the police authority. It also held that even if section 41 could not be construed in this way, the Home Secretary's actions would have been lawful under the prerogative.

Policing at a national level. It would be wrong to view police forces as acting always in isolation. Chief Constables can seek mutual aid from other forces,[39] and a number of national policing organizations have been created over the years. The Serious Organised Crime Agency is an important recent example. This body was formed by the amalgamation of the National Criminal Intelligence Service, the National Crime Squad, and parts of the Immigration Service and Her Majesty's Revenue and Customs.[40] Billed as 'an FBI for the UK', it began operating in 2006 and its remit extends throughout the United Kingdom. Its focus is on tackling drugs and people trafficking, money laundering, major fraud and other serious offences. It also has an important role in combating the financing of terrorism and it has a range of new investigative powers at its disposal.[41]

A further example of the move towards greater centralization is provided by the creation of the National Policing Improvement Agency. Established under section 1 of the Police and Justice Act 2006, the objects of this body include 'the identification, development and promulgation of good practice in policing', the provision of expert advice on operational and other matters, and the provision of support in connection with

---

[30] Ibid, ss 6A and 8. (These provisions will be repealed and policing plans and reports will be governed by new sections 6ZB and 6ZC of the Act when the Police and Justice Act 2006 is brought into force.)

[31] Ibid, s 54.   [32] Ibid, ss 40 and 40A.   [33] Ibid, s 46.

[34] Ibid, s 37A.   [35] Ibid, s 38.

[36] Ibid, ss 39 and 39A (codes for police authorities and chief officers); Police and Criminal Evidence Act 1984, ss 60, 60A and 66 (codes for the exercise of police powers and duties); Serious Organised Crime and Police Act 2005, s 10 (codes for SOCA).

[37] Police Reform Act 2002, s 6.   [38] [1989] QB 26, [1988] 1 All ER 556.

[39] Police Act 1996, s 24.   [40] Serious Organised Crime and Police Act 2005, s 1.

[41] See Part 1 of the Act and *One Step Ahead: A 21st Century Strategy to Defeat Organised Crime* (Cm 6167, 2004). See also, p 415, *ante*.

information technology, training and the procurement of equipment and services.[42] The Agency has already assumed responsibility for the Police National Computer, the National DNA Database, and the national fingerprint and palm print system (IDENT1). It also provides specialist training and operational advice to assist forces in dealing with major incidents and murder investigations. The Agency is required to submit annual plans and reports to the Secretary of State,[43] who in turn has the power to determine the Agency's strategic objectives.[44]

The creation of the National Reporting Centre during the miners' strike in the mid-1980s provides an example of a less formal centralized body.[45]

(b) Police authorities and Chief Constables

A Chief Constable is required to produce drafts of policing plans for his police authority to finalize,[46] and he must also submit a general report to the authority at the end of each financial year.[47] Beyond this, the police authority's rights are limited, and it has sometimes been said that a Chief Constable cannot be challenged on operational matters. In reality the position is not so straightforward, but the law does recognize that the Chief Constable has a wide discretion to determine strategy and other matters. The scope for judicially reviewing a Chief Constable's decisions is thus extremely limited, and neither the deployment of police resources nor individual policing decisions are normally matters for the courts. In *R v Commissioner of Police for the Metropolis, ex parte Blackburn* the Court of Appeal considered the legality of a policy by which the Commissioner had directed his officers to enforce the Gaming Acts only in certain circumstances. Lord Denning MR stated:[48]

> [It is the duty of the Commissioner], as it is of every Chief Constable, to enforce the law of the land. He must take steps so to post his men that crimes may be detected; and that honest citizens may go about their affairs in peace. He must decide whether or not suspected persons are to be prosecuted ... but in all these things he is not the servant of anyone, save of the law itself. No Minister of the Crown can tell him that he must, or must not ... prosecute this man or that one. Nor can any police authority tell him so. The responsibility for law enforcement lies on him. He is answerable to the law and to the law alone [but] there are many fields in which [a chief police officer has] a discretion with which the law will not interfere. For instance, it is [for him] to decide in any particular case whether enquiries should be pursued, or whether an arrest should be made ... It must be for him to decide on the disposition of his force and the concentration of his resources on any particular crime or area. No court can or should give him direction on such a matter.

The court added that it could intervene if what was at issue was effectively an abdication of duty, but the matter was not put to the test because the policy statement had

---

[42] 2006 Act, Schedule 1, para 1.   [43] Ibid, Schedule 1, paras 5 and 28.
[44] Ibid, Schedule 1, para 6.   [45] See generally, Freeman, 'Law an\d Order in 1984' [1984] CLP 175.
[46] Police Act 1996, s 8. (This provision will be repealed and policing plans will be governed by a new section 6ZB of the Act when the Police and Justice Act 2006 is brought into force.)
[47] Ibid, s 22.   [48] [1968] 2 QB 118 at 136, [1968] 1 All ER 763 at 769.

already been withdrawn. In another case the House of Lords accepted that police discretion could be the subject of judicial review, but it stressed that as long as it was used for a legitimate purpose, the courts would not interfere with the exercise of that discretion.[49] Although these cases do not deal directly with the relationship between the Chief Constable and his police authority, they clearly illustrate the extent of a Chief Constable's discretion and the level of autonomy that he has.

(c) Chief Constables and individual officers

Constables are office holders under the Crown, though they are not Crown servants or employees of the Chief Constable. As stated previously, all police officers derive their powers from their status as constables, though certain powers can only be exercised by officers holding a particular rank. An intimate search of a suspect, for example, can only be authorized by an officer of at least the rank of inspector.[50]

The reality of modern policing is that each force has its own policies and command structure, and all officers are subject to rules governing their employment, personal conduct and discipline.[51] However, when exercising the powers of a constable an officer is legally responsible for his own actions, and he cannot be directed to exercise them in a particular way. In *Lindley* v *Rutter*[52] it was held that a police officer had acted unlawfully in removing an item of underwear from a drunken, arrested woman. The officer had wrongly regarded a standing instruction as depriving her of any discretion as to whether such garments should be removed. Although there was a common law power which could have provided the authority for the officer's conduct, she had not considered whether the conditions for exercising this power were satisfied: her actions were therefore unlawful. This does not mean that it will always be improper to rely on a policy or standing instruction; what matters is whether there has been a genuine exercise of discretion.[53]

3 'THE EXTENDED POLICE FAMILY'[54]

(a) Civilian officers

The Police Reform Act 2002 allows Chief Constables to confer limited law enforcement powers on civilians employed by police authorities. The idea is that if civilians are able to perform basic public order and support functions, constables can be given more time

---

[49] *Holgate-Mohammed* v *Duke* [1984] AC 437, [1984] 1 All ER 1054; cf. *R* v *Chief Constable of Devon & Cornwall, ex parte Central Electricity Generating Board* [1982] QB 458, [1981] 3 All ER 826.

[50] Police and Criminal Evidence Act 1984, s 55.

[51] Police Regulations 2003, SI 2003/527; Police (Conduct) Regulations 2004, SI 2004/645.

[52] [1981] QB 128, [1980] 3 WLR 660.

[53] See e.g. *R* v *Chief Constable of Avon and Somerset Constabulary, ex parte Robinson* [1989] 2 All ER 15, [1989] 1 WLR 793.

[54] See *Policing in the New Century: A Blueprint for Reform* (Cm 5326, 2001); Morris, 'Extending the Police Family: Issues and Anomalies' [2002] PL 670; Ormerod and Roberts, 'The Police Reform Act 2002 – Increasing Centralisation, Maintaining Confidence and Contracting out Crime' [2003] Crim LR 141; Jason-Lloyd, *Quasi-Policing* (2003).

to focus on their core policing role. Section 38(2) of the Act provides that a civilian employee may be designated as one or more of the following: (a) a community support officer, (b) an investigating officer, (c) a detention officer, or (d) an escort officer.[55]

The main role of community support officers (CSOs) is to help tackle low-level disorder and anti-social behaviour problems, and they are given a range of specific powers for this purpose.[56] The list of available powers is set out in Schedule 4, Part 1 of the 2002 Act, and initially it was left to individual Chief Officers to determine which of these powers should be conferred on their CSOs. Perhaps inevitably there was wide variation in the approaches taken by different forces, and this was a source of considerable confusion for members of the public. There was also a concern that CSOs in some areas did not have sufficient powers to be able to contribute effectively to local policing.[57] The 2002 Act was amended in response to these concerns,[58] and the Secretary of State can now confer a standard set of powers on all CSOs. These powers currently include: the power to require a person suspected of anti-social behaviour or a designated offence to give his name and address; powers to deal with alcohol consumption in public places; the power to seize controlled drugs; and the power to issue fixed penalty notices in respect of littering, cycling on the footway, and offences under dog control orders.[59] Chief Officers still have a discretion as to whether to confer any of the additional powers listed in Schedule 4 of the Act, and perhaps the most controversial of these is the power to use reasonable force to detain persons in certain circumstances.

Investigating officers are essentially civilian scene of crime officers: they have the power to apply for and execute search warrants, and once a suspect has been lawfully arrested they can exercise many of the search and seizure powers available to constables.[60] Detention officers perform various functions with regard to persons in police custody, and they have powers to search, photograph and fingerprint suspects.[61] Escort officers, on the other hand, are primarily involved in transporting detainees to and from police stations, and their powers are limited accordingly.[62]

(b) Non-police employees

Some police powers can be conferred on civilians who are not employed by police authorities. Thus, where a police force has contracted a private company to provide some of its escort and detention services, the Chief Constable can designate employees of that company as escort or detention officers.[63] The Act also enables Chief Constables to establish schemes whereby other non-police employees, such as security guards and traffic wardens, may be accredited to perform community safety functions. Accredited

[55] An amendment made by the Serious Organised Crime and Police Act 2005 will also allow civilians to be appointed as 'staff custody officers', but at the time of writing this amendment has not been brought into force.

[56] Police Reform Act 2002, ss 38 and 38A.

[57] Home Office, *Consultation on the Standard Powers of Community Support Officers* (2005), para 3.

[58] By the Police and Justice Act 2006.

[59] Police Reform Act 2002 (Standard Powers and Duties of Community Support Officers) Order 2007, SI 2007/3202.

[60] Police Reform Act 2002, s 38(6); Schedule 4, Part 2.   [61] Ibid, s 38(6); Schedule 4, Part 3.

[62] Ibid, s 38(6); Schedule 4, Part 4.   [63] Ibid, s 39.

persons cannot exercise the full range of powers available to CSOs, but they can, for example, issue fixed penalty notices for littering and dog-fouling, and in some circumstances they can also require a person to provide his name and address.[64]

Before any powers under the Act can be conferred on a non-police employee, the Chief Constable must be satisfied that he is a suitable person to exercise those powers, and that he is capable and adequately trained.[65] He must also be satisfied that the person's employer is a 'fit and proper person' to supervise him for these purposes.[66]

(c) Accountability

Private sector employees designated as detention or escort officers are subject to the police complaints regime, as are civilian officers employed by police authorities.[67] There is also little doubt that all those who exercise police powers, including those accredited under community safety schemes, will be liable under the Human Rights Act 1998 if they infringe Convention rights.[68] Nevertheless, the idea of extending police powers to persons who are not trained as constables remains controversial, particularly where those persons are not employed by the police authority and are not directly subject to police control. Paradoxically, some critics have also suggested that the new powers do not go far enough. As Jason-Lloyd has noted:[69]

> [I]t is wrong to give civilians limited police powers when they are likely to face unlimited situations on the streets. The present structure of their powers is restricted to certain incidents, but this will not prevent other incidents from occurring within the same scenario where they have not been given specific powers to deal with them.

POLICE ACCOUNTABILITY

The accountability of Chief Constables to police authorities and the Home Secretary has already been discussed, but police accountability is also achieved through a variety of other mechanisms.

1 RULES OF EVIDENCE

In general, English courts adhere to the principle that it is no part of their task to punish the police by excluding evidence. Crompton J once observed that, 'it matters not how you get it; if you steal it even, it would be admissible',[70] but the modern reality is

---

[64] Ibid, ss 40–41; Schedule 5.   [65] Ibid, ss 39(4) and 41(4).

[66] Ibid, ss 39(5) and 41(4).   [67] Police (Complaints and Misconduct) Regulations 2004, SI 2004/643.

[68] See the discussion of section 6 of this Act at p 164, *ante*.

[69] 'Police Reform – A Better Way?' (2003) 167 JP 805.

[70] *R v Leatham* [1861–73] All ER Rep Ext 1646.

that in some circumstances improperly obtained evidence may be excluded by the rules governing admissibility.

(a) Confession evidence

Confession evidence is only admissible if the prosecution can show beyond reasonable doubt that it was not obtained (a) by oppression of the person who made it;[71] or (b) in consequence of anything said or done which was likely to render it unreliable.[72] 'Oppression' is defined in section 76(8) of PACE to include 'torture, inhuman or degrading treatment, and the use or threat of violence (whether or not amounting to torture)'. Beyond this, the term carries its ordinary, natural meaning, and in *R v Fulling* the Court of Appeal adopted a definition from the Oxford English Dictionary:[73]

> the exercise of authority or power in a burdensome, harsh or wrongful manner; unjust or cruel treatment of subjects, inferiors, etc.; the imposition of unreasonable or unjust burdens.

In *R v Miller* the Court of Appeal had no doubt that the confession of a defendant 'on the borderline of mental handicap' had been obtained by oppression:[74]

> We are bound to say that on hearing [the interview tape], each member of this Court was horrified. Miller was bullied and hectored. The officers...were not questioning him so much as shouting at him what they wanted him to say. Short of physical violence, it is hard to conceive of a more hostile and intimidating approach by officers to a suspect.

Miller had denied being involved in any offence over 300 times before finally 'confessing' to murder, and the finding that his confession had been obtained by oppression led to his conviction being quashed. It is rare, however, for a court to find that a confession has been obtained by oppression, and where police misconduct does result in confession evidence being excluded it is usually on the grounds of unreliability. Thus, in *R v Trussler* a drug addict's confession was excluded because he had been denied access to a solicitor and had been interviewed after 18 hours in custody without a rest period.[75] In another case, it was held that confession evidence should have been excluded from the defendant's trial because his interview had not been properly recorded. Although this could not have caused him to make unreliable admissions,[76] it had deprived the court of cogent evidence as to what had happened during the interview, and this made it impossible to be sure that section 76(2)(b) had not been breached. The officers had also offered improper inducements to persuade the defendant to admit his guilt, and this was a further reason for excluding the evidence. By contrast, section 76 did not provide

---

[71] PACE, s 76(2)(a). The term 'confession' is defined in section 82(1) to mean a statement wholly or partly adverse to the person who made it.

[72] Ibid, s 76(2)(b).

[73] [1987] QB 426 at 432, [1987] 2 All ER 65 at 69, per Lord Lane CJ. On the facts, telling the defendant that her lover had been having an affair was held not to constitute oppression.

[74] (1993) 97 Cr App R 99 at 103, per Lord Taylor CJ. Cf. *R v Emmerson* (1991) 92 Cr App R 284: an officer raising his voice and using bad language did not amount to oppression.

[75] [1988] Crim LR 446.   [76] *R v Delaney* (1989) 88 Cr App R 338.

a basis for excluding the confession of a heroin addict who claimed that he would have said anything to get bail and get access to drugs: he had not been offered any inducements to confess and his admissions were not made 'in consequence of anything said or done'.[77]

(b) Excluding evidence on the grounds of unfairness

Section 78 of PACE is another important provision and is potentially far wider in scope than section 76. It gives the court a discretion to exclude evidence on which the prosecution proposes to rely, where to admit it would create unfairness to the proceedings. It applies to both confession and non-confession evidence and may provide a basis for excluding evidence obtained in breach of PACE and the Codes of Practice. In *R v Samuel* for example, the Court of Appeal quashed the conviction of a man who confessed after being denied access to a lawyer. The Court noted that section 78 requires a judge to take account of how disputed evidence has been obtained, and in this case the police had acted in breach of a 'fundamental' right.[78] Improperly obtained evidence will not always be excluded, however, and the courts have often asserted that their exclusionary powers should not be used as a way of disciplining the police. Thus in *R v Alladice* it was not 'unfair' to admit a confession made in breach of the right to legal advice, because the defendant conceded that he had understood his rights and coped well with police interviews.[79] In *R v Mason*, evidence obtained by placing a covert listening device in the defendants' cells was also held to have been properly admitted.[80] The lack of regulation of such surveillance meant that Article 8 of the ECHR had undoubtedly been breached, but the defendants had not been oppressed or tricked into making their admissions and the use of the evidence did not render the proceedings unfair. This approach reflects that adopted in *Khan v UK*, where the use of a similar device in a suspect's house was found to breach the right to respect for private life, but not the right to a fair trial under Article 6.[81]

(c) Issues of propriety and reliability

It has been argued that despite statements to the contrary, judges often adopt a disciplinary approach to the exclusion of evidence in practice. In one case a suspect confessed after he and his solicitor were falsely told that his fingerprints had been found on incriminating evidence. In quashing his conviction the Court of Appeal stated that its decision was not about police discipline; yet it was undoubtedly influenced by the fact that the police had acted in bad faith and had deliberately set out to deceive.[82] In *R v Canale* it was held that confession evidence should have been excluded because of 'flagrant...deliberate and cynical' breaches of the recording requirements in PACE;[83]

---

[77] *R v Goldenberg* (1989) 88 Cr App R 285.   [78] *R v Samuel* [1988] QB 615, [1988] 2 All ER 135.

[79] (1988) 87 Cr App R 380; see also, *R v Dunford* (1990) 91 Cr App R 150.

[80] *R v Mason (Adrian Craig)* [2002] EWCA Crim 385, [2002] 2 Cr App R 38.

[81] (2001) 31 EHRR 45.

[82] *R v Mason (Carl)* [1987] 3 All ER 481, [1988] 1 WLR 139; see Birch, 'The Pace Hots Up: Confessions and Confusions Under the 1984 Act' [1989] Crim LR 95 at 107.

[83] *R v Canale* [1990] 2 All ER 187; see also, *R v Keenan* [1990] 2 QB 54, [1989] 3 All ER 598.

yet in *R v Sanghera (Rashpal)* the defendant's trial was held to have been fair despite the admission of evidence obtained during an improper search.[84] In the latter case the Court of Appeal noted that the police had acted in a bona fide manner, and that at the time of the search they had believed the defendant to be a victim rather than a suspect. As this last case demonstrates, judges are generally reluctant to exclude 'real' evidence on the grounds of impropriety, because there is often little doubt about its reliability. With confession evidence on the other hand, the issues of propriety and reliability cannot always be so easily separated. It should also be remembered that section 78 is concerned with 'fairness to the proceedings', rather than simply with fairness to the accused: the court in *Sanghera* clearly felt that a greater injustice might be done if the evidence was excluded from the jury.[85] Similarly, evidence that a witness in *R v Forbes* had made an 'unequivocal' identification of the accused was held to have been fairly admitted. This was despite the fact that the police had breached Code of Practice D by failing to hold a formal identification parade.[86]

(d) Abuse of process

Police misconduct may also provide the basis for an application to dismiss a prosecution on the grounds of an abuse of process.[87] The defendant in *DPP v Ara* had made an admission in the absence of a lawyer, and had subsequently made numerous unsuccessful requests to obtain a copy of the interview tape. His solicitor stated that without the tape he was unable to advise his client whether to accept a police caution, and the defendant was eventually charged with an offence of assault occasioning actual bodily harm. At a hearing before magistrates it was decided that it would be an abuse of process to proceed with the prosecution.[88] In general, it will also be an abuse of process to proceed with a case where police entrapment has caused a suspect to commit a crime which would not otherwise have occurred.[89]

2 CRIMINAL PROCEEDINGS

Quite apart from its possible effect on the prosecution of a suspect, police misconduct can sometimes amount to a criminal offence in itself. A number of highly publicized miscarriages of justice have involved allegations of police misconduct,[90] and in some

---

[84] [2001] 1 Cr App R 20, [2000] All ER (D) 1415.

[85] Cf. *R v Veneroso* [2002] Crim LR 306: drugs found while officers were on premises illegally were held to be inadmissible on the basis of Article 8, ECHR. The judge indicated, however, that the outcome might have been different if semtex had been found.

[86] [2001] 1 AC 473, [2001] 1 All ER 686.

[87] *R v Horseferry Road Magistrates' Court, ex parte Bennett*; sub nom *Bennett v Horseferry Road Magistrates' Court* [1994] AC 42, [1993] 1 All ER 138.

[88] [2001] EWHC 493 (Admin), [2002] 1 WLR 815. The magistrates were held to have acted lawfully.

[89] *R v Looseley*; sub nom *Attorney-General's Reference (No 3 of 2000)* [2001] UKHL 53, [2001] 4 All ER 897. Cf. *Smurthwaite v Gill* [1994] 1 All ER 898, (1994) 98 Cr App R 437: no grounds for a stay of proceedings or the exclusion of evidence where officers had merely provided a suspect with the opportunity to offend.

[90] Some of these are discussed in Walker and Starmer, *Miscarriages of Justice: A Review of Justice in Error* (1999).

cases officers have been prosecuted for perjury or conspiracy to pervert the course of justice. In one recent case the Metropolitan Police were successfully prosecuted under health and safety laws, following the fatal shooting of a man wrongly suspected of being a suicide bomber.[91] More often, the legality of police conduct has been tested in prosecutions brought under section 89 of the Police Act 1996. This section makes it an offence to assault, or to resist or wilfully obstruct, a constable acting in the execution of his duty. The expression 'execution of duty' has a technical meaning for these purposes: an officer who infringes the rights of an individual in the absence of some legal authority will have acted outside the execution of his duty. The effect of such action is that any prosecution under section 89 must fail. Thus, a police officer who is trespassing and who is ejected from the premises using reasonable force will not succeed in a prosecution under section 89.[92] Similarly, a person who is being unlawfully restrained will not be committing a section 89 offence if he uses physical force to secure his release.[93] The key to each of these situations is the concept of unlawful interference with individual rights. If there is no interference with individual rights, or if there is some authority in law for the interference, the constable remains within the execution of duty.

3 CIVIL ACTIONS

Police misconduct may give rise to a civil action for assault, trespass or false imprisonment. The legality of police detention may also be tested by applying for a writ of habeas corpus.

A Chief Constable is liable for any unlawful conduct of an officer acting in the performance of police functions.[94] Police authorities have a duty to indemnify Chief Constables in such cases, and at their discretion they may also indemnify any member of the police force against whom unlawful conduct is alleged.[95] What is within 'the performance of police functions' was considered in *Makanjuola* v *Commissioner of Police for the Metropolis*,[96] where an off-duty officer committed a serious sexual assault after using his warrant card to gain entry to premises. The Chief Constable was held not liable in damages for the assault, because it was not a fraudulent performance of what the constable had the authority to do honestly. Exemplary damages were awarded against the constable. The fact remains though, that the effectiveness of the civil law remedy may depend upon the liability of the Chief Constable, since an individual officer may be of modest means and not worth suing.

Unless a police authority is itself in breach of a statutory or common law obligation, it will not be directly liable for the actions of its officers. Moreover, it owes no general

---

[91] See *The Guardian*, 1 November 2007. No individual officer was prosecuted but the force was fined £175,000 after being found guilty of exposing non-employees to health and safety risks, contrary to section 3(1) of the Health and Safety and Work etc. Act 1974.

[92] *Davis* v *Lisle* [1936] 2 KB 434, [1936] 2 All ER 213.

[93] *Kenlin* v *Gardiner* [1967] 2 QB 510, [1966] 3 All ER 931; *Collins* v *Wilcock* [1984] 3 All ER 374, [1984] 1 WLR 1172. Cf *Mepstead* v *DPP* [1996] Crim LR 111: a constable who took a person by the arm to calm him and to emphasise what was being said was acting within the execution of his duty.

[94] Police Act 1996, s 88(1).   [95] Ibid, s 88(2), (4).   [96] [1992] 3 All ER 617.

duty of care to members of the public in respect of the investigation and prevention of crime.[97] However, a duty of care may be established if a special relationship with a particular member of the public can be identified, and in *Swinney* v *Chief Constable of the Northumbria Police* it was said to be arguable that a special relationship had arisen between the police and a police informant.[98] Police officers and police authorities also have a duty under the Human Rights Act 1998 to act compatibly with Convention rights, and at least some of these rights may be breached by a failure to respond to a 'real and immediate risk' to an identified individual.[99] In one recent case, for example, the High Court awarded damages to the parents of a witness murdered following inadequate police protection.[100]

4 JUDICIAL REVIEW

It has already been seen that the exercise of police discretion is judicially reviewable.[101] However, the restricted role of the courts in judicial review means that this is not always a satisfactory way of challenging police actions.

5 COMPLAINTS AGAINST THE POLICE

The police complaints system provides a non-legal mechanism for dealing with allegations of police misconduct. Pressure for such a system led to the creation of the Police Complaints Board in 1976,[102] but this body was widely regarded as unsatisfactory because the investigation of complaints was handled by the police themselves. In an attempt to address this concern the Police and Criminal Evidence Act 1984 established a new regime under the supervision of the Police Complaints Authority.[103] However, although the creation of this new, independent body was generally welcomed, critics pointed out that its role was largely supervisory and that there was still no independent mechanism by which complaints could actually be investigated. As the Macpherson Inquiry noted in 1999:[104]

> [The] investigation of police officers by their own or another Police Service is widely regarded as unjust, and does not inspire public confidence.

---

[97] *Hill* v *Chief Constable of West Yorkshire* [1989] AC 53, [1988] 2 All ER 238.

[98] [1997] QB 464, [1996] 3 All ER 449: the police were accused of allowing the informant's identity to fall into the public domain.

[99] *Osman* v *UK* (2000) 29 EHRR 245. This case concerned the failure of the police to prevent the death of a man who was murdered by his son's teacher. The teacher was known to have formed an obsessive attachment to the son, and the Court of Human Rights confirmed that Article 2 may impose a positive duty to protect life. It did not, however, find a breach of Article 2 on the facts.

[100] *Van Colle* v *Chief Constable of Hertfordshire* [2006] EWHC 360 (QB), [2006] 3 All ER 963. The £50,000 awarded was reduced to £25,000 on appeal: [2007] EWCA Civ 325, [2007] 1 WLR 1821, [2007] 3 All ER 122.

[101] See p 220, *ante*.   [102] Police Act 1976.

[103] The system was subsequently governed by provisions in the Police Act 1996.

[104] *Report of the Stephen Lawrence Inquiry* (Cm 4262-I, 1999) at ch 47, para 58.

The Independent Police Complaints Commission (IPCC)

In response to criticism in the Macpherson Report and elsewhere, the Police Complaints Authority was replaced by the Independent Police Complaints Commission.[105] The IPCC was formally launched in April 2004, and it handles complaints about both officers and civilians who serve with the police. It is also required to record incidents involving criminal conduct on the part of such persons, in addition to recording behaviour justifying disciplinary proceedings.[106] Alongside those who have experienced or witnessed alleged misconduct, any other person who has been adversely affected by it has the right to complain to the Commission.[107] The Commission itself has a Chairman and fifteen regional Commissioners,[108] and it has the power to temporarily second officers from any police force in the UK.[109] Chief Police Officers have a duty to co-operate with any IPCC investigation, and they must ensure that the Commission is provided with access to police premises and relevant evidence.[110] Most complaints continue to be investigated locally by individual police forces, but the IPCC has the power to supervise or manage investigations where appropriate.[111] A report must be submitted to the Commission at the end of any investigation that it has supervised, managed or conducted, and a copy of this report must also be sent to the relevant police force.[112] The complainant has a right to be informed about the progress and outcome of the investigation,[113] and if evidence of criminal activity or misconduct is found, criminal or disciplinary proceedings will normally follow.

POLICE POWERS

Police officers derive their powers from a wide range of sources, both common law and statutory. The detail of such powers is beyond the scope of this book, but a discussion of the general framework is set out below. A crucial issue is whether the system achieves the right balance between protecting the public on the one hand, and maintaining safeguards for individuals on the other. The need to secure this balance has been highlighted by several miscarriage of justice cases, and it has assumed particular importance since the rights to liberty and to a fair trial were given explicit recognition by the Human Rights Act 1998.

Historically, police powers were piecemeal and ill-defined, creating problems for both the police and suspects. The Royal Commission on Criminal Procedure, which reported in 1981,[114] carried out a major review of the investigative powers of the police, and the questioning and treatment of suspects. The Report provided the basis for the

---

[105] Police Reform Act 2002, s 9.   [106] Ibid, s 10.
[107] Ibid, s 12. A complaint may also be made by a representative acting on behalf of such a person.
[108] The minimum requirement is for a Chairman and ten Commissioners: Ibid, s 9(2).
[109] Ibid, Schedule 2, para 6.   [110] Ibid, ss 17 and 18.   [111] Ibid, Schedule 3, para 15.
[112] Ibid, Schedule 3, para 22.   [113] Section 20.   [114] Cmnd 8092, 1981.

Police and Criminal Evidence Act 1984 (PACE), though not all of its recommendations were accepted in their entirety.

1 GENERAL CONSIDERATIONS

Before looking at the legal framework in more detail, certain matters merit further discussion: (a) the common law concept of breach of the peace; (b) the concepts of 'reasonable suspicion' and 'reasonable belief'; (c) the use of force in the exercise of police powers; and (d) the role of the Codes of Practice.

(a) Breaches of the peace

At common law, a police officer is entitled to take any action necessary to prevent an imminent breach of the peace or to restrain a breach of the peace that is actually occurring.[115] Where a breach of the peace has already happened and there is a likelihood of reoccurrence, it would appear that an officer may also take reasonable steps to prevent such reoccurrence. In *Chief Constable of Cleveland* v *McGrogan*[116] it was held that the police had not acted unlawfully in detaining a man for almost 24 hours, because there was a real apprehension that if released sooner he would have committed a further breach of the peace within a short time. Definitions of what constitutes a breach of the peace have varied,[117] but it is now generally accepted that the correct approach is that identified in *R* v *Howell*:[118]

> We cannot accept that there can be a breach of the peace unless there has been an act done or threatened to be done which either actually harms a person, or in his presence his property, or is likely to cause such harm, or which puts somebody in fear of such harm being done.

Once the likelihood of an imminent breach of the peace is established, a police officer has the power to take reasonable steps to prevent it from happening or continuing. This may involve restraining and temporarily detaining an individual,[119] removing an item from his possession[120] or entering on to private property.[121] It may also mean requiring an individual to carry on his activities elsewhere or in a different way,[122] or requiring him not to travel along a certain route.[123] However, regardless of whether an officer is seeking to make an arrest or to take other preventative action, a breach of the peace must reasonably be believed to be imminent and the steps taken to prevent it must be no

---

[115] *Albert* v *Lavin* [1982] AC 546, [1981] 3 All ER 878.

[116] [2002] EWCA Civ 86, [2002] 1 FLR 707.

[117] See e.g. the approach of Lord Denning in *R* v *Chief Constable of Devon & Cornwall, ex parte Central Electricity Generating Board* [1982] QB 458 at 471, [1981] 3 All ER 826 at 832.

[118] [1982] QB 416 at 426, [1981] 3 All ER 383 at 389, per Watkins LJ.

[119] *Albert* v *Lavin* [1982] AC 546, [1981] 3 All ER 878.

[120] *Humphries* v *Connor* (1864) 17 ICLR 1.

[121] *McConnell* v *Chief Constable of the Greater Manchester Police* [1990] 1 All ER 423, [1990] 1 WLR 364.

[122] *Duncan* v *Jones* [1936] 1 KB 218, [1935] All ER Rep 710; *Piddington* v *Bates* [1960] 3 All ER 660, [1961] 1 WLR 162.

[123] *Moss* v *McLachlan* (1984) 149 JP 167.

more than necessary. Thus in the recent case of *Laporte*, it was held that when officers searched three coaches carrying anti-war protesters and concluded that a breach of the peace was not imminent, they had no power to prevent the coaches from continuing to the site of a demonstration or to compel the protesters to return to London with a police escort.[124]

Where a breach of the peace *is* reasonably apprehended, a person may be arrested and taken before a magistrates' court, where he may then be bound over to be of good behaviour and to keep the peace.[125] This binding over power has been criticized by the European Court of Human Rights for its uncertainty,[126] and the Law Commission has recommended its abolition.[127] However, a recent Home Office consultation paper argued that 'it would be better to resolve the underlying issues of certainty and fairness', rather than to remove the power altogether.[128] It also recommended that the sanction for non-compliance should be a fine rather than imprisonment.[129]

It will be apparent that alongside the extensive body of police powers conferred by Acts of Parliament, the police also have a wide measure of discretionary power that is still governed by the common law. It will be equally apparent that the use of this power can impinge upon conduct which in itself is perfectly lawful. In the Irish case of *Humphries* v *Connor* for example, an officer was held to have acted lawfully when he removed a political emblem from the lapel of a woman who was attracting a hostile crowd.[130] More recently, however, the courts have emphasized that where a person is not acting unlawfully and is not himself 'threatening' to breach the peace, the power of arrest should only be used exceptionally.[131]

The use of the breach of the peace power may also contravene the Human Rights Act if it interferes with a Convention right in a manner that is not proportionate to a legitimate purpose. For example, detention for longer than is necessary to prevent an imminent breach of the peace or to bring a person before magistrates could amount to an unlawful interference with the right to liberty. Moreover, if through such detention a person is prevented from participating in a demonstration, there may also be an interference with the rights to freedom of expression and freedom of assembly. Whether the detention is unlawful in this respect will depend on whether it can be justified under Articles 10(2) and 11(2) of the ECHR.[132]

---

[124] *R (on the application of Laporte)* v *Chief Constable of Gloucester* [2006] UKHL 55, [2007] 2 AC 105, [2007] 2 WLR 46.

[125] For a review of the law, see Law Commission Working Paper 103.

[126] See *Steel* v *UK* (1999) 28 EHRR 603. The Court also ruled that binding over proceedings must be regarded as 'criminal proceedings' for the purposes of the Convention. Note, however, that breach of the peace in itself is not a crime: *Williamson* v *Chief Constable of West Midlands* [2003] EWCA Civ 337, [2004] 1 WLR 14. See further, p 183, *ante*.

[127] *Binding Over*, Law Commission Report No 222 (1994).

[128] Home Office, *Bind Overs: A Power for the 21st Century* (2003) consultation paper, at para 9.4.

[129] Ibid, at para 7.10.7.   [130] (1864) 17 ICLR 1: the emblem in question was an orange lily.

[131] *R (on the application of Laporte)* v *Chief Constable of Gloucester* [2006] UKHL 55, [2007] 2 AC 105, [2007] 2 WLR 46; *Foulkes* v *Chief Constable for Merseyside* [1998] 3 All ER 705, [1998] 2 FLR 789; *Bibby* v *Chief Constable of Essex* (2000) 164 JP 297.

[132] *R (on the application of Laporte)* v *Chief Constable of Gloucester* [2006] UKHL 55, [2007] 2 AC 105, [2007] 2 WLR 46.

(b) Reasonable suspicion and reasonable belief

Most police powers depend for their rightful exercise on the officer having a particular state of mind at the relevant time. The usual requirement is for a 'reasonable suspicion' of certain facts,[133] and this provides an essential safeguard against the arbitrary use of power. In *Shaaban Bin Hussien* v *Chong Fook Kam*[134] Lord Devlin observed that 'suspicion in its ordinary meaning is a state of conjecture or surmise where proof is lacking: "I suspect but cannot prove"'. In the later case of *Castorina* v *Chief Constable of Surrey*[135] the Court of Appeal stated that an honest belief was not a necessary pre-condition. By contrast, an arrest which is based solely on an honest belief that an offence has been committed may not satisfy the requirements of Article 5 of the ECHR.[136]

Whether or not a reasonable suspicion exists is a matter to be determined objectively by the court. In order to be reasonable a suspicion must be based on evidence, but this need not be evidence that would be acceptable in a court of law. A suspicion may also be reasonable if based on information from an informant or a fellow officer: it need not be based entirely on the officer's own observations.[137] However, in the context of stop and search powers, PACE Code of Practice A makes it clear that a suspicion will not be reasonable if it is based solely on personal factors:[138]

> Reasonable suspicion can never be supported on the basis of personal factors alone without reliable supporting intelligence or information or some specific behaviour by the person concerned. For example, a person's race, age, appearance, or the fact that the person is known to have a previous conviction, cannot be used alone or in combination with each other as the reason for searching that person. Reasonable suspicion cannot be based on generalizations or stereotypical images of certain groups or categories of people as more likely to be involved in criminal activity.

(c) Force

The law allows reasonable force to be used, where necessary, in the exercise of police powers. Section 3 of the Criminal Law Act 1967 provides that a person may use such force as is reasonable in the circumstances, to: (a) prevent crime; or (b) effect or assist in the lawful arrest of an offender, suspected offender, or person unlawfully at large. In addition, section 117 of the Police and Criminal Evidence Act 1984 provides that any power under the Act may be exercised using no more force than is reasonably necessary. Both provisions permit the use of force against property as well as persons. For example, an officer seeking to execute a lawful power of arrest may use

---

[133] For examples of exceptions, see the powers conferred by the Criminal Justice and Public Order Act 1994, s 60 and the Terrorism Act 2000, s 44.

[134] [1970] AC 942 at 948, [1969] 3 All ER 1626 at 1630.   [135] [1988] NLJR 180.

[136] *Fox, Campbell and Hartley* v *UK* (1991) 13 EHRR 157; cf. *Murray* v *UK* (1995) 19 EHRR 193 (mere suspicion sufficient in circumstances where officers could demonstrate an objective basis). For further discussion of Article 5, see p 182, *ante*.

[137] *O'Hara* v *Chief Constable of the Royal Ulster Constabulary* [1997] AC 286, [1997] 1 All ER 129; *O'Hara* v *UK* (2002) 34 EHRR 32.

[138] At para 2.2.

reasonable force to gain entry on to premises, as long as he can demonstrate the necessity of his actions.[139]

(d) Codes of Practice

Section 66 of PACE authorizes the Home Secretary to make Codes of Practice dealing with the different stages of police investigations. Codes dealing with the exercise of stop and search powers (Code A), the execution of search powers (Code B), the treatment and questioning of suspects (Code C), the identification of suspects (Code D), the tape-recording of police interviews (Code E), the visual recording of interviews (Code F), statutory powers of arrest (Code G), and the detention, treatment and questioning of terror suspects (Code H) have all been introduced.[140]

The PACE Codes are important to both the practitioner and the police, and as noted above, if there is a 'significant and substantial' breach of the Codes, evidence obtained as a result of that breach may be excluded from consideration by the courts.[141] A breach of the Codes can also form the basis for disciplinary action against an officer.

2 STOP AND SEARCH POWERS

Stop and search powers are amongst the most controversial of police powers. On the one hand they authorize action which some consider necessary for the prevention and detection of crime. On the other, they provide the potential for misuse and for the harassment of minority groups. Before 1984 there existed a wide range of stop and search powers, which were exercisable on different criteria, in different circumstances and by different people. However, the Royal Commission on Criminal Procedure expressed concern at the potential for these powers to be abused,[142] and following its recommendations general powers of stop and search were included in the Police and Criminal Evidence Act 1984.

Section 1 of PACE provides that any person or vehicle may be detained and searched by a constable if he has reasonable grounds to suspect that he will find stolen or prohibited articles.[143] An offensive weapon constitutes a 'prohibited article' for these purposes, and this term covers any article made or adapted for causing injury to a person, or any article intended to cause injury by the person who is carrying it with him.[144] The other

---

[139] *O'Loughlin* v *Chief Constable of Essex* [1998] 1 WLR 374: on the facts of the case the use of force was not lawful, as the officer had not first made it clear that he wanted to enter to make an arrest.

[140] Code F was issued under the authority of s 60A of PACE. The latest version of Codes A–E came into effect on 1 February 2008. The current Codes F and G came into effect on 1 January 2006, and Code H has been in force since 24 July 2006. See also, p 40, *ante.*

[141] See p 424, *ante.* See also, *R* v *Walsh* (1990) 91 Cr App R 161, [1989] Crim LR 822; *R* v *Aspinall* [1999] 2 Cr App R 115, (1999) 96(7) LSG 35.

[142] Cmnd 8092, 1981, at p 1011.

[143] Section 163 of the Road Traffic Act 1988 provides uniformed constables and traffic officers with a general power to require a person driving a vehicle on a road to stop. It does not in itself authorize the detention or search of the vehicle, though in some circumstances the power to detain may be implied by the courts: see *Lodwick* v *Sanders* [1985] 1 All ER 577, [1985] 1 WLR 382.

[144] Sections 1(7)(a) and 1(9).

articles prohibited by section 1 are articles made, adapted or intended for use in connection with burglary, theft, taking a motor vehicle without authority, obtaining property by deception, or destroying or damaging property.[145] Prohibited fireworks and articles with a blade or point may also be the subject of a stop and search, even if they do not constitute offensive weapons.[146]

The power to stop and search is exercisable in any place to which the public have access,[147] and any stolen or prohibited article found may be seized.[148] There is no specific power to seize any other item discovered, but an officer can make an arrest if he finds anything that he reasonably believes to be evidence of a crime.[149] Care must be taken to ensure that the stop and search powers are not abused, and the requirement for reasonable suspicion is thus an important safeguard. In addition, before carrying out a search the officer must inform the person concerned of his name, the name of the police station to which he is attached, the object of the search, and his grounds for proposing to make it. If he is not in uniform, he must also provide documentary evidence that he is, in fact, a police officer.[150] A further safeguard is the requirement for the officer to make a written record of the search, either at the time or as soon as practicable afterwards.[151] The person searched is entitled to a copy of this record if he requests one within 12 months. Sir Ronnie Flanagan's recent *Review of Policing* recommended using new technology to streamline these recording requirements, and the government has indicated that this recommendation will be adopted.[152]

Not all stop and search powers are so precisely circumscribed. Where a senior officer anticipates violence in a particular locality, he can authorize what amounts to a random power of stop and search for a period not exceeding twenty-four hours.[153] Under such an authorization, a constable may stop and search any person or vehicle for offensive weapons or dangerous instruments. The officer does not need to reasonably suspect the person of being in possession of such an article, and thus for a limited period there is a power to stop and search that is effectively unchallengeable. An even more extensive power may be authorized under section 44 of the Terrorism Act 2000. This power can only be authorized by an officer of at least the rank of assistant chief constable,[154] and only where it is considered expedient for the prevention of acts of terrorism.[155] Once such an authorization is in place, any person or vehicle in the locality may be

---

[145] Sections 1(7)(b) and 1(8), as amended. [146] Sections 1(8A) and 1(8B).

[147] Section 1(1).   [148] Section 1(6).   [149] Powers of arrest are discussed at p 436, *post.*

[150] Section 2.   [151] Section 3.

[152] *The Review of Policing: Final Report* (2008), at para. 5.59. The report also recommended scrapping the form used to record 'stop and account' encounters, and replacing it with digital record-keeping and a requirement to issue a simple receipt: see paras 5.60–62.

[153] Criminal Justice and Public Order Act 1994, s 60. In future, senior officers will also be able to authorize searches where it is reasonably believed that: (a) an incident involving serious violence has taken place, and (b) it is expedient to issue an authorization in order to find a dangerous instrument or offensive weapon used in it – see section 60(1)(aa), as inserted by the Serious Crime Act 2007.

[154] Or, in the case of the Metropolitan Police district and the City of London, an officer of at least the rank of commander.

[155] In *R (on the application of Gillan)* v *Commissioner of Police for the Metropolis* [2006] UKHL 12, [2006] 2 AC 307, [2006] 4 All ER 1041, the House of Lords confirmed that 'expedient' does not mean the same as 'necessary' for these purposes.

searched for articles that could be used in connection with terrorism.[156] The authorization can last for up to twenty-eight days and may be renewed at the end of this period. Section 45(1)(b) expressly states that the power may be exercised 'whether or not the constable has grounds for suspecting the presence of articles of that kind', and doubts have been raised about the compatibility of such powers with Article 5 of the ECHR. However, the House of Lords recently held that stop and search powers will not normally engage Article 5 at all, on the basis that the brief period of detention involved does not amount to a deprivation of liberty.[157]

The exercise of stop and search powers is subject to more detailed guidance in PACE Code of Practice A.[158] This provides that a person searched under section 1 of PACE cannot be required to remove any clothing in public other than an outer coat, jacket or gloves, although a person searched under the terrorism powers may also be required to remove headgear or footwear. The Code also makes it clear that for searches which require a reasonable suspicion, that suspicion cannot be based on personal factors alone unless there is reliable supporting intelligence or information or some specific behaviour by the person concerned. Despite this, however, studies have repeatedly shown that black and Asian people are disproportionately more likely to be stopped and searched than those from other ethnic groups.[159] Moreover, research carried out by one police force showed that a reduction in the use of stop and search had had little effect on levels of crime in the area: the force's detection rate had actually increased during the same period.[160] Throughout the UK the proportion of searches that result in an arrest is consistently low, and Lustgarten has concluded that 'it is hard to see how a suspicion which misfires so often and so consistently can be credibly described as "reasonable"'.[161]

PACE does not affect the capacity of an officer to speak to or question a person in the normal course of his duties, as long as there is no attempt to detain and no element of compulsion.[162] Frequently, routine questioning will provide the reasonable suspicion needed to justify detention for the purposes of a search. However, the converse is equally true: the Act allows reasonable suspicion to be eliminated by questioning, and in these circumstances there is no obligation to search. A written record of the encounter should still be made, however, and police officers and staff are also required to record any incident where a person in a public place is asked to account for himself.[163]

---

[156] Section 45(1)(a).

[157] *R (on the application of Gillan)* v *Commissioner of Police for the Metropolis* [2006] UKHL 12, [2006] 2 AC 307, [2006] 4 All ER 1041.

[158] The latest version of the Code came into force on 1 February 2008.

[159] *Report of the Stephen Lawrence Inquiry*, Cm. 4262-I, 1999 at para. 45.8; Miller, Bland and Quinton, *The Impact of Stops and Searches on Crime and the Community*, Police Research Series Paper No 130 (2000), ch 4; Home Office, *Statistics on Race and the Criminal Justice System*, 2000, ch 3.

[160] Lustgarten, 'The Future of Stop and Search' [2002] Crim LR 603, at p 614.

[161] Ibid, at p 615.

[162] For the general principles, see *Rice* v *Connolly* [1966] 2 QB 414, [1966] 2 All ER 649 (refusal to answer police questions not a wilful obstruction of a constable acting in the execution of duty).

[163] See Code of Practice A, paras 4.7 and 4.12. See also n 152, *supra*.

3 SURVEILLANCE

The police sometimes need to use surreptitious means of investigation, and this may involve the use of technical devices such as eavesdropping equipment. Police telephone tapping has been regulated by statute since 1986,[164] but until 1997 there was no statutory regime covering the use of other forms of surveillance. Covert surveillance interfering with property or wireless telegraphy is now regulated by Part IV of the Police Act 1997. Section 93(1) of the Act provides that an 'authorising officer'[165] may authorize 'the taking of such action as he may specify', if he believes that:

(a) the action is necessary for the purpose of preventing or detecting serious crime;[166] and

(b) the taking of the action is proportionate to what it seeks to achieve.

Authorizations relating to property used mainly as a dwelling, hotel bedroom or office premises must be approved by a Commissioner appointed under section 91 of the Act. Authorizations which are likely to result in the acquisition of legal, journalistic or confidential personal information also require approval.[167]

Other forms of covert surveillance are subject to the provisions of the Regulation of Investigatory Powers Act 2000. Surveillance involving interference with postal or communications systems is governed by Part 1 of the Act. Under section 5, the Secretary of State may issue a warrant for the interception of communications if he believes that it is necessary for national security, for the prevention and detection of crime, or for safeguarding the economic well-being of the UK. A warrant can only be requested by one of the high-ranking officers listed in section 6, and section 17 prevents intercept material from being disclosed or adduced in connection with legal proceedings. The effect of the latter provision is that such surveillance can be used for intelligence purposes but is inadmissible as evidence at any trial. In this respect it can be argued that the Act fails to satisfy the ECHR with regard to both the fair trial requirements in Article 6 and the privacy provisions in Article 8.[168] However, having previously ruled out a change in the law the government has apparently had a rethink, and following the recommendations of the Chilcot Report[169] it is now proposing to allow intercept evidence to be used in criminal trials.[170]

Part II of the 2000 Act regulates the use of covert human intelligence and other forms of surveillance. Intrusive surveillance – that which involves physical intrusion

---

[164] Interception of Communications Act 1985; since repealed and replaced by the more extensive provisions in the Police Act 1997 and the Regulation of Investigatory Powers Act 2000.

[165] A chief constable or one of the other high ranking officials listed in s 93(5).

[166] 'Serious crime' is defined for these purposes by s 93(4).   [167] Section 97.

[168] See Ormerod and McKay, 'Telephone Intercepts and their Admissibility' [2004] Crim LR 15. Section 17 has been interpreted as allowing a limited enquiry where it is alleged that communications within a private system have been intercepted with the consent of the owner: *Attorney-General's Reference (No 5 of 2002)* [2004] UKHL 20, [2005] 1 AC 167, [2004] 4 All ER 901.

[169] *Privy Council Review of Intercept as Evidence: Report to the Prime Minister and the Home Secretary* (Cm 7324, 2008).

[170] Gordon Brown MP (Prime Minister), 471 HC Official Report (6th series), col 959, 6 February 2008.

on to residential premises or into a private vehicle – can only be authorized by the Secretary of State or a 'senior authorising officer'. The person making the authorization must be satisfied that such intrusion is necessary for national security, for the prevention and detection of crime, or for safeguarding the economic well-being of the UK.[171] Non-intrusive surveillance can be authorized on a much wider range of grounds, and authorization can be granted can by a police superintendent or by certain other senior officials designated by the Secretary of State.[172] Rules for the conduct of covert operations involving human intelligence sources are set out in section 29 of the Act.

4 ARREST

Arrest is a matter of fact rather than a legal concept, though it does have legal consequences. The essence of arrest is the deprivation of liberty, as explained by Lord Diplock in *Holgate-Mohammed* v *Duke*:[173]

> [A]rrest is a continuing act: it starts with the arrester taking a person into his custody (by action or words restraining him from moving elsewhere beyond the arrester's control) and it continues until the person so restrained is either released from custody, or...is remanded in custody by the magistrate's judicial act.

In that case an officer arrested a person on reasonable suspicion of burglary because he wanted to continue questioning her at the police station. As the power to arrest existed, its use to facilitate further questioning was held to be a legitimate use of police discretion: although the suspect could not simply be 'detained' for the purpose of questioning, there was nothing to prevent the officer from exercising a lawful power of arrest in order to achieve this objective.[174]

In order for an arrest to be lawful, the arresting officer must be able to point to a specific power of arrest, and he must comply with any necessary procedural requirements.

(a) Powers of arrest

An arrest may be lawfully made with or without a warrant. In respect of the former, the Magistrates' Courts Act 1980 confers a power on magistrates to issue a warrant of arrest.[175] In relation to arrest without warrant, the Police and Criminal Evidence Act 1984 made radical changes. Section 26 repealed all statutory powers authorizing arrest without a warrant, with the exception of 21 specific powers which were expressly

---

[171] Sections 26(3) and 32.
[172] Sections 26(2) and 28; Regulation of Investigatory Powers (Directed Surveillance and Covert Human Intelligence Sources) Order 2003, SI 2003/3171.
[173] [1984] AC 437, [1984] 1 All ER 1054.
[174] But see the discussion of the amended section 24 of PACE at p 437, *post*.
[175] Section 1.

preserved by schedule 2.[176] The common law power to arrest for breach of the peace was also preserved.[177]

Before 2006, section 24 of PACE conferred general powers of arrest in respect of serious or 'arrestable' offences. These powers applied in relation to past, present and future offences, and in some situations were available to both police officers and members of the public. By contrast, an arrest without a warrant for a 'non-arrestable' offence could only be made by a police officer, and only where one or more of the 'general arrest conditions' set out in section 25 of the Act were satisfied.

A constable's powers of arrest under the new regime. In 2006, amendments made by the Serious Organised Crime and Police Act 2005 were implemented. The principal effect of these amendments is to remove the idea of a distinction between arrestable and non-arrestable offences and to make all arrests subject to a test of necessity. The circumstances in which a citizen's arrest can be made have also been narrowed.

In many respects, the powers conferred on constables by the amended section 24 are unchanged. Thus, a constable has the power to arrest without a warrant:

(a) any person who has already committed an offence, or who is suspected on reasonable grounds of having done so;

(b) any person who is (or is reasonably suspected to be) in the act of committing an offence; or

(c) any person who is (or is reasonably suspected to be) about to commit an offence.

A constable can also make an arrest if he reasonably suspects that an offence has been committed and that a particular individual was responsible. As under the previous system, this means that it is possible for an officer to make a lawful arrest in circumstances where it later transpires that no crime has occurred.

Whereas the original section 24 applied only to 'arrestable' offences, the power set out in the amended provision can be exercised in respect of *any* offence. It is, however, now subject to a test of necessity: in order for an arrest without a warrant to be made, the constable must have reasonable grounds for believing that the arrest is necessary for one of the reasons listed in section 24(5). Most of these reasons replicate the general arrest conditions previously found in section 25. Thus, an arrest may be necessary:

(a) to enable the name or address of the person in question to be ascertained (in cases where the constable does not know and cannot readily ascertain these details, or has reasonable grounds for doubting whether details provided by the person are genuine);

---

[176] A number of these powers have been repealed subsequently, and new statutory arrest powers have also been created: section 41 of the Terrorism Act 2000 for example, empowers a constable to arrest a person 'whom he reasonably suspects to be a terrorist'.

[177] This was the effect of PACE, s 25(6).

(b) to prevent the person in question from causing injury to himself or another, suffering physical injury, causing loss or damage to property, committing an offence against public decency; or causing an unlawful obstruction of the highway; or

(c) to protect a child or other vulnerable person from the person in question.

The other lawful reasons for making an arrest under section 24 had no equivalent under the old system:

(d) to allow the prompt and effective investigation of the offence or the person's conduct; or

(e) to prevent the prosecution of an offence from being hindered by the person's disappearance.

It will be apparent that reason (d) in particular is potentially very wide, and in this respect the new section 24 appears to extend the arrest powers available to police officers. On the other hand, a constable's scope for exercising these powers is now limited by the requirement of necessity, and it could be argued that the overall effect of this is to restrict the discretion outlined in *Holgate-Mohammed* v *Duke*.[178]

> 'Necessary' means that there is no alternative to arrest; that enabling or preventing, as the case may be, one or more of the arrest conditions set out in s 24(5), cannot be achieved by any other means short of arrest. Thus the extremely broad common law discretion, whether or not to arrest, appears to have been replaced by a much narrower statutory discretion, limited by the necessity requirement and the arrest conditions...[179]

Guidance as to the circumstances in which an arrest might be considered necessary is set out in Code of Practice G, but it remains to be seen how the new criteria will be interpreted by the courts.

Citizens' arrests. The arrest powers of the private citizen have always been more limited than those available to police officers, since they only apply where it is reasonably believed that a person has committed or is in the act of committing an offence. Thus, a citizen has no power to arrest a person who is *about* to commit an offence, and he will also be acting unlawfully if he makes an arrest in the *mistaken* belief that an offence has already been committed. In *R* v *Self*[180] for example, the defendant was charged with assault to escape lawful arrest. The arrest had been made by a citizen assisting a store detective, but the defendant was able to show that he had not in fact stolen the goods in question. Since no offence had been committed by anyone, the arrest was held to be unlawful and the defendant was not guilty of the assault.

---

[178] See p 436, *ante*.

[179] Austin, 'The New Powers of Arrest: Plus CA Change: More of the Same or Major Change?' [2007] Crim LR 459 at p 464.

[180] [1992] 3 All ER 476, [1992] 1 WLR 657. See also: *Walters* v *WH Smith & Son Ltd* [1914] 1 KB 595, [1911–13] All ER Rep 170.

The recent amendments to PACE mean that the scope for making a citizen's arrest has been further restricted. The effect of the new section 24A is that citizens only have a power of arrest in respect of indictable offences, and this power may only be exercised where it is not reasonably practicable for a constable to make the arrest instead. In addition, the person making the arrest must have reasonable grounds for believing that his actions are necessary to prevent injury, to prevent loss of or damage to property, or to prevent the suspect from making off before a constable can assume responsibility for him.

Even before these reforms it was unwise for a citizen to attempt an arrest unless he was absolutely sure of his facts. Now, in addition to being sure that an offence has been (or is being) committed, he also needs to know whether the offence in question is indictable and he must make an assessment as to whether it would be practicable for a police officer to make the arrest instead. As one critic has suggested, these changes 'will deter all but the most foolhardy citizens from exercising the power, and impose upon those citizens who need to exercise it, unacceptable risks of consequent liability'.[181]

(b) Mechanics of arrest

Even where a power of arrest exists, an arrest will only be lawful if the person arrested is told (a) that he is under arrest,[182] and (b) on what grounds he has been arrested. This information must be given at the time of the arrest or as soon as practicable afterwards.[183] Thus if a suspect manages to escape before a constable is able to explain the grounds for his arrest, the arrest will nevertheless be lawful. Once the suspect is re-captured and the situation is under control, any further delay in explaining the grounds will render the arrest invalid, but only from that moment onwards.[184] Similarly, where an arrest is initially unlawful because of a failure to comply with these requirements, it will become lawful subsequently once the reasons for the arrest are given. In *Lewis and another* v *Chief Constable of the South Wales Constabulary*[185] the Court of Appeal identified arrest as a continuing act: the claimants' action for damages failed because they had only been unlawfully detained for a short period.

The statement of reasons does not have to specify a particular crime, or give a technical definition of the offence charged. What is needed is sufficient information to enable the arrested person to know why his liberty is being interfered with. In *Abbassy* v *Commissioner of Police*[186] the plaintiff was told that he was being arrested for 'unlawful possession' of a vehicle. He had been asked four times about ownership of the vehicle, but had responded in a rude and abusive fashion. Police inquiries later showed that he was in fact authorized to drive the vehicle. The claimant was charged with wilfully obstructing a constable in the execution of his duty, contrary to what is now section 89 of the Police Act 1996. The charges were later dropped and the claimant sought damages for unlawful arrest and false imprisonment. However, the court ruled that it had been

---

[181] Austin (2007), *supra* n 179, at p 438.   [182] Section 28(1).   [183] Section 28(3).
[184] *DPP* v *Hawkins* [1988] 3 All ER 673, [1988] 1 WLR 1166.   [185] [1991] 1 All ER 206.
[186] [1990] 1 All ER 193, [1990] 1 WLR 385. The decision confirms that the approach outlined in the pre-PACE case of *Christie* v *Leachinsky* [1947] AC 573, [1947] 1 All ER 567 is still correct.

made clear to him that the arrest was for unlawful possession of the vehicle. The fact that the officer had not specifically mentioned the vehicle in his statement of reasons was irrelevant. The judge had therefore misdirected the jury on a matter of law, and a re-trial was ordered. The claimant in *Taylor* v *Chief Constable of Thames Valley Police*[187] was a ten year old child who was arrested 'on suspicion of violent disorder': he had been throwing stones whilst participating in a demonstration. The child brought an action for false imprisonment and trespass to the person, alleging that he had not been given sufficient information for the arrest to be lawful. The Court of Appeal held that in order for an arrest to comply with section 28 of PACE and Article 5(2) of the ECHR,[188] a person had to be informed of the basis for the arrest in non-technical language that he could understand. The information given to the claimant in this case had been sufficient for these purposes, and the trial judge had been wrong to direct that a reference to throwing stones was needed.

An arrest also has certain physical requirements: it comprises compulsion and submission to that compulsion. There must either be a touching symbolic of seizure of the body, or alternatively, words of compulsion to which there is submission.[189]

(c) The consequences of arrest

By sections 30 and 30A, an arrested person must be taken to a police station or released on bail as soon as practicable after the arrest. However, these steps may be delayed if it is necessary to the investigation for the arrestee to be present elsewhere.[190] By section 32, an arrested person may be searched if the constable has reasonable grounds to believe that (a) he may present a danger to himself or others, (b) he may have concealed on him an article that may assist him in escaping from lawful custody, or (c) he may have concealed on him an article which is evidence relating to an offence.

If the offence for which the arrest was made is indictable, section 32(2)(b) also confers the power to enter and search the premises where the suspect was arrested, or where he was immediately prior to his arrest. Section 18 confers a similar power in respect of premises occupied or controlled by the arrested person. However, under the former provision the officer can only search for evidence of the offence for which the arrest was made, whereas under section 18 the officer may also search for evidence of 'connected' or 'similar' offences. The exercise of both powers is dependent on a lawful arrest having been made.

5 DETENTION

The custody officer performs a key role in relation to the detention, treatment and questioning of suspects. Each designated police station must have at least one custody

---

[187] [2004] EWCA Civ 858, [2004] 1 WLR 3155, [2004] 3 All ER 503.
[188] See p 182, *ante* for a discussion of Article 5(2).
[189] *Alderson* v *Booth* [1969] 2 QB 216, [1969] 2 All ER 271.
[190] Section 30(10); (10A). Section 30A was inserted by the Criminal Justice Act 2003, and it confers a discretion on constables to release an arrested person on what is informally known as 'street bail' – i.e. bail granted elsewhere than at a police station.

officer,[191] and it is to a 'designated station' that an arrested person should normally be taken. Until now, section 36 of PACE has required the person appointed to this role to be a police officer with at least the rank of sergeant. However, amendments made by the Serious Organised Crime and Police Act 2005 pave the way for civilian 'staff custody officers' to be appointed.[192] The main functions of a custody officer are set out in sections 36, 38, 39 and 40 of PACE. They broadly encompass a duty to ensure that the treatment of all detained persons is in accordance with the requirements of the Act, and that the record-keeping required by the Act actually occurs. If these requirements are not complied with, the detention of the suspect is likely to become unlawful. The custody officer also has an important role in ensuring compliance with PACE Code of Practice C, which provides more detailed guidance for the detention, treatment and questioning of those in police custody.

In order to protect the interests of the suspect, PACE envisages a separation of functions between the custody officer and those investigating the offence. However, whether this concept is sustainable in practice is a moot point. Quite apart from the loyalties and pressures that membership of the same force might create, a custody officer may sometimes find it difficult to cure a natural desire to assist in an investigation himself.[193]

In determining the legality of a suspect's detention and treatment in custody, several points must be considered:

(a) A person who attends a police station voluntarily is free to leave at any time, unless and until he is arrested.[194]

(b) A custody record must be kept, detailing all actions taken in respect of the arrested person. The custody officer is responsible for the accuracy and completeness of this record, and the timing of each entry must be noted. A solicitor or appropriate adult representing the detainee must be permitted to consult the record at any time.[195]

(c) If an investigating officer concludes that there is sufficient evidence to provide a realistic prospect of conviction, he must refer the case to the custody officer. It is for the custody officer to determine whether the suspect should be charged or released, and whether or not police bail should be granted.[196]

(d) Within six hours of a suspect's detention being authorized, there must be a review to determine whether that detention continues to be necessary. Further reviews should be conducted at intervals of nine hours or less for as long as the detainee remains in police custody.[197]

(e) There are strict limits on how long an arrested person can be detained before being either charged or released. The basic rule is that detention shall not last

---

[191] *Vince* v *Chief Constable of the Dorset Police* [1993] 2 All ER 321, [1993] 1 WLR 415.

[192] Sections 120 and 121. See further, p 420, *ante*.

[193] See e.g. *R* v *Absolam* (1989) 88 Cr App Rep 332.   [194] PACE, s 29.

[195] Code C, para 2. There are references throughout PACE to the various matters that must be recorded.

[196] PACE, s 37; Code C, paras 16.1–16.2.

[197] PACE, s 40; Code C, para 15. This review should be carried out by the custody officer if the arrestee has been charged; otherwise, the review officer must be an officer of at least the rank of inspector who has not been directly involved in the investigation.

longer than 24 hours from the time of arrest, or time of arrival at the police station, whichever is earlier.[198] This 24-hour period may be extended by a further 12 hours (i.e. 36 hours in total) by an officer of at least the rank of superintendent.[199] The officer must have reasonable grounds to believe that: (a) detention is necessary to secure or preserve evidence relating to the offence for which the arrest was made, or to obtain such evidence by questioning; (b) that the offence is an indictable offence; and (c) that the offence is being investigated diligently and expeditiously.

If the police wish to detain a person beyond 36 hours, a warrant of further detention must be obtained from a magistrates' court. The period of further detention granted by such a warrant cannot exceed 36 hours, though at the end of this period the police can apply to extend the warrant for a further 36 hours.[200] Four days (or 96 hours) is therefore the maximum permitted period of detention without charge.[201] The grounds for issuing or extending a warrant of further detention are the same as those for authorizing an initial extension of detention by a senior officer.

(f) Once a person has been charged with an offence, the custody officer must order his release unless one of the conditions in section 38 applies. These conditions are that:

(i)   the person's name or address cannot be ascertained, or is reasonably believed to be false;

(ii) it is reasonably believed that the person will fail to appear in court to answer bail;

(iii) in the case of a person arrested for an imprisonable offence, it is reasonably believed that detention is necessary to prevent him from committing a further offence;

(iv) detention is necessary to enable a urine or non-intimate sample to be taken for the purposes of a drugs test;

(v)   it is reasonably believed that detention is necessary for the protection of, or to prevent physical injury to, any other person or property;

(vi) detention is necessary to prevent the arrestee from interfering with the administration of justice or with police investigations of that or other offences; or

(vii) detention is necessary for his own protection.

6 TREATMENT OF SUSPECTS

The Police and Criminal Evidence Act 1984 includes provisions designed to give proper protection to a suspect in the police station. The objective is to ensure not only that suspects are treated in accordance with minimum standards, but also that admissions and other evidence are obtained in such a way that they can safely be relied upon in court.

---

[198] PACE, s 41.   [199] Ibid, s 42(1).   [200] PACE, s 43.
[201] This period is longer for those detained under the Terrorism Act 2000: see Schedule 8 of that Act.

The courts also regard the right of silence as important, and amongst other things, Code of Practice C seeks to prevent improperly induced self-incrimination.

(a) Search

Section 54 of PACE requires the custody officer to ascertain everything that a detained person has with him when he is brought to the police station. He may cause the person to be searched for this purpose (although such a search is not obligatory), and a search may also be carried out to ascertain whether the detainee is in possession of an item that could be seized under section 54(4).[202] Articles covered by this provision are those which the custody officer believes might be used to: (a) cause physical injury; (b) damage property; (c) interfere with evidence; or (d) assist an escape. The same provision allows the custody officer to seize items in the detainee's possession if he has reasonable grounds for believing them to be evidence of an offence.[203] If necessary, a detained person can also be searched or examined for the purposes of identification.[204] However, the extent of any search must be strictly limited to what is necessary in the circumstances. A detainee should not be strip searched, for example, unless the officer reasonably believes that he might have concealed an article which he would not be allowed to keep.[205]

Intimate searches – those which involve the physical examination of body orifices other than the mouth[206] – are governed by different rules. An intimate search can only be authorized by an officer of at least the rank of inspector, and only where there are reasonable grounds to believe that the detainee may have concealed a Class A drug or an item which he might use to injure himself or others.[207] Intimate searches should normally be carried out by a registered nurse or medical practitioner. Any search conducted by a police officer or civilian detention officer, whether intimate or otherwise, must be performed by an officer of the same gender as the detainee.[208]

(b) Information about rights

The arrested person must be informed of the right to have someone notified of his arrest. Section 56 provides that a person held in custody is entitled, at his request, to have a friend, relative or other person notified of his whereabouts as soon as practicable. If the person named by the detainee is unobtainable he may nominate two others, and the police may extend the right further if they wish. The right is an important one, to be denied only in limited circumstances where to grant it would interfere with the investigation. Even if grounds for denying contact with an individual exist, they are

---

[202] Section 54(6A.)

[203] Cf. the pre-PACE position as stated in *Lindley v Rutter* [1981] QB 128, [1980] 3 WLR 660.

[204] PACE, s54A. Such a search can only be authorized by an officer of at least the rank of inspector.

[205] Code C, Annex A, para B.10.

[206] PACE, s 65(1).This definition was amended to make it easier for the police to deal with suspects who concealed drugs in their mouths. In *R v Hughes* [1994] 1 WLR 876 the holding of a suspect's nose and jaw, causing the extrusion of articles in the mouth, was held to be a search, but not an intimate search.

[207] Ibid, s 55.   [208] Ibid, ss 54(9) and 55(7).

unlikely to apply to making contact with a solicitor.[209] The arrested person also has the right to consult the Codes of Practice.[210]

(c) The taking of fingerprints and other samples

Until recently a person who had not been charged with an offence could only be finger-printed in limited circumstances, but the position now is that any person who has been arrested or charged in respect of a recordable offence may have his fingerprints taken, either by conventional or electronic means.[211]

An 'intimate sample' is defined by section 65 of PACE to mean: (a) a sample of blood, semen or any other tissue fluid, urine, or pubic hair; (b) a dental impression; or (c) a swab taken from a person's genitals or from a body orifice other than the mouth. Before an intimate sample can be taken, an officer must have both the written consent of the detainee and the authorization of a senior officer.[212] Such authorization can only be granted where the officer has reasonable grounds for (a) suspecting the detainee of involvement in a recordable offence, and (b) believing that the sample will tend to prove or disprove his involvement. An intimate sample may also be taken from a person who is not in police custody, but who has provided at least two non-intimate samples during the course of an investigation which have proved insufficient for the purpose of analysis.[213] Where a detainee refuses, without good cause, to consent to the taking of an intimate sample, adverse inferences may be drawn from this in any subsequent criminal proceedings.[214] By creating a legal framework for such samples to be taken, PACE paved the way for the introduction of a national DNA database in 1995. By April 2006 this database held over 4 million DNA profiles.[215]

Hair samples (other than pubic hair), samples taken from the nails, swabs taken from body parts not covered by section 65, saliva, and skin impressions, constitute 'non-intimate samples' for the purposes of PACE. Section 63 provides that where a person has been arrested for a recordable offence, a non-intimate sample may be taken without his consent and without the need for authorization from a senior officer. There is also a power to take a non-intimate sample from a person held in police custody on the authority of a court, although in this case the authorization of a senior officer is required.

(d) Conditions of detention

Minimum standards for the conditions of police detention are set out in parts 8 and 9 of Code of Practice C. They provide that cells should be adequately heated, cleaned

---

[209] *R* v *Samuel* [1988] QB 615, [1988] 2 All ER 135.

[210] Code C, para 3.1; *DPP* v *Skinner* [1990] RTR 254.

[211] PACE, s 61, as amended. More recent amendments will, once implemented, allow fingerprints to be taken at a place *away* from a police station where an officer has doubts about the identity of a suspect: Serious Organised Crime and Police Act 2005, s 117.

[212] PACE, s 62(1).   [213] Ibid, s 62(1A).   [214] Ibid, s 62(10).

[215] *The National DNA Database Annual Report 2005–2006*, at p 28. The human rights issues arising from the retention of DNA samples were considered in *R (on the application of S)* v *Chief Constable of South Yorkshire; R (on the application of Marper)* v *Chief Constable of South Yorkshire* [2004] UKHL 39, [2004] 1 WLR 2196, [2004] 4 All ER 139. See also Roberts and Taylor, 'Privacy and the DNA Database' [2005] EHRLR 373.

and ventilated, that clean bedding should be supplied, and that access to toilet and washing facilities should be granted. They also stipulate that a replacement must be supplied for any item of clothing taken away for investigation, and that adequate meals must be provided. Brief outdoor exercise should be permitted where practicable, and suspects should be visited at least once an hour (or once every half an hour if a suspect is intoxicated). The custody officer must call for medical treatment if a suspect appears to be suffering from an illness, injury or mental disorder, or is otherwise in need of clinical attention.

A serious failure to maintain adequate standards could amount to a breach of Article 3 of the ECHR, which prohibits torture and inhuman or degrading treatment. In an extreme case such a failure could also constitute a breach of Article 10 of the Bill of Rights, which prohibits 'cruel and unusual punishments'.

(e) Vulnerable suspects

Special rules apply to vulnerable persons. If the custody officer cannot establish effective communication with a detainee who appears to be deaf, or if there are doubts about the detainee's ability to hear, speak, or understand English, the officer must call for the assistance of an interpreter.[216]

If the person arrested is a juvenile, the 'appropriate adult' must be told of the arrest as soon as possible, and he must be asked to come to the police station.[217] Where the appropriate adult is not the person normally responsible for the juvenile's welfare, the latter party must also be informed of the situation.[218] Similar rules apply to those who are mentally disordered or otherwise mentally vulnerable.

7 ACCESS TO LEGAL ADVICE

In *R v Samuel*[219] the right of access to legal advice was described as 'fundamental'. The key provision is section 58 of PACE, which states that a person who is in police detention 'shall be entitled, if he so requests, to consult a solicitor privately at any time'. Access to a solicitor can only be delayed in respect of a person arrested for an indictable offence, and such a delay can only be authorized by an officer of at least the rank of superintendent.[220] Before authorizing a delay, an officer must reasonably believe that the exercise of the right will do one of the following: (a) lead to interference with or harm to evidence connected with an indictable offence; (b) lead to interference with or physical injury to other persons; (c) lead to the alerting of other persons suspected of having committed such an offence; (d) hinder the recovery of any property obtained as a result of such an offence; or (e) hinder the recovery of the value of any property obtained by criminal conduct.[221] In the case of a person arrested under the terrorism provisions, the scope for restricting access to legal advice is greater.

---

[216] Code C, para 13.10. [217] Code C, para 3.15. For the meaning of 'appropriate adult', see para 1.7.
[218] Code C, para 3.13. [219] [1988] QB 615, [1988] 2 All ER 135. [220] PACE, s 58(6).
[221] Ibid, ss 58(8); (8A).

These powers of delay have been construed very narrowly by the courts. In *R* v *Samuel*[222] the accused was denied access to a solicitor because the police feared that the solicitor might unwittingly alert other suspects. The court held that the police had failed to demonstrate a reasonable belief that the solicitor in question might jeopardize their investigation: even if he had presented such a risk, the appropriate response would have been to ask the suspect to nominate an alternative, or to call the duty solicitor instead. The court also made it clear that legal advice cannot be delayed on the grounds that a solicitor might advise silence or make the investigation harder.[223]

More detailed rules are set out in part 6 of Code of Practice C. This states that a suspect under arrest at a police station must be informed clearly of his right to consult privately with a solicitor, free of charge, at any time during his period in custody. Posters with this information must be displayed prominently in the charging area of each police station, and at certain stages in the process the suspect must be reminded of the right. There is no obligation on the police to request a solicitor on their own initiative, though if a solicitor attends at the request of the suspect's family, the suspect has the right to see him. The police must not take any action to discourage the exercise of the right, and they must not misrepresent the position.[224]

Once it has been requested, the police must generally wait until legal advice has been tendered before proceeding with an interview. The advice may be given over the telephone or in person, and may come either from a solicitor or from an 'accredited or probationary representative'.[225] Such a representative may be refused access if an officer of at least the rank of inspector considers that his presence would hinder the investigation:[226] the officer may take into account whether the representative's identity has been properly established, and whether he has a criminal record or is otherwise an unsuitable character. Restricting the presence of a solicitor is a far more serious step, but a solicitor may be asked to leave an interview if his conduct is preventing the police from being able to properly put questions to the suspect.[227]

The impact of the right under section 58 has been much debated. It seems likely that the mere presence of a lawyer at the police station will reduce the incidence of procedural irregularities, but research suggests that the quality of legal advice received by those in custody is variable.[228] Moreover, whilst the proportion of detainees obtaining legal advice has undoubtedly increased since PACE was introduced, the figure is still quite low. Research by Bucke and Brown found that legal advice was requested by around 40% of detainees in 1997,[229] with most of the other 60% taking the view that they simply did not need a lawyer.[230] The precise reasons for this low uptake are unclear but it seems that a variety of ploys, whether inadvertent or intentional, can dissuade

---

[222] [1988] QB 615, [1988] 2 All ER 135.   [223] Ibid. See also *R* v *Alladice* (1988) 87 Cr App R 380.
[224] See *R* v *Beycan* [1990] Crim LR 185.   [225] See Code C, para 6.12.
[226] Ibid, para 6.12A.   [227] Code C, paras 6.9–6.11.
[228] McConville and Bridges, *Custodial Advice and the Right to Silence* (1993) RCCJ Research Study No 16. See also the Legal Services Commission's Evaluation of the Public Defender Service, which was conducted by Bridges and Sherr: http://www.legalservices.gov.uk/criminal/pds/evaluation.asp.
[229] *In Police Custody: Police Powers and Suspects' Rights under the Revised PACE Codes of Practice* (1997) HORS 174, at p 19.
[230] Ibid, at p 22.

suspects from taking advantage of their rights. For example, many of the detainees in Bucke and Browne's study said that they would wait until later before deciding whether they needed a lawyer: the authors suggest that custody officers may have encouraged this by emphasizing that suspects could change their minds about seeking legal advice at any time.[231] Similarly, Phillips and Brown found that some of the suspects in their study had declined legal advice after being told that they probably would not be charged.[232] The effectiveness of the right to legal advice also depends on the availability of suitably qualified legal advisers, and the duty solicitor scheme funded by the Legal Services Commission has an important role here.[233]

The courts generally take any denial of the right to legal advice very seriously, and a confession made whilst the police are in breach of their obligations is likely to be excluded from evidence under section 78 of PACE.[234] The importance of the right is also recognized by Article 6 of the ECHR.[235]

8 INTERVIEWS

One of the most serious problems identified in recent years is the possibility that confessions made by suspects may not always be reliable. The 1984 Act and Code of Practice C provide a detailed framework for the conduct and recording of interviews, the importance of which was explained in *R v Canale:*[236]

> The object is two-fold: not merely to ensure that the suspect's remarks are accurately recorded and that he has an opportunity when he goes through the contemporaneous record afterwards of checking each answer and initialling each answer, but likewise it is a protection for the police, to ensure, so far as possible, that it cannot be suggested that they induced the suspect to confess by improper approaches or improper promises. If the contemporaneous note is not made then each of those two laudable objects is apt to be stultified.

Initially, there was a danger that the police might seek to circumvent the rules governing interviews by questioning suspects before they were brought to the police station. Amendments to Code C mean that the term 'interview' now covers any questioning of a person regarding his involvement or suspected involvement in a criminal offence or offences.[237] It does not, however, cover routine questioning in the ordinary course of an officer's duties.[238]

---

[231] Ibid.

[232] *Entry into the Criminal Justice System: A Survey of Police Arrests and their Outcomes* (1998) HORS 185, at p 159.

[233] See p 409, *ante.*   [234] See p 424, *ante.*   [235] See p 185, *ante.*

[236] [1990] 2 All ER 187 at 190, per Lord Lane CJ.

[237] For an interpretation of this, see *R v Cox* (1993) 96 Cr App R 464.

[238] Distinguishing between interviews and other forms of questioning is not always easy in practice: see *R v Absolam* (1989) 88 Cr App R 332; *R v Gill (Sewa Singh)* [2003] EWCA Crim 2256, [2004] 1 WLR 469, [2003] 4 All ER 681.

(a) The right of silence

The notion of the right of silence is closely linked to the idea of freedom from self-incrimination. A suspect has the right not to be required to self-incriminate, which means that he cannot generally be compelled to answer questions put to him by a police officer[239] or to testify at any subsequent trial. Before 1994, a jury could not be invited to draw any adverse inference from the fact that a defendant had elected to remain silent during police questioning. This has now changed, however, following the enactment of the Criminal Justice and Public Order Act 1994. If a person who is being questioned under caution fails to mention a fact later relied on in his defence, section 34 of this Act provides that a court or jury may draw such inferences from this failure as appear proper. Similar inferences may be drawn from a failure to account for certain matters during questioning,[240] or from the failure of a defendant to testify in his own defence at trial.[241]

Though the right to silence is not expressly mentioned in the European Convention on Human Rights, the watering down of this right does have implications for Article 6 and the right to a fair trial. In *Murray* v *UK* the Court held that the right to silence was not essential to a fair trial: indeed, there was no breach of Article 6 on the facts of the case because the weight of evidence against the accused meant that the drawing of inferences was not unfair.[242] On the other hand, a judge must ensure that appropriate weight is given to any explanation offered by the defendant, and Article 6 would clearly be breached if a defendant was convicted solely on the basis of his silence.[243] Where a suspect has remained silent on the basis of legal advice the effect of this advice must be taken into account, but it will not necessarily preclude the court from drawing adverse inferences. Conversely, the risk of inferences being drawn from silence means that any delay in granting access to lawyer will be regarded as a particularly serious matter.[244] Indeed, section 34(2A) of the 1994 Act provides that if a suspect is questioned before he has had the opportunity to consult a lawyer, no adverse inferences may be drawn from any failure to answer police questions.

(b) Cautions

A caution must be administered before a suspect is questioned with a view to obtaining evidence which may be given in court. A caution must also be administered on arrest. The standard wording of this caution was modified in 1994 to reflect changes in the right to silence. It now states:[245]

> You do not have to say anything. But it may harm your defence if you do not mention when questioned something which you later rely on in court. Anything you do say may be given in evidence.

---

[239] There are some limited exceptions to this rule. Section 172 of the Road Traffic Act 1988, for example, imposes a duty to give information about the driver of a vehicle in certain circumstances: see *Brown* v *Stott* [2003] 1 AC 681, [2001] 2 All ER 97.

[240] Sections 36 (failure to account for objects, substances or marks) and 37 (failure to account for presence at a particular place).

[241] Section 35.   [242] (1996) 22 EHRR 29.

[243] *Condron* v *UK* (2001) 31 EHRR 1; *Beckles* v *UK* (2003) 36 EHRR 13.

[244] Ibid; *Murray* v *UK* (1996) 22 EHRR 29.   [245] Code C, para 10.5.

(c) The conduct of interviews

Interviews must take place at a police station, unless delay would lead to: (a) interference with or harm to evidence connected with an offence; (b) interference with or harm to other people; (c) serious loss of, or damage to, property; (d) the alerting of other persons suspected of committing an offence; or (e) hindrance to the recovery of property obtained in consequence of the commission of an offence.[246]

Code C requires that the suspect should be reminded of his right to free legal advice before any interview is conducted. It also contains specific requirements about breaks from questioning, maximum periods of questioning, and the provision of proper food and refreshments as appropriate. Perhaps more importantly, section 76 of PACE provides that a confession obtained by oppression or in circumstances likely to lead to unreliability must be excluded from evidence at any trial.[247]

(d) Records of interviews

Code C requires the police to keep an accurate record of all interviews with suspects, including details of the time, date, location, breaks, and the names of all persons present.[248] Any interview conducted at a police station with a person suspected of an indictable offence must now be tape-recorded in accordance with Code of Practice E.[249] The recording must be carried out openly and two copies must be made. The master copy must be sealed in the suspect's presence,[250] and if the suspect is to be charged or prosecuted, he must be supplied with his own copy as soon as practicable after the conclusion of the interview. Where a suspect objects to being tape-recorded his objections must be recorded on the tape, but the interviewer may then turn off the tape and record the interview in writing.[251]

Where an interview is recorded in writing, the record must be made contemporaneously with the interview or as soon as possible afterwards.[252] Unless it is impracticable, the suspect should be shown the record for the purposes of verification, and he should be given the opportunity to sign it as correct.[253] If he declines to do so, this must itself be recorded, along with any unsolicited comments made.[254]

The visual recording of interviews is a more recent innovation, which was given a statutory basis in 2001.[255] Visual recording is not yet mandatory,[256] but where it is carried out it must comply with Code of Practice F.

(e) Vulnerable suspects

There is a recognition that certain groups require additional safeguards, and specific rules exist for the protection of juveniles and those who are mentally disordered or

---

[246] Code C, para 11.1.   [247] See p 392, *ante*.   [248] Code C, para 11.7.

[249] A separate Code of Practice governs the recording of interviews with persons detained under the terrorism provisions.

[250] Code E, para 2.2.   [251] Ibid, para 4.8.   [252] Code C, para 11.8.

[253] Ibid, para 11.11.   [254] Ibid, paras 11.13–11.14.

[255] PACE, s 60A, as amended by the Criminal Justice and Police Act 2001.

[256] A pilot study was conducted between 2002 and 2003, which made visual recording compulsory in certain police areas: Police and Criminal Evidence Act 1984 (Visual Recording of Interviews) (Certain Police Areas) Order 2002, SI 2002/1266.

otherwise mentally vulnerable. Such persons should not be interviewed or asked to sign an interview record in the absence of an appropriate adult[257] unless the criteria governing urgent interviews are satisfied. Specifically, the police must wait for an appropriate adult unless an officer of at least the rank of superintendent considers that a delay would do one of the following: (a) lead to interference with or harm to evidence connected with an offence; (b) lead to interference with or physical harm to persons or property; (c) lead to the alerting of other persons suspected of having committed an offence; or (d) hinder the recovery of any property obtained as a result of an offence.[258] The officer must also be satisfied that the person's physical or mental state will not be significantly harmed by the interview.[259]

Those suffering temporary disability due to drink, drugs or illness should not normally be interviewed until they are fit, though the courts are generally willing to leave this judgment to the police.[260]

9 IDENTIFICATION

Following a series of wrongful convictions, the Devlin Committee was established to investigate how the law dealt with identification evidence. The Committee recommended[261] that in all but the most exceptional cases, juries should be directed not to convict on the basis of eye-witness testimony unless it was supported by substantial other evidence. No legislation followed, but the Court of Appeal in *R v Turnbull* laid down certain guidelines.[262] The guidelines suggest that identification evidence can be split into good and poor quality identification. If, for example, the identification was made in good conditions of light and weather, with ample opportunity to observe, the matter can safely be left to the jury. On the other hand, if the identification is of poor quality, the case should be withdrawn from the jury unless it is supported and confirmed by other evidence. In all cases that depend wholly or substantially on identification evidence, the judge should direct the jury to proceed with special caution. In addition, there is no difference for these purposes between recognition evidence and evidence involving the identification of a stranger: although it might be assumed that the former would be more reliable, the witness in each case is using his particular knowledge of a person to identify him, and the *Turnbull* guidelines therefore apply.

To minimize the risks associated with identification evidence, Code of Practice D sets out specific rules as to how suspects are to be identified. Failure to comply with this Code is likely to result in the evidence being excluded from any trial. If the identity of a suspect is not known, a witness may be shown photographs or taken to a par-

---

[257] Code C, para 11.15. See para 1.7 of this Code for the meaning of 'appropriate adult'.

[258] Ibid, para 11.1.   [259] Ibid, para 11.18.

[260] *R v Lamont* [1989] Crim LR 813; *R v Moss* (1990) 91 Cr App R 371.

[261] *Report to the Secretary of State for the Home Department of the Departmental Committee on Evidence of Identification in Criminal Cases* (1976, HC 338).

[262] [1977] QB 224, [1976] 3 All ER 549. Note that the guidelines appear to apply only to the identification of humans, and not to the identification of vehicles and other objects.

ticular locality to observe possible candidates, but certain safeguards must be met.[263] Once the identity of the suspect *is* known, a video identification, group identification or identification parade may be organized. Unless such a procedure would not be practicable or would serve no useful purpose in proving or disproving his involvement in the offence, one of these procedures *must* be offered if a suspect disputes an identification.[264] Such a procedure may also be organized if the officer in charge of the investigation considers that it would be useful. The preferred method of identification in either case is video identification. Paragraph 3.14 of the Code states that a suspect should be offered video identification unless one of the other procedures would be a more suitable and practicable alternative. In all cases a suspect must be reminded of his entitlement to free legal advice, and his consent to the procedure must be sought. In the absence of consent the police may use covert or other means of identification, and the suspect's refusal to participate may be given in evidence at any subsequent trial.[265]

FURTHER READING

AUSTIN, 'The New Powers of Arrest: Plus CA Change: More of the Same or Major Change?' [2007] Crim LR 459

BIRCH, 'The Pace Hots Up: Confessions and Confusions under the 1984 Act' [1989] Crim LR 95

BUCKE and BROWN, *In Police Custody: Police Powers and Suspects' Rights under the Revised PACE Codes of Practice* (1997) HORS 174

ENGLISH and CARD, *Police Law* (Oxford University Press: 10th edn, 2007)

Home Office, *Policing in the New Century: A Blueprint for Reform* (Cm 5326, 2001)

Home Office, *One Step Ahead: A 21st Century Strategy to Defeat Organised Crime* (Cm 6167, 2004)

JASON-LLOYD, *Quasi-Policing* (Cavendish: 2003)

JASON-LLOYD, 'Police Reform – A Better Way?' (2003) 167 JP 805

LUSTGARTEN, *The Governance of the Police* (Sweet & Maxwell: 1986)

LUSTGARTEN, 'The Future of Stop and Search' [2002] Crim LR 603

McCONVILLE and BRIDGES, *Custodial Advice and the Right to Silence* (1993) RCCJ Research Study No 16

MILLER, BLAND and QUINTON, *The Impact of Stops and Searches on Crime and the Community*, Police Research Series Paper No 130 (2000)

MORRIS, 'Extending the Police Family: Issues and Anomalies' [2002] PL 670

NEWBURN (ed), *Handbook of Policing* (Willan: 2003)

NEWBURN and REINER, 'From PC Dixon to Dixon plc: Policing and Policing Powers since 1954' [2004] Crim LR 601

ORMEROD and McKAY, 'Telephone Intercepts and their Admissibility' [2004] Crim LR 15

---

[263] Code D, paras 3.2–3.3.

[264] In *R v Forbes* [2001] 1 AC 473, [2001] 1 All ER 686 an earlier version of the Code was interpreted to mean that an identification procedure had to be held in all cases, even where the suspect was already well known to the witness. The wording adopted since 2002 ensures that parades need not be held in cases where they would serve no useful purpose.

[265] Code D, para 3.17.

ORMEROD and ROBERTS, 'The Police Reform Act 2002 – Increasing Centralisation, Maintaining Confidence and Contracting out Crime' [2003] Crim LR 141

REINER, *The Politics of the Police* (Oxford University Press: 3rd edn, 2000)

ROBERTS and TAYLOR, 'Privacy and the DNA Database' [2005] EHRLR 373

WALKER and STARMER, *Miscarriages of Justice: A Review of Justice in Error* (Blackstone: 1999)

PART III

CIVIL PROCEDURE

14

THE CIVIL PROCESS

INTRODUCTION

This purpose of this chapter is to give an overview of the process of civil litigation. Civil process has undergone radical reform in the last fifteen years, following the implementation of the reforms recommended by the Woolf Committee. At the same time, growth has occurred in the range and availability of alternative dispute resolution. Specific areas addressed will include:

- The reasons for the recommendations of the Woolf Report.
- It main recommendations.
- How those recommendations have been implemented.
- How the civil justice system is administered.
- Alternative forms of dispute resolution, including arbitration and mediation.

THE CONTEXT

Access to justice is a fundamental right. It has even been described as a constitutional right, insofar as such rights exist.[1] For society to operate effectively, there must be means whereby disputes between individuals, and between the state and individuals, can be resolved. The civil justice process provides those means, but must be accessible to those who need such access. Procedural, financial, or other restrictions defeat the whole purpose of the civil justice process, as does unnecessary delay or length.

Civil litigation has, for the most part,[2] traditionally been regarded as adversarial in nature.[3] Within a framework of substantive and procedural law established by the state for the resolution of civil disputes, the main responsibility for the initiation and conduct

---

[1] See Laws J in *R v Lord Chancellor, ex parte Witham* [1998] QB 575, [1997] 2 All ER 779. The significance of the constitutional right is that it should only be abrogated by the clear words of an Act of Parliament. For the detail of this case, see p 403, *ante*.

[2] Proceedings involving children might be regarded as an exception.

[3] Access to Justice: Interim Report to the Lord Chancellor on the Civil Justice System in England and Wales, June 1995 ('the Woolf Interim Report'), at para 3. See also the Final Report (the 'Woolf Final Report', 1996).

of proceedings has traditionally rested with the parties to each individual case, with the person bringing the action (the claimant)[4] setting the pace at which the litigation proceeds. The parties to the litigation controlled the commencement of the action, the setting of the legal agenda within which the case was to be decided,[5] the progress of the case, the question of interim relief whilst the case was in progress, the settlement or otherwise of the case, and the acquisition and adducing of evidence. The role of the judge was to adjudicate on issues selected by the parties when they chose to present them to the court. That approach is not intended to have survived the reforms of the 1990s and early 2000s, which followed two landmark reports by Lord Woolf. The Woolf Interim Report and the Woolf Final Report[6] were the foundations on which reform of the civil justice system was built, culminating in the new Civil Procedure Rules (CPR).[7] The success of the Woolf Reforms of course remains to be fully evaluated but have been endorsed by subsequent reports.[8]

The civil justice process has long been criticized for its cost, delay, and complexity.[9] Since the mid-nineteenth century there have been some sixty or so reports on aspects of procedure, including the Civil Justice Review.[10] In 1993 (the year before Lord Woolf's review was commissioned) that civil justice process was condemned by a report published by the Bar Council and Law Society,[11] and was described as 'fragmented and confusing' by the Middleton Report[12] in 1997. The Woolf Interim Report identified a key reason for this as being the absence of effective judicial control. Without this, the adversarial process was likely to encourage an adversarial culture and to degenerate into an environment in which the litigation process was too often seen as a battlefield where no rules apply. In this environment, questions of expense, delay, compromise, and fairness might have only low priority. The consequence was that expense is often excessive, disproportionate, and unpredictable; and delay is frequently unreasonable.[13]

THE WOOLF ANALYSIS

The fact that the Woolf Interim and Final Reports identified fundamental shortcomings in the civil justice process has already been noted above. At the heart of the problems were the adversarial approach of litigation, the expense and complexity of litigation, and

---

[4] Formerly known as the '*plaintiff*'. For changes in nomenclature, see p 465, *post*.

[5] The 'pleadings'.

[6] *Access to Justice: Final Report*. For general comment and reference, see Zuckerman and Cranston *Reform of Civil Procedure: Essays on Access to Justice* (1995); Zander *The Government's Plans on Civil Justice* (1998) 61 MLR 383; Zander 'Forwards or Backwards for the New Lord Chancellor' (1997) 16 CJQ 208. Note that not all comment was dismissive of the pre-existing process: see, e.g. Conrad Dehn QC Reform of Civil Justice: Essays on 'Access to Justice' (1995) at pp 149–61.

[7] See p 463, *post*.   [8] See p 463, *post*.   [9] Woolf Interim Report, *op cit*, para 8.

[10] Report of the Review Body on Civil Justice, Cm 394, 1988, HMSO.

[11] *Civil Justice on Trial: The Case for Change*, 1993.

[12] Review of Civil Justice and Legal Aid: Report to the Lord Chancellor by Sir Peter Middleton GCB ('the Middleton Report'), Lord Chancellor's Dept, September 1997, at para 1.7.

[13] Woolf Interim Report, *op cit*, para 4.

the delays with which it was surrounded, although not all such criticisms applied to all proceedings. We have already noted the existence of specialist courts or jurisdictions.[14] For example, the Commercial Court developed specialist procedures and protocols to facilitate the handling of cases within its remit. So, too, with judicial review, where[15] the procedures and processes under Order 53 of the old Rules of the Supreme Court provided speedy (if not necessarily inexpensive) means for the challenge of actions and decisions of public bodies. The question of choice of court also was an important factor contributing to delay, inefficiency, and cost.

1 DELAY AND ADVERSARIAL NATURE OF CIVIL LITIGATION

As already noted, the conduct of civil litigation has, historically, been in the hands of the parties, operating within a framework of rules of court, creating the potential for delay. In *Rastin v British Steel plc*,[16] Sir Thomas Bingham pointed out that 'delay has long been recognised as the enemy of justice'. An adversarial process encourages an adversarial culture, and this worked well where all parties were keen to see the case progress, were appropriately represented, and the court had little need to intervene.[17] But the adversarial system in civil litigation has not always in the past delivered that. In one analysis, extra-judicially, Sir Gavin Lightman[18] identified a number of 'disturbing features for those who are more interested in the achievement of justice than playing the game'.[19] These included the fact that success depends very much on the events at court itself, which in turn turns on the investment made by the respective parties in the litigation – 'money talks loud and clear' – and the judge has limited opportunity to redress the balance. The quality of advice varies enormously, from (to quote the metaphor used) 'fine wine' to 'unfit to drink'. The judge has to achieve fairness on the material put before him. Above all, Lightman concluded that the system was expensive and time-consuming: 'you must purchase your "champions" for the tournament, and champions do not come cheap'. This disenchantment with the adversarial system was heightened by the plethora of judicial pronouncements on matters of substantive law. The Woolf reforms were viewed as advances, but substantial litigation remains 'extravagantly expensive and unpredictable...'.

Clearly, whatever the pros and cons of the system, the rules governing preparation for trial often highlighted these problems. The Woolf Interim Report observed that the whole process could be much like a battleground, with the parties waging 'war' often devoid of judicial intervention or control.[20] In 1994, High Court cases on average took 163 weeks in London and 189 weeks elsewhere to progress from commencement

---

[14] See p 259 *et seq, ante*.   [15] See chapter 7, *ante*.

[16] [1994] 2 All ER 641, [1994] 1 WLR 732.

[17] See Andrews, *English Civil Procedure* (2003) at paras 2.22–2.23.

[18] High Court judge, in Edward Bramley Memorial Lecture: see (2003) 22 CJQ 235.

[19] His comments were focused on the criminal justice system but may be thought, by some, to have some value in the context of the criminal justice system. For the adversarial system, see p 551, *post*.

[20] Interim Report, *op cit*, paras 29 *et seq*.

of the action to trial. The great majority of this time was between commencement and setting down: 123 weeks in London and 148 weeks elsewhere. The equivalent county court figures were around eighty weeks overall from commencement to trial, with typically around sixty weeks elapsing. In the majority of cases the delay arose from a failure to progress the case efficiently, wasting time on peripheral issues, or from procedural skirmishing to wear down an opponent or to excuse failure to get on with the case.[21] Woolf considered that this approach was too often condoned by the courts, paradoxically for fear of disadvantaging the litigant. Excessive discovery,[22] the use of experts in heavy demand, and the exertion of partisan pressure on experts also each contributed to delay.

Delay, Woolf concluded, was of more benefit to the lawyers than to the parties.[23] It allowed litigators to carry excessive caseloads in which the 'minimum possible action occurs over the maximum possible timescale'. The process of case settlement was addressed at a very late stage, not facilitating speed but, by contrast, creating extra costs. Rules of court were flouted on a vast scale. The timetables they contained were generally ignored and their other requirements complied with when convenient to the interests of one of the parties and not otherwise. Woolf considered that the powers of the courts had fallen behind the more sophisticated and aggressive tactics of some litigators. Orders for costs which resulted[24] were of little value, applied after the damage was done. The delay in being able to obtain effective intervention by the court encouraged rule-breaking and discouraged the party who would be prejudiced from applying for preventive measures. The main procedural tools for conducting litigation efficiently had become subverted from their proper purpose. Pleadings often failed to state the facts as the rules require, leading to a fundamental deficiency, namely the failure to establish the issues in the case at a reasonably early stage, and from which many problems resulted.[25] New procedures had become bogged down in technicalities or excesses, especially in respect to expert evidence and discovery.

The Report also focused on equally fundamental issues that result. He wrote:[26]

> Delay is an additional source of distress to parties who have already suffered damage. It postpones the compensation or other remedy to which they may be entitled. It interferes with the normal existence of both individuals and businesses. In personal injury cases, it can exacerbate or prolong the original injury. It can lead to the collapse of relationships and businesses. It makes it more difficult to establish the facts because memories fade and witnesses cannot be traced. It postpones settlement but may lead parties to settle for inadequate compensation because they are worn down by delay or cannot afford to continue.

Many of his recommendations address directly issues of delay.

---

[21] For condemnation of the culture, see Lightman, 'Civil Litigation in the 21st Century' (1998) 17 CJQ 383.
[22] The process whereby documents in the hands of one party are made available to other parties in the litigation, and now known as disclosure.
[23] Interim Report, Ch 3, para 31.   [24] See p 519, post.
[25] Interim Report, para 9.   [26] Interim Report, para 30.

2 EXPENSE

Delay and expense are, of course, inextricably linked. If litigation is unaffordable then there is a denial of justice.[27] This problem has not, historically, been fully addressed by the civil legal aid system, which has often catered for the needs of those on the lowest income levels, leaving a range of middle-income earners unable to seek redress in the courts and thus with unmet legal needs. This is a situation addressed by the growth of conditional fee agreements following the gradual phasing-out of civil legal aid.[28] Disproportionality was also a problem: a claim which can only be pursued, or defended, at disproportionate cost is one that cannot in reality be brought or defended easily. Woolf noted that the costs in some cases, particularly smaller value cases, were often in excess of the value of what was in dispute. Research undertaken for the Woolf Inquiry showed that in half of the cases examined by the research team, the costs for one party to litigation equalled or exceeded the value of the claim disproportionately.[29] It considered that disproportionate costs permeated many aspects of the civil justice process. In part, this flowed from the cost of legal services, and the level of fees charged by lawyers. It also stemmed from the fact that solicitors generally charge by an hourly rate, thus compounding the effect of cumbersome rules, procedures, or structures that allow the parties to dictate the pace of litigation, and issues to be determined. The question of the awards of costs was also relevant.[30] As noted earlier, if no effective rules apply, priority is not always given to the taking of steps to settle the litigation, or to progress it quicker, and therefore more cheaply. Woolf concluded[31] that the expense of litigation is one of the most fundamental problems confronting the civil justice system. He quoted Sir Thomas Bingham, the Master of the Rolls, as describing it as 'a cancer eating at the heart of the administration of justice'. The problem of cost is fuelled by the combative environment in which litigation is conducted.

Excessive cost deters people from making or defending claims. A number of businesses told the Woolf Inquiry that it is often cheaper to pay up, irrespective of the merits, than to defend an action.[32] This is particularly true at the lower end of the scale of litigation. For individual litigants the unaffordable cost of litigation constitutes a denial of access to justice. This problem of disproportionate cost is most acute in smaller cases where the costs of litigation, for one side alone, frequently equal or exceed the value of what is at issue. The result is often that it was impossible for ordinary people to take or defend smaller cases unless they are legally aided, have insurance backing, or believe they can be certain of winning their case and their costs. Like the Middleton Report was to do, Woolf also focused on the overall costs to the state, with inexorable rises in the costs of legal aid. This has now of course been reversed by the expedient of removing state funding for many classes of litigation. For individual legally aided litigants, the high cost of litigation impacted through the increased contributions which they had to pay throughout the duration of the case and the statutory charge on any compensation they recover. The Report concluded that this approach to litigation which then applied

---

[27] Ibid, Ch 3, para 13.   [28] See p 404, *ante.*
[29] Ibid, para 19, citing research of Professor Hazel Genn.
[30] See p 519, *post.*   [31] Interim Report, *op cit*, Ch 1.   [32] Ibid, para 13.

usually resulted in total uncertainty for the parties as to what litigation will require, and consequently increased the amount of expenditure in which they may be involved and the timescale of that involvement. This arose from a number of factors:

(a) the rule that costs normally follow the event and the inevitable uncertainty as to the outcome of litigation;

(b) the procedures when management of the case is primarily a matter for the parties and that either side could influence not only its own costs but also its opponent's;

(c) the requirement of the adversarial system that every aspect of a case be fully investigated. This encouraged excessive work and cost on issues which were often recognized from an early stage as peripheral;

(d) the charging system, on a daily or hourly basis, which meant that the more that is done on a case, the more lawyers were paid;

(e) the lack of continuity in the handling of cases, resulting in the additional work necessary to refresh memories.

3 COMPLEXITY

Alongside delay and expense is complexity – what one writer has described as 'the unholy trinity of consequences which flow once a lawyer gets hold of a dispute'.[33] Woolf concluded that unnecessary complexity was caused by the then state of the rules of court, the multiplicity of procedures and jurisdictions, the multiplicity of methods of commencing actions, and the multiplicity of Practice Directions. None of the above was helped by 'obscure and uncertain' substantive law.[34] All these factors created additional problems where, whether for financial or other reasons, there was a growth in the number of unrepresented parties.

4 COURT OF TRIAL

Allied to all of the above are issues relating to the structure of the various courts of trial.[35] The question of which court tries an action was at the forefront of the various factors which contribute to current problems about delay, inefficiency, and cost. The jurisdictions of the county court and High Court were separate, but overlapping, with each having similar, but different, regimes of procedure and rules, adding to the complexity and other related problems.

Historically, determination of civil claims has been undertaken by the High Court and the county courts. In some matters, the jurisdiction of the High Court was exclusive, in others concurrent with the county court, in the sense that an action could be commenced in either. The jurisdiction of the county court in respect of which the

---

[33] Andrews, *English Civil Procedure* (2003), at para 2.6. The author was reflecting on what was identified as a possibly cynical response of a layman.

[34] Interim Report Ch 3, para 44.   [35] As to which, see p 464, *et seq*.

Queen's Bench Division has jurisdiction had been limited by the financial value of the claim. Prior to 1991, in contract or tort actions, the value of the claim had to be no greater than £5,000. In equity and property matters the figure was £30,000. If the amount of the claim exceeded the jurisdiction of the county court then the matter had to be dealt with by the High Court, subject to statutory powers of transfer between the two courts. Proceedings in the county court were potentially cheaper, but the proceedures followed in the county court were not always either speedy or effective. It was hardly surprising, therefore, that the Review Body on Civil Justice[36] found that much of the work tried at High Court level was not of sufficient importance, complexity, and substance to justify the time and expense involved in High Court proceedings. It identified the types of cases that did in fact justify proceedings at High Court level. These included:

(a) public law matters, which should be dealt with by way of judicial review;[37]

(b) those matters dealt with in specialist jurisdictions, especially the Commercial Court;[38]

(c) ordinary cases, which were important, complex, or which involved a substantial claim. The Review recommended changes to the jurisdiction of the county court, and improved mechanisms for transfer between the two jurisdictions.

As a result of this Review, the Courts and Legal Services Act 1990 altered the whole basis of distribution of work between High Court and county court, although did not adopt in their entirety the recommendations of the Review Body. In 1991 the Lord Chancellor made the High Court and County Court Jurisdiction Order,[39] which adjusted fundamentally the distribution of work between the two courts. By virtue of this order, there was no longer to be any limit to the jurisdiction of the county court in contract or tort. The general principle was that a claimant should be free to choose whichever court is preferred, although in deciding where in fact to commence an action a claimant will usually have regard to the court by which such an action will ultimately be tried. The general principle of freedom of choice expressed above was subject to one important qualification: any action of a value less than £50,000 and involving a claim of damages for personal injuries, had to be commenced in the county court. There was also a presumption that a non-personal injuries claim of the value between £25,000 and £50,000 would be started in the county court.

Woolf recognized the value of such changes, but saw the need to go much further, as part of his philosophy that some of the problems identified above stemmed from in the then inability of the court itself to manage the progress and conduct of the case. As noted later,[40] this has led to changes where the jurisdiction of the court is to be determined through a multi-track approach whereby the court of trial, and the procedure followed, will be determined by the nature of the claim, including its financial value.

---

[36] See Civil Justice Review, *op cit*, p 456, *ante*.   [37] See p 215, *ante*.
[38] See p 262, *ante*.   [39] SI 1991/724.   [40] See p 494, *post*.

5 RECOMMENDATIONS

Woolf did not consider the situation analysed above to be inevitable. The Woolf Report analysed the whole civil process, particularly case management, and the procedures adopted both prior to, and at, trial. In his recommendations he sought to increase the speed proceedings should achieve, to simplify both the language and the process itself, to ensure greater accessibility, to promote settlement and out-of-court resolution of disputes, and to make litigation more efficient and cost effective. In particular, his approach envisaged that pre-trial process and procedure should be managed and overseen by the court, to ensure that proceedings are conducted at the appropriate speed.

Amongst the detailed recommendations were:

(a) an expanded small claims jurisdiction;

(b) a new fast track for straightforward cases not exceeding £10,000 to be a strictly limited procedure designed to take cases to trial within a short but reasonable timescale;

(c) a new multi-track, for cases above £10,000, spanning both High Court and county court cases, and providing appropriate and proportionate case management. Individual hands-on case management was concentrated on those cases which require significant attention and which most benefit from it. Other cases in the multi-track would proceed on standard or individually tailored timetables, according to standard or individual directions;

(d) within the multi-track there would be effective case management, through case management conferences and pre-trial review;

(e) the most complex and important cases were to be heard only by High Court judges and not by deputies. Other cases would be managed and heard by the appropriate level of judge and able to move flexibly within the system to ensure this.

The implementation and effect of the Woolf recommendations are noted at the appropriate part of our discussion about the new system.

The Woolf recommendations were broadly endorsed by the Middleton Report,[41] and accepted generally by the government. To facilitate these fundamental changes, the government took through Parliament what is now the Civil Procedure Act 1997. That Act paved the way for detailed changes. It does so by, in section 1, providing for a new set of procedural rules (the Civil Procedure Rules) which apply to Court of Appeal, High Court, and county court proceedings. The power to make new rules is to be exercised with a view to securing that the civil justice system is accessible, fair, and efficient.[42] Civil Procedure Rules are made by a Civil Procedure Rule Committee. In addition, a Civil Justice Council is established by section 6 of the 1997 Act.

---

[41] See p 456, *ante.*   [42] 1997 Act, s 1(3).

ADMINISTRATION OF THE CIVIL
JUSTICE SYSTEM

The growing impetus for change was also driven by the need to achieve efficiency and cost-effectiveness. As the Middleton Report put it:[43]

> The civil justice system as a whole is not managed coherently, nor do its individual parts seem to be managed with efficiency much in mind. There is indeed a view that efficiency might be incompatible with justice: that it is always desirable and necessary to take infinite pains in order to achieve the best possible result in each case. Desirable though this may seem as a principle, it inevitably comes up against the limitation of available resources...I have therefore concentrated on efficiency. I take that to mean getting more out of a given level of resources, or the same amount at lower cost.

Responsibility for administration of civil justice now lies with the Lord Chancellor and the Department of Constitutional Affairs.[44] The Woolf Report[45] recommended the establishment of a Civil Justice Council as a body with ongoing responsibility for overseeing and co-ordinating the proposals for reform contained in that Report. Such a Council was established in 1998. Its primary task is to advise the Lord Chancellor on how the civil justice system can be improved. Section 6 of the Civil Procedure Act imposes a duty on the Council to keep the civil justice system under review, to consider how to make the civil justice system more accessible fair and efficient, to advise the Lord Chancellor and the judiciary on the development of the civil justice system, and to refer proposals for change to the Lord Chancellor and the Civil Procedure Rule Committee.

The Council comprised representatives from the judiciary, the legal profession, civil servants with knowledge of the administration of justice, persons with experience and knowledge of consumer affairs, individuals with knowledge and experience of the lay advice sector, and those able to represent the interests of particular kinds of litigants (for example, companies or business).[46]

1 RULES OF COURT

Civil litigation is conducted by the parties in accordance with rules of court. Prior to the implementation of the Woolf recommendations separate rules existed in respect of the county court (County Court Rules) and the Supreme Court (the Rules of the Supreme Court). The Civil Procedure Rules (CPR) replace both, and amount to a new procedural code.[47] They are intended to be free-standing, applied individually to the facts of the case, and certainly not limited by pre-CPR case law.[48] That does not mean that the development of principles in pre-CPR case law should be ignored, still less that

---

[43] See p 456, *ante*.

[44] Formerly with the Lord Chancellor's Department. For issues relating to this, see p 19, *ante*.

[45] *Op cit*, para 19.

[46] For general information about the Council, see http://www.civiljusticecouncil.gov.uk.

[47] CPR 1.1(1).   [48] *Hamblin* v *Field, The Times*, 26 April 2000; *Purdy* v *Cambran* [1999] CPLR 843.

the appeal courts should not continue to develop principles as to how the rules should be used.[49]

The rules do not directly affect rules of substantive law.[50] Nor do the rules prevent the courts within their own jurisdiction, from innovating where the rules are silent on a point,[51] or deprive the courts of any inherent jurisdiction. In *Grobbelaar* v *News Group Newspapers*[52] Lord Bingham described this as follows:

> ...the inherent jurisdiction of the court may be defined as the reserve or fund of powers, a residual source of powers, which the court may draw upon as necessary whenever it is just and equitable to do so, and in particular to ensure the observance of the due process of law to prevent improper vexation or oppression, to do justice between the parties and to secure a fair trial between them.

The power of a judge to refuse to hear persons who have no right of audience before the court, or counsel who are improperly dressed, or to sit in camera, or to abort a trial and start a new one where a procedural irregularity has occurred, or to adjourn the proceedings are all inherent powers. The important development of *Mareva* injunctions[53] and *Anton Piller* orders[54] (under the old regime) derived from the inherent jurisdiction of the court, and there is no reason to doubt that such judicial creativity can continue under the new regime. Likewise, the court has always had inherent power to regulate its own procedure. In *Langley* v *North West Water Authority*[55] the Court of Appeal held that a Liverpool solicitor was bound to comply with a Code of Practice issued by the Liverpool County Court. This amounted to a local Practice Direction which the court was entitled to issue under its inherent jurisdiction, except to the extent that it was concurrent with statute law or rules of court. There is probably no reason why action consistent with the CPR, and in particular the *Overriding Objective*, cannot continue.

2 THE OVERRIDING OBJECTIVE

The CPR commence with the statement of an *Overriding Objective* to which any court must seek to give effect when exercising any power given by the rules, or when

---

[49] See, e.g. *Ford* v *GKR Construction* [2000] 1 All ER 802.

[50] The comments of Henn Collins MR in *Re Coles and Ravenshear* [1907] 1 KB 1, at 4, to the effect that 'the relation of the rules of practice to the work of justice is intended to be that of handmaiden rather than mistress' remains true in concept, but must be viewed in accordance with the *Overriding Objective*, as to which see p 465.

[51] See Andrews, *English Civil Procedure* (2003), at para 1.10 citing as an example *Venables* v *News Group Newspapers Ltd* [2001] 1 All ER 908: perpetual injunction to restrain publication of details of T and V being revealed. T and V had been convicted of the notorious murder of James Bulger, a crime attracting outrage and vigilantism.

[52] [2002] 4 All ER 732, citing Jacob 'The Inherent Jurisdiction of the Court' (1970) CLP 23.

[53] *Mareva Compania Naviera SA* v *International Bulkcarriers SA* [1980] 1 All ER 213. These are known as Freezing orders: see p 491, *post*.

[54] *Anton Pillar KG* v *Manufacturing Processes Ltd* [1976] Ch 55, [1976] 1 All ER 779. These are now known as Search Orders: see p 488, *post*.

[55] [1997] 2 FLR 841. See also Sir John Donaldson in *R* v *Secretary of State for the Home Department, ex parte Swati* [1986] 1 All ER 717, [1986] 1 WLR 477. See now CPR, 3.1.

it interprets any rule (CPR 1.2). At the start this code defines what dealing with cases 'justly' means. It includes, so far as practicable:

(a) ensuring that the parties are on an equal footing;

(b) saving expense;

(c) dealing with the case in ways that are proportionate –

    (i) to the amount of money involved;

    (ii) to the importance of the case;

    (iii) to the complexity of the issues;

    (iv) to the financial position of each party

(d) ensuring that it is dealt with fairly and expeditiously;

(e) allotting it to an appropriate share of the court's resources, whilst taking into account the need to allocate resources to other cases.

It is the duty of all parties, and their lawyers, to comply with this objective.[56] It may on occasion guide how a court actually decides a case, or how it deals with questions of costs. One key example of this is the debate that has been ongoing as to whether a court has the right to compel unwilling parties to engage in Alternative Dispute Resolution (ADR) and whether a failure to do so could, and should, be penalized by a refusal to award costs that otherwise the party would expect to receive.[57]

The CPR contain the relevant rules. They also contain *Practice Directions*, which amount to guides to the interpretation of the rules themselves[58] and also pre-action protocols, with which a court will expect a party to comply. A failure to do so may be reflected by a court in the grant, or refusal, of a discretionary remedy or procedure, or may be reflected in any orders for costs (CPR 3.1(4)).

3 THE TERMINOLOGY

As part of the process of seeking to simplify and demystify civil litigation recommended by Woolf, the CPR change many of the names, terms, and expressions formerly used, and to be found in the pre-CPR case law and texts. Whether the changes achieve their objective, or are simply change for change's sake, is a matter of taste and opinion. Where necessary these are dealt with at the appropriate part of the text, but the following should be noted at the outset:

- Plaintiff – now **claimant**
- Guardian ad litem – now **litigation friend**
- Writ – now **claim form**

---

[56] CPR, 1.3; Access to Justice Act 1969, s 42.

[57] For discussion of this important issue, see p 466, *post*, and see, e.g., *Dunnett v Railtrack (Practice Note)* [2002] 1 WLR 2434. For the rules relating to costs, see p 518, *post*.

[58] *Godwin* v *Swindon BC* [2001] EWCA Civ 1478 per May LJ.

- Leave – now **permission**
- Pleadings – now **statement of case**
- Interlocutory relief – now **interim remedies**
- Ex parte – now **without notice**

SETTLEMENT AND ALTERNATIVE MEANS OF DISPUTE RESOLUTION

1   INTRODUCTION

Increasingly, those with disputes have sought alternative means of dispute resolution. As noted above, litigation, particularly in the High Court, is both time-consuming and expensive, and suffers the disadvantage of, generally, being conducted in public. Arbitration has long been seen as an accepted alternative to court procedures, particularly in the sphere of commerce and business, and involves a binding resolution of a dispute by an arbitrator. The principle of arbitration was adopted in respect of small claims in the county court, evolving into the small-claims track introduced as part of the Woolf reforms.[59] In addition, there has begun a tendency to look for other, more informal forms of mechanism for the resolution of disputes, generally known as Alternative Dispute Resolution (ADR).

Unlike arbitration, the characteristics of such mechanisms are, often, those of conciliation, mediation, and negotiation, and which by their nature will not generally involve the imposition of the verdict or conclusion. Such means of avoiding full-scale litigation are particularly helpful to parties to disputes in the commercial or business sectors. As long ago as 1994,[60] the Commercial Court encouraged alternative dispute resolution, particularly where the costs of litigation were likely to be wholly disproportionate to the amount at stake, and cost-effective.[61] Woolf envisaged a 'landscape of civil litigation...fundamentally different from what it is now', starting with the premise that litigation should be avoided where possible, but, if it occurred, less adversarial and more cooperative. He urged the use of ADR in the civil justice process, a fact reflected in the provisions of the CPR. 'Active case management' is one of the key principles introduced by the CPR, and that includes a court's 'encouraging parties to use an alternative dispute resolution procedure if it considers that appropriate, and facilitating the use of such a procedure'.[62] ADR is a 'method of resolving disputes otherwise than through the

---

[59] See p 496, *post*.

[60] *Practice Note (Commercial Court Alternative Dispute Resolution)* [1994] 1 All ER 34, 1 WLR 14.

[61] See, generally, Partington, 'Alternative Dispute Resolution: Recent Developments, Future Challenges' (2004) 23 CJQ 99; Genn, 'Court-Based Initiative for Non Family Civil Disputes: The Commercial Court and the Court of Appeal', Research Report for LCD, 2002.

[62] CPR 4 (2)(e).

use of such a procedure'.[63] Pre-action protocols[64] emphasize the exchange of information at an early stage and promotion of negotiations leading to settlement. Parties are
required to follow a 'reasonable procedure' intended to avoid litigation, and the parties
must state whether they are willing to enter into ADR.[65] The effect of decisions elsewhere
in the civil justice system also should not be overlooked. Section 4(4)(c) of the Access to
Justice Act 1999 requires persons carrying out functions under the Community Legal
Service[66] to do so with a view to achieving 'the swift and fair resolution of disputes
without unnecessary or unduly protracted proceedings in court'. There are thus financial incentives, which may be increased with changes to the Community Legal Services
approach to legal aid.[67] The legal aid scheme has not always encouraged litigation to be
seen as a last resort, because of the higher rates lawyers have been paid for representation as opposed to Legal Help (which provides support for early resolution of disputes),
and because most legal aid remuneration has been based on hourly rates (with therefore
greater rewards for more adversarial processes).[68]

Distinctions must be made between the different forms of process mentioned above.
Arbitration is an alternative form of dispute adjudication, with the result usually
binding on both sides. Mediation, conciliation, and negotiation are, in effect, means
of assisted dispute settlement:[69] no settlement can be imposed and the onus is on the
parties to come to an agreement. The nature of the process may vary: it can be a process 'designed to facilitate agreement'[70] or can be evaluative by encouraging settlement
through evaluation of the parties' rights and case. Different mediators adopt different
styles and approaches.[71] And the mediation may not be wholly voluntary: distinctions
can be drawn between ADR which forms an alternative to the commencement of proceedings in the first place, and court-ordered ADR once proceedings are under way.[72]

We now turn to discuss these different strands.

2 ARBITRATION

Arbitration is one, long-standing alternative form of dispute resolution used by parties
to contracts, particularly contracts involving the construction industry, and favoured
as a form of dispute resolution by parties to international commercial contracts. The law
hitherto has been governed by statutory provision, principally the Arbitration Acts of
1950 and 1979, as explained and developed by common law. In 1996 a new Arbitration

---

[63] Glossary, CPR.   [64] See p 478, *post.*

[65] *Practice Direction for Pre Action Protocols*, para 4.2. Some specific pre-action protocols specifically
require such consideration: e.g. clinical negligence protocol.

[66] As to which, see p 406, *ante.*

[67] See Consultation Paper, 'A New Focus for Civil Legal Aid – Encouraging Early Resolution, Discouraging
Unnecessary Litigation', Department for Constitutional Affairs, 2004.

[68] *Consultation Paper, op cit*, n 67, at p 8.

[69] *Alternative Dispute Resolution: A Discussion Paper*, LCD November 1999, at 2.4.

[70] See also Department of Constitutional Affairs Public Service Agreement 3 which aims to reduce the
proportion of disputes resolved by resort to the courts.

[71] See the analysis by Prince in *Court-based Mediation: A Preliminary Analysis of the small Claims Mediation
Scheme at Exeter Crown Court*, Research Report for the Civil Justice Council, March 2004, at p 12.

[72] For court-ordered ADR and its implications, see p 473, *post.*

Act was passed, which repealed earlier legislation, and which was designed to provide a statutory statement of the relevant statutory and common law principles, in clear and comprehensible language, complying where appropriate with international rules and principles governing arbitration.[73]

Section 1 of that Act states the general principles governing arbitration:

(a) the object of arbitration is to obtain the fair resolution of disputes by an impartial tribunal without unnecessary delay or expense;

(b) the parties should be free to agree how their disputes are resolved, subject only to such safeguards as are necessary in the public interest;

(c) in matters governed by Part I of the Act (which governs arbitration under an arbitration agreement) the court should not intervene except as the Act provides. The Act applies where the 'seat' of the arbitration is in England and Wales, in other words, that England and Wales is the jurisdiction designated by the parties to the arbitration agreement, or by or in accordance with that agreement.

The jurisdiction of arbitrators usually arises out of contract, though there are numerous statutory provisions which provide for the reference of disputes to arbitration. An agreement to refer disputes to arbitration is a contract and, as such, is subject to the ordinary law of contract. Such an agreement must be in writing if the provisions of the 1996 Act are to apply.[74] Any provision purporting to oust the jurisdiction of the courts is not effective to do so,[75] though there is no objection to a clause which makes reference to arbitration a condition precedent to a right of action. The effect of such a clause, traditionally known as a *Scott* v *Avery*[76] clause, is that if a party does institute proceedings without referring the dispute to arbitration, the clause may be pleaded as a defence in those proceedings and the other party may, after acknowledging service of the writ but before taking any other step in the proceedings, apply to the court for an order staying the proceedings.[77] The court must grant a stay unless satisfied that the arbitration agreement is null and void, inoperative, or incapable of being performed. Unlike the position at common law (which sometimes applies) the poverty or insolvency of such a claimant is not a ground for refusing a stay.[78]

(a) Procedure

Procedure on arbitrations is governed (except, in relation to statutory references, where the statute in question otherwise provides) by the Arbitration Act 1996. The issues arising must (in the absence of contrary agreement) be decided according to the rules of law considered by the court to be applicable, decided in accordance with

---

[73] See Report of the Department of Trade and Industry Departmental Advisory Committee on International Commercial Arbitration, 1985 (the Mustill Report). That Committee prepared the draft Bill in 1995.

[74] 1996 Act, s 5(1).   [75] Ibid, s 87.

[76] (1856) 5 HL Cas 811.   [77] Arbitration Act 1996, s 9.

[78] Cf. *Fakes* v *Taylor Woodrow Construction Ltd* [1973] QB 436, [1973] 1 All ER 670. The 1996 Act, s 9, does not include the limited grounds accepted as just reason for a stay in this case.

the principles of conflict of laws.[79] The arbitrator must act fairly and impartially as between the parties, giving each party a reasonable opportunity of putting his case, and for dealing with his opponents' case, and must adopt procedures suitable to the circumstances of the particular case, avoiding unnecessary delay and expense.[80] The arbitrator must decide all procedural and evidential matters, subject to the right of the parties to agree any matter. The arbitrator may thus decide when and where proceedings are to be held, in what language, what documents should be produced and disclosed, what questions should be put to and answered by the parties, whether to apply strict rules of evidence, the extent to which there should be oral or written submissions, and whether the tribunal should take the initiative in ascertaining the facts and the law.[81] In other words, the arbitrator has complete discretion to depart from traditional procedures, and to act inquisitorially. Arbitrators may appoint experts, legal advisers, or assessors to advise them.[82] Parties to arbitration are entitled to legal representation unless they agree otherwise.[83] They can also obtain a witness summons to secure the attendance of a witness.[84] Since 1990,[85] an arbitrator had no power to dismiss an arbitration for want of prosecution. Section 41 of the 1996 Act entitles an arbitrator to dismiss a claim where:

(a) there has been inordinate and inexcusable delay on the part of the claimant in pursuing the claim; and

(b) the delay

   (i) will give rise to a substantial risk that it is not possible to have a fair resolution of the issues in that claim; or

   (ii) has caused, or is likely to cause or have caused, serious prejudice to the respondent.

In the absence of specific provision reference to arbitration connotes reference to a single arbitrator.[86] Where specific provision is made for the appointment of two arbitrators there is a requirement to appoint an additional person as chairman. Under section 18 of the 1996 Act the High Court has various powers to appoint arbitrators and umpires in default of appointment by the parties, the Act specifying in detail the various powers that arise so that disputes are resolved without recourse to the court. The High Court also has power to revoke the authority of an arbitrator or umpire on the ground of delay, bias, or improper conduct[87] and has inherent jurisdiction to stay arbitration proceedings by injunction. There used to be provision whereby an arbitrator might, and, if directed by the court, had to, state in the form of a 'special case' for the opinion of the High Court, either his award or any question of law arising in the reference.[88] The power to apply for a special case was sometimes exercised by a party to delay unduly the resolution of the dispute and to add needlessly to costs. This was altered in 1979, the current provision being found in section 87 of the 1996 Act. This provides that the parties may enter into an 'exclusion agreement', but only if they do so after the arbitration has commenced.

[79] 1996 Act, s 46(3). [80] Ibid, s 33(1). [81] Ibid, s 34(1).
[82] Ibid, s 37(1). [83] Ibid, s 36(1). [84] *Ibid*, s 43(1), CPR 34.2.
[85] Introduced by the Courts and Legal Services Act 1990, s 102.
[86] 1996 Act, s 15(3). [87] Ibid, s 24. [88] Arbitration Act 1950, s 21.

There will then be no power in the High Court to consider a question of law arising in the course of the arbitration; nor will there be any right of appeal. Therefore (subject to the limited power of the High Court to set aside or remit an award for misconduct the arbitrator's decision will be final. Exclusion agreements entered into before the arbitration is commenced are effective only in a limited class of cases and in particular, are invalid in the case of a 'domestic arbitration agreement', that is, basically, an agreement which does not provide for arbitration outside the United Kingdom and is not one to which no United Kingdom national or resident is a party.[89] The decision of the arbitrator is in the form of an 'award', dealing with all the issues on which reference was made. The award may contain provision for the payment of money, costs, or an order of specific performance (except of a contract relating to land).[90] As between the parties the award binds the parties in relation to the issues decided, thus extinguishing any cause of action in relation thereto.

(b) Intervention by the court

The court's powers over arbitrations are governed by the 1996 Act. The court may hear application, and section 44 gives to the court the power to make certain orders during an arbitration, unless the parties otherwise agree. These powers relate to the taking, inspection or preservation of evidence.[91]

The power of the court in respect of completed arbitrations is set out in section 69 of the 1996 Act. The court may hear an application challenging the award if there has been an error by the arbitrator as to a matter relating to substantive jurisdiction, or where there has been a serious irregularity.[92] A right of appeal on any question of law arising out of an award made on an arbitration agreement exists (unless excluded by a valid 'exclusion agreement' (*ante*)) but only by consent of all parties or with leave of the court; the court may not grant leave unless it considers that the determination of the question of law could affect substantially the rights of the parties, that the question was one the arbitrator was asked to determine, that on the basis of the findings of fact the decision is obviously wrong or one of general public importance and the arbitrator's decision is open to serious doubt, and, finally that it is just and proper in all the circumstances for the court to determine the question. It may attach conditions to the grant of leave (for example the provision of security for the amount claimed). In addition to the right of appeal, there is jurisdiction in the High Court (save where there is a valid exclusion agreement) to determine any question of law arising in the course of the reference,[93] but

---

[89] 1996 Act, s 85.   [90] Ibid, s 67.

[91] See *Cetelem SA v Roust Holdings Ltd* [2005] EWCA Civ 18, [2005] 4 All ER 52, disapproving *Hiscox Underwriting Ltd v Dixon, Manchester & Co Ltd* [2004] EWHC 479.

[92] Ibid, s 68. The term 'serious irregularity' is broadly defined by s 68(2) and includes one or more of the following matters which the court considers has caused or will cause substantial injustice to the applicant: failure to comply with general duties under s 33, exceeding its powers, failure to conduct proceedings in accordance with agreed procedures, uncertainty or ambiguity about its award, the award being obtained by fraud, or irregularity in the conduct of the proceedings.

[93] Ibid, s 45. A court may deal with an application for a witness summons and third party disclosure of documents: see *Tajik Aluminium v Hydro Aluminium* [2005] EWCA Civ 1218, [2005] 4 All ER 1232.

only with the consent of the arbitrator or of all the parties. There is an appeal from the High Court to the Court of Appeal, from decisions under Act, but only

(a) with leave of the High Court; and

(b) if the High Court certifies that the question of law is one of general public importance or one which for some other special reason should be considered by the Court of Appeal.[94]

Where an arbitrator has misconducted himself or the proceedings the court may remove him and may set aside the award, or may remit it for reconsideration. The parties may nominate any person they wish to act as arbitrator. Members of the Bar are not infrequently appointed. In addition, by section 93 of the Arbitration Act 1996 a judge of the Commercial Court may, if in all the circumstances he thinks fit, accept appointment as sole arbitrator or as umpire where the dispute appears to him to be of a commercial character and provided the Lord Chief Justice has informed him that, having regard to the state of business in the High Court, he can be made available to do so. Similar powers exist in respect of official referees. Where a judge has acted as arbitrator or umpire under this section appeal lies by case stated to the Court of Appeal.

3 MEDIATION AND NEGOTIATION

(a) Family matters

Conciliation and mediation plays a significant role in divorce proceedings.[95] The trend generally is towards less court intervention in matrimonial matters. Divorce itself is basically a paper exercise, and the majority of financial matters, and matters relating to children, are dealt with by consent. The 1990s saw a general trend towards encouraging, and requiring, mediation in the context of families. The Family Law Act 1996 encourages and requires mediation to occur. The same philosophy applies in the context of cases involving children, and a range of projects aimed to complement the judicial process through alternative dispute resolution in child care cases, by identifying and exploring the issues to be determined and exploring options on which the parties could agree. Pilot projects have been run in child care cases involving public law issues: these include a joint Alternative Dispute Resolution Project run by National Family Mediation and the Tavistock Centre, funded by the Department of Health, aiming to provide mediation as an alternative to the court process in child protection, fostering, adoption, or contact cases where there is a dispute between parents, carers, and local authority social workers.[96] National Family Mediation has also developed policies involving mediation in domestic violence cases. Since section 29 of the Family Law Act 1996 was introduced, the Legal Services Commission will require divorcing or separating couples who are eligible for legal aid and who are in dispute on matters relating to children, to attend an

---

[94] Ibid, s 69(8).

[95] In this and other forms of mediation the quality is important. The Civil Mediation Council in December 2005 introduced an accredited scheme for court mediation: see Fry, 'It's Good to Talk' (2006) 156 NLJ 132.

[96] See Walsh, 'Working in the Family System' [1997] Fam Law at 109–10.

interview with a mediator as a pre-condition to the consideration of an application for legal aid. Mediation services are available at a growing number of major centres.

Changes in legal funding contribute to this process. The Community Legal Service has restructured Legal Help, General Family Help, and Help with Mediation,[97] with a single level of service called Family Help, intended to cover all non-adversarial family dispute resolution, coupled with a further reduction in funding for representation in contested proceedings.[98] This is now being piloted and rolled out through the Family Advice and Information Service. The philosophy of diverting from the courts was well summarized as follows:[99]

> [Research] has highlighted parents' awareness of the negative impact of conflict and sub-optimal contact arrangements on their children and their desire to find a better way of sorting these issues out . . . most do not want to resort to the courts. They are led or feel pressed there. Courts are not possibly the best equipped to deal with the emotional and practical problems being brought before them. The process can be (and is) criticised for being too backward-looking and focused on fact-finding: it is adversarial and may actually increase and prolong conflict . . . Courts certainly have a place in this – for those cases where safety is an issue or where no amount of help will reduce the conflict – but we estimate that there might be up to 60 per cent of the current court caseload that need not and should not really be there.

(b) Other court-based mediation

Court based mediation schemes are now normal, and a key way of diverting cases from the long and expensive road to full trial.[100] An example is the Court of Appeal Mediation scheme for non-family appeals, conducted by the Centre of Excellence for Dispute Resolution (CEDR Solve). Judges of the Court of Appeal may recommend mediation when dealing with permission to appeal: in its first year, a settlement rate of 68 per cent of cases referred to it was achieved.

Another example is the Court Settlement Process (CSP) in the Technology and Construction Court. Since June 2006, specially trained judges offer CSP, where, following a request from the parties, a case-managing judge feels that the parties should be able to achieve an amicable settlement.

(c) Contractual and regulatory disputes

Some contracts specify a form of dispute resolution which, at any rate initially, requires disputes to be arbitrated or decided by an arbitrator or complaint resolution procedure. Examples of this are many, and include not only standard building agreements, but also more consumer-orientated matters such as some disputes between holidaymaker and travel company. Such agreements do not necessarily oust the jurisdiction of the

---

[97] As to which see p 471, *ante*.

[98] Parental disputes about arrangements for their children amount to some 28 per cent of the civil legal aid budget.

[99] *Community Legal Service Consultation Paper, op cit*, at p 18.

[100] See generally Genn, *Court-Based Mediation for non-Family Civil Disputes*. Research Report for Lord Chancellor's Department, 2002.

courts. In addition, a range of dispute resolution mechanisms may exist, and are on the increase.[101] The Confederation of British Industry has established the Centre for Effective Dispute Resolution (CEDR). The City Disputes Panel was created to deal with disputes in the banking and finance sector.

In the public sector, the government has sought to increase the use of ADR as an alternative to litigation. The Environment Council offers an ADR service for public interest and environmental disputes. The NHS has been involved in pilot mediation projects. The Housing Ombudsman refers disputes in relation to public sector housing. The Planning Inspectorate has a pilot project in the context of planning appeals. Indeed, Woolf in his Final Report[102] identified the fact that applicants for judicial review should be encouraged to settle their disputes without recourse to the courts, through grievance procedures and ombudsman remedies which are increasingly available. Such complaints mechanisms exist increasingly in the sphere of public law, for example the National Health Service complaints procedure or the independent Housing Ombudsman noted above.[103]

All these mechanisms may have consequences for the availability of judicial remedies. For example, section 26 of the Children Act 1989 provided for a mechanism for dealing with complaints. In *R v Birmingham City Council, ex parte A*,[104] the applicant sought judicial review of the actions of the local authority in failing to provide suitable accommodation for a severely disturbed child. The application failed, the court holding that the appropriate response was to utilize the statutory complaints mechanism, not to seek judicial review. Again, and more recently, in *Frank Cowell* v *Plymouth City Council*[105] Lord Woolf himself criticized the abuse of judicial review in a case involving the re-housing of elderly residents of a care home, describing the process as 'over judicialised'.

(d) Court based schemes and court-led ADR requirements

It will be clear from the above that some courts have played a role in the development of ADR. Since 1993 the Commercial Court has been identifying cases regarded as appropriate for ADR. In some cases judges have suggested ADR. In others an order has been made requiring the parties to attempt ADR, a position that needs now to be reviewed in the light of the decision in *Halsey* v *Milton Keynes General NHS Trust*.[106] It stops short of compulsion. It was described as follows in *Halsey*:

> It is the strongest form of encouragement. It requires the parties to exchange lists of neutral individuals who are available to conduct 'ADR procedures', to endeavour in good faith to agree a neutral individual or panel and to 'take such reasonable steps they may be advised to resolve their disputes by ADR procedures before the neutral individual or panel so chosen...' The order also provides that if the case is

---

[101] See Nesic, 'Mediation – On the Rise in the United Kingdom?' to be found at http://www.adr.civiljusticecouncil.gov.uk/updocs

[102] At p 251.   [103] See Nichol, 'Available Dispute Resolution', Legal Action, December 1997, p 6.

[104] [1991] 3 All ER 610, [1991] 1 WLR 697.   [105] *The Times*, 8 January 2002.

[106] See p 475, *post*.

not settled 'the parties shall inform the court what steps towards ADR have been taken and (without prejudice to matters of privilege) why such steps have failed'.

If following an ADR order there has been a failure to settle the parties must explain what steps were taken towards ADR, and why they failed. By 2000 the number of such orders had reached sixty-eight in a six-month period.[107] Typically, ADR occurred in about 50 per cent of cases where such an order was made, with a success rate for settlement in those cases of about 52 per cent. The research showed that ADR had some impact in reducing the proportion of cases going to trial, even if the ADR itself had proved unsuccessful. It identified the fact that orders can have a positive effect in opening up communication between the parties and avoiding the fear of one side showing weakness in being the first to suggest settlement.

Many other court-based initiatives can be identified. They include schemes at the Patents Court and the Central London County Court, a scheme in Exeter,[108] and in several other centres.

Given the growth in interest and activity in ADR since the early 1990s, and now the positive obligation to seek to avoid litigation contained in the CPR, key questions remain as to whether the parties can be forced to engage in mediation. Of course, the parties to a contract may have stipulated that a negotiated settlement or mediation is the first step, before litigation may be considered. An agreement to negotiate has been held not to be enforceable, because of the lack of sufficient certainty as to what is means,[109] but, by contrast, the House of Lords in *Channel Tunnel Group Ltd* v *Balfour Beatty Construction Ltd*[110] held that a court has a discretionary power to stay proceedings[111] if there is a dispute mediation clause equivalent to an agreement to arbitrate. Although the matter may not be completely clear,[112] a prior agreement is likely, if it is sufficiently clear and certain, to be binding.[113]

That conclusion is probably inevitable given the attitude of the courts since the introduction of the CPR and its requirement to consider ADR. A contrary conclusion would fly in the face of public policy.[114] Under the CPR parties may seek a stay to attempt ADR[115] and a failure to engage in ADR following a court's direction may be reflected in any costs order sought or made. In *Dunnet* v *Railtrack plc*[116] a defendant's application for costs was refused because of a failure to mediate. If parties 'turned down out of hand the chance of alternative dispute resolution when suggested by the court...they may have to face uncomfortable costs consequences...'.[117] Another court considered that the right question to ask was: is there on an objective viewpoint any real chance of mediation

---

[107] See Genn, *Court-Based Initiatives for Non-Family Civil Disputes*. Research Report for Lord Chancellor's Department, 2002.

[108] See Interim Research Report by Prince: *Court-Based Mediation – A Preliminary Analysis of Small Claims Mediation Scheme at Exeter County Court*, Civil Justice Council, March 2004.

[109] *Walford* v *Miles* [1992] 1 All ER 453.

[110] [1993] AC 334. See also *Scott UK Ltd* v *F E Barber Ltd* [1997] 3 All ER 540.

[111] As to which, see p 498, *post*.

[112] See *Halifax Financial Services Ltd* v *Intuitive Systems Ltd* [1999] 1 All ER (Comm) 303.

[113] The key question may be the mandatory nature of the procedure agreed: see *Cable & Wireless* v *IBM* [2002] EWHC 2059 (Comm).

[114] *Cable & Wireless* v *IBM* per Colman J.   [115] CPR, 26.4(1).   [116] [2002] CP Rep 35.

[117] *Dunnet* v *Railtrack plc, supra*, per Brooke LJ.

succeeding?[118] On the particular facts the court did not think so, and therefore did not deprive the claimant of his costs.

The authorities generally have proved inconsistent.[119] For that reason the guidance given in two cases in the Court of Appeal, *Halsey v Milton Keynes General NHS Trust* and *Steel v Joy*[120] is to be welcomed. In neither case was a party deprived of costs because of a failure to mediate. In *Halsey*, a clinical medical case, the defendant believed that it had a very strong case, that mediation costs would be disproportionately high, and the claimant's requests in pre-action correspondence was highly tactical. In *Steel*, a personal injury case, the claim involved a point of law which it was reasonable to wish to be resolved by the court. The case was probably intrinsically unsuitable for mediation.

The court gave general guidance. It does not have power to order reluctant litigants to mediate. To do so would violate Article 6 of the Convention, because it would be an unacceptable obstruction to right of access to the courts. The court can encourage, not compel. All those involved in litigation should routinely consider whether the dispute is suitable for ADR. If a party refuses to mediate, the court can displace the normal costs rule and order that party to pay the costs despite winning at trial. This should occur only if that party has acted unreasonably in refusing ADR. The burden of showing that lies with the unsuccessful party. If the case *is* mediated the parties are entitled to adopt whatever position they want, and the court is not, later, entitled to ask why that position was in fact adopted. This thus preserves the confidentiality of mediation. Above all, although most cases are suitable for ADR there is not a presumption in favour of mediation. In deciding what cases are suitable, regard should be had to the nature of the case, its merits, the extent to which other settlement methods have been attempted, whether the costs of mediation are disproportionately high and whether delay in arranging mediation would be prejudicial.

None of the above prevents a court from a court imposing an order requiring the parties to consider the suitability of mediate. Refusal will still carry the risk of deprivation of costs.

FURTHER READING

ANDREWS, *English Civil Procedure* (Oxford University Press: 2004)

Department for Constitutional Affairs Consultation Paper, *A New Focus for Civil Legal Aid – Encouraging Early Resolution, Discouraging Unnecessary Litigation* (2004)

DHEN et al, *Reform of Civil Procedure: Essays on Access to Justice*, ed. Zuckerman and Cranston (Clarendon Press: 1995)

LIGHTMAN, 'Civil Litigation in the 21st Century' (1998) 17 CJQ 383

WOOLF, *Access to Justice* (Lord Chancellor's Department: 1995) – the 'Woolf Report'

---

[118] See *Hurst v Leeming* [2002] C P Rep 59; cf. *Leicester Circuits v Coates* [2003] EWCA Civ 333.

[119] *Neal v Jones; Société Internationale de Télécommunications Aéronautiques v Wyatt* [2002] EWHC 2401.

[120] [2004] EWCA (Civ) 576. See also *Burchell v Ballard* [2005] EWCA Civ 358.

15

PRE-TRIAL PROCESS[1]

INTRODUCTION

This chapter will examine the important first stage of civil process – the pre-trial process. The right approach before an action is begun, the choice of the right court, and the early procedures are each crucial. Specific areas covered will include:

- The purpose of pre-action protocols and their importance in attempting to avoid proceedings, or in identifying the issues that arise.
- How civil actions are commenced.
- The early procedural issues.

CHOICE OF COURT

The Woolf Civil Justice Reforms[2] made fundamental changes to the commencement of actions. As already noted,[3] jurisdiction in civil matters has historically been divided between the county court and High Court.[4] The latter has had almost unlimited jurisdiction, unless statute has given jurisdiction exclusively to a county court. The jurisdiction of the county court has been limited historically by value, or by the nature of the subject matter. For example, the county court has not had (and does not have) jurisdiction to deal with claims in libel or slander.[5]

Within that structure, the choice of where to commence the action turned on what was the appropriate court of trial. If the matter was within the exclusive jurisdiction of either the High Court, or of the county court, it was in that court that the action should have been commenced, usually by writ (in the case of the High Court) or summons (in the case of the county court). If the matters fell to be regarded as a small claim, the county court was the appropriate forum for the case. If judicial review[6] was sought an application had to be made to the Administrative Court (formerly, the Queen's Bench Divisional Court). Increasingly, though, the High Court and county court have had concurrent

---

[1] See, generally, Zuckerman, *Civil Procedure* (2003); Andrews, *English Civil Procedure* (2002); Loughlin and Gerlis, *Civil Procedure* (2004).

[2] See p 456, *ante*.   [3] See p 264, *ante*.   [4] See p 264, *ante*.

[5] County Courts Act 1984, s 15(2).   [6] See p 264, *ante*.

jurisdiction in respect of most matters. The county court can now deal with any matters that are founded on contract or tort whatever the financial value or complexity, jurisdiction over claims in equity and contentious probate where the value involved does not exceed £30,000[7] and unlimited jurisdiction to hear cases for the recovery of land.[8] The county court now has many of the same powers in respect of procedure and remedies as does the High Court. Yet, despite the concurrence of many aspects of jurisdiction the intention has been to keep the High Court for only the most valuable, complex, or important cases. Section 1 of the Courts and Legal Services Act 1990 empowers the Lord Chancellor to make provision for the allocation of business. Article 7 of the High Court and County Court Jurisdiction Order 1991[9] creates a presumption that cases of a value less than £25,000 must be tried in the county court: a claim of less than £15,000 *cannot* be commenced in the High Court. The presumption is that a claim of a value of £50,000 or more *will* be eligible for High Court trial. The position will be otherwise if the application of certain criteria shows that a different court of trial is in fact appropriate. These criteria also apply in deciding in which court cases falling between these two financial figures should be tried, with one proviso. Cases involving personal injury claims of an estimated amount less than £50,000 must be commenced in the county court (except in the case of clinical medical negligence claims). The criteria mentioned above are set out in Article 7(5) of the order, which deals primarily with the transfer of cases between the two jurisdictions.[10] However, they are equally relevant to the question of initial choice of jurisdiction. The factors identified are as follows:

(i)   the financial substance of the action, including that of any counter-claim;

(ii) whether the action is otherwise important, for example by raising issues of general public importance, or where the case will amount to a test case;

(iii) the complexity of the facts, legal issues, remedies, or procedures involved. Complex cases are more suitable for High Court trial;

(iv) whether transfer of the case will lead to more speedy trial, although this alone should not be a determining factor.

To facilitate the greater use of the county court jurisdiction, section 38 of the County Courts Act 1984 gave to the county court, generally speaking, the power to make any order which could be made by the High Court if the proceedings were in that court. That power is subject to any limitation imposed by regulations, and examples of such matters are freezing orders[11] or search orders.[12] In substantial cases where such orders may be crucial to the obtaining of information or prevention of dissipation of assets, these restrictions may conclusively influence the choice of High Court rather than county court jurisdiction. Some cases, such as professional negligence, claims under the Fatal Accidents Act 1976, claims of fraud or of undue influence, malicious prosecution, and false imprisonment, claims against the police, and contentious probate may be particularly suitable for High Court trial.[13] All concerned are bound by the Civil Procedure Rules. A claim should be started in the High Court only if by reason of

---

[7] County Courts Act 1984, ss 23, 32; County Courts Jurisdiction Order 1981, SI 1981/123.
[8] 1984 Act, s 21.   [9] SI 1991/724.   [10] See CPR, 30.3(1), 30.3(2).
[11] See p 491 *post*.   [12] See p 488, *post*.   [13] Practice Direction 29, para 2.6.

its financial value and the amount in dispute and/or the complexity of the facts, legal issues, or procedures involved, and/or the public importance of the matters involved the claimant believes the claim should be dealt with by a High Court judge.[14] If a case does not fall within these criteria, nor is required to be tried in the High Court by statute or falls within a specialist jurisdiction (such as the Administrative Court)[15] it will be transferred to the county court.[16] In a case where the choice of court was known to be wrong, and intended to intimidate the opponent, or to run up costs, a court might strike out the case.[17] This should not happen where there has been a bona fide error or misjudgment, because this would not only be contrary to the spirit of the 'overriding objective'[18] but possibly a breach of the fair trial provisions of Article 6 of the European Convention which encompasses the right of access to the court. A further sanction may be a reduction in the costs allowed at the conclusion of the case.[19]

The total effect of these changes is that the vast majority of actions, some 90 per cent, commence in the county court. The High Court is the forum for the more specialist and difficult cases.[20] The general powers to transfer between the two levels of court must be exercised having regard to the matters identified in the Civil Procedure Rules. These include:[21]

(a) the financial value of the claim, or the amount in dispute;

(b) the convenience or fairness of hearings being held in another court;

(c) the availability of a judge specializing in the type of claims in question;

(d) the complexity of facts, legal issues, remedies, or procedures;

(e) the public ignorance of the claim; the facilities available at the court where the claim is being dealt with, in particular with regard to the disabilities of a party or witness;

(f) whether any possibility of the making of a declaration of incompatibility.[22]

The court may have regard to matters as diverse as the convenience of the defendant[23] and the suitability of the court.

PRE-ACTION PROTOCOLS

We have already seen that Pre-Action Protocols supplement the Civil Procedure Rules.[24] Their purpose was well explained by Brooke LJ in *Carlson* v *Townsend*[25] as 'guides to good litigation and pre-litigation practice, drafted by those who know the difference

---

[14] Practice Direction 7, para 2.4.   [15] For judicial review, see p 215, *ante*.
[16] Count Court Act 1984, s 40; Practice Direction 29, para 2.6. Similar powers exist to transfer cases from the county court to the High Court if the latter is the more appropriate venue.
[17] *Restrick* v *Crickmore* [1994] 2 All ER 112.   [18] As to which, see p 464, *ante*.
[19] Supreme Court Act 1981, s 51(8), (9). For costs, see p 522, *post*.
[20] See Report of the Review Body on Civil Justice, Cm 394, 1988, HMSO.
[21] CPR, 30.3(2).   [22] As to which, see p 158, *ante*.   [23] *Pepin* v *Taylor* [2002] EWCA Civ 1522.
[24] See p 463, *ante*.   [25] [2001] 3 All ER 663.

between good and bad practice...'. There is not one general protocol: a government Consultation Paper that mooted that possibility[26] came in the end to the conclusion that it was better to proceed by way of Practice Direction setting out a general framework within which parties in dispute should act prior to the commencement of formal action.[27] The essential elements are that the claimant should set out details of the matter in question, copies of essential documents relied on, and a response within a stated period (a period of one month is identified as a standard). Such a pre-action letter should indicate whether Alternative Dispute Resolution (ADR)[28] is sought. It should also give details of any conditional fee agreement.[29] A response should then follow from the defendant, with an acknowledgement within twenty-one days. This will set out (if that be the case) why the claim is not accepted, again with relevant detail. Clearly the objective is to avoid litigation if that is possible, and the Protocol envisages negotiation to try to avoid litigation prior to the actual commencement of proceedings.[30]

Specific pre-action protocols have been developed for particular kinds of litigation. These include Protocols in respect of personal injury cases, clinical disputes, construction and engineering disputes, defamation cases, professional negligence cases, and judicial review. The detail of them is beyond the scope of this book,[31] but the common features of clear statements designed to identify what matters are in dispute, what matters are claimed, and the extent to which the parties disagree are all evident. What is also important is their impact on the courts. They are intended to assist the process of negotiation and settlement before costly proceedings are begun. The main sanction for their disregard lies in the area of costs.[32] The Civil Procedure Rules seek to encourage pre-action settlement, and, as noted below,[33] Part 36 of CPR sets out a procedure where one party can offer to settle by making an offer or payment. If this is not accepted, and the ultimate judgment or award of the court at trial is not as generous as that offered under the Part 36 procedure, the party who refused the Part 36 offer may be penalized in costs for the expense of a trial unnecessarily incurred. The effect of this may be to increase the chances of settlement and the avoidance of litigation, but it may, perhaps, also 'front-load' some costs, bringing forward some costs from the litigation to the pre-litigation stage.[34]

COMMENCING A CIVIL ACTION

Prior to the introduction of the Woolf Reforms a complex range of methods of commencement of civil action existed. A county court action was, generally, commenced by summons. An action in the Queen's Bench Division was in most cases commenced

---

[26] *Consultation Paper: General Pre-Action Protocol*, 2002, www.dca.gov.uk/consult/preactionresp.htm
[27] Practice Direction Protocols para 4.1.
[28] See p 473, *ante*.   [29] See p 400, *ante*.   [30] Protocol, *op cit*, para 4.7.
[31] For a convenient summary, see Loughlin and Gerlis, *Civil Procedure*, 2nd edn (2004), at pp 87–97.
[32] See, e.g., *Ford* v *GKR Construction Ltd* [2000] 1 All ER 802.
[33] See p 501, *post*.   [34] See *Andrews op cit*, para 1.17.

by writ of summons, generally referred to as a writ. The last writ was issued on 24 April 1999.[35] Alternative methods of commencement also existed, of which the most important was the originating summons. This was an appropriate method of proceeding in the High Court where the parties' dispute was such that it could be determined without evidence on matters of fact. Woolf recommended that one form should be used for every civil dispute.[36] This in fact has not been completely achieved, but the basis of all procedure is, now, that the *main* way of commencing a civil action, whether in the High Court or county court, is by the issue of a claim form (Part 7 procedure).[37] But not all proceedings are begun by a claim. As noted above, it was possible to commence an action by way of originating summons. This procedure was used, for example, where the matter involved the question of the construction of a statute, or document, or where an application was made to the High Court other than one in pending proceedings and where no other procedure was specified, such as for discovery of documents before commencement of an action.[38] An equivalent procedure was introduced by Part 8 of the Civil Procedure Rules (Part 8 procedure). This is a process used where a decision is sought from the court on a question unlikely to involve a substantial dispute of fact. This could, again, involve the construction of a statute, contract, deed, or will. Part 8 may also be used in other circumstances specified in the CPR, such as the agreement by the court of a settlement agreed on behalf of a child.[39] The choice is not that of the parties alone: the court may overturn the decision of the claimant,[40] if the Part 7 procedure is thought more appropriate because of the way it identifies complex issues to be determined.

1 THE CONTENTS OF THE CLAIM

A Part 7 claim identifies the claimant and defendant, although, exceptionally, it may be valid despite a failure to name the defendant provided it identifies those included in the action with sufficient particularity. One example was seen in *Bloomsbury Publishing Group Ltd* v *News Group Newspapers Ltd*,[41] where the question in issue centred on whether the defendants had been adequately identified. Copies of the well-known Harry Potter children's novels had been taken from the printers, pre-publication, by unauthorized persons. The court, in upholding the validity of an order against 'the person (or persons) who have offered [the books] for sale', observed that the overriding objective of the Civil Procedure Rules[42] was inconsistent with any rule that preferred form to substance.

The claim instructs the defendant to satisfy the claim, or, alternatively, acknowledge service and state whether the claim will be contested. Without this, the claimant may obtain judgment in default without giving further notice to the defendant. The claim will contain a concise statement of its nature, a description of the remedy sought although, when it comes to trial the court may grant such remedy to which the defendant

---

[35] Andrews, *op cit*, para 10.2.
[36] Woolf Final Report, *op cit*, Ch 2, para 3, Ch 12, para 1.   [37] CPR 7.2.
[38] Under Supreme Court Act 1981, s 33(2). For the equivalent post-Woolf procedure, see p 486, *post*.
[39] CPR Practice Direction 8A, 1.4.   [40] CPR, 8.1(3).
[41] [2003] 3 All ER 736.   [42] See p 463, *ante*.

is entitled.[43] The claim will state the amount of any money claimed, or contain a statement of value, which then allows the court to allocate the case to the correct court and track.[44] Importantly, a party who has entered into a conditional fee agreement and who will wish to recover a success fee[45] or an after-the-event insurance premium, must file details of those arrangements so that the defendant is aware of the possible financial effects should he lose.

A Part 8 claim will set out the nature of the issue or question the claimant wishes the court to resolve, the remedies sought, and the basis on which such remedies might be granted. The evidence supporting the claim, in the form of written statements or affidavits (sworn statements) must accompany the claim. The defence respond in kind. There is, though, no power to strike out an application in default of such a response.[46]

2 PARTIES TO PROCEEDINGS

A single claim form may start several claims that can conveniently be disposed of in the same proceedings.[47] This may amount to several claims against a single defendant, or may involve multiple defendants. An action may be representative in nature: where more than one person has the same interest, an action may be conducted by or against the same interest as representative of any other persons who have that same interest.[48] Thus, where several persons have the same interest, whether as claimants or defendants, one or more persons may be authorized to appear on behalf of all persons so interested. However, a representative action is only appropriate where all the persons to be represented have a common grievance and will all benefit from the relief claimed if claimants[49] or are jointly liable if defendants.[50] Thus where the liability of defendants is several, for example in conspiracy[51] or defamation, they cannot be represented and must be sued in their own names. Nevertheless an action for negligence has been allowed to proceed against representatives of the members of a club on the ground that they were joint occupiers of the club premises.[52] A judgment against representative defendants is binding on them all.

3 REPRESENTATIVE AND MULTI-PARTY ACTIONS

(a) Background

Representative actions have been somewhat circumvented by group actions whereby several actions out of a large number of potential claims are litigated to establish liability

[43] CPR, 16.2(5).   [44] CPR, 16.3.   [45] See p 526, *post*.
[46] CPR, 8.1(5).   [47] CPR, 7.3.   [48] CPR, 19.6.
[49] *Smith* v *Cardiff Corporation* [1954] 1 QB 210, [1953] 2 All ER 1373, distinguished in *John* v *Rees* [1970] Ch 345, [1969] 2 All ER 274.
[50] *Mercantile Marine Service Association* v *Toms* [1916] 2 KB 243.
[51] *Hardie & Lane* v *Chilton* [1928] KB 663.
[52] *Campbell* v *Thompson* [1953] QB 445, [1953] 1 All ER 831; see also *Wallersteiner* v *Moir (No 2)* [1975] QB 373, [1975] 1 All ER 849, where a minority shareholders' action was likened to a representative action on behalf of the company and it was stated by the Court of Appeal that the shareholder, after issuing proceedings, should in effect apply to the court for an order sanctioning the proceedings, the effect of which would be to give the shareholder a right to have the company pay his costs.

and the principles for the award of damages. The types of situations suitable for multi-party actions were summarized in 1997[53] as follows:

(a) Major one-off disaster claims (such as the ferry disaster at Zeebrugge and the King's Cross tube station fire disaster) where causation is generally common to all the cases and may not be in dispute and where the class of those affected is clearly defined from the outset. In many cases the number of individuals in the class will be high.

(b) Product liability claims (especially those involving pharmaceutical products such as Opren and benzodiazepine) where liability may be difficult to determine and common issues may be difficult to identify. Such claims are frequently complicated by a multiplicity of defendants who all manufactured similar products as well as by a multiplicity of claimants. In a case involving the drug Opren there were some 1,500 claimants against a drug company, which were litigated on the basis of a 'master' statement of claim, and with certain 'lead cases' to determine different aspects of the overall issue

(c) Multiple claims relating to industrial diseases deriving from the same cause, such as asbestosis claims, industrial deafness, and vibration white finger claims.

(d) Environmental cases deriving not only from specific incidents but also from damage occurring over a period of time, such as seepage from an industrial plant, or a nuclear installation, or prolonged use of chemicals in particular circumstances. These types of claim may involve both personal injury and property damage as well as, in some cases, loss of amenity.

(e) Claims relating to use or consumption of defective goods or services causing damage to property, or personal injury and/or financial loss. Examples are claims by tenants of a block of flats or an estate for a landlord's failure to repair; shareholders against a company or its auditors for disseminating misleading information; residents of a neighbourhood against a public authority's decision to build a road or to permit development in their area; a group of package holiday customers against a tour operator; a group of customers who have bought defective goods; or for professional negligence claims. Often, but by no means always, the claims may be individually small, but together quite substantial.

Development of group actions in the UK has centred on a variety of types of case. There are cases involving 'mass disasters' involving large numbers of individual claims. Instead of having to try separately a whole series of cases arising out of the same 'disaster' it was more efficient for the courts to try the common questions as one action. As a result, the evolution of multi-party actions has largely occurred because of 'an innovative approach by the courts and practitioners to procedure rules, in particular those relating to lead actions, or test cases, and the joining of parties to the action'. Their development was well summarized by Longmore LJ in *Afrika and others* v

[53] *Multi-Party Actions: Consultation Paper from Civil Justice Working Group*, Lord Chancellor's Department, 1997.

Cape Plc; X, Y and Z and others v *Schering Healthcare Ltd; Sayers and others* v *Merck & Smithkline Beecham plc:*[54]

> Multi-party actions are a comparatively novel feature of English litigation and the courts have attempted over recent years to fashion new types of order to enable viable actions to be brought in situations where a single individual would find it prohibitively expensive to bring proceedings on his or her own. The present appeals arise in three separate multi-party actions: the first is what is known as the MMR/MR litigation in which claims are made for injuries allegedly suffered by children as a result of the administration of vaccine against measles, mumps and rubella (or just measles rubella); the second action is the oral contraception litigation in which claimants seek damages for injuries sustained by the taking of oral contraceptives; the third action is brought by workers in South Africa against the English holding company of the South Africa subsidiary, which employed them, for injuries suffered as a result of exposure to asbestos. Typically defendants are drug manufacturers, health trusts on whose behalf drugs are prescribed, or other large corporations some of whom (or whose insurers) have deep pockets. Claimants are typically individuals who could not contemplate financing litigation themselves, and obtain assistance for that purpose from the Legal Services Commission or, perhaps, under a Conditional Fee Agreements... These actions are difficult, as well as expensive, to run and impose great burdens on the practitioners who conduct them and the judges who try them. They can, however, be a service to many who suffer severe injuries and it is the policy of the courts to facilitate such actions in appropriate cases and adapt traditional procedures accordingly...

The impact of the actions of the Legal Services Commission contracting representation in this type of case has already been noted.[55]

(b) The Woolf Report and Group Litigation Order

The Woolf Report identified objectives that any new system for multi-party actions should aim to achieve. Firstly, it should provide access to justice where large numbers of people have been affected by another's conduct, but individual loss is so small that it makes an individual action economically unviable. Secondly, it should provide expeditious, effective, and proportionate methods of resolving cases, where individual damages are large enough to justify individual action but where the number of claimants and the nature of the issues involved mean that the cases cannot be managed satisfactorily in accordance with normal procedure. Thirdly, the rules should achieve a balance between the normal rights of claimants and defendants, to pursue and defend cases individually, and the interests of a group of parties to litigate the action as a whole in an effective manner. Rules seek to achieve these objectives.

Part 19 of the Civil Procedure Rules makes provision for Group Litigation pursuant to a Group Litigation Order. Solicitors representing claimants in such a potential case are encouraged to form a Solicitor's Group, and to appoint one of their number as the

---

[54] [2001] EWCA Civ 2017.   [55] See p 405, *ante*.

lead in seeking a Group Litigation Order.[56] An application is made to the court. When made, such an order provides for the registration of all the claims in being, and identifies the court which is to manage the case under the case management approach envisaged by Woolf. In the early days of group actions, pre-Woolf, the courts had to be innovative. In *AB v John Wyeth & Brother Ltd*[57] Steyn LJ observed:

> The procedural powers of a judge in control of a group case are not tied to trad-itional procedures. Subject to the duty to act fairly, the judge may and often must improvise: sometimes this will involve the adoption of an entirely new procedure.

One problem is the question of who joins the group: litigants have to opt-in, and there can often be some disagreement as to how big a class of potential litigants actually is.[58] Some argue that the process would be better if the class was identified, with those falling within it, having to opt-out.[59]

The rules permit a judge to set a timetable, give directions, and generally manage the case through its often difficult and long processes. The judge will identify the lead solici-tor, provide for a cut-off date for joining the group, and identify test claims. The court can order that parties be joined.[60] A judgment given relating to a Group Litigation Order issue is binding on the parties to all other claims on the group register at the time the judgment or order is made, unless the court orders otherwise.[61] An individual adversely affected may, however, seek permission to appeal.

4 ISSUE AND SERVICE OF THE CLAIM[62]

Once issued the claim is normally valid for four months beginning with the date of issue.[63] However, it may on application be renewed for a further period not exceeding twelve months if the court is satisfied that it has not been possible to serve it during that period. Such an application is made without giving notice to the other party. An extension will only be granted where the application for extension has been made promptly, and only if the court has been unable to serve the claim form, or the claimant has taken all reasonable steps to serve it, but has been unable to do so.[64] There are pro-visions in the rules which provide for a series of dates for 'deemed service'. For example, where service is by first-class post, service is deemed to have been effected on the sec-ond day[65] after the claim form was posted. These dates are applied rigidly. In *Godwin v Swindon BC*[66] the court recognized this as a total fiction. Service was deemed to

---

[56] Practice Direction 19B.   [57] (1992) 12 BMLR 452.

[58] See *Autologic Holdings plc v Inland Revenue Commissioners* [2005] UKHL 54, [2006] 1 All ER 118; *Hobson v Ashton Martin Slack Solicitors* [2006] EWCA Civ 134 (QB); *Owen v Ministry of Defence* [2006] EWHC 990 (QB); *Davies v Department of Trade and Industry* [2007] 1 WLR 3232, [2006] EWCA Civ 1360.

[59] Mulheran, 'Justice Enhanced: An Opt-Out Class Action for England' (2007) MLR 550.

[60] *Davies and others v Department of Trade and Industry* [2007] 1 All ER 518, [2006] EWCA Civ 1360.

[61] CPR, 19.12(1)(a).   [62] See, generally, *Collier v Williams* [2006] EWCA Civ 20.

[63] CPR, 7.5(2). See, e.g., *Dickins v Solicitors' Indemnity Fund* [2005] EWHC 2754.

[64] CPR, 7.6(3).

[65] This includes *all* days, and not simply working days: *Anderton v Clwydd CC (No 2)* [1992] 1 WLR 374.

[66] [2002] 1 WLR 997.

have occurred on Monday 11 September 2000, it having been posted on Thursday 7 September 2000, and thus out-of-time, even though the letter was in fact received on Friday 8 September, which was within time. This extraordinary result can be justified only on the basis of simplicity and certainty, and raises some issues about whether the individual's right of access to the courts is being limited in an unreasonable and disproportionate way, possibly infringing the fair trial provisions of Article 6 of the European Convention.[67]

The claim is served on the defendant by the court unless the claimant informs the court that he wishes to serve the claim himself, or unless there is a rule, order, or practice direction releasing the court from this obligation.[68] The Civil Procedure Rules specify the mode of service.[69] This may be by whatever means are agreed, by personal service, by leaving the claim at an address provided by the defendant for that purpose, leaving the claim at the usual or last-known address of an individual,[70] or through a document exchange system. However, service by post is permitted and is the normal method of service by the court.[71] Electronic service by e-mail or fax is also envisaged in some circumstances where it has been indicated in writing by an individual that this will be accepted.

The court also has the power to order service by some other means, a process known as 'substituted service'. This might take, for example, the form of service by registered or recorded delivery post to the defendant's last known address, service on the defendant's solicitor or agent, or service by advertisement in the press. It also has the power to dispense totally with service,[72] but this power should not be used to validate late service.[73]

5 PUBLIC OR PRIVATE LAW

A second preliminary factor of importance which must be considered is whether the proposed action involves questions of public law. Where in reality an action raises issues of public law, the normal procedure for determination of those questions is by an application for judicial review under Part 54 of the Civil Procedure Rules.[74] A failure to use the Part 54 procedure, with its time limits and the requirement to obtain permission, may result subsequently in an application by the defendant to have the action struck out as an abuse of process of the court. The courts have developed a much more liberal approach to these matters, as was seen earlier.[75]

6 ADDITIONAL CLAIMS

Although additional claims (formerly known as counterclaims, contributions, and indemnities) logically are issues and procedures that arise once the proceedings have

---

[67] See *Andrews op cit*, at para 10.48. See also *Sealy v Consignia plc* [2002] 3 All ER 801; *Vinos v Marks and Spencer plc* [2001] 3 All ER 784; *Naglegan v Royal Free Hospital NHS Trust* [2002] 1 WLR 1043.
[68] CPR, 6.3, 6.13.   [69] See, generally, CPR, 6.8–6.9.
[70] Not a property let by him: *O'Hare and another v McDougal* (2005) [2005] EWCA (Civ) 1628.
[71] Practice Direction 6, para 8.1.   [72] CPR 6.9.
[73] *Godwin v Swindon BC* [2001] 4 All ER 641, disapproving *Infantino v Maclean* [2001] 4 All ER 641.
[74] Formerly Ord 53 RSC.   [75] See chapter 7, *ante*.

been commenced, it is convenient to deal with them here. We have noted the Part 7 and Part 8 procedures for the commencement of actions. Where a party wishes to advance a new claim within existing procedures, Part 20 applies. It permits the making of an additional claim (i.e. a claim that the claimant, or the claimant and others, is himself liable to the defendant). Thus if the supplier of goods is suing for the unpaid price, a counter-claim might claim damages of defective goods. But an additional claim can be against a third party, although the permission of the court will be needed to bring in as a further defendant a third party.[76] Thus a purchaser who is defending an action brought by the retailer of a motor vehicle might wish to bring into the action the manufacturer of the car if the defendant wishes to allege gross design or construction faults. Such a claim can be served as of right against the claimant at the same time as the service of the defence, but otherwise permission is required.

A contribution may be sought from someone who is liable to pay part of any damages awarded. Thus a driver potentially liable in damages for injuries caused to a pedestrian may seek a contribution from another driver considered to be partly at fault and responsible for the accident giving rise to the claim. By contrast a defendant may see an indemnity, usually from an insurance company. Part 20 provides for the procedure to be followed in such cases. This involves the service of a notice setting out the nature and grounds of the claim for a contribution of indemnity. Permission of the court is not required.

PRE-COMMENCEMENT ORDERS
AND PROCEDURES

Questions concerning disclosure and inspection of documents and the inspection, preservation, and the like of property are dealt with during the course of proceedings, usually after the statements of case and defence, and these matters are dealt with below in that context.[77] However, statutory provisions enable parties to obtain orders of this type prior to the commencement of proceedings. There are two distinct procedures of this type, set out below. There are also common law powers.

1 DISCLOSURE AND INSPECTION OF DOCUMENTS

A potential litigant often will not know whether a cause of action exists, or a cause of action with realistic prospects of success exists, without knowing the contents of documents held by the potential defendant. For example, the strength of a potential claim in medical negligence against a hospital trust may turn on the contents of medical records held by the hospital. In 1991 a power was introduced by section 33(2) of the Supreme

---

[76] CPR, 20.5.   [77] See p 505, *post.*

Court Act 1981, which provided that a person who appears to the High Court to be likely to be a party to subsequent proceedings in respect of a claim of personal injuries or death could apply for pre-trial discovery of documents in the possession, custody, or power of a person. The Woolf Report recommended the extension of this power to all categories of case.[78] This was achieved in the Civil Procedure Rules.

For an order to be made, the following conditions must be satisfied:[79]

(a) The person against whom the order is sought must be a likely party to the proceedings; it is not enough that that person is a potential witness.

(b) The document or documents sought would be disclosable under the standard rules of disclosure if the action was in progress.[80]

(c) Pre-action disclosure is desirable in order to dispose fairly of the anticipated proceedings, or to assist the dispute to be resolved without proceedings, or to save costs.

That party may be ordered to disclose whether those documents are in his custody, possession, and power and, if so, to produce them to the applicant, unless they are protected from disclosure by the doctrine of privilege. It is immaterial that the likelihood of the claim being made is dependent upon the outcome of the disclosure; the words 'likely' in the rules is to be construed as meaning 'may or may well be made' if, on disclosure, the documents in question indicate that the applicant has a good cause of action.[81] On the other hand a 'thin and fragile case' in *Snowstar Shipping Co Ltd* v *Graig Shipping Co*[82] was the context when a too widely drawn application was refused.

If the relevant evidence is not in the possession of a person who is likely to be a party, rule 34 applies. If the pre-conditions are satisfied the court can order disclosure of documents in the possession of a person or body who is not a party or not likely to be so. The preconditions are that the documents must be likely to support the case of the applicant or adversely affect one of the parties to it.

2 INSPECTION, ETC OF PROPERTY

Section 33(1) of the Supreme Court Act 1981 empowers the High Court, in some circumstances, to make an order providing for the inspection, photographing, preservation, custody, or detention of property (including land or chattels) which appears to the court to be property which may become the subject matter of subsequent proceedings in the court, or as to which any question may arise in such proceedings, or for the taking of samples of any such property and the carrying out of any experiment on or with any such property. This is not limited to articles in the possession of a party, a position which may be contrasted with that that exists after commencement of proceedings.

---

[78] Woolf Final Report, *op cit.*   [79] See, generally, CPR, 31.   [80] See p 507, *post.*

[81] This was the position under pre-existing law: see *Dunning* v *United Liverpool Hospital's Board of Governors* [1973] 2 All ER 454, [1973] 1 WLR 586. See, now *Swain* v *Hillman* [2001] 1 All ER 91; *Three Rivers DC and others* v *HM Treasury and Governor and & Co of the Bank of England* [2002] EWCA Civ 1182.

[82] [2003] EWHC 1367.

The relationship between the power of inspection and that of disclosure was examined in *Huddleston* v *Control Risks Information Services Ltd.*[83] The court drew a distinction between a party wishing to examine 'the medium' (i.e. the document itself) as opposed to being concerned with 'the message' (i.e. with the contents of the document). Section 33(1), inspection, applied to the former, section 33(2), discovery, to the latter. Since in this case the claimant's concern was for the contents, which were believed to be defamatory, what was being sought was discovery, for which the relevant conditions, described above, did not apply. The power of inspection could not be used to circumvent these criteria.

3 THE *NORWICH PHARMACAL* PRINCIPLE

In addition to the powers described above, a court may in some circumstances order disclosure against a third party who has information. If it does so it is doing so as part of its inherent jurisdiction. Whilst this will often be during litigation, it may be appropriate to obtain such disclosure prior to action, in order to discover whether a basis of action exists, and against whom. The principle, which was first stated by the court in *Norwich Pharmacal Co* v *Commissioners of Customs and Excise* does not permit disclosure in all circumstances: it is only where the third party is in some way involved in the wrongdoing alleged that the court will order disclosure against that third party.[84] However, the rule has been extended to cases where a third party has information necessary for locating and recovering missing funds,[85] and to a case where the defendant (which ran a discussion board on an internet site), knew the identity of an individual posting allegedly defamatory material in respect of the claimant.[86]

4 SEARCH ORDERS

The High Court developed what was known as an *Anton Piller* order, named after the case in which the Court of Appeal first sanctioned the making of such an order.[87] This allowed a court to order a defendant to permit a claimant to enter the defendant's premises in order to inspect, remove, or make copies of documents belonging to the claimant or relating to the claimant's property. The procedure and power is now governed by section 7 of the Civil Procedure Act 1997. An order may be obtained without notice, but will only be made where the claimant shows that there is a grave danger of property being smuggled away or vital evidence destroyed; it is usually applicable to infringement of copyright cases, passing off, or breaches of confidence, or cases of that sort.[88]

[83] [1987] 2 All ER 1035, [1987] 1 WLR 701.
[84] *Harrington* v *North London Polytechnic* [1984] 3 All ER 666; [1984] 1 WLR 1293. In *Ricci* v *Chow* [1987] 3 All ER 534, [1987] 1 WLR 1658 the Court of Appeal decided that disclosure of the identity of the publisher and printer of an alleged defamatory article would not be ordered against the defendant, a person involved in no way in the publication, but who knew the publisher's name.
[85] *Arab Monetary Fund* v *Hashim (No 5)* [1992] 2 All ER 911; *Bankers Trust* v *Shapira* [1980] 3 All ER 353.
[86] *Totalise plc* v *Motley Fool Ltd* [2001] EWCA Civ 1897.
[87] *Anton Piller KG* v *Manufacturing Processes Ltd* [1976] Ch 55.
[88] See, e.g., *ex parte Island Records Ltd* [1978] Ch 122, [1978] 3 All ER 824.

A search order may, at first sight, appear to be in the nature of a search warrant issued to a private individual, but in fact it is not; it confers upon the claimant no right to enter the defendant's premises, but rather imposes a duty on a defendant to permit the claimant to enter his premises. Failure on the part of the defendant to comply will, however, be a contempt of court. The use of the power has become extremely popular with claimants and their advisers. By its very nature it may enable a claimant to strike gold in relation to wrongful acts, such as misuse of confidential information or infringement of copyright, which but for the order the claimant might possibly never have been in a position to prove (defendants in these matters frequently being less than frank as to voluntary disclosure); all that the claimant risks is having to pay his opponent's costs of the application and damages if any are caused.

There are three pre-conditions for the making of a search order. First, there must be a strong prima facie case. Secondly, the damage or potential damage to the applicant must be very serious. Thirdly, there must be clear evidence that the defendants have in their possession incriminating documents or things, and there must be evidence of a real possibility that the defendant may destroy such material before any application on notice can be heard.

In order to minimize speculative and oppressive applications the courts have formulated several procedural safeguards. Thus the claimant's solicitor should attend when the order is executed; if permission to enter premises is refused no force should be used; the defendant should have the opportunity to contact his solicitor, and should be advised of his right to obtain legal advice.[89] The requirement to allow entry does not in fact operate immediately, despite the use of the word 'forthwith' in an order, but operates only after there has been a reasonable period of time to obtain legal advice. The applicant must make full disclosure to the court of all matters relevant to his application and if material facts are omitted the order will be discharged. The nature of the search order is exceptional, and creates potential for abuse. In *Universal Thermosensors Ltd* v *Hibben*[90] Sir Donald Nicholls V-C identified certain key points, that are now reflected in Practice Direction 25:

(1) An order should normally contain a term that, before compliance, the defendant may obtain legal advice, if this is done forthwith. If such a term is to be of use, generally such order should be executed only on working days in office hours, when a solicitor can be expected to be available.

(2) If an order is to be executed on private premises and a woman may be at the house alone, the solicitor serving the order must be, or be accompanied by, a woman.

(3) The order should expressly provide that, unless seriously impracticable, a detailed list of the items being removed should be prepared at the time of removal, with the defendant being given the opportunity to check that list.

(4) Orders sometimes contain a restraining order restraining those on whom they are served from informing others of the existence of the order for a limited period, subject to an exception in respect of communication with a lawyer to gain legal

---

[89] Practice Direction 25.   [90] [1992] 3 All ER 257, [1992] 1 WLR 840.

advice. The length of time governed by the restraining order should not be an excessively long period. In the instant case, one week was too long.

(5) An order should not be executed at business premises without a responsible officer or representative being present.

(6) Consideration should be given as to how a competitor of the business subject to the order can be prevented from having unlimited access to the documents of that business.

(7) An order should, where possible, be served by a solicitor other than a member of the firm of solicitors acting for the claimant. That solicitor should also have experience of the search order procedure. The defendant against whom an *ex parte* order has been made may apply to have the order set aside (as can any litigant against whom an *ex parte* order is made); he may even refuse compliance with the order and apply urgently to have it set aside but he does so at his peril since if his application fails he will be in contempt of court and liable to severe penalties if he has in the interim breached the order, for example by destroying records.

It was held by the House of Lords in *Rank Film Distributors Ltd* v *Video Information Centre*[91] that defendants could resist the making of an order on the ground of privilege against self-incrimination.[92] This was a serious inroad into the scope of what were then known as *Anton Piller* orders since, in the nature of things, persons against whom such orders are made are frequently engaged in fraudulent activity. To remedy this, section 72 of the Supreme Court Act 1981 withdrew the privilege in relation to High Court proceedings for infringement of rights pertaining to any intellectual property or for passing-off, including proceedings brought to prevent any apprehended such infringement or passing-off and proceedings brought to obtain disclosure of information relating thereto. Other exceptions to the privilege also exist. However, it has become clear that, since the passage of the Human Rights Act 1998,[93] that the privilege does not apply in criminal proceedings in relation to independent evidence.[94] This is evidence which came into effect independently of compulsory questioning or disclosure process. It has been held that, for that reason, the rule in civil cases ought to be the same.[95]

The extent to which such orders can be resisted on the grounds of the privilege against self-incrimination was considered by the House of Lords in *AT & T Istel Ltd* v *Tully.*[96] The House was of the opinion that the privilege, which itself in a civil case was an 'archaic and unjustifiable survival from the past', only protected the defendant if compliance with the order would provide evidence against him in a criminal trial. If the defendant could be protected against being exposed to the reasonable risk of the information to be disclosed being used in a criminal prosecution by other means, then the courts were entitled to rely on those other means. In that case the Crown Prosecution Service had agreed not to seek to use in criminal proceedings the documents disclosed.

---

[91] [1982] AC 380, [1981] 2 All ER 76.   [92] As for this, see below.
[93] See p 79, *ante.*   [94] *Saunders* v *United Kingdom* (1998) 23 EHRR 313.
[95] *C plc* v *P (Secretary of State for the Home Department and another intervening)* [2007] EWCA Civ 493, [2007] 3 All ER 1034.
[96] [1993] AC 45, [1992] 3 All ER 523.

5 FREEZING ORDERS

(a) Jurisdiction

It will be appreciated that the prospective claimant in an action for debt or damages faces two distinct obstacles. The first is to obtain a judgment (or settlement) in his favour; the second is to enforce that judgment. It is of little consolation to most litigants to succeed in the action and yet be unable to enforce the judgment. Regrettably, where a defendant is uninsured against his liability this is a situation which often arises. Where the defendant is simply insolvent this is a misfortune that the claimant must bear. However, the courts can and will intervene to prevent a defendant from avoiding his liability to the claimant by disposing of his assets, and in particular removing them outside the jurisdiction of the English courts. The jurisdiction to issue an injunction to restrain a defendant from removing assets was developed in the *Mareva*[97] case, are now to be found in the Civil Procedure Rules, and which reflect principles developed by case law.[98] The purpose of the injunction is to prevent the defendant from evading justice by disposing of assets. The claimant must show a good arguable case in relation to the substantive claim.[99] The defendant must have assets, whether inside or outside the jurisdiction. There must also be proved a real risk that, if the court does not grant an order, the defendant will take the opportunity to dissipate those assets or otherwise put them beyond the reach of the court. The standard is a high one: it will be insufficient to show that the defendant is short of money.[100]

The words 'dealing with' encompass disposing of, selling or charging assets. Until recently it had been thought that one important restriction on the court's power to grant a freezing injunction lay in the fact that the injunction is ancillary to a cause of action; it is not a cause of action in itself. Thus, if a claimant's claim is not justiciable in the English courts he cannot obtain an injunction. For example, if the defendant is domiciled in a country to which section 25 of the Civil Jurisdiction and Judgments Act 1982 does not apply, leave to serve a writ outside the jurisdiction will be required. If this was not granted, there would be no basis for a successful application for a freezing injunction. This view was supported by the Court of Appeal in *The Veracruz I*[101] where it was stressed that the powers of the High Court to grant an injunction derived from section 37 of the Supreme Court Act 1981, and were to grant an injunction in all cases where it was just and convenient to do so. The right to obtain an interim injunction was not a cause of action in itself. However, this conclusion is called into doubt by the decision of the House of Lords in *Channel Tunnel Group Ltd* v *Balfour Beatty Construction Ltd*.[102] In that case Lord Mustill indicated that the fact that proceedings in an English court could be the subject of a stay did not prevent the court from granting interim relief. Lord Browne-Wilkinson doubted whether the authority on which this restriction was based remained good law.

---

[97] *Mareva Compania SA* v *International Bulkcarriers SA* [1975] 2 Lloyds Rep 509.
[98] CPR, 25.1.   [99] *Derby* v *Weldon* [1990] Ch 48.
[100] *Midas Merchant Bank plc* v *Bello* [2002] EWCA Civ 274.
[101] [1992] Lloyds Rep 353.   [102] [1993] AC 334, [1993] 1 All ER 664.

(b) Procedure

An applicant for a freezing order is well advised to act quickly. To this end the customary practice is to apply without notice in the first instance, sometimes even before issuing a claim[103] (in which case the claimant will be required to undertake to issue a claim within a specified period or 'forthwith'). Such an application must be made to the High Court.[104] That court can make an order which will be made to take effect until the return date on the claim which the claimant will have issued or undertaken to issue. The claimant must swear an affidavit in support of his application. In *Third Chandris Shipping Corporation* v *Unimarine SA*[105] the Court of Appeal stated guidelines that judges should follow on such applications:

> (i) the claimant should make full and frank disclosure of all matters in his knowledge which are material for the judge to know;
>
> (ii) the claimant should give particulars of this claim and the amount thereof and of the defendant's case against it;
>
> (iii) the claimant should give some grounds for believing that the defendant has assets within the jurisdiction;
>
> (iv) the claimant should give some grounds (not merely that the defendant is abroad) for believing that there is a risk of the assets of the defendant being removed before the judgment is satisfied;
>
> (v) the claimant should give an undertaking in damages, in a suitable case to be supported by a bond or security.

The court has power to order disclosure of documents or to administer interrogatories as to the amount, whereabouts or other details of the defendant's assets, with a view to securing the efficacy of the injunction. Such an order can operate worldwide.[106] Copies of the injunction will generally be served upon the defendant's bank or other body having custody of his assets, so as to fix such body with knowledge of the injunction (since such body would itself be guilty of contempt of court if it assisted the defendant to act in breach of the injunction, knowing that it is probable that the asset is being disposed of in breach of the injunction). The receipt by a bank of such notice overrides its customer's instructions, e.g. to honour cheques.

(c) Principles upon which the court acts

By section 37(1) of the Supreme Court Act 1981 the High Court may grant an order 'in all cases in which it appears to the court to be just and convenient to do so'. However, although not subject to statutory fetters, the courts have developed principles on the basis of which to grant or refuse injunctions. The general principles affecting the discretion whether to grant or refuse an interlocutory injunction are those laid down by the House

---

[103] See *Fourie* v *Le Roux and another* [2007] UKHL 1, [2007] 1 All ER 1087.
[104] *Schmidt* v *Wong* [2005] EWCA Civ 1506.   [105] [1979] QB 645.
[106] For enforceability, see *Daqdouria Group Intervention Inc and others* v *Simmons* [2006] EWCA Civ 399.

of Lords in *American Cyanamid Co* v *Ethicon Ltd*[107] and will be considered in due course. However, there are additional principles which particularly apply to *Mareva* applications. As a first step the claimant must satisfy the court (i) that he has at least a good arguable case; and (ii) that the refusal of an injunction would involve a real risk that a judgment or award in the claimant's favour would remain unsatisfied because of the defendant's removal of assets from the jurisdiction or dissipation of assets within the jurisdiction. An injunction will not be granted merely for the purpose of providing a claimant with security for a claim, even where it appears likely to succeed and even where the granting of the injunction will not cause hardship to the defendant. An injunction will not be granted so as to give the claimant priority over other creditors, nor to prevent the defendant from paying his debts as they fall due or carrying on his legitimate business. It is also common for the injunction to be expressed so as to exclude periodical payments of reasonable amounts to provide for the living or other expenses of the defendant, including amounts to be paid to his legal advisers to contest the litigation.

(d) Position of third parties

It has been noted that service of a copy of the order upon a third party, such as a bank, operates in effect to freeze the account. This has led to problems and the courts are vigilant to ensure that banks and other third parties do not suffer in consequence of the grant of a freezing order. Thus, a bank is entitled to a variation of the injunction to enable it to set off against any funds which it holds any right that it has in respect of facilities granted to the client, for example bank charges, interest, or the balance on another account. Similarly, an order will not be granted, or will be discharged, where the effect would be to interfere substantially with the business of a third party. In *Polly Peck International plc* v *Nadir (No 2)*[108] the court indicated that a freezing injunction ought not to be granted against a bank, except where that bank was likely to act so as to avoid judgment. Where a bank or third party is compelled to enter the proceedings in order to obtain an order, or discharge of an order, the claimant will ordinarily be required to pay its cost on an indemnity basis.

FURTHER READING

ANDREWS, *English Civil Procedure* (Oxford University Press: 2004)

Lord Chancellor's Department, *Multi Party Actions: Consultation Paper from Civil Justice Working Group* (1997)

ROBERTS, 'Settlement as Civil Justice' (2000) 63 MLR 739

WARD, 'New Carrots and Sticks: Proposals for Reform of CPR Part 36' (2007) 70 MLR 278

WOOLF, *Access to Justice* (1995) – the 'Woolf Report'

---

[107] See p 503, *post*.   [108] [1992] 4 All ER 769.

16

CIVIL TRIALS

INTRODUCTION

This chapter will examine the process of trial itself. The landscape has changed in a major way since the Woolf Reforms and the much more case-management approach inherent in the Civil Procedure Rules. The hearing itself is just a part of the process. Specific areas covered will include:

- The three-track approach to allocation of court – *Small Claims*, *Fast Track*, *Multi-Track*.
- The settlement and discontinuance of cases.
- How issues to be decided are identified.
- The sharing of relevant information through disclosure.
- The trial itself.

THE COURT OF TRIAL

In previous chapters we have examined the nature of the new landscape for civil litigation, introduced following the Woolf Report,[1] and the process that applies in respect of avoiding disputes and in commencing them if that is inevitable. With the Woolf Reforms in place it is neither possible, or appropriate, to discuss the civil pre-trial and trial procedure simply, for the complexity of the Civil Procedure Rules, and their applicability in many different ways to different types of action, prevents this within the scope of a general text on the English legal system. This chapter concentrates on key principles, issues, and processes.

1 THE THREE-TRACK APPROACH

The Woolf Report proposed[2] that cases be allocated to one of three tracks – the *Small Claims* track, the *Fast* Track, and the *Multi-Track*, except where the procedural judge

---

[1] See generally chapter 14 at p 456, *ante*.
[2] See *Access to Justice: Judicial Case Management: The Fast track and Multi Track, A Working Paper*, July 1997; See also Middleton Report, *op cit*, at paras 2.24–2.27.

believed that particular characteristics of the individual case made it appropriate for it to be allocated to a different track: This approach reflects the general thrust of the Woolf Report, and of the civil justice reforms, in trying to ensure that the processes undertaken, the requirements made of the parties, that the mode of trial reflect the nature and complexity of what has to be decided and that procedural requirements (and costs)[3] are proportionate to the dispute with which the law has to deal. In part the pre-existing structures did that by defining specific jurisdictions for the county court and High Court, with powers of transfer between the two. The new procedures under the Civil Procedure Rules address these issues in the context of a common form of commencement of civil process, by reference to criteria that are likely to be good indicators as to the level appropriate to the dispute.

Allocation to the appropriate track is done by a district judge or master, following the completion of an allocation questionnaire. Parties completing an allocation questionnaire can request a stay to pursue settlement, or the court can impose a stay of its own initiative,[4] reflecting the philosophy that where cases can be resolved without course to a hearing they should be. Decisions about the allocation of some matters are automatic: Part 8 proceedings (the old originating summons procedure)[5] go automatically to the multi-track. So too with proceedings destined for one of specialist lists – the Commercial Court and the Technology and Construction Court, which provide specialist adjudication in their respective areas.[6] The scope of each track is defined by the Rules,[7] but there is no inevitability about that allocation. However, the process in many instances will be almost automatic. The court has to consider the appropriateness of the relevant track, and, in deciding that, must have regard to the following:[8]

(a) the financial value of the claim;

(b) the nature of the remedy sought;

(c) the complexity of facts, law; or evidence;

(d) the number of parties;

(e) the value of any counterclaim, and its complexity;

(f) the likely amount of oral evidence;

(g) the importance of the claim to those who are not parties;

(h) the views expressed by the parties;

(i) the circumstances of the parties.

Special rules apply in respect of multiple claims: they will normally be allocated to the track appropriate to that of highest value, but the parties may agree otherwise.[9]

---

[3] It will later be noted that costs recovery in the small claims and fast tracks are limited: see p 496, *post*.
[4] CPR, 26.4(2).   [5] See p 480, *ante*.
[6] See p 262, *ante*.   [7] CPR, 26.6.
[8] CPR, 26.8(1).   [9] CPR, 26.7(3).

2 SMALL CLAIMS TRACK

This is the small claims jurisdiction of the county court, and designed to provide a procedurally simple and inexpensive means of disposing of small claims. It is the track to which cases with a financial value of £5,000 or less will normally be allocated, including personal injury claims within that where the element of compensation sought for pain and suffering is less than £1,000. Its jurisdiction extends to tenant claims against landlords in relation to defective premises where the cost of repairs does not exceed £1,000. It also has power to deal with cases where counterclaims exceed £5,000.

The procedure adopted in this track is simplified. No interim relief is available except interim injunctions; disclosure is limited; expert evidence may not be called without the leave of the court. When notified of a hearing date parties are required to exchange all documents on which each intends to rely. Costs are not generally recoverable.[10]

3 FAST TRACK

This normally apply to all claims above £5,000, but less than £15,000,[11] and claims under that limit that are excluded from the small claims jurisdiction (for example personal injuries claims where in excess of £1,000 is sought for pain and suffering). The trial must be likely to last no more than one day, and will generally be in the county court. The amount of expert evidence that may be called is limited to one, or in some cases two, expert per party.[12] The rules provide for directions about the appointment of a joint expert or for experts to try and agree matters. However, where there is a justifiable need for oral expert evidence and the trial is likely to last more than one day, allocation to 'multi-track' may be more appropriate.[13]

When a case is allocated to the fast track directions relating to disclosure, service of witness statements, expert evidence, and as to date of trial will be given. A timetable will be set with the aim of ensuring trial within thirty weeks. A directions hearing will not generally be held.[14] A pre-trial process will occur to ensure that the timetable imposed and directions made have been complied with,[15] to ensure that parties give notice of any applications that are to be made to the court and to ensure that an estimate of likely costs is given to the court.

If it becomes evident that the case is no longer suitable for the fast-track procedure because it is of a greater value than anticipated or for any other reason, the court may (though does not have to) reallocate to the multi-track.[16]

4 MULTI-TRACK

The multi-track will normally apply to all defended claims valued at more than the fast track limit, all clinical negligence claims, all claims in categories in respect of High Court jurisdiction, e.g. judicial review, test cases, cases where there is a right to a jury

---

[10] See p 519, *post.*   [11] CPR, 26.6(4).   [12] CPR, 26.6(5).
[13] *Kearsley* v *Karfield* [2005] EWCA Civ 1510.   [14] CPR, 28.2, 28.3.
[15] CPR, 28.5.   [16] CPR, 26.10.

trial, or cases where fraud is alleged against a party. Effective case management, which is inherent in the civil justice reforms,[17] is obviously crucial at the highest level, dealing with a wide variety of the most difficult or complex cases, but the extent to which the court needs to get involved beyond the issuing of standard directions will depend on the nature, complexity, and value of the matter. Directions without a hearing may be given at the allocation stage. The court can require further information from the parties beyond the statement of case, and may give directions relating to disclosure, case management timetables, and expert evidence. A case management conference may be necessary in an appropriate case, and must be held if the court proposes to appoint a joint expert or assessor.[18] At such a conference the court will consider a range of matters, including whether the issues are clear, whether amendments to the claim are needed, what disclosure of documents is necessary, what expert evidence is required, what evidence should be obtained and disclosed, and how matters of law and fact should be tried.[19] Necessary directions will be given, all designed to secure the achievement of minimizing delay and cost and ensuring compliance with the overriding objective. In due course (which may in cases of real complexity be after a very long process) a pre-trial checklist is completed, and in some cases a pre-trial review occurs, shortly before trial.

The above snapshot of the different forms of procedure anticipated in the different tracks serves only to demonstrate the key principle: that processes should be appropriate and proportionate to the matter being litigated, within the overall principle of active case management. As noted earlier, effective case-management aims to achieve early settlement where that is possible, the diversion of cases to alternative methods for the resolution of disputes, the encouragement of a spirit of co-operation between the parties, the identification of the issues, and progressing a case to trial as quickly and cheaply as possible.

Only the most complex and important cases are heard by High Court judges. Other cases will be managed and heard by the appropriate level of judge and the system permits cases to move flexibly within it to ensure this. As noted earlier, most claims will fall within the jurisdiction of the county court. Case management conferences and other interim hearings may now be conducted by telephone, following successful pilot schemes.[20] The case management role is managed by procedural judges who will generally be Masters or district judges working in teams with High Court and Circuit judges. For the heavier cases, requiring full 'hands-on' judicial control, the procedural judge may be a High Court or Circuit judge. The procedural judge will:

(a) conduct the initial scrutiny of all cases to allocate them to the appropriate management track;

(b) conduct the case management conference unless it is more appropriate for the trial judge to do so;

---

[17] See p 465, *ante*.   [18] Practice Direction 29, para 4.13.
[19] Practice Direction 29, para 5.3.   [20] In Newcastle, Luton and Bedford.

(c) generally monitor the progress of the case and investigate if parties are failing to comply with timetables or directions; and

(d) draw the existence of Alternative Dispute Resolution (ADR) to the parties' attention where this is appropriate or desirable.

The trial judge will normally conduct the pre-trial review.

The salient features of the 'fast track' will be a set timetable of twenty–thirty weeks, with a fixed date or 'warned week' set at the outset for trial; limited discovery, short trials (not exceeding one half day); no oral evidence from experts; and limited evidence from non-experts, and a firm timetable for all actions.

DISCONTINUANCE AND STRIKING OUT

A party may wish to discontinue an action. The parties and their solicitors, at every stage of the proceedings, will generally be attempting to resolve their dispute without the expense of a trial. In fact very few actions come to trial. If the claimant is satisfied that his cause of action was misconceived or has ceased to exist he may at any time consent to judgment being entered against him with costs. The result will be to determine finally the issues he has raised in his claim. However, the claimant is better advised simply to discontinue his action since this course will not prevent him from suing again at a more convenient time. This can be done, usually as of right, under Part 38 of the Civil Procedure Rules. However, the permission of the court will be needed to discontinue a claim, or any part of a claim, in respect of which the court has issued an interim injunction, given an undertaking to the court, or has received an interim payment.[21] If the claimant serves notice of discontinuance the defendant has the power to apply, within twenty-eight days, to have that set aside.[22] The court will then have to decide whether the defendant has suffered any injustice as a result of the discontinuance. This power to strike out a notice of discontinuance will be exercised rarely, and then in cases where it effectively amounts to an abuse of process of the court. Such was the case in *Gilham* v *Browning*[23] where the counterclaim that was being discontinued was raised only to circumvent an evidential restriction in that case. A party who discontinues is usually going to be liable in costs.[24]

A court also has the power to strike out a statement of case.[25] This it may do if the case discloses no reasonable grounds to bring or defend the claim, that the statement of claim amounts to an abuse of the court's process, or there have been failures to comply with a rule, practice direction, or court order. This provision is in addition to the power preserved by section 49(3) of the Supreme Court Act 1981, to stay proceedings as part

---

[21] CPR, 38.2.   [22] CPR, 38.4.   [23] [1998] 2 All ER 68.
[24] CPR, 38.6. For costs, see p 518, *post*.   [25] CPR, 3.4.

of its inherent jurisdiction, which may perhaps be exercised where there are concurrent proceedings in another country.[26]

The question of striking out for delay or 'want of prosecution' is a key one especially because one of the objectives of the Civil Justice reforms was to remove unnecessary delay from civil proceedings, to secure justice within a reasonable time. Questions of default and delay can, under the Civil Procedure Rules, be dealt with by sanctions,[27] from which the parties can seek relief, a power to be exercised in the light of the matters identified in rule 3.9 as those to which the court should have regard. The decision appears to be that which the court considers just in all the circumstances,[28] but in a way which respects the overriding objective[29] but which also respects the fair trial provisions of Article 6 of the European Convention.[30] One way of achieving compliance is through a peremptory ('or unless') order of the court; in such cases the action is liable to be dismissed on account of the conduct of the party in failing to comply with the court's peremptory order; But the power to strike out a case for delay is an extreme one. Prior to the Civil Procedure Rules, the traditional position of the courts was not generally to use the striking out power in cases of delay. In *Birkett* v *James*[31] the House of Lords held that in cases in which the limitation period had not expired (so that if the action were dismissed the plaintiff could simply issue a fresh writ), the court would not, save in rare and exceptional cases, dismiss an action for want of prosecution, unless some factors other than mere delay have prejudiced the defendant. As stated above, such cases are likely to be very rare. Such a position grew increasingly under challenge,[32] In *Arbuthnot Latham Bank Ltd* v *Trafalgar Holdings Ltd*[33] Lord Woolf MR observed:

> In *Birkett* v *James* the consequences to other litigants and to the courts of inordinate delay was not a consideration which was in issue. From now on it is going to be a consideration of increasing significance. Litigants and their legal advisers must recognise that any delay which occurs from now on will be assessed not only from the point of view of the prejudice caused to the particular litigants whose case it is, but also in relation to the effect it can have on other litigants who are wishing to have their cases heard and the prejudice which is caused to the due administration of justice....

There has thus been a 'change of culture'.[34] The fact that there may be another way of penalizing the delay is not inevitably decisive against a striking out for delay, although, arguably, is a matter that the court has to bear in mind.[35]

---

[26] *The Abadin Daver* [1984] AC 398, [1984] 1 All ER 470.

[27] See CPR 3.3–3.9.   [28] *Purdy* v *Cambran* [1999] CPLR 843.

[29] See p 464, *ante*.   [30] Zuckerman, *Civil Procedure, op cit*, para 10.97.

[31] [1978] AC 297; [1977] 2 All ER 801. For exceptions at common law, see, e.g., *Spring Grove Services Ltd* v *Deane* (1972) 116 Sol Jo 844, which case was exceptional in that the defence depended essentially on the evidence of two witnesses who were no longer available to the defendant when the second action was brought; cf. *Department of Health and Social Security* v *Ereira* [1973] 3 All ER 421. The matter is one for the discretion of the court: *Arbuthnot Latham Bank Ltd* v *Trafalgar Holdings Ltd* [1998] 2 All ER 181 [1998] 1 WLR 1426.

[32] See, e.g., *Grovit* v *Doctor* [1997] 2 All ER 417.   [33] [1998] 2 All ER 181.

[34] Per Chadwick LJ in *Securum Finance Lyd* v *Ashton* [2001] Ch 291 at 310.

[35] *UCB Corporate Services Ltd (formerly UCB Bank plc)* v *Halifax SW Ltd* [2000] LS Gaz R 24.

SETTLEMENT

The importance of settling any claim without it reaching the stage of a hearing has already been noted.[36] The overriding objective and the pre-action protocols, and indeed the case management arrangements put in place by the CPR, all lay emphasis at attempting to resolve disputes outside the courtroom. It is usually also in the interests of the parties (or their insurance companies) who are likely to be in constant communication to effect a settlement of the action. This they may do with complete candour since letters which pass between them are privileged from production and any offer or admission of liability made therein is said to be made 'without prejudice'. The nature of a settlement is that it is a contract whereby the parties abandon their previous rights and obligations in return for the creation of new rights and obligations.

The parties may effect a settlement without the consent of the court by giving notice of withdrawal before trial. Where an order of the court is required, which will usually be the case when the action is settled during the trial, the required terms will be drawn up and indorsed on counsels' briefs, or, more usually, the parties will submit to judgment on agreed terms. The settlement of any action on behalf of an infant or patient must be approved by the court.

SUMMARY JUDGMENT

A party to proceedings may have little or no prospect of successfully succeeding in his claim or defence. Part 24 of the Civil Procedure Rules permits summary judgment to be given, either on the application of the claimant or of the defendant, or on the court's own initiative. The court has to be satisfied that there is no real prospect of success on the claim or issue, or no real prospect of successfully defending the claim or issue, and, in either situation, there is no other compelling reason why the claim or issue should be disposed of at a trial.[37]

The power is an important one in the context of active case management.[38] A judge should, in an appropriate case consider of his own initiative the merits of a case, and if it has no prospects of success it should not be allowed to continue.[39] The power should, though, be exercised with caution in the context of a litigant in person.[40]

---

[36] See p 498, *ante*.

[37] CPR, r 24.2. *Three Rivers District Council and others* v *Governor and Company of the Bank of England (No 3)* [2001] 2 All ER 513; *Celador Production Ltd* v *Melville* [2004] EWHC 2362.

[38] See *Harris* v *Bolt Burdon* (2000) *The Times*, 8 December; *Swain* v *Hillman & Gay* [2001] 1 All ER 91.

[39] *Peter John O'Donnell and others* v *Charly Holdings Inc (A Company Incorporated under the Laws of Burma) and another.* Unreported, 14 March 2000.

[40] *Orford* v *Rasmi Electronics* and others [2002] EWCA Civ 1672.

PART 36 PAYMENTS AND OFFERS TO SETTLE

1 THE PRINCIPLE

In any action for debt or damages the defendant has been able at any time to pay money into court in satisfaction of any or all of the claims being pursued in the action by the claimant. Prior to the Civil Procedure Rules these were known as 'payments into court', but now are known as Part 36 payments. Part 36 also deals with offers to settle.[41] Offers to settle which are not backed by payments may, and sometimes must, be treated as falling within this principle.[42]

Part 36 has been described as 'one of the cornerstones of procedure made by the CPR'.[43] This statement serves only to emphasize the key principle, noted throughout, that the promotion of settlement is one of the key aims, which the conduct of litigation should seek to promote, facilitate, and encourage.[44] We have already noted[45] that Part 36 provides for pre-action offers to settle. An offer to settle can be made at any time before proceedings are commenced. Whilst this might seem self-evident, its recognition in Part 36 and in the Pre-Action Protocols is significant: if a party to proceedings unreasonably fails to accept a pre-action Part 36 offer, that is a matter to which the courts can have regard on questions of cost.[46] However, in *Daniels v Commissioner of Police for the Metropolis*[47] the court stressed that the normal rule is that the unsuccessful party pays costs. It is incumbent on the unsuccessful party to demonstrate that the conduct of the other party in refusing a Part 36 offer was so unreasonable as to justify departure from that rule. In that case the unsuccessful claimant sought to appeal against costs on the basis that the other party should have negotiated. In rejecting that argument, the court concluded that it is not unreasonable to decline to pay a claim that is in fact dismissed.

A party may make a Part 36 payment into court at any stage in the proceedings, or may make an offer to settle, although if the claim is one for money the appropriate action is a payment under Part 36 rather than an offer. Offers to settle are appropriate in respect of proceedings where non-pecuniary relief is being sought (for example, an injunction). This was made clear in *Amber v Stacey*[48] where the defendant had made an offer of settlement in the sum of £4,000, followed, later, by a payment into court. When the judge eventually made a judgment for a sum less than that paid into court he made a costs order in favour of the defendant as from the date of offer of settlement.[49] This was held to be wrong in principle, the court varying the costs order made.

---

[41] Formerly known as *Calderbank* offers. See, now, CPR, 36.5.

[42] *Crouch v King's Healthcare NHS Trust* [2004] EWCA Civ 1332; [2005] 1 All ER 207; *Trustees of Stokes Pension Fund v Western Power Distribution (South West) plc* [2005] EWCA Civ 854, [2005] 3 All ER 775. See r. 36.

[43] *Petrotrade Inc v Texaco Ltd* [2001] 4 All ER 853.

[44] Woolf, *Final Report, op cit*, Ch 10, para 2.   [45] See p 500, *ante*.

[46] *Ford v GKR Construction* [2000] 1 All ER 802. For costs generally, see p 518, *post*.

[47] [2005] EWCA Civ 1312.   [48] [2001] 1 WLR 1225.

[49] For the costs implications, see p 518 *et seq*.

Significant changes were made to Part 36 in 2007. In particular, public and insured defendants are now excepted from the requirement of making a payment into court, reflecting approaches taken in some case law.[50]

2 EFFECTS OF A PAYMENT INTO COURT OR OFFER

Unless the court considers it unjust to do so, the court will order the claimant to pay any costs incurred by the defendant after the latest date on which the payment or offer could have been accepted without needing the permission of the court.[51]

A Part 36 offer or payment will have been made by notice being given to the claimant and other parties. The notice will state various details prescribed by the Rule and Practice Directions It can be given at any time, but if that is given less than twenty-one days before trial the payment or offer can only be accepted if the parties agree liability for costs or the court gives permission.[52] Thus, within twenty-one days of the trial the court permission or agreement of the parties is a key prerequisite. The court has discretion in the matter which is not simply confined to the application of the costs sanction envisaged by Part 36. In *Barclays Bank plc Martin and Mortimer*[53] the court stressed that it had to consider whether unfairness to the defendant, potentially caused by a change in the circumstances of the litigation, would arise if the claimant was allowed, late, to accept a Part 36 payment.

If an offer is wrongly rejected the issue of costs arise. Costs will be given to a claimant who, having failed to accept a payment or offer to settle, fails to 'beat' the payment (i.e. obtain more by way of monetary sum) or fails to obtain more advantageous terms of judgment than those contained in the offer to settle.[54] Those costs will usually, but not inevitably be on the standard basis.[55] On occasion, if the conduct of the claimant was wholly unjustified, costs might be on an indemnity basis,[56] although such cases are likely to be rare. This costs sanction is not, though, automatic. Whether the defendant gets his costs after a failure by the claimant to beat the payment-in is a matter of judicial discretion.[57] That discretion should, though, normally be exercised in accordance with the general principle that, in this situation, a defendant should receive his costs. Thus in *Factortame Ltd* v *Secretary of State for the Environment, Transport and the Regions*[58] the defendant was entitled to his costs after the rejection of a Part 36 offer, even though the defendant had not provided accurate figures as to matters which would have affected the levels of compensation. It was, in each, case a matter for the discretion of the trial judge.

---

[50] *Crouch* v *King's Healthcare NHS Trust* [2004] EWCA Civ 1332, [2005] 1 WLR 2015; *Stokes Pension Fund* v *Western Power Distribution plc* [2005] 1 WLR 3595.

[51] CPR, 36.20(2). *Ede Walker Residential Ltd* v *Davis* [2005] EWHC 3483.

[52] CPR, 36.5(7).   [53] (2002) *The Times*, 19 August.

[54] CPR, 36.20. See *Daniels* v *Commissioner of Police for the Metropolis* [2005] EWCA 1312.

[55] See p 524, *post*.

[56] *Excelsior Commercial & Industrial Holdings Ltd* v *Salisbury Hammer Asbden & Johnson*, unreported, 12 June 2002. For the indemnity principle, see p 524, *post*.

[57] See *Ford* v *GR Construction* [2000] 1 All ER 802.

[58] [2002] 3 WLR 104. For other aspects of the *Factortame* litigation, see p 130, *ante*.

INTERIM RELIEF

1 INTERLOCUTORY INJUNCTION

An injunction is 'a court order prohibiting a person from doing something or requiring a person to do something'.[59] The power of the High Court to issue injunctions is, of course, inherited from the jurisdiction in equity,[60] but now extends to both High Court and county court by virtue of statutory provisions. In addition to the court's inherent power to grant an injunction by way of final remedy, section 37(1) of the Supreme Court Act 1981[61] empowers the court to grant an injunction by an interlocutory order 'in all cases in which it appears to the court to be just or convenient so to do'.[62] It may be noted that the injunction need not be directed at achieving the same relief as that which is sought by way of final relief in the proceedings. Their purpose was well explained by Lord Oliver in *Attorney-General* v *Times Newspapers*:[63]

> interlocutory injunctions are designed to ensure the effective administration of justice, so that the rights which it is the duty of the courts to protect can fairly be determined and effectively protected and enforced by the courts.

Procedures for obtaining such interim relief are governed by the Civil Procedure Rules, Part 23 and reflect the key principles for the grant of an interim injunction explained in the leading case of *American Cyanamid Co* v *Ethicon Ltd*.[64] Lord Diplock stated that the approach referred to above was incorrect and, in a speech with which the remainder of their Lordships agreed, laid down the following principles:

(1) The claimant must first satisfy the court 'that the claim is not frivolous or vexatious; in other words that there is a serious question to be tried'.

(2) The court should then go on to consider the 'balance of convenience'.

(3) As to that, the court should first consider whether, if the claimant were to succeed at the trial in establishing his right to a permanent injunction, he would be adequately compensated by an award of damages for the loss he would have sustained by refusal of an interlocutory injunction.

(4) If damages would not provide an adequate remedy (for example because the defendant may be impecunious) the court should consider whether the defendant would be adequately compensated by the claimant's undertaking as to damages (*infra*) in the event of an interlocutory injunction being granted but a permanent injunction being refused at the trial.

---

[59] Glossary to CPR.   [60] See p 6, *ante*.   [61] See County Courts Act 1984, s 38.

[62] The position of the Crown was discussed in *Factortame* v *Secretary of State for Transport* [1990] 2 AC 85, [1989] 2 All ER 692.

[63] [1992] 1 AC 191, see also *Attorney-General* v *Punch Ltd* [2002] UKHL 50.

[64] [1975] AC 396, [1975] 1 All ER 504.

(5) Where other matters are equal, it is a 'counsel of prudence to take such measures as are calculated to preserve the status quo'.

(6) Finally, 'if the extent of the uncompensatable disadvantage to each party would not differ widely, it may not be improper to take into account in tipping the balance the relative strength of each party's case as revealed by the affidavit evidence'. By this is meant that the court should consider whether the strength of the case of one party is disproportionate to the other.[65]

Lord Diplock made it clear that there may be special factors which operate in 'individual cases' in addition to the principles enumerated above. Nevertheless it is clear that the courts should not embark on anything resembling a trial of the action.

The Court of Appeal initially showed little enthusiasm for these principles. In *Cayne* v *Global Natural Resources plc*[66] the Court of Appeal pointed out that where the grant or refusal of an interlocutory injunction will have the practical effect of putting an end to the action the task of the court is to do its best to avoid injustice, and to balance the risk of doing an injustice to either party. In such cases the *American Cyanamid* guidelines cannot apply and unless the claimant can show an overwhelming case he will not be granted an injunction the effect of which would be tantamount to shutting the defendant out from contesting the action. May LJ justified this departure by observing:

> I think that one must be very careful to apply the relevant passages from Lord Diplock's familiar speech in the *Cyanamid* case not as rules but only as guidelines, which is what I am certain Lord Diplock intended them to be.

Special issues arise in the context of publications, and attempts to restrain them by interim injunction. That arises because of the special emphasis that has to be given by a court to the right of freedom of expression, pursuant to section 12 of the Human Rights Act 1998.[67] In *Cream Holdings Ltd* v *Banerjee*[68] the Court of Appeal held that, in such a case, it was insufficient that there was a serious issue to be tried. Section 12(3) required the courts to look at the merits, putting the *American Cyanamid* test on one side.

Application for an interim injunction must be made to a judge. In cases of extreme urgency application can be made without leave on affidavit, in which event an injunction will be granted for a very short period until an application by summons or motion can be brought before the court.

As an alternative to injunction the court will usually accept an undertaking from the defendant (which has precisely the same effect). In addition, as a condition of being granted an interim injunction the claimant is customarily required to give his undertaking as to damages, that is an undertaking to indemnify the defendant in respect of any damages which the latter sustains by reason of the injunction in the event of the action

---

[65] See *Series 5 Software Ltd* v *Clarke* [1996] 1 All ER 853. A court should not grant interim relief where a new cause of action is relied on: see *Khorasandjian* v *Bush* [1993] QB 727.

[66] [1984] 1 All ER at 237. The *Cyanamid* principles do not apply to mandatory injunctions: *Locabail International Finance Ltd* v *Agroexport* [1986] 1 All ER 901, [1986] 1 WLR 657. The factors to be taken into account in the context of mandatory injunctions were set out in *Zockell Group Ltd* v *Mercury Communications Ltd* [1998] FSR 354. See also *Services Ltd* v *Merent Psychometric International Ltd* [2002] FSR 8.

[67] As to which, see p 153, *ante*.   [68] [2003] EWCA Civ 103.

failing. For this reason it is generally improvident for a claimant to apply for an inter-locutory injunction unless he has a strong case in circumstances in which the interim will cause the defendant heavy expense, for example by delaying building works.

2 INTERIM PAYMENT OF DAMAGES

One long-standing criticism of civil procedure in the English courts was that wholly innocent parties, such as injured passengers in road accidents, had to wait for long periods for their damages while disputes between other parties, such as the car drivers (in fact, their insurers) were being resolved. The Report of the Committee on Personal Injuries Litigation[69] recommended that in such litigation, courts should have power to make interim payments and effect was given to this recommendation by the Administration of Justice Act 1969. This was replaced by section 32(1) of the Supreme Court Act 1981[70] which authorizes rules of court enabling the High Court:

> in such circumstances as may be prescribed to make an order requiring a party to the proceedings to make an interim payment of such amount as may be specified in the order, with provision for the payment to be made to such other party to the proceedings as may be so specified or, if the order so provides, by paying it into court.

The power is regulated in detail by rule 25 of the Civil Procedure Rules. An interim payment may only be made if the defendant admits liability in whole or in part, or judgment that damages be assessed has already been obtained, or the court is satisfied that if the matter went to trial the claimant would receive a sum of money substantial in nature. Additional criteria apply in personal injury cases.

STATEMENTS OF CASE

1 BACKGROUND

Statements of case replace the old pre-Woolf system of pleadings. These were written statements served by each party on his opponent, containing the allegations of fact on which the party pleadings relied. They were supposed to serve various purposes. Principally they enabled each party to determine exactly which facts are alleged against him. This could save a party from preparing evidence to meet allegations which are not being made against him. Also it enabled parties to establish their 'common ground', that is to say facts on which they are in agreement, thus saving the expense of proving these matters at the trial. Secondly, the action was decided upon the pleadings. Thus the parties and their successors could, by reference to the pleadings, determine in the future exactly what the case decided, so that they may not have to, and indeed may not be allowed to, fight the same issues again. Similarly reference to the pleadings in an

---

[69] Cmnd 3691 of 1968 (the Pearson Committee). [70] See also County Courts Act 1984, s 50.

action might disclose the *ratio decidendi* of the case for the purpose of the doctrine of precedent, since any fact not pleaded would not usually be regarded as a fact upon which a judgment is based.

Whether pleadings always in fact fulfilled these objectives is a matter of doubt. The Woolf Report[71] considered that the use of pleadings by claimants often had the effect not of clarifying the issues, but of merely adding to the adversarial conflict responsible for delay. The system caused extra and unnecessary cost, complications and delays. The Report recommended that pleadings should have to spell out the facts relied on so that the parties can identify and define the matters in issue. Their content needed to be verified by the parties, so enabling the court to determine the range and scale of material required to progress the case and the necessary extent of disclosure, witness statements, and the use of experts. In short, this important part of the process should be such as to enable the court adequately to make decisions as to how a case should be managed, in accordance with the overriding objective.[72]

The old 'pleadings' are replaced by the new 'statements of case', a term defined widely to include a claim form,[73] particulars of claim, a defence, a Part 20 claim,[74] a reply to a defence, and any other information supplied either voluntarily or under a court order.[75] They should be characterized by conciseness, and by their capacity to clarify rather an obscure the issues,[76] but obviously have to be sufficiently clear and detailed to achieve that.[77] In *McPhileny v Times Newspapers Ltd*[78] Lord Woolf MR observed:

> [Statements of case] mark out the parameters of the case that is being advanced by each party [and] identify the issues and the extent of the dispute between the parties. The need for extensive [statements of case] including particulars should be reduced by the requirement that witness statements are now exchanged. In the majority of pleadings identification of the documents upon which a party relies, together with copies of that party's witness statements, will make clear the detail of the nature of the case the other side has to meet obvious.

The new regime for civil procedure from the outset seeks to achieve these aims. The information disclosed pre-action,[79] the contents of the claim form[80] and duties to exchange documents and information[81] all form part and parcel of this process. Specific types of claim require specific types of information to be supplied. A few examples suffice. A claim under a contract requires a copy of the documents relied on to be attached to, or served with, the particulars of claim.[82] A Fatal Accidents Act 1976 claim should identify details of the dependant. In a personal injury claim, which relies on medical evidence, a report from a medical practitioner about the injuries sustained should be attached with the particulars of claim or otherwise served. A defendant who

---

[71] *Op cit*, paras 153–164.   [72] See p 464, *ante*.

[73] See p 480, *ante*.   [74] See p 486, *ante*.

[75] CPR, 2.3 Part 16. The Part 16 procedure does not apply to Part 8 proceedings (as to which see p 480, *ante*).

[76] *McPhilemy v Times Newspapers Ltd* [1999] 3 All ER 775, per Lord Woolf MR.

[77] *The Royal Brompton Hospital NHS Trust v Hammond and others* (2001) 76 Con LR 148.

[78] [1999] 3 All ER 775.   [79] See p 486, *ante*.   [80] See p 480, *ante*.

[81] See p 480, *ante*, and p 507, *post*.   [82] Practice Direction 16.

wishes to resist the claim will need to serve details of his defence. This will address every allegation made in the particulars of claim, with admissions or non-admissions (as appropriate). These admissions will identify facts which are agreed or not in dispute, as well as the response on the issues of liability. The basis and detail of any denials or non-admissions must be set out.[83] A claimant is entitled to serve a reply to a defence, but is not obliged to do so.

All statements of case must be accompanied by a statement of truth, a statement that the party putting it forward believes it to be true.[84] A party must also supply relevant details of any conditional fee agreements.[85]

Statements of case may be amended by consent or with permission.[86] Amendments made by agreement will be formally dealt with by means of a consent order, but otherwise the permission of the court will be required. The court has a discretion in the matter, to be exercised in accordance with the overriding objective.[87] Amendments which allow the court to adjudicate on the real issues in the case will generally be allowed, provided they are not inconsistent with facts which have already been asserted as part of the statement of case.[88] But prejudice might arise if the statement of case is amended in a way that affects the track in which the case is dealt with, or the defendant's response to the case. One example is *Maguire* v *Molin*[89] where the amendment sought and refused was to increase the value claimed from £15,000 (the maximum for the fast track) to £80,000. Amendments which introduce effectively new claims after the expiration of any limitation period will not generally be permitted, for otherwise the limitation periods themselves would be circumvented.[90] However, questions of the operation of the Human Rights Act 1998[91] arose in *Goode* v *Martin*[92] where, although the court recognized a limitation period as potentially compatible with Article 6 of the Convention, the court used section 3 of the 1998 Act to interpret the requirement so as to allow a new claim beyond the limitation period where it was based on facts which were already in issue.

DISCLOSURE AND INSPECTION OF DOCUMENTS

1 RELEVANT PRINCIPLES AND BACKGROUND

Disclosure (formerly known as discovery) is the procedure whereby a party discloses, to the court or to any other party, the relevant documents in the action that he has, or has had, in his possession, custody, or power. Documentary evidence plays an important part in nearly all civil cases. Its purpose was explained by Sir John Donaldson as follows:[93]

> In plain language litigation is conducted 'cards face up on the table'. Some people from other lands regard this as incomprehensible. 'Why' they ask 'should I be

---

[83] CPR, 16.5.2.   [84] CPR, 22.1(6).   [85] See p 402, *ante*, and p 525, *post*.
[86] CPR, 17.1(2).   [87] See p 464, *ante*.   [88] *Cobbold* v *Greenwich LBC*, unreported, 24 May 2001.
[89] [2002] EWCA Civ 1083.   [90] CPR, 17.4(2).   [91] See p 150, *ante*.
[92] [2001] EWCA Civ 1899.   [93] *Davies* v *Eli Lilly & Co* [1987] 1 All ER 801, [1987] 1 WLR 428.

expected to provide my opponent with the means of defeating me?' The answer, of course, is that litigation is not a war or even a game. It is designed to do real justice between opposing parties and, if the court does not have all the relevant information, it cannot achieve this object.

In an action for breach of contract, for example, the transactions between the parties may be contained entirely in letters which have passed between them. One party's letters may not be intelligible unless read in conjunction with letters in the possession of the other party. Similarly, in an industrial injuries action, the employers are likely to have internal accident reports, machine maintenance records, records of complaints, and the like which it is very much in the claimant's interests to see, while, on the other hand, the claimant may have documents relating to his medical condition, or to his earnings since the accident or state benefits which he has received, all of which may be highly relevant to the quantification of his claim by the defendants.

Accordingly a party will want to have his opponent disclose which documents the latter has, or has had, in his possession (disclosure), and, secondly, to inspect and take copies of those documents in his opponent's possession (inspection).[94] Sometimes a party may have documents which are relevant to the litigation, and therefore disclosable, but which he wishes to safeguard against circulation either to third parties, or occasionally to the claimant himself for extraneous reasons. As to this point, the traditional position has been that on disclosure each party impliedly undertakes not to use the documents which are disclosed for any ulterior or improper purpose. The use of such documents in breach of that implied undertaking has been held to be a contempt of court. Thus in *Home Office* v *Harman*[95] a solicitor who passed documents to a journalist to assist in the preparation of an article was held to be in contempt, even though the documents had been read in open court. Nor can a party generally rely upon such documents in other proceedings. Thus where a claimant in proceedings against his employers obtained discovery of a memorandum about him which contained an alleged libel, the court held that he could not found a libel action on that publication since that would be an abuse of the process of the court.[96] In *Crest Homes plc* v *Marks*[97] the court indicated that it would release a party from that undertaking if the applicant could demonstrate 'cogent and persuasive reasons' for such a release, and that the release did not cause injustice. If there is a real risk of the claimant using documents for an improper collateral purpose, the court could restrict inspection, for example to a party's legal advisers.

---

[94] 'Inspection' is not limited to ocular inspection but includes examination by any of the senses. Thus, a tape-recording is a document, inspection of which would be effected by playing the same upon a tape-recorder to the inspecting party: *Grant* v *Southwestern and County Properties Ltd* [1975] Ch 185, [1974] 2 All ER 465; similar considerations apply to untransmitted television film: *Senior* v *Holdsworth, ex parte Independent Television News Ltd* [1976] QB 23, [1975] 2 All ER 1009.

[95] [1983] 1 AC 280, [1982] 1 All ER 532. This finding was held to be in breach of the European Convention of Human Rights, Article 10 by the Court of Human Rights in *Harman* v *United Kingdom*, in that it infringed the right of freedom of expression and the right to impart and receive information under Article 10.

[96] *Riddick* v *Thames Board Mills Ltd* [1977] QB 881, [1977] 3 All ER 677.

[97] [1987] AC 829, [1987] 2 All ER 1074.

The position is now governed by the Civil Procedure Rules.[98] A party to whom a document is disclosed may use it only for the purposes of the proceedings and not for any other purpose, except where the document has been read to or by the court, or referred to at a public hearing, the court gives permission, or those who disclosed and received agree. Despite these exceptions the court nonetheless has discretion to restrict or prohibit the use of a document. The presumption will be that a document produced in open court will be disclosable.[99] If as in the *Lilly Icos* case the document was of only peripheral importance in the hearing and the contained highly sensitive commercial information there might be a case for restricting disclosure.

The pre-existing system of discovery was roundly condemned by the Woolf Report. One overseas judge observed:

> If there was a hell to which disputatious, uncivil, vituperative lawyers go, let it be one in which the damned are eternally locked in discovery disputes with other lawyers of equally repugnant attributes.

Whatever the element of overstatement, reform was another key objective of the civil justice reforms. The pre-existing law allowed discovery not only of relevant documents, but of others which might lead to the production of relevant documents.[100] It should be borne in mind that the greater the level of disclosure the greater burden is imposed on parties to identify and produce information. This can potentially add to the length of time litigation takes, and its cost. It is for this reason that the Woolf Report recommended that disclosure should be controlled by the court as part of its case-management function, it being regulated with regard to the size of the case, the cost of disclosure, and the likely cost. For the future it is envisaged that disclosure on the scale that it used to happen will rarely take place.

The rules[101] now define 'standard disclosure' as involving documents on which the party will rely, documents which adversely affect his own case, which adversely affect another parties' case, or which support that case. In addition documents which are required to be disclosed by any Practice Direction must be disclosed. An ongoing duty to disclose exists. The rules governing disclosure apply to fast-track and multi-track litigation, but not claims in the small claims track.

Obligations to disclose can arise pre-action. The Court of Appeal in *Black* v *Sumitomo*[102] considered pre-action disclosure to be important, particularly where the claim had not been fully established enabling a potential claimant to decide whether a claim might succeed and on what basis. This was particularly the case in personal injury and medical negligence cases. It was also a necessary prerequisite in some cases in order to obtain funding, to establish what the likelihood of success is in a case potentially the

---

[98] CPR, 31.22.   [99] *Lilly Icos Ltd* v *Pfizer Ltd* [2002] EWCA Civ 2.

[100] See *Compagnie Financire* v *Peruvian Guano Co* (1882) 11 QBD 55. Interesting parallels exist with the development of disclosure in criminal cases.

[101] CPR, 31.6.

[102] [2002] 1 WLR 1562. The court reviewed earlier case law including *Dunning* v *United Liverpool Hospitals Board of Governors* [1973] 1 WLR 586; *Shaw* v *Vauxhall Motors Ltd* [1974] 2 All ER 1185; *Burns* v *Shuttlehurst* [1999] 1 WLR 1449.

subject of a conditional fee agreement. On the other hand the court must discourage 'fishing expeditions'. Pre-trial protocols govern what should, ideally, be disclosed voluntarily. But the CPR make provision for an order requiring pre-trial disclosure.[103] This was discussed in chapter 15.[104]

2 DISCLOSURE AND INSPECTION AGAINST OTHER PERSONS

We have already noted the procedure whereby orders for disclosure and inspection of documents against proposed parties may be made before the commencement of proceedings. Under section 34 of the Supreme Court Act 1981 there is, in addition, power, in actions for damages for death or personal injuries, to order a person who is not a party to the proceedings and who appears to be likely to have or have had in his possession, custody, or power any documents which are relevant to an issue arising out of the action to disclose whether these documents are in his possession, custody, or power and to produce those which he has to the applicant. This power is exercisable only after the commencement of proceedings, the application being by summons (which must be served on the person against whom the order is sought and on all parties to the action) supported by affidavit and now applies to all proceedings.

3 ACTION FOR DISCLOSURE

Save for the limited exception, in personal injuries actions, discussed above, there is, as a rule, no procedure for obtaining discovery against persons who are not parties to an action. They can, of course, be compelled to attend the trial and to produce, at that stage, documents in their possession (by means of court order) but there is a rule, sometimes known as the 'mere witness' rule, whereby discovery cannot be obtained against a person against whom no relief is sought but who might be a witness in an action. It follows that if a party wishes to inspect documents in the possession of a person against whom he has no cause of action, he cannot sue that person simply for the purpose of obtaining evidence, by way of disclosure of documents, for use against the party against whom there is a cause of action. This rule appears to have little in the way of logic to commend it but it is, nevertheless, too firmly entrenched to be altered save by way of legislation.

However, it has already been seen that a limited exception to the rule was formulated by the House of Lords in the case of *Norwich Pharmacal Co* v *Customs and Excise Commissioners*.[105] The facts of the case were unusual. The appellants, who were the owners of a patent covering a chemical compound, learned from information published by the respondents that a number of consignments of the compound had been

---

[103] CPR, 31.16.   [104] See p 486, *ante*.

[105] 1974] AC 133, [1973] 2 All ER 943, applied in *Loose v Williamson* [1978] 3 All ER 89, [1978] 1 WLR 639, [1974] AC, at 175, [1973] 2 All ER, at 948; see also, on the *Norwich Pharmacal* principle, *Arab Monetary Fund* v *Hashim (No 5)* [1992] 2 All ER 911.

imported between 1960 and 1970, none of which had been licensed by the appellants. The appellants therefore knew that others were infringing their patent but did not know their identity. The respondents refused to disclose the identity of the importers whereupon the appellants brought an action against the respondents seeking an order for discovery of documents relating to the importations. The House of Lords granted such an order; the reasoning behind the decision was expressed by Lord Reid, as follows:

> if through no fault of his own a person gets mixed up in the tortious acts of others so as to facilitate their wrong-doing he may incur no personal liability but he comes under a duty to assist the person who has been wronged by giving him full information and disclosing the identity of the wrongdoers.

In *Ashworth Hospital Authority* v *MGN Ltd*[106] Lord Woolf stressed that the court should start from the proposition that a non-party should not be subjected to the civil process and made to disclose information. He should at least be 'involved', however innocently, in another person's wrongdoing.

DIRECTIONS

It will be evident from the above that the case-management role of the court throughout the case will give the courts the opportunity to make directions relating to the whole management, conduct, and progress of the case. Amongst those already identified are matters of disclosure, evidence, expert evidence, place, time, and mode of trial. Unlike the pre-Woolf system there is not simply one time when these matters will be considered. They are ongoing issues. The involvement of the court will in part depend on the nature and complexity of the matters in issue, and the track the case is on.

TRIAL

1 PREPARATION OF EVIDENCE

At an early stage of the action the papers will usually have been sent to counsel or solicitor (as appropriate).[107] Counsel will normally settle the statement of case but, in any event, will advise appropriately through the progress of the case through its various stages. Cases are won and lost in their preparation. Counsel will therefore wish to consider which applications should be made, whether the statement of case requires amendment, and similar matters. The first consideration upon preparing an action for trial is on whom the burden of proof rests. The general rule is that where any allegation

---

[106] [2002] 1 WLR 2033.   [107] For rights of audience, see p 377, *ante*.

of fact is in issue the party who alleges that fact must prove it. The statement of case will disclose where the general burden lies. If an allegation in the statement of case is admitted (expressly or impliedly) it need not be proved at all. If it is denied then the burden rests on the claimant. If the defendant denies liability because of other facts, the burden of proving them lies on him. Throughout, the standard of proof is the balance of probabilities (the 51 per cent rule), although it must be noted that this is a variable and not absolute standard.[108] However, the burden may shift during the action by the effect of presumptions. If a presumption is raised in favour of a party, the effect is to shift the burden of disproving the matter presumed to his opponent.

Having decided which matters he must prove, counsel will decide how he proposes to prove them. The two principal methods of proof are by witnesses and by documents.

(a) Witnesses

Counsel or solicitor will name the witnesses whom he requires. There is no property in a witness, so that there is no objection to interviewing or calling any witness even if he has been served with a witness summons by an opponent.[109] It is, of course, wrong to call a witness whose testimony is unlikely to support one's case, since a party cannot cross-examine a witness he has called, unless the court gives leave to treat the witness as hostile. Also, to intimidate or otherwise tamper with a witness amounts to a contempt of court.[110] Usually a witness will be prepared to attend voluntarily if he is tendered a reasonable fee. Where he will not, his attendance may be compelled by order. A witness who fails to comply may be committed for contempt of court.

(b) Evidence

Facts to be proved in a civil case are proved by the testimony of a witness in person and in open court. To that basic rule there are exceptions. Facts can be proved by formal admissions at trial, although a pre-trial admission of liability is not binding.[111] A party need produce no proof of any matter admitted in his favour. Admissions may also be made in answer to interrogatories. A useful means of compelling an opponent to admit a fact is to serve him with a 'notice to admit facts', calling upon him to admit the facts listed in the notice. If he will not admit these facts and they are proved at the trial, unless the court otherwise orders, he will bear the costs of proof. This is, of course, a powerful weapon but it must not be abused. A party should not be asked to admit the facts in issue or any inference of fact, such as negligence. He should only, in practice, be asked to admit facts of a formal nature or facts which can easily be proved against him if he does not admit them. If admissions are made which clearly establish one party's liability the other party may, without waiting for a trial, apply for judgment based on

---

[108] See p 13, *ante*.
[109] See observations of Lord Denning MR in *Fullam v Newcastle Chronicle and Journal Ltd* [1977] 3 All ER 32, [1977] 1 WLR 651; see also *Harmony Shipping Co SA v Davis* [1979] 3 All ER 177, [1979] 1 WLR 1380.
[110] *Chapman v Honig* [1963] 2 QB 502, [1963] 2 All ER 513.
[111] *Sowerby v Charlton* [2005] EWCA Civ 1610.

those admissions.[112] Similar to such a notice is a 'notice to admit documents', calling upon the party served to admit the authenticity of the documents listed, though not the truth of their contents. The effect of failure to admit is, again, that the party who was served with the notice has to pay the costs of proving the documents at the trial, unless the court otherwise orders, which may involve an extra witness, such as a handwriting expert.

Wide powers are conferred on the judge by the Civil Procedure Rules as to the means of proof. Thus he may order evidence to be given at the trial by affidavit or in any other specified manner. For example, he may order the date on which an important event occurred to be proved by production of a newspaper containing a report of the event. In addition he may restrict the number of medical or other expert witnesses who may be called at the trial. In the fast-track procedure there should be a single joint expert.[113] Finally, it should be noted that a court may direct that a written statement be treated as the evidence in chief of the witness, including previous inconsistent statements.[114]

(c) Documents

Documentary evidence, especially in contract cases, frequently forms the basis of a party's case. Where he is in possession of the documents himself, he is in no difficulty. However, the documents which are needed by a party may be in the possession of an opponent or of a third party. That problem may be overcome through the revised rules relating to disclosure, which should identify relevant documents in the hands of opponents or third parties.[115] If they are in the possession of a third party, the proper course is to serve him with an order requiring the witness to attend and produce the relevant documents.

(d) Notices under the Civil Evidence Act 1995

Where it is desired to put in evidence at the trial statements admissible under the provisions of the Civil Evidence Act 1995, the party desiring to do so must within twenty-one days after setting down serve on every other party a notice containing prescribed particulars of (if the statement is oral) the time, place, and circumstances in which the statement was made, the persons by whom and to whom it was made and the substance of the statement or, if material, the words used. In the case of written statements admissible by virtue of the Act, the notice must annex a copy of the document in question as well as contain certain prescribed particulars relating to the circumstances of its compilation. If the party giving the notice alleges that the maker cannot be called as a witness at the trial because he is dead, beyond the seas, unfit by reason of his bodily or mental condition to attend as a witness, cannot be found, or cannot reasonably be expected to have any recollection of matters relevant to the accuracy of his statement, the notice must contain a statement to this effect otherwise a party served with a notice

[112] For summary judgment see p 500, *ante*.   [113] R 35.7.
[114] *Fifield v Denton Hall Legal Services* [2006] EWCA Civ 169.   [115] See p 507, *ante*.

may within twenty-one days serve a counter-notice requiring the maker of any state-ment to be called as a witness by the party who served the original notice, in which event if that person is not called as a witness, his statement is not admissible under the 1995 Act.

When the evidence for each side has been prepared the parties must await trial. Neither party need serve any notice of the date of trial on his opponent. Accordingly (unless the case has been given a fixed date) all parties must watch carefully the lists. The Week's List is published on Mondays and contains the cases expected to be tried in that week. Each day there is published a Daily Cause List containing the actions to be heard that day and a Warned List consisting of actions likely to be tried in the near future. Thus neither side has any excuse if his case is not ready when the action comes on for trial. If one party fails to appeal, the trial may proceed in his absence. However, if application is made within seven days, a judgment obtained in the absence of a party may be set aside, generally on condition that he pay the costs thrown away. Although adjournment is possible, last minute postponements are looked upon with disfavour by the judge in charge of the list and may result in the offending firm of solicitors being penalized personally with the extra costs incurred.

2 PROCEDURE AT THE TRIAL

Jury trials are now rare in civil proceedings,[116] so a trial is almost certainly by judge and judge alone. It must also be borne in mind that procedures in respect of the small claims track will be very informal and very different from procedures in a complex multi-track case. The following gives some indication of the procedure followed in a High Court or contested county court action in the multi-track, or, to some extent, fast track.

(a) Right to begin

If damages are unliquidated or the burden of proving any single issue on the pleadings rests on the claimant, then the claimant begins. Thus the only case where the defendant has the right to begin is a case in which the claimant claims only liquidated damages and the defendant has not traversed any allegation in the statement of claim. The right to begin and the right to the last word are advantages which are probably exaggerated, especially in the absence of a jury.

(b) Case for the claimant

Counsel for the claimant opens his case stating the facts on which the claimant relies The court will already have a large amount of information in the case 'bundle' contain-ing skeleton arguments, statement of case, relevant documents, and other appropriate documents. It will be assumed that these have been read and thus the style and content of the advocacy will be very different from that in jury trial. The advocate should not rely upon any fact which he is not permitted to prove, which means, of course, that he

---

[116] See p 362, *ante.*

cannot allege any fact not pleaded, although he may, even at this late stage, be allowed to amend the statement of case. The claimant's witnesses are then called and sworn. They are examined and may be cross-examined and re-examined. In the course of cross-examining the claimant's witnesses, counsel for the defendant must 'put his case' which includes making clear which part of the claimant's case is challenged and what positive allegations are being made in relation to the evidence of the claimant's witnesses, so that they may have the opportunity of dealing with those allegations. This is important to the efficient conduct of trials because if counsel for the claimant calls a witness whose evidence is not challenged on a particular point, then he is entitled to assume that the point is not in issue and he will not call any other witnesses to deal with it. If the defence lead evidence as to matters which should have been put but were not put to the claimant's witnesses, judicial rebuke is virtually inevitable and, unless counsel was responsible for the oversight (in which event he will, in the interests of his client, immediately accept responsibility for it), the judge is likely to infer, and find, that the evidence in question is a recent invention. His documents, including answers to interrogatories which he wishes to put in, are then put in evidence. Finally, counsel argues the propositions of law upon which he relies, citing to the court all relevant authorities on the point whether they support his own case or that of his opponent. If they tend to support his opponent's case, he must attempt to distinguish them from the present case on their facts. He cannot, however, ignore them, since this would infringe his duty to the court.

(c) Case for the defence

At the close of the claimant's case the defendant has the following courses open to him:

(1) he may submit 'no case to answer'. This is a submission that the claimant has failed to make out a prima facie case, or to establish the elements of a recognized cause of action. The submission is rare in a civil action since the objection will usually have been taken long before the trial. If it is made, the judge, before deciding, may require the defendant to 'stand on his submission', which means that he can call no evidence if his submission fails. Counsel for the claimant has a right to reply to the submission. If it succeeds, judgment is entered for the defendant. If it fails and the defendant has been put to his election, judgment is entered for the claimant.

(2) He may state that he intends to call no evidence, oral or documentary. Counsel for the claimant will then address the court followed by defence counsel who thus obtains the right to the last word.

(3) In most cases the defence will be a mixture of law and fact and the defendant will want to put in some evidence. In this event defence counsel may make an opening speech outlining his defence. His witnesses give their evidence in the same way as those of the claimant followed by the defendant's documents and legal submissions. The claimant may be permitted to adduce evidence in rebuttal where the defence case has raised matters which could not reasonably have been foreseen. Defence counsel then makes a closing speech, following which counsel for the claimant has a right to make a closing speech in reply. Where a party in his

closing speech raises any fresh point of law, the other party is entitled to reply but only in relation to that point.

(d) Expert testimony

The whole subject of expert testimony is of importance: if the trial is to be efficient, the situation where the trial becomes a 'battle of experts' should be avoided, where possible. In the fast-track, there will be a single joint expert. Generally neither party should meet the expert witness without the other.[117]

Real difficulties arise where there is disputed expert evidence. It is important that the expert be independent and objective, and keep within his or her area of competence.[118] The issues are common to both civil and criminal procedure, and are discussed in more depth later.

(e) Verdict and judgment

At the conclusion of all the evidence and the legal argument for both sides the judge sums up (in the rare case where there is a jury) or gives judgment, or reserves his judgment if there is not. He must direct the jury (if there is one) as to the issues in the case, stating on whom the burden of proving the individual issues rests, and outlining the evidence in support of those issues. He must also direct upon the standard of proof required from the party on whom the burden rests. He will direct on the law applicable to the issues of fact, for example, whether the words are capable of bearing the defamatory meaning alleged or whether the defendant owes the claimant a duty of care in negligence. He must leave the actual issues of fact and the assessment of damages to the jury, but, now, following a series of cases involving disproportionate damages awards, may give them guidance as to the appropriate level of damages that may be awarded. A modern tendency is for the judge to pose a series of questions to the jury calling for their decision on the facts and, if they find for the claimant on any issue, the amount of damages. Where the claimant has sought an equitable remedy as an alternative or in addition to damages, the grant of this remedy is in the discretion of the judge.

It remains for judgment to be entered in accordance with the verdict. A judgment crystallizes the rights of the parties in respect of the subject matter of the action. Thus they are estopped from litigating the same issues of fact again. Even if fresh damage becomes apparent the claimant cannot sue because his right is extinguished. Counsel for the unsuccessful party may apply for a stay of execution pending an appeal. This may be granted on terms. After judgment on the issues of liability and damages the judge may make orders as to interest and costs.

Historically damages have always been expressed in English currency. This has caused hardship in cases in which sterling has been devalued, so a party who bargained for payment in foreign currency has been awarded damages in sterling, the rate of exchange

---

[117] *Peet* v *Mid-Kent Healthcare Trust (Practice Note)* [2001] EWCA Civ 1703; cf. *Childs* v *Vernon* [2007] EWCA Civ 305.

[118] *National Justice Cia Naviera SA* v *Prudential Assurance Co Ltd (Ikaria Reefer)* [1993] 2 Lloyds Rep 68; *Re AB (Child Abuse: Expert Witnesses)* [1995] 1 All ER 181.

being calculated at the date upon which his entitlement to payment arose (the 'breach-date' rule). Accordingly in 1975 the House of Lords changed this rule. Since 1975 the English courts have shown an increasing willingness to give judgment in foreign currency. At first limited to contract actions where the sum was due under the contract in a foreign currency and the proper law of the contract was the law of that country in whose currency the obligation was expressed, the power is now exercised in cases where the claimant's loss would be most truly expressed in a foreign currency, in which case judgment will be given in that currency, and in tort actions, where damages may be awarded in a currency which the claimant has used to make good the loss which he has suffered. Nevertheless, a judgment can only be enforced in terms of sterling. Accordingly, if enforcement becomes necessary the judgment will be converted into its sterling equivalent at the date when leave is given to enforce the judgment.

Finally, there is, save in personal injuries actions, no procedure for successive awards of damages in the same action. Damages have to be assessed once and for all at the trial. This may cause hardship to either side, since subsequent events may demonstrate the hypotheses upon which the award of damages were based to be false with the result that the damages were too high or too low. This is particularly so in personal injury actions where, for example, an award of damages for loss of future earnings capacity must necessarily be highly speculative. To remedy this situation section 32A of the Supreme Court Act contains provision for 'provisional damages' in personal injury actions.

Section 35A of the Supreme Court Act 1981 empowers the court to award simple (but not compound) interest on debts or damages 'at such rate as the court thinks fit or as rules of court may provide'. In commercial cases the usual rate is 1 per cent above United Kingdom clearing banks' base rates over the relevant period. Different rules exist in respect of personal injury actions, where on most awards, the court must grant interest:

(1) the claimant is awarded interest on general damages for pain, suffering and loss of amenities from the date of service of the writ to the date of trial at a conventional rate of 2 per cent per annum;

(2) the claimant is awarded interest on special damages from the date of the accident to the date of trial at half the rates which during that period were payable on money in court placed on special account;

(3) no interest is awarded on future loss of earnings or other prospective financial losses.

FURTHER READING

ANDREWS, *English Civil Procedure* (Oxford University Press: 2004)

WOOLF, *Access to Justice* (1995) – the 'Woolf Report'

17

COSTS

INTRODUCTION

The financing of litigation and the provision of legal services are major issues that were discussed in Chapter 12. The question of costs is inextricably linked to those issues: who pays – which is what 'costs' are about – is linked to the question of how a party is able to pay. This chapter will therefore focus on the rules and principles governing the award of costs, in addition to considering how costs are quantified.

THE POWER TO AWARD COSTS

In his Report, Lord Woolf identified the question of costs as one of the key problems that the civil justice system had to address.[1] Much of his Report was addressing how litigation could be made more efficient, less cumbersome, and thus cheaper and more affordable. At the same time the move to Conditional Fee Agreements[2] has created new funding opportunities in respect of many types of litigation, but raises important issues about costs.[3]

The basic rule is that costs are within the discretion of the court. In most cases the judge will order one side to pay all or a proportion of the costs of his opponent. At common law a successful litigant had a right to costs but this right has been virtually removed by legislation so that at the present day the award of costs is discretionary. A court has discretion as to whether costs are payable by one party, the amount to be paid, and when they are to be paid.[4] It is not, of course, an absolute discretion and it is a wrong exercise of the discretion to deprive a party of his costs if he has been completely successful and guilty of no misconduct.[5] Unless there are special factors present, a successful party may expect his costs from an unsuccessful opponent. This is the basic

---

[1] See Interim Report, *op cit* Ch 25, para 1.
[2] See p 400, *ante.*   [3] See p 525, *post.*
[4] CPR, 44.3(1). This may include costs against an unincorporated association: see *Huntingdon Life Sciences Group plc* v *Cass* [2005] EWHC 2233 (QB), [2005] 4 All ER 899.
[5] *Donald Campbell & Co Ltd* v *Pollack* [1927] AC 732, per Viscount Cave at 811–12.

rule that costs normally follow the event, on an indemnity basis.[6] Further, there are some circumstances where a party is generally entitled to costs unless the court orders otherwise. A defendant is prima facie entitled to costs if the claim is struck out for non-payment of fees, or the claim is discontinued.[7] A claimant is likewise entitled to costs where he accepts a Part 36 offer or payment.[8]

1 THE DISCRETION

When deciding how this discretion is to be used, the court will have regard to the conduct of the parties. It will need to have regard to the overriding objective[9] and the extent, for example, to which Pre-Action Protocols have been followed, with appropriate disclosure, or the extent to which the parties have engaged in ADR.[10] CPR, 44.3 provides that the relevant conduct includes:

(a) pre-action conduct;[11]

(b) whether it was reasonable for a party to consider, raise, or contest a particular allegation or issue;

(c) the manner in which a case has been pursued or defended, or how a particular issue or issues has been produced;

(d) whether a claimant has exaggerated his claim.[12]

The issues will turn on the particular facts of the case. But, in the context of ADR,[13] the court in *Halsey* v *Milton Keynes General NHS Trust, Steel* v *Joy*[14] observed:

> In deciding whether to deprive a successful party of some or all of his costs on the grounds that he has refused to agree to ADR, it must be borne in mind that such an order is an exception to the general rule that costs should follow the event. In our view the burden is on the successful party to show why there should be a departure from that general rule. The fundamental principle is that such departure is not justified unless it is shown (the burden being on the successful party) that the successful party acted unreasonably in refusing to agree to ADR.

The rules envisage that costs may be awarded, or not awarded, in respect of specific issues within the litigation. Lord Woolf in *AEI Rediffusion Music Ltd* v *Phonographic Performance Ltd*[15] observed:

> It is now clear that too robust an application of the 'follow the event' principle encourages litigants to increase the costs of litigation, since it discourages from being selective as to the points they take. If you recover all your costs as long as you win, you are encouraged to leave no stone unturned in your effort to do so.

---

[6] CPR, 44.3(2); see p 523, *post*.   [7] CPR, r 38.6.

[8] CPR, 36.13(1).   [9] See p 464, *ante*.   [10] See p 467, *ante*.

[11] For an example see *Dunnett* v *Railtrack* [2002] EWCA Civ 302, *Reed Executive plc* v *Business Information Ltd* [2004] 4 All ER 943, where it could not be established without reference in inadmissible evidence whether ADR was justified (though the court concluded on other evidence that it was not).

[12] See, e.g., *Booth* v *Brittania Hotels Ltd* [2002] EWCA 579.

[13] As to which, see p 518, *ante*.   [14] [2004] 4 All ER 920.   [15] [1999] 1 WLR 1507.

CPR, 44.3(6) provides that a party may be ordered to pay a proportion of other party's costs, a stated amount, costs from or to a certain date, costs incurred before the proceedings were begun, costs in respect of particular steps, costs relating to distinct parts of the proceedings, or interest on costs. Where the court considers that only parts of the costs should be recoverable, it is good practice where possible to express that in percentage terms (e.g. 60 per cent of the total) rather than on specific issues, in order to avoid difficulties in calculation and apportionment.[16] However, such an order should be made where possible by the trial judge who has knowledge of the conduct of the case.[17]

There has been a considerable volume of litigation as to what is 'the event' in an action.[18] In a simple action involving one claimant, one defendant, and a single issue, no difficulty arises; the event is judgment on that issue. However, where there are several parties or several issues the situation is more complex, and the court will have to deal with costs where appropriate on an issue basis. In the context of multi-party actions special provisions apply.[19]

2   ORDERS AGAINST NON-PARTIES

As already noted costs are completely within the discretion of the court. In *Aiden Shipping Co Ltd* v *Interbulk Ltd*[20] the House of Lords stressed that section 51 of the Supreme Court Act 1981 permitted the ordering of costs against non-parties, and that:

> Courts of first instance are…well capable of exercising their discretion under the statute in accordance with reason and justice.

It should, however, be noted that this was a case where a close relationship existed between the third party (who was in fact a party to a related action) and the parties to the cause in respect of which the costs were awarded.[21] Extensive guidance as to how the power to award costs in such cases should be used was given by the Court of Appeal in *Symphony Group plc* v *Hodgson*:[22] it was established that it was exceptional for a non-party to be ordered to pay such costs, particularly if the party had a cause of action against the non-party. Fair procedures should be followed to ensure that the non-party had the opportunity to make representations, and to ensure that cross-examination of a non-party is not simply being directed to the issue as to whether the court should make a costs order against that non-party. These procedures are now contained in CPR r 48.2.

A good example of the scope and limits of the power can be seen in two recent cases. The first is *Hamilton* v *Al Fayed*[23] where the well-known defendant, who had proved

---

[16] *Verrechia* v *Commissioner of Police for the Metropolis* [2002] EWCA Civ 605; see also *AEI Rediffusion* v *Phonographic Performance Ltd* [1999] 2 All ER 299; *Firle Investments Ltd* v *Datapoint International Ltd* [2001] EWCA Civ 1106; *Mars UK Ltd* v *Technology Ltd (No 2)* [1999] TLR 501.
[17] *Aaron* v *Shelton* [2004] 3 All ER 561.   [18] *Reid, Hewitt & Co* v *Joseph* [1918] AC 717.
[19] See p 527, *post*.   [20] [1986] AC 965, [1986] 2 All ER 409.
[21] See [1986] 2 All ER 416; *Steele, Ford and Newton* v *Crown Prosecution Service* [1994] 1 AC 22, [1993] 2 All ER 769; *Shah* v *Karanjia* [1993] 4 All ER 792.
[22] [1994] QB 179, [1993] 4 All ER 143.   [23] [2002] EWCA Civ 665.

successful in a libel action, was unable to recover his costs from the claimant, who was declared bankrupt. The defendant then sought a section 51 order against the group of individuals who had funded the claimant in the litigation. In rejecting the application for a section 51 costs order, the court confirmed that a general principle protects a person who funds litigation from being made the subject of a section 51 order, a principle which extends to any person whose reasons for funding are either familial, out of natural affection, but also where the contribution was motivated to see that a genuine dispute was not lost by default. The right of the defendant to recover his costs had to give way to the public interest in access to the courts. However, in *Phillips v Symes*[24] the court considered whether the potential exists for costs to be awarded against an expert witness. It accepted that a costs order could be made against an expert who, by his or her evidence, causes significant expense to be incurred, although the particular question here in that case was one of potential liability, the question of actual liability being left for a later hearing. The question was whether the witness was in flagrant disregard of his or her duties to the court.

3 COSTS ORDER FOR MISCONDUCT AND WASTED COSTS ORDERS

The court may disallow all or any part of costs being claimed, or order a party of his legal representative personally to pay the costs incurred by the other party, if the party or the legal representative is at fault because of failure to comply with a rule, practice direction, or court order, or if he has behaved unreasonably or improperly before or during the proceedings.[25] This can include an attempt to inhibit the court from furthering the overriding objective,[26] and is additional to the power to make a wasted costs direction, discussed below.

Section 51(6) of the Supreme Court Act 1981 (as substituted) permits the court to make a 'wasted costs' order against a legal or other representative. It permits the court to disallow costs incurred, or to make an order requiring personal payment, as a result of improper, unreasonable, or negligent acts or omissions by such representatives, or in respect of costs which, in the light of such an act or omission, it would be unreasonable to expect the party on whose behalf they were incurred to pay.

This provision was the subject of judicial scrutiny and comment in *Re a Barrister (Wasted Costs Order) (No 1 of 1991)*.[27] The court identified a three-stage test, now reflected in a Practice Direction.[28]

(a) Had the legal representative of whom complaint was made acted improperly, unreasonably, or negligently?

(b) If so, did such conduct cause the applicant to incur unnecessary costs?

(c) If so, was it in all the circumstances just to order the legal representative to compensate the applicant for the whole or part of the relevant costs?

---

[24] [2004] EWHC 2330 (Ch), [2005] 4 All ER 519.   [25] CPR, 44.14.
[26] See p 464, *ante*.   [27] [1993] QB 293, [1992] 3 All ER 429.   [28] PD 48, para 53.4.

However, in *Ridehalgh* v *Horsefield*[29] the court stressed that care should be taken not to create a new and costly form of satellite litigation, a point reinforced by the House of Lords in *Metcalfe* v *Wetherill*,[30] where it was stressed that the discretion to make a wasted costs order should be reserved for those cases where the unjustifiable conduct can be demonstrated without recourse to disproportionate procedures. It is 'the last resort'.

'Improper conduct' is conduct which would justify disciplinary action; 'unreasonable', means not permitting of reasonable explanation. Sometimes, of course, the legal representative may not be in a position to give a full explanation as to why a particular course of action was undertaken, or not undertaken, because of the doctrine of legal professional privilege. The court should in these circumstances be slow to invoke the wasted costs jurisdiction.[31]

'Negligent' bears the meaning of a failure to act with the competence to be reasonably expected of ordinary members of the profession. It is not improper to pursue a hopeless case, unless that amounts to an abuse of process. Nor is any distinction to be drawn between legally aided and self-financing litigants. A wasted costs order may well be justified where an advocate's conduct of court proceedings is quite plainly unjustifiable. Above all, such applications should not be used as a means of intimidation, and should normally be dealt with at the conclusion of the trial.

Having considered the question of which side must pay costs, the judge must decide what is to be the basis on which the costs are to be assessed, in order to determine how much of an opponent's costs the loser will have to pay.

THE ASSESSMENT OF COSTS

1 THE PROCESS

'Assessment of costs' is the new term for what was traditionally known as 'taxation of costs', and is the process by which the amount due under a costs order is determined. It takes one of two forms: 'summary assessment' and 'detailed assessment'. Summary assessment is the assessment by the court at the end of the hearing of the costs due, without consideration of the detailed components of the amount claimed. At certain stages during proceedings a party must serve a costs estimate on other parties. These costs estimates identify the potential costs liability of other parties. In particular, a costs estimate has to be filed with the documentation dealing with court allocation.[32] This will give the client, and the parties, advance notice of likely potential costs liability under the indemnity principle.[33] Under the rules, a claimant for costs will need to account for any

---

[29] [1994] Ch 205, [1994] 3 All ER 848.   [30] [2002] UKHL 27.

[31] See *Ridehalgh* v *Horsefield* [1994] 3 All ER 848; *Metcalfe* v *Wetherill*, see p 388, *ante*.

[32] Part 43.

[33] *Leigh* v *Michelin Tyres* [2003] EWCA Civ 1766, [2004] 2 All ER 175; *Gabutt* v *Edwards* [2005] EWCA Civ 1206.

difference of 20 per cent or more between the costs estimate and the costs on detailed assessment.

The costs estimate will be used to inform the court as to the appropriate costs order to make on summary assessment. However, an inadequate costs estimate will not inevitably mean that the party claiming costs fails to recover what he ultimately claims.[34] Detailed assessment by contrast involves the detailed scrutiny of a party's costs by a costs officer.[35]

A summary assessment will, unless there is good reason to do otherwise, occur[36] in respect of:

(a) the whole claim for costs following a fast-track trial;[37]

(b) any hearing which has lasted no longer than one day;

(c) some hearings in the Court of Appeal.

The objective is to try and reduce the amount of time, effort, and cost involved in determining issues relating to costs where it is possible to do so. The summary assessment of cost, will consider the costs estimates and a statement of costs which will set out the number of hours claimed, the hourly charging rate of the lawyers involved in handling the case, the level of fee earner (i.e. his seniority and experience) disbursements, and costs for attending the hearing. A failure to supply such a statement may not totally deprive a party of costs under summary assessment, but may affect the nature and content of the costs order made.[38] A detailed assessment involves a detailed consideration of a Bill of costs following the commencement of assessment proceedings after the conclusion of the trial, and within three months of that trial. After a variety of procedural steps, the detailed assessment hearing will occur (unless the parties reach agreement and appropriate orders are made) and a final costs certificate issued.

2 THE AMOUNT OF COSTS

At the outset, one must distinguish between costs between a solicitor and his own client, which amount to a contract debt, and costs between the parties with which, here, we are concerned. Regarding costs between a solicitor and his own client, each party must pay his own solicitor's costs,[39] although the advent of conditional fee agreements creates an important, and relatively new, context. The effect is that costs will be permitted on an indemnity basis.[40] This means that 'all costs shall be allowed except in so far as they are unreasonable in amount or have been unreasonably incurred'. All costs incurred with the express or implied approval of the client are deemed to be reasonable. This may be significantly more than the amounts recoverable under a costs order, which perhaps may amount only to 75–80 per cent of the total costs calculated on an indemnity basis.[41] Of course, if there is a conditional fee agreement the problem becomes theoretical,

[34] *Leigh* v *Michelin Tyre plc* [2004] 2 All ER 173.   [35] CPR, 43.4.
[36] Practice Direction 44.   [37] As to which, see p 496, *ante*.
[38] *Macdonald* v *Taree Holdings Ltd* (2000), Unreported.   [39] See p 378, *ante*.
[40] See p 525, *post*.   [41] See Andrews, *English Civil Procedure, op cit*, para 36.22.

because the funding arrangements are designed to secure that the litigant is not liable to pay costs.

In respect of costs between parties under a costs order, these will be assessed on either the 'standard basis' or the 'indemnity basis', but within the established principle that no party is liable to pay more than the expense and costs incurred by the party claiming costs.[42] Standard costs provide for the recovery of expenditure and costs which have been reasonably incurred.[43] By contrast indemnity costs are more generous, allowing the recovery of all costs not unreasonably incurred. The benefit of the doubt is given to the party who is entitled to costs, and the doctrine of proportionality does not apply.[44] There are, though, some cases where the costs that can be recovered are limited. Small claims[45] costs are restricted to court fees, travelling expenses, and loss of earnings through attendance at court, limitations that are self-evidently necessary if the purpose of a small claims jurisdiction free from large potential costs is to be realized. In fast track proceedings,[46] the costs that may be recovered for advocacy at court are limited depending on the amount of the claim.

(a) Standard costs

Costs on the standard basis is the normal basis of calculation for party and party costs. It requires costs not only to have been incurred necessarily, but also proportionally.[47] The facts of *Lownds* v *Home Office* illustrate the issue, with costs of approximately £17,000 being incurred in respect of a claim compromised at £3,000 damages. Although the appeal failed for transitional reasons in respect of the introduction of the Civil Procedure Rules, the case demonstrates vividly the fact that what is appropriate depends on the whole context of the case. In guidance given in its judgment, the court stated that the question of costs must be assessed (in the context of the claimant's costs) in terms of the proportionality of the expenditure to the likely amounts at stake and recoverable. By contrast the proportionality of the defendant's expenditure will be in relation to the amount claimed, for the defendant is entitled to take the claim at face value.

But even if the total costs may be proportionate, that of itself will not suffice. The court will look at each item on the statement of costs and determine whether it was reasonably incurred, and of a reasonable amount. On the other hand, if the total bill was disproportionate, the court would allow items which were necessary (as opposed to reasonable) to incur, to the extent that the amount of such items was reasonable.

The Civil Procedure Rules[48] identify the factors to be taken into account in deciding whether expenditure is reasonably or unreasonably incurred:

(a) the conduct of all the parties, including pre-commencement conduct, and the efforts made to resolve the dispute before and during proceedings;

(b) the amount or value of the money or property involved;

[42] Confusingly called 'the indemnity principle'. See *Harold* v *Smith* (1860) 17 ER 1229; *Gundry* v *Sainsbury* [1910] 1 KB 645; *General of Berne Insurance Co* v *Jardine Reinsurance Management Ltd* [1998] 2 All ER 301.
[43] See CPR, r 43, 44.   [44] *Lownds* v *Home Office* [2002] 1 WLR 2450.
[45] See p 496, *ante*.   [46] See p 496, *ante*.
[47] *Lownds* v *Home Office, ante* n 44.   [48] CPR, 44.5(3).

(c) the importance of the matter to all the parties;

(d) the particular complexity of the matter or the difficulty or novelty of the questions raised;

(e) the skill, effort, specialized knowledge, and responsibility involved;

(f) the time spent on the case;

(g) the place where and the circumstances in which work or any part of it was done. In particular it may be unreasonable to employ more expensive London lawyers if it was unnecessary to do so.[49]

(b) Indemnity costs

As noted above, these provide a more generous measure of cost recovery. The courts have a wide discretion as to whether, and in what circumstances, to award costs on an indemnity basis.[50] Despite the fact that the courts have sometimes held that indemnity costs ought only to be awarded if a party has been engaged in culpable misconduct in the conduct of the litigation,[51] there is no need for moral misconduct or lack of probity. Any conduct might be considered by a judge to justify an indemnity costs order, and it was not for the appeal court to limit that discretion. Arguing a case devoid of merit might be one example, or clear breaches of the Civil Procedure Rules another.[52]

Indemnity costs are also awarded in certain other situations apart from the court's discretion: these include costs awarded in favour of a trustee or personal representative of an estate, where the parties have entered into an agreement regarding the payment of 'all costs', or a claimant has made an offer to settle the case under the Civil Procedure Rules, Part 36, and it was reasonable for the defendant to have accepted that offer.

COSTS AND CONDITIONAL FEE AGREEMENTS

We have already noted the development of conditional fee agreements as a means of securing funding for litigation and access to justice.[53] These agreements have largely superseded legal aid as a means of funding most types of litigation, were authorized by the Courts and Legal Services Act 1990 (as amended in 1999 by the Access to Justice Act 1999), and allow litigation to be entered into by a claimant on a somewhat inaccurately so-called 'no win, no fee basis'. They achieve this by providing for the client's fees

---

[49] *Sullivan* v *Co-operative Insurance Company Ltd*, *The Times* 19 May 1999; *Wraith* v *Sheffield Forgemasters Ltd* [1998] 1 WLR 132.

[50] *Excelsior Commercial & Industrial Holdings Ltd* v *Salisbury Hammere Aspden & Johnson* 12 June 2002, unreported.

[51] *See Kiam* v *MGN Ltd (No 2)* [2002] 2 All ER 242.

[52] *Barron* v *Lovell* [1999] CPLR 630.   [53] See p 400, *ante*.

and expenses to be payable only in certain specified circumstances.[54] The agreement specifies a 'success fee' which is chargeable if the case is won, and which provides an uplift to the costs that would normally be charged. The costs and the success fee will be, in principle, recoverable from the losing party (subject to the court's discretion already discussed). There is, though, the prospect of lack of success. For that reason, the claimant will also incur the cost of pre-action insurance to cover costs should the claim fail and costs be awarded against the claimant. It is also possible to purchase insurance (After the Event legal expenses insurance) to cover potential liability for the claimant's own costs. The premium payable will reflect the strength of the case and may be structured so that different sums are payable at different stages.[55] To prove liability for such matters the claimant will have to produce a copy of the agreement, with non-relevant confidential detail obscured or deleted.[56]

The reasons for this development are well documented, and reflect the modern movement away from state-funded civil litigation through the legal aid scheme. They also potentially widen access to justice.[57] But they also clearly have a significant impact on questions of costs between parties because of the potential liability of a losing defendant for the success fee and the insurance premium. That is one cogent reason for the requirement that details of any Conditional Fee Agreement funding arrangement be given at the commencement of proceedings by the claimant to the defendant.[58]

The principles to be applied in determining costs due in such circumstances have been worked through in a series of cases. One basic issue is the enforceability of the agreement, which must comply with section 58 of the 1990 Act and the Conditional Fee Agreements Regulations of 2000.[59] Insurers have been increasingly concerned to challenge agreements where breach of the regulations and statutory requirements could be shown. The point was eventually disposed of in *Sharratt* v *London Central Bus Co Ltd (The Accident Group Test Cases)*,[60] where the court held that only where departure from the requirements had a material adverse effect on either the protection afforded to the client or upon the proper administration of justice would a conditional fee agreement be unenforceable. If the client would have no cause for complaint then the costs basis inherent in the agreement would apply.

Another issue is the level of success fee recoverable from the losing party. The general principle in respect of costs is that they should be reasonable and proportionate. However, the proportionality of the success fee must be considered separately from the normal costs incurred. The court will not simply look at the total sum of costs and success fee, and reach a conclusion as to the proportionality of the total sum. A good

[54] 1990 Act, s 58(1) (as substituted by Access to Justice Act 1999, s 27). For a good summary of the legislative history, and the development of a principle discussed in *Thai Trading Co (A Firm)* v *Taylor* [1998] 3 All ER 65, see *Sharratt* v *London Central Bus Co Ltd (The Accident Group Test Cases)* [2003] 4 All ER 590 (CA), [2004] 3 All ER 325.
[55] *Rogers* v *Merthyr Tydfil CBC* [2006] EWCA Civ 134.
[56] *Sharratt* v *London Central Bus Co Ltd, ante,* n xx.
[57] See, e.g., Lord Phillips MR in *R (Factortame Ltd)* v *Secretary of State for the Environment, Transport and the Regions (No 8)* [2002] 3 WLR 104.
[58] See p 480, *ante.*   [59] SI 2000/692.   [60] [2003] 4 All ER 590.

example is a defamation case, *Campbell* v *MGN (No 2)*.[61] The success fees in respect of costs attributable to an appeal to the House of Lords, were 95 per cent and 100 per cent respectively for solicitor and counsel. The defendant challenged these, arguing that, in a defamation case, such sums were a disproportionate interference with the right to freedom of expression. The claim failed, the levels of success fee having to be considered separately, not as part of the overall level of costs.

The success fee can be reduced if itself it is disproportionate and, in determining that, regard must be had to the risk that the fee would not be payable, to the legal representative's liability for disbursements, and the availability of other forms of funding.[62] These are not easy issues: the Court of Appeal in *Callery* v *Gray (No 1)*[63] pointed to a reasonable success fee in a road traffic personal injury claim being no more than 20 per cent, bearing in mind that 99 per cent of such cases succeed. The facts of that case demonstrate the problem. The agreed success fee in the agreement was 60 per cent. An after the event insurance policy cost £367. The amount of compensation agreed by way of settlement was approximately £1,500. The costs judge reduced the success fee to 40 per cent, a figure, as noted above, reduced to 20 per cent on appeal. Yet in *Halloran* v *Delaney*[64] it was said that the appropriate success fee in such cases would normally use a figure of 5 per cent as a starting point, unless persuaded otherwise by the particular circumstances of the case, a conclusion supported by the House of Lords in *Callery* v *Gray*[65] in the context of modest and straightforward cases of this type. It also recognized the need, perhaps, for different success fee uplifts for different costs or different parts of the litigation.

There remains the question of the insurance fee. In deciding whether the recovery of such costs is permissible, the court will have regard to the availability of any pre-existing insurance cover, level and extent of the cover provided, whether any part of the premium was debateable in the event of early settlement, and any commission received by the claimant or his agents.[66] The stage at which it is appropriate to take out the insurance cover will be a matter for the court to decide on an individual basis.

COSTS IN MULTI-PARTY PROCEEDINGS

The use of multi-party actions to determine complex issues has already been discussed.[67] They can, though, raise difficult issues. The Woolf Report observed:[68]

If the treatment of costs is not examined from the outset, the result is either subsidiary litigation or protracted problems when the matter comes to [assessment]. My general proposals for information on costs to be made available at every stage

[61] *Op cit*, p 401, *ante*. [62] Practice Direction (44) 11.8.
[63] [2001] 1 WLR 2112. [64] [2003] 1 WLR 28. [65] [2002] 3 All ER 652.
[66] Practice Direction (44), para 11.100. See also *Samonini* v *London General Transport Services Ltd* [2005] EWHC 90001 (Costs).
[67] See p 481, *ante*. [68] Final Report, *op cit*, at Ch 17, para 57.

when the managing judge is involved are all the more important in relation to multi-party actions, where many claimants will be legally aided and have no direct control over costs and where costs can escalate dramatically. At every stage of the [multi-party situation] the judge should consider, with the help of the parties, the potential impact on costs of the directions that are contemplated and whether they are justified in relation to what is at issue. Parties and their legal representatives, as in other cases on the multi-track, should provide information on cost already incurred and be prepared to estimate the cost of proposed further work....

Rule 48.6A of the Civil Procedure Rules provides for costs where a Group Litigation Order has been made. This provides for cost sharing orders in respect of common costs, which are divided equally, an approach that was developed further by the court in *Davies v Eli Lilly*, applied in *Ward v Guinness Mahon plc*.[69] Procedures have also been developed to allow quarterly calculation of costs, relevant to those parties who discontinue their own claim or who settle.[70]

FURTHER READING

ANDREWS, *English Civil Procedure* (Oxford University Press: 2004)

COOK, 'That Was the Costs Year that Was' (2007) 26 CJQ 134

EVANS, 'Wasted Costs' (2001) 64 MLR 51

WOOLF, *Access to Justice* (1995) – *the Woolf Report*

---

[69] [1996] 4 All ER 112. See *Afrika and others v Cape plc, and other related case* [2003] 3 All ER 631.
[70] *Foster v Roussel Laboratories*, Unreported, 29 January 1997.

18

APPEALS

INTRODUCTION

This chapter will explore the final stage of civil process – the right to appeal. It will address:

- When an appeal can be brought.
- The courts that deal with appeals.
- The powers of the Court of Appeal.
- The approach of the Court of Appeal.

THE CONTEXT

The modern appellate process in civil cases has, like all other aspects of civil procedure, undergone significant change.[1] Prior to the implementation of the Woolf interim and final reports[2] the process was governed by the Supreme Court Act 1981. Now, Part 52 of the Civil Procedure Rules governs appeals both from the High Court and from the county court as well as in respect of certain other specialist appeals. These include jurisdiction to hear appeals from the Employment Appeal Tribunal,[3] the Lands Tribunal,[4] and various other statutory tribunals.[5]

Prior to the civil justice reforms, the Court of Appeal (Civil Division) was the fulcrum of the civil appellate system, with it dealing with all matters arising from the High Court. The Court of Appeal had jurisdiction to hear appeals from any judgment or order of the High Court, except where appeal went direct to the House of Lords under what was known as the 'leapfrog' procedure.[6] Likewise appeals from the county courts generally, but not always,[7] went to the Court of Appeal.[8]

---

[1] See the remarks of Brooke LJ in *Tanfern v Cameron-McDonald* [2000] 2 All ER 801.
[2] As to which, see p 456, *ante.*   [3] See p 307, *ante.*
[4] See chapter 9, *ante.*   [5] See chapter 9, *ante.*
[6] Supreme Court Act 1981, s 16. For appeal to the House of Lords, see p 532, *post.*
[7] Appeals from orders in bankruptcy matters lay in the first instance to a Divisional Court of the Chancery Division, and then with leave to the Court of Appeal.
[8] County Courts Act 1984, s 77.

The new structure creates a hierarchy, with appeals normally going to the next level. Which court will deal with which appeals is dealt with by the Access to Justice (Destination of Appeals) Order 2000.[9] Thus an appeal from the decision of a county court district judge will normally go to a circuit judge.[10] All appeals from a county court judge are normally dealt with by a High Court judge. Decisions of the High Court Master or District Judge[11] will, again, normally lie to a High Court judge. As before, decisions of High Court judges lie to the Court of Appeal. The purpose is clear: to ensure that the ever-increasing burden on the Court of Appeal prior to the Woolf reforms[12] was addressed by ensuring that only cases that need to be dealt with by the full Court of Appeal should be. However, such an approach might sometimes exclude from Court of Appeal consideration important points of law or practice. Accordingly, a 'leapfrog' procedure permits some cases to be transferred directly to the Court of Appeal. This is where an appeal would otherwise lie to a Circuit Judge or High Court judge, but the appeal raises important points of principle or practice, or there is some other compelling reason.[13] The Master of the Rolls also has the power to require a direct first appeal to the Court of Appeal.[14] And despite this hierarchy one important further exception exists: a 'final decision' can proceed to the Court of Appeal. A 'final decision' is one which would finally determine the entire proceedings.[15] This might include points of law, or evidence, such as limitation periods, but does not include striking out the proceedings or a statement of case.[16]

Appeals from the Court of Appeal in limited circumstances lie to the House of Lords.[17] As noted above, there may, exceptionally, be an appeal directly from the High Court to the House of Lords.[18]

RIGHTS OF APPEAL

Until the implementation of the civil justice reforms many rights of appeal existed as of right, with permission ('leave') to appeal needed only in a minority of cases.[19] The changed procedures now generally require 'permission'[20] to appeal to be granted.[21] That is not the case if a statutory scheme of appeal exists, because the scheme of appeal

---

[9] SI 2000/1071.   [10] See p 317, *ante.*   [11] See p 319, *ante.*

[12] See *Review of the Court of Appeal (Civil Division)* (the Bowman Report) to be found at www.dca.gov.uk/civil/. For commentary see Jacob at (1998) 61 MLR 390.

[13] CPR, 52.14(1).   [14] Access to Justice Act 1999, s 57(1)(a).

[15] Destination of Appeals Order. *Op cit*, art. 1(2)(c).

[16] *Tanfern* v *Cameron-McDonald* [2000] 1 WLR 1315.   [17] See p 532, *post.*

[18] Administration of Justice Act 1969. See, further, p 532, *post.*

[19] The more important cases included: appeals from Divisional Courts of the High Court; appeals from consent orders or orders solely as to costs; from interim orders or judgments; from decisions of a county court judge where the value of the claim in contract, tort or certain other monetary claims did not exceed £5,000 (£15,000 in equity or probate); from a commercial judge on an arbitration appeal.

[20] For the change in terminology made by CPR, see p 465, *ante.*   [21] CPR, 52.3.

permits appeal as of right,[22] nor does it apply in certain situations where the liberty of the individual is at stake. The cases that fall within this category include orders committing an individual to prison, secure accommodation orders made under section 25 of the Children Act 1989, or cases where an application for an order of habeas corpus is refused.[23]

A party wishing to appeal must make an oral application to the court whose decision he seeks to appeal.[24] That is made to the relevant appeal court, or, if that application is refused, an application for permission can be made to the relevant appeal court provided the procedures that have been prescribed are followed.[25] These require an appeal notice and an 'appeal bundle' to be prepared. Unless statute provides otherwise, the time period for the lodging of the appeal notice is fourteen days. Leave to extend the time for the filing of an appeal notice may be granted by the court whose decision or order is being appealed, or by the appeal court provided the relevant procedure is complied with.[26] The question of extension is one for the court, not for the parties, a position reflecting the obligation of the courts under the Civil Procedure Rules to manage effectively the progress of cases. The decision not to grant an extension is itself a matter that is appealable.[27]

The appeal bundle will include copies of the appeal notice, a skeleton legal argument,[28] a copy of the order being appealed, a copy of the reasons for the decision, any written statements in support of the application,[29] and any other documents reasonably considered to be necessary to enable the appeal court to reach its decision. If there are relevant documents which are not available, for example the judgment giving written reasons for the decision, an explanation must be given. The record of the judgment or ruling being appealed is crucial if the appeal court is to be able to take an informed view of the appeal.[30] More limited documentation is needed if the appeal is one arising from a decision in the small claims track.[31]

The appeal court has various powers in respect of an appeal notice. It may, of course, grant permission. The criteria the court will apply will be to ask whether the appeal would have a real prospect of success, or whether there is some other compelling reason why the appeal should be heard.[32] Where there has already been an appeal, the criteria are even more strict: the case must raise an important issue of principle, or there must be other compelling reasons why a further appeal should be permitted. This is designed to facilitate the speedier resolution of disputes by making second appeals a rarity.[33]

Permission is unlikely to be granted in respect of case management decisions. In *Thermawear Ltd* v *Linton*[34] Lord Bingham MR stressed that procedural initiatives would be futile if every decision or initiative could be appealed.

---

[22] *Colley* v *Council for Licensed Conveyancers* [2001] 4 All ER 998.
[23] As to which, see p 215, *ante*.   [24] CPR, 53.2(3).
[25] See CPR, 53.2; Practice Direction 52.   [26] See CPR, 52.4.
[27] *Foenander* v *Bond Lewis* & Co [2001] EWCA Civ 759.
[28] Not required from a litigant in person: Practice Direction 52, para 7.7A.
[29] See p 533, *post*.   [30] *Plender* v *Hyams* [2001] 2 All ER 179.
[31] See Practice Direction 52. For the small claims track see p 496, *ante*.
[32] CPR, 52.3(6).   [33] *Tanfer Ltd* v *Cameron-McDonald* [2000] 1 WLR 1311.
[34] *The Times*, 20 October 1995.

No right to appeal lies against a refusal of permission to appeal,[35] nor, apparently, are reasons for the refusal of permission needed to be given.[36] Alternatively it may:[37]

(a) strike out the whole or part of an appeal notice;

(b) set aside permission to appeal either in whole or in part;

(c) impose conditions, or vary conditions, upon which an appeal may be brought.

A notice will be struck out only rarely, and usually if the court has been misled or the point at issue is clearly dealt with by statutory provision which had been overlooked.[38] Conditions should only be imposed where there is a 'compelling reason' to do so.[39] These might include security for costs, as in *Aoun* v *Bahri*, where such a requirement in respect of the costs of the lower court proceedings was held unreasonable. Other examples are an order to pay a judgment debt,[40] or the payment of money into court.[41] The discretion of the court is not in any way limited, subject to questions of reasonableness.

Appeal lies from the civil division of the Court of Appeal to the House of Lords only with permission of the Court of Appeal or of the House of Lords.[42] There is no requirement that the appeal be based on a point of law, though almost always appeal to the House of Lords is based upon a point of law rather than on an issue of fact or an award of damages. Although permission is the only prerequisite for appealing, no appeal lies from the decision of the Court of Appeal where any statute expresses the decision of the Court of Appeal to be final. As noted earlier, the Administration of Justice Act 1969, Part II provided for a 'leapfrog' appeal direct from the High Court to the House of Lords subject to the grant of a certificate by the trial judge and of leave by the House of Lords in any case in which appeal lies to the Court of Appeal (with or without permission). The criteria which apply as pre-conditions to the grant of such a certificate were stated by the House of Lords in the first 'leapfrog' case under the 1969 Act procedure, *American Cyanamid* v *Upjohn Co.*[43] These are – (1) the consent of all parties must be given, and (2) the case must involve a point of law of general public importance either relating to the construction of an enactment or is a point on which the judge was bound by precedent.

For the purpose of European Community law the House of Lords is clearly 'a court or tribunal of a Member State, against whose decision there is no judicial remedy under national law', so that where a question arises concerning:

(a) the interpretation of the Treaty;

(b) the validity and interpretation of acts of the institutions of the Community; or

---

[35] Access to Justice Act 1999, s 54(4).

[36] *North Range Shipping Ltd* v *Seatrans Shipping Corporation* [2002] 1 WLR 2397; *X* v *Federal Republic of Germany* (1981) 25 DR 240; *Nerva* v *United Kingdom* App No 42295/98, 11 July 2000.

[37] CPR, 52.9(1).

[38] *Nathan* v *Smilovich* [2002] EWCA Civ 759; *Barings Bank plc (in liquidation)* v *Coopers & Lybrand* EWCA Civ 1155.

[39] Per *Brooke LJ* in *Aoun* v *Bahri* EWCA Civ 1141.

[40] *Hammond Suddards Solicitors* v *Agrichem International Holdings Ltd* [2001] EWCA Civ 1915.

[41] *Bell Electric Ltd* v *Aweco Appliance Systems GmbH & Co* [2002] EWCA Civ 501.

[42] Administration of Justice (Appeals) Act 1934, s 1.   [43] [1970] 3 All ER 785.

(c) the interpretation of the statutes of bodies established by an Act of the Council,
     where those statutes so provide,

the House of Lords is bound to refer that question to the European Court for a preliminary ruling (unless, of course, the High Court or Court of Appeal has already
referred the question in the same case) and, having obtained the ruling, is bound to
follow it.[44]

PROCEDURE AND POWERS ON APPEAL

The purpose of an appeal is to review the decision of the lower court, and not, generally, a rehearing of the original argument. In *Audergon* v *La Baguette Ltd*[45] the Court
of Appeal held that it was undesirable to formulate criteria to be applied when deciding
whether to rehear the case, but the Court must have good reason for ordering such a
re-hearing. In that case the judge hearing the appeal did not have such a good reason,
because the Master who had conducted the original matter had considered all the relevant evidence. But good reason might exist if the judge had given inadequate, or no,
reasons, because then the process of review would be impossible.[46]

Appeals in the Court of Appeal have traditionally been heard by two or three judges
of the Court, the court may now consist of a single judge.[47] The Court hears full legal
argument from both sides and may substitute its own judgment for that of the court
below. Even though it is not a complete rehearing, In addition, the appellant is normally
confined to the points of law which he raised in the court below. He may in certain circumstances, discussed below, be allowed to take new points on appeal but he cannot,
except with leave of the Court of Appeal, rely on any grounds of appeal or apply for any
relief not specified in his notice of appeal.[48]

The Court of Appeal has all the powers, authority, and jurisdiction of the court or
tribunal from which the appeal was brought in any matter before it. An appeal court
will not generally admit evidence not before the lower court, but does have the power to
admit new evidence.[49] This discretion must be exercised in accordance with the overriding objective,[50] in the light of all the circumstances of the case. The Civil Procedure
Rules state[51] that appeal courts will not receive oral evidence or evidence that was not
before the lower courts, unless it orders otherwise.

---

[44] See p 138, *ante*.   [45] [2002] EWCA Civ 10.

[46] *Ansari* v *Puffin Investment Co Ltd* [2002] EWCA 234; cf. *Dyson Ltd* v *Registrar of Trademarks* [2003]
EWCHC 1062.

[47] Supreme Court Act 1981, s 54(2)–(4), substituted by Access to Justice Act 1999, s 59.

[48] CPR, 52.   [49] CPR, 52.11.

[50] *Gillingham* v *Gillingham* [2001] EWCA Civ 906. *Hamilton* v *Al-Fayed* (2002), EWCA Civ, 605. For the
overriding objective, see p 464, *ante*. For discussion of *Ladd* v *Marshall*, see *Pearce* v *Ove Harup Partnership*
[1999] 1 All ER 769; *Shaker* v *Al-Bedrawi* [2002] 4 All ER 835.

[51] CPR, 52.11.

The Court has power to examine trial witnesses though it rarely does so, being content in most cases to rely upon the judge's note or a transcript of the official short-hand note. It has power to receive further evidence orally, by affidavit or by deposition taken before an examiner but, where there was a trial or hearing on the merits, but, as noted above, the Court will not admit further evidence (other than evidence as to matters which have occurred since the trial) except on special grounds. In *Ladd* v *Marshall*,[52] Denning LJ prescribed the following three conditions for the reception of fresh evidence in the Court of Appeal:

> first, it must be shown that the evidence could not have been obtained with reason-able diligence for use at the trial; secondly, the evidence must be such that, if given, it would probably have an important influence on the result of the case, though it need not be decisive; thirdly, the evidence must be such as is presumably to be believed, or, in other words, it must be apparently credible though it need not be incontrovertible.

This statement was approved by the House of Lords in *Skone* v *Skone*[53] where the evidence consisted of a bundle of love letters written by the co-respondent in a divorce suit to the wife which tended to prove adultery between them. The trial judge had dismissed the husband's petition and accepted the co-respondent's evidence to the effect that adultery had not taken place. It was argued that these letters (which were in the possession of the wife) could have been obtained by seeking discovery of documents from the wife. The House of Lords rejected this argument on the basis that the husband had no reason to suspect the existence of such letters, that the letters, if genuine, falsified the judge's finding to such an extent that it would be unjust to leave matters where they were and, furthermore, that there was a strong prima facie case of deception of the court. It must be emphasized that these rigorous conditions need not be satisfied in respect of evidence of matters occurring after the trial. Evidence will be admitted of matters occurring after the trial where the basis on which the trial judge gave his decision has been clearly falsified by subsequent events.

Of course, such authorities pre-date the civil justice reforms, and the approach to the old case law is that it is often no longer relevant or appropriate.[54] But in *Gillingham* v *Gillingham*[55] the principles in *Ladd* v *Marshall* were considered to remain good law, not as rules but, rather, as indicators of matters which should be taken into account. In *Gillingham* the evidence was forgotten correspondence, which had not been disclosed by the other party. Although, with reasonable diligence it might have been discovered, the matter could not fairly or satisfactorily be resolved without it, and it was therefore right to allow the appeal and order a new trial.

On appeal the Court has full power to make any order which should have been made in the court below and to substitute its own order as to liability, quantum, or costs for that of the court below. In addition the Court of Appeal is not confined to the points raised in the notice of appeal or respondent's notice. It may, though it rarely does, take

---

[52] [1954] 3 All ER 745, applied in *Roe* v *Robert McGregor & Sons Ltd* [1968] 2 All ER 636.
[53] [1971] 2 All ER 582.   [54] See p 464, *ante*.   [55] See n 50, *ante*.

any point of law or fact so far as is necessary to ensure the determination on the merits of the real question in issue between the parties. Should the Court of Appeal wish to decide an issue of fact which has not been raised in the statement of case, an extremely infrequent contingency, it may allow the grounds of appeal to be amended.

THE APPROACH TO THE DETERMINATION
OF APPEALS

1 APPEAL ON A POINT OF LAW

Most appeals are based on a point of law. It has already been stated that, notwithstanding the general power to take a point not raised therein, the Court usually confines itself to the points raised in the notice of appeal or respondent's notice. Furthermore there is a general rule that a party cannot take on appeal a point which he did not take in the court below.[56]

To this rule there are two important exceptions. The first occurs where the point of law was expressly reserved in the court below. This might occur where the court below was not free to consider the point because it was bound by precedent on that point, whereas the Court of Appeal might be free to reconsider the precedent in question. Secondly, an appeal court will allow a point to be taken, and indeed will take the point itself, where not to do so would result in an abuse of the court's process. Thus the illegality of a contract may be raised on appeal even though the point was overlooked in the court below.[57]

2 APPEAL AGAINST A FINDING OF FACT

An appeal is not, generally, by way of rehearing, and thus an appeal court will be reluctant to interfere with findings of fact made by the judge. However, an appeal court can allow an appeal where the decision being appealed was 'wrong' and make draw such inference of fact which it considers justified on the evidence.[58] This has been held to mean that an appeal court must consider and make up its mind about findings of fact.[59] Whether a judge on appeal will overturn findings of fact, or inferences from fact, will depend on all the circumstances: did the trial judge reach the conclusion based on assessment or oral testimony, in which circumstance the trial judge will have had the advantage of hearing the evidence. By contrast inferences from primary facts may be more susceptible to the appeal court taking a different view.[60] Appeal is by way of rehearing, the Court of

---

[56] See *Meco Pak AB v Electropaint Ltd* [2001] EWCA Civ 1537.
[57] See *Snell v Unity Finance Ltd* [1964] 2 QB 203; *Oscroft v Benabo* [1967] 2 All ER 548.
[58] CPR, 52.11.   [59] See *Todd v Adam* [2002] EWCA Civ 509.
[60] *Assicurazioni Generali Spa v Arab Insurance Group BSC* [2002] EWCA 1642.

Appeal has power to substitute its own finding of fact, direct or inferential, for that of the trial judge or jury. However, the appeal court does not have the advantage, which the judge, or, occasionally judge and jury had, of seeing the trial witnesses and observing their demeanour. Consequently the jurisdiction exercised by the Court of Appeal in relation to findings of fact is confined to inferential findings of fact. The Court has the power to substitute its own inference from the facts as found for that of the trial judge or jury and will not hesitate to do so. In a pre-CPR case, involving a claim of medical negligence, where the crucial issue of fact was whether a hospital registrar had pulled 'too long and too hard' on the head of the infant plaintiff in the course of his birth, Lord Bridge explained his willingness to uphold an appeal from the trial judge's finding in the plaintiff's favour in the following words:[61]

> My Lords, I recognise that this is a question of pure fact and that in the realm of fact, as the authorities repeatedly emphasise, the advantages which the judge derives from seeing and hearing the witnesses must always be respected by an appellate court. At the same time the importance of the part played by those advantages in assisting the judge to any particular conclusion of fact varies through a wide spectrum from, at one end, a straight conflict of primary fact between witnesses, where credibility is crucial and the appellate court can hardly ever interfere, to, at the other end, an inference from undisputed primary facts, where the appellate court is in just as good a position as the trial judge to make the decision.

Where a jury has returned a general verdict it is impossible to distinguish direct findings of fact from inferential findings and, indeed, the jury cannot be asked, after they have returned a general verdict, to state what their direct findings of fact were. An appeal court, therefore, can only upset the general verdict of a jury if it cannot be supported by the evidence or is a verdict which no reasonable men could have reached. In *Grobbelaar v News Group Newspapers*[62] an attempt by the Court of Appeal to overturn a defamation finding because it flew in the face of the evidence as it was read by the Court of Appeal was overturned by the House of Lords. The jury's verdict could not be dismissed as irrational or perverse, though the House of Lords reduced the damages award from £88,000 to a derisory £1.

3 APPEAL AGAINST THE EXERCISE OF A DISCRETION

In many circumstances the judge has a discretion as to whether, and in what manner, to exercise his powers. Commonly encountered instances of judicial discretion are the discretion as to costs, the discretion whether to grant or refuse an injunction, and the discretion as to the mode of trial, in particular in relation to the question of whether or not to order jury trial. However, no discretion is absolute and there may be a successful appeal in relation to the exercise of a judicial discretion if the appellant can show that the judge exercised his discretion under a mistake of law, or under a misapprehension as to the facts, or that he took into account irrelevant matters or gave insufficient weight, or too

---

[61] *Whitehouse* v *Jordan* [1981] 1 All ER 267 at 286.
[62] [2002] 1 WLR 3024, HL, overturning [2001] 2 All ER 437.

much weight, to certain factors, or that he failed to exercise his discretion at all.[63] If the judge gives no reasons, or insufficient reasons for the exercise of his discretion, the court may infer that he has gone wrong in one respect or another, and, indeed, the conclusion may be that there is a breach of the fair trial provisions of Article 6 of the Convention.[64] It is vital for proper reasons to be stated, not only because of the requirements of fairness to the parties but also that the appellate court can perform its function of review.

The burden of proof is on the party who alleges that the discretion was wrongly exercised and, in any event, the Court of Appeal will only allow the appeal if satisfied that the judge's conclusion is one which involves injustice or was clearly wrong. In *Hadmor Productions Ltd* v *Hamilton* Lord Diplock explained the extent of an appellate court's powers as follows:[65]

> Before adverting to the evidence that was before the judge and the additional evidence that was before the Court of Appeal, it is I think appropriate to remind your Lordships of the limited function of an appellate court in an appeal of this kind. An interlocutory injunction is a discretionary relief and the discretion whether or not to grant it is vested in the High Court judge by whom the application for it is heard. On an appeal from the judge's grant or refusal of an interlocutory injunction the function of an appellate court, whether it be the Court of Appeal or your Lordships' House, is not to exercise an independent discretion of its own. It must defer to the judge's exercise of his discretion and must not interfere with it merely on the ground that the members of the appellate court would have exercised the discretion differently. The function of the appellate court is initially one of review only. It may set aside the judge's exercise of his discretion on the ground that it was based on a misunderstanding of the law or of the evidence before him or on an inference that particular facts existed or did not exist, which, although it was one that might legitimately have been drawn on the evidence that was before the judge, can be demonstrated to be wrong by further evidence that has become available by the time of the appeal, or on the ground that there has been a change of circumstances after the judge made his order that would have justified his acceding to an application to vary it. Since reasons given by judges for granting or refusing interlocutory injunctions may sometimes be sketchy, there may also be occasional cases where even though no erroneous assumption of law or fact can be identified the judge's decision to grant or refuse the injunction is so aberrant that it must be set aside on the ground that no reasonable judge regardful of his duty to act judicially could have reached it. It is only if and after the appellate court has reached the conclusion that the judge's exercise of his discretion must be set aside for one or other of these reasons that it becomes entitled to exercise an original discretion of its own.

4 APPEAL AGAINST AN AWARD OF DAMAGES

The approach adopted when determining an appeal against an award of damages differs according to whether the award was made by a jury or by a judge sitting alone. Where

[63] For challenge on judicial review to the exercise of discretionary powers, see p 223, *ante*.
[64] See p 185, *ante*, and p 571, *post*. [65] [1983] 1 AC 191 at 220.

unliquidated damages are claimed, historically the Court has not interfered with the award of a jury unless the damages awarded were so large or, more rarely, so small that no jury could reasonably have given them.[66]

However, a new trial may be ordered if it appears to the Court either that the jury took into account irrelevant factors or failed to consider matters which it ought to have considered and in consequence awarded damages which were excessive or inadequate. The case of *Lewis* v *Daily Telegraph Ltd*[67] provides a good example. In that case two national newspapers published on the same day paragraphs alleged to be defamatory of the plaintiffs. The jury in the first action awarded the plaintiffs a total of £100,000; in the second action two days later in which there were factors which a jury might be entitled to take into account as aggravating damages, a different jury awarded the plaintiffs a further £117,000. New trials of both actions were ordered on the ground (inter alia) that the damages in each case were excessive. The House of Lords, affirming the decision of the Court of Appeal, stated that in such a case, pursuant to section 12 of the Defamation Act 1952, each jury should be directed to consider how far the damage suffered can reasonably be attributed solely to the libel with which they are concerned, and how far it ought to be regarded as the joint result of the two libels, bearing in mind that the plaintiff ought not to be compensated twice for the same loss. In *Rantzen* v *Mirror Group Newspapers (1986) Ltd*[68] the plaintiff, a well-known television presenter, had been awarded £250,000 damages for defamation. The defendant appealed, on the basis that the award was excessive, and sought an order under section 8 of the Courts and Legal Services At 1990, which now provides that where the court has the power to order a new trial on the basis of excessive or inadequate damages, it may be given the power to substitute the proper sum instead of ordering that new trial. The Court of Appeal concluded that this power had to be exercised in the context of Article 10 of the European Convention on Human Rights, which permitted restrictions on freedom of expression only where they were necessary in a democratic society to meet a pressing social need. On this basis large awards of damages were to be subjected to very close scrutiny. The question now to be asked is whether a reasonable jury could have thought the award necessary to compensate the plaintiff. On the facts the award was excessive by any objective standard of reasonable compensation, and an award of £110,000 was substituted for that of the jury. Where the award of damages appealed against was made by a judge sitting alone the Court of Appeal will not hesitate to interfere with the assessment, not only on the ground that the judge applied a wrong principle of law in making the assessment, but also on the ground that the award is out of scale with awards in similar cases.

The matter was considered again by the Court of Appeal in *John* v *MGN Ltd*,[69] where the Court held that when assessing compensatory damages in a defamation case a jury could in future properly be referred by way of comparison to the conventional

---

[66] *Johnson* v *Great Western Railway Co* [1904] KB 250; *Cassell & Co Ltd* v *Broome* [1972] AC 1027, [1972] 1 All ER 801.

[67] [1964] AC 234, [1963] 2 All ER 975.   [68] [1994] 2 QB 670, [1993] 4 All ER 975.

[69] [1996] 2 All ER 35.

compensation scales in personal injury cases as well as to previous libel awards made or approved by the Court of Appeal, and there was no reason why the judge, in his directions, or counsel, should not indicate to the jury the level of award which they considered appropriate. Those changes of practice would not undermine but rather buttress the constitutional role of the libel jury by rendering their proceedings more rational and so more acceptable to public opinion. The same principle also applies in actions against the police for unlawful conduct.

There is, of course, no prescribed scale of damages in any type of action but, nevertheless, there is a certain degree of parity in awards in respect of similar types of damage particularly in actions for damages for personal injuries. In such cases the Court of Appeal will not make small adjustments to the sum awarded though it will make a substantial adjustment if that is found necessary. In practice the Court will rarely interfere unless an adjustment of at least 20 per cent or 25 per cent is envisaged. It is this diversity of approach to awards of damages made by judges and juries respectively that has led to the virtual disappearance of jury trial in personal injuries actions.

The Court of Appeal has power under section 17 of the Supreme Court Act 1981 to order a new trial. It may exercise this power on an appeal from a judge and jury or from a judge alone just as it can on a motion for a new trial following a trial with a jury. A new trial may be ordered on any one issue without disturbing the finding of the court below on any other issue. Thus the Court of Appeal may order a new trial on the issue of damages while affirming the decision on the question of liability. Indeed if the only ground of application is the amount of damages the court should limit the new trial to that issue and leave the findings as to liability undisturbed. If there is a new trial, that trial is completely independent of the first trial. The mode of trial need not be the same, no estoppel arises as a result of the first trial and the parties may raise new points and may contest issues left uncontested at the first trial. The costs of the first trial are sometimes ordered to await the outcome of the new trial though, as a rule, the successful applicant ought to be allowed the costs of his application.

FURTHER READING

ANDREWS, *English Civil Procedure* (Oxford University Press: 2004)

BOWMAN, *Review of the Court of Appeal (Civil Division),* Lord Chancellor's Department, September 1997

LEGGATT, 'The Future of the Oral Tradition in the Court of Appeal' (1995) 14 CJQ 148

WOOLF, *Access to Justice* (1995) – the 'Woolf Report'

PART IV

CRIMINAL PROCEEDINGS

19

CRIMINAL PROCEEDINGS AND THE CRIMINAL JUSTICE SYSTEM

INTRODUCTION

It is only relatively recently that there has been a coherent 'system' of criminal justice. Even now it is characterized by a multiplicity of departments, boards and organizations. This chapter will examine some of the issues arising from this, focusing specifically on:

- How the criminal justice system is managed.

- The adversarial nature of the process.

- The increasing pressure and trend toward case management to ensure fair and efficient determination of charges.

- The concept of a fair trial as required by Article 6 of the Convention on Human Rights.

MANAGEMENT OF THE CRIMINAL JUSTICE PROCESS

1 THE 'SYSTEM'

The use of the word 'system' in the context of the English criminal justice system may be misleading. With a multitude of different government departments, agencies, and others making 'separate and sometimes conflicting'[1] contributions, and in excess of 400,000 staff,[2] the problem of consistent and coherent planning and action is obvious.

---

[1] See Auld Review, *op cit*, Ch 8, para 1.
[2] See http://www.cjsonline.gov.uk/the_cjs/departments_of_the_cjs

In the recent past, several government departments (principally the Home Office and Department of Constitutional Affairs),[3] some forty-two police forces, the Crown Prosecution Service, Magistrates' Courts Committees, the Prison Service, and Courts Service have each had major roles, quite apart from the roles that defence lawyers and defendants themselves play. The Auld Review observed that administrative complexities and muddle of responsibilities had a practical and visible effect on the efficient and effective working of the 'system'.[4] It considered that efficiency and effectiveness are as important as the formal procedural and substantive rules in ensuring that the aims of the criminal justice system are in fact achieved. This objective is not always easily achieved in the current 'system'.

More recently, emphasis has been placed on the achievement of a more 'joined-up', co-ordinated, approach. A new National Criminal Justice Committee was established following the Auld Review and publication of the White Paper *Justice for All*.[5] It comprises leading civil servants from relevant Government Departments, comprising the Director of Public Prosecutions, the Chief Executives of relevant Criminal Justice agencies, a representative of the Association of Chief Police Officers, and a senior judge. The Committee reports to a Cabinet Committee and is responsible for overall criminal justice system delivery. For wider involvement of all those involved in the criminal justice system, a new National Criminal Justice Board comprises representatives not only of the Bar, magistracy, and judiciary, but also the representatives of the Commission for Racial Equality, the Law Society, victim and witness organizations, and senior academics. It acts as a consultative and advisory body on the criminal justice system, and gives a voice to a wide range of interests within the criminal justice system, advising on criminal justice reform so that all who work within, or with, the 'system' can have their say and influence decision-making. Some forty-two local Criminal Justice Boards were established during 2002–2003.

A variety of other initiatives have, in recent years, been launched. The Youth Justice Board[6] was established in 1998,[7] with its objectives including monitoring the operation of the youth justice system, to publish information about that system, to advise on necessary changes, and to promote good practice. The Courts Act 2003 established a unified court service and management structure,[8] aiming to establish decentralized management and local accountability within a national framework.[9] A National Courts Agency has functions which include setting performance indicators, monitoring performance standards, and managing projects for common systems (such as information technology). All criminal justice agencies will be able to exchange case information electronically, with victims being able to follow the progress of their case online. Through overall co-ordination and liaison, common IT systems, and better case management it is expected that cases will be dealt with quicker, more efficiently, and in a more consistent way. Changes in police structures and organization,[10] the creation of the National

[3] Formerly the preserve of the Lord Chancellor's Department: see chapter 1, *ante*.
[4] Auld Review, Ch 8, para 12.   [5] *Op cit*, Ch 9, para 5.   [6] See p 675, *post*.
[7] Crime and Disorder Act 1998, s 41.   [8] See p 18, *ante*.   [9] *Justice for All, op cit*, 9.17.
[10] See chapter 15, *ante*.

Probation Service,[11] and its proposed merger with the Prison Agency into the National Offender Management Service are each a response to the need for a co-ordinated, efficient and consistent management of process and of punishments.[12]

So where, then, does actual responsibility lie in this complex structure? Within central government, there are three government departments who have responsibility for 'the system':

(a) Home Office

Oversees the Police and the National Offender Management Service, and sponsors the Youth Justice Board, Criminal Injuries Compensation Authority, and the Criminal Cases Review Commission.

(b) Ministry of Justice

Oversees the magistrates' courts, the Crown Court, the Appeal Courts and the Legal Service Commission.

(c) Office of the Attorney-General

Oversees the Crown Prosecution Service, the Serious Fraud Office, and Customs and Excise prosecutors.

The work of these three Departments is co-ordinated by yet another government body, the Office for Criminal Justice Reform, a cross-departmental organization which reports to Ministers in each of the three government departments. Its task is to drive through improvements set out by the National Criminal Justice Board described above. One recent example is the publication by the OCJR of the Victims Code of Practice.[13]

2 THE AIMS OF THE CRIMINAL JUSTICE SYSTEM

The Auld Review identified two main aims that were set by government for the criminal justice system.[14] One was the reduction of crime and the fear of crime and its social and economic costs. The other was the dispensing of justice fairly and efficiently, to promote confidence in the law. This second aim had several more specific objectives: to secure just processes and just and effective outcomes; to deal with cases with appropriate speed; to meet the needs of victims, witnesses and jurors within the system; to respect the rights of defendants and treat them fairly; and to promote confidence in the criminal justice system.

These aims and objectives were accepted by that Review as an appropriate starting point, although it counselled against expecting too much of the criminal justice system, and in particular urged that the courts should not be seen as 'a medium for curing the ills

---

[11] Criminal Justice and Courts Services Act 2000, s 2, creates, inter alia, a National Probation Service. Section 2 states that the Home Secretary, local probation boards and probation officers must have regard to (1) the protection of the public; (2) the reduction of re-offending, and (3) the proper punishment of offenders.

[12] See chapter 23, *post.*   [13] See p 549, *post.*   [14] *Op cit*, Ch 1, para 7.

of society'.[15] Nonetheless, as noted above, the trend of recent legislation has been to seek greater co-ordination between the different agencies who deal with the administration of the criminal justice system and those who have some responsibility for policies that may diminish criminal activity, or which might divert persons from the criminal justice system. We have already noted the co-ordinating role of the Youth Justice Board.[16] The Crime and Disorder Act 1998 created a new framework for the development and management of crime and disorder strategies, requiring police authorities and chief police officers to act in co-operation with each other, and formulate strategies for the reduction of crime and disorder.[17] It also placed an obligation on local authorities to consider the crime and disorder implications of what they do. Section 37 of the 1998 Act states a clear aim for the youth justice system, which deals with those under the age of eighteen: the principal aim of the youth justice system is to prevent offending by children and young persons. It is the duty of all persons and bodies carrying out functions in relation to the youth justice system to have regard to that aim.

More recent legislation has identified for the first time the purposes of sentencing. Section 126 of the Criminal Justice Act 2003 states that these are:[18] (a) the punishment of offenders, (b) the reduction of crime (including its reduction by deterrence and its reduction by the reform and rehabilitation of offenders), (c) the protection of the public, and (d) the making of reparation by offenders to persons affected by their offences. Of course, the statement of aims and purposes tells us nothing about how different aims or purposes can be reconciled, or how the detailed processes, rules, and punishments should be used.

All these examples demonstrate that there are many interested parties affected by the criminal justice system, and who may view the purpose of what they are doing in different lights. Clearly, ensuring a fair trial for a defendant is fundamental, and a right enshrined in Article 6 of the European Convention.[19] There are, though, other legitimate interests: those of prosecutors, in ensuring that the guilty are in fact convicted; those of victims, in receiving 'justice'; those of government and other public authorities, in reducing the incidence of crime. These competing interests have to be balanced, and this is reflected in the trial and in pre-trial processes. Ensuring that some of these wider aims are achieved may, however, mean adopting approaches such as diverting offenders away from the criminal process to address offending behaviour, through cautioning or youth offender programmes, or using a combination of criminal and civil process to prevent repeat offending behaviour. The White Paper *Justice for All*[20] identified what were seen as weaknesses in critical areas throughout the criminal justice system: the police only detected 23 per cent of the 5.5 million offences recorded during 2000–2001; too many defendants offend whilst on bail;[21] the system brings defendants to trial too slowly; too many go unconvicted; and too many are not given the sentence

[15] Ibid, Ch 1, para 9.   [16] *Ante*, and see p 548, *post*.

[17] Crime and Disorder Act 1998, ss 5–6, based largely on the Report of the Morgan Committee, *Safer Communities: The Local Delivery of Crime Prevention through the Partnership Approach*, Home Office, 1991.

[18] See p 691, *post*.   [19] See p 185, *ante*, and p 555, *post*.

[20] 2002, Cm 5563, Home Office.

[21] Some 25 per cent, rising to 38 per cent of under-18s: ibid, para 1.6.

they need. It recommended a more integrated strategy to reduce crime and deliver justice, through a 'virtuous circle'[22] of prevention, detection, prosecution, punishment, and rehabilitation.

In this context, the trial process is fundamental, but forms only a part of a wider system designed to meet these diverse interests and objectives. The extent to which the failings identified above can be overcome depends crucially on the success or otherwise of the large number of provisions contained in the extremely complex Criminal Justice Act 2003,[23] many of which were brought into force between 2004 and 2007. Yet despite all these provisions there continue to be major challenges to achieving a fair, speedy and effective system for determining all cases. The fact that in 2007 a terrorism trial lasted 13 months, twice as long as expected, with the jury then deliberating for some 27 days,[24] is a vivid and cogent reminder that there continue to be major challenges that have to be addressed.

3 YOUTH JUSTICE[25]

Distinct issues arise in the context of juveniles (those aged under eighteen). Section 44 of the Children and Young Persons Act 1933 requires any court, in fulfilling its duties, to take account of the welfare of the child or young person before it. More recently, considerable debate has occurred as to the role and functions of the youth justice system. In a Consultation Paper,[26] the government stated its belief that action was needed to bring about greater consistency in the approach to working with young offenders in the community and to ensure that all the relevant local agencies play a full part. It also believed that the youth justice system should seek to prevent crime. For that reason, section 37 of the Crime and Disorder Act 1998 states that:

> It shall be the principal aim of the youth justice system to prevent offending by children and young persons.

It is the duty of all persons and bodies carrying out functions in relation to the youth justice system to have regard to that aim. This is a broad statement of an overall duty that applies not only to local authorities, health authorities, probation services, voluntary agencies, and the police, but also to the courts in dealing with young offenders after conviction.

The role of local authorities in establishing youth offending teams and creating youth justice strategies should be noted. Each local authority is under a duty to secure that, to such extent as is appropriate for their area, all youth justice services are available,[27] performed in partnership with other agencies such as the police. Local authorities

---

[22] Ibid, para 1.12.

[23] Containing some 339 sections and thirty-eight Schedules. Only some of the provisions had been brought into force as at the date of going to press.

[24] See *The Times*, 3 May 2007.   [25] See, generally, Ward, *Young Offenders* (Jordans 2001).

[26] *No More Excuses – A New Approach to Tackling Youth Crime in England and Wales*, Cm 3809, 1997.

[27] 1998 Act, s 38.

operate within the overall guidance given by the Youth Justice Board.[28] This comprises ten, eleven, or twelve members, appointed by the Home Secretary, and includes persons with extensive recent experience of the youth justice system. Its functions are set out by section 42(5) of the Crime and Disorder Act 1998, and include:

(a) the monitoring of the operation of the youth justice and the provision of youth justice services;

(b) advising the Home Secretary on the operation of that system and the provision of such services; how the principal aim of that system might most effectively be pursued; the content of any national standards he may see fit to set with respect to the provision of such services, or the accommodation in which children and young persons are kept in custody; and the steps that might be taken to prevent offending by children and young persons;

(c) the monitoring and collection of information about the youth justice system and the provision of services by local authorities;

(d) the identification and promotion of good practice in the context of the operation of the youth justice system and the provision of youth justice services, the prevention of offending by children and young persons; and in respect of working with children and young persons who are or are at risk of becoming offenders.

Central to the implementation of strategy in relation to young offenders are Youth Offending Teams (YOTs). These teams are expected to 'pull together all the relevant local agencies in delivering community-based interventions with, and supervision of, young offenders'.[29] At least one team has been established in each local authority area, and include at least one probation officer, local authority social worker, police officer, and nominee of a health authority and of the local education authority. They are under a duty to co-ordinate the provision of youth justice services within the local authority area, and to carry out such functions as are assigned to the team in the local authority's youth justice plan made under section 41.[30] Not only should youth offending teams co-ordinate local provision relating to work with young offenders, but they also play a key role in the reprimand and caution system introduced by the 1998 Act,[31] and in respect of various of the orders that may be made by a court when dealing with young offenders. Their primary functions include report-writing for courts, the preparation of reparation or action plans, and the supervision of young offenders within the community, based upon an inter-agency partnership philosophy.[32]

---

[28] Ibid, s 41.

[29] *No More Excuses: New National and Local Focus on Youth Crime*, Home Office, 1997, para 1.21. See also Morgan Report, *Safer Communities: The Local Delivery of Crime Prevention through the Partnership Approach*, Home Office, 1991.

[30] *Ante.*   [31] See p 563, *post.* Note, in particular, the role of Youth Offender Panels.

[32] Consultation Paper, *op cit*; see also Morgan Report, *Safer Communities: The Local Delivery of Crime Prevention through the Partnership Approach* (1991).

4 VICTIMS OF CRIME

For the lawyer, the primary emphasis of the criminal justice system has traditionally been on the detection of crime, and the prosecution of those accused of it. The objectives of that process have, of course, always been the prevention of crime, and the punishment of those who engage in it. Yet the victims of criminal conduct have not always been regarded as fundamental players within the criminal justice 'system'. Although the power to have regard to the injury or loss suffered by the victim is reflected in the power of the court to make a compensation order,[33] or to receive compensation through the Criminal Injuries Compensation Authority,[34] victims have generally had little role in the criminal justice process, beyond giving evidence. Even in that regard, the process has not always been 'victim friendly'. The White Paper *Justice for All*[35] observed:

> Justice is not simply about punishment for its own sake. Many victims, when asked, say that they simply want to ensure that no one else has to go through the kind of experience they themselves have. And the best way of ensuring that is to catch, convict and rehabilitate offenders and prevent further crime. Victim's own evidence is crucial in bringing offenders to justice. They must be nurtured and not subject to a host of delays, postponements and barriers…The criminal justice agencies have a particular responsibility to support victims and witnesses…This includes ensuring that they are protected, if vulnerable from intimidation or further crime, and taking into account the impact of the offence on victims when sentencing offenders.…

To address this, another White Paper, *A Better Deal for Victims and Witnesses*[36] reviewed what was working well, and what was not. Amongst the positive developments identified were the development of victim support, which, in 2004, helped in excess of one million victims, and the special measures provisions introduced by the Youth Justice and Criminal Evidence Act 1999 to help vulnerable witnesses.[37] Yet a range of problems remained: the need to abandon trials because witnesses and victims refuse to testify, the fact that many victims and witnesses felt badly treated by the criminal justice process, in particular by failure to keep them informed of the progress of cases, or informed of significant events such as the release of an offender from prison. Some of these problems have arisen because responsibility for victims and witnesses is distributed too widely across the criminal justice system, causing confusion, inefficiency and delay. Whatever, victim satisfaction with the police in particular fell from 67 per cent in 1984 to 58 per cent in 2000. The White Paper observed:[38]

> Everyone has the right to justice including those accused of crime. But many victims feel that the rights of defendants take precedence over theirs. Public confidence in [the criminal justice system] is dependent on how people perceive that they, or

---

[33] See p 709, *post.*   [34] See p 709, *post.*

[35] Cm 5074, July 2002 (available at www.homeoffice.gov.uk) at paras 2.11–2.12.

[36] Home Office, 2003.   [37] By means of special measures directions: see p 646, *post.*

[38] *Op cit*, p 2.

their family or friends, will be treated as a victim or witness to a crime. Too often the perceptions are that victims and witnesses are the ones on trial rather than the suspect.

A variety of measures – administrative and evidential – have been introduced to address some of the problems that lead to this perception. Greater powers for the police to impose conditions on police bail,[39] greater protection for witnesses,[40] the use of witness statements in some cases to avoid vulnerable witnesses having to go to court,[41] the greater regard for the victim in the sentencing process,[42] and a range of pilot projects and initiatives, often in liaison with the voluntary sector are examples of the types of measures put in place. A pilot scheme is under way in London to permit relatives of the victims of murder to make a statement to the trial court prior to the sentencing of a convicted defendant.[43]

This need to address issues relating to victims was recognized by the passage of the Domestic Violence, Crime and Victims Act 2004, which requires the Home Secretary to issue a Code of Practice as to the services to be provided to a victim of criminal conduct by a person who appears to have functions relating to the victims of criminal conduct, or in respect of any aspect of the criminal justice system.[44] These include the Courts Service, Magistrates' Courts Committees, the Courts Agency, the Criminal Cases Review Commission, the Criminal Injuries Compensation Authority, the Criminal Injuries Compensation Appeals Panel, Crown Prosecution Service, the police, the Parole Board, probation boards, the National Association of Victim Support Schemes, and Youth Offending teams.

Those who have responsibilities under the code are under an obligation to provide services and information to specified classes of victims of crime, particularly victims of offences against the person (including sexual offences) and victims of some offences against property. Special protections will be given to vulnerable victims: a victim falls within this class if he or she is under seventeen, mentally disordered, has experienced domestic violence, been the subject of harassment or religious or racially aggravated crime, or has been the subject of intimidation. The general nature of the duty was described as follows:[45]

> Under the [Code] all the services that come into contact with victims…have new responsibilities to ensure that the needs of victims are met…The police…will be responsible for providing information if a suspect is arrested, cautioned or charged; telling them whether the suspect is on bail; protecting them from intimidation; informing them promptly of the date of any court hearing and ensuring that the victim is put in touch with Victim Support Services. The National Probation Service is responsible for keeping victims informed about a prisoner's release and arrangements for their supervision and any licence conditions.

Particular responsibilities are placed on the Crown Prosecution Service.[46] Under a scheme funded by some £11 million by government the CPS already provides victims

[39] See p 565, *post.*   [40] See p 646, *post.*   [41] See p 647, *post.*
[42] See p 549 et seq.   [43] See p 694, post.   [44] 2004 Act, s 32(1).
[45] *Justice for All, op cit*, para 2.43.   [46] For the CPS, see p 383, *ante.*

with an explanation when the prosecution decision is to discontinue the case or to alter the charges substantially. In certain sex offences or racially aggravated crime in serious cases such as those involving a death or child abuse the CPS offer to meet the victim or victim's family to explain the basis of the decision.

Amongst the rights conferred upon some (though not all) victims are the right to be informed of key stages and decisions, the right to make representations on certain matters relating to release of offenders on licence,[47] and the right to make complaint to the Parliamentary Commissioner for Administration.[48] Section 48 and Schedule 8 of the 2004 Act create the office of Commissioner for Victims and Witnesses. The functions of the Commissioner are (under section 49) the promotion of the interests of victims and witnesses, the taking of necessary steps with a view to encouraging good practice in the treatment of victims and witnesses, and the keeping under review of the operation of the code of practice.

THE CRIMINAL PROCESS

1 ADVERSARIAL NATURE

Despite the trend towards diverting offenders away from the criminal justice process, the trial remains at the heart of the criminal justice process. It is, essentially, adversarial in nature.[49] The process of investigation and evidence-gathering is conducted by the police or other investigating body, but with the Crown Prosecution Service (CPS)[50] playing an increased role in supervising the investigation and determining what charges, if any, are to be brought.[51] Traditionally the court plays no significant part in the preparation of the case. The trial itself is not an investigation into events or allegations, but rather a hearing to decide, within complex rules of evidence,[52] whether the prosecution has proved, to the appropriate standard,[53] whether the defendant is guilty of the particular offences with which the prosecution have charged him.[54] By contrast, in many civil law

---

[47] See p 702, *post.*

[48] 2004 Act, s 47, Schedule 7, amending the Parliamentary Commissioner Act 1967.

[49] For assessment generally of the adversarial process, see the various submissions of evidence to the Royal Commission on Criminal Justice, 1993, Cm 2263, HMSO, and the Royal Commission on Criminal Procedure, 1981, Cmn 8292, HMSO, at para 1.8.

[50] See p 383, *ante.*

[51] See p 567, *post.* When in force, Police and Criminal Evidence Act 1984 (PACE), s 37B, inserted by Criminal Justice Act 2003, Schedule 3, para 2, will give the decision as to whether to charge, and with what, to the CPS.

[52] Detailed consideration of the rules of evidence is beyond the scope of this book. See, generally, Dennis, *The Law of Evidence* (3nd edn, 2007).

[53] The criminal standard is often described that the court must be satisfied of the defendant's guilt beyond any reasonable doubt. For difficulties in establishing the nature of the standard, see chapter 1, *ante,* and p 12, *ante.*

[54] Whilst a judge has a discretion to call witnesses not called by the prosecution or defence, this power should be used sparingly, and only where necessary in the interests of justice: *R v Roberts* (1984) 80 Cr App R 89.

jurisdictions the process is inquisitorial in nature. This term is used to describe systems where judges or magistrates supervise the pre-trial investigations and preparation of the case, to a greater or lesser extent, and play a significant part in the questioning of the witness at trial, and in the decisions as to what evidence should be considered by the court. Simply put, the trial is much more of an investigation than a contest, although some inquisitorial systems have adversarial characteristics, and over-rigid distinctions should be avoided.

This adversarial characteristic has often been viewed as one of the strengths of the English system. These strengths were identified by the Court of Appeal in *R* v *McIlkenny*:[55]

> Another feature of our law, which goes hand in hand with trial by jury, is the adversarial nature of criminal proceedings. Clearly a jury cannot embark on a judicial investigation. So the material must be placed before the jury. It is sometimes said that the adversarial system leaves too much power in the hands of the police. But that criticism has been met, at least in part, by the creation of the Crown Prosecution Service. The great advantage of the adversarial system is that it enables the defendant to test the prosecution case in open court. Once there is sufficient evidence to commit a defendant for trial, the prosecution has to prove the case against him by calling witnesses to give oral testimony in the presence of the jury. We doubt whether there is a better example of exposing the weaknesses in the prosecution case, whether the witness be a policeman, a scientist or a bystander, than by cross examination.

Yet, despite these perceived advantages, in recent years focus has turned to whether the criminal trial in fact achieves its purpose, and, more fundamentally, whether the criminal justice system itself delivers what society expects of it. The adversarial approach of the trial, best exemplified by jury trial in the Crown Court,[56] has not seriously been challenged. The Royal Commission on Criminal Procedure,[57] Royal Commission on Criminal Justice,[58] and the Review of the Criminal Courts of England and Wales[59] (the Auld Review) each considered that:

> there is no persuasive case for a general move away from our adversarial process. Not only is it the norm throughout the common law world, it is beginning to find favour in a number of civil law jurisdictions which have become disenchanted with their inquisitorial tradition.[60]

In part, this debate about the nature of the criminal trial and trial process arose because of a series of causes célèbres[61] where the trial, and indeed pre-trial, process failed to operate in a way to prevent injustice and miscarriage of justice. That was the situation

---

[55] [1992] 2 All ER 417, at 425–6. [56] See chapter 11, *ante*.

[57] *Op cit*, para 1.8. [58] *Op cit*, paras 11–14.

[59] The Auld Review, 2001, HMSO. [60] Ibid, Ch 1, para 28.

[61] See, e.g., *R* v *McIlkenny*, *ante*; *R* v *Maguire* [1992] QB 936, [1992] 2 All ER 433; *R* v *Silcott, Braithwaite and Raghip*, *The Times*, 9 December 1991; *R* v *Kisko* (1992), unreported. See, generally, Walker and Starmer, *Justice in Error* (1994). For a host of examples see the various annual reports of the Criminal Cases Review Commission, at http://ccrc.gov.uk, and p 716, *post*.

in *Ward*. In *R* v *McIlkenny* itself, the appeal court identified some of the weaknesses of the adversarial process, such as the imbalance in resources between prosecution and defence, and the need for proper disclosure of prosecution evidence to the defence. Above all, the effectiveness of any system depends upon it not being abused by those who work within it. Many, though not all, of the miscarriages of justice that made headline news stemmed not from failures in the trial process itself, but, rather from failures in the investigation process or from failures to apply properly the processes designed to protect the fairness of the trial itself.[62]

Concerns about the workings of the wider criminal justice process, and the balance between its competing aims, have been increasing in recent years. Back in 1993 the Royal Commission on Criminal Justice made some 352 separate recommendations.[63] As already noted, it did not recommend a fundamental change of approach, doubting whether a general move away from the adversarial approach would be desirable. It concluded that a system which keeps separate the roles of the police, prosecutor, and judge offers a basic protection against the risk of 'unnecessarily prolonged detention prior to trial'.[64] Instead, its recommendations were intended to make the pre-existing system 'more capable of serving the interests of justice and efficiency', and intended to deal with matters that seemed to the Commission to turn what ought to be a search for the truth into 'a contest played between opposing players according to a set of rules which the jury does not necessarily accept or even understand'.[65] It recognized that the criminal trial and the criminal justice process had a wider purpose other than simply to protect defendants, although that is a fundamental characteristic of a 'fair trial'. In achieving this balance, the Commission identified certain principles against which detailed rules, and any suggested changes to those rules, had to be judged: 'Are they fair'? 'Are they open?' 'Are they workable?'

Some, though not all, of the recommendations of the Royal Commission formed the basis of subsequent legislation, or informed the deliberations of other committees, commissions or working groups. The 1990s saw a plethora of government and parliamentary activity, with significant quantities of criminal justice legislation,[66] and culminating in the Auld Committee Report in 2000.[67] That Report, with its 328 recommendations, has itself informed the most recent legislation, the Criminal Justice Act 2003. This constant flow of legislation addressed not only changes to the adversarial pre-trial, trial, and sentencing powers and processes, but also wider and more fundamental questions about the structure and aims of the criminal justice system.

---

[62] Many of the cases in question involved alleged police malpractice: see, e.g. *R* v *Maguire, ante*.

[63] The Commission did not consider police powers (which had been the subject of change in PACE following the Royal Commission on Criminal Procedure, 1981, Cmnd 2263, HMSO), the rules relating to bail or sentencing. The various Research Studies published by the Royal Commission are a valuable source of data relating to, and analysis of, the trial system.

[64] Ibid, Ch 1, para 14.   [65] Ibid, Ch 1, para 11.

[66] See, e.g., Criminal Justice Act 1991; Criminal Justice Act 1993; Criminal Justice and Public Order Act 1994; Criminal Procedure and Investigations Act 1996; Crime (Sentences) Act 1997; Crime and Disorder Act 1998, Youth Justice and Criminal Evidence Act 1999.

[67] See n 59, *ante*.

2 CASE MANAGEMENT

This general acceptance of a broadly adversarial approach should not disguise the fact that an increasing degree of case management by the court itself has developed. Examples of this are the process of pleas and directions hearings and preparatory hearings,[68] the increased duties of disclosure of evidence on both prosecution and defence,[69] the courts' role in protecting witnesses through special measures directions,[70] and in dealing with applications to withhold evidence.[71] These together constitute a significant inroad in the basic principle that the court does not get involved in what is put before it, and how that is done. In fact, the basic duty on a trial judge to ensure a fair trial, and, now, the wider right to a fair trial under Article 6 of the European Convention on Human Rights,[72] require a judge to perform a key role.[73] In *R* v *Ward*[74] the appeal court, in quashing a conviction wrongly obtained, stated that it was the responsibility of a trial judge to ensure a fair trial, to reduce the risk of wrongful conviction to a minimum.

3 CRIMINAL PROCEDURE RULES

As noted above, a fair trial for the defendant must be the prime objective of the criminal trial. In a note written to the Lord Chancellor, Lord Woolf CJ wrote that 'the presumption of innocence and a robust adversarial process are essential features of English legal tradition and of the defendant's right to a fair trial . . .'. However, the efficient and effective management of cases is crucial if, on the one hand, a defendant is to be tried fairly and expeditiously, and, on the other, that the process is efficient, and effective in ensuring that those who *are* guilty are convicted and punished. To this end, one important precondition are procedural rules which are clear and concisely expressed, and which can be changed without complex legislative intervention.[75] To achieve this, new Criminal Procedure Rules which came into force on 4 April 2005, were introduced, and aim to consolidate the rules and practices that govern the process from beginning to end. They are intended to create a culture change, making everybody involved in a case responsible for helping to make the case go ahead efficiently, under the supervision of the court,[76] and are the first step in the creation of a 'comprehensive criminal procedural code'. The Rules have been made by a new Criminal Procedure Rule Committee.[77] Reference is made in this book to these Rules during detailed consideration of the trial process, where it is necessary to do so. Rule 1.2 imposes a duty on every participant in the case to prepare

---

[68] See p 629, *post*.   [69] See p 606, *post*.   [70] See p 646, *post*.

[71] A court may allow relevant evidence to be withheld if a claim of public interest immunity is made out. For the procedure to be followed, see in particular, *R* v *H, R* v *C, The Times*, 6 February 2004, following the decision of ECHR in *Edwards and Lewis* v *United Kingdom, The Times*, 29 July 2003.

[72] See chapter 5, *ante*, and p 555, *post*.   [73] See p 555, post.

[74] [1993] 2 All ER 577.   [75] Auld Review, *op cit*, Ch 10.

[76] http://www.dca.gov.uk/criminal/crimpr.htm.

[77] For the relevant legislative framework, see Courts Act 2003, ss 69–74.

and conduct the case in accordance with a new overriding objective. This is that 'criminal cases be dealt with justly'.[78] This is, by rule 1.2, to comprise seven elements:

(a) acquitting the innocent and convicting the guilty;

(b) dealing with the prosecution and the defence fairly;

(c) recognizing the rights of a defendant, particularly those arising under Article 6;

(d) respecting the interests of witnesses, victims, and jurors and keeping them informed of the progress of the case;

(e) dealing with the case efficiently and expeditiously;

(f) ensuring that appropriate information is available to the court when bail and sentence are being considered;

(g) dealing with a case in ways that take into account the gravity of the offence charged, the complexity of the matters in issue, the severity of the consequences for the defendant and others affected, and the needs of other cases.

These may be thought not to be controversial, although (g) above gives to the possible danger of the downgrading of the procedural standards in cases perceived as less serious. The Rules place a duty on all those involved to ensure compliance with their provisions, and to report any 'significant failure', defined as being a failure which might hinder the court in furthering the overriding objective.

In future the courts will look to trying to avoid deciding cases on the basis solely of procedural irregularities. The aim, under the Rules, is to decide cases on their merits.[79]

THE RIGHT TO A FAIR TRIAL

1 ARTICLE 6

However we characterize the nature of the process, the right to a fair trial is fundamental, and enshrined in Article 6 of the European Convention on Human Rights.[80] Article 6 states:

(1) In the determination of his civil rights and obligations or of any criminal charge against him, everyone is entitled to a fair and public hearing within a reasonable time by an independent and impartial tribunal established by law. Judgment shall be pronounced publicly but the press and public may be excluded from all or part of the trial in the interest of morals, public order or national security in a democratic society, where the interests of juveniles or the protection of the private life of the parties so require, or to the extent strictly necessary in the opinion of the court in special circumstances where publicity would prejudice the interests of justice.

---

[78] CPR 2005, 1.1.　　[79] *R v Ashton* [2006] EWCA Crim 794.　　[80] See also, p 285, *ante*.

(2) Everyone charged with a criminal offence shall be presumed innocent until proved guilty according to law.

(3) Everyone charged with a criminal offence has the following minimum rights:

(a) to be informed properly, in a language which he understands and in detail, of the nature and cause of the accusation against him;

(b) to have adequate time and facilities for the preparation of his defence;

(c) to defend himself in person or through legal assistance of his own choosing or, if he has no sufficient means to pay for legal assistance, to be given it free when the interests of justice so require;

(d) to examine or have examined witnesses against him, and to obtain the attendance and examination of witnesses on his behalf under the same conditions as witnesses against him; to have the free assistance of an interpreter if he cannot understand or speak the language used in court.

It confers protection on those who are subject to a determination of a criminal charge (Article 6(1)). Whether a matter involves a criminal charge will depend on the classification of the proceedings in domestic law, the nature of the offence; and the nature and degree of severity of the penalty that the person concerned risks incurring.[81] Amongst the instances of matters being classified as criminal are the investigation of an allegation of assault with no formal punishment,[82] penalties imposed for breach of military discipline,[83] a regulatory traffic offence,[84] administrative proceedings for customs regulations,[85] and fines imposed by tax authorities.[86] Recent English authorities serve to demonstrate the types of issue that arise. In *R v M; Kerr; H*,[87] it was held that Article 6 does not apply to proceedings under sections 4 and 4A of the Criminal Procedure (Insanity) Act 1964, which relate to the fitness to plead of a defendant. Such proceedings are not criminal, because they do not result in a conviction or a penalty, but merely determine whether the defendant can stand trial. Even if they were criminal, provided the disadvantages to a defendant under a disability are minimized, the trial could be fair and the defendant's disability would not usually, of itself, found an application for abuse of process.[88] Again, in *Han and another v Commissioners of Customs and Excise*[89] the issue arose as to whether the imposition of penalties on taxpayers for dishonest evasion of VAT (described as civil penalties) gave rise to criminal charges for the purpose of Article 6 of the Convention. It was held by the VAT and Duties Tribunal that they did, and that the taxpayers were entitled to the minimum rights contained in Article 6(3). On appeal, the Commissioners of Customs and Excise argued that the classification of the penalty was a civil penalty, that civil penalties had been introduced deliberately to decriminalize the VAT system, and there was an absence of any threat of imprisonment. In rejecting this argument, the Court noted in particular that alternative regimes existed under the legislation (one of them clearly criminal in nature) and with routes to

---

[81] *Engel v Netherlands (No 1)* (1976) 1 EHRR 647; *AP v Switzerland* (1997) 26 EHRR 541.
[82] *Adolf v Austria* (1982) 4 EHRR 313.   [83] *Engel v Netherlands (No 1), ante.*
[84] *Ozturk v Germany* (1984) 6 EHRR 409.   [85] *Benedenoun v France* (1994) 18 EHRR 54.
[86] *AP v Switzerland, ante.*   [87] [2001] All ER (D) 67.
[88] See p 572, *post.*   [89] [2001] 4 All ER 687.

move from one to another. A further example is the administration of a reprimand or warning under section 65 of the Crime and Disorder Act 1998,[90] which was held in *R (on the Application of U) v Metropolitan Police Commissioner*[91] to be the determination of a criminal charge. Because the offender had not been told that the effect of a reprimand would be registration as a sex offender,[92] there was a breach of Article 6.

Article 6 is not concerned with the fairness of provisions of substantive law. For that reason a challenge in *R v G*[93] to the test of recklessness in respect of the crime of arson failed. The question that Article 6 requires a court to answer is simply: 'is the trial fair'. Nor does Article 6 prescribe rules for the admissibility of evidence:[94] In *Khan (Sultan) v United Kingdom*[95] the Court of Human Rights found there to be no breach of Article 6 in admitting evidence obtained by interception of conversations obtained by an interference with the property rights of the applicant, even though there might in some circumstances be a breach of the Article 8 rights of the applicant. There was no evidence of unreliability or unfairness. Article 6 does not directly address questions of errors of law or misuse of judicial discretion, unless a wider Convention right is infringed.[96]

2 LIMITS TO THE RIGHT?

The right to a fair trial cannot be limited.[97] A court must, though, be mindful that, although it should not accord a margin of appreciation[98] to the national authority, it should give weight to the decisions of a representative legislature and democratic government within the areas of discretionary judgment accorded to them. In deciding what the right to a fair trial involves, a court may ask whether a limit on a right is reasonable, directed by national authorities towards a clear and proper public objective and proportionate to that objective. Thus in *Brown v Stott (Procurator Fiscal: Dunfermline)*[99] the Privy Council, on an appeal from Scotland, held that provisions in section 172 of the Road Traffic Act 1988 requiring the registered owner of a motor vehicle to supply information as to the driver of a vehicle at any date and time did not infringe Article 6 rights protection against being required to self-incriminate. There was a clear public interest in dealing with driving that imperils the safety of others.

The concept of applying legal rules to secure a fair trial is, of course, not one that is new, and which only arises under Article 6: English criminal procedure and evidential rules has long proceeded on this basis.[100] Both at common law and under section 78 of the Police and Criminal Evidence Act 1984 (PACE), a trial court must always act to secure a fair trial. It has been described as an 'elementary right of every defendant',[101] and

---

[90] See p 563, *post*.   [91] [2003] 1 All ER 419.
[92] Under Sexual Offences Act 2003.   [93] [2002] EWCA 1992.
[94] *Schenk v Switzerland* (1998) 13 EHRR 242; *Doorson v The Netherlands* (1996) 22 EHRR 330; *Trivedi v United Kingdom* [1997] EHRLR 520.
[95] [2000] Crim LR 683.   [96] *Ali v United Kingdom* (1997).
[97] See p 185, *ante*.   [98] See p 176, *ante*.   [99] [2001] 2 All ER 97.
[100] In a Scottish case the same principle (ie that fairness does not depend necessarily on *art 6*) was confirmed: *Robertson (Stewart) v H.M.Advocate* [2007] HCJAC 63.
[101] Per Lord Hope in *R v Brown (Winston)* [1998] AC 367.

as a 'constitutional right'.[102] One mechanism for achieving this has long been the basic common law discretion, which exists to permit the exclusion of evidence, the probative value of which is low compared with its prejudicial effects.[103] However, Article 6 does raise certain key issues in the context of the criminal process. Amongst these are questions as to the presumption of innocence,[104] the principle against self-incrimination,[105] the right to legal advice and representation,[106] and the obligation to employ rules and procedures in a fair way. It also impacts significantly on issues relating to sentence.[107] The detailed issues that it raises are discussed as they arise.

Most fundamental of all, though, is the right to be tried by an independent and impartial tribunal. Justice must not only be done, but be seen to be done. If it can be shown that a court is the subject of actual bias, or, much more likely, gives the appearance of bias or lack of impartiality (judged objectively) then Article 6 rights will be infringed.[108] The question is whether there is a real danger of bias.[109] A court should ascertain the circumstances, and then 'ask itself whether, having regard to those circumstances, there was a real danger of bias on the part of the relevant member of the tribunal in question, in the sense that he might unfairly regard (or have unfairly regarded) with favour, or disfavour, the case of a party to an issue under consideration'. The matter must be viewed from the perspective of the 'informed observer'.[110] *R v Gough* is a good example. The brother of the appellant was the next-door neighbour of one member of the jury. The House of Lords concluded that there was not a real danger that the appellant had received a trial that was unfair, the juror having sworn a statement that she was unaware of the connection until after the jury had delivered its verdict.

In a criminal case, one aspect of the problem is whether a judge who has made pre-trial rulings or findings can, fairly, preside over the trial itself. There will usually be a legitimate doubt about impartiality if the judge has been involved in the case before trial in a way that involves the formulation of an opinion as to the guilt or innocence of the defendant.[111] There will also be a breach of Article 6 where the prosecuting authority appointed the judge.[112]

Another aspect is potential bias in respect of the jury.[113] Again, the test is to ask: what would a fair-minded observer think? A conviction is likely to be quashed if a reasonable possibility or danger of bias might be thought to exist.[114] This may be an increasing problem now that serving police officers and solicitors are eligible to serve on juries.[115] In

---

[102] Ibid per Lord Steyn.   [103] *R v Sang* [1980] AC 402.   [104] See p 648, *post.*
[105] See p 185, *post.*   [106] See p 186, *ante.*   [107] See ch 23.
[108] See *Piersack v Belgium* (1982) 5 EHRR 69; *De Cubber v Belgium* (1984) 7 EHRR 236; *Hauschildt v Denmark* (1989) 12 EHRR 416; *Langborger v Sweden* (1989) 12 EHRR 416.
[109] *R v Gough* [1993] AC 646.
[110] *Locabail (UK) Ltd v Bayfield Properties* [2000] 2 WLR 870; *Porter v Magill* [2001] UKHL 67, [2002] 2 AC 357; *Lawal v Northern Spirit Ltd* [2003] UKHL 35. See also *Director General of Fair Trading v Proprietary Association of Great Britain* [2001] 1 WLR 700.
[111] *Brown v United Kingdom* (1985) 8 EHRR 272.
[112] *Findlay v United Kingdom* (1997) 24 EHRR 221; *De Cubber v Belgium* (1984) 7 EHRR 236 (trial judge was previously the investigating judge).
[113] For juries, see p 349, *ante.*   [114] *R v Evans (Lyn Harris)* [2005] EWCA Crim 766.
[115] See p 350, *ante.*

R v Abdroikov (Nurlon) and associated appeals[116] one conviction was quashed because it was not clear that justice was seen to be done when one of the jurors was a full-time, salaried, long-serving employee of the prosecutor. However, the dissenting speeches of Lords Rodger and Carswell serve only to illustrate that the application of this seemingly simple principle is far from easy.

FURTHER READING

Annual Reports of the Criminal Cases Review Commission

Ashworth and Redmayne, *The Criminal Process*, 3rd edn (Oxford University Press: 2000)

Auld Review, *Review of the Criminal Courts of England & Wales* (http://www.criminal-courts-review.org.uk)

Belloni and Hodgson, *Criminal Injustice* (Palgrave: 2000)

---

[116] [2007] UKHL 37, [2007] 1 WLR 2679.

20

PRE-TRIAL PROCEDURE

INTRODUCTION

Pre-trial procedure is crucial. It is at this stage that, if the decision to prosecute is taken, the charge or charges will be decided. Selection of the right charges is a key decision, and can, if wrong, significantly weaken the chances of successful prosecution. Decisions also have to be made about the mode of trial, and whether bail is to be granted. This chapter will therefore examine:

- The choices that have to be made as to whether to prosecute, and who makes them.
- The role of the Crown Prosecution Service in deciding the charge.
- The classification of offences.
- Decisions as to mode of trial.
- The right to grant bail and the ground on which it may be refused.

THE DECISION TO COMMENCE PROCEEDINGS

1 DISCRETION AND CAUTIONING

The fact that an offence is believed to have been committed does not mean that the commencement of a prosecution is inevitable. Discretion exists at various stages as to whether a prosecution should be commenced, or the suspect cautioned formally or informally. The police and the Crown Prosecution Service or other prosecution authority each has discretion at appropriate times. That discretion may be reviewable on normal judicial review principles.[1] It is also the duty of prosecuting authorities to keep under review the decision whether or not to prosecute.

At the policing level, an individual officer has discretion as to what action, if any, he should take. He can informally caution, make an arrest,[2] or formally report a suspect

---

[1] See p 215, *ante*.

[2] Arrest for the purposes of cautioning is lawful only if the grounds for arrest in fact exist, and are being used. There is no power to detain for the purposes of cautioning: *Collins* v *Wilcock* [1984] 3 All ER 374, and p 416, *ante*.

with a view to prosecution. These decisions will often be made in the light of the overall policies adopted by the police force of which the officer is a part. At a later stage a decision will have to be taken whether an individual should be charged, and, if so, with what offence, or whether a caution should be administered. That practice was originally non-statutory: now the Criminal Justice Act 2003 has introduced a statutory scheme. Whatever, a caution is intended to replace charge and prosecution, although it cannot prevent a private prosecution[3] from being commenced.[4]

2 THE NON-STATUTORY BACKGROUND

The practice of formally cautioning, rather than prosecuting, can be traced back to 1929, but until 2003 never had a statutory basis. It was first regulated in 1978,[5] but despite these attempts to achieve greater consistency, cautioning practices varied widely between individual police forces and were confined in the main to elderly offenders, those suffering mental stress and young first offenders who had committed minor offences.[6] In 1991, some 279,000 offenders were dealt with by way of caution, some 179,000 of these relating to indictable or either-way offences. The Royal Commission on Criminal Justice[7] recommended an extension of cautioning to more petty offenders, but also recognized a need for national guidelines within which cautioning could occur, thus achieving greater consistency. It recommended that consideration should be given to combining cautions with other support, through social services or the probation service but recognized that a failure to prosecute an individual can itself damage confidence in the criminal justice system.

In 1994, Circular 18/1994 was issued. It encouraged the police to caution formally rather than prosecute in some circumstances. It required there to be clear and reliable evidence of the suspect's guilt relating to the material elements of the offence, sufficient to raise a reasonable prospect of conviction: the suspect must have admitted guilt.[8] The caution amounts to a conviction for the purposes of registration under the provisions of the Sex Offender Notification Requirements.[9] In *R* v *Metropolitan Police Commissioner, ex parte Thompson*[10] Schiemann LJ stated:

> A formal caution is not something to be regarded lightly. Records are kept of the admininistering of cautions...Such a caution while carrying no immediate disagreeable consequence for the recipient, has potential adverse consequences for him should he be accused of offending on a future occasion. He is more likely to be prosecuted for that offence and he will not be able to claim good character

---

[3] As to which see p 384, *ante*.

[4] *R* v *Jones & Whally* [2005] EWHC 931, [2006] Crim LR 67.

[5] Home Office Circular 70/1978, replaced by Circular 14/1985.

[6] See Wilkinson and Evans, 'Police Cautioning of Juveniles: The Impact of Circular 14/1985' [1990] Crim LR 165; Westwood, 'The Effects of Home Office Guidelines on the Cautioning of Offenders' [1991] Crim LR 591; Evans, 'Police Cautioning and the Young Offender' [1991] Crim LR 598.

[7] *Op cit*, Ch 5, para 57.

[8] *R (on the application of W)* v *Chief Constable of Hampshire Constabulary* [2006] EWHC 1904 (Admin).

[9] *R (On the application of U)* v *MPC* [2002] 4 All ER 593.

[10] [1997] 1 WLR 1519 at 1521.

before the trial court. If convicted, the existence of a prior formal caution may affect his sentence...

The Auld Review observed that some 260,000 cautions were issued in 1999, amounting to some 25 per cent of 'solved' offences.[11] The offences were mainly, but not totally, in respect of less serious offences, with cautioning rates significantly high in respect of minor thefts and drug offences, but, paradoxically, the cautioning rate for summary-only offences was lower than for either-way offences. This may change under the 'caution-plus' provisions introduced by the Criminal Justice Act 2003 following the recommendations of the Auld Review. The incidence of cautioning was also higher in respect of juveniles. Juveniles are now dealt with under a separate scheme of reprimands and warnings introduced by the Crime and Disorder Act 1998.[12]

This extra-statutory scheme had its drawbacks. There was no sanction in respect of the original offence for an offender who re-offends. The power to caution did not have a power associated with it requiring an offender to engage in activities such as reparation to the victim, to pay compensation, or attend appropriate activities such as a drug or alcohol treatment programme, or sex offender programme. The Auld Review concluded that the cautioning system paid no regard to the feelings of the victim, lacked rigour, and posed a temptation to hard-pressed police forces to use cautions to effect a better clear-up rate. It therefore proposed, for adult offenders, a new system of 'caution-plus', which forms the basis for the conditional caution provisions of the Criminal Justice Act 2003.

3 CONDITIONAL CAUTIONS FOR ADULT OFFENDERS

As noted above, until the passage of the 2003 Act,[13] no statutory power existed governing the cautioning of adult offenders at all, still less one which permitted the imposition of a requirement that the offender should make reparation for his offending behaviour, such as the payment of compensation for the damage done by vandalism, or apology to the victim, or a requirement of attendance at particular forms of activity which could address the offending behaviour. This was in stark contrast to the approach taken in respect of young offenders by the Crime and Disorder Act 1998.

Section 22 of the 2003 Act defines a conditional caution as one 'given in respect of an offence and which has conditions attached with which the offender must comply'. Conditions can be imposed only to the extent that they either ensure or facilitate the rehabilitation of the offender or to make sure that he makes some reparation. The caution (which amounts to a criminal conviction) is to be administered by the police, or by the CPS, or by any other designated person,[14] thus allowing cautioning in respect

---

[11] *Op cit*, Ch 10, paras 41–47. The equivalent figures for 2000, excluding motoring offences, was 239,000 offenders: *Cautions Court Proceedings and Sentencing 2000* Home Office Statistical Bulletin 20/01, Nov 2001.
[12] See p 563, *post*.
[13] The conditional caution provisions are being piloted, and not universally in force.
[14] 2003 Act, s 22(4).

of minor offences investigated by non-police bodies, such as the Department of Social Security, or the RSPCA.

There are five prerequisites prescribed by section 23, which must each be satisfied:

(1) The cautioner must have evidence that the suspect committed the crime.

(2) The CPS must be satisfied that there is sufficient evidence to charge the suspect with the offence, and that a caution should be given. The CPS thus is the decisive decision-maker, and no doubt will be reluctant to caution in serious cases, or where the suspect has similar convictions, a poor record, or where the offence merits imprisonment.

(3) The suspect must admit the offence to the cautioner.

(4) The nature of the caution, and the consequences of the breach must be made clear to the suspect.[15]

(5) The suspect must sign a document recording the details of the offence and the admission of it by him. This in law amounts to a confession,[16] and will be evidence against the offender if he is subsequently prosecuted following non-compliance with the conditions attached to the caution.

The Act does not prescribe any limits to the conditions that may be imposed. Guidance under a Code of Practice has been issued, but any conditions must be compliant with the Article 8 rights of the offender (right to respect for private and family life, etc).[17] Clearly, if the conditions impose any restrictions or requirements that affect the Article 8 rights of the offender, those conditions must be necessary and proportionate to ensure Convention-compliance, but, if justified, could include a requirement to clean up graffiti, make financial reparation, or attend treatment or behaviour programmes. If they are broken, the power exists to prosecute the offender for the original offence, a powerful sanction that may well make the conditional caution an effective way of dealing with the lower-level type of offence, whilst at the same time reducing the workload on the courts.

4 REPRIMANDS AND WARNINGS FOR JUVENILES

Circular 18/94 created a presumption in favour of cautioning of juveniles (i.e. those aged under eighteen).[18] Under the Circular, juveniles were more likely to be cautioned than adults, but no support for the juvenile to address the offending behaviour was linked to the caution, at any rate in a formal sense. The Royal Commission on Criminal Justice[19] concluded that consideration should be given to combining cautions with other support, through social services or the probation service. It also recognized that failure to prosecute can damage confidence in the criminal justice system. Research showed that

---

[15] See by analogy, *R v R and R* [2002] Crim LR 349, where there was a failure to explain that acceptance of a caution would result in registration under the sex offender legislation.

[16] Defined by PACE, s 82(3) as a statement wholly or partly adverse to its maker.

[17] See p 190, *ante.*   [18] See p 561, *ante.*

[19] *Op cit*, at Ch 5, paras 57 *et seq.*

those children who display criminal behaviour at an early age are more likely to become serious or persistent offenders.[20] Cautions could best work for young offenders, diverting them from the criminal justice system if the response was clear and firm: cautions were shown to be of decreasing effectiveness as they are repeated.[21] It was to achieve a more effective and consistent scheme that the Crime and Disorder Act 1998 introduced reprimands and final warnings. However, the power to issue a conditional caution to a child or young person is given by section 98 of the Criminal Justice and Immigration Act 2008. There is often a choice to be made.

Under the 1998 Act, a constable may administer either a reprimand or a final warning where he has evidence that a child or young person[22] has committed an offence, and he considers that the evidence is such that, if the offender were prosecuted for the offence, there would be a realistic prospect of him being convicted.[23] The power only arises if the offender admits to the constable that he committed the offence, has not previously been convicted of an offence, and the constable is satisfied that it would not be in the public interest for the offender to be prosecuted.

The constable may reprimand the offender if the offender has not previously been reprimanded or warned. The offender must be warned rather than given a reprimand if the constable considers the offence to be so serious to require a warning, but an offender may not be warned more than once. Guidance exists as to when a reprimand or a warning is appropriate, and the form of the reprimand or warning. The scheme envisages that a first offence might be met with a reprimand, provided it is not too serious. Any further offence should be met with a warning: no offender should receive two reprimands, and any offence after a warning should result in prosecution, except where it is minor in nature and at least two years have elapsed since the administration of the warning.

The reprimand or warning is given at the police station by the constable in the presence of an appropriate adult, who will be a parent, guardian, representative of the local authority if the juvenile is in care, local authority social worker, or other responsible adult other than a police employee. The effect is the same as a conviction although reprimands and final warnings do not become 'spent' under the Rehabilitation of Offenders Act 1974.[24] It may therefore have the consequence of requiring the offender to register under the Sex Offenders legislation.[25] Where a warning is given the constable must refer the juvenile to a youth offending team,[26] which will assess the juvenile referred and, may lead to that juvenile participating in a rehabilitation programme. This might include, for example, meeting the victim, apologizing for the crime and hearing about its effects, a programme of work, or payment of compensation. A failure to comply with the rehabilitation programme is not of itself punishment, but a 'failure to

---

[20] *Young People and Crime* Home Office Research Study No 145, 1996.

[21] *No More Excuses – A New Approach to Tackling Youth Crime in England and Wales* Cm 3809, 1997, para 5.9.

[22] Probably to be determined as at the date of the offence, not court proceedings: see *Ghafour* [2002] Crim LR 739.

[23] 1998 Act, s 65(1).

[24] Which treats certain convictions as 'spent' after periods specified in the Act.

[25] See *R (on the application of R)* v *Durham Constabulary* [2005] UKHL 21, [2005] 2 All ER 369.

[26] 1998 Act, s 66(1). For youth offending teams, see p 548, *ante*.

participate' in the programme may be cited in criminal proceedings just like a previous conviction.[27] That appears to relate only to total non-participation, not inadequate participation.

It is clear that a reprimand or final warning can have significant consequences. It did in *R (on the application of R) v Durham Constabulary*[28] where the consequences of a warning (of which he was not told) was registration on the sex offender register. He sought to challenge the warning on the basis that it infringed his Article 6 rights: it amounted, he argued, to the determination of a criminal charge by a police officer who was not an independent and impartial tribunal as Article 6 requires. That argument was rejected. The warning was not a finding of guilt of a criminal offence, even though significant consequences might flow from it.

5 JUDICIAL SCRUTINY OF THE DECISION TO PROSECUTE OR CAUTION

The decision to caution, or to prosecute instead of cautioning, is not beyond judicial scrutiny.[29] In *R v Chief Constable of Kent County Constabulary, ex parte L*,[30] the Divisional Court considered that a decision to prosecute a twelve-year-old girl, which was claimed to be in breach of the policy for cautioning of juveniles, was susceptible to judicial review, although on the facts it was found to be a proper exercise of discretion. Watkins LJ considered that the policy of cautioning, instead of prosecuting, was well settled and played a prominent part in the process of decision-making in an individual case. Care should be taken, however, to avoid 'the danger of opening too wide the door of review of the discretion to continue a prosecution', and the Court appeared to draw a distinction between decisions involving adults and those involving juveniles. Another Divisional Court in *R v Inland Revenue Commissioners, ex parte Mead*[31] has stressed that decisions relating to adults are not beyond judicial review, although the situations in which the courts would in fact intervene will be rare.[32] The criteria for the administration of reprimands and final warnings, and conditional cautions, are now set out in statutory form. An individual will have a legitimate expectation that Guidance issued will be adhered to.[33]

6 POLICE BAIL

Questions of bail arise at various stages of the criminal process. An arrested person need not, now,[34] always be taken to the police station. Where a suspect's identity and

---

[27] Ibid, s 66(5).   [28] See n 25, *supra*.

[29] There are distinct limits to judicial review of the decisions of a prosecution authority: see Watkin LJ in *R v General Council of the Bar, ex parte Percival* [1991] 1 QB 212, [1990] 3 All ER 137.

[30] [1993] 1 All ER 756.   [31] [1993] 1 All ER 772.

[32] The fact that there are alternative remedies, for example, to challenge for abuse of process, does not prevent the exercise of discretion itself from being challenged by way of judicial review.

[33] See p 564, *ante*.

[34] From 20 January 2004, when Criminal Justice Act 2003, s 4, came into force.

address are known and the offence is minor, there is often no need to go through the time-consuming process of the custody process at the police station. New provisions in PACE[35] permit a constable to release a suspect on 'street bail' before reaching the police station. The change is intended to simplify procedures, reduce administrative burden, save police resources, and speed up the process.[36] The bailed person must be given, or sent a notice telling him when and where he must answer to his bail, which may be at any time in the future, although it is anticipated that a period of two weeks should be the norm, and should not in any event exceed six weeks.[37] A constable should, in deciding whether to use this power, have regard to the nature of the offence, the ability to progress the case at the police station, the level of confidence in the suspect answering bail, and the level of understanding and awareness of the suspect. The likelihood of further offending, risk to the safety or welfare of the suspect, and the age of the suspect are also relevant.[38]

If an arrested person is in fact taken to the police station, a custody officer must order his release from police detention either on bail or without bail, in which case he goes to prison. The powers and duties of the police when dealing with the continued detention of those in custody have already been discussed.[39] The power to order bail is subject to limitations, which apply where the name and address of the arrested person is unknown, if detention is necessary for his protection or for the protection of other persons or property, if the defendant is not likely to answer to his bail, or is likely to interfere with the administration of justice, or, in the case of an imprisonable offence, detention is necessary to prevent his committing further offences.[40]

THE DECISION TO PROSECUTE

1 CRIMINAL JUSTICE ACT 2003

Until the passage of the 2003 Act, the decision to commence proceedings was generally in the hands of the police, although other organizations have law enforcement powers as well. In most cases the police have charged, taken a suspect into custody, or provided the information for the issue of a summons or warrant for arrest. It was though, the duty of the Director of Public Prosecutions to take over the conduct of all criminal proceedings instituted on behalf of a police force.[41] In reality, the DPP and Crown Prosecution Service played a central role in the decision-making process, as have, in

---

[35] PACE, ss 30A–30D. The Criminal Justice Act 2003, s 4, also amends PACE, ss 30, 34–36, 41, and 47.
[36] *Justice for All, op cit*, para 3.10.
[37] Home Office Circular 61/2003, *Bail Elsewhere than at a Police Station.*
[38] Circular 61/2003, *ante.*   [39] See p 440, *ante.*   [40] PACE, s 38(1).
[41] Prosecution of Offences Act 1985, s 3(2)(a). In difficult, important or otherwise appropriate cases the DPP may institute proceedings: s 3(2)(b). For the office of the DPP, see p 383, *ante.*

the case of serious or complex fraud, the Serious Fraud Office. The role of the CPS has now changed radically[42] through a new scheme created by the 2003 Act.

Persons or bodies other than the police have been entitled to institute proceedings, and that position is not changed by the new arrangements discussed below. The Royal Commission on Criminal Procedure[43] in 1981 concluded that it would be both impracticable and undesirable to bring all prosecutions within the ambit of the CPS, although it suggested that a private prosecutor should first be under a duty to notify the Crown Prosecutor, who should then decide whether to take over the prosecution. That latter suggestion was not implemented. The Auld Review[44] likewise considered that the right of private prosecution should remain, even though it is rarely used. Section 6 of the Prosecution of Offences Act 1985 states that nothing in the Act precludes any person from instituting any criminal proceedings to which the Director's duty under the Act does not apply. There are, though, safeguards. By section 42 of the Supreme Court Act 1981, if on an application by the Attorney-General the High Court is satisfied that any person has habitually and persistently and without any reasonable ground instituted vexatious prosecutions (whether against the same or different persons) the court may make a criminal proceedings order. This has the effect that no information shall be laid before a justice of the peace, and no application for leave to prefer a Bill of indictment shall be made by that person without the leave of the court. Leave is not to be granted unless the High Court is satisfied that the institution of proceedings does not amount to an abuse of process. In addition, in some cases the consent of the Attorney-General is needed.[45]

The Auld Review rejected any system of pre-charge check or approval. It did, though, endorse the recommendation of the Law Commission[46] that any court before which a private prosecution is initiated should be under a duty forthwith to notify the DPP in writing. The DPP could decide whether to take over the proceedings, or take them over and then discontinue them. That recommendation has not been implemented, but since private prosecutions will in reality be known to Crown Prosecutors at some stage, there is nothing to prevent this practice from occurring routinely.

2 THE NEW PROCEDURE

The 2003 Act gives the CPS much greater involvement in the decision to prosecute and choice of charge. The Auld Review took the view that the CPS 'has still to fill its proper role which…should be closer to the more highly regarded Procurator Fiscal in Scotland or the Office of the Director of Public Prosecutions in Northern Ireland'.[47] It recommended that the CPS should, generally, determine the initial charge. Following

---

[42] *Infra.*   [43] *Op cit*, paras 7.40–7.52.   [44] *Op cit*, Ch 12, paras 46–51.

[45] See, e.g., offences of incitement to racial hatred (Public Order Act 1986, s 27); offences under the Terrorism Act 2000. Some 150 statutes require the consent of either the Attorney-General or the DPP. See p 383, *ante*. The Law Commission, and the Auld Review recommended general abolition of these requirements.

[46] Auld Review, *op cit*, Ch 12, para 50, citing Law Commission, *Consents to Prosecution*, Law Comm No 255, paras 7.4–7.8.

[47] *Op cit*, Ch 12, para 12. For the CPS generally, and recent reforms see p 383, *ante*.

implementation of changes recommended by the Glidewell Report[48] and the Narey Report,[49] with CPS staff increasingly located in or close to police stations ('co-location'), or on call, greater CPS involvement is, for the first time, a practical proposition. Studies showed, however, that a voluntary approach did not inevitably create the closer involvement in the charging process.[50] Given the automatic sending for trial procedure now in place for trial on indictment,[51] the need for speed and efficiency, and the obligation in the Code for Crown Prosecutors not only to consider whether there is sufficient evidence (the 'sufficiency of evidence' test) but also whether it is in the public interest to prosecute (the 'public interest' test),[52] the Auld Review considered that change was essential.

That recommendation has to be viewed in the context of a continuing failure always to get the charge right in the first place. The Government White Paper *Justice for All*[53] stated that some 13 per cent of cases have to be discontinued by the CPS, either because there was not enough evidence to convict or because it is not in the public interest to proceed. Some 45 per cent of police files submitted to the CPS are not properly compiled, leading to the collapse of some cases, due to lack of evidence.[54] A failure to get the charge right early also makes the plea before venue procedure[55] less useful that it could be. *Justice for All* reported that pilot co-location projects saved, in cost, some 14 per cent of what would otherwise have been spent in monetary terms, and the number of cases disposed of at first hearing increased by some 20 per cent.

A new section 37B of PACE[56] sets out the duties of the police. Except in minor and road traffic cases, the police must supply the CPS with information specified in Guidance. The CPS will then decide whether a charge should be laid, and, if so, whether it should be using the sufficiency of evidence and public interest test. Alternatively, the CPS may decide that a conditional caution[57] is appropriate. The decision will be communicated in writing on the police and be binding on them. Co-location should make this process relatively speedy, but no time-limit is specified by section 37B, and section 37 of PACE has been amended to allow bail to be granted to a suspect whilst this decision-making process occurs.

3 THE CRITERIA

By section 10 of the Prosecution of Offences Act 1985, the Director of Public Prosecutions is under a duty to issue a Code for Crown Prosecutors, giving guidance on the general

[48] *A Review of the Crown Prosecution Service*, HMSO, 1998: see p 383, *ante*.

[49] *Review of Delay in the Criminal Justice System*, Home Office, 1997.

[50] *Reducing Delay in the Criminal Justice System: Evaluation of Pilot Schemes*, Ernst & Young, Home Office, 1999.

[51] See p 599, *post*.

[52] See p 569, *post*. The police in charging have regard, under Code C, only to the sufficiency of evidence.

[53] *Op cit*, Ch 3, p 52. The CPS Inspectorate in its Annual Report 1999–2000 found that some 22 per cent of police charges relating to assault, public order and road traffic were incorrect.

[54] See Ward and Davies, *Practitioners' Guide to the Criminal Justice Act 2003* (2004) para 3.2.

[55] See p 580, *post*, and Herbert, 'Mode of Trial and Magistrates' Sentencing Powers: Will Increased Powers Inevitably Lead to a Reduction in the Committal Rate?' [2003] Crim LR 314.

[56] Created by Criminal Justice Act 2003, s 28 and Schedule 2. The provisions came into force on 29 January 2004.

[57] See p 562, *ante*.

principles to be applied by them in determining, in any case, whether proceedings should be instituted, discontinued, or what charges should be made. The is to be found in works such as *Archbold* or *Blackstone's Criminal Practice* or on the COPS web site.

The first question to be decided is whether there is sufficient evidence. There must be admissible, substantial and reliable evidence that a criminal offence has been committed by an identified individual. In deciding this, a prima facie case is not enough: the test is whether there is a realistic prospect of conviction. This is an objective test. It means that a jury, or bench of magistrates (or district judge), properly directed in law is more likely than not to convict the defendant of the charge alleged.[58] In deciding that, a careful study of the available evidence will be undertaken. The possibility that evidence might be inadmissible in law, nor be excluded because of failure to comply with relevant rules, the possibility that a confession may be unreliable, the possibility that a witness may be hostile or likely to be unreliable, or not likely to tell the truth, the impression a witness will make in court, the availability of all necessary witnesses or the likelihood of the court accepting documentary evidence and competence of young children are all factors which are relevant. The prosecutor will look at the overall weight of the case, whether dangers of concoction of evidence exists, whether a case can be sustained against more than one defendant (if there is more than one), and whether the public might consider a prosecution to be oppressive. The prosecutor will also consider what the defence case may be.

Having decided whether there is a sufficiency of evidence, the prosecutor is then required to consider the wider public interest, although the interests of the victim also should be borne in mind. The graver the offence the less likelihood there will be that the public interest will permit the case to be dealt with by anything other than prosecution, although the Code does urge prosecutors to strive to ensure that the spirit of cautioning guidelines is observed, where the seriousness of the offence allows. In particular the following factors may provide an indication that prosecution may not be required –

(a) where a court is likely to impose a small or nominal penalty only;

(b) where the offence was committed as a result of a genuine mistake or misunderstanding (balanced against the seriousness of the offence);

(c) where the loss or harm is minor, and results from a single incident (and particularly if it was caused by misjudgment);

(d) where the offences are stale. However, the staleness may have been caused by the offender himself, the offences may only just have come to light, there may have been the need for a long, complex investigation, or the offences may be serious;

(e) prosecution may have a very bad effect on the health of the victim, again bearing in mind the seriousness of the offence;

(f) old-age or infirmity;

(g) mental disorder at the time of the commission of the offence. Where the effect of proceedings on the health of the accused is not outweighed by a wider public

---

[58] The so-called '51 per cent' rule.

interest in favour of prosecution, proceedings should not be commenced, or may be discontinued. In this type of case other relevant factors will be the nature of the mental condition and the likelihood of further offending;

(h) changes in attitude by the complainant, including the making of reparation or putting right loss. However, prosecution cannot be avoided simply by an ability to pay compensation.

In addition to the Code of Practice, the CPS and police have developed charging standards for certain types of offence. These include certain assaults and other offences against the person, driving offences, and public order offences. The intention is to ensure fairness and consistency in the approach to certain types of offence. Certain principles are stated in all the charging standards. Charges should accurately reflect the extent of the defendant's involvement and responsibility, the choice of charges should accurately reflect the defendant's involvement and responsibility, the choice of charges should ensure the clear and simple presentation of the case; it is wrong to encourage a defendant to plead guilty to a few charges by selecting more charges than are necessary, and it is wrong to select a more serious charge not supported by the evidence in order to encourage a plea of guilty to a lesser allegation.

4 DISCONTINUANCE

Under section 23 of the Prosecution of Offences Act 1985 notice of discontinuance can be issued, provided this is done in summary cases before the hearing of the evidence, or, in cases to be tried on indictment, before sending for trial. This can be done by correspondence, and without the expense and inconvenience of a court hearing. It does not replace the power of a prosecutor to go before a court and offer no evidence or withdraw a charge, both of which remain options[59] although the leave of the court is needed.[60] Nor does it interfere with the power of the Attorney-General to prevent proceedings from continuing by the issue of a writ of *nolle prosequi*.

In deciding how to use these powers it is the duty of prosecutors to keep a case under review. In the case of juveniles it may become clear that a reprimand or final warning is a more appropriate way of dealing with the matter. In respect of those suffering illness the effect on health may make it appropriate for the case to be withdrawn.[61]

This power of review has been shown to be important. Since the creation of the Crown Prosecution Service in 1985 the incidence of discontinuance or withdrawal has risen from 7 per cent in 1985 to 13 per cent in 2001. In part this is due to the defects in the charging process, now addressed by the 2003 Act. The Narey Report considered[62] that

[59] *R v Director of Public Prosecutions, ex parte Cooke* (1991) 95 Cr App R 233.
[60] The Royal Commission on Criminal Justice recommended that the CPS should have the power to discontinue a case without the leave of the court at any time prior to the start of the trial: *op cit*, Ch 5, para 37.
[61] This power to discontinue remains throughout the trial itself. In *R v Seelig* (1993) the defendant was discharged because he was medically unable to cope with the strains of a long trial in which he was defending himself: see *The Times*, 15 February 1993.
[62] *Op cit*, p 460.

the CPS should not be permitted to discontinue cases on public interest grounds because they consider the offence is not serious. This recommendation, designed to resolve differences between police and CPS, is unlikely to be implemented given the key role in charging is now given to the CPS itself.

TIME LIMITS FOR PROSECUTION AND ABUSE OF PROCESS

1 REQUIREMENTS OF ARTICLE 6

The right to trial within a reasonable time is part of the Article 6 rights of a defendant, that period being judged from the date on which the defendant is charged or officially notified that he is to be prosecuted,[63] and which continues all the way through the proceedings until a sentence is fixed.[64] Thus, it applies to decisions in respect of the enforcement of compensation orders or fines.[65] The reasonableness of the length of proceedings must be assessed in the light of all the circumstances of the case, having regard to the complexity of the case, the conduct of the applicant and of the prosecution authorities, and the importance of what is at stake. Where there is a breach of Article 6 there must be such remedy as is just, effective, and proportionate.[66]

Increasing concern has arisen about delays in the criminal justice system.[67] In general there is no time limit on the prosecution of an indictable offence, although by contrast, summary proceedings must be brought within six months from the date of commission of the offence.[68] Even in some cases triable on indictment Parliament has, for reasons of policy, imposed a time limit: thus a prosecution for unlawful sexual intercourse with a girl under the age of sixteen may not be commenced more than twelve months after the commission of the offence.[69] However, even where no specific time limit exists the court is not powerless, and can intervene to correct abuse of process caused by delay. The elapsing of time may also be a ground leading to a conviction being quashed. In *R v B*[70] it was held that a residual discretion existed to set aside a conviction considered to be unsafe because of the elapsing of time between offence and prosecution. That decision, though, was exceptional, and distinguished in *R v E(T)*[71] where there was a twelve-year gap between alleged sexual offences against children and their prosecution. The crucial factor in *E(T)* was that there was supporting evidence independent of the allegations

---

[63] *Eckle v Germany* (1982) 5 EHRR 1; *Ewing v United Kingdom* (1986) 10 EHRR 141.

[64] *Findlay v United Kingdom* (1997) 24 EHRR 221; *Phillips v United Kingdom* (2001).

[65] *Crowther v United Kingdom* [2005] All ER (D) 06 (Feb); *Lloyd v Bow Street Magistrates' Court* [2003] EWHC 2294.

[66] *Attorney-General's Reference (No 2 of 2001)* [2004] 1 Cr App R 25.

[67] See p 553, *ante*.

[68] Or six months from when the matter of complaint arose: see Magistrates' Courts Act 1980, s 127.

[69] See Sexual Offences Act 2003, s 9.   [70] [2003] 2 Cr App R 197.

[71] [2004] 2 Cr App R 36.

by the complainant, and unlike *B*, it was possible for the defendant to defend himself by cross-examination of the complainant.

2 ABUSE OF PROCESS

A court can, as part of its inherent power, order a stay to prevent abuse of process.[72] Thus if the prosecution has manipulated or misused the process of the court:

> so as to deprive the defendant of a protection provided by the law or if there has been such delay so that prejudice or unfairness to the defendant arises...[73]

then the court can order that the prosecution does not proceed. This is a power 'of great constitutional importance',[74] and arises in two classes, which may, of course, overlap. But, whichever class into which the case falls, the crucial factor is the public interest. In *Attorney-General's Reference (No 2 of 2001)*[75] the majority of the House of Lords held that it was not appropriate to stay proceedings unless (a) there could no longer be a fair hearing, or (b) it would be otherwise unfair to try the defendant. If the proposed trial would actually be unfair, then there would be an infringement of the fair trial provisions of Article 6. However, where matters of fairness can be dealt with at the trial they should be, rather than the proceedings being stayed for an abuse of process. In *Attorney-General's Reference (No 2 of 2001)* the court observed that a charge should not be stayed or dismissed if any lesser remedy would be just and proportionate. This was the case in *R v Hopkins*,[76] where an application to stay proceedings for abuse of process failed. Despite the fact that the prosecution was in respect of complaints of sexual abuse and violence which the police had originally investigated and decided not to proceed with the subsequent investigation and prosecution did not create unfairness that could not be dealt with at the trial.

The second class of case is where, although the fairness of the trial is not in question, nevertheless it would be unfair to the defendant because of the abuse that has occurred. In *R v Croydon Justices, ex parte Dean*[77] this was applied and a conviction quashed, the accused having been assured that he would not be prosecuted. Again, in *R v Horseferry Road MC, ex parte Bennett*[78] the House of Lords held that the doctrine of abuse of process applied to prevent the trial of an accused who had been brought to the United Kingdom through the collusion of the UK and South African authorities, in breach of extradition procedures. Despite the fact that the fairness of the trial itself was not in issue, the court considered that the judiciary had a responsibility for the maintenance of the rule of law. A third example is where criminal proceedings are brought vexatiously

---

[72] *Connolly v Director of Public Prosecutions* [1964] AC 1254, (1964) 48 Cr App R 183.
[73] *R v Derby Magistrates' Court, ex parte Brooks* (1984) 80 Cr App R 164.
[74] Per Lord Salmon in *DPP v Humphrys* [1976] 2 All ER 479, at 527.
[75] [2004] 1 Cr App R 25.   [76] [2004] All ER (D) 356 (Feb).
[77] [1993] QB 769, [1993] 3 All ER 129; see also *R v Bow Street Stipendiary Magistrates' ex parte Director of Public Prosecutions* (1989) 91 Cr App R 283; *R v Crown Court at Norwich, ex parte Belsham* [1992] 1 All ER 394, [1992] 1 WLR 54.
[78] [1994] 1 AC 42; see also *R v Beckford* [1996] 1 Cr App R 94.

by a private prosecutor.[79] Nonetheless, the ultimate objective of the discretionary power to stay proceedings is to ensure that there should be a fair trial. It is usually only in cases where there has been prosecution misconduct that the proceedings will be stayed under this second class, as *ex parte Dean* and *ex parte Bennett* illustrate.[80]

Dealing with a case involving delay, Viscount Dilhorne in *Director of Public Prosecutions* v *Humphrys*[81] warned that use of this power should only occur 'in the most exceptional circumstances'. This was an approach echoed by Lord Lane CJ in *A-G's Reference (No 1 of 1990)*[82] where he stated that even if delay was unjustifiable the imposition of a stay:[83]

> should be the exception rather than the rule. Still more rare should be cases where a stay can properly be imposed in the absence of any fault on the part of the complainant or prosecution.

This remains true despite the provisions of the Human Rights Act 1998, which incorporate the right to a fair trial within a reasonable time.[84] The defendant must show on the balance of probabilities that, owing to the delay, he will suffer serious prejudice to the extent that no fair trial can be held. In deciding this, the ability of the court through the rules of evidence to regulate what is placed before it, and the ability of the judge to warn and to give appropriate directions to the jury, should both be borne in mind. The reasons for delay may also be relevant. Prosecution inefficiency is one factor,[85] as is the nature of the case. A longer period of preparation for the prosecution is only to be expected in complex cases, particularly fraud cases.[86] Delay may also arise because of the nature of the offence alleged, and the reluctance of a victim to come forward.[87] Whatever the reason, long delay is not, inevitably, a justification for a stay. In *R* v *Central Criminal Court, ex parte Randle and Pottle*[88] a delay of twenty years in a case of assisting the Soviet spy, George Blake, in escaping from lawful custody was held, on the facts, not to justify a stay. Again, in *R* v *V*[89] a twenty-year gap between alleged acts of sexual abuse and the prosecution was held to be no bar to prosecution, the court stressing that staying proceedings for delay should be exceptional. The delay could be explained by the fact that the complainant of the sexual offence was seven years younger than the defendant (his brother) and the defendant had threatened the complainant, had been violent in the past, and the complainant had been reluctant to tell because of the effect on her family.

Statute has created a framework within which prosecutors must work. By section 2 of the Prosecution of Offences Act 1985, and regulations made hereunder, there are

---

[79] See, e.g., *R* v *Belmarsh Magistrates' Court, ex parte Watts* [1999] 2 Cr App R 198.
[80] See *R (On the application of Ebrahim)* v *Feltham MC; Muoat* v *DPP* [2001] 3 All ER 381.
[81] [1977] AC 1, [1976] 2 All ER 497.
[82] [1992] QB 630, [1992] 3 All ER 169; *R* v *H* [2003] All ER (D) 403 (Feb).
[83] See *The Reasonable Time Limit Requirement: An Independent and Meaningful Right* [2005] Crim LR 5.
[84] *R* v *H* [2003] All ER (D) 403. For Article 6, see p 185 and p 171, *ante*.
[85] *R* v *West London Magistrates' Court, ex parte Anderson* (1984) 80 Cr App R 143.
[86] See Narey Report, *op cit*.
[87] *R* v *LPB* (1990) 91 Cr App R 359.; *R* v *Evans (T.M)* [2004] EWCA Crim 1441.
[88] (1992) 92 Cr App R 323.
[89] [2004] All ER (D) 207 (Feb); see also *R* v *V* [2004] All ER (D) 207 (Feb).

time limits regulating how long a defendant may be kept in custody pending the start of summary trial, between the first appearance at court and sending for trial, and between sending for trial and the start of the trial.[90] These are seventy days between first appearance and sending for trial,[91] eighty-six days from date of first appearance to the opening day of the trial and 112 days from sending for trial until arraignment.[92] Application can be made for extension of those limits, and a right of appeal exists in respect of the decision of a magistrates' court to extend, or a refusal to extend, these time limits. By contrast, no power exists in respect of such an order made by the Crown Court, but since this is not a matter 'relating to trial on indictment' an aggrieved person could seek judicial review of the decision.

Of course, delay may arise not only in respect of the commencement of the proceedings but also in their conduct. The reduction of delays in the criminal justice system is regarded by the government as a matter of high priority. Despite a significant reduction in the number of cases coming before the courts, custody time limits are not always met.[93] This issue is discussed in due course.[94]

BRINGING THE SUSPECT BEFORE THE COURT

A suspect could of course have been charged, and thus brought before the court, or alternatively, bailed, and under a duty to surrender to bail. Otherwise proceedings could, prior to the implementation of provisions of the Criminal Justice Act 2003, be commenced by the defendant being brought before the court in one of three ways. Firstly, by a summons; secondly, by warrant for arrest; thirdly by arrest without warrant. In respect of arrest without warrant, the available powers have already been discussed.[95]

The Auld Review pointed to the antiquated and inefficient nature of the system described above.[96] Many cases begun by summons were adjourned at the first hearing due to the non-appearance of the accused, which could be compelled only by the issue of a warrant, resulting in a further adjournment. Some cases could in fact be dealt with in the absence of the defendant: they are, however, limited to cases where the charges are summary-only and carried a maximum punishment of no greater than three months imprisonment.[97]

Sections 28 to 31 of the Criminal Justice Act 2003 implement the recommendations of the Auld Review, and bring both greater simplicity and efficiency to the commencement of proceedings. A prosecutor will issue a *written charge* setting out the allegation, issue a *requisition* requiring the accused to appear before the magistrates' court at the specified date, and serve both on the court and defendant. It is hoped to cut out wasted first

---

[90] See Prosecution of Offences (Custody Time Limits) Regulations 1987, SI 1987/698.
[91] See p 599, *post.*   [92] See p 631, *post.*   [93] See Narey Report, *op cit.*
[94] See p 605, *post.*   [95] See Ch 13.   [96] *Op cit*, Ch 10, paras 416–422.
[97] Magistrates' Courts Act 1980, s 12.

and second appearances in motoring, local authority, and breach of community penalty cases.[98] Informations as a means of obtaining a summons are abolished, but remain as an option of obtaining a warrant, and for private prosecutors.

Section 308 of the 2003 Act removes some of the restrictions on dealing with a case in the absence of the defendant. However, this change is not as sweeping as may first appear, because a court must require those whom it is considering dealing with in a manner greater than an absolute discharge or fine to attend in person.

CLASSIFICATION OF OFFENCES

Some 95 per cent of all criminal cases are tried summarily in the magistrates' or youth court. It is only a small minority of cases that are tried on indictment in the Crown Court.[99] The decision as to whether a charge is tried in the magistrates' court, with its advantages of speed, relative informality, and cost, or on indictment by judge and jury turns initially on the classification of the offence charged. Prior to the implementation of Part III of the Criminal Law Act 1977 the law relating to the classification of criminal offences and the determination of the appropriate Mode of Trial, summary or on indictment, was complex. Thus there were provisions for summary offences to be tried on indictment and for indictable offences to be tried summarily, while there was a third class of offences, colloquially (though not by statute) called 'hybrid' offences which might take on the character of either summary offences or indictable offences according to the election of the parties. These classifications were reviewed by the James Committee in 1975,[100] which had as its twin aims a simplification of the procedure and possible reduction in the case loads of the Crown Court. Its recommendations were in part controversial, but the majority of them were adopted, and implemented by Part III of the Criminal Law Act 1977.

As regards Mode of Trial there are now three classes of offence namely:

(a) offences triable only on indictment;[101]

(b) offences triable only summarily;[102] and

(c) offences triable either way.[103]

---

[98] Ward and Davies, *op cit*, para 3.24.

[99] See the admonition by Darbyshire in 'An Essay on the Importance and Neglect of the Magistracy' [1997] Crim LR 639.

[100] *The Distribution of Criminal Business between the Crown Court and Magistrates' Courts*, Cmnd 6323, HMSO.

[101] This should be distinguished from the phrase 'indictable offences', which means offences which, if committed by an adult, are triable on indictment, either exclusively or because they are 'either-way' offences: Interpretation Act 1978, s 5, Schedule 1.

[102] A 'summary offence' means an offence which, if committed by an adult, is triable only summarily.

[103] An offence 'triable either way' means an offence which, if committed by an adult, is triable either on indictment or summarily.

1 OFFENCES TRIABLE ONLY ON INDICTMENT

Because offences can only fall within one of the other two categories if statute so provides, it follows that where there is no express statutory provision an offence is triable only on indictment. This involves a trial by judge and jury[104] in the Crown Court. The case will not now require committal proceedings and will be sent or transferred for trial.[105]

In practice only the gravest indictable offences are triable only on indictment; these include murder, genocide, manslaughter, infanticide, child destruction, abortion, serious sexual offences, sedition, mutiny, piracy, offences under section 1 of the Official Secrets Act 1911, robbery, wounding or causing grievous bodily harm 'with intent', blackmail, assault with intent to rob, aggravated burglary, and burglary comprising the commission of, or an intention to commit, an offence triable only on indictment. It will, however, be recalled that these are triable only on indictment if committed by an adult. As we shall see, in the case of children and young persons, all indictable offences (other than homicide) may, and in most cases must, be tried summarily.[106]

2 OFFENCES TRIABLE ONLY SUMMARILY

The expressions 'summary offence' and 'offence triable only summarily' may be taken as synonymous. A statute creating a summary offence will first define the offence and then state that it is punishable 'on summary conviction' with a particular penalty, thereby indicating that the offence is a summary one. In addition a number of offences which, prior to the Criminal Law Act 1977, were not summary offences according to the statute creating them, became so.[107]

Special rules apply to some offences under the Criminal Damage Act 1971: offences under section 1 of this Act (excluding arson) are triable only summarily if the 'value involved' does not exceed £5,000. Section 22 of the Magistrates' Courts Act 1980 prescribes a procedure for determining whether such offences are to be regarded as summary or as triable either way (if the value involved exceeds £5,000). The court begins by hearing any representations made by the prosecutor or the accused as to the value involved; if it appears to the court clear that the value involved does not exceed the prescribed sum, it will proceed to summary trial. If it is clear that it does exceed that sum, then it will treat the offence as triable either way (which, of course, it then is).[108] If it is

---

[104] For limited exceptions, see pp 624 and 626, *post.*
[105] See p 599, *post.*   [106] See p 677, *post.*
[107] See, now, Magistrates' Courts Act 1980, s 17 and Schedule 1.
[108] The court must hear 'representations', meaning submissions, assertions of fact and sometimes production of documents; however, the court is not bound to hear evidence of the value involved: *R v Canterbury and St Augustine Justices, ex parte Klisiak* [1982] QB 398, [1981] 2 All ER 129. Moreover, it is possible in cases of doubt for the prosecution to limit the charge to certain items clearly below the prescribed value, even though in fact other damaged items would take the value above the prescribed value (so as to ensure summary trial). In *R (DPP) v Prestatyn Magistrates' Court* [2002] Law Society Gazette, 1 July 2002, it was held, in the case of genetically modified maize that it was impossible to ascribe a value, and thus the offence was triable either-way.

not clear whether or not the value involved does exceed the prescribed sum, then the defendant is given the choice and told that if he consents to summary trial, his liability to imprisonment or to a fine will be limited to the maximum that magistrates have power to impose; the nature of the offence will then be determined in accordance with the accused's decision. If a person is convicted, either by a magistrates' court or by the Crown Court, he cannot appeal on the ground that the magistrates were mistaken as to the value involved.[109]

3 OFFENCES TRIABLE EITHER WAY

The third class of offence is offences triable either way. In respect of these offences, the court has to determine whether the case is suitable for summary trial, or should be sent to the Crown Court. The defendant must, though, agree to summary trial if the court considers that summary trial is appropriate, and can himself elect jury trial, a right not generally open to a defendant until 1855.[110] The perceived inadequacy of prosecution disclosure, the potential for offence negotiation, the fact that mode of trial is often agreed informally between prosecutor and defendant and the perception, justified or not, the Crown Court process is superior have all been cited as factors which have encouraged defendants to elect for trial by jury.[111]

The offences which are either way are listed in Schedule 1 to the Magistrates' Courts Act 1980, which consists of thirty-five paragraphs incorporating some sixty-six separate offences; these include unlawful wounding or inflicting grievous bodily harm, with or without a weapon, assault occasioning actual bodily harm, common assault, bigamy, certain forms of perjury and forgery, all indictable offences under the Theft Act 1968 (except robbery, blackmail, assault with intent to rob and certain burglaries), arson, offences under section 1 of the Criminal Damage Act 1971 where the value exceeds £5,000 (*ante*), and indecent assault. In addition many other statutes expressly provide for an offence to be triable either summarily or on indictment (the former 'hybrid' offences) and these are now triable either way.[112]

4 POSSIBLE REFORM

This division of functions between Crown Court and magistrates' court has been the subject of continued discussion over many years. The James Committee[113] recommended the creation of the three-fold division outlined above,[114] though noted that the English system was 'unusual' in giving a defendant a right to choose his court of trial.[115] It also considered that it was appropriate to reclassify offences of low value theft as summary offences, thus restricting the right to jury trial. This proposal met considerable resistance, in the light of the impact any conviction for theft might have

---

[109] Magistrates' Courts Act 1980, s 22(8).   [110] *Op cit*, Ch 5, para 123.
[111] See, e.g., Herbert, 'Mode of Trial and Magistrates' Sentencing Powers' [2003] Crim LR 315.
[112] Ibid, s 17(2).   [113] *Op cit*, Cmnd 6323.
[114] Implemented by the Criminal Law Act 1977.   [115] *Op cit*, para 60.

on a person's reputation and career. The Royal Commission on Criminal Justice[116] concluded that the distribution of work between magistrates' court and Crown Court was neither rational, nor always amounted to an efficient use of resources recommending that the decision should be by agreement, or, where there was a dispute as to mode of trial, the magistrates' court should determine the matter. This, it anticipated, would lead to fewer mode of trial hearings and fewer cases going to the Crown Court than the 37 per cent of cases the Commission found were electing jury trial. The Commission 'found that those electing trial had one of three or more main objectives: first a wish to put off trial with a view to securing in the meantime the advantages of a more liberal prison regime which would count towards a sentence if convicted and imprisoned; second, a well-founded belief that there was a better chance of acquittal in the Crown Court than before magistrates; and third, a mistaken belief that, if convicted the sentence would be lighter.'[117]

(a) Proposals for change

A government consultation paper in 1995[118] placed emphasis on the resource implications. It identified a large increase in the proportion of cases involving either-way offences being committed to the Crown Court for trial.[119] In relation to defendants aged seventeen or over, the proportion of such cases rose from 15 per cent in 1980 to 23 per cent in 1987, before falling to 17 per cent in 1992. A significant proportion of these cases were committed to the Crown Court because the magistrates themselves declined jurisdiction. In 1987 the relevant percentage was 47 per cent, rising to 64 per cent in 1991 and then falling to 63 per cent in 1992. This increase in committals had an affect not only on the workload of the court itself, but upon the size of the prison population, on the police, the Crown Prosecution Service and the Legal Aid Fund. The Consultation Paper considered one option to be a reclassification of the mode of trial of minor thefts and certain other offences. In doing so it mirrored the approach taken by the James Committee. Two other options related not so much to the classifications themselves, but rather to the decision-making process as to where 'either-way' offences should be tried. The first option came from the Royal Commission on Criminal Justice. It recommended that a person accused of an either-way offence should no longer be entitled to insist on trial in the Crown Court, but that the mode of trial should be a matter of agreement between the accused and the Crown Prosecution Service, and, in the absence of such agreement, be determined by magistrates. The other option considered was a change in the law relating to the mechanics of the decision-making process, so that magistrates could be aware, at the time of making the choice of mode of trial, of how the accused intends to plead at trial. The Consultation Paper estimated that a significant number of cases (38,000 in the year ending June 1993) were sent for trial in the Crown Court only for the accused to plead guilty on arraignment, and be given a sentence which the magistrates themselves could have imposed. It identified the fact

---

[116] *Op cit*, Ch 6, para 13–19.   [117] *Op cit*, Ch 6, paras 6–8.
[118] *Mode of Trial: A Consultation Paper* 1995, Cm 2908, HMSO.
[119] Ibid, para 2.

that a 'significant proportion' of accused falling into that category would in fact be prepared to plead guilty in a magistrates' court to an either-way charge and be dealt with by the magistrates. Such cases were often sent to the Crown Court because magistrates declined jurisdiction. It was this last option that found favour. Amended procedures (Plea before Venue) were introduced by the Criminal Procedure and Investigations Act 1996.[120]

(b) The Auld Review

The question of either-way offences was one of the major issues addressed by the Auld Review[121] whose consideration of this issue followed hard on the heels of two Mode of Trial Bills which had attempted, in effect, to give the decision-making power as to mode of trial of either-way offences to the magistrates' court, not the defendant.[122] Auld, like the Royal Commission on Criminal Justice and Narey Report[123] before him, took the view that it was for the court, not the defendant to determine mode of trial. The Review rejected the notion that there was some 'ancient, constitutional, fundamental or even broad right of the citizen to jury trial'.[124] The right to elect in fact began as a right to elect summary trial to avoid the rigour of trial on indictment in a limited number of cases, in the context of a harsh system which provided few protections for defendants. The Review considered that the public has 'a legitimate interest in the financial and human cost of the criminal justice system and how best to apply its finite resources and with justice to all'. It is for the court to determine whether the circumstances of the case merit the more elaborate, costly, and time-consuming procedures of the Crown Court. It also concluded that the fact that some defendants perceive juries as more ready to acquit than magistrates is not a sound reason for leaving the power to elect with the defendant. There may be many reasons why juries are more ready to acquit. If procedures in the magistrates' courts are unfair these should be addressed.[125] The Review's recommendations, that the court should decide with a limited right of appeal, that committal proceedings for either-way offences and committals for sentence should be abolished, have, however, only been partially implemented. The most recent interventions in this area, contained in the Criminal Justice Act 2003, do not proceed along the same lines as the ill-fated Modes of Trial Bills. Instead they sought to address the issue by modified Plea before Venue procedures and powers,[126] and by increased powers of sentencing for magistrates.[127]

---

[120] See, generally, procedure for mode of trial.   [121] *Op cit*, Ch 5, paras 119–172.

[122] Both Bills (Mode of Trial and Mode of Trial (No 2)) were rejected by the House of Lords essentially on the grounds that they diminished the fundamental right to trial by jury for a serious offence, although considerable criticism of their detail was made.

[123] *Op cit*, Ch 1 p 2, and Ch 8, p 33.

[124] *Op cit*, Ch 5, para 166. All references in this discussion are to paras 66 *et seq*.

[125] Citing Ashworth, *The Criminal Process: An Evaluation Study* (1998), p 262, and Darbyshire; 'For the New Lord Chancellor – Some Causes for Concern about Magistrates' [1997] Crim LR 869.

[126] See p 581, *post*.   [127] See p 700, *post*.

PROCEDURE FOR DETERMINING
MODE OF TRIAL

The procedure for determining the Mode of Trial differs according to whether or not the accused is an adult. If he is, then, as has been noted, he will always be tried on indictment for an offence triable only on indictment and will always be tried summarily for a summary offence; only in the case of an 'either-way' offence are there alternative possibilities (see Fig. 2). In the case of juveniles the position is quite different. Before considering these procedures it should be noted that if magistrates mistakenly adopt a procedure which is not permitted, for example by 'trying' a case which is triable only on indictment or by sending for trial in the case of an offence triable only summarily, then their 'trial' or 'committal' will be a complete nullity. Even if the defendant has been 'sentenced' he may later be committed for trial and properly tried, if the offence was triable only on indictment.[128]

The choice of charge is that of the prosecution. If the charge preferred is appropriate on the facts given their seriousness, then the defence cannot challenge that charge on the basis that the preferment of another, different charge would have permitted trial on indictment. Problems may also arise where fresh charges are levelled by the prosecutor, which, in reality, amount to attempts to deprive the justices of jurisdiction to try the case themselves. In *R v Brooks (Christopher)*[129] the appellant appeared before magistrates on a charge under section 20 of the Offences against the Person Act 1861. The appellant was content to be tried summarily, and the justices so ordered. The chief prosecuting

Fig. 2 Decisions as to mode of trial

---

[128] See, e.g., *R v West* [1964] 1 QB 15; [1962] 2 All ER 624.   [129] [1985] Crim LR 385.

solicitor then advised the bringing of a new charge under section 18 of the 1861 Act. In quashing the conviction obtained on such a charge O'Connor LJ observed that the prosecutor was seeking:

> to act as an appellate tribunal from the justices. There is no other explanation for it, and he said as much.

However, in *R v Redbridge Justices, ex parte Whitehouse*[130] it was made clear that it was the abuse of power that led to the irregularity in *Brooks*. If the facts are capable of supporting a fresh charge, the justices must decide whether it is both proper and appropriate. If they have already decided on summary trial, any further charge which would have the effect of making summary trial impossible should be scrutinized with care, but is not totally prohibited. The operation of this principle was seen in *R v Sheffield Justices, ex parte Director of Public Prosecutions*[131] where the defendant elected trial on a charge of assault occasioning actual bodily harm. The Crown then substituted a charge of common assault. Upon the magistrates staying the proceedings, the prosecutor successfully applied for judicial review. The substitution was a proper one, despite the fact that it deprived the accused of his right to trial by jury. There was no evidence of manipulation, and the defence had been notified of the proposal at an earlier stage. It was an appropriate charge on the facts.

1 THE PLEA BEFORE VENUE PROCESS – ADULTS

As noted above, the plea before venue process is the means by which the decision is taken as to whether an either-way offence is tried by the magistrates' court or sent to the Crown Court for trial by jury. Amended by the Criminal Procedure and Investigations Act 1996 to allow an indication of plea to be given, so that cases where a guilty plea is forthcoming are not sent unnecessarily to the Crown Court, but retained at magistrates' courts level, significant further amendments have been made by the Criminal Justice Act 2003. These amendments are part of a strategy to retain more either-way offences at magistrates' court level. These provisions recognize the inextricable links between mode of trial and sentencing powers, and are designed to achieve fewer cases going to the Crown Court. The Royal Commission on Criminal Justice found[132] that Crown Courts were imposing sentences that were within the powers of the magistrates' court. The amended plea before venue system was not working as it should.[133] The early plea provisions introduced in 1996 were not overcoming some of the objections to, or reservations about, summary trial. The 2003 Act will, when fully in force, allow a suspect to seek an indication of likely sentence, so that he can gauge what is his likely fate if he pleads guilty. At the same time the sentencing powers of magistrates are to be extended,[134] committals for sentence largely abolished,[135] and magistrates allowed to

---

[130] (1991) 94 Cr App R 332.   [131] [1993] Crim LR 136.

[132] *Op cit*, para 6.12, relying on research conducted by Hedderman and Moxon, *Magistrates' Court or Crown Court? Mode of Trial Decisions and Sentencing*, Home Office Research Study No 125, HMSO, 1992.

[133] See also Herbert, 'Mode of Trial and Magistrates' Courts Powers' [2003] Crim LR 315.

[134] Not yet in force: see p 700, *post*.   [135] See p 672, *post*.

take into account previous convictions of the defendant.[136] By this combination of measures it is hoped to achieve a greater number of guilty pleas and significantly reduce the number of cases going to the Crown Court, with a consequent cost saving.

(a) Procedure

Before any evidence is called, a magistrates' court before whom a person aged seventeen or over appears charged with an offence triable either way must adopt the following procedure:

(1) If the prosecution is being carried on by the Attorney-General, the Solicitor-General, or the Director of Public Prosecutions and he applies for the offence to be tried on indictment, then it must be tried in that way and send the case for trial. In any other case the following steps apply.

(2) The court must first cause the charge to be written down, if this has not already been done, and read to the accused.

(3) The court must explain to the defendant in ordinary language that he may indicate whether (if the offence were to proceed to trial) he would plead guilty or not guilty (1980 Act, section 17A).

(4) The defendant must also be warned that if he indicates that he intends to plead guilty the court will proceed to summary trial.

(5) If the defendant does indicate he would plead guilty then the court must proceed to summary trial with, of course, the power to commit for sentence which exists under section 3 of the Powers of Criminal Courts (Sentencing) Act 2000,[137] though if the court has given an indication of sentence (see below) this is a power which is unlikely to be used often. This indication of plea does not indicate the formal taking of a plea (1980 Act, section 17A(9)). Thus, if the accused indicates that he intends to plead not guilty, then, if the case is committed for trial, it is necessary for a formal plea to be taken in the Crown Court.

(6) If the accused indicates that his intention is to plead not guilty, then the magistrates' court proceeds to determine Mode of Trial, in accordance with the procedure set out below (section 18 of the 1980 Act, as amended).

(7) The prosecutor and then the accused are given an opportunity to make representations as to which Mode of Trial would be more suitable. The prosecutor will be invited to give details of the defendant's previous convictions (1980 Act, section 19(2)).[138]

---

[136] This is part of a wider theme of the 2003 Act in allowing a greater use of evidence of bad character at trial. See p 652, *post*.

[137] A new s 3 is substituted for the pre-existing provision, by Schedule 3, para 22 of Criminal Justice Act 2003. For changes to power to commit for sentence, see p 672, *post*.

[138] As substituted by Criminal Justice Act 2003, Schedule 3. This provision amounts to a change from the pre-existing position: see *R v Colchester Justices, ex parte North Essex Building Co Ltd* [1977] 3 All ER 567; *R v Doncaster Magistrates' Court, ex parte Goulding* [1993] 1 All ER 435; *R v South Hackney Juvenile Court, ex parte RB and C* (1983) 4 Cr App R 294.

(8) The court then considers whether the offence appears more suitable for summary trial or for trial on indictment, having regard to the representations referred to in (7) above, to the nature of the case, whether the circumstances make the offence one of serious character, whether the punishment which a magistrates' court would have power to inflict for it would be adequate, and 'any other circumstances which appear to the court to make it more suitable for the offence to be tried in one way rather than the other'.[139] The Court must also have regard to allocation guidelines made by the new Sentencing Guidance Council.[140] These Allocation Guidelines, replacing the pre-existing Mode of Trial Guidelines, are intended to promote consistency in decisions made as to mode of trial.[141]

(9) If, following consideration as above, it appears to the court that the offence is more suitable for trial on indictment, then it must tell the defendant that it has so decided and will then proceed to send the case for trial, the defendant having no power to prevent this course even if neither he nor the prosecution has requested it.

(10) If, on the other hand, it appears to the court that the offence is 'more suitable for summary trial', then the court must explain to the defendant in ordinary language that he can either consent to summary trial or, if he wishes, be tried by a jury. Magistrates' courts have increasingly limited powers to commit to the Crown Court for sentence, if, having dealt with the case summarily, they consider their sentencing powers inadequate.[142] The magistrates' court must inform the defendant of that power. Those powers have mostly been abolished by the Criminal Justice Act 2003,[143] the power to commit to be (when the provision is brought into force) under a new section 3A of the Powers of Criminal Court (Sentencing) Act 2000, introduced by the 2003 Act. This will permit committal for sentence only if the defendant is found convicted of a 'specified offence'.[144] The effect of this is that once a magistrates' court accepts jurisdiction it must, in most cases, sentence the defendant, if convicted, within its own sentencing powers, reducing the number of cases that end up at the Crown Court.

(11) After explaining to the defendant his options, the court must ask him whether he consents to be tried summarily or wishes to be tried in the Crown Court. Before making his choice, the defendant may (when a new section 20 of the 1980 Act is fully brought into force)[145] ask the court for an indication of likely sentence. The rationale for this new provision is that if the defendant receives an indication of likely sentence, particularly if it amounts to a statement that the defendant does not face a custodial sentence, he may be more willing to accept summary trial and not exercise his right to elect for jury trial. Again, this is part of the overall strategy of reducing jury trial.

---

[139] 1980 Act, s 19(4).   [140] See p 693, *post*.
[141] Criminal Justice Act 2003, s 170(5).
[142] Powers of Criminal Courts (Sentencing) Act 2000, s 3.
[143] Schedule 3. That provision is not yet in force.   [144] See, further, p 704, *post*.
[145] Introduced by Schedule 3, Criminal Justice Act 2003.

A court is not bound to give such an indication, and some courts may be unwilling in the early stages of operation of the new provisions to do so. An indication is not the taking of a plea,[146] and a defendant may elect trial by jury, or maintain his initial not guilty plea if the indication is one that is not favourable to him.

The defendant may, after the indication of likely sentence, reconsider his initial indication of plea. If he does, he will again be invited to give such an indication (1980 Act, section 20(5),(6)). The court will then deal with the mode of trial issues in the way outlined above.

(12) If the defendant consents to summary trial, the magistrates proceed to try him; if he does not consent, they deal with matters such as bail and send him for trial (see below).

There are provisions in section 25 of the 1980 Act whereby the magistrates may change from summary trial to proceed to decline jurisdiction. Where the court has begun to try an either-way offence summarily it may, at any time before the conclusion of the evidence for the prosecution, discontinue the summary trial and proceed to send for trial. This will necessitate starting all over again and the court must adjourn the hearing, and is not required to remand the defendant.

The defendant must usually be present in court in person during the proceedings at which the Mode of Trial is determined.[147] However, the court may proceed in the absence of the defendant if they consider that by reason of his disorderly conduct before them it is not practicable for the proceedings to be conducted in his presence. In addition, where the defendant is represented by counsel or a solicitor who in his absence signifies to the court the defendant's consent to the proceedings for determining how he is to be tried for the offence being conducted in his absence, and the court is satisfied that there is good reason for proceeding in the absence of the defendant, then the court may proceed in the defendant's absence.[148] In either case the consents required either to summary trial may be given by the defendant's counsel or solicitor.[149]

2 CHILDREN AND YOUNG PERSONS

The law has given significant protection to children and young persons. An attempt was made by the Children and Young Persons Act 1969 to prohibit the prosecution of children[150] for all crimes except murder, and severely limit the prosecution of young persons. However, these provisions were never brought into force, and were repealed in 1991,[151] leaving children and young persons open to prosecution, but with restrictions as to how proceedings shall be heard. Cases involving juveniles are nearly always tried in the Youth Court.[152]

---

[146] 1980 Act, s 20A(4), not yet in force.   [147] 1980 Act, s 18(2).
[148] Ibid, s 18(3), 23(1).   [149] Ibid, ss 23(3), (4).
[150] A child is a person aged ten–thirteen inclusive. A young person is a person aged fourteen–seventeen.
[151] Criminal Justice Act 1991, Schedule 13.   [152] See p 274, *ante.*

A child under the age of ten is irrebuttably presumed to be *doli incapax*, that is, incapable in law of committing a criminal offence.[153] This minimum age of criminal responsibility has been criticized[154] and was unsuccessfully challenged in the Court of Human Rights in *T* v *United Kingdom, V* v *United Kingdom*.[155] The Court concluded that there was no clear common standard amongst the countries who were signatories to the Convention: even if the age of ten could be said to be low, it could not be regarded as so disproportionate to the stance taken by some other countries.

Whenever a child or young person appears before a youth court charged with any indictable offence except 'homicide' he must, subject to certain exceptions, be tried summarily.[156] This rule does not apply to an offence of homicide. Nor does it apply:

(a) in the case of a young person charged with an offence for which the penalty is in the case of an adult fourteen years' imprisonment or more, not being an offence for which the sentence is fixed by law, or certain sexual or firearms offences, and the court considers that if he is found guilty it ought to be possible to sentence him to detention under section 91 of the Powers of Criminal Court (Sentencing) Act 2000;[157] or

(b) in the case of a child or young person charged jointly with an adult if the court considers it necessary in the interests of justice to commit them both for trial.[158] In this case the court may also commit the child or young person for any other indictable offence with which he is charged at the same time (whether jointly with an adult or not) if that other offence arises out of circumstances which are the same as or connected with those giving rise to the first offence.[159]

The power to try a juvenile in an adult court was criticized by the Court of Human Rights in *T* v *United Kingdom* and *V* v *United Kingdom*. In this notorious case, where two juveniles were tried and convicted of the murder of a young boy in circumstances that aroused public disgust and anger, the two defendants were tried in an adult Crown Court. The Court concluded that the nature of the proceedings against each of the defendants was a breach of Article 6, in that the defendants were, in the context of a public hearing in the Crown Court, unable to participate effectively in the criminal proceedings. Despite the special measures taken, the formality and ritual of a Crown Court trial must have seemed incomprehensible to the defendants. As a result, a Practice

---

[153] The rebuttable presumption that a child under fourteen was incapable of committing an offence unless it was proved that the child knew that what he had dome was seriously wrong was abolished by Crime and Disorder Act 1998, s 34.

[154] See, e.g. Family Studies Centre Briefing Paper No 3, 1998.

[155] [2000] 2 All ER 1024, (2000) 30 EHRR 121.

[156] Magistrates' Courts Act 1980, s 24(1): 'appears' means appears or is brought before the court when the court makes its decision as to mode of trial, so that a defendant who attains the age of eighteen before this occasion is treated as an adult despite the fact that he was a young person when he appeared at an earlier remand hearing: *R v Islington North Juvenile Court, ex parte Daley* [1983] 1 AC 347; *sub nom Re Daley* [1982] 2 All ER 974, approving *R v St Albans Juvenile Court, ex parte Goodman* [1981] 2 All ER 311 and disapproving *R v Amersham Juvenile Court, ex parte Wilson* [1981 2 All ER 315, which suggested otherwise. Under the Crime and Disorder Act 1998, s 47, where a person attains the age of eighteen before the start of the trial it may send the case to the Crown Court for trial.

[157] See p 680, *post*.   [158] Magistrates' Courts Act 1980, s 24.   [159] Ibid, s 24(2).

Direction was issued.[160] It is clear from that Practice Direction that separate trial, rather than joint trial in an adult court should be held where the interests of justice did not necessitate a joint trial.[161]

A child or young person not accused jointly with an adult will be tried in a youth court. However, if charged jointly with an adult he will be tried in an ordinary magistrates' court unless the adult pleads guilty or is not tried summarily (so that they are no longer jointly charged) in which event the court may before any evidence is called in the case of the child or young person remit him to a youth court for trial.[162]

The provisions set out above regarding plea before venue apply equally to juveniles in respect of the limited circumstances when a case can in fact be dealt with in an adult court.[163]

3 FACTORS THAT INFLUENCE MODE OF TRIAL

It has been noted that, in respect of 'either-way' offences, the mode of trial is determined both by the magistrates' court and by the defendant. Magistrates were given specific guidance as to how these powers should be used by the National Mode of Trial Guidelines, and, now, the Allocation Guidelines.[164] Certain key principles apply:[165]

(a) the court should never make a decision on the ground of convenience or expedition;

(b) the court should assume that the prosecution version of the facts is correct;

(c) the fact that the offences are specimen charges is relevant. By contrast, the fact that the defendant will be asking for other offences to be taken into consideration is not;

(d) where complex questions of fact, or difficult points of law, arise, the court should consider sending for trial;[166]

(e) where two or more defendants are jointly charged with an offence, each has an individual right to elect his mode of trial;

(f) either-way offences should be tried summarily unless the particular case has one of the specified features, and the court considers that its sentencing powers are insufficient;

---

[160] *Practice Direction (Crown Court: Trial of Children and Young Persons)* [2000] 2 All ER 285. See now *Practice Direction (Consolidated Criminal Practice)* [2002] 3 All ER 904.

[161] See, further, p 680, *post*.

[162] Ibid, s 29. This is a power to remit for trial, not for mode of trial to be determined: *R v Tottenham Youth Court, ex parte Fawzy* [1998] 1 All ER 365.

[163] Magistrates' Courts Act 1980, ss 24A–24D, inserted by Criminal Justice Act 2003, Schedule 3 (not yet in force).

[164] See p 693, *post*.

[165] See Magistrates' Courts Act 1980, s 19, and the various guidelines set out as the Mode of Trial decisions.

[166] Committals for trial (the phrase used by the Practice Direction) are abolished by Criminal Justice Act 2003, Schedule 3 (not yet in force). Cases can now either be sent or transferred for trial.

(g) the court should consider its power to commit for sentence if evidence arises during the course of the hearing which leads the court to conclude that the offence is so serious, or the offender such a risk to the public, that its powers to sentence him are inadequate.[167]

COURT BAIL

1 NATURE OF BAIL

A person is 'granted bail' when he is released from the custody of the law subject to a duty to surrender to custody at some future time. The 'custody' is the custody of a court unless bail was granted by a police officer, in which event it is the custody of the officer. Considerable changes in the law were effected by the Bail Act 1976, which gave effect to many, though not all, of the recommendations of a Home Office Working Party Report[168] which identified the deficiencies of the old law. Previously, bail involved entering into a 'recognizance' which is an acknowledgement of a debt to the Queen payable on default of compliance with the conditions of the recognizance. The 1976 Act abolished personal recognizances from the defendant but preserved them for sureties (where these are required). If granted bail the defendant is under a duty to surrender to custody when required; if he fails without reasonable cause to do so he commits an offence under section 6(1) of the 1976 Act, punishable either on summary conviction or as a contempt of court.[169]

Bail may be granted either unconditionally or, in some circumstances, subject to conditions. Before any conditions can be imposed it must appear to the court that such conditions are necessary to prevent a failure to surrender to custody, to prevent the commission of an offence while on bail, to prevent interference with witnesses or an obstruction of the course of justice, or to allow inquiries or reports to be made to assist the court in dealing with him for the offence.[170] A court, in the future, may also impose a condition on a defendant for his own protection or welfare, irrespective of the age of the defendant.[171] These factors are, in fact, similar to those a court may rely upon in refusing bail where the court believes that 'substantial grounds' to believe that any of them apply exist,[172] and in *R v Mansfield Justices, ex parte Sharkey*[173] it was argued that 'substantial grounds' likewise had to exist before a court could impose conditions. This argument was rejected by the Court of Appeal. It was enough that a court considered that there was a real and not fanciful risk of an offence being committed whilst the defendant was on bail. In this case, the justices were entitled to impose conditions preventing the

---

[167] But note that the power to commit for sentence is heavily restricted by the provisions of Criminal Justice Act 2003 (not yet in force). See p 582, *ante* and p 672, *post*.

[168] *Bail Procedures in Magistrates' Courts*, Home Office, 1974.

[169] Bail Act 1976, s 3(2).   [170] Ibid, s 3(6).

[171] Bail Act 1976, s 3, as amended by Criminal Justice Act 2003, s 13.

[172] Ibid, Schedule 1, para 1.   [173] [1985] QB 613, [1985] 1 All ER 193.

PART IV CRIMINAL PROCEEDINGS

defendants from picketing or demonstrating at places other than their own places of work, during a major industrial dispute in the coal industry and where the court knew that disturbances at coal pits had occurred.

Where conditions can be imposed, they may cover a wide variety of matters. They may comprise the provision of a surety or sureties to secure the person's surrender to custody; the provision of security (if it appears that he is unlikely to remain in Great Britain until the time appointed for him to surrender to custody); requirements to secure that he surrenders to custody, does not commit any offence while on bail, does not interfere with witnesses or otherwise obstruct the course of justice or make himself available for the purpose of enabling inquiries or a report to be made to assist the court in dealing with him for the offence.[174] A court can also impose a condition requiring a defendant to attend an interview with a legal representative.[175] Failure to obtain legal advice or representation is one of the most common reasons for delay, because the necessary steps to enable the case to proceed have not been taken. What is clear is that any condition must be necessary and proportionate, because the restriction of liberty invokes Convention rights under Article 5 and Article 8, and thus the restrictions must be justifiable.[176] Conditions commonly imposed include conditions of residence, as to surrender of passport, reporting to a police station at prescribed times, not visiting specified premises, and not approaching specified persons. Such conditions can be onerous in their effect. They can be varied by a court on the application of the person bailed, the prosecutor or a constable. In addition, section 16 of the Criminal Justice Act 2003 confers a right of appeal to the Crown Court against certain conditions. These are:

(a) that the person reside away from a particular place or area;

(b) that the person resides at a particular place other than a bail hostel;

(c) for the provision of a surety or the giving of a security;

(d) that the person concerned remains indoors between certain hours;

(e) requirements in respect of electronic monitoring; that the person makes no contact with another person.

The Crown Court may vary any such condition, a power that previously belonged to the High Court. Presumably, it is open to the Crown Court to vary conditions by deleting a condition entirely, or by adding new, alternative conditions.

2 OCCASIONS FOR THE GRANT OF BAIL

The question of when bail may be granted to a person may arise at various stages of his case, from the moment that he is arrested to the final determination of any appeal

---

[174] Bail Act 1976. These conditions may now be imposed not only by a court but by a police officer. In murder cases, unless satisfactory reports on the defendant's mental condition have already been obtained, the court must impose as conditions of bail (a) a requirement that the defendant shall undergo examination by two medical practitioners for the purpose of enabling such reports to be prepared, and (b) a requirement that he shall for that purpose attend such an institution or place as the court directs (ibid, s 3(6A)).

[175] Crime and Disorder Act 1998, s 54(2).   [176] See p 182, *ante.*

arising out of his conviction. Bail in cases of treason can only be granted by order of a High Court judge or the Home Secretary.[177] We have also noted the powers of the police regarding bail. In the context of the courts, bail may be granted as follows.

(a) By magistrates

Magistrates have power to grant bail at various stages of proceedings, subject to certain restrictions. When a defendant is first brought before a magistrates' court charged with an offence it quite often happens that the prosecution is not ready to proceed, in which event the proceedings are adjourned and the accused is remanded, either in custody or on bail. This may arise in the course of summary proceedings or where the offence is triable only on indictment (in which event the magistrates will eventually send the case for trial) or where it is triable 'either way'.[178] If magistrates decide to send a defendant to the Crown Court for trial, that sending for trial may be in custody or on bail.[179] Following summary conviction, the magistrates have (now) limited power to commit the defendant to the Crown Court for sentence.[180] If they do they may commit in custody or on bail.[181] Finally, following conviction, if the magistrates adjourn for the purpose of considering sentence they may remand the defendant on bail or in custody[182] and, having imposed a custodial sentence, they may, if a person has given notice of appeal or applied to the magistrates to state a case,[183] grant bail.[184]

If bail is refused on a remand, the maximum period of remand is eight clear days[185] unless the accused is already serving a custodial sentence, in which event it is twenty-eight clear days.[186] There may, of course, be further remands thereafter.[187]

Where magistrates adjourn a summary trial, or the determination of the method of trial of any either-way offence and remand the defendant in custody, they may, if the defendant is an adult, order that he be brought up for any subsequent remands before an alternative magistrates' court nearer to the prison where he is to be confined on remand. If the defendant's presence is required, this may be achievable through a live television link.[188] This is, again, designed to reduce delays, in this instance delays which arise where escorted prisoners arrive late at court.

Although successive applications for bail may be made to a magistrates' court (or to any court having power to grant bail), the Bail Act 1976 restricts the scope for continued applications. If bail has been refused a second application for bail can be supported with any

---

[177] Magistrates' Courts Act 1980, s 41.   [178] See p 577, *ante.*
[179] Bail Act 1976, s 6(3).   [180] See p 582, *ante,* and p 672, *post.*
[181] See the terms of ss 3A and 4 of the Powers of Criminal Courts (Sentencing) Act 2000, as amended by Criminal Justice Act 2003.
[182] Magistrates' Courts Act 1980, s 128(1). If the remand is for medical examination and report it must not be for more than three weeks, if in custody, for four weeks, if on bail, and, if on bail, conditions as to undertaking medical examination must be imposed (ibid, s 30).
[183] See p 684, *post.*   [184] Magistrates' Courts Act 1980, s 113.
[185] Ibid, s 128(6): 'clear days' means omitting the day of the remand and the day fixed for the appearance. In certain circumstances this may be exceeded – see 1980 Act, s 128A. The key condition is that a previous remand must have been made.
[186] 1980 Act, s 131(1).   [187] Ibid, s 129(1).   [188] Crime and Disorder Act 1998, s 57.

argument that is desired, whether or not put before the court before. At any subsequent hearings the court need not hear arguments as to fact or law that it has heard previously.[189]

(b) By the Crown Court

The Crown Court may grant bail to any person:[190]

(a) who has been committed in custody for appearance (trial or sentence) before the Crown Court; or

(b) who is in custody pursuant to a sentence imposed by a magistrates' court and has appealed against conviction or sentence; or

(c) who is in the custody of the Crown Court pending the disposal of his case by the Crown Court; or

(d) who, after the decision of the Crown Court in his case, has applied to the Crown Court to state a case for the High Court;[191] or

(e) who has applied to the High Court for an order of certiorari, or for leave to apply, in respect of proceedings in the Crown Court;[192] or

(f) to whom the Crown Court has granted a certificate under the Criminal Appeal Act 1968 (case fit for appeal); or

(g) who has been remanded in custody by a magistrates' court, where he has been refused bail by that court after hearing full argument.

The prosecution also has some rights of appeal against the grant of bail, first introduced in 1993,[193] in respect of an offence punishable by imprisonment for a term of five years or more. That has been changed to extend to any offence punishable with imprisonment,[194] a change designed to overcome the problem of mistaken grant of bail at a time when it can be rectified. For this right to exist the prosecution must have objected to bail at the hearing before the magistrates' court, and have to show that there is a risk to the public of serious harm if the defendant is bailed. The appeal is by way of rehearing.[195] The Crown Court may remand the defendant in custody or on bail subject to such conditions as it thinks fit.

(c) By the High Court

Hitherto, an appeal against a magistrates' court withholding bail, or the imposition of conditions, lay to the High Court. That jurisdiction has largely been abolished.[196]

---

[189] Even if refused bail on remand, a defendant is entitled to have his right to bail fully reviewed at the stage of sending for trial: *R v Reading Crown Court, ex parte Malik* [1981] QB 451, [1981] 1 All ER 249.

[190] Supreme Court Act 1981, s 81 (as amended).   [191] See p 684, *post.*

[192] This only applies to appellate proceedings in the Crown Court, because whilst it is sitting as a court of first instance it is not amenable to judicial review: see p 215, *ante.*

[193] Bail (Amendment) Act 1993.   [194] Criminal Justice Act 2003, s 16.

[195] For the relevant procedure, see Supreme Court Act 1981, s 18(2). Where notice of appeal is given orally, the magistrates' court must remand the defendant in custody pending hearing of the appeal.

[196] See Criminal Justice Act 2004, s 17. For the original jurisdiction, see Criminal Justice Act 1967, s 22, as amended by Bail Act 1976, Schedule 2.

(d) By the Court of Appeal

The Court of Appeal has power to grant bail pending appeal to that court or pending a retrial ordered by that court following such an appeal[197] or pending appeal from that court to the House of Lords.[198] It is rare for the Court of Appeal to grant bail, but it occasionally does so, for example where the sentence appealed against is a short one so that it might be served by the time the appeal comes on for hearing, or where there is a strong prima facie likelihood of success.[199]

3 THE RIGHT TO BAIL

The marginal note to section 4 of the Bail Act 1976 is 'General right to bail of accused persons and others' (the 'others' being persons who are brought up for breach of the requirements of certain community orders,[200] or persons who have been remanded following conviction for reports). The section created a statutory presumption in favour of granting bail and provides that, except as provided in Schedule 1 to the Act, bail shall be granted to a person who appears before a magistrates' court or the Crown Court in the course of or in connection with proceedings or who applies for bail in connection with proceedings. It does not apply (save in the case of remand for reports) after conviction.

The right to bail was restricted by section 25 of the Criminal Justice and Public Order Act 1994, which originally provided that a person charged with, or convicted of, murder, attempted murder, manslaughter, rape, or attempted rape must not be granted bail. This provision, intended to prevent repeat offences being committed by a person whilst on bail, was introduced despite the lack of clear empirical evidence that it was needed. It is now being modified, to restore an element of discretion in the hands of the court. Section 56 of the Crime and Disorder Act 1998 modified this to permit a grant of bail where 'exceptional circumstances' exist. The Act carefully avoided defining what might be regarded as exceptional circumstances.

Schedule 1 contains detailed provisions relating to circumstances in which bail may justifiably be withheld. The wider Human Rights Act context should not be overlooked. Article 5 of the Convention does indeed permit the deprivation of liberty, but the presumption is in favour of liberty and the state must show that there are 'relevant and sufficient' reasons to justify detention.[201] The period of pre-trial detention must be limited to a reasonable period of time, the public interest in detention must be balanced with the presumption of innocence, and the withholding of bail must be based on individual circumstances and not stereotypes.[202] There is a need to balance the competing interests in

---

[197] Criminal Appeal Act 1968, ss 8(2), 19; the power may be exercised by a single judge (ibid, ss 31, 45(2)).

[198] Ibid, s 36. By s 37, if the prosecutor is appealing to the House of Lords and, but for the decision of the Court of Appeal, the appellant would be liable to be detained, the Court of Appeal may make an order providing for his detention or directing that he shall not be released except on bail; there is similar provision on prosecution appeals from the Queen's Bench Divisional Court (Administration of Justice Act 1960, s 5).

[199] *R* v *Wattam* (1978) 68 Cr App R 293.

[200] See s 4(3), as amended by Criminal Justice Act 1991. For these orders, see p 707, *post*.

[201] *Letellier* v *France* (1991) 14 EHRR 83.

[202] *Yagci and Sargan* v *Turkey* (1995) 20 EHRR 505; *A* v *France* [1999] 17 EHRR 462.

preventing interference with the administration of justice, preservation of public order, and the need to protect the defendant. It is in this context that the following grounds permitting refusal of bail, and in some cases the presumption against bail, must be judged. These vary according to whether the accused is charged with an 'imprisonable offence' or a 'non-imprisonable offence', that is to say whether or not the offence is punishable with imprisonment (even if the accused himself, for example by reason of his age, would not be liable to be imprisoned for it).

(a) Refusal of bail for non-imprisonable offences

If the offence is non-imprisonable the only circumstances in which bail may be withheld are:

(1) if the defendant having previously been granted bail, has failed to comply with his obligation to surrender to custody and the court believes that he would so fail again;

(2) if the court is satisfied that the defendant should be kept in custody for his own protection or, if he is a child or young person, for his own welfare;

(3) if he is already in custody pursuant to a court sentence;[203]

(4) if, having been granted bail in the instant proceedings, he has been arrested for absconding or breaking the conditions of his bail.[204]

(b) Refusal of bail for imprisonable offences

If the offence is imprisonable, there is a much wider range of circumstances in which bail may be justifiably withheld, in addition to those listed above.[205] These provisions were significantly amended by the Criminal Justice Act 2003 in the light of research conducted for the White Paper *Justice for All*, which showed that some 18 per cent of adults and 38 per cent of under eighteens, and 12 per cent of all those bailed subsequently fail to attend court or offend whilst on bail.[206] The Auld Review[207] reported police disenchantment at the lack of CPS vigour (as it was perceived) in respect of those who abscond, or re-offend, and are later granted bail. The amended Schedule 1 to the Bail Act 1976 addresses some of these issues. A court may refuse bail in the following circumstances:

(5) the court is satisfied that there are substantial grounds for believing that the defendant, if released on bail (whether subject to conditions or not) would:

   (a) fail to surrender to custody; or

   (b) commit an offence while on bail; or

   (c) interfere with witnesses or otherwise obstruct the course of justice;

(6) where it has not been practicable for want of time to obtain sufficient information to enable the court to make its decision;

---

[203] Or a sentence of an authority acting under the Armed Forces Act 1996 (or its predecessors).
[204] Bail Act 1976, Schedule 1, Part II.   [205] Ibid, Schedule 1, Part I.
[206] *Justice for All*, Cm 5563, at Ch 3.   [207] *Op cit*, p 429, para 81.

(7) where a case is adjourned for inquiries or report and it appears that it would be impracticable to complete the inquiries or make the report without keeping the defendant in custody.

In considering the grounds referred to under (5) above the court must have regard to the nature and seriousness of the offence or default, the character, antecedents, associations, and community ties of the defendant, the defendant's record in relation to fulfilling his obligations under previous grants of bail in criminal proceedings, the strength of the evidence against him and any other considerations which appear to be relevant.[208] A further restriction was introduced into Schedule 1 in 1994[209] in an attempt to reduce the incidence of offending by persons on bail. In 1993, a study conducted by the Metropolitan Police showed that some 40 per cent of suspects arrested in one week were already on bail.[210] Further amendments made by the 2003 Act mean that a court must 'give weight' to the fact that the defendant is already on bail when assessing whether there is a substantial risk that the defendant would commit a further offence if released on bail.[211] This applies in respect of a person accused of any imprisonable offence. It effectively amounts to a presumption against bail. A court should re-bail such a defendant only if it is satisfied that there is no significant risk of committing an offence whilst on bail. It is by no means certain that this presumption complies in all circumstances with Article 5 of the Convention. As the Parliamentary Joint Committee observed in 2003:[212]

> ...the court would be prevented from granting bail in at least some circumstances even though it is not satisfied that there is a sufficient public interest in detaining the defendant pending trial...In some cases (for example, where a minor offence has been committed and the defendant poses no real risk to the community) the court would be prevented from granting bail where detaining the defendant in custody would be self-evidently disproportionate to any purpose, and in other cases it might be clear that the public interest in detaining the defendant is outweighed by other considerations...[such as] the other Convention rights of the defendant, members of his or her family or other dependants....

Further, section 15 of the 2003 Act requires a court to refuse to bail an adult defendant who fails without reasonable cause to answer bail in the same proceedings unless the court is satisfied that there is no significant risk that the defendant would fail to surrender if released on bail. In respect of juveniles there is no such presumption against bail, but the fact of absconding is a relevant fact for the court to consider in deciding whether there is a substantial risk that the juvenile would fail to surrender to bail.

A still further restriction on bail is contained in Schedule 1 to the Bail Act 1976[213] as part of a range of measures introduced to address the issue of drug-taking and drug-related crime. A court may deny bail, unless the court is satisfied that there is no signifi-

---

[208] Schedule 1, para 9.   [209] Criminal Justice and Public Order Act 1994, s 26.
[210] Debates in 1994 Act, Mr Robert McLennan MP, HC Cmttee.
[211] Bail Act 1976, Schedule 1, Part I, para 2A, inserted by Criminal Justice Act 2003, s 14.
[212] Cited by Ward and Davies, *Criminal Justice Act 2004 – A Practitioners' Guide* (2004), at para 3.30.
[213] Inserted by Criminal Justice Act 2003, s 19.

cant risk of re-offending whilst on bail, or the defendant declines to take up the offer of a 'relevant assessment' in respect of his drug-taking, or, having agreed to one, fails to comply with it. In order for this power to exist:

(a) the defendant must be aged eighteen or over;

(b) the presence in his body of Class A drugs must have been detected;

(c) either he has been charged with an offence under section 5(2) or 5(3) of the Misuse of Drugs Act 1971, or the court is satisfied that his misuse of Class A drugs caused or contributed to his behaviour, or his offending was wholly or partly motivated by his intended misuse of a Class A drug.

The Act[214] contains detailed provisions for recording the decisions of both courts and police officers in relation to bail and entitling defendants to copies of records of such decisions. Where a court withholds bail or imposes or varies conditions of bail in the case of a person who has a 'right to bail' in criminal proceedings, it must give reasons and these are recorded with the record of the decision.[215]

4 SURETIES

As already noted, the 1976 Act abolished personal recognizances from defendants (although a person may be required to provide security[216]). Recognizances still exist, however, in relation to sureties; these are persons who are sometimes colloquially said to 'stand bail' for the accused. If a person is granted bail subject to the provision of sureties, the court must fix the amounts of the sureties and must also be satisfied that the proposed sureties are suitable having regard to their financial resources, character, and any previous convictions and proximity (whether in point of kinship, place of residence, or otherwise) to the defendant.[217] In practice courts are usually guided by the police in matters relating to the suitability of proposed sureties.

Before sureties are taken it is the practice to explain the nature of the obligations being undertaken so as to ensure that the proposed surety understands them and to warn of the consequences of the defendant failing to answer to his bail. These are, prima facie, forfeiture of the amount of the recognizance and possible imprisonment in default. The court has power to order the surety, in the event of default by the defendant, to forfeit the whole of the amount of the recognizance or part thereof.[218] Before exercising its discretion the court must, in some circumstances,[219] give the surety the opportunity to be heard and must take into account circumstances relating either to means or to the surety's culpability for the non-appearance of the defendant which might make it fair and just for the surety not to be ordered to forfeit the whole amount of the recognizance. Although not decisive, the conduct of the surety will be an important factor in the deci-

---

[214] Bail Act 1976, s 5.   [215] Ibid, s 5(3), (4).

[216] Hitherto limited to persons unlikely to remain in the United Kingdom, but, now, see Crime and Disorder Act 1998, s 54.

[217] Ibid, s 8(2).   [218] Magistrates' Courts Act 1980, s 120(3).

[219] See Crime and Disorder Act 1998: where recognizances not conditioned for the appearance of the defendant, the court is not bound.

sion of the court as to whether or not to order forfeiture, either in whole or in part. In *R v Southampton Justices, ex parte Green*[220] Lord Denning MR stated that if the surety was guilty of no want of diligence and used every effort to secure the appearance of the accused it might be proper to remit the sum entirely. Imprisonment may be ordered in default of payment, of up to twelve months.

It is an offence, punishable on summary conviction or as a contempt of court, to agree to indemnify a surety in criminal proceedings (or, in the case of the surety himself, to be indemnified).[221]

An order of the Crown Court entreating the recognizance of a surety for a defendant who has failed to surrender to his bail to stand trial is not a 'matter relating to trial on indictment' (within section 29(3) of the Supreme Court Act 1981) so that the order is subject to judicial review.[222]

FURTHER READING

ASHWORTH and REDMAYNE, *The Criminal Process*, 3rd edn (Oxford University Press: 2000)

Auld Review – *Review of the Criminal Courts of England & Wales* (http://www.criminal-courts-review.org.uk)

The Distribution of Criminal Business between the Crown Court and the Magistrates' Court, 1988, Cmnd 6323

Review of the Crown Prosecution Service (HMSO: 1988)

---

[220] [1976] QB 11, [1975] 2 All ER 1073.   [221] Bail Act 1976, s 9.
[222] *Re Smalley* [1985] AC 622, *sub nom Smalley* v *Crown Court at Warwick* [1985] 1 All ER 769.

21

TRIAL ON INDICTMENT

INTRODUCTION

Although the proportion of cases that are actually tried by this method is small, trial on indictment indicates the real nature of the criminal trial, and it is the procedure adopted in serious cases tried by judge and jury. This chapter will examine the nature of trial on indictment, looking specifically at:

- How cases are sent for trial by the magistrates' court to the Crown Court.
- The duties of disclosure that the law places on both prosecution and defence, and how disclosure may be resisted.
- The problems that expert evidence creates.
- Long trials and the difficulties they cause.
- The procedure to be followed at trial.
- The protections for defendants.

SENDING AND TRANSFER FOR TRIAL

1 INTRODUCTION

The first stage of the trial of an indictable offence has, in recent legal history, been the committal for trial, or, as it is sometimes known, the preliminary inquiry before justices. Increasingly this has been only of a formal nature. Over the years the nature of committal for trial has significantly changed, with numerous legislative attempts to change its nature and purpose: indeed, the whole legislative history might be regarded as a case study into governmental and legislative indecision. That history is set out below. Now, cases are sent for trial, following major changes made by the Criminal Justice Act 2003. Committal proceedings will have been abolished.[1] However, the long history serves as

---

[1] Up until the bringing into force of the provisions of Sch 3 to the Criminal Justice Act 2003, either-way offences to be tried in the Crown Court were committed for trial, without consideration of the evidence. For the position with regard to cases of serious or complex fraud, of children, a sending for trial procedure has long existed.

a case study as to how changes in criminal procedure often occur piecemeal, as well as enabling an understanding of some of the earlier authorities.

2 THE BACKGROUND

Prior to 1967, oral committal proceedings were always held. They provided a mechanism for initial scrutiny by a court of the prosecution case against the defendant, so as to ensure that sufficient evidence exists to justify requiring the defendant to stand trial on indictment, with the expense and personal suffering that inevitably follows. Fundamental changes were made by the Criminal Justice Act 1967. The procedure had to be followed even where the sufficiency of the prosecution evidence was not being questioned, even by the defendant. Furthermore, since the magistrates often sat in open court, the resulting publicity in notorious cases sometimes gave rise to the creation of a real risk of prejudice to the trial itself. The 1967 Act therefore introduced new procedures, permitting committal for trial without the consideration of the evidence, thus saving much time and expense. It also introduced changes limiting the publicity that can be given to the evidence or the details of the offence.

As long ago as 1981 the Royal Commission on Criminal Procedure[2] concluded that committal proceedings did not operate as an effective filter to prevent weak cases from reaching court. It proposed their abolition and replacement by a new procedure, to be known as an 'application for discharge'. This procedure would have given the defence the option of a hearing before magistrates at which to make a submission of no case to answer, after the prosecution had disclosed its case in writing. These proposals were not implemented at that time.

In 1986 the matter was considered further by the Fraud Trials Committee,[3] which identified a whole series of objections to committal proceedings. These included the length of time taken by full committals, with the consequent delays, the potential for abuse, whereby proceedings were undertaken in the hope of acquiring material to use as a defence, in the hope that advantage could be gained if witnesses die, go abroad, or suffer from fading memories. In addition, the difficulties magistrates had in dealing with serious fraud cases, the cost of such proceedings, and the small number of defendants discharged in fraud cases were all noted. The committee recommended an interim procedural reform, until action might be taken by government on the Royal Commission recommendations in respect of serious fraud cases. The resulting changes were introduced in the Criminal Justice Act 1987,[4] which introduced a notice of transfer procedure. Four years later, in 1991, a similar procedure was introduced in some cases involving children.[5] Where these provisions apply, a notice of transfer can be served which effectively deprives the magistrates of jurisdiction and leads to automatic transfer to the Crown Court. As already noted these cases involving transfer to the Crown Court remain in force.

This approach commended itself to the Royal Commission on Criminal Justice,[6] which, in its research, found that full committal proceedings involving a hearing

---

[2] Cmnd 8092, HMSO, 1981.   [3] HMSO, 1986.   [4] Criminal Justice Act 1987, s 4.
[5] Criminal Justice Act 1991, s 53.   [6] Report, Ch 6, paras 26–32.

occurred in only about eight per cent of cases tried on indictment, and recommended abolition of the full committal procedure, but with the defence being able to make oral submissions of no case to answer, to be considered on the evidence contained in the case papers. In respect of either-way offences, submissions would have been to a magistrates' court, and be dealt with by a stipendiary magistrate, but in respect of offences triable only on indictment such submissions would be to the Crown Court.[7]

The principle of limiting committal proceedings was accepted by the government, who, however, took a different view on the detail. The Criminal Justice and Public Order Act 1994 introduced a new scheme of transfers for trial,[8] subject to rights to make written representations to dismiss the case. These provisions were never implemented. The government found it difficult to create a scheme that would work effectively, and met strong criticism from professional bodies. It sought to remedy some of these difficulties by further provisions in the Criminal Procedure and Investigations Act 1996. The provisions initially contained in that Act had themselves to be abandoned, again because of practical difficulties and of representations by professional bodies. There followed the extraordinary spectacle of the government then abandoning the original proposals of the 1994 Act, and abandoning its proposals to amend the 1994 Act in the 1996 Act, and, instead, introducing revised provisions into the 1996 Act.[9] These revised provisions, ultimately enacted, kept committal proceedings in place, but modified the rules under which they are conducted.

The result was that committal proceedings remained, subject to the changes in the 1996 Act. These had the effect of limiting the evidence to be considered at such proceedings to documentary evidence and exhibits tendered by the prosecution. However, the right to a hearing remained, and magistrates continued to be able to consider any representations made by either the defence or the prosecution, to assist the court in reaching its decision as to whether the case should be committed for trial. This modified procedure did not, however, remain unchanged for long. The Crime and Disorder Act 1998 abolished committal proceedings in cases where an adult is charged with an indictable only offence.[10] Instead a scheme was introduced which basically requires service of the prosecution case in writing, followed by an opportunity for the defendant to make an application to the Crown Court for the case to be dismissed. Such an application may in some circumstances be an oral application. This new procedure governed cases of serious or complex fraud, or which involve children, in indictable-only cases, hitherto which had been within the notice of transfer procedures. The effect was to achieve a scheme not dissimilar from that recommended by the Royal Commission on Criminal Justice, with three distinct processes:

(a) the automatic transfer to the Crown Court of cases of an adult which include an indictable only offence, under the 1998 Act;

---

[7] The Royal Commission made consequential recommendations about the appropriate court for an application for bail, and in respect of the time limits for making such applications of no case to answer: paras 29 and 31.

[8] 1994 Act, s 44 and Schedule 4.   [9] 1996 Act, ss 51–52, and Schedule 3.

[10] 1998 Act, s 51–52, and Schedule 3.

   (b) committal proceedings in respect of most either-way offences, subject to the limitations as to evidence introduced in the 1996 Act;

   (c) the notice of transfer procedures contained in the 1987 and 1991 Acts, when they apply, in cases other than indictable-only offences.

As noted above, the Criminal Justice Act 2003 made further changes.[11] The changes were intended to give effect to the recommendations of the Auld Review and the White Paper *Justice for All*, to create greater speed and efficiency in the handling of criminal cases. Their effect is to provide for common offences (i.e. those linked together) and linked offenders to be sent to the Crown Court automatically. The court will not have to wait for committal papers to be prepared, although arraignment in the Crown Court will not occur until service of the prosecution's evidence, normally within forty-two days.[12]

3 PROCEDURE

(a) Indictable only offences

Under the provisions contained in the Crime and Disorder Act 1998, where an adult is charged with an indictable only offence (other than one to which the transfer for trial provisions apply) he must be sent forthwith to the Crown Court.[13] The person committed will be committed also in respect of any either-way offences or summary offences with which he is also charged which:

   (a) appear to the court to be related to the indictable only offence, and

   (b) in the case of summary offences, are punishable with imprisonment or involve obligatory or discretionary disqualification from driving.[14] A summary offence is related to an indictable only offence if it arises out of circumstances which are the same as, or connected with, those giving rise to the indictable only offence.[15] In cases where an adult is jointly charged with an either-way offence that appears to be related to the indictable only offence he also must be sent for trial. 'Related to' in this context means if the offence could be joined in the same indictment.[16] By contrast if a child or young person is jointly charged with that same indictable only offence the court may send for trial, but is not required to do so.

A person who has been sent for trial under the 1998 Act is entitled to receive copies of the documents containing the evidence on which the charge or charges are based.[17] When he has received that evidence, and before arraignment, he may apply either orally

---

[11] 2003 Act, Schedule 3. These provisions are not yet in force.

[12] Crime and Disorder Act (Service of Prosecution Evidence) Regulations 2000, SI 2000/3305.

[13] 1998 Act, ss 51–52 and Schedule 3. When in force s 51 will be as substituted by the Criminal Justice Act 2003, Schedule 3, para 18.

[14] Ibid, s 51(2), (4), (6), (11).

[15] Ibid, s 51(11). When the 2003 Act is in force the relevant provision is a new s 51E of the 1998 Act.

[16] For joinder of counts in an indictment, see p 620, *post*.

[17] Ibid, Schedule 3, para 1.

(provided he has given notice of intention to so) or in writing to the Crown Court sitting in the place specified, for the charge, or any of them, to be dismissed.[18] A defendant is only entitled to adduce oral evidence at such a hearing if he is granted leave to do so, and that will only be granted if it appears to the judge, having regard to any matters stated in the application for leave, that the interests of justice require him to do so. The 1998 Act contains detailed provisions that govern the power of the Crown Court to deal with any summary offence.[19] A Crown Court has the power to take a plea of guilty, but not to try such an offence if a plea of not guilty is entered. It can dismiss such a charge if the CPS does not propose to offer evidence on that charge. A complex procedure applies where, for whatever reason, there ceases to be an indictable only offence before the court, but an either-way offence remains. In such a case, following an inquiry as to the intended plea, the court has to decide whether trial on indictment or summary trial is more suitable.[20]

When a case is sent for trial the court must specify in a notice, the offence or offences which are being sent, and the place at which he is to be tried.[21]

(b) Either-way offences

The Criminal Procedure and Investigations Act 1996 introduced significant modifications to the relevant provisions of the Magistrates' Courts Act 1980. Under these provisions, as amended,[22] it has been open for a magistrates' court (which comprises for this purpose a single justice, or in some circumstances a justices' clerk or member of his staff)[23] to commit the accused for trial without consideration of the evidence, where the parties agree. Where, however, committal for trial is contested, the magistrates had to consider the evidence, that evidence being confined to documentary evidence and exhibits tendered by the prosecution, provided these meet the conditions set out in the 1980 Act.[24]

These provisions are repealed by the Criminal Justice Act 2003, which substituted new provisions into the Crime and Disorder Act 1998. The effect of a new section 50A of the 1998 Act[25] is that, in the case of an either-way offence not sent for trial because it is related to an indictable only offence, the court having followed the normal procedure for determining mode of trial, must send the defendant for trial on that charge unless it is transferred for trial (see below). The sending for trial procedure is the same as that for indictable only offences.

(c) Notices of transfer

In certain cases involving serious or complex fraud, the notice of transfer provisions that were contained in the Criminal Justice Act 1987 apply. When in force these provisions are superseded by new provisions in the Crime and Disorder Act 1998.

---

[18] Ibid, para 2.   [19] Ibid, paras 5–6.   [20] Ibid, para 6.
[21] See p 603, post.   [22] See Magistrates' Courts Act 1980, s 6.   [23] See p 663, *post*.
[24] Magistrates' Courts Act 1980, ss 5A–5F, introduced by 1996 Act, s 47 and Schedule 1. Those provisions are repealed by Criminal Justice Act 2003, Schedule 32.
[25] Inserted by 2003 Act, Schedule 3, para 17.

As already noted, committal proceedings in serious fraud cases were abolished in 1987, section 46 of the Criminal Justice Act 1987 providing for some such cases to be automatically transferred to the Crown Court. If in the opinion of an appropriate officer[26] there is sufficient evidence for the accused to be committed for trial and the evidence reveals a case of fraud of such seriousness or complexity[27] that it is appropriate that the management of the case should without delay be taken over by the Crown Court, then a notice of transfer could be served. This must be done before the magistrates' court begins any summary trial, or before the case is sent for trial under section 51 of the 1998 Act: when the notice is served, the magistrates' court loses all jurisdiction. The decision to serve the notice of transfer appears to be beyond judicial challenge or appeal.[28] These provisions are repealed and substantially re-enacted by the creation of a new section 51B of the Crime and Disorder Act 1998 in 2003.[29] The one difference of substance is the removal of the procedure introduced in 1987 which permitted a defendant to make an application for dismissal. Such a procedure would be anomalous following the general re-jigging of the sending for trial procedures, which contain no such right.

The Criminal Justice Act 1991 introduced similar provisions in cases where a child was the victim of, or witnessed, certain offences of violence or of a sexual nature, and where the case should be taken over and proceeded with by the Crown Court to avoid prejudice to the welfare of the child.[30] Again, these provisions are repealed and similarly re-enacted by the Criminal Justice Act 2003, which creates a new section 51A of the Crime and Disorder Act 1998. Where they apply,[31] the Director of Public Prosecutions can serve a notice of transfer. The evidence must be sufficient for the person charged to be committed for trial. Similar provisions did exist in respect of war crimes, but have now been repealed.[32]

(d) Voluntary bills of indictment

Historically there has been one way by which a case could reach the Crown Court without committal, sending or transfer for trial. By a procedure known as the voluntary Bill procedure, the prosecution can apply to a High Court judge[33] for leave to prefer a Bill

---

[26] A term given a wide meaning by 1987 Act, s 4(2) to include the DPP, Director of the Serious Fraud Office, Commissioners of Inland Revenue, Commissioners of Customs and Excise, and the Secretary of State. The definition is re-enacted in identical terms by Crime and Disorder Act 1998, s 51B(9), as introduced by Criminal Justice Act 2003, Schedule 3, para 17.

[27] These terms reflect amendments made by the Criminal Justice and Public Order Act 1994, Schedule 9, in response to recommendations made by the Royal Commission on Criminal Justice.

[28] Criminal Justice Act 1987, s 6(2): see, now, 1998 Act, s 51B(8).

[29] See Criminal Justice Act 2003, Schedule 3, para 17.

[30] Criminal Justice Act 2001, s 53.

[31] The provisions apply to cases involving specified violent or sexual offences, defined now by 1998 Act, s 51C(3), where a child under seventeen would be called as a witness and the DPP is of the opinion that for the purpose of avoiding any prejudice to the welfare of the child the case should be taken over and proceeded with without delay by the Crown Court.

[32] War Crimes Act 1991, Schedule 1, para 4, repealed by the Criminal Procedure and Investigations Act 1996, s 47 and Schedule 5.

[33] A circuit judge has no power to grant leave to prefer a Bill of indictment: *R v Thompson* [1975] 2 All ER 1028, [1975] 1 WLR 1425.

of indictment against the accused. The judge in his discretion grants or refuses leave,[34] with the result that if leave is granted the Bill is preferred forthwith and there is no need for any proceedings. The defendant lost the advantage of knowing in advance the substance of the case against him. The applicant himself cannot attend unless permitted by the judge to do so, whilst the defendant is not entitled to attend at all. Even where there is a hearing it is not in open court.[35]

The use of this power has always been problematic[36] because it by-passed normal procedures and safeguards. To overcome this, the law now provides safeguards.[37] Except where there is good reason for doing otherwise, a defendant must receive notice of an application to seek a voluntary Bill, with supporting documentation, and must have an opportunity to make representations, in writing, and if desirable, orally. It is, though, exceptional, to be used only when the interests of justice rather than administrative convenience justify it. In one case,[38] the DPP had sought a voluntary Bill of indictment when he was concerned at the failure of a youth court to commit a young person to the Crown Court for sentence.[39] It was held that proceedings by way of judicial review[40] were more appropriate than seeking to obtain a voluntary Bill of indictment.

(e) Publicity

Following a well-publicized murder trial where pre-trial publicity created a severe risk of prejudice to the trial itself,[41] restrictions on the reporting of committal proceedings were introduced in 1967,[42] and are now contained in the Magistrates' Courts Act 1980. Those provisions are now in turn replaced by those introduced into the Crime and Disorder Act 1998,[43] designed to reflect the regime described above.

The effect of these provisions is that it is unlawful to publish anything other than the matters specified in section 52A(7) of the 1998 Act. These are:

(a) the identity of the court and the name of the justice or justices;

(b) the name, age, home address, and occupation of the defendant;

(c) in the case of a defendant charged with a case being transferred under section 51B (serious or complex fraud), and relevant business information;

---

[34] See, e.g., *Re Roberts* [1967] 1 WLR n474. The issue of a voluntary Bill is not susceptible to judicial review: *R v Manchester Crown Court, ex parte Williams* (1990) 154 JP 589.

[35] See, generally, *R v Raymond* [1981] QB 910, [1981] 2 All ER 246, where an attempt to challenge the validity of the voluntary Bill procedure (on the grounds that it infringed standards of procedural fairness) was rejected by the Court of Appeal. Such conclusions might, now, have to be reconsidered in the light of the terms of Article 6 but, for the reasons stated in the body of the text the issue is unlikely to arise.

[36] See, e.g. *Practice Direction* [1990] 1 WLR 633.

[37] *Consolidated Criminal Practice Direction* [2002] 1 WLR 2870, paras 35.5–35.6.

[38] *R (Director of Public Prosecutions) v Camberwell Youth Court* [2004] EWCA 1805 [2005] 1 Cr App R 6.

[39] As to which, see, p 671, *post*.   [40] See chapter 7, *ante*.

[41] The trial of Dr John Bodkin Adams in 1957. Devlin J stated that it would have been far better if the preliminary proceedings were held in private.

[42] Criminal Justice Act 1967, implementing the recommendations of the Tucker Report, Cmnd 479, HMSO, 1958.

[43] Crime and Disorder Act 1998, s 52A, introduced by Criminal Justice Act 2003, Schedule 3, para 17.

(d) details of the offence or offences;

(e) the name of counsel or solicitors engaged in the proceedings;

(f) the date and place of any adjournment;

(g) the arrangements as to bail;

(h) whether a right to representation funded by the Legal Services Commission[44] has been granted.

This limitation can be lifted by the court, though, if the defendant objects, the court must consider such a course of action to be in the interests of justice.[45] In such cases any wider restrictions on reporting may come into effect.[46] Of course, the process of sending for trial (when fully in force) will render such provision unnecessary.

4 SENDING FOR TRIAL

When a case is sent for trial, it will be in respect of the offences with which the defendant is charged, in accordance with the principles already discussed. The notice of sending for trial will specify those offences, and the place at which the defendant is to be tried. In the selection of the place of trial the court must have regard to the convenience of the defence, the prosecution, and the witnesses, the desirability of expediting the trial, and any direction given by or on behalf of the Lord Chief Justice in respect of location for trial.[47]

The structure of the Crown Court has already been discussed.[48] It is not a single court but sits in a number of different locations. These are described as first-tier, second-tier, and third-tier centres. First-tier centres deal with both civil and criminal cases and are visited by High Court and circuit judges; second-tier centres deal with criminal cases only but are visited by both High Court and circuit judges, while third-tier centres deal with criminal cases only and are visited only by circuit judges. Each circuit contains a number of each type of centre. Offences in turn are divided into four classes,[49] each containing a number of offences. Offences in Class 1 must normally be tried by a High Court judge although cases of murder may be released by the presiding judge, for trial by a circuit judge approved for that purpose by the Lord Chief Justice; examples are murder and the rare offences for which a person may be sentenced to death. Offences in Class 2 must be tried by a High Court judge unless a presiding judge of the circuit releases any particular case for trial by a circuit judge or recorder; examples are manslaughter, abortion, and rape. Offences in Class 3 may be tried by a High Court judge, or by a circuit judge or recorder; these are all offences triable only on indictment not falling within any other class.

---

[44] For details of funding in criminal cases, see p 409, *ante*.

[45] 1998 Act, s 52A(2).   [46] See chapter 10, *ante*.

[47] 1998 Act, s 51D(4), inserted by Criminal Justice Act 2003, Schedule 3, para 17.

[48] See p 266, *ante*.

[49] By the directions set out in *The Consolidated Practice Direction*. See now Criminal Procedure Rules, *op cit*, p 554, *ante*.

Offences in Class 4 will normally be tried by a circuit judge or recorder, although they may also be tried by a High Court judge; examples are wounding or causing grievous bodily harm with intent, conspiracy, and all offences triable either way.

Therefore, when a magistrates' court sends for trial a person charged with any offence within Classes 1 or 2, it must specify, as the place of trial, the location of the Crown Court where a High Court judge regularly sits. In the case of an offence in Class 4 the magistrates' court must simply specify the most convenient location of the Crown Court. In selecting the most convenient location, the justices must have regard to the location of the Crown Court designated by the presiding judge as the location to which cases should normally be committed from their petty sessions area.[50] The magistrates will also need to have regard to whether live TV link facilities exist, if this is likely to be necessary because of a special measures direction or for any other reason.[51]

The magistrates must consider whether to release the defendant on bail, or to send in custody. Factors which must be considered, including the imposition of conditions, have already been explained.[52]

DELAY AND TIME LIMITS

1 BACKGROUND

It has already been seen that the Prosecution of Offences Act 1985 imposes time-limits upon the length of time an accused person may be held in custody.[53] The potential for delay to lead to application to stay the proceedings because of abuse of process also exists, although it will only be an exceptional case where delay is likely to lead to a successful application.[54]

Trial within a reasonable time is one important characteristic of the right to a fair trial under Article 6. Delay is a particular matter of concern in criminal proceedings, leading to the potential for an unfair trial, because of the time between the event in question and the determination of guilt. It also prolongs the effect of the alleged crime on the victim, witnesses and, indeed, the defendant. It was because of increasing, and unacceptable, delays that the government in 1996 established the Narey Committee to review delays within the criminal justice system. The Narey Report was published in February 1997,[55] and contained some thirty-three different recommendations. These recommendations, discussed at the appropriate parts of this book,[56] ranged over a wide area, including the operation and powers of the CPS, the role of justices' clerks, limitations on trial by jury, abolition of committal proceedings in respect of indictable only offences, changes to the pleas-and-direction hearing, and major changes to the youth justice system. Many

---

[50] Ibid, para 3.   [51] See p 646, *post.*   [52] See p 591, *ante.*

[53] See p 573, *ante.*   [54] See p 572, *ante.*

[55] *Review of Delay in the Criminal Justice System*, 27 February 1997, HMSO.

[56] See chapters 19, 20, 22.

of them, although not all, have been accepted and are the subject of implementation through legislative and administrative changes.[57] Many of the procedural changes made by the Criminal Justice Act 2003, including the revised provisions relating to charging and sending for trial, are based on proposals made by the Auld Review and the White Paper *Justice for All*, intended to create efficiency and reduce delay.

2 TIME LIMITS

One area of importance is the question of time limits under the 1985 Act. The effect of the custody time limits is that, if a defendant is in custody, proceedings need to be commenced within the prescribed limits. If, for whatever reason, delay occurs, the prosecution has to obtain an extension of time from the court under section 22(3) of the 1985 Act. The power to make regulations under section 22 of that Act permits time limits generally to be set and to provide sanctions for non-compliance. Power exists to extend the regulations beyond custody time limits. Section 40 of the Crime and Disorder Act 1998 confers a wider power to make regulations which govern different types of offence, of accused, or different areas of the country. Statutory time limits will be set for all non-custodial cases, both in relation to adults and to juveniles, although with tougher time limits in cases involving persistent young offenders, and young offenders on bail.[58] This latter proposal is part of the general reform of the youth justice system, with the objective of halving the time from arrest to sentence.[59] For adults, it is proposed that statutory time limits be set for the pre-trial stage of all proceedings, both indictable and summary, broken down into three stages: the first listing of the case to start of summary trial; first appearance to committal or transfer; committal or transfer to start of Crown Court trial. It is not intended to set time limits for the period between trial and conviction. To do so would, of course, place the fairness of proceedings in individual cases at risk.

Accompanying this extension of time-limit provision are changes in the rules governing enforcement, contained in the Crime and Disorder Act 1988. Section 22(3) of the 1985 Act now provides that an extension of the time limit may be granted by a court, before the expiration of the time limit, provided the court is satisfied that the need for the extension is due to:

(i)   the illness or absence of the accused, a necessary witness, a judge or magistrate; or

(ii) a postponement which is occasioned by the ordering by the court of separate trials in the case of two or more accused; or

(iii) what is some other good and sufficient cause. In addition the court will have to be satisfied that the prosecution has acted with all due diligence and expedition, which will be a question of fact for the court to consider in the context of the individual application and its effects. No extension of time limits will be

---

[57] See, in particular, Crime and Disorder Act 1998, ss 43–47.
[58] Ibid, s 41.   [59] See p 674, *post.*

needed in respect of periods during which the accused is unlawfully at large.[60] If, because of prosecution delay, proceedings are stayed, fresh proceedings may in some circumstances be commenced, in cases where the stay is by a Crown Court, by the preferment of a voluntary Bill or indictment,[61] and in other cases by the laying of a new charge.[62]

DISCLOSURE OF EVIDENCE

1 INTRODUCTION

The effective working of the adversarial system depends, in part, upon proper disclosure.[63] Unlike in civil proceedings where production and disclosure of evidence generally is available, the duties of pre-trial disclosure in criminal cases have in the past been limited. The prosecution has always been under a duty to disclose at the stage of committal, or to serve within a certain period in the case of sending for trial,[64] the evidence upon which it proposes to rely, subject only to the right to call additional evidence in some circumstances and subject to certain conditions.[65] Historically, a defendant has been under no general duty to disclose his defence. A defendant, or a suspect, in criminal proceedings, has a 'right of silence'. This 'right of silence'[66] has traditionally permitted the defence at any stage to adduce evidence without notice, and without adverse inferences being drawn in law from that non-disclosure. That rule was modified in 1967 in respect of evidence of alibi,[67] in respect of the adducing of expert evidence,[68] and, more recently, by the provisions that permit inferences from silence in respect of certain matters in particular circumstances.[69] The general right to silence remains, although the practical effect of recent changes in the law may well be to limit or reduce reliance on the right.

A common law duty of disclosure on the prosecution in respect of unused material[70] reflected the fact that fairness to a defendant depends on material that might assist his case, or weaken that of the prosecution being made known, and produced, to him. The

---

[60] Ibid, s 40(5).   [61] See p 601, *ante.*   [62] See s 40.

[63] See p 551, *ante,* and note, in particular, *R* v *Mcllkenny* [1992] 2 All ER 417.

[64] See Crime and Disorder (Service of Prosecution Evidence) Regulations 2000, SI 2000/3305. The specified period thereunder is forty-two days, although authorities conflict as to whether this is mandatory: see *Gallagher, White Burke and Morris* (2002) Criminal Law Weekly (CLW) 20/05; *R* v *Haynes* (2002) CLW 25/6; *Re Fehily* (2002) CLW 26/9.

[65] Service of the witness statements.

[66] For the various meanings of this term, see Lord Mustill in *R* v *Director of Serious Fraud Office, ex parte Smith* [1993] AC 1, *sub nom Smith* v *Director of Serious Fraud Office* [1992] 3 All ER 456.

[67] Criminal Justice Act 1967, s 12.

[68] By Crown Court (Advance Disclosure of Expert Evidence) Rules 1987. See now Criminal Procedure Rules.

[69] Criminal Justice and Public Order Act 1994, ss 34–38.

[70] See *R* v *Bryant and Dickson* (1946) 31 Cr App R 146.

precise extent of that duty was, though, uncertain,[71] and Guidelines were issued by the Attorney-General[72] to rectify that. These formed the corner-stone of the rules relating to disclosure, and were regarded as 'to all intents and purposes' as having the force of law,[73] until the scope of the common law obligations was settled by the Court of Appeal.[74]

The effect of this change of approach was to meet some of the concerns of the Royal Commission on Criminal Justice, which, in 1993, stated[75] that:

> the defence can require the police and prosecution to comb through large masses of material in the hope either of causing delay or chancing upon something which will induce the prosecution to drop the case rather than to have to disclose the material concerned. The defence may do this by successive requests for more material, far beyond the stage at which it could be reasonably claimed that the information was likely to cast a doubt upon the prosecution case. Although it may be time consuming and wasteful of the sources for the police to check all the materials requested they may have to do so if they are to be sure that it can properly be released.

Despite the development by the common law of a modified approach, in 1995 a government consultation paper[76] proposed the introduction of a statutory scheme of disclosure, governing both prosecution and defence. This scheme was implemented by the Criminal Procedure and Investigations Act 1996. The 1996 Act introduced a new and complex scheme of disclosure, applicable to both prosecution and defence, supplemented by a Code of Practice made by the Home Secretary.[77] This now governs how material acquired during an investigation is recorded, preserved, and produced to the prosecutor by the investigator, and provides for the recording of material generally, and for the separate recording of what is known as 'sensitive material'. This Code is important, because, self-evidently, only if the prosecutor is in possession, or has access to, all the potentially relevant material can he make a judgment as to what, if anything, should be disclosed.

The 1996 Act creates a scheme of disclosure which is basically constructed in three stages. The first is primary prosecution disclosure. The second is the giving of a defence statement, to be followed by the third and final stage, secondary prosecution disclosure. This three-stage process was itself significantly modified by provisions contained in the Criminal Justice Act 2003 mostly brought into force on 4 April 2005. Despite the youth of the 1996 Act provisions, the Auld Review found them to be unsatisfactory in key respects, and not working as Parliament had intended. It also considered that the duties

---

[71] See Royal Commission on Criminal Procedure, Cmnd 8092, HMSO, 1981, which found the practices of police forces to be inconsistent and variable.

[72] (1981) 74 Cr App R 302. [73] Royal Commission on Criminal Justice.

[74] *R v Melvin and Dingle* 20 September 1993, unreported; *R v Brown* [1995] 1 Cr App R 191; *R v Keane* (1994) 99 Cr App R 1. The test adopted was as follows – 'I would judge to be material in the realm of disclosure that which can be seen on a sensible appraisal by the prosecution: (1) to be relevant or possibly relevant to an issue in the case; (2) to raise or possibly raise a new issue whose existence is not apparent from the evidence the prosecution proposes to use; (3) to hold out a real (as opposed to fanciful) prospect of providing a lead on evidence which goes to (1) or (2)'.

[75] *Op cit*, Ch 6, para 42. [76] Cm 2262, HMSO, 1993.

[77] Under Part II of the Criminal Procedure and Investigations Act 1996.

Fig. 3 Process of disclosure

imposed on the defence did not go far enough. These issues are addressed as we deal with the detailed provisions below.

2 PROSECUTION DISCLOSURE

Section 3(1) originally provided that the prosecutor (i.e. the CPS) must disclose to the accused any prosecution material[78] which has not been previously disclosed to the accused, and which, *in the prosecutor's opinion*, might undermine the case for the prosecution against the accused. Alternatively, he must give to the accused a written statement that there is no such material. At the same time, the prosecutor gives to the accused a schedule of non-sensitive material which he has received from the disclosure officer. By these means, the accused should be provided with relevant unused material, together with a schedule of material which is relevant and which has been acquired by the prosecutor, and, through these documents, judge what further documents may, or should, be disclosable in the light of the needs of the defence. Thus, statements by witnesses who contradict the testimony of those who will be called to testify for the prosecution, inconsistent forensic evidence, the previous convictions of prosecution witnesses, matters relating to the credibility of prosecution witnesses, and inconsistent versions of the events in question are all examples of material that fall within the scope of section 3.

This first stage, known originally as *primary prosecution disclosure* but renamed *initial prosecution disclosure* by the Criminal Justice Act 2003, made the test at this stage essentially subjective. That, though, was open to criticism, putting the judgment of the prosecutor on this matter effectively beyond judicial scrutiny, and is changed by the 2003 Act.[79] The words in section 3 (highlighted above in italics) are repealed, and the

---

[78] Defined by 1996 Act, s 8. See *DPP v Wood, DPP v McGillicuddy* [2005] EWHC 2986 (Admin).
[79] Criminal Justice Act 2003, s 32.

duty extended to include evidence that might be considered capable of assisting the defence's case. The decision of the prosecutor is, henceforth, reviewable if any challenge is made by the defence.

3 SENSITIVE MATERIAL

(a) Introduction

A court has the power to refuse to disclose certain types of information in the public interest. The rule of evidence known as public interest immunity permits the withholding of otherwise relevant material from a party to proceedings on the grounds that its disclosure is not in the public interest.[80] For example, it may deal with matters relating to national security, or reveal the identity of a member of the security services thus rendering that person operationally ineffective. One general class of case where the courts have been prepared to uphold claims of public interest immunity is that relating to information concerning law enforcement. The right of the police to withhold information concerning police informers was recognized in *Marks* v *Beyfus*,[81] and has been extended to the location, and identity of occupants, of police observation posts.[82] Other successful claims of public interest immunity have related to records relating to the welfare of children.[83] The 1996 Act leaves the substantive rules governing disclosure of sensitive material unchanged, but changes the procedure to be followed. Provisions in the 1996 Act[84] permit such material to be withheld where disclosure would be contrary to the public interest.

(b) Definition

The definition of sensitive material goes beyond that protected by public interest immunity, and extends to material that is confidential in nature. What is, or is not sensitive material, will initially be determined by the disclosure officer, but subject to the ultimate decision of the court. Examples of such material given by the Code of Practice include the following:

(a) material relating to national security;

(b) material received from the intelligence and security agencies;

(c) material relating to intelligence from foreign sources which reveals intelligence gathering methods which are sensitive;

(d) material such as telephone subscriber cheques and itemized billing which is supplied to an investigator for intelligence purposes only;

(e) material given in confidence;

---

[80] See, generally, *Conway* v *Rimmer* [1968] AC 910; *Air Canada* v *Secretary of State for Trade* [1983] 1 All ER 96; *Makanjuola* v *Commissioner of Police for the Metropolis* [1992] 3 All ER 617.
[81] (1890) 25 QBD 494.
[82] See *R* v *Hackett* [1986] Crim LR 462; *R* v *Hennessy* (1979) 68 Cr App R 419; *R* v *Agar* [1990] Crim LR 183; *R* v *Rankine* [1986] 2 All ER 566.
[83] *R* v *K (Trevor Douglas)* (1993) 97 Cr App R 342; *Re D (An Infant)* [1970] 1 All ER 1088.
[84] See ss 3(6), 7(5), 8(5), 9(8).

(f)   material relating to the identity or activities of informants, or undercover police officers, or other persons supplying information to the police who may be in danger if their identities are revealed;

(g)   material revealing the location of premises or other places used for police surveillance or the identity of any person allowing a police officer to use them for surveillance;

(h)   material revealing, either directly or indirectly, techniques and methods relied on by a police officer in the course of a criminal investigation, for example covert surveillance techniques, or other methods of detecting crime;

(i)   material whose disclosure might facilitate the commission of other offences or hinder the prevention and detection of crime;

(j)   internal police communications such as management minutes;

(k)   material on the strength of which search warrants were obtained;

(l)   material containing details of persons taking part in identification parades;

(m)   material supplied to an investigator during a criminal investigation which has been generated by an official other body concerned with the regulation or supervision of bodies corporate or of persons engaged in financial activities;

(n)   material supplied to an investigator during a criminal investigation which relates to a child witness and which has been generated by a local authority social services department or other party contacted by the investigator during the investigation.

The disclosure officer in the first instance compiles a list of sensitive material, which is supplied to the prosecutor. It is for the prosecutor to decide whether or not a claim to withhold relevant material is to be made. Clearly, if a document is not relevant and material, it need not be disclosed, and issues of public interest immunity do not arise. Where a claim of immunity is made in respect of documents that are relevant, the court has to balance the respective public interest in maintaining the sensitivity of the document, on the one hand, and in ensuring a fair trial of an accused, on the other. This balancing function, in a criminal case, is not at all easy, and, although the case law[85] suggests that relevant material can be withheld in a criminal case, it is unlikely to be withheld where material may assist the defence. The Scott Report into the Arms for Iraq scandal observed that there was no reported case:

> in which the judge has concluded that documents would be of assistance to the defendant that is none the less declined on public interest immunity grounds to order them to be disclosed. The firm conclusion is, in my opinion justified, that in criminal cases the only question should be whether the documents might be of assistance to the defendant.

---

[85] See *R v Chief Constable of the West Midlands Police, ex parte Wiley* [1995] 1 AC 274, [1994] 3 All ER 420. *R v Governor of Brixton Prison, ex parte Osman* [1992] 1 All ER 108, [1991] 1 WLR 281; *R v Clowes* [1992] 3 All ER 440.

(c) The issues

This obviously raises fundamental issues, both in terms of the principle of withholding material and the decision-making process to determine the matter. At common law the law recognized that the prosecution might have to make an application without the defendant being present, or, exceptionally, without even knowing about the application (known as an *ex parte* application).[86] The 1996 Act sets out a similar procedure for dealing with applications to withhold sensitive material. The question as to how such cases are to be dealt with, consistent with the Article 6 rights of a defendant, was authoritatively dealt with by the House of Lords in *R v H and C*,[87] in dealing with an appeal where the appellant contended that the trial judge was right to require the Attorney-General to appoint special counsel to represent the defendants in an *ex parte* hearing held in their absence and that of their own lawyers.[88] The court considered that derogation from the principle of full disclosure might be justified where there is a risk to an important public interest, but only to the minimum necessary to protect that public interest and never at the expense of the overall fairness of the trial itself. If material did not weaken the prosecution case, or strengthen that of the defence, there was no obligation to disclose it. If it were neutral, again no obligation to disclose existed, but it should be brought to the attention of the court. There would be very few cases where the prosecution could not make some measure of disclosure to the defence, even if that is confined to telling the defendant that an *ex parte* application is being made. If material is of serious help to a defendant, there was a serious question as to whether a defendant could receive a fair trial at all, even if special counsel were, wholly exceptionally, appointed by the Attorney-General to safeguard the interests of the defendant. Special counsel should only be appointed where the trial judge was satisfied that no other course would adequately meet the overriding requirement of fairness to the defendant. On the particular facts, in a drugs case turning on observation evidence and alleged police impropriety, the trial judge had not fully examined the nature of the prosecution evidence and the basis of the claim, and thus the decision to appoint special counsel was premature. However, the special counsel procedures do not of themselves infringe Article 6 of the Convention.[89]

4 DEFENCE DISCLOSURE

(a) Background

The law has, since 1967, required an accused to give seven days' notice of his intention to adduce evidence in support of an alibi.[90] A failure to do so meant that the evidence

---

[86] *R v Ward* [1993] 2 All ER 577.   [87] [2004] 2 Cr App R 10.
[88] Relying on *Edwards and Lewis v United Kingdom*, App 396457/98 and 40451/98, unreported, 22 July 2003.
[89] See *R v H & C, supra.*
[90] An 'alibi' is an assertion that the accused person was elsewhere at the time of the commission of the offence.

could not be adduced without the leave of the court.[91] The purpose of the rule is to enable checks to be made by the prosecution as to the truth or otherwise of the claims of the accused that he was elsewhere at the time of the commission of the offence. Further, in cases of serious or complex fraud where a preparatory hearing is held,[92] the defence might have been required to disclose the general nature of its defence (though not the names of the witnesses it proposes to call), and the principal areas of disagreement.

Apart from these cases, and the obligation to disclose expert evidence, discussed above, there was no general duty on the defence to disclose in advance the nature and content of the defence upon which it is proposed to rely. This so-called 'right to silence' meant that it was not open to a court to invite a jury to draw adverse inferences from a failure to disclose pre-trial the facts relied upon by the defence.[93] Various calls for change were made. In 1972, the 11th Report of the Criminal Law Revision Committee recommended that a court should be permitted to draw inferences from silence in court, or from a failure to disclose facts subsequently relied upon by the defence.[94] The report was highly controversial,[95] and not acted upon. More recently, the Court of Appeal in *R v Alladice*[96] considered that it was 'high time' that some change in the law was made. This was indeed recommended in 1988 by the Working Group on the Right to Silence,[97] established by the Home Secretary. The question of defence disclosure was one of the most controversial issues considered by the Royal Commission on Criminal Justice. It took the view that no change should be made in respect of the 'right to silence', except in respect of disclosure of the defence proposed to be relied upon. The majority[98] believed that those who intended to contest the charges against them should be obliged to disclose the substance of their defence in advance of trial, or indicate that they would not be calling any evidence but simply argue that the prosecution has failed to prove its case.[99] A failure to do so, or an explanation at trial different from the one given in advance, or the advancing of mutually exclusive alternative defences, should be a matter from which the jury could draw adverse inferences, subject to the discretion of the court to prevent this where good reasons existed. A defendant who did not disclose would not generally be entitled to further disclosure of material from the prosecution.

The rationale for such proposals was a desire to reduce 'trial by ambush' involving springing a defence upon the prosecution without warning. The Royal Commission did not consider the proposals to infringe the right of defendants not to incriminate themselves, but accepted that a problem existed only in a minority of cases.[100] By contrast, the dissenting opinion in essence questioned whether the fundamental right of the defence not to respond until trial, and to require the prosecution to prove its case, should be changed where no real problem exists. It also pointed to the ineffectiveness of

---

[91] Criminal Justice Act 1967, s 11.   [92] See p 629, *post*.   [93] *R v Gilbert* (1977) 66 Cr App R 237.
[94] Cmnd 4991 (HMSO, 1972).   [95] See, e.g., MacKenna at [1972] Crim LR 605.
[96] (1988) 87 Cr App R 380.
[97] See Zuckerman, 'Trial By Unfair Means – The Report of the Working Group on the Right to Silence' [1989] Crim LR 855.
[98] With one dissentient: see RCCJ, pp 221–35.   [99] Ibid, Ch 6, paras 56–73.
[100] Ch 4, para 19, relying on data from the Crown Court survey.

the advance disclosure powers in serious fraud cases.[101] These recommendations were, broadly, implemented by the 'right to silence' provisions contained in the Criminal Justice and Public Order Act 1994.

(b) Defence disclosure under the 1996 Act

The scheme of disclosure introduced by the Criminal Procedure and Investigations Act 1996 contained provisions relating to defence disclosure. The Act made a significant change by requiring defence disclosure following primary prosecution disclosure. Under the original section 5, once the prosecutor has complied or purported to comply, with the duty of primary prosecution disclosure, the accused was under a duty to serve on the prosecutor a defence statement. A defence statement was defined as a written statement:

(a) setting out in general terms the nature of the accused's defence;

(b) indicating the matters on which he takes issue with the prosecution;

(c) setting out, in the case of each such matter, the reason why he takes issue with the prosecution.

The purpose of this scheme was to avoid so called 'trial by ambush', with the accused coming up with a defence at a late stage[102] but also was intended to permit a prosecutor to reassess what has been disclosed, and what further needs to be disclosed, in the light of positive knowledge as to what the defence actually is. Similar provisions applied specifically in the context of alibi evidence.[103] Yet even these provisions were considered inadequate by the Auld Review, which observed:[104]

> I can understand why, as a matter of tactics, a defendant might wish to prefer to keep his cards close to his chest. But that is not a valid reason for preventing a full and fair hearing on the issues canvassed at the trial. A criminal trial is not a game under which a defendant should be presented with a sporting chance. It is a search for the truth.

It concluded that defence statements under pre-existing provisions disclosed very little. Further, despite section 11(3) of the 1996 Act (which allows inferences to be drawn from a failure to make adequate defence disclosure, similar to those in the Criminal Justice Act 1987 concerning cases of serious or complex fraud,[105] and to the provisions in sections 34, 36, and 37 of the Criminal Justice and Public Order Act 1994 governing silence at or before trial)[106] there were few effective sanctions for failure to comply. The results were sometimes aborted trials, poorly prepared prosecution files, wasted witness or victim time through unnecessary attendance at court, and consequential knock-on financial costs to the courts, CPS, and Criminal Defence Service. Changes were thus

---

[101] Page 222, para 8, relying on Levi, *The Investigation, Prosecution and Trial of Serious Fraud* (Royal Commission on Criminal Justice Research Study No 14, HMSO, 1993).

[102] See p 601, *ante*.   [103] Section 11 of the Criminal Justice Act 1967 is repealed.

[104] Auld Review Ch 10, para 154.   [105] See Criminal Justice Act 1987, s 10.

[106] See p 606, *ante*.

introduced by the Criminal Justice Act 2003, the effect of which is to widen the requirement for defence disclosure.

A new section 6A of the 1996 Act[107] amends the definition of a defence statement. It must be in writing[108] and:

(a) set out the nature of the accused's defence including any particular defences on which he intends to rely;

(b) indicate the matters of fact on which he takes issue with the prosecution;

(c) set out, in the case of each matter, why he takes issue with the prosecution; and

(d) indicate any point of law (including any point as to the admissibility of evidence) which he wishes to take, and any authority on which he intends to rely for that purpose.

Further, a new section 6C[109] requires a defendant to indicate whether he intends to call any persons (other than himself) as witnesses, unless that detail has already been given as part of the details of an alibi. The details to be given include names, addresses, and dates of birth (where known). A failure to give this detail does not prevent the witness being called, but, rather, allows comment to be made and inferences to be drawn from a failure to do so. The purpose of this additional detail is so that investigators can run checks on proposed defence witnesses to look at any criminal record or antecedents, as well as to diminish the effects of 'surprise witnesses'. It facilitates the prosecution examining the veracity of any potential witnesses, although, on the other hand, may deter some potential witnesses from coming forward (not wishing to have details given, in advance, to the police). Because of concerns that witnesses may be, or feel, intimidated, new provisions impose obligations on the Home Secretary to issue a Code of Practice for police interviews of defence witnesses.[110]

Thus a greater measure or more specific information is required by the new law. The Royal Commission on Criminal Justice had envisaged only brief details as to the offence[111] and the Auld Review itself did not think that changes of this type to defence statement provisions were necessary.[112] The practical difficulties involved in providing this level of detail, within tight time limits, may be substantial. Which facts are in dispute and what points of law are to be taken often will not be clear because of the need to evaluate and investigate the prosecution case, and even changes to legal representation may complicate matters, without always being necessary. Relevant points of law may be obvious on the face of the documentation, or from pleas and directions hearings or preparatory hearings. The provisions as a whole perhaps mark an ongoing trend towards the criminal trial becoming more inquisitorial in nature and less of a 'contest', perhaps a conclusion supported also by the additional provisions on expert evidence.[113]

---

[107] See Criminal Justice Act 2003, s 33(3).

[108] Such a statement is deemed to be given with the authority of the defendant: see 1996 Act, s 6E, inserted by Criminal Justice Act 2003, s 38.

[109] See Criminal Justice Act 2003, s 34.

[110] 1996 Act, s 21A, inserted by Criminal Justice Act 2003, s 40.

[111] Royal Commission, *op cit*, para 68, p 99.

[112] *Op cit*, Ch 10, para 180.   [113] See p 615, *post*.

5 FURTHER PROSECUTION DISCLOSURE

The third stage of the disclosure scheme is further prosecution disclosure. Once the defence has engaged in defence disclosure, it is the duty of the prosecutor to keep the issue of disclosure under review. This duty, formally marked by secondary prosecution disclosure under section 7 of the 1996 Act[114] requires the disclosure of prosecution material which might reasonably be considered capable of undermining the case for the prosecution or assisting the case for the defence (i.e. the same test as for initial prosecution disclosure). Material must be disclosed as soon as practicable. This test is objective in nature, i.e. it is open to a court to review the judgment made and its reasonableness, but judged by the state of affairs existing at the time.

6 EXPERT EVIDENCE

(a) Introduction

Section 81 of the Police and Criminal Evidence Act 1984 authorizes the making of rules regarding the disclosure of expert evidence. The Crown Court (Advance Notice of Expert Evidence) Rules 1987 were made under that power, and apply to trials on indictment.[115] Following committal or sending for trial the party who is seeking to rely on expert evidence, whether of fact or opinion, must furnish to the other party a statement in writing of any finding or opinion upon which he proposes to rely, and, on request in writing, provide a copy of (or access to, if that is more practicable) the records of any observation, test, calculation, or other procedure in respect of which the finding or opinion is based. A failure to disclose means that the evidence cannot be adduced without the leave of the court.

This obligation of disclosure is not the only obligation. In *R* v *Ward*[116] the Court of Appeal stressed that there is a common law obligation upon a government forensic scientist to act impartially, and to disclose any scientific evidence that might arguably assist the defence. Failure to comply with this obligation was one of the principal reasons for quashing the convictions of the defendant in that case. It was failure to disclose fully in this way that caused problems in *R* v *Ward* and other cases.[117] Such an obligation to disclose does not meet the criticism of those who argue that the trial process is unfairly tilted in favour of the prosecution because of its command of forensic science and other scientific facilities,[118] and generally the imbalance of resources. Some argue that the court itself should appoint its own expert witnesses, to report impartially to the court.[119] The whole question was examined extensively by the Royal Commission on Criminal Justice.[120]

---

[114] Repealed and replaced by a new s 7A by Criminal Justice Act 2003, s 33.

[115] The power to make rules in respect of expert evidence in summary cases has been conferred by the Criminal Procedure and Investigations Act 1996, s 19. See now the Criminal Procedure Rules 2005.

[116] [1993] 2 All ER 577, [1993] 1 WLR 619.

[117] See, e.g. *R* v *Maguire* [1992] QB 936, [1992] 2 All ER 433.

[118] For a description of the organization of forensic science facilities, see the RCCJ, *op cit*, Ch 7, para 6–36.

[119] See *Spencer* [1992] Crim LR.   [120] Report, Ch 9.

The Commission considered, but rejected, a proposal to create an independent forensic science agency, as opposed to one being part of a government department or police authority. Instead, it proposed[121] the establishment of a Forensic Science Advisory Council to report to the Home Secretary on the performance, achievements, and efficiency of the forensic science laboratories, in both the private and public sectors. Subject to a rule that the same laboratory should not take on work for both prosecution and defence in the same case, public sector laboratories should look on themselves as equally available to defence and prosecution. This is important in the light of research findings[122] that defence solicitors sometimes encounter difficulty in finding suitable independent experts to interpret prosecution findings.[123] In respect of the general duty of disclosure, the Royal Commission welcomed the approach taken in *R* v *Ward*.[124] It also recommended streamlining legal aid provision to assist in this respect.

(b)   The problems – a more inquisitorial approach?

Of significance is the approach taken by the majority of the Commission towards a more inquisitorial system in respect of forensic science evidence. The Royal Commission found[125] that a sizeable minority of contested Crown Court cases involve scientific evidence. In approximately 25 per cent of such cases there was a defence challenge to such evidence, and in some 800 cases a year not only was such a challenge made but also expert evidence was called on behalf of the defence. In these cases the duty of disclosure applies equally to the defence as to the prosecution. Hitherto, however, the defence has been under no duty to disclose the evidence it has obtained from experts whom it does not intend to call, perhaps because it is unfavourable. Nor was there a duty to disclose expert evidence acquired by the defence for the purposes of discrediting prosecution evidence through cross-examination. The Royal Commission recommended changes which would have had the effect of requiring a greater measure of pre-trial discussion between experts, and imposed a duty to indicate the areas of prosecution expert evidence which are not agreed.[126] It also made recommendations as to the handling of expert evidence at the trial.[127] It emphatically rejected the appointment of a court expert, or an assessor, whose views would not be susceptible to examination or cross-examination.

Changes to the law were not made until the passage of the Criminal Justice Act 2003 following the recommendations of the Auld Review. Section 35 of the 2003 Act inserted into the Criminal Procedure and Investigations Act 1996 a new section 6D, which provides that if the accused instructs a person with a view to his providing an expert opinion for possible use as evidence at the trial of the accused, he must give to the court

---

[121] Ch 7, para 3.2.

[122] Roberts and Willmore, *The Role of Forensic Science Evidence in Criminal Proceedings* (Royal Commission on Criminal Justice Research Study No 11 (HMSO, 1992)); Steventon, *The Ability to Challenge DNA Evidence* (Royal Commission on Criminal Justice Research Study No 9 (HMSO, 1992)).

[123] See RCCJ, Ch 9, paras 50–53.   [124] Ibid, para 47.

[125] Crown Court Survey: see RCCJ, para 57. The estimates ranged from 30–40 per cent of cases, in quantity some 10,000 cases per year.

[126] Royal Commission, *op cit*, paras 62–64.   [127] Ibid, Ch 9, para 4.

and the prosecutor a notice specifying that person's name and address unless that has already been specified in the defence statement. This duty is confined to the supply of details as to the name and address of the possible witness. It does not require disclosure of the expert's report, which is likely to be protected from disclosure by the doctrine of legal professional privilege.[128] Curiously, section 11 of the 1996 Act (inferences from failure to supply defence statement) does not apply to the new section 6D, and there is no sanction for non-compliance, which may lead to patchy compliance. Concerns also arise about how this requirement may affect the way defence lawyers interact with experts, in particular as to the amount and type of privileged information given to the expert instructed.

The real difficulties in relation to disputed expert evidence were vividly illustrated in *R v Harris, Rock, Chery, Faulder*.[129] In relation to the controversial and disputed 'Shaken Baby syndrome'[130], when four convictions were reviewed, the Court of Appeal heard from no less than 25 medical expert witnesses. The Court of Appeal reviewed and adopted principles as to how expert evidence should be presented and dealt with. These are of equal validity in criminal and civil cases.

- Expert evidence should be seen to be the independent product of the expert, uninfluenced as to form or content by the case itself.[131]

- The expert should provide an independent assessment by way of objective unbiased opinion in relation to matters only within his expertise.

- The facts and assumptions should be clearly stated.

- If the data on which the evidence is based is inadequate, the expert should say so, and make only a provisional assessment.

- Any change of opinion should be disclosed.

- The basis of any hypothesis on which the opinion is based should be explained, and any controversy about it referred to.[132]

The Criminal Procedure Rules[133] require experts to consult together, to agree points of agreement and disagreement.

7 ADEQUACY OF DISCLOSURE RULES

The effectiveness of any scheme of prosecution disclosure depends on those whose duty it is to decide such questions being aware of the full extent of evidence available. Research shows that the regime under the 1996 Act may still have problems, with a

---

[128] As to which, see p 379, *ante*.   [129] [2006] 1 Cr App R 5.

[130] On this, see, in particular, *R v Clark (Sally)* [2003] EWCA Crim 1020. For other issues regarding expert evidence see *R v Cannings* [2004] EWCA Crim 1.

[131] For this and other statements see *dicta* of Cresswell J in *National Justice Cia Naviera SA v Prudential Assurance Co Ltd (Ikaria Reefer)* [1993] 2 Lloyds Rep 68.

[132] *In re AB (Child Abuse: Expert Witnesses)* [1995] 1 FLR 181.

[133] R 24. See also Guidance given by Attorney-General in February 2006.

lack of effective judicial enforcement.[134] The findings show that, generally, there is a lack of resources for both prosecutors and police; a lack of training; police conflicts of interest; reliance on defective schedules; the increasing lack of defence or Crown Court experience of CPS staff; the lack of adequate remuneration for members of the Bar to read unused material. These findings point to issues other than the disclosure rules themselves as being the key factors if the 1996 Act provisions are to fully achieve their objectives.

THE INDICTMENT

1 INTRODUCTION

A Bill of indictment is a written or printed accusation of crime made at the suit of the Crown against one or more persons. A Bill of indictment may be preferred by any person[135] against any other person before the Crown Court, generally within twenty-eight days of sending for trial or notice of transfer, or within a period to be specified following a person being sent for trial under Schedule 3 of the 1998 Act.[136] However, a Bill of indictment is of no legal validity in itself. It only becomes a legal document when it is turned into an indictment proper by being signed by the appropriate officer of the court, who in turn can only sign the draft Bill if he is satisfied that the accused is validly before the court.[137] The judge of the court may direct the appropriate officer to sign the Bill, either on his own motion or on the application of the prosecution. After it has been signed, the proper officer must on request supply to the defendant a copy free of charge.[138]

Where the Bill is preferred following sending for trial it may charge any offence which appears on the statements, in addition to or in place of the offence or offences for which he was committed, subject to the normal rules as to joinder of offences.[139] It is immaterial that the 'added' offences involve a higher penalty than the original charge or charges. Although the accused will necessarily have knowledge of the facts alleged to constitute the offence, if not of the precise charge based on those facts, there are obvious possibilities of injustice, and the Court of Appeal has said[140] that whenever it is decided to bring such 'fresh' charges, the police ought to see the defendant and

---

[134] See Disclosure: A Protocol for the Control and Management of Unused Material in the Crown Court, 2005, available at www.hmcourts-service.gov.uk. See Zander, *Mission Impossible* (2006) 156 NLJ 618. For relevant case law, see *R v Harris* [2006] 1 Cr App R 5; *R v B* [2006] EWCA Crim 417, [2006] Crim LR 745.

[135] Except in those cases where a private person has no right to institute proceedings: see p 567, *ante*.

[136] See p 603, *ante*.

[137] Through notice of transfer, voluntary Bill, or by direction of the Court of Appeal. An alternative procedure under the Perjury Act 1911, s 9, existed until abolished by the Prosecution of Offences Act 1985, s 28.

[138] Indictment Rules 1971, r 10(1).   [139] See p 620, *post*.

[140] In *R v Dickson* [1969] 1 All ER 729, [1969] 1 WLR 405, where the defendant's solicitors had six days' notice of 'fresh' charges.

warn him of the charges under caution, so that he may make a statement in answer if he wishes.

The whole of the indictment may consist of such 'substitute' charge or charges. If the defendant considers that one or more of such charges does not fairly arise out of the facts in the depositions he may move to quash the indictment. It is then for the trial judge to rule on the sufficiency of the indictment. Where, however, the defendant was sent for trial in respect of two offences which had been repealed by statute, it was held that he was never lawfully committed at all, and it was immaterial that the third count of the indictment was in respect of an offence which both existed and was disclosed by the depositions.[141]

2 FORM AND CONTENTS

The rules as to the form of indictments are now contained in the Indictments Act 1915 and the Indictment Rules 1971. The drafting of the indictment is the responsibility of counsel for the prosecution,[142] whose duty it is to ensure that it is in proper form for the particular case. In most cases, other than those of complexity or difficulty, the actual drafting is undertaken by, or on behalf of, the Crown Prosecution Service.

An indictment is in three parts; introductory matters, statement of offence, and particulars of offence. The introductory matters are twofold, first the court of trial and secondly the name of the defendant, appearing in the form:

THE QUEEN v [Defendant] charged as follows:

As regards the statement of offence and particulars of offence, the rules provide[143] that every indictment must contain, and need not contain more than, a statement of the specific offence with which the defendant is charged, describing the offence shortly, together with such particulars as are necessary to give reasonable information as to the nature of the charge. Where, however, the offence is created by statute, there must be a reference to the statute and to the relevant section, and all the essential elements of the offence must be disclosed in the particulars, unless the defendant is not prejudiced or embarrassed by failure to describe any such element.[144] The fact that an indictment is defective does not render the trial a nullity. Whether a conviction obtained on an indictment that is deficient can stand will turn, ultimately, upon whether injustice or unfairness has been caused to the defendant. Whether these provisions are effective is open to doubt. The Royal Commission on Criminal Justice observed[145] that indictments were largely formal in nature, giving little information. It found widespread evidence of

---

[141] *R v Lamb* [1969] 1 All ER 45, [1968] 1 WLR 1946.

[142] *R v Newland* [1988] QB 402; [1988] 2 All ER 891.

[143] Indictment Rules 1971, r 5(1) and, now, Criminal Procedure Rules. Cf. the rules for the content of an information: see p 657, *post*. There may also be approved forms of indictment for individual offences: ibid.

[144] Ibid, r 6. It is not necessary for the indictment to specify or negative any exception, exemption, excuse, proviso, or qualification. There is, again, an analogy with the rules for the content of an information.

[145] Ch 8, para 5.

a failure to comply with the duty to give reasonable information as to the nature of the charge, and agreed with the Law Commission when that body observed:

> There are strong reasons of justice and efficiency why the particulars in each count in an indictment should contain sufficiently clear factual allegations to inform the jury of the issues it will have to decide, and more generally, to enable the indictment to operate as a practical agenda for the trial.[146]

3 JOINDER; SEPARATE TRIALS

Hitherto we have considered an indictment charging one offence only. However, within certain limits, a single indictment may charge more than one offence, or be drawn in respect of more than one defendant, or both. This is known as joinder.

(a) Joinder of offenders

The basic rule is that where two or more persons join in the commission of an offence, all or any number of them may be jointly indicted for that offence, or each may be indicted separately. If they are in fact indicted separately there would be no power in any court to order 'consolidation' of the indictments, however desirable this might seem from the point of view of saving time and expense,[147] but, of course, the same result could be achieved through the use of the voluntary Bill procedure[148] to supersede existing indictments. However, joinder is now very common. The matter is one of judicial discretion, and what is in the interests of justice. Where the individual offences of the different accused are related to each other by virtue of time or some other link, then it may well be appropriate for them to be tried together.[149] The fact that evidence against one accused is inadmissible against another will be a relevant factor, though not necessarily decisive. Another consideration will be the length of the trial that will ensue should they be tried together. This is returned to later.[150]

(b) Joinder of offences

The basic rule is as follows:

> Charges for any offences may be joined in the same indictment if those charges are found on the same facts or form or are a part of a series of offences of the same or a similar character.

It should also be noted that in some limited circumstances summary offences may be tried with offences that are to be tried on indictment.[151]

It is a matter of fact and degree in each case as to whether this rule is satisfied, in accordance with principles set out in the cases. In *Ludlow* v *Metropolitan Police*

---

[146] Counts in an Indictment (Law Commission, 1992).
[147] *Crane* v *Director of Public Prosecutions* [1921] 2 AC 299.   [148] See p 601, *ante.*
[149] *R* v *Assim* [1966] 2 QB 249, [1966] 2 All ER 881.   [150] See p 622, *post.*
[151] Criminal Justice Act 1988, s 40. The charge must be founded on the same facts or evidence, or be part of a series of offences.

Commissioner[152] the House of Lords indicated that in deciding whether offences were of a similar character, regard should be had both to their legal and factual characteristics. To show a 'series of offences' the prosecution must be able to show some nexus between them, a 'feature of similarity which in all the circumstances of the case enables the offences to be tried together'. It is not necessary that the evidence in respect of one charge should be admissible on another, a conclusion left ambiguous and unclear by the House of Lords in *Director of Public Prosecutions* v *P*,[153] where the tests for the use of evidence relevant to one count to prove another were reviewed and clarified, but appeared to conclude that the tests for admissibility and joinder in a sexual case were the same.[154]

The application of the principle was seen in a non-sexual case in *R* v *Cannan*[155] where the Court of Appeal held that a trial judge was entitled in his discretion to order the trial together of six offences involving three separate women. Three counts involved abduction, rape and buggery against one woman, another alleged attempted kidnapping against a second, and two more counts of alleged abduction and murder of a third. Sexual cases, by contrast, are particularly difficult because of the prejudice that may arise. In *Director of Public Prosecutions* v *Boardman*[156] Lord Cross seemed to equate the test for joinder of offences with their admissibility as evidence. He stated that if each count was inadmissible in respect of the other offences then they ought to be tried separately. It is, he said, asking too much of any jury to disregard the other charges when considering each individual charge.

This approach is contrary to the wording of rule 9 itself. Despite the House of Lords not putting the matter beyond doubt in *DPP* v *P*, the wording of rule 9 is clear. In *R* v *Christou*[157] the House of Lords held that where an accused person was charged with sexual offences against more than one person, where the evidence of one complainant was not admissible on charges concerning other complainants, the trial judge had a discretion to order that the charges be tried together. The judge is not obliged to exercise that discretion in favour of the accused simply because the evidence is not admissible on more than one count of the indictment. The key issue is simply: can the issues be resolved fairly? In that case the appellant was charged with sexual offences against his two young female cousins, C and M, with whom he had been living at the time of the alleged offences. The House of Lords concluded that the trial judge had acted properly in requiring that they be tried together, notwithstanding the fact that the evidence of C was not admissible on the counts that related solely to M. Further, in the case of *R* v *West*,[158] the court had to consider the same issue in the context of a non-sexual offence. The appellant had been

---

[152] [1971] AC 29, [1970] 1 All ER 567. The House was considering the appropriate provision of the 1915 Rules, which were materially the same as r 9. See also: *R* v *Kray* [1970] 1 QB 125, [1969] 3 All ER 941.

[153] [1991] 2 AC 447; *sub nom R* v *P* [1991] 3 All ER 337. See *R* v *Tickner* [1992] Crim LR 44.

[154] Evidence can only be considered if it is both relevant and admissible. Admissibility in these circumstances depended on the operation of the so-called similar fact evidence rule. This rule, and others relating to bad character, were significantly altered by Criminal Justice Act 2003, ss 98–114 which came into effect in December 2004.

[155] (1990) 92 Cr App R 16.

[156] [1975] AC 421; *sub nom Boardman* v *Director of Public Prosecutions* [1974] 3 All ER 887.

[157] [1997] AC 117.   [158] [1996] 2 Cr App R 375.

tried and convicted of ten counts of murder. The evidence on many of these counts was admissible on other counts, under the so-called similar fact evidence rule. The Court of Appeal held, however, that the trial judge had acted properly in declining to sever the indictment and order separate trials in respect of three counts which were unaffected by similar fact evidence. This was a matter for the judge's discretion, which he had not exercised improperly.[159]

4 LONG TRIALS: THE NUMBER OF COUNTS AND ACCUSED

(a) The reasons for long trials

It has already been seen that the joinder of offenders, and of charges, is permissible. The danger exists that an indictment may become so overloaded that, as a result, the trial becomes too complex in terms of the issues the jury has to comprehend and decide, or unmanageable in terms of time. On many occasions the courts have complained of indictments which are overloaded.

In *R v Novac*[160] where a large number of counts of sexual offences were laid against four defendants, Bridge LJ observed:

> whatever advantages were expected to accrue from one long trial they were heavily outweighed by the disadvantages. A trial of such dimensions puts an immense burden on both judge and jury. In the course of a four or five day summing up the most careful and conscientious judge may so easily overlook some essential matter. Even if the summing up is faultless, it is by no means cynical to doubt whether the average juror can be expected to take it all in and apply all the directions given. Some criminal prosecutions involve considerations of matters so plainly inextricable and indivisible that a long and complex trial is an ineluctable necessity. But we are convinced that nothing short of the criterion of absolute necessity can justify the imposition of the burden of a very long trial on the court.

The problem has arisen particularly in two different situations. The first concerns the use of conspiracy charges. There may be both evidential and tactical reasons why prosecutors may wish to lay a count of conspiracy in addition to counts alleging specific offences. This practice was disapproved in a Practice Note in 1977.[161] The onus is on the prosecution to justify a joinder of a conspiracy charge with other substantive offences. If it cannot, it must elect to proceed either upon the conspiracy charge or the substantive offences. Justification might exist where the substantive offences which the prosecution is in a position to prove do not adequately reflect the extent and persistence of the defendants' criminality. Thus, for example, there might be evidence to show that a person had been engaged for some time in the importation of drugs of various kinds, although the prosecution might only be able to prove one specific importation.

[159] *R v Trew* (1996).   [160] (1976) 65 Cr App R 107.
[161] [1977] 2 All ER 540; *sub nom Practice Direction* [1977] 1 WLR 537.

Secondly, a number of long complex fraud cases has placed great strain upon the jury trial system.[162] In *R v Cohen*[163] the trial was so long that the judge's summing-up (itself of considerable length) dealt only with one of the issues before the court. In passing sentence following convictions, later quashed on appeal, McKinnon J observed:

> All involved in this case have been called upon to achieve what no-one in our courts should be asked to achieve. That applies to the defendants, to the jury and to me.

Even more startling, a recent fraud case collapsed after over two years, at a cost estimated at over £60 million, having 'lurched from problem to problem, finally [folding] after sickness, jury problems, lengthy delays and disruptions'.[164] Following that fiasco, a Protocol was issued providing detailed guidance as to how such cases should be managed.[165]

But it is not only problems with the subject matter or the indictment. Sometimes it is due to inevitable problems that arise during a trial, and how they are managed. In one recent case a terrorist trial, involving seven defendants, lasted thirteen months, with the jury taking some twenty-seven days – a record – to deliver its verdicts.[166] Reports characterized the trial as plagued by sickness, technical problems, religious holidays and legal wrangles.

(b) Reform

The Roskill Report on Fraud Trials[167] advocated the abolition of jury trial in complex fraud cases to be replaced by trial by judge and two specialist assessors. Such recommendations were a response to a recognition that such trials are inevitably long, causing unacceptable disruption to the lives of jurors, and unduly complex, the evidence often being beyond the comprehension of jurors. Such claims are, of course, difficult to gauge in the light of the prohibition on study of how in fact juries reach their verdicts, and upon what evidence.[168] By contrast, others have argued for the simplification of such cases. In its evidence to the Royal Commission, the Law Society[169] argued that such trials should be simplified by not including superfluous counts, and by keeping prosecution evidence within strict limits, principally by limiting the number of accused in the indictment. The Royal Commission itself considered the restriction of jury trial to be beyond its scope, but echoed the calls set out above for the number of counts or particulars on an indictment to be kept to a minimum.[170] In that regard, its recommendation for a review of the relationship between the criminal law and non-criminal action by

---

[162] See, generally, the Roskill Committee, *op cit*, and Royal Commission on Criminal Justice Report, Ch 7, paras 59–67.

[163] [1992] NLJR 1267. The jury retired on the 184th day of the trial.

[164] *The Times*, 23 March 2005.

[165] See chapter 10, *ante*. Protocol for the control and management of heavy fraud and other complex cases [2005] 2 All ER 249.

[166] See *The Times*, 23 May 2007.   [167] See n 162, *supra*.

[168] Contempt of Court Act 1981, s 8. For discussion of jury trial generally, see p 367, *ante*.

[169] Evidence of the Law Society to the Royal Commission on Criminal Justice (1992).

[170] Ch 8, para 79.

financial regulators may be important in reducing the scope of criminal trials in such cases.[171] The Auld Review recommended trial on indictment without a jury.

5 NON-JURY TRIAL ON INDICTMENT

(a) Long or complex cases

Section 43 of the Criminal Justice Act 2003[172] will permit a prosecutor to apply for a judge-only trial where the subject matter is likely to be complex, the trial long or both long and complex. This change was supported by the Auld Review, which envisaged specialist fraud judge, trial by judge and experts, or trial by judge and lay assessors.[173] A White Paper[174] identified the great strain that long trials imposed on many jurors. Such trials may last for many months, with the juror away from work, perhaps with childcare problems, unable to talk with non-jurors about the case in question, unable to make future plans, or to take time off without adjournments granted by the court. The subject matter may be dry and technical, even tedious.

Examples of failure of high-profile fraud trials are well known. During the period 1988 to 1993, long trials following trials relating to the take-over of the company Guinness led to the conviction of only two of four defendants. In 1995 to 1996, trials of defendants arising out of the dealings of the publisher Robert Maxwell were unsuccessful, costs of up to £30 million having been incurred. And of course the spectacular collapse of the Jubilee line case involving six defendants, after two years and at an estimated cost of £60 million, seemingly makes the case for reform irresistible. Yet, despite these problems, the success rate in cases of serious fraud has been good, in 2002 around 86 per cent.[175] It is a moot question as to whether the system should be judged by the conviction rate alone, but even on that basis the above statistics show that there are many aspects to this problem, particularly as one of the key questions that arises is whether a jury can ever understand a long and complex case. It was, though, the fact that non-jury trial in the Crown Court was seen as wrong in principle by opponents of the change being proposed by the legislation in 2003 that caused this change, and another in section 44, to be so fiercely resisted. Whether in fact it is brought into effect could have been a matter of some doubt in the light of new provisions in Domestic Violence, Crime and Victims Act 2004,[176] although the latest causes célèbres have reignited the debate.

Section 43 will permit non-jury trial where because of length or complexity, the trial would be too burdensome for a jury. What that amounts to will be a matter for a judge to decide when an application is made for a non-jury trial at a preparatory hearing.[177] Many shorter cases can involve issues of complexity, and length alone does not signify

---

[171] Ch 7, para 64.
[172] The government gave an undertaking to review further the whole question of non-jury trial before s 43 is brought into effect.
[173] Auld Review, *op cit*, Ch. 5, para 1097.   [174] *Justice for All*, Cm 5563, 2002.
[175] See HC Cmtte debate on Criminal Justice Bill, HC Cmtte, 4 January 2003, col 321.
[176] As to which, see p 626, *post*.
[177] As to which, see p 629, *post*, and Criminal Justice Act 2003, s 45. An order for non-jury trial will require the approval of the Lord Chief Justice.

complexity. They are, though, alternatives. When deciding an application, the judge must look at ways in which the trial could be simplified so that the length or complexity may be reduced. However, no step is to be regarded as reasonable if it would significantly disadvantage the prosecution.[178]

(b) Danger of jury interference

Section 44 of the Criminal Justice Act 2003 addresses the issue of jury 'nobbling', allowing the prosecution to apply for trial by judge alone in cases where there is, first, a real and present danger of interference with the jury, and, secondly, there is a risk that despite the fact that steps could be taken to protect from these malign influences, the prospect of jury tampering is so substantial that a non-jury trial is necessary in the interests of justice.

This change was prompted by a perceived increase[179] in the numbers of trials collapsing, particularly but not exclusively in London, with interference, or attempted interference, with the jury necessitating the discharge of the jury and the re-commencement of the trial. Section 43 requires there to be a danger of jury tampering. There must be a real and present danger of tampering, and the judge on an application must be satisfied that protection of the jury will not alleviate that risk. Section 44(6) gives examples of where there may be a real and present danger of jury tampering:

(a) where the trial is a re-trial and the jury in the previous trial was discharged because of jury tampering;

(b) where tampering has taken place in previous criminal proceedings involving the defendant or any of the defendants;

(c) where there has been intimidation, or attempted intimidation of any person who is likely to be a witness at the trial.

This last example is extremely wide, with witness intimidation, regrettably, not being uncommon. Its breadth may perhaps be reduced by the fact that the prosecution must show that that risk exists even though steps could be taken to protect the witness. A court will also consider whether that danger can be reduced by adoption of special measures,[180] or by using as evidence the out-of-court statements given to the police by the witness.[181]

The jury tampering may occur during a trial. The effect of section 44 is that the judge will have the power to discharge the jury and continue the trial without a jury, subject to first allowing the parties to make representations. In such cases the judge will be the judge both of fact and law, and of course will be aware of evidence that the jury might not have been allowed to be aware of. This is likely to raise Article 6 issues in the future, following the decision of the Court of Human Rights in *Edwards and Lewis* v *United Kingdom*[182] that the trial judge might have been influenced, unconsciously, by material

---

[178] 2003 Act, s 43(6), (7).
[179] The White Paper, *Justice for All*, *op cit*, contained no statistical evidence on this point.
[180] See p 646, *post*.   [181] Under Criminal Justice Act 2003, s 116. See p 647, *post*.
[182] *The Times*, 29 July 2003.

he was aware of because of an application for public interest immunity which he had dealt with and of which the defence were unaware.

(c) The non-jury trial

Where a non-jury trial is ordered under either section 43 or section 44, the judge decides the case in exactly the same way as the jury would have done, and has all the powers, duties, and rights of the jury.[183] There is, though, one difference: unlike a jury, the judge must state reasons for his decision.

(d) Trial of multiple counts without a jury

The provisions in the Domestic Violence, Crime and Victims Act 2004 which permit trial in the Crown Court without a jury in certain circumstances were far less controversial than those discussed above, for several reasons. First, they implement a Law Commission Report[184] designed to overcome practical problems caused by the Court of Appeal decision in *R v Kidd*.[185] Secondly, they do not dispense with the role of the jury totally in any one case.

The problem faced by a jury in trying a case with many, multiple, counts (particularly in fraud cases) has already been noted. To overcome those problems, prosecutors have been encouraged to indict on sample counts, counts which are indicative of the nature and type of offending. It was long the practice of courts to try a defendant on sample counts, and then to sentence for the totality of the offending identified by the court. However, in *R v Kidd* it was decided that it was improper for a court to have regard, when sentencing, to offences for which the defendant had not been tried and convicted, or had not admitted. That had the effect in some cases of limiting the power of a sentencing court to reflect in the total sentence the multiple nature of the offending. For example, in a case of multiple benefit fraud the totality of the offending may involve many individual procurements of benefit cheques of a total value far in excess of anything that could be adequately reflected by sample counts.[186]

To overcome this problem section 17 of the 2004 Act permits a prosecutor to apply, at a preparatory hearing,[187] that the trial of some, but not all, counts on an indictment be conducted without a jury. The judge must be satisfied that the number of counts on the indictment is likely to mean that trial by jury on all of them would be impracticable, that sample counts could be identified, and that it is in the interests of justice for an order to be made. The effect is that the sample counts will be tried by judge with a jury in the normal way, and then, at the conclusion of that trial the judge is able to order trial of the remaining counts (which are reflected by the sample counts) by a judge without a jury. The judge is not to be bound by the verdict of the jury, but clearly it is highly unlikely that trial by judge only would occur in respect of multiple counts where the defendant had been acquitted on the relevant sample counts. On the other hand, the normal rules

---

[183] Criminal Justice Act 2003, s 48.
[184] Law Com No 277, October 2002, *The Effective Prosecution of Multiple Offending*.
[185] [1998] 1 WLR 604 (otherwise known as *R v Canavan*).
[186] The facts of a pre-*Kidd* case, *R v Evans* [1992] NLJR 1267.   [187] See p 629, *post*.

of evidence will apply: evidence of the multiple offences may well be admissible at the trial before the jury,[188] and convictions in respect of the sample counts will certainly be admissible at the trial without a jury of the multiple examples. The nature of the judge only trial is the same as that identified above.

It remains to be seen what the effect of section 17 is. It may, paradoxically, have the effect of encouraging prosecutors to include more counts in indictments, not less as the courts have consistently urged. And it *could* render unnecessary the introduction of the more controversial powers contained in section 43 of the Criminal Justice Act 2003 unnecessary.

6 DUPLICITY

Where two or more offences are joined in one indictment each one must be alleged in a separate count or paragraph of the indictment.[189] If an indictment in fact charges more than one offence in a single count then it is bad for duplicity. This must be distinguished from the analogous situation which, more accurately, may be described as uncertainty. This arises where a statutory provision contains one offence, which may be committed by a variety of means, or by virtue of different states of mind. Whether a count in an indictment may charge simply by reference to the statutory provision, or must allege the specific ingredients in each count, charging more than one count if necessary, is a question of construction of the relevant statute.[190]

A good example of the problem is contained in section 5 of the Domestic Violence, Crime and Victims Act 2004,[191] which creates an offence of allowing the death of a child or vulnerable adult. The offence can be committed in various ways, and section 5(2) provides that the prosecution do not have to prove which. The question arises as to whether one count in an indictment can allege all or any of the different variants. Of course, a prosecutor can avoid the whole problem in indicting on different counts.

In deciding whether a count is bad for duplicity, regard should be had to the question of whether different maximum punishments exist according to the presence or absence of specific factual ingredients.[192] Where that is so, it is likely that a court will consider the statute to create separate offences, which should therefore be indicated separately. In *Courtie*[193] Lord Diplock (with whom the other Law Lords concurred) held that where one provision involved the imposition of different penalties depending on whether the prosecution established particular factual ingredients then Parliament had created two different offences, which should be the subject of separate counts or informations.[194]

---

[188] See Criminal Justice Act 2003, s 101.

[189] Indictment Rules 1971, r 4(2), see Criminal Procedure Rules now, 2. Each count is equivalent to a separate indictment. Counts must be numbered consecutively.

[190] See p 660, *post*, for similar issues in respect of duplicity of charges of summary offences.

[191] Which came into force on 21 March 2005. [192] *R v Courtie* [1984] AC 463, [1984] 1 All ER 740.

[193] See n 192, above. [194] See p 660, *post*.

7   OBJECTING TO THE INDICTMENT: AMENDMENT

If the defendant desires to object to the validity of the indictment he should do so before he is arraigned. The grounds of objection have already been explained[195] though the power of the court to quash an indictment to prevent abuse of the process of the court should also be noted.

The Court of Appeal does not readily hear objections to the validity of an indictment where the objection was not taken at the trial, although failure to take it is not insuperable. When objection is taken the court may (unless it rules against the objection altogether) either quash the indictment or amend it. The Indictments Act 1915 permits a court to make such order of amendment as it thinks necessary to meet the circumstances of the case, unless amendment cannot be made without injustice.[196]

A new count may be added before the defendant is arraigned, and even after arraignment a count can be added charging a completely new offence;[197] the question is one of degree depending on the facts of the particular case.[198]

Application for amendment may be made by either side and at any time or amendment made by the judge of his own motion. Since counsel for the prosecution has general responsibility for the correctness of the indictment he should not open his case without being satisfied on the point and should make any necessary application for amendment before the defendant is arraigned, having inspected the indictment for the purpose. Defending counsel should also inspect, in his own client's interests.

PRE-TRIAL REVIEW

Except in cases of serious or complex fraud[199] no formal system for pre-trial review by the court of trial existed until 1996, although informal arrangements operated. Pre-trial reviews in fact operated in Crown Courts across the country, providing a basis for voluntary discussion of matters affecting a forthcoming trial, such as the plea to be entered, length of trial, points of law, or admissibility of evidence.[200] Such reviews appear to have occurred in approximately 25 per cent of cases.[201] The Royal Commission considered one trial project that had involved all cases being listed for a 'pleas and directions' hearing.[202] The majority of the Commission considered such a scheme to be both

---

[195] See p 627, *ante*.   [196] Section 5(1).

[197] *R v Radley* (1973) 58 Cr App R 394, where the amendment was made at the conclusion of the prosecution opening; cf. *R v Tirado* (1974) 59 Cr App R 80.

[198] It seems that an amendment on immaterial matter may be made at or after verdict: *R v Dossi* (1918) 87 LJKB 1024.

[199] See Criminal Justice Act 1987, s 7(1).

[200] The Royal Commission on Criminal Justice (at Ch 7, para 10) identified also a scheme based on the exchange of forms, recommended by a Working Party chaired by Watkins LJ. The results obtained in a pilot scheme were disappointing.

[201] Ibid, para 11, relying on the Crown Court Survey.

[202] Working Group on Pre-trial Issues: Recommendation 92 (cited by RCCJ, Ch 7, para 12).

unnecessary and impracticable. Instead it proposed a scheme based on the automatic completion of forms with details of plea. The disclosure obligations recommended by the Commission[203] would then have been complied with, and both prosecution and defence would then indicate whether a preparatory hearing was needed and for what purpose.[204] Such hearings would occur in a minority of cases, usually those anticipated to last at least five days, although it would be open to the parties to require a hearing in shorter cases.[205] Such hearings would deal with plea, matters of evidence (including issues of admissibility), and expert opinion, matters generally relating to the trial. Such decisions would be binding on the trial judge and counsel. For this reason the Royal Commission was concerned that the practice of returned briefs be minimized as much as possible.[206]

Pleas and directions hearings ('PDH') in Crown Court cases have become in effect mandatory. The advantages of the hearing lie in the ability of the court to engage in effective case management, to the benefit not only of the workload of the court in general but also to the effective handling of individual cases. However, the Narey Report[207] did accept that there may be some merit in the claim that PDH should not be mandatory in all cases since in straightforward ones they may involve an additional and unnecessary burden.

Following the recommendations of the Royal Commission, the government published in 1995 a consultation paper.[208] This paper recognized the desirability of achieving the objectives identified by the Royal Commission, namely the achievement of shorter and more efficient trials. However, it did not adopt the Royal Commission's proposals for pre-trial exchange of papers in less complex cases, and considered that the way forward was creation of a system based on a mixture of binding rulings at pleas and directions hearings, coupled with preparatory hearings to be held in complex or potentially lengthy cases. The government's approach was given statutory effect by Parts III and IV of the Criminal Procedure and Investigations Act of 1996.

By section 40 of the 1996 Act, a judge may, at a pre-trial hearing make a binding ruling as to:

(a) any question as to the admissibility of evidence;

(b) any other question of law relating to the case concerned.

A 'pre-trial hearing' can be held after sending for trial and before the commencement of the trial itself. In respect of the former, it can be dealt with if necessary by written submissions or limited oral submissions.[209] Pre trial hearings permit not simply questions of law to be determined, but also whether material should be disclosed, whether counts on an indictment should be quashed, and whether or not orders should be made, for example, under section 4 of the Contempt of Court Act 1981.

---

[203] See p 606, *ante.*   [204] RCCJ, para 20.   [205] Ibid, para 17.

[206] Ibid, para 36.   [207] See p 579, *ante.*

[208] *Improving the Effectiveness of Pre-trial Hearings in the Crown Court* (HMSO, 1995, Cm 2924).

[209] *R* v *K* [2006] EWCA Crim 724.

In addition, by section 29(1) of the 1996 Act, where it appears to a Crown Court judge that an indictment reveals a case of such complexity, or a case whose trial is likely to be of such length, that substantial benefits are likely to accrue from a preparatory hearing, such a hearing may be held. The purpose of the preparatory hearing is defined by section 29(2) as:

   (a) identifying issues which are likely to be material to the verdict of the jury;

   (b) assisting the comprehension of any such issues;

   (c) expediting the proceedings before the jury;

   (d) assisting the judge's management of the trial;

   (e) determining applications for non-jury trial.[210]

These provisions are not, in principle, new, and are similar to those found in section 7 of the Criminal Justice Act of 1987, dealing with cases of serious or complex fraud. The significance of a preparatory hearing is made clear by section 31(4). Under that subsection, a judge at a preparatory hearing may order the prosecutor:

   (1) to give to the court and the accused a written statement of certain matters which include the principal facts of the case for the prosecution, the witnesses who will speak to them, any exhibits relevant to those facts, any proposition of law on which the prosecutor proposes to rely, and the consequences that flow from any of those matters;

   (2) to prepare the prosecution evidence and any explanatory material in such a form as required by the court;

   (3) to give to the court and the accused written notice of documents the truth of contents of which ought in the prosecutor's view to be admitted, and of any such matters which in his view ought to be agreed;

   (4) to make any amendments of any case statement given as appear to the judge to be appropriate.

ARRAIGNMENT AND PLEAS

1 ATTENDANCE OF THE ACCUSED

On the day fixed the accused will, if he has been detained in custody, be brought from the prison or remand centre where he has been detained and lodged in the cells. If he has been on bail he must surrender to his bail and will then be placed in the cells to await his trial. It may be that the defendant has been on bail and does not appear, in which case the court of trial may issue a warrant, called a 'bench warrant' for the arrest of the

---

[210] See p 626, *ante.*

defendant; this is a summary procedure and will not normally be used unless the arrest of the defendant is a matter of urgency.

Still further powers are provided by section 7(3) of the Bail Act 1976 by which a constable may arrest without a warrant any person who has been released on bail in criminal proceedings if, inter alia, he has reasonable grounds for believing that the person is unlikely to appear at the time and place required.

2 ARRAIGNMENT

Assuming that the defendant has appeared at, or has been brought to, the court, the first formal step in his trial will be the arraignment, which is the process of calling an accused forward to answer an indictment. The defendant will be brought from the cells into the dock[211] and the proper officer will first ask him his name. Assuming that he is the person named in the indictment he will then be asked to plead. The indictment will be read to him (omitting only the introductory matters) and he will be asked to plead to it; further, where the indictment contains more than one count, each should be put to the defendant separately and he should be asked to plead separately, for each count is equivalent to a separate indictment.[212]

On arraignment the defendant may, of course, simply say nothing. If this occurs, the first question is whether the defendant is mute of malice, that is to say, able to speak but refusing to do so, or whether he is mute by visitation of God, that is to say, temporarily or permanently unable to speak. If there is any doubt a jury must be sworn to try the issue. Witnesses may be called on either side and counsel may address the jury; the judge will then sum up the case to the jury, who will retire if necessary and then give a verdict.[213] If the finding is that the defendant is mute of malice the court may then order the proper officer of the court to enter a plea of not guilty on behalf of the defendant (assuming that he still declines to speak);[214] the trial will then proceed as if the defendant had himself pleaded not guilty. If, however, the finding is that the defendant is mute by visitation of God, the defendant may yet be perfectly well able to defend himself, and a plea of not guilty should be entered by the court and the trial should proceed in the ordinary way.

However, there may well be some question of whether the defendant is fit to plead, the test for which is whether he is fit to challenge jurors, instruct counsel, understand the evidence, and give evidence himself.[215] The procedure to be followed is contained in the Criminal Procedure (Insanity) Act 1964, which was substantially amended in 2004.[216] Such matters used to be dealt with by a jury, but are now generally to be dealt

---

[211] The Royal Commission did not recommend that docks be abolished. It considered that they should be situated as near as possible to the accused's legal representatives: Ch 8, para 109.

[212] *R v Boyle* [1954] 2 QB 292, [1954] 2 All ER 721.

[213] This may in some circumstances be by a majority: see p 653, *post*.

[214] Criminal Law Act 1967, s 6(1)(c).

[215] *R v Berry* (1977) 66 Cr App R 156; not whether he is able to defend himself properly or well: *R v Robertson* [1968] 3 All ER 557, [1968] 1 WLR 1767.

[216] As amended by the Criminal Procedure (Insanity and Unfitness to Plead) Act 1991. See ss 4, 4a, and 5 of the 1964 Act. The provisions were also substantially amended by Domestic Violence, Crime and Victims Act 2004, s 22.

with by a judge, research showing that in the vast majority of cases the function of the jury was largely ritualistic, with the clear majority of questions of unfitness not being contested.[217] Evidence may be called by either side and speeches will be made; the judge will direct the jury, who will return a verdict. If the finding is that the defendant is unfit to plead, the trial does not proceed, but the defendant is not free to go; he is liable to be detained in hospital or made subject to various orders.[218] The court has power, in the interests of the accused, to postpone trial of the issue of fitness to plead until any time up to the opening of the case for the defence. If, before such time, the defendant is acquitted (on a submission of no case to answer) his fitness or otherwise will not be determined.[219] This is to ensure that the case against the person being detained is in fact tested, and to ensure that an innocent person is not subject to detention. If the finding is one of fitness to plead, the defendant will then be called upon to plead to the indictment; if he still declines to answer, a plea of not guilty will be entered on his behalf.

3 PLEAS

Assuming that all questions of fitness to plead have been disposed of adversely to the defendant, in the sense that the trial on the substantive issues must go on, various pleas are open to the defendant. In the vast majority of cases the alternatives are pleas of guilty or not guilty.

The decision to accept a plea to a lesser charge is that of the prosecutor, and does not require the consent of the court unless the decision arises after the prosecution has called its evidence and a case to answer has been found.[220] Such decisions may often assist in avoiding the time and expense of a trial, and are one explanation for the problem of 'cracked trials'. These are cases that are listed for trial but where on the day of trial the defendant pleads guilty.[221] By contrast, the holding of discussions informally with the trial judge to ascertain attitudes to likely sentence is a practice that has been heavily criticized by the Court of Appeal.[222] Out-of-court discussions with the trial judge should not occur unless absolutely essential, and then subject to various conditions. The Royal Commission proposed[223] a modification to this rule, so that judges may indicate the highest sentence that they would impose at that point on the basis of the facts put to them.[224] This might occur at pre-hearing, and encourage an accused to plead guilty. There is, of course, a danger that some defendants might plead guilty when they were,

---

[217] See Mackay and Kearns, 'The Trial of the Issue of Unfitness to Plead' [2000] Crim LR 536.

[218] Criminal Procedure (Insanity and Unfitness to Plead) Act 1991, s 5.

[219] Ibid, s 4; see, for such a case, *R v Burles* [1970] 2 QB 191, [1970] 1 All ER 642.

[220] *R v Grafton* [1993] QB 101, [1992] 4 All ER 609. The position is different if counsel expressly asks for the approval of the judge: *R v Broad* (1978) 68 Cr App R 281. See, generally, Farquharson Committee Report (1986) LS Gaz 3599.

[221] RCCJ, Ch 7, para 13. The Crown Court Study showed that 'cracked' trials were 26 per cent of all cases, creating serious problems (para 45).

[222] *R v Turner* [1970] 2 QB 321, [1970] 2 All ER 281; *R v Coward* (1979) 70 Cr App R 70.

[223] *Op cit.*   [224] Report, Ch 7, para 50.

in fact, innocent.[225] The Crown Court Survey[226] found some evidence of this, but the significance of the data obtained is open to doubt.[227]

In fact the majority of accused persons at Crown Court plead guilty.[228] Therefore they obtain a 'discount' on the otherwise justified sentence.[229] The Royal Commission proposed a formalized system, of graduated discounts, to encourage early pleas of guilty.[230] In 1994, changes were made to allow credit to be given for an early plea of guilty, and are now to be found in section 144 of the Criminal Justice Act 2003. It does not formally enact that those offenders who fall within its terms must receive a discount on sentence, but that is the effect of sentencing policy and practice.[231] On the other hand, the research shows that approximately 50 per cent of those pleading not guilty are in fact acquitted,[232] with a significant number of 'non-jury' acquittals. These non-jury acquittals merit further mention: the statistical evidence suggests that discharge, usually where the prosecution offers no evidence, is far more common than judges directing a jury to enter a 'not guilty' verdict because of the inadequacy of the evidence before the court.[233]

(a) Plea of guilty

On the assumption that the plea covers the whole indictment, counsel briefed for the prosecution will give a brief outline of the facts and then call a police officer to give the antecedent history of the defendant, in the form of a sheet setting out the defendant's home and educational background, previous jobs, criminal record, and anything else thought to be relevant. He may be cross-examined by defending counsel. The court will then usually consider a pre-sentence report,[234] presented usually on behalf of a probation officer, and, sometimes, a victim impact statement. There is then a plea in mitigation made by counsel for the defence, sometimes supported by witnesses (very rarely the defendant). The defendant will then usually be given the opportunity of saying something himself to the court, after which sentence will be passed. If there are two defendants, one of whom is pleading guilty and the other not guilty, the one pleading guilty will not normally be sentenced until the trial of the other defendant is concluded.[235]

It is customary for the normal rules of evidence to be relaxed at proceedings following a plea of guilty. The rules of evidence do not apply to 'antecedent evidence', which is invariably given by a single police officer on the basis of files concerning the defendant which the officer has in court. Nevertheless, the officer should not make allegations against the defendant which he has reason to think that the latter would deny and which he cannot

---

[225] It is for this reason that an accused must plead personally, not through counsel.
[226] See generally Ashworth, 'Plea, Venue and Discontinuance' [1993] Crim LR 830.
[227] RCCJ, Ch 7, para 45.   [228] *Op cit*, Ch 6.
[229] See, e.g., *R v Hollington and Emmens* (1985) 82 Cr App R 281.   [230] Ibid, para 47.
[231] See p 696, *post* and Reduction in Sentence for Guilty Plea (Sentencing Guidelines Council, 2005).
[232] Vennard, 'The Outcome of Contested Trials' in Moxon (ed) *Managing Criminal Justice* (1985).
[233] Ordered and Directed Acquittals in the Crown Court, RCCJ Research Study No 15 (HMSO, 1993).
[234] Criminal Justice Act 1991, s 3. These were formerly known as Social Inquiry Reports. See further, p 698, *post*.
[235] *R v Weekes* (1982) 74 Cr App R 161. The position may be different if the accused is going to give evidence for the prosecution against his co-accused.

properly prove.[236] Of course, if matters of importance are disputed, then the court may require them to be formally proved. In addition, where despite the plea of guilty there is a factual dispute that will affect the basis upon which the court will sentence the accused, the trial judge will hear evidence to determine that question, a so called 'Newton' hearing.[237]

If the defendant pleads guilty to some, but not all, counts or pleads guilty to a lesser offence, the prosecution must decide whether to proceed on the remaining counts or 'accept' the defendant's pleas, in which event the counts to which he has not pleaded guilty will be left 'on the file'. Although the defendant will never have been in peril of conviction on those counts, so that he could theoretically be tried on them, in practice this would not be permitted without leave of the court and, indeed, the counts on the file are sometimes ordered to be marked with words such as 'not to be proceeded with without the leave of this court or of the Court of Appeal'. However, even if the prosecution is content to adopt this course, the judge must, if asked, consent to it and, if he does not, he may order the trial to proceed.[238]

(b) Plea of not guilty

It should be noted that this is not necessarily a positive assertion that the defendant is innocent but merely a request or a challenge to the prosecution to prove the case against him. A defendant may plead guilty to one count in the indictment but not guilty to another, or even admit part of an offence contained in a single count but not the rest of the offence.[239] He may also plead not guilty to the offence charged but guilty to some other offence of which he may lawfully be convicted by way of alternative verdict; thus he may plead not guilty to murder but guilty to manslaughter. The whole question of alternative verdicts is now regulated by section 6(3) of the Criminal Law Act 1967. This enables the jury to acquit of the offence charged, but to convict of another offence which the court has jurisdiction to try and which is expressly or by implication alleged in the indictment.[240]

The point arises, often acutely, when the judge comes to sum up the case to the jury. Where nothing appears on the statements which can be said to reduce the crime charged to the lesser offence of which the defendant wishes to plead guilty, it is the duty of counsel for the Crown to present the offence charged in the indictment, leaving it to the jury 'in the exercise of their undoubted prerogative' to return a verdict of guilty of the lesser offence.[241] Even where there is material on the statements capable of sustaining a lesser charge, the prosecution is entitled to formulate its charges as it thinks fit. However, it is for the discretion of the trial judge whether to direct the jury as to the potential for an alternative verdict.

---

[236] Cf. *R* v *Robinson* (1969) 53 Cr App R 314, where the officer described the defendant as 'the principal drug pusher' in the Midlands, evidence the reception of which the Court of Appeal described as a 'clear and obvious injustice'. See also *R* v *Wilkins* (1977) 66 Cr App R 49.

[237] *R* v *Newton* (1982) 77 Cr App R 13.   [238] *R* v *Broad* (1978) 68 Cr App R 281.

[239] *Machent* v *Quinn* [1970] 2 All ER 255.

[240] What is included 'by implication' is often difficult to decide. The test is whether the allegations in the indictment are capable of including the elements of the alternative offence: *Metropolitan Police Commissioner* v *Wilson* [1984] AC 242; *sub nom R* v *Wilson* [1983] 3 All ER 448.

[241] *R* v *Soanes* [1948] 1 All ER 289.

Secondly, the defendant may change his plea once the trial has started but in this case the appropriate verdict must be returned by the jury which will have been sworn to try the case;[242] it may seem a formality that if the defendant changes his plea, for example, from 'not guilty' to 'guilty', the foreman of the jury should be required to stand up and say that the defendant is guilty, but:

> once a prisoner is in charge of a jury he can only be either convicted or discharged by the verdict of the jury.[243]

(c) Autrefois acquit and autrefois convict

These are by far the most important of a number of so-called 'special pleas in bar' which can be raised by the defendant when the indictment is put to him.[244] The substance of the pleas in bar is that there is some reason why the court should not proceed to try the defendant, which should be made the subject of immediate inquiry, so that if the reason is found to be a valid one the defendant should be released and further proceedings stayed.[245] The general principle of the two pleas of *autrefois acquit* and *autrefois convict* is that the same person should not be put in jeopardy twice for the same offence founded on the same facts, not merely for the same facts. This principle has been subject to important qualification following the passage of re-trial provisions contained in the Criminal Justice Act 2003.[246] Nonetheless, the principle remains important.

Autrefois acquit was well explained by a United States judge[247] as follows:

> The underlying idea ... is that the state with all its resources and power should not be allowed to make repeated attempts to convict an individual for an alleged offence, thereby subjecting him to embarrassment, expense and ordeal and compelling him to live in a continuing state of anxiety and insecurity, as well as enhancing the possibility that even though innocent he may be found guilty.

The principles to be applied are discussed below.

(d) Autrefois acquit and convict – the principles

The two pleas were extensively considered by the House of Lords in *Connelly v Director of Public Prosecutions*.[248] The following principles emerge from that and subsequent cases:

(1) A man cannot be tried for a crime in respect of which he has previously been convicted or acquitted. The reason for this is that an accused should not be put in peril twice. It is for this reason that the doctrine does not apply where the accused was never in fact in jeopardy. In *R v Dabhade*[249] a charge was formally

---

[242] *R v Heyes* [1951] 1 KB 29, [1950] 2 All ER 587.

[243] Ibid per Lord Goddard CJ [1951] 1 KB at 30, [1950] 2 All ER at 588.

[244] Others are demurrer (that the facts alleged do not constitute the offence charged); plea to the jurisdiction (that the court has no jurisdiction to try); pardon (that a pardon has been granted). These are extremely rare.

[245] See the remarks of Lord Goddard CJ in *R v County of London Quarter Sessions, ex parte Downes* [1954] 1 QB 1 at 5–6; [1953] 2 All ER at 750.

[246] See p 258, *ante*.

[247] Justice Black in *Green v United Kingdom* 355 US 184 (1957), 2 Led 2nd 199 at 201.

[248] [1964] AC 1254, [1964] 2 All ER 401.   [249] [1993] QB 329, [1992] 4 All ER 796.

dismissed, because in law it was defective. The accused was committed for trial on a substituted charge of theft. In dismissing an appeal against conviction, based upon the principle of *autrefois acquit*, the Court of Appeal indicated that where a charge was dismissed because it was defective, or because the evidence was insufficient to sustain a conviction, or because of a rationalization of the prosecution case, the appellant was never in fact in jeopardy.

(2) The same rule applies where a person could have been convicted of the alleged offence on a previous indictment. In this context the rule as to alternative verdict offences is of importance. As has already been seen,[250] a defendant on being charged with certain crimes may plead, or be found, guilty of certain other crimes and not guilty of the offence charged, without the need for a fresh indictment. Thus on a charge of murder the accused may be convicted of manslaughter. The doctrines of *autrefois acquit* and *autrefois convict* apply to any offence which was an alternative verdict offence to the original offence, and of which the accused was acquitted or convicted. Thus if the defendant is acquitted of murder, the defence of *autrefois acquit* will be open to him if charged with manslaughter or attempted murder arising out of the death of the same person.

(3) The rule applies if the crime in respect of which he is charged is in effect, or substantially the same as, the crime of which he was earlier acquitted or could have been (or was) convicted. This is in reality a matter for the common sense of the court.

(4) One test[251] of when the rule applies is to ask whether the evidence necessary to support the second indictment, or whether the facts which constitute the second offence, would have been sufficient to procure a legal conviction on the first indictment either as to the offence charged or of an offence of which the accused could have been found guilty.

(5) The matter is not decided simply by comparing indictments, but on the overall facts. The accused may adduce evidence as to the identity of the persons involved, and as to dates and other facts necessary to show that the doctrine applies.

(6) It is not within the doctrine that the facts under examination, or the witnesses being called in the later proceedings, are the same as those in the earlier proceedings.

(7) Irrespective of the above, a person may be able to show that a matter has in fact been decided already by a court competent to decide it, in the sense of a finding or plea of guilty and a sentence passed pursuant to that finding or plea. The matter must, though, in fact have been decided. In *Richards* v *R*[252] the accused pleaded guilty to manslaughter, but had not been sentenced. At a resumed hearing the

---

[250] See p 634, *ante*.

[251] Lords Pearce and Devlin disagreed on this point, identifying this as abuse of process rather than *autrefois acquit*. See, in support, *R v Beedie* [1997] 2 Cr App R 167, adding that both the third and fourth principle amounts to an abuse of process, the difference being that *autrefois* is a complete answer to the prosecution case, whereas an abuse of process argument is launched to persuade the judge that it is unfair to try the defendant, the quashing of the indictment being a discretionary remedy not one available.

[252] [1993] AC 217, [1992] 4 All ER 807.

prosecution was halted, and the appellant subsequently tried and convicted and sentenced to death[253] for murder. In dismissing the appeal against conviction the Privy Council was of the view that the plea of *autrefois convict* did not assist the accused, because the adjudication was not in fact complete.

The Law Commission considered the rule in 1999,[254] and recommended change, which occurred in 2003. Section 75 of the Criminal Justice Act 2003 allows a prosecutor to apply to the Court of Appeal for an order that an individual be retried for a qualifying offence[255] of which he has been acquitted.[256] Clearly, if such an order is made, *autrefois acquit* is no bar, but the terms of section 84 of the 2003 Act apply. The re-trial must be on an indictment preferred by direction of the Court of Appeal, and on which the defendant is arraigned within two months of the order of the Court of Appeal. Such a power is not likely to be often used, but provides an important route for dealing with cases where new evidence arises, or new procedures allow new analysis of existing evidence, such as DNA profiling. Departure from the principle of *autrefois acquit* may appear to offend a long-established principle, but a rule which prevented a person being re-tried in the face of cogent new evidence might be viewed equally as unjust.[257]

4 MOTION TO QUASH THE INDICTMENT

Instead of entering any plea, general or special, the defendant may move to quash the indictment. This may be done on several grounds. If any of the rules, already described,[258] as to the framing of the indictment have not been followed this may be made the ground for a motion to quash; however, it has already been seen that the court possesses ample power to amend the indictment and it will only be rarely that a motion to quash on this ground will succeed. It could only do so on the ground of some grave defect of substance, such as the insufficiency of the particulars of offence, or duplicity. An indictment may also be quashed on the ground that the offence charged in it is not one known to the law. Yet another ground is that the appropriate officer did not have jurisdiction to sign it; as has already been seen he can sign it only if certain conditions are satisfied. An indictment can also be quashed if it amounts to an abuse of the process of the court.[259]

5 PRELIMINARY POINTS OF LAW

It sometimes happens that there is a point of law involved in a case the decision of which may effectively dispose of the whole case. Thus, for example, the basic facts alleged by the prosecution may be admitted by the defence, the sole issue being whether those

---

[253] It was a Privy Council appeal from Jamaica, where the death penalty still exists.

[254] Law Com No 156, 1999, *Double Jeopardy*.

[255] Defined by Criminal Justice Act 2003, Schedule 5, and include serious offences against the person, some sexual offences, serious drugs offences and some criminal damage offences.

[256] See p 638, *post*.

[257] See Criminal Justice Act 2003. For examples of where such powers might be used see, e.g., the ongoing history of the Stephen Lawrence affair, as to which see p 258, *ante*.

[258] See p 627, *ante*.   [259] See p 572, *ante*.

admitted facts amount to the offence charged. In cases of this sort it is obviously a sterile exercise to go through the motions of trial by jury when the outcome of the case will depend entirely upon the judge's decision as to the law. The judge hears argument upon the law (before empanelling a jury); if a ruling is given which, in the view of the accused and his advisers, is fatal to the defence, the accused can then change his plea.[260] The point may, in fact, be dealt with at a preliminary hearing, or through a pre-trial ruling.[261] However, it is necessary for a plea of not guilty to be taken before the point of law is argued.

If points of law are taken successfully at the commencement of the case in this way (or indeed, at any other time) the ruling may prevent the case from continuing. This is known as a terminating ruling. A terminating ruling is any ruling whether on law or evidence that is fatal to the prosecution case: a dismissal for abuse of process, a ruling of *autrefois acquit*, a successful submission of no case to answer, a ruling of public interest immunity adverse to the Crown, and a ruling that the conduct alleged does not form a known criminal offence are each examples. The Auld Review[262] and the Law Commission[263] each recommended changes in the law: as the latter put it:

> If a case is to fall on a legal argument it is better for public confidence in the criminal justice system that it should be susceptible to the second opinion of a higher court, that it be appealable.

That is achieved by provisions in the Criminal Justice Act 2003 which confer rights of appeal against terminating rulings.[264]

6 EMPANELLING THE JURY: CHALLENGES

Assuming that there is a plea of not guilty to some part of the indictment the next stage of the trial will be the swearing of the jury. The Juries Act confers on the Lord Chancellor general responsibility for the summoning of jurors,[265] a function in reality performed locally. From all the jurors summoned, twelve will be chosen by ballot; a jury should be randomly selected[266] and a court has no power to interfere with the selection of a jury except in the rarest of cases, and for cause, for example relating to the physical or mental fitness of the proposed juror.[267] The selected jurors will take their places in the jury box. Before the jury is sworn the defendant is given the opportunity to challenge members of the jury for cause, either to the whole panel summoned or to an individual juror. The burden is on the party making the challenge to show such a cause, the issue being tried by the trial judge. Prior to 1988 an accused had a right of peremptory challenge of up to three jurors, which meant that, unlike for cause, the defendant did not have to state

[260] See, e.g., *Director of Public Prosecutions* v *Doot* [1973] AC 807, [1973] 1 All ER 940. An accused who has pleaded guilty in such circumstances can appeal against his conviction on the ground that the preliminary point of law was wrongly decided against him.
[261] See p 628, *ante*.   [262] *Op cit*, Ch 12, paras 47–65.
[263] Report on *Double Jeopardy and Prosecution Appeals, op cit*.
[264] 2003 Act, ss 57–66. See, further, p 721, *post*.   [265] Juries Act 1974, s 2.
[266] See RCCJ, Ch 8, paras 52–64.   [267] See p 352, *ante*.

any reason for challenge. This right was abolished by the Criminal Justice Act 1988. By contrast the right of the Crown to require jurors to 'stand by' still exists.[268] By this procedure, the juror is asked to stand down, but consideration of the cause of challenge (since a challenge by the Crown must be for cause) is postponed. It will usually then happen that there are enough 'spare' jurors for a whole jury to be assembled, however many more challenges are made, so that the trial can proceed and the cause of the Crown's challenge is never made the subject of enquiry. The Crown will usually act on the basis of knowledge of a potential juror's criminal record[269] or, in exceptional cases of other matters disclosed on an authorized check of police records.[270]

Each member of the jury having been sworn individually, the appropriate officer of the court then tells the jury of the terms of the offences to which the defendant has pleaded not guilty and informs them that it is their duty, having heard the evidence, to say whether he is guilty or not. The trial judge may also explain certain features about a criminal trial to the jury.[271]

COURSE OF THE TRIAL

1 PUBLICITY

English law regards 'open justice' as a fundamental principle[272] which therefore means that the trial, including the process of arraignment described above, should be open to the public, and may be reported. Despite this, the principle is not unlimited, and may be departed from where necessary where openness or publicity would harm the interests of justice.[273] Powers exist to postpone the reporting of all or part of a trial,[274] to prevent reporting,[275] or in some situations to sit in camera. In addition, a variety of statutory powers exist that limit the principle.[276]

2 PROCEDURE AT THE HEARING

(a) Speeches

Prosecuting counsel starts by making an opening speech. This will be an outline of the allegations against the defendant and of the evidence which it is proposed to call in support of the allegations. No reference should be made to any item of evidence if counsel has been informed that there is going to be an objection to the admissibility of that

---

[268] See Attorney General's Guidelines [1988] 3 All ER 1086.
[269] These may disqualify a juror from service: see chapter 11, *ante*.
[270] *Attorney General's Guidelines on Jury Checks* [1988] 3 All ER 1086, and p 352, *ante*.
[271] Royal Commission on Criminal Procedure, Cmnd 8092 (HMSO, 1981), para 67.
[272] *Scott* v *Scott* [1913] AC 417, [1911–13] All ER Rep 1.   [273] See p 240, *ante*.
[274] Contempt of Court Act 1981, s 4(2). A right of appeal against such an order exists: Criminal Justice Act 1988, s 159.
[275] Contempt of Court Act 1981, s 11.   [276] See p 240, *ante*.

evidence. The fact that evidence is relevant[277] is not sufficient: for it to be considered at a trial it must also be admissible, and there are a number of rules of evidence which exclude evidence that might be thought to be relevant. Examples of these include evidence of the character of the accused unless it is directly relevant to the issue before the court and evidence of out-of-court statements.[278] A judge may also exclude from evidence relevant material where the fairness of the trial demands that that be done.[279] Therefore, in opening the case prosecuting counsel must take care not to refer to evidence that is not admissible, or which is likely to be excluded. Objections to the admissibility of evidence, or for the exclusion of evidence will be tried by the judge, usually (although not always) in the absence of the jury, at the time in the trial when the evidence would otherwise have been called. This procedure is known as a 'voir dire', taking its name from the name of the oath taken by witnesses during that hearing.

The institution of the opening speech has been criticized on the ground that counsel may make allegations which are not borne out by the evidence of his witnesses (even before they are the subject of cross-examination) yet the jury may recollect only the statements of counsel, since they came first. It is a strict rule that prosecuting counsel should limit his observations to what appears in the depositions, or witness statements. The only exception arises in the case of those witnesses in respect of whom a notice of additional evidence has been served. Even this practice is not strictly required by law, but the court has an inherent discretion to prevent oppressive conduct towards the defendant[280] and it is most unlikely that a judge would allow additional evidence to be called unless a notice of additional evidence, setting out a summary of that witness's evidence, had been served on the defendant.

(b) Witnesses

Prosecution witnesses will then be called[281] and will be subject to examination in chief by prosecuting counsel, cross-examination by defending counsel, and re-examination

---

[277] 'Relevance' was defined in *Stephen's Digest* as meaning that '...any two facts to which it is applied are so related to each other that according to the common course of events one either taken by itself or in connection with other facts proves or renders probable the past, present or future existence or non existence of the other.' For the difficulties in determining whether evidence is sufficiently relevant, see *R v Blastland* [1986] AC 41, [1985] 2 All ER 1095; *R v Kearley* [1992] 2 AC 228, [1992] 2 All ER 345.

[278] The use of out-of-court statements as proof of their contents has traditionally been prohibited by the hearsay rule, subject to a number of statutory and common law exceptions. The law relating to hearsay has been significantly changed by Criminal Justice Act 2003, ss 114–131, and is beyond the scope of this book. The effect of the changes may be to allow out-of-court statements in lieu of oral testimony in a greater number of circumstances.

[279] See, in particular PACE, s 78, discussed at p 424, *ante*.

[280] See the remarks of Lord Devlin in *Connelly v Director of Public Prosecutions* [1964] AC 1254 at 1346 *et seq*.

[281] It is the duty of the prosecution to take all reasonable steps to secure the attendance at the trial of all witnesses (other than those subject to a conditional witness order) named on the back of the indictment (*R v Cavanagh* [1972] 2 All ER 704, [1972] 1 WLR 676). However, the prosecution has a discretion whether to call a particular witness and, having called him, whether to adduce his evidence-in-chief or merely to tender him for cross-examination. Where the witness's evidence is capable of belief the prosecution should call him even though his evidence is unfavourable to the prosecution case and if they do not do so, the judge may intervene and direct that he be called; on the other hand if the witness's evidence does not appear to be capable of belief the prosecution need not call him and it will then be for the defence to call him if they wish to do so; *R v Oliva* [1965] 3 All ER 116, [1965] 1 WLR 1028.

by prosecuting counsel. Examination in chief is the first stage in the examination of a witness, and is carried out by the party calling the witness. The purpose of examination in chief is to elicit the testimony the witness has to give on the relevant matters. An advocate cannot ask the witness leading questions. A leading question is one which suggests to the witness the answer that is expected or which assumes a fact still to be proved. It is sometimes said that any question that can be answered with a simple 'Yes' or 'No' is a leading question. This is often, although not invariably, true. Leading questions are often permitted on formal matters, such as name, address, and occupation, and it is permissible for a party to lead a witness with the concurrence of the other parties and the court. Nor can an advocate cross-examine his own witness by putting previous inconsistent statements to the witness, unless the court rules that that witness is 'hostile'. A witness is hostile if that witness is 'not desirous of telling the truth at the instance of the party calling him'.[282] Some hostility or animosity is called for: it is not enough that the evidence is unfavourable to the party calling him. If the witness is hostile, then, at common law, he may be asked leading questions by the party calling him, and, under section 3 of the Criminal Procedure Act 1865, previous inconsistent statements may be put to him, which will affect the 'credit' of the witness in the eyes of the jury, and, now, may in some circumstances be evidence of the truth of their contents.[283] More usually, a witness will ask, or be invited, to refresh his memory from an out-of-court statement made when the events were still fresh in the mind.[284] The answers of a witness must be accepted by the advocate calling that witness, even if the witness has 'not come up to proof' (i.e. not testified as anticipated).

Following examination in chief, a witness will be cross-examined by the advocate for the party not calling that witness. The purpose of cross-examination is to weaken the testimony of the witness, either by casting doubt about his testimony, or by eliciting facts favourable to the cross-examiner, or by discrediting the credit of the witness in the eyes of the jury. An advocate may, for this purpose, ask leading questions and, indeed, there are few limits on what may be asked in cross-examination: normally, any question relevant to the issues in the case will be allowed.[285] Exceptions to this general rule exist in respect of questions relating to the interception of communications,[286] in respect of matters for which a claim of public interest immunity is successfully made.[287] By contrast, the law imposes limits on questions that may be asked and which affect the credit or credibility of the witness. The basic rule is that the question must, if asked, relate to the likely standing of the witness in the eyes of the court.[288] There are complex and special rules about the questions that may be asked about the bad character of both

---

[282] *Ewer* v *Ambrose* (1825) 3 B & C 746.   [283] See Criminal Justice Act 2003, s 119.

[284] *R* v *Da Silva* [1990] 1 All ER 29, [1990] 1 WLR 31. If the witness wishes to refresh his memory, and have the document with him, actually whilst testifying, it must be contemporaneous, i.e. made whilst the events were still fresh in the mind of the maker of the statement: *R* v *Richardson* [1971] 2 QB 484. See also *A-G's Reference (No 3 of 1979)* (1979) 69 Cr App R 411 and cf. *R* v *Chisnell* [1992] Crim LR 507 (police officers allowed to refresh memory from notes transcribed many months earlier, but at a time when the events were still fresh in the mind). See, now, Criminal Justice Act 2003, s 120.

[285] *CT Hobbs* v *Tinling & Co* [1929] 2 KB 1; *R* v *Funderburk* [1990] 2 All ER 482.

[286] Regulation of Investigatory Powers Act 2000, s 17.

[287] See p 608, *ante*.   [288] See *Hobbs* v *Tinling*, *ante*, n 274.

non-defendants and defendants alike,[289] and in sexual cases section 41 of the Youth Justice and Criminal Evidence Act 1999 imposes strict limits on what may or may not be asked in a sexual case. A complainant may not, subject to limited exceptions, be asked questions relating to his or her sexual experience. Such limitations are designed to give some protection for the witness, and to ensure that rape complainants in particular are not deterred from coming forward by the potential of unnecessary and intrusive questioning. One key authority, *R v A (No 2)*, highlights the restrictive nature of section 41. In a preliminary ruling, the House of Lords ruled that, potentially, section 41 did not prevent questions about the sexual relationship that the appellant and complainant had had, if that was necessary to secure a fair trial. The 'reading down' of section 41 to ensure compliance with Article 6 has already been noted.[290]

Even where questions relating to credit are permitted, the law imposes strict limits as to how far the cross-examiner may adduce other evidence to contradict (i.e. rebut) the testimony of that witness. The reason for this is that there is a need to keep the trial to the issues at hand, and to prevent the trial from becoming an exploration of a multiplicity of other matters. This is known as the collateral evidence rule: the answers of a witness in cross-examination to matters that relate to credit are regarded as final, and can only be rebutted if one of the exceptions to the rule exists.[291] There are four such exceptions that potentially arise. The first is if the witness denies a previous conviction: the denial may be rebutted.[292] Secondly, if the witness denies making a previous inconsistent statement, that denial may be rebutted.[293] Thirdly, the cross-examiner may rebut a denial of bias.[294] Finally, if the witness denies having a general reputation for untruthfulness, that denial may be rebutted.[295]

Cross-examination is followed, sometimes, by re-examination by the advocate for the party calling the witness. The purpose of re-examination is limited to clarifying matters that have arisen out of the testimony the witness has given to the court, usually in the hope of bolstering testimony which has been shaken under cross-examination. As in examination in chief, leading questions may not be asked. Furthermore, a party cannot use re-examination as an opportunity for raising matters which he omitted to raise in examination in chief unless the form of the cross-examination justifies this.

(c) 'No case to answer'

When all the witnesses for the prosecution have been examined, prosecuting counsel will close his case by saying 'that is the case for the prosecution' or words to that effect. There may then be a submission by defending counsel that there is no case to answer as regards the whole or some part of the indictment. This may be put in two ways; first that there is no evidence that the crime alleged against the accused was committed by him; secondly that the evidence, taken at its highest, is so tenuous that a jury could not

---

[289] See Criminal Justice Act 2003, s 98, s 100, s 101.
[290] See p 156, *ante.*   [291] *Harris* v *Tippett* (1810) 2 Camp 637.
[292] Criminal Procedure Act 1865, s 6.   [293] Ibid, s 4.
[294] *A-G* v *Hitchcock* (1847) 1 Exch 91.   [295] *R* v *Richardson* (1977) 66 Cr App R 6.

properly convict on it.[296] This is a matter for the judge to determine and, although there is no set rule, it is usually regarded as desirable that the argument on the submission should take place in the absence of the jury. Prosecuting counsel has, of course, a right to reply to defending counsel's submission. If the submission is upheld the trial will end as regards that part of the indictment at least, though that will be a terminating ruling potentially giving right to a possible right of appeal.[297] The jury should in such a case be instructed to return a formal verdict of not guilty; this is analogous to the case where the defendant changes his plea to guilty in the course of the trial. Even if no formal verdict is taken, the case, once withdrawn from the jury, is completely 'dead' and cannot be revived by the defendant's own evidence or evidence given by a prosecution witness who is allowed to be recalled.[298] Similarly where two men are jointly charged, and a successful submission is made on behalf of one of them, he is to be regarded as no longer charged during what remains of the trial.[299]

The role of the judge at this stage is crucial. If the prosecution evidence is such that no properly directed jury could convict upon it then it is the duty of the judge to stop the case.[300] This is particularly so where the prosecution rely wholly on the confession of a person who suffers a significant degree of mental handicap, the confession itself being unconvincing. Such a case should be withdrawn from the jury.[301] By contrast, if the case is one where the strengths or weaknesses of the case depend upon the view to be taken as to the reliability of a witness or other matters properly within the remit of the jury, then the case should be left to the jury to decide. If the submission is simply rejected, the trial will proceed. Even if no submission is made the judge may at any time after the close of the prosecution's case ask the jury whether they think that the prosecution case has been proved and invite them to return a verdict of not guilty if they think that it has not;[302] the more desirable practice is for the judge to take the initiative and direct the jury to return a verdict of not guilty.

(d) Defence case

The defence case will then open, assuming that the trial is proceeding as to part or all of the indictment. Defence counsel has no right to make an opening speech to the jury unless he is calling witnesses as to fact other than the defendant (whether or not he is also calling the defendant); even then the matter is in his discretion.[303] Witnesses for the defence are then called. If the defendant is giving evidence it is the general rule that he must give evidence before other witnesses; he must be in court, and if he heard the evidence of other witnesses before him,[304] he might be tempted to 'trim' his own evidence.

---

[296] R v Galbraith [1981] 2 All ER 1060.   [297] Under the Criminal Justice Act 2003.
[298] R v Plain [1967] 1 All ER 614, [1967] 1 WLR 565. The corollary of this is that if the submission is wrongly rejected the accused is entitled to have his subsequent conviction quashed by the Court of Appeal, even though evidence subsequently given would support that conviction; R v Cockley [1984] Crim LR 429.
[299] R v Meek (1996) 110 Sol J 867.   [300] R v Galbraith n 296, ante.
[301] R v McKenzie [1993] 1 WLR 453.   [302] R v Young [1964] 2 All ER 480.
[303] The Royal Commission recommended that the right of the defence to make a speech at the commencement of the case should be extended to all cases, in substitution for the right here described.
[304] PACE, s 79.

A witness about whose evidence there could be no controversy may of course be taken before the defendant. What evidence is called for the defence depends on the nature of the case. An accused person is not a compellable witness in his own defence.[305] However, if he fails to testify in his own defence without good cause, or refuses without good cause to answer any question, the court may draw such inference as it thinks proper.[306] An exception to this is where it appears to the court that the physical or mental condition of the accused makes it undesirable for him to give evidence.

Whether an inference is in fact drawn is a matter for the jury, based on their own perception of common sense.[307] If good cause is argued by the accused, an evidential basis to establish it must exist: it is not enough for the accused simply to assert.[308] Age is not a barrier. Until 1998, no inference could be drawn in respect of an accused aged under fourteen. This was considered illogical by the government, in the light of the fact that an inference can be drawn from the silence of a suspect aged under fourteen at the investigatory stage, and the Crime and Disorder Act 1998 removed the age limitation.

All defence witnesses are subject to examination in chief, cross-examination, and re-examination in the normal way. Where there is more than one defendant, cross-examination of prosecution witnesses and speeches will normally be taken in the order in which the defendants' names appear on the indictment, although there is no fixed rule on the matter. Once the case for the defence has been closed the prosecution may be allowed to call rebutting evidence, in the discretion of the judge. The general rule is that rebutting evidence should be allowed only where evidence has been called on behalf of the defendant which could not fairly have been foreseen by the prosecution.[309] In determining this it should be borne in mind that in most cases the defence will have given a defence statement pursuant to section 5 of the Criminal Procedure and Investigations Act 1996.[310] Rebutting evidence may be called at any time up to the conclusion of the summing-up and retirement of the jury and defending counsel has a right to cross-examine the witnesses called in rebuttal. Further, if evidence is called after the conclusion of the speeches, counsel may deliver supplemental speeches dealing with the new evidence.

The judge has a right to recall witnesses himself or even call witnesses whom neither side has called; he may also question witnesses to clarify matters of doubt or to probe further into matters which he thinks have not been sufficiently investigated. However, a judge must be careful not to overstep the mark. In *R* v *Grafton* prosecuting counsel decided during his case to offer no further evidence. The trial judge disagreed with that decision, and called the one remaining prosecution witness. In quashing the resulting conviction, the Court of Appeal stressed that the judge's power to call witnesses should be used sparingly, and only to advance the ends of fairness and justice. Until the case for the Crown is complete it is the Crown's decision as to whether or not the prosecution should proceed.

Closing speeches and the summing-up then follow. These are dealt with later.[311]

---

[305] PACE, s 80.   [306] Criminal Justice and Public Order Act 1994, s 35.
[307] *R* v *Cowan* [1996] QB 373; *Murray* v *DPP* [1999] 1 WLR 1.
[308] See *Practice Direction: Crown Court (Defendants Evidence)* [1995] 2 Cr App R 192.
[309] *R* v *Picher* (1974) 60 Cr App R 1.   [310] See p 611, *ante*.   [311] See p 652, *post*.

3 WITNESSES

The procedure to be followed in the calling of evidence has been noted above. The general rule is that any person who is capable of giving intelligible testimony is a competent witness. A person who is incapable of such testimony because of mental capacity, whether of a permanent or temporary nature,[312] will not be competent and thus will not be heard. Until recently, it was thought that special rules applied to young children, but widespread criticism led to changes in the law. These have the effect of applying the same test of competence to a child as to an adult.[313] Special rules continue to apply to accused persons: an accused is not a competent witness for the prosecution, although he is competent in his own defence.

A witness who is competent is usually compellable. In other words, the witness can be required to attend court to testify, on pain of being punished for contempt of court. The attendance of a witness at the Crown Court is compelled by the issue of a witness order or witness summons, issued by the Crown Court.[314] A witness can resist the granting of a witness summons only if he has no relevant evidence to give, or if the witness is entitled to claim public interest immunity to resist the claim that he should testify or produce relevant documents.[315] To the general rule that a witness is compellable there are certain exceptions. An accused person is never compellable in his own defence. The spouse of the accused is only compellable in certain limited situations, contained in section 80(3) of the Police and Criminal Evidence Act 1984. These situations are as follows:

(1) where the offence charged involves an assault on, or injury or threat of injury to, the spouse or a person at the time of the offence under the age of sixteen years;

(2) a sexual offence alleged to have been committed against a person under the age of sixteen years;

(3) an offence of attempting, conspiring, aiding or abetting, counselling, or inciting such an offence.

Where the spouse is competent but not compellable the trial judge is under a duty to inform the witness of that witness's right not to testify.[316] If the witness then decides to give evidence, that witness can then be treated in the normal way, for example, he or she may be declared hostile.

Various other persons are not compellable witnesses. This includes the sovereign, as well as foreign sovereigns, ambassadors, High Commissioners, and various grades of diplomatic staff. In any legal proceedings to which a bank is not a party, a bank or bank officer cannot be compelled to produce any banker's book the contents of which can be proved by secondary evidence, e.g. by the production of documentary evidence.[317]

---

[312] *R v Baines* [1987] Crim LR 508.

[313] *DPP v M* [1997] 2 All ER 749; *G v DPP* [1997] 2 All ER 755; *R v McPherson* [2006] 1 Cr App R 30; *R v Powell* [2006] Cr App R 468; *DPP v R* [2007] EWHC 852 (Admin).

[314] Criminal Procedure (Attendance of Witnesess) Act 1965, s 2.

[315] See p 609, *ante*.   [316] *R v Thompson* (1976) 64 Cr App R 96.

[317] Bankers Book Evidence Act 1879.

Where a witness testifies he usually does so orally. The general rule is that all witnesses must give evidence on oath, but a child under the age of fourteen always gives unsworn evidence.[318] Any person having authority to hear evidence has the power to administer an oath,[319] but it is usually administered by the clerk to the court. The usual form of oath runs as follows:

> I swear by Almighty God that the evidence I shall give shall be the truth, the whole truth and nothing but the truth.

The witness holds the New Testament, or in the case of Jews the Old Testament, in his uplifted hand.[320] This form of oath is only appropriate to members of the Christian and Jewish faiths. Any person who objects to taking the usual oath may take any other form of oath, according to his religious beliefs, which he declares to be binding on his conscience. As an alternative, a person who objects to being sworn is permitted to 'make his solemn affirmation' instead of taking the oath. This substitutes the words 'I (name) do solemnly sincerely and truly declare and affirm' for 'I swear by Almighty God...'. A witness is also permitted to affirm if it is not reasonably practicable without inconvenience or delay to administer the form of oath appropriate to the witness's beliefs (for example, because the book on which the witness wishes to swear is not available).[321] An affirmation is not unsworn testimony: it is equivalent to an oath and a false statement on affirmation amounts to perjury.[322]

Once sworn, or having affirmed, a witness gives evidence orally, usually in open court. Exceptions to this are permitted where it is essential for the administration of justice, or where statute specifically authorizes. In 1999, the Youth Justice and Criminal Evidence Act conferred the power to make special measures directions in respect of children or vulnerable witnesses in some circumstances,[323] although not, generally, in respect of a defendant.[324] For example, a witness may give evidence from behind a screen, so that the witness does not have to face the alleged perpetrator of the offence, or through a live TV link. The use of video links is particularly important in cases involving children's evidence, especially where it is alleged that the child is the victim of abuse. In such cases the law is increasingly concerned to ensure that the child does not have the damage of the alleged offence compounded by the experience of having to face the alleged perpetrator in open court. This power to take evidence through a live TV link also extends to cases where an adult witness is outside the United Kingdom. In addition, a video recorded interview with a child may sometimes be admissible as the evidence in chief of that child, provided it was possible for a jury, properly directed, to conclude that it was a

---

[318] Criminal Justice Act 1991, Camberwell Green Youth Court [2005] UKHL 2; [2005] Crim LR 497. See also Crime and Justice Act 2007.

[319] Evidence Act 1851, s 16.   [320] Oaths Act 1978, s 1.

[321] Oaths Act 1978, s 5(2).   [322] Ibid, s 5(4).

[323] See Home Office Report of the Advisory Group on Video Evidence , Home Office, 1989 (the *Pigot Report*); Birch, *A Better Deal for Vulnerable Witnesses* [2000] Crim LR 849; Hotano, *The Child Witness Review: Much Ado About Too Little* [2007] Crim LR 849.

[324] See *R (on application of D)* v *Camberwell Green Youth Court; R (on Application of DPP)* v *Cambridge MC* [2005] UKHL 4.

credible account.[325] However, the power to permit a video-recorded cross-examination, recommended by the Pigot Report and contained in section 27 of the Youth Justice and Criminal Evidence Act has not been implemented, and is unlikely to be so, because, amongst other reasons, of the difficulty in making it work appropriately and fairly.[326]

(a) Out of court statements

Normally, the evidence given by a witness is oral in nature. Historically, a technical rule of evidence, the hearsay rule, prevents the out-of-court statements of a person being adduced to prove the truth of the assertions contained in those statements. The reasons for this general rule reflect the oral nature of the criminal trial: an out-of-court statement may, if it is made orally, be prone to distortion or inaccuracy. If the maker of the statement is available to testify, his out-of-court statement is self-serving and adds nothing to what he can tell the court. If, by contrast, the maker of the statement is unavailable to testify, the witness cannot be cross-examined on what is alleged to have been said in that statement.

Yet it can clearly be seen that the out-of-court statements of an individual may be both relevant and reliable, often made at a time when the events or matters in issue were fresh in the mind of that person. For that reason the hearsay rule has been severely criticized, and is subject to a wide range of exceptions. Changes have been made by the Criminal Justice Act 2003. Section 114 of that Act has recast the rule to preserve some of the common law and statutory exceptions that existed prior to the 2003 Act, and created a new 'safety valve' that can be used to admit evidence of out-of-court statements that infringes the rule but which it is in the interests of justice to receive. These new rules do not, of themselves, infringe Article 6.[327] As a result of this recasting of the rules the following are the main forms of evidence now potentially admissible in evidence:

(1) Statements made by a witness who is unavailable for a variety of reasons. These include death, the fact that the person is physically or mentally unfit to be a witness, the fact that the witness is outside the UK and it is not reasonably practicable to secure his attendance, or cannot be found, or the witness does testify because of fear.[328]

(2) Where statements contained in documents are made or received in the course of a trade business or profession.[329]

(3) Statements in public documents.

(4) Spontaneous statements made by individuals where events dominate the mind of the individual (known as *res gestae statements*).[330]

---

[325] See *R v K (Evidence: Child Video Interview* [2006] EWCA Crim 472.

[326] See Cooper *Pigot Unfulfilled* [2005] Crim LR 456.

[327] See *R v Labri* [2005] EWCA Crim 3135.

[328] Criminal Justice Act 2003, s 115. This largely replicates the provisions of Criminal Justice Act 1968, s 23, but extends to both documentary and oral statements.

[329] Criminal Justice Act 2003, s 116. This largely replicates the provisions of Criminal Justice Act 1968, s 24.

[330] For the pre-existing common law see *R v Andrews* [1987] AC 281.

(5) Confessions made by a defendant.[331]

(6) Statements used to refresh memory.[332]

(7) Some previous consistent or inconsistent statements.[333]

(8) Statements within the 'safety valve' described above. A good example may be a confession to the crime made by a person other than the defendant, which would technically be hearsay but nonetheless of strong evidential value.

One particular exception to the rule, mentioned above, is the power to consider a video recording of an interview with a child. In cases involving offences of violence, or sexual offences, the video recording of the interview with a child may, with leave of the court, be adduced. If such a video is shown, what the child says is evidence and can be used to prove the truth of the matters to which the child speaks. Leave will be granted unless:

(a) it appears to the court that the child will not be available for cross-examination;

(b) rules of court governing disclosure of the circumstances in which the recording was made have not been complied with;

(c) the court is of the opinion that, in the interests of justice, the recording ought not to be admitted. In considering whether or not leave should be granted, the court must consider whether any prejudice to the accused which might result is outweighed by the desirability of showing the whole, or substantially the whole, of the video. A *Memorandum of Good Practice* was adopted intended to govern how such video recorded interviews should be conducted so as to ensure that the interview can safely be relied on.

4 THE BURDEN OF PROOF AND THE RIGHT OF SILENCE

(a) The 'golden thread'

The burden of proof in a criminal case is on the prosecution. The prosecution must prove each element of the crime charged. This includes, subject to certain limited exceptions,[334] disproving any defence that is raised. This fundamental principle was well demonstrated in *Woolmington v Director of Public Prosecutions*[335] where the accused, charged with murdering his wife, claimed that the killing was an accident. The trial judge in his summing up directed the jury that if the Crown proved that the accused killed the deceased the burden rested on the accused to prove provocation or accident.

---

[331] Subject to the requirements of PACE s 76 being satisfied.

[332] Criminal Justice Act 2003, s 139.   [333] 2003 Act, ss 119–120.

[334] These include the burden of proving a plea in bar (e.g. *autrefois acquit*) insanity, diminished responsibility, unfitness to plead as well as under certain specific statutory exceptions.

[335] [1935] AC 462. Cf. *R v Bone* [1968] 2 All ER 644, [1968] 1 WLR 983 in which the defendant's conviction was quashed because of the trial judge's failure to direct that, in relation to the defence of duress, it was for the prosecution to disprove the defence rather than for the defendant to prove it.

The conviction was quashed in the House of Lords because of this misdirection. In the famous words of Lord Sankey LC:

> ...throughout the web of the English criminal law one golden thread is always to be seen, that is the duty of the prosecution to prove the prisoner's guilt, subject to.... The defence of insanity and subject also to any statutory exception.[336]

The circumstances in which the law departs from the principle are limited. The burden of proving a special plea in bar is on the accused. Thus, if it is claimed that the accused has been previously acquitted on the same charge, then the doctrine of *autrefois acquit* will apply.[337] The burden of proof on this point will be on the accused. Another example is the defence of insanity: the burden of proving insanity is on the defence where this issue is raised by the defence, as is the burden of proving diminished responsibility or unfitness to plead.[338] Certain statutory exceptions also exist, which raises important issues in the context of Article 6, discussed below.[339] Whenever a burden of proof is placed on the accused, the standard of proof is not that normally imposed on the prosecution ('beyond reasonable doubt') but the lesser, civil, standard of the balance of probabilities.[340]

(b) Article 6 of the Convention

The fact that the burden of proof is on the prosecution is crucially connected with the basic principle that an accused person has the right not to self-incriminate. As already noted,[341] this is a right recognized both by English law and by the European Convention of Human Rights.[342] It is for this reason that an accused person cannot, generally, be required to self-incriminate or required to testify in his own defence. An accused is a competent, but not compellable, witness in his own defence. Further, if self-incriminatory statements are obtained from an accused person unfairly, or by a trick, or in circumstances where they should not be relied on because safeguards created by the law have been evaded or ignored,[343] they will be excluded for evidence. Inroads into these principles have in recent years been made by Parliament. The fact that inferences may now be drawn from a failure to mention facts at the investigatory stage, or from a failure to disclose the nature of the defence later relied on, has already been seen, but, as already noted, section 35 of the Criminal Justice and Public Order Act 1994 permits a court to draw such inference as it thinks proper from a failure of an accused to give evidence or

---

[336] Ibid, at p 481.   [337] See p 635, *ante.*

[338] Homicide Act 1957, s 2(2); *R v Dunbar* [1958] 1 QB 1, [1957] 2 All ER 737.

[339] See, e.g. Road Traffic Act 1988, s 5(2); Prevention of Crime Act 1953, s 1. For a general, and important statutory exception, see Magistrates' Courts Act 1980, s 101 which provides that, on summary trial, where an enactment makes the commission of a particular act an offence subject to a proviso, exception, excuse or qualification, the burden of proving that falls on the accused. For the application of s 101, see *R v Hunt* [1987] AC 352, [1987] 1 All ER 1.

[340] *R v Carr-Briant* [1943] KB 607, [1943] 2 All ER 156. Note though that the civil standard may not be absolute, and may vary according to the nature of what has to be proved.

[341] See pp 185 and 555, *ante.*

[342] *Murray* v *United Kingdom* (1966) 22 EHRR 29; *Condron* v *United Kingdom* [2000] Crim LR 679.

[343] *R v Mason* [1987] 3 All ER 481, [1988] 1 WLR 139.

his refusal, without good cause, to answer any question. Whether an inference is in fact drawn will depend on all the circumstances and whether an evidential basis has been established to explain the failure to testify or to answer the relevant question.[344]

This right not to be required to self-incriminate is at the heart of the debate as to whether burdens of proof which raise a presumption of guilt, and place a burden of proof on a defendant are consistent with Article 6. In *Saliabaku* v *France*[345] the Court of Human Rights observed:

> Presumptions of fact or of law operate in every legal system. Clearly the Convention does not prohibit such presumptions in principle. It does, however, require the Contracting States to remain within certain limits… art 6(2) does not regard presumptions of fact or of law provided for in the criminal law with indifference. It requires States to confine them within reasonable limits which take into account the importance of what is at stake and maintain the rights of the defence….

The effect of this is to require the court in each case to take a view as to whether the legislative interference with the presumption of innocence is justified and proportionate.[346] The constituent rights in Article 6 are not absolutes.[347] In respect of any statutory provision the first step is to determine whether it does in fact impose a burden of proof on the defendant.[348] If it does not, then clearly no issue arises. But if it does the court must be assessed in the context of Article 6(2). Whilst Article 6 does not inevitably prohibit a burden of proof being placed on a defendant, it will be open to challenge.

Although these principles appear straightforward, they have generated significant debate and disagreement as the courts have sought to implement them in a principled but pragmatic way.[349] In *Lambert* conflicting opinions were delivered by the House of Lords, when it concluded that section 28 of the Misuse of Drugs Act 1971 was to be read as imposing only an evidential burden on the defendant, leaving on the prosecution the legal burden (i.e. of satisfying the court so that it is sure of the guilt of the accused). A five-strong Court of Appeal in *Attorney-General's Reference (No 1 of 12004, R* v *Edwards and others*[350] examined and explained *Lambert*, but preferred statements made by Lord Nichols made in yet another case, *R* v *Johnstone*.[351] These differences of emphasis were described by Lord Bingham in *Sheldrake* v *DPP*[352] as explicable in the light of differences in the subject matter of the two cases. Section 5 of the 1971 Act (*Lambert*) and section 91 of the 1994 Act *(Johnstone)* were directed to serious social and economic problems, but

---

[344] See *R* v *Cowan* [1996] QB373; [1995] 3WLR 818.   [345] (1988) 13 EHRR 379.
[346] See Lord Steyn in *R* v *Lambert* [2001] 3 All ER 577 at 590.
[347] See Lord Bingham in *Brown* v *Stott (Procurator Fiscal, Dunfermline)* [2001] 2 All ER 97.
[348] See *R* v *Hunt* [1987] 1 All ER 1; Magistrates' Courts Act 1980, s 101.
[349] Amongst the authorities to which regard should be had are the following: *R* v *Lambert, ante* n 330; *R* v *DPP, ex parte Kebiline* [1999] 4 All ER 801; *L* v *DPP* [2002] 1 Cr App R 420; *R* v *Drummond* [2002] All ER (D) 70; *R* v *Johnstone* [2003] 3 All ER 884; *R (On application of Grundy & Co Excavations Ltd)* v *Halton Division Magistrates' Court* (2003) 167 JP; *Attorney-General's Reference (No 1 of 2004), R* v *Edwards* [2004] All ER (D) 318.
[350] See n 349, *ante.*
[351] See n 349, *ante.* Trade Marks Act 1994, s 91(5) held not to infringe Article 6.
[352] [2005] 1 All ER 337.

the justifiability and fairness of the respective reverse-onus provisions had to be judged in the particular context of each case. In the latter case the offence was committed by dealers and traders of goods who might be expected to exercise some care about the provenance of goods in which they dealt. The correct approach, concluded the House of Lords in *Sheldrake*, is never to decide whether a reverse burden should be imposed on a defendant, but always to assess whether a burden imposed by Parliament unjustifiably infringes the presumption of innocence. It should not inevitably be assumed that 'Parliament would not have made an exception without good reason': that approach may lead the court to give too much weight to the enactment under review and too little to the presumption of innocence and the obligation imposed on it by section 3 of the Human Rights Act 1998.[353] Applying these principles, the court in *Shedrake* held that section 5 of the Road Traffic Act 1988[354] imposed a reverse onus, but was plainly directed to a legitimate objective, the prevention of death, injury and damage on the roads. By contrast, the reverse burden provision in section 12 of the Terrorism Act 2000 was not a proportionate and legitimate response to the problem being addressed. Although a defendant might reasonably be expected to show that an organization of which he was a member was not proscribed for the purpose of the offence under section 11 of the 2000 Act, it would be all but impossible for him to show that he had not taken part in activities of the organization at the time when it was proscribed. It thus was to be read as imposing only an evidential burden.

The clear effect of this mass of case law is to leave cases to be dealt with on their own particular facts, a conclusion that is likely to mean an ongoing stream of case law.[355]

5 PROTECTION OF THE DEFENDANT

An accused has always had special protections. The right not to be required to self-incriminate has already been noted. It extends not only to the trial itself but to the pre-trial process. In *Saunders* v *United Kingdom*[356] the Court of Human Rights concluded that the principle against self-incrimination extended to the prosecution not being allowed to use evidence obtained through methods of coercion or oppression. That does not mean to say that the use of evidence obtained through self-incrimination by an accused is prohibited. A confession obtained from an accused is admissible provided it has been obtained fairly and in compliance with the terms of section 76 of PACE.[357] Again, a requirement for information, obtained on pain of penalty, as to the identity of the driver of a motor vehicle was held not to contravene Article 6

---

[353] Per Lord Bingham in *Sheldrake* v *DPP, ante*, disapproving dicta of the Court of Appeal in *A-G's Reference (No 1 of 2004)*. For the role of the court in applying Human Rights Act 1998, s 3, see p 155, *ante*.

[354] In respect of excess alcohol in blood, defence to prove no likelihood of driving whilst over prescribed limit.

[355] See Ashworth, *The Presumption of Innocence in English Law* [1996] Crim LR 30; *Reverse Onuses and the Presumption of Innocence: In Search of Principle* [2005] Crim LR 901.

[356] (1997) 2 BHRC 358.

[357] Evidence obtained by torture is always inadmissible, even if that torture was not inflicted in the United Kingdom: *A(FC) and others* v *Secretary of State for the Home Department* [2005] UKHL 71.

in *Brown v Stott (Procurator Fiscal, Dunfermiline)*[358] because it was a necessary and proportionate limitation of the basic right not to be required to self-incriminate. The provisions in sections 34, 37, and 38 of the Criminal Justice and Public Order Act 1994, which permit inferences to be drawn from a failure, in some circumstances, to supply information are, again, within Article 6 provided they do not provide the sole or main evidence against the accused.

At trial, the right of the accused not to testify has already been noted.[359] It used to be the case that, under section 1(3) of the Criminal Evidence Act 1898, an accused had a unique 'shield' about being asked questions about previous convictions or bad character. This has been significantly changed by the passage of sections 98 and 101 of the Criminal Justice Act 2003, which still give the accused some protections, but place him or her on a much more similar basis to other witnesses. Those rules are complex and outside the scope of this book.

6 CONCLUSION OF THE CASE

Each side may address the jury, except that where a defendant is unrepresented and either gives no evidence at all or only gives evidence himself the prosecution have no right to sum up their case.[360] In all cases the rule is that prosecuting counsel speaks first and is then followed by counsel for the defendant. The judge will then sum up.

The purpose of the summing-up is to instruct the jury as to the burden and standard of proof, the role of judge and jury, and to give directions on points of law where it is necessary to do so. The Judicial Studies Board has prepared model directions on common issues and points of law for the benefit of judges. The judge will also usually give a summary of the facts: indeed, in *R v Gregory*[361] the Court of Appeal suggested that there must be a reminder of the facts in all cases. However, in *R v Wilson*[362] the Court of Appeal upheld a conviction in a case where a judge considered the trial so short that a summary of the facts was unnecessary. Nor can the judge dictate what verdict the jury should reach, even if he or she considers it to be obvious or inescapable.[363]

Criticism of this part of the judicial function has from time to time been made,[364] that summings-up can unwittingly, and occasionally deliberately, influence the jury's view of the facts. Some suggested to the Royal Commission that, as in the United States, no summing-up of the facts should be given. This was rejected, but the Commission did disagree with the approach taken in *R v Gregory*, and indicated that it is in each case a question of fairness and balance.[365]

---

[358] [2001] 2 All ER 97.   [359] See p 649, *ante.*

[360] *R v Harrison* (1923) 17 Cr App R 156. Where the defendant is represented but calls no evidence, counsel for the prosecution has a right to make a closing speech but the Court of Appeal has stated that it is a right which it should rarely be necessary to exercise save in long and complex cases: *R v Bryant* [1979] QB 108; [1978] 2 All ER 689, an instructive case on the history of the procedure relating to speeches in criminal trials.

[361] [1993] Crim LR 623.   [362] [1991] Crim LR 838.

[363] [2005] UKHL 9, [2005] 2 Cr App R 8.

[364] See RCCJ, Ch 8, para 20.   [365] Ibid, para 22.

7 VERDICT

No pressure should be placed on a jury to reach a verdict.[366] The jury generally retire to the jury room to consider their verdict. They are put in charge of officers of the court called jury bailiffs who must take an oath not, without the leave of the court, to allow any person to speak to the jury or to speak to them themselves without such leave, except only to ask them if they are agreed upon their verdict. Once they have retired to consider their verdict, the jury can separate only with leave of the court, which in turn can be given only in cases of 'evident necessity' such as a juror being taken ill in the course of the jury's deliberations. They do not have to stay in the same jury room until they have reached a conclusion, but they must not separate, subject to the very limited exception noted above, and it is desirable if not essential for them always to be in the custody of one of the court bailiffs while, for example, staying at a hotel overnight.[367] The jury may, of course, ask for further guidance from the judge upon any point of law or evidence arising in the case, but both the request for information and the answer to it must be given in open court; if the jury have asked for guidance in the form of a note sent to the judge, this note should be read out verbatim and then the answer given.[368]

When the jury have concluded their deliberations they will return to court and one of their number, whom they have appointed foreman, will stand up and, subject to the possibility of a majority verdict, in answer to questions put by the appropriate officer of the court, deliver the verdict of the jury. The Criminal Justice Act 1967 introduced into English law the majority verdict. A verdict need not be unanimous if when there are not less than eleven jurors, ten agree on the verdict, and when there are ten, if nine agree. The law cannot accept any majority verdict unless the jury have had not less than two hours of deliberation, or such longer period as the court thinks reasonable having regard to the nature and complexity of the case,[369] nor can the court accept a majority verdict of guilty unless the foreman of the jury states in open court the number of jurors who agreed on, and dissented from, the verdict.[370] A Practice Direction contains procedure whereby it is hoped to conceal the fact that an acquittal was by a majority. In *R v Pigg*[371] the House of Lords held that the words 'ten agreed' (in answer to the question how many agreed and how many dissented) was sufficient

---

[366] *R v McKenna* [1960] 1 QB 411, [1960] 1 All ER 326: judge told jury that they would be kept overnight if they failed to agree a verdict within ten minutes. A guilty verdict was returned after six minutes. The resulting conviction was quashed on appeal. See also: *Bushell's case* (1670) Vaugh 135, 124 ER 1006.

[367] It may be necessary to restrict their reading or television viewing: see *Re Central Independent Television* [1991] 1 All ER 347, [1991] 1 WLR 4.

[368] *R v Neal* [1949] 2 KB 590, [1949] 2 All ER 438. Breach of this rule will almost invariably amount to a material irregularity resulting in a subsequent conviction being quashed; *R v Goodson* [1975] 1 All ER 760, [1975] 1 WLR 549 (where a juror, after retirement, was permitted by the jury bailiff to leave the jury room, following which he was seen making a telephone call); but compare *R v Alexander* [1974] 1 All ER 539, [1974] 1 WLR 422 in which the irregularity was a trifling one (juror returned to court simply to collect one or more of the exhibits and was observed throughout) and was held to be of insufficient gravity to justify quashing the conviction.

[369] Juries Act 1974, s 17(4).

[370] Ibid, s 17(3). The requirement of this subsection is mandatory so that if, for whatever reason, the foreman does not so state the conviction will inevitably be quashed: *R v Barry* [1975] 2 All ER 760, [1975] 1 WLR 1190.

[371] [1983] 1 All ER 56, [1983] 1 WLR 6.

compliance with the statute. If after such discussion as is practicable in the circumstances the jury still cannot reach the necessary measure of agreement the judge has no option but to discharge them. The defendant will then be remanded in custody or on bail to be tried afresh. Theoretically this could happen several times, but if successive juries disagree the practice is for the prosecution to offer no evidence at a third trial. On a re-trial, the fact that there has been a previous trial is usually irrelevant and inadmissible, but it may become necessary to refer to it, for example for the purpose of proving that the defendant or a witness made some particular statement or admission. Thus in *R v McGregor*,[372] the defendant was charged with receiving. At an earlier, abortive, trial he had admitted possession. A police officer was allowed to give evidence of this admission.

Other circumstances in which the jury may be discharged are:[373]

(1) illness. If during the course of a criminal trial a juror falls ill he may be discharged by the judge from further service, and depending on the facts, normally will be so discharged. The judge may then discharge the whole jury, but does not have to do so; neither is discharge of the single juror fatal to the continuance of the trial, since statute now provides that when, in the course of a trial, any member of the jury dies or is discharged the trial may nevertheless continue provided that the number of jurors does not fall below nine. If, however, the charge is murder or any offence punishable by death the prosecution and every accused must consent in writing to the trial continuing, even if only one juror is discharged or dies;

(2) misconduct of a juror, such as holding improper conversations with a member of the public about the case or absenting himself from his colleagues at the time when the jury were in the course of retiring to consider their verdict; and

(3) improper revelation to the jury of the defendant's past criminal record. In such a case the jury is frequently discharged.

In some circumstance there is the power for a jury to convict of a lesser, and different offence.[374]

8 POST VERDICT ORDERS AND SENTENCE

If the defendant pleads guilty, or is convicted by the jury, questions of sentence arise. That is dealt with in chapter 23. But even if the defendant is acquitted that may not, now, quite be the end of it, because the Domestic Violence, Crime and Victims Act 2004

---

[372] [1968] 1 QB 371, [1967] 2 All ER 267.

[373] Juries Act 1974, s 16. The judge may discharge a juror who 'being through illness incapable of continuing to act or for any other reason' (s 16(1)). This is a matter left to the discretion of the trial judge, although the Court of Appeal will interfere if injustice has resulted. In *R v Hambery* [1977] QB 924, [1977] 3 All ER 561 the trial judge discharged a lady juror in order to permit her to go away on holiday, a course which the Court of Appeal saw no reason to criticize.

[374] See *R v Coutts* [2006] UKHL 39; *R v Foster* [2007] EWCA Crim 2869; p 634, *ante*.

has given courts the right to impose restraining orders in some circumstances, despite the fact that the defendant has been acquitted. For convenience those are dealt with later.[375]

FURTHER READING

ASHWORTH and BLAKE, 'The Presumption of Innocence in English Law' [1996] Crim LR 849

ASHWORTH and REDMAYNE, *The Criminal Process*, 3rd edn (Oxford University Press: 2000)

Auld Review – *Review of the Criminal Courts of England & Wales* (http://www.criminal-courts-review.org.uk)

DENNIS, 'Reverse Onuses and the Presumption of Innocence' [2005] Crim LR 901

Home Office Report of the Advisory Group on Video Evidence (1989)

The Roskill Report on Fraud Trials (1987)

---

[375] See p 711, *post.*

22

SUMMARY PROCEDURE
AND APPEALS

INTRODUCTION

Summary trial accounts for the vast majority of all criminal cases that are dealt with by the courts. The basis of pre-trial procedure and the adversarial nature of criminal trials have already been noted, but summary trial is quicker and more informal than trial on indictment. This chapter will highlight some of the key differences between the two modes of criminal trial, focusing specifically on:

- How cases to be tried summarily are commenced.
- The time limits.
- Differences in pre-trial procedure.
- Hearings on summary trial.
- The system of youth justice.

JURISDICTION

1 INTRODUCTION

The often forgotten,[1] central role of the magistrates' courts[2] in dealing with criminal cases has already been noted.[3] In excess of 95 per cent of criminal business is dealt with summarily,[4] including virtually all cases involving children and young persons which are dealt with in the youth court. This level of work is increasing in the light of recent legislation and practice changes.[5] The issues raised by this, in terms of the composition

---

[1] See the admonition of Darbyshire, 'An Essay on the Importance and Neglect of the Magistracy' [1997] Crim LR 639.

[2] For this purpose we can include the youth courts.   [3] See chapter 20, *ante.*

[4] Auld Review Ch 3, para 2. This may be an underestimate: see Auld Review *op cit*, and Darbyshire, *op cit*, n 1.

[5] See p 580, *ante.*

of the court and the choice of mode of trial have already been noted.[6] The growth of the summary jurisdiction is, as already noted,[7] part of a continued wish by government to reduce the proportions of cases tried on indictment, with consequent benefits in terms of speed, cost and efficiency.

At the outset of any discussion of summary procedure two basic points must be noted. First, the overarching purpose of the Criminal Procedure Rules. These rules[8] provide a detailed framework for the operation of magistrates' court procedure and practice, as have in the past the various Magistrates' Courts Rules.[9] Secondly, note should be taken of the wide, and increasing, role of the justices' clerk, or legal adviser, discussed below.[10]

2 PROCESS

Summary procedure is commenced by process. The way an accused person may be brought before a court has already been discussed,[11] and the Criminal Justice Act 2003 introduced significant changes.[12] Under the pre-2003 Act current procedure, as the result of the laying of an information,[13] either a summons to appear in court or a warrant to arrest the accused could be obtained. Alternatively, the criminal proceedings could be commenced by bringing the offender to court following arrest,[14] assuming the power of arrest to be available. A warrant could not be issued in any case where a summons has already been issued. In any event, as has already been noted, a warrant cannot be issued for the arrest of an adult in the case of a summary offence, unless the offence is punishable with imprisonment or the defendant's address is 'not sufficiently established' for a summons to be served on him. Even where a warrant may lawfully be issued, it was rarely thought necessary in the case of any summary offence.

The Auld Review considered this procedure to be 'antiquated'.[15] A prosecutor could charge, summons, or lay an information, but only a charge brings with it an obligation to attend court, and many cases in fact begun by summons have to be adjourned due to the non-appearance of the defendant. This was because the issue of a summons does not place the defendant on bail, and thus create an obligation to surrender to bail. This analysis led the Auld Review to recommend change, which is achieved by the Criminal Justice Act 2003. A new system of requisition and written charge is created.[16] The power to issue an information is abolished,[17] though will remain an option for public prosecutors as a means of obtaining a warrant under section 1 of the Magistrates' Courts Act 1980 (issue of summons or warrant for arrest) to bring a charge against someone

---

[6] See p 576, *ante*.   [7] See p 577, *ante*.

[8] See, generally, p 554, *ante*. Made pursuant to Courts Act 2003, s 63. See SI 2005/384.

[9] See Magistrates' Courts Rules 1981, SI 1881/552 and related rules.

[10] See p 663, *post*.   [11] See p 574, *ante*.

[12] See p 574, *ante*.

[13] For this see Criminal Procedure Rules 2005, r 7.1.

[14] As to which, see chapter 14, *ante*.

[15] Auld Review, *op cit*, Ch 10 paras 416–422.

[16] See p 574, *ante*.   [17] Criminal Justice Act 2003, s 29(4).

already in custody, or for someone other than a public prosecutor to obtain a summons or warrant.[18] A clear simplification has been achieved.

3 JURISDICTION

A magistrates' court for an area[19] has jurisdiction to try summary offences committed within that area. It also has jurisdiction as a court of trial in the following circumstances:

(1) where a person is brought before the court on a summons or warrant issued to be tried jointly with another person over whom the court has jurisdiction);[20]

(2) in relation to either-way offences, in any case where it has jurisdiction to conduct preliminary hearings;[21]

(3) in relation to the trial of a young defendant for an indictable offence, in any case where it has jurisdiction to conduct preliminary hearings;

(4) where it has jurisdiction to try a defendant for a summary offence, it can also try him for any other summary offence.

THE COURSE OF THE TRIAL

1 TIME-LIMIT

Unless expressly provided to the contrary a magistrates' court cannot try a summary offence unless the prosecution process (by requisition and charge, formerly by information or summons) was commenced within six months from the time when the offence was committed.[22] However, it may try summarily an either-way offence outside that period, because this statutory time limit is confined to summary offences.[23] Time runs from the time of commission of the offence, not from the time of its discovery; however, it is sufficient if the process is commenced within the six months, even if the trial takes place outside that time. It is in each case a question of construction of the statute whether the offence in question is a continuing offence, that is, committed each day that the act or state of affairs in question continues, or whether it is a 'once and for all' offence in that it is committed on one day and one day only. Thus in *R v Wimbledon Justices, ex parte Derwent*[24] a statute made it an offence to let or offer to let a house in excess of a certain rent. The Divisional Court held that a person lets a house once and

---

[18] For private prosecutions generally, see p 567, *ante*.
[19] County, a London commission area, or the City of London (Magistrates' Courts Act 1980, s 2(1)).
[20] See p 273, *ante*.   [21] See p 577 et seq, *ante*.
[22] Magistrates' Courts Act 1980, s 127(1).
[23] Ibid, s 127(2); see also *Kemp v Liebherr (Great Britain) Ltd* [1987] 1 All ER 885, [1987] 1 WLR 607.
[24] [1953] 1 QB 380, [1953] 1 All ER 390.

for all when he demises it by means of a lease and that an information laid six months after the date of the demise was out of time. Proceedings could therefore be restrained by prohibition since:

> If in a case brought before justices it can be seen on the face of the proceedings that the offence is alleged to have been committed more than six months before the information was laid, justices have no power to commence dealing with the case at all, because they have no jurisdiction to sit on a court of summary jurisdiction in the case of an offence alleged to have been committed more than six months before the proceedings were instituted.[25]

Even where the offence is continuing it seems that the time limit runs from each day, so that the magistrates cannot hear any charge in respect of an offence as occurring more than six months before the date of the information;[26] in other words the matter is to be regarded as if the defendant committed the offence once every day. Where an information or charge and requisition is laid in time it may be amended to charge a different offence, after the expiry of six months from the commission of that offence, provided that this does not cause injustice.[27]

The general need to avoid delay in criminal proceedings has already been noted.[28] So, too, has the doctrine of abuse of process.[29] This doctrine applies to summary proceedings equally as to proceedings on indictment. In *R v Willesden Justices, ex parte Clemmings*,[30] Lord Bingham CJ indicated that magistrates had the power to stop a prosecution where there was an abuse of process, because:

(a) the prosecution have manipulated or misused the process of the court so as to deprive the accused of a protection provided by law or to take unfair advantage of a technicality; or

(b) the accused has been, or would be, prejudiced in the preparation or conduct of his defence by delay on the part of the prosecution, which was unjustifiable.

The principles on which these rules will be exercised are broadly those as apply more generally.[31] The court will consider whether the wrongdoing is deliberate, whether prejudice has been caused or the potential for it arises.[32] One example is *R v Brentford Justices, ex parte Wong*[33] In that case an information for careless driving was laid two days before the expiration of the statutory six-months time limit. At the time the information was laid the prosecution had not decided whether or not to prosecute and did not advise the defendant of the decision to do so until he was informed (by letter) some two months later. The summons consequent on the information was not served until some five months after the laying of the information, and the trial did not commence

---

[25] [1953] 1 QB 380, at 385, [1953] 1 All ER 390, at 391, per Lord Goddard CJ.

[26] *R v Chertsey Justices, ex parte Franks* [1961] 2 QB 152, [1961] 1 All ER 825.

[27] *R v Newcastle-upon-Tyne Justices, ex parte John Bryce (Contractors) Ltd* [1976] 2 All ER 611, [1976] 1 WLR 517.

[28] See p 571, *ante*.   [29] See p 580, *ante*.   [30] (1987) 87 Cr App R 280.   [31] See p 580, *ante*.

[32] See generally, *R v Oxford City Justices, ex parte Smith* (1987) 75 Cr App R 200, *R v Canterbury and St Augustine Justices, ex parte Turner* (1983) 147 JP 193; *R v Watford Justices, ex parte Outrim* [1983] RTR 26.

[33] [1981] 1 QB 445.

until some nine months after the laying of the information. On appeal for the refusal of the magistrates' court to stay the proceedings for abuse of process, the Divisional Court held that the police conduct amounted to 'a deliberate attempt to gain further time...', and stayed the proceedings.

2 NUMBER OF OFFENCES

A magistrates' court must not proceed to the trial of a charge which charges more than one offence.[34] This is a natural rule, because the charge fulfils the same function in summary trial as the indictment in the case of trial at the Crown Court; the same considerations of, inter alia, fairness to the defendant, which prohibit duplicity in an indictment, also prohibit the charging of more than one offence as one charge. Thus in *Ware* v *Fox*[35] an information charged the defendant with being concerned in the management of premises which were used for the purpose of smoking cannabis or cannabis resin or dealing in cannabis or cannabis resin. The Queen's Bench Divisional Court held that on the proper construction of the relevant statute[36] the information alleged two offences, namely managing premises used for smoking and managing premises used for dealing and was bad for duplicity. By contrast, section 5 of the Public Order Act 1936 created[37] the offence of using 'threatening, abusive or insulting words or behaviour with intent to provoke a breach of the peace or whereby a breach of the peace is likely to be occasioned'. It was held in *Vernon* v *Paddon*[38] that the section created one offence, the essential feature of which is conduct intended to provoke a breach of the peace or whereby such a breach was likely to be occasioned.

The issue as to whether an information is bad for duplicity is not always easy to decide. In *R* v *Courtie*[39] Lord Diplock suggested that where one provision involved the imposition of different penalties depending on whether the prosecution established particular factual ingredients then Parliament had created two separate offences, and these should be the subject of separate informations. Applying this principle a Divisional Court in *Director of Public Prosecutions* v *Corcoran*[40] held that an information charging an offence of failure, without reasonable excuse, to provide a specimen of breath, blood, or urine, contrary to section 7(6) of the Road Traffic Act 1988, was bad for duplicity, because the maximum punishment for this offence depended on the purpose for which the specimen was being sought. However, a short time later a differently constituted Divisional Court, in dismissing appeals in several cases,[41] overruled the earlier ruling and distinguished *R* v *Courtie*. On a construction of the statutory provisions, this was one offence; the question of punishment was relevant to sentence only.

---

[34] Criminal Proceedings Rules, r 7.3. However, two or more informations may be set out in a single document (ibid, r 7.3(3)); see *Shah* v *Swallow* [1984] 2 All ER 528; *sub nom Director of Public Prosecutions* v *Shah* [1984] 1 WLR 886.

[35] [1967] 1 All ER 100, [1967] 1 WLR 379.   [36] Dangerous Drugs Act 1965, s 5.

[37] Now repealed and replaced by Public Order Act 1986, s 5.

[38] [1973] 3 All ER 302, [1973] 1 WLR 663.   [39] [1984] AC 463, [1984] 1 All ER 740.

[40] [1993] 1 All ER 912.

[41] *Shaw* v *Director of Public Prosecutions (and other cases)* [1993] 1 All ER 918.

Where a charge amounts to more than one offence the prosecutor should be called on to elect before the trial begins on which offence to proceed; if he declines to make his election the charge should be dismissed.[42] It is important that the matter should be put right at the outset, since, as will be noted below, the magistrates must state the substance of it to the defendant and ask him to plead to it. However, even after a trial has started a charge bad for duplicity can be cured, by the court requiring the prosecutor to elect, just as it can prior to the trial itself.[43] The prosecutor will elect as to which offence he wishes to proceed on, the remainder will be struck out and the trial begun afresh. Again, if the prosecutor declines to elect, the charge as a whole will be struck out.

Details of the charge will be before the court.[44] It is quite permissible, however, and indeed common, for two informations against the same defendant, or (where the cases are related) against different defendants, to be tried together. It was formerly thought that this could only be done by consent but the House of Lords in *Chief Constable of Norfolk* v *Clayton*[45] held that, although magistrates should first seek consent to such a course, they could nevertheless in the exercise of their discretion order a joint trial even without the consent of the parties, although they should not do so where it would not be fair and just to a defendant.[46]

Where the charges allege an offence and an attempt to commit that offence, these may be ordered to be tried together without the consent of the defendant[47] and this will usually be done.

3 PRE-TRIAL PROCEDURES

(a) Administrative hearings

The general approach now being pursued in respect of the criminal justice process is the need to ensure that delay is reduced and kept to a minimum. It was with this aim that the Narey Report[48] recommended a wide range of structural and procedural reforms, including reforms to summary process. In particular, it recommended the establishment of procedures that will permit administrative hearings, giving case-management powers to justices' clerks in much the same way as, on indictment, the court may engage in pleas and directions hearings and preparatory hearings. Clearly such hearings could deal with a variety of administrative matters, thus saving court time, and reducing its waste through unnecessary adjournments. Although experiments along these lines

---

[42] *Edwards* v *Jones* [1947] KB 659, [1947] 1 All ER 830. See now Criminal Procedure Rules r 7.3(4).

[43] Criminal Procedure Rules, r 7.3(3).

[44] Per Lord Parker CJ and Salmon J (as he then was) in *Hargreaves* v *Alderson* [1964] 2 QB 159, [1962] 3 All ER 1019; see also *Garman* v *Plaice* [1969] 1 All ER 62, [1969] 1 WLR 19.

[45] [1983] 2 AC 473; *sub nom Clayton* v *Chief Constable of Norfolk* [1983] 1 All ER 984. This does not, however, enable a summons and cross-summons to be tried together; this cannot be done semble even by consent: *R* v *Epsom Justices, ex parte Gibbons* [1984] QB 574, [1983] 3 All ER 523.

[46] The wishes of the parties should not lightly be overruled: *R* v *Highbury Corner Magistrates' Court, ex parte McGinley* (1986) 150 JP 257.

[47] Criminal Attempts Act 1981, s 4(2).

[48] Review of Delay in the Criminal Justice System, 27 February 1997.

had from time to time occurred,[49] the basis on which they had been conducted was open to some doubt, and necessary changes were introduced by the Crime and Disorder Act 1998. It did this in two ways.

The first was by early administrative hearings. Section 47 of the 1998 Act provides that the first hearing before a magistrates' court following the charging of a person with an offence at a police station may be conducted by a single justice. Justices' clerks were also given some case management functions.[50] At such a hearing the accused must be asked whether he wishes to receive legal aid, if he does his eligibility is to be determined and, if he is in fact eligible, the necessary arrangement must be put in hand for him to obtain it. The single justice may also exercise any other power exercisable by a single justice (see below). The second was the extension of the powers which may be exercised by a single justice. By section 49 of the Crime and Disorder Act 1998, a range of powers was conferred on a single justice, or, where rules provide,[51] on a justices' clerk (or legal adviser).

(b) Powers of a single justice or justices' clerk

These powers comprise authority:

(a) to extend bail or to impose or vary conditions of bail;

(b) to mark an information as withdrawn;

(c) to dismiss an information or discharge an accused where no evidence is offered by the prosecution;

(d) to make an order for the payment of the accused's costs out of central funds;

(e) to request a pre-sentence report[52] following a guilty plea, and, for that purpose, to give an indication of the seriousness of the offence;

(f) to request a medical report and, for that purpose to remand the accused in custody or on bail;

(g) to remit an offender to another court for sentence;

(h) to determine mode of trial on an amended charge;

(i) to vary the time for appearance at court specified by police bail;

(j) to extend, with the consent of the accused, a custody or other time limit;

(k) to grant representation for the Crown Court under the Legal Aid Act 1988;

(l) to order production of a driving licence;

(m) to give a direction prohibiting the publication or disclosure of certain matters;

(n) to give, vary or revoke directions, which may include directions as to a timetable for the proceedings, the attendance of the parties, the service of documents, and the manner in which evidence is to be given.

---

[49] Although with no clear basis in law.
[50] Powers to extend this jurisdiction to justices' clerks were conferred by s 48(2). See further, p 663, *post.*
[51] See *ante*, n 50.   [52] Where required by Criminal Justice Act 1991, s 3.

Further changes to the range of powers exercisable by a single justice were made by the Criminal Justice Act 2003. A single justice will be able to deal with the revised process for determination of mode of trial for either-way offences.[53]

These changes individually focus on matters of considerable detail. Together, they provided a means whereby summary cases are not subject to continual or unnecessary adjournments or unnecessary hearings on what are important, but often administrative or preparatory, matters and are conducted efficiently and, so far as possible, speedily. The practice as to how they have in fact been used has varied, in particular as to the respective roles of the single justice and the justices' clerk or legal adviser. The Auld Review noted[54] that courts in two-thirds of magistrates' courts commission areas held at least some early administrative hearing presided over by a single magistrate nor clerk or adviser. It noted:

> Some sit in the normal way with a bench of magistrates and a clerk, but the clerk deals with the directions and the magistrates deal with matters reserved to them. Some sit in split session, starting with the clerk alone and then bring in the magistrates to deal with anything outside the clerk's jurisdiction. And some sit, as they always have, as a full directions court, consisting of a bench of magistrates and the clerk, with the magistrates' dealing both with matters reserved to them and otherwise exercisable by the clerk.

(c) Powers of justices' clerk

The powers of justices' clerks are now to found specified by rules made in 1999 and re-enacted with amendments in 2005.[55] These powers now extend to dealing with informations, summonses, and (in some cases) the issue of warrants of arrest. Adjournments by consent, the ascertaining of plea, the issue of directions, requests for pre-sentence reports, and varying or amendment of some community orders are amongst the long list of matters in respect of which power is conferred on a clerk, all designed to ensure effective case-management and disposal. This is not crucial in the light of the provisions of the Criminal Procedure Rules. In pursuit of the overriding objective that applies now to all criminal proceedings,[56] a magistrates' court must actively manage a case.[57] This includes:

(a) the early identification of the real issues;

(b) the early identification of the needs of witnesses;

(c) achieving certainty as to what must be done, by whom and when, in particular by the early setting of a timetable for the progress of the case;

(d) monitoring the progress of the case and compliance with directions;

(e) ensuring that evidence, whether disputed or not, is presented in the shortest and clearest way;

---

[53] Criminal Justice Act 2003, Schedule 3. For mode of trial, see, p 575, *ante*.
[54] *Op cit*, Ch 4, para 56.
[55] See Justices' Clerks Rules 2005 SI 2005 No 545, replacing Justices Clerks Rules 1999.
[56] See p 555, *ante*.   [57] Criminal Procedure Rules, 3.2.

(f) discouraging delay, dealing with as many aspects of the case as possible on the same occasion, and avoiding unnecessary hearings;

(g) encouraging the participants to co-operate in the progression of the case; and

(h) making use of technology.

These are, of course, matters that apply equally to trial on indictment.[58] In their fulfilment each party must nominate a person responsible for the progression of the case (a 'case progression officer'), which may cause some organizational difficulties for smaller defence teams. He monitors compliance with directions, keeps the court informed, and must be available during normal working hours. A court may nominate a magistrate, or clerk to manage the case, and to make and deal with directions, including matters as to the date and length of a hearing. The rules provide for matters relating to case preparation and progression, readiness for trial, and identification of matters relevant to the trial itself, such as the witnesses to be called and points of law to be raised. In short, the framework for active case management is established, supplemented by a whole host of other relevant regulations and provisions.

(d) Disclosure

The regime for the disclosure of unused material by the prosecution and for defence disclosure, both contained in the Criminal Procedure and Investigations Act 1996, has already been discussed.[59] Until the passage of that Act the position regarding prosecution disclosure in summary proceedings had been unclear. In one case[60] a Divisional Court decided that the interests of justice required that decisions as to whether material should be disclosed should be restricted to the Crown Courts and were not matters for consideration by magistrates. However, that was a case concerned with committal proceedings, and did not address the more general question of disclosure on summary trial. Logically, there should be no fundamental difference between trial on indictment and summary trial in this respect, although various practical issues arise, and the position was clarified by another Divisional Court in *R v Bromley Magistrates' Court, ex parte Smithy and Wilkins*,[61] where Simon Brown LJH observed that an accused in a summary case is as much entitled to the safeguards designed to secure a fair trial in a magistrates' court as in the Crown Court.

Section 1 of the 1996 Act applies the disclosure provisions of that Act (i.e. prosecution and defence disclosure) to cases where a person is charged with a summary offence in which a court proceeds to summary trial and the accused pleads not guilty, and to cases where a magistrates' court proceeds to summary trial on an either-way offence to which the accused pleads not guilty. It also applies to the trial in the youth court of an indictable offence in respect of a person under the age of eighteen. The effect of this is that the duty of prosecution initial disclosure and further prosecution disclosure arises.[62] A court will also have powers to determine questions as to whether material

---

[58] See p 628, *ante*.   [59] See p 606, *ante*.
[60] *R v South Worcestershire Magistrates, ex parte Lilley* [1995] 4 All ER 186, (1995) 159 JP 598.
[61] [1995] 4 All ER 146, (1994) 159 JP 251.   [62] See p 606, *ante*.

should be withheld in the public interest.[63] In respect of defence disclosure, the position is slightly different. There is no obligation on the defence to disclose the nature of the defence. However, section 6 of the 1996 Act creates a power for voluntary defence disclosure in summary cases, with the potential for an inference to be drawn[64] for inadequate or incomplete disclosure. The advantage for the accused in engaging in voluntary defence disclosure is that only if he does so will the prosecutor be under an obligation to engage in further prosecution disclosure.[65] If, of course, there is voluntary defence disclosure under section 6, then the extended obligations created by the Criminal Justice Act 2003[66] will apply.

One further change made by the 1996 Act should be noted. In cases of trial on indictment the law requires advance notice to be given of expert evidence that is to be called. No such obligation has existed hitherto in summary cases. There can be no real justification for this distinction, and the 1996 Act rectifies the omission by authorizing the making of rules which will extend to summary cases.[67] No such rules have yet been made. The new section 6D of the 1996 Act,[68] which requires details to be given as to experts who have been consulted is, read literally, wide enough to extend to summary proceedings but it is far from clear that it does so.

4 HEARING

If the defendant appears at the hearing, the court must state to him the substance of the information and ask him whether he pleads guilty or not guilty. In spite of these words, the same pleas as are open to a defendant charged with an indictable offence may be raised by a defendant charged with a summary offence. If the plea is one of not guilty the prosecutor may make an opening speech, and will then call his evidence. Where the prosecutor is unrepresented, it is open to the magistrates, in their discretion, to permit their clerk to examine prosecution witnesses.[69] Section 97 of the Magistrates' Courts Act 1980 will apply, and the witnesses will be subject to cross-examination and re-examination according to the circumstances of the case, and in accordance with the procedures and rules of evidence already noted.[70] If necessary, a witness can be summonsed to the court to give evidence by witness summons issued under section 97 of the 1980 Act. Alternatively, in some circumstances the written statement of the witness may be considered by the court.[71] Clearly, such out-of-court statements may infringe the rule of evidence relating to hearsay[72] and the relevant exceptions, whether statutory or common law, will need to be considered.

---

[63] Criminal Procedure and Investigations Act 1996, s 3(6) and s 14. See, further, p 606, *ante*.

[64] See 1996 Act, s 11. The inference will be of the same type as may be drawn under Criminal Justice and Public Order Act 1994, ss 34–38, as to which see p 644, *ante*.

[65] Under 1996 Act, s 7. See p 607, *ante*.   [66] See p 615, *ante*.

[67] 1996 Act, s 19(1).   [68] As to which see p 616, *ante*.

[69] *Simms v Moore* [1970] 2 QB 327, [1970] 3 All ER 1.   [70] See p 639, *ante*.

[71] Under Criminal Justice Act 2003, s 114; see also Magistrates' Courts Act 1980, s 102; Criminal Justice Act 1967, s 9.

[72] Under the Criminal Justice Act 2003, which significantly amended the pre-existing rules relating to hearsay.

The procedure followed during the examination and cross-examination of witnesses mirrors that in trial on indictment, although rules of evidence may sometimes be applied less strictly there are, of course, important differences. Detailed matters of procedure are dealt with by Part 37 of the Criminal Procedure Rules 2005. Since there is no jury, the magistrates are both the tribunal of law and tribunal of fact: in other words, all decisions are for them irrespective of whether they are matters of fact or law. Thus the magistrates will decide questions of admissibility of evidence, although the procedures for doing so (which are quite clear in trial on indictment) are less clear on summary trial. It has been noted[73] that a Crown Court may hold a hearing (known as a *voir dire*, after the name of the oath taken by witnesses who testify at such a hearing) in order to decide questions of admissibility of evidence. Such a hearing is held in the absence of the jury, so that the jury does not hear evidence which may later be ruled inadmissible. The concept of a *voir dire* in magistrates' courts is wholly artificial, and the cases leave unclear the extent to which a magistrates' court, on summary trial, must conduct a 'trial within a trial' in order to decide whether evidence is admissible.[74]

It is also pertinent to consider the role of the justices' clerk. The functions of justices' clerks are considered elsewhere.[75] The clerk will generally advise on matters of law and procedure, and ensure that the trial is conducted properly, but must take great care to ensure that he plays no part in decisions on matters of fact, which are for the justices themselves.[76] The clerk may assist a party to present his case.[77] Care should be taken to avoid influencing the decisions of the justices on matters of fact or sentence, or to avoid giving the appearance of doing so.

At the conclusion of the evidence for the prosecution the defendant may address the court, whether or not he calls evidence; if he is calling evidence it will follow at once. The defendant may then address the court a second time but only if he himself has given evidence, another witness has been called on his behalf, and the court gives leave.[78] If the defendant addresses the court twice the prosecutor has a right to address the court a second time immediately before the defendant's second speech. The court will then retire if necessary and convict the defendant or dismiss the charge. If on the other hand the defendant pleads guilty the court may convict him without hearing evidence.[79] The wording of the subsection shows that it is often desirable to hear some evidence, particularly where it is part of the prosecution's case that the offence was committed in circumstances of aggravation, or perhaps if a committal for sentence to the Crown Court is contemplated or if the plea of guilty tendered may be 'equivocal'.[80] In any event the court retains full power over the case until sentence is passed and has discretion to allow a change of plea until that time if justice so requires.[81] Whether there is a plea of guilty or finding of guilt, there will normally be such an inquiry into the past record of

---

[73] See p 640, *ante*.

[74] See, in particular, *R v Liverpool Juvenile Court, ex parte R* [1988] QB 1, which provides that a *voir dire* should be held in respect of confession evidence.

[75] See p 663, *ante*.   [76] *R v Sussex Justices, ex parte MacCarthy* [1924] 1 KB 256.

[77] See *ante*.   [78] Criminal Procedure Rules 2005, r 37.1.

[79] Magistrates' Courts Act 1980, s 9(3).   [80] See p 631, *ante*.

[81] *S (An Infant) v Manchester City Recorder* [1971] AC 481, [1969] 3 All ER 1230.

the defendant as follows conviction of an indictable offence; the court may then adjourn, for not more than four weeks at a time, for inquiries to be made or for the purpose of determining the best way to deal with the case.[82] When the court resumes it need not be composed of the same magistrates; if, however, there are any newcomers the court which sentences or deals with the offender must make such inquiry into the facts and circumstances of the case as are necessary to acquaint the newcomers fully with those facts and circumstances.[83] This must be done even though the court will have held some such inquiry before; the use of the words 'the court' seems to prohibit the newcomers being given information privately before the court sits.[84]

Finally, note should be taken of the power which magistrates have under the Justices of the Peace Act 1361 to bind over a defendant to keep the peace or be of good behaviour even where he is acquitted.[85]

ABSENCES

1 GENERAL EFFECTS OF ABSENCE[86]

It sometimes happens that one or both of the parties fails to appear at the trial or adjourned trial of the information. If the defendant does not appear the court may, and sometimes must, hear the case in his absence provided that either the court is satisfied that the defendant was served with notice of the charge within what appears to be a reasonable time before the hearing, or the defendant appeared on a previous occasion to answer the charge.[87] Alternatively the court may adjourn the hearing, with or without issuing a warrant for the arrest of the defendant; but a warrant can only be issued if the court is satisfied as to the matters stated above. There is a further restriction on the issue of a warrant; if the court adjourns the trial after hearing evidence, or convicting the defendant without hearing evidence on a plea of guilty, the court must not issue a warrant unless it thinks it undesirable, by reason of the gravity of the offence, to continue the hearing in his absence. In any event, a warrant cannot be issued unless the offence

---

[82] Magistrates' Courts Act 1980, s 10(3); the period is three weeks if the defendant is in custody.

[83] Magistrates' Courts Act 1980, s 98(7). This is perhaps the nearest that English law comes to allowing special 'sentencing tribunals'.

[84] In the event of a question arising which might require reference to the European Court for a preliminary ruling the justices may, on application or otherwise, order the question to be referred and the hearing will then be adjourned pending receipt of the European Court's ruling; for a case in which this was done, and observations as to the approach which magistrates should adopt to this problem, see *R v Plymouth Justices, ex parte Rogers* [1982] QB 863, [1982] 2 All ER 175.

[85] See *Veater v G* [1981] 2 All ER 304, [1981] 1 WLR 567; *Hughes v Holley* (1986) 86 Cr App R 130.

[86] Magistrates' Courts Act 1980, ss 11–16. As to absence during the initial procedure on information for an offence triable either way, see p 584, *ante*. See now Magistrates' Courts (Procedure) Act 1998.

[87] The mode of service is prescribed by the Criminal Procedure Rules. If the court proceeds in the absence of the defendant in a case where he has not been duly served in accordance with this rule, the 'hearing' is a complete nullity: *R v Seisdon Justices, ex parte Dougan* [1983] 1 All ER 6, [1982] 1 WLR 1476.

is punishable by imprisonment or unless the court, having convicted the defendant, proposes to disqualify him.

The accused may be represented at the hearing by solicitor or counsel,[88] in such circumstances the accused being deemed to be present even if not physically in court. If the accused in fact is present he may be assisted by another person,[89] although the court may decline this if the level or nature of the assistance is unreasonable.

If the prosecutor fails to appear the court may dismiss the information or, if evidence has been received on a previous occasion, continue the hearing.[90] This is one example of the importance of the stage of the trial at which the justices begin to hear evidence. Alternatively the court may adjourn the trial, or may in an appropriate case dismiss the information for want of prosecution under section 15(1) of the Magistrates' Courts Act 1980. However, this power should not be used for this purpose save in exceptional cases. In *R v Hendon Justices, ex parte Director of Public Prosecutions*[91] a magistrates' court dismissed an information for want of prosecution when the defendants, their advocates, and the prosecution witnesses were all at court, but the prosecuting solicitor was not. This absence occurred because of an error in court administration, and the court was aware that a solicitor was on his way to rectify the position. In quashing the order of the justices the Divisional Court stressed that the duty of the magistrates' court is to hear informations properly brought before it. The prosecution had a right to be heard; the proper course was to adjourn until the hearing could proceed.

If neither side appears, the court may again dismiss the information or, if evidence has been received on a previous occasion, continue the hearing;[92] alternatively the hearing may simply be adjourned.

2 PLEADING GUILTY BY POST

The Magistrates' Courts Act 1957 provided a new and convenient procedure whereby the defendant can plead guilty in cases where his appearance at court would be no more than a formality, if not a serious waste of time and money. It is now governed by section 12 of the 1980 Act. The procedure laid down by the Act is generally acknowledged to have worked well and is extensively used, particularly in motoring cases; however, it has no application at all to: (1) youth court proceedings in respect of persons under sixteen years; (2) offences triable either way; or (3) offences for which the accused is liable to be sentenced to imprisonment for a term exceeding three months. Where the Act does apply, the procedure is as follows. The prosecutor will serve with the summons a notice in prescribed terms as to the effect of section 12 of the Act and a concise statement of such facts as he will place before the court if the defendant does decide to plead guilty by post. Although the Act is silent on the point it seems that it is entirely within the discretion of the prosecutor as to whether he will make use of the Act and serve the

---

[88] Magistrates' Courts Act 1980, s 12.
[89] *R v Leicester City Justices, ex parte Barrow* [1991] 2 QB 60, [1991] 3 All ER 935.
[90] Magistrates' Courts Act 1980, s 15.   [91] [1994] QB 167, [1993] 1 All ER 411.
[92] Magistrates' Courts Act 1980, s 16.

above documents with the summons, even on the assumption that the Act applies to the offence charged. Where, however, the prosecutor does elect to use the procedure, he must serve the documents and then inform the clerk to the justices that he has done so. It is then for the defendant or his solicitor to inform the clerk that he desires to plead guilty without appearing, if that is so, by sending, appropriately completed, the part of the notice described above. He does not, of course, have to use the procedure, and even if he does at first give notification that he is not going to appear he may change his mind and appear.

If, however, he does not appear the court may proceed to hear the case in his absence (whether or not the prosecutor is also absent) provided that it is satisfied that the notice and statement of facts were served on the defendant with the summons. Before accepting the plea of guilty and convicting the defendant in his absence the court must cause to be read out aloud the defendant's notification that he is going to plead guilty, the statement of facts served on the defendant, and any statement by way of mitigation which the defendant himself may have submitted. The statement of facts read out must be precisely the same as that served upon the defendant. These rules must be meticulously observed, and breach of them may be a ground for quashing the conviction by means of certiorari:

> we all know that these matters have to be dealt with expeditiously.[93] It seems to me, however, to be quite clear that, before the magistrates can exercise jurisdiction in a case of this sort, they must strictly observe the conditions of the statute. Mere knowledge of the contents of the accused's submission, the mere reading of it themselves, is not sufficient; the submission must be read in open court.[94]

The rule that the precise statement of facts must be read out is also important, because after hearing it the magistrates may decide that the case is too grave to be dealt with in the way contemplated by the parties and may adjourn the case for the defendant to be present.

Assuming that, after hearing the notification of intention to plead guilty, the statement of facts and the submissions in mitigation, the magistrates accept the plea, they will record a conviction and (in the majority of cases to which the Act applies) impose a fine. Where they think it desirable to imprison the defendant or to impose any disqualification on him they must adjourn the hearing[95] without imposing any penalty whatever. There must then be sent to the defendant a notice stating the time and place of the adjourned hearing and the reason for the present adjournment (that is that the court is considering imprisonment or disqualification). If he chooses not to appear after receiving notice of what the court has in mind the court can proceed to disqualify him

---

[93] Section 12, as amended by the Criminal Justice Act 1991, s 69.

[94] *R v Oldham Justices, ex parte Morrissey* [1958] 3 All ER 559n, at 560, [1959] 1 WLR 58, at 59, per Lord Parker CJ.

[95] Under the Magistrates' Courts Act 1980, s 10(3). This applies even if disqualification is mandatory under the 'totting-up' provisions; further there may even in this case be grounds for mitigating the normal consequences of conviction, which the defendant should have the chance to state: *R v Llandrindod Wells Justices, ex parte Gibson* [1968] 2 All ER 20, [1968] 1 WLR 598.

in his absence;[96] they cannot, however, sentence him to imprisonment or detention in his absence.[97] In such a case the proper course is to issue a warrant for the defendant's arrest.[98] Thus a person can never be sentenced to imprisonment in his absence and can only be disqualified in his absence following an adjournment for the purpose of giving him an opportunity to appear. However, a person may be committed to prison, for default in payment of a fine, in his absence.[99]

SENTENCE

The types of sentence imposable by magistrates are basically similar to those available to the Crown Court, although the extent of magistrates' powers in relation to severity of sentence is more limited. They can, at the moment, normally only sentence to imprisonment for up to six months in respect of any one offence[100] (or twelve months in the case of consecutive sentences),[101] although that is to change when the provisions of Criminal Justice Act 2003 are brought into force.[102]

Their powers relating to the imposition of fines and the making of compensation orders are restricted. Since all summary jurisdiction derives from statute the amount of the maximum fine for any offence is prescribed by statute. However, where a statute provides for imprisonment or other detention but makes no express provision for a fine, there is a general power to fine instead of imposing a custodial sentence.[103]

As a result of inflation statutory fines may quickly become too low and, to combat this phenomenon, the Criminal Justice Act 1982, section 37 introduced 'the standard scale' of fines for summary offences. This scale consists of five levels and the ensuing sections of the 1982 Act provided for the substitution of a level on the standard scale for the figures prescribed by existing statutory provisions. Thus, for example, a summary offence formerly punishable with a fine of £100 became punishable with a fine up to level 3. To keep pace with inflation these levels may be increased by order of the Secretary of State,[104] although it should be remembered that the fine that may be imposed in respect of an either-way offence will be determined by the terms of the specific statutory provision. The maximum compensation that magistrates can order under a compensation order is similarly limited.[105]

The position regarding the appropriate level of fines for summary offences has proved somewhat controversial. In an attempt to create some equal impact of fines upon those

---

[96] Ibid, s 11(4). But, now, see Magistrates' Courts (Procedure) Act 1998.

[97] Ibid, s 11(3).   [98] Ibid, s 13(3).

[99] Ibid, s 82(5); *R v Dudley Magistrates' Court, ex parte Payne* [1979] 2 All ER 1089, [1979] 1 WLR 891.

[100] Magistrates' Courts Act 1980, s 31(1); they can, of course, commit to the Crown Court for sentence in the circumstances noted at p 671, *post.*

[101] Ibid, s 133.   [102] See p 672, *post.*   [103] Magistrates' Courts Act 1980, s 34(3).

[104] Magistrates' Courts Act 1980, s 143 (as amended by the Criminal Justice Act 1982, s 48). They were increased by the Criminal Justice Act 1991, s 17, under which the maximum fine for a level 5 offence is £5,000.

[105] Ibid, s 40(1); s 143 applies to s 40(1).

of different incomes, the Criminal Justice Act 1991 introduced[106] a system of 'unit fines', whereby the actual amount of a fine depended upon a complex formula that sought to multiply an amount related to the seriousness of the offence with a multiple reflecting the level of disposable income of the defendant. After widespread public concern, the scheme was abandoned. The position is now governed by a revised section 18 of the Criminal Justice Act 1991,[107] which requires the sentencing court to take into account both the seriousness of the offence and the ability of the defendant to pay.[108]

Finally, reference should be made to the provisions, now contained in section 39 of the 1980 Act, whereby a person aged seventeen or over who has been convicted before different magistrates' courts of two or more offences punishable with imprisonment or disqualification from driving, may be remitted to be dealt with by one of the courts concerned.

A wide range of special rules govern the sentencing and treatment of young offenders by the youth court. These are dealt with later.[109]

COMMITTALS FOR SENTENCE

1 INTRODUCTION

In some instances a defendant who has been tried in the magistrates' court may be committed to the Crown Court to be sentenced or otherwise dealt with. The case then becomes:

> a sort of composite case in which power is given to one court to convict and to another to give judgment; and until the judgment is given the hearing of the case is not complete.[110]

The basic justification for the power to commit for sentence has been that a magistrates' court, having accepted jurisdiction in respect of an either-way offence, may consider, after conviction, that its sentencing powers are inadequate. Currently its powers of imprisonment are limited, in respect of a single offence, of six months, and in total twelve months in respect of multiple offences.[111] Section 3 of the Powers of Criminal Courts (Sentencing) Act 2000 (as amended currently) provides for committal to the Crown Court where the magistrates' court considers that the offence, or the combination of the offence and other offences associated with it,[112] is so serious that greater punishment should be inflicted than the magistrates' court has power to impose. A power to commit also arises in respect of an offence in respect of which the defendant

---

[106] Criminal Justice Act 1991, ss 18–19.   [107] As substituted by Criminal Justice Act 1993, s 65(1).
[108] Powers of Criminal Courts (Sentencing) Act 2000, s 128.   [109] See p 680, *post*.
[110] Lord Goddard CJ in *R v Norfolk Justices, ex parte Director of Public Prosecutions* [1950] 2 KB 558, at 568; *sub nom R v Greenhoe Justices, ex parte Director of Public Prosecutions* [1950] 2 All ER 42, at 46.
[111] See p 672, *post*.   [112] See p 700, *post*.

has already indicated a guilty plea where the defendant is sent for trial on one or more related offences.[113]

As already noted,[114] the Royal Commission on Criminal Justice in 1993 observed[115] that the Crown Court was often passing sentences that were within the powers of the Crown Court. It was to address this issue that the Criminal Justice Act 2003 has altered mode of trial provisions,[116] and (when fully implemented) will increase magistrates' sentencing powers.[117] When these new provisions are fully in force, changes to the power to commit for sentence will be implemented. The 2003 Act inserts a new section 3 into the Powers of Criminal Courts (Sentencing) Act 2000.[118] Under this new section 3, the power to commit for sentence will only apply where the offender is convicted having indicated, when venue was determined, that he would plead guilty. There will be no power to commit for sentence where a defendant is convicted, the magistrates' court having accepted jurisdiction and convicted him after a non-guilty plea. The intention is that magistrates retain a greater proportion of cases, confident that their increased sentencing powers will be sufficient to deal with the more serious cases that it is anticipated that they will retain. However, there is, of course, a danger that magistrates will not retain those more serious cases, but instead simply impose greater levels of sentence. For that reason, adherence to sentencing guidelines will be even more crucial.[119]

2 PROCEDURE FOR COMMITTAL

Committal will normally be to the most convenient location of the Crown Court. In selecting this the justices may have regard to directions given by the presiding judge or judges of the circuit. Committal may be in custody or on bail, but the Court of Appeal has indicated that:

> the cases must be rare when magistrates' courts can properly commit for [sentence] on bail because the whole purpose of the committal is to have the man sent to prison, and have him sent to prison for a longer period than the magistrates' court could impose.[120]

However, the defendant may give notice of appeal against conviction and may then, *qua* appellant, be released on bail, although, where a possibly severe sentence awaits him, bail will only be granted 'with extreme care, and only in really exceptional cases'.[121] There is no appeal against the order of committal as such;[122] if the defendant thinks that the committal was bad in law, for example because he was not warned that he might be

---

[113] Powers of Criminal Courts (Sentencing) Act 2000, s 4.   [114] See p 578, *ante*.

[115] Royal Commission, *op cit*, para 6.12, relying on research conducted by Hedderman and Moxon, *Magistrates' Court or Crown Court: Mode of Trial Decisions and Sentencing*, Home Office Research Study No 125, HMSO 1982. See now Herbert, 'Mode of Trial and Magistrates' Sentencing Powers' [2003] Crim LR 315.

[116] See p 580, *ante*.   [117] See p 580, *ante*.

[118] 2003 Act, Schedule 3, para 22.   [119] See p 692, *post*.

[120] *R v Coe* [1969] 1 All ER 65, at 68, [1968] 1 WLR 1950, at 1954.

[121] *Re Whitehouse* [1951] 1 KB 673, at 675, [1951] 1 All ER 353, at 354.

[122] *R v London Sessions Appeal Committee, ex parte Rogers* [1951] 2 KB 74, [1951] 1 All ER 343.

committed, he should apply to a Divisional Court of the Queen's Bench Division for a quashing order or prohibition order; the Crown Court will not, of course, sentence him until the result of his application is known, since the order of committal may be held to be a nullity. On such an application the Divisional Court can only hear argument as to the legality of the committal and cannot entertain any suggestion that the committal was too harsh a step to take having regard to the facts; this is an argument to be addressed (although not in so many words) to the Crown Court when the defendant appears there for sentence.

On such appearance, procedure is as if the defendant had been committed for trial to the Crown Court and had pleaded guilty to the charge. No actual plea will be taken, since that stage of the trial is concluded, but otherwise the position is as if the defendant had pleaded guilty at the Crown Court itself. Thus notices required to be served 'three days before the trial' may be served three days before the hearing at the Crown Court,[123] and, if the defendant has been granted bail, but fails to surrender, the Crown Court may issue a bench warrant.[124] It might then be thought that the Crown Court could allow the defendant to withdraw his plea of guilty (if such was tendered) in the magistrates' court, before he was sentenced, and it is now clear from *R v Mutford and Lothingland Justices, ex parte Harber*[125] following the decision of the House of Lords in *S (An Infant) v Manchester City Recorder*[126] that this is permissible. The Crown Court certainly has such a power when trying a case on indictment.[127]

At the hearing there should be formal identification by the police of the defendant as the person who appeared at the magistrates' court and was committed; if there is no police officer present who can give this information, the defendant may, it seems, be asked whether he was the person who appeared and was committed. The Crown Court will inquire into the circumstances of the case as it would following a plea of guilty before itself; prosecuting counsel will give the court an outline of the facts. It should be noted that if there is a dispute as to the facts of the offence upon which the defendant has been committed for sentence, the Crown Court can either resolve that matter itself, if necessary by hearing evidence, or can remit the case to the magistrates' court for such dispute to be resolved.[128] The court will then consider the defendant's antecedents, and usually a pre-sentence report;[129] defending counsel (or solicitor) will then address the court in mitigation. The Crown Court can then pass any sentence up to the maximum which the particular indictable offence carries and can deal with the defendant in any manner in which it could deal with him if he had just been convicted of the offence on indictment before the court.[130] The position as to appeal itself against this sentence is considered later.[131]

---

[123] *R v Grant* [1951] 1 KB 500, [1951] 1 All ER 28.   [124] Bail Act 1976, s 7.

[125] [1971] 2 QB 291, [1971] 1 All ER 81. The Crown Court can only take into consideration what took place in the magistrates' court: *R v Marylebone Justices, ex parte Westminster City Council* [1971] 1 All ER 1025, [1971] 1 WLR 567.

[126] [1971] AC 481, [1969] 3 All ER 1230.   [127] See p 632, *ante*.

[128] *Munroe v Crown Prosecution Service* [1988] Crim LR 823.

[129] See p 698, *post*.   [130] Powers of Criminal Courts Act 1973, s 42.   [131] See p 716, *post*.

If the defendant appeals against conviction, as well as being committed for sentence, the Crown Court will of course hear his appeal first, since, if this succeeds, there will be no cause to sentence him.

YOUTH JUSTICE

Procedures in the youth court mirror those that apply on summary trial in the magistrates' court, although a clear division between the two courts exists,[132] those who sit in the youth court are members of a youth court panel,[133] and special restrictions apply on the reporting of proceedings.[134] The child or young person will be accompanied by parent, guardian, or social worker, and the proceedings will be very much more informal than those in the magistrates' court, clearly essential because of the age of the person before the court.

1 AIMS AND PROVISION OF YOUTH JUSTICE

Although no fundamental differences exist in terms of procedure, youth justice raises very distinct issues which are reflected in the powers, and objectives of the youth court (and of the Crown Court when dealing with children and young persons). Section 44 of the Children and Young Persons Act 1933 requires any court, in fulfilling its duties, to take account of the welfare of the child or young person before it. More recently considerable debate has occurred as to the role and functions of the youth justice system. In a Consultation Paper,[135] the government stated its belief that action was needed to bring about greater consistency in the approach to work with young offenders in the community and to ensure that all the relevant local agencies play a full part. It also believed that the youth justice system should seek to prevent crime. For that reason, section 37 of the Crime and Disorder Act 1998 states that:

> It shall be the principal aim of the youth justice system to prevent offending by children and young persons.

By section 37(2) it shall be the duty of all persons and bodies carrying out functions in relation to the youth justice system to have regard to that aim. This is a broad statement of an overall duty that will apply not only to local authorities, health authorities, probation services, voluntary agencies, and the police, but also to the courts in dealing with young offenders after conviction.

The role of local authorities in establishing youth offending teams and creating youth justice strategies should be noted. Each local authority is under a duty to secure that, to such extent as is appropriate for their area, all youth justice services are available

---

[132] See generally chapter 10.   [133] Ibid.   [134] See p 678, *post.*
[135] *No More Excuses – A New Approach to Tackling Youth Crime in England and Wales,* Cm 3809 (1997).

there,[136] performed in partnership with other agencies such as the police. Local authorities will operate within the overall guidance given by a new Youth Justice Board.[137] This will comprise ten, eleven, or twelve members, appointed by the Home Secretary, and who will include persons with extensive recent experience of the youth justice system. Its functions are set out by section 42(5) of the Crime and Disorder Act 1998, and include:

(a) the monitoring of the operation of the youth justice and the provision of youth justice services;

(b) advising the Home Secretary on the operation of that system and the provision of such services; how the principal aim of that system might most effectively be pursued; the content of any national standards he may see fit to set with respect to the provision of such services, or the accommodation in which children and young persons are kept in custody; and the steps that might be taken to prevent offending by children and young persons;

(c) the monitoring and collection of information about the youth justice system and the provision of services by local authorities;

(d) the identification and promotion of good practice in the context of the operation of the youth justice system and the provision of youth justice services, the prevention of offending by children and young persons; and in respect of working with children and young persons who are or are at risk of becoming offenders.

Youth justice teams are an important element in the strategy to deal with youth offending which was introduced by the Crime and Disorder Act 1998. At least one team exists in each local authority area, and includes at least one probation officer, local authority social worker, police officer, and nominee of a health authority and of the local education authority. These youth justice teams are under a duty to co-ordinate the provision of youth justice services within the local authority area, and to carry out such functions as are assigned to the team in the local authority's youth justice plan made under section 41. Not only is it intended that youth offending teams should co-ordinate local provision relating to work with young offenders, but they also play a key role in the reprimand and caution system introduced by the 1998 Act, and in respect of several of the orders that may be made by a court when dealing with young offenders. Their primary functions include report-writing for courts, the preparation of reparation or action plans, and the supervision of young offenders within the community, based upon an inter-agency partnership philosophy.[138]

---

[136] 1998 Act, s 38.

[137] Ibid, s 41. For an insight into the workings of the youth justice system, see the Annual Reports of the Youth Justice Board, to be found at www.youthjustice.org.uk

[138] Consultation Paper, *op cit*; see also Morgan Report, *Safer Communities: The Local Delivery of Crime Prevention through the Partnership Approach* (1991).

2 COURT OF TRIAL

(a) Committal to the Crown Court

Young defendants (i.e. those aged under eighteen when the mode of trial decision is made)[139] must generally be tried in the youth court. The exceptions to this are in respect of murder,[140] and those cases which fall within section 91 of the 2000 Act. These exceptions are:

(1) where the young defendant has attained the age of fourteen, and the offence is one to which section 91 of the Powers of Criminal Courts (Sentencing) Act 2000 applies. These are offences which, if committed by an adult, attract a maximum term of imprisonment of fourteen years or more, or indecent assault on a woman, and certain other specified offences.[141] The offence must not be one for which the sentence is fixed by law;

(2) where the young defendant is charged jointly with a person who has attained the age of eighteen and the court considers it necessary in the interests of justice to commit the young defendant for trial.

In addition where a young defendant is sent for trial under section 91, the court may also send for trial any other indictable offences with which he is charged at the same time, whether jointly with an adult or not, if that offence could be joined on the same indictment.[142]

These provisions have to be considered in the light of the fact that the maximum term of detention (under a detention and training order) that a youth court can impose is two years. If it considers longer detention is appropriate, the powers under section 91 must be used. When deciding whether to commit the young defendant for trial in respect of a grave offence (as defined above) the court should not consider what sentence should be imposed if the young defendant is convicted, but, instead, should consider whether the court that sentences the defendant if convicted should have the option to impose a greater term of detention than generally available. In *R v Devizes Youth Court, ex parte M*[143] the charge was one of arson. The Divisional Court concluded that the right course was to consider whether the Crown Court should have the power to order detention to impose a term of indefinite detention under what is now section 91.[144] That, though, has to be considered in the context of the basic principle inherent in *T v United Kingdom; V v United Kingdom*[145] that the application of adult trial procedures to young defendants may potentially give rise to a breach of Article 6 (and possibly other provisions) of the European Convention.

---

[139] *R v Islington North Juvenile Court, ex parte Daley* [1983] 1 AC 487, *sub nom Re Daley* [1982] 2 All ER 974.

[140] Which includes murder, manslaughter, causing death by reckless driving, killing in pursuance of a suicide pact, and infanticide: Magistrates' Courts Act 1980, s 24.

[141] Indecent assault on a woman, an offence of causing death by dangerous driving, an offence of causing death by careless driving whilst under the influence of drink or drugs.

[142] For joinder, see p 620, *ante*.   [143] 22 January 2000, unreported.

[144] The case was decided under the predecessor Children and Young Persons Act 1933, s 53.

[145] [2000] 2 All ER 1024.

(b) European Convention

The position of a young defendant was considered by the Court of Human Rights in *SC v United Kingdom*.[146] The child must be able to participate in the trial. This presupposes that a defendant has a broad understanding of the nature of the trial process, and of what is at stake for him or her, including the significance of any penalty. It means that, if necessary with help, the defendant should be able to understand the general thrust of what is said in court. In this case the court concluded that an eleven-year-old could not do this. The child had learning difficulties and the reading age of a child of eight. The charge of attempted robbery should have been tried in a specialist court, able to give proper consideration to the child's age and handicap.

Magistrates should therefore start with a presumption that the case will not be sent to the Crown Court, unless that is clearly required, either because their powers to order detention under a detention and training order[147] are inadequate or, alternatively, the likely sentence approaches the maximum of two years.[148] A committal under section 91 in respect of a defendant under fifteen years should only rarely occur.[149] Because detention is not available to a youth court in respect of a defendant under fifteen, the presumption is that a non-custodial sentence is the appropriate response unless a sentence of two years or more could be justified.

(c) Trial in an adult magistrates' court – the general policy

The general policy to be applied was summarized by the court in *R (on application of H, A and O)* v *Southampton Youth Court*[150] as follows:

- There is a general policy of Parliament that defendants under the age of eighteen, and particularly under fifteen, should if possible be tried in a youth court.

- There is a policy that first-time offenders aged twelve to fourteen years, and all offenders under twelve, should not be detained in custody, and the power to detain for grave offences should not be used to water down that policy.

- In each case the court should ask itself whether there was any real prospect, having regard to the defendant's age, that the defendant might receive a sentence of two years or more.

Within these principles the normal rule is, therefore, that a young defendant will be tried in the youth court, unless committed to the Crown Court, which should be the only alternative. To that rule, there is an exception where a young defendant is jointly charged with an adult. Such a case must be heard in the adult court,[151] but the case may

---

[146] [2005] Crim LR 131. See also *R (on application of S)* v *Waltham Forest Youth Court* [2004] EWHC 71; *R (on application of H, A and O)* v *Southampton Youth Court* [2004] EWHC 2912.

[147] See p 681, *post*.

[148] *R v Southampton Crown Court, ex parte K* [2002] EWHC 1640 (Admin). *R (on application of H, A and O)* v *Southampton Youth Court* [2004] EWHC 2912.

[149] *R (on the application of M)* v *Waltham Forest Youth Court and the DPP; R (on the application of W)* v *Thetford Youth Court and the DPP* (2002) 166 JP 453.

[150] [2004] EWHC 2912.   [151] Children and Young Persons Act 1933, s 46.

be remitted to the youth court if the adult pleads guilty and the young defendant pleads not guilty, or where the adult is committed for trial or is discharged and the young defendant pleads not guilty.[152]

(d) Violent offences

Special sentencing arrangements apply in respect of 'specified violent offences'.[153] Some confusion has arisen as to where such defendants should be tried, given that the relevant provisions appear to suggest that such offences should be tried in the Crown Court. Like many aspects of sentencing law, the position is by no means clear, and the fact that a court in *Crown Prosecution Service* v *South East Surrey Youth Court*[154] was led to conclude that it was required to retain jurisdiction by other legislation, despite the seemingly clear provisions of the Criminal Justice Act 2003, speaks volumes for the complexity of the legislation. The principles, the court concluded, were clear. Where a defendant was under eighteen he should, where possible, be tried in the youth court. The court should be particularly rigorous to ensure, before committing to the Crown Court, that there is a significant risk of serious harm by the commission of further offences. That is unlikely to be satisfied unless a pre-sentence report prepared by a youth offending team assessing the defendant has been considered.

3 THE TRIAL

One of the key purposes of the youth court is to ensure process and procedure which is appropriate to the age of the defendant. Trying the young defendant in an adult court, especially the Crown Court, raises difficult issues. The European Convention on Human Rights, the United Nations Standard Minimum Rules for the Administration of Juvenile Justice (the Beijing Rules), the United Nation Convention on the Rights of the Child, and Article 14 of the International Covenant on Civil and Political Rights of 1966 all focus on the essential principle that the age and welfare of the child or young person are key matters to which the courts must have regard.[155] That is also inherent in domestic law, section 44 of the Children and Young Persons Act 1933 requiring a court to have regard to the welfare of the child.

The trial process in the youth court reflects the needs of the child or young person. Limitations exist on publicity (including restrictions on publishing the name of the defendant) and limitations on those entitled to be present in court.[156] The limitation on reporting can be lifted if it is in the interests of justice to do so, but not simply for the purpose of adding to the punishment of the defendant by publishing his name.[157] The trial itself will follow normal procedures, and be conducted under the normal rules of evidence, but should reflect the age and maturity of the defendant. In some

---

[152] Magistrates' Court Act 1980, s 29.   [153] See p 704, *post*.
[154] [2005] EWHC Admin 2929.
[155] For recognition in domestic law of these international obligations, see *McKerry* v *Teesdale and Wear Valley Justices* [2000] Crim LR 594.
[156] Children and Young Persons Act 1933, ss 43, 47.
[157] *McKerry* v *Teesdale and Wear Valley Justices* [2000] Crim LR 594.

circumstances it may be possible to proceed in the absence of the child himself, provided that attendance is not essential to the just hearing of the case, in the context of the rights to a fair trial.[158]

Particular problems arise in the Crown Court, as was vividly demonstrated by *T* v *United Kingdom; V* v *United Kingdom*.[159] T and V were tried, and convicted, for murder in the Crown Court. The Court of Human Rights concluded that whilst not all the complaints made by T and V were justified,[160] the nature of the proceedings amounted to a breach of Article 6, in that T and V were, in the context of a public hearing in the Crown Court, unable to participate effectively in the criminal proceedings. At the trial of T and V special measures were taken in the light of the age of the defendants (eleven years), and to promote understanding of the nature of the proceedings. The defendants had trial procedures explained to them, and shown the courtroom in advance of the trial itself. The hearing times were shortened in order not to tire the defendants excessively. Despite this the Court of Human Rights concluded that the formality and ritual of the Crown Court must have seemed incomprehensible and intimidating to a child aged eleven. There was evidence that certain of the modifications to the court room, particularly the raised dock (designed to allow the defendants to see what was going on, had the effect of increasing the defendant's sense of discomfort during the trial, leaving them exposed to the scrutiny of press and public. The trial generated high levels of press interest, given the notoriety of the alleged crime (the murder of B, a three-year-old boy). There was also evidence that T suffered from post-traumatic stress disorder, which, combined with the lack of therapeutic work since the date of the offence, had limited T's ability to consult his lawyers and adequately testify in his own defence. It was insufficient that T was represented by skilled and experienced lawyers. The Court considered it unlikely that T would have felt able to adequately consult with them whilst under public scrutiny in a tense courtroom, or in the light of his lack of maturity.

These findings highlighted the difficulties faced in attempting to try young defendants in adult courts. A Practice Direction was issued in response, addressing the needs of young defendants in the Crown Court.[161] It requires henceforth appropriate steps addressing these issues, in terms of the layout of the courtroom and the familiarization of the defendant with it; the hours the court sits, and the need to dispense with the formal court dress of wigs and gowns; and appropriate measures to control attendance by the public or press. Above all, a young defendant should, where at all possible, be tried separately from an adult. This, of course, then raises the issue as to whether the charge should be tried in the youth court or Crown Court. Clearly, in the case of T, only Crown Court trial was appropriate given the nature of the charge, but that will not always be the case.

---

[158] 1933 Act, s 42. For the requirements of the 'fair trial' provisions of Article 6, see chapter 6, and p 555, *ante*.

[159] [2000] 2 All ER 1024.

[160] In particular, the Court rejected a submission that the procedure amounted to inhuman or degrading treatment under Article 3. The Court did also find that there *was* also a breach of Article 5, in that the procedure for determining and reviewing the tariff for the indeterminate sentence imposed was unfair and contravened Article 5. For this latter issue, see p 705, *post*.

[161] See also Criminal Procedure Rules, *op cit*, p 554, *ante*.

4 YOUTH OFFENDER CONTRACTS

In 1999 a new method of dealing with young offenders was introduced, and now to be found in Part III of the Powers of Criminal Courts (Sentencing) Act 2000. Section 16 provides that a youth court or magistrates' court may, and in some cases must, refer a young offender to a youth offender panel, where the pre-conditions it creates are satisfied. Essentially, the power to make a referral arises when it is proposing to impose a non-custodial sentence. The duty to refer arises when an offender, who has never before been convicted of an offence, pleads guilty.[162] The objective of the procedure is to address the causes of the offending behaviour. A youth offender panel, created by section 21, will agree a contract with the young offender, which may involve reparation to the victim and measures to address the needs of the offender, in the hope of removing or reducing the causes of the offending behaviour. If a contract cannot be agreed, or is broken, the offender is returned to the sentencing court to be sentenced for the original offence.

The power to make a referral is one vested in the youth court or magistrates' court. The Crown Court has no such power. The power to refer, as already noted, is the means for dealing with the offender without a custodial term, and cannot be combined with any community order.[163]

5 IMPRISONMENT AND COMMUNITY PUNISHMENT

The Crown Court, following trial on indictment, has various powers. Section 90 of the Powers of Criminal Courts (Sentencing) Act 2000 prescribes a mandatory detention during Her Majesty's Pleasure for conviction for murder scommitted by an offender under eighteen at the time of the offence, and a term of detention for certain specified offences of seriousness, where the court is satisfied that no other method of dealing with the case is appropriate. However, the powers of the youth court have historically been limited. In respect of offenders aged under fifteen, no power of detention exists, other than to require detention in secure accommodation under a supervision order. In respect of those aged fifteen and under eighteen, section 100 of the 2000 Act provides for detention under a detention and training order. This allows a court to sentence a young offender to a detention and training order requiring the offender to be subject to a period of detention and training, followed by a period of supervision. Where a child or young person is convicted of an offence which is punishable with imprisonment in the case of a person aged twenty-one or over, and the court is satisfied that a custodial sentence is justified by the seriousness of the offence or the need to protect the public,[164] the sentence that the court can pass is a detention and training order. There are also pre-conditions on the imposition of the order on certain offenders: in the case of an offender under the age of fifteen at the time of the conviction, the court must be of the opinion that he is a persistent offender; in the case of an offender under the age of twelve at that time, the court must consider that only a custodial sentence would be adequate

---

[162] 2000 Act, s 17, amended by Criminal Justice and Immigration Act 2008, Part 4.
[163] For sentences generally, see p 701, *post*.   [164] See p 700, *post*.

to protect the public from further offending by him; and the offence was committed on or after such date as the Home Secretary may appoint.

A detention and training order is an order that the offender in respect of whom it is made shall be subject, for the term specified in the order, to a period of detention and training followed by a period of supervision. The term of a detention and training order shall be four, six, eight, ten, twelve, eighteen, or twenty-four months. Thus the length of sentence that a youth court may impose has been increased. The order will be served in such secure accommodation as may be determined by the Secretary of State or by such other person as may be authorized by him for that purpose. The period of detention is half the length of the order.[165] The other half of the order is a period of supervision by a probation officer, local authority social worker, or member of a youth offending team.[166] Where a detention and training order is in force in respect of an offender and it appears on information to a justice of the peace acting for a relevant petty sessions area that the offender is in breach of the order, a summons may be issued, and the youth court may order the offender to be detained, in such secure accommodation as the Home Secretary may determine, for such period, not exceeding the shorter of three months or the remainder of the term of the detention and training order, as the court may specify; or impose on the offender a fine not exceeding level 3 on the standard scale.

A range of community or other orders exists[167] and is available in respect of young offenders. These rehabilitation orders (in respect of offenders aged sixteen or over), are now, youth rahibilitation orders, following the Criminal Justice and Immigration Act 2008.[168] Other available orders include a reparation order, a sentence requiring a young offender to make reparation to the victim of the offence or a person otherwise affected by it, or to the community at large. The order is intended to help show young offenders the harm which they have done to the community and to their victims, and enable the courts to impose punishments which make some amends to the victim, or to the community generally. Another order is the action plan order.[169] This requires a young offender to comply with an action plan intended to address his offending behaviour. The intention is that the action plan order should provide the opportunity for a short but intensive programme of work with the young offender constructed by or on behalf of the youth offending team, in consultation with the offender's parents, to tackle the causes of offending at an early stage.

6 OTHER ORDERS

A youth court may fine a young offender an amount not exceeding £1,000, and may order the fine to be paid by a parent or guardian.[170] It may impose absolute or conditional discharges,[171] make compensation orders,[172] or impose disqualifications.[173]

---

[165] 2000 Act, s 100.   [166] As to which, see p 675, *ante*.   [167] See generally, p 709, *post*.

[168] See p 709, *post*.   [169] 2000 Act, s 12.

[170] 2000 Act, s 137.   [171] See p 709, *post*.

[172] See p 709, *post*.   [173] See p 710, *post*.

APPEALS FOLLOWING SUMMARY TRIAL

Wider issues relating to the appellate system are dealt with later.[174] Here we address specific procedures which apply in cases of summary trial.

A defendant convicted by a magistrates' court may appeal either:

(1) to the Crown Court, and thence by way of case stated to the Queen's Bench Division of the High Court; or

(2) by case stated to the Queen's Bench Division of the High Court;

(3) from the Queen's Bench Divisional Court to the House of Lords, in certain circumstances.

In addition to those rights of appeal there is the possibility of applying for judicial review. Each of these will be considered in turn.

1   APPEAL TO THE CROWN COURT

Where the defendant has been convicted in the magistrates' court of either a summary offence or an either-way offence tried summarily he may appeal to the Crown Court, if he pleaded guilty against his sentence only, or if he pleaded not guilty against both conviction and sentence.[175] It will be seen that there is an express statutory prohibition against an appeal against conviction if the defendant pleaded guilty. This may be contrasted with the position following trial on indictment, where there is nothing in the Criminal Appeal Act to prevent an appeal against conviction to the Court of Appeal even if the defendant pleaded guilty.[176] It has been observed that the judges have laid down that appeals against conviction following a plea of guilty will only be entertained by the Court of Appeal in certain exceptional circumstances; so in the case of appeals to the Crown Court also, the judges have given a construction to the statute which evades the effect of the exact words used by Parliament, but on this occasion in favour of the defendant. It has been held that to make a plea of guilty binding and effective it must be unambiguous;[177] if therefore the defendant says the actual word 'guilty' but adds to it a statement which, if true, amounts to a defence to the charge, or if from the circumstances it is clear that he is denying the charge but has pleaded guilty through ignorance of the law, a plea of guilty accepted in these circumstances is a nullity.[178] The Crown Court can, therefore, hear an appeal against the 'conviction' which is equally a nullity, and under powers presently to be considered can remit the case to the magistrates with an expression of opinion that a plea of not guilty ought to be entered. Where on the other hand there has been a deliberate and unequivocal plea of guilty, no appeal against conviction can be entertained.[179]

---

[174] See p 712, *post*.   [175] Magistrates' Courts Act 1980, s 108(1).   [176] See p 715, *post*.
[177] R v *Durham Quarter Sessions, ex parte Virgo* [1952] 2 QB 1, [1952] 1 All ER 466.
[178] R v *Blandford Justices, ex parte G* [1967] 1 QB 82, [1966] 1 All ER 1021.
[179] *P Foster (Haulage) Ltd* v *Roberts* [1978] 2 All ER 751.

The expression 'sentence' includes any order made on conviction by a magistrates' court, with an exception in respect of an order for absolute or conditional discharge, although if on a later date sentence is passed in respect of the offence for which the order for conditional discharge was made, that is following 'breach' of the order, there may be:

(1) an appeal against that later sentence;

(2) an order for the payment of costs;

(3) an order for the destruction of an animal, made under the Protection of Animals Act 1911; and

(4) any order, if the court has no discretion as to the making of the order or its terms, for example if the court is bound to order endorsement of a driving licence.[180] It has already been noted that there is no appeal against a committal for sentence, in the cases already discussed in which there may be such a committal, although there may be an appeal against the conviction on which the committal is based.

There is a right of appeal against an order to enter into recognizances to keep the peace or be of good behaviour,[181] and this right exists where such an order has been made following acquittal.[182]

With limited exceptions only the defendant may appeal. The procedure[183] is that an appeal must be commenced by giving notice of appeal, to the clerk of the magistrates' court, and to the other party, within twenty-one days after the day on which the decision of the magistrates' court was given (meaning the day on which sentence is passed if there is an adjournment of the case after conviction). The Crown Court may extend the time, either in relation to a notice not yet given or to a notice already given but out of time.

Proceedings before the Crown Court on an appeal against conviction take the form of a complete rehearing of the case;[184] the prosecution must open the case and call its witnesses afresh and either side may introduce fresh evidence without any leave. This is of course in sharp contrast to proceedings in the Court of Appeal. The Crown Court may confirm, reverse, or vary the decision of the magistrates' court,[185] or remit the case with an expression of their opinion;[186] as already seen this latter procedure will be appropriate where an 'equivocal' plea of guilty has been entered, which in all the circumstances the Crown Court considers should have been treated as a plea of not guilty. The Crown Court must give reasons for its decision except where they are obvious.[187] As regards appeals against sentence, the Crown Court may impose any sentence which the magistrates' court could have passed, whether more or less severe than that which they

---

[180] Magistrates' Courts Act 1980, s 108(3).
[181] Magistrates' Courts (Appeals from Binding Over Orders) Act 1956.
[182] *Shaw* v *Hamilton* [1982] 2 All ER 718, [1982] 1 WLR 1308.
[183] See Criminal Procedure Rules, r 63.
[184] Supreme Court Act 1981, s 48. Although the prosecution cannot alter the case by amending the information (*Garfield* v *Maddocks* [1974] QB 7, [1973] 2 All ER 303).
[185] Supreme Court Act 1981, s 48(2)(a).   [186] Ibid, s 48(2)(b).
[187] *R* v *Snaresbrook Crown Court, ex parte Input Management Ltd* (1999) 163) JP 533; *R* v *Kingston Crown Court, ex parte Bell* (200) 164 JP 901.

actually passed. The court may also do this if the appeal is against conviction only.[188] Again, there is a sharp contrast between appeals to the Crown Court and appeals to the Court of Appeal following trial on indictment, since the Court of Appeal never has had the power to interfere with the sentence in any way if the appeal is against conviction only and, in addition, cannot now increase sentence;[189] the Crown Court can do both. Finally, the Crown Court may:

> make such other order in the matter as the court thinks just, and by such order exercise any power which the said authority might have exercised.[190]

The wording is liberal, but it was held[191] on an almost identical provision in the previous legislation, that quarter sessions had no power to vary the sentence by quashing the sentence passed at the magistrates' court and committing to itself for sentence. The reason lies in the point already noted[192] that committal for sentence is not itself a sentence; if therefore magistrates elect to sit as a sentencing court instead of as a committing court quarter sessions could not go behind that election. Their power was to interfere with a sentence, not a decision as to whether the defendant should be committed or sentenced. This is presumably still true for the Crown Court.

If the appeal is against sentence only it may proceed on the basis of the facts relevant to sentence produced before the magistrates, if counsel for the appellant agrees to that course; there will then be no need for any evidence whatever to be called before the Crown Court. The same strictness of proof is not demanded in matters relevant to sentence as in matters relevant to conviction. In fact proceedings on an appeal against sentence normally take the same course as if the defendant had just been convicted, or had pleaded guilty, before the court.[193]

From the Crown Court a further appeal lies by way of case stated to the Queen's Bench Division of the High Court; this will be considered below.

2 APPEAL BY CASE STATED TO THE QUEEN'S BENCH DIVISION FROM MAGISTRATES' COURTS AND THE CROWN COURT

(a) Magistrates' courts and youth courts

Any person who was a party to proceedings before a magistrates' court (or youth court) or (although not a party) is aggrieved by the conviction, order, determination, or other

---

[188] Ibid, s 9(4). However, the Crown Court cannot impose a sentence which the magistrates could not have imposed. Thus an unrepresented defendant who has not previously been sentenced to imprisonment cannot (subject to minor exceptions) be sentenced to imprisonment (Powers of Criminal Courts Act 1973, s 21(1)). Accordingly, on appeal in such a case, the Crown Court cannot impose a sentence of imprisonment even though the accused is legally represented on his appeal: R v Birmingham Justices, ex parte Wyatt [1975] 3 All ER 897, [1976] 1 WLR 260. It can also vary a sentence passed at the same time and not appealed: R v London Crown Court, ex parte Mentesh [2001] 1 Cr App R (S) 323.
[189] See p 716, post.   [190] Supreme Court Act 1981, s 48(2)(c).
[191] In R v Bullock [1964] 1 QB 481, [1963] 3 All ER 506.
[192] See p 671, ante.   [193] See p 722, post.

proceeding may appeal against the proceeding on the ground that it is wrong in law or in excess of jurisdiction by applying to the magistrates' court to state a case for the opinion of a Divisional Court of the Queen's Bench Division of the High Court.[194] The power to appeal by way of case stated is not normally a proper way of challenging a sentence that has been imposed, the proper procedure for which is appeal to the Crown Court.[195] Only where the sentence is, by any acceptable standard 'astonishing' will proceedings by way of case stated be entertained.[196]

Thus, either the defendant or the prosecutor in a criminal case may make application for a case to be stated. Application may also be made by a person aggrieved, but:

> the words 'person aggrieved' do not really mean a man who is disappointed of a benefit which he might have received if some other order had been made (still less does it mean someone having a merely sympathetic interest in the proceedings). A 'person aggrieved' must be a man who has suffered a legal grievance, a man against whom a decision has been pronounced which has wrongfully deprived him of something, or wrongfully refused him something, or wrongfully affected his title to something.[197]

A party to proceedings who has succeeded in part only may appeal against the incompleteness of his success. Executors of a person who has died since the hearing of the case in the magistrates' court are 'interested', at any rate if a fine has been imposed, since the money to pay this would come out of the estate of the deceased; they may accordingly bring an appeal by way of case stated.[198] If the deceased had been sentenced to imprisonment the executors appear not to be 'interested'.[199]

Application must be made in writing, within twenty-one days after the day on which the decision of the magistrates' court was given;[200] again, if the magistrates adjourn after conviction, the day on which sentence is actually passed is the first day on which time begins to run.[201] The application should be delivered to the clerk of the magistrates' court whose decision is being questioned or sent to him by post; the names of the magistrates constituting the court do not have to be given and it is therefore immaterial that there is an error in their names.[202]

The application must identify the point of law on which the opinion of the High Court is sought.[203]

The magistrates may refuse to state a case only on the ground that the application is in their opinion frivolous, and may not refuse to state a case if the application is made by or under the direction of the Attorney-General, even in the unlikely event of such

---

[194] Magistrates' Courts Act 1980, s 111(1).

[195] *Tucker v Director of Public Prosecutions* [1992] 4 All ER 901.   [196] Ibid, per Pill J.

[197] *Ex parte Sidebotham* (1880) 14 Ch D 458, at 465, per James LJ, described as 'the best definition of the expression "aggrieved"' in *R v London Sessions, ex parte Westminster Corporation* [1951] 2 KB 508, at 511, [1951] 1 All ER 1032, at 1033, per Lord Goddard CJ.

[198] *Hodgson v Lakeman* [1943] 1 KB 15. The position is otherwise in an appeal following trial on indictment: *R v Jefferies* [1969] 1 QB 120, [1968] 3 All ER 238.

[199] *R v Rowe* [1955] 1 QB 573, [1955] 2 All ER 234.   [200] Magistrates' Courts Act 1980, s 111(2), (3).

[201] Ibid.   [202] *R v Oxford (Bullingdon) Justices, ex parte Bird* [1948] 1 KB 100.

[203] Magistrates' Courts Rules 1981, r 76(1).

an application being considered frivolous.[204] On refusal the magistrates must give the applicant a certificate of refusal if he so requires; he may then apply to the High Court for an order directing the justices to state a case.[205] On the making of the application, whether granted or refused, the applicant loses his right to appeal to the Crown Court.[206]

A 'case' will normally contain a statement of the information as laid, the facts found, the contentions of the parties, the cases cited, the decision, and the question or questions for the decision of the High Court. If one or other of the parties is contending that there was no evidence on which the magistrates could come to their decision, a statement of the evidence should be included. This form, originally settled by Lord Goddard CJ, should always be used. The case may be stated by all the justices whose decision is questioned or by any two of them[207] and may be stated in relation to a number of different prosecutions, even against different defendants on different days, provided that they raise precisely the same point. Under no circumstances should the case state that the decision was that of a majority, if that was the position.[208] The case should in any event be submitted to both parties for their consideration and in the event of any difficulty it should be left to the parties themselves to produce a draft and submit it to the magistrates for their consideration.[209] If, in spite of this, a party to an appeal considers that the facts have been improperly stated in the case he may apply to the Queen's Bench Division for the case to be remitted to the justices for restatement of the facts, the application being accompanied by an affidavit setting out the facts which it is alleged should go in the case.[210] Periods of twenty-one days are allowed for delivering the draft case to the parties, for the parties to make representations and for the justices to prepare the final case.[211] These time limits are not inflexible and may be extended, but in such event a written statement of the reasons for the delay must accompany the final case.[212]

On the hearing the court will hear and determine the questions of law arising, after argument by counsel for the parties. The court may allow argument on a point not raised in the court below or even take such a point itself,[213] provided that in each case the point is one of pure law, not requiring any evidence. The magistrates themselves may file an affidavit, setting out the grounds of the decision and any facts which they may consider to have a bearing on the issues;[214] in view of the existence of the case this procedure will rarely be appropriate. Unless misconduct is alleged there is no need for the justices to be

---

[204] Magistrates' Courts Act 1980, s 111(5). See *R v Mildenhall Magistrates' Court, ex parte Forest Heath District Council* (1997) 161 JP 401.

[205] Magistrates' Courts Act 1980, s 111(6).

[206] Ibid, s 111(4). See *Sunworld Ltd v Hammersmith & Fulham LBC; R v Blackfriars Crown Court, ex parte Sunworld Ltd* [2000] 2 All ER 837.

[207] Criminal Procedure Rules 2005, r 64.

[208] *More O'Ferrall Ltd v Harrow Urban District Council* [1947] KB 66, at 70, [1946] 2 All ER 489, at 491.

[209] *Cowlishaw v Chalkley* [1955] 1 All ER 367n, [1955] 119 JP 171.

[210] *Spicer v Warbey* [1953] 1 All ER 284, [1953] 1 WLR 334.

[211] Criminal Procedure Rules 2005, r 68.   [212] Ibid, r 68.

[213] *Whitehead v Haines* [1965] 1 QB 200, [1964] 2 All ER 530.

[214] Review of Justices Decisions Act 1872.

represented by counsel. The court may reverse, affirm, or amend the decision in respect of which the case has been stated, or may remit the matter to the magistrates with its opinion, or make such other order as it sees fit.[215]

(b) The Crown Court

The Crown Court may also state a case for the opinion of the High Court. Either party to any order, judgment, or other decision of the Crown Court, other than one relating solely to trial on indictment, may apply for a case to be stated on the ground that the decision is wrong in law or in excess of jurisdiction.[216] Thus, either party to an appeal from the magistrates' court, against conviction or sentence may apply, as (apparently) may a person sentenced at the Crown Court after committal for sentence from a magistrates' court. These provisions are in several respects an extension of the old law; however, a person aggrieved by the Crown Court's decision, but not a party, still has no right of appeal. Application should be made in writing to the appropriate officer of the Crown Court within twenty-one days after the decision; again, the Crown Court may only refuse to state a case if the application is considered frivolous.[217] The powers of the Queen's Bench Division appear to be the same as those exercisable on an appeal from the magistrates.[218]

3 APPEAL TO THE HOUSE OF LORDS

Finally it should be noted that an appeal to the House of Lords may be made from the Divisional Court of the Queen's Bench Division, subject to the same conditions as those governing appeals from the Court of Appeal in the case of trial on indictment.[219] Thus there must be a certificate from the Divisional Court that a point of law of general public importance is involved in its decision and either the Divisional Court or the House of Lords must give leave to appeal on the ground that the point is one which ought to be considered by the House of Lords. In this way a summary offence may be considered

---

[215] Summary Jurisdiction Act 1857, s 6. If a question arises which is appropriate to be referred to the European Court for a preliminary ruling (as to which, see p 138, *ante*) the court may, of its own motion or on application, make an order whereupon proceedings will be stayed pending receipt of the ruling, unless the Divisional Court otherwise orders: RSC, Ord 114. A rehearing is only appropriate where a fair trial is still possible; cf. *Griffith v Jenkins* [1992] 2 AC 76, [1992] 1 All ER 65 in which case the House of Lords laid down guidelines as to the circumstances in which the power to order a rehearing should be exercised.

[216] Supreme Court Act 1981, s 28. Certain decisions of the Crown Court are made final; see s 28(2)(b).

[217] Criminal Procedure Rules 2005, r 64.

[218] The case of *Harris, Simon & Co Ltd v Manchester City Council* [1975] 1 All ER 412, [1975] 1 WLR 100 demonstrated a little known legal oddity whereby under the Manchester General Improvement Act 1851 an objection to the Manchester City Council's resolution to stop up two streets was made by way of appeal to the Crown Court (as successor to the jurisdiction of quarter sessions) where the objection is heard as an appeal by judge and jury. Since juries do not make detailed findings of fact, the Divisional Court on an appeal by way of case stated approached the case on the basis that the appeal could succeed only if the judge had misdirected the jury or if their conclusion was perverse, in the sense of being a conclusion which no reasonable jury could have reached. This instance of an appeal by way of case stated of the verdict of a jury appears to be unique.

[219] Administration of Justice Act 1960, s 1.

by four courts; the magistrates' court, the Crown Court, the Divisional Court of the Queen's Bench Division and the House of Lords.[220]

JUDICIAL REVIEW

Magistrates' courts and the Crown Court, in the exercise of their jurisdiction over summary offences, are inferior courts and therefore their proceedings are amenable to judicial review by the High Court.[221] This procedure may be appropriate where there is no right of appeal. Thus, for example, it has been noted that there is no right of appeal from an order for the payment of costs; nevertheless the High Court has on *Wednesbury* principles[222] been prepared to quash an order for costs which was so far outside the normal sum imposed as to involve an error of law.[223] Similarly, following an appeal against sentence from a magistrates' court to the Crown Court, there is no further appeal (except by way of case stated if a point of law is involved); nevertheless in *R v St Albans Crown Court, ex parte Cinnamond*[224] a disqualification of eighteen months for careless driving, although within the jurisdiction of the court, was quashed as being so far outside the normal sentence imposed by courts for this offence as to enable the Divisional Court to hold that it must have involved an error of law.

FURTHER READING

ASHWORTH and REDMAYNE, *The Criminal Process*, 3rd edn (Oxford University Press: 2000)

Auld Review – *Review of the Criminal Courts of England & Wales* (http://www.criminal-courts-review.org.uk)

DARBYSHIRE, 'An Essay on the Importance and Neglect of the Magistracy' [1997] Crim LR 639

No More Excuses – A New Approach to Tackling Youth Crime in England & Wales (1997) HMSO Cm 1809

---

[220] *Spicer v Holt* [1977] AC 987, [1976] 3 All ER 71 is a case in which this happened. It might, in addition, be considered by the European Court, to the extent that a question arising in the proceedings was referred to that court for a preliminary ruling; see p 138, *ante*.

[221] See chapter 6, *ante* for details of this jurisdiction and procedure.

[222] As to which see p 223, *ante*.

[223] *R v Tottenham Justices, ex parte Joshi* [1982] 2 All ER 507, [1982] 1 WLR 631.

[224] [1981] QB 480, [1981] 1 All ER 802.

23

SENTENCES

INTRODUCTION

The law relating to sentences is complicated, confused, highly technical, and constantly changing. A detailed consideration of sentencing powers and practices is beyond the scope of this book, and the aim of this chapter is simply to paint a picture of the main features and principles. For a detailed analysis of the particular sentences and case law, reference should be made to the specialist sentencing practitioners' texts. The focus of this chapter will be on:

- General sentencing principles.
- The influence, if any, of the views of victims.
- The sentencing process.
- The main types of sentence.

GENERAL PRINCIPLES

The law governing the sentencing of offenders has undergone frequent, and radical, changes in recent years. In part these changes have been a response to the stated desire of political parties to reduce the incidence of crime, and in part due to the often competing philosophies as to the purpose of custodial sentences. The result has been a plethora of statutes making new provision, or amending existing provision, or even substituting new changes for those that reached the statute book but which never were fully implemented.[1] The position in respect of sentencing legislation reached such a level of complexity that Lord Bingham CJ in *R* v *Governor of Brockhill Prison, ex parte Evans*[2] was moved to observe (in the context of the date of release of prisoners) as follows:

> The Law Commission has described it as an important feature of any criminal justice system that sentencing provisions should be accessible and comprehensible

---

[1] See, e.g. Crime and Disorder Act 1998, ss 69–74, which introduced the new detention and training orders (as to which see p 706, *post*) for the never implemented secure training order provisions in Criminal Justice and Public Order Act 1994, ss 1–18.

[2] [1997] QB 443, [1997] 1 All ER 439.

and has recommended the enactment of a comprehensive statutory consolidation of such provisions...We hope that this may be seen as a task commanding a high degree of priority....

That consolidation occurred in 2000, with the passage of the Powers of Criminal Courts (Sentencing) Act 2000. Any belief that that would provide the desired clarity and ease of access to the statutory provisions was misplaced, with at least one amendment of the 2000 Act before it came into effect,[3] and significant further changes made by the Criminal Justice Act 2003. Those pieces of legislation have served only to create a mass of case law, not easy to apply, and occasionally contradictory.

1 THE HALLIDAY REPORT

At the heart of current approaches to the sentencing process are the recommendations of the Halliday Report,[4] the latest in a long line of reports and studies examining aspects of the sentencing framework. It was born out of a belief that the then existing sentencing structure suffered from serious deficiencies that reduced its effectiveness to contribute to crime reduction and public confidence. Amongst those deficiencies were the lack of any clear message about the effect that repeat offending should have on sentence, the absence of reality as to what sentences in fact mean, and unexplored opportunities for non-custodial sentences, including reparation for victims.[5] The Criminal Justice Act 1991 had required sentencers to concentrate on the nature of the offences (the principle of 'just deserts'), and although that approach was diluted by various legislative inroads (such as the taking into account of previous convictions of offenders when sentencing, or requirements relating to mandatory or minimum sentences) the basic approach was proportionality of the sentence to the offence. That did not encourage sentencers to think wider, and address the needs of crime reduction or reparation. Community sentences were perceived as weak and ineffective.

Those were not the only perceived deficiencies. Despite the work done by the Sentencing Advisory Panel, in partnership with the Court of Appeal, sentencing law was confusing and obscure, and was not such as to inspire public confidence. There needed to be a more accessible framework, and decisions in individual cases needed to be understood. Community punishments[6] were not considered as sufficiently punitive or protective. Arrangements for the enforcement of community punishments were, again, uncertain and unclear. Yet, at the same time structural re-organization provided real opportunities. Management of offenders in custody was the responsibility of the Prison Service. Management of those offenders serving punishments within the community was the responsibility of the probation service. By means of the new National Offender Management Service, integrating the two,[7] and the development

---

[3] See Criminal Justice and Courts Services Act 2000.

[4] *Making Punishments Work: Report of a Review of the Sentencing Framework for England and Wales*, Home Office 2001, available at www.homeoffice.gov.uk/docs/halliday.html.

[5] Ibid, Introduction.   [6] See p 707, *post*.

[7] As to which see *Correctional Services Review* (the Carter Review), 11 December 2003, available at www.homeoffice.gov.uk.

of sophisticated risk assessment techniques and of programmes of treatment accredited by the Home Office there were real opportunities to address offending behaviour. Research considered by Halliday confirmed the potential benefits of such programmes, but an appropriate sentencing framework was needed to maximize their chances of success.

A change in framework might also help achieve changes in sentencing behaviour,[8] by placing emphasis on the incapacitation of persistent and dangerous offenders, and on reparation and reform for others. Resources should be targeted on those most likely to re-offend and on those who commit offences serious enough to re-offend. This approach led Halliday to conclude that there should be clear principles of sentencing, clear sentencing guidelines, and a mass of important detailed changes in sentencing law. Many of the recent changes dealt with hereafter owe their origin, in whole or in part, to the Halliday Report.

2 PRINCIPLES OF SENTENCING

The Crime and Disorder Act 1998 had, in the context of young offenders, set out the basic objective of the prevention of re-offending.[9] Surprisingly, no statutory statement existed of the principles to which a sentencer should have regard when dealing with an adult.[10] Section 142 of the Criminal Justice Act 2003 now requires a court when passing sentence[11] to have regard to the purposes of sentencing it identifies. These are:

(a) the punishment of offenders;

(b) the reduction of crime (including its reduction by deterrence);

(c) the reform and rehabilitation of offenders;

(d) the protection of the public;

(e) the making of reparation by offenders to persons affected by their offences. In this context reparation might be financial or non-financial, and those affected might by individuals such as a victim, or the public more generally.

It is not intended that the principles will be applied uniformly. Sentencing courts will retain the right to reflect local conditions, problems, and issues, but, paradoxically, that may limit the worth of general statements such as these, because section 142 does not (and cannot) specify what weight is to be given in an individual case by the sentencing court. Nor do the principles apply to offences which have mandatory sentences (e.g. murder) or minimum sentences.[12] They did, however, provide challenges for the courts in seeking to reconcile them and their application in individual cases. Often the needs of one militates against another, and care must be taken in reading individual decisions.[13]

---

[8] Halliday Report, *op cit*, para 1.25.   [9] 1998 Act, s 37: see p 674, *ante.*

[10] i.e. a person aged eighteen or over.

[11] Which includes any order made by a court made when dealing with the offender. This is wide enough to include compensation orders, sex offender orders, and restraining orders. In respect of young offender, see 2003 Act, s 142A, inserted by Criminal Justice and Immigration Act 2008, s 9.

[12] 2003 Act, s 142(2). For minimum sentences, see p 702 , *post.*   [13] See p 692, *post.*

3 CONSISTENCY OF SENTENCING AND APPROPRIATE SENTENCE

As already noted, it is of considerable importance that different courts sentence consistently for the same type of offence, and impose a penalty appropriate to the level of seriousness of the offence of which the offender is convicted. On the other hand, the fact that a sentencing court has, or should have, a discretion to sentence in accordance with the circumstances of the particular offence is equally important and, to some, a basic constitutional principle. It was well explained as follows:

> Attempts by the executive arm of government to influence sentencing are unconstitutional, attempts by the legislature to interfere with the discretion of the courts are, even if not strictly unconstitutional, bound to result in potential confusion and injustice to defendants, the sentencing powers of the courts should therefore be left to the wisdom of the courts under the guidance of the Court of Appeal.[14]

It was this last concern that led to trenchant opposition to the introduction in the Crime (Sentences) Act 1997 of mandatory and minimum sentences.[15] Certain offences carry a mandatory sentence. Others carry a minimum sentence.[16] Consistency is also achieved through the Attorney-General's power to make a reference to the Court of Appeal in a case where the sentence imposed is considered to be unduly lenient,[17] and through the practice of the Court of Appeal of issuing guideline judgments setting out the appropriate approach to offences of similar types.[18] In respect of summary offences the Magistrates' Association issued Guidelines in respect of a wide range of offences.[19]

Nonetheless, existing mechanisms to ensure sentencing consistency proved inadequate. For that reason the Crime and Disorder Act 1998 created a Sentencing Advisory Panel.[20] It also imposed a duty on the Court of Appeal to issue guidance on appropriate sentences for specific types of offence.[21] The Sentencing Advisory Panel had the power to propose to the Court of Appeal (Criminal Division) that guidelines for sentencing in particular categories of indictable offence be framed or revised. It was required to do so if so directed by the Home Secretary. The Panel was under a duty to consult, to formulate its own views, and communicate them to the Court of Appeal and to furnish information to the Court of Appeal about the sentences imposed by courts in England

---

[14] Ashworth, *Sentencing and Penal Policy* (1983) at p 54. See also Ashworth, *Sentencing and Criminal Justice* (2nd edn, 1995) at pp 40–51; cf. Walker and Padfield, *Sentencing Theory, Law and Practice* (1996) at p 380, who see no constitutional principle which forbids or even discourages Parliament from limiting the discretion of sentences if that has advantages.

[15] See, e.g. Lord Woolf CJ, in the 2nd Reading, Debate of Crime (Sentences) Act 1997, *op cit*, col 997 where he complained of 'the legislature taking over what has been accepted to be the proper role of the judiciary'.

[16] See p 702, *post*.   [17] See p 693, *post*.

[18] See the following guideline cases for examples: see, e.g. *R v Billham; R v Bibi* (1980) 71 Cr App R 360; *R v Willis* (1974) 60 Cr App R 146; *R v Taylor, Roberts and Simons* (1977) 64 Cr App R 182.

[19] See p 693, *post*.

[20] Crime and Disorder Act 1998, s 81. Both s 80 and s 81 are repealed by the 2003 Act, but s 169 provides for the continuation of the Panel.

[21] Ibid, s 80.

and Wales for offences of the relevant category, the cost of different sentences, and their relative effectiveness in preventing re-offending.[22] The recommendations of the Panel did not in any way bind the Court of Appeal but have a highly persuasive effect. Likewise the 1998 Act[23] imposed a duty on the Court of Appeal to consider whether to frame guidelines as to the sentencing of offences of particular categories.

This process worked seemingly well, with a series of guideline judgments following consideration by the Council.[24] However, section 167 of the Criminal Justice Act 2003 established a Sentencing Guidelines Council, whilst the Panel is preserved (by section 169). This Council has a mixed judicial and non-judicial membership,[25] is chaired by the Lord Chief Justice, and with the non-judicial element intended to reflect wider interests of society. It remains unclear as to why this non-judicial element was not equally reflected in the composition of the Panel.

The purpose of the Council is to develop the work done by the Court of Appeal through guideline judgments and the Magistrates' Association through its sentencing guidelines. Now, it is the Council which will issue sentencing and allocation guidelines. Nothing in the 2003 Act regulates the interaction of the Council and Panel, who will, presumably report to the Council. The task of the Council will be to formulate sentencing guidelines, having regard to the need to promote consistency in sentencing. It will also formulate allocation guidelines to provide consistency in decision making as to the allocation of mode of trial for either-way offences.[26] A sentencing court will be obliged to have regard to the sentencing guidelines.[27] The first such guidelines were published in December 2004, when it produced guidelines on discounts for early guilty pleas, offence seriousness, and the implementation of new sentences. Since then a large number of guidelines has been published, covering a wide range of offences.[28] The Lord Chief Justice has been at pains to stress the improved quality of the guidelines following input of the non-judicial members of the Council.

4 THE ROLE OF THE ATTORNEY-GENERAL

The prosecution has a limited role in the sentencing process. It is under a duty to bring to the attention of the sentencing court matters relating to the power of the court, and has the right to correct misstatements of fact that may be made by an accused during the sentencing process. However, the prosecution has no specific right of appeal in an individual case against a sentence perceived as being unduly lenient. It was to permit some higher court review of such sentences that the Criminal Justice Act 1988 introduced powers which entitle the Attorney-General to refer to the Court of Appeal cases

---

[22] Ibid, s 81.   [23] Section 75.

[24] There include: *R v Millberry, Morgan and Lackenby* [2003] Crim LR 561 (rape); *R v Oliver, Hartley and Baldwin* [2003] Crim LR 127 (child pornography); *R v Celaire and Poulton* [2003] Crim LR 124 (possession of offensive weapons); *R v McInerney and Keating* [2003] Crim LR 209 (domestic burglary); *R v R* [2003] EWCA Crim 2199.

[25] Four non-judicial members will reflect the experience of the police, criminal prosecution, criminal defence, and welfare services. The DPP will also be annex officio member.

[26] See p 586, *ante*.   [27] 2003 Act, s 172(1).

[28] In respect, in particular of violent and sexual offences.

in which he considers an over-lenient sentence to have been imposed. Where such a reference is made the Court of Appeal may quash any sentence imposed and, in its place, impose such sentence as it thinks appropriate, within the powers that were available to the sentencing court. The Court of Appeal will not intervene unless the sentencing judge's sentence was wrong in principle, so that public confidence would be damaged if the sentence were not altered.[29]

5 VICTIMS

Traditionally, the victims of crime had not had a significant formal role within the process of the offender being convicted and dealt with. A government White Paper, *Justice for All*[30] observed:

> Justice is not simply about punishment for its own sake. Many victims, when asked, say they simply want to ensure that no-one else has to go through the kind of experience they themselves have. And the best way of ensuring that is to catch, convict and rehabilitate offenders and prevent further crime. Victim's own evidence is crucial in bringing offenders to justice. They must be nurtured and not subject to a host of delays, postponement and barriers...the criminal justice agencies have a particular responsibility to support victims and witnesses...This includes...taking into account the impact of the offence on victims when sentencing offenders...

In recent years, a variety of measures have been taken to improve the position of victims and how they are treated. Victim Support has been developed, and assists in excess of one million victims each year; witnesses when giving evidence are now eligible for special measures to protect them;[31] the Witness Service assists those who have to testify; and the police and Crown Prosecution Service have received better training in respect of how better to deal with vulnerable witnesses. Yet various studies demonstrated that more could be done, in particular as to informing victims of the progress of their case, the verdict, or plea, the sentence, if any, imposed, and the disposition and release of those sent to prison.[32] To remedy this, the Domestic Violence, Crime and Victims Act 2004 contained major provisions aimed at supporting the victims of crime. The provisions are 'intended to give victims guaranteed[33] and consistent levels of advice support and information...'.

The 2004 Act requires the Home Secretary to issue a Code of Practice setting out the minimum standards expected of individuals and agencies who deal with victims of crime, particularly the police and Crown Prosecution Service. It will primarily concentrate on victims of violence and sexual offences, the victims of property crime, and vulnerable victims. The detailed provisions of the Code will set minimum standards for the transmission of information about charge, date of hearings, progress of the case, the

---

[29] *Attorney-General's Reference (No 5 of 1989) (R v Hill-Trevor)* (1989) 90 Cr App R 358.

[30] *Op cit*, paras 2.11b–2.12.   [31] See p 645, *ante*.

[32] See, in particular, *A Better Deal for Victims and Witnesses*, Home Office Consultation Paper, 2003; *Compensation and Support for the Victims of Crime*, Home Office Consultation Paper, 2004.

[33] Baroness Scotland, Minister of State, Home Office, HL 2nd Reading, 15 December 2003.

result, and sentence. Victims of violent or sexual offences will have the right to receive information and make representations about the treatment of the offender after sentence and his potential release, including as to matters relating to conditions of licence,[34] and in respect of matters relating to hospital orders.[35]

Provisions also exist for financial support for victims of crime. The Criminal Injuries Compensation Act 1995 placed on a statutory footing the arrangements for the compensation of some victims of crime, and which had been formerly dealt with on a non-statutory basis.[36] The 2004 Act envisages the creation of a victims' fund, which will be created from surcharges imposed on offenders following conviction,[37] and partly by money recovered from offenders in respect of compensation paid by the Criminal Injuries Compensation Scheme.[38] Statutory powers are being changed to permit a greater number of compensation orders.[39] But it is often not possible for such an order to be made or paid and the victim of a crime of violence may depend on compensation being paid from the Criminal Injuries Compensation scheme. To that end the 2004 Act creates powers that enable the recovery of compensation paid by the Criminal Injuries Compensation Scheme.

A variety of other statutory changes have been made to support victims, including access to the Parliamentary Commissioner for Administration in respect of complaints of maladministration, and the creation of the office of Commissioner for Victims and Witnesses to champion their cause.

THE SENTENCING PROCESS AT THE CROWN COURT

A judge will sentence on the basis of the guilty plea or verdict of the jury. If there is a significant dispute about what factually occurred, then, following a plea of guilty, unless the prosecution accepts the defence version, a hearing is held to decide any dispute.[40] However, if there is a verdict (as opposed to a plea) of guilty, the judge sentences on the basis of the facts as they appear to him, provided that that view is consistent with the verdict of the jury.

1 PASSING SENTENCE

If the defendant has been found guilty on any part of the indictment the court will then proceed to sentence, in a similar manner to that following a plea of guilty. There is first

---

[34] 2004 Act, s 45(2), replacing and extending Criminal Justice and Courts Services Act 2000, s 69.
[35] Hospital orders may be made following a finding of disability under Criminal Procedure (Insanity) Act 1964.
[36] See *R v Criminal Injuries Compensation Board, ex parte Lain* [1967] 2 All ER 770.
[37] See p 710, *post.*   [38] See p 710, *post.*   [39] See Courts Act 2003.
[40] Known as a Newton hearing: *R v Newton* (1982) 77 Cr App R 13.

an inquiry into the defendant's antecedents. A pre-sentence report[41] is then considered. The defendant, through his advocate, makes a speech in mitigation. In the course of this part of the trial it not infrequently happens that the defendant asks for other offences to be taken into consideration. This practice is based on convention and has no statutory foundation; yet at the same time it is extremely convenient both from the point of view of the police and of the defendant. If there are other offences which the defendant has committed but which are still untried (or unknown), then the defendant may admit them to the court of trial and ask the judge to take them into consideration when sentencing him for the offence of which he has just been convicted. In practice he will probably tell the police well before the hearing that he wishes certain offences to be taken into consideration or the police may suggest the matter to him and he will then be supplied with an appropriate form of admission; however, there seems to be nothing to prevent a court taking an offence into consideration even if the defendant does not either admit it or ask for it to be taken into consideration until the actual trial. However:

> If justice is to be done it is essential that the practice should not be followed except with the express and unequivocal assent of the offender himself. Accordingly, he should be informed explicitly of each offence which the judge proposes to take into consideration; and should explicitly admit that he committed them and should state his desire that they should be taken into consideration in determining the sentence to be passed on him.[42]

Once the defendant has served his sentence he will not, by long established custom, be prosecuted in respect of any of the offences which have been taken into consideration, although if he were prosecuted the defence of *autrefois convict* would not be open to him, there having been no trial, let alone conviction, in respect of those offences.[43] If, however, his conviction were quashed, a prosecution might be brought. The mere fact that the defendant asks for the offence to be taken into consideration does not, of course, compel the court to do so. Certain limitations have been laid down in the cases. Broadly, the offence to be taken into consideration should be of the same character as the offence of which the defendant has been convicted; if the defendant has already been separately committed for trial in respect of the offence to be taken into consideration the judge should obtain the consent of the prosecution before doing so.[44] Even if the prosecution does consent, the judge ought to consider whether the public interest requires a separate inquiry. Neither ought the court to take into consideration an offence carrying disqualification from driving.[45] The reason is that in very many cases it will be desirable if not obligatory to disqualify the defendant, yet there can only be a disqualification on conviction, and taking other offences into consideration does not amount to a conviction in respect of them.

---

[41] See p 698, *post*.

[42] *Anderson v Director of Public Prosecutions* [1978] AC 964 at 977; *sub nom Director of Public Prosecutions v Anderson* [1978] 2 All ER 512, at 515–16, per Lord Diplock.

[43] *R v Nicholson* [1947] 2 All ER 535.   [44] *R v McLean* [1911] 1 KB 332.

[45] *R v Williams* [1962] 3 All ER 639, [1962] 1 WLR 1268.

A sentence takes effect from the beginning of the day on which it is imposed, unless the court otherwise directs. The court should make clear whether any terms of imprisonment are concurrent or consecutive. Any sentence imposed, or other order made, by the Crown Court may, under section 47(2) of the Supreme Court Act 1981, be varied or rescinded by the Crown Court within the period of twenty-eight days from the date of such sentence or order.

2 DEFERMENT OF SENTENCE

As an alternative to passing sentence immediately upon an offender, the judge has power to defer sentence for the purpose of enabling the court or any other court to which it falls to deal with him to have regard, in dealing with him to his conduct after conviction (including, where appropriate, the making by him of reparation for his offence) or to any change in his circumstances.[46] The deferment can only be made if the offender consents and the court is satisfied, having regard to the nature of the offence and the character and circumstances of the offender that it would be in the interests of justice to do so. The offender must also agree to comply with such requirements as to his conduct during the period of deferment that the court considers it appropriate to impose. There are no statutory limits as to what requirements may be imposed, although a court will need to ensure that any such requirements are necessary, proportionate, and reasonable in order to prevent arguments as to whether they infringe Article 8 of the European Convention.[47] A court will monitor the offender's progress against those requirements. Progress will continue to act as a mitigating factor in respect of the final sentence, and might, for example, persuade a court that a community sentence rather than a custodial term is appropriate.

The power to defer sentence is intended for cases such as those in which a persistent offender has at last shown an inclination to settle down and work or those in which persons have, under domestic or financial pressure, stolen from their employers sums which they say they propose to repay. Accordingly it will not be appropriate to defer sentence where the offence is so minor that it would not merit a sentence of imprisonment in any event. Nor is it appropriate to do so where the offence is so serious that it must inevitably result in a substantial custodial sentence. This is because it would not be appropriate to impose a custodial sentence if the information before the court about the offender's conduct during the period of deferment is favourable to him. The period of deferment may be anything up to six months and there must not be a further deferment on the specified date.[48] Furthermore, where sentence is deferred, all aspects of the sentence should be deferred; the sentence must not be 'split' by, for example, imposing an immediate disqualification from driving, but deferring the remainder of the sentence.

---

[46] See Powers of Criminal Courts (Sentencing) Act 2000, ss 1, 1A–1F, 2, as amended and substituted by Criminal Justice Act 2003, s 278 and Schedule 23.

[47] See p 190, *ante*.

[48] *R v Fairhead* [1975] 2 All ER 737. However, a restitution order may be made under the Theft Act 1968, even if the passing of the sentence is in other respects deferred: Theft Act 1968, s 28(1) (as amended by the Criminal Law Act 1977, Schedule 12).

3 PRE-SENTENCE REPORTS AND OTHER REPORTS

A court must generally consider a pre-sentence report ('PSR')[49] before sentencing an offender to a custodial sentence. Such a report will also be a pre-condition to the imposition of certain community orders, or requirements in them.[50] A PSR is a written report usually prepared by the probation service, although it may well be prepared by a social worker or other member of the youth offending team[51] if the offender is under the age of eighteen. Failure to consider such a report does not invalidate a sentence passed, but in the event of an appeal the court must obtain one. The report, prepared in accordance with National Standards, will contain an assessment of the offence and its seriousness, of any factors that relate to the offender which may affect the assessment of seriousness, and especially of any risk that the offender poses. It should address the attitudes of the offender and other matters which may be relevant to the sentence ultimately imposed. It is not the practice of probation to prepare PSR in respect of those accused who indicate an intention to deny the offence. In such a case there will need to be an adjournment in order for a report to be prepared, causing delay. It was for this reason that the requirement to obtain a PSR was modified in 1994,[52] to permit a court to sentence without one where such a report is considered unnecessary. This exception does not apply in respect of offenders aged under eighteen, unless the offence for which the offender is being sentenced is triable only on indictment, and it is considered that sufficient information is available.

In addition to a PSR a court may wish, or be required, to consider other reports. Thus, a court may require a specialist report indicating the risk to the community that a sex offender poses. Other orders may require a report from a doctor or psychologist setting out details of a particular condition or addiction as a prerequisite to the making of a particular order. Thus, for example, before a court can impose a community rehabilitation order with a requirement for medical treatment, it must first consider a report from a qualified medical practitioner. Where a PSR has been obtained a copy is given to the offender or his solicitor, the prosecutor, although statute limits the use to which the report may be put. The court has the power to require a financial circumstances statement,[53] which it will use where it is contemplating the imposition of a fine and wishes to find out the means of the offender.

4 PRE-SENTENCE DRUG TESTING

Drug misuse has long been recognized as one of the major causes of offending. On its back comes a range of acquisitive or violent offences.[54] Knowledge of the fact of addition

---

[49] For the relevant statutory provisions, see Criminal Justice Act 2003, ss 156–159 re-enacting, with amendments, Powers of Criminal Courts (Sentencing) Act 2000, s 156.

[50] Where additional requirements are being considered: see s 156(2) of the 2003 Act.

[51] See p 674, *ante*.

[52] Criminal Justice and Public Order Act 1994, Schedule 9, paras 40–42.

[53] Criminal Justice Act 2003, s 162, re-enacting with amendments Powers of Criminal Courts (Sentencing) Act 2000, s 126.

[54] See Home Office Research Study 183, *Drugs and Crime*, 2002.

or misuse may therefore be crucial if offending behaviour is to be addressed. Section 161 of the Criminal Justice Act 2003 confers a wide power to order a pre-sentence drug test. The court can make an order in respect of anyone aged fourteen or over, where the court is considering imposing a community sentence and, in the case of an adult, where it is considering a suspended sentence. The consent of the offender is not required: if the offender does not comply, and there is no reasonable excuse of that failure, a criminal offence is committed. In addition the court may draw its own conclusions, which may affect the nature and requirements of any order made on sentencing.

5 RESTRAINING ORDERS

Section 5 of the Protection from Harassment Act 1997 has, since 1997, permitted a court, when sentencing a defendant convicted of an offence under section 2 or section 4 of that Act,[55] to make a restraining order. That power has now been extended to any defendant, irrespective of the offence for which the defendant was convicted, and irrespective of whether the conviction is on indictment or on summary trial. The nature of the order is discussed later.[56] But, importantly, it also applies in some circumstances to cases even where the defendant was acquitted. A court will, in all relevant cases, irrespective of verdict, have to give consideration to the making of such an order.

THE SENTENCING PROCESS IN THE MAGISTRATES' COURT

The sentencing process itself does not, in principle, differ in cases tried summarily rather than on indictment, though the particular role of the youth court in dealing with young defendants should be borne in mind.[57] But the sentencing powers of the magistrates' courts are limited by statute. Those limitations, upon the maximum term of imprisonment or maximum fine, are important not only in respect of how the defendant is

---

[55] A s 2 offence is committed by a person who pursues a course of conduct (a) which amounts to harassment of another, and (b) which he knows or ought to know amounts to harassment of another . . . A course of conduct does not fall within the above if the defendant shows – (a) that it was pursued for the purpose of preventing or detecting crime, (b) that it was pursued under any enactment or rule of law or to comply with any condition or requirement imposed by any person under any enactment; or (c) that in the particular circumstances the pursuit of the course of conduct was reasonable (see s 1 of the 1997 Act).

A s 4 offence is committed by a person whose course of conduct causes another to fear, on at least two occasions, that violence will be used against him, if the defendant knows or ought to know that his course of conduct will cause the other so to fear on each of those occasions. The exceptions stated in n 6 above (in the context of s 2) apply equally to s 4.

'Harassment' is further defined by 1997 Act, s 7 which states that references to 'harassment' include alarming the person or causing the person distress. A 'course of conduct' must involve conduct on at least two occasions.

[56] See p 711, *post*.   [57] See p 586, *ante*.

dealt with, but in wider issues about the proportion of cases that are sent for trial by the magistrates' courts.

Currently, magistrates' courts do not have the power to impose a term of imprisonment of more than six months in respect of any one offence and twelve months in total for multiple offences. Powers of committal for sentence exist, where the sentencing powers of the magistrates' court are considered to be inadequate. Those limits are set to change when section 154 of the Criminal Justice Act 2003 is implemented. When that happens, magistrates' courts will have the power to impose a sentence of no more than fifty-one weeks[58] in respect of any one offence and a total, in the case of multiple offences, of sixty-five weeks. The rationale for this significant change is inextricably bound up with decisions relating to mode of trial.[59] The government wished to see fewer cases going for trial to the Crown Court. Whether inadequate sentencing powers is a primary reason for the numbers of cases being sent to trial at the Crown Court is arguable, with some evidence existing to show that significant cases which are committed attract sentences that the magistrates' court itself could in fact have imposed.[60]

As a consequential but necessary change, if the magistrates' court is to retain a greater number of cases for sentence, the powers of the magistrates' court to commit for sentence are restricted.

OFFENCE SERIOUSNESS AND SENTENCING THRESHOLDS

The Criminal Justice Act 1991, which has provided the basis for approaches to sentencing in recent years, was primarily based on the concept of 'just deserts', a fact reflected in the basic principles stated in the Powers of Criminal Courts (Sentencing) Act 2000. Under that Act, a custodial sentence could not generally be imposed unless the offence, together with any associated offences,[61] were so serious that only a custodial sentence could be justified,[62] or that a custodial sentence (in the case of a violent or sexual offence) was necessary to protect the public. Further, a community sentence could only be imposed if the court was of the opinion that the offence, together with any associated offences, was serious enough to warrant such a sentence.

---

[58] For the significance of the period of fifty-one weeks, see p 703, *post*.

[59] See p 578, *ante*.

[60] See Herbert, 'Mode of Trial and Magistrates' Sentencing Powers' [2003] Crim LR 315; Royal Commission on Criminal Justice, *op cit*, para 6.12, citing research conducted by Hedderman and Moxon, *Magistrates' Court or Crown Court: Mode of Trial Decisions and Sentencing* Research Study No 125, HMSO, 1992.

[61] An 'associated offence' was an offence for which the offender is being dealt with on the same sentencing occasion, or which the offender is asking to be taken into consideration on that occasion.

[62] 2000 Act, s 79(2). For discussion of the custody threshold, see Ashworth and von Hirsch, 'Recognising Elephants: The Problem of the Custody Threshold' [1997] Crim LR 187.

A hierarchy of seriousness was thus created. That hierarchy is maintained by new, replacement, provisions contained in the Criminal Justice Act 2003, but with amended wording.[63] The amended custody threshold is described to be where the offence and any associated with it '...was so serious that neither a fine alone or a community sentence can be justified...', the revised wording being intended to signify that custody really should be the sentence of last resort. Nothing, though, prevents the imposition of a custodial sentence where the defendant fails to signify his willingness to comply with a requirement proposed to be inserted into a community order.

By section 143 a court must, in considering the seriousness of any offence, consider the offender's culpability, and the harm or risk of harm that the offence was intended to cause. Culpability therefore does not depend solely on the consequences of the offence. The court must take into account the fact and nature of any previous convictions, and the fact (if that was the case) that the offence was committed whilst on bail.[64] The seriousness of an offence is aggravated by racial or religious motivation,[65] but mitigated by an early guilty plea.[66] The court must also have regard to sentencing guidelines issued by the Sentencing Guidelines Council[67] in determining levels of seriousness and how the offence is dealt with in terms of type and length of sentence.

IMPRISONMENT

1 SUSPENDED SENTENCE

A sentence of imprisonment may be imposed but suspended, i.e. ordered not to take effect immediately.[68] The sentence must not be for more than two years and the period of suspension must be between one and two years. The effect of a suspended sentence is that so far as that sentence is concerned, the defendant is not liable to be imprisoned unless (1) during the period of suspension he commits another offence punishable with imprisonment, and thereafter (2) a court order that the sentence shall take effect. When suspended sentences were first introduced there was a tendency for courts to impose a suspended sentence upon persons who, but for the existence of the power to impose suspended sentences, would not have received a sentence of imprisonment at all. However, suspended sentences are custodial sentences, and therefore the criteria for the imposition of a custodial sentence (*ante*) must be satisfied before the decision whether it should be suspended is taken. In addition the Criminal Justice Act 1991[69] had made it harder for a court to impose a suspended sentence. Now, the power to suspend a sentence of imprisonment should only be used where the exceptional circumstances of the case justify it. The Act provides no guidance at to what might amount to exceptional circumstances for this purpose.

---

[63] 2003 Act, s 152. For amendments relating to community orders, see 2000 Act, s 150A, inserted by Criminal Justice and Immigration Act 2008, s 11.

[64] 2003 Act, s 143. [65] 2003 Act, s 145. [66] 2003 Act, s 144.

[67] See p 692, *ante*. [68] 2000 Act, s 118. [69] See now 2000 Act, s 118.

2 LENGTH OF CUSTODIAL SENTENCE

In cases of murder, a sentence of life imprisonment is mandatory. Life sentences are dealt with below.[70]

In any other case, the length of any custodial sentence imposed will be such as is commensurate with the seriousness of the offence, and in the light of sentencing guidelines. This does not prevent a sentence being imposed to deter future offences. In *R* v *Cunningham*[71] Lord Taylor CJ observed:

> the sentence commensurate with the seriousness of the offence of this kind will be substantial to reflect the need both for punishment and deterrence. What [the Act] does prohibit is adding an extra length to the sentence by which those criteria is commensurate with the seriousness of the offence simply to make a special example of the defendant.

Special provisions apply to dangerous offenders, which replace pre-existing provisions introduced by the Criminal Justice Act 1991. It used to be the case that a longer than commensurate custodial sentence could be imposed if necessary, in the case of a violent or sexual offence, to protect the public from serious harm. Those provisions were repealed by the Criminal Justice Act 2003.

There are also special provisions relating to minimum sentences in some cases. The Crime (Sentences) Act 1997 introduced minimum sentences in respect of repeat drug trafficking and repeat burglary offences, although the provisions relating to burglary were never implemented. Where an offender aged eighteen or over commits a drug trafficking offence, having at that date already two separate and consecutive convictions for such offences, a court must impose a minimum term of seven years' imprisonment unless there are specific circumstances relating to the offence or the offender which justify it not so doing. Again, the rationale for the provision is open to doubt: the majority of such offences will in any event attract a long sentence.

The fact that an offender is sentenced to a particular term of imprisonment does not mean that that is the period actually served in prison or detention. Under provisions introduced in 1991,[72] a distinction was drawn between short-term prisoners (serving up to four years) and long-term prisoners. Short-term prisoners served half of their sentence, with release on licence then automatic, subject only to the possibility of earlier release under home detention curfew, which could contain curfew conditions and provide for electronic tagging if appropriate. Long-term prisoners (those serving four years or more) became eligible for release on licence by the Parole Board after having served half the term, and generally had the right to automatic release after two-thirds of the term. This regime lacked clarity, was not well understood by the public and did not engage with the need to continue to work with the offender in respect of his offending behaviour.[73] A new regime was introduced by the Criminal Justice Act 2003.[74] This abolished the distinction between short-term and long-term prisoners. Now, prisoners serve one half of their

---

[70] See p 705, *post.*   [71] (1993) 14 Cr App R (S) 444.   [72] Criminal Justice Act 1991.

[73] Halliday Report, *op cit*, paras 4.1–4.10.

[74] 2003 Act, ss 237–68, amended by Criminal Justice and Immigration Act 2008, s 21.

sentence in prison or detention, subject to eligibility for home detention curfew for those who are eligible up to 135 days early.[75] The remaining part of the sentence will be spent on licence, which may be subject to licence conditions. Special provisions apply in respect of 'custody plus', intermittent custody, extended sentences, and life prisoners.

3 CUSTODY PLUS

New provisions, known as 'custody plus' address issues relating to the usefulness of short sentences. The Halliday Report[76] highlighted the lack of utility as one of the significant weaknesses of the sentencing framework. Only half of a term of imprisonment is ever served, because of automatic release at the halfway stage[77] and no power to impose conditions on the second six-month period existed. This is exacerbated by the fact that release under home detention curfew, permits release on licence at an even earlier stage. All this at a time when the number of short-term sentences of less than twelve months was increasing – by 67 per cent in the period 1989 and 1999. In that same period there was an increase of 176 per cent in respect of the shortest sentences of three months or less. Halliday concluded that greater use could be made of community sentences, of intermittent custody,[78] but also of a scheme that combined custody with a period served, under supervision, in the community and subject to conditions.

Custody plus applies to offenders aged eighteen, and comprises[79] a custodial period of a minimum of two weeks and a maximum of thirteen in respect of any one offence.[80] This is to be followed by a licence period, of a period comprised by the remainder of the term once the custodial term has been served (i.e. the total sentence length less the custodial term). The total length of the sentence must not be less than twenty-eight weeks or more than fifty-one weeks in respect of any one offence,[81] a fact that explains the curious new maximum limit on magistrates' court sentencing powers.[82] Licence conditions can be imposed in respect of the licence period.

4 DANGEROUS OFFENDERS

We have already noted the repeal of the 'longer than commensurate sentence' provision that existed in respect of violent or sexual offence.[83] As part of the strategy, inherent in the Halliday Report and the Criminal Justice Act 2003, of concentrating on prioritizing resource and imprisonment on those who pose a danger to society, new indeterminate sentences (i.e. life imprisonment or detention for life) are introduced. The 1991 Act regime already discussed provided no protection once the normal release date for such offenders had passed. Different approaches were tried in the Crime (Sentences)

---

[75] See 2003 Act, s 246.   [76] *Op cit*, para 3.1 *et seq*.
[77] Criminal Justice Act 1991, s 33(1)(a).   [78] See below.
[79] Criminal Justice Act 2003, s 181. The provisions are not yet in force and not likely to be so for some time, probably 2007.
[80] Twenty-six weeks maximum for aggregate offences.
[81] Maximum sixty-five weeks for aggregate offences.
[82] See p 700, *ante*.   [83] See p 702, *ante*.

Act 1997,[84] but never brought into force, and the Crime and Disorder Act 1998 modified but did not replace the 1991 Act scheme. This governmental indecision is ended by the 2003 Act.

The new powers apply to 'serious offences', defined by a long schedule of offences,[85] and which comprise more than sixty violent and more than forty sexual offences (known as '*specified offences*') ranging (in the case of violent offences) from manslaughter, soliciting murder, and wounding with intent to causing grievous bodily harm to causing death by careless driving while under the influence of drink or drugs, carrying a firearm with criminal intent, racially aggravated assaults or racially aggravated public order offences. In respect of sexual offences the net is again cast widely, and includes rape, unlawful sexual intercourse, incest, indecent assault, the offence of causing prostitution of women, and possession of indecent photographs of children.

Four situations are identified and dealt with:

(a) Life sentence or imprisonment for public protection for serious offences by a person aged over eighteen[86]

If the court is of the opinion that there is significant risk to members of the public of serious harm[87] caused by the commission of further 'specified offences'[88] then the court must decide whether the offence is punishable by life or a fixed term of at least ten years. If a life sentence is available and appropriate on normal sentencing principles, that sentence must be imposed. If it is not, the court must determine whether the normal determinate sentence is adequate to protect the public. If it is not, it must pass a sentence for public protection, which is an indeterminate sentence, treated for release purposes in the same way as a life sentence.

(b) Detention for life or for public protection for serious offences committed by a person aged under eighteen[89]

This replicates, with necessary textual amendments to reflect that those under eighteen are subject to detention for life, the sentence discussed at (a) above in relation to adults.

(c) Extended sentence for violent or sexual offences committed by a person aged eighteen or over[90]

This applies where the mandatory life sentence of imprisonment for public protection does not. Where there is a significant risk of serious harm to members of the public caused by the commission of further specified offences, and the term of imprisonment which it would pass would otherwise not be adequate for the purpose of protecting the

---

[84] Which provided for an extended supervision regime.

[85] 2003 Act, Schedule 15.

[86] 2003 Act, s 225, amended by Criminal Justice and Immigration Act 2008, s 13.

[87] Defined as death or serious personal injury, whether physical or psychological: s 224(3).

[88] The specified offence in respect of the risk in question does not have to be the same (or even the same type) as that which triggers the provision.

[89] 2003 Act, s 226.   [90] 2003 Act, s 227.

public from serious harm from the commission of further specified offences, the court may impose an extended sentence. This is a term which equals the appropriate custodial term (defined by normal principles) and a further period (the 'extension period') for which the offender is to be subject to licence. The length of that licence will be of such length as the court considers necessary to prevent the commission of further specified offences, subject to the total period of the sentence not exceeding the maximum for the offence. The appropriate sentence on normal sentencing principles is six years, and if the maximum for the offence is ten years, the extended period must be no longer than four years. No automatic early release licence provisions apply to extended sentences: early release from the custodial term depends upon it being granted by the Parole Board.[91]

(d) Extended sentence for violent or sexual offences committed by a person aged under eighteen[92]

This replicates, with necessary textual amendments, the sentence discussed at (c) above in relation to adults.

These provisions are a significant addition to the armoury of the court, but care will need to be taken to ensure that the sentence imposed can be justified and is proportionate to the risk that the public face.

5 LIFE SENTENCES

We have seen that a life sentence in the case of a dangerous offender can be mandatory. That is always the situation in cases of murder, the death penalty having been effectively abolished in 1965.[93]

Prior to December 2002, guidance as to the minimum period to be served by a mandatory life sentence was given to the Home Secretary by the judiciary. Since 1983, a tariff for mandatory life prisoners had been set by the Home Office, following recommendations by the trial judge and Lord Chief Justice. The Home Secretary's role was the subject of repeated challenge in domestic courts and under the Convention on Human Rights at Strasbourg.[94] Following a decision (in a case relating to a discretionary life sentence) that the setting of the 'tariff' was a judicial not an executive function[95] the law was changed so that the trial judge set the tariff.[96] Following a series of subsequent challenges,[97] the House of Lords ruled in *R (Anderson)* v *Secretary of State for the Home Department*[98] that the Home Secretary should play no part in fixing the tariff of a convicted murderer, even

---

[91] 2003 Act, ss 247, 249.   [92] 2003 Act, s 228.

[93] It was not finally abolished for treason and piracy with violence until 1991.

[94] For the history, see Lord Bingham in *R (Anderson)* v *Secretary of State for Home Affairs* [2002] 4 All ER 1089 at 1097.

[95] *Thynne* v *United Kingdom* (1991) 13 EHRR 666.

[96] Crime (Sentences) Act 1997, s 28.

[97] *V* v *United Kingdom* [2002] All ER 1024: breach of Article 6 in setting tariff for young offender; *R* v *Secretary of State for the Home Department, ex parte Venables* [1997] 3 All ER 97 unfair for Home Secretary to set tariff in respect of individual detained during Her Majesty's Pleasure; *Stafford* v *United Kingdom* (2002) 13 BHRC 360.

[98] [200] 4 All ER 1089.

if he did no more than confirm what the trial judge had recommended. The fixing of the tariff was a sentencing exercise involving a question of the quantum of punishment. Section 29 of the Crime (Sentences) Act 1967 could not be read in a way compatible with Article 6 of the Convention,[99] the court thus making a declaration of incompatibility. This was the catalyst for change, first by judicial sentencing guidelines as to the minimum terms to be served by life prisoners,[100] and then by the passage of section 269 of the Criminal Justice Act 2003.

The effect of section 269 is that the sentencing court must, in most cases, specify a minimum period of sentence. This must be done in open court, and set out the reasons why the order is made. As soon as the prisoner has served the specified period, he is eligible for release on licence, and must be released if the Parole Board (the body responsible for determining early release questions) so directs.[101] The length of time specified by the court is that which the court considers appropriate, taking into account the nature of the offence and any associated offences.[102] This leaves the question as to how the court is to determine the seriousness of the offence. Schedule 21 of the 2003 Act sets out the starting-points for different offences. For example, it identifies a starting point for murder of two or more persons as thirty years. It then identifies a range of aggravating and mitigating factors, such as pre-meditation, vulnerable victim, abuse of trust, concealment, destruction or dismemberment of the body (all aggravating), and an intention to cause serious harm rather than kill, the age of the offender, belief that the murder was an act of mercy (all mitigating). These principles are now being developed in detail by a series of guidelines and judicial decisions.[103]

6 YOUNG OFFENDERS

Generally, although not always, young offenders are dealt with in the youth court. However, for the most serious crimes they will be tried on indictment and, if found guilty, sentenced by that court. The general considerations that apply to young offenders have already been noted.[104] Irrespective of whether an offender is a young offender (i.e. under eighteen) there are restrictions on the power of a court to impose a custodial sentence on a person aged under twenty-one. Where an offender is not less than eighteen but under twenty-one, and a custodial sentence is justified, he may be sentenced to detention in a young offenders' institution. Where an offender is aged between twelve and eighteen, he may be sentenced to a detention and training order, which couples a period in custody in secure accommodation amounting to one-half of the length of the order, with an equivalent period of supervision. This order, introduced by the Crime and Disorder

---

[99] See *Easterbrook v United Kingdom, The Times*, 18 June 2003 which confirmed the correctness of that conclusion in the context of ECHR.

[100] See *Practice Statement (Crime: Life Sentences)* [2002] 1 WLR 1789.

[101] Crime (Sentences) Act 1997, s 28.   [102] See p 700, *ante*.

[103] See, in particular, *The Consolidated Criminal Practice Direction (Amendment No 8) (Mandatory Life Sentences)* [2005] 1 Cr App R 8.

[104] See p 680, *ante*.

Act 1998,[105] is discussed in more detail in due course. That Act conferred the power to extend the operation of this order to ten- and eleven-year-olds, but such powers have never been brought into effect.

Two other provisions should be noted. Section 90 of the Powers of Criminal Courts (Sentencing) Act 2000[106] provides that a person convicted of an offence who appears to the court to have been under the age of eighteen years at the time the offence was committed shall not, if he is convicted of murder, be sentenced to imprisonment for life, but instead the court must sentence him to be detained during Her Majesty's Pleasure. If he is sentenced in that way, he is detained in such place and under such conditions as the Home Secretary directs. Section 90(2) provides that where:

(a) a young person is convicted on indictment of any offence punishable in the case of an adult with imprisonment for fourteen years or more, not being an offence the sentence for which is fixed by law; or

(b) a child is convicted of manslaughter, and the court is of opinion that none of the other methods in which the case may legally be dealt with is suitable, the court may sentence the offender to be detained for such period (not exceeding the maximum term of imprisonment with which the offence is punishable in the case of an adult) as may be specified in the sentence. Where such a sentence has been passed, the child or young person will be liable to be detained in such place and on such conditions as the Home Secretary directs.

The second special provision is that contained in section 93 of the 2000 Act. This provides that where a person aged eighteen or over but under the age of twenty-one years is convicted of any offence other than murder for which a person aged twenty-one years or over would be liable to imprisonment for life, the court shall, if it considers that a custodial sentence for life would be appropriate, sentence him to custody for life.

COMMUNITY SENTENCES

If an offence is serious enough to warrant the passing of a community sentence, but not so serious so as to require a custodial sentence, the court may pass such a sentence. A community sentence is, now[107] a single sentence which can comprise one or more community orders.[108] These are as follows:

(1) Community rehabilitation order (formerly known as Probation): where an offender, aged not less than sixteen years, is placed under the supervision of a probation officer for a period not exceeding three years. Such an order may contain

---

[105] See now Powers of Criminal Courts (Sentencing) Act 2000, ss 100–107.
[106] Re-enacting Children and Young Persons Act 1933, s 53.
[107] Since the implementation of Criminal Justice Act 2003, s 147.
[108] Defined by Criminal Justice Act 2003, s 177.

requirements to keep in touch with a supervising officer, for the general purpose of securing the rehabilitation of the offender and for the protection of the public from him.

(2) Community punishment orders (formerly known as Community Service Orders): where an offender, aged not less than sixteen years, is required to perform work in the community for periods not less than forty hours or not more than 240 hours;

(3) Community punishment and rehabilitation order (formerly known as a combination order): these are a combination of community rehabilitation and community punishment orders, which may be imposed on a person aged at least sixteen years. It is an order which requires the offender:

    (a) to be under the supervision of a probation officer for a period not less than twelve months or more than three years, and

    (b) to perform unpaid work for a specified number of hours, not less than forty or more than 100.

(4) Drug treatment and testing orders: where a court considers that a person, aged not less than sixteen at the date of conviction for an offence, is dependent on or has a propensity to misuse drugs, and his dependency is such as requires and may be susceptible to treatment, the court may make a drug treatment and testing order. Such an order may include requirements that the offender submit to treatment, with a view to reduce or eliminate the dependency or propensity. The idea behind these orders is that offenders should be both punished and rehabilitated within the community. The particular order or orders forming part of the sentence must be commensurate with the seriousness of the offence and other offences associated with it, and be the most suitable for the offender, although the scope of such orders has been extended to include the use of community service and attendance centre orders for fine default, despite the fact that the normal threshold for the imposition of a community order has not been reached. Further, a community service order or a curfew order may be made in respect of persistent petty offenders. There are certain limits as to which community orders can be combined. Such orders have historically been viewed as being dependent on the offender being willing to consent to the making of such an order. The consent of the offender to the making of a probation order or community service or supervision order is no longer required.

Changes were made to the legislative regime governing community orders by the Criminal Justice Act 2003 to allow different requirements to be imposed as considered necessary by the court to reflect offence seriousness or the measures necessary to address the causes of the offending. Amongst the matters that can be included are unpaid work requirements, activity requirements, a requirement to attend specific programmes designed to tackle offending behaviour or the causes of offending, impose curfews and prohibit activities, provide for a residence requirement, or an exclusion requirement, or a drug rehabilitation requirement.

In respect of offenders under the age of 18, a court may make a Youth Rehabilitation Order, which enables a court to make one order comprising one or more of the requirements specified in section 1 of the Criminal Justice and Immigration Act 2008.

Failure to comply with the requirements of a community order or a youth rahabilitation order can result in the offender being punished, or being re-sentenced for the original offence.[109]

FINES

A court may impose a fine in lieu of, or in addition to, dealing with him in any other way. Unless a limit is fixed by the statute prescribing the offence (as it will usually be in the case of matters tried summarily, there is no limit to the amount of the fine. The court is obliged to fix a period of imprisonment or detention in default of payment.

ABSOLUTE AND CONDITIONAL DISCHARGES

Where a court thinks it inappropriate to pass any sentence, or make a probation order, it may discharge the offender either absolutely, without any condition, or subject to the condition that he does not commit any further offence for a period fixed by the court, not exceeding three years. If he commits another offence in that period he is liable to be sentenced for his original offence.

COMPENSATION AND RESTITUTION

A court by or before which a person is convicted of an offence may, instead of or in addition to dealing with him in any other way, make an order requiring him to pay compensation for any personal injury, loss, or damage resulting from that offence (or any other offence which is taken into consideration).[110] Some 14 per cent of those sentenced

---

[109] For the enforcement regime, see Criminal Justice Act 2003, Schedule 8, Criminal Justice and Immigration Act 2008, Schedule 2.

[110] Powers of Criminal Courts (Sentencing) Act 2000, s 130.

in the magistrates' court and 7 per cent of those sentenced at the Crown Court are ordered to pay compensation, most usually to those who receive a non-custodial sentence. In 2001, the average amount ordered to be paid was £144 in the magistrates' court and £1,444 at the Crown Court.[111]

No compensation order may be made in favour of the dependants of a deceased person in consequence of his death, nor in respect of injury, loss, or damage due to a road accident. In determining whether to make an order and the amount of such order the court must have regard to the offender's means. In practice the power to make compensation orders has been exercised somewhat sparingly. In particular, the Court of Appeal has repeatedly stated that no order should be made where it might result in the accused committing further offences in order to discharge his obligations; for this reason a substantial compensation order will not usually be appropriate where the offender is imprisoned since the need to discharge the order may hinder his rehabilitation on his release.[112]

If there are subsequent civil proceedings, the damages are assessed without reference to the order, but the order is taken into account when enforcing the judgment.[113] Compensation is of such amount as the court considers appropriate, having regard to any evidence and to any representations made by or on behalf of the accused or the prosecutor.

In future[114] an offender may be liable to pay a surcharge. These provisions are part of a strategy to ensure that funds are contributed by offenders to resource measures designed to support victims of crime.[115] Such surcharges are likely to vary from £5 to £30, and to be regarded as separate and distinct from any fine imposed. Surcharges are also liable to be paid in respect of on-the-spot penalties issued for disorderly behaviour,[116] and in respect of repeat road traffic offences.[117] 'Repeat' for this purpose means a second or subsequent offence.

MISCELLANEOUS ORDERS[118]

The principal sentences and orders the court has power to make have been considered above. There are, in addition, various other forms of order which may be made, detailed consideration of which is beyond the scope of this work. However, it may be noted that the Crown Court has, in addition to the powers detailed above, power to make orders

---

[111] *Consultation Paper, op cit*, p 11.
[112] See *R v Oddy* [1974] 2 All ER 666, and the cases therein cited.　　[113] 2000 Act, s 134.
[114] When the provisions of Domestic Violence Crime and Victims Act 2004, ss 14–16 are brought into force.
[115] See chapter 19, *ante*.
[116] See Domestic Violence Crime and Victims Act 2004, s 15; Criminal Justice and Police Act 2001.
[117] 2004 Act, s 16.
[118] See generally Powers of Criminal Courts (Sentencing) Act 2000.

for costs[119] either out of central funds or inter partes, orders depriving offenders of property used, or intended for use, for the purpose of crime, orders disqualifying an offender from holding or obtaining a licence to drive a motor vehicle, orders authorizing the admission to and detention in specified hospitals of offenders suffering from mental illness, psychopathic disorder, subnormality, or severe subnormality,[120] and recommendations for deportation.[121] Significant powers of confiscation and forfeiture also exist under the Drug Trafficking Offences Act 1986.

Where the Crown Court imposes a fine, forfeits a recognizance or makes an order for costs, it may order the person concerned to be searched and any money found on him to be applied towards payment of the fine or other sum.

RESTRAINING ORDERS

The power to make a restraining order whether on sentencing or even after a defendant has been acquitted has already been noted.[122] Restraining orders are made under the terms of section 5 of the Protection from Harassment Act 1997. The effect of section 12 of the Domestic Violence and Crime Act 2004 is to permit such an order to be made when a person is convicted of *any* offence. The order must be 'for the purpose of protecting the victim of the offence'. Such an order may well be appropriate where future conduct might involve stalking, burglary, or criminal damage. Such an order may even be made following acquittal, for the same purpose. That raises important questions of proof. When an individual has been convicted, evidence can be heard as part of the sentencing process. By contrast the acquittal is, technically, the end of the case. Nonetheless, a court will be entitled to receive evidence about the level of risk or danger for the future. Such proceedings will be civil in nature. By contrast, breach of a restraining order is a criminal offence.

FURTHER READING

ASHWORTH and REDMAYNE, *The Criminal Process*, 3rd edn (Oxford University Press: 2000)

HALLIDAY, *Making Punishments Work: Report of a Review of the Sentencing Framework for England & Wales* (2001) (www.homeoffice.gov.uk/docs/halliday)

WALKER and PADFIELD, *Sentencing: Theory, Law and Practice* (Butterworths: 1996)

---

[119] *Practice Direction on Costs in Criminal Proceedings* [2004] 2 Cr App R 26.
[120] Mental Health Act 1983, s 37.   [121] Immigration Act 1971, s 6.   [122] See p 699, *ante*.

24

APPEALS AND MISCARRIAGES OF JUSTICE

INTRODUCTION

In some ways the appellate system is the most important element of the entire judicial system: however good a trial process may be, there will rarely be complete certainty as to matters of 'fact', and because of the inevitable risk of human error, the potential for miscarriages of justice arises. Over the years the criminal justice system has been dogged by a series of miscarriages of justice – some well known but others not so. The existence of strong processes for investigating and dealing with suspected wrongful convictions is therefore crucial. This chapter will examine:

- The role of the Court of Appeal (Criminal Division).
- The powers of the Court of Appeal (Criminal Division).
- The role and powers of the Criminal Cases Review Commission.

THE COURT OF APPEAL

If a defendant is convicted on indictment at the Crown Court his appeal lies, if at all, to the Court of Appeal (Criminal Division). Appeals from the decisions of the magistrates' court acting summarily, and from the Crown Court acting in its appellate capacity, lie to the Divisional Court of the Queen's Bench Division.

The role and powers of the Court of Appeal (Criminal Division) have been the subject of a great deal of debate in recent years,[1] largely generated by a series of cases where convictions have had to be overturned, often some years after conviction and subsequent appeal.[2] In particular, the question of when the court should be able to

---

[1] See O'Connor, 'The Court of Appeal: Re-Trials & Tribulations' [1990] Crim LR 615; JUSTICE Report on Miscarriages of Justice (1989). See also, and generally, Spencer, 'Does our Present Court of Appeal System Make Sense?' [2006] Crim LR 677.

[2] See e.g. *R v Maguire* [1992] QB 936, [1992] 2 All ER 433; *R v McIlkenny* [1992] 2 All ER 417.

overturn a conviction, how it should treat fresh evidence, and whether it should have greater powers to order re-trials following an appeal, and whether the Court of Appeal should have the right to order a retrial of a defendant who has, in fact, been acquitted, have each been raised, and the subject of consideration by the Royal Commission on Criminal Justice[3] and the Auld Review.[4] However, it is important to remember that controversy about the criminal appellate system is not new.

1 THE DEVELOPMENT OF THE COURT OF APPEAL (CRIMINAL DIVISION)

Until 1907 there was, in fact, no right of appeal at all. Where points of law arose on trial on indictment the trial judge could, but was not obliged to, refer such points for consideration by a court known as the Court for Crown Cases Reserved. Not until the passage of the Criminal Appeal Act 1907 was a formal appellate system introduced, and that Act was passed largely in response to a miscarriage of justice caused by the mistaken identification of an accused.[5] The 1907 Act created the Court of Criminal Appeal, which was given powers to allow appeals against conviction if that conviction was unreasonable or could not be supported having regard to the evidence, or if there was a wrong decision on a question of law. No power to order a re-trial existed at that time. The Criminal Appeal Act 1964 created a power to order a new trial, although only on the ground of 'fresh evidence',[6] a restriction that was not removed until the passing of the Criminal Justice Act 1988.[7] By the Criminal Appeal Act 1966, the jurisdiction of the Court of Criminal Appeal was transferred to the Court of Appeal (Criminal Division).[8]

The whole of the pre-existing legislation was consolidated in the Criminal Appeal Act 1968. However, the powers of, and the use of such powers by, the Court of Appeal attracted considerable attention, and concern, as miscarriages of justice came to light. The Royal Commission on Criminal Justice therefore considered the powers and functions of the Court of Appeal (Criminal Division). The result was a government consultation paper, followed by the passage of the Criminal Appeal Act 1995. That Act, based on the recommendations of the Royal Commission, significantly amends the existing legislation.

Before looking at the substance of the powers themselves, three general points need to be remembered:

(a) The right of appeal has traditionally been that of the defendant, except in cases referred to the court by the Home Secretary.[9] The prosecution has had no right of appeal against acquittal, or against unfavourable legal rulings although there is a limited power for points of law, and lenient sentences to be referred to the Court

---

[3] Cm 2263 (1993, HMSO).   [4] *Op cit*, Ch 9.   [5] The Adolph Beck case.
[6] Section 1, re-enacted in Criminal Appeal Act 1968, s 7.   [7] See p 726, *post*.
[8] Being one of two divisions of the Court of Appeal: Supreme Court Act 1981, s 3(1).
[9] See p 717, *post*.

of Appeal by the Attorney-General.[10] Major changes in that context have now been introduced.[11]

(b) The court's powers derive solely from statute. The court has no inherent or residual power which entitles it to fill gaps in the statutory provisions. Criticism can fairly be made of the statutory provisions, not only in the obvious cases where the court's role has been limited, but also in other areas where gaps in the appellate system exist.

(c) The recent controversies about the actions of the court must be viewed in the light of the overall function and role of the court. This is dealt with below.

2 THE ROLE OF THE COURT OF APPEAL

The Court has been at pains to stress the limits of its powers. In *R v McIlkenny*[12] Lloyd, Mustill and Farquharson LJJ in a joint judgment observed:

> Under jury trial juries not only find the facts; they also apply the law. Since they are not experts in the law, they are directed as to the relevant law by the judge. But the task of applying the law to the facts, and so reaching a verdict, belongs to the jury and the jury alone. The primacy of the jury in the English criminal justice system explains why, historically, the Court of Appeal had so limited a function Since justice is as much concerned with the conviction of the guilty as the acquittal of the innocent, and the task of convicting the guilty belongs constitutionally to the jury, not to us, the role [of the Court] is necessarily limited. Hence it is true to say that whereas the Civil Division of the Court of Appeal has appellate jurisdiction in the full sense, the Criminal Division is perhaps more accurately described as a court of review.

The point has also cogently been made that not only is the Court subordinate to the jury; also the jury's role is itself limited.[13] It is not the task of the jury within the adversarial system to pronounce innocence or guilt, but rather whether it has been proved, according to law, that the accused is guilty as charged. For these reasons the Court of Appeal has considered itself constrained in dealing with appeals, particularly those based upon new evidence. The extent to which these constraints are justifiable, or in the public interest, is a matter for debate. The Royal Commission on Criminal Justice concluded that such considerations as to the role of the jury have too heavily influenced the Court, and that the Court of Appeal should be 'readier to overturn jury verdicts than it has shown itself in the past'.[14] In particular it should be more prepared to consider arguments that a jury has made a mistake, and to admit evidence that might favour a defendant even if it was, or could have been, available at the trial. It is debatable as to how far the various legislative changes will, in fact, result in a greater willingness by the Court of Appeal to follow a more liberal approach.

---

[10] See p 720, post.   [11] See p 721, *post.*   [12] [1992] 2 All ER 417.
[13] See p 551, *ante.*   [14] Report, Ch 10.

THE GROUNDS OF APPEAL

1 APPEAL AGAINST CONVICTION

By section 1 of the Criminal Appeal Act 1968, a person convicted on indictment may appeal to the Court of Appeal:

(a) against his conviction, on any ground which involves a question of law alone;

(b) with the leave of the Court of Appeal, against his conviction on any ground which involves a question of fact alone, or a question of mixed law and fact, or any other ground which appears to the court to be a sufficient ground of appeal.

Where leave to appeal is required, it may be granted in the first instance by a single judge of the Court; if he refuses, the applicant may have his case considered by the Court itself.[15] This process excludes a large proportion of cases, although the proportion of cases where leave is granted is increasing, with in 2004 leave being granted in some 34 per cent of cases.[16] The Royal Commission found that the chances of success are distinctly higher where the defendant is represented. In this regard the Commission found uneven and unsatisfactory provision for the giving of legal advice on appeal, which is part of the professional duty of solicitor and counsel. Initial advice after the case on appeal is within the scope of criminal legal aid (99 per cent of cases within the Crown Court). The research also found misunderstandings about the powers of the Court regarding length of sentence. The Commission concluded that interpreter facilities should be made available by the Prison Service to facilitate the giving of advice to those who do not understand English. The present requirement to obtain leave should be kept, and legal aid extended to cover advice as to whether an application should be renewed.

The trial judge may also grant a certificate that the case is fit for appeal, on a question of fact or mixed law and fact. This should only be done where the trial judge is satisfied that there is a substantial point, and one worthy of consideration by the Court of Appeal.[17]

Nothing in the Act prevents an appeal against conviction in a case where the accused in fact pleaded guilty at his trial. However, an appeal in such circumstances will only succeed if: (i) the defendant did not appreciate the nature of the charge; or (ii) he did not intend to admit that he was guilty of it; or (iii) on the admitted facts, he could not in law have been guilty of the offence to which he pleaded guilty. Such cases are rare, but not unknown.[18] In *R* v *Boal*[19] the Court was prepared to entertain an appeal where the

---

[15] Criminal Appeal Act 1968, s 31(3).

[16] See, generally, Spencer, 'Does the Present Criminal Appeal System Make Sense?' [2006] Crim LR 677.

[17] *R* v *Eyles* (1963) 47 Cr App R 260; cf. *R* v *Smith* [1974] QB 354, [1974] 1 All ER 6.32.

[18] *R* v *Forde* [1923] 2 KB 400, at 403; *R* v *Gould* [1968] 2 QB 65 [1968] 1 All ER 849; cf. *R* v *Vickers* [1975] 2 All ER 945, [1975] 1 WLR 811.

[19] [1992] QB 591; [1992] 3 All ER 177.

defendant had pleaded guilty as a result of advice based upon a misunderstanding of the law by his barrister.

2 APPEAL AGAINST SENTENCE

The defendant may appeal against the sentence passed on him after conviction unless the sentence is one fixed by law. Such an appeal requires the leave of a single judge, or, if refused, of the full court.[20] The appeal can be not only against the sentence, but also against any order that forms part of the sentence, such as a compensation order,[21] disqualification from driving, a binding over order,[22] or recommendation for deportation.[23] There is no right of appeal against a recommendation that a defendant convicted of murder should serve a certain number of years, because this is not a recommendation binding on the Home Secretary.[24] By contrast, if a judge makes an order, in respect of a discretionary life sentence, specifying what part of the sentence must expire before the offender is able to have his case referred to the Parole Board, this has legal consequences and would appear to be a matter which can be subject to an appeal.[25]

The prosecution also has the right to have the sentence of a court reviewed.[26] If it appears to the Attorney-General that the sentencing of a person in a proceeding in the Crown Court has been unduly lenient, in respect of an offence triable only on indictment (or such other offence as the Secretary of State may order) then, with leave of the Court of Appeal, the case may be referred to them for the sentence to be reviewed.[27] The application must be made within twenty-eight days of the sentence being passed.[28]

Concern was expressed at the time this power was introduced that a defendant is in jeopardy twice.[29] The power to review granted by the Act is in respect of a sentence perceived to be unduly lenient, not simply in respect of a sentence with which the court disagrees. The power is used where the judge has erred as a matter of sentencing principle, and thus is a means of achieving consistent application of sentencing policy.[30]

3 CRIMINAL CASES REVIEW COMMISSION

Once the avenues of appeal outlined above have been exhausted then, unless a final appeal to the House of Lords is permitted, the one remaining formal option open to an accused is the making of an application to the Criminal Cases Review Commission. The Commission was established by the 1995 Act following consistent, and justified,

---

[20] Criminal Appeal Act 1968, s 1.   [21] Se p 709, *ante*.

[22] *R v Williams* [1982] 3 All ER 1092, [1982] 1 WLR 1398.

[23] See the Criminal Appeal Act 1968, s 50(1), defining sentence to include 'any order made by a court when dealing with an offender'.

[24] *R v Aitken* [1966] 2 All ER 453n, [1966] 1 WLR 1076.

[25] See the terms of Criminal Justice Act 1991, s 34(2).

[26] Introduced by Criminal Justice Act 1988, s 36.

[27] See *Criminal Justice Act 1988 (Review of Sentencing) Order 2006*, SI 2006/1116.

[28] Criminal Justice Act 1988, Schedule 3.   [29] See p 637, *post*.

[30] For wider issues in this context, see p 692, *ante*.

criticism of the pre-existing system under section 17 of the 1968 Act whereby a convicted person might apply to the Home Secretary for his case to be referred back to the Court of Appeal, or whereby the Home Secretary might of his own motion refer back a case, on a point arising in a case.[31] This is what occurred in *R v Berry (No 2)*[32] where a finding on a point of law by the Court of Appeal led to that court quashing a conviction, the court not determining another ground of appeal that was before the court. On appeal to the House of Lords by the prosecution, the decision of the Court of Appeal was reversed. The Court of Appeal now being without jurisdiction to deal with this further point, the only way in which it could now be dealt with by the Court was for the Home Secretary to make a reference under section 17, which is in fact what occurred. Yet the approach of the Home Office was on the whole slow and cautious, showing 'too great a constitutional deference' to the Court of Appeal.[33]

The operation of section 17, and, generally the role of the Home Office, was considered by the Royal Commission on Criminal Justice.[34] It noted that the Royal Prerogative of mercy in respect of trials on indictment was 'seldom exercised',[35] and it noted also that section 17 references were made in only a small proportion of the cases of those brought to the attention of the Home Office by the parties, or by campaigning groups such as JUSTICE.[36] The restrictive nature of the test[37] used by the Home Secretary to decide whether a reference should be made had been identified by the May Committee,[38] which also criticized the Home Office for not being pro-active in miscarriage cases. References back were only made in cases where fresh evidence had emerged since the trial and appeal. The view of the May Committee that there was a need for change was supported by the Royal Commission. It recommended that the Home Secretary's power to make references under section 17 should be abolished. Instead, the role now performed by the Home Office should be given to an independent body, a new Criminal Cases Review Authority. This authority, to comprise both lawyers and lay persons, would oversee any further investigations needed into cases referred to it by complainants, although it would not appear to have powers to instigate investigations on its own motion.

This recommendation was accepted in principle. The result was the creation, by the 1995 Act, of the Criminal Cases Review Commission. At least one-third of the members of the Commission must be lawyers,[39] and two-thirds persons who have knowledge or expertise of any part of the criminal justice system.[40] Members are appointed by the Crown on the advice of the Prime Minister,[41] and hold office for an initial term of five

[31] 1968 Act, s 17(1)(a).

[32] [1991] 2 All ER 789, [1991] 1 WLR 125; for the resulting decision, see *R v Berry* (3 April 1992, unreported).

[33] See Nobles and Schiff, 'The Criminal Cases Review Commission: Establishing a Workable Relationship with the Court of Appeal' [2005] Crim LR 173; *The Criminal Cases Review Commission & The Court of Appeal: The Commissions' Perspective* [2005] Crim LR 937.

[34] *Op cit*, Ch 11.   [35] Ibid, para 3.

[36] A campaigning organization with a primary aim of investigation of, and campaigning against, miscarriages of justice. See, in particular, JUSTICE, *Miscarriages of Justice*, 1989.

[37] Royal Commission Report, *op cit*, Ch 1.

[38] Established to report on the miscarriage of justice in the Guildford and Woolwich pub bombings cases.

[39] Criminal Appeal Act 1995, s 8(5).   [40] Ibid, s 8(6).   [41] Ibid, s 8(4).

years, renewable only once. The Commissioners are aided by caseworkers, and have a general power to undertake, or to arrange the undertaking by others, of inquiries.[42] The number, and type of cases, can be discovered by looking at the Annual Reports for the Commission. In evaluating that work, it is worth observing that legal aid is not available to lawyers pursuing miscarriage cases – a significant gap – convicted persons therefore being highly dependent on the public spiritedness of lawyers undertaking what amounts to *pro bono* work (i.e. without payment).

(a) The use of the powers

The Annual Report for 2005–2006 is illustrative. The Commission received 932 cases, making a cumulative intake of 10,254 since it was established. It referred twenty-one convictions and four sentences to the Court of Appeal. On the conviction referrals, eight were for murder, seven for dishonesty, four for sexual offences, two for non-fatal violence, two for drugs offences, one for manslaughter, one for possession of a firearm, and one for membership of a proscribed organization. Of the cases decided by the Court of Appeal following reference, nine convictions were upheld. Referral of murder cases shows the greatest proportion of appeals which are dismissed.[43] Where convictions are overturned, the most common reason was fresh evidence casting doubt on the reliability of prosecution witnesses.[44] Flawed or doubtful expert evidence is also an issue, as demonstrated vividly in a series of case relating to deaths of babies.[45] The Commission observed:[46]

> The reasons for referral have been diverse but a strong underlying theme can be identified. In most cases there has been fresh evidence casting doubt on the reliability of prosecution witnesses. Concerns were identified about the way in which original exhibits had been handled in a rape case. Doubt was raised about the original medical evidence in a shaken baby case.
> Psychological evidence suggests that a confession was unreliable...In other cases, referral resulted from the identification of defects in the investigative or trial process...In four cases the applicant had pleaded guilty and in three of those cases there had been no previous appeal but the Commission decided there were exceptional grounds to justify referral. This illustrates the fact that even though there may be no new evidence, careful analysis of the facts and circumstances at the time of trial can provide compelling reasons for referral on the basis of new argument.

Although the Commission has the power to undertake inquiries, this is likely to be exceptional. Rather, the intention is that inquiries be carried out by the police under the supervision and instruction of the Commission, a position regarded as inevitable by the Royal Commission on Criminal Justice. The Review Commission has the power to require the original investigatory body to appoint an investigating officer to report back to the Commission,[47] or to appoint an investigator from another police force.[48]

[42] Ibid, s 21.   [43] CCRC Annual Report 2003–2004, p 14.
[44] See *R v Mills and Poole* (1978) 68 Cr App R 154; *R v Cooper and McMahon* [1969] 1 QB 267.
[45] *R v Cannings*, [2004] 2 Cr App R 7, *R v Clark* [2000] EWCA Crim 54.
[46] CCCRC, Annual Report, *op cit*, p 18.   [47] Ibid, s 19.   [48] Ibid, s 2.

(b) The criteria

The Commission takes over the powers formerly exercised by the Home Secretary under section 17 of the 1968 Act. The powers to refer cases (which now include convictions on summary trial) are contained in section 13 of the 1995 Act. Firstly, there must be a real possibility that a conviction would not be upheld if a reference were made. Secondly, the reason for this must be that an argument or evidence was not raised at trial or on appeal. Finally, an appeal must have been heard or leave to appeal refused. The second and third criteria are not absolutes: the Commission can, despite them, refer a case where exceptional circumstances exist.[49]

The judgment therefore required of the Commission is a difficult one, and it is theirs alone.[50] It involves a prediction of the view the Court of Appeal may take, which may in turn require the Commission to assess what attitude the Court will take on a fresh evidence application.[51] The key words are therefore 'real possibility', because it is at best a judgment. The Commission has to make this judgment even though the criteria applied by the Court include a power to hear evidence when it is necessary or expedient in the interests of justice to do so.[52] One good example of the interrelationship between Commission and Court of Appeal is R v Mills and Poole.[53] In that case the Commission had decided not to refer a case following a libel case where a detective whose testimony was crucial was disbelieved. The Commission did so because it considered that the facts, which had been thoroughly examined at trial and on appeal, had not changed. On judicial review of the Commission's refusal the Divisional Court accepted the propriety of the Commission's decision but nonetheless invited a reference. That was duly made, and the Court of Appeal did not regard the situation as unfair, but quashed the conviction for a previously undiscovered legal error.

Another problem for the Commission is how it should deal with cases where there has been a change in the law or practice of the Court of Appeal. The Divisional Court in R (on the application of the Director of Public Prosecutions) v Criminal Cases Review Commission[54] suggested that the Commission should ignore any aspect of the law or practice applied by the court. That view was rejected by the Court of Appeal,[55] which concluded that, except in exceptional circumstances, a conviction should not normally be referred to the Court of Appeal on the basis of a change in the law. Any other conclusion would lead to conflict with the approach of the Court of Appeal itself, and between the Court and the Commission. The Criminal Justice and Immigration Act 2008 reinforces this approach, by permitting the Court of Appeal to disregard the development of the law since the date of conviction.[56] However, that still leaves the Commission with the difficult judgment, in an exceptional case, to determine whether to uphold a conviction would cause 'substantial injustice'.

[49] Ibid, s 13(2). Perhaps a good example is the referral of the case of Mills (1978) 68 Cr App R 154.
[50] See R v Criminal Cases Review Commission, ex parte Pierson (1999).
[51] For the powers of the Court of Appeal, see p 722, post.
[52] See, generally, powers of the Court.
[53] See [1998] 1 Cr App R 43, [2001] EWCA Crim 753, [2004] 1 Cr App R 7.
[54] [2007] 1 Cr App R 30.   [55] See [2008] Crim LR 50.   [56] 2008 Act, s 42.

If the Commission decides to make a reference, then the case returns to the Court of Appeal to be dealt with in the normal way. The appeal may not be on any ground other than one related to reasons given by the Commission for making the reference.[57] There are no legal obstacles to old cases being referred. Cases have been referred that go back many years,[58] although the utility of referring old cases has been criticized, both judicially and extra-judicially.

The Court has the power itself to refer a case to the Commission for investigation and report.[59] Eleven such referrals have been made since the establishment of the Commission,[60] and the work of the Commission is likely to increase now that Court referrals may be made at the stage of application of leave to appeal, rather than simply at the appeal itself.[61] For that reason, the changes made by the 1995 Act to the powers of the Court are just as important as the creation of the Commission itself. If the Commission decides not to make a reference, it is required to state the reasons why it has so decided.[62]

4 REFERENCE FOLLOWING ACQUITTAL

The prosecution does not have any right to appeal against acquittal, unlike the position in cases of summary trial. However, the Criminal Justice Act 1972[63] gives to the prosecution a limited right to have points of law which arose during a trial resulting in an acquittal reconsidered by the Court of Appeal. The nature of the procedure is that of a reference of a point of law, rather than an appeal, for the outcome of the reference has no effect on the acquittal in the case.

The Act and the rules made hereunder go to great lengths to protect the acquitted person. Not only is his acquittal unaffected, he may appear to present argument in the Court of Appeal, is entitled to be represented by counsel, and have his costs paid out of central funds. His identity must not be disclosed during the proceedings in the Court of Appeal except by his consent.

The purpose of the power is to enable clarification of points of law which are important, and before wrong interpretations of law become entrenched at trial court level. The Court may, of its own motion or on application, refer the point to the House of Lords.

5 PROSECUTION RIGHTS OF APPEAL

Although defendants have many rights of appeal, the prosecutor has had only the extremely limited rights noted above. The position differed somewhat in the case of

---

[57] Criminal Appeal Act 1965, s 14(4A) inserted by Criminal Justice Act 2003, s 315. This followed a case where the appeal went far beyond the reference: see *R v Day* [2003] EWCA Crim 1060.

[58] See, e.g., *R v Mattan, The Times*, 5 March 1998; *R v Hanratty* [2002] 2 Cr App R 30; *Ellis* [2003] EWCA Crim 3556; *Knighton* [2002] EWCA Crim 2227 (a seventy-five year-old conviction).

[59] Ibid, s 15.   [60] CCRC Annual Report, 2003–2004, p 46.

[61] See Criminal Justice Act 2003, s 315.

[62] Ibid, s 14(6). See, generally, *R v Secretary of State for the Home Department, ex parte Hickey (No 2)* [1995] 1 All ER 490, [1995] 1 WLR 734.

[63] 1972 Act, s 36(1).

summary trial, where there has always been the power to apply to the High Court by way of case stated,[64] a right exercisable both by defence and the prosecution. That lack of a general means whereby the prosecution could seek recourse to appeal courts to correct legal error has been the subject of increasing concern. The Law Commission in 2001 observed:[65]

> If a case falls on legal argument it is better for public confidence in the criminal justice system that it should be susceptible to the second opinion of a higher court, than it be unappealable.

The Auld Review likewise regarded the position as unsatisfactory.[66] It recommended that the prosecution should have three new rights: appeals from preparatory hearings against potentially terminating rulings; then a right to appeal against an acquittal resulting from a terminating ruling up to the end of the prosecution case; and a right of appeal against a finding of no case to answer. Those recommendations form for the basis of provisions in Part 9 of the Criminal Justice Act 2003. They apply to trials on indictment.

The general right of prosecution appeal in respect of rulings, subject to the leave of the trial judge or the Court of Appeal, are contained in section 58 of the 2003 Act. Section 58 does not use the expression 'terminating rulings', but it is such matters which section 58 is intended to address, although also a phrase best avoided. The Solicitor-General in debate, put the matter graphically by observing:[67]

> A terminating ruling is like an elephant. One can recognize it when it comes lumbering through the doors of the court. If it looks like a terminal ruling it is appealable.

The type of matters that are likely to 'lumber through the door' are matters which are so fatal to the prosecution case, and mean that it cannot, effectively, succeed. This might include stays for abuse of process,[68] a successful argument of *autrefois acquit* or *autrefois convict*;[69] a successful submission of no case to answer;[70] an adverse public interest immunity ruling;[71] or a ruling that the facts alleged disclose no offence known to English law. The effect of this power may be that a trial has to adjourn whilst the appeal is dealt with, presumably as a matter of some urgency.

A second prosecution right of appeal is in respect of evidentiary rulings, defined by section 62(2) as such rulings that significantly weaken the prosecution case. These need not be rulings that effectively are 'terminating' and thus fall within section 58.

Finally, although not technically a right of appeal, we have already noted that in limited circumstances the prosecution may apply to the Court of Appeal for leave to permit the prosecution to proceed to a second prosecution of a defendant who has already

---

[64] Magistrates' Courts Act 1980, s 111. This is not technically an appeal but a review on certain grounds.

[65] *Double Jeopardy and Prosecution Appeals* Law Com No 267, 2001.

[66] Auld Review, *op cit*, Ch 12, paras 47–65.

[67] HC Cmttee, 25 February 2003. For guidance, see *R v Clarke* [2007] EWCA Crim 2532; *R v Y* [2008] EWCA Crim 10.

[68] See p 572, *ante.*   [69] See p 637, *ante.*

[70] In such a situation, the procedure to be adopted is dealt with by 2003 Act, s 58(7).

[71] See p 609, *ante.*

been acquitted.[72] This is an exceptional course of action and runs counter to the general principle that an individual should not be tried again for an offence of which he has been acquitted.

POWERS OF THE COURT

1 POWER TO QUASH A CONVICTION

The powers to quash a conviction are contained in section 2 of the 1968 Act. In its *original* form, section 2 set out three grounds. These were as follows:

(a) under all the circumstances of the case the conviction[73] is unsafe and unsatisfactory;

(b) there was a wrong decision on a point of law;

(c) there was a material irregularity in the course of the trial.

In addition, section 2 contained a proviso. The Court of Appeal might, on an appeal against conviction, dismiss the appeal, even though of the opinion that the point raised might be decided in favour of the appellant, if it is considered that no miscarriage of justice has actually occurred. The test was whether a reasonable jury, after a proper summing-up, could have failed to convict the appellant:[74] in other words, the Court was putting itself in the place of the jury. It was often applied where there has been misdirection on a matter of law.

The relationship between the proviso and the powers contained in section 2(1) of the 1968 Act discussed was complex.[75] For this reason it was argued that there was really only one test that the court should apply in deciding the use of section 2(1): has there been a miscarriage of justice?[76]

The majority of the Royal Commission took the view:[77]

(1) if a conviction was safe despite an error, then the appeal should be dismissed;

(2) if an error was made that rendered the conviction unsafe, then the conviction should be quashed;

---

[72] See p 258, *ante*.

[73] 'Conviction' was substituted for 'verdict of the jury' by the Criminal Law Act 1977, s 44. The previous wording appeared to preclude an appeal if the accused pleaded guilty, unless the count to which the accused pleaded guilty disclosed no offence known to the law or (perhaps) on the admitted facts he could not in point of law have been guilty of the offence; this, presumably erroneous, drafting in the 1968 Act went judicially unnoticed until *Director of Public Prosecutions* v *Shannon* [1975] AC 717; *sub nom R* v *Shannon* [1974] 2 All ER 1009, in which case Lord Salmon drew attention to the need for some amendment to s 2(1) of the 1968 Act.

[74] *Stirland* v *Director of Public Prosecutions* [1944] AC 315, [1944] 2 All ER 13; see also (among many cases) *R* v *Haddy* [1944] KB 442, [1944] 1 All ER 319. For the proper attitude to application of the proviso in a murder case, see *Anderson* v *R* [1972] AC 100, [1971] 3 All ER 768.

[75] See *R* v *Maguire* [1992] QB 936, [1992] 2 All ER 433.

[76] See O'Connor, *op cit* at [1990] Crim LR 615.   [77] Report, *op cit*, Ch 10, para 38.

(3) if an error may render a conviction unsafe, then the conviction should be quashed and a re-trial ordered. This would render the proviso redundant.

The majority also took the view that this should be the case even where appeals are based upon pre-trial malpractice or procedural irregularity. It is not the purpose of the appellate process to discipline the police or prosecution – the judge will have excluded tainted evidence anyway.

In 1995 the Criminal Appeal Act changed the law, by introducing a single test. The proviso was abolished. Under the new section 2 the test is this: the Court must allow an appeal against conviction if they think that the conviction is 'unsafe'. This formulation should be compared with the recommendation of the Royal Commission that the single ground be 'the conviction is or may be unsafe'.[78] The difference in wording is of little consequence, in the light of the tests adopted by the courts to the question as to whether a conviction is unsafe, and in the light of parliamentary intent.

The key issue is how the words in section 2 are interpreted and used by the Court of Appeal. The wording of the original section 2 ('unsafe or unsatisfactory') was considered by the House of Lords in *Stafford* v *Director of Public Prosecutions*,[79] where Viscount Dilhorne cited with approval a passage from the judgment of the court in *R* v *Cooper*:[80]

> The court must in the end ask itself a subjective question, whether we are content to let the matter stand as it is, or whether there is not some lurking doubt in our minds which makes us wonder whether an injustice has been done. This is a reaction which may not be based strictly on the evidence as such; it is a reaction that can be produced by the general feeling of the case as the court experiences it to be.

The Royal Commission received conflicting evidence about the application of this 'lurking doubt' approach. Research indicated that between 1968 and 1989 only six cases applied the test, and in 1989 one out of 114 appeals. Yet the more recent research for the years 1991–92 showed a greater use of this power (fourteen out of 102).[81] However, the language of lurking doubt was not always used by the Court. For the Court to conclude that a verdict was unsatisfactory because of an injustice in the case and in the verdict was no different from an application of the 'lurking doubt' test. Nevertheless, the Court in *R* v *Maguire*[82] stressed that it is the words of the Act that have to be applied, not some other reformulation of the question. Despite the fact that the word 'or' was used, the weight of authority suggests that 'unsafe' and 'unsatisfactory' in fact were regarded as bearing the same meaning.[83] This was a view supported by the Royal Commission. On this basis, the change in wording in section 2 does not change or limit the scope of the role of the Court.[84] Not only will the Court be able to interfere where the verdict of the jury is unsatisfactory on the evidence, but also on the various other grounds relating to errors of law, misdirections, and the like which underpinned the majority of successful appeals. Errors in summing up, misdirection on matters of law, a failure in appropriate cases to withdraw

---

[78] Ibid, para 46.   [79] 1974] AC 878, [1973] 3 All ER 762.
[80] [1969] 1 QB 267, at 271, [1969] 1 All ER 32, at 34, per Widgery LJ (as he then was).
[81] Report, Ch 10 para 43.   [82] *R* v *Maguire* [1992] QB 936, [1992] 2 All ER 433.
[83] See O'Connor, *op cit*, n 1, p 722, *ante*; cf. Smith, 'The Criminal Appeal Act 1995' [1995] Crim LR 920.
[84] See Smith, *op cit*, at p 924, as to parliamentary intent.

the case from the jury are all instances where section 2(1)(a) operate and will continue to do so. The unsafeness of the conviction may have arisen because of the way the case was conducted. In respect of appeals based upon error by lawyers, the test identified in *R v Ensor*[85] was whether injustice had been suffered as a result of flagrantly incompetent advocacy. This was, in the view of the Royal Commission,[86] too narrow:

> It cannot possibly be right that there should be defendants serving prison sentences for no other reason than that their lawyers made a decision which later turns out to have been mistaken. What matters is not the degree to which the lawyers were at fault, but whether the particular decision, whether reasonable or unreasonable, caused a miscarriage of justice.

A wide variety of errors, usually of a procedural nature, may cause a conviction to be unsafe. These might include unfair conduct or undue interruption by the judge, improper disclosure to the jury of the defendant's character, tampering with a juror, misconduct on the part of a juror and failure to inform an undefended person of his right to call witnesses. In *R v Maguire*[87] it was held that a failure to comply with the requirements concerning disclosure of unused material amounted to a 'material irregularity'. However, the central question should be: what is the impact on the safety of the conviction of the procedural error? Does it render the conviction 'unsafe'?[88] The balance of authority suggests that a conviction is not rendered unsafe simply because the court is dissatisfied at what went on at trial.[89] In *R v Mullen*[90] a conviction obtained as a result of a trial which should not have taken place, because of illegality in bringing the appellant to the United Kingdom to face trial, was unsafe. A broad approach to the meaning of 'unsafe' should be adopted. This difference from the approach in *Chalkey* is supported by more recent cases, In *R v Rabdall*[91] Lord Bingham said:

> it is not every departure from good practice which renders a trial unfair. But the right of a defendant to a fair trial is absolute. There will come a point when the departure from good practice is so gross, or so persistent, or so prejudicial, or so irremediable that an appellant court will have no choice but to condemn a trial as unfair and quash a conviction as unsafe, however strong the grounds for believing the defendant to be guilty.

This position is regarded as unsatisfactory by the government, concerned about 'guilty' persons being acquitted.[92] The government is introducing provisions into what will be the Criminal Justice and Immigration Act 2008, to reverse this approach, and to re-instate the approach adopted in *Chalkey*.

---

[85] 1989] 2 All ER 586, [1989] 1 WLR 497.   [86] Report, para 59.

[87] [1992] QB 936, [1992] 2 All ER 433.   [88] *R v Renda* [2005] EWCA Crim 2827.

[89] *R v Chalkey* [1997] EWCA Crim 3416. See also *R v Rajcoomar* [1999] EWCA Crim 447; *R v Thomas* [1999] EWCA Crim 1266.

[90] [1999] EWCA Crim 278. See also *R v Smith* [1999] 2 Cr App R 238.

[91] [2002] 1 WLR 2237; see also *R v Abdroikov* [2005] EWCA 470; *R v O'Hare* [2006] EWCA Crim 471; *R v Russell* [2006] EWCA Crim 470.

[92] *Quashing Convictions* – Report of a Review by the Lord Chancellor, the Home Secretary and the Attorney-General (2007), to be found at www.cjsonline.gov.uk

Another area of uncertainty that remains are cases where a conviction for an offence, other than that for which the accused was tried, is upheld on appeal by virtue of the proviso. One such case was *R v Pickford*[93] where the accused had pleaded guilty to an offence that, in law, he could not have committed as charged. The Court of Appeal upheld the conviction, applying the proviso, on the grounds that although the appellant had not in law committed the offence charged (incitement of a boy to commit incest with the boy's mother) he had in fact incited the mother to commit the incest (which was in law an offence). It is unclear as to whether this type of case is no longer good law on the grounds that the proviso has been abolished, or whether such a conviction would be regarded as 'safe'. The fact that the Court felt constrained to use the proviso provides clear evidence that such a conviction cannot be regarded as 'safe'.

It might also be noted that the conclusion that a conviction is 'unsafe' does not necessarily reflect on the trial process itself. In *R v B*[94] a conviction for sexual assault was overturned even though the trial had been conducted perfectly properly, because it had taken thirty years for the complainant to make the allegation.

2 POWER TO SUBSTITUTE AN ALTERNATIVE VERDICT

Where the defendant has been convicted of an offence and (1) the jury could on the same indictment have found him guilty of some other offence; and (2) it appears to the Court of Appeal that the jury must have been satisfied of the facts proving him guilty of that other offence, the Court may, instead of allowing or dismissing the appeal against conviction, substitute a verdict of guilty of that other offence and pass sentence on the defendant for it.[95] The sentence must not be greater than that passed on the defendant at the trial, and must not, of course, exceed the maximum permitted by law for the substituted offence.[96] The Court exercises this power with care, particularly in the light of (2) above, which involves some consideration of a verdict of a jury for which no reasons are given. Further, it is a material, though not decisive, point against exercising the power if the jury were not given any direction as to the alternative offence.[97] Where the indictment contains counts for two offences (such as theft and handling) which are in the circumstances alternative to each other, and the jury convict of one but acquit of the other, the court cannot substitute a verdict of guilty of the latter, even if that seems the correct verdict, since the jury expressly acquitted. The proper course, if there is a conviction on one, is for the jury to be discharged from giving a verdict on the other whereupon the Court of Appeal may substitute a verdict of guilty.[98] This may also be important from the point of view of a re-trial.

---

[93] [1995] 1 Cr App R 420. For other authorities in similar vein, see *R v Boal* [1992] QB 591; *R v Ayres* (1984) 78 Cr App R 232; *R v McHugh* (1976) 64 Cr App R 92.

[94] [2003] EWCA Crim 319.   [95] Criminal Appeal Act 1968, s 3(1).   [96] Ibid, s 3(2).

[97] See, generally, *R v Caslin* [1961] 1 All ER 246, [1961] 1 WLR 59. This case was decided under the corresponding provisions of the Criminal Appeal Act 1907, but appears still to be good law.

[98] *R v Melvin and Eden* [1953] 1 QB 481, [1953] 1 All ER 294.

3 POWER TO RECEIVE FRESH EVIDENCE AND
TO ORDER A NEW TRIAL

The power to receive fresh evidence was contained in the 1907 Act, and is now to be found in section 23 of the 1968 Act, as now amended by the Criminal Appeal Act of 1995. This section contains both a duty and discretion. Originally worded in a restrictive way, which set too high a threshold,[99] section 23 was amended by the 1995 Act. Section 23(2) creates *a right* to admit fresh evidence (i.e. evidence not adduced at the trial) if they think it necessary or expedient in the interests of justice. It imposes a *duty* to do so if:

(a) the evidence is likely to be credible, and would have been admissible at the trial; and

(b) there is a reasonable explanation for the evidence not being adduced at trial.

Thus the intent of the change is that the Court now, when considering the exercise of the duty has to consider whether such evidence is capable of being believed without having to take a view as to whether, on the facts, it is likely to be so. The Court may decline to receive such evidence if it is satisfied that the evidence, if received, would not afford any ground for allowing the appeal.[100]

As noted, by section 23(1) the Court has a discretion to admit the evidence of any witness or document if it thinks it necessary or expedient in the interests of justice to do so. It may be thought curious to have a discretion that in fact allows the Court to bypass the more detailed criteria in section 23(2). That, though, simply reflects the basic role of the Court of Appeal in the criminal justice system, namely to ensure fairness and justice. It does, however, make the role of the Criminal Cases Review Commission more difficult in trying to predict how the Court of Appeal will deal with any particular case.[101] In this situation the evidence does not have to satisfy the criteria in section 23(2) of not being tendered at the trial. An example of the use of this discretion was seen in *R v Lattimore*,[102] where some of the evidence was in fact given at the trial, and all of it was in fact available. It was allowed to be heard because it cast doubt upon the confession evidence upon which the prosecution case largely depended. The Court will only exceptionally allow the discretion to be used as a means of different defences being put forward at the appellate stage. In *R v Ahluwalia*[103] the Court, exceptionally, allowed fresh medical evidence to be adduced to support a defence of diminished responsibility to the charge of murder of the appellant's husband, a defence which had not been raised at trial, an approach that did not reflect the balance of earlier authority[104] but which demonstrates the concern of the Court to ensure that any conviction is in fact safe. Although the Court warned against running defences on appeal that had not been advanced at trial, the particular facts were such as to justify the course in fact taken.

---

[99] And which required the evidence to be 'likely to be credible'.
[100] Criminal Appeal Act 1968, s 23(2).   [101] See p 719, *ante*.
[102] (1975) 62 Cr App R 53.   [103] [1992] 4 All ER 889.
[104] See *R v Dodd* (1971, Unreported); *R v Melville* [1976] 1 WLR 181; *R v Straw* [1995] 1 All ER 187 (decided in 1987, but not reported until 1995).

Appeals on the grounds of fresh evidence used to be relatively rare, but of increasing importance given the role of the Criminal Cases Review Commission, and the nature of the cases it handles.[105] The case law has continued to demonstrate the real problems the courts face in this area in deciding whether to admit the evidence, how to evaluate it, what judgments to make, whether to quash a conviction, and whether or not to order a retrial. The power to order a new trial was first introduced in 1964.[106] The Court may order a new trial if it considers that the interests of justice so require.[107] This power to order re-trial is not now confined to fresh evidence cases.[108] The power to order re-trials is at the heart of the debate as to how cases where fresh evidence comes to light should be dealt with. It was argued by Lord Devlin[109] that a conviction should always be quashed where fresh evidence has been received, since a conviction is bound to be unsafe or unsatisfactory if not based on all the evidence. That, though, is not the approach of the courts. In *Stafford* v *Director of Public Prosecutions*[110] the House of Lords considered that the verdict should be quashed if the Court itself considers the verdict to be unsafe or unsatisfactory, thus requiring the Court to take a view of the effect of the fresh evidence tendered. Viscount Dilhorne stated that:

> While . . . the Court of Appeal and this House may find it a convenient approach to consider what a jury might have done if they had heard the fresh evidence, the ultimate responsibility rests with them and them alone for dealing with the question . . . .[111]

This approach was criticized as restricting the use of the re-trial powers,[112] but was considered and affirmed in the definitive re-statement of the law by the House of Lords in *R* v *Pendleton*.[113]

In *R* v *McIlkenny*[114] the Court of Appeal had described its approach as follows:

> Nor is there any difficulty in fresh evidence cases, where the fresh evidence is discovered soon after the trial. If the evidence is incredible, or inadmissible, or would not afford a ground for allowing the appeal, we decline to receive it. If the fresh evidence surmounts that preliminary hurdle, we first quash the conviction, if we think it unsafe or unsatisfactory, and then order a retrial if the interests of justice so require. Where new evidence is conclusive, we quash the conviction without ordering a retrial. The difficulty becomes acute when there is no contest. For then we have to make up our minds whether the convictions are unsafe or unsatisfactory without having the benefit of having the evidence tested by cross-examination. Where a retrial is still possible, the quashing of the conviction is only the first half of a two stage process. Where a retrial is no longer possible, it is the end of the road.

Some ten years later the approach of the House of Lords in *Pendleton* was very much the same. If the Court is sure of innocence it should quash the conviction. If it is sure

---

[105] See p 719, *ante*.　　　[106] Criminal Appeal Act 1964, s 1.

[107] Criminal Appeal Act 1968 ss 7–8.　　　[108] See 1968 Act, s 7, amended by Criminal Justice Act 1988.

[109] See Royal Commission on Criminal Justice, Report, *op cit*, Ch 10, para 62.

[110] [1974] AC 898, [1973] 3 All ER 762.

[111] Applied in *R* v *Hakala* [2002] EWCA Crim 730; *R* v *Hanratty (decd)* [2002] 3 All ER 534; *R* v *Ishtiaq Ahmed* [2002] EWCA Crim 2781. Approved in *Dial and another* v *State of Trinidad & Tobago* [2005] UKPC 4, [2005] 1 WLR 1660. See also *R* v *Cannings* [2004] 2 Cr App R 7.

[112] See Royal Commission, ibid, at para 66.　　　[113] [2002] 1 All ER 72.　　　[114] [1992] 2 All ER 417.

of guilt it should uphold the conviction. In less clear-cut cases it should ask itself the question: what might have been the effect of this evidence on the jury? The Court of Appeal should be aware that the primary decision maker is the jury, and that it may have an incomplete understanding of the full process that led the jury to convict. The Court of Appeal can make its own assessment, but it would usually be wise to test that assessment against the question: if the evidence had been tendered at trial, it might reasonably be thought that the conclusion would have been affected.

What is clear is that the courts, now, take the view that its discretion cannot be fettered by inflexible mechanistic rules.[115] The Court is also more likely to be generous in cases of expert medical evidence.[116]

4 *VENIRE DE NOVO*

The appeal court has always had the power to order a *venire de novo* where proceedings in the court of trial were so defective as to amount to a nullity. To the defendant this no doubt seems very like ordering a new trial, but strictly the Court is ordering not a new trial but a proper one. It has not, unfortunately, been established what degree of irregularity suffices to render proceedings a nullity; there are only particular examples in the cases of proceedings which have been held to be a nullity. This has been held to be so where the judge at the trial was not properly qualified,[117] where the defendant specifically asked for but was denied his right of peremptory challenges,[118] or where a plea of not guilty was misheard and dealt with as a plea of guilty.[119]

5 HOSPITAL ORDERS

The Court has certain powers to consider whether a hospital order was rightly made, and in some circumstances can substitute a verdict of guilty for an offence which was charged at the trial, of which the defendant could have been convicted, for the special verdict of not guilty by reason of insanity or against a finding of unfitness to plead reached at the trial.[120]

APPEALS AGAINST SENTENCE

On an appeal against sentence the court may reduce the sentence, or may vary it, by substituting one form of detention for another. The Court will interfere with a sentence where it is 'wrong in principle', an approach that applies also to references made by the

---

[115] See *R v Mackerney and Pinfold* [2003] EWCA Crim 3643; *R v Gee, The Times*, 22 April 2006.
[116] *R v O'Brian*, 2000, unreported.   [117] *R v Cronin* [1940] 1 All ER 618.
[118] But no such right now exists: see p 352, *ante*.
[119] *R v Scothern* [1961] Crim LR 326.   [120] See p 654, *ante*.

Attorney-General. Where the sentence is against conviction only there is no power to interfere with the sentence in any way. Nor, except on an Attorney-General's reference, has the Court the power to increase sentence, a power that once existed but was rarely used.

PROCEDURE

Under section 9(d) and (e) of the Criminal Appeal Act 1907 the Court had the power to appoint a special commissioner to conduct an inquiry into documents and to appoint assessors where their special expert knowledge was likely to be required for the determination of a case. These powers were little, if ever used, and not re-enacted by the 1968 Act. The Royal Commission considered that the Court of Appeal is not well constituted to supervise or direct police or other investigations. Nor should the same body exercise judicial and investigatory functions.[121]

As noted above, some appeals to the Court may be brought without leave, but in most cases there must be an application to the Court itself for leave. The time limit for giving notice of appeal, or application for leave to appeal, is twenty-eight days from the date of conviction or sentence. This time may be extended by the Court. Such application is made in the first instance to a single judge of the Court, who considers it in private. A single judge has most of the powers of a Court of three judges (besides, of course, the power to grant leave); exceptionally he does not have any of the powers relating to fresh evidence. An application may of course be abandoned, and notice of abandonment cannot be withdrawn although it may be treated as a nullity if the abandonment was not the result of a deliberate and informed decision in the sense that 'the mind of the appellant did not go with his act of abandonment.'[122] For example, where an application for leave to appeal was granted but, because of a postal strike, was not communicated to the applicant before he gave notice of abandonment, he was permitted to withdraw his notice.[123] If the single judge refuses leave to appeal (or to exercise any other of his powers) the applicant may be considered by a Court of two judges. Both the single judge and the Court may grant legal aid and bail. Bail, for obvious reasons, is very rarely granted; indeed almost the only cases where it will be granted are where the defendant has obtained (or does not need) leave to appeal and has a very good chance of succeeding on appeal, or where the defendant has been given a comparatively short sentence after a long and complex trial. In the latter case he might otherwise have served much of his sentence before the appeal was heard.

---

[121] Report, *op cit*, Ch 11, para 11.   [122] *R v Medway* [1976] QB 799.
[123] *R v Noble* [1971] 3 All ER 361.

APPEAL TO THE HOUSE OF LORDS

A further appeal lies by either prosecution or defence from the Court of Appeal (Criminal Division) to the House of Lords if:

(1) the Court of Appeal certifies that a point of law of general public importance is involved in the decision; and

(2) either the Court of Appeal or the House of Lords gives leave to appeal on the ground that the point is one which ought to be considered by the House.

The certificate was considered a necessary condition, to avoid the House of Lords being inundated with hopeless applications. This justification was not accepted by the Royal Commission, which recommended its abolition.[124] If the Court of Appeal is satisfied that there is a point of law of general public importance involved it will give the certificate, as it were, automatically. There will always, nevertheless, be an element of discretion as to whether an appeal is allowed to proceed, since even if the point were of general public importance it might still not be worthy of consideration by the House of Lords in the particular case; for example, it might already be the subject of clear and satisfactory decisions of lower courts. This element of discretion is preserved by the requirement that there can be no further proceedings. On the other hand, the Court of Appeal may give a certificate and yet refuse leave, in which case a petition may be made to the House of Lords for leave to appeal, the petition being heard by the Appeals Committee of the House.

It is proper and convenient that the certificate should state what the point of law of general public importance is;[125] however, it seems likely that other points may be raised by either side once the case is before the House of Lords on the point certified.[126] However, the grant of a certificate on some point affecting the validity of the conviction does not enable the appellant to argue that the sentence is invalid. The House of Lords may exercise similar powers to those of the court below.

The procedure described above does not apply following the hearing of an Attorney-General's reference after acquittal. In these cases the Court of Appeal may of its own motion or in pursuance of an application refer the point of law in the case to the House of Lords 'if they appear to the court that the point ought to be considered by that House' and there is, accordingly, no need for a certificate that a point of law of general public importance is involved. Indeed the point of law need not be a point of general public importance, although no doubt the Court of Appeal would only refer such a point to the House as a matter of practice.

---

124 Report, *op cit*, Ch 10, para 79.
125 *Jones* v *Director of Public Prosecutions* [1962] AC 635, [1962] 1 All ER 569.
126 *A-G for Northern Ireland* v *Gallagher* [1963] AC 349, [1961] 3 All ER 299.

FURTHER READING

Ashworth and Redmayne, *The Criminal Process*, 3rd edn (Oxford University Press: 2000)

Auld Review – *Review of the Criminal Courts of England & Wales* (http://www.criminal-courts-review.org.uk)

JUSTICE, *Report on Miscarriages of Justice* (1989)

Spencer, 'Does the Present Criminal Appeal System Make Sense?' [2006] Crim LR 677

INDEX